HANDBOOK
of
MATERIAL CULTURE

HANDBOOK
of
MATERIAL CULTURE

Edited by
CHRISTOPHER TILLEY,
WEBB KEANE,
SUSANNE KÜCHLER,
MIKE ROWLANDS
AND
PATRICIA SPYER

Los Angeles | London | New Delhi
Singapore | Washington DC

SAGE Publications Ltd
1 Oliver's Yard
55 City Road
London EC1Y 1SP

SAGE Publications Inc.
2455 Teller Road
Thousand Oaks, California 91320

SAGE Publications India Pvt Ltd
B 1/I 1, Mohan Cooperative Industrial Area
Mathura Road
New Delhi 110 044

SAGE Publications Asia-Pacific Pte Ltd
33 Pekin Street #02-01
Far East Square
Singapore 048763

British Library Cataloguing in Publication data

A catalogue record for this book is available from the British Library

ISBN 978-1-4129-0039-3

Library of Congress Control Number available

Typeset by C&M Digitals (P) Ltd, Chennai, India
Printed on paper from sustainable resources
Printed in Great Britain by the MPG Books Group

Mixed Sources
Product group from well-managed forests and other controlled sources
www.fsc.org Cert no. SA-COC-1565
© 1996 Forest Stewardship Council

CONTENTS

LIST OF ILLUSTRATIONS AND TABLES

ILLUSTRATIONS

TABLES

NOTES ON CONTRIBUTORS

Russell Belk is the N. Eldon Tanner Professor of Business Administration at the University of Utah. He has published widely on consumer behaviour, marketing and elite consumption. He is also a specialist in the use of qualitative research techniques in consumer behaviour and has published extensively on the methods of field research and interpretation of consumers. His publications include *Collecting in a Consumer Society* (Routledge, 2001).

Barbara Bender is Emeritus Professor of Heritage Anthropology in the Department of Anthropology, University College London. Both an archaeologist and an anthropologist, her early work was on the beginning of farming and the emergence of social inequality. Her more recent work has been on issues of landscape: politics, contestation, and landscapes of movement and exile. Her books include *Landscape: Politics and Perspectives* (ed., 1993), *Stonehenge: Making Space* (1998), *Contested Landscapes: Movement, Exile and Place* (ed., with M. Winer, 2001), *Stone Worlds: Narrative and Reflexive Approaches to Landscape Archaeology* (with Sue Hamilton and Chris Tilley, 2005).

Suzanne Preston Blier is Allen Whitehill Clowes Professor of Fine Arts and Professor of African and African-American Studies at Harvard University. The recipient of numerous grants (Guggenheim, Social Science Research Council, Fulbright and Getty), she has authored a range of books and articles on African art and architecture, among them, *The Anatomy of Architecture: Ontology and Metaphor in Batammaliba Architectural Expression* (1997), *African Vodun: Art, Psychology, and Form* (1995), *Royal Arts of Africa* (1998), *Butabu: Adobe Architecture of West Africa* (with James Morris, 2003) and *Art of the Science: Masterpieces from the Teel Collection* (editor, 2004).

Victor Buchli is Reader in Material Culture in the Department of Anthropology, University College London. He is the author of *An Archaeology of Socialism* (1999) and, with Gavin Lucas, *Archaeologies of the Contemporary Past* (2001). His other edited volumes are *Material Culture: Critical Concepts* (2004) and *The Material Culture Reader* (2002). He is also managing editor with Alison Clarke and Dell Upton of the interdisciplinary journal of the domestic sphere *Home Cultures*.

Beverley Butler is a lecturer in Museum Studies and Cultural Heritage at the Institute of Archaeology, University College London. She has carried out fieldwork in Egypt and Palestine on the social impact of cultural heritage projects, most recently involving a study of the building of the new library at Alexandria. She has published most recently on cultural heritage theory and on the Alexandria museum.

James Carrier has taught and done research in Papua New Guinea, the United States and Britain. He is Senior Research Associate at Oxford Brookes University and Adjunct Professor of Anthropology at the University of Indiana. His main publications in economic anthropology include *Wage, Trade and Exchange in Melanesia* (with A. Carrier, 1989), *Gifts and Commodities: Exchange and Western Capitalism since 1700* (1995), *Meanings of the Market* (ed., 1997), *Virtualism: a New Political Economy* (ed., with D. Miller, 1998) and *Handbook of Economic Anthropology* (ed., 2005).

Margaret Conkey is the Class of 1960 Professor of Anthropology and Director of the Archaeological Research Facility at the University of California, Berkeley. She has worked with the materiality and material culture of the Upper Paleolithic, written on the uses of style in archaeology, and contributed a number of publications to the field of gender and feminist archaeology.

Paul Connerton is Honorary Fellow in the German and Romance Studies Institute at the University of London and Research Associate in the Department of Social Anthropology at the University of Cambridge. He has been Visiting Fellow at the Australian National University and Simon Senior Research Fellow at the University of Manchester. He is the author of *The Tragedy of Enlightenment: an Essay on the Frankfurt School* (1980) and *How Societies Remember* (1989).

Dinah Eastop is Senior Lecturer in Textile Conservation at the Textile Conservation Centre, University of Southampton. She is also an Associate Director of the AHRC Research Centre for Textile Conservation and Textile Studies. She is a member of the editorial board of the International Institute of Conservation's *Reviews in Conservation* and is conducting research on garments concealed in buildings (http://www.concealedgarments.org).

Ron Eglash holds a B.Sc. in Cybernetics, an M.Sc. in Systems Engineering and a Ph.D. in History of Consciousness, all from the University of California. A Fulbright postdoctoral fellowship enabled his field research on African ethnomathematics, which was published in 1999 as *African Fractals: Modern Computing and Indigenous Design*. He is an associate professor of Science and Technology Studies at Rensselaer Polytechnic Institute. His current project, funded by the NSF, HUD and Department of Education, translates the mathematical concepts embedded in cultural designs of African, African-American, Native American and Latino communities into software design tools for secondary school education. The software is available online at http://www.rpi.edu/~eglash/csdt.html.

Judith Farquhar is Professor of Anthropology at the University of Chicago. She is the author of *Knowing Practice: the Clinical Encounter of Chinese Medicine* (1994) and *Appetites: Food and Sex in Post-socialist China* (2002). Her current research, undertaken in collaboration with Qicheng Zhang of the Beijing University of Chinese Medicine, is an investigation of popular self-care practices in Beijing.

Robert J. Foster is Professor of Anthropology at the University of Rochester. He is the author of *Social Reproduction and History in Melanesia: Mortuary Ritual, Gift Exchange and Custom in the Tanga Islands* (1995) and *Materializing the Nation:*

Commodities, Consumption, and Media in Papua New Guinea (2002), and editor of *Nation Making: Emergent Identities in Postcolonial Melanesia* (1995). His research interests include globalization, material culture and comparative modernities. He is working on a book tentatively entitled *Worldly Things: Soft Drink Perspectives on Globalization*.

Chris Gosden is a lecturer/curator in the School of Archaeology and the Pitt Rivers Museum, University of Oxford, where he teaches archaeology and anthropology. He has carried out fieldwork in Papua New Guinea, Turkmenistan and Britain. His main interests are in material culture and colonialism; his two most recent works in the area are *Collecting Colonialism* (with Chantal Knowles, 2002) and *Archaeology and Colonialism* (2004). He leads the Relational Museum Project on the history of collections in the Pitt Rivers Museum, using the museum as a privileged means of exploring the links between people and things. He is developing a project on material culture and human intelligence.

Janet Hoskins is Professor of Anthropology at the University of Southern California, Los Angeles. She is the author of *The Play of Time* (1994, awarded the Benda Prize in Southeast Asian Studies) and *Biographical Objects: How Things tell the Stories of People's Lives* (1998) and editor of *Headhunting and the Social Imagination in Southeast Asia* (1996). She did research in Indonesia from 1979 to 2000 and has been working in California and Vietnam since 2002.

David Howes is Professor of Anthropology at Concordia University, Montreal. He is the editor of *Empire of the Senses: the Sensual Culture Reader* (2004), the lead volume in the Sensory Formations series, as well as the co-author (with Constance Classen and Anthony Synnott) of *Aroma: the Cultural History of Smell* (1994) and author of *Sensual Relations: Engaging the Senses in Culture and Social Theory* (2003). His other research interests include the anthropology of consumption, legal anthropology, and the constitution of the Canadian imaginary.

Webb Keane is an Associate Professor in the Department of Anthropology at the University of Michigan, Ann Arbor. He is the author of *Signs of Recognition: Powers and Hazards of Representation in an Indonesian Society* (1997) and of articles on cultural theory, language, exchange and religion. Among his writings on material culture are 'The hazards of new clothes: what signs make possible' (in *The Art of Clothing*, ed. Küchler and Were, 2005), 'Semiotics and the social analysis of material things' (in *Language and Communication*, 2003), 'Money is no object: materiality, desire, and modernity in an Indonesian society' (in *The Empire of Things*, ed. Myers, 2001), 'Materialism, missionaries, and modern subjects in colonial Indonesia' (in *Conversion to Modernities*, ed. van der Veer, 1996) and 'The spoken house: text, act, and object in eastern Indonesia' (*American Ethnologist*, 1995). His forthcoming volume *Between Freedom and Fetish* is about subjects and objects in Christian modernities.

Susanne Küchler is Reader in Material Culture Studies in the Department of Anthropology at University College London. She has conducted long-term field research in Papua New Guinea on objectification and remembering and has written on issues of art, memory and sacrifice from an ethnographic and theoretical perspective. More recently she has directed comparative research into clothing and innovation in Polynesia, which has now developed into a project on artefactual intelligence. Her publications include *Malanggan Art, Memory and Sacrifice* (2002) and *Pacific Pattern* (in press).

Paul Lane is Director of the British Institute in Eastern Africa, Nairobi, and specializes in African archaeology and material culture. His Ph.D. was an ethno-archaeological study of space and time among the Dogon of Mali, and he has published widely on this topic and more generally on ethnoarchaeological research in Africa. His recent work has encompassed archaeological studies of Tswana responses to European colonialism and conversion to Christianity, and the historical archaeology of Luo settlement. His most recent book is *African Historical Archaeologies* (ed., with Andrew Reid, 2004).

Robert Layton is Professor of Anthropology at the University of Durham. His main research interests are in art, indigenous rights, social change and social evolution. He has carried out fieldwork in France (1969, 1985, 1995) and Australia (1974-81, 1993, 1994). His publications include *The Anthropology of Art* (1991), *Conflict in the Archaeology of Living Traditions* (1994), *An Introduction to Theory in Anthropology* (1997) and *Anthropology and History in Franche-Comté* (2000).

Bill Maurer is Associate Professor of Anthropology at the University of California, Irvine. He is the author of *Mutual Life, Limited: Islamic Banking, Alternative Currencies, Lateral Reason* (2005) and *Recharting the Caribbean: Land, Law and Citizenship in the British Virgin Islands* (1997). He conducts research on the anthropology of money, finance and law, and also writes on anthropological theory and globalization.

Daniel Miller is Professor of Material Culture in the Department of Anthropology, University College London. Recent publications include *Materiality* (ed., 2005), *Clothing as Material Culture* (ed. with S. Küchler, 2005), with Mukulika Banerjee, *The Sari* (2003), and with Heather Horst, *The Cell Phone: An Anthropology of Communication* (in press).

Jon P. Mitchell is Reader in Anthropology at the University of Sussex. He has written on the anthropology of performance, ritual, religion, memory and politics, primarily in the Mediterranean context of Malta. His books include *Ambivalent Europeans: Ritual, Memory and the Public Sphere in Malta* (2002), *Powers of Good and Evil: Social Transformation and Popular Belief* (ed., with Paul Clough, 2002) and a special issue of *Journal of Mediterranean Studies*, 'Modernity in the Mediterranean' (2002).

Fred Myers is Silver Professor and Chair of Anthropology at New York University. He has carried out research with Western Desert Aboriginal people in Australia. He is interested in exchange theory and material culture, the intercultural production and circulation of culture, in contemporary art worlds, in identity and personhood, and in how these are related to theories of value and practices of signification. He is the co-editor of *The Traffic in Culture: Refiguring Art and Anthropology* (with George Marcus, 1995). His interests in material culture, circulation and value are developed in an edited volume, *The Empire of Things:*

Regimes of Value and Material Culture (2001), and a study of the development and circulation of Aboriginal acrylic painting, *Painting Culture: the Making of an Aboriginal High Art* (2002).

Bjørnar Olsen is Professor of Archaeology at the University of Tromsø. His research interests include archaeological theory, material culture, Saami history and ethnography, and north Scandinavian archaeology. He has written several books and numerous papers on these topics, including *Camera archaeologica: rapport fra et feltarbeid* (with J.E. Larsen, A. Hesjedal and I. Storli, 1993), *Bosetning og samfunn i Finnmarks forhistorie* (1994), *Fra ting til tekst: teoretiske perspektiv i arkeologisk forskning* (1997) and *Samenes historie fram til 1750* (with L.I. Hansen, 2004). He is directing a research project on dwellings and cultural interfaces in medieval arctic Norway as well as conducting research on the ontology of things.

Christopher Pinney is Professor of Anthropology and Visual Culture at University College London. He has held visiting positions at the Australian National University, the University of Chicago and the University of Cape Town. His most recent book is *Photos of the Gods: the Printed Image and Political Struggle in India* (2004).

Mike Rowlands is Professor of Anthropology and Material Culture at University College London. His earlier research was in long-term social change and the archaeology of colonialism in prehistoric Europe and West Africa. More recently he has focused on cultural heritage issues and ethnographic studies of heritage projects in Mali and Cameroon. Recent publications include *Social Transformations in Archaeology* (with Kristian Kristiansen, 1998).

Jane Schneider is Professor of Anthropology at the City University of New York Graduate Center. She is the co-editor with Annette B. Weiner of *Cloth and Human Experience* (1987) and the author of several essays on cloth and clothing. In 1998 she edited *Italy's Southern Question; Orientalism in one Country* and in 2003 co-edited (with Ida Susser) *Wounded Cities: Destruction and Reconstruction in a Globalized World*. Her anthropological field research in Sicily has led to three books, co-authored with Peter Schneider: *Culture and Political Economy in Western Sicily* (1976), *Festival of the Poor: Fertility Decline and the Ideology of Class in Sicily* (1996) and *Reversible Destiny: Mafia, Antimafia and the Struggle for Palermo* (2003).

Anthony Shelton is Director of the Museum of Anthropology and Professor of Anthropology at the University of British Columbia, Vancouver. He was previously Professor of Anthropology at the University of Coimbra and Keeper of Ethnography at the Horniman Museum, London. His most recent exhibition is 'African Worlds' at the Horniman Museum and he has published extensively on museum theory and museum history and material culture styles in Mexico and the South-Western United States.

Marilyn Strathern, currently Professor of Social Anthropology at the University of Cambridge and Mistress of Girton College, has had a longstanding ethnographic interest in gender relations (*Women in Between*, 1972) and kinship (*Kinship at the Core*, 1981). This led to a critical appraisal of ownership and control in models of Melanesian societies (*The Gender of the Gift*, 1988), and, to some extent, of consumer society in Britain (*After Nature*, 1992). Interest in reproductive technologies (*Reproducing the Future*, 1992 and the co-authored *Technologies of Procreation*, 1993) sharpened a concern with new property forms, a collection of essays, *Property, Substance and Effect*, appearing in 1999. Most recently she has been involved with colleagues, in PNG and the UK, in another collaborative study, this time of debates over intellectual and cultural property under the general title 'Property, Transactions and Creations' (*Transactions and Creations*, edited with E. Hirsch, 2004).

Patricia Spyer is Professor of Anthropology at Leiden University. She is the author of *The Memory of Trade: Modernity's Entanglements on an Eastern Indonesian Island* (2000) and editor of *Border Fetishisms: Material Objects in Unstable Spaces* (1998). She has published, among other topics, on violence, the media and photography, historical consciousness, materiality and religion.

Robert St. George teaches in the history department at the University of Pennsylvania. His research focuses on American cultural history, material culture, vernacular landscapes and heritage productions in North America, England, Ireland and Iceland. Among his publications are *The Wrought Covenant: Source Materials for the Study of Craftsmen and Community in South-eastern New England, 1620–1700* (1979), *Material Life in America, 1600–1860* (1988), *Conversing by Signs: Poetics of Implivation in Colonial New England Culture* (1998) and *Possible Pasts: Becoming Colonial in early America* (2000). He is completing a book on popular violence, law and lived religion in eighteenth-century Maine.

Julian Thomas is Professor of Archaeology in the School of Arts, Histories and Cultures at the University of Manchester. His research is principally concerned with the Neolithic archaeology of Britain and north-west Europe, the philosophy of archaeology and material culture studies. He has a particular interest in the role of modern thought in the formation of archaeology as a discipline, and he is a member of the Council of the Royal Anthropological Institute and an Associate Director of the AHRC Research Centre for Textile Conservation Textile Studies. His publications include *Understanding the Neolithic* (1999) and *Archaeology and Modernity* (2004).

Christopher Tilley is Professor of Material Culture in the Department of Anthropology and Institute of Archaeology, University College London. His research interests are in anthropological theory and material culture studies, phenomenological approaches to landscape, the anthropology and archaeology of 'art', and the Neolithic and Bronze Age of Britain and Europe. He has carried out fieldwork in Scandinavia, Britain, France and Vanuatu. Recent books include *An Ethnography of the Neolithic* (1996), *Metaphor and Material Culture* (1999) and *The Materiality of Stone: Explorations in Landscape Phenomenology* (2004). He is a series editor of the *Journal of Material Culture*.

Peter van Dommelen is Senior Lecturer in Mediterranean archaeology at the University of Glasgow. His research interests are in postcolonial approaches to ancient and (early) modern colonialism as well as survey archaeology and rural settlement in the late prehistoric and early historical western Mediterranean. Colonialism and peasant societies feature prominently in his research on rural organization, Carthaginian expansion and the role of the island of Sardinia in the wider Punic world, where he has carried out extensive fieldwork (2002–). He is founding co-editor of the journal *Archaeological Dialogues*.

Jean-Pierre Warnier is a Professor of Ethnology at the University of Paris V (Sorbonne). He has done extensive research in the kingdoms of western Cameroon, with particular emphasis on their economic history since 1700, on the local and regional hierarchies, and on the embodiment of power in their material culture cum bodily conducts. He taught for three years in Nigeria and for six years in Cameroon. For the last ten years he has been developing a praxeological and political approach to material culture. His recent publications include *Construire la culture matérielle. L' homme qui pensait avec ses doigts* (1999) and *Matiére à politique. Le pouvoir, les corps et les choses* (2004, co-edited with J.-F. Bayart).

Diana Young is a Research fellow at the centre for Cross-Cultural Research, Australian National University. Her interests are in the area of visual and material culture and the development of an anthropology of design with particular regard to the built environment. Since 1996 she has carried out fieldwork among Pitjantjatjara and Yankunytjatjara people and has written about contemporary Australian Aboriginal material culture and the expressive potential of consumer goods such as clothing and cars. She co-curated the Australian exhibition *Art on a String; threaded objects from the central desert and Arnhem Land* and is co-author of the accompanying book. She is writing a book called *The Desire for Colour* about the re-visualization of traditional concepts using novel coloured materials, among Aboriginal people in the Western Desert.

INTRODUCTION

Studies of material culture have undergone a profound transformation during the past twenty years and are now among the most dynamic and wide-ranging areas of contemporary scholarship in the human sciences. This is reflected in an impressive volume of research activity, and a flood of books, edited collections, review articles and papers devoted to this field. An international journal, the *Journal of Material Culture*, first published in 1996, reaches an audience of archaeologists, anthropologists, sociologists, geographers, historians and people working in cultural, design and technological studies. Although questions of materiality pervade a wide range of disciplines in the social and human sciences, no single academic discipline unifies the various approaches to material culture and gives them an institutional identity. One consequence is that questions broached and solutions proposed in different venues are not always brought to bear on those in others. The editors consider the field of material studies to have reached a sufficient degree of maturity that the time has come for a single comprehensive review of the field. To that end, we have commissioned the chapters that follow from leading scholars of material culture in its various dimensions.

At present, material culture studies form a diffuse and relatively uncharted interdisciplinary field of study in which a concept of materiality provides both the starting point and the justification. This field of study centres on the idea that materiality is an integral dimension of culture, and that there are dimensions of social existence that cannot be fully understood without it. Yet the 'material' and the 'cultural' are commonly regarded as fundamentally opposed, for instance, as the physical to the intellectual. The thrust of this *Handbook* is to emphasize that the study of the material dimension is as fundamental to understanding culture as is a focus on language (formalized in the discipline of linguistics and linguistic anthropology) or social relations (formalized in sociology and social

anthropology) or time (archaeology and history) or space (geography) or representations (literary and art historical studies) or a focus on relations of production, exchange and consumption (economics). Material culture studies may be held simultaneously to intersect with and to transcend the special concerns of these and other disciplines. Such an intellectual field of study is inevitably eclectic: relatively unbounded and unconstrained, fluid, dispersed and anarchic rather than constricted. In short, it is undisciplined rather than disciplined. This we regard as a strength rather than a weakness and an alternative to the inevitable disciplinary restrictions with regard to research which is validated, or otherwise, as valuable, serious or appropriate.

In this sense, and in relation to other disciplines with their in-built hierarchies and legitimizing powers and ancestors, material culture studies might be regarded as an academic manifestation of characterizations of our contemporary cultural condition as 'postmodern', involving indeterminacy, immanence or becoming, ambiguity, heterodoxy and pluralism. As a field of research transcending established disciplines material culture studies are always changing and developing, redefining both themselves and their objects of study, cross-fertilizing various other 'disciplined' ideas and influences: impure, contingent, dynamic. Historically, however, they do have a primary disciplinary 'home' and point of origin within the disciplines of archaeology and anthropology. Prehistoric archaeology, has of course, material culture as its principal source of evidence about the human past while the study of material culture has always been a component of social anthropological studies, which have historically been to a greater or lesser extent highlighted and foregrounded or neglected and dismissed. However, neither discipline has sought to define itself in terms of the study of things and their relations to persons in quite the same way as envisaged in the structure and organization of this *Handbook*. By bringing together a wide range of approaches to material culture, this volume seeks to sharpen scholarly awareness of the nature of materiality and its implications for cultural, social, and historical knowledge.

A concern with collecting, classifying and studying artefacts formed the core of much anthropological research from the nineteenth-century birth of the discipline until the 1920s. In the wake of Western colonial expansion there was a concern to rescue, or salvage, what was perceived to be left of 'primitive' culture throughout the world. This was a time in which the great museum collections were established through systematic collecting. The first scientific anthropological expedition to the Torres Strait led by Haddon in 1898 had the collection of artefacts as one of its major goals. Many more collecting expeditions were to follow throughout the world. Given the assumption that natives and their ceremonies and belief systems could not be saved, at least the material residues might be preserved for posterity. The study of material culture formed a fundamental part of the major theoretical preoccupations and debates of the day. Artefact studies, organized by measures of technological progress, provided the empirical basis for grand schemes of social evolution, diffusion, acculturation and change. In North America material culture had an especially prominent place in the research of Franz Boas and his early students. The West came to know itself and its place in the world primarily through a study of the artefactual Other. Museums became the great showcases for the display of a vanishing world.

This focus on the artefact changed with the advent of the fieldwork revolution in anthropology from the 1920s and the replacement of evolutionism with functionalist and structural-functionalist theories. For example, Radcliffe Brown's major study of the Andaman Islanders relegated the study of material culture to an appendix. The primary concern was now with social relations rather than things. A study of artefacts could no longer supposedly theoretically inform a study of culture. Conceived as dead inert matter, things were primarily conceived as having a utilitarian significance fulfilling the basic needs of human adaptation to different environments as tools, a technological substrate of life, or alternatively, as passive markers of social status and ethnic difference. A study of artefacts became reduced to a dry discussion of technologies or a description of material form illustrating social context. Artefacts became reflections of that which was deemed fundamental: social relations, political

and economic systems. Thus the academic study of things largely retreated out of university departments of social anthropology and became entrenched in museums, whose primary goals remained collecting and cataloguing and setting up displays in which artefacts were made to signify different peoples on a comparative basis. In the process Melanesian, Polynesian, African and indigenous North American cultures became reified *as* things.

Schematic and abstracted views of social relations have given the standard ethnographic monograph, from the1920s onwards, a somewhat surreal character. One sometimes reads of a world of social interactions where things are either absent, or simply provide a kind of backdrop to relations between persons. Of course, virtually all ethnographies have had to describe and discuss material culture and consider social relations in a material setting, but this has all too often been by default rather than design. Despite a stress on social relations we would maintain that what is, in fact, implied by all the results of anthropological research, whether this has been a principal concern of the anthropologist or not, is that persons cannot be understood apart from things. Much of material culture studies is concerned with deepening our insight into how persons make things and things make persons.

A post-1960s shift from the theoretical dominance of functionalist to that of structuralist and symbolic anthropology paved the way for a reintroduction of the study of material culture into the mainstream of anthropological research. From a functionalist perspective things were only good to use, props for the social. Now they could become reconceptualized as 'good to think' in Lévi-Strauss's felicitous phrase. The 'symbolic turn' in social anthropology led to the re-emergence of an emphasis on material culture with important sub-disciplines developing concerning themselves specifically with art, vernacular architecture and, more broadly, the social uses of artefacts and in the contexts of ceremonial performances and display, death rituals, technologies and exchange.

In archaeology, until the 1960s, material culture was primarily regarded as reflecting ethnic identities, the diffusion of ideas among different groups, invasion, migration and social change. Artefacts provided spatial and temporal markers of ethnic identities and primarily reflected ideas in the minds of their makers. Alternatively they were studied in terms of the technologies required to make them, and understood in terms of grand schemes of social evolution. The 'new archaeology' of the 1960s saw the rise to prominence of precisely the kinds of positivist and functionalist approaches which had largely been abandoned in mainstream ethnographic studies. Material culture came primarily to be seen in terms of its contribution to environmental adaption or the smooth functioning of social systems. This functionalism contributed to a growing disciplinary divergence between ethnographic and archaeological approaches to material culture. However, it also led to two very important developments which to a certain extent directly reintegrated ethnographic and archaeological approaches in ethnoarchaeological studies and archaeological studies of contemporary or modern material culture. From the 1980s onwards the development of symbolic, structural, structural-Marxist archaeologies had the effect of reintegrating ethnographic and archaeological conceptualizations of material culture, effectively giving birth to the broader field of material culture studies represented in this *Handbook*.

In the past, archaeology, with a few exceptions, has been concerned with the past and considered itself, alternatively, as being an extension of history, a science of the past seeking laws and generalizations about human social behaviour, a social interpretation of the past, and so on. Before the advent of a distinctive field of material culture studies most archaeologists generally read anthropology not because they were interested in material culture *per se* as a project of study important in and for itself, but in order to provide better ideas for the interpretation of the past. Similarly, most social and cultural anthropologists, until recently, have rarely been interested in archaeological studies in terms of how they might inform considerations of materiality and material culture in general, but more as a means of providing a historical background to their contemporary cultural concerns. A distinct field of material culture studies transcending both disciplines has, we believe, enormous potential in transforming their relationship in terms of a common focus on materiality and material culture, and with shared epistemological and methodological problems raised by material things. One of the primary objectives of this *Handbook* is to contribute to a new relationship between sociocultural and archaeological anthropology.

The intellectual background of both the editors and the contributors to the *Handbook* is primarily in the disciplines of archaeology and anthropology and, inevitably, some chapters are more 'archaeological' or 'anthropological' than others. However, the various contributors also frequently cite, review and discuss material culture studies in both disciplines and in a wide variety of others, in their discussions of either particular theoretical positions and traditions of research in Part I, such as phenomenology or postcolonial theories, or particular domains and areas of study such as visual culture, exchange, architecture or landscape as in Parts II, III and IV or the problems of representation and heritage discussed in Part V.

Having arisen out of a wide variety of disciplines and research traditions, material culture studies are inevitably diverse. In addition to this the very concept of materiality is itself heterogeneous and ambiguous. Attempts at rigorous definition are entangled with deep metaphorical roots and cultural connotations. According to various dictionary definitions materiality can mean *substance*, something comprised of elements or constituents, of variously composed matter: the tangible, the existing or concrete, the substantial, the worldly and real as opposed to the imaginary, ideal and value-laden aspects of human existence. The concept of materiality is thus typically used to refer to the fleshy, corporeal and physical, as opposed to spiritual, ideal and value-laden aspects of human existence. Materiality can also be taken to refer to individual *things*, or collections of things, rather than to persons or societies. Things are typically referred to in terms of material possessions and to physical and economic well-being. Things thus have material *benefits* for persons. The object and the objectivity of things supposedly stand opposed to the subject and the subjectivity of persons. From this perspective, persons are animated and alive, while the things, whatever they may be, are simply static and dead: kick a stone or a pot and you won't hurt or offend it. Yet even in simple empirical terms, a host of borderline cases, such as animals or technological extensions of persons, challenge the opposition. Furthermore notions of materiality in everday talk are frequently linked with commonsense ideas about data, facts or objective evidence, rather than anything to do with human subjectivity and bias, the mind, ideas or values. In this other empirical sense materiality is something important to us. It is consequential, something of *value*. Concomitantly, people can be metaphorically regarded as possessing the best materials, *qualities*, for the job.

Empirically material culture studies involve the analysis of a domain of things, or objects, which are endlessly diverse: anything from a packet of fast food to a house to an entire landscape, and either in the past or in the present, within contemporary urban and industrial cultures in the United States and Europe to small-scale societies in Africa, Asia or the Pacific. Contemporary material culture studies may take as their principal concern, and starting point for analysis, particular properties of objects or things: things as material matter, as found or made, as static or mobile, rare or ubiquitous, local or exotic, new or old, ordinary or special, small or monumental, traditional or modern, simple or complex.

Alternatively, material culture studies may take the human subject or the social as their starting point: the manner in which people think through themselves, and their lives and identities through the medium of different kinds of things. Material culture studies in various ways inevitably have to emphasize the dialectical and recursive relationship between persons and things: that persons make and use things and that the things make persons. Subjects and objects are indelibly linked. Through considering one, we find the other. Material culture is part and parcel of human culture in general, and just as the concept of culture has hundreds of potential definitions and manifestations and is never just one entity or 'thing' so has the material component of culture. Where a thing or an object and a person, or culture and material culture, 'begin' or 'end' can never be defined in the abstract. All depends on the context of analysis and research.

The studies in this *Handbook* are all variously concerned with the concept of materiality and the conceptualization of things, of which some of the main ones are as follows:

1 Things as materially existing and having a significance in the world independent of any human action or intervention (e.g. a stone, a mountain, an animal or a tree).
2 Things as created by persons: artefacts.
3 The matter or component substances, or materials, of which these things are composed: their origins, associations and combinations.
4 The technologies required to produce things, the manner in which these things may be moved and exchanged and consumed.
5 The manner in which things relate to conscious ideas and intentions held by persons or subjects.
6 The manner in which things relate to unconscious structures of thought and affect, unacknowledged conditions, habits or experiences, and unintended consequences of social life going beyond individual intentional consciousness.

7 The relationship of things, material culture in general, with human culture or society: things as an integral part of being human and living together with others.
8 The relationship of things to value systems, cosmologies, beliefs and emotions, more broadly to personal and social identities.
9 The relationship of things to history and tradition, individual and collective memories, social stasis and social change, and to concepts of space, place, concept and locality.
10 The relationship of things to the human body: the body itself as a cultural and sensuous thing which may move, present and display itself in various ways, and the manner in which things produce, constrain, extend and limit bodily capacities.

Precisely because the terms 'materiality' and 'material culture' defy any strict definitions, that which is incorporated in, or left out of, any *Handbook* such as this is always likely to remain contentious and a matter of debate. In every part of the *Handbook* the editors collectively have selected studies intended to exemplify a much wider field. It would, of course, be impossible to cover everything. In the initial outlines of the book we listed around forty chapter topics; the reviewers suggested some twenty more, and surely other reviewers would have added yet others. The *Handbook* provides a selection of what, over the course of our discussion, the editors agreed to regard as some of the most important, significant and well-researched perspectives and domains or areas of interest, from an enormous field of potential studies which has no real limit or boundary.

The individual chapters in the *Handbook*, and their organization, reflect the fact that substantive studies of material culture have generally been of three types: (1) those that make a particular material domain such as vernacular architecture, basketry, clothing, food, domestic furnishing, etc., their object of study within specific cultural and historical contexts; (2) those that attempt to generalize beyond the specificity of the particular case towards theorizing the significance, meaning and power of material forms in understanding the constitution of social relations by examining broader categories such as studies of art, landscape, memory, technology, exchange and consumption either in relation to specific case studies or cross-culturally; (3) more holistic cultural studies attempting to analyse a plethora of material domains (e.g. architecture, food, technology and landscape) within the ambit of particular archaeological or ethnographic case studies. The *Handbook* reflects all these concerns and interests. In doing so, it principally attempts to promote a *critical* survey of the theories, concepts, intellectual debates and traditions of study characterizing material culture studies. The book thus goes far beyond providing a simple literature review of various empirical or conceptual domains. Rather than simply describing and discussing the field as it currently exists, the *Handbook* also attempts to chart the future: the manner in which material culture studies may be extended and further developed.

ORGANIZATION OF THE HANDBOOK

The *Handbook* is divided into five parts. The first maps material culture studies as a theoretical and conceptual field. These chapters lay out the theoretical terrain for the study of things, covering the history and development of various approaches, the philosophical and conceptual background, key authors, concepts and texts. The individual chapters relate various theoretical perspectives to the study of materiality and material culture in relation to discussions of specific examples. As should be clear, the *Handbook* does not claim to represent one single theoretical or disciplinary perspective or methodological approach but a wide range, reflecting current modes of thinking and research in the field.

The second part covers the relationship between material forms, the body and the senses. It aims to show that material culture cannot be understood apart from the body. Therefore a theory of materiality requires a theorization of the embodied subject and the multiple ways in which the world is sensed and experienced.

The third part focuses on subject-object relations. It considers the manner in which a wide variety of material forms are related to differing kinds of subjectivities and social relations. These chapters work out from the positioning of the subject to consider the manner in which material forms produce, and become integrated in, a particular perspective on the world. This part includes highly specific discussions of both particular material domains

such as cloth and clothing, architecture and art and more general perspectives on materiality and its significance in relation to discussions of globalization, memory and landscape. It aims to show how general processes can be understood and illuminated from the specific perspective of the study of particular material forms. It also works the other way round by illustrating the manner in which the particularity of material forms can be understood from the perspective of general processes. It aims to illustrate the dialectic of subjectivity and objectivity in the constitution of the meanings and significances of things. This section includes discussions of many of the major topics that have traditionally made up the core of empirical material culture case studies.

The fourth part of the book, on process and transformation, considers material culture studies from the perspective of a basic tripartite biography of things: things made, things exchanged, things consumed. It then moves on to consider the manner in which things and their meanings become transformed in performative context and issues of time and decay and physical transformation processes to considering transformations over the very long term from a specifically archaeological perspective.

The fifth and final part considers the contemporary politics and poetics of displaying, representing and conserving material forms in the present and the manner in which this impacts on notions of tradition and social identity.

Each of the individual chapters provides a historical overview of the topic and a critical review of the principal literature, emphasizing conceptual and theoretical issues. Going beyond these general reviews they also crucially suggest future directions for research. The *Handbook* is thus intended not only to survey the field as currently constituted but also to be future oriented and provide a guide to future empirical research. We hope that it may stimulate developments in material culture studies both within individual disciplines and in relation to the wider interdisciplinary field sketched here. The aim is to act as a stimulus to future research that focuses specifically on the materiality of the social worlds people inhabit rather than this being considered a peripheral issue to other concerns. It is an insistence on the significance and importance of investigating material domains that links what otherwise might be regarded as very diverse approaches and topics together.

The new focus represented in this volume is on material culture as a specific category of concern and analysis worthy of investigation in its own right rather than something which becomes subsumed within a pre-existing mode of academic categorization. The fidelity of these studies is first and foremost to the study of material culture itself: an insistence that things matter, that the study of things makes a difference to the way in which we understand the social world and can make a unique and valuable contribution to the broader concerns of the social and historical sciences in general.

PART I

THEORETICAL PERSPECTIVES

The chapters in this section of the *Handbook* have been chosen to reflect the diversity of theoretical perspectives which have profoundly influenced the development of material culture studies and conceptualizations of materiality since the early 1970s. A healthy theoretical pluralism and debate with regard to the significance and interpretation of material forms in relation to social relations has never been greater. This is itself a reflection of both wider developments in the social sciences as a whole and the nature of material culture studies as constituting an inter-disciplinary field of interest.

The first three chapters discussing Marxism, structuralism and semiotics, and phenomenology may be considered 'foundational' theoretical perspectives in so far as it is impossible to imagine either the existence of a notion of materiality or a field labelling itself material culture studies without their existence. All these three perspectives are 'living' and developing theoretical traditions, themselves providing multiple perspectives on material forms which differ. Thus Marx's own voluminous writings offer quite different perspectives, from an earlier humanistic concern with the sensuous character of life and the production and social uses of things to the more abstract 'structural' concerns of his later writings. In Marx's writings we variously encounter (1) a way to understand long-term historical change in an evolutionary manner, (2) a particular ontological perspective on the nature of human praxis or labour and the ramifications of the dialectical method linking together human consciousness and practical action, (3) a theory of ideology and (4) a theory of the constitution of society in relation to contradictions between 'base' and 'super-structure'. Going beyond Marx's own work, a Marxist perspective has been married to a succession of different structuralist and phenomenological brides throughout the latter half of the twentieth century and has had a profound influence in relation to the development of

the objectification perspectives discussed in Chapter 4 and postcolonial theories considered by van Dommelen (Chapter 7) as well as in relation to post-structuralist positions (Olsen, Chapter 6), if only in its denial. As Maurer (Chapter 1) shows, throughout their history material culture studies have an indelible Marxist heritage, from the earlier archaeological work of Childe to the structural-Marxist perspectives which became intellectually dominant in anthropological and archaeological studies during the 1970s and 1980s to current concern with globalization, cultural 'hybridity' diasporas, and capital and material cultural 'flows'.

While Marxist positions ground considerations of material culture in relation to material resources, labour, production, consumption and exchange, the structuralist and semiotic approaches discussed by Layton (Chapter 2) stress the significance of objects and their relation to social action in relation to cognition and symbolization. Things are meaningful and significant not only because they are necessary to sustain life and society, to reproduce or transform social relations and mediate differential interests and values, but because they provide essential tools for thought. Material forms are essential vehicles for the (conscious or unconscious) self-realization of the identities of individuals and groups because they provide a fundamental non-discursive mode of communication. We 'talk' and 'think' about ourselves through things: their integral components, (e.g. the various elements of a textile design) articulations and associations of different things (e.g. furniture in a house). Artefacts, from such a perspective, are signs bearing meaning, signifying beyond themselves. Material culture becomes, from a structuralist perspective, a form of 'text', something to be read and decoded, its grammer revealed.

In anthropology, and in post-processual archaeology (see Olsen, Chapter 6) a semiotic perspective, while sharing some of the same fundamental tenets of structuralism, developed as a critique of the anti-historical and universalist tendencies found in Lévi-Strauss's version of structuralism. Sign systems were to be investigated and understood as historically and culturally variable, with homologies and transformations traced between them. Semiotic analyses of a broad variety of material domains, from art and architecture to food and clothing, to ritual performances and 'totemic' (classificatory) practices, to death rituals have played a fundamental role in the development of material culture studies from the 1960s onwards, attempting to throw light on the fundamental principles or rules by means of which people order their lives through the ordering of their things. The idea that there is a language of things has become enormously influential.

Both Marxist and structuralist and semiotic approaches, and their various combinations, provide us with *depth* epistemological and ontological frameworks for understanding material forms. In other words the surface appearances of both things and social relations are regarded as relatively trivial and superficial. In order to conduct a successful analysis we need to delve below the surfaces of things and persons in order to reveal the fundamental structuring and structured rules and generative principles at work – contradictions between the social forces and relations of production in relation to human labour and its organization, for the former; grammars and codes for the latter. By contrast, the phenomenological perspectives discussed by Thomas (Chapter 3) return us to the 'surface', to the detailed description and analysis of things as we directly experience and perceive them, from a distinctively human and sensuous perspective. This is to stress material forms as encountered through the multiple sensuous and socialized subjective apparatus of our bodies (sight, sound, touch, smell, taste): the manner in which we comprehend both things and persons though our embodied being in a lived world which we share with others.

Marxist and structuralist/semiotic approaches have undoubtably been far more influential in relation to the past development of material culture studies than phenomenological approaches, which have been explicitly developed only during the past decade or so. The reason may be, as Thomas suggests, that unlike Marxism or structuralism, a phenomenological perspective provides in fact no clear or obvious methodology with which to approach the study of things. While one can readily, and

almost mechanically, produce an analysis of things that both 'work' (i.e. make some coherent sense or understanding of them) and that are recognizably 'Marxist' or 'structuralist', the influence of phenomenological thought in relation to material culture studies has been both more subtle and contextually dependent.

One of the abiding problems shared by both structuralist/semiotic approaches and various post-structuralist positions (see Olsen, Chapter 6) from the point of view of material culture studies is the primacy granted to sign systems, language, 'text' or discourse, in rather different ways, as a model or analogue for understanding culture in general and material forms in particular. While we may be obviously obliged to speak and write about things in words, in the act of doing so we are almost inevitably required to evoke their difference, in short the very materiality of their presence in the world beyond the word: their sonorous and tactile, olfactory and three-dimensional visible presence – words don't bleed. This is one reason why the 'objectification' perspectives of Bourdieu and Munn drew so heavily on the semiotic concepts of iconicity and indexicality because these concepts are non-arbitrary and help us to put things back into the material world of causes, effects and resemblances. Thus things have a material dimension and significance which are far more than simply a matter of mind, cognition and communication (see Tilley, Chapter 4). Attempting to cope with these multidimensional sensuous and corporeal aspects of things and persons is very much at the forefront of a phenomenological approach.

A phenomenological perspective on both persons and material forms, and a broad semiotic perspective, form an essential component of many of the objectification perspectives on material forms discussed in Chapter 4. It is found most explicitly in the work of Bourdieu and Munn, both of whom emphasize the sensuous characteristics of human practice, and equally the sensuous characteristics and qualities of things. The theoretical perspectives considered here, developed in relation to material culture studies during the 1970s and 1980s as a response to perceived shortcomings in 'classical' Marxist, structuralist/semiotic and, to a certain extent, various heremeneutic (interpretative)/phenomenological positions within the wider social sciences. In various ways these theories attempt to combine key insights from these three traditions of thought while avoiding some of the principal pitfalls: economic and technicist reductionism in some versions of Marxism, timeless synchronism of a supposedly invariant human mind (in Lévi-Strauss's version of structuralism) and lack of consideration of power, exploitation and domination in much phenomenological thought.

Bourdieu's work on Kabyle society has heavily influenced a host of archaeological and anthropological material culture studies of relatively undifferentiated small-scale societies, while his studies of French society in his book *Distinction* (1984) and elsewhere have provided a springboard for numerous anthropological studies of contemporary consumption. The thrust of analysis shifts here from a traditional Marxist emphasis on processes of production and exchange to the manner in which practices of consumption are actively used to fashion personal and social identities through the differential uses, appropriation and meanings of things. But, for Bourdieu, consumption is far more than an appropriation of things. Things also shape people through their effects in relation to the reproduction of habitus in relation to class.

At a disciplinary level, in archaeology ideas drawn from Bourdieu's approach to objectification provided part of the impetus to the critique of, and the development of an alternative to, 'new', 'scientific' or 'post-processual' archaeology with its emphasis on laws, functional systems, social evolutionism and so on advocated during the 1960s and 1970s. Together with insights drawn from structural-Marxist, structuralist and semiotic approaches it heavily influenced a paradigm shift, within Anglo-American archaeology at least, during the 1980s to what became known as 'post-processual' or, somewhat later, during the 1990s, 'interpretative' archaeology. In the process prehistory, as a study of material forms, was rewritten. In anthropology, by contrast, a widespread rejection of functionalist, positivist and empiricist approaches had taken place long before as a result of the post-1960s influence of structuralist and symbolic approaches. Here Bourdieu's work was so influential because it provided a clear break with and critique of the dominance of atemporal structuralist and symbolic approaches based primarily on Lévi-Strauss's appropriation of structural linguistics to study society and material forms. Bourdieu argued that agency is mediated through practical embodied routinized activity in the world. He stresses in particular the contingent, improvised and provisional character of action in relation to 'structural' rules and principles resulting in habitual dispositions to behave in particular ways.

The significance of individuals, their agency and capacity to make a difference to the understanding of either culture in general, or material culture in particular, has characteristically been either dismissed altogether, or downplayed in both Marxist and structuralist accounts. Bourdieu's work, and in a rather different way Giddens's 'structuration' framework, provided a novel solution to the abiding problem of how to conceptualize the relationship between structure and action, society and the individual, drawing the individual back, as a significant element, into the frame of analysis. Persons and their doings are regarded as being both the medium and the outcome of, for Giddens, structural rules and principles 'generating' social action or 'habitus' (dispositional frameworks to act in a certain manner) for Bourdieu.

In relation to material culture studies the insight developed, discussed by Hoskins (Chapter 5), that the social lives of persons found its parallel in the social lives of things. Just as persons have biographies and life cycles, the same notion can be applied to things. The focus of study shifts to the interwining and entangled identities of persons and the things they make, exchange, use and consume. Things provide a powerful medium for materializing and objectifying the self, containing and preserving memories and embodying personal and social experiences. This perspective emphasizes the manner in which things have a fluid significance. Their meanings change through time and in relation to the manner in which they are circulated and exchanged and pass through different social contexts. Things labelled as commodities are not a single kind of thing (as opposed to a gift) but mark only a temporary moment in the contextualization and understanding of a thing.

The manner in which persons and things are to be understood in relation to each other depends crucially on the manner in which we conceptualize both these things – as commodities, gifts, resources, markers of identity, etc. – and the way in which we conceptualize human agency or subjectivity. If things become problematic in so far as their meaning is often shifting, ambiguous and contested, then it has to be appreciated that the same is true of the notion of agency. Agency has different meaning and import in different cultural contexts. One (modernist) view of agency regards agents as more or less discrete, if nevertheless socially constructed, centres of consciousness, action and being, each with its own individual biological human lives. However, agency need not simply be located at this personal level and may transcend the individual person and be located collectively in ceremonial performances, houses, death rituals and alliances, transcending individual lives and aspirations. Furthermore, individual personhood may be 'distributed' in relation to things, as Gell has argued (see Hoskins, Chapter 5).

If things may be held to possess their own biographies it is but a short step to consider these things as possessing their own agency and actively having *effects* in relation to persons: altering their consciousness, systems of values and actions. This is Gell's argument, discussed by Hoskins, that things are significant in relation not so much to what they *mean* in the world (the structuralist and semiotic position) as to what they *do*: the influence they exert on persons. Things intervene, they make a difference in the world, altering the minds of others. Thus the war shield created by a warrior will frighten the enemy, and the prowboard of the boat used in *kula* shell exchanges will dazzle the exchange partner and induce him to give up his shells. Above all, what this perspective stresses is not only the fluidity of the temporal meaning of things but that they intervene in the social world: they make a difference. Things do not just represent meanings or reflect, or 'ideologically' invert, persons, social relations or processes. They play animated roles in the formation of persons, institutions or cultures. How we think, and how we act, depend as much on the objects we surround ourselves with, and encounter, as on the languages we may use, or the intentions we may have. We find ourselves through the medium of the things: a basic and fundamental phenomenological standpoint in the consideration of subject-object relations (see the introduction to Part III).

The first five chapters of this part of the *Handbook* present particular, and to some extent competing, views with regard to the significance of material forms and the manner in which they may best be studied and understood. Thus we can adopt a broadly Marxist or semiotic approach or a phenomenological approach or produce some kind of variable synthesis of insights drawn from them as in objectification and biographical/agency approaches in any particular substantive study. We may feel comfortable with, or comforted by, the availability of such perspectives. By contrast, the poststructuralist perspectives discussed by Olsen in Chapter 6 provide no such clear guidance, and their impact is primarily unsettling and discomfiting. The primary concern here is to radically problematize our relationship with

the things themselves in academic study, to continually ask the questions 'What are we doing?' and 'Why are we doing it?'

One fundamental argument, in this respect, is that there is not, and can never be, one 'correct' or 'right' theoretical position which we may choose to study material forms or to exhaust their potential for informing us about the constitution of culture and society. The ways in which individual and social identities are realized and cognized, manifested or concealed, negotiated or imposed, reproduced or transformed, through the realm of things are peculiarly complex and embedded. Different theoretical positions inevitably emphasize alternative aspects of materiality and the significance of things for persons, groups, institutions and societies. Adopting any particular theory is like wearing tinted sunglasses. The world inevitably becomes coloured and variously illuminated, from a particular perspective dependent on a set of always questionable presuppositions with regard to the way that world is. Other aspects of that world are inevitably blurred or obscured and the imposition of one theoretical framework, such as Marxism, is ultimately totalitarian in its consequences. This is simply to recognize that whatever particular theoretical position we may adopt, or any synthesis between them that we may attempt to achieve, we cannot simultaneously and comprehensively explore all aspects of materiality, leaving nothing out. We cannot pin the world down in this manner and blissfully apply theories to 'data'.

Theories are like toolboxes. Depending on their contents, particular perspectives can only represent ('fix') aspects of the world from a particular and always limited perspective. They are always vehicles of power. Positively, they orientate us in a particular direction, showing us where to go and what to look for. Some may be on a larger scale, or more comprehensive, than others. Negatively, they blind, limit and constrain us. None is actually capable of reproducing 'reality' except in terms of abstractions and generalizations which may as often as not provide a poor guide as to how to actually carry out substantive empirical research. Thus theories are not just sets of discursive 'presences', i.e. particular sets of 'visible' concepts, variously articulated. They are also defined by their 'absences', that which they push to one side, fail to deal with, subsume or ignore.

However, it is quite clear that abandoning theory, rather than working with it, is a futile and naive response to the realization that no one position, or any present or future possible combination of them, could ever provide a comprehensive understanding of either materiality in general or particular sub-sets of material forms such as clothing, domestic architecture or 'art'. Our various theories of materiality and material culture may inevitably be rather rusty and blunt tools but without them any but the most 'innocent' and unreflective empirical research would be well nigh impossible.

Theory, from a post-structuralist perspective, is useful only in so far as it is continually being contextualized, worked through, altered and changed, in relation to particular empirical studies and problems. Rather than being applied from the top down in order to organize, discuss, describe and then interpret a particular set of data, the post-structuralist imperative is instead to set theory to 'work' from the bottom up and alter it and, in the process, our self-understanding of the world through the process of empirical research. It is also to understand that facts and values cannot be clearly separated, that the values and interests we hold will, in part, determine what we believe to be facts. Rather than believing that our studies enable us to arrive at certain truths with regard to the nature of material forms, we have a more limited aspiration: to make *sense* of them in a particular way, something which always has to be argued for, and can be argued against: a dialogic relationship. Post-structuralism requires us to be far more self-reflexive with regard to the personal and institutional conditions of academic research and the effects of representing things in particular ways: what does it mean to re-present objects in words? Is this not a domestication of their difference? How can we cope with the sensory and experiential domain of human experience in a text? Can images substitute for words? In what manner should we write: linear narratives, double texts? How do we cope with different perspectives, different voices, with multiple perspectives on materiality,

with the sheer ambiguity of material forms? Uncomfortable questions with no easy answers.

Most of the postcolonial theories discussed by van Dommelen (Chapter 7), and most particularly the work of Said, Spivak and Bhabba, are directly inspired by the more general post-structuralist positions discussed by Olsen in Chapter 6. The primary concern has been to analyse structures of materiality, power and discourse in relation to colonialism, which itself, of course, is intimately related to the birth of modern ethnographic studies of material culture. In a disciplinary sense we have moved full circle from the birth of the ethnographic collection and study of things under colonialism and many archaeological studies to the analysis of the nature and effects of this today. This leads us to further reflect on key issues with regard to issues of power, representation and authority in both written and material discourses. The materiality of colonialism as manifested in art and architecture, clothing and hygiene, settlement layout, representations of landscape, ideas about nature and culture, etc., form a rich and relatively little pursued domain for empirical study. As van Dommelen shows, such a perspective is not only relevant to understanding the 'hybridity' of notions of materiality and material culture in relation to the recent history of European colonialism but can also provide a valuable perspective for the interpretation of the much more distant past.

Post-structuralism goes hand in hand with the theoretical pluralism in relation to material culture studies manifested in the various contributions to this section of the *Handbook*. The field is not one but many. Theoretical pluralism is here to stay, something to celebrate, rather than being considered somehow inadequate, a failure or a dilemma to be resolved through a future synthesis grander than all the others. It is in this spirit that the various chapters in this part are written and presented.

Christopher Tilley

1

IN THE MATTER OF MARXISM

Bill Maurer

The real unity of the world consists in its materiality, and this is proved not only by a few juggled phrases, but by a long and wearisome development of philosophy and natural science.

(Engels, *Anti-Dühring*, 1877)

You make me feel mighty real.

(Sylvester, 1978)

WHAT'S THE MATTER WITH MARXISM?

It is difficult to think about materiality, or to think materially about the social, without thinking about Marxism. The Cold War led many scholars in the West to use 'materialism' as a code word for Marxism for much of the twentieth century. More recently, in certain quarters of social scientific thought, materiality stands in for the empirical or the real, as against abstract theory or discourse. Materiality is also invoked as causal and determinative, as moving things and ideas toward other states of being. Invoked in this sense, materiality, with a nod or more to Marxism, is sometimes offered as a corrective to the idea that concepts or ideas are autonomous and causal, or as an attack against presumed extravagances of 'postmodernism' or other forms of 'idealism'.

This review of Marxism and the problem of materiality is concerned with the supposed limits of critical reflection for dealing with actually existing materialities embodied in living, human agents as well as the sedimented histories and concrete objects that occupy the world. Historically, Marxist-oriented scholars have insisted on an account of actually existing 'men' in their real, material conditions of existence. Reactions against abstraction in theory more recently often explicitly or implicitly invoke the Marxist heritage as both a theoretical formation and an agenda for oppositional political practice. As Marx wrote in his eleventh thesis on Feuerbach, 'The philosophers have only interpreted the world, in various ways; the point is to change it.' Or, as a colleague once put it to me, 'Derrida never helped save a Guatemalan peasant.'

This chapter uses a narrow delineation of the field of Marxist-inspired debate and critique, emphasizing those anthropologists (and, to a lesser extent, archaeologists) who explicitly invoke Marxism in its various guises and who seek in Marxist theories a method and a theory for thinking materially about the social. The chapter pays particular attention to the instances when such authors attempt to think critically about what difference it makes to stress materiality and to think 'materially'. Such an exercise, however, while admittedly also bounded by the partiality imposed by the imperatives of the essay format, cannot escape replicating the antinomies of Marxist thought itself.

Perhaps the greatest of these is the tension between the dialectical method and historical materialism that inflected subsequent arguments about the nature and analytical standing of materiality. This tension derives from Marx's assertion of the practical and objective basis of humans' subjective consciousness, his inversion of Hegel's dialectic, and the reductionist tendencies that Marx shared with many nineteenth-century social and natural philosophers as diverse as Auguste Comte and Charles Darwin. In the nineteenth century various materialisms sprung up in reaction to, or were enlisted against, G.W.F. Hegel's idealist theory of history. For Hegel, the Absolute, the universal spirit, moved people to perceive the contradictions in the governing ideas of the age; through the dialectic between each idea and its opposite, men achieve new understandings and move human history ultimately to culminate in a Christian state. For Marx, material forces and relations of production moved people to realize the contradictions of their material existence, culminating in revolutionary transformation. Inverting Hegel – placing matter over thought in a determinative albeit dialectical position – opened the door to a solidification, as it were, of materiality itself as irreducibly real regardless of any human effort to conceptualize it; as autonomous; and as determinative, in the last instance, of everything else. Dialectics gave way to reductionist causality even as that causal argument gave Marx a means of seeing human ideas and human societies unfolding in history without relying on the Christian metaphysics implicit in Hegel's universal spirit.

Although writers on Marx have sometimes argued that his writings betray a dialectical phase ('the early Marx') and a historical materialist phase ('the late Marx', or, sometimes, 'the works written with Engels'), within *Capital* itself one finds evidence of the tension between dialectial and historical materialism. In distinguishing the labor of humans from that of animals, Marx emphasized humans' capacity for projective consciousness, humans' ability to plan a material world in advance of their own shaping of it:

> A spider conducts operations that resemble those of a weaver, and a bee puts to shame many an architect in the construction of her cells. But what distinguishes the worst architect from the best of bees is this, that the architect raises his structure in imagination before he erects it in reality.
>
> (1978: 174)

This passage nicely demonstrates the dialectic between human consciousness and practical activity that Marx borrowed from Hegel. It is not simply that people imagine things separately from the things themselves, but that their practical activity in turn shapes their consciousness. The worst architect projects his will into material constructions that then not only reflect that will but operate back upon it to shift it in another direction. Elsewhere in *Capital*, however, one reads that '[t]he ideal is nothing else than the material world reflected by the human mind' (1978: 27). Here, the architect's imagination is simply a reflection of his material reality, his material conditions of existence. There is no dialectical movement. So, where the dialectic between consciousness and practice distinguishes the worker from the bee, still the worker's ideational or subjective reality ultimately 'reflects' the material world in the last instance.

Marx laid the groundwork for both his dialectical method and his materialist theory of history in responding to Ludwig Feuerbach's rejection of Hegelian idealism. For Feuerbach, Hegel's theory of history as the unfolding of the absolute idea neglected sensuous and empirically perceptible reality in all its multifarious particularity, by positing that that reality was the expression of spirit, much as in Christianity Jesus is the material incarnation of divinity. Thus, according to Feuerbach, '[t]he Hegelian philosophy is the last magnificent attempt to restore Christianity, which was lost and wrecked, through philosophy' (Feuerbach 1966: 34).

Marx is often said to have married Feuerbach's materialism to Hegel's dialectic. Indeed, the *Theses on Feuerbach* bear out this claim. 'Feuerbach wants sensuous objects, really distinct from the thought objects, but he does not conceive human activity itself as *objective* activity' (Marx, *Theses on Feuerbach*). For Marx, in contrast, 'The question whether objective truth can be attributed to human thinking is not a question of theory but is a practical question.' Marx here criticized Feuerbach's materialism for its refusal to see human thought as a material process, a practical, dialectical engagement with the sensuous world.

The dialectic is difficult to sustain, however, given the imperatives of the new 'science' of Marxism in the nineteenth and twentieth centuries, and the social and humanistic fields that would try to adopt it. In a review essay on Marx and anthropology, William Roseberry (1997) spent considerable time worrying over the distinctions and relations among 'what men say or imagine, how they are narrated, and men in the flesh' (p. 29), taking his cue from the famous passage of *The German Ideology*:

> [W]e do not set out from what men say, imagine, conceive, nor from men as narrated, thought of, imagined, conceived, in order to arrive at men in the flesh. We set out from real, active men, and on the basis of their real life-processes we demonstrate the development of the ideological reflexes and echoes of this life-process.
>
> (Marx and Engels 1970: 47)

In order to resolve the ultimate epistemological status of these 'real men' *vis-à-vis* the conceptual schemes within which they operate (what they say, conceive, or what is said or imagined about them), Roseberry suggested a 'modest' reading of the text that would see these elements as 'constitut[ing] an indissoluble unity' (Roseberry 1997: 30), echoing the Engels of the *Anti-Dühring* as quoted in the first epigraph to this chapter. Roseberry also gestured toward the critical reflexivity that apprehension of this unity entails, since the analyst also occupies a position in an analogous unity, which of necessity emphasizes 'certain "real individuals" and not others, or certain "purely empirical" relationships and not others' (p. 30). Thinking about the indissoluble unity of real 'men' and their (and our) conceptual schemes gets to the heart of one of the problems of Marxist critique: the extent to which, as a strong reading of Marx would argue, Marxism is of necessity internal to its object, the capitalist society of Marx's day (Postone 1993). This, in turn, gets to the heart of the problem of the application of Marxist theory in anthropological analyses of materiality in other social formations. This is the problem faced by most of the writers whose work is reviewed in this chapter as they attempted to fit Marxist concepts to the empirical relationships of actually existing people – 'real men' (and women) – and the material world of non- or pre-capitalist contexts.

We are faced, then, with two distinct problems. The first is the unresolved tension between Marx's use of the dialectic and his materialist reductionism. The second is the applicability of Marxist concepts outside of the world for which they were imagined – or outside of the world that compelled the mind of Marx to reflect the material conditions and contradictions of capitalism in his dialectical and historical materialisms. I argue in this chapter that these two problems wended their way through anthropological and other social scientific accounts of materiality in such as way as to bring a series of otherwise independent oppositions into alignment. The first is the opposition between the ideal and the material, where the former is taken to reference the subjective world 'inside' consciousness and the latter the objective world 'outside' consciousness. The second is the opposition between theoretical discourse or abstraction and what we might call 'plain speech'. Where the former reflects on found materialities to seek potentially hidden or latent content, the latter claims to reflect them 'directly' in language, and purports to reduce or even eliminate the gap between

mind and thing. The final opposition is that between realism and empiricism. This may not at first be self-evident, but I use these terms in the particular sense developed by philosophers of science. Realism strives for knowledge independent of any theory or any sensory act, and discounts the perceptible as the only or the privileged route to the truth. Empiricism discounts anything not perceptible to the senses or beyond the range of the human sensorum. Realism posits an observer-independent world, and its Platonic presuppositions – that universal forms or laws exist autonomously from human history or consciousness – permit a kind of theoretical abstraction disallowed by strict empiricism, which depends on the immediately perceptible. (One could thus equate realism with positivism, the doctrine of universal, generalizable laws separate from any subjective human understanding or encounter with the world.)

The aligning of the ideal, the theoretical, and the real, on the one hand, and the material, plain speech and empiricism, on the other, was a contingent articulation of a kind of social scientific 'common sense'. It did not occur seamlessly or without contradiction (or confusion). In looking chronologically at materialist theories of society in anthropology and archaeology, this chapter charts the shifts among these concepts and their generative potential for thinking materially about the social in spite of their inherent instability. The quest for a science that would explain causal relations among material and social variables looms large in my story. Such a quest for causality occupied Marx, as well, and helps explain his deep interest in the work of natural and social evolutionists like Charles Darwin and Lewis Henry Morgan.

How did Marxism's convergence with other materialisms of the nineteenth and twentieth centuries encourage the denunciation of abstraction in favor of plain speech, that is, in favor of a critical metalanguage that denies its status as such by purporting to reveal the deeper reality, the 'real men', and their histories behind the veils of ideological abstraction of which 'theory' is a component?

If I overdraw the terms, it is because anthropological debates over materiality and history have done so, as well. Consider, for example, two responses to the work of Jean and John Comaroff. In their work on the historical anthropology of southern Africa, the Comaroffs have attempted to correlate shifts in consciousness with shifts in material culture, daily practices, and routines. For example, they show how mission school architecture encouraged certain kinds of movement that in turn shaped people's self-understandings. Critics have taken them to task on the causal assumptions of their argument and on the level of speculation necessary for them to make such arguments. Sally Falk Moore, for example, worries that their 'imaginative sociologies' run too far ahead of actual 'cases' – empirically observable instances – to support any claims of 'causality' (Moore 1999: 304). Donald Donham argues that the Comaroffs employ 'a *post hoc* rhetoric' of cultural difference to the detriment of the analysis of 'actual events' and Tswana agents' own narratives (Donham 2001: 144). The Comaroffs reply, to both critics, that they seek a methodology that is 'empirical without being narrowly empiricist' (Comaroff and Comaroff 1999: 307). By this, they mean to capture sensuous material realities without imputing to them the kind of autonomy or causal determination that some materialisms presuppose. They write that they sought, in *Of Revelation and Revolution* (1991, 1997) to:

> underscore the need to transcend a procrustean opposition: to separate ourselves, on the one hand, from postmodern theoreticism and, on the other, from those more conventional colonial historians who have sought to avoid theory via the empiricist strategy of finding order in events by putting events in order.
>
> (Comaroff and Comaroff 2001: 159)

It seems that the unity of which both Marx and Engels wrote has difficulty maintaining its integrity, that it is continually unbundling itself into the neat dichotomies of the material and the ideal, the empirical and the real, the directly apprehensible and the theoretical. Marxist-inspired theories tend to equate each pole of these oppositions with one another despite the friction this might cause for causal or dialectical forms of argumentation. Hence, it has become routine in anthropology and elsewhere to stress, when dealing with materiality, that one is neither valorizing nor rejecting outright the empirical; that one is appreciative of the discursive constitution of the material even as one is attentive to the 'significance intrinsic to material life' (Farquhar 2002: 8); that one is steering between the rocks of high theory and the shoals of naive empiricism.

Whence the conflation between the empirical and the material, and all those categories that can stand in for those concepts, such as history, the body, people's 'actual lives', objects, geographies, nature, and so forth? As Roseberry and others have noted, there is a tension in Marxism between the historical and

the formal analysis of capitalism. The former tends to rely on empirically observable evidence for the postulation of a *telos* to world historical development; the latter tends to model underlying causal relationships at the expense of the empirically observable. So, for example, those Marxisms (like structural Marxism, discussed below) that attempted to discover the motor driving a particular social formation did not have to rely on empirical evidence but could still claim realism; those that were steered by empirical data could reject the abstractions of structural Marxism as part of the ideological obfuscation of capitalism. Indeed, the history of Marxist anthropology in the twentieth century has seen this opposition play itself out, between the evolutionary and cultural materialist approaches that made a strong claim to empirical verifiability and to the status of science, on the one hand, and the various approaches tracing a lineage to Louis Althusser that worried less about verifiability than logical consistency and another sort of claim to the status of science, on the other. Post-Althusserians (and I would include here followers of Pierre Bourdieu and Michel Foucault) face the charge of abstraction from the inheritors of the more reductionist cultural materialist approaches (even if those heirs do not always recognize themselves as such; although few may cite Marvin Harris in the early 2000s, there is a sense in which his cultural materialism, discussed below, has been naturalized as common currency for many anthropologists, especially for lay audiences, or before undergraduates). And the latter, realist Marxisms, can surprise when they pair up with empiricist Marxisms in arguments over whether anthropology is a 'science' and the supposed bourgeois romanticism and aestheticism of 'postmodern' discourse.

A specter is haunting anthropologies of materiality; the specter of empiricism. It should be clear by now that mine is an interested review that has an exorcism in mind. It is borne of analytical frustration with the tools available for thinking materially about social formations, a frustration that also has to do with the way 'data', 'the facts', and 'materiality' are first conflated and then asked to speak for themselves in readily-accessible causal languages that as a matter of course reject the need for any 'theory'; the way that evolutionary and cultural materialist Marxism has been deployed as just such a language; and the way that structural Marxisms sometimes play along by eliding their realism with empiricism. Approaching the problem of materiality through the specter of empiricism haunting anthropology places anthropological knowledge production at the center of the discussion, as it calls into questions the material on which anthropology makes its analytical claims as well as the very opposition between the material and the theoretical.

In what follows, I review four moments in the history of anthropological and archaeological engagement with Marxism on the question of materiality. The story begins with Engels and the consolidation of historical materialism in the various theories that posited distinct social forms occupying specific evolutionary stages. After a brief detour through the Manchester school, which had more affinities with the dialectical method than contemporaneous evolutionisms (especially those on the other side of the Atlantic), I consider the French structural Marxists. The structural Marxists eschewed some of the more reductionist aspects of evolutionary theory and worried less about evolutionary stages than the causal relationships among structural components of a society: the economic base, including the material conditions and relations of subsistence; the ideological superstructure, including all the stuff of 'culture' as it has been defined by other anthropologists; and the structures mediating the two, especially kinship. Next, I explore Marxisms of the 1970s and 1980s that reformulated mid-century evolutionisms in terms of world histories and world systems. Such Marxisms increased anthropologists' attention to commodities' circulation and the spatial formations such circulations engendered. Finally, I consider work done in the 1990s and the early 2000s that attempts to tackle globalization and transnationalism and that is working in the tracks of critiques of Marxist and other grand narratives. Some of this work relies on heirs of Althusser, such as Bourdieu and Foucault. Some of it is beginning to unpack the oppositions between abstract and concrete, real and empirical, theory and practice by drawing attention to how the poles of these oppositions continually merge into one another in the coproduction of subjects and objects.

What's the matter in Marxism? Can there be a Marxist anthropology of materiality that obviates the antinomies between the concrete and the abstract, empiricism and realism, world and word? Can there be a Marxist approach to materiality that recuperates the dialectic without falling into idealism and without replicating the teleology and temporality of historical materialism? I return to this question in the conclusion.

ENGELS, EVOLUTION AND ENERGY

Engels can be credited with the elevation of historical materialism to the status of science after Marx's death. Using the ethnological data that were beginning to filter into Europe from explorers, missionaries, and others around the world, Engels posited discrete stages in the evolution of social formations. 'Men can be distinguished from animals by consciousness, by religion or anything else you like. They themselves begin to distinguish themselves from animals as soon as they begin to produce their means of subsistence' (Marx and Engels 1970: 42). In acting on nature to procure their subsistence, people at the same time change their own natures, and so make history (see O'Laughlin 1975: 346). The dialectical relationship between human consciousness and nature is such that consciousness as such must always be understood materially, as praxis, not just contemplation. As I have indicated above, Marx made this clear in his attack on Feuerbach's materialism. Contemplation, then, thought itself, 'therefore part of the material world and governed by the same law of dialectical movement that characterizes nature' (O'Laughlin 1975: 343).

The standard account of Marx's materialism is that changing relationships with nature determine the shifts in consciousness that define the stages of social evolution. Yet the theoretical impulse toward evolutionism itself then places those changing relations with nature in a position of ontological priority despite Marx's unity of thought and matter. Hence Engels's deterministic account of human evolutionary change in *The Origin of the Family, Private Property and the State* (1884/1972). In it, Engels appropriated Lewis Henry Morgan's (1877/1963) *Ancient Society* because it so readily suggested a correlation between different forms of the organization of subsistence and different forms of the organization of family. The suture between Engels and Morgan is near pefect, more so than in Marx's own writings; indeed, the first word of Engels's book is 'Morgan', and the name appears in the first sentence of each of the first three chapters. Where, in *The German Ideology*, Marx and Engels were able to posit 'various stages of development in the division of labor' (Marx and Engels 1970: 43), now, with Morgan's data, Engels could more precisely chart those various stages, and provide an evolutionary account for the appearance of private property. And Morgan's text was perfectly amenable to this task. As Morgan wrote, and Engels quoted, 'the great epochs of human progress have been identified, more or less directly, with the enlargement of the sources of subsistence' (Morgan 1963: 19). More or less directly, then, Engels outlines the history of this enlargement: from 'man' as a 'tree-dweller' living on 'fruits, nuts and roots', to 'the utilization of fish for food … and … the use of fire', to 'the invention of the bow and arrow', to 'the introduction of pottery', to 'the domestication of animals', to 'the smelting of iron ore' (Engels 1972: 87–92); we have here a history of social formation in terms of material appropriations from nature using new technologies developed in tandem with nature and with the dialectical evolution of human consciousness.

The emphasis on food can be found in Bronislaw Malinowski's materialism (see Kuper 1996: 29), as, for Malinowski, all of society and culture ultimately boiled down to satisfying one's basic human needs (having sex and filling one's belly, according to Malinowski). The emphasis on material culture can be found in Franz Boas's corpus; despite his reluctance toward Marxism, Boas found the material record of signal importance in demonstrating that Native Americans had histories marked by change and development and in providing the new science of anthropology an untapped field to collect, record, and document. This emphasis on material culture was an archaeologist's dream. In the early twentieth century, V. Gordon Childe (1936) could posit a theory of universal evolution in terms of archaeological data that neatly fit into the framework of historical materialism. 'Progressive changes' in social evolutionary time 'came from the base' (Trigger 1981/1984: 72). Using archaeological data on subsistence, tools, trade, and house construction, Childe could test Marxist theory and refine it (by supplementing evolutionary theory with diffusionist theories from other quarters in anthropology, for example). The result was a research strategy that took particular kinds of data – amenable both to archaeological discovery and collection and to incorporation in the Marxist evolutionary framework – and deduced from them specific social arrangements.

Childe's research strategy brought the problem of causality into relief, as it made an explicit scientific program of material determination. The professionalization of the discipline and its practitioners' quest to have it accorded the status of a 'science' permitted the complete obviation of Marx's dialectics in favor of strictly reductive material determination. Leslie White, for example, reintroduced

nineteenth-century evolutionary concepts and a focus on technology to mid-century American anthropology. Placing the emphasis on the acquisition of subsistence, White argued that human culture evolves as the amount of energy harnessed from nature in the form of plants, animals, and other material objects increases. The science of culture should seek data that might verify this formula. Hence, the emphasis on technological aspects of culture – the tools used to procure energy from the environment. As for cultural conceptions, myths, ideas: 'there is a type of philosophy proper to every type of technology' (White 1949: 366). Julian Steward's (1955) counterpoint to White was that universal evolution could not explain either variation or parallel emergence of similar traits in widely geographically separated societies. For Steward's multilinear evolution, then, human relationships with their specific environments produce specific cultures. The kinds of data necessary for the analysis were similar to those required by White, but also included environmental variables. Marshall Sahlins and Elman Service (1960) brought the two theories together in their delineation of 'general' and 'specific' evolution, the former the grand story of the evolution of Culture, the latter the smaller stories of the evolution of cultures. Various cultural ecological approaches (e.g., Rappaport 1968, Vayda 1969) extended and refined the framework, sometimes displacing its evolutionary pretensions altogether, and sometimes vociferously discounting any concern that the directions of causation might be multiple, as with Marvin Harris's (1979) cultural materialism. Imported into archaeology via the 'New Archaeology' of the 1960s and 1970s, such perspectives, as Bruce Trigger (himself an exponent of Childe) writes, helped maximize 'the explanatory potential of archaeological data' (Trigger 1978: x).

Regardless, then, and despite the lengthy debates among them, in each of these Marxist-inflected materialisms there was a clear distinction between data gathering and theory building, one that replicated the causality presumed in Engels's materialist historiography from tools and food to families and philosophies. These mid-century evolutionisms were exercises in hypothesis building and hypothesis testing with the positivist aim of building generalizable laws. Still, despite the deductive orientation – or precisely because of its positivist inclinations – it was taken as a matter of course that one could simply see, collect, and measure the data, since the data were material facts that did not require any theory for their apprehension. The materialist theory of the social was not a theory of materiality. Instead, it was an effort to ground anthropology and archaeology in certain empirical facts amenable to the scientific method; and to proceed deductively even as one leaped inductively from material objects or measurable forces like energy to grand theories of the evolution of society.

DEEP AND DEEPER STRUCTURES

If Marx's totality got unbundled in cultural materialist evolutionisms of the mid-twentieth century, it was reified in the contemporaneous Manchester school. Although it left questions of ultimate determination aside, Max Gluckman's (1955) theory of functional conflict bore more than a passing resemblance to the dialectical method. Peter Worsley's (1956) Marxist reanalysis of the Tallensi studied by Meyer Fortes (1945) placed signal importance on rights to arable land, a scarce commodity that Worsley revealed to be the basis of elder men's authority. Attention to the material conditions of production allowed Worsley to illuminate the lineage system. In its implicit apprehension of a socio-material totality, Worsley's re-evaluation of the Tallensi resembled and prefigured the structural Marxists of the 1960s and 1970s. If mid-century Marxisms in anglophone anthropology remained resolutely if sometimes vulgarly materialist (as Friedman (1974) claimed of Harris, because of the latter's insistence on a direct causal relationship between the determining base and the epiphenomenal superstructure), those developed in France strove for a realism that sometimes left the empirical to one side. The influence of Louis Althusser cannot be overstated. Turning to Marx's writings on ideology as opposed to his statements on evolution, and by way of the psychoanalytic theory of Jacques Lacan, Althusser (1971, 1977) moved the discussion of ideology beyond its role in covering over the really real (i.e., subject to universal laws, if not empirically observable) economic base, and as dialectically constitutive of subjects, productive forces and relations of production themselves. Like Lacan, Althusser argued that ideology was less like a dream (a 'purely imaginary, i.e. null, result of the "day's residues"', 1977: 108) and more like a language that structured access to an always-just-out-of-reach reality. Ideology is also always performative: Althusser referred back to Pascal on how belief for the Christian

does not pre-exist the act of prayer but is rather its effect (p. 114).

Take, for example, Maurice Godelier, on the Inca:

> religious ideology is not merely the superficial, phantasmic reflection of social relations. It is an element internal to the social relations of production; it functions as one of the internal components of the politico-economic relation of exploitation between the peasantry and an aristocracy holding State power. This belief in the Inca's supernatural abilities ... was not merely a legitimizing ideology, after the fact, for the relations of production; it was part of the internal armature of these relations of production.
>
> (Godelier 1977: 10)

Godelier, and the other so-called structural Marxists, folded superstructure into the base and laid the groundwork for a critique of ideology in 'primitive' and ancient societies not simply reducible to the unmasking of a ground or base of empirically observable relations and forces of production. Widely influential in sociocultural anthropology and imported into some quarters of archaeology (Friedman and Rowlands 1977; Miller and Tilley 1984), the structural Marxists represent a different relation to Marx's corpus than that of, say, Leslie White and others whose reception was more directly via Engels. Something deeper than surface appearance is sought, but not necessarily in the spirit of unmasking. For our imbrication in our own social formation ever removes the really real – here, the supposedly autonomous material world separate from our empirical perception of it – from our grasp. 'All science would be superfluous if the outward appearance and the essence of things directly coincided' (Marx, quoted in Spriggs 1984: 3). Indeed, this structuralist element places naive empiricism to one side, but at the expense, perhaps, of reinvigorating the material/ideal dichotomy, an aspect of Althusserian Marxism that vexed archaeologists (see Rowlands 1984: 109).

Another aspect of Althusser that proved problematic to archaeology was its ascription of the institutions of the state, and the accretions of state power in material objects, to a society's powerful members – the so-called dominant ideology thesis – permitting 'only the powerful to make statements with artifacts' (Beaudry et al. 1991: 156). Although it led to a new focus on elites and material culture, ideological analysis in archaeology tended to assume rather than explain how certain categories of objects came to signify prestige (see Robb 1998: 333–4). Here, artifacts were taken as 'symbolic' unless they were clearly functional, and 'ideological power' came to be seen as 'an elite tactic' analogous to other more straightforward forms of elite power (*ibid.*). Thus, Elizabeth Brumfiel (1995) criticized Mary Helms's (1993) interpretation of skilled crafts and long-distance trade items as linked to political leadership for being insufficiently attentive to the situated negotiations and relationships of prestige and power. Still, Brumfiel notes the importance of Helms's insight that style horizons can be used to demonstrate the connection between skilled crafts and the development of symbolic systems that diffuse over space and time. The question is whether to see style horizons as simply evidence for the geographic and temporal extension of power, or, possibly, the symbolic inversion of power relationships and the formation of new kinds of resistance (see, e.g., Brumfiel 1992, 1996). Thus, despite some limitations, the structural Marxist orientation provided new ideas for the analysis of material culture, more notably in archaeology than sociocultural anthropology, I think, drawing from the humanist Marxist toolkit of concepts such as hegemony, dominance and ideology (Rowlands and Kristiansen 1998).

In sociocultural anthropology, structural Marxism had an impact in rethinking the structural and material position of kinship in the forces and relations of production. Works by Claude Meillassoux (1972) and Pierre Philippe Rey (1971) explored how non-productive elder elites extract surplus labor in lineage systems. Meillassoux argued that senior men seek control over the means of reproduction – women. Women here were reduced to their bare, or, one should say fertile, materiality, and not treated as social subjects (see Harris and Young 1981); indeed, one could argue that Meillassoux treated land in those societies where land is the subject of labor (as opposed to its instrument) as having more of the qualities of subjecthood than women. Ian Hodder (1984) was able to read Meillassoux into the archaeological record by comparing Neolithic central and western European megaliths with central European longhouses. Hodder argued that the tombs represented a symbolic and material transformation of the longhouses that took place as the productive base of societies shifted. When labor was more determinative than land, emphasis was on the domestic and the naturalization of women's reproductive abilities; 'material culture [was] used to form a world in which women [were] to be emphasized, celebrated but controlled' (Hodder 1984: 66). As

land became more determinative, emphasis shifted to control over the ideological meaning and perpetuation of the lineage and the mediation of supernatural powers expressed by megaliths; women's importance declined and the megalithic burial takes the symbolic and ideological place of the longhouse (*ibid.*).

Meillassoux, like Rey (1971) and Terray (1972), was also interested in the relations among different modes of production coexisting in a society; Althusser's acceptance of overdetermination or multiple determination aided this analysis, although it left it open to the charge of muddying the distinction between base, superstructure, and the totality a more orthodox Marxist would insist obtains between them. The concept of overdetermination was first used by Sigmund Freud in rejecting simple material reductionisms to explain phenomena like hysteria in favor of the idea that observable symptoms might have multiple, interacting causes. For Althusser, overdetermination meant that the contradictions in a social formation were not strictly speaking always reducible to the economic base. Needless to say, some Marxists did not take to the structural Marxists' seeming rejection of the base-structure-superstructure model of society. Thus, Bridget O'Laughlin on Terray: 'There is a confusion here of concepts and concrete reality,' the latter, the base, which of necessity 'can be realized within a social totality' such that 'every mode of production describes not only a base but corresponding forms of superstructure' (O'Laughlin 1975: 358).

WORLD HISTORY, NEO-SMITHIAN MARXISM AND THE COMMODITY

The idea that more than one mode of production might exist within a society, theorized in the work of the structural Marxists, informed analyses of colonialism that began to shape the discipline of anthropology in the 1970s and into the 1980s. Maurice Bloch's (1983) survey of Marxism and anthropology made use of the concept of the 'social formation' to describe such situations. Talal Asad's (1972) critique of Frederik Barth's (1959) ethnography of Swat Pathans attempted to excise the economistic, functionalist and bourgeois assumptions of British functionalism by introducing the same concerns over land and labor highlighted by the structural Marxists, as well as introducing the problem of history as the sediment or residue of past material relations. Asad argued that Barth had overlooked the history of British colonialism, its impact on land tenure, and its indirect enrichment of certain elite landholders because of Barth's implicit adherence to what Asad called a 'market model' of society. This Asad explained with reference to the Enlightenment thinker Thomas Hobbes, who argued that men in the state of nature competed with one another over scarce resources and that, without the firm hand of a sovereign, life was nasty, brutish, and short. While Hobbes may have accurately described the competitive market society emerging in his own day, Asad argued, he also conveniently naturalized the individualist and competitive nature of capitalism, which Barth then inadvertently imported into his account of Swat.

Indeed, with the work of Sidney Mintz and Eric Wolf, students of Julian Steward, the 'concrete reality' that occupied O'Laughlin took on a decidedly historical cast, and history, historical process, or historical transformation provided a necessary supplement to materiality. Rather than simply looking for material culture, the economic base, or what have you, and using them in causal arguments about the formation of societies, Mintz and Wolf paid attention to historical processes that brought new material formations into existence and made old ones obsolete. Wolf's (1982) 'kin-ordered' and 'tributary' modes of production emphasized the flow of material goods within lineages and tribute-based political economic orders, respectively, and enabled a retelling of the histories of traditional anthropological subjects in terms of a grand narrative of the development of extractive colonialism, industrial capitalism, and the making of peasants and proletarians that did not suffer from the Eurocentrism of world-systems theory. Mintz's *Sweetness and Power* (1985) traced the intertwined emergence of peasant, proletarian, and bourgeois through the history of a particular commodity, sugar, richly describing it in all its material and symbolic dimensions as it moved in the circuits of trade and the culinary table. Mintz is interested in the materiality of sugar itself, demonstrating how sweetness as a sensory experience shifts its modality such that it becomes associated with *sugar* to the exclusion of other sweet-tasting substances. As a history of the sense of taste, and ultimately of 'taste' itself as a mark of 'civilization,' Mintz's study links an emerging commodity not only to histories of slave labor and nascent forms of industrialized production but also to a generalized culture of taste that associated sweetness with sugar and sugar with essential markers of Britishness like tea drinking. Tea also remade time; the new daily ritual was itself the material instantiation of new regimes of work discipline and abstract, universal time.

Sahlins (1976) would berate the Marxists for elevating 'practical reason' to the status of the transcendent real and being ultimately bourgeois utilitarians. Sahlins argued that ideas are autonomous of any prior causes that could be found in a separate 'material' domain and that ideas themselves have material consequences. In a different vein, Taussig (1989) attacked the work of Mintz and Wolf for making of history a fetish, and creating for anthropology 'a mode of representation which denies the act of representing' (1989: 11). In Mintz and Wolf's histories, Taussig wrote, quoting Barthes, 'everything happens ... as if the discourse or the linguistic existence was merely a pure and simple "copy" of another existence, situated in an extra-structural field, the "real"' (*ibid.*). Mintz and Wolf, for their part, read Taussig's critique as preoccupied with 'subjectivity and reflexivity' (1989: 25), rejected the implicit charge that they are 'positivist, naturalizing devils' (*ibid.*), and attacked Taussig's 'nihilism' (p. 29). Defending their work as providing histories of how 'particular things became commodities' (*ibid.*), however, they opened themselves up to the further charge, levied against Wallersteinian world-systems analysis, of what Robert Brenner (1977) had called 'neo-Smithian Marxism'. Brenner argued that the work of Wallerstein and his acolytes was Marxist in name only, as it elevated the circulation and exchange, rather than the production, of commodities as explanatory of social, political and cultural formations.

Such criticisms would also dog new attention to commodities as things and commodification as a process. The idea that things had a 'social history' or 'cultural biographies' smacked of commodity fetishism even as it was offered by Arjun Appadurai (1986) and others as a means of softening the gift/commodity distinction and refusing the progressivist teleology implied in many discussions of the commodity form up to that point. The conceptual separation of gift economies from commodity economies in anthropological theory took attention away from those moments in non-capitalist societies when a thing's exchangeability became its most 'socially relevant feature' (Appadurai 1986: 13). Looking at things this way introduced a temporal dimension to the study of material objects, their 'life course', as it were, the ways they can move into and out of relations of exchange and formations of value (see Hoskins, Chapter 5).

The commodity is thus 'not one kind of thing rather than another, but one phase in the life of some things' (p. 17). The commodity form is thus, for Appadurai, only contingently materialized in objects. This realization allowed Appadurai and others analytically to separate commodification from reification, and to open up the possibility of reification – the making-material of a thing – without commodification.

Renewed attention to the commodity form as a contingent stage in the life of a thing, together with attempts to escape Marx's use value/exchange value dichotomy, helped invigorate the field of material culture studies. With a dose of Bourdieu's or Giddens's theories of practice, anthropologists, archaeologists (e.g., Rowlands and Kristiansen 1998) and others were initiating a discussion about the coproduction of subjects and objects in specific and mobile social formations (see Miller 1998, 2001). In archaeology, for example, some older interpretations of Paleolithic European cave art assumed the paintings to be human attempts to represent their relationship with nature, symbolically to mediate it. More recent interpretations reject the firm delineation between symbolic and material/technological systems this implies. As Margaret Conkey summarizes, in this approach 'material culture is produced ... not just to use or not even just to "mean." Rather, technology is viewed *as* ideology, production *as* meaning' (Conkey 1987: 424). Similarly, Christopher Tilley writes, 'Material culture may be physically embedded but it is at the same time culturally emergent ... [T]here can be no simple or formal demarcation between what is internal to, or is in, and that which is external to, or outside, the object' (Tilley 1993: 5). Work on the coproduction of subjects and objects through material symbolic practices bridges the intellectual and institutional divides between anthropology, archaeology, material culture studies, design, architecture, fashion theory, and geography, and contributes to discussions about global and transnational material/social fields.

SPECTERS OF MARX

It is just such discussions about globalization and transnationalism that have brought the commodity form and its materialization in objects and in persons to the forefront of contemporary anthropologies of capitalism. Rejecting earlier developmentalist frameworks, figures like James Ferguson (1999), Lisa

Rofel (1999), Katherine Verdery (1996, 2003), Anna Tsing (2000), and Akhil Gupta (1998) challenge the modernist aesthetic and analytic of both development discourse and anthropology, and make a case for a richer understanding of the many forms of contemporary capitalisms, post-socialisms, as well as the non-capitalist social formations operating within or alongside dominant ones (Gibson-Graham 1995). Although materiality is rarely foregrounded as such in these works, attention to the built environment, the manner in which architecture and planning interface with and make material ideologies of dominance and rule (e.g., Bourdieu 1977 on the Kabyle house; Caldeira 2000; Holston 1989; Pemberton 1994), and practices of embodiment, dress, and habit (Bourdieu 1977) characterize this kind of work. It is best exemplified, perhaps, in the Comaroffs' corpus cited at the outset of this chapter.

What in an earlier moment would have been separated out as 'political economic' versus 'historical' approaches now cohabit – indeed, intermingle – to the extent that the one is not dissociable from the other. Ara Wilson's work on the 'intimacies of capitalism' through the global commodities of Avon stitches together the world of consumer goods with what she calls 'folk' economies and 'market' economies deeply in the bodies and desires of Thai women (2004: 193). Alan Klima (2002) and Rosalind Morris (2000) attend to money, materiality, magic, and mediumship in exploring other modalities of fetishism via, or sometimes askance, its theorization in Marxist thought. In this, their work resonates with a tradition of scholarship in anthropology on exchange and money (Parry and Bloch 1989), gift and commodity (Gregory 1982) property (for a recent collection, see Verdery and Humphrey 2004), and consumption (e.g., Foster 2002).

If attention to material forms, forces, or objects seems to slip away in such works, however, it is because Marxist legacies, realist pretensions, and empiricist ghosts still haunt such endeavors, because we have not, 'even now, escaped the ontological division of the world into "spirit" and "matter"' (Keane 2003: 409). Archaeologist Elizabeth Brumfiel (2003) can claim that 'it's a material world' by emphasizing artifacts and excavations but without questioning either the separation of spirit and matter that allows her to 'abstract signs from the soil' (Masri 2004) or the linguistic ideology that understands words unproblematically to refer to things in the world. The movement from object to knowledge proceeds as if the object pre-exists its enlistment – an assumption warranting both realism and empiricism and allowing them to blur into one another – and as if its enlistment in language is a straightforward referential affair. Attempts to revivify Marxism often resituate a materialist analysis of social formations and reanimate its old reductionisms and dichotomies: the causal determination afforded the economic base or the forces of production; the dichotomy between material and ideal, practice and theory. The material/ideal impasse mirrors the structure/agency problems of an earlier era. Writings densely attentive to materiality, the pressing back of the material on the ideal or the coconstitution of objects and subjects (and objects as subjects and vice versa) nonetheless neatly replicate the magic of willful and moving commodities and the reduction of 'real, active men' to their labor power.

Alongside such work is an emergent attention to abstraction, ephemerality, virtuality, and the apparent dematerialization of political economic forms. Authors speculate on the increasing detachment between money and 'real' commodities or labor power, the virtualization of money and finance, and the fantasy work that seemingly animates contemporary capitalisms after the end of the gold standard and the Bretton Woods agreements. There is no unity on how best to approach such phenomena or what their implications might be, but there have been a number of forays into these fields (e.g., Miyazaki 2003; Tsing 2000; Maurer 2004; LiPuma and Lee 2004; Miller 1998). Miller (1998) makes explicit the relation between the apparent abstraction of the economy, the work of abstraction of capital hypothesized in Marx, and analytical abstraction as an intellectual enterprise. Those seeking a new Marxism for a new set of problems presented by dematerialized property offer grand theory less attentive to materiality and more concerned with the effectivity of political argument and action in the academy and beyond in a world where there are seemingly no alternatives to capitalism (e.g., Jameson 2002; Hardt and Negri 2000). Derrida's (1994) extensive consideration of capitalist time and the time of Marx's *Capital* stands as a signal contribution to the contemporary rethinking of ideological abstraction and commodity fetishism.

Marx illustrated the concept of commodity fetishism with the example of a table, and referenced the nineteenth-century craze for mystical parlor games in which objects apparently move without any human intervention:

> The form of wood, for instance, is altered, by making a table out of it. Yet, for all that, the table

continues to be that common, everyday thing, wood. But, so soon as it steps forth as a commodity, it is changed into something transcendent. It not only stands with its feet on the ground, but, in relation to all other commodities, it stands on its head, and evolves out of its wooden brain grotesque ideas, far more wonderful than 'table-turning' ever was.

> (Marx 1978: 71)

Lingering over Marx's image of the turning table at the opening of *Capital*, Derrida writes:

> The capital contradiction does not have to do simply with the incredible conjunction of the sensuous and the supersensible in the same Thing; it is the contradiction of *automatic autonomy*, mechanical freedom, technical life. Like every thing, from the moment it comes onto the stage of a market, the table resembles a prosthesis of itself. Autonomy *and* automatism, *but* automatism of this wooden table that spontaneously puts itself into motion, to be sure, and seems thus to animate, animalize, spiritualize, *spiritize* itself, but while remaining an artifactual body, a sort of automaton, a puppet, a stiff and mechanical doll whose dance obeys the technical rigidity of a program. Two genres, two generations of movement intersect with each other in it, and that is why it figures the apparition of a spectre.

> (1994: 153)

The living, moving commodity haunts the thing's use value (p. 151) and renders it 'not sensuous *and* non-sensuous, or sensuous *but* non-sensuous; [Marx] says: sensuous non-sensuous, sensuously super-sensible' (*ibid*.). Derrida thus finds in Marx a different kind of unity of matter and thought than posited by Engels in the first epigraph to this chapter. Engels's unity was ultimately the subordination of thought into matter. In Derrida's reading of Marx, the relation between matter and thought is not dialectical – as thesis/antithesis or contradictory poles whose tension and resolution create a new conjuncture no longer legible as 'matter' and 'thought' – but spectral. A specter is a shadow from another time, whose time has gone, but yet manifests itself in *this* time. It is *out of synch* with the rest of today's time-space, not in opposition to it, not contradicting it, just not quite fully in or out of it. 'Two genres, two generations of movement intersect' in the ghost, as in the commodity-table.

Despite their apparent self-evidence, then, matter and thought, thing and person, are continually infolding and intertwining, a dense web that momentarily and for particular purposes congeals subjects and objects with elements of willfulness or agentive power. This is essentially Bruno Latour's (1993) position on the ontological status of non-human agents in *We have Never been Modern*. But to continue with Derrida: 'The wood comes alive and is peopled with spirits: credulity, occultism, obscurantism, lack of maturity before Enlightenment, childish or primitive humanity': believing commodities to take on value in relation to other commodities, believing commodities to move of their own accord or to reach out to us and pique our desire, we demonstrate childish credulity in spite of our better Enlightened selves. And yet such childish, primitive credulity is integral to – indeed, constitutive of – the market itself, and 'what would Enlightenment be without the market' (1994: 152)? The paradoxes compound themselves in that the super-sensibility of the sensuous – our inability to grasp the real – also warrants the practical and intellectual techniques at our disposal to make the attempt. 'Empiricist' and 'bourgeois', one might say (and Marilyn Strathern practically does, 1992: 173), are analogues of analytical practice in capitalism and its techniques of self-reflection and autodocumentation, the sciences.

Including Marxism. As Dipesh Chakrabarty reminds us, echoing Alfred Sohn-Rethel (1978) and Moishe Postone (1993), Marx's concept of abstract labor, the 'secret of the expression of value' that places all activity, human or otherwise, on one scale of quantifiable value, 'could not be deciphered … until the concept of human equality had already acquired the permanence of a fixed popular opinion' (Marx, quoted by Chakrabarty 2000: 52). 'The generalization of contractual equality under bourgeois hegemony,' Chakrabarty summarizes, 'created the historical conditions for the birth of Marx's insights' (*ibid.*). Chakrabarty goes on to emphasize that the abstraction entailed in abstract labor was 'a concrete performance of the work of abstraction' (p. 54) – abstraction as concrete practice, the historical unity with which Marx (and Hegel) began his inquiry into history, the formulation subtending the effort to keep the Marxian totality bundled together despite its continual unravellings.

In the meantime, however, the very realization of capitalist time's specificity and the formal dynamics of contractual equality provide occasions to rethink the materiality of the capitalist landscape. Mark Leone's (1984) analysis of a formal Georgian garden in Annapolis, MD, shows how the use of perspective and scale as well as classical quotations and botanical science created both a representation of universal history and abstract, evenly segmented capitalist time, as well as an instrument for inculcating the 'rationality' of that notion of time as well as natural order. In addition, by carefully arranging plants based on detailed knowledge of their growing behavior the garden planner was able to map knowledge of precedents – based on systematic observation and temporal demarcation – that redounded into juridical order. As Leone writes, 'just as precedent inserted into law allowed the established order to protect its own position by making that position appear historically valued, so that same social position seemed to be more fixed when it appeared to be served by optical, astronomical, and geometrical phenomena displayed in the garden's *allées* and vistas' (1984: 29). Here, capitalist time, abstract labor, and juridical order come together in the materiality and embodied experience of a formalized landscape.

CONCLUSION: DOES MARXISM MATTER?

Here's the rub for studies of materiality elsewhere and in other times: if abstract labor provides 'the key to the hermeneutic grid through which capital requires us to read the world' (Chakrabarty 2000: 55) then how are we to read 'other' worlds? Marilyn Strathern provides a case in point in her analysis of Melanesian exchange and the Maussian legacy apparent in how anthropologists have understood it. By assuming that Melanesian exchange operates according to a 'barter theory of value' (so many pigs equals so much *taro*, a comparison of quantities) anthropologists continually misread the nature of the gift. 'I suspect we have been dazzled … by the precision of the counting,' she writes, and have missed that the counting is less about establishing ratios based on aggregations of items, than about creating analogies between them (Strathern 1992: 171). Strathern refuses to take for granted the discreteness of subjects and objects, much less persons and things, and instead asks how transacting brings the persons and things into being and into embodiment or materiality. The work of Bruno Latour, and actor-network theory in general, has inspired similar work on the networks of human and non-human actors that materialize persons and things as distinct in spite of their continual blurring. Anthropologists adopting while sometimes chafing against this sort of approach are doing research on science (Raffles 2002; Hayden 2004), bureaucracy (Riles 2000; Fortun 2003), activism (Jean-Klein 2003), money (Maurer 2005), law (Reed 2004), and anthropological reflection itself (Crook 2005). Fred Myers's research on the creation of markets for Australian Aboriginal art demonstrates that the materialities at issue are not necessarily the art works themselves so much as the dense set of curatorial events, the 'material practices through which these objects have moved' (Myers 2001: 167, punctuation omitted). Such practices include the mundane materialities of a printed 'number on a painting that link[s] it to a document on file' (p. 202).

Research agendas for Marxist-inspired studies of materiality, I am suggesting, should continually work to unground their own perceptual foundations, their own empiric, since the Marxist paradigm insists on the situatedness of perception itself (and its objectification as such, as a separable element of consciousness) in capitalist modalities of time, space, subject, object, and evaluation. So, were one to study a commodity chain today, for example, one would also want to understand the networked processes and subjects/objects that constitute the commodity *as well as* the perceptual apparatus warranting its stabilization as such. This would include the research enterprise that materializes forth the object in the material/discursive terrain of scholarship itself.

Taking the lead from new objects of ethnographic scrutiny, the kind of contemporary research agenda I am suggesting would focus as much on the form as on the content of the work. New Marxist-inspired attention to materiality brings into its purview the materiality of the presentation of research. No longer simply experimentations with textual and discursive strategies, such exercises in form make explicit the mutual imbrication of research objects, research processes and research results. Examples can be found in work like Christopher Kelty's (2001), which queries the 'freedom' and 'openness' of new virtual materialities such as open-source software. Despite its apparent separation from the market of commodities, open-source code relies on a strict set of citational practices required to be on display whenever and wherever it is appropriated. These mirror academic practices of the creation and circulation of reputation and regard manifest in databases like the Social Sciences Citation Index (see Kelty 2001). Publishing in a free-access 'virtual' journal/database makes explicit the relationship between form and content in both the object and Kelty's own representation of it in an 'open source' venue. Kelty's virtualization of open source and academic citationality reminds me of Tilley et al.'s (2000)

experiments with the interface among rocks, landscape art, and archaeology which seek to transform experiences of the materiality of place by highlighting the way rock, art, and archaeology formally replicate one another. One might see the objects here – dematerialized databases and code, on the one hand, and rock and stone, on the other – as opposite ends of a virtual-material continuum. However, like Kelty's work, Tilly et al.'s experiment ungrounds, as it were, the perceptual bases of empiricist modes of knowledge generation. 'An awareness and interpretation of the significance of different stones on the hill is ultimately a relationship between the body and the object. ... performing art is a process of engagement that allows us to see the hill, its stones and the prehistoric architecture in a new way' (Tilley et al. 2000: 60). I am suggesting a performative scholarly engagement the enactment of which constitutes its critical currency.

Lurking everywhere, of course, is still the 'fissure of the consciousness into "practical" and "theoretical"', which Slavoj Žižek (1989: 20) views as the product of the abstraction of exchange. This leads Žižek away from the classical Marxist conception of ideology as false consciousness of the real conditions of existence and toward a conception of ideology as the real conditions of existence themselves. Like Sohn-Rethel and, to a lesser extent perhaps, Chakrabarty, this also leads Žižek to a peculiar form of stage theory, in which it is not until commodity exchange is 'generalized' and 'universalized' that it 'brings about its symptom' of hiding the real within it (1989: 22–3). The ghosts of stage theory lurk in the temporal phrases of Žižek's account: pre-capitalist societies have not 'yet' witnessed the universalization of the production of commodities, but 'as soon as' the generalization takes place, labor is abstracted and the 'freedom' to exchange 'becomes its own negation' (p. 22). It is as if one could go and measure whether or not a pre-capitalist had 'yet' achieved – progress! – the general equivalent of the commodity form in abstract labor, abstract human equality, and universal exchangeability.

It seems, then, that even if we open up the material analysis of the social to the instability, the uncanniness attending the tendentious purification of hybrid subjects/objects, we cannot escape capitalist time and its attendant teleologies and empirics. And this is a problem not just with Marxism, but with the symptom that Marxism identified in its internal critique of its own social formation. It would seem to make the apprehension of 'other' worlds impossible, even as it sets for itself the very task, as an imperative that justifies and defines itself, of locating such other non- or pre-capitalist worlds.

Does it matter? I am not sure that it does. Writing against the apocalyptic narrative of feminism's failure, and the frequently heard lament that academic feminism has abandoned 'real women's lives' to take up complex theory, Robyn Wiegman makes a case for a feminism not identical to itself, that is, a feminism that is not correlative with actually existing women's subjectivities and that therefore 'demands something other from the political than what we already know' (Wiegman 2000: 822). Such a feminism recognizes that theory 'will exceed its contemporary emplottment as the critical container of US feminism's activist subjectivity' (*ibid.*). I have been making a case for an analogous, non-identical Marxism: it 'will not be efficient; it will not have the clarity of productive order; it will not guarantee that feminist [or any other] struggle culminates in a present that is without waste to the future. This is the case because the future is itself the excess of productive time: elusive, unimaginable, and ultimately unable to be guaranteed or owned' (*ibid.*). If Marxism is capitalism's critique, it is also its definition. And if Marxism can be a moving and emergent critique, then it can abandon without apologies its empiricist and realist pretensions and instead allow itself to trundle along, to muddle through, its own potentialities as they emerge together with its objects, material, immaterial, and everything in between.

REFERENCES

Althusser, Louis (1971) *Lenin and Philosophy, and other Essays*. New York: Monthly Review Press.

Althusser, Louis (1977) *For Marx*. London: Verso.

Appadurai, Arjun (ed.) (1986) *The Social Life of Things*. Cambridge: Cambridge University Press.

Asad, Talal (1972) 'Market model, class structure, and consent'. *Man*, 7: 74–94.

Barth, Frederik (1959) *Political Leadership among Swat Pathans*. London: Athlone Press.

Beaudry, Mary, Cook, Lauren J. and Mrozowski, Stephen (1991) 'Artifacts and active voices: material culture as a social discourse', in Randall McGuire and Robert Paynter (eds), *The Archaeology of Inequality*. Oxford: Blackwell, pp. 150–91.

Bloch, Maurice (1983) *Marxism and Anthropology: the History of a Relationship*. Oxford: Oxford University Press.

Bourdieu, Pierre (1977) *Outline of a Theory of Practice*. Cambridge: Cambridge University Press.

Brenner, Robert (1977) 'The origins of capitalist development: a critique of neo-Smithian Marxism', *New Left Review*, 104: 25–92.

Brumfiel, Elizabeth (1992) 'Distinguished lecture in archaeology: breaking and entering the ecosystem – gender, class and faction steal the show', *American Anthropologist*, 94: 551–67.

Brumfiel, Elizabeth (1995) Review of Mary Helm, *Craft and the Kingly Ideal*, in *Ethnohistory*, 42 (2): 330–2.

Brumfiel, Elizabeth (1996) 'Figurines and the Aztec state: testing the effectiveness of ideological domination', in R. Wright (ed.), *Gender and Archaeology* Pittsburgh, PA: University. of Pittsburgh Press, pp. 143–66.

Brumfiel, Elizabeth (2003) 'It's a material world: history, artifacts, and anthropology', *Annual Review of Anthropology*, 32: 205–23.

Caldeira, Teresa (2000) *City of Walls: Crime, Segregation and Citizenship in São Paolo*. Berkeley, CA: University of California Press.

Chakrabarty, Dipesh (2000) *Provincializing Europe*. Princeton, NJ: Princeton University Press.

Childe, V. Gordon (1936) *Man Makes Himself*. London: Watts.

Comaroff, Jean and Comaroff, John (1991) *Of Revelation and Revolution: Christianity, Colonialism, and Consciousness in South Africa* I. Chicago: University of Chicago Press.

Comaroff, Jean and Comaroff, John (1997) *Of Revelation and Revolution: Christianity, Colonialism, and Consciousness in South Africa* II. Chicago: University of Chicago Press.

Comaroff, Jean and Comaroff, John (1999) 'Second thoughts: a response to Sally Falk Moore', *American Ethnologist*, 26 (2): 307–9.

Comaroff, John and Comaroff, Jean (2001) 'Of fallacies and fetishes: a rejoinder to Donham', *American Anthropologist*, 103 (1): 150–60.

Conkey, Margaret (1987) 'New approaches in the search for meaning? A review of research in "Paleolithic art"', *Journal of Field Archaeology*, 14 (4): 413–30.

Crook, Tony (2005) 'Kim Kurukuru'.Unpublished MS.

Derrida, Jacques (1994) *Specters of Marx*. New York: Routledge.

Donham, Donald (2001) 'Thinking temporally or modernizing anthropology', *American Anthropologist*, 103 (1): 134–49.

Engels, Frederick ([1877] 1962) *The Anti-Dühring: Herr Dühring's Revolution in Science*. Moscow: Foreign Languages Publishing House.

Engels, Frederick ([1884] 1972) *The Origin of the Family, Private Property and the State*. New York: International Publishers.

Farquhar, Judith (2002) *Appetites: Food and Sex in Post-socialist China*. Durham, NC: Duke University Press.

Ferguson, James G. (1999) *Expectations of Modernity: Myths and Meanings of Urban Life on the Zambian Copperbelt*. Berkeley, CA: University of California Press.

Feuerbach, Ludwig (1966) *Principles of the Philosophy of the Future*. Indianapolis, IN: Bobbs-Merrill.

Fortes, Meyer (1945) *The Dynamics of Clanship among the Tallensi*. London: Oxford University Press.

Fortun, Kim (2003) *Advocacy after Bhopal*. Chicago: University of Chicago Press.

Foster, Robert J. (2002) *Materializing the Nation: Commodities, Consumption and Media in Papua New Guinea*. Bloomington, IN: Indiana University Press.

Friedman, Jonathan (1974) 'Marxism, structuralism and vulgar materialism', *Man* (n.s.), 9: 444–69.

Friedman, J. and Rowlands, M.J. (eds) (1977) *The Evolution of Social Systems*. London: Duckworth.

Gibson-Graham, J.K. (1995) *The End of Capitalism (As we Knew it): a Feminist Critique of Political Economy*. Oxford: Blackwell.

Gluckman, Max (1955) *The Judicial Process among the Barotse of Northern Rhodesia*. Manchester: Manchester University Press/Rhodes-Livingstone Institute.

Godelier, Maurice (1977) 'Economy and religion: an evolutionary optical illusion', in J. Friedman and M.J. Rowlands (eds), *The Evolution of Social Systems*. London: Duckworth, pp. 3–11.

Gregory, C.A. (1982) *Gifts and Commodities*. London: Academic Press.

Gupta, Akhil (1998) *Postcolonial Development*. Durham, NC: Duke University Press.

Hardt, Michael and Negri, Antonio (2000) *Empire*. Cambridge: Harvard University Press.

Harris, Marvin (1979) *Cultural Materialism: the Struggle for a Science of Culture*. New York: Random House.

Harris, Olivia and Young, Kate (1981) 'Engendered structures: some problems in the analysis of reproduction', in Joel S. Kahn and Josep R. Llobera (eds), *The Anthropology of Pre-capitalist Societies* London: Macmillan, pp. 109–47.

Hayden, Corinne (2004) *When Nature Goes Public*. Berkeley, CA: University of California Press.

Helms, Mary (1993) *Craft and the Kingly Ideal: Art, Trade and Power*. Austin, TX: University. of Texas Press.

Hodder, Ian (1984) 'Burials, houses, women and men in the European Neolithic', in Daniel Miller and Christopher Tilley (eds), *Ideology, Power and Prehistory*. Cambridge: Cambridge University Press, pp. 51–68.

Holston, James (1989) *The Modernist City: an Anthropological Critique of Brasilia*. Chicago: University of Chicago Press.

Jameson, Frederic (2002) *A Singular Modernity*. New York: Verso.

Jean-Klein, Iris (2003) 'Into committees, out of the house? Familiar forms in the organization of Palestinian committee activism during the first intifada', *American Ethnologist*, 30 (4): 556–77.

Keane, Webb (2003) 'Semiotics and the social analysis of material things', *Language and Communication*, 23: 409–25.

Kelty, Christopher (2001) 'Free software/free science', *First Monday*, 6 (12), available at http://firstmonday.org/issues/issue6_12/kelty/index.html, last accessed 21 November, 2004.

Klima, Alan (2002) *The Funeral Casino: Meditation, Massacre and Exchange with the Dead in Thailand*. Princeton, NJ: Princeton University Press.

Kuper, Adam (1996) *Anthropology and Anthropologists: the Modern British School*. New York: Routledge.

Latour, Bruno (1993) *We have Never been Modern*. Cambridge, MA: Harvard University Press.

Leone, Mark (1984) 'Interpreting ideology in historical archaeology: using the rules of perspective in the William Paca Garden in Annapolis, Maryland', in Daniel Miller and Christopher Tilley (eds), *Ideology, Power and Prehistory*. Cambridge: Cambridge University Press, pp. 25–35.

LiPuma, Edward and Lee, Benjamin (2004) *Financial Derivatives and the Globalization of Risk*. Durham, NC: Duke University Press.

Marx, Karl (1978) *Capital*, I. New York: Viking.

Marx, Karl and Engels, Frederick (1970) *The German Ideology*. New York: International Publishers.

Masri, Shelli (2004) 'Abstracting signs from the soil'. Unpublished MS. Irvine, CA: Department of Anthropology, University of California.

Maurer, Bill (2004) 'Cyberspatial properties: taxing questions about proprietary regimes', in C. Humphrey and K. Verdery (eds), *Property in Question: Value Transformation in the Global Economy*. Oxford: Berg, pp. 297–318.

Maurer, Bill (2005) *Mutual Life, Limited: Islamic Banking, Alternative Currencies, Lateral Reason*. Princeton, NJ: Princeton University Press.

Meillassoux, Claude (1972) 'From reproduction to production', *Economy and Society*, 1: 93–105.

Miller, Daniel (1998) *A Theory of Shopping*. Cambridge: Polity Press.

Miller, Daniel (2001) 'Conclusion: a theory of virtualism', in James G. Carrier and Daniel Miller (eds), *Virtualism: a New Political Economy*. Oxford: Berg, pp. 187–215.

Miller, Daniel and Tilley, Christopher (eds) (1984) *Ideology, Power and Prehistory*. Cambridge: Cambridge University Press.

Mintz, Sidney (1985) *Sweetness and Power: the Place of Sugar in Modern History*. New York: Viking.

Mintz, Sidney and Wolf, Eric (1989) 'Reply to Michael Taussig', *Critique of Anthropology*, 9 (1): 25–31.

Miyazaki, Hirokazu (2003) 'The temporalities of the market', *American Anthropologist*, 105: 255–65.

Moore, Sally Falk (1999) 'Reflections on the Comaroff lecture', *American Ethnologist*, 26 (2): 304–6.

Morgan, Lewis Henry ([1877] 1963) *Ancient Society*. New York: World Publishing.

Morris, Rosalind C. (2000) *In the Place of Origins: Modernity and its Mediums in Northern Thailand*. Durham, NC: Duke University Press.

Myers, Fred (2001) 'The Wizards of Oz: Nation, state, and the production of Aboriginal fine art', in Fred Myers (ed.), *The Empire of Things: Regimes of Value and Material Culture*. Santa Fe, NM: School of American Research Press, pp. 165–204.

O'Laughlin, Bridget (1975) 'Marxist approaches in anthropology', *Annual Review of Anthropology*, 341–70.

Parry, Jonathan and Bloch, Marc (1989) 'Introduction: Money and the morality of exchange', in J. Parry and M. Bloch (eds), *Money and the Morality of Exchange*. Cambridge: Cambridge University Press, pp. 1–32.

Pemberton, John (1994) *On the Subject of 'Java'*. Ithaca, NY: Cornell University Press.

Postone, Moishe (1993) *Time, Labor and Social Domination*. Cambridge: Cambridge University Press.

Raffles, Hugh (2002) *In Amazonia*. Princeton, NJ: Princeton University Press.

Rappaport, Roy (1968) *Pigs for the Ancestors*. New Haven, CT: Yale University Press.

Reed, Adam (2004) *Papua New Guinea's Last Place: the Aesthetics of Incarceration in Post-colonial Melanesia*. Oxford: Berghahn Books.

Rey, Pierre Philippe (1971) *Colonialisme, néo-colonialisme et transition au capitalisme: example de la Comilog au Congo-Brazzaville*. Paris: Maspéro.

Riles, Annelise (2000) *The Network Inside-out*. Ann Arbor, MI: University of Michigan Press.

Robb, John E. (1998) 'The archaeology of symbols', *Annual Review of Anthropology*, 27: 329–46.

Rofel, Lisa (1999) *Other Modernities: Gendered Yearnings in China after Socialism*. Berkeley, CA: University of California Press.

Roseberry, William (1997) 'Marx and anthropology', *Annual Review of Anthropology*, 26: 25–46.

Rowlands, Michael and Kristian Kristiansen (1998) 'Introduction', in K. Kristiansen and M. Rowlands (eds), *Social Transformations in Archaeology*. London: Routledge, pp. 1–26.

Rowlands, Mike (1984) 'Objectivity and subjectivity in archaeology', in Matthew Spriggs (ed.), *Marxist Directions in Archaeology*. Cambridge: Cambridge University Press, pp. 108–13.

Sahlins, Marshall (1976) *Culture and Practical Reason*. Chicago: University of Chicago Press.

Sahlins, Marshall and Service, Elman (eds) (1960) *Evolution and Culture*. Ann Arbor, MI: University of Michigan Press.

Sohn-Rethel, Alfred (1978) *Intellectual and Manual Labor: a Critique of Epistemology*. Atlantic Highlands, NJ: Humanities Press.

Spriggs, Matthew (1984) 'Another way of telling: Marxist perspectives in archaeology', in Matthew Spriggs (ed.), *Marxist Directions in Archaeology*. Cambridge: Cambridge University Press, pp. 1–9.

Steward, Julian (1955) *Theory of Culture Change*. Urbana, IL: University of Illinois Press.

Strathern, Marilyn (1992) 'Qualified value: the perspective of gift exchange', in Caroline Humphrey and Stephen Hugh-Jones (eds), *Barter, Exchange and Value: An Anthropological Approach*. Cambridge: Cambridge University Press, pp. 169–91.

Sylvester (1978) 'You Make me Feel mighty Real', *Step II*. San Francisco: Fantasy Records. [audio recording].

Taussig, Michael (1989) 'History as commodity in some recent American (anthropological) literature', *Critique of Anthropology*, 9 (1): 7–23.

Terray, Emmanuel (1972) *Marxism and 'Primitive' Society*. New York: Monthly Review Press.

Tilley, Christopher (ed.) (1993) *Interpretative Archaeology*. Oxford: Berg.

Tilley, Christopher, Hamilton, Sue and Bender, Barbara (2000) 'Art and the re-presentation of the past', *Journal of the Royal Anthropological Institute* (n.s.), 6: 35–62.

Trigger, Bruce (1978) *Time and Traditions: Essays in Archaeological Interpretation*. New York: Columbia University Press.

Trigger, Bruce (1981/1984) 'Marxism and archaeology', in Jacques Maquet and Nancy Daniels (eds), *On Marxian Perspectives in Anthropology: Essays in Honor of Harry Hoijer*. Malibu: Undena Publications, pp. 59–97.

Tsing, Anna (2000) 'Inside the economy of appearances', *Public Culture*, 12: 115–44.

Vayda, Andrew P. (ed.) (1969) *Environment and Cultural Behavior*. Garden City, NJ: Natural History Press.

Verdery, Katherine (1996) *What was Socialism, and What comes Next?* Princeton, NJ: Princeton University Press.

Verdery, Katherine (2003) *The Vanishing Hectare: Property and Value in Postsocialist Transylvania*. Ithaca, NY: Cornell University Press.

Verdery, Katherine and Humphrey, Caroline (eds) (2004) *Property in Question: Value Transformation in the Global Economy*. Oxford: Berg.

White, Leslie (1949) *The Science of Culture*. New York: Farrar Straus.

Wiegman, Robyn (2000) 'Feminism's apocalyptic futures', *New Literary History*, 31 (4): 805–25.

Wilson, Ara (2004) *The Intimate Economies of Bangkok: Tomboys, Tycoons and Avon Ladies in the Global City*. Berkeley, CA: University of California Press.

Wolf, Eric (1982) *Europe and the People without History*. Berkeley, CA: University of California Press.

Worsley, Peter (1956) 'The kinship system of the Tallensi: a revaluation', *Journal of the Royal Anthropological Institute*, 86: 37–73.

Žižek, Slavoj (1989) *The Sublime Object of Ideology*. London: Verso.

2

STRUCTURALISM AND SEMIOTICS

Robert Layton

Structuralism and semiotics provide ways of studying human cognition and communication. They examine the way meaning is constructed and used in cultural traditions. Applications of structuralist and semiotic method have raised questions concerning the extent to which cultural understandings are stable and shared, or changeable and ambiguous. Structuralism contends that the cultural significance of objects and actions derives from their place in a *cognitive* system. Structuralism was first advocated by the French sociologists Durkheim and Mauss (1903/1963). It became the dominant theory in the social sciences during the 1960s and 1970s (e.g. Douglas 1973; Glucksmann 1974; Hawkes 1977; Lane 1970; Robey 1973; Sturrock 1979; Wittig 1975). In 1968/1971 the psychologist Piaget argued for the relevance of structuralism to an even wider range of disciplines, from mathematics to philosophy. Piaget anticipated some of the criticisms of more formalized versions of structuralism. The failure of early structuralists to consider temporal process was addressed by Bourdieu (1977) and Giddens (1979, 1984), giving rise to what has been termed 'post-structuralism'. Foucault (e.g. 1972, 1977) and Derrida (1976) drew attention to the relationship between meaning and power. More recently, the anthropologist Gell has challenged the claim that that anything except language 'has "meaning" in the intended sense' (Gell 1998: 6). He is particularly critical of the structuralist semiotic anthropology in the 1970s (p. 163). At that period, Gell writes, 'it was customary to discuss systems of all kinds as "languages". ... Art was the (cultural) "language of visual forms"' (Gell 1998: 164, A.G.'s parenthesis). Gell singles out Faris (1971) and Korn (1978), who argued for rather

complex vocabularies of visual elements and grammatical rules for combining them into well formed motifs or compositions in the art of East Africa and New Guinea.

THE THEORETICAL FRAMEWORK

The Foundations of Structuralism and Semiotics

Early structuralists reacted against previous writers who had interpreted non-Western customs as survivals from supposed archaic stages in human social evolution. They argued that the significance of a custom depends on its place in the structure of contemporary culture. In *The Rites of Passage* (1905), for example, van Gennep criticized the popular procedure of taking rituals out of their ceremonial context and considering them in isolation, as historical survivals, 'thus removing them from a context which gives them meaning and reveals their position in a dynamic whole' (Gennep [1905] 1960: 89). Van Gennep contended that there is a general tendency among human societies to conceive of a change in status on the model of a journey from one town or country to another or, as he expressed it, a 'territorial passage' (Gennep 1960: 18). Van Gennep argued that territorial passage had three aspects, separation from the place of origin, transition (*la marge*), and incorporation into the destination. Territorial passage could therefore stand for any change of status in society, but each phase in the ceremony made sense only in terms of its place along the journey from old to new status. 'Marriage by capture', where the groom and his brothers ride to the bride's house, snatch her and carry her back to the wedding, is not a survival from some original condition of Hobbsian anarchy. It dramatizes the separation of the bride from her position as an unmarried girl in her parents' house, and her incorporation into the groom's household as a married woman. Through a series of case studies, Van Gennep demonstrated that rituals of birth, entry into adulthood and death can all have the same structure.

In 1912 Durkheim provided a more formalized and theoretically productive structural analysis in his examination of Aboriginal totemism. Since some totemic species seemed insignificant in themselves, Durkheim deduced they gained significance from their place in the totemic system. The classification of animal species parallels the classification of social groups. The marsupial rat and the witchetty grub were valued not because they had some intrinsic significance, but because each stood for the concept of a particular clan as one segment in the social system. The species itself was, moreover, less sacred than its representation in totemic art. This, Durkheim argued, was because the artistic motif represented the clan's identity in concrete form. He argued that the existence of society depended on such symbols. 'Individual consciences … can communicate only by means of signs which express their internal states' (Durkheim 1915: 230). Art and writing therefore originated to fulfil the same purpose: 'man commenced designing … [so] as to translate his thought into matter' (Durkheim 1915: 127. n). Painted depictions of totemic animals were so simple (consisting predominantly of circles, arcs and dotted lines) that Durkheim took them to be arbitrary and non-representational.

The Swiss linguist Saussure (1915/1959) applied the reasoning used in Durkheim's analysis of totemism to the explanation of communication through language. The sounds of speech, like the animal species depicted in totemic art, have no intrinsic meaning. The meaning of words is established by their place in the vocabulary. The linguistic sign has two components, the *signified* or idea, and the *signifier*, the spoken sound(s) that conventionally express that idea, equivalent to the idea of the clan and its expression in the totemic emblem. Saussure realised that there were many other sign systems in human culture that could be studied using the same methods: 'A science that studies the life of signs within society is conceivable. … I shall call it *semiology*' (Saussure 1959: 16). Saussure acknowledged that some

semiological systems might include signs that seem to have intrinsic significance, such as bowing submissively to a superior, but emphasized that even these gestures are based on social convention.

A semiotic system is thus made up of two parallel structures: a set of ideas that divide up experience into discrete units, and a set of material signifiers that stand for those ideas. The signifiers may be sounds, pictures or gestures. Signifiers may be completely conventional, or there may be an iconic or associative connection between the signifier and the object, the idea of which it signifies.

Saussure introduced an important refinement to Durkheim's totemic model for structuralism, the distinction between *language* and *speech*. Speech draws upon the vocabulary and grammar of the language to construct a limitless series of statements. Speech consists of what Saussure called a syntagmatic chain comprising, for example, a subject, verb and object. Each element also belongs to a paradigmatic series of alternative subjects, verbs and objects that could have been selected instead:

The child chases the ball.

The dog catches the stick. …

Sense, Reference and Abduction

Saussure's primary concern was with *sense*, or *signification*: how sounds are conventionally related to ideas thanks to the structure of the language. The US philosopher Peirce classified signs according to the way they *refer* to objects in the environment. (See also Barthes 1967: 38, and Piaget 1968/1971: 115 n. 8, who identifies a similar set of terms in Saussure's work.) Peirce identified three types of reference. An indexical sign has something in common with what it refers to: smoke is naturally associated with, and therefore points to, fire; a weather vane is an index of wind direction (Peirce 1955: 102–3). Icons (such as the motifs in representational art) look like what they refer to. As long as we can 'read' the style, we can recognize what is depicted. Peirce used the term 'symbol', for signs such as the words of language that are associated with the objects they refer to purely according to cultural convention.

Gell (1998) argues that, because art makes use of representation (iconic) images, and may be constructed from materials intrinsically associated with their subject matter (particular woods or pigments), art does not depend on convention and is therefore not a semiological system. Gell argued that art objects take effect not by communicating ideas, but by extending their maker's or user's agency through references to the world of objects (see Hoskins, Chapter 5 below). Agency is the ability to choose between different courses of action. I exert my agency by restricting or enabling yours (see Giddens 1984: 9, 15). According to Gell, an art object can extend its maker's or user's agency in several ways. Sometimes the agency is psychological, as when an enemy is frightened by an awesome shield. The *kula* valuables exchanged between leading men on the Trobriand Islands of the Pacific circulate well beyond the personal reach of previous custodians, but their association with a powerful man makes them indexes of his bodily presence even after others have received and passed on those valuables.

Gell argues that art objects are not construed as meaningful; their references are construed through the process of 'abduction'. Abduction is a form of inference practised in 'the grey area where semiotic inference (of meaning from signs) merges with *hypothetical inferences* of a non-semiotic (or not conventionally semiotic) kind' (Gell 1998: 14, parenthesis and italics in original). It is true that icons and indexes do not rely as completely on cultural convention as arbitrary verbal sounds (signs). Nonetheless, what icons and indexes signify, and what they refer to, will almost certainly be established by convention. Campbell spells this out very clearly in her analysis of the art on the canoes used to travel between islands in the *kula* network. Animals whose culturally defined qualities correspond to the values of the *kula* are represented as icons, but according to the conventions of local style. The appropriateness of the chosen animals is determined through local cultural symbolism (Campbell 2001). In contrast to Gell, the archaeologist Dobres (2000: 142) accepts that agency can take effect semiotically. She defines agency as 'an inter-subjective quality and unfolding process of knowing, acting and being-in-the-world', a world that 'is mediated by cultural reason, symbolic sensibilities, and personal and collective history' (Dobres 2000: 151).

While Gell's attempt to develop a non-semiological theory of art is questionable, his use of the term 'abduction' is fruitful. Meaning in some art systems is highly codified, while in others it is scarce and questionable. This creates a continuum between semiology and abduction in Gell's sense, that is, a continuum between highly codified meanings and situations where it is unclear whether something is intended to be meaningful or not and, if meaningful, how it should be construed.

Durkheim understood the importance of differentiating the totemic designs of different clans. Totemic art is indeed a good example of a clearly structured system. As one Aboriginal man explained to me while discussing totemic body paintings, to dance at a ceremony wearing another clan's design 'would be to steal their land and their life'. It was an offence punishable by death. Panofsky showed how European Renaissance viewers would recognize a painting of a male figure with a knife in his hand as St Batholomew, a female figure holding a peach as the personification of veracity (Panofsky 1955: 54). The lily is a symbol of purity or virginity, and therefore often carried by St Mary. Traditional Chinese art also relies heavily on a codified series of images. Here, the peach is an image of long life, the peony an image of riches and honour. A Qing dynasty New Year's painting from Suzhou Province shows a boy pulling a cap and belt on a toy cart. Cap and belt are essential parts of the official uniform of ancient China, and different ranks of officials wore distinctive styles of cap and belt. The painting signified the parents' wish that their children would grow up to pass the imperial examinations and become officials (see Wang 1985; I'm grateful to Dr Biao Xu for teaching me about this tradition). Other traditions are much less codified. Gombrich (1972) challenged the idea that the artist could evoke the emotions s/he intended in the viewer by comparing two paintings by Van Gogh, the bedroom that expressed tranquillity and the café where the artist felt he could go mad. We know the artist's feelings, Gombrich argued, only through letters Van Gogh wrote to his brother.

Roland Barthes's semiological study of mid-twentieth century French culture invites reanalysis in terms of the concept of abduction, since he deals with cultural traditions where meaning is suspected but uncertain. Barthes characterized semiology as the study of:

> Any system of signs, whatever their substance and limits; images, gestures, musical sounds, objects, and the complex associations of all these, which form the content of ritual, convention and public entertainment: these constitute, if not *languages*, at least systems of signification.
>
> (Barthes 1967: 9)

Barthes applied this approach to advertising, clothing and food. In the 'garment system', he claimed, there is a 'language' that consists of a set of named items of clothing. Assembling one's clothing for the day is a form of self-expression:

to choose to wear a beret rather than a bowler hat is to make a particular statement, as it is to wear jeans or corduroy trousers. 'Speech' or 'usage' consists of the individual way of wearing clothes. Food comprises a similar system: there are syntagmatic chains realized by assembling a meal, and there are choices to be made between alternative dishes at each course. Bad choices may produce an 'ungrammatical' meal – starting with jelly and ending with soup, for example, or serving gravy with fish (cf. Douglas 1975: 249–59). Barthes also writes of furniture having 'meanings' (1967: 29). Barthes recognized that the identity of the signifying units needs to be studied empirically: does the choice of white or brown bread convey a different message, or are they equivalent? He does not, however, consider that for some people wearing a beret or dungarees is simply a practical decision even if for others it makes a statement.

The mere presence of sequences of actions entailing choice is not proof of a semiological system. It has been suggested that the ability to make a series of choices in the shaping of a stone tool is evidence of prehistoric mental mastery of grammar (Gowlett 1984). To make any implement, the craftsman has to put together a sequence of actions – the *chaîne opératoire* – that may embody practical choices at several steps. While such cognitive skills may be a precondition for modern human speech, stone tool manufacture in the Lower Palaeolithic is not proof that early hominids could represent what they were doing verbally and there is even less reason to assume each component of a prehistoric tool itself signified ideas – such, for example, as male : female, culture : nature, etc. (Dobres 2000: 155–6).

Barthes's contemporary Georges Mounin was rightly critical of Barthes's imprecise use of semiological terminology. Mounin readily accepted that highly codified systems such as heraldry, railway signalling, the highway code and cartography are genuine semiological systems. Road signs categorize the world into opposed ideas (advice/instruction, locomotive crossing/children crossing), each of which is represented by a sign. The use of a triangle to signify advice and a circle to signify instruction is arbitrary, but locomotives and children are represented iconically. Ordnance Survey maps in Britain codify landscape features into deciduous woodland versus coniferous woodland, church with spire versus church with tower, and represent these concepts with conventional icons such round tree/conical tree. However, Mounin argued that when Barthes writes of the signification of clothing, he is using the word in a medical sense (as in 'the spots on your body show you have measles'). In other words, clothes are symptomatic or indexical of a cultural situation, but do not necessarily signify ideas about that situation. Mounin agreed this did not make clothing uninteresting, but clothes should rather be studied as 'diagnostic symptoms of the psychosocial ills' of bourgeois society (Mounin 1970: 193). Barthes uses the term 'sign' indiscriminately, even when he is in fact discussing Peircian indices (Mounin 1970: 196), thus confusing meaning and reference. When he wrote of the semiology of clothing, moreover, Barthes suggested 'one may say, for instance, that a certain sweater means *long autumn walks in the woods*' (Barthes 1967: 43). But to whom does the sweater have this association? Possibly just Barthes and his dog! Given the human propensity constantly to be interpreting and making sense of the world, it is likely that everything around us will evoke some mental response, but many of these 'meanings' may be idiosyncratic to the individual.

Barthes also argued that 'every usage is converted into a sign of itself' (Barthes 1967: 41), a claim that seems to defy the fundamental tenets of semiology set out by Durkheim and Saussure; a sign system, by definition, uses *tokens* of objects (words, pictures, gestures) to refer to those objects. It is the words we choose to talk about things that reveals their meaning for us (as Barthes understood; see Olsen 1990: 172). Objects can nonetheless be used as signifiers of *something else*. To take a local example, some shops in my home town still have oversized, nineteenth-century metal representations of artefacts hanging outside. A former café has a 4 ft wide teapot, a former shoe shop a 6 ft high boot (cf. Ruesch and Kees 1970). The boot and teapot do not signify themselves, they represent the trade conducted from the building and this would be the case even if real artefacts were used. One must have the idea of 'teashop' versus 'shoe shop' to understand their significance.

Korsmeyer argues items of food *can*, but do not necessarily, have meaning: croissants were first made by Viennese bakers to celebrate the Austrian victory over the Turks, while Thanksgiving and Passover are both celebratory meals. Korsmeyer (2002: 36) contends that the food eaten by a Norwegian when they get up in the morning 'does not mean breakfast' to a US citizen. While Korsmeyer is right to point out that breakfast is a cultural artefact, 'meaning' is used here in a similar way to Barthes's notion of a sweater 'meaning' long autumn walks in the woods; US citizens do not associate pickled herring with breakfast. Meanings must be shown to be current. All Jews know that Passover celebrates the sparing of their ancestors' firstborn sons in Egypt, but not all US citizens may recall that Thanksgiving is held to honour the native people who saved the lives of the *Mayflower* colonists during their first winter in North America. Few people eating croissants will be aware that they once signified the defeat of a people whose emblem was the crescent moon. Meanings may be lost, and normally meaningless food items can suddenly acquire signification: when France refused to back the 2003 US invasion of Iraq, over-patriotic Americans renamed 'french fries' 'freedom fries'.

From Structure to Process and Post-structuralism

Such evidence that elements of culture can gain, lose or change meaning leads one to ask whether structural systems must be stable if they are to be mutually intelligible. Saussure recognized that a language gradually changes. However, like Durkheim, he saw change as evolution in the system, rather than the result of innovations introduced by individuals. He argued that individual idiosyncrasies can have no meaning, because they are not part of the conventional system. Individuals *use* the system, but it exists independently of them. Piaget (1968/1971: 76) attributes the predominantly synchronic character of Saussure's structuralism to the influence of current economic and biological theory on his thought. Economists had come to appreciate that the price of tobacco in 1910 depended, not on its price in 1890 or 1920, but on then current market conditions (cf. Barthes 1967: 54–5). Equally, the function of an organ depends on its relation to other organs in the body, not on its evolutionary history. In the same way, Saussure evidently reasoned, a word's significance depends on its relation to other words in the current vocabulary. When we look up the meaning of a word in a dictionary, we find it defined in relation to other words. A track is a well beaten path; a road is a track with a prepared surface. Saussure was unable to integrate analysis of the 'synchronic' state of a language at any moment and the 'diachronic' process by which it changed over time. It seemed as if the language must be stable if it is the function as a medium for communication.

Lévi-Strauss later struggled with the same paradox. Lévi-Strauss followed Durkheim in arguing that art can communicate only if it forms a stable system. He thus perpetuated the synchronic, even timeless, quality of structural analysis. Lévi-Strauss explained to Georges Charbonnier (Charbonnier 1961) that artists in 'primitive' society are careful to defend their group's own 'language' because, if foreign elements were incorporated too liberally, the semantic function of the art and its role within the society would be destroyed. Lévi-Strauss saw free choice in Western marriage undermining the ability of kinship to structure social relationships and attacked the frequent proliferation of new styles among some contemporary Western artists that made it impossible to re-establish a visual language (Lévi-Strauss, in Charbonnier 1961: 93–4).

Lévi-Strauss has clearly been uneasy about the difficulty of analysing change from a structuralist perspective, and has returned to this problem in a number of his publications. He argues that certain cultures are more likely than others to achieve a stable symbolic system. The simple societies studied by anthropologists have little taste for novelty (Lévi-Strauss 1987: 275). Complex societies are more susceptible to innovation and change than simple ones. Lévi-Strauss characterized the difference as one between 'cold' and 'hot' societies. Cold societies seek to counter the effects of history on their equilibrium and continuity (Lévi-Strauss 1966: 234), while hot societies make history the moving power of their development. All societies are *in* history, the difference lies in how they respond to it. Those who want to sustain a stable structure must fight the contingent, non-repetitive events of history, whose cumulative effects are to produce economic and social upheavals that undermine the existing structure of culture (Lévi-Strauss 1966: 234–5).

Piaget drew a distinction between the logical structures studied in mathematics, which genuinely exist outside of time and are reversible (in the sense that subtraction reverses addition, division reverses multiplication), and the types of structure that unfold through time that are studied in linguistics, sociology and psychology. The latter are not strictly reversible, but rather subject to feedback mechanisms that either preserve or modify their structure. Unlike Lévi-Strauss, Piaget therefore did not treat stability as the normal or necessarily desirable condition. He anticipated (Piaget 1968/1971: 104) that game theory would provide a more dynamic approach to the generation of economic systems by treating them as the outcome of negotiations between players in the economy, and argued that analysis of the evolution of language must similarly take into account the fact that the individual develops speech through interaction with other individuals.

Bourdieu and Giddens were both critical of the timeless quality of structural analysis (Bourdieu 1977: 5; Giddens 1984: 25). Lévi-Strauss uses a single text for each South American myth that he analyses. Bourdieu argued that structural analysis of this type tends to treat variation in individual performances as though they were deviations from an unwritten score. In fact, however, there is no single, transcendent 'myth', only a limitless set of tellings performed by individuals on particular occasions. (For two case studies from Australia see Layton 1992: 40–4, and for a case from India see Narayan 1993.)

Turning the Durkheimian position on its head, the linguist Searle (1969) argued that language does not have any real existence outside people's heads. A competent speaker has, by trial and error, internalized a vocabulary and set of rules for using speech, which allow meaningful and predictable interaction. Dictionaries can only report on current usage. How, then, is consensus negotiated and sustained within a speech community? Lévi-Strauss argued that, in the structure of any particular culture, 'what we witness and try to describe are attempts to realise a sort of compromise between certain historical trends and special characteristics of the environment ... and mental requirements' (Lévi-Strauss 1987: 104). Bourdieu developed the concept of habitus to represent how this process occurred (Bourdieu 1977). Giddens and Bourdieu reject the Durkheimian notion that there is a supra-organic entity, 'society' or 'culture', which tries to maintain its own structure. Social systems are a by-product of agents pursuing their own ends through cultural strategies. (On Ricoeur's parallel critique of Lévi-Strauss, see Tilley 1990: 58–60.) Agents use the repertoire of social strategies they have learned to construct relationships with others. In doing so, social networks are generated that, as Marx appreciated, are beyond agents' control but enable or constrain their subsequent actions. Participants in exchange experience it as a sequence of transactions, in which each transaction is prompted by the previous offering and seeks to influence subsequent exchanges to the actor's advantage (Bourdieu 1977: 25). Participants have a 'practical mastery' of how to handle social relationships. Structural-functionalists such as Parsons

and Radcliffe-Brown treated social structure as a constraining force, external to human action, but it is, in fact, the agents' activities which reproduce the conditions that make those activities possible, a process that Giddens called 'structuration' (Giddens 1984: 27, 162, 176).

Bourdieu studied the Kabyle people of Algeria. He describes how he and his Kabyle field assistant set out to discover the structure of the Kabyle seasonal calendar and the rituals that accompanied each phase of the agricultural cycle. Everybody gave them a slightly different answer, because each individual carried their own mental habitus. While aspects of Bourdieu's work owe a lot to Durkheim and Lévi-Strauss, this was a radical break with their concept of the collective culture imposing its vision upon individual members. What, then, prevents individual habituses from diverging so far that no one can understand anyone else? Bourdieu argued that public rituals tend to create consensus. The culturally constructed environment had a similar effect. In the traditional Kabyle house men sit on a raised area at the back, women in a lower area in front. Children therefore grow up in a cultural environment that predisposes them to think of men as superior to women. When children grow up and build their own houses, they reproduce the material structure. Bourdieu also recognized that kin groups persist because they share a common interest in managing the group's inherited property. Since many activities would be impossible without the help of other members of the group, ostracism is a terrible sanction and the threat of it encourages conformity (Bourdieu 1977: 35, 60, 1980/1990: 136–40; see Tilley, Chapter 4).

Agency and the Control of Knowledge

Although Lévi-Strauss has occasionally entered political debate (e.g. Lévi-Strauss 1994), his structuralism is characteristically apolitical (Tilley 1990: 56–7). Foucault took post-structuralism further by highlighting the hidden role of power in the way that we speak or write about the world, let alone how we act. A discourse, he wrote, is not 'an innocent intersection of words and things' (1972: 49). Each discourse (such as the technical language used in an academic discipline) shapes the way we experience the world. The conventions of a discourse specify the objects it talks or writes about by giving them names such as madness or witchcraft. Discourse defines the topics that are worth discussing and, most important, who can speak on them with authority. The rules of a discourse also determine what positions the subject can take towards the object of discourse: as direct questioner, observer, interpreter, etc., and defines which statements are deemed valid, marginal or irrelevant. Derrida more pointedly criticized Lévi-Strauss's naive approach to the objectivity of scientific writing. The anthropologist has the power to describe his subjects as 'primitive', 'tribal', 'non-literate', both through his authority as an expert on his subject and through the subjects' inability to answer back. The indigenous cultural space 'is shaped and reoriented by the gaze of the foreigner' (Derrida 1976: 113). Anthropologists have become increasingly sensitive to this issue (e.g. Clifford 1986), and some at least have moved to involve their subjects as collaborators in writing anthropological accounts (see Olsen, Chapter 6).

STRUCTURALISM AND SEMIOTICS IN ANTHROPOLOGY: HISTORY, CURRENT RESEARCH AND PROSPECTS

Structuralism became the dominant school in anthropology during the 1960s and '70s largely thanks to the prolific work of Lévi-Strauss. Lévi-Strauss argued that it was the structure of human cognition that generated structure in social relationships. Humans conceive of social relationships in terms of an opposition between self and other, or us and them. The exchange of gifts and the exchange of marriage partners were forms of communication between us and them that made statements about the social relationships between individuals or groups. They should therefore be treated like language, the best-studied medium of human communication (Lévi-Strauss 1952). In his mid-career work on South American mythology, Lévi-Strauss moved away from the Durkheimian/ Saussurian tradition and ceased emphasizing the arbitrariness of cultural symbolism. He had discovered certain recurrent themes in the verbal imagery of the Amazon region. Legends describing the transition from nature to culture repeatedly characterized the animal condition as one in which food was eaten raw, and individuals mated at random, while the cultural condition was one in which food was cooked, and men exchanged their sisters to create political alliances (see, for example, Lévi-Strauss 1970). My own view is that, even if certain

images are recurrent, they are not universal. Despite van Gennep's demonstration that the territorial model for status change is widespread there are other common images, such as rebirth. Saussure's observation that even signs which seem to have intrinsic significance depend on cultural convention remains valid.

Van Gennep's *The Rites of Passage* was translated into English in 1960, and also contributed to the rise of structuralism in British anthropology. Mary Douglas used van Gennep's ideas in her book *Purity and Danger* (1966). Douglas argued that concepts of 'dirt' are based not on hygiene, but on matter that is out of its proper place in the scheme of the culture. The phase of transition is the most dangerous stage in an initiation rite because it takes people out of their stable social roles. Animals that do not fall neatly into categories (such as the pangolin, a mammal with reptile-like scales) are similarly considered dangerous and polluting. 'The whole cultural repertoire of ideas concerning pollution and purification are used to mark the gravity of the event' (Douglas 1966: 96).

Victor Turner also highlighted the suspension of normal social regulations while initiates are secluded during ritual. People in a such a 'liminal' state evade or slip through the networks of classifications that normally locate positions in cultural space. They exist in a state of 'communitas' (Turner 1969: 95). Turner took a more positive view of this condition than Douglas, and later argued that the most creative ideas occur not during daily routines but in liminal moments such as play and joking, that facilitate fresh perceptions of social life (Turner 1990).

Structuralism has been used in numerous studies of art in small-scale societies. Rosman and Rubel (1990), for example, carried out a structural analysis of Kwakiutl art and ritual on the north-west coast of North America using ethnographic data Boas collected between 1890 and 1895. Boas documented an elaborate iconography that made it possible to identify the totemic guardian species depicted on masks and totem poles that identify the wearer's social affiliation, lending support to Durkheim's theory. The beaver, for example, was depicted with large incisor teeth, the hawk with a curved beak, the killer whale with a dorsal fin (see Layton 1981/1991: 151–7). Rosman and Rubel take this analysis a step further. They identify a basic division in Kwakuitl art and culture between *baxus*, the secular condition, and *tsetsequa*, the sacred condition. *Baxus* was associated with the totemic, land-owning descent groups. *Baxus* held sway during the summer, while *tsetsequa* was 'on top' during the winter. During the harsh winters, several totemic lineages congregated in defended villages, where they lived on food that had been collected and preserved during the summer. The spirit world, associated with ancestors during the summer, becomes immanent in the village during winter. Descent groups were replaced by secret societies whose membership cuts across the lineages. Unlike the benign lineage guardians, the winter spirits are fearsome cannibals or their assistants. A liminal period (cf. van Gennep) between the two seasons was signalled by the whistling sound of spirits moving closer through the forest. Finally, the spirits entered the village and captured the young people who were to be initiated that winter into the secret societies. In contrast to totemic carvings, the winter masks convey the grotesque and exaggerated world that the shaman experienced during trance. The beaks of eagle and raven masks are grotesquely elongated, embodying spirits that have come to peck the brains from the skulls of initiates.

Following Foucault, many recent writers have highlighted the role of power in the imposition of particular interpretations upon artefacts, particularly the power of colonizing peoples, and the efforts of the colonized to subvert the interpretations of the dominant community. Indigenous artefacts have undergone transformations of value as they are appropriated by different cultural traditions. The S. BLACK bag (Peers 1999) was made in western North America during the era of the fur trade. The four decorative tassels that hang from the bag are an ancient form of Native American artefact. According to Peers, such bags were often used for carrying personal possessions. But the floral patterns embroidered on both sides of the bag are of European origin, adopted by native women from around the year 1800. On the side worn next to the body, a heart is embroidered amid the flowers, probably to be read in the European sense as a sign of affection between a woman of mixed descent and her white husband (S. Black). In 1842, after its owner's death, the bag was bought by George Simpson, Governor of the Hudson's Bay Company, or by his assistant Hopkins. It was brought back to England as a souvenir of frontier life and belonged to the Hopkins family for forty years, then was given to the Pitt-Rivers Museum. As long as the museum's policy was to conserve 'authentic' tribal artefacts the bag's value to the collection was tenuous and it was fortunate not to be thrown out as an 'inauthentic' product of cultural mixing. More recently it has become appreciated as

'illustrating' (i.e. being symptomatic/indexical of) fur-trade society and cultural hybridity (Peers 1999: 299).

Even more complex is the history of artefacts made for the potlatch on the north-west coast of North America, that have been returned to native communities. Saunders describes how two Kwakwaka'wakw (Kwakiutl) groups arrived at different solutions for the display of artefacts returned from the Victoria Museum in Ottawa to local museums. At Alert Bay the regalia are displayed on three sides of the interior as if at a traditional potlatch, 'mutating into priceless Art as symbols of Kwakwaka'wakw greatness – a finely wrought fabric of historical and mythological geopolitical time frames' (Saunders 1997: 109). Saunders infers the display is directed primarily at reshaping a white audience's perception of native culture. The Cape Mudge museum, by contrast, is 'a cosy little place' (Saunders 1997: 111). The artefacts have not been 'museumized'. Each cluttered case contains the objects owned by a different family and there are no explanatory captions. To the local community the meanings are clear and carefully nurtured, but this knowledge is confined to the community, just as traditional knowledge was, and not publicly displayed.

Povinelli (1993) shows how the Aboriginal women of Belyuen, in northern Australia, live in a meaningful cultural landscape, but are conscious of the uncertainty of the meanings embodied in the behaviour of plants and animals around them. The totemic 'dreamings' communicate through the behaviour of animals, but the messages are unclear. 'People must discriminate among the numerous events that occur in the countryside and decide what is a sign and what is not' (Povinelli 1993: 692). Was the call of a dove the cry of a deceased woman to her living namesake? Was a successful yam harvest a gift from the yam ancestor? Women confirmed their egalitarianism by not asserting authoritative readings of the landscape, but made fun of a younger woman who risked a display of competence by proposing an interpretation. Povinelli's case study exemplifies Bourdieu's and Giddens's arguments about negotiation and structuration. It underlines the need for future research to test the degree of consensus in any community, and how agreement is negotiated.

Two studies indicate the direction such research might take. Derrida accepted Saussure's argument that the linguistic sign consists of a purely conventional association of sound and meaning. If, then, language is constructed through practice, and each discourse constructs a different way of giving meaning to experience, so knowledge itself is an artefact of language and as arbitrary as language (Derrida 1976: 49–50). Webb Keane (forthcoming) argues that icons and indexes are to some extent exempt from Derrida's indeterminacy because they are anchored to their referents by similarity or association. Material objects can become meaningful, but they also exercise constraints and opportunities on their users. Keane gives the example of middle-class Indonesian men who choose different clothes for different occasions. It is easier to kneel in a sarong, and sarongs are therefore worn for Friday prayers. It is easier to sit on a chair in trousers, therefore safari suits are worn at official meetings. Thus, while meanings are still open to negotiation, clothing has an inherent potential to signify adherence to Islamic or to Western values.

Rowlands's study of war memorials gives an excellent example of a more loosely formalized and contested tradition. Memorials function, as Lévi-Strauss might have put it, to suppress time in a 'hot' society by representing recent events according to the structure of classic prototypes (cf. Rowlands 1999: 132). Rowlands asks why some monuments enable people to experience healing and reconciliation while others evoke distaste and condemnation. He identifies two types of memorial: the national or triumphalist type and the type that demands recognition of what was done, to whom and by whom. Controversies over the aptness of visual form therefore partly concern competing policies, one seeking to celebrate national or ethnic prowess, the other seeking confession, expiation and reparation. Rather in the manner that Rosman and Rubel contrasted the summer and winter art of the Kwakiutl, Rowlands contrasts the Lincoln and Vietnam Memorials in Washington as examples of structurally opposed genres. The Vietnam memorial is sunken into the ground, while the Lincoln memorial is raised up. The Vietnam memorial is made of black granite, the Lincoln memorial of white marble. The former is modernist in form, rather than the classical Greek style of the Lincoln memorial. The listing of the 58,132 names of those US citizens who died in Vietnam emphasizes the reality and individuality of the deaths. The Vietnam memorial asks questions, while the Lincoln memorial 'is an act of closure'; it does not mention slavery or the Civil War.

Rowlands shows how controversy may arise over the aptness of the chosen images for the intended message. There are guidelines for designing an appropriate memorial, but no precise rules for success. He cites the rejected design for an Australian war memorial in which a single, naked female figure was to be depicted, hanging from a cross over the broken bodies of dead soldiers. He argues the design evoked two unpalatable ideas: that the nation itself (the naked female) had been sacrificed, and that the dead soldiers remained unsanctified. Lévi-Strauss (1970: 12) assumed the mind of the analyst can discover what meanings such structural oppositions have for others, because myth operates alike in all our minds. It is important in such innovative situations not to make any such assumption, but to interview the sculptor and the users. Rowlands quotes the architect's intentions, and relies on the observed behaviour of visitors to the Vietnam memorial to deduce their feelings.

The extent to which individual habituses overlap will vary according to the way knowledge is held and transmitted, and this is a research area that urgently needs further study. Extrapolating from Bourdieu, it could be said that there are three preconditions for the persistence of a cultural system (or should that be 'a congeries of habituses'?):

1 *It must generate behaviour appropriate to the environment.* Totemism, for example, is associated with hunter-gatherer territoriality, and expresses the association between groups and areas of land (see Layton 1986). Kwakiutl lineages came together in their winter villages for mutual defence against warfare (Maschner 1997), and therefore benefited from rituals that helped to merge their separate identities.
2 *It must make sense of experience.* Rowlands's study of war memorials shows how memorials attempt to make sense of the loss of life in warfare.
3 *It must be mutually intelligible and transmissible.* Artists, for example, learn how to read the style and iconography of existing performances and use that knowledge to create new performances within the cultural idiom. These new works are in turn 'read' by an audience, whose expectations are shaped by their experiences. Where artist and audience share a similar habitus, readings will be more or less consistent, but the degree of consistency of readings needs to be verified and explained through fieldwork.

A good example of this phenomenon is given in Mulvaney's (1996) and Merlan's (1989) studies of rock art in the Victoria River district of northern Australia. Mulvaney was able to work with the children of known artists. These people were in their seventies and eighties when Mulvaney interviewed them. He found the paintings were 'memory triggers for whole stories, events and remembering people of the past' (Mulvaney 1996: 18). The paper deals only with paintings attributed to named people who were witnessed painting by Mulvaney's instructors. Some depicted memorable incidents that befell particular people while foraging, others portrayed ancestral and legendary beings. Totemic beings are typically depicted as large figures, and placed in shelters associated with the travels of the ancestor in question. Painting was only ever practised within one's own country.

Coupled with the tendency to depict ancestral beings at sites on their track, this facilitated interpretation by succeeding generations. Once incidents have faded from living memory, little can be said about paintings that record individual cases of hunting success other than general remarks on traditional hunting techniques and the importance of particular species in the diet (see Layton 1995). The Wardaman people Merlan (1989) worked with had been displaced during the violent years of early pastoral colonization (c. 1880–1930). When confronted with an unfamiliar site, Wardaman rely on the style and iconography of the art, their knowledge of the totemic landscape in which the art is placed, and the legends describing the ancestors' travels to interpret it. They were relatively confident about arriving, through discussion, at the identity of ancestral figures. However, while a minority of the man-made figures were attributed to named individuals or categories of people, the majority were simply described as the work of 'old people', specific incidents having been forgotten.

Further work on the durability of interpretative traditions will clearly help elucidate the transmission of habitus in different cultural contexts.

STRUCTURALISM AND SEMIOTICS IN ARCHAEOLOGY

During the first half of the twentieth century the dominant interpretation of Upper Palaeolithic rock art, advocated by Breuil (1952), was that paintings and engravings had accumulated more or less randomly in the caves as the product of sympathetic magic. In the late 1950s,

Laming and Leroi-Gourhan proposed a radically different, structuralist interpretation. They argued that figures were deliberately placed in certain regions of the cave and that the juxtaposition of different species expressed cognitive oppositions in Palaeolithic culture. In the French cave of Lascaux many panels seemed to repeat the same juxtapositioning of different species: horse and bison, mammoth and wild cattle. Predatory animals seemed to be confined to inaccessible locations (Laming 1962: 271–85). Leroi-Gourhan surveyed Palaeolithic cave art in France and Spain, and claimed that some species (deer, ibex, horse) always occurred in narrow passages, while others (bison and wild cattle) occurred in large chambers. Where the two classes occurred on the same panel, deer, etc., were peripheral, bison and cattle at the centre. Leroi-Gourhan claimed to have found the means to interpret these oppositions in the simple geometric 'signs' that earlier writers had construed as weapons or huts. In his view, they were all simplified representations of human sexual organs; 'female' signs were associated with bison and cattle, 'male' signs with the periphery (Leroi-Gourhan 1958a, b, 1964).

Leroi-Gourhan's claims were re-examined, and rejected, by Ucko and Rosenfeld (1967). His distribution patterns failed to be replicated in caves that were discovered later. While his particular interpretations have since been abandoned, there is no doubt that only a few of the possible pairings of species actually occur in Upper Palaeolithic caves (Sauvet and Wlodarczyk 2000–01). Sauvet et al. (1977) classified signs strictly according to visual similarities in their form, without making any attempt to guess what they represented. They found statistical regularities in the association of different 'signs', reporting that only a limited number of the mathematically possible combinations are actually found. This led them to conclude that each of their twelve categories of sign probably constituted a single unit of signification in a system governed by 'grammatical' rules, but they did not attempt to infer what the meaning of the signs might be.

Following Barthes's lead, the study of clothes and artefacts as signifiers – particularly of ethnic identity – has been taken up by several archaeologists (Wobst 1977; Hodder 1982; Wiessner 1983). There remains plenty of scope for ethno-archaeology to elucidate how the use of artefacts as signifiers is negotiated, held constant or reinterpreted. Such findings can allow a more fine-grained interpretation of the archaeological record.

A number of archaeologists, including Tilley (1991) and Richards (1996), have extrapolated from Bourdieu's analysis of the Kabyle house to reread archaeological landscapes as the material construction of messages about power and gender. However, the relative indeterminacy of cultural meanings, both between cultures and (as post-structural studies emphasize) within cultures, makes interpretation difficult. Tilley (1990: 67) noted the potential value for archaeology of Lévi-Strauss's structural analyses of the relationship between native American social organization and settlement structure. Colin Richards's study of the Neolithic landscape on the Orkney Islands of Scotland offers a definitive interpretation of one prehistoric settlement. Late Neolithic houses on Orkney have the same cruciform layout as the nearby tomb of Maes Howe. As Richards puts it, people dwelled around the 'life-maintaining' central hearth of the house. The tomb of Maes Howe has the same cruciform structure, but lacked a central hearth: it was a house of the dead. Maes Howe was covered by a clay mound that 'positions the dead as being below the surface of the humanly inhabited world' (Richards 1996: 202). Remarkably, the entrance passage is oriented so that, just before and just after the midwinter solstice, the sun shines directly into the tomb. Richards draws, not unreasonably, upon the kind of widespread imagery recorded by van Gennep, and by Lévi-Strauss in South America, to infer ideas signified by the opposition of tomb to settlement, and its orientation to the sun. The direction of the entrance is interpreted as signifying a passage rite, the death of the old year and the birth of the new; a time of celebration.

It is unlikely that most prehistoric sites will be as unambiguous as Maes Howe. Tilley used ethnographic evidence for the significance of the distribution of rock art in the landscape to derive several possible readings of 4,000 year old rock engravings at the Swedish site of Namforsen. Tilley acknowledged that 'one of the features of the Namforsen rock carvings … is their inherent ambiguity' (Tilley 1991: 78). He was conscious of the power that lies in the hands of archaeologists when the site's original creators cannot dispute much later archaeological interpretation. To 'read' Namforsen, Tilley argues, one must first identify the units of signification and rules for their combination into statements. The panels are complex, but certain recognizable motifs such as ships, elk and human footprints appear many times and each therefore probably conveyed a discrete meaning within a cultural structure. The juxtaposition

of elk and fish, for example, seems to signify a cognitive opposition between land and sea. One interpretation of the various oppositions is to read them, following Lévi-Strauss, as the expression of a totemic system in which (for example) a land-oriented clan is juxtaposed to a sea-oriented clan. However, no single reading can be persuasive because the text does not seem to match what that reading predicts. 'Understanding is a process in which we need to try out alternative readings of the text in order to see how to make sense of it from different positions' (1991: 117). Tilley therefore turns to the ethnography of the Evenk, recent hunter-gatherers from the same region, and tries a second interpretation, of Namforsen as the liminal space occupied by shamans. Tilley finds many of the features that Turner considered diagnostic of liminality reproduced in the distribution of images.

Looking for structure in the distribution of rock art sites and the intensity of occupation, Bruno David has discussed how far into the past the 'archaeological signature' of Australian Aboriginal beliefs can be traced. For example, Ngarrabullgan (Mount Mulligan), in north Queensland, was avoided by local Aboriginal people during colonial times. People have lived in the region for more than 35,000 years. Ngarrabullgan was intensively occupied from 5400 BP to 900 BP, but rock shelters on the top of the mountain were then abandoned, even though other rock shelters in the region continued to be used. Current beliefs must therefore be only about 900 years old. 'Abandonment … appears to have been mediated by the onset of a new *system* of signification that rendered the mountain inappropriate for habitation' (David 2002: 46, my emphasis). Abandonment of the single site of Ngarrabullgan carries less weight than the regional rise in rock painting at contemporary sacred sites in central Australia, which David also discusses, between 900 and 600 years ago. Here, a much older stylistic tradition of geometric motifs becomes distributed across the landscape in a new pattern. In my view (Layton 1992: 231. ff), the ethnographically documented modes of mapping on to the landscape expressed through clan totemism can be traced to the appearance of the Australian 'small tool' tradition, associated with more permanent base camps, about 5,000 years ago. I consider David is unlikely to be correct when he claims the very foundations of the Aboriginal theory of being are no more than a few hundred years old, but do see his method for tracking change in Aboriginal cultural practices as fruitful.

In the field of structuralism and semiotics, I believe the most pressing research questions for anthropology concern the ways in which mutual understandings are negotiated and the extent to which they are achieved. Archaeological research can benefit from Anthropology, but must address different questions. Archaeology needs to consider what conditions make cognitive structures apparent in the patterning of the archaeological record, and question carefully the extent to which researchers can 'decode' the material expression of prehistoric cultures. Archaeologists cannot gain the intersubjective insights that come from participant observation, but they can investigate how uniformity of practice is sustained for a sufficiently long time to become archaeologically visible and, potentially, what kinds of political process lead to the expression of cognitive structures in the landscape.

Archaeology needs to develop systematic procedures for assessing reconstructions of meanings from past cultures. While the physical structure of monuments and distributions of rock art in the landscape can sometimes be identified beyond reasonable doubt, are there any criteria for deciding which readings are merely possible and which are likely on the balance of probabilities to be correct? Bourdieu's explanation for the transmission of habitus through the construction of the Kabyle house proposes a two-way process. The Kabyle house refers to men and women, and it signifies their relative status. Richards's 'reading' of Maes Howe somewhat similarly depends first on identifying references that artefacts such as tombs and houses make to things in the real world (the hearth in the Orkney house, the winter sun). The meanings of these things are then inferred from plausibly universal cognitive structures. This is by no means always possible. Tilley's analysis of Namforsen takes us further into plausible conjecture, and can draw on regional ethnography that may well have some continuity from the period when the rock art he discusses was created.

By the time we extend research as far back as the Upper Palaeolithic, the structure of meaning is irrecoverable. We can recognize paintings in Upper Palaeolithic art that refer to horse and bison, but we do not know what horse and bison signified in the cultures of the Upper Palaeolithic. Breuil's assumption that Upper Palaeolithic cave art accumulated randomly can be challenged through statistical analysis, but Leroi-Gourhan's interpretation of simple, variable and ambiguous geometric motifs as signifiers of gender was hopelessly optimistic. Shamanism has been argued as a *motive* for Upper Palaeolithic art (e.g. Lewis-Williams 2002), and this line of research has offered another way of investigating the distinctive cognitive structure of Upper Palaeolithic culture. Since the Upper Palaeolithic art of France and Spain represents the earliest incontestable art tradition, and is associated with the arrival of fully modern humans in western Europe, the structure of the art (expressed in the range of motifs and their distribution within and between sites) and the evidence that gives of cognitive skills, are probably of more interest to modern researchers than the specific meaning any images may have held in their original cultural context.

REFERENCES

Barthes, R. (1967) *Elements of Semiology*, trans. A. Lavers and C. Smith. London: Cape.

Bourdieu, P. (1977) *Outline of a Theory of Practice*, trans. R. Nice. Cambridge: Cambridge University Press.

Bourdieu, P. (1980/1990) *The Logic of Practice*, trans. R. Nice. Stanford, CA: Stanford University Press.

Breuil, H. (1952) *Four Hundred Centuries of Cave Art*, trans. M. Boyle. Montignac: Centre d'Études et de Documentation Préhistoriques.

Campbell, S. (2001) 'The captivating agency of art: many ways of seeing', in C. Pinney and N. Thomas (eds), *Beyond Aesthetics: Art and the Technology of Enchantment*. Oxford: Berg, pp. 117–35.

Charbonnier, G. (1961) *Entretiens avec Claude Lévi-Strauss*. Paris: Plon.

Clifford, J. (1986) 'On ethnographic allegory', in J. Clifford and G. Marcus (eds), *Writing Culture*, Berkeley, CA: University of California Press, pp. 98–107.

David, Bruno (2002) *Landscapes, Rock-art and the Dreaming: an Archaeology of Preunderstanding*. Leicester: Leicester University Press.

Derrida, J. (1976) *Of Grammatology*, trans. G.C. Spivak. Baltimore, MD: Johns Hopkins University Press.

Dobres, M.-A. (2000) *Technology and Social Agency*. Oxford: Blackwell.

Douglas, M. (1966) *Purity and Danger*. London: Routledge.

Douglas, M., ed. (1973) *Rules and Meanings*. Harmondsworth: Penguin Books.

Douglas, M. (1975): 'Deciphering a meal', in M. Douglas, *Implicit Meanings*. London: Routledge, pp. 249–75.

Durkheim, E. (1915) *The Elementary Forms of the Religious Life*, trans. J.W. Swain. London: Unwin.

Durkheim, E. and Mauss, M. (1903/1963) *Primitive Classification*, trans. Rodney Needham. London: Cohen & West.

Faris, J. (1971) *Nuba Personal Art*. London: Duckworth.

Foucault, F. (1977) *Discipline and Punish: the Birth of the Prison*. London: Penguin.

Foucault, M. (1972) *The Archaeology of Knowledge*, trans. A.M. Sheridan Smith. London: Tavistock.

Gell, A. (1998) *Art and Agency: an Anthropological Theory*. Oxford: Oxford University Press.

Gennep, A. van (1960) *The Rites of Passage*, trans. M.B. Vizedom and G.L. Caffee. London: Routledge.

Giddens, A. (1979) *Central Problems in Social Theory: Action, Structure and Contradiction in Social Analysis*. London: Macmillan.

Giddens, A. (1984) *The Constitution of Society*. Cambridge: Polity Press.

Glucksmann, M. (1974) *Structural Analysis in Contemporary Social Thought: a Comparison of the Theories of Claude Lévi-Strauss and Louis Althusser*. London: Routledge.

Gombrich, E. (1972) 'The visual image,' *Scientific American*, September, pp. 82–96.

Gowlett, J. (1984) 'Mental abilities of early man: a look at some hard evidence', in R. Foley (ed.), *Hominid Evolution and Community Ecology*. London: Academic Press, pp. 167–92.

Hawkes, T. (1977) *Structuralism and Semiotics*. London: Methuen.

Hodder, I. (1982) *Symbols in Action*. Cambridge: Cambridge University Press.

Keane, W. (forthcoming) 'Signs are not the garb of meaning: on the social analysis of material things', in D. Miller (ed.), *Materiality*. Durham, NC: Duke University Press.

Korn, S. (1978) 'The formal analysis of visual systems as exemplified by a study of Abelam (Papua New Guinea) painting', in M. Greenhalgh and V. Megaw (eds), *Art in Society: Studies in Style, Culture and Aesthetics*. London: Duckworth, pp. 161–73.

Korsmeyer, C. (2002) 'The meaning of taste and the taste of meaning', in A. Neill and A. Ridley (eds), *Arguing about Art: Contemporary Debates*. London: Routledge, pp. 28–48.

Laming, A. (1962) *La Signification de l'art rupestre paléolithique*. Paris: Picard.

Lane, M., ed. (1970) *Structuralism: a Reader*. London: Cape.

Layton, R. (1981/1991). *The Anthropology of Art*. St Albans: Granada. Cambridge: Cambridge University Press.

Layton, R. (1986) 'Political and territorial structures among hunter-gatherers', *Man*, 21: 18–33.

Layton, R. (1992) *Australian Rock Art*. Cambridge: Cambridge University Press.

Layton, R. (1995) 'Rereading rock art: text and discourse', in K. Helskog and B. Olsen (eds), *Perceiving Rock Art: Social and Political Perspectives*. Oslo: Novus, pp. 183–93.

Layton, R. (2000) *Anthropology and History in Franche Comté: A Critque of Social Theory*. Oxford: Oxford University Press.

Leroi-Gourhan, A. (1958a) 'La fonction des signes dans les sanctuaires paléolithiques', *Bulletin de la Société Préhistorique Française*, 55: 307–21.

Leroi-Gourhan, A. (1958b) 'Le symbolisme des grands signes dans les sanctuaires paléolithiques', *Bulletin de la Société Préhistorique Française*, 55: 384–98.

Leroi-Gourhan, A. (1964) *Les Religions de la préhistoire*. Paris: Presses Universitaires de France.

Lévi-Strauss, C. (1952) 'Social structure', in A.L. Kroeber (ed.), *Anthropology Today*. Chicago: University of Chicago Press.

Lévi-Strauss, C. (1966) *The Savage Mind*, trans. anon. London: Weidenfeld & Nicolson.

Lévi-Strauss, C. (1970) *The Raw and the Cooked: Introduction to a Science of Mythology*. London: Cape.

Lévi-Strauss, C. (1987) *The View from Afar*, trans. J. Neugroschel and P. Hoss. Harmondsworth: Penguin Books.

Lévi-Strauss, C. (1994) *Saudades do Brasil*. Paris: Plon.

Lewis-Williams, D. (2002) *The Mind in the Cave: Consciousness and the Origins of Art*. London: Thames & Hudson.

Maschner, H. (1997) 'The evolution of Northwest Coast warfare', in D.L. Martin and D.W. Frayer (eds), *Troubled Times: Violence and Warfare in the Past*. Amsterdam: Gordon & Breach, pp. 267–302.

Merlan, F. (1989) 'The interpretive framework of Wardaman rock art: a preliminary framework', *Australian Aboriginal Studies*, 1989 (2): 14–24.

Mounin, G. (1970) *Introduction à la sémiologie*. Paris: Minuit.

Mulvaney, K. (1996) 'What to do on a rainy day: reminiscences of Mirriuwung and Gadjerong artists', *Rock Art Research*, 13: 3–20.

Narayan, K. (1993) 'On nosecutters, gurus and story-tellers', in S. Lavie, K. Narayan and R. Rosaldo (eds), *Creativity/Anthropology*. Ithaca, NY: Cornell University Press, pp. 30–53.

Olsen, B. (1990) 'Roland Barthes: from sign to text', in C. Tilley (ed.), *Reading Material Culture*. Oxford: Blackwell, pp. 163–205.

Panofsky, E. (1955) *Meaning in the Visual Arts*. Harmondsworth: Penguin.

Peers, L.L. (1999) 'Many tender ties: the shifting contexts and meaning of the S. Black bag', *World Archaeology*, 31 (2): 288–302.

Peirce, C.S. (1955) 'Logic as semiotic: the theory of Signs', in J. Buchler (ed.), *The Philosophy of Peirce: Selected Writings*. London: Kegan Paul, pp. 98–119.

Piaget, J. (1968/1971) *Structuralism*, trans. C. Maschler. London: Routledge.

Povinelli, E.A. (1993) '"Might be something": the language of indeterminacy in Australian Aboriginal land use', *Man* (n.s.), 28: 679–704.

Richards, C. (1996) 'Monuments as landscape: creating the centre of the world in late Noelithic Orkney', *World Archaeology*, 28 (2): 190–208.

Robey, D. (1973) *Structuralism: an Introduction.* Oxford: Clarendon Press.

Rosman, A. and Rubel, P. (1990) 'Structural patterning in Kwakiutl art and ritual', *Man* (n.s.) 25: 620–39.

Rowlands, M. (1999) 'Remembering to forget: sublimation as sacrifice in war memorials', in A. Forty and S. Kuechler (eds), *The Art of Forgetting.* Oxford: Berg, pp. 129–45.

Ruesch, J. and Kees, W. (1970) *Nonverbal Communication: Notes on the Visual Perception of Human Relations.* Berkeley, CA: University of California Press.

Saunders, B. (1997) 'Contested *Ethnie* in two Kwakwaka'wakw museums', in J. MacClancy (ed.), *Contesting Art: Art, Politics and Identity in the Modern World.* Oxford: Berg, pp. 85–130.

Saussure, F. de (1915/1959) *Course in General Linguistics,* trans. C. Bally and A. Sechehaye. London: Owen.

Sauvet, G. and Wlodarczyk, A. (2000–01) 'L'art pariétal, miroir des sociétés paléolithiques', *Zephyrus* (University of Salamanca), 53–3: 217–40.

Sauvet, G., Sauvet, S. and Wlodarczyk, A. (1977) 'Essai de sémiologie préhistorique', *Bulletin de la Société Préhistorique Française,* 74: 545–58.

Searle, J.R. (1969) *Speech Acts: an Essay in the Philosophy of Language.* Cambridge: Cambridge University Press.

Spencer, B. and Gillen, F.J. (1899) *The Native Tribes of Central Australia.* London: Macmillan.

Sturrock, J., ed. (1979) *Structuralism and since: from Lévi-Strauss to Derrida.* Oxford: Oxford University Press.

Tilley, C. (1990) 'Claude Lévi-Strauss: structuralism and beyond', in C. Tilley (ed.), *Reading Material Culture.* Oxford: Blackwell, pp. 3–81.

Tilley, C. (1991) *Material Culture and Text: the Art of Ambiguity.* London: Routledge.

Turner, V.W. (1969) *The Ritual Process: Structure and Anti-Structure.* London: Routledge.

Turner, V.W. (1990) 'Are there any universals of performance in myth, ritual and drama?' in R. Schechner and W. Appel (eds), *By Means of Performance: Intercultural Studies of Theatre and Ritual.* Cambridge: Cambridge University Press, pp. 8–13.

Ucko, P. and Rosenfeld, A. (1967) *Palaeolithic Cave Art.* London: Weidenfeld & Nicolson.

Wang, Shucun, ed. (1985) *Corpora of Chinese Fine Arts, Fascicule of Painting XXI, Folk New Year's Painting.* Beijing: Wenwu Press.

Wiessner, P. (1983) 'Style and information in Kalahari San projectile points', *American Antiquity,* 48 (2): 253–76.

Wittig, S., ed. (1975) *Structuralism: an Interdisciplinary Study.* Pittsburgh, PA: Pickwick.

Wobst, M. (1977) 'Stylistic behaviour and information exchange', in C.E. Cleland (ed.), *Papers for the Director: Anthropology Papers of the Museum of Anthropology, University of Michigan,* 61: 317–42.

3

PHENOMENOLOGY AND MATERIAL CULTURE

Julian Thomas

While it may be relatively easy to isolate examples of Marxist, structuralist or feminist analyses of material culture, studies that openly identify themselves as phenomenological are a little scarcer. This is surprising, given that phenomenology is sometimes represented as a 'method', and is predominantly concerned with the human experience of 'things'. In this chapter I will argue that the ideas of the phenomenological tradition have been highly influential in the study of material culture, although their source has not always been explicitly acknowledged. Phenomenological insights have been readily adopted within other schools of thought, and they also amount to far more than an epistemology. Yet this latter point has been overlooked by some recent 'phenomenological' approaches, which understand the term to mean little more than a methodology in which the investigator bases their interpretation of a place or object upon their unbridled subjective experience. As I will hope to demonstrate, this does little justice to the subtlety of phenomenological thought. This chapter will draw out some of the principal strands of the tradition, demonstrating along the way the extent to which they have informed the study of material things, and focusing in particular on some of the studies that have been professedly phenomenological in character.

Phenomenology is concerned with the human encounter, experience and understanding of worldly things, and with how these happenings come to be possible. While empiricism and positivism take the *givenness* of material objects as an unquestioned first principle, phenomenologists from Edmund Husserl onwards have argued that if science is to concern itself with the acquisition of information through the physical senses (in laboratory experiments or field observations) then the character of experience needs to be problematized. Rationalists like Descartes had sought to overcome scepticism about our knowledge of the phenomenal world by starting from the reality of the human subject's thought processes. If we cannot doubt that we think, we can construct logical procedures and instruments for evaluating the veracity of our sense-impressions. Yet Husserl wanted to achieve a still greater degree of conviction, by understanding precisely what happens in the process through which some conception of an encountered thing is generated. If Descartes had sought to arrive at certainty through radical doubt, Husserl wanted to question all of his own assumptions and prejudices about the world in order to approach the purest essence of experience. Yet this same imperative to cast doubt on all presumptions would lead phenomenology towards a much more fundamental question: why is it that there is *something* instead of just nothing? (Heidegger 2001: 1).

Heidegger's question is a characteristically phenomenological one, even if by the time he asked it he had broken with his mentor and established a 'hermeneutic phenomenology' that was radically removed from Husserl's work. For what distinguishes phenomenology is not simply a concern with experience and understanding, but an unstinting demand that no aspect of either can be taken for granted. In the work of Heidegger, Merleau-Ponty and others the source of many of the unexamined assumptions about human existence came to be identified as the Western philosophical tradition itself, which phenomenology had originally been intended to strengthen. A consequence of this has been that one of the hallmarks of phenomenological thinking is the way that it commonly reverses the causal relationships presumed by contemporary 'common sense', such as those between substance and meaning, or essence and manifestation. Putting this another way, phenomenological arguments are often 'counter-intuitive', but they are constructed under the understanding that our 'intuition' is the product of a contingent order of things.

THE EMERGENCE OF PHENOMENOLOGICAL THOUGHT

Phenomenology in the accepted sense began with the work of Franz Brentano in the later nineteenth century. Brentano proposed what he called a 'descriptive psychology', which was to be differentiated from the neurological study of mental processes, and concerned with the significance and content of cognitive acts (Moran 2000: 9). Brentano pointed out that mental phenomena differ from physical ones in that they are always *directed* at something (Schuhmann 2004: 281). Anything that does not refer to something else is rightfully the subject matter of the natural sciences, but a different approach was required to address the directionality of conscious activity, which Brentano referred to as 'intentionality'. Intentionality always takes a form in which individual mental events are connected to one another relationally, so that a single episode of sense-perception is never just the acquisition of an atomized unit of information. In thought and perception, objects appear as 'presentations', which form the basic elements of consciousness (Rollinger 2004: 259). The intentionality of mental activity forms a whole or horizon, which renders these presentations comprehensible.

Brentano's account of intentionality greatly influenced Husserl, who originally intended his phenomenology to be a form of descriptive psychology. Husserl wanted to establish a science which could identify the fundamental structures of consciousness, thereby unravelling the problem of perception (Moran 2000: 60). Intentionality was central to this project, for Husserl held that consciousness is always directed towards some object, whether real or imagined. Consciousness is always consciousness-of-something, although this something may be as abstract as a number or a mathematical formula. The implication of this is that intentionality provides the basis for the relationship between people and their world, which is bodily as well as cognitive, although the objects to which we direct ourselves are objects-as-conceptualized. Husserl wanted to address these cognitive objects in their purest form: not mental processes but the ideal entities to which these refer and direct themselves (Matthews 2002: 24). For Husserl, this was what the 'phenomena' of phenomenology amounted to, things that appeared as such in consciousness. It would be easy to argue that this amounts to a form of idealism, yet Husserl's view was that, in the process of the directing of consciousness toward its objects, something about the world beyond the mind is given to us (Hintikka 1995: 82). For while in some senses the phenomena that Husserl was attempting to isolate were attributes of the mind, they were also the means by which 'intuition' is possible. Intuition is the kind of insight that occurs when one recognizes that something is the case (Moran 2000: 10). Intuition is the experience of 'getting the point' and recognizing how things are. This is what happens when we understand material things. It was the purity of these moments of insight that Husserl's phenomenology sought to capture, in which we cannot doubt that we have apprehended the real nature of things through our mental apparatus. Husserl claimed that his phenomenology was governed by a 'principle of propositionlessness', and dealt not in abstract theories but with the attempt to address 'the things themselves' (2000: 9). He stressed that material things are always revealed *to* someone, and thus stressed the importance of human beings as subjects of experience.

Husserl's emphasis on identifying experiences in their purest possible state led him by the first decade of the twentieth century to establish a working procedure that he referred to as the 'phenomenological reduction'. This was intended to lead the investigator from episodes of perception to the universal essences that underlay them, by 'bracketing' the prejudicial assumptions that surrounded any particular experience and exposing the core of pure consciousness and the phenomena immanent within it. These assumptions made up what Husserl called the 'natural attitude': the average, unquestioning, everyday perspective from which we generally approach the world. The reduction involved a radical self-questioning, in which the investigator attempted to strip away all of the conceptual clutter that tied the core experience to a contingent set of circumstances. By this means, it should be possible to identify precisely what consciousness was directing itself towards in the course of an experience: its intentional object.

Husserl's term for the raw material of experience, gathered from the material world, was 'hyle'. Like Kant before him, he argued that this material was chaotic and formless, and impossible to apprehend in its native state. It is the ordering capabilities of human beings that render hyletic data comprehensible, through the way that we direct our attention to particular things, in the process rendering them as objects of consciousness (Hintikka 1995: 88). This can happen because the human mind has at its disposal a series of ideal objects, or *noema*, which are 'filled' by experience, thereby providing it with a structure. The noema are objects-as-they-are-intended, the vehicles of intentionality, which specify the expectations that enable a particular phenomenon to be identified. Thus, for instance, a noemon for the colour red might be composed of a series of conditions which allowed the colour to be identified when encountered in experience. Husserl considered these noema to be *a priori* structures of consciousness, while still providing a bridge between consciousness and the physical world.

As a new foundation for the sciences, Husserl intended that the phenomenological reduction should identify a series of structures that have priority over scientific observation and scientific explanation (Matthews 2002: 32). The causal relationships that natural science deals in are relations between entities whose character has *already* been established before explanation can begin, and this requires that their significance or meaning must already have been grasped. Husserl's phenomenology was thus concerned with the 'pre-scientific'. Implicit in this view is the recognition that science is a worldly practice, carried out by human subjects in the phenomenal world, and containing contingent elements which must themselves be bracketed if one is to approach the fundamental structures of consciousness. This bracketing should attempt to set aside all aspects of the lived world, in order to grasp how the abstract essences of phenomena might appear to a pure consciousness. Everything else is epiphenomenal and non-essential. Needless to say, this approach committed Husserl to the belief that particular aspects of mental functioning are

transcendental. The 'natural attitude' was to be associated with the particular and the historical, and even the assumption of the existence of a world needed to be bracketed in order to access the horizon of pure subjectivity (Moran 2000: 2).

If phenomenology was to be pre-scientific, the criteria of explanatory adequacy used in science could not apply to it. 'Facts' could not provide any basis for the verification of phenomenological insights (Husserl 1983: 44), since facts were actually constructed in the processes that phenomenology sought to illuminate. What had been grasped intuitively could only be verified through further intuitive insights. As we have seen, Husserl's faith in the security of such insights was connected with the incontestable reality of thought, itself linked with the notion of a transcendental subject. Eventually, Husserl would come to argue that since science was built upon theoretical abstractions that were secondary to the structures of experience, the world of lived engagement (the 'life-world') had priority over scientific explanation. While it is common to imagine that science deals in the fundamental realities of things, Husserl would claim that the truths of science were abstracted from more basic structures (Ricoeur 1974: 8).

None of this, however, should encourage us to believe that Husserl was anti-scientific. His phenomenology aspired to achieve the status of an 'eidetic' rather than a factual science. Such eidetic sciences included geometry and mathematics, which concerned themselves with abstract essences instead of factual observations. Their truths were demonstrated by logic and reason, as opposed to inductive or deductive treatments of evidence. Just as physics and chemistry depend upon the insights of mathematics and geometry, Husserl believed that phenomenology could become an eidetic science of consciousness, essential to the reform of the natural sciences. To this end, he proposed that the phenomenological reduction should be complemented by an 'eidetic reduction', in which the investigator moved beyond the bracketing of everyday experience to an appreciation of the universal essence of reality (Moran 2000: 134).

HEIDEGGER AND HERMENEUTIC PHENOMENOLOGY

While Husserl brought the modern phenomenological tradition into being, it was his pupil

Martin Heidegger who radically transformed that tradition. Heidegger's phenomenology is at once one that has had many more points of contact with other modes of inquiry (mainstream philosophy, hermeneutics, theology, *gestalt* psychology and eventually post-structuralism), and that has had more influence on the study of material culture. Heidegger's project began with Husserl's insight that natural science is a way of finding out very particular things about the world, rather than a source of universal grounding truths. In particular, the sciences are relatively powerless to understand the fundamental character of human existence (Zimmerman 1990: 19). As we have seen, science is grounded upon a deeper understanding of worldly things: entities are already comprehensible before we begin to explain them. Heidegger drew upon hermeneutics to address the character of human understanding. But while hermeneutics had hitherto concentrated on the interpretation of scripture and historical texts, Heidegger argued that understanding was fundamental to all human existence. To experience, understand and interpret is not just a method of inquiry, it is a mode of being (Ricoeur 1974: 3). For Heidegger, phenomenology was not a science at all, but a means of addressing whatever shows itself to us, and whatever seems to be something (Heidegger 1962: 51).

To Heidegger, a thing's being is its *disclosure* or revelation, and this depends upon its being understood-as (Frede 1993: 57). To be intelligible, any entity must be recognizable-as-something. Phenomenology is therefore concerned not just with consciousness, but with the way that the human world is constituted as a structure of intelligibility. While Husserl wanted to reduce experience down to its fundamental atoms by bracketing the everyday world, Heidegger is emphatic that things can reveal themselves to us only *in a world*. Worldly things are not just objects in consciousness: they are always embedded in a complex network of relations between people and things, and they are only comprehensible as such (1993: 53). Furthermore, the disclosure of things is not a matter of isolated objects being observed by a transcendental subject. Things show themselves only to a particular kind of being: a mortal human who always finds themselves embedded in cultural tradition, enmeshed in social relations with others, and engaged in pursuing projects for the future. The world cannot be bracketed at all, because it forms the horizon within which things

disclose themselves, while human beings have a form of existence which is inconceivable without its being located in multiple contexts and relationships: this is *being-in-the-world*. This means that Heidegger radically reassesses the 'natural attitude' and the life-world, arguing that the 'ordinary everydayness' of human existence is actually constitutive of what Husserl would call 'intentionality' (Critchley 2000: 102).

Husserl had maintained the Cartesian relationship between object and subject, and along with it had accepted what Heidegger would refer to as the 'substance ontology' of Western thought. This is the view that what distinguishes worldly things is their 'object givenness', their physical existence as lumps of matter. The world thus comes to be understood as a collection of independently existing entities, which can be perceived by human subjects, who are themselves lumps of matter to which minds are in some way connected. Heidegger's conception of 'being-in-the-world' is a means of repudiating the separation of mind and body, and rejecting the view that phenomena are given as substantial entities that are represented in consciousness (Frede 1993: 60). For Heidegger, the Western philosophical tradition has assumed that there is only one possible relationship between people and things: that between subject and object, in which we observe some entity in a distanced, dispassionate and analytical fashion. But, in reality, things can show themselves to us in a variety of different ways, depending on the kind of involvement that we have with them (Heidegger 1962: 51). In particular, we can draw a distinction between the 'present-at-hand' and the 'ready-to-hand'. The former is the situation in which the passive observer looks on something as an object of knowledge or contemplation, while the latter denotes an engagement in which a thing is put to use, perhaps as a tool in some task (Hall 1993: 125). Heidegger's classic example of this is the hammer, which 'recedes' from our explicit concern as we use it to hammer in a nail. We focus on the task rather than the tool, and in the process we achieve a much more primordial and instinctual communion with it than if we merely stared at the hammer from a distance (Heidegger 1962: 97). In *Being and Time* (1962) Heidegger explains that when we use something as a piece of equipment, a 'thing-for', it is always part of an 'equipmental totality', so that, as well as being submerged in the practice of use, the thing is also bound in to a network of reference and connection. The hammer is in the first instance known as part of a constellation that includes the nail, the roof tile, the rafter, and so on. Our everyday understanding is of totalities, contexts, projects and relationships, rather than of isolated objects. Only when the hammer fails in use, malfunctioning or breaking down (the head comes off, the handle breaks, or the tool is simply not heavy enough for the task), does it become present-at-hand, something that we just look at and contemplate in its uselessness.

What is significant here is that readiness-to-hand and presence-to-hand are both ways in which things can be disclosed to us, although they engender quite different kinds of familiarity. So the same object or artefact can become known to us in a series of distinct ways. The ring which is a family heirloom can be at one moment reassuring and at another depressing, depending upon how we are feeling (Guignon 2001: 54). Cartesian thought would hold that these feelings about an object are entirely secondary to its existence as a material thing, and have no bearing upon its 'facticity'. Heidegger would suggest on the contrary that our moods or attunements are 'world-disclosing'; they are implicated in the way that things show up to us in the first place. Indeed, in particularly nihilistic or angst-ridden moods, the world fails to reveal itself at all. It presents us with no possibilities. Yet as Heidegger points out, we have no choice over which mood we will find ourselves in at a given time: we are 'delivered over' to our mood. This involvement of mood in the disclosure of things underlines the way that phenomena can only be 'there' for humans, who are finite beings caught between past, present and future in a concrete situation (Polt 2001: 59). Yet this is not to argue that the appearance of material things as recognizable entities is a human 'achievement' or willed practice. Human beings 'ground the presence' of things whether they like it or not (Heidegger 1993: 234). It might be more accurate to say that humans provide the space in which things can appear, which is quite different from willing them into being (Zimmerman 1993: 244).

While Heidegger's early arguments about the position of things as tools in an equipmental totality may be flawed, in a broader sense the way that people gain an understanding of material entities depends upon a *background* or horizon. This background is composed of a variety of embodied skills and means of coping, cultural traditions, a general conception of how the world is ordered, and a variety of

human projects and requirements (Wrathall 2000: 94). It is in the context of this network of entities and practices that things reveal themselves, not for the most part as puzzling or requiring explanation but as always-already understood. It is therefore a mistake to imagine that human beings wander around the world, encountering isolated packages of information and rendering them meaningful. Things are revealed *in their meaningfulness* in the first instance, and the notion of a pure Cartesian object which has only physical extension and density is actually abstracted from a significant entity.

MERLEAU-PONTY AND LEVINAS

Although Heidegger's work intersects with material culture studies most directly, another phenomenologist whose ideas are of relevance was Maurice Merleau-Ponty. We have seen that Heidegger used phenomenology as a springboard for a series of reflections on what he would call 'fundamental ontology'. For Heidegger, the adoption of a phenomenological approach, and the challenging of conventional suppositions that it requires, lead us inevitably into a consideration of far-reaching philosophical issues. In particular, Heidegger was preoccupied with the question of Being, and the contrast between Being in general and the existence of particular creatures (the 'ontological difference'). Merleau-Ponty, on the other hand, restricted himself to attempting to understand how human beings conduct themselves under particular contingent conditions (Matthews 2002: 31). Like Heidegger, Merleau-Ponty rejected Husserl's search for universal, transcendental structures of consciousness, and indeed denied the existence of any such thing. This was partly because he understood perception to be culturally formed (Ihde 1993: 76). Merleau-Ponty also shared Heidegger's concern with the lived world of everyday activity, rather than attempting to create some form of science of human experience.

Merleau-Ponty's focus was perception, which (like Husserl) he took to be pre-scientific in character. Perception is experience that takes place before reflection and theorizing (Merleau-Ponty 1962: 131). It is unlike symbolic communication, for it is not concerned with representation, and it cannot be explained in a scientific manner, for it is not an object (Matthews 2002: 47). Perception is not simply a cognitive activity, for the subject who engages in experience is always embodied (Merleau-Ponty 1962: 203). This argument requires a rather different view of intentionality from that proposed by Brentano and Husserl, for Merleau-Ponty implies that it is the incarnated being that directs it attention to things in the world. An embodied human being can see, and can move around, position itself in relation to things, and handle them. Sight, touch and movement provide quite particular ways of entering into relationships with things, and none of these can be achieved by a disembodied mind. So intentionality is dispersed throughout the body rather than concentrated in a cognitive realm. Merleau-Ponty's treatment of perception is distinctively phenomenological, in that he argues that sensations are not isolated or atomized sense-events. They can be understood only in the wider context of a person's immersion in the world. Perception is inherently meaningful, and people apprehend sensations in terms of what they signify ('my leg is itchy') rather than as pure sense-data, which are somehow given significance after they have been identified ('the nerve endings on my lower leg are registering some kind of signal – I guess it must be an itch'). The body's relationship with the world that it inhabits is charged with meaning, and each sensory episode both draws from and contributes to our experience and comprehension of the totality.

Merleau-Ponty's emphasis on the embodied person as the subject of experience finds an echo in the work of Emmanuel Levinas, who perhaps even more than Heidegger explored the broader repercussions of the phenomenological approach. Contradicting the Western philosophical tradition that afforded a grounding status to epistemology, Levinas maintained that ethics should be recognized as 'first philosophy' (Levinas 1998: 100). Levinas's ethics is founded upon a phenomenology of the other person, concerned with the experience of being face to face with another human being. Like Merleau-Ponty, Levinas insists that we understand the other person to be corporeal, and as a being who can experience hunger, thirst, pain, pleasure, lust and enjoyment (Waldenfels 2002: 65). Our ethical relationships are not with abstract universal subjects, but with the kind of being who knows the pleasure of eating. The face-to-face relation with the other is inherently ethical, as it brings us directly into contact with a living being to whom we are responsible (Wyschogrod 2002: 191). Just as Merleau-Ponty

places embodied perception before the scientific explanation of conceptual objects, Levinas argued that the relationship with the other precedes and extends beyond comprehension. Following Heidegger, he saw being alongside others as constitutive of our identity as human beings – one can have no sense of oneself as a self without the presence of another. Yet I can never be the other person, and I can never see the world through their eyes. There is always something about the other person that escapes my understanding. Because I cannot be at all, in the absence of the other person, and because the speaking person addresses me directly, I am compelled to offer solicitude to the other in their suffering. Ethical duty is embedded in relationships which precede reason and science.

GEOGRAPHY, ARCHITECTURE AND PLANNING

The concerns of Merleau-Ponty and Levinas ostensibly draw us away from this chapter's focus on material culture studies. But both demonstrate that it is impossible to insulate the phenomenological approach, and present it as a neatly packaged 'methodology', which can be straightforwardly applied to a given body of evidence. Because phenomenology systematically undermines the modern West's prioritization of epistemology and the demand that ethics, aesthetics, rhetoric and politics be purged from analysis and explanation, these concerns are forever on the brink of erupting into any phenomenological investigation. Phenomenology deals in world disclosure, in which an engagement with a particular entity leads us into an expanding web of relationships. No matter how restricted the frame of inquiry, phenomenology will tend to lead towards more extensive reflections.

It was precisely this reflexive dimension of phenomenological thought that attracted geographers and architects during the 1960s and 1970s. In both disciplines, the earlier twentieth century had seen a growing emphasis on a Cartesian conception of space, in which the relationships between objects could be discussed in purely geometrical terms (Gregory 1978: 131). This perspective appeared to evict human beings from their lived world, repositioning them as viewers and interpreters of a domain of objects. The so-called 'humanistic geography' presented an alternative which focused on the question of *place*, a phenomenon which is arguably difficult to account for in quantitative or geometrical terms. A place is not simply a region of space, but is experienced by people as having meaning (Tuan 1974: 213; Relph 1976: 15). This meaning is culturally specific, and needs to be understood from an insider's point of view (Lynch 1972: 29). Much of this debate proceeded on the basis that meaningless space is transformed into meaningful place through human intervention, and thus risked simply reproducing the Cartesian framework of an inert world which is rendered meaningful by humanity. Nonetheless, Yi-Fu Tuan presented an account of place and landscape that was more authentically phenomenological. Tuan's critically important insight was that the geometrical space of 'scientific' geography was not a given, but was itself a sophisticated cultural construction (1974: 215). This means that there is no founding knowledge of space that is meaning-free, and to which meaning is added. On the contrary, people discover their world in the process of understanding it, and Tuan lays much stress on the role of the human body in this process.

Although Tuan's account tends toward the archetypal, his attempts to identify fundamental spatial experiences have much to commend them. He suggests that it is the presence of the body that gives places their structure and orientation, and that this affects the way that we characteristically create architecture. Thus, most rooms are divided into a back and a front, and are accessed by a human-sized portal (1977: 40). In the same way, people create a spatial understanding of the world in general (including parts of it that they have never directly experienced) by elaborating on the spatiality of the body. 'Mythical space' can thus use the body as a microcosm, or present a cosmology ordered around the cardinal points, which are themselves centred on the body (Tuan 1977: 96). Places are most significant to us when they are associated with a human presence (that of ourselves or others), and consequentially Tuan argues that buildings and monuments are in some senses substitutes for human beings, in that they constitute centres of meaning (1974: 239). In pre-modern societies, Tuan suggests, such places are differentiated from the chaotic and formless state of the cosmos at large by the presumed presence of spirits and deities, so that temples and shrines are instrumental in the development of a structured conception of the world (1974: 234).

At the same time, the development of a built environment transforms the way that human beings interact with their world, because architecture refines and sharpens our experience of place (Tuan 1977: 107).

Ideas like Tuan's eventually had some impact on discussions of the design and planning of urban spaces. In the post-war era, town planning was often based upon principles of rationality and efficiency, resulting in developments that were often anonymous and alienating (Relph 1993: 28). The modernist prescription that an ideal society or living space could be designed in the abstract and then constructed in material form appeared to be contradicted by the reality that dwellings created on an 'intuitive' or 'organic' basis promoted a more harmonious existence than contemporary 'machines for living'. Where concrete tower blocks seemed disconnected with the human scale, a phenomenological approach advocated an architecture that served as an extension of the human body (Jäger 1985: 215). The 'primitive geography' of embodied experience described by Tuan could thus provide the point of departure for a kind of planning that worked outward from people's everyday involvement in the world, rather than imposing a totalitarian spatial order from above. Under these circumstances, the connection between people and buildings would be a seamless one, in much the same way as in Heidegger's description of tool use: an authentic form of dwelling. By facilitating people's harmonization with their lived world architecture might become more than a set of aesthetic objects, and contribute to human well-being (Dovey 1993: 249).

A number of authors stressed that a phenomenological approach to planning and architecture could not limit itself to considerations of form, but had to address the relationship between the building and the dweller (Dovey 1985: 34). This might mean either that architecture should emerge out of the commitment to place and the established dwelling practices of a community, or that buildings should themselves be capable of engendering a relationship between people and place. Kimberley Dovey, for instance, argued that buildings are more likely to enable people to enter into an authentic relationship with their world when they themselves possess authenticity (1985: 33). So rather than being adorned with window shutters that don't actually close, or non-functional chimneys, buildings have forms that articulate with life as it is lived.

Precisely how this approach to the built environment would work in practice is made a little clearer by Violich's comparative analysis of four Dalmatian coastal towns (1985: 114). This is presented as an 'intuitive urban reading', but it is actually an attempt to distil from the experience of walking the town streets those elements that render the built landscape welcoming, inclusive or alienating. The obvious problem with such a project is that it is undertaken from a first-person perspective, yet makes no attempt to theorize the conditions that contribute to the specificity of a particular person's experience of place. Nonetheless, Violich's account produces a series of insights that could not have been extracted from maps or plans alone. In seeking clues to the distinctive identities of the four towns, he points to the combination of topographic and historical/cultural elements (Violich 1985: 114). Given that they are all harbour settlements, particular stress is laid on the way that land and water meet in relation to the urban form (Figure 3.1). Thus Pucisce and Hvar wrap around their harbours, while Bol lies side-by-side with the sea, and Korcula thrusts out into the ocean (Figure 3.2). The consequence of this set of relationships is that Bol has developed into an 'urban ladder' or grid of streets running parallel with

the sea, Pucisce rises up its hills like a theatre from the stage-like harbour, and Korcula's architectural qualities are set off against the surrounding water (Figure 3.3). Korcula's enclosed quality is further enhanced by the mountainscape beyond the sea channel, and its old centre is distinct from newer development inland. Visiting Korcula therefore has the particular quality of moving from the present into the past, and back again (Violich 1985: 129). Violich's point is that the constellation of social, cultural and physical phenomena that make up that character of a place can be discovered only from within.

THE DAYAK LONGHOUSE

Violich's 'reading' of Dalmatian coastal towns finds an interesting comparison in Christine Helliwell's investigation of the domestic architecture of the Gerai Dayak of Borneo (1996). Violich insists that the various strands of urban identity can be integrated only through the pedestrian's experience of moving through the streets, revealing them from inside. Similarly, Helliwell argues that the search for formal social structures that correspond with an

Figure 3.1   *A typical Dalmatian harbour: Supetar, Brac.* Photo *Julian Thomas*

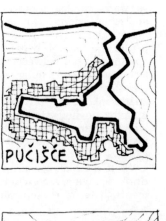
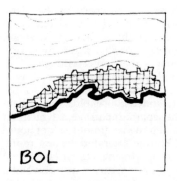
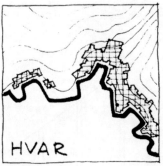

Figure 3.2   *Four Dalmatian towns*
Source: Violich (1985)

Figure 3.3   *Korcula, from the sea.* Photo *Julian Thomas*

abstract mapping of the space of the Gerai longhouse has obscured the social reality. In experiencing the longhouse as a lived space, she also discovers a sociality that is more protean and seamless than other ethnographies might suggest. Such analyses present Dayak society as being composed of a series of independent and bounded households, each inhabiting one of the separate apartments which run side by side along the length of the longhouse (Figure 3.4). Yet the lateral divisions represented by these apartments are cross-cut by a series of named linear spaces which run along the entire building. The most important division of the longhouse is a vertical wall, which separates the partitioned sleeping, cooking and eating space of the apartments from the outer gallery. This means that the primary distinction is not between the individual apartments, but between the apartments collectively and this outer space. While, from a Western point of view, it is easy to misread the apartments as the 'private' space of a family unit, the longhouse community is a collectivity which distinguishes itself from the Malay people who are granted access to the outer gallery.

While the Malay, who neither eat pork nor drink rice wine, are excluded from the apartments, these are less separate from one another

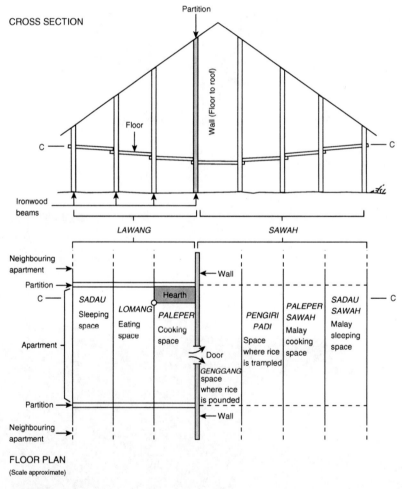

Figure 3.4   *The Gerai Dayak longhouse*
Source: Helliwell (1996)

than a schematic plan would suggest. Although each apartment is occupied by a distinct family group, the partitions that separate them are flimsy and permeable (Helliwell 1996: 134). They are riddled with holes, through which children and animals pass between apartments, and which afford glimpses from one space into another. Yet the Western privileging of vision over the other senses could lead one to underestimate the extent to which an unbroken field of sociability encompasses the entire longhouse. For even if they are on their own in the apartment, the inhabitants of the longhouse are never alone. Helliwell records that she often saw people seemingly talking to themselves, and that only after some time did she recognize that such apparent monologues were always overheard (1996: 141). In this sense the Gerai constantly 'audit' each other, and their habitual activity takes into account the continual possibility of the members of one 'household' intervening in the affairs of another. Just as Violich's perambulations reveal aspects of urban identity that cannot be appreciated on the map, so Helliwell's immersion in the 'field of voices' within the longhouse uncovers unexpected dimensions of Gerai social life.

TIM INGOLD: MAKING A BASKET

A further example of how phenomenological ideas might inform our thinking about material culture is provided by Tim Ingold, in an essay that dwells on the weaving of a basket (Ingold 2000: 339–48). Ingold may not describe himself as a phenomenologist, but the way in which he uses insights drawn from the close observation of things as a starting point for a wider argument is characteristic of the tradition. He addresses the question of 'making' from a perspective informed to some extent by Heidegger, and directly questions our reliance upon the oppositions between culture and nature, and form and substance. In nature organisms grow, while cultural artefacts are made. But what is the difference between these forms of coming-into-being? Ingold's suggestion is that a consideration of the crafting of baskets collapses some of our accepted distinctions.

Natural forms like the shells of marine creatures are generally considered to have been grown from within, directed by a genetic pattern, while artefacts are formed from without. Artefacts have form imposed on them by

human agency. In both cases some kind of 'blueprint' is presumed to exist, whether specified by DNA or lodged in the mind of an artisan. The difference lies in whether the pattern originates above or below the surface of the object, yet the assumption that the surface forms a critical boundary is broadly accepted. The surface is where substance meets action, and the growth of natural things is immanent within the substance itself. The crucial question that Ingold asks is whether a beehive is made or grown (2000: 340). Karl Marx once remarked that the worst of architects is better than the best of bees, for he has always already built the structure in his mind before the first stone is laid (see Maurer, Chapter 1). Yet this contrasts with Heidegger's argument that, in order to build, we must first learn how to dwell on earth. We build because we are dwellers (1977a: 326). Heidegger wrote this in the context of the housing shortage that followed the Second World War, and in the knowledge that its likely solution would be the construction of endless anonymous blocks of flats. These would represent the imposition on to the earth of entities that had been planned in the abstract, but which had no organic connection with their location. His counter-example of the Black Forest cottage is undoubtedly romantic and nostalgic, but it makes the point that an architecture can grow out of an authentic relationship of dwelling on the earth.

Ingold distils from Heidegger a distinction between a 'building perspective' and a 'dwelling perspective', and argues that our habitual error lies in imagining that making is rather like the process of representation in reverse: a fully formed image in the mind is reproduced in material form. This is the 'building perspective', in which artefacts are thought of as surfaces upon which the mind has stamped a preconceived form. Form is cultural and substance is natural, so that culture appears to be a cognitive phenomenon which floats over the surface of the material world without ever penetrating it. It is worth noting at this point that Ingold describes the surface of the artefact as the point where culture *confronts* nature. This seems to echo Heidegger's account (1977b) of the *Gestell* or 'enframing' as a mode of occasioning that *challenges* nature. Heidegger argued that the modern era in the West was characterized by a vision of the world as a stock of raw materials that could be subjected to the human will. The modern era admitted only a single way for material things to reveal themselves: as inert matter. In a strong sense, Ingold's building perspective appears to be related to Heidegger's *Gestell*.

For Ingold, the building perspective is challenged by any detailed consideration of basket weaving. A basket is not made by imposing force from outside upon a body of mute substance. The 'surface' of the basket does not exist before the weaving begins: it is actually built up, and emerges, in the practice of making. For this reason, the basket does not clearly have an 'inside' and an 'outside' at all. The individual reeds or canes that make up the basket might each be said to have an exterior, but they lace into and out of the woven surface, and this in turn is to be distinguished from the interior and exterior of the basket in its capacity as a vessel. The individual elements of the basket may be 'transformed' to a very limited extent in the process of making; it is more accurate to say that they are *incorporated*. The structure that develops through the weaving is not one that is imprinted or stamped (like molten metal in a mould or a coin in a die) by external force: it is the developing tensile stress of the basket itself that gives it its shape (Ingold 2000: 342). It follows from this that the basket weaver has only a general grasp of the form that she is intending to achieve before she begins work. She does not have a mental template, but a series of skills or a body of know-how which inform her engagement with the material. Form grows out of this involvement, rather than issuing out of the artisan's mind.

The broader argument that Ingold draws out from these points is that the forces involved in the making of both artefacts and organisms are not contained within any surface or boundary, and actually extend between any entity and its environment (2000: 345). Effectively, this reiterates the phenomenological message that no kind of being can exist without a background. The basket weaver, like any maker, is positioned in a field of forces that is composed of skills and dispositions as well as muscle power. Such a field exists in nature as much as in the human world, and both artefacts and organisms are generated through morphogenetic processes that have a narrative structure. They are not necessarily mapped out in advance, and each episode of growth builds on what has gone before. When human beings make things, they work within a world rather than acting upon a material world from outside. Weaving is therefore a paradigm of what human beings do when

they create artefacts, a skilful crafting that knits things together. We could go on to argue that when a modern motor car has been designed on a computer screen and the component parts are assembled in a precise and automated manner on a robotic production line, this is a most unusual kind of making. It is not even a simulation of what happens when an artisan works with her materials, for the outcome is always decided in advance, and there is no sense of a dialogue with material things. This kind of production is abstracted and impoverished, derived from and secondary to weaving, just as scientific analysis is derived and abstracted from the everyday.

PHENOMENOLOGIES OF LANDSCAPE AND MONUMENTALITY

The clearest example of a debate over the usefulness of phenomenology to the investigation of material culture can be found in relation to recent experiential studies of landscape and monumentality, which are primarily archaeological in their subject matter (see Corcos 2001; Chapman and Geary 2000; Cummings and Whittle 2000; Fleming 1999; Hamilton 1999; Witcher 1998 and among many others, Bender this volume). The principal inspiration for this burst of activity has been Christopher Tilley's *A Phenomenology of Landscape* (1994). In this work Tilley's arguments are informed by ethnography at least as much as by phenomenological philosophy, but the two strands harmonize to the extent that they both cast doubt on the universality of contemporary Western conceptions of space and place. A survey of the anthropological literature reveals that for many non-Western societies supernatural powers and ancestral presences are immanent in the landscape, and are implicated in the way that people understand their own place in the life-world (Tilley 1994: 59). Particular landmarks are often identified as places of ancestral or metaphysical influence, and these may serve as reminders of the past which serve to stabilize contemporary identities and social relationships. On this basis, Tilley argues that there is every reason to suppose that the prehistoric communities of Britain also understood the landscapes that they frequented to be inherently meaningful and filled with spiritual power. Present-day archaeologists, however, are accustomed to thinking about the land in Cartesian terms, as an inert spatial resource that can be bought and sold and adequately represented on maps and aerial photographs.

It is Tilley's proposed remedy for this state of affairs that draws his study closer to the mainstream of phenomenological thought. If we have allowed ourselves to think of prehistoric monuments and dwellings as dots on maps, or at best as brief 'heritage experiences' sandwiched between car journeys, we should learn to encounter them differently by approaching them in the course of an extensive walk through the countryside. Tilley explicitly states that this focus on the site as we experience it within the broader landscape is not intended as a form of empathy, which might try to share the thoughts and feelings of prehistoric people (1994: 74). It is simply that, by using our own body as a means of addressing a megalithic tomb or a standing stone and establishing relationships between structure and topography, we generate an understanding in the present which stands as an analogy or allegory for those of the past. It is a basis for hypothesis and argument, rather than a revealed truth about the landscape and its past. Our experience of the monument in its modern landscape is informed by an entirely different cultural tradition from that of past people, and moreover the land itself has altered irrevocably over the past 6,000 years. The landscape is itself a record of generations of human activity, which have added field boundaries, houses, roads and telegraph poles to its surface. Yet Tilley argues that there is still something about the land that remains stable over time:

> The skin of the land has gone for good, and can only be partially recovered through the most diligent of scientific analyses; but not its shape. The bones of the land – the mountains, hills, rocks and valleys, escarpments and ridges – have remained substantially the same since the Mesolithic, and can still be observed.

> (Tilley 1994: 73–4)

Some critics have argued that although Tilley forswears empathy, he implicitly relies on a degree of essentialism in claiming that we share a common physiognomy with prehistoric people, and that consequentially aspects of our worldly experience are comparable (Karlsson 1998: 188). Alternatively, it is suggested that Tilley's accounts of the landscape

context of the megalithic tombs of south-west Wales and the Black Mountains, and of the Dorset Cursus, are specific to a white, middle-class man. If one were disabled or pregnant, one's physical engagement with these places might be quite different (Brück 1998: 28). On the other hand, a first-hand experience of a place can be undertaken only from a single subject position. It has what Heidegger would call a quality of 'mineness'. I can hypothesize how different a past person's experience might be, but only from my own located embodiment. What is undeniable is that there are insights in Tilley's book that could not have been generated in any other way. His description of walking the Neolithic linear earthwork of the Dorset Cursus as a kind of spatial narrative that leads through a series of unexpected encounters could be developed only out of an embodied practice of being in place. Regrettably, as we noted above, the fresh and compelling character of the analyses presented in *A Phenomenology of Landscape* has inspired an outbreak of 'landscape phenomenologies' which sometimes lack the philosophical grounding of the original.

In a parallel and related development, archaeologists have also become interested in the experiential dimensions of the interior spaces of prehistoric monuments (e.g. Barrett 1994: 9–69; Pollard 1995; Richards 1993; Thomas 1993; 1999: 34–61). These studies share some common ground with the architectural analyses of Violich and Helliwell, but focus in particular on the ways that constructed spaces both constrain and facilitate performance, interaction and experience. Ceremonial monuments such as the megalithic tombs of earlier Neolithic Britain (c. 4000–3000 BC), or the henge enclosures of the later Neolithic (c. 2500 BC) were at once elaborate architectural forms and locations that afforded intense sensory stimulation. A megalithic tomb like that at West Kennet (Figure 3.5) contained the remains of the dead, which were apparently subject to periodic handling and reordering, while also providing the setting or 'stage' for encounters and activities of consumption on the part of the living. Such an architecture may have choreographed and restricted the acts and movement of persons inside the monument, but they may equally have provided guidance or 'cues' in the reproduction of ritual activities. Moreover, as well as saturating the senses of the participants (smells of rotting bodies; tastes of mortuary

Figure 3.5   *The entrance to the megalithic tomb at West Kennett, north Wiltshire.* Photo *Julian Thomas*

feasts; vocal sounds enhanced by the restricted space; lights flickering in the dark tomb interior), the monument establishes positions in which people can stand in relation to one another, and thus helps to construct subject positions from which people can speak in an authoritative fashion. Investigations of this kind have been criticized on the ground that they are somewhat anonymous, and that while they are concerned with bodily experience they do not address the particular identities of the people involved (e.g. Hodder 2000: 24–5). However, it might be fair to reply that the point of these studies is to document experiential worlds and forms of subjectification that are remote from our own, rather than to attempt to recover 'individuals' who are comparable with those of the modern West.

CONCLUSION AND SUGGESTIONS FOR FURTHER RESEARCH

Phenomenology developed out of an imperative to secure Western science by ascertaining the precise relationship between consciousness and the material world. Yet the recognition that science is secondary to or derived from the structures of human existence that phenomenology revealed had profound consequences. Since the scientific revolution of the seventeenth century Western thought had relied on the notion that science had privileged access to the fundamental nature of the universe. Husserl had implicitly claimed that phenomenology was concerned with an order of reality that was more primordial than that addressed by the natural sciences. Heidegger and Merleau-Ponty, by arguing that our most basic understandings can only be generated in the context of a social and phenomenal world, transformed phenomenology from a search for abstract essences to an interrogation of the everyday. This shift from the transcendental to the immanent can be understood as part of a more general twentieth-century trend, which acknowledges the importance of ordinary life. In turn, we could identify the emergence of material culture studies with this growing interest in the quotidian. What distinguishes phenomenology, however, is a desire to see the everyday as an appropriate location for attending to the deepest of existential questions. A meditation on a discarded shoe can lead into a questioning of the nature of art, and so on. This is because the tradition refuses to separate philosophical knowledge from the world of things, while viewing thinking as an embodied practice, and sees no observation, however mundane, as immune from an unending critique. Phenomenology consequentially has an invaluable contribution to make to the investigation of material culture, but it must do this without relinquishing its critical spirit.

In more specific terms, it is clear that the full potential of phenomenological approaches to material culture is far from having been realized. While experiential analyses of architecture and landscape in present and past contexts have been undertaken, these have often concentrated on the visual and (to a lesser extent) the tactile aspects of human engagements with space and place. As Helliwell's account of the Gerai longhouse demonstrates, a concern with sound and smell can significantly enhance our understanding of the sense of place, as well as enabling us to address the role of memory in everyday experience. By comparison, portable artefacts have been less intensively studied from a phenomenological standpoint than places and structures. Ingold's account of basket weaving opens the way for new approaches to a variety of forms of 'making'. While the appositeness of these ideas to the study of textiles is obvious, the relinquishment of an attachment to the culture/nature dichotomy and the substance ontology might have dramatic consequences for our conception of (for instance) flint knapping. Moving beyond the conventional focus on production and consumption, an investigation of the haptic qualities of objects might prove productive, particularly in the context of the mass-produced material culture of the contemporary West, where the impact of phenomenological thought has been slim. Finally, a keystone of the phenomenological approach is the understanding that the 'subjective' aspects of experience are not superficial elements constructed on the bedrock of an invariant materiality, but are the means through which the material world reveals itself to us. It might therefore be instructive to consider the question of the variable ways in which the (presumably culturally constructed) moods, attunements and emotional states of people in a variety of contexts disclose their material surroundings and conditions to them.

REFERENCES

Barrett, J.C. (1994) *Fragments from Antiquity*. Oxford: Blackwell.

Brück, J. (1998) In the footsteps of the ancestors: a review of Christopher Tilley's *A Phenomenology of Landscape: Places, Paths and Monuments*, *Archaeological Review from Cambridge*, 15: 23–36.

Chapman, H.P. and Gearey, B.R. (2000) 'Paleoecology and the perception of prehistoric landscapes: some comments on visual approaches to phenomenology', *Antiquity*, 74: 316–19.

Corcos, N. (2001) 'Churches as prehistoric ritual monuments: a review and phenomenological perspective from Somerset', *Assemblage*, 6, www.shef.ac.uk/assem/issue6.

Critchley, S. (2000) 'Heidegger for beginners', in J.E. Faulconer and M.A. Wrathall (eds), *Appropriating Heidegger*. Cambridge: Cambridge University Press, pp. 101–18.

Cummings, V. and Whittle, A. (2000) 'Tombs with a view: landscape, monuments and trees', *Antiquity*, 77: 255–66.

Dovey, K. (1985) 'The quest for authenticity and the replication of environmental meaning', in D. Seamon and R. Mugerauer (eds), *Dwelling, Place and Environment*. New York: Columbia University Press, pp. 33–49.

Dovey, K. (1993) 'Putting geometry in its place: towards a phenomenology of the design process', in D. Seamon (ed.), *Dwelling, Seeing and Designing*. Albany, NY: State University of New York Press, pp. 247–69.

Fleming, A. (1999) 'Phenomenology and the megaliths of Wales: a dreaming too far?' *Oxford Journal of Archaeology*, 18: 119–25.

Frede, D. (1993) 'The question of Being: Heidegger's project', in C. Guignon (ed.), *The Cambridge Companion to Heidegger*. Cambridge: Cambridge University Press, pp. 42–69.

Gregory, D. (1978) *Ideology, Science and Human Geography*. London: Hutchinson.

Guignon, C. (2001) 'Being as appearing: retrieving the Greek experience of *Phusis*', in R. Polt and G. Fried (eds), *A Companion to Heidegger's Introduction to Metaphysics*. New Haven, CT: Yale University Press, pp. 34–56.

Hall, H. (1993) 'Intentionality and world: Division I of *Being and Time*', in C. Guignon (ed.), *The Cambridge Companion to Heidegger*. Cambridge: Cambridge University Press, pp. 122–40.

Hamilton, S. (1999) 'Using the surface: inter- and intra-site visibility', *Sussex Archaeological Collections*, 137: 11–15.

Heidegger, M. (1962) *Being and Time*, trans. J. Macquarrie and E. Robinson. Oxford: Blackwell.

Heidegger, M. (1977a) 'Building dwelling thinking', in D.F. Krell (ed.), *Martin Heidegger: Basic Writings*. London: Routledge, pp. 319–40.

Heidegger, M. (1977b) 'The question concerning technology', in M. Heidegger, *The Question Concerning Technology and other Essays*. New York: Harper & Row, pp. 3–35.

Heidegger, M. (1982) *The Basic Problems of Phenomenology*. Bloomington, IN: Indiana University Press.

Heidegger, M. (1993) 'Letter on humanism', in D.F. Krell (ed.), *Martin Heidegger: Basic Writings*, 2nd edn. London: Routledge, pp. 213–65.

Heidegger, M. (2001) *Introduction to Metaphysics*. New Haven, CT: Yale University Press.

Helliwell, C. (1996) 'Space and society in a Dayak longhouse', in M. Jackson (ed.), *Things as They Are: New Directions in Phenomenological Anthropology*. Bloomington, IN: Indiana University Press, pp. 128–48.

Hintikka, J. (1995) 'The phenomenological dimension', in B. Smith and D.W. Smith (eds), *The Cambridge Companion to Husserl*. Cambridge: Cambridge University Press, pp. 78–105.

Hodder, I. (2000) 'Agency and individuals in long-term processes', in M-A. Dobres and J.E. Robb (eds), *Agency in Archaeology*. London: Routledge, pp. 21–33.

Husserl, E. (1983) *Ideas Pertaining to a Pure Phenomenology and to a Phenomenological Philosophy, First Book*. Dordrecht: Kluwer.

Ihde, D. (1993) *Postphenomenology Essays in the Post-modern Context*. Evanston, IL: Northwestern University Press.

Ingold, T. (2000) *The Perception of the Environment: Essays in Livelihood, Dwelling and Skill*. London: Routledge.

Jäger, B. (1985) 'Body, house and city: the intertwinings of embodiment, inhabitation and civilisation', in D. Seamon and R. Mugerauer (eds), *Dwelling, Place and Environment*. New York: Columbia University Press, pp. 215–25.

Karlsson, H. (1998) *Re-thinking Archaeology*. Gothenberg: Gothenburg University.

Levinas, E. (1998) *Entre nous: Thinking-of-the-Other*. New York: Columbia University Press.

Lynch, K. (1972) *What Time is this Place?* Cambridge, MA: MIT Press.

Matthews, E. (2002) *The Philosophy of Merleau-Ponty*. Chesham: Acumen.

Merleau-Ponty, M. (1962) *Phenomenology of Perception*. London: Routledge.

Moran, D. (2000) *Introduction to Phenomenology*. London: Routledge.

Pollard, J. (1995) 'Inscribing space: formal deposition at the later Neolithic monument of Woodhenge, Wiltshire', *Proceedings of the Prehistoric Society*, 61: 137–56.

Polt, R. (2001) 'The question of nothing', in R. Polt and G. Fried (eds), *A Companion to Heidegger's Introduction to Metaphysics*. New Haven, CT: Yale University Press, pp. 57–82.

Relph, E. (1976) *Place and Placelessness*. London: Pion.

Relph, E. (1993) 'Modernity and the reclamation of place', in D. Seamon (ed.), *Dwelling, Seeing and Designing*. Albany, NY: State University of New York Press, pp. 25–40.

Richards, C.C. (1993) 'Monumental choreography: architecture and spatial representation in late Neolithic Orkney', in C. Tilley (ed.), *Interpretative Archaeology*. London: Berg, pp. 143–80.

Ricoeur, P. (1974) *The Conflict of Interpretations: Essays in Hermeneutics*. Evanston, IL: Northwestern University Press.

Rollinger, R.D. (2004) 'Brentano and Husserl', in D. Jacquette (ed.), *The Cambridge Companion to Brentano*. Cambridge: Cambridge University Press, pp. 255–76.

Schuhmann, K. (2004) 'Brentano's impact on twentieth-century philosophy', in D. Jacquette (ed.), *The Cambridge Companion to Brentano*. Cambridge: Cambridge University Press, pp. 277–97.

Thomas, J.S. (1993) 'The hermeneutics of megalithic space', in C. Tilley (ed.), *Interpretative Archaeology*. London: Berg, pp. 73–98.

Thomas, J.S. (1999) *Understanding the Neolithic*. London: Routledge.

Tilley, C. (1994) *A Phenomenology of Landscape: Paths, Places and Monuments*. Oxford: Berg.

Tuan, Y.F. (1974) 'Space and place: humanistic perspective', *Progress in Geography*, 6: 211–52.

Tuan, Y.F. (1977) *Space and Place: the Perspective of Experience*. Minneapolis, MN: University of Minnesota Press.

Violich, F. (1985) 'Towards revealing the sense of place: an intuitive reading of four Dalmatian towns', in D. Seamon and R. Mugerauer (eds), *Dwelling, Place and Environment*. New York: Columbia University Press, pp. 113–36.

Waldenfels, B. (2002) 'Levinas and the face of the other', in S. Critchley and R. Bernasconi (eds), *The Cambridge Companion to Levinas*. Cambridge: Cambridge University Press, pp. 63–81.

Witcher, R. (1998) 'Roman roads: phenomenological perspectives on roads in the landscape', in C. Forcey, J. Hawthorne and R. Witcher (eds), *TRAC 97: Proceedings of the Seventh Annual Theoretical Roman Archaeology Conference, Nottingham, 1997*. Oxford: Oxbow Books, pp. 60–70.

Wrathall, M. (2000) 'Background practices, capacities, and Heideggerian disclosure', in M. Wrathall and J. Malpas (eds), *Heidegger, Coping, and*

Cognitive Science. Cambridge, MA: MIT Press, pp. 93–114.

Wyschogrod, E. (2002) 'Language and alterity in the thought of Levinas', in S. Critchley and R. Bernasconi (eds), *The Cambridge Companion to Levinas*. Cambridge: Cambridge University Press, pp. 188–205.

Zimmerman, M. (1990) *Heidegger's Confrontation with Modernity: Technology, Politics, Art*. Bloomington, IN: Indiana University Press.

Zimmerman, M.E. (1993) 'Heidegger, Buddhism and deep ecology', in C. Guignon (ed.), *The Cambridge Companion to Heidegger*. Cambridge: Cambridge University Press, pp. 240–69.

4

OBJECTIFICATION

Christopher Tilley

The concept of objectification may be held to be, in a profound sense, at the heart of all studies of material culture. A concern with objectification is simultaneously a concern with the nature of materiality itself. Is the very notion of a category, 'material culture', misguided and essentially arbitrary, an eclectic grouping together of very different kinds of things or objects whose only superficial resemblance is that they share a property of materiality? Or is the materiality of things a significant and important attribute that makes, say, a consideration of houses and pianos, glass beads and food intrinsically important and meaningful in itself, a category to be taken seriously in social analysis? An objectification perspective provides an answer to both these basic questions, as it is to do with what things are and what things do in the social world: the manner in which objects or material forms are embedded in the life worlds of individuals, groups, institutions or, more broadly, culture and society.

In one sense to consider objectification is simultaneously to consider the entire disciplines of archaeology and anthropology, in relation to the study of material forms, an impossible task. This is both the beauty, and the danger, of discussing the concept, such is its generality. What remains of animals, when they die, is usually just the remains of their bodies. By contrast humans leave behind a vast array of artefacts which, quite literally, objectify their past presence. Most animals do not alter the world to any great extent and their global distribution is determined by environmental constraints. People, by contrast, are found everywhere and actively serve to create, or objectify, the environments of which they are a part.

The concept of objectification can be traced back to Hegel's *Phenomenology of the Spirit* (1807/1977) and Marx's later materialist appropriation and inversion of the Hegelian notion of the dialectic (see Miller 1987; Maurer; Chapter 1). Keane (1997) has noted that in anthropology a notion of objectification as mimesis was central to the idea, formulated by Durkheim and Mauss ([1903] 1963), of collective representation. Classes of things in the world reflect pre-existing social groups. Material forms, such as the arrangement of houses in a village, are objectifications that serve the self-knowledge of individuals and groups. They are isomorphic with a 'true' or desired state. Objectification in such a perspective is the concrete embodiment of an idea. The idea comes first and becomes realized in the form of a material thing. Such a notion also underpinned the traditional archaeological concept of culture: different kinds of artefacts distributed across space and time reflected different groups of people. Changes in these artefacts reflected movement of peoples or the diffusion of ideas (see Shanks and Tilley 1987: 79 ff. for a discussion).

The idealism of this position and the manner in which it priveledges mind over body and produces a split between the two is self-evident. By contrast, the accounts of Hegel and Marx situate objectification as a temporal moment in a much broader dialectical process. It is implicated in action, in the physical production of things which are therefore active in the self-constitution of identities, and interactions between people. But, as Miller has argued (1987), things are not just objectifications at the point of their production but throughout their life cycles, in moments of exchange, appropriation and consumption. Objects circulate through people's activities and can contextually produce new types of activities, objects and events.

Theoretical discussions of the concept specifically in relation to the study of material culture have been relatively few. For Bourdieu (1977, 1984, 1990) objectification processes form a central part of his 'theory of practice' which has had a major influence on the recent development of material culture studies in archaeology and anthropology since the 1980s, which, for this reason, is discussed in some detail below together with some other influential studies. Miller, for whom Bourdieu is a central influence, has written by far the most substantive discussion of the birth and development of this concept in the literature in relation to the study of material culture, attempting to develop a general theory of material forms in relation to objectification processes (Miller 1987). The central ideas can be simply put as follows.

Objectification, considered in the most general way, is a concept that provides a particular way of understanding the relationship between subjects and objects, the central concern of material culture studies. It attempts to overcome the dualism in modern empiricist thought in which subjects and objects are regarded as utterly different and opposed entities, respectively human and non-human, living and inert, active and passive, and so on. Through making, using, exchanging, consuming, interacting and living with things people make themselves in the process. The object world is thus absolutely central to an understanding of the identities of individual persons and societies. Or, to put it another way, without the things – material culture – we could neither be ourselves nor know ourselves. Material culture is thus inseparable from culture and human society. It is not a sub-set of either, a part or a domain of something that is bigger, broader or more significant, but constitutive. Culture and material culture are the two sides of the same coin. They are related dialectically, in a constant process of being and becoming: processual in nature rather than static or fixed entities. Persons and things, in dynamic relation, are constitutive of human culture in general, societies and communities in particular, and in the agency of groups and individuals. Ideas, values and social relations do not exist prior to culture forms which then become merely passive reflections of them, but are themselves actively created through the processes in which these forms themselves come into being.

Thus material forms do not simply mirror pre-existing social distinctions, sets of ideas or symbolic systems. They are instead the very medium through which these values, ideas and social distinctions are constantly reproduced and legitimized, or transformed. So differing forms of sociality and different ways of identity construction are produced through the medium of living with and through a medium we call 'material culture'. The meanings and significance of things for people are part and parcel of their lives. To use a phenomenological description of this process: we touch the things and the things simultaneously touch us. The relationship is reciprocal. Object and subject are indelibly conjoined in a dialectical relationship. They form part of each other while not collapsing into or being subsumed into the other. Subject and object are both the same, yet different. The ontological relationship between the two embodies this contradiction or ambiguity: same and different, constituted and constituting. Personal, social and cultural identity is embodied in our persons and objectified in our things. Through the things we can understand ourselves and others, not because they are externalizations of ourselves or others, reflecting something prior and more basic in our consciousness or social relations but because these things are the very medium through which we make and know ourselves.

OBJECTIFICATION: THINGS AND WORDS

Given the domination of linguistic analyses in anthropology, and the social sciences more generally, it has always been tempting for those interested in the study of material culture to oppose a world of things to language as very different kinds of objectified representation. Keane (1995, 1997) usefully discusses both in relation to objectification and embodiment in public performances stressing their mutual intertwining in social practices which go beyond simply an expression of 'meaning' as normally understood. He stresses the manner in which public performances bind the objectifying powers of words and the objectifying powers of things together. To choose to investigate either one or the other therefore inevitably results in a partial account. The 'hazards' of representation are bound up with the vicissitudes of social interaction, with the unintended, as well as the intended, consequences of the uses of words and things with inevitable political, economic and historical entailments.

Another way to understand the relationship between speech or language and material forms is to suggest that metaphor is central to both, to the manner in which particular meanings are communicated and synaesthetic links are established between seemingly disparate social and material domains (Tilley 1999). Material forms, as objectifications of social relations and gendered identities, often 'talk' silently about these relationships in ways impossible in speech or formal discourses. The things themselves mediate between persons at a silent and unconscious level of discourse, that which Miller (1987) refers to as the 'humility of things'. The material object may be a powerful metaphorical medium through which people may reflect on their world in and through their material practice. Through the artefact, layered and often contradictory sets of meanings can be conveyed simultaneously. The artefact may be inherently ambiguous in its meaning contents precisely because it acts to convey information about a variety of symbolic domains through the same media (Tilley 1991), and because it may perform the cultural work of revealing fundamental tensions and contradictions in human social experience. In other words 'the artefact through its "silent" speech and "written" presence, speaks what cannot be spoken, writes what cannot be written, and articulates that which remains conceptually separated in social practice' (Tilley 1999: 260 ff.). Material forms complement what can be communicated in language rather than duplicating or reflecting what can be said in words in a material form. If material culture simply reified in a material medium that which could be communicated in words it would be quite redundant. The non-verbal materiality of the medium is thus of central importance.

OBJECTIFICATION AND SOCIALIZATION

Consider the following diary entry:

Sunday 21 March 1998, 9.15 a.m. They run outside into the conservatory from the kitchen. Alice carries her red jacket. She falls over and bangs her head on the kitchen door. Terrible howl. Benjamin opens the garage door, closes it, opens it, closes it, opens it and starts fiddling with the key. K. opens a drawer in the kitchen. B. immediately runs up and removes a yellow plastic chicken leg and a coat hook and throws them on the floor. A. swings her red jacket around and drops it. B. runs out of the kitchen, through the conservatory and opens the door to the garage and starts altering the thermostat on the boiler. He is stopped. He starts to suck the end of the chicken leg. A. goes into the garage and removes a box containing a tile cutter and carries it into the kitchen and drops it on the floor. She then picks up her red jacket and starts to shake the kitchen door. B. starts to hit the tile cutter box with the chicken leg. A. stands on the box and starts to jump up and down. She removes the box to the lounge. B. rummages with dirty clothes on the kitchen floor that A. had deposited earlier in a heap. *9.30 a.m.* Both go into K.'s study. B. starts opening the desk drawers and pulling things out. A. fiddles with the knobs on the radio ...

(Tilley: personal diary)

This somewhat typical sixteen-minute sequence of events records the activities of my twins when they were nineteen months old. Neither could speak a word. They were learning through manipulating things, through bodily interaction with things and through exploring different kinds of domestic places and their contents: rooms, doors, drawers, knobs, and so on. This world of ordinary things is a complex multidimensional sensuous space of forms and colours, tastes and textures, sounds and smells, stasis and motion. The child is the original participant observer who pieces together and makes sense of the world through being a part of it. In the intellectual development of the child things come first, words are second, and many of the first words to be used attach a name to a thing: 'bed', or refer to a thing: 'there!' Material culture forms a primary aspect of child socialization. The child is massively confronted with a material world of things which objectify values, etc., through which they learn who they are and where they are. And if my children had been brought up in contemporary Bali or Australia or eighteenth-century Holland or in the Neolithic of southern England the character of the domestic spaces, objects and their properties would powerfully betoken a very different world and set of values and social relations.

OBJECTIFICATION AND PRODUCTION

The *qualities* of artefacts may objectify the persons who have made and used them. So for the Telefol of Papua New Guinea 'a good *bilum* [net bag] is like a good woman' (MacKenzie 1991: 127). It embodies her personal weaving skills and energy. A good *bilum* enhances the appearance of the carrier, is essential for a feeling of self-worth and to impress outsiders. Similarly among the Yekuana of Venezula people talk of the development of manual skills in basket making as indicative of spiritual qualities: 'The fact that those who create the most skillfully crafted objects are also the most ritually knowledgable members of the community is a truism every Yekuana recognizes' (Guss 1989: 70). Creating things is thus a fabrication of the social self. The corollary of this, of course, is that in many societies destroying these same things marks the end of this social self. Many studies have been concerned with investigating these kinds of links between persons and things (e.g. Jolly 1991; Pandya 1998; Riggins 1984; Fowler 2004; J. Thomas 2000).

A primary component of the consideration of objectification processes involves gender relations, the manner in which these are constructed through things. This has frequently involved consideration of 'male' or 'female' artefacts and domains of practice. However, Mackenzie (1991) argues that certain classes of *bilums*, used by men among the Telefol, are androgynous objects, both male and female. Men appropriate the *bilum* made by women, which is an objectification of women's work, and procede to decorate it with feathers, thus turning it into an object associated with male identity, and simultaneously concealing, or hiding, the female labour that is at the base. MacKenzie argues that the male feather elaborations on the basic female *bilum* are adjuncts to wider associations of the net bag to wider associations between it and female fecundity and biological motherhood secretly mainfested in male rituals. Another way of conceptualizing the gendered identities that the male net bag symbolizes is to suggest that rather than being androgynous it is doubly gendered, an argument that Hoskins makes in relation to the gendering of material forms in Indonesia (Hoskins 1998). The general theme of the objectification of gendered identities and what forms these may take has promoted much archaeological debate (see e.g. Gosden 1999; Gilchrist 1994; Moore 1986, 1994; Holliman 2000; Prine 2000; Thomas 2000; Sørensen 2000; Yates and Nordbladh 1990; Yates 1993)

OBJECTIFICATION AND BIOGRAPHIES

The *personification* or anthropomorphic representation of people through things is one powerful and typical form objectification processes

take. The things so personified may be to do with wider social relations and ties, the socially created person, or they may be referents for the person as he or she is experienced through the objects that represent them. The biographies of particular persons and particular things may be intertwined. The thing is the person and the person is the thing. An obvious corrolary of this position is Gell's argument that objectification processes are bound up not only with the agency of persons but with the agency of things in relation to these persons (Gell 1992, 1996, 1998; Hoskins 1998, Chapter 5 in this volume), a theme explored in the archaeological literature (Tilley 1996; J. Thomas 1996; Jones 2002; Fowler 2004). Thus the circulation of valuables such as beautifully polished axes or highly decorated pots, or bronze swords, which may have been heavily anthropomorphized, with individual, names, histories and a gender, and referred to in terms of human body parts, in the manner of *kula* shells, become part and parcel of the creation of the identities of persons of renown.

OBJECTIFICATION AND EXCHANGE

Gift giving in ritual contexts is one of the most powerful ways in which the identity of people in relation to others is created. People are objectified as affines or members of the same clan through the gifts they give at a particular occasion. Battaglia (1990: 136 ff.) gives an excellent example from Sabarl island, Melanesia, of the way in which the body of a dead person is reconstructed and then deconstructed through 'corpses' of artefacts and food, gifts by men and women kin and affines as part of the *segaiya* or series of mortuary feasts. The rites and feasts while commemorating others also commemorate the self, since, according to Battaglia, Sabarl personhood is relational and dialogical in nature. The ceremonies are ways of both remembering the dead and his or her social ties through bringing together corpses of things and ways of forgetting through dismantling and deconstructing these corpses. 'Marrying', 'complementing' and 'matching' things are central to the mortuary transactions. Battagalia notes that:

in the feast of Moni, the symbolic intercourse and subsequent conflation of the 'corpses' of objects and food makes the point dramatically. Objects are said to add 'grease' to the food. Consuming objects and food alike releases the reproductive potential of particular individuals and the community ... Axe blades become more like food, and both of these 'more like people'.

(1990: 189–90)

The important point made here is that objectification processes have the effect of breaking down simplistic dyadic distinctions between object and subject worlds. Things and food can become persons in the ceremonies and the consumption of these things is a necessary precondition for the reproduction of persons.

Keane notes that formal exchange in Sumba, Indonesia:

extracts certain kinds of objects, principally metal artefacts and cloth, from the general economy of production, utility and consumption and imposes constraints on how they can properly be handled. The act of exchange is a moment into their transformation into things that circulate … the transactors of valuables can hope that, eventually, the social agency that they construct … can be incorporated into ancestral identities that stand out above the risks to which ongoing activity is prone: concretized in tombs and villages, recalled in names and histories.

(Keane 1997: 68)

Simmel stresses that objects are desirable because they objectify the self, they are extensions of the self, yet they are separate and can never be fully encompassed by the self (Simmel 1990: 66–7). As Keane points out this perspective has certain profound consequences in understanding Sumbanese exchange, its promise and risk. Things can both extend the agency and identity of their transactors but they may also become lost in this process. The capacity of the thing to 'work' in favour of its transactor is not an inherent property but must be continually sustained by human interactions and speech acts (Keane 1997: 93). These are all integral to objectification.

OBJECTIFICATION AND A MODEL OF CULTURE: BOURDIEU'S LOGIC OF PRACTICE

In societies where educational practice is not clearly institutionalized everything the child learns about the world comes about through the medium of the things encountered in it and through imitating the ongoing social practices and actions he or she sees. So this is not an abstract or theoretical knowledge, a matter of learning formalized cultural rules and principles. It is concrete and practical. For Bourdieu

this is the 'logic of practice' for which he tries to provide an abstract and generalized 'outline of a theory of practice', the titles of his two major ethnographic and theoretical works on Kabyle society in Algeria (Bourdieu 1977, 1990). The child learns about bodily postures and techniques (bodily *hexis*), how to make and use tools as an extension of the body, how to cultivate crops, a style of speech – in short an entire subjective experience of the world or *habitus*. This knowledge is repetitive and routinized, part of a cultural tradition. It becomes embodied in the child's very being. So there is a dialectic at work between objectification and embodiment. Such knowledge, knowing how to go on, having a practical mastery of the world in which one lives, does not require discursive formalization but is nevertheless structured and structuring, providing principles which generate the actions of individual persons in particular material contexts. These structuring principles are not fixed and invariant but are essentially improvisations within a wider cultural logic of practice, liable to modification as individual agents act in relation to each other and pursue their own particular social interests and strategies. The habitus is a structured structuring structure which exists only in and through the material practice of agents, a disposition to act in a particular kind of way.

PRACTICAL LOGIC AND MATERIAL CULTURE

What are the implications of Bourdieu's stress on social life as both a practical logic and a logic subject to improvisation for the study of material forms? He argues that the Kabyle house is the principal locus for the objectification of the generative schemes that make up the habitus (Bourdieu 1977: 89 ff., 1992: appendix). The house 'through the intermediary of the divisions and hierarchies it sets up between things, persons and practices, this tangible classifying system, continuously inculcates and reinforces the taxonomic principles underlying all the arbitrary provisions of this culture' (Bourdieu 1977: 89). The house is the objectification of the habitus, which is simultaneously embodied in the practices of those who dwell in it, which becomes inculcated in the earliest learning processes of children. The material manifestation of the habitus finds tangible material expression in the spatial divisions of the house and arrangements of material culture within it according to a set of homologous oppositions: fire : water :: cooked : raw :: high : low :: light : shade :: male : female :: *nif* : *hurma* : fertilizing : able to be fertilized (1977: 90).

The most important of these oppositions is that between male and female. According to Bourdieu these same oppositions are established between the house as a whole and the rest of the Kabyle universe. One or other of the two sets of oppositions either with regard to the internal organization of the house or with regard to the opposition between the house and the outside world is foregrounded depending on whether the house is considered from a female or male point of view so that 'whereas for the man, the house is not so much a place he enters as a place he comes out of, movement inwards properly befits the woman' (1977: 91). He argues that the same generative schemes organize magical rites and representations and rituals. They give meaning and significance to basic operations such as moving to the left or the right, going east or west, filling or emptying containers, and so forth. The opposition between movement outwards to the fields or the circulation of exchange items and movement inwards, towards the accumulation and consumption of things, corresponds with a male body, self-enclosed and directed outwards, and a female body resembling the dark, dank house with its food, children, animals and utensils (1977: 92). It is:

> through the magic of a world of objects which is the product of the application of the same schemes to the most diverse domains, a world in which everything speaks metaphorically of all the others, each practice comes to be invested with an objective meaning ... the mental structures which construct the world of objects are constructed in the practice of a world of objects constructed according to the same structures. The mind born of the world of objects does not arise as a subjectivity confronting an objectivity: the objective universe is made up of objects which are the product of objectifying operations structured according to the very operations that the mind applies to it. The mind is a metaphor of the world of objects which is itself but an endless circle of mutually reflecting metaphors.
>
> (1977: 91)

Social practice in the object world arises from the habitus or generative schemes and dispositions which are themselves the product of this world. We do not move from mind to material objectifications of that mind because the mind that is predisposed to think in a certain way is itself a product of these material objectifications. Both the mind and material forms are fundamentally metaphorical in character.

For Bourdieu, the habitus has an endless generative capacity to produce thoughts, actions, ideas, perceptions and emotions, giving social life its relative predictability and relative freedom. The limits to this are the weight of historical tradition and the material environment, which both constrain and condition people's access to material and non-material resources alike. Specific rites, for example, may in a mimetic way relate to a natural process that needs to be facilitated, establishing analogical relations of resemblance between the way grain swells in a cooking pot, the swelling of the belly of a pregnant woman and the germination of wheat in the ground (1977: 116).

The habitus produces objectified homologies between what may initially appear to be entirely different domains within the constraints of the agrarian cycle of the seasons. Thus in Kabylia a fundamental opposition exists between dry foods (cereals, dried vegetables, dried meat) and raw, green or fresh foods. Dry foods are boiled in water indoors in cooking pots and are not spiced. This makes the food *swell*. These foods are eaten during the late autumn and winter when it rains and the dry land is fertilized and begins to swell and the bodies of women are expected to swell. Green or fresh foods are eaten raw or grilled and heavily spiced. These are eaten during spring and summer, the period when the land dries out and crops previously developing inwardly open out and ripen in the light of day (1977: 143 ff.).

The manufacture of pottery is similarly intimately linked to the agrarian season by a series of homologies:

> the clay is collected in autumn but it is never worked in that season, nor in winter, when the earth is pregnant, but in spring. The unfired pottery dries slowly in the sun (wet-dry) while the ears of corn are ripening (the wet-dry period). So long as the earth bears the ears it cannot be baked; it is only after the harvest, when the earth is bare and no longer producing, and fire is no longer liable to dry up the ears (the dry-dry period) that baking can be carried out, in the open air (dry-dry).
>
> (1977: 146)

The whole of human existence, being the product of the *habitus*, is organized in a manner homologous to the agrarian year and other temporal series such as the opposition between day and night, morning and evening. For example, procreation is associated with evening, autumn and the damp nocturnal part of the house, gestation relates to the underground life of grain, and so on (1977: 154). Everything has its proper time and its proper rhythm. Above all what Bourdieu stresses is a continuous dialectic between the generative structures of the habitus, action, agency and signification.

OBJECTIFICATION, DOMINATION, SYMBOLIC CAPITAL

Bourdieu stresses that the social world, objectified and manifested through material forms, is always an essentially arbitrary construction in so far as there is never just one way to order human social relations, build houses, use tools, decorate pots, etc. However, the reproduction of every social order requires beliefs to be legitimized through ideological means. One of the primary means of achieving this is through naturalization, i.e. making the social order appear inevitable and timeless or part of an order of nature rather than culture. According to Bourdieu this is part of the hidden (because it is never discussed) significance of the homologies between the passage of the seasons and the agrarian calendar and their linkage with a whole host of seasonal rites and specific practices such as food preparation and pot making for the Kabyle. It has always been like this; how could things be otherwise? This is what Bourdieu refers to as *doxa* (1977: 164. ff.).

The world of tradition is experienced as a 'natural world'. It is self-evident and cannot be disputed. In Kabyle society *doxa* legitimates social divisions and inequalities in relation to sex and age materially objectified by clothing and cosmetics, decoration and ornamentation, tokens and emblems. Such a world 'goes without saying because it comes without saying' (1977: 167). There are no competing discourses or opinions. In this world material culture, far from passively symbolizing social divisions and inequalities, plays an active and fundamental role in legitimizing and reproducing them. The male pursuit of symbolic capital, or prestige and social honour, can be readily converted back into the material medium of economic capital: goods and resources. Relations of domination have themselves the opacity and permanence of things. Bourdieu argues that in societies without any self-regulating market, educational or juridical system, relations of domination can be set up and maintained only by strategies that must be endlessly renewed and repeated because there are no

lasting conditions for them to be mediated and maintained. Gentle or hidden exploitation (symbolic violence) is at the heart of every social relationship, present in the gift and the debt which acceptance of the gift entails.

In such a social world it is the most economical mode of domination because it fits in perfectly with the economy of the system by concealing that it is a form of violence done to persons through the objectified medium of transacting things (1977: 192). The gift governed by an ethic of honour and shame transmutes economic capital into social capital. An interested relationship is misrecognized as a disinterested gratuitous relationship. The acquisition of social capital is the only way of accumulating economic capital. So gifts must endlessly be given to create debts and lasting social bonds: giving becomes a way of possessing the labour of others. If gift giving involves an endless sequence of conversions between economic capital and symbolic capital, rituals and rites affirming sexual and social divisions, hierachies and statuses must also be endlessly repeated and naturalized in relation to the seasonal calendar. Essential to both is the objectified domain of material forms.

OBJECTIFICATION AND ART

Morphy's (1991) rich and subtle analysis of Yolngu aboriginal paintings from Arnhem Land, north-east Australia, provides an excellent example of objectification in art. Morphy shows both what an important social institution Yolngu art is and how it objectifies essential features of the structure of Yolngu society and the system of restricted knowledge. Paintings, dances and songs are collectively the *mardayin* or sacred law through which knowledge of the ancestral past is transmitted and re-enacted. Paintings do not just represent the ancestral past, they are a dimension of it, powerful and active in relation to persons in the present. This past is an integral part of the processes of socialization and categorization by means of which the Yolngu know themselves and their culture. The art provides a way of 'socializing people into a particular worldview in which certain themes become meaningful, in which certain values are created, and by which certain things can be done' (Morphy 1991: 293). They provide, in particular, a means of ordering the relationships between people, ancestors and land. The paintings are powerful because of their association, in a clan-based gerontocracy, with powerful individuals, because they are used to discriminate between different areas of owned land and because they are used to mark status differences between men and women, the initiated and the non-initiated. Although they are regarded as having intrinsic value and worth in themselves their use to mediate claims among the living to power and authority contributes dialectically to their own significance and power. By encoding meaning and being integrated with a system of restricted knowledge that is only gradually revealed through the course of a person's life, and through their articulation with the political system, the paintings, Morphy argues, serve to connect (1) the particular with the general; (2) the individual with the collective and (3) the outside to the inside. People move from having the world defined for them by others, through the agency of the objectified images, to eventually playing a creative role in fashioning for others this world themselves.

Different forms of paintings play different roles. They may have iconic, indexical or purely symbolic elements. The power of geometric art lies in its multivalency and its ability to express polysemous relationships between things not possible in iconic representations which have more restricted meaning ranges. It establishes relationships between objects and events that otherwise may remain unconnected. Morphy comments that the 'paradox of Yolngu art is that the geometric representations are multivalent, but their interpretation is initially obscured by the non-iconic nature of the elements, whereas the figurative representations obscure the multiplex relations between things by orienting interpretations in a particular direction' (1991: 296). Different artistic forms in which the world is objectified have different consequences and powers. Some are more appropriate in one social context, others in another. In the final analysis Yolngu art is very far from being a passive reflection of ideas or social relations and has played a key role in the reproduction of Yolngu identity, part and parcel of a creative response and resistance to colonization.

OBJECTIFICATION: 'TASTE' AND LIFESTYLE

Bourdieu's book *Distinction* (1984) has had a major impact on anthropological studies of modern industrial societies. In it he builds on his earlier ethnographic work to extend the concept of the 'habitus' to include an analysis of French society in the 1960s in an analysis of the cultural basis of 'taste'. Different social classes are argued to possess distinct dispositions to purchase various kinds of food and other consumer goods, read particular kinds of newspapers and books, engage in different kinds of sport, listen to different kinds of music, visit art galleries or museums, or not. People are argued to be involved in a never-ending struggle with regard to different forms of capital: economic (money, access to material resources), social (networks, relations with other persons), cultural (legitimate and legitimated knowledges), symbolic (prestige and social honour). These forms of capital can be converted into each other. Thus money can buy private education and access to different social networks and prestige. People's tastes and preferences, their lifestyles and patterns of consumption are objectified through the clothes they buy and how they wear them, the foods they eat and their table manners, the kinds of cars they drive and so on, in a systematic and predictable manner. Bourdieu is interested not just in documenting differences in 'tastes' and lifestyles, but in how these are mobilized in struggles for status and prestige and naturalized in various ways, made to appear to be self-evident and non-arbitrary. The possession of high Culture, a mark of social distinction, gets collapsed into culture. Cultured individuals regard their own cultural distinction as something that is taken for granted, natural, an inherent marker of their inherent social value and status.

The importance of Bourdieu's *Distinction* for material culture studies ultimately resides in the claims made that there are systematic homologies in people's lifestyle choices objectified through an entire gamut of material forms and activities *without* which social status could not be marked and recognized and that the qualities of the things consumed enter into the very manner in which people think and feel about themselves and their relation to others. For example, tastes in food:

> depend on the idea each class has of the body and of the effects of food on the body, that is, on its strengths, health and beauty; and on the categories it uses to evaluate these effects, some of which may be more important for one class and ignored by another, and which the different classes may rank in different ways. Thus, whereas the working classes are more attentive to the strength of the (male) body than its shape, and tend to go for products that are cheap and nutritious, the professions

prefer foods that are tasty, health-giving, light and not fattening. Taste, a class culture turned into nature, that is, *embodied*, helps to shape the class body.

(Bourdieu 1984: 190, emphasis in original)

Read today, and from an English perspective, Bourdieu's analysis of French society seems peculiarly stereotyped. If the world of tastes, cultural distinctions and lifestyles he portrays was ever really like this it has changed out of all recognition in an era of globalization and transnational societies. Mapping objectifications of identities in the twenty-first century requires a much more complex and subtle analysis which is beginning to be addressed in recent anthroplogical studies of consumption.

OBJECTIFICATION AND CONSUMPTION

There are fundamental differences between things and their relationships to persons in industrial consumer societies and the small-scale communities that archaeologists and anthropologists have typically studied until recently. Hoskins (1998: 192) has summarized these differences in terms of:

1   Investment in form.
2   Investment in work.
3   Novelty versus age.
4   Exchange histories and paths.

A person's relationship to an object is obviously very different when they have made it themselves, or provided the raw materials, or in other ways participated in its production in ways discussed above in relation to Telefol net bags and Yekuana basketry. It is easy to see the manner in which the self becomes part of the thing and vice versa. By contrast almost all the things surrounding us in consumer societies are bought ready-made and their conditions of production are concealed from the consumer. The things thus appear to have a price and a value in themselves rather than their value being socially created. This is, of course, the basis for Marx's analysis of commodity fetishism and the distinction he draws between the use value of a thing and its exchange value. As a consequence almost all discussions of commodities have centred on our intrinsic alienation from them and this has consistently been linked with moralistic discussions of 'materialistic' and acquisitive values in late capitalist

societies in which buying things becomes an end in itself but is ultimately unfulfilling. Persons are dupes of a system which encourages us to buy more and more and the endless production of novelty – new types of consumer goods and the inbuilt obsolescence of the old – stimulates this consumption. It is novelty rather than tradition that is significant, and the manner in which things are exchanged is impersonal as opposed to the ceremony and face-to-face encounters characteristic of small-scale societies.

The thrust of some anthropological studies of consumption (see Miller, Chapter 22 in this volume) has been to challenge many of these assumptions. Miller, in particular (1987, 1988, 1995, 1998, 2001; see also Carrier 1995), has stressed the manner in which persons actively appropriate consumer goods, objectify and fashion their identities through, for example, altering kitchens, home furnishings, consuming particular types of drink, styles of clothing, going shopping for food in a supermarket, and so on. Once bought, home consumer products can be endlessly personalized and become as much part of the modern self as craft products in small-scale societies. But the very important point here is that the thrust of the analysis of objectification processes shifts from production and exchange being primary to consumption. Rather than focusing on the negative consequences of consumerism in relation to personal and social identities Miller's work focuses on its positive aspects in fashioning personal and social relations, 'the myriad strategies of recontextualization and consumption which have been used to overcome the alienatory consequences of mass consumer culture' (Miller 1987: 229).

OBJECTIFICATION AND THE CREATION OF VALUE IN SPACE-TIME

Munn's *The Fame of Gawa* (1986) is a symbolic study of value transformations in the Massim society of the Milne Bay area, Papua New Guinea. She analyses a complex nexus of time-space-person relations in which positive and negative values are created and transformed. The central premise of her study is that 'actors construct this meaningful order in the process of being constructed in its terms' (1986: 2). This involves the analysis of cultural meanings implicated in social practices through the objective and intersubjective media of material forms and bodily states. Gawan society is understood in terms of its grounding in an inter-island world involving *kula* exchange of armbands and necklaces circulating in opposite directions (Leach and Leach 1983; Malinowski 1922). Engagement in the *kula* results in the fame of Gawa, in the positive evaluation of Gawans, by others with whom they have few or no face-to-face relationships. The circulation of the shells effectively converts material forms into an immaterial essence, the renown of Gawa, which is ultimately about the self-esteem and self-worth of Gawans. This fame can be achieved only by an externalizing process involving the production of material forms, such as garden crops and canoes, and their transaction into an inter-island world. The self-identity of Gawans is thus produced on Gawa and in relation to a wider world. Both on Gawa and beyond, the production and exchange of material culture make this possible. The agency of Gawans is thus achieved through the medium of the active possibilities afforded by things as they circulate between individuals and groups.

The production of value involves, on the one hand, consideration of the phenomenal form of practices and, on the other, underlying structures or 'generative schema' that characterize this process, as in Bourdieu's work on Kabylia (Munn 1986: 7). The lived world is both an arena for action and constructed through the actions of persons, a dialectic of objectification and embodiment. Agents engaging in social actions are themselves 'acted upon' by these very acts, which are thus both constituting and constituted. Actions such as the exchange of food produce desirable outcomes or effects as well as sometimes having more latent undesirable properties. Key types of acts have positive outcomes; others, involving witchcraft, are negative in their effect. Social acts, and the material forms implicated in these acts, can thus have relative degrees of potency in the creation of value. As in Bourdieu's work sociocultural practices do not take place in space and in time but create the space-time in which they go on. Space-time is thus action objectified in relation to a system of value (1986: 11 ff.). Different degrees of extension of intersubjective space-time are intimately related to different material media. For example, the kind of space-time created by the annual internal transmission of yam tubers from a woman's kinsmen to affines is very limited compared with canoe transactions. The latter have much greater depth in space-time, i.e. their spatio-temporal reach, and therefore their value is far greater.

Munn stresses that value is generated by particular *types* of acts and practices. A key part of her argument is that this value is also signified through specific *qualities* that characterize particular material forms such as the body itself, food, *kula* shells and canoes. She uses the term, derived from Pierce (1955), *qualisign* to denote the positive or negative values different kinds of things signify. For Gawans, she argues, these qualisigns can be understood in terms of fundamental binary oppositions involving motion, speed : slowness or stasis, weight : lightweightedness, heaviness and lightness, light : darkness. They may also have associations with directionality such as upwards versus downwards movement. These qualisigns are, in turn, linked to gender divisions between male and female and the environment. The land is slow and heavy, the sea is swift and buoyant. Processes of production transform the qualities of things. Canoe manufacture on Gawa transforms a heavy rooted thing, the tree, into a buoyant mobile object that is a fundamental medium for extending Gawan space-time in inter-island exchange.

Keane (2003, n.d.) has cogently argued that what this amounts to is a materialist rather than a linguistically grounded notion of semiotics or the process of signification which shakes off Saussure's radical separation of the sign from the material world with the *assumption* that the relationship is always arbitrary: 'the qualities of things consumed enter into the certain qualities of subjectivity, regardless of whether those things ever become available for interpretation as "signs." As embodied subjectivity, they mediate future possibilities' (Keane 2003: 418).

Let us return to some of the specifics of Gawan material culture to more closely examine the objectification processes involved in Gawan intersubjective space-time and its relation to the body. In different contexts and material media qualities such as lightness or heaviness may be positively or negatively evaluated in terms of their outcomes or effects. So heavy stones are positively evaluated because they weigh down the gardens whose immobility is symbolically condensed in the stones that are essential to their fertility and growth (Munn 1986: 80 ff.). The antithesis of both mobility and immobility is unregulated eating. Excessive eating weighs down the body and makes it slow, only good for sleep, an inappropriate state during daylight. It wastes yams which otherwise could be given in feasts to others, demonstrating prodigality with visitors, acts that will be remembered, thus extending the space-time of individuals and groups. Gardens and *kula* shells represent two poles of spatiotemporal potency:

> stones assure renewal and long-term spatiotemporal continuities through internal fixity ... Kula shells, on the other hand, are the most expansive of the circulatory media that create ... 'an emergent space-time of their own' by means of release and mobility, that is, by the continuous changing (exchanging) of shells in inter-island transmission.
>
> (1986: 104)

OBJECTIFICATION: HISTORY, PLACE, LANDSCAPE

Objectification theories of material culture have almost always privileged the manner in which artefacts relate to the identities of individuals and groups and cultural systems of value in the manner discussed above. However, this does not end their entanglements. In transcultural and colonial contexts these forms of identification can readily be made by outsiders. As N. Thomas has pointed out, things to which local people attach no particular importance can be regarded as resonant of local distinctiveness or badges of identity by outsiders (Thomas 1991: 163). This is, of course, precisely what archaeologists and anthropologists have always tended to do. In these 'mixed' contexts of interactions artefacts can also objectify particular events and transactions in a much more specific way. For example, Marquesans and some other Polynesians treated guns, whether received through purchase, barter or as gifts, as though they manifested elements of the person who gave them and the power of foreign warriors (1991: 98 ff.). The adoption of a new clothing style, the 'poncho', by western Polynesian Christians did not merely express their new found modesty. The clothing style made this modesty possible (N. Thomas 1999).

In particular contexts of interaction and exchange people by presenting themselves to others may simultaneously present or objectify themselves to themselves and be surprised by the result (Strathern 1991). Their self-objectifications can thus be revelatory. Artefacts may thus objectify a particular event of transaction or aspects of the identity of the transactor. They can also objectify particular places where they were made or transacted or places from which the raw materials were obtained. The artefact can thus be a place, a landscape, a story or an event, and concomitantly people's different relationships with places, landscapes, paths and types of dwellings are primary ways in which individual and group biographies and identities become objectified (Appadurai 1995; Barrett 1994; Bradley 2000; Basso and Feld 1996; Hodder 1990; Lovell 1998; Low and Lawrence-Zuniga 2003; Tilley 1994; Hirsch and O'Hanlon 1995).

Artefacts considered as particular kinds of substances, bone, clay, stone, wood, flint, quartz, shell, local or exotic, whether they were deposited whole or fragmented in particular ways, their textures, colours, forms, and their depositional relationships in different contexts (burials, houses, ritual and ceremonial monuments, settlements, pits, etc.), can be fruitfully analysed in terms of the manner in which they objectify particular kinds of social relationships and conceptions of the world, as a growing number of archaeological studies have demonstrated (Bradley 2000; Brück 2001; Chapman 2000; Fowler and Cummings 2003; Fowler 2004; Parker-Pearson and Ramilisonina 1998; Jones 2002; Jones and MacGregor 2002; Richards 1996; J. Thomas 1996; 1999, Tilley 1996, 2004).

CONCLUSION: SOME NOTES FOR FUTURE RESEARCH

Detailed ethnographic studies of the importance of things in early childhood socialization are conspicuously absent from the anthropological literature and comparative investigation of these processes is required. Similarly studies of material culture in relation to movement and loss represent an almost novel area of research: the objectifications of transnational and diasporic communites, elderly people forced to move into nursing homes, or mental patients in institutions, and so on (Belk 1992; Marcoux 2001; Parkin 1999).

It has often been claimed that certain material forms – in particular, houses and the layout of villages or tombs and mortuary practices or art – are privileged sites for the objectification of cultural meanings, but this may just be a bias of what has been investigated. There is a pressing need to examine in more detail the role of ordinary artefacts as part of the flow of everyday life rather than concentrating analyses on what are assumed to be key objectifications. We need to further investigate the banal and the everyday as well as the extraordinary. For example, virtually all academic studies of gardens and gardening in industrialized societies have focused on the grand public gardens, the gardens of the privileged, the rich and the powerful. A rather different perspective on the personal and cultural significance of the garden is emerging from research I am conducting on ordinary people's gardens and allotments (Tilley n.d.).

Another persistent theme in the literature has been to link different forms of objectication with different types of societies, principally capitalist and non-capitalist. However, recent consumption studies have shown that blanket distinctions between types of things such as gifts and commodities are fairly meaningless. Things change their meanings through their life cycles and according to the way they are used and appropriated and in the manner in which individuals and groups identify themselves with them. Further studies need to be undertaken of these kinds of value transformations, and their possible linkage with generative structures or cultural schemes that result in generative homologies between different material domains, both in the past and in the present.

In colonial and postcolonial 'contact' situations an 'inappropriate' relationship between persons and things has frequently posed problems for missionaries in particular and others. The aim was often to create a new human 'native' subject independent of a world of things, of dead matter, to free people from a false relationship with things, as in fetishism and animism, to abstract persons from their entanglements with things in the name of enlightenment, freedom and autonomy (Keane 2001, 2004a). But as Keane points out the irony of all this is that the overall premise is false: people can never be free from objectification, since people must always work, use, transact, possess and consume objects. Studies of the role of different Christian religous cults, missionary work and the values of traders and settlers in colonial and postcolonial contexts provide a fertile domain for further exploration of objectification processes and how they transform people's relationship with things in historical perspective.

Objectifications can take on myriad forms, from tombs to houses to pots to paintings to ritual speech and cultural performances to sacrifice and hunting rites, and so on. Some will be more important in one social context, others in another, some foregrounded, others backgrounded. We need to take these differences seriously and analyse their similarities and differences cross-culturally and in the past and

in the present, investigate more fully *kinds* of temporal linkages between kinds of things, types of action and forms of sociability. We also need to analyse, in relation to this, in far greater detail than at present, the manifold sensuous qualities of things from a broad phenomenological perspective: their sounds, textures, smells, tastes as well as their visual appearance and form, which have always dominated discussion. This is, as yet, a relatively underdeveloped area of the analysis of material culture in which detailed work, particularly in relation to the archaeological past, is only just beginning (Tilley 2004; Howes 2004 and Chapter 11 in this volume).

A focus on *materiality* necessarily involves consideration of objectification processes and embodiment. By refining our empirical understanding of the manner in which these processes work in relation to the manifold sensuous qualities of things, and of our human experience of them, we may reach a fuller critical appreciation of the manner in which those things are ontologically constitutive of our social being.

REFERENCES

Appadurai, A. (1995) 'The production of locality', in A. Appadurai, *Modernity at Large*. Minneapolis, MN: University of Minnesota Press.

Barrett, J. (1994) *Fragments from Antiquity: an Archaeology of Social Life in Britain, 2900–1200 BC*. Oxford: Blackwell.

Basso, K. and Feld, S., eds. (1996) *Senses of Place*. Albuquerque, NM: University of New Mexico Press.

Battaglia, D. (1990) *On the Bones of the Serpent*. Chicago: University of Chicago Press.

Belk, R. (1992) 'Moving possessions: an analysis based on personal documents from the 1847–1869 Mormon migration', *Journal of Consumer Research*, 19: 339–61.

Bourdieu, P. (1977) *Outline of a Theory of Practice*. Cambridge: Cambridge University Press.

Bourdieu, P. (1984) *Distinction*. London: Routledge.

Bourdieu, P. (1990) *The Logic of Practice*. Cambridge: Polity Press.

Bradley, R. (2000) *An Archaeology of Natural Places*. London: Routledge.

Brück, J. (2001) 'Body metaphors and technologies of transformation in the English middle and late Bronze Age', in J. Brück (ed.) *Bronze Age Landscapes: Tradition and Transformation*. Oxford: Oxbow.

Carrier, J. (1995) *Gifts and Commodities*. London: Routledge.

Chapman, J. (2000) *Fragmentation in Archaeology: People, Places and Broken Objects in the Prehistory of South-east Europe.* London: Routledge.

Durkheim, E. and Mauss, M. (1903/1963) *Primitive Classification.* Chicago: University of Chicago Press.

Fowler, C. (2004) *The Archaeology of Personhood,* London: Routledge.

Fowler, C. and Cummings, V. (2003) 'Places of transformation: building monuments from water and stone in the Neolithic of the Irish sea', *Journal of the Royal Anthropological Institute,* 9: 1–20.

Gell, A. (1992) 'The technology of enchantment and the enchantment of technology', in J. Coote and A. Sheldon (eds), *Anthropology, Art and Aesthetics.* Oxford: Clarendon Press.

Gell, A. (1996) 'Vogel's net: traps as artworks and artworks as traps', *Journal of Material Culture,* 1 (1): 15–38.

Gell, A. (1998) *Art and Agency.* Oxford: Clarendon Press.

Gilchrist, R. (1994) *Gender and Material Culture: the Archaeology of Religious Women.* London: Routledge.

Gosden, C. (1999) *Anthropology and Archaeology: a Changing Relationship.* London: Routledge.

Guss, D. (1989) *To Weave and Sing: Art, Symbol and Narrative in the South American Rainforest.* Berkeley, CA: University of California Press.

Hegel, G. (1807/1977) *Phenomenology of Spirit.* Oxford: Oxford University Press.

Hirsch, E. and O'Hanlon, M., eds. (1995) *The Anthropology of Landscape.* Oxford: Clarendon Press.

Hodder, I. (1990) *The Domestication of Europe.* Oxford: Blackwell.

Holliman, S. (2000) 'Archaeology of the 'Aqi: gender and sexuality in prehistoric Chumash society', in R. Schmidt and B. Voss (eds), *The Archaeology of Sexuality.* London: Routledge.

Hoskins, J. (1998) *Biographical Objects.* London: Routledge.

Howes, D., ed. (2004) *Empire of the Senses.* Oxford: Berg.

Jolly, M. (1991) 'Gifts, commodities and corporeality: food and gender in South Pentecost, Vanuatu', *Canberra Anthropology,* 14: 45–66.

Jones, A. (2002) *Archaeological Theory and Scientific Practice.* Cambridge: Cambridge University Press.

Jones, A. and MacGregor, G., eds. (2002) *Colouring the Past.* Oxford: Berg.

Keane, W. (1995) 'The spoken house: text, act, and object in eastern Indonesia', *American Ethnologist,* 22: 102–24.

Keane, W. (1997) *Signs of Recognition: Powers and Hazards of Representation in an Indonesian Society.* Berkeley, CA: University of California Press.

Keane, W. (2001) 'Money is no object: materiality, desire and modernity in an Indonesian society', in F. Myers (ed.), *The Empire of Things.* Santa Fe, NM: School of American Research Press.

Keane, W. (2003) 'Semiotics and the social analysis of material things', *Language and Communication,* 23: 409–25.

Keane, W. (2004a) 'Signs are not the garb of meaning: on the social analysis of material things', in D. Miller (ed.), *Materiality.* Durham, NC: Duke University Press.

Keane, W. (2004b) 'Epilogue: anxious transcendence', in F. Cannell (ed.), *Words and Things in the Anthropology of Christianity.* Durham, NC: Duke University Press.

Leach, J. and Leach, E., eds. (1983) *The Kula: New Perspectives on Massim Exchange.* Cambridge: Cambridge University Press.

Lovell, N., ed. (1998) *Locality and Belonging.* London: Routledge.

Low, S. and Lawrence-Zuniga, D., eds (2003) *The Anthropology of Space and Place.* Oxford: Blackwell.

MacKenzie, M. (1991) *Androgynous Objects: String Bags and Gender in Central New Guinea.* Melbourne: Harwood Academic Press.

Malinowski, B. (1922) *Argonauts of the Western Pacific.* London: Routledge.

Marcoux, J. (2001) 'The *casser maison* ritual: constructing the self by emptying the home', *Journal of Material Culture,* 6: 213–35.

Miller, D. (1987) *Material Culture and Mass Consumption.* Oxford: Blackwell.

Miller, D. (1988) 'Appropriating the state on the council estate', *Man,* 23: 353–73.

Miller, D., ed. (1995) *Acknowledging Consumption.* London: Routledge.

Miller, D. (1998) *A Theory of Shopping.* Cambridge: Polity Press.

Miller, D., ed. (2001) *Home Possessions.* Oxford: Berg.

Moore, H. (1986) *Space, Text and Gender.* Cambridge: Cambridge University Press.

Moore, H. (1994) *A Passion for Difference.* Cambridge: Polity Press.

Morphy, H. (1991) *Ancestral Connections.* Chicago: University of Chicago Press.

Munn, N. (1983) 'Gawan kula: spatiotemporal control and the symbolism of influence', in J. Leach and E. Leach (eds), *The Kula.* Cambridge: Cambridge University Press.

Munn, N. (1986) *The Fame of Gawa.* Cambridge: Cambridge University Press.

Pandya, V. (1998) 'Hot scorpions, sweet peacocks: Kachchhe art, architecture and action', *Journal of Material Culture,* 3 (1): 51–76.

Parker-Pearson, M. and Ramilisonina, (1998) 'Stonehenge for the ancestors: the stones pass on the message', *Antiquity,* 72: 308–26.

Parkin, D. (1999) 'Mementoes as transitional objects in human displacement', *Journal of Material Culture,* 4: 303–20.

Pierce, C. (1955) *Philosophical Writings of Pierce,* ed. J. Buchler. New York: Dover Publications.

Prine, E. (2000) 'Searching for third genders: towards a prehistory of domestic space in middle Missouri villages', in R. Schmidt and B. Voss (eds), *The Archaeology of Sexuality*. London: Routledge.

Richards, C. (1996) 'Henges and water: towards an elemental understanding of monumentality and landscape', *Journal of Material Culture*, 1: 313–36.

Riggins, H., ed. (1994) *The Socialness of Things*. Berlin: Mouton de Gruyter.

Shanks. M. and Tilley, C. (1987) *Social Theory and Archaeology*. Cambridge: Polity Press.

Simmel, G. (1990) *The Philosophy of Money*. London: Routledge.

Sørensen, M-L. (2000) *Gender Archaeology*. Cambridge: Polity Press.

Strathern, M. (1991) 'Artefacts of history: events and the interpretation of images', in J. Siikala (ed.), *Culture and History in the Pacific*. Finnish Anthropological Society Transactions 27. Helsinki: Finish Anthropological Society.

Thomas, J. (1996) *Time, Culture and Identity*. London: Routledge.

Thomas, J. (1999) 'An economy of substances in late Neolithic Britain', in J. Robb (ed.), *Material Symbols: Culture and Economy in Prehistory*. Carbondale, IL: Southern Illinois University Press.

Thomas, J. (2000) 'Death, identity and the body in Neolithic Britain', *Journal of the Royal Anthropological Institute*, 6: 603–17.

Thomas, N. (1991) *Entangled Objects*. Cambridge, MA: Harvard University Press.

Thomas, N. (1999) 'The case of the misplaced poncho: speculations concerning the history of cloth in Melanesia', *Journal of Material Culture*, 4: 5–20.

Tilley, C. (1991) *Material Culture and Text: the Art of Ambiguity*. London: Routledge.

Tilley, C. (1994) *A Phenomenology of Landscape*. Oxford: Berg.

Tilley, C. (1996) *An Ethnography of the Neolithic*. Cambridge: Cambridge University Press.

Tilley, C. (1999) *Metaphor and Material Culture*. Oxford: Blackwell.

Tilley, C. (2004) *The Materiality of Stone: Explorations in Landscape Pheonomenology* I. Oxford: Berg.

Tilley, C. (n.d.) 'Gardens and Gardening: an Ethnographic perspective'. MS in preparation.

Yates, T. (1993) 'Frameworks for an archaeology of the body', in C. Tilley (ed.), *Interpretative Archaeology*. Oxford: Berg.

Yates, T. and Nordbladh, J. (1990) 'This perfect body, this virgin text', in I. Bapty and T. Yates (eds), *Archaeology after Structuralism*. London: Routledge.

ACKNOWLEDGEMENTS

I am grateful to Webb Keane, Howard Morphy and Mike Rowlands for advice and comments on this chapter.

5

AGENCY, BIOGRAPHY AND OBJECTS

Janet Hoskins

Anthropologists since Mauss (1924/1954) and Malinowski (1922) have asserted that the lines between persons and things are culturally variable, and not drawn in the same way in all societies. In certain contexts, persons can seem to take on the attributes of things and things can seem to act almost as persons. Studies of traditional exchange systems (from Boas and Malinowski to Strathern, Munn and Campbell) have elaborated on this insight by detailing how objects can be given a gender, name, history and ritual function. Some objects can be so closely associated with persons as to seem inalienable (Weiner 1992), and some persons – slaves, dependants – can have their own humanity depreciated so as to approach the status of simple possessions. Within this framework, things can be said to have 'biographies' as they go through a series of transformations from gift to commodity to inalienable possessions, and persons can also be said to invest aspects of their own biographies in things.

AGENCY AND OBJECTS

The recent agentive turn in social theory had led a number of theorists to speak in new ways about the agency of objects. It might be useful to trace the genealogy of this particular usage in order to clarify its antecedents and its currently controversial status. Laura Ahern sees the new interest in agency at the turn of the twenty first century as following on the heels of critical social movements and critiques that have questioned:

> impersonal master narratives that leave no room for tensions, contradictions, or oppositional actions

on the part of individuals and collectivities. It is because questions about agency are so central to contemporary political and theoretical debates that the concept arouses so much interest and why it is therefore so crucial to define clearly.

(2001: 109)

Her definition, in which agency is 'the socio-culturally mediated capacity to act' (2001: 110), is deliberately not restricted to persons, and may include spirits, machines, signs and collective entities (ancestors, corporations, social groups). It is also deliberately relative, since just as different societies have varying notions of social action, they may have diverse ideas about who and what is capable of acting in a particular context.

An open definition raises the question of exactly what is meant by an agent. Does the capacity to act imply individuality and distinctiveness? Can it also apply to relatively generic classes of objects? Can the agency of objects be dissolved and decentred (as certain structuralists and post-structuralists have argued) or does the notion of agency by itself imply an idiosyncratic power to change the world? Such questions need to be explored in relation to an ethnographic study of objects as agents in the world.

The proposition that things can be said to have 'social lives' was developed in an influential edited collection (Appadurai 1986), which drew attention to the ways in which passive objects were successively moved about and recontextualized. Appadurai's essay in that volume framed this explicitly as a process of commodification and decommodification, although of course 'commodity' is only one of a wider range of different 'identities' (gift, talisman, art work, heirloom, ancestral legacy, ritual sacra, memento) that an object can assume. He was concerned with showing how the capitalist spirit of calculation is still often present in the gift (as Mauss was well aware, since he spoke of its coercive power), and in analysing the shifts in object identity created by trajectories that took them through different regimes of value. Fifteen years later, another collection titled *The Empire of Things: Regimes of Value and Material Culture* (Fred Myers 2001) tried to carry that notion further by focusing on contradictions among objects' shifting meanings for different constituencies.

Both of these collections emphasize commerce and external constraints over local meanings and internal configurations, in keeping with a broader disciplinary change from 'local' levels to 'global' ones, and from single-sited field projects to multi-sited ones in order to trace persons and things as they move through space and time. The relationship between objects and individual subjectivity was given relatively short shrift, as was the relation between objects and gender or personality. Objects do indeed pass through many transformations, and Appadurai's call for a study of the 'paths' and 'life histories' of things inspired a whole series of new studies which looked at the 'mutability of things in recontextualization' (Nick Thomas 1989: 49). This involves a form of 'methodological fetishism' which looks at the ways in which things may be drawn into significant diversions from familiar paths:

> It is only through the analysis of these trajectories that we can interpret the human transactions and calculation that enliven things. Thus, even though from a *theoretical* point of view human actors encode things with significance, from a *methodological* point of view it is the things-in-motion that illuminate their human and social context.
>
> (Appadurai 1986: 5)

Kopytoff's essay 'The cultural biography of things' in the same volume focused these questions on particular objects, asking, Who makes it? In what conditions? From what materials? For what purpose? What are the recognized stages of development? How does it move from hand to hand? What other contexts and uses can it have? In effect, his essay encouraged researchers to ask the same questions of a thing that they would of people.

Christopher Steiner argues (Steiner 2001: 209) that anthropologists who focused on the agentive elements of objects had misinterpreted the seminal idea of the 'cultural biography of things' articulated in Kopytoff's article in *The Social Life of Things* (1986). The processual model of commoditization that Kopytoff proposed, he argues, had an impact in anthropology because it coincided with a broadening of research paradigms to include transnational movement and connection.

> Yet in their zeal to explore the social identity of material culture, many authors have attributed too much power to the 'things' themselves, and in so doing have diminished the significance of human agency and the role of individuals and systems that construct and imbue material goods with value, significance and meaning. Thus, commodity fetishism has been inscribed as the *object* of the model rather than its *subject* ... . The point is not that 'things' are any more animated than we used to believe, but rather that they are infinitely malleable to the shifting and contested meanings constructed *for them* through human agency.
>
> (Steiner 2001: 210)

It is perhaps more accurate to see these as two separate directions of interpretation, one stressing the ways in which things are commodified and lose personality, the other looking at the processes by which they are invested with personality and may have an impact. The malleability of objects, and the many different ways they may be perceived, are linked to what Gell might call their 'instrumentality' or even – in his provocative new use of the term – their 'agency', the ways in which they stimulate an emotional responses and are invested with some of the intentionality of their creators. Others have also looked at the ways in which things actively constitute new social contexts, working as technologies (such as clothing) that can make religious change (conversion to Christianity) or political allegiance visible as a feature of people's behavior and domestic life.

Gell has formulated a theory about the creation of art objects that could in fact be a theory about the creation of all forms of material culture. He asserts that things are made as a form of instrumental action: Art (and other objects) is produced in order to influence the thoughts and actions of others. Even those objects which seem to be without a directly identifiable function – that is, objects which have previously been theorized as simple objects of aesthetic contemplation – are in fact made in order to act upon the world and to act upon other persons. Material objects thus embody complex intentionalities and mediate social agency. The psychology of art needs to look at how patterns and perception have specific effects on viewers, and are designed to arouse fear, desire, admiration or confusion.

His work suggests a more active model of an object's biography, in which the object may not only assume a number of different identities as imported wealth, ancestral valuable or commodity but may also 'interact' with the people who gaze upon it, use it and try to possess it. Gendering objects in itself allocates aspects of agency and identity to things (Strathern 1988, 1992), and Gell's model of the 'distributed mind' which we find scattered through objects has a strong kinship with Strathern's notion of the 'partible person' who is divisible into things that circulate along specific exchange trajectories.

The equivalence suggested between the agency of persons and of things calls into question the borders of individual persons and collective representations in a number of ways. It implies that we need to pay more attention to the phenomenological dimension of our interactions with the material world, and interrogate the objects which fascinate us as well as our reasons for feeling this fascination.

The theoretical frame that he elaborates for making new sense of these objects – both the 'traditional ones' like cloth and the new ones like photographs – comes from Gell's ideas about the technology of enchantment and the enchantment of technology. He defines his concept of technical difficulty as producing a 'halo effect' of resistance (a notion related to, but still somewhat different from, Walter Benjamin's notion of the 'aura'). Works of art make it difficult for us to possess them in an intellectual rather than a material sense, so their effect on our minds is 'magical' – it is a form of enchantment.

In *Art and Agency* (1998), Gell takes this argument further by arguing that anthropological theories of art objects have to be primarily concerned with social relations over the time frame of biographies. He rejects the linguistic analogies of semiotic theories and insists that art is about doing things, that it is a system of social action – and that we have to look at how people act through objects by distributing parts of their personhood into things. These things have agency because they produce effects, they cause us to feel happy, angry, fearful or lustful. They have an impact, and we as artists produce them as ways of distributing elements of our own efficacy in the form of things. Art objects use formal complexity and technical virtuosity to create 'a certain cognitive indecipherability' (1998: 95) which may

tantalize and frustrate the viewer in trying to recognize wholes and parts, continuity and discontinuity, synchrony and succession. He analyses involuted designs intended to entrance and ward off dangerous spirits, tattoos and shields in Polynesia, and idols which are animated in a variety of ways, and able to bestow fertility, sickness, cures or misfortunes.

Gell argues that an object acts as an agent when the artist's skill is so great that the viewer simply cannot comprehend it and is therefore captivated by the image. This notion of captivation asserts that an object is art on the basis of what it does, not what it is. Gell's approach allows him to sidestep the problematic distinction between Western and non-Western art, and to present a theory about the efficacy of an object's appearance – about cross-cultural visuality, in other words – rather than specifically about art. Objects which are often treated as material culture or crafts, rather than art (like textiles, betel bags, etc.) therefore deserve equal attention, since their making is a 'particularly salient feature of their agency' (Gell 1998: 68).

Gell defines captivation as 'the demoralisation produced by the spectacle of unimaginable virtuosity' (1998: 71), an effect created by our being unable to figure out how an object came into being. Many imported objects in remote locations in Melanesia or South East Asia emerge as 'captivating' – the smooth, shiny surfaces of porcelain ceramics (given ritual status as the anchors of the polity, Hoskins 1993), the explosive sounds and fatal bullets of guns, and of course the mysterious lifelike two-dimensional images of the camera. In the 1990s, when tourists began to come to this once remote area in substantial numbers, they were considered predatory voyeurs, 'foreigners with metal boxes' who used the hose-like aperture of their zoom lenses to extract blood from children and take it home to power electronic devices in the industrial West. The cameras that every tourist brings to capture images of headhunters and primitive violence became the very emblems of the exotic violence that they were designed to capture (Hoskins 2002).

Rather than using these stories to produce yet another version of the colonial cliché of the credulous native, Gell's theory provides us with the insight that there is nothing irrational or even particularly 'primitive' in seeing the camera as a technology of enchantment – all forms of visual representation share this trait. Photographs themselves were rarely shared with their subjects in 'tribal' or 'adventure tourism' – instead, people in remote villages saw a parade of intimidating gadgets which seemed to steal away some aspect of their lives that they had no access to or control over. The story of the bloodthirsty camera encodes a critical awareness of global inequities in access to and use of technology. Gell's notion of captivation helps us to isolate a realm of specifically *visual* power, which – while obviously embedded in a wider political economic context of unequal access to technology – is also enchanting in its own way.

Looking at photographs and paintings in the context of ancestor worship and animism helps us to isolate the 'agentive elements' of certain technologies, and disengage these elements from simple differences in representation between a hand-drawn image, say, and one produced by chemicals working to record lines of light and shadow. Much of Gell's argument builds on what was left unsaid in Walter Benjamin's 'A short history of photography', where he first criticized the 'fetishistic and fundamentally anti-technical concept of art with which the theoreticians of photography sought to grapple for almost a hundred years' (Benjamin 1978: 241).

In fact, Gell acknowledges his debt to Benjamin only through his spectral reincarnation as Michael Taussig, who has seized on Benjamin's insight that 'it is through photography that we first discover the existence of this optical unconscious' (1978: 243) – which is the secret that shows us how our own eyes work to construct coherent visual images. Benjamin described the new visual worlds produced by photography to 'waking dreams … which, enlarged and capable of formulation, make the difference between technology and magic visible as a thoroughly historical variable' (1978: 244). Benjamin argued that 'The first people to be reproduced entered the visual space of photography with their innocence intact, uncompromised by captions' (1978: 244). While sitting for long exposures they had to focus on life in the moment rather than hurrying past it, and thus 'the subject as it were grew into the picture' (1978: 245) and felt a sort of participation in the process that is no longer true of the quick snapshot.

Rather than seeing the celluloid image as the 'last refuge of the cult value of the picture', it is possible to see it instead as the wedge of a postcolonial perspective on modernity. Photographs of revered figures from the past, ancestors and heroes, can be used not only to commemorate them in traditional ways, but also to recreate them visually for a new world of globalized imagery. The 'resistance' which

Gell talks about in art objects – their ability to challenge us and captivate us visually – suggests that the 'magic' of mechanical reproduction will not remove the aura of art objects but only enhance it. John Berger makes a similar argument when he notes that 'The bogus religiosity which now surrounds original works of art, and which is ultimately dependent upon their market value, has become the substitute for what paintings lost when the camera made them reproducible' (Berger 1972: 230). The new craze for photography in the Third World stems from a global political economy in which mechanical visuality is restricted to certain peoples and certain institutions, and these lines of access are marked by differences of race and culture as well as class.

FROM AGENCY TO BIOGRAPHY

Asking questions about the agency of objects has led to the development of a more biographical approach, particularly in Melanesia, where Malinowski (1922) first described the distinctive 'personalities' of shell valuables. The *malanggan*, an intricate wooden carving produced for mortuary ceremonies in New Ireland, is the most widely collected object in the global world of 'primitive art'. They are laboriously produced, then displayed for a few hours at the end of a ceremony. It is only the internalized memory of the object which is locally valued, so it can be 'killed' with gifts of shell money – and then made available for sale to collectors. Gell describes this process as making the *malanggan* 'an index of agency of an explicitly temporary nature' (1998: 225). By providing the 'skin' for a deceased relative, the process of carving objectifies social relationships and brings together the dispersed agency of the deceased – visualizing his social effectiveness as 'a kind of body that accumulates, like a charged battery, the potential energy of the deceased' (Gell 1998: 225). Küchler, in the most detailed ethnography of *malanggan*, says it serves as a container for ancestral life force, which mediates and transmits agency from one generation to another (2002), as a visualized memory which is publicly transacted. The 'cognitive stickiness' of art works, which allows them to be the vehicles of a technology of enchantment, lies in their ability to absorb death and represent it as a new form of life.

Küchler's work finishes with the observation that *malanggan* themselves are memory objects which work in the opposite way to our own museum displays. She notes that 'the extraordinary theatre of memory that we have enshrined in our museums is the result of a laborious and systematic work of displacement of objects by images' (2002: 190). While we value objects because of the memories attached to them, the people of New Ireland value them instead for their work in detaching memories, undoing and displacing relations between persons and things. In this way, 'surfaces can be vehicles of thought in ways that we ascribe to living kinds only' (Küchler 2002: 193). The 'animated skins' of New Ireland are made deliberately to affect the thinking and feeling of those who look upon them.

Gell argues that consciousness is a mental process through which subjective temporality is constituted through transformations over time. Nancy Munn's (1986) work on Gawa canoes and wealth objects describes this as 'value creation' over a biographical cycle, in which the canoes start life as trees grown on clan land, are then transferred to other clans to be carved, then sailed and traded against yams or shell valuables. The canoe itself is dematerialized but still 'owned', although in another form, and it is ultimately converted into what Munn calls 'sociotemporal space-time'. A famous *kula* operator is able to 'move minds' at great distances and becomes so enchantingly attractive and so irresistibly persuasive that the exchange paths of all the most desirable valuables converge in his direction. His personhood is distributed through a series of objects linked by his strategic actions and calculated interventions, which anticipate the future to guide each transaction to the most useful end.

Gell's review of the politics of Melanesian exchange leads him back to the idea that the *oeuvre* of a Western artist can be seen as a form of distributed personhood, a way of collecting 'a life' through collecting representations which cull the memories of that life and give them visual expression. His argument recalls the distinction made by French sociologist Violette Morin (1969) between a 'biographical object' and a 'protocol object', or a standardized commodity. Though both sorts of objects maybe produced for mass consumption, the relation that a person establishes with a biographical object gives it an identity that is localized, particular and individual, while those established with an object generated by an outside protocol are globalized, generalized and mechanically reproduced. Morin distinguishes three levels of mediation as characteristic of biographical objects – their relation to time, space and the owner or consumer.

In relation to time, the biographical object grows old, and may become worn and tattered along the life span of its owner, while the public commodity is eternally youthful and not used up but replaced. In relation to space, the biographical object limits the concrete space of its owner and sinks its roots deep into the soil. It anchors the owner to a particular time and space. The protocol object, on the other hand, is everywhere and nowhere, marking not a personal experience but a purchasing opportunity. The biographical object 'imposes itself as the witness of the fundamental unity of its user, his or her everyday experience made into a thing' (Morin, 1969: 137–8), while the public commodity is in no way formative of its user's or owner's identity, which is both singular and universal at the same time. People who surround themselves with biographical objects do so to develop their personalities and reflect on them, while consumers of public commodities are decentred and fragmented by their acquisition of things, and do not use them as part of a narrative process of self-definition.

OBJECTS AS THE SUBJECT OF BIOGRAPHIES

Thinking about objects as in some ways similar to persons has led to several experiments with biographical writing about objects. These various experiments have taken two dominant forms: (1) those 'object biographies' which begin with ethnographic research, and which thus try to render a narrative of how certain objects are perceived by the persons that they are linked to, and (2) efforts to 'interrogate objects themselves' which begin with historical or archaeological research, and try to make mute objects 'speak' by placing them in a historical context, linking them to written sources such as diaries, store inventories, trade records, etc. The first has been primarily the domain of anthropologists (MacKenzie 1991; Hoskins 1993, 1998; Keane 1997; Ferme 2001), the second primarily the domain of art historians (Arnold 2002), historians (Saunders 2002; Ulrich 2001) and archeologists (Bradley 1990; Meskell 2004; Fontijn 2002; Tilley 1996, 1999; J. Thomas 1996, 1999). Breaking up that comfortable symmetry has been the work of a few anthropologists who have worked extensively with archives (Edwards 2001; Stoler 2002) or with museum collections (Errington 1998; Kirshenblatt-Gimblett 1998).

Among the first anthropologists to explicitly take a biographical approach to the study of objects was Maureen Mackenzie in *Androgynous Objects: String Bags and Gender in Central New Guinea* (1991). She explicitly focuses on the 'the lifecycle of an object' in order to 'uncover the relations and meanings which surround it' (1991: 27). The objects she examines, bags made of looped twine from bark fibres (*bilum*), are used to hold young children, vegetables, fish, firewood, and carried by both men and women, with women carrying them from the head and men carrying them from the shoulders. As 'the most hard-worked accessory of daily life' (1991: 1) in Papua New Guinea, the string bag mediates and manifests a whole series of social relationships for the Tekefol people – nurturance, decoration, supernatural protection, spirit divination, gift exchange, etc. A new tourist and export market has also given the string bag value as a trade commodity, and it can be spotted on the shoulders of teenage girls in American shopping malls as well as Melanesian villages. Particular styles of string bags are badges of regional identity, initiatory grades and ritual status. By looking at this 'seemingly insignificant domestic carryall', MacKenzie concentrates 'on the different types of agency and the different competences which gender demarcates' (1991: 22), rejecting an earlier suggestion from Annette Weiner (1976: 13) that the string bag represents a domain of female control and autonomy. Her theoretical contribution is to present a case study of an object which crosses over from male to female worlds: 'My biographical focus on a single artefact ... as a complete object made by women and men, will give me a technological and sociological understanding of its combinatory symbolism, and reveal spheres of activity that an analysis of either female work or male cult activity would miss' (1991: 28).

The approach taken in a series of studies of material culture, history and exchange on Sumba is also ethnographic, but it focuses more on narrative elaboration than variations in physical form (Hoskins 1993, 1998; Keane 1997). The Kodi people of Sumba, eastern Indonesia, have a series of named 'history objects' which demarcate and preserve a sense of the past and collective memory. These are called the 'traces of the hands and feet' (*oro limya oro witti*) of the ancestors, and consist of heirloom gold valuables, porcelain urns, spiritually potent weapons, and musical instruments used to communicate with the spirit world. *The Play of Time: Kodi Perspectives on Calendars, History and Exchange* (Hoskins 1993)

examined the use of prestigious objects in the annual cycle of ritual ceremonies, and their significance in preserving and authenticating memories of ancestral exploits. Recent encounters between traditional objects like a supposedly unmovable urn containing holy water and the colonial 'staff of office' bestowed by Dutch invaders on local leaders (*rajas*) were traced to show local perceptions that prestigious objects could help to make history by 'choosing' their proper location and exerting a mysterious influence on their human guardians to assure that they ended up there. Certain ritual tools – the 'possessions of the ancestors' – were believed to be repositories of magical power which could affect the processes that they came to represent: 'Power objectified in a concrete object preserves an impression of stability even when the object comes into the possession of a rival; thus, it can legitimate usurpation while maintaining a fiction of continuity' (1993: 119).

In more private, domestic spheres ordinary objects like a spindle, a betel bag, and a woven cloak also used as a funeral shroud illustrate connections between people and things that are less ritualized but equally intimate. In *Biographical Objects: How Things Tell the Stories of People's Lives* (Hoskins 1998) six women and men narrate their own lives by talking about their possessions, using these objects as a pivot for introspection and a tool for reflexive autobiography. The metaphoric properties are deeply gendered, and established through the conventional use of paired couplets in ritual language, which portray the betel bag as containing the fertile folds of a woman's body, or the spindle and the spear as the probing force of masculine penetration. The desire to possess another person in a sexual sense may be deflected on to the possession of a beloved thing, often a surrogate companion or spouse (sometimes actually buried with an unmarried person 'to make the grave complete'). Pervasive themes of dualism and the search for the counterpart are projected on to the object world, where fantasies of wholeness and completion are more easily fulfilled.

Webb Keane's *Signs of Recognition: Power and Hazards of Representation in an Indonesian Society* (1997) examines similar themes in the exchange transactions of Anakalang, another Sumbanese domain. His approach is less biographical – in that it does not address many individual lives – and more processual. He looks at the ways in which words and things are invested with social value as they are transacted in tandem, introducing an economic dimension to speech events, so that verbal descriptions are part of a complex political economy in which things are not always what they seem. He argues that agency should not necessarily be located in biologically discrete individuals, but is instead most salient in formal ceremonial contexts, which 'display and tap into an agency that is assumed to transcend the particular individuals present and the temporal moment in which they act' (1997: 7). So agency on Sumba can be located in disembodied ancestors, lineage houses, inter-clan alliances, and even heirloom valuables, all of which are subject to ongoing construction and transformation.

Material objects can be used to both reveal and conceal secret histories, as explored in Mariane Ferme's *The Underneath of Things: Violence, History and the Everyday in Sierra Leone* (2001). Looking at the connections between cola nuts, cloth, palm oil, clay, houses and hair styles, she finds a hidden history of slavery and oppression, which has left its mark on gender relations as well. As 'the material bearers of collective memory' (Ferme 2001: 9) these everyday objects are inscribed with biographical and historical resonances. Clay and oil, for instance, are 'biographical substances that inscribe temporality on the body' (Ferme 2001: 17), producing heat or coolness in various life-cycle rituals which socially construct gender and maintain its force through bodily memories. Ferme argues, 'the material world matters, but ... the life that objects and substances take on, from circumstances not of their own making but of their made-ness, produces unstable meanings and unpredictable events' (2001: 21). The circulation of everyday objects takes place within not only a visible political economy but also 'an occult economy' in which hairstyles and clothing patterns fix the significance of historical events in time and act as 'mnemonic clues' to secret strategies developed by people used to living close to death. An 'aesthetics of ambiguity' has developed as a way to live with permanent danger. The civil war that has raged throughout the country since 1991 has created new narratives around objects linked to pain and violence, objects which hide their real meanings underneath the surface. Ferme suggests that there are stories in the shadows of this African nation which need to be retrieved and understood in relation to many different levels of concealment and circulation.

Ferme's study is inspired, in part, by the micro-history of Carlo Ginzburg, which focuses on tiny details as clues to wider social processes and transformations, constructing a complex social reality from apparently insignificant material data (Ginzburg 1989). A similar agenda lies behind historian Laurel Thatcher Ulrich's *The Age of Homespun: Objects and Stories in the Creation of an American Myth* (2001). Shifting from studying the lives of ordinary people, through wills and diaries, to studying their artefacts, Ulrich looks at baskets, spinning wheels, needlework and cloth to interrogate a total of fourteen objects and uncover details about their makers and users and the communities they built. She portrays eighteenth-century New England as a battleground of Indian, colonist, slave and European cultures, each leaving its mark on the design of these 'surviving objects'. Ulrich also examines the construction of cultural memory, by quoting the work of theologian Horace Bushell and examining the perennial American nostalgia for the 'good old days', when clothing and other necessities were mostly made at home by family labour. Aiming to study 'the flow of common life', in order 'to discover the electricity of history', Ulrich identifies many individuals involved with these artefacts. But it is objects themselves that emerge as the strongest 'personalities' in the book. We learn that American Indians (like Ferme's Sierra Leone women) saw wigwams and house construction (as well as hair plaiting) as forms of 'weaving', that French stitchery inspired needlepoint framed in Boston homes, and that wealth objects were displayed in coveted Hadley cupboards to document and preserve family prestige. Questions of provenance are explored in a series of detective stories, which then lead to further linkages of geography, genealogy and history.

Dana Arnold brings together a series of essays in *The Metropolis and its Image: Constructing Identities for London, c. 1750–1950* (2002) that present the biography of a city on the model of a human life story. The collection looks at key moments in the emergence of London as a metropolis and different ways its image has been conceived and represented. The complexity of London's different identities is revealed in the tensions and contradictions between manifestations of civic and national pride, the relationship between private and governmental institutions and urban planning issues. Specific questions of architectural style are examined in the context of the relationship between the City of London and London as a metropolis. Urban identities are explored with a methodology which looks at how the city has been anthropomorphized as it is pictured in the visual arts, planned by the architects and urbanists, and studied by historians who interpret its various *alter egos* and former identities.

Archeologists have also adapted biographical methods. Lynne Meskell's *Object Worlds in*

Ancient Egypt: Material Biographies in Past and Present (2004) looks at how excavated objects reveal ancient Egyptians' lives and preoccupations. What do Egyptian burial practices tell us about their notions of the person, gender and bodily experience? Do giant pyramids and the preservation of the body through mummification signal a particular concern with embodiment and memory, so that the physical body is required for the social legacy? Meskell's notion of the 'material biography' brings together questions of personhood and the meanings of objects in relation to an ancient culture that is heavily documented but still incompletely understood. She also asks comparative questions about why Egyptian antiquity has been of such great popular interest, from Parisian landmarks to the modern temples of commerce that are Las Vegas casinos. The mysteries provoked by this vanished world suggest ways in which ancient objects are used to mediate between past and present, and to summon up an alternative cultural space to explore contemporary concerns with mortality and materiality.

David Fontijn's *Sacrificial Landscapes: Cultural Biographies of Persons, Objects and 'Natural' Places in the Bronze Age of the Southern Netherlands* (2002) looks at elaborate metal valuables which were left behind in various watery locations. Why did the communities that buried them never return to retrieve them? Controlled excavations of local settlements and cemeteries have revealed few of these objects, while more remote streams and marshes have them in great abundance. The selective deposition of these bronze objects is related in his argument to the construction of various forms of social identity, such as male or female, or of belonging to local or non-local communities. He then discusses the 'cultural biographies' of weapons (axes, spears, daggers), ornaments and dress fittings, and tries to reconstruct the social contexts in which these objects once 'lived'.

Somewhat further afield, a recent collection on the history of scientific knowledge looks at the *Biographies of Scientific Objects* (Daston 2000) and asks, Why does an object or phenomenon become the subject of scientific inquiry? Why do some of these objects remain provocative, while others fade from centre stage? Why do some objects return as the focus of research long after they were once abandoned? Dreams, atoms, monsters, culture, society, mortality and the self are among the objects addressed, and the book ranges from the sixteenth century to the twentieth, exploring the ways in which scientific objects are both real and historical. Marshall Sahlins has a

contribution entitled 'Sentimental pessimism and ethnographic experience: or, Why culture is not a disappearing object'. While the notion of 'biography' here is obviously to some extent a rhetorical conceit, it is used deliberately to suggest a life trajectory, a process in which a concept or diagnosis can have a 'youth', a period of 'mature development' and even a 'death', so that its life span resembles that of an individual. Objects of inquiry are discovered and invented, become popular for a period and then may experience a waning of their influence, and they grow more 'real' as they become entangled in webs of cultural significance.

Cloth has attracted particular attention as a biographical object, because it is worn on the body and is often a marker of identity. *Between the Folds: Stories of Cloth, Lives and Travels from Sumba* (Forshee 2001) begins each chapter with a photograph of a textile, and follows it with a description of the individual who designed and wove the textile, showing how motifs and colours can reflect the creator's personality. The new development of trade, tourism and a commercial market on the island reviews how these cloths have travelled as commodities as well as expressions of artistic inventiveness. *Clothing the Pacific* (Colchester 2003) looks less at the issue of authorship and more at shifting social and historical contexts, particularly influences from missionary and colonial authorities who had their own ideas of how Pacific Islanders should be dressed. Conversion to Christianity is often marked by changes in dress, and new composite styles are prominent in diasporic communities, suggesting that a new way of dress is also a new fashioning of the self, a biographic process of changing the inner person to fit new outer garments. Clothing is analysed as a technology that 'recreated certain contexts anew' (Colchester 2003: 15) in the hybrid forms of modest 'Sunday best' costumes in Tahiti and Samoa, Cook Islands appliqué quilts and even T-shirts in Polynesian Auckland.

CONCLUSION

Anthropologists have long argued that things can, in certain conditions, be or act like persons: they can be said to have a personality, to show volition, to accept certain locations and reject others, and thus to have agency. Often, these attributes of agency are linked to the anthropomorphizing process by which things are said to have social lives like persons and thus to be appropriate subjects for biographies. Gell's challenge to anthropological theory came from a phenomenological perspective. In an earlier reflection on theories of the occult (Gell 1974: 26) he argued that 'magical thought is seduced by the images it makes of something that by definition cannot be represented', but ritual acts try to represent it anyway. In a similar fashion, his theories of the technology of enchantment suggest that objects that challenge our senses or our comprehension have their most powerful effects on our imaginations.

His approach has proved controversial. While some collections have obviously been inspired by its challenges (Pinney and Thomas 2001), others have been more critical (Campbell 2002), or have seemed to react by largely ignoring it (Myers and Marcus 1995; Phillips and Steiner 1999). In *The Art of Kula* (2002) Campbell examines the layers of encoded meaning on the carved and painted prow boards of Trobriand canoes, arguing that colour associations and other formal elements 'speak' to the islanders about emotional and spiritual issues. This would seem close to Gell's arguments about the agency of art objects, but Campbell finds his approach ultimately too restrictive. While she applauds the interest in intention, causation, result and transformation that is part of seeing art as a vehicle for social action, she hesitates to cast aside 'those approaches that examine the way formal elements encode meanings and the processes of representing significant relationships and the context in which these communicate' (2002: 8). Art has long been investigated as a visual code of communication, and the problem of indigenous aesthetics is an important component of this. She does say that the biographic elements of art, and the ways in which it may provide an abstracted or indirect 'visual biography', must remain central to the discipline.

Gell argued that a biographical approach to the study of objects is also a particularly anthropological approach, because 'the view taken by anthropology of social agents attempts to replicate the time perspective of these agents themselves' (Gell 1998: 10). In contrast, history or sociology could be described as supra-biographical and social and cognitive psychology as infra-biographical. Because anthropology tends to concentrate on 'the act' in the context of 'the life' – or a particular stage of 'the life' – it is necessarily preoccupied with the life cycle and the individual agent. The specifically biographical depth of focus defines a methodology that works best in the spaces traversed by agents in the course of their biographies. Anthropology studies social relationships over the life course, and its approach to the study of art objects should, accordingly, focus on their relations to the persons who produce and circulate them.

The large number of works which have tried to present cultural biographies of objects or to talk about the social lives of things testifies to the fact that it is not only anthropologists who have been inspired by the biographical frame. But they also show that the notion of biography – borrowed from literary theory – has provided new perspectives on the study of material culture, and prompted new questions about how people are involved with the things they make and consume. While anthropological research has expanded beyond the study of small societies to larger global contexts and connections, the emphasis on the individual agent and stages of the life cycle remains important in the discipline, and is perhaps a trademark of even multi-sited fieldwork. When historians, philosophers of science and art historians borrow certain methods and concepts from anthropology, they are paying homage to insights developed in a biographical context and expanded to account for wider social and cultural movements. The agentive turn which has become prominent in various forms of practice theory requires attention to biographical frames of meaning and individual relations established through things with other persons. Future research will continue to question the cultural contexts established for whole classes of objects (clothing, jewellery, body parts, etc.) and the assumptions that their contexts entail. Objects themselves may not be animated, but their relations have certainly animated many debates about the ways to understand society, culture and human lives.

REFERENCES

Ahern, Laura (2001) 'Language and agency', *Annual Review of Anthropology*, 30: 109–37.

Appadurai, Arjun, ed. (1986) *The Social Life of Things: Commodities in Cultural Perspective*. Cambridge: Cambridge University Press.

Arnold, Dana, ed. (2002) *The Metropolis and its Image: Constructing Identities for London, c. 1750–1950*. London: Blackwell.

Benjamin, Walter (1978) *One Way Street and other Writings*. New York: Harcourt Brace.

Berger, John (1972) *Ways of Seeing*. London: BBC.

Bradley, R. (1990) *The Passage of Arms*. Cambridge: Cambridge University Press.

Campbell, Shirley (2002) *The Art of Kula*. London: Berg.

Colchester, Chloe, ed. (2003) *Clothing the Pacific*. London: Berg.

Daston, Lorraine, ed. (2000) *Biographies of Scientific Objects*. Chicago: University of Chicago Press.

Edwards, Elizabeth (2001) *Raw Histories: Photographs, Anthropology and Museums*. London: Berg.

Errington, Shelly (1998) *The Death of Authentic Primitive Art and other Tales of Progress*. Berkeley, CA: University of California Press.

Ferme, Mariane (2001) *The Underneath of Things: Violence, History and the Everyday in Sierra Leone*. Berkeley, CA: University of California Press.

Fontijn, David (2002) *Sacrificial Landscapes: Cultural Biographies of Persons, Objects and 'Natural' Places in the Bronze Age of the Southern Netherlands*. Leiden: Leiden University Press.

Forshee, Jill (2001) *Between the Folds: Stories of Cloth, Lives and Travel from Lumba*. Honolulu, HA: University of Hawaii Press.

Gell, Alfred (1974) 'Understanding the occult', *Radical Philosophy*, 9 (winter): 17–26.

Gell, Alfred (1992) 'The technology of enchantment and the enchantment of technology', in J. Coote and A. Shelton (eds), *Art, Anthropology and Aesthetics*. Oxford: Oxford University Press, pp. 40–67.

Gell, Alfred (1998) *Art and Agency: a New Anthropological Theory*. Oxford: Oxford University Press.

Ginzburg, Carlo (1989) *Clues, Myths, and the Historical Method*, trans. John and Ann T. Tedeschi. Baltimore, MD: Johns Hopkins University Press.

Hoskins, Janet (1993) *The Play of Time: Kodi Perspectives on Calendars, Exchange and History*. Berkeley, CA: University of California Press.

Hoskins, Janet, ed. (1996) *Headhunting and the Social Imagination in Southeast Asia*. Stanford, CA: Stanford University Press.

Hoskins, Janet (1998) *Biographical Objects: How Things Tell the Stories of People's Lives*. London: Routledge.

Hoskins, Janet (2002) 'Predatory voyeurs: Tourists and "Tribal violence" in remote Indonesia', *American Ethnologist*, 29 (4): 603–30.

Keane, E. Webb (1997) *Signs of Recognition: Powers and Hazards of Representation in an Indonesian Society*. Berkeley, CA: University of California Press.

Kirschenblatt-Gimblett, Barbara (1998) *Destination Culture: Tourism, Museums and Heritage*. Berkeley, CA: University of California Press.

Kopytoff, Igor (1986) 'The cultural biography of things: Commoditization as process', in Arjun Appadurai (ed.) *The Social Life of Things: Commodities in Cultural Perspective*. Cambridge: Cambridge University Press.

Küchler, Susanne (2002) *Malanggan: Art, Memory and Sacrifice*. London: Berg.

MacKenzie, Maureen (1991) *Androgynous Object: String Bags and Gender in Central New Guinea*. London: Harwood Academic Publishers.

Malinowski, Bronislaw (1922) *Argonauts of the Western Pacific*. London: Routledge.

Mauss, Marcel (1924/1954) *The Gift*. London: Cohen & West.

Mauss, Marcel (1968–69) *Oeuvres*, 3 vols. Paris: Minuit.

Meskell, Lynne (2004) *Object Worlds in Ancient Egypt: Material Biographies in Past and Present*. London: Berg.

Morin, Violette (1969) 'L'objet biographique', *Communications*, 13: 131–39. Paris: École Pratiques des Hautes Études, Centre d'Études des Communications de Masse.

Munn, Nancy (1986) *The Fame of Gawa*. Cambridge: Cambridge University Press.

Myers, Fred, ed. (2001) *The Empire of Things: Regimes of Value and Material Culture*. Santa Fe, NM: SAR Press.

Myers, Fred and George Marcus, ed. (1995) *The Traffic in Culture: Refiguring Art and Anthropology*.

Phillips, R.B. and Steiner, Christopher (1999) *Unpacking Culture: Art and Commodity in Colonial and Postcolonial Worlds*. Berkeley, CA: University of California Press.

Pinney, Christopher and Thomas, Nick, ed. (2001) *Beyond Aesthetics: Art and the Technologies of Enchantment*. Oxford: Berg.

Saunders, N. (2002) 'Bodies of metal, shells of memory: "trench art" and the Great War recycled', in V. Buchli (ed.), *The Material Culture Reader*. Oxford: Berg.

Sharp, Lesley A. (2000) 'The commodificiation of the body and its parts', *Annual Review of Anthropology*, 29: 287–328.

Steiner, Christopher (2001) 'Rights of passage: On the liminal identity of art in the border zone', in Fred Myers (ed.), *The Empire of Things: Regimes of Value and Material Culture*. Santa Fe, NM: School of American Research Press, pp. 207–31.

Stoler, Ann (2003) *Carnal Knowledge and Imperial Power: Race and the Intimate in Colonial Rule*. Berkeley, CA: University of California Press.

Strathern, Marilyn (1988) *The Gender of the Gift: Problems with Women and Problems with Society in Melanesia*. Berkeley, CA: University of California Press.

Strathern, Marilyn (1992) *Partial Connections*. ASAO Special Publications 3. Savage, MD: Rowman & Littlefield.

Strathern, Marilyn (2004) 'The patent and the Malanggan', in C. Pinney and N. Thomas (eds), *Beyond Aesthetics: Art and the Technologies of Enchantment*. Oxford: Berg, pp. 259-87.

Thomas, J. (1996) *Time, Culture and Identity*. London: Routledge.

Thomas, J. (1999) 'An economy of substances in earlier Neolithic Britain', in J. Robb (ed.), *Material Symbols*. Carbondale, IL: Southern Illinois University.

Thomas, Nick (1989) 'Material culture and colonial power: ethnological collecting and the establishment of colonial rule in Fiji', *Man* (n.s.), 24 (1): 41–56.

Thomas, Nick (1991) *Entangled Objects: Exchange, Material Culture and Colonialism in the Pacific.* Cambridge, MA: Harvard University Press.

Thomas, Nick (1993) 'Related things', *Social Analysis,* 34: 132–41.

Thomas, Nick and Pinney, Christopher, eds (2001) *Beyond Aesthetics: Art and the Technologies of Enchantment.* Oxford: Berg.

Tilley, Christopher (1996) *An Ethnography of the Neolithic: Early Prehistoric Societies in Southern Scandinavia.* Cambridge: Cambridge University Press.

Tilley, Christopher (1999) *Metaphor and Material Culture.* Oxford: Blackwell.

Ulrich, Laurel Thatcher (2001) *The Age of Homespun: Objects and Stories in the Creation of an American Myth.* New York: Knopf.

Weiner, Annette (1976) *Women of Value, Men of Renown: New Perspectives in Trobriand Exchange.* Austin: University of Texas Press.

Weiner, Annette (1992) *Inalienable Possessions: The Paradox of Giving-while-Keeping.* Berkeley, CA: University of California Press.

6

SCENES FROM A TROUBLED ENGAGEMENT

Post-Structuralism and Material Culture Studies

Bjørnar Olsen

As signified by their common prefix, post-structuralism belongs to the number of oppositional intellectual projects that emerged in the (late) twentieth century. Despite the fact that most of these enterprises were united in opposing dominant regimes of power/knowledge and associated essentialist conceptions of truth, their differences should not be underrated. This even counts for post-structuralism's relations to its closest relative, postmodernism, with which it is often confused. Although postmodernism as a concept has proved extremely elusive (which may actually be seen as representative of the very condition it is meant to signify), some identifying distinctions can nonetheless be noted. Writ large, postmodernism can be conceived of as an epistemic rupture that has shaken the foundational pillars on which modern life was built, announcing a new condition tellingly signified by the numerous 'ends' it became associated with (of grand narratives, the nation state, universal reason, authenticity, history, etc.). Probably more conspicuously, however, postmodernism has surfaced as a new aesthetic or 'style' characterized by a playful allusiveness that stresses irony, genre mixing, eclecticism and ambiguity (Connor 1997; Jameson 1984; Lyotard 1984).

Although clearly related to the wider orbit of postmodernism (like fish to water, to paraphrase Foucault), post-structuralism is distinctive in being confined mainly to academic discourses and more firmly located within a defined body of knowledge. As an intellectual project, it became heavily marked by its close (although

oppositional) relations with the structuralist programme which constituted the breeding ground for most early dissenters. Moreover, the fact that post-structuralism emerged within a niche of French post-war intellectual environment, and (directly and indirectly) was conditioned by the anti-essentialist philosophy of Nietzsche and Heidegger (whose thoughts it effectively inherited), contributes further to its confinement within academic communities.

The 'post' added to structuralism by a new generation of intellectuals should not be understood in any antithetical or purely negative way. Post-structuralism shared several basic conceptions with its 'relational other'. Firstly, a non-essential conception of how meaning is constituted: that it is a product of the difference between entities rather than some inherent quality of the entities themselves. Second, that language (or texts) constitutes a 'model world' for any system of signification; and third, a distaste for the dominant Cartesian ontology, identifying being (and self) with consciousness.

The post-structuralist revolt, however, was grounded in a much more far-reaching critique of Western metaphysics, a metaphysics that was still supposed to infiltrate structuralism. More specifically, Western thought was claimed to be dominated by a 'metaphysics of presence', in which truth, knowledge and being were argued and secured by reference to some foundational essence, a transcendent originary instance or centre located outside discourse and practice (Derrida 1977, 1978). While the structuralist credo of meaning as a product of the 'play of difference' (rather than being the inherent property of the individual entities) effectively challenged this metaphysics, this achievement was undermined by structuralism's own conception of language as an ordered and closed system: that the actual utterances (*parole*) were nothing but the pre-coded result of a fixed underlying structure or grammar (*langue*). This opposition between an arbitrary surface expression and a firm, hidden foundational content was manifested even in the very Saussurian concept of the sign (also as reflected in the signifier-signified split) in which the sign itself was always reduced to something secondary, a representation *of* or *for* something invariable and more 'real' located outside discourse and difference (cf. Derrida 1977: 43–4, 1978: 18–24).

SCOPE AND LIMITATIONS

Throughout the last decades of the Twentieth century the term 'post-structuralism' became associated with a large number of topics and approaches within philosophy, literary criticism and feminist studies. However, only a few of them become significant within the disciplines concerned with material culture. The most important influence may be labelled as 'textualism' – a term coined to characterize new modes of reading and analysing texts. Thus, a main focus of this chapter will be to explore features of this new textual approach, and in particular how the deconstruction of textual unity, origin and authorial control 'worked' when exported to non-textual domains, such as things and materialities at large. This also includes a discussion of how things are written, i.e. how things are transformed into written discourse and, more generally, the relationship this establishes between things and texts. The final section discusses some of the problems with this textual regime and some possible steps to overcome the limitation built into it.

A note regarding selection: some readers may react to the fact that my choice of cases and works is archaeologically biased. Even if archaeology has provided post-structuralism with one of its most celebrated and saleable metaphors (*pace* Foucault), the archaeologists themselves may look as relevant to the topic as an entrenched race of disciplinary dinosaurs. The reason for my modest sectarianism arises partly out of my own location but is more due to the fact that archaeologists, even if only a fringe

minority among them, were instrumental in introducing post-structuralist (as well as structuralist) theory to the study of material culture. I also trust the readers have the intertextual capacity to transpose the relevance of what is discussed here into their own fields of study.

Having revealed my disciplinary sympathies it seems appropriate to continue with some remarks on chronologies – and confusions.

CHRONOLOGIES AND CONFUSIONS

The emergence of structuralism and post-structuralism are set wide apart chronologically. Structuralism originates in the early twentieth century work of linguist Ferdinand de Saussure and was later modified and formalized by a number of scholars throughout the first half of the century, notably Roman Jakobson, Louis Hjelmslev and Vladimir Propp. Somewhat ironically, at the point when structuralism began to gain academic fame outside its normal site of linguistics, thanks largely to the work of Claude Lévi-Strauss, it had simultaneously begun to come under attack on its own home ground. During the 1960s a group of French philosophers and literary theorists such as Jacques Derrida, Michel Foucault, Julia Kristeva and Roland Barthes launched the critique to which the label 'post-structuralism' later was added (cf. Sturrock 1979; Tilley 1990a).

It would be a grave exaggeration to claim that this revolt produced much of a stir within the disciplines devoted to the study of material culture. Understandable, to be sure, given that a decade would pass before structuralism itself would begin to make its way into this field (see, however, Leroi-Gourhan 1964, 1965, 1968; Deetz 1967). When this actually happened, most notably in American ethnology and historical archaeology (Glassie 1975; Deetz 1977; Leone 1977; Beaudry 1978), and British 'post-processual' archaeology (Hodder 1982a, b, Shanks and Tilley 1982), it was soon to be overtaken by scholars freshly familiar with the post-structuralist critique. This compression is most evident in early post-processual archaeology (cf. Hodder 1985, 1986), where both structuralist and post-structuralist theories and approaches were advocated rather simultaneously from the mid-1980s onwards and sometimes even by the very same authors (cf. Shanks and Tilley 1987; Olsen 1987; Tilley 1991).

Thus, while structuralism and its 'post' are separated by close to six decades of research, their impact on material culture studies occurred late and almost simultaneously. It is hardly surprising that this partly overlapping chronology caused some confusion. What became known as the 'textual analogy', the idea that material culture could be conceived of and 'read' as text (cf. Patrik 1985; Hodder 1986; Moore 1986; Tilley 1990a, 1991; Buchli 1995), proved to be especially vulnerable. While the concept of text clearly was attached to the post-structuralist repertoire, involving a new, reader-centred epistemology, in material culture studies it was often confused with the structuralist conception of language and the idea of texts as structured and linear systems (cf. Patrik 1985; Hodder 1986; Parker Pearson 1995; Preucel and Bauer 2001). This confusion of a textual (post-structuralist) analogy with a linguistic (structuralist) one may well have provoked the feeling that the analogy was 'fraught with danger' (Renfrew 1989):

> I can see that an artistic cycle, such as the glyphs on a Maya stele, or the paintings in an Egyptian tomb, may be read as a text. I can even concede that a building, the work of a single architect or designer, may be seen is this light … as the product of a single human mind, the analogue of the 'writer' of the text. Even here, the analogue is not a strong one, for it is a feature of written text that they are in essence linear: the words need to be in the right order. One of the distinguishing features of the visual arts is that the lineal order need not matter … when we turn to an archaeological site consisting of a palimpsest of structures and rubbish pits, constructed and deposited at different periods, the analogy breaks down altogether.
>
> (Renfrew 1989: 35–36)[1]

To understand why such criticism is utterly misplaced as an attack on the post-structuralist textual approach – which it was intended as – we need to consider this approach in more detail.

A ROUGH GUIDE TO POST-STRUCTURALISM

Even if mostly a summarizing term-of-convenience, textualism can be regarded as a key nominative for the early post-structuralist movement. Despite the fact that it also carried serious ontological implications it is most commonly associated with a new epistemology of reading that radically challenged existing interpretive premises. The transition to this new epistemology was marked by two important sacrifices: that of the author and that of structure.

In traditional literary criticism, as well as in the traditional hermeneutic conception of understanding, the author and the world of the author were regarded as the main entrance to a qualified interpretation of the text. Interpretation largely rested on the ability to grasp the author's intentions, to reveal him and his world 'beneath' the text: once the author is found, the text is explained (Barthes 1977: 147). As noted by Roland Barthes:

> The author, it is believed, has certain rights over the reader, he constrains him to certain meanings of the work, and this meaning is of course the right one, the real meaning: whence a critical morality of the right meaning (and of its defect, 'misreading'): we try to establish *what the author meant*, and not at all *what the reader understands*.
>
> (1986: 30, emphasis in original)

Post-structuralism did away with the traditional notions of authors as producers and readers as consumers of text. Interpretation or reading was claimed to be much more than recovering a preconceived message. It was a creative and productive task that involved a redistribution of power and responsibility from the author to the reader. This process of democratization, however, conditioned that the orthodox idea of the author as the father and owner of the work was dismantled. Thus, a new epistemology of reading – and the birth of the reader – could happen only at the cost of 'the death of the author' (Barthes 1977: 142–9).

Put in less absolute terms, this approach suggests that even the most self-conscious author can circumscribe only some aspects of meaning. Those who read the text – often in different historical and cultural settings – bring to it other voices, other texts, and create meanings far beyond the author's intention. It is inconceivable that a play by Shakespeare, for example, should have a present meaning identical to the one it had at the moment of production, or should conform to the author's intentions. We translate into the text the effective history of sociocultural development, we expose it to new conditions, new regimes of meaning and truth, and transform it into a present product. Thus, the reader becomes an actor, a producer of meaning (cf. Olsen 1990: 181).

The decentring of the author, however, was not in itself an attack on the structuralist approach; on the contrary, such a decentring may be argued to be well in concordance with the structuralist anti-subjective agenda. The departure and 'post' are evident, however, in another operation involved in this new epistemology of reading and were launched precisely as a critique of the grounding principle of the structural approach. In a famous introductory remark to his book *S/Z*(1975), Roland Barthes launches a veritable attack on the structuralist procedure, the purpose of which, he claims, was to heal the 'wounds' of the text (or narrative), to recover its meaning by repatriating it to the greater structural scheme which it emanates from. In his own words, the structuralist fallacy consisted in seeing:

> all the world's stories within a single structure: we shall, they thought, extract from each tale its model, then out of these models we shall make a great narrative structure, which we shall reapply (for verification) to any one narrative: a task as exhaustive as it is ultimately undesirable, because the text thereby loses its difference.
>
> (Barthes 1975: 3)

Thus, the new epistemology of reading conditioned more than the assassination of the author. The main act of the structuralist constitution, proclaiming that the text is just a manifestation of an underlying structure or grammar, also had to be sacrificed. The script of this act was sameness, not difference.

The latter concept – or *différance*[2] – became a major mantra in post-structuralism, and especially in Derrida's embrace of it. To put it in very simple terms, in his version difference denies the possibility that a single element, a sign, can be present in and of itself, referring only to itself. It always refers to some 'other' outside itself, which is not present, and which is itself constituted through this difference. Thus, every element is constituted on the basis of the trace it carries of other members of the signifying system, a 'differential network, a fabric of traces referring endlessly to something other than itself, to other differential traces' (Derrida 1979: 84, cf. Derrida 1973: 138–40, 1987: 26; see also Yates 1990: 114 ff. for a more detailed discussion). When Barthes (above) refers to the 'difference' of the text, he did not refer to its identity (its difference from other texts), but rather to its fragmentation as a product woven of quotation and traces from other texts (Barthes 1986: 60). All boundaries and divisions of the text are blurred, provoking those who want to set up strict limits for the text: 'speech, life, the world, the real, history, and what not, every field of reference – to body or mind, conscious or unconscious, politics, economics, and so forth' (Derrida 1979: 84).

Difference is closely related to another key concept that emerged out of the early post-structuralist work, that of 'intertext' as introduced by Julia Kristeva. According to her, intertextuality refers to the transportation (or transposition) of textual material within the matrix of all texts, including non-written ones:

> the term *intertextuality* denotes this transposition of one (or several) sign-system(s) into another ... If one grants that every signifying practice is a field of transpositions of various signifying systems (an intertextuality), one then understands that its 'place' of enunciation and its denoted 'object' are never single, complete and identical to themselves, but always plural, shattered, capable of being tabulated.
>
> (Kristeva 1986: 111, emphasis in original)

Thus, every text may be conceived of as the site of intersection of other texts, a 'multidimensional space in which a variety of writings, none of them original, blend and clash' (Barthes 1977: 146, cf. Derrida 1987: 33). Every text is a work of translation, making the closure of any text impossible.

Intertextuality reaffirms the crucial role of the reader in the production of the text, since the reader is claimed to be the node that facilitates the transportation and exchange of textual material.[3] Former readings and experiences are read into the text, it is the reader who brings these texts together. As nicely summarized by Barthes:

> A text is made of multiple writings, drawn from many cultures and entering into mutual relations of dialogue, parody and contestation, but there is one place where this multiplicity is focused and that place is the reader, not as hitherto was said, the author. The reader is the space on which all the quotations that make up a writing are inscribed without any of them being lost; a text unity lies not in its origin but in its destination.
>
> (Barthes 1977: 148)

This new epistemology of reading, or deconstructive reading, did not aim at destroying the text, but at shaking up its unity and individuality; to reveal its polyvalence as a tissue of quotation from innumerable other texts (including the non-written texts of the world). This transgression was more than an interpretative turn: it clearly involved an ontological rupture, since any strict division between the world and the text was denied. Or rather, it was a denial of the possibility of living outside the infinite (inter)text. This inevitably brings us to probably the most debated and ridiculed dictums of post-structuralism, Derrida's 'there is nothing outside of the text'.

Contrary to the many vulgar and simplistic interpretations of Derrida's claim, it does not assert that there is no world or being outside texts or narratives. Rather, it opposes the idea of a strict divide between the world (or reality) on one side, and the textual representation of it on the other. It proposes an ontology of the 'limitless text', in which the meaning-constitutive quality of the text – the play of difference – is as relevant (and inevitable) to speech, thought and the 'world itself' as to writing. There is no meaning or significance outside the play of difference. Both in texts and in our lived experiences meanings are created within this web of innumerable relations of differentiation, where signs refer to signs, and 'where nothing is anywhere simply present or absent. There are only, everywhere, differences and traces of traces' (Derrida 1987: 26). With special reference to the relationship between language and the materiality, Judith Butler has captured this argument in the following way:

> On the one hand, the process of signification is always material; signs work *by appearing* (visibly, aurally), and appearing through material means, although what appears only signifies by virtue of those non-phenomenal relations, i.e., relations of differentiation, that tacitly structure and propel signification itself ... what allows for a signifier to signify will never be its materiality alone; that materiality will be at once an instrumentality and deployment of a set of larger linguistic relations.
>
> (Butler 1993: 68)

Thus, to write is not a parasitic act, or a dangerous and incidental supplement to a primordial unitary world. In fact, 'there have never been anything but supplements' (Derrida 1978: 159). Writing, interpretation, or science, may be conceived of as replacing one signifying chain with another. In this sense, the world has always-already been written; difference as the meaning-constitutive quality has always existed. Hence, the futility of craving for an origin and presence outside this play of difference, in other words, an authentic invariable world where things have meaning without referring to other things and other systems of signification (Derrida 1977: 158–9, 1987: 28–9; Norris 1982: 32–41).

MATERIAL CULTURE AS TEXT

The brief sketch outlined above distils the post-structuralist legacy in the state it started to influence material culture studies during the 1980s. Clearly, there were other intellectual linkages and strands, and Michel Foucault's studies of power and disciplinary practices in particular, given their concern with the materiality of discourse, might have been expected to become more influential than they actually did. One of his important contributions to social theory was to show how systems of ideas and the exercise of regulatory power can never become effective without a material disciplinary and normalizing technology that ontologizes and fixes the desired categories and norms (i.e. by making them 'visible' within a hierarchical and efficiently spatial organization) (Foucault 1973, 1979; Tilley 1990b).

This explicitly very materialistic approach, however, received far less enthusiasm among students of things than the textual approach did. Even if it is beyond the scope of this chapter to elaborate on this in detail, I am inclined to believe that the more pleasing appeal of the latter paradoxically was grounded in it being (mis)conceived as more 'subjective' and 'humanistic'. The general public and intellectual attraction for the symbolic, the aestheticized and the plastic, mixed with the late-twentieth-century obsession with the active individual, clearly made the 'free' reader-centred interpretative approach more attractive than Foucault's somewhat dismal analysis of alienating disciplinary technologies (cf. Olsen 2003: 88–94).

To all this must be added that very few material culture studies can be claimed to be grounded explicitly in post-structuralist theory (for exceptions see Yates 1990). Very often the approaches were eclectic, with some references to aspects of post-structuralism, stressing multivocality, openness to interpretation, small stories, etc. (cf. Hodder 1989, 1999; Shanks 1992, 1999; Holtorf 1998; Bouquet 1991; Edmonds 1999). Thus, any compartmentalizing of them as 'post-structuralist' must be seen as a retrospective choice of convenience rather than suggesting that there actually existed (or exists) a post-structuralist camp in material culture studies, which clearly is not the case. It is more appropriate to talk about different degrees of influence.

Probably the most identifiable post-structuralist influence within this field is well captured in the notion *material culture as text*. The claim was that material culture could be seen as analogous to text, or, rather, it could be read as text. Despite certain conceptual confusions (as noted above), the textual analogy proper was based on the disjunction between textual meaning and authorial intention. As a written text becomes separated from its author, things also become detached from their context of production and enter into dialogue with other texts through the dynamic act of interpretation. Related interpretive ideas had been presented in other theoretical camps, such as among late hermeneuticans (Gadamer 1975; Ricoeur 1981) and reception theorists (cf. Iser 1974, 1978), and the sources of inspiration for the textual analogy were somewhat mixed (cf. Johnsen and Olsen 1992).[4]

Traditionally, material culture has been approached as carrying a final signified to be disclosed through the act of interpretation. What does this awl mean? What is the significance of this design? Why is this pot decorated this way? The intentional act of producing/using endows the object with a grounding layer of meaning that can be exposed with the aid of proper methodological procedures. Central among these was the contextual approach[5] of bounding things within their appropriate context (or/and to put oneself in the place of – or close to – the producer/users). Actually, to some scholars this procedure was so imperative to interpretation that it legitimitized the claim that 'an object out of context is not readable' (Hodder 1986: 141). Unsurprisingly, this origin-centred contextualism became an easy target for the post-structuralist counter-claims: how can we limit or close off a text or a context? How can it be bounded and shut off from readers and other text? What is 'outside' context? To Yates (1990: 270–2) this traditional hermeneutics was a claim to totality and determination, a restrictive approach that limited the signifying potential of material culture. It was, in short, an attempt to endow things with a final signified outside the play of difference.

A post-structuralist approach works rather differently: it emphasizes *how* things mean, what thoughts they stimulate; it investigates and affirms the plurality of meanings obtained by things being re-read by new people in new contexts. Such readings are more a matter of translation and negotiation than of recovering. Consider the life history of a Neolithic megalith: this monument has continuously meant (or been read) since it was created 6,000 years ago. It still means something to tourists, farmers, archaeologists, artists, television producers and advertising agents. Due to its veritable duration this material text has opened itself to infinite readings by continuously confronting new readers in altered historical situations. Rather than being endowed with a pre-given signified to be disclosed (burial, ancestral house, monument of power, etc.), its effective

history of interpretation proves it as a receptive and open site to signification. This openness to signification allows the megalith to establish ties to any historical moment and culture. Actually, this material text can be claimed to be more radically plural, carnivalesque and out of authorial control than any written text. In this sense, its origin was lost by its own creation. Only the material signifier remains more or less constant; the signified are repeatedly created and lost through the historical act of re-reading (Olsen 1990: 197–200; cf. Holtorf 1998).

Another example, if not post-structuralist by intention, may exemplify this perspective further. In his excellent book *Material Culture* (1999), Henry Glassie discusses processes of material creation, communication and consumption in relation to handicrafts and local communities in northern Turkey. He is especially concerned with how certain artefacts, the carpets produced by the weaver Aysel, through their life processes assemble history and contexts. Although 'inalienable' in their domestic origin, carrying memories, aesthetics and tradition, Glassie depicts how the carpets made by Aysel, through processes of economic exchange, escape the circle of the village, leaving her, never to be seen again (Glassie 1999: 45–58). The close and infiltrated (but not univocal) meanings attached to their cultural *Heimat* are replaced or extended as the carpets embark on a new life. Hence the beautiful biography:

> A German couple buy a carpet in the Covered Bazaar in Istanbul. It becomes a souvenir of their trip to Turkey, a reminder of sun on the beach, and it becomes one element in the décor of their home, a part of the assembly that signals their taste. Their son saves it as a family heirloom. To him it means childhood. Germany replaces Turkey. The weaver's memories of village life give way to memories of an aging psychiatrist in Munich for whom the carpet recalls a quiet moment when he lay upon it and marshalled his bright tin troops on a rainy afternoon. Then his son, finding the carped worn, wads it into a bed for a dog, and his son, finding it tattered in his father's estate, throws it out. It becomes a rag in a landfill, awaiting its archaeologists.
>
> (Glassie 1999: 58)

To decide what meaning is the right or proper one, what context of interpretation is appropriate for interpretation, or even to decide when the carpet is 'out of context', seem futile (cf. McGuckin 1997). Even if the carpet stayed in Aysel's village, it would still be translated and intersected with other texts. The folklorist or anthropologist studying them as a manifestation of local material culture would bring to his analysis knowledge of other motifs; he would compare them with design patterns from other parts of the world, his former readings and studies would intersect, networks of theoretical and methodological resources would be activated, etc. Then, when his studies of the carpets finally became processed into finished products (paper, books or Web pages) they would take on new and accumulated trajectories, enmeshing the carpets into new networks of readings. Even if the interpreter never made his way to the remote village, the carpets would still be intertextual products, patchworks that interweave materials, memories, kinship, inspirations, religious beliefs, etc. Old carpets would be re-read as the transformation of society, knowledge and the global-local interface would supply the readers with new links, making possible the transposition of other signifying material. Thus, the imperative of an invariable context, or an authentic object that escapes difference, seems impossible to maintain.

MATERIALIZED TEXTS

Post-structuralism brought an important dimension to the epistemology of interpretation, emphasizing the processes by which meaning is produced rather than passively recovered. Interpretation is a never-ending task, a creative act of production, not the disclosure of some fossil strata of meaning. Within material cultural studies the criticism it brought forward of narrow contextual hermeneutics was clearly an important and liberating turn. However, the somewhat biased enthusiasm for selected aspects of post-structuralist theory, especially those stressing multivocality and the plurality of meanings, seems to have encouraged a somewhat game-like – even numerical – attitude towards interpretation: how many ways can a thing come to mean? How many layers of meaning can be accumulated? Furthermore, and despite stressing the relational foundation of meaning (as activated by the 'free play of the signifier'), the important sources of meaning seem always located *outside* the signifier (the object, the text) in question: in the reader, in other readings, other texts, who/which donate to it these new dimensions of meaning. And finally, even if the textual analogy was powerful and productive, few asked about the *difference* in the way things and texts mean. Do we experience a city, a house or a landscape in the

same manner as we *read* a textual or spoken statement? What is the difference between the somatic and non-discursive experience of the former and the conscious intellectual engagement with the latter? Can the textual analogy be broadened to embrace the somatic experiences of matter?

Despite the obvious difficulties (and contradictions) involved, if material culture is to be compared to – and analysed as – text in a more sophisticated and 'material' manner we need to complicate and extend the conception of text – maybe to such a degree that the text is as much an analogy of the material as vice versa. Trying to accomplish this within the theoretical orbit of post-structuralism, one productive step may be to consider the (material) text as 'writerly' rather than 'readerly'. Roland Barthes coined this distinction to separate those texts that pretend (even if futilely) to have only representative functions, leaving the reader with no choice but passive consumption, from those texts that resist such simplistic mimesis and offer some kind of active co-authorship (Barthes 1977: 155–64). While the readerly text strives to erase itself to become as transparent and innocent as possible, the writerly text insists on being something more than a medium for communicating a preconceived meaning. Neither is it a mere blank slate for inscription, or an arena for the free play of our imagination; in other words, that we can read anything we like into – or out of – it, the often claimed fallacy of post-structuralist interpretation (cf. Hall 1996: 218). Rather, it implies a necessary redistribution of power and 'agency' – not to the author, but to the text itself.

In striving towards symmetry, the writerly text neither admits any smooth passage between signifier or signified nor provides an empty site where we may embody our own subjective and culturally dependent meanings. Contrary to any normal conception of texts, it has no beginning or linearity; it is a reversible structure offering numerous entrances, of which none can be claimed to be the primary. By acknowledging the text's materiality and non-transparency, it loses its status as a passive medium and becomes a site of contestation and negotiation, something to be worked upon, considered, struggled with. To read such text is more than a purely intellectual enterprise, it entails somatic experience, a kind of wrestling, in which the outcome is not given. It provides a sensation that is not one of a pleasing experience, the 'comforting stimulation for weakened nerves', to paraphrase Simmel (1978: 474), but one that unsettles and distorts (Barthes 1976: 14).

Thus, if there is a 'pleasure of the text', in Barthes's subtle conception of the term, it consists in materializing it, 'to abolish the false opposition of practical and contemplative life. The pleasure of the text is just that: a claim lodged against the separation of the text' (Barthes 1976: 58–9). To read is not to take the reader to something or somewhere else, a world beyond the text (be it the author's or the reader's). Such texts may rather be seen as operating in an undifferentiated space that unhinges such oppositions, an intermediate role that, in some aspects at least, comes close to Kristeva's notion of the *chora* – the in-between (1986: 93 ff.; cf. Grosz 2002).

This involvement with a text that resists domination and transparency can be conceived of as based on a reversed analogy: on text as thing, as materiality. Undoubtedly a target for another claim of mimetic aspiration (cf. the discussion below), but not one fraught with the same embarrassment. Barthes's notion of writerly text involves negotiation, a plea for symmetry, something that resembles the reciprocity involved in Benjamin's mimetic (and auratic) relationship to things (as well as in Bergson's notion of 'intellectual sympathy' and the 'chiasm' of the late Merleau-Ponty). This is a relationship that cares for things' difference, and this otherness (or impenetrability) is precisely what makes them 'speak' to us. This 'conversation' is not intellectual rhetoric, it can be activated only by a 'physiognometic' dialogue that restores to things their own materiality:

> this bursting forth of the mass of the body towards the things, which makes a vibration of my skin become the sleek and the rough, makes me follow with my eyes the movements and the contours of the things themselves, this magical relations, this pact between them and me according to which I lend them my body in order that they inscribe upon it and lend me their resemblance.
>
> (Merleau-Ponty 1968: 146)

To perceive the writerly character of an object means to accord it the ability to look back at us, to return our gazes and to speak to us in its own language (cf. Merleau-Ponty 1968: 133–40, Benjamin 1973: 147–8).

This perspective also challenges the current dominant interpretative doctrine in which things, monuments and landscapes primarily are conceived of as sites of 'inscription', i.e. as metaphorical 'stand-ins' for socially and culturally constituted meanings (implicitly conceived of as extra-material in their origin).[6] Despite much talk about somatic experience and bodily practice in recent anthropological and archaeological discourses, things and landscapes seem to have little to offer to processes of 'embodiment' beyond being plastic, open-ended and receptive. One implication of the 'writerly' approach, however – at least in my conception of it – is precisely a concern also for the properties possessed by the material world itself. In other words, we are dealing with entities that do not just sit in silence waiting to be embodied with socially constituted meanings, but possess their own unique qualities and competences which they bring to our cohabitation (and co-constitution) with them.

WRITING THINGS

Post-structuralist textualism worked both ways; thus it also triggered a debate and a series of reflections on the ways in which material culture was *written* and the formation processes that are activated as we move from things to text (cf. Tilley 1989; Baker and Thomas 1990; Olsen 1990; Hodder et al. 1995, Joyce 1994; Joyce et al. 2002). Studying material culture is of necessity to engage in textual activity. A thing becomes an anthropological or archaeological object basically by being realized as texts (field reports, catalogues, journal articles, books). Every description and classification analysis, ranging from the labelling of artefacts (Bouquet 1991) to social and historical synthesis (White 1973, 1978), involves textualization and the use of (oral/written) language. Even the photographed and exhibited item gets most of its identity from the meta-text (the caption) that accompanies it (Olsen 1990: 192).

Most researchers, however, regard language and writing mainly as means of communication, and the dominant style or genre guiding scholarly authorship has been 'clarity'. ('Write so that people can understand you!') Writing academic texts is to write *about* a subject matter, a transformation that always is supposed to involve the hierarchical and irreversible move from signified to signifier, from content to form, and from idea to text. The aspired-to ideal seems to be that of an erased or transparent signifier that allows the content 'to present itself as what it is, referring to nothing other than its presence' (Derrida 1978: 22). Thus, the common conception of academic language has been that it is:

> merely an instrument, which is chooses to make as transparent, as neutral as possible, subjugated to scientific matters (operations, hypothesis, results),

which are said to exist outside it and to precede it: on one side and *first of all*, the contents of the scientific message which are everything, and on the other and *afterwards*, the verbal form entrusted with expressing these contents, which is nothing.

(Barthes 1986: 4)

One of the most profound post-structuralist contributions was to challenge this transitive conception of language and writing. Post-structuralists seriously problematized the simplistic representational attitude evident in realist novels as well as academic discourse in which the text is believed unconditionally to mirror the world, constituting its simulacrum. All texts, they claimed, including scientific ones, are products of the multitudes of codes and voices related to history and textual production itself. As discourse, anthropological and archaeological texts, for example, participate in the same structure as the epic, the novel and the drama, and to write is to make ourselves subject to narrative formation processes, to literary techniques and conventions (rhetorics, allegories, plots). Thus, the strict border between scientific text and fictional literature is blurred, simultaneously making way for the provocative claim that philosophical and scientific texts could be analysed – and 'deconstructed' – using the same literary devices as applied to fiction (cf. Derrida 1977, 1978).

This emphasis on science and research as textual practices, as writing, had an important impact on the theoretical debate in disciplines concerned with material culture. This debate, which also was inspired by the meta-historical works of Hayden White (1973, 1978), caused a new awareness of how literary form intervenes in the construction of the object. This was most noticeable in anthropology, where the recognition of the constitutive character of ethnographical writing led to a debate on the representation and construction of the 'other' (Clifford and Marcus 1986; Clifford 1988; Geertz 1988; Hastrup 1992; Hastrup and Hervik 1994; see also Edmonds 1999). Much emphasis was initially placed on the way ethnographic texts were presented, stressing autobiography and the rhetorical devices applied in writing the field. Poetry (or 'poetic' writing) and other experiments with literary forms were proposed as alternative and more adequate representations of the complexities and hybridities encountered in the field (cf. Prattis 1985; Fischer 1986; Giles 2001). According to Marcus and Fischer, the objective of experimental writing was to produce a more authentic representation of cultural differences (Marcus and Fischer 1986: 42–3), as well as 'to involve the reader in the work of analysis' (Marcus and Fischer 1986: 67).

The sudden focus on autobiography, style and aesthetics probably made an amount of narcissism unavoidable (cf. Campbell and Hansson 2000). Both archaeology and anthropology produced works where the issue of content clearly seems of less regard than the celebration of style, what Clifford once referred to as 'our fetishizing of form' (Clifford 1986: 21). The new imperative of creating polyphonic texts also caused some questionable (although memorable) solutions. The discrediting of the 'tyrannical' authorial voice, and of the author as the centre and source of discourse, led to numerous homespun attempts at infusing dialogue and multivocality into the text. Since the archaeologist or ethnographer could no longer 'remain in unchallenged control of his narrative' (Marcus and Fischer 1986: 67), other voices had to be added.

The devices applied to achieve this often boiled down to a adding a section with dialogue or conversation in an otherwise quite conventional narrative (featuring the author and one or more opponents as participants, a solution probably inspired by Foucault's dialogic conclusion in *The Archaeology of Knowledge*) (Foucault 1970: 199–211; cf. Tilley 1991; Hodder et al. 1995; Hodder and Preucel 1996; Hodder 1999; Karlsson 1998; Joyce et al. 2002). Even if encountering such a dialogue in scientific texts may have provoked some reflection, it hardly paid more than lip service to the ideal of multivocality. More seriously, many of these attempts can actually be read as a way of safeguarding against criticism by controlling reader responses (producing both questions and answers), and thus actually reinstalling the author as the centre of discourse. It is as if the author takes on the reader's and critic's role, producing texts that are already fragmented and ready-made deconstructed (cf. Shaw and Stewart 1994: 22–3). A less deceptive attempt at creating texts that relates openly and experimentally to our experience of material culture is to be found in the work of Michael Shanks (1992, 1999, 2004; Pearson and Shanks 2001). By seriously engaging in how this experience may be written and visualized, Shanks effectively utilizes imagery, simulation and narrative to provoke reflection on how we experience the material.

An interesting turn has recently been witnessed in archaeology where a more 'reflexive' approach to fieldwork is called for. In concordance with the textual turn in ethnography, this approach also challenges the 'production line' conception of research and writing (cf. Fabian 1990: 769), running irreversibly (and spatially unidirectionally) from 'raw' data collection (away), through analysis, interpretation and writing (back home) (cf. Hodder 1999; Berggren and Burström 2002; Chadwick 2003; Hodder and Berggren 2003). The conventional monological site report was conceived of as an archive of the archaeological record excavated, ignoring processes of interpretation, emotions and power relations at work during fieldwork. By its simplistic narrative form it also seriously misrepresented the palimpsests of structures and things excavated. Since the 1990s, however, new means of representing this experience utilizing the possibilities offered by visual media and electronic information technology have been proposed (cf. Larsen et al. 1993; Tringham 2000; Holtorf 2000–01). Especially promising are the possibilities offered for linking texts and textured fragments in complex hypertextual networks (including pictures, sounds etc., i.e. hypermedia). These electronic means enable – and force – the reader to be creative; you have to make your own choices when exploring the rhizome-like paths of the intertextual networks. Actually, the hypertextual possibilities offered by the new productive forces of information technology are clearly in concordance with some of the theoretical positions of poststructuralism (fragmentation, multivocality, intertextuality) (cf. Landow 1992; Holtorf 2000–01; see also the collaborative authoring forums of the MetaMedia Lab, Stanford, at metamedia. Stanford.edu).

MIMESIS REGAINED?

The new emphasis on dialogue and plurality was clearly intended as a liberating turn. In ethnography is was partly a project of empowering the 'other' as more than an 'informant', or in James Clifford's more modest words 'to loosen at least somewhat the monological control of the executive writer/anthropologist and to open for discussion ethnography's hierarchy and negotiation of discourses in power-charged, unequal situations' (Clifford 1997: 23). *Things* are maybe less likely to be cared for as complex, historical agents or in need of emancipation. However, their treatment in scientific discourses is somehow analogous to Western blindness towards the other (cf. Olsen 2003, 2004). This even includes a certain ambiguity (cf. Young 1995), being at the same time objects of ignorance (and contempt) and of desire. As noted by several commentators (Simmel, Benjamin), the modern attitude to things was characterized by this ambiguity: a fear of things in their brute materiality and simultaneously a redemptive longing for the atomized, aestheticized and romanticized object (Simmel 1978: 404, 478; Andersson 2001: 47–51).

Clearly, the polysemous and 'uncontrollable' character of things poses a problem in a modern world which is obsessed with material *signs* 'but likes them to be clear' (Barthes 1977: 29), privatized or subjective. Things' otherness and ambiguity unsettle and distort us, and urge means for domestication and subordination. Language and writings have clearly functioned to counter this disquieting material obstinacy by introducing its totalitarian regime of meaning. One outcome is a world less and less sensitive to the way things articulate themselves, making their domestic 'language' increasingly incomprehensible to us. Commenting on this situation, Walter Benjamin once said that if things were assigned the property of aural (human) language they would immediately start to complain, a complaint directed against the betrayal committed by this wordy language in ignoring the tacit speech of things and thereby depriving them of their right to express themselves (Benjamin 1980a: 138–9, cf. Andersson 2001: 166).

Intellectually (or present-at-hand, to use Heidegger's concept) we encounter things as (pre)labelled, as enveloped by layers of linguistic meaning. As noted by Barthes, 'the text directs the reader through the signifieds of the image, causing him to avoid some and receive others; by means of an often subtle dispatching, it remote-controls him towards a meaning chosen in advance' (Barthes 1977: 40). Even an innocent catalogue label or figure caption ('Spear-thrower from Mas d'Azil', 'The sorcerer of Trois-Frères', 'The beautiful Bronze Age warrior: chiefly Urnfield equipment from northern Italy'[7]), loads the object with a preconceived signified, burdens it with a culture and moral that clearly reduce its possible signification (Olsen 1990: 195).

Against this background of sameness and uniformism, it is understandable that the introduction of new ways of writing things, which are more ambiguous and multi-layered (such as double texts, experiments with hypertext and -media, poetics, irony, etc.), was conceived of (and motivated as) an act of liberation. Such presentations clearly appear to be more appropriate means of securing, realizing or *making manifest* (cf. Shanks 1999) things' material diversity and polyphonic character. One (if not *the*) *raison d'être* beyond all this seems to be that whereas the former, realist writings misrepresented the world as simplistic and straightforward, post-structuralist (and postmodern) writings and presentations let the presumed complexity and hybridity shine through (cf. Marcus and Fischer 1986: 31, 42–3). This point of motivation is well expressed by Hayden White in relation to historiography:

> Since the second half of the nineteenth century, history has become increasingly the refuge of all those 'sane' men who excel at finding the simple in the complex, the familiar in the strange ... The historian serves no one well by constructing a specious continuity between the present world and that which preceded it. On the contrary, we require a history that will educate us to discontinuity, more than ever before; for discontinuity, disruption and chaos are our lot.

(White 1978: 50)

What is rarely discussed, however, is how this new plea for a more complex and diverse representation can be conceived of as advocacy of a new *mimesis*. Although normally claimed to be the great fallacy of realism (which conflated a literary form with an epistemological stance), experimental writings and presentations may actually be a new way of creating 'representations that are (or pretend to be) isomorphic with that which is being represented' (Fabian 1990: 765). Even if the aspiration of creating better (or more realistic) representations should not necessarily be the cause of great embarrassment, it clearly seems odd in relation to a theoretical legacy that precisely questions such mimicry and any representationist stance altogether.

THE TYRANNY OF THE TEXT

There is also another issue at stake here, similarly submerged in the ongoing debate about things and texts. This concerns how the textual approach campaigned for by post-structuralists may have reinforced the hegemony of the text, allowing (and in a very literal sense) no space outside it. Finally fully conquered, the materiality of things ended up as little more than an arbitrary quality in a dematerialized discourse (Beek 1991: 359). Following in the wake of an idealist intellectual tradition that has continuously devalued, stigmatized and demonized

the material (as always bypassed, always made transcendental), to conceive of any material experience that is outside language becomes the subject of suspicion. As claimed by Julian Thomas, '[a]ny notion of a pre-discursive materiality is incomprehensible, since we cannot articulate the pre-discursive other than in discursive concepts' (Thomas 2004: 143). This suspicion exemplifies what Ian Hacking has termed 'linguistic idealism' (or the Richard Nixon doctrine), 'that only what is talked about exists; nothing has a reality unless it is spoken of, or written about' (Hacking 2001: 24). One consequence is, of course, that 'we miss the wordless experience of all people, rich and poor, near or far' (Glassie 1999: 44).

An example of how post-structuralism came to campaign for a textual (and linguistic) colonialism against things is provided by the work of Judith Butler, whose work has been hailed by a number of archaeologists and anthropologists as providing a new framework for understanding materiality (despite rarely addressing non-human matters). Discussing the differentiation between sex and gender, Butler (1993) convincingly argues how the latter term (by being conceived of as socially and culturally constructed) came to reinforce the naturalness and 'given' quality of the former. Sex constitutes the invariable material bedrock on which gender is moulded. Thus, by being conceived of as matter, the biological (sexual) body escapes cultural construction. According to Butler, however, this escape is precisely a product of the metaphysics of a material first instance, an originary *a priori*, in other words based on a deceptive conception of materiality as existing prior to, or outside of, language. Unmasked, this ontologized matter (as opposed to the culturally constructed) is revealed as nothing but a linguistic construct itself, something always discursively articulated. Thus, there is no materiality existing outside of language: 'We may seek to return to matter as prior to discourse to ground our claims about sexual difference only to discover that matter is fully sedimented with discourses on sex and sexuality that prefigure and constrain the uses to which that term can be put' (Butler 1993: 28).

Following Butler, materiality is nothing given, being a site or a substance, but a 'process of materialization that stabilizes over time to produce the effect of boundary, fixity, and surface we call matter' (Butler 1993: 9). This interesting thought, however, is based on an inverted hierarchy of opposition in which materialization is seen solely as a process in service (or an effect) of power. Thus, sex is a forcible materialization of a 'regulatory ideal' (heterosexuality): to materialize the body's sex is 'to materialize sexual difference in the service of the consolidation of the heterosexual imperative' (1993: 2). Materialization and its by-product matter end up as epiphenomena of something more primary (power, regulatory ideals, etc.). And, well in concordance with the effective history of modern Western thought, materiality continues to be viewed with suspicion and contempt, entailing the old vision of freedom and emancipation as that which escapes the material (cf. Latour 1993: 137–8, 2002). Thus the conspiracy theory claiming that '"[m]ateriality" appears only when its status as contingently constituted through discourse is erased, concealed, covered over. Materiality is the dissimulated effect of power' (Butler 1993: 35).

Despite Butler's promising introductory quotation from Donna Haraway's cyborg manifesto ('Why should our bodies end at the skin, or include at best other beings encapsulated by skin?' Butler 1993: 1), her discussion and conception of materiality are entirely anthropocentric, leaving little room for other 'carnal beings' not covered with skin. Taking those non-human beings seriously should not be conflated with any imperative or desire of subjugating oneself to materiality as a transcendental centre or final signified to which all discourse may be anchored. Such either/or logic seems utterly misplaced. It is rather a claim to do away with all such hierarchies or centres, and thus to acknowledge the otherness of things and of materiality as providing a distinct sphere of experience – sometimes closely related to language, but sometime very remote from it. As Gosewijn van Beek points out in his pertinent comment to the prophets of linguistic absolutism:

> Certainly, there is no escape from language when analysing and talking about material culture, especially as language is the preferred medium of scientific exchange. But this does not mean that the material aspect we necessarily talk about *in* language has no locus in other media of experience. The 'hegemony of linguistic approaches to the object world' surely is a reification of the dominant form of scientific discourse which then is constructed as the substance of things we talk about.
>
>   (Beek 1991: 359)

Material things are not experienced solely as linguistic signs or signifiers, despite their ability of being transposed and represented in other media. We may talk and write about the city, for example, as a concept or an 'idea', as a mental construct, as something social, symbolic or purely textual. Still this concept relates to, and emerges from, a complex material infrastructure of streets, walls, buildings, sewer pipes, public transport, people, cars, etc. As noted by Hacking, with a different point of reference (the material infrastructure surrounding the idea of 'women refugees'), you may want to call these structures 'social' because their meanings are what matter to us, 'but they are material, and in their sheer materiality make substantial differences to people' (Hacking 2001: 10).

The hegemony of the text may be seen as related to a general asymmetry in academia, and especially in the humanities, where material life (technology, manual labour, dirt) has always been an object of contempt and thus utterly marginalized.[8] This regime of subordination may actually be related to a central aspect of Derrida's deconstructionist theory: the hierarchies of opposites (Derrida 1977). In Western culture pairs of opposites such as body/soul, matter/mind, form/content, nature/culture play a fundamental role in ordering discourses. As Derrida points out, this is a hierarchy of value (even of violence) in which one side is always given priority over the other (here, the left side) which is conceived of as marginal, derivative, a supplement. His favourite example (even if a questionable one) is the way speech is prioritized over writing – the latter being conceived of as redundant, a dangerous supplement to speech (and thus to thought). However, another opposition of subordination is less talked about, that of writing (and speech) over things. This hierarchy of value in which matter is subordinate to text and language is well in accordance with a logocentric tradition that always privileges the human side (thought, speech, writing) and renders matter passive, meaningless or negative (cf. Olsen 2003; Thomas 2004: Chapter 9).

CONCLUSION: WAYS OUT?

Some of the initial criticism directed at the textual analogy in material culture studies was based on the traditional assumption of written texts as linear (and irreversible) structures and thus their incompatibility with the material world, with its chaotic palimpsest of things. Even if this criticism clearly was based on a misunderstanding of the post-structuralist conception of text, which was precisely palimpsestial in nature, one may still question why students of material culture needed the textual detour to discover their own subject matter's far more fragmented, reversible, and polysemic nature? One obvious answer is of course provided by the textual hegemony discussed above, including the disciplinary hierarchy attached to it. As we learned from Foucault, the authority of a statement, i.e. its status as a serious speech act, depends as much on who is uttering it – and from what institutional site – as on its actual content (Foucault 1970).

However, this not to say that the textual turn was just an ideologically enforced curve made in vain. Rather, the value and impact of this peculiar version of the 'logic of the supplementary' must be evaluated also using other and more generous criteria of judgement. First and foremost post-structuralist textualism constituted a vital source of theoretical inspiration. By questioning the obviousness of the traditional hermeneutic approach to interpretation, it provoked reflection on how we interpret things, on what entities are involved in the meaning-creative process and on their mutual relationship. The post-structuralist discourse on these issues was far more advanced than any contemporary debate in the disciplines devoted to things, and offered if not a free at least a cheap ride along the road of theoretical maturation.

A major fault, however, was to conflate the textual and the material as ontological entities. Many of us inspired by post-structuralism all too easily came to ignore the *differences* between things and text; to ignore that material culture *is* in the world in a fundamentally different constitutive way from texts and language. As noted by Joerges (1988: 224), things do far more than speak and express meanings. Actually, only a minor part of the material world is 'read' or interpreted in the way we deal with linguistic means of communication. Our dealings with most things take place in a mode of 'inconspicuous familiarity', we live our lives as 'thrown' into an entangled ready-to-hand material world that fundamentally orientates our everyday life in a predominantly non-discursive manner (Heidegger 1962: 85–105; cf. Thomas, Chapter 3 in this volume). Thus, our being-*in* this world is a concrete existence of involvement that unites us with the world. As Merleau-Ponty's latest work suggests, the thingly aspect of our own being (our common 'fabric' as 'flesh') is essential for this unity. The body and things correspond to each other 'as the two halves of an orange', we can touch and be touched, see and

be seen, in the process acting upon things and at the same time being acted upon by them (Merleau-Ponty 1968: 133–43).

Even if these practical dealings with things are to be kept separate from the way we as scholars epistemologically relate to our source material (which of necessity implies making them present-at-hand), to acknowledge that things and texts have different modes of being is necessarily also of vital importance to how we interpret them. To conceive of our dealing with material culture as primarily an intellectual encounter, as signs or texts to be consciously read, is to deprive things of their otherness. It is to turn them into readerly, non-auratic, domesticated objects unable to 'speak back' in their own somatic way. Simmel once diagnosed the modern tendency to fragmentize and aestheticize the material world as an act of redemption. According to him, the curiosity about the fragment, the atomized and 'aestheti-sized' thing (including the interest in antiquities, in turning objects into art), was a way of escaping the materiality of things, a response to 'the fear of coming into too close a contact with objects' (Simmel 1978: 474). Unfortunately, much recent work in material culture studies is akin to this attitude, in which the repugnant task of digging into the substance of things seems far less feasible than contemplating the readerly veil that envelops them (cf. Ingold 2000: 340–2; Olsen 2003: 93–4).

If our living with things is a predominantly somatic experience, a dialogue between material entities, then we also have to envisage a poetics that, although not untranslatable – which is not the case – is clearly of a very different kind (cf. Benjamin 1980b: 156). If things were invested with the ability to use ordinary language they would on the one hand talk to us in ways very banal, but also very imperative and effective: walk here, sit there, eat there, use that entrance, stop, move, turn, bow, lie down, gather, depart, etc. All our everyday conduct, from the morning toilet, through work, rest to bedtime is monitored by brigades of material actors uttering such messages. Our habitual practices, memory, what is spoken of as social and cultural form, cannot be conceived of as separate from this 'physiognometic' rhetoric. At the same time, our dialogue with the material world is a sophisticated discourse about closeness, familiarity, about bodily belonging and remembering, extremely rich and poly-semic, involving all our senses. Walking through a forest, for example, involves encountering the 'numberless vibration' (*pace* Bergson) of the material world. We hear and smell the trees as much as we see them, we are touched by their branches, moistened by the dewfall. Sounds, smells and touches admit proximity with the world, more than seeing they mediate the corporeality and symmetry of our being in the world (Heidegger 1971: 25–6; cf. Welsch 1997: 158; Ingold 2000: 249 ff.).

This cacophony of sensations involved in our material living is well expressed in the writings of authors such as Proust, James and Borges, making manifest a nearness to things, a kind of topographical mode of experience (cf. Andersson 2001; Brown 2003). Fortunately, this (for most of us unobtainable) level of authorship is not the only means by which to make manifest our intimacy with things. Today, the new media reality has equipped us with tools to create new and far more complex interfaces than words. The hypermedia linking of text, sound, video clips addressed above represents one such option that emancipates representation from the constraints of pure narrativity. Moving beyond conventional forms of documentation and inscription, some scholars have started exploring the hybrid space between art and scholarship to express (or manifest) the 'ineffable' experience of place and materiality (cf. Pearson and Shanks 2001; Witmore 2004; see also Tilley et al. 2000; Renfrew 2003). Rather than thinking of this as a new mode of representation, with the effective historical burdens implied, the concept of *mediation* is proposed as a way of translating between material presence and media, a process that 'allows us to attain richer and fuller translations of bodily experience and materiality that are located, multitextured, reflexive, sensory, and polysemous' (Witmore 2004). Drawing on the work of media artist Janet Cardiff, Christopher Witmore, for example, has utilized 'peripatetic video' (or video walks) as a mode of engaging with materiality and bodily experience at archaeological sites in Greece. By infusing the aural and visual experience into the corporeal activities of movement and interaction his work exemplifies a new concern with media as an active mode of engagement through which the full realm of bodily sensation is implicated.

Exploring the hybridized space where scholarship and art cohabit creates a possible interface where things and bodily practices can be articulated outside the realms of wordy languages. However, even if experimental and non-literary ways of making manifest our engagement with material culture are very important and to be encouraged, this is not to claim that the study of material culture needs to be some kind of art or handicraft – where the only legitimate utterances are those performed or made in stone or wood. Although words and things are different, this is not to say that they are separated by a yawning abyss (making any statement a linguistic construction). If we conceive of things as possible to articulate, even to contain their own articulation, they may be transformed (and translated) also into discursive knowledge, even if this may take us through many links and to crossing many small gaps (Latour 1999: 67–79, 141–4). Avoiding the absolutism of the 'whereof one cannot speak, thereof one must be silent' (Wittgenstein), or any other linguistic (and material) idealism, the crucial point is rather to become sensitive to the way things *articulate themselves* – and to our own somatic competence of listening to, and responding to, their call.

To what extent post-structuralism can help develop such sensitivity is doubtful. As argued elsewhere (Olsen 2003, 2004), a major obstacle to the development of a sensitive and symmetrical approach to things is found in the limitations imposed by the current territorial circumscription of knowledge and expressions. Modelled on its essentialist ontology, the legacy of the modern constitution was a rifted and polarized disciplinary landscape inhospitable to the needs of things. Being mixtures of cultures-natures, works of translation, things ended up as matters out of place, an exclusion which at least partly explains their oblivion in twentieth-century academic discourses (cf. Latour 1993: 59). At first sight, the role of post-structuralism in countering this modernist legacy may seem heroic and promising as manifested by its programmatic tenets of blurring boundaries, investigating spaces in between and exploring intertextual networks. However the primacy given to language as a 'model world', and the unwillingness to acknowledge non-discursive realms of reality and experience (cf. Butler 1993), make post-structuralism an unreliable ally in the defence of things.

This is not to say that it is *un*helpful. The best we can do is to approach it with a *bricoleur* attitude, picking those bits and pieces we need and joining them with the appropriate spare parts from other projects. Post-structuralism (*pace* Saussure) campaigned for the notion of the relationality of signifiers, that meanings are produced in relations. This important lesson relates it to the more thingly disposed approaches of phenomenology and network theory, likewise stressing the relational character of our being-in-the-world[9] (Heidegger 1962; Merleau-Ponty 1968; Law and Hassard 1999; Latour 1993, 1999). Despite internal controversies and contradiction, such an eclectic approach seems far more fitted to deal with the complex hybridity we call 'things'. Moreover, if we avoid the fundamentalist trap of swearing allegiance to this or that theoretical regime, in other words caring more for things' needs than for the purity of philosophies, we may also dare to develop a relational approach that acknowledges that there are qualities immanent to the signifiers (beings, actants) themselves, properties that are not accidental or only a product of their position in a relational web. A bridge or an axe does have competences that cannot be replaced by just any other signifier. Thus even if their qualities are activated or realized as part of a relational whole, the immanent properties of the material signifiers do matter.

NOTES

1 Even if this argument is considered relevant on the condition that texts are linear and material culture is not, it remains somewhat enigmatic that those who advocate it seem so little concerned with its implications for the opposite move: in other words, how this proclaimed palimpsest of structures and fragments can be consistently and unproblematically transformed into linear scientific texts (cf. Parker Pearson 1995: 370; Olsen 1997: 119–20).

2 The concept of *différance* is a hybrid of the concepts of *différence* and *differé*, thus combining the notion of 'differing' with 'deferral'. By doing this Derrida adds a dimension of postponement (and dispersal) to the concept of difference.

3 It remains somewhat enigmatic, however, why the author could not also be credited with such a role. If not assigned any role in creating the text's difference and intertextuality, every notion of experimental and poetic 'writerly' writings becomes futile.

4 The interpretive perspective of the reader-oriented reception aesthetic (*Rezeptionäs-thetik*) is closer to the late hermeneutics of Hans Georg Gadamer than to post-structuralism. Reception aesthetic, especially an advocated by Jauss, differs from post-structuralism by granting the text greater independence of subjective intentions thus suggesting that the possible

range of readings to a large extent is determined by the individual text itself (c.f. Iser 1978: 49ff).

5 As argued elsewhere (Johnsen and Olsen 1992), this approach both as conducted within different schools of archaeology (Müller 1884, Hodder 1986) and in anthropology (participant observation), is basically a legacy of the early (romantic) hermeneutic conception of understanding.

6 To a large extent itself a legacy of the post-structuralist thinking (even if narrowly conceived – and often misnamed 'phenomenology').

7 Figure captions borrowed from Thomas (2004).

8 Academia was an arena for pure thought to be kept apart, distinct from, any repugnant trivia of labour and production. Only the aesthetisized material, the fine art, the exotic – and the book – were allowed access, keeping the oily, smelling object at arm's length. The difficulties of technological disciplines and engineering in gaining acceptance as 'real' academic disciplines is but another aspect of this story.

9 As outlined by Heidegger, in our everydayness we are always dealing with things and beings in their relatedness. In this (ready-to-hand) mode, things only 'show' themselves in their interconnectedness, as chains of reference 'of something to something' (Heidegger 1962: 97). Likewise, network theory may be understood as 'a *semiotics of materiality*. It takes the semiotic insight, that of the relationality of entities … and applies this ruthlessly to all materials – and not simply to those that are linguistic (Law 1999: 4).

REFERENCES

Andersson, Dag T. (2001) *Tingenes taushet, tingenes tale*. Oslo: Solum Forlag.

Baker, Fredrick and Thomas, Julian eds (1990) *Writing the Past in the Present*. Lampeter: St David's University College.

Barthes, Roland (1975) *S/Z*, trans. R. Miller. London: Cape.

Barthes, Roland (1976) *The Pleasure of the Text*, trans. R. Miller. London: Cape.

Barthes, Roland (1977) *Image-Music-Text*, essays selected and translated by S. Heath. London: Fontana.

Barthes, Roland (1986) *The Rustle of Language* ed. F. Wahl, trans. R. Howard. Oxford: Blackwell.

Beaudry, Mary (1978) 'Worth its weight in iron: categories of material culture in early Virginia probate inventories', Archeological Society of Virginia, *Quarterly Bulletin,* 33 (1): 19–26.

Beek, Gosewijn van (1991) 'Words and things: a comment on Bouquet's "Images of artefacts"', *Critique of Anthropology,* 11 (4): 357–360.

Benjamin, Walter (1973) *Charles Baudelaire: a Lyric Poet in the Era of High Capitalism,* trans. Harry Zohn. London: New Left Books.

Benjamin, Walter (1980a) 'Die Bedeutung de Sprache in Trauerspiel und Tragödie, in Walter Benjamin *Gesammelte Schriften* II (1). Frankfurt am Main: Suhrkamp.

Benjamin, Walter (1980b) 'Über Sprache überhaubt und über die Sprache des Menschen', in Walter Benjamin, *Gesammelte Schriften* II (1). Frankfurt am Main: Suhrkamp.

Berggren, Åsa and Burström, Mats, eds (2002) *Reflexiv fältarkeologi?* Malmö: Rikantikvarieämbetet, Malmö Kulturmiljö.

Bouquet, Mary (1991) 'Images of artefacts', *Critique of Anthropology,* 11 (4): 333–56.

Brown, Bill (2003) *A Sense of Things: the Object Matter of American Literature.* Chicago and London: University of Chicago Press.

Buchli, Victor (1995) 'Interpreting material culture: the trouble with the text', in I. Hodder, M. Shanks, A. Alessandri, V. Buchli, J. Carman, J. Last and G. Lucas (eds), *Interpreting Archaeology: Finding Meaning in the Past.* London: Routledge.

Butler, Judith (1993). *Bodies that Matter: On the Discursive Limits of Sex.* London: Routledge.

Campbell, Fiona and Hansson, Jonna (2000) *Archaeological Sensibilities.* Göteborg: Gotarc Series C. Arkeologiska Skrifter 38.

Chadwick, Adrian (2003) 'Post-processualism, professionalization and archaeological methodologies: towards reflective and radical practice', *Archaeological Dialogues,* 10 (1): 97–117.

Clifford, James (1986) 'Introduction: Partial Truths', in James Clifford and George E. Marcus (eds) *Writing Culture: the Poetics and Politics of Ethnography.* Berkeley, CA and Los Angeles: University of California Press.

Clifford, James (1988) *The Predicament of Culture: Twentieth-Century Ethnography, Literature, and Art.* Cambridge, MA: Harvard University Press.

Clifford, James (1997) *Routes: Travel and Translation in the late Twentieth Century.* Cambridge, MA: Harvard University Press.

Clifford, James and Marcus, George E. (1986) *Writing Culture: the Poetics and Politics of Ethnography.* Berkeley, CA and Los Angeles: University of California Press.

Connor, Steven (1997) *Postmodernist Culture.* Oxford: Blackwell.

Deetz, James (1967) *Invitation to Archaeology.* New York: Natural History Press.

Deetz, James (1977) *In Small Things Forgotten: The Archaeology of early American Life.* New York: Anchor Books.

Derrida, Jacques (1973) *Speech and Phenomena,* trans. D.B. Allison. Evanston, IL: Northwestern University Press.

Derrida, Jacques (1977) *Of Grammatology,* trans. G.C. Spivak. Baltimore, MD: Johns Hopkins University Press.

Derrida, Jacques (1978) *Writing and Difference,* trans. A. Bass. London: Routledge.

Derrida, Jacques (1979) 'Living on: border lines', in Harold Bloom, Paul de Man, Jacques Derrida, Geoffrey H. Hartman and J. Hillis Miller, *Deconstruction and Criticism.* New York: Continuum.

Derrida, Jacques. (1987) *Positions,* trans. A. Bass. London: Athlone Press.

Edmonds, Mark (1999) *Ancestral Geographies in the Neolithic.* London: Routledge.

Fabian, Johannes (1990) 'Presence and representation: the other and anthropological writing', *Critical Inquiry,* 16: 753–72.

Fischer, Michael M.J. (1986) 'Ethnicity and the postmodern arts of memory', in James Clifford and George E. Marcus, *Writing Culture: the Poetics and Politics of Ethnography.* Berkeley, CA and Los Angeles: University of California Press.

Foucault, Michel (1970) *The Archaeology of Knowledge,* trans. A Sheridan. London: Tavistock.

Foucault, Michel (1973) *The Birth of the Clinic: an Archaeology of Medical Perception,* trans. A Sheridan. London: Tavistock.

Foucault, Michel (1979) *Discipline and Punish: the Birth of the Prison,* trans. A Sheridan. Harmondsworth: Penguin Books.

Gadamer, Hans Georg (1975) *Truth and Method.* London: Sheed & Ward.

Geertz, Clifford (1988) *Works and Lives: the Anthropologist as Author.* Cambridge: Polity Press.

Giles, Melanie (2001) 'Taking hands: archaeology, poetry and photography', *Staple,* 51: 28–31.

Glassie, Henry (1975) *Folk Housing in Middle Virginia: a Structural Analysis of Historical Artifacts.* Knoxville, TN: University of Tennessee Press.

Glassie, Henry (1999) *Material Culture.* Bloomington and Indianapolis, IN: Indiana University Press.

Grosz, Elisabeth (2002) *Architecture from the Outside: Essays on Virtual and Real Space.* Cambridge, MA: MIT Press.

Hacking, Ian (2001) *The Social Construction of What?* Cambridge, MA and London: Harvard University Press.

Hall, Martin (1996) *Archaeology Africa.* Cape Town: David Philip.

Hastrup, Kirsten (1992) 'Writing ethnography: state of the art', in Judith Okely and Helen Callaway (eds), *Anthropology and Autobiography*. London: Routledge.

Hastrup, Kirsten and Hervik, Peter, eds (1994) *Social Experience and Anthropological Knowledge*. London: Routledge.

Heidegger, Martin (1962) *Being and Time*. New York: Harper & Row.

Heidegger, Martin (1971) 'The origin of the work of art', in Martin Heidegger, *Poetry, Language, Thought*. New York: Harper & Row.

Hodder, Ian (1982a) 'Theoretical archaeology: a reactionary view', in Ian Hodder (ed.), *Structural and Symbolic Archaeology*. Cambridge: Cambridge University Press.

Hodder, Ian (1982b) *Symbols in Action*. Cambridge: Cambridge University Press.

Hodder, Ian (1985) 'Post-processual archaeology', *Advances in Archaeological Method and Theory*, 8: 1–26.

Hodder, Ian (1986) *Reading the Past: Current Approaches to Interpretation in Archaeology*. Cambridge: Cambridge University Press.

Hodder, Ian (1989) 'This is not an article about material culture as text', *Journal of Anthropological Archaeology*, 8: 250–69.

Hodder, Ian (1999) *The Archaeological Process: an Introduction*. Oxford: Blackwell.

Hodder, I. and Berggren, Å. (2003) 'Social practice, method, and some problems of field archaeology', *American Antiquity*, 68 (3): 421–34.

Hodder, I. and Preucel, R.W. eds (1996) *Contemporary Archaeology in Theory: a Reader*. Oxford: Blackwell.

Hodder, I., Shanks, M., Alessandri, A., Buchli, V., Carman, J., Last, J., and Lucas, G., eds (1995) *Interpreting Archaeology: Finding Meaning in the Past*. London: Routledge.

Holtorf, Cornelius (1998) 'The life-history of megaliths in Mecklenburg-Vorpommern (Germany)', *World Archaeology*, 30 (1): 23–38.

Holtorf, Cornelius (2000–01) *Monumental Past: The Life-histories of Megalithic Monuments in Mecklenburg-Vorpommern (Germany)*. Electronic monograph, University of Toronto at Scarborough: CITDPress, http://cidtpress.utsc.utoronto.ca/holtorf.

Ingold, Tim (2000) *Perception of the Environment: Essays in Livelihood, Dwelling and Skill*. London: Routledge.

Iser, Wolfgang (1974) *The Implied Reader*. Baltimore, MD: Johns Hopkins University Press.

Iser Wolfgang (1978) *The Act of Reading: a Theory of Aesthetic Response*. Baltimore, MD: Johns Hopkins University Press.

Jameson, Fredric (1984) 'Postmodernism, or the cultural logic of late capitalism', *New Left Review*, 146: 53–92.

Joerges, Bernward (1988) 'Technology in everyday life: conceptual queries', *Journal for the Theory of Social Behaviour*, 18 (2): 219–37.

Johnsen, Harald and Olsen, Bjørnar (1992) 'Hermeneutics and archaeology: on the philosophy of contextual archaeology', *Americal Antiquity*, 57 (3): 419–36.

Joyce, Rosemary (1994) 'Dorothy Hughes Popenoe: Eve in an archaeological garden', in C. Claasen (ed.), *Women in Archaeology*. Philadelphia, PA: University of Pennsylvania Press.

Joyce, R., with Preucel, R.W. and Lopiparo, J. (2002) *The Languages of Archaeology: Dialogue, Narrative and Writing*. Oxford: Blackwell.

Karlsson, Håkan (1998) *Re-thinking Archaeology*. Göteborg: Gotarc Series B, Archaeological Theses 8.

Kristeva, Julia (1986) *The Kristeva Reader*, ed. Toril Moi. Oxford: Blackwell.

Landow, George P. (1992) *Hyper-text*. Baltimore, MD: Johns Hopkins University Press.

Larsen, Jens-Eirik, Olsen, Bjørnar, Hesjedal, Anders, and Storli, Inger (1993) *Camera archaeologica: rapport fra et feltarbeid*. Tromsø: Tromsø Museums Skrifter XXIII.

Latour, Bruno (1993) *We have Never been Modern*. London and Cambridge, MA: Harvard University Press.

Latour, Bruno (1999) *Pandora's Hope: Essays on the Reality of Science Studies*. London and Cambridge, MA: Harvard University Press.

Latour, Bruno (2002) 'Bodies, cyborgs and the politics of incarnation', in Sean T. Sweeney and Ian Hodder (eds), *The Body*. Cambridge: Cambridge University Press.

Law, John (1999) 'After ANT: complexity, naming and topology', in John Law and John Hassard (eds), *Actor Network Theory and After*. Oxford: Blackwell.

Law, John and Hassard, John, eds (1999) *Actor Network Theory and After*. Oxford: Blackwell.

Leone, Mark (1977) 'The new Mormon temple in Washington DC', in L. Ferguson (ed.) *Historical Archaeology and the Importance of Material Things*. Society for Historical Archaeology, Special Series 2.

Leroi-Gourhan, André (1964) *Le Geste et la parole* I, *Technique et langage*. Paris: Albin Michel.

Leroi-Gourhan, André (1965) *Le Geste et la parole* II. *La Mémoire et les rythmes*. Paris: Albin Michel.

Leroi-Gourhan, André (1968) 'The evolution of Paleolithic art', *Scientific American*, 218 (2): 58–68.

Lyotard, Jean-François (1984) *The Postmodern Condition: a Report on Knowledge*. Manchester: Manchester University Press.

McGuckin, Eric (1997) 'Tibetan carpets: from folk art to global community', *Journal of Material Culture*, 2 (3): 291–310.

Marcus, George and Fischer, Michael (1986) *Anthropology as Cultural Critique*. Chicago: University of Chicago Press.

Merleau-Ponty, Maurice (1968) *The Visible and the Invisible*. Evanston, IL: Northwestern University Press.

Moore, Henrietta (1986) *Space, Text and Gender: An Archaeological Study of the Marakwet of Kenya*, Cambridge: Cambridge University Press.

Müller, Sofus (1884) 'Mindre Bidrag til den forhistoriske Archæologis Methode II. Den archæologiske Sammenligning som Grundlag for Slutning og Hypothese', *Aarbøger for nordisk Oldkyndighed og Historie* 1884: 183–203.

Norris, Christopher (1982) *The Deconstructive Turn: Essays in the Rhetoric of Philosophy*. London and New York: Methuen.

Olsen, Bjørnar (1987) *Arkeologi, tekst, samfunn: Fragmenter til en post-prosessuell arkeologi.* Stensilserie B, historie/arkeologi 24. Tromsø: ISV, University of Tromsø.

Olsen, Bjørnar (1990) 'Roland Barthes: from sign to text', in Christopher Tilley (ed.), *Reading Material Culture*. Oxford: Blackwell.

Olsen, Bjørnar (1997) *Fra ting til tekst: teoretiske perspektiv i arkeologisk forskning*. Oslo: Universitetsforlaget.

Olsen, Bjørnar (2003) 'Material culture after text: remembering things', *Norwegian Archaeological Review*, 36 (2): 87–104.

Olsen, Bjørnar (2004) 'Momenter til et forsvar av tingene', *Nordisk Museologi*, 2004 (2): 25–36.

Parker Pearson, Michael (1995) 'Tombs and territories: material culture and multiple interpretation', in I. Hodder, M. Shanks, A. Alessandri, V. Buchli, J. Carman, J. Last and G. Lucas (eds), *Interpreting Archaeology: Finding Meaning in the Past*. London: Routledge.

Patrik, Linda (1985) 'Is there an archaeological record?' *Advances in Archaeological Method and Theory*, 8: 27–62.

Pearson, Mike and Shanks, Michael (2001) *Theatre/Archaeology*. London: Routledge.

Prattis, J. Iain (1985) 'Dialectics and experience in fieldwork: the poetic diemension', in J. Iain Prattis (ed.), *Reflections: the Anthropological Muse*. Washington, DC: American Anthropological Association.

Preucel, Robert W. and Bauer, Alexander A. (2001) 'Archaeological pragmatics', *Norwegian Archaeological Review*, 34 (2): 85–96.

Renfrew, Colin (1989) 'Comments', *Norwegian Archaeological Review*, 22 (1): 33–41.

Renfrew, Colin (2003) *Figuring it out: What are we? Where do we come from? The Parallel Visions of Artists and Archaeologists*. London: Thames & Hudson.

Ricoeur, Paul (1981) *Hermeneutics and the Human Sciences*. Cambridge: Cambridge University Press.

Shanks, Michael (1992) *Experiencing the Past: On the Character of Archaeology*. London: Routledge.

Shanks, Michael (1999) *Art and the Early Greek State: Experiences of the Discipline*. London: Routledge.

Shanks, Michael (2004) 'Three rooms: archaeology and performance', *Journal of Social Archaeology*, 4 (2): 147–80.

Shanks, Michael and Tilley, Christopher (1982) 'Ideology, symbolic power and ritual communication: a reinterpretation of Neolithic mortuary practices', in Ian Hodder (ed.), *Structural and Symbolic Archaeology*. Cambridge: Cambridge University Press.

Shanks, Michael and Tilley, Christopher (1987) *Reconstructing Archaeology: Theory and Practice*. Cambridge: Cambridge University Press.

Shaw, Rosalind, and Stewart, Charles (1994) 'Introduction: problematizing syncretism', in Charles Stewart and Rosalind Shaw (eds), *Syncretism/Anti-syncretism: the Politics of Religious Synthesis*. London: Routledge.

Simmel, Georg (1907/1978) *The Philosophy of Money*. London: Routledge.

Sturrock, John, ed. (1979) *Structuralism and Since: From Lévi-Strauss to Derrida*. Oxford: Oxford University Press.

Thomas, Julian (2004) *Archaeology and Modernity*. London: Routledge.

Tilley, Christopher (1989) 'Discourse as power: the genre of the Cambridge inaugural lecture', in Daniel Miller, Michael Rowlands and Christopher Tilley (eds), *Dominance and Resistance*. London: Unwin Hyman.

Tilley, Christopher, ed. (1990a) *Reading Material Culture: Structuralism, Hermeneutics and Post-structuralism*. Oxford: Blackwell.

Tilley, Christopher (1990b) 'Michel Foucault: towards an archaeology of archaeology', in Christopher Tilley (ed.), *Reading Material Culture: Structuralism, Hermeneutics and Post-structuralism*. Oxford: Blackwell.

Tilley, Christopher (1991) *Material Culture and Text: the Art of Ambiguity*. London: Routledge.

Tilley, Christopher (1994) *A Phenomenology of Landscape*. London: Berg.

Tilley, C., Hamilton, S. and Bender, B. (2000) 'Art and the re-presentation of the past', *Journal of the Royal Anthropological Institute* (n.s.), 6 (1): 36–62.

Tringham, Ruth (2000) 'Expressing the feminist practice of archaeology through hypermedia opera', in Margareth W. Conkey and Alison Whylie (eds), *Practicing Archaeology as a Feminist*. Santa Fe, NM: School of American Research Press.

Welsch, Wolfgang (1997) *Undoing Aesthetics*. London: Sage.

White, Hayden (1973) *Metahistory: the Historical Imagination of Nineteenth-Century Europe*. Baltimore, MD: Johns Hopkins University Press.

White, Hayden (1978) *Tropics of Discourse: Essays in Cultural Criticism*. Baltimore, MD: Johns Hopkins University Press.

Witmore, Christopher (2004) 'Four archaeological engagements with place: mediating bodily experience through peripatetic video', *Visual Anthropology Review*, 20 (2): 57–72.

Yates, Timothy (1990) 'Jacques Derrida: "There is nothing outside of the text"', in Christopher Tilley (ed.), *Reading Material Culture: Structuralism, Hermeneutics and Post-structuralism*. Oxford: Blackwell.

Young, Robert J.C. (1995) *Colonial Desire: Hybridity in Theory, Culture and Race*. London: Routledge.

ACKNOWLEDGEMENTS

I wish to thank Chris Tilley and Chris Witmore for comments on earlier versions of this chapter. I also pay homage to Orvar Löfgren – and Ingmar Bergman – for providing inspiration for its title.

7

COLONIAL MATTERS

Material Culture and Postcolonial Theory in Colonial Situations

Peter van Dommelen

Definitions of major theoretical perspectives are, even at the best of times, always going to be as much slippery and vague as wrapped in controversy and attempts to pinpoint what postcolonial theory is about or what it tries to achieve usually do not fare much better. If anything, postcolonialism defies any such effort right from the start, as there is widespread debate about the very term that can or should be used to refer to the body of concepts and tenets that have by and large become grouped together under the banner of 'postcolonial theory'.

Disagreement erupts from the outset when writing out the very term 'postcolonial': should postcolonial be spelled with a hyphen or written as one word? And does the prefix 'post' signal the same things as in 'postmodern' (Appiah 1991)? The hyphenated version is the oldest of the two spellings. It was first used in the 1960s and 1970s by economists, political scientists and anthropologists who were discussing decolonization in Third World countries that had been occupied by Western colonial powers. In this straightforwardly chronological use of the term, the prefix must be understood literally and the neologism as a whole simply refers to the period after colonialism. In recent years, however, deletion of the hyphen has gradually gained currency in academic circles, especially in literary studies (cf. below), in order to signal an endeavour to go beyond colonialism in a metaphorical and ideological rather than simply chronological sense. As a result, the unhyphenated version of the term denotes nothing

simple at all, as the hyphen has in practice been displaced by a host of associated but not necessarily coherent connotations that are assumed to amount to a particular analytical and theoretical perspective on colonialism (Barker et al. 1994: 1; Loomba 1998: 7–8). Adding to the confusion is that the chronological sense of the term has not entirely been supplanted either, as there is a general recognition that the academic postcolonial perspective roots directly in the 'post-colonial condition' of the wider world and that the former cannot, and indeed should not, be separated from the latter (Jacobs 1996: 22–9; Young 2003: 45–68).

Although the absence of a coherent set of basic principles has led to the increasing insistence that 'there is no single entity called "postcolonial theory"' (Young 2003: 7), the multitude of introductions to, handbooks on and readers of postcolonialism that have appeared as well as the launch of two major academic journals suggest a rather different situation in practice.[1] In academic terms at least, there certainly does appear to be a distinct way of thinking or perspective that is subscribed to by substantial numbers of academics and other intellectuals alike, whose primary academic basis is to be found in literary and cultural studies. Leaving aside for the moment the finer details of the origins, coherence and scope of postcolonial theory, I note that postcolonial studies can at the very least be characterized, if not defined, as a specifically Western analytical perspective about representing colonial situations and structures and I will use the term in that sense throughout the chapter. Where this leaves the term 'postcolonialism' is another matter which I will consider in more detail below.

While this simple observation alone would warrant exploration of these ideas and insights and consideration of their relevance to and connections with material culture studies, it is worth noting that the rise of postcolonial studies has been accompanied by a renewed interest in colonialism and colonial situations more generally, that has not had much follow-up in material culture studies. This is all the more remarkable, as material culture has gained substantial prominence in discussions of globalization, which is a theme that is inherently intertwined with post-colonial developments (in the chronological sense), and which has not escaped the attention of postcolonial studies. Because globalization studies constitute a substantial field in themselves at the interface between geography and anthropology that has not failed to note the significance of material culture, I will limit my discussion in this chapter to colonial situations (Eriksen 2003; cf. below).

It is therefore my aim in this chapter first to discuss postcolonialism and the wide-ranging views of postcolonial studies as well as to consider their background and characteristics. I will then go on to explore how and to what extent they can inform material culture studies and how an emphasis on the role of material culture may contribute to postcolonial theory and studies of colonialism. Throughout the chapter I will draw on archaeological and anthropological examples from colonial situations across the world, albeit with a bias towards the Mediterranean.

POSTCOLONIAL ORIGINS: DECOLONIZATION, COLONIAL REPRESENTATION AND SUBALTERN RESISTANCE

While the suggestion that the Algerian war of independence (1954–62) represented a critical moment in the emergence of postcolonial studies may be difficult to substantiate (Young 1990: 1), there can be little doubt that their origins hark back to the early post-World War II decades, when the European nations were dismantling their overseas colonial networks. As formal decolonization, for a variety of reasons, was slow or failed to be matched by economic and cultural independence, Western neo-colonialism was denounced by both political activists and scholars. Economic relationships between the recently independent countries and north-west Europe and North America were also increasingly analysed academically, from which sprang scholarly concepts such as dependency theory and world systems theory (Frank 1967; Wallerstein 1974; Amin 1976).

The cultural critique of Western neo-colonialism was by contrast mostly fronted by writers outside the academy. Authors like Leopold Sédar Sengor, Wole Soyinka and Aimé Césaire led the way for (francophone) authors in Africa and the Caribbean to extol indigenous values, traditions and cultural achievement under the banner of the so-called *nègritude* movement and to insist on the cultural liberation of their countries. Other intellectuals, among them Franz Fanon, Albert Memmi, Amilcar Cabral and Mahatma Gandhi, soon joined these demands, insisting that the formerly colonized countries and peoples should become aware of the cultural and historical legacies of Western colonialism (Young 2001: 159–334). Fanon in particular pointed out that colonialism 'turns to the past of the oppressed people, and distorts, disfigures and destroys it' (1967: 169) and emphasized the importance of writing 'decolonized histories' in which indigenous people are fully represented and play an active part. How this advice could be put into practice was brilliantly demonstrated by the Moroccan historian Abdellah Laroui, who wrote an 'alternative' *History of the Maghreb* (1970, 1977). In this study, he foregrounded the role of the Berber inhabitants as opposed to the Roman and French contributions to the region emphasized in conventional colonialist histories. Shortly afterwards, the Algerian historian Marcel Bénabou published his study of Roman North Africa (1976), in which he explored this period from an indigenous perspective and emphasized local resistance to Roman rule and culture. He particularly drew attention to the fact that many allegedly Roman features of and contributions to North Africa, as diverse as certain deities and rituals, funerary and domestic architecture and irrigation and other related hydraulic engineering systems, can actually be traced back to pre-colonial times and argued that Roman North Africa maintained a substantial indigenous dimension (Bénabou 1976; cf. Mattingly 1996). Slightly later, and taking his lead separately from Marxism and world systems theory, Eric Wolf proposed an alternative global history of the early modern period (1982).

Postcolonial theory has subsequently developed as an academic discipline from the study of the writings of these pioneering authors into what has been summarized as 'a certain kind of interdisciplinary political, theoretical and historical work that sets out to serve as a transnational forum for studies grounded in the historical context of colonialism as well as in the political context of contemporary problems of globalization' (Young 1998: 4). This rather loose definition reflects a frequently expressed view that postcolonial studies are not and should not be limited to academics alone. To many people, the postcolonial critique of colonialist concepts and stereotypes should be voiced in the wider world, too, especially because the consequences of colonization continue to be felt in a range of ways. Hence the claim that 'postcolonialism is about a changing world, a world that has been changed by struggle and which its practitioners intend to change further' (Young 2003: 7).

It should also be noted that in this view the relevance of postcolonial theories is explicitly not restricted to colonial situations proper but that they apply just as much to contemporary decolonized or post-colonial contexts and their specific economic, political and cultural dependences that derive from older colonial connections.

The honour to have galvanized these widespread feelings of unease about the post-colonial world is unanimously awarded to Edward Said, whose *Orientalism* (1978) is widely recognized as the founding text of postcolonial studies (e.g. Quayson 2000: 3; Loomba 1998: 43). While postcolonial studies draw on a wide range of influences, it is Said's merit to have woven the various strands together into a more or less coherent ensemble. Among these threads, two in particular have been elaborated upon and added to in many respects. These are known under the labels of 'colonial discourse analysis' and the 'subaltern studies group'. In the remainder of this section, I will briefly discuss these constitutive influences on postcolonial studies.

Edward Said and the Power of Culture

The basic thesis put forward by Said in *Orientalism* (1978) and elaborated in more general terms in *Culture and Imperialism* (1993) is that colonial domination does not rely on violence and exploitation alone but is 'supported and perhaps even impelled by impressive ideological formations ... as well as forms of knowledge affiliated with domination' (Said 1993: 8). Following Foucault's insistence that 'power and knowledge directly imply one another' (Said 1978: 27), Said argued that 'ideas, cultures and histories cannot seriously be studied without their force, or more precisely their configurations of power, also being studied' (Said 1978: 5). With regard to the Middle East, this meant that British and French colonial rule was greatly assisted by the creation and cultivation of Western prejudices and stereotypes about the region and its inhabitants. Representing them variously as primitive, unreliable and lascivious not only morally justified European occupation of the region – at least in Western terms – but also discouraged local people from actively resisting European rule. As Said demonstrated in a careful examination of a wide range of media varying from novels, scholarly accounts and popular journals to paintings, school books and political speeches, these stereotypes became a permanent feature of life in the colonies and the home countries alike and effectively made Western representation so persistent and pervasive that resistance became literally inconceivable.

Theoretically, Said based these arguments on Foucault's contention that specialized knowledge must be expressed in a specific way as part of a particular 'discourse' in order to be acceptable to the specific tradition or 'discursive formation' of the relevant field or institution. Because 'Orientalism can be discussed and analysed as the corporate institution for dealing with the Orient', as Said explicitly argued (1978: 3), the seemingly disparate range of Orientalist representations he had examined thus turned out to constitute a coherent 'system of knowledge about the Orient', in which 'the Orient is less a place than a *topos*, a set of references, a congeries of characteristics ...' (Said 1978: 177). In essence, it is therefore the hidden coherence of the various representations that explains their impact on the 'real' world outside the texts (cf. Young 2001: 395–410).

The influence of Said's work on postcolonial studies is best demonstrated by the fact that his emphasis on discourse has basically created an entirely new field which is now called 'colonial discourse analysis' and which in literary circles has practically become shorthand for postcolonial analysis. Given Said's literary background – he taught English literature – it is also fitting that his work has contributed much to the present literary focus of postcolonial studies.

Representation and Colonial Discourse

While it is clearly Said's merit to have placed representation at the heart of postcolonial studies, the latter have been influenced no less by Gayatri Spivak and Homi Bhabha, and it is a measure of their impact that the three of them have been dubbed the 'holy trinity' of postcolonial theory (Young 1995: 165). Practically all handbooks follow suit and dedicate a chapter to each of the three theorists.

The literary orientation already evident in Said's work has strongly been reinforced by Spivak and Bhabha, not least because both are literary theorists, too (Moore-Gilbert 1997: 74–151; cf. Thomas 1994: 51–60). In theoretical terms, they have both elaborated on the textual nature of discourse and representation, drawing attention to its fragmented and incoherent if not contradictory nature. In doing so, they have also tended to emphasize the autonomy of colonial discourse from its authors and often the external world altogether. This is particularly evident in Bhabha's work, as he pays little attention to the economic, political and indeed material world in which the texts were produced. He has accordingly repeatedly been accused of 'an "exhorbitation of discourse" [and] of neglecting material conditions of colonial rule by concentrating on colonial representation' (Loomba 1998: 96; cf. Moore-Gilbert 1997: 147–8). This critique holds only partially true for Spivak, who has taken up Derrida's notion of deconstruction to read texts of colonial discourse 'against the grain', because she emphasizes that the hidden voices she exposes relate to 'real' groups of people in the colonial world. On the whole, however, there is no denying that postcolonial studies have adopted an ever-increasing focus on literary critique and literary representations that is evidently at odds with Said's insistence on the systematic and institutionalized nature of colonial discourse and its intimate connections with social and political power (Loomba 1998: 69–103; Young 2001: 389–94; cf. below).

Spivak and Bhabha's major contribution to postcolonial thinking concerns the coherence of colonial discourse, which was a key issue for Said. As Spivak has made clear in her seminal essay 'Can the subaltern speak?' (1985), the alleged uniformity of colonial discourse is interspersed with implicit references to and statements by groups of people who are denied an official voice, like peasants and women. While Spivak has elaborated on Said's lack of attention to the colonized and attempts to retrieve an alternative history from the colonizers'

representations, Bhabha has called into question the strong opposition between colonizers and colonized, emphasizing the common ground bridging the alleged 'colonial divide' between the two sides. Highlighting the ambiguities of colonial discourse, he explores what he calls the 'third space' of colonial situations (Bhabha 1989), where he finds 'processes of interaction that create new social spaces to which new meanings are given' (Young 2003: 79). Bhabha's discussion of these processes of interaction in terms of hybridization has given rise to a major theme in postcolonial studies (Young 1990: 141–56; Werbner and Modood 1997).

While Spivak and Bhabha have led the way with ever more sophisticated analyses of colonial discourse and representation, the critique of widespread textualism in postcolonial studies 'at the expense of materialist historical inquiry and politicized understanding' (Young 1995: 161, 2001: 390) has steadily become louder. In response, Robert Young has begun to explore the roots of postcolonial studies beyond literary studies, insisting on the intimate connections between culture and politics, representation and domination – effectively going back to Foucault's tenet that 'there is no power relation without the correlative constitution of a field of knowledge, nor any knowledge that does not presuppose and constitute at the same time power relations' (1979: 27; Young 2001, 2003).

Alternative Histories and Subaltern Resistance

There is another strand of postcolonial studies that goes back as far as *Orientalism*: in the late 1970s a group of historians began regular meetings in Cambridge to discuss South Asian historiography, because they were dissatisfied with its elitist and colonialist bias. Their joint publication in 1982 became the first of a series of (so far) eleven volumes published under the banner of the subaltern studies group (Guha 1982b; see Chaturvedi 2000; Young 2001: 352–6).

In the programmatic opening essay of that volume, Ranajit Guha explicitly spelled out their intention to highlight 'the subaltern classes and groups constituting the mass of the labouring population and the intermediate strata in town and country – that is, the people' who had so far consistently been refused a place in Indian and Asian history (Guha 1982a: 4).

The subaltern scholars share their emancipatory goal to write alternative histories 'from below' with post-colonial intellectuals like

Césaire, Cabral and Laroui. As with many proponents of dependency or world systems theory like Wolf or Amin, Marxism looms very large in their conceptual baggage. As signalled by the prominent use of the term 'subaltern', the 'subaltern scholars' draw in particular on the work of Antonio Gramsci, whose inspiration was also explicitly invoked by Said (1978: 6–7, 1993: 56–9). They have in particular borrowed Gramsci's notion of subalternity as a means to restore agency to the peasants and colonized alike and to insist on their autonomy: 'subaltern politics ... was an *autonomous* domain ... It neither originated in elite politics nor did its existence depend on the latter' (Guha 1982a: 4, original emphasis).

In order to redress the colonialist stereotypes of the passive and irrational peasant and their alleged 'inability to make their own history' (O'Hanlon 1988: 192), the subaltern scholars and other historians in their wake have seized on the theme of rebellion and resistance, exploring the role and significance of rioting, banditry and forms of 'silent resistance' such as tax dodging, poaching, evasion, etc. (Scott 1985; Haynes and Prakash 1991; Adas 1991). Despite numerous references, Gramsci's views on hegemony and resistance have, however, received much less attention, perhaps because their theoretical implications are at odds with the much acclaimed peasant autonomy (Arnold 1984). This is unfortunate, because Gramsci's discussion of the ways in which the subaltern 'common sense' is shaped by hegemonic culture but may also give rise to forms of silent resistance gets close to the postcolonial notion of hybridity as proposed by Bhabha and others (Mitchell 1990; van Dommelen 1998: 28–9).

On the whole, the subaltern studies volumes have been very influential, as they have not only succeeded in opening up new debates in South Asian historiography but because they have also inspired alternative perspectives on colonial history elsewhere in the world, notably in South America (Young 2001: 356–9; cf. Prakash 1995; Schmidt and Patterson 1995).

Representing Colonialism

If ever there was one term that expressed what postcolonial studies are about, it would have to be 'representation'. In the first place of course because of their heavy literary bias but in the second place also, and probably more importantly so, because of their concern with the place of the colonized in colonial societies, bearing in mind Said's assertion that knowing the Orient was key to European rule.

From this perspective, a number of key postcolonial themes can be identified that are loosely connected by a shared 'contestation of colonialism and the legacies of colonialism' (Loomba 1998: 12). These concern:

1 The writing of alternative histories 'from below', in particular those of subaltern groups and communities, who make up the people 'without history', to use Wolf's celebrated term (1982: 385).
2 The awareness that colonial situations cannot be reduced to neat dualist representations of colonizers versus colonized, because there are always many groups and communities that find themselves to varying degrees in between these extremes.
3 The recognition that hybrid cultures are common, if not inherent, features of colonial situations because of the constant and usually intense interaction between people.

Given its roots in Western (neo)colonialism, postcolonial theory is undoubtedly a Western perspective, and a largely intellectual and academic one at that. Nevertheless, the broad terms outlined above do not necessarily apply to Western modern colonialism alone, even if that tends to dominate research. These general principles can be applied equally fruitfully to the analysis of earlier pre-modern colonial situations, such as ancient Greek colonialism or the early Spanish occupation of Central America, or indeed contemporary, formally decolonized situations such as twenty-first-century West Africa (van Dommelen 2002: 126–9; Mignolo 2000: 93–100).

CONTEXTUALIZING POSTCOLONIALISM

Outside literary studies, postcolonial theory has not become a distinct field anywhere else. There is nevertheless no shortage in other disciplines of research inspired by or drawing on postcolonial theory, especially not in history, as one might expect, given the historical background of the subaltern studies group (Cohn 1990; Washbrook 1999).[2] In anthropology and archaeology, where most attention to material culture may be expected, postcolonial ideas have certainly not passed unnoticed, especially as colonialism has again come to the fore as an increasingly prominent research topic

(Thomas 1994; Gosden 1999: 197–203, 2004; cf. Pels 1997; Lyons and Papadopoulos 2002).

In both anthropology and archaeology, colonialism has long remained – and to some extent continues to be – a theme of limited interest in general. It is only in specific fields, such as Pacific ethnography and classical and historical archaeology, where colonial situations play a central part, that colonialism has been the subject of substantial debates. This is somewhat surprising, because colonialism has been such a widespread phenomenon across the globe and through the ages that it has arguably been a manifest feature of many situations (Gosden 2004). As pointed out earlier, this contrasts markedly with the attention given in anthropology to globalization (Eriksen 2003).

While the renewed anthropological archaeological interest in colonialism has certainly resulted in a number of fine studies of the significance of specific categories of material culture in colonial situations (see below), it is nevertheless the representation of colonial situations that has figured most prominently in anthropological and archaeological studies of colonialism, alongside occasional more specific approaches such as a long-term perspective in archaeological studies. In this section I will first discuss how these two disciplines have responded to postcolonial theory. I will then focus more specifically on material culture and examine, first of all, how it has been studied in relation to colonialism and postcolonial theory. Because of the very different ways in which material culture and consumption have been taken up in globalization studies I will limit this discussion to colonial situations only. Second, I will explore some theoretical issues of relevance to material culture studies and postcolonial theory alike.

Archaeological and Anthropological Representations

In both anthropology and archaeology, most attention has been focused on the connections between the disciplines and contemporary colonialism. Although the awareness of the colonial entanglements of academic research in both disciplines is ultimately related to the political and cultural decolonization of the Third World, it is only anthropological inquiries into the active involvement of anthropologists in colonial administrations that can be traced back to the 1950s and 1960s (Asad 1973; Stocking 1991; Pels and Salemink 1999; Gosden 1999: 15–32; 58–9). While the actual contribution of anthropologists

to the establishment and maintaining of colonial power was fairly minor, this certainly does not hold for the reverse: as Talal Asad points out, it was not simply that colonial connections facilitated fieldwork, the heart of the matter surely is the recognition that 'the fact of European power, as discourse and practice, was always part of the reality anthropologists sought to understand' (Asad 1991: 315). With the debates about the 'crisis of representation' and 'critical reflexivity' in recent decades, anthropologists have realized the impact of many colonialist concepts and discourses that remained influential after decolonization, and have accordingly shifted attention from examining practical and direct collaboration with colonial administrators, missionaries or military officials to considering issues of representation and authority in general. A key study in this respect has been Johannes Fabian's *Time and the Other* (1983) that demonstrated how the denial of time and change in anthropological studies continued to contribute to a notion of Western superiority (Pels 1997: 165–6). It is finally worth noting that parallel developments in postcolonial theory have not gone unnoticed by anthropologists (e.g. Thomas 1994), while the same cannot be said of postcolonial studies, which remain slow to pick up on research outside literary studies.

Archaeology, in contrast, has been much slower to wake up and own up to its colonial baggage. In evident contrast to anthropology, it did not examine its specific colonial roots and more general Western biases until quite recently. That does not mean that no archaeologist has ever noticed or commented on the implications of their disciplinary past, as Bruce Trigger had already drawn attention to the colonialist and nationalist biases of archaeological representations in 1984 (Trigger 1984). At the same time, Michael Rowlands exposed Western prejudice in representations of European prehistory (1984, 1986). But well known and much cited as these papers are, most people have taken them not to apply to their particular field and it was not until a more general interest in disciplinary history developed in the later 1990s that archaeologists began a critical self-examination of their colonial inheritance.

Postcolonial theory has played a significant part in this process, which has been most prominent in Mediterranean and classical archaeology.[3] One of the best examples can be found in North Africa, in Algeria in particular, where the abundance and high quality of monumental remains of the Roman period (second and first centuries BC to fifth and sixth centuries AD) has always attracted much attention, both from archaeologists and the French colonial authorities. Inspired by colonial discourse theory, the one-sided colonialist bias of the histories written by (mostly French) archaeologists and historians has recently been laid bare, and the active and sustained involvement of the French military in archaeological fieldwork and publication has been made evident (Mattingly 1996, 1997; cf. Webster 1996 and Hingley 2000: 1–27 for a British perspective). The latter not only facilitated archaeological research but also actively appropriated the Roman past of the Maghreb by comparing themselves to the Roman army and presenting themselves as their rightful successors. This is evident from the myriad references to Roman military feats in accounts of the French occupation as well as from the frequent comparisons between the Roman and French armies and their respective achievements in an authoritative study of the Roman army in North Africa by the historian René Cagnat (published in 1832: Dondin-Payre, 1991). These ideas also influenced French military activities on the ground and led to the active involvement of troops in the excavation and restoration of Roman remains. This is best demonstrated by the Roman military camp of Lambaesis in the Batna region of north-east Algeria, which was largely excavated by the French military, who had begun to construct a prison on the site (Figure 7.1). Under the direction of Colonel Carbuccia, the Roman camp was unearthed between 1848 and 1852. These activities included the reconstruction of the tomb of T. Flavius Maximus, the commander of the Roman third legion based in Lambaesis, and adding a French inscription commemorating these restorations. When the monument was formally inaugurated in 1849, Colonel Carbuccia extensively praised the Roman officer as his illustrious predecessor, while his troops saluted them both with a rifle volley and march-past (Dondin-Payre 1991: 148–149).

Throughout Algeria in particular, there are plenty of examples where the French colonial authorities used Roman remains to suggest, if not to claim explicitly, that they had returned to land that was legitimately theirs, thereby ignoring and often cancelling thirteen centuries of Muslim settlement and much longer Berber presence (Prochaska 1990: 212). As more attention is gradually being paid to indigenous traditions and contributions before and during the Roman period, it is fitting that it was precisely in the Maghreb that calls for such an alternative history were first voiced with regard to (Roman) archaeology. It nevertheless remains a demonstration of the strength of colonial representations that it is only now that Marcel Bénabou's work has been rediscovered: when he wrote his La Résistance africaine (1976) in the wake of the Algerian war of independence, it was all but ignored by Western archaeologists (van Dommelen 1998: 20–1).

Its colonial roots have also been brought home to archaeology, especially in North America and Australia, by indigenous people's claims of ancestral objects and bodies which had been recovered in the name of science or which had simply been looted (Gosden 2001: 249–57). Overall, it is obvious that postcolonial theory has certainly not gone unnoticed in archaeology and anthropology, although it is the former discipline in particular which has been influenced most directly.

Colonial Contexts in Practice: Hegemony, Resistance and Material Culture

Despite the recognition that postcolonial theory suggests radically new ways of looking at colonial situations, there have been relatively few archaeological or anthropological studies that have really engaged with these ideas and that have placed them at the heart of their approach; and even fewer have made the explicit connection between material culture and postcolonial theory. As a consequence, the literary bias of postcolonial study has imposed itself on the social and human sciences, instead of being redressed by an emphasis on social practice, human agency and, of course, material culture.

As mentioned earlier, the 'weak contextualizations' of postcolonial theory have already repeatedly been criticized because of the tendency in postcolonial theory to ignore the often harsh realities of colonialism on the ground (Turner 1995: 204; Parry 1987, 2002). Several anthropologists have taken this observation to its logical conclusion and have argued that colonial projects cannot be reduced to either economic exploitation or cultural domination and that both coercion and persuasion are part of the colonial equation, because, as Nicholas Thomas has said, 'even the purest moments of profit and violence have been mediated and enframed by structures of meaning' (1994: 2).

While Thomas's book Colonialism's Culture has perhaps most explicitly called for more attention to 'the competence of actors' in the shaping of colonial situations (1994: 58; cf. Turner 1995: 206–10), the most extensive ethnographic elaboration of the specific ways in which

Figure 7.1   *Overview of the site of the Roman military camp of Lambaesis, as shown on a nineteenth-century postcard*
Source: Afrique Française du Nord, http://afn.collections.free.fr/)

people's daily activities were part and parcel of the colonial process is surely provided by the two volumes of John and Jean Comaroff's *Of Revelation and Revolution* that have so far appeared (Comaroff and Comaroff 1991, 1997). In this study, they highlight the roles of the various actors involved in the colonial context of Tswana land in northern South Africa, in particular the missionaries and the local Tswana people. They are at pains to distinguish between the different positions and perspectives among the local Tswana as embodied by 'the humble prophetess Sabina, the iconoclastic, *nouveau-riche* Molema, the "heathen" chief Montshiwa and many others' (Comaroff and Comaroff 2001: 116). All these actors voiced their views in what the Comaroffs call the 'long conversation' between Methodist missionaries and Tswana people, and they all tried to have things their own way. A key argument developed throughout both volumes is that it was not so much the overt attempts of the missionaries to impose themselves that had the greatest impact on the colonial situation but rather that most changes occurred unconsciously under hegemonic colonial influence (Comaroff and Comaroff 1991: 23–7; cf. Piot and Auslander 2001).

It is Gramsci's notion of hegemony, 'updated' as it were with ample reference to Bourdieu's theory of practice, that several anthropologists

have invoked as a conceptual means to connect local practices with the wider colonial structures of domination and exploitation (most notably Keesing 1994; Comaroff 1985; Comaroff and Comaroff 1991). Unlike the subaltern scholars, however, they focus on the extent to which subaltern consciousness is (or is not) swayed under hegemonic influence. Particular attention is given to what Gramsci called the 'practical activity' of people, of which they have 'no clear theoretical consciousness' but which 'nonetheless involves understanding the world in so far as it transforms it' (*Quaderni* 11.12).[4] It is again the Comaroffs' work that exemplifies how practice, theory and postcolonial views about resistance and hybridity can meaningfully be brought together. They use both concepts to capture the 'in-betweenness' of many indigenous and colonial activities and processes, as local people actively transformed changes that colonizers attempted to impose, emphasizing that 'processes of cultural appropriation and admixture … occurred on all sides, and on the middle ground, of the colonial encounter' (Comaroff and Comaroff 2001: 113). As argued by the Comaroffs, these processes constitute a dialectic that lies at the heart of colonial situations, because it 'altered everyone and everything involved, if not all in the same manner and measure' through 'an intricate mix of visible and invisible agency, of word and gesture, of subtle persuasion and brute force on the part of all concerned' (Comaroff and Comaroff 1997: 5, 28; see van Dommelen 1998: 28–32 for a detailed discussion).

Because of their emphasis on daily life and routine practices, such an approach inevitably touches on material culture as constituting an integral feature of the shaping of everyday experiences and practice (Bourdieu 1990: 52–65; Appadurai 1986; Miller 1987). This observation is all the more relevant to colonial situations, that are after all largely defined by the physical co-presence of colonizers and colonized (Thomas 1994; Pels 1999: 1–43). Material culture plays a critical, if rarely acknowledged, role in these 'contact zones', because it frames everyday colonial life and colonial interaction in general (Comaroff and Comaroff 1991: 274–8; cf. Pratt 1992). Material culture can also be argued to be particularly prominent in colonial situations, because of the usually strong and inevitably very visible contrasts between colonial and indigenous objects (Thomas 1991: 205–6). Another quite different reason for examining material culture in conjunction with postcolonial ideas is the insights it may give into the lives and practices of those people who are usually absent from historical documents and novels, i.e. those better known as the 'subaltern'.

POSTCOLONIAL MATTERS

Whilst colonial situations may differ substantially from other social contexts in a variety of ways, social interaction in such contexts is not intrinsically different from that in general (Pels 1997: 166–9; Prochaska 1990: 6–26). There is consequently no reason why material culture would play a less significant role in colonial situations than anywhere else. The basic insight that 'things matter' consequently applies just as much to colonial contexts as to any other situation (Miller 1998: 3).

While there is a remarkable lack of archaeological and anthropological studies that have taken up the role of material culture in relation to postcolonial theory, as discussed above, the significance of material culture in colonial contexts has nevertheless been highlighted or commented on in one way or another by a number of archaeologists, anthropologists, art historians and geographers. Most of these studies are unrelated to one another, as they consider colonial situations that differ widely in time and place, and only few refer explicitly to postcolonial theories. At the same time, they do share several broad themes that relate to postcolonial thinking in general. Some of these themes may be associated with more widely shared concerns of our time but others can arguably be ascribed to a shared interest in material culture which has led these studies to investigate the various colonial situations along similar lines.

In this final section I will discuss a range of colonial studies with a particular focus on material culture and argue why and how they demonstrate ways forward to draw on postcolonial ideas in material culture studies. By and large, three broad themes can be distinguished that relate closely to the key postcolonial ideas outlined above (p. 108) and that I suggest offer as many promising avenues for examining material culture in (post)colonial studies. These three themes concern the material dimensions of representation, the use of material culture for writing alternative histories 'from below' and the material expressions of hybridization processes. It should be noted, however, that these strands are not strictly separate and indeed do intertwine.

Material Discourse and Representation

One particularly exciting and promising avenue for new research that is being pioneered by material culture studies in colonial situations regards discourse and representation: while the literary bias of postcolonial studies is increasingly being noted and redressed by an increasing interest in other genres and media of representation such as school books, engravings and paintings (Douglas 1999; Young 2001: 390–1, 408–10), material culture constitutes another, so far largely unexplored, dimension of representation. More specifically, it is houses and settlement layouts that are being explored as related to and indicative of people's perceptions of and actual responses to colonial contexts (Chattopadhyay 1997: 1). Domestic architecture and settlement planning feature particularly prominently among the studies exploring this strand, because there are well established and profound links between how people organize their living spaces in practical terms and their views of how life should properly be lived (Miller 1994: 135–202; Robben 1989; cf. Carsten and Hugh-Jones 1995).

A powerful example is provided by Chattopadhyay's study of colonial houses in (late) nineteenth-century Calcutta, in which she demonstrates that the domestic life of the British residents in this city was organized in ways that diverged quite markedly from the

Victorian ideal as usually expressed in public (2000, 2002). General historical wisdom has it that the colonial world of British India was dominated by the strict separation of public and private spheres, in which men and women led strictly separate lives. Keeping up the distinction and literally keeping a distance from the indigenous inhabitants was deemed to be equally important, and it was the women's task to realize this in the domestic context. Novels and housekeeping guides are the key sources from which evidence is sought to support this representation (Chattopadhyay 2002: 243–6).

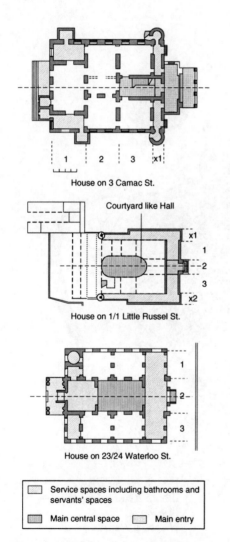

Figure 7.2 *Three examples of colonial house plans in nineteenth-century Calcutta that clearly show the central place of the grand hall*
Source: Chattopadhyay (2002: figure 1)

On closer inspection of the actual houses occupied by the colonial inhabitants of Calcutta, however, it turns out that colonial life on the ground was rather different. For a start, the layout of houses was typically very much open-plan, organized as it was around a grand central hall with multiple aligned doorways to promote ventilation (Figure 7.2). In many cases, the rooms could be closed off from the hall only by a curtain and, even if there were doors, they could not normally be locked. In most cases the hallway was used as both drawing and dining room, because it was the largest space available, and the direct access from there to the bedrooms was a common cause of complaint among colonial inhabitants of Calcutta. While separate spaces at the back of the house were usually reserved for servants, the open structure made it difficult to maintain any strict separation between residents and servants. Any such distinction was often blurred even further by the use of the veranda as an extension of the hall to enjoy a cool breeze, because it literally extended the residential spaces among the storage and working areas of the servants (Chattopadhyay 2000: 158–66).

Taking material culture into account not only provides an alternative source of evidence, demonstrating why colonial discourse analysis can be problematic in historical and anthropological terms, but also allows us to consider representations of the colonial situation in another light and effectively to contextualize them. This point can again be demonstrated with evidence from Calcutta, which was (and is) generally represented as a typical colonial city, where colonizers and colonized lived entirely separate lives in distinct 'black' and 'white' towns. The widespread occurrence of neoclassical architecture is usually highlighted to underscore the colonial nature of the city. Scrutiny of residential patterns and of the spatial organization of the city, however, suggests that these architectural features merely provide a colonialist facade, behind which colonial and indigenous lives were lived in much less strictly separate ways than publicly suggested (Chattopadhyay 2000: 154–7). What is interesting in this instance is that material culture – neoclassical architecture – was used to prop up a representation of the colonial context that was contradicted, if not challenged, by the situation on the ground.

A comparable case has been documented in Morocco under French rule (1912–56), where the colonial authorities created 'dual' or segregated cities by building modern European-style *villes nouveaux* next to and in many ways in opposition to the existing indigenous *medinas*

(Abu-Lughod 1980: 131–73). The professed motivations of Lyautey, the governor-general of the French protectorate of Morocco between 1912 and 1925, for spearheading large-scale urban transformation alternated between modernist planning concerns and the desire to preserve indigenous architecture (Rabinow 1989: 104–25). At the same time, they also served the colonial interests of the French colonial elites particularly well.

The modern capital of Rabat is a clear case in point, as the centuries-old town became literally surrounded by new French developments in less than a decade after the French take-over. As the new city plan shows, the city centre was shifted away from the indigenous old town, which was literally bypassed by the spacious new boulevards (Abu-Lughod 1980: 155–62; Figure 7.3). In addition, the obvious contrast between the latter and the narrow and dark alleys of the *medina*, as well as that between the indigenous architecture with its dark mud bricks and irregular outlines and the straight lines and brightness of the concrete tower blocks in the *ville nouvelle* actively reinforced the colonialist representation of the indigenous

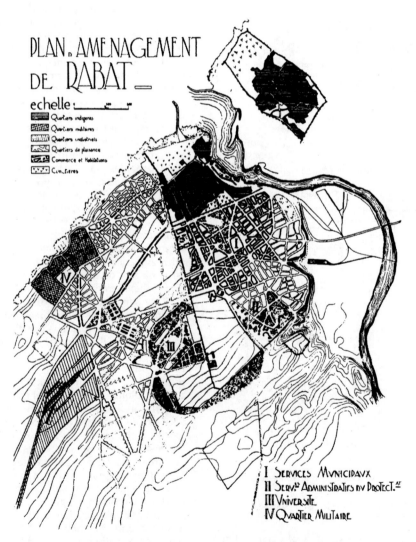

Figure 7.3   *Rabat around 1920, showing the colonial expansion of the city*
Source: Abu-Lughod (1980: figure 6)

Moroccans as backward and by implication in need of Western and modern(ist) stewardship. As underscored by the stark contrast between the modernist boulevards and the mud-brick city walls in Rabat as well as by the use of terms such as *cordon sanitaire*, referring to the open spaces between the indigenous and European quarters, colonialist representation was supported as much by material culture as by discourse.

This contrast, however, stood in obvious contradiction to developments in the urban centres of neighbouring Algeria, which had been under French rule since 1831. Those places witnessed the creation of a distinct French North African settler culture and in these hybridization processes well established distinctions between colonizers and colonized were gradually being lost (Abu-Lughod 1980: 152–5; Prochaska 1990: 206–29). These developments were actively countered by the French colonial elites, who coined for instance the disparaging term *pied noir* to refer to North African-born French settlers. The large-scale urban planning efforts can be seen in the same light as an attempt by the French colonial elites actively to use the material culture of the urban fabric to put the inhabitants of French Morocco literally in their place. Lyautey in fact admitted as much when he declared that he was keen to avoid the mistakes made in Algeria (Rabinow 1989: 288–90).

Alternative Histories

As the previous section has already demonstrated, material culture studies can unlock information about social groups who normally remain out of sight when considering colonial contexts through written documents, regardless of whether these are novels or other types of documents. As might be expected, archaeological research looms particularly large in this respect (Given 2004).

The point has most forcefully been made by the work in and around Fort Ross, which was a Russian trading and hunting settlement established in 1812 on the coast of northern California (Figure 7.4). The history and occupation of the fort itself are relatively well known from archival Russian sources and these show that close to the fort an indigenous settlement had been located, where native Alaskan workers were housed, who had been brought in by the Russian company as a labour force. Excavations in this settlement and careful analysis of the archaeological remains have, however, shown that the Alaskans were not the only inhabitants of the village. Because the evidence of the daily routines of food preparation and refuse disposal presents many affinities with indigenous Californian practices and because substantial quantities of indigenous Californian material culture like chipped-stone tools and milling stones were used in the village, it is evident that the Alaskans interacted quite closely with the local Kashaya Pomo people, forging, as has been suggested, quite intensive relationships. It seems indeed likely that Kashaya women formed households with Alaskan men (Lightfoot et al. 1998: 203–15; Lightfoot 2003: 20–4).

Farther south along the Californian coast, a string of Spanish missions had been established between 1769 and 1835 with obviously very different intentions (Figure 7.4). Conversion and acculturation ranked most prominently among the aims of the missions and explain for instance the absence of indigenous settlements like the Alaskan village at Fort Ross: although documents attest that substantial numbers of indigenous people went to live at the missions, they all stayed within the colonial compound under the close supervision of the priests. Detailed analysis of the remains of some of the mission houses suggests, however, that within this colonial setting, many indigenous practices persisted nonetheless, especially those regarding food preparation and hunting (Lightfoot 2005a, 2005b).

While the documentary evidence emphasizes the differences between the two colonial situations in coastal California, the archaeological evidence demonstrates that that is not the whole story, because it was largely shaped by the colonizers' perspective. Examination of the material culture actually in use on the ground allows us to refocus on indigenous and other groups that make up those colonial contexts. It also makes it patently clear that the colonial situations were far more complex than initially suggested and that, most of all, in both cases, despite the apparent differences, people of very different cultural and ethnic background lived together very closely without entirely losing their own traditions (Lightfoot 1995, 2005b; cf. below).

Alternative histories do not follow naturally from archaeological evidence, however, as much archaeological research is often heavily biased towards written evidence and works of art as well as guided by an elite perspective. This is most evident in the ancient Mediterranean, where colonialism played a prominent role throughout its history. In combination with the implicit identification of

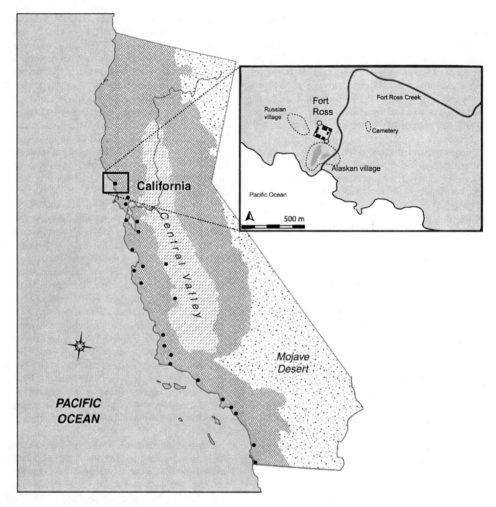

Figure 7.4   *California, showing the location of Fort Ross and the Spanish missions. The detail map shows the area around Fort Ross and the Alaskan village*
Source: After Lightfoot et al. (1998: figure 1)

Western scholars with Greek, Roman or Phoenician colonizers, the colonial situations of classical antiquity have generally been presented in terms of colonizers bringing civilization and wealth, while the indigenous inhabitants of the colonized regions have routinely been ignored (van Dommelen 1997: 305–10).

The Carthaginian colonial occupation of southern Sardinia between the fifth and third centuries BC is a case in point: documentary sources suggest that the Carthaginians controlled the southern regions of the island very closely and brought over large numbers of North African settlers to work on the great

estates they had created to secure a steady supply of grain to the city of Carthage. While the impressive archaeological remains of the colonial cities on the coast and the widespread occurrence of Punic material culture in the interior regions of Sardinia have usually been taken to confirm this picture, intensive archaeological survey and careful analysis of the distribution of archaeological remains have brought to light a far more complicated colonial situation. While both the houses built and the household items used from the late fifth century BC onwards were of identical colonial Punic types, usually produced locally, their relative numbers as well as their distribution in and relationships with the landscape differed greatly between the coastal lowlands and the interior (Figures 7.5–6). In the former areas, very high numbers of individual farmsteads were established *ex novo* in close proximity to colonial towns, whereas in the interior houses mostly clustered together into hamlets and villages (Figure 7.5). They were moreover usually built on the sites of long-established indigenous settlements that were clearly marked by monumental settlement towers called *nuraghi* (Figure 7.7). In many cases, the Punic houses simply continued earlier settlement patterns in a different guise. More important, no indications of elite-run estates have been encountered, as small-scale peasant cultivation appears to have been the dominant mode of agrarian production in the Punic period. The differences between the coastal and interior areas therefore suggest that Carthaginian settlers were dominant in the lowlands only, in proximity to the large colonial settlements, and that indigenous settlement patterns and landscape perceptions continued to be prominent in the inland hills and plains (van Dommelen 1998: 115–59, 2002).

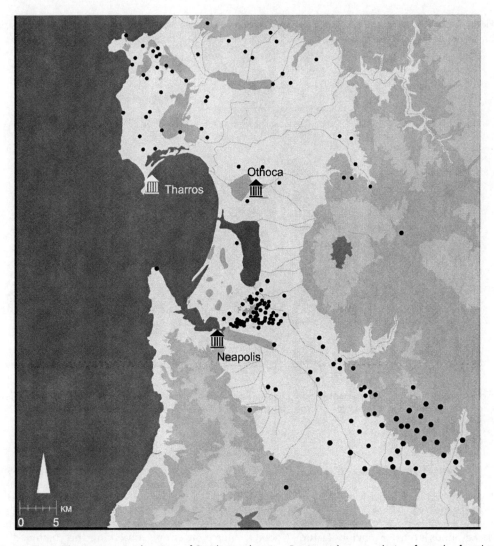

Figure 7.5   *The west central region of Sardinia, showing Punic settlements dating from the fourth to the second centuries* BC. Drawing *Peter van Dommelen*

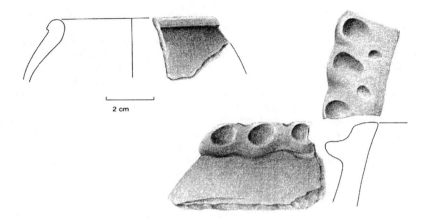

Figure 7.6   *Two typically Punic locally produced domestic items from Punic sites in the Terralba district: an amphora and a tabuna, or cooking stand.* Drawings *Riu Mannu survey*

Figure 7.7   *View of the nuraghe San Luxori (Pabillonis) immediately to the left of the medieval church dedicated to St Luxorius, with the site of the Punic–Roman settlement in the foreground.* Photo Peter van Dommelen

Hybridizing Material Culture

Hybridity ranks particularly prominently among material culture studies of colonial situations, as the combined use of objects with different backgrounds is often an obvious feature. A good example is the combination of Alaskan-style houses ('flattened cabins') and settlement layout with local Kashaya stone tools in the so-called 'Alaskan' village of Fort Ross (Lightfoot et al. 1998: 209–15; cf. above). In this very basic sense, however, hybridity has little analytical force, as simply observing the combined use of diverse objects hardly contributes to an improved understanding of colonial contexts. If, however, the concept is connected to cultural practice and hybridization is redefined as the process underlying the 'cultural mixture [which] is the effect of the practice of mixed origins' (Friedman 1997: 88), it does provide a conceptual tool that allows Bhabha's ideas about ambivalence and the 'third space' to be meaningfully related to social practice and material culture (Nederveen Pieterse 1995; Friedman 1997; van Dommelen forthcoming).

In the case of the Alaskan village at Fort Ross, it is clear that the 'mixing' of material culture was not random but on the contrary highly structured: all indigenous objects can be associated with basic domestic practices like food preparation and cleaning the house while practices like the building of the house and hunting were all carried out in line with 'Alaskan' customs. This pattern confirms documentary evidence that the village had been set up by Alaskan men from Kodiak island who had been brought in by the Russians as marine hunters and labourers and that in time these men had formed households with local indigenous women, chiefly from the Kashaya Pomo tribe. Most significant is the observation that the diet in these 'interethnic households' was truly new, as it included foodstuffs that previously had not been consumed by either Alutiiq people (venison, Californian rockfish) or Kashaya people (seal, whale: Lightfoot et al. 1998: 212). This shows that the joint households of people from different ethnic background led to the creation of new hybrid practices.

Of key importance for understanding such hybridization processes is the realization that the meanings of the objects involved could not and did not remain unchanged. While this point has been forcefully made by Nicholas Thomas for colonial situations in general (Thomas 1991; 1997a), it is a critical feature of hybridization processes, in which existing practices and objects are recombined into new ones. This point is nicely made by Thomas in his discussion of the introduction of cloth in the Pacific, and in particular by the use of bark cloth in Samoa (1999, 2002). While cloth gradually replaced traditional bark clothes throughout Polynesia in the course of the late eighteenth century, the latter has continued to be used, albeit not as regular clothing, in various parts of western Polynesia. A particularly interesting case is Samoa, where bark cloth had never been common, but where the so-called *tiputa*, a type of bark cloth typical of Tahiti, was adopted in the early to mid-nineteenth century. What

appears to have happened is that the inhabitants of Samoa regarded *tiputa* in local terms as empowering their bearers, while the missionaries promoted them as symbols of Christian modesty. The interesting point is that these missionaries were mainly Tahitan converts who had adopted an indigenous garment from their own traditions and adapted it to their new needs and beliefs. In the Samoan context, the *tiputa* were yet again given a new meaning and could thus coexist with the earlier introduced cloth (Thomas 2002: 196).

Similar consecutive reinterpretations and reconfigurations of the meaning of material culture have been noted in Punic Sardinia. In the interior of the island, a series of shrines have been recorded that were apparently dedicated to the Greek goddess Demeter. All documented cases reused a previously abandoned *nuraghe*. Careful excavation and detailed analysis of the finds associated with the Demeter shrine in *nuraghe* Genna Maria of Villanovaforru have painted a complex picture. The objects offered or otherwise used in the cult leave little doubt that the rituals performed in the shrine from the early fourth century BC onwards were not dedicated to the well known Greek goddess Demeter. There are first of all items such as incense burners that refer to Punic ritual traditions and show that the shrine represented a colonial introduction. This is supported by the fact that Demeter was adopted in the Punic pantheon in the early fourth century BC and the ensuing spread of a Punic version of her cult. The ritual assemblage is, however, dominated by oil lamps, which were alien to Punic rituals but which are known from a range of contemporary Sardinian sanctuaries, as well as several pre-colonial Iron Age ones. Interestingly, the many hundreds of oil lamps found are practically all Greek and later Roman imports from the Italian mainland but include a few hand-made ones resembling indigenous types (Figure 7.8).

It is obvious that, amid this multitude of influences and imports, no single 'original' meaning could have been kept intact and that the cult that was practised at Genna Maria represented a new 'invention' drawing on a range of locally available materials which were reinterpreted in the process. As underscored by the fact that the ritual of lighting or otherwise offering a lamp was important but that the type of lamp that was used was of no significance and that even incense burners may have been used in this role, the original provenance and connotations of the objects were superseded by the new meanings constructed in the

Figure 7.8 *An oil lamp, incense burner and female portrait (of Demeter?) from the Punic shrine in the* nuraghe *Genna Maria*
Source: Lilliu et al. (1993: figure 1)

new colonial and ritual setting (van Dommelen 1997: 314–16, 1998: 153–4, forthcoming).

CONCLUSION: COLONIAL MATTERS AND POSTCOLONIAL THEORY

While there may have been little interaction so far between postcolonial studies and material culture studies, I hope to have demonstrated that there surely is ample scope for joining up these fields. On the one hand, from a postcolonial perspective, paying more attention to material culture is important in two respects: in the first place, because it will help redress the literary bias in studying colonial situations while nicely complementing the present trend to examine colonial practices. And second, because it expands the range of the media in which colonial situations are represented beyond texts and illustrations. On the other hand, from the point of view of material culture studies, postcolonial theory offers the potential to explore the field of colonialism, while also providing innovative conceptual tools to look into globalization.

As the preceding case studies may have demonstrated, hybridization in particular can already be seen to emerge as a prominent theme in material culture studies, in both colonial situations and contemporary contexts of globalization. Nicholas Thomas's work on the use and perception of material culture in colonial contexts and on colonialism more generally is clearly leading this way (Thomas 1991, 1994, 1997b). At the same time, a distinct field of archaeological colonial studies is emerging, in which the potential to construct alternative histories is realized in various exciting ways (Rowlands 1998; Hall 2000; Given 2004). Representation is finally the third key theme, in which anthropology and archaeology have begun fruitfully to explore how material culture can expand and add to the conventional literary bias of postcolonial studies (Thomas 1997b).

NOTES

1 The two journals are *Interventions: International Journal of Postcolonial Studies* and *Post-colonial studies: Culture, Politics, Economy* (both

published since 1999 and 1998 respectively). In addition, the Web-based journal *Jouvert: Journal of Postcolonial Studies* was launched in 1997 from North Carolina state University (http://social.chass.ncsu.edu/jouvert/). Among the many handbooks, the most frequently referenced ones are Ashcroft et al. (1989, 1995), Barker et al. (1994), Chambers and Curti (1996), Loomba (1998), Moore-Gilbert (1997), Quayson (2000) and Young (1995, 2001, 2003).

2 The journal *Comparative Studies in Society and History* is particularly important in publishing such work.

3 While there has been little reflection on the colonial roots of historical archaeology, which is the other field most explicitly engaged with colonialism, there has been increasing interest in the archaeology of slavery (cf. below).

4 English translation by Hoare and Nowell Smith (1971: 333); Italian edition, Gerratana (1975: 1385).

REFERENCES

Abu-Lughod, J. (1980) *Rabat: Urban Apartheid in Morocco*. Princeton: Princeton University Press.

Adas, M. (1991) 'South Asian resistance in comparative perspective', in D. Haynes and G. Prakash (eds), *Contesting Power: Resistance and Everyday Social Relations in South Asia*. Berkeley, CA: University of California Press, pp. 290–305.

Amin, S. (1976) *Unequal Development: an Essay on the Social Formations of Peripheral Capitalism*. Marxist Theory and Contemporary Capitalism. Hassocks: Harvester Press.

Appadurai, A. (1986) 'Introduction: commodities and the politics of value', in A. Appadurai (ed.), *The Social Life of Things*. Cambridge: Cambridge University Press, pp. 3–63.

Appiah, K. (1991) 'Is the post- in postmodernism the post- in postcolonial?' *Critical Inquiry*, 17: 336–57.

Arnold, D. (1984) 'Gramsci and peasant subalternity in India', *Journal of Peasant Studies*, 11: 155–77.

Asad, T., ed. (1973) *Anthropology & the Colonial Encounter*. London: Ithaca Press.

Asad, T. (1991) 'From the history of colonial anthropology to the anthropology of Western hegemony', in G. Stocking (ed.), *Colonial Situations: Essays on the Contextualization of Ethnographic Knowledge*. History of Anthropology 7. Madison: University of Wisconsin Press, pp. 314–24.

Ashcroft, B., Griffiths, G. and Tiffin, H. (1989) *The Empire writes back: Theory and Practice in Postcolonial Literature*. London: Routledge.

Ashcroft, B., Griffiths, G. and Tiffin, H. (1995) *The Post-colonial Studies Reader*. London: Routledge.

Barker, F., Hulme, P. and Iversen, M. (1994) 'Introduction', in F. Barker, P. Hulme and M. Iversen (eds), *Colonial Discourse/Postcolonial Theory*. Manchester: Manchester University Press, pp. 1–23.

Bénabou, M. (1976) *La Résistance africaine à la romanisation*. Paris: Maspéro.

Bhabha, H. (1989) 'The commitment to theory', in *The Location of Culture*. London: Routledge, pp. 19–39.

Bourdieu, P. (1990) *The Logic of Practice*. Cambridge: Polity Press.

Carsten, J. and Hugh-Jones, S., eds (1995) *About the House: Lévi-Strauss and Beyond*. Cambridge: Cambridge University Press.

Chambers, I. and Curti, L., eds (1996) *The Postcolonial Question: Common Skies and Divided Horizons*. London and New York: Routledge.

Chattopadhyay, S. (1997) 'A critical history of architecture in a post-colonial world: a view from Indian history', *Architronic: the Electronic Journal of Architecture*, 6 (1): http://architronic.saed.kent.edu.

Chattopadhyay, S. (2000) 'Blurring boundaries: the limits of the "white town" in colonial Calcutta', *Journal of the Society of Architectural Historians*, 59 (2): 154–79.

Chattopadhyay, S. (2002) '"Goods, chattels and sundry items": constructing nineteenth-century Anglo-Indian domestic life', *Journal of Material Culture*, 7 (3): 243–71.

Chaturvedi, V. (2000) 'Introduction', in V. Chaturvedi (ed.), *Mapping Subaltern Studies and the Postcolonial*. Mapping series. London: Verso, pp. vii–xix.

Cohn, B. (1990) *An Anthropologist among the Historians and other Essays*. Oxford India Paperbacks. Dehli: Oxford University Press.

Comaroff, J. (1985) *Body of Power, Spirit of Resistance: the Culture and History of an African People*. Chicago: University of Chicago Press.

Comaroff, J. and Comaroff, J. (1991) *Of Revelation and Revolution* I, *Christianity, Colonialism and Consciousness in South Africa*. Chicago and London: University of Chicago Press.

Comaroff, J. and Comaroff, J. (1997) *Of Revelation and Revolution* II, *The Dialectics of Modernity on a South African Frontier*. Chicago and London: University of Chicago Press.

Comaroff, J. and Comaroff, J. (2001) 'Revelations upon Revelation', *Interventions: International Journal of Postcolonial Studies*, 3 (1): 100–26.

Dondin-Payre, M. (1991) 'L'*Exercitus Africae*, inspiration de l'armée française: *ense et aratro*', *Antiquités africaines*, 27: 141–9.

Douglas, B. (1999) 'Art as ethno-historical text: science, representation and indigenous presence in eighteenth and nineteenth-century oceanic voyage literature', in N. Thomas and D. Losche (eds),

Double Vision: Art Histories and Colonial Histories in the Pacific. Cambridge: Cambridge University Press, pp. 65–99.

Eriksen, T. (2003) 'Introduction', in T. Eriksen (ed.), *Globalisation: Studies in Anthropology.* Anthropology, Culture and Society. London: Pluto Press, pp. 1–17.

Fabian, J. (1983) *Time and the Other: how Anthropology makes its Object.* New York: Columbia University Press.

Fanon, F. (1967) *The Wretched of the Earth.* Penguin Twentieth-century Classics. Harmondsworth: Penguin Books.

Foucault, M. (1979) *Discipline and Punish: the Birth of the Prison.* Harmondsworth: Peregrine.

Frank, A. (1967) *Capitalism and Underdevelopment in Latin America: Historical Studies of Chile and Brazil.* New York: Monthly Review Press.

Friedman, J. (1997) 'Global crises, the struggle for cultural identity and intellectual porkbarrelling: cosmopolitans versus locals, ethnics and nationals in an era of dehegemonisation', in P. Werbner and T. Modood (eds), *Debating Cultural Hybridity: Multi-cultural Identities and the Politics of Anti-racism.* Postcolonial Encounters. London: Zed Books, pp. 70–89.

Gerratana, V., ed. (1975) *Antonio Gramsci, Quaderni del carcere: Edizione critica dell'Istituto Gramsci.* Turin: Einaudi.

Given, M. (2004) *The Archaeology of the Colonized.* London: Routledge.

Gosden, C. (1999) *Anthropology and Archaeology: a Changing Relationship.* London and New York: Routledge.

Gosden, C. (2001) 'Postcolonial archaeology: issues of culture, identity, and knowledge', in I. Hodder (ed.), *Archaeological Theory Today.* Cambridge: Polity Press, pp. 241–61.

Gosden, C. (2004) *Archaeology and Colonialism: Cultural Contact from 5000 BC to the Present.* Cambridge: Cambridge University Press.

Guha, R. (1982a) 'On some aspects of the historiography of colonial India', in R. Guha (ed.), *Writings on South Asian History and Society.* Subaltern Studies 1. Dehli: Oxford University Press, pp. 1–8.

Guha, R., ed. (1982b) *Subaltern Studies I. Writings on South Asian History and Society.* Oxford India Paperbacks. Dehli: Oxford University Press.

Hall, M. (2000) *Archaeology and the Modern World: Colonial Transcripts in South Africa and the Chesapeake.* London: Routledge.

Haynes, D. and Prakash, G. (1991) 'Introduction: the entanglement of power and resistance', in D. Haynes and G. Prakash (eds), *Contesting Power: Resistance and Everyday Social Relations in South Asia.* Berkeley, CA: University of California Press, pp. 1–22.

Hingley, R. (2000) *Roman Officers and English Gentlemen: the Imperial Origins of Roman Archaeology.* London: Routledge.

Hoare, Q. and Nowell Smith, G., eds (1971) *Selection from the Prison Notebooks of Antonio Gramsci.* London: Lawrence & Wishart.

Jacobs, J. (1996) *Edge of Empire: Postcolonialism and the City.* London: Routledge.

Keesing, R. (1994) 'Colonial and counter-colonial discourse in Melanesia', *Critique of Anthropology,* 14: 41–58.

Laroui, A. (1970) *L'Histoire du Maghreb: un essai de synthèse.* Paris: Maspéro.

Laroui, A. (1977) *The History of the Maghreb: an Interpretive Essay.* Princeton, NJ: Princeton University Press.

Lightfoot, K. (1995) 'Culture contact studies: redefining the relationship between prehistoric and historical archaeology', *American Antiquity,* 60 (2): 199–217.

Lightfoot, K. (2003) 'Russian colonization: the implications of mercantile colonial practices in the North Pacific', *Historical Archaeology,* 37 (4): 14–28.

Lightfoot, K. (2004) *Indians, Missionaries, and Merchants: the Legacy of Colonial Encounters on the California Frontiers.* Berkeley, CA: University of California Press.

Lightfoot, K. (2005) 'The archaeology of colonial encounters: comparative perspectives', in G. Stein (ed.), *The Archaeology of Colonies in Cross-cultural Perspective.* School of American Research Advanced Research Seminar Series. Sante Fe, NM: School of American Research.

Lightfoot, K., Martinez, A. and Schiff, A. (1998) 'Daily practice and material culture in pluralistic social settings: an archaeological study of culture change and persistence from Fort Ross, California', *American Antiquity,* 63 (2): 199–222.

Lilliu, C. et al. (1993) *Genna Maria II, 1: il deposito votivo del mastio e del cortile.* Cagliari: Stef.

Loomba, A. (1998) *Colonialism/postcolonialism.* The New Critical Idiom. London and New York: Routledge.

Lyons, C. and Papadopoulos, J., eds (2002) *The Archaeology of Colonialism.* Issues and Debates. Los Angeles: Getty Research Institute.

Mattingly, D. (1996) 'From one imperialism to another: imperialism in the Maghreb', in J. Webster and N. Cooper (eds), *Roman Imperialism: Post-colonial Perspectives.* Leicester Archaeology Monographs 3. Leicester: Leicester University Press, pp. 49–69.

Mattingly, D. (1997) 'Dialogues of power and experience in the Roman Empire', in D. Mattingly (ed.), *Dialogues in Roman imperialism: Power, Discourse, and Discrepant Experience in the Roman Empire.* Journal of Roman archaeology Supplementary Series 23. Portsmouth, RI: Journal of Roman Archaeology, pp. 7–24.

Mignolo, W. (2000) *Local Histories/Global Designs: Coloniality, Subaltern Knowledges, and Border Thinking.*

Princeton Studies in Culture/Power/History. Princeton, NJ: Princeton University Press.

Miller, D. (1987) *Material Culture and Mass Consumption.* Oxford: Blackwell.

Miller, D. (1994) *Modernity: an Ethnographic Approach: Dualism and Mass Consumption in Trinidad.* Oxford and Providence, RI: Berg.

Miller, D. (1998) 'Why some things matter', in D. Miller (ed.), *Material Culture: Why Some Things Matter.* Consumption and Space. London: UCL Press, pp. 3–21.

Mitchell, T. (1990) 'Everyday metaphors of power', *Theory and Society*, 19: 545–77.

Moore-Gilbert, B. (1997) *Postcolonial Theory: Contexts, Practices, Policies.* London: Verso.

Nederveen Pieterse, J. (1995) 'Globalization as hybridization', in M. Featherstone, L. Lash and R. Robertson (eds), *Global Modernities.* Theory, Culture and Society. London: Sage, pp. 45–68.

O'Hanlon, R. (1988) 'Recovering the subject: Subaltern Studies and histories of resistance in colonial South Asia', *Modern Asian Studies*, 22: 189–224.

Parry, B. (1987) 'Problems in current theories of colonial discourse', *Oxford Literary Review*, 9 (1–2): 27–58.

Parry, B. (2002) 'Directions and dead ends in postcolonial studies', in D. Goldberg and A. Quayson (eds), *Relocating Postcolonialism.* Oxford: Blackwell, pp. 66–81.

Pels, P. (1997) 'The anthropology of colonialism: culture, history, and the emergence of Western governmentality', *Annual Review of Anthropology*, 26: 163–83.

Pels, P. (1999) *A Politics of Presence: Contacts between Missionaries and Waluguru in late colonial Tanganyika.* History and Anthropology 22. Amsterdam: Harwood Academic.

Pels, P. and Salemink, O., eds (1999) *Colonial Subjects: Essays on the Practical History of Anthropology.* Ann Arbor, MI: University of Michigan Press.

Piot, C. and Auslander, M. (2001) 'On *Of Revelation and Revolution*', *Interventions: International Journal of Postcolonial Studies*, 3 (1): 1–4.

Prakash, G. (1995) 'Introduction: after colonialism', in G. Prakash (ed.), *After Colonialism: Imperial Histories and Postcolonial Displacements.* Princeton Studies in Culture/Power/History. Princeton, NJ: Princeton University Press, pp. 3–17.

Pratt, M.-L. (1992) *Imperial Eyes: Travel Writing and Transculturation.* New York and London: Routledge.

Prochaska, D. (1990) *Making Algeria French. Colonialism in Bône, 1870–1920.* Cambridge: Cambridge University Press.

Quayson, A. (2000) *Postcolonialism: Theory, Practice or Process?* Oxford: Polity Press.

Rabinow, P. (1989) *French Modern: Norms and Forms of the Social Environment.* Chicago: University of Chicago Press.

Robben, A. (1989) 'Habits of the home: spatial hegemony and the structuration of house and society in Brazil', *American Anthropologist*, 91 (3): 570–88.

Rowlands, M. (1984) 'Conceptualizing the European Bronze and early Iron Age', in J. Bintliff (ed.), *European Social Evolution: Archaeological Perspectives.* Bradford: University of Bradford, pp. 147–56.

Rowlands, M. (1986) 'Modernist fantasies in prehistory?' *Man*, 21: 745–6.

Rowlands, M. (1998) 'The archaeology of colonialism', in K. Kristiansen and M. Rowlands (eds), *Social Transformations in Archaeology: global and Local Perspectives.* Material Cultures: Interdisciplinary Studies in the Material Construction of Social Worlds, pp. 327–3. London: Routledge.

Said, E. (1978) *Orientalism.* New York: Vintage Books.

Said, E. (1993) *Culture and Imperialism.* London: Chatto & Windus.

Schmidt, P. and Patterson, T. (1995) 'Introduction: from constructing to making alternative histories', in P. Schmidt and T. Patterson (eds), *Making Alternative Histories: the Practice of Archaeology and History in non-Western Settings*, pp. 1–24. Santa Fe, NM: School of American Research Press.

Scott, J. (1985) *Weapons of the Weak: Everyday Forms of Peasant resistance.* New Haven, CT: Yale University Press.

Spivak, G. (1985/1999) 'Can the subaltern speak? Speculations on widow sacrifice', *Wedge*, 7–8: 120–30; revised version in G. Spivak, *A Critique of Postcolonial Reason*, Cambridge, MA: Harvard University Press.

Stocking, G., ed. (1991) *Colonial Situations: Essays on the Contextualization of Ethnographic Knowledge.* History of Anthropology 7. Madison, WI: University of Wisconsin Press.

Thomas, N. (1991) *Entangled Objects: Exchange, Colonialism and Material Culture in the Pacific.* Cambridge, MA: Harvard University Press.

Thomas, N. (1994) *Colonialism's Culture: Anthropology, Travel and Government.* Cambridge: Polity Press.

Thomas, N. (1997a) 'The inversion of tradition', in *In Oceania: Vision, Artifacts, Histories.* Durham, NC and London: Duke University Press, pp. 186–209.

Thomas, N. (1997b) *In Oceania: Vision, Artifacts, Histories.* Durham, NC and London: Duke University Press.

Thomas, N. (1999) 'The case of the misplaced ponchos: speculations concerning the history of cloth in Polynesia', *Journal of Material Culture*, 4 (1): 5–20.

Thomas, N. (2002) 'Colonizing cloth: interpreting the material culture of nineteenth-century Oceania', in C. Lyons and J. Papadopoulos (eds), *The Archaeology of Colonialism.* Issues & Debates. Los Angeles: Getty Research Institute, pp. 182–98.

Trigger, B. (1984) 'Alternative archaeologies: nationalist, colonialist, imperialist', *Man*, 19: 355–70.

Turner, L. (1995) 'Consuming colonialism', *Critique of Anthropology*, 15: 203–12.

Van Dommelen, P. (1997) 'Colonial constructs: colonialism and archaeology in the Mediterranean', *World Archaeology*, 28 (3): 305–23.

Van Dommelen, P. (1998) *On Colonial Grounds: a Comparative Study of Colonialism and Rural Settlement in first Millennium BC west central Sardinia.* Archaeological Studies Leiden University 2. Leiden: Faculty of Archaeology, Leiden University.

Van Dommelen, P. (2002) 'Ambiguous matters: colonialism and local identities in Punic Sardinia', in C. Lyons and J. Papadopoulos (eds), *The Archaeology of Colonialism.* Issues & Debates. Los Angeles: Getty Research Institute, pp. 121–47.

Van Dommelen, P. (forthcoming) 'The orientalising phenomenon: hybridity and material culture in the western Mediterranean', in C. Riva and N. Vella (eds), *Approaching Orientalisation.* Monographs in Mediterranean Archaeology. London: Equinox.

Wallerstein, I. (1974) *The Modern world System.* New York: Academic Press.

Washbrook, D. (1999) 'Orients and Occidents: colonial discourse theory and the historiography of the British Empire', in R. Winks (ed.), *Historiography.* Oxford History of the British Empire 5. Oxford: Oxford University Press, pp. 596–611.

Webster, J. (1996) 'Roman imperialism and the post-imperial age', in J. Webster and N. Cooper (eds), *Roman Imperialism: Post-colonial Perspectives.* Leicester Archaeology Monographs 3. Leicester: Leicester University Press, pp. 1–18.

Werbner, P. and Modood, T., eds (1997) *Debating Cultural Hybridity: Multi-cultural Identities and the Politics of Anti-racism.* Postcolonial Encounters. London: Zed Books.

Wolf, E. (1982) *Europe and the People without History.* Berkeley, CA: University of California Press.

Young, R. (1990) *White Mythologies: Writing History and the West.* London and New York: Routledge.

Young, R. (1995) *Colonial Desire: Hybridity in Theory, Culture and Race.* London and New York: Routledge.

Young, R. (1998) 'Ideologies of the postcolonial', *Interventions: International Journal of Postcolonial Studies*, 1 (1): 4–8.

Young, R. (2001) *Postcolonialism: An Historical Introduction.* Oxford: Blackwell.

Young, R. (2003) *Postcolonialism: A very short Introduction.* Very Short Introductions 98. Oxford: Oxford University Press.

ACKNOWLEDGEMENTS

I would like to thank the editors for inviting me to contribute this chapter to this volume and Chris Tilley in particular for his helpful comments.

PART II

THE BODY, MATERIALITY AND THE SENSES

How is a place sensed? Are the limits of my language the limits of my world? What sort of agency can be ascribed to food or colour? Should the visual be seen as a primary mode of communication, relatively free of language? Can anthropology expand on the pleasures of eating while acknowledging its relationship to privation, inequality and exploitation? In what ways are color relationships used to animate things and produce a sense of movement? Does moving as part of a crowd in New York, Rome or Shanghai, or alone in dwellings of different architectural orderings, constitute the same kind of experience? How do the micro-technologies of the self tacit in material practices of, say, 'wrapping' or 'containment' contribute to governmentality and state formation in particular places and times? And might analysing commodities as bundles of sensual relations help explain the often innovative appropriations of foreign products in contexts of 'cross-cultural' consumption?

The chapters in this part collectively stage a theory of materiality that, at one and the same time, is a theory of the embodied subject and the multiple, concomitant ways of sensing, feeling, knowing, experiencing and performing or the sensuous particularities of corporeal being and acting, broadly conceived. To think the body here is not to think *the body* but, rather, to engage embodiment or the body in all its sensuous and visceral specificities commingled, entangled and enmeshed, acting upon and being acted upon in material life worlds of differing character and composition. Inevitably, these approaches to embodiment analytically place the body relationally, as itself often internally hierarchicized and divided up into privileged versus 'subaltern' parts and faculties, and as hyphenated with respect to wider space-time, material and agentive co-ordinates: the subject-acting-with-its-incorporated objects (Warnier); the agency of

things-as-material caught in intimate, often tacit, collaborative 'craftwork' with embodied subjects (Farquhar), as put into play in variously coloured contexts and mobile within the ebb and flow of colour (Young); active within an ontology of materiality linking humans and non-humans through visceral forms of identification and embodied reciprocities (Pinney); or 'emplaced' as distinct from (though inclusive of) their embodiment through the sensuous reaction of persons to place in association with material artifacts in multisensorial settings (Howes).

Such artefacts, in turn, may serve as 'extensions of the senses', for instance through body decorations like the ear and lip discs worn by Suyà Amerindians that project prioritized body parts linked with valued faculties of speech and hearing outwards or virtually extend an embodied subject's space-time as in the desired transformation in the *kula* ceremonial exchange system from being a 'face with no name', admired for one's visual and olfactory presence in face-to-face transactions, to 'a name with no face' when a man's name circulates apart from his body through the medium of the named kula shells that have passed through his possession, thereby building his fame in tandem with that of shells (Howes; Munn 1986). The material complexes, networks, bodily conducts and sensescapes extending out from and accommodating the exchanges among embodied subjects and sensuous things described here are invariably contingent, unstable and dynamic, and not necessarily or exclusively human-centred or derived.

A veritable 'sensual revolution' (Howes), these newly conceptualized fields of multisensoriality, interconnectedness and revalued assessments of agency propose renewed forms of engagement with – perhaps even a re-enchantment of – the *irreducible materiality* of things (Pietz 1985) and, by extension, their libidinous, affective, visceral, aesthetic, expressive modalities. In different ways, the authors here take distance from 'the totemization of language as a godlike agency in Western culture' (Stafford, in Pinney) and linguistic-derived theoretical models like semiology and structuralism. For some, this means attending to what 'discourse is unable to say' (Carroll in Pinney), to assumed as opposed to articulated forms of knowledge (Farquhar), or, somewhat differently, a *rapprochement* with the cognitive and neuro-sciences (Warnier). Relatedly, the dematerializations of colour science, the iconological 'codes' of art history, reduction to 'social context', culture, history or other explanatory frames, the alleged transcendence of 'meaning' and, more generally, theoretical appeals that evacuate embodied subjects and material artefacts of their sensuous particularities come in for sustained criticism.

To be sensuous is to suffer, in the sense of being acted upon (Marx, in Pietz 1993: 144). The pervasive logocentrism, ocularcentrism and appeals to pure 'presence' in the theoretical models critiqued here attest not only to the dominant epistemological assumptions of Euro-american academia during the greater part of the last century but, much more widely, to the management and negotiation of 'suffering' in historically situated ways. Attempts to contain the expressive potentiality of colour (Young), the fear of touch (Howes) and the anxiety provoked by images (Pinney) describe a world long beholden to 'the impossible project of the transcendental subject, a subject constituted by no place, no object' and, by extension, a corresponding suspicion or even fear of the power exerted by tangible, sensuous things (Stallybrass 1998: 186). While gender is touched upon only in passing in some of the chapters here, the gendered character of this transcendental subject, according to which 'woman' is always already closer to sensuous nature and thus, by definition, less transcendental, is worth noting. If the fear of the sensuous is also a fear of the loss of self then the imagination of this loss is a gender-inflected one (Staten 1995).

Whether implicitly or more explicitly the authors in this part displace the autonomous subject of liberal secular theory. Such displacement follows from an emphasis on embodiment described by a cluster of expressive potentialities reminiscent of the original Greek term for aesthetics – *aesthikos* or 'perceptive by feeling' (Buck-Morss, in Pinney) – as itself part of a wider semantic circuit comprising the word for senses, *aesthísis*; emotion-feeling and

aesthetics, respectively *aésthima* and *aesthitikí*; *aesthesis* or action/power through the medium of the senses, and the media or *semia* (tracks, marks) by which one senses (Seremetakis 1994: 5). It should be evident that the approaches to materiality and embodiment offered here dramatically refigure or efface such conventionally posed distinctions as mind and body, voluntary and involuntary, the affective and the aesthetic, passivity and action. Potentially, they also open up embodied subjects to the wider calculus of human sufferings and joys understood, once again, within the minute material and sensory transactions within which such subjects not only act but are acted upon in myriad ways.

But what constellation of agency or agencies is at work here? Farquhar's micro-histories of the 'cultivation of life' by contemporary Beijing residents are finely textured accounts that intimate how the crafting of a material form of life interweaves different varieties of agency. Involving the taste, pleasures and embodied knowledge of foods, the material qualities of foodstuffs, correlated talk about food, and notions of health, comfort, virtue, thrift, gender and friendship, such a palimpsest, in turn, is shot through with the contingencies and struggles of personal biography and the macro-histories of widespread famine and deprivation as mediated by multiple movements of desire, memory and pain. Relevant here is also the notion of 'corpothetics', or embodied, corporeal aesthetics as opposed to 'disinterested' representation which overcerebralizes and overtextualizes (Pinney 2004: 8) or, similarly, Poole's 'gut aesthetics', sedimented and aroused by photographs, in her particular example, in addition to the pleasures these provide. More generally, 'gut aesthetics' speaks to the appearance of race as something that historically came to be *seen* (Poole 1997) but also, much as class, to be sensed and even smelled in so far as class, race, gender and other power-inflected distinctions are commonly sutured to differently valued physiological sensations (Howes; Spyer 2000: 57).

At issue here is by no means simply the embodied beholder or subject. In this regard, the current resurgence of interest in Goya animated by the sense that in the post-1989 global proliferation of war and violence he 'is part of our own time' is revealing (Hughes 2003: 10; cf. Castelli 2004). Depriving the viewer of the possibility of an 'estranged beholding gaze' (Petrovskaya, in Buck-Morss 1994: 56) – or, in other words, the cinematic/televisual gaze through which the vast majority of people in

Euro-america experience violence – *Los desastres de la guerra* exert an expressive force characteristic of Lyotard's energetic domain of the 'figure' as opposed to the closed, knowable domain of 'discourse' (Lyotard, in Pinney). In this capacity, the copperplates act 'as a node of alterity where intensities are felt rather than communicated' (Pinney), an effect that is not diminished by the testimonial *Yo lo vi*, 'I saw it,' scratched by Goya under them (Hughes 2003: 5).

In his book-length evaluation of *Formations of the Secular* Talal Asad criticizes the secular assumption that to suffer is to lack agency and be in a passive state – to be an object rather than a subject. Thus, he takes issue with Scary's secular characterization of the body in pain as inscrutable, resistant to language and thought, and therefore both private and universal. Instead, he proposes that while pain-in-itself does not constitute 'language' in any conventional sense it may be subject to various kinds of structuration which while not necessarily bestowing 'meaning' on pain offer ways of engaging it (Asad 2003: 79–80). Being musical and mathematical, the examples he provides of such structuration are thus not 'language' but rather other modalities of structuring experience. Forms of 'agentive pain', suffering like fear or terror, or the experience of violent pain-pleasure are sought-after forms of agency within different religious traditions and subcultures (Asad 2003: 67–124). The sensual dimensions of late medieval affective Christian piety and new mnemonic techniques of pious contemplation harnessed to visual and textual depictions of the bloody body of 'The Man of Sorrows' and the bloody signs of the Passion – the switch, lance, crown of thorns, wounds – entailed a work of the 'imagination' that is a far cry from its modern connotations of fantasy and personal creativity (Groebner 2004: 95). When Luther heard the word 'Christ', he wrote, 'the picture of a man hanging on the Cross is sketched in my heart', underscoring not only the not wholly voluntary imaginative work involved here but also the interpenetration of an 'elaborate schooling of perception and training of the emotions on the one side and sheer terror on the other' (2004: 97).

Yet if the Middle Ages are conventionally construed as a time when life was nasty, brutish and short, it would be a mistake not to relativize the alterity of such practices. It might be more fruitful, following Pinney, to approach these and other alternative structurings of the senses, affect and religiosity less as essentialized different expressive modalities than as latent possibilities in all cultural production.

In our own times such 'subaltern' modalities exist at the margins of normative practice – as embodied reciprocity 'among adolescents the world over who desire portraits of sport and music celebrities characterized by a high degree of frontality' (Pinney); in the sought-after violent pain-pleasure of S/M; or in the sensory shut-down, an agentive 'playing dead', *dystoposthesia* or 'incompatibility of bodies to the space they inhabit' (Fletcher, in Howes) identified as a strategy among homeless people in Boston (Howes; cf. Buchli, Chapter 16).

Future research will undoubtedly continue to flesh out and complicate our understanding of forms of situated embodiment as well as, where appropriate, the often concomitant processes of 'ensoulment' (Asad 2003: 89; Hirschkind 2006; Mahmood 2005). Equally important, gender and queer studies, critical disability studies, and science and technology studies challenge and unsettle in different ways any notion of the normatively defined body understood in all its wholeness and health and, by extension, the related hegemonically inscribed forms of corporeal being and agency. It is crucial, moreover, to be sensitive and attuned to how different traditions and subcultures home in on the specificities of particular senses, body parts and capabilities while ignoring others and how, in turn, the relation between elaboration and attention, on the one hand, and depreciation and/or inattention, on the other, are inflected not only by the varying predispositions of time and place but, crucially, by the workings of power relations. Examples of such heightened attention or, in some instances, even fetishism of specific body parts include the bloody attacks on people's noses as a sexually charged form of defacement in the late Middle Ages (Groebner 2004: 67–86), the unpaired gloves and gloved hands of Renaissance portraiture, enabling of a 'fetishizing' movement (Derrida, in Stallybrass and Jones 2001: 120), the missionary and medical focus on foot binding in nineteenth-century China (Zito n.d., 2005), the children's faces proliferating in pro-peace public service announcements and documentaries in post-Suharto Indonesia (Spyer n.d.), or the insistence in consumer culture, especially for women, on breaking down and scrutinizing all body parts (Fraser and Greco 2005: 27).

Scholars are also refining analytically their approach to the 'scapes', 'fields' or 'economies' associated with embodiment, materiality, and the senses – by attending, for instance, to the marked differences in, say, the practice and evaluation of hearing in even such closely related, neighbouring 'oral/aural societies' as the Amerindian Suyá and Kayapo (Howes), the subtle differentiations in 'ethical audition' and thus, also, reception within the same tradition – to wit, cassette-tape sermon listening versus Quranic recitation in contemporary Egypt (Hirschkind 2006), the layered and diversified embodiments of visuality from the reciprocity of embodied vision characteristic of Hindu *darshan* (Pinney; cf. Spyer 2001) to a Benjamin-inspired focus on the tactility of visual perception and the somatic impact of images (Buck-Morss 1989; Taussig 1993), to name only a few. Besides the refinement and fleshing-out of sound and visuality along these lines, tactility (Pels 1998, 1999) and, more generally, the relation between distance and proximity, the virtual and the sensuous are understudied directions for future research – as implied, for instance, by the concluding example in Diana Young's chapter.

Analytically at stake in these examples, as in the chapters of this part, are less 'types' of visual, auditory, colour, tactical, etc., perception and experience (Pinney) than the complex movements and propensities characteristic of material life-worlds from their most intimate, sensuous particularities to their contingent location within larger global processes and networks. What they intimate is a refiguring of the social and of social experience such that, at its most radical, the theory of materiality staged here offers a renewed understanding of what social theory can be. And this may involve anything from a rejection of such well worn categories as class, gender and race as too crude to convey the intricacies of agentive, sensuously informed social differentiation, or a recasting of such things as governmentality or the workings of late capitalist or non-capitalist formations once the agencies through which these operate are no longer assumed to be exclusively human – not even in such an oblique manner as Marx's commodity fetishism.

Patricia Spyer

REFERENCES

Asad, Talal (2003) *Formations of the Secular: Christianity, Islam, Modernity*. Stanford, CA: Stanford University Press.

Buck-Morss, Susan (1989) *The Dialectics of Seeing: Walter Benjamin and the Arcades Project*. Cambridge, MA: MIT Press.

Buck-Morss, Susan (1994) 'The cinema screen as prosthesis of perception: a historical account', in C. Nadia Seremetakis (ed.), *The Senses Still: Perception and Memory as Material Culture in Modernity*. Chicago: University of Chicago Press.

Castelli, Elizabeth A. (2004) 'Introduction', in Elizabeth A. Castelli (ed.), *Reverberations: On Violence*. The Scholar and Feminist Online, 2 (2): 1–4.

Fraser, Mariam and Greco, Monica (eds) (2005) 'Introduction', in *The Body: a Reader*. London: Routledge.

Groebner, Valentin (2004) *Defaced: the Visual Culture of Violence in the late Middle Ages*, trans. Pamela Selwyn. New York: Zone Books.

Hirschkind, Charles (2006) *The Ethics of Listening: Affect, Media and the Islamic Counterpublic*. New York: Columbia University Press.

Hughes, Robert (2003) *Goya*. New York: Knopf.

Mahmood, Saba (2005) *Politics of Piety: the Islamic Revival and the Feminist Subject*. Princeton, NJ: Princeton University Press.

Munn, Nancy D. (1986) *The Fame of Gawa: A Symbolic Study of Value Transformation in a Massim (Papua New Guinea) Society*. Cambridge: Cambridge University Press.

Pels, Peter (1998) 'The spirit of matter: on fetish, rarity, fact, and fancy', in Patricia Spyer (ed.), *Border Fetishisms: Material Objects in Unstable Spaces*. New York: Routledge.

Pels, Peter (1999) *A Politics of Presence: Contacts between Missionaries and Walugugu in late Colonial Tanganyika*. Amsterdam: Harwood Academic.

Pietz, William (1985) 'The Problem of the Fetish' I, *Res* 9: 5–17.

Pietz, William (1993) 'Fetishism and materialism: the limits of theory in Marx', in Emily Apter and William Pietz (eds), *Fetishism as Cultural Discourse*. Ithaca, NY: Cornell University Press.

Pinney, Christopher (2004) *'Photos of the Gods': the Printed Image and Political Struggle in India*. London: Reaktion Books.

Poole, Deborah (1997) *Vision, Race, and Modernity: a Visual Economy of the Andean Image World*.

Seremetakis, C. Nadia (1994) 'The memory of the senses', I, 'Marks of the transitory', in Nadia C. Seremetakis (ed.), *The Senses Still: Perception and Memory as Material Culture in Modernity*. Chicago: University of Chicago Press.

Spyer, Patricia (2000) *The Memory of Trade: Modernity's Entanglements on an Eastern Indonesian Island*. Durham, NC: Duke University Press.

Spyer, Patricia (2001) 'Photography's framings and unframings: a review article', *Comparative Studies in Society and History*, 43 (1): 181–92.

Spyer, Patricia n.d. 'Orphaning the Nation: Violence, Sentimentality, and Media in the Wake of Ambon's War.' Unpublished MS.

Stallybrass, Peter (1998) 'Marx's coat', in Patricia Spyer (ed.), *Border Fetishisms: Material Objects in Unstable Spaces*. New York: Routledge.

Stallybrass, Peter and Jones, Ann Rosalind (2001) 'Fetishizing the glove in Renaissance Europe', *Critical Inquiry*, 28: 114–32.

Staten, Henry (1995) *Eros in Mourning: Homer to Lacan*. Baltimore, MD: Johns Hopkins University Press.

Taussig, Michael (1993) *Mimesis and Alterity: a Particular History of the Senses*. New York: Routledge.

Zito, Angela (2005) 'Bound to be represented', in Larissa Heinrich and Fran Martin (eds), *Modernity Incarnate: Refiguring Chinese Body Politics*. Honolulu, HI: University of Hawaii Press.

Zito, Angela (n.d.) 'Secularizing the pain of footbinding in China: missionary and medical stagings of the universal body', unpublished ms.

8

FOUR TYPES OF VISUAL CULTURE

Christopher Pinney

The problem of visual culture parallels the problem of material culture. Should we treat the visual as a screen on to which knowledges and practices which have been formulated 'elsewhere' are projected? Or should the visual be seen as a primary mode of communication, relatively free of language? This chapter explores different approaches to the problem.

'Visual culture' first acquired critical currency in the art historian Svetlana Alpers's *The Art of Describing* (1983) in which she examined Dutch painting in the wider context of notions and practices of vision, optical devices and visual skills such as map making. These collectively constituted a repertoire of expectation and potentiality – an encompassing visual culture – within which specific painting traditions might be understood. Alpers derived the term from the art historian Michael Baxandall who in *Painting and Experience in Fifteenth Century Italy* (1972) and *The Limewood Sculptors of Renaissance Germany* (1980) developed ideas such as the 'period eye' and the visual 'demotic' (Kaufmann 1996: 45). These 'anthropological' gestures directed attention from the art object to the culture of perception, and from elite traditions to more diffuse everyday practices and interactions. The move from 'art' to 'visual culture' signalled a greater inclusivity of subject matter (from formal aesthetics to quotidian visual representation) and a theoretical readjustment that emphasized cultural practice rather than artists' intentionalities and aesthetic virtue. W.J.T. Mitchell suggests that one of the central tasks of visual culture should be to 'make seeing show itself' in a process he terms 'showing seeing' (2002: 86). To give vision a culture is to attach it to 'human societies, with the ethics and politics, aesthetics and epistemology of seeing and being seen' (2002: 87).

The term 'visual culture' hence bears the mark of an 'anthropological' move away from art history. This was acknowledged, albeit sceptically, by the editors of the journal *October* who in a 'Visual Culture Questionnaire' sent to sundry art historians, film theorists, literary critics and artists noted that 'It has been suggested that the interdisciplinary project of "visual culture" is no longer organized on the model of history (as were the disciplines of art history, architectural history, film history, etc.) but on the model of anthropology' (Mitchell 1996: 25).

For the *October* editors there was a positive dimension to this interdisciplinary 'anthropological' aspect, as well as a negative aspect. On the plus side, they suggested, it opened the possibility of a return to a breadth of inquiry that characterized the work of, for instance, Riegl and Warburg. This breadth was lost, the editors proposed, with the growth of 'medium-based historical disciplines, such as art, architecture, and cinema histories' (1996: 25). The renewal of these inquiries depended on a return to an 'earlier intellectual possibility'.

In briefly tracing a history of work within visual culture it consequently makes little sense to reinscribe those disciplinary frontiers which a new practice of visual culture has done so much to erode. There is no single practice of visual culture: what I delineate here are four loose paradigms which I hope will usefully indicate the huge differences in the theoretical modalities of engagement with visual culture. These differences can be dramatic, but they are rarely differences founded on a disciplinary inheritance.

Four different paradigms will be considered: the visual as language; as transcendent; its relation to power; and the visual as presence. In all of these we will see certain anthropologists, art historians, and others united in common concerns and approaches and opposed to certain other anthropologists, art historians and others with commitments to contrasting paradigms.

THE VISUAL AS LANGUAGE

The 'linguistic turn' (Rorty 1979: 263) that so transformed the humanities from the 1960s through to the 1980s also had marked consequences for the study of visual culture. In most cases, the origins of visuality's linguistic turn, like that of the humanities more generally, lie in the delayed impact of Saussurean linguistics. However, there are other, earlier, antecedents.

The idea of the visual as a code in need of decoding, in a linguistic fashion, emerges theoretically within art history through the work of Aby Warburg and Erwin Panofsky. Warburg invoked contemporary texts (such as Cesare Ripa's *Iconologia* of 1593) as code books, linguistic manuals which facilitated the decipherment of Renaissance visual representation. The first instance of a strategy that would come to dominate much twentieth-century art history occurs in Warburg's 1891 dissertation on Botticelli in which he attempted to discover the identity of the mysterious figure standing on the shore on the right side of 'Birth of Venus'. Vicenzo Cartari is cited, the first reference, Warburg's biographer E.H. Gombrich notes, 'to a mythographic handbook which was to play such an important part in the tradition begun by Warburg' (1986: 61). Indeed, Warburg's iconographic method found a physical manifestation in a huge library. Assembled first in his native city of Hamburg and transferred to London in late 1933, where they would become the physical instantiation of the Warburg Institute, these texts constituted a partial grammar for the decipherment of the coded rediscovery of classical antiquity in the Renaissance (Gombrich and Eribon 1993: 48–9).

Panofsky, Warburg's student, who exported the method to the United States, explicitly defined art historical inquiry as a concern with 'meaning' and elaborated in his programme of *iconology* a form of proto-semiotics. To understand the meaning of a man lifting his hat entailed a contextual grasp of the conventional, language-like, codes of culture, he argued. The primary mode might be said to be a matter of factual description (the man lifts his hat). The

more interesting second level was dependent on a set of conventional, cultural, understandings: within Europe at a certain time this gesture signified politeness (Howells 2003: 24–31).

Another way of describing the different levels that concerned Panofsky would be in terms of the Danish semiotician Louis Helmslev's notions of denotation and connotation. As tools of cultural analysis they were disseminated through Roland Barthes whose structuralist semiology sought language-like patterns in non-linguistic signifiers. Having attacked the 'innocence' of bourgeois *écriture* in his first book, *Writing Degree Zero*, Barthes increasingly focused on visual aspects of contemporary consumer culture. Taking *langue* and *parole*, signifier and signified, and syntagm and system from Saussure, Barthes added a dash of Helmslev to develop powerful analyses of aspects of visual culture such as photography, cooking and fashion. Language came to colonize the visual: 'though working at the outset on non-linguistic substances, Semiology is required, sooner or later, to find language ... in its path ...' (*Elements of Semiology*, 1967: 10–11, cited by Burgin 1982: 50 see Layton Chapter 2 this volume). Semiology invoked language in its study of the visual in two senses, first through its assumption that visual marks had (in most cases) an arbitrary relation to what they signified, just as phonemes did, and second through its assumption that the visual was essentially 'translatable', capable of an unravelling or decoding as a result of which 'meaning' would appear. Just as Saussure had maintained that in language 'there are only differences', so too in cultural production. The code was what mattered, this was the mechanism that allowed pictures to be 'read' (cf. Elkins 1999: 55).

'Reading' also became a form of critical decoding for many who took up the Brechtian aspect of Barthesian semiology. Just as Brecht had sought to destroy bourgeois naturalism in literary and theatrical practices, so Barthes, in *Mythologies* (1957), sought to unravel the mythic naturalization of capitalism and nationalism with its idioms of consumption and identification. Within photographic theory Victor Burgin invoked Saussure and Helmslev in an attempt to shatter claims to the natural articulated through an exclusive concern with technology and aesthetics rather that social determinations (1982: 46 ff.). This Brechtian strategy acquired a particular valency through the rise of a cultural studies paradigm (associated in particular with Stuart Hall) which invoked metaphors of coding and decoding in order to reveal the contingency, and hence changeability, of the political order and its imaginary (a topic dealt with in more detail in the section after next). Image practices which make the world appear 'palpable, irreducible and unquestionable' (Evans and Hall 1999: 4) demand a political/critical response.

The version of French semiology mediated to Anglo-American art history in large part by Norman Bryson (which achieved a near hegemonic theoretical currency) produced an expectation that 'the visual arts are "sign systems" informed by "conventions", that paintings, photographs, sculptural objects, and architectural monuments are fraught with "textuality" and "discourse"' (Mitchell 1994: 14; see also Bryson 1991). The problem of form is dissolved in history and culture, with the image/artefact rendered void and awaiting an influx of discursive meaning. Benjamin's declaration in the 1930s that in future 'the caption [will become] the most important part of the shot' (cited by Evans and Hall 1999: 7) serves to authorize the movement from the image to the frame. Within anthropology, approaches to the volatility of objects which stress their 'social life' (Appadurai 1986) or their 'promiscuity' (Thomas 1991) invoke a similar set of assumptions about the triumph of culture and history over materiality.

Analyses emerging from the French tradition have tended to structure debate around a binary of whether the visual *tout court* should be considered linguistic or not, although the later work of Roland Barthes, especially in *Camera Lucida* (1982), betrays an epiphanal longing for the transcendence of signs. (In that book he yearns for the 'impossible science' of photography's ability to capture, through portraiture, a Proustian involuntary memory.) It is easy to agree with Bryson's claim that 'Signs are subject to historical process; their meaning can never escape historical determinations' (1991: 72), but this is not the same as claiming that *all* signs are *equally* the reflection of this determination.

That all signs are not equally so determined was argued by the logician C.S. Peirce, whose century-old work is increasingly cited in debates around visual culture (e.g. Keane 1997). Peirce proposed a trichotomy of signs: symbols which had an arbitrary relation to their referent; icons which had a relationship of resemblance; and indexes which had a relationship of contiguity. Under this scheme most language would be deemed 'symbolic', i.e. marked by a purely conventional relationship between signifier and signified. Whether onomatopoeia is more properly thought of as iconic (configured

through resemblance – having the quality of the object it denotes) has been the subject of much debate. However, one might say that most figurative painting is iconic as opposed to the indexicality of the photograph, which has been affected by its referent: they are, as Rosalind Krauss writes, parallel to 'fingerprints or footprints or the rings of water that cold glasses leave on tables' (1986: 31).

Peirce's theoretical vocabulary has largely displaced that of an earlier debate which was concerned with many of the same issues. E.H. Gombrich has been central to this, earlier in his career as a strong conventionalist arguing in *Art and Illusion* (1960) that there was a language of pictorial representation, and later as an advocate that certain signs had a natural element that escaped the symbolic nature of language. In this later incarnation he sought to distance himself from what he saw as Nelson Goodman's extreme relativism. Whereas for Goodman all was arbitrary, and realism simply 'a matter of habit', Gombrich sought to place limits on this conventionalism. Photographs may be difficult to 'read' by members of cultures with no experience of photography but this, Gombrich argues, should not lead us to conclude that they are entirely conventional. They are transformations, certainly, but not arbitrary, and we should expect that cultures might easily learn to read photographs much as they would learn how to use a pair of binoculars (a claim which most ethnography sustains, though cf. Weiner 1997).

In his later writing Gombrich focused on what he saw as a biological recognition of certain shapes and motifs which absolutely transcended convention. Considering the famous Pompeii mosaic depicting a snarling dog captioned *cave canum* ('beware of the dog') Gombrich suggests that in order to understand the text one needs to know Latin, whereas in order to understand the picture of the dog one needs only to know about dogs. The picture is a natural sign, not conventional in the way that the linguistic caption is. In a similar fashion he claims that 'The fish which snaps at the artificial fly does not ask the logician in what respect it is like a fly and in what respect unlike'. Responding to this, W.J.T. Mitchell wittily noted that such reasoning ignores such facts as that 'a dog will fetch a stick and ignore a photograph of a duck, that it will ignore its own image in a mirror, but respond instantly to the call of its name or other (arbitrary) verbal commands' (1986: 88).

Mitchell's brilliant discussion, in *Iconology* (1986), demonstrates not so much a commitment to the linguistic model so much as hostility to Gombrich's invocation of the natural as something entirely removed from the domain of the social. The anxiety generated by any claim to transcendence finds its most articulate form in Derridean deconstruction. Whereas for Barthes the claim to the ontic was essentially political, for Derrida it is the consequence of a philosophical tradition that is unable to relinquish its attachment to forms of transcendent signification. These invocations of a pure presence, self-sufficient in itself, necessarily reveal their own impossibility through deconstruction. In this sense deconstruction is always 'auto-deconstruction': the fractures that run through invocations of presence render such claims inherently unstable and unsustainable and the task of the analyst is to tease out and emphasize processes that are always, already at work. The hesitancy of visual culture's engagement with Derrida is on the face of it surprising, for there is much, especially in his major early work *Of Grammatology* (1976), that speaks directly to its concerns (cf. Brunette and Wills 1994). It is striking that none of the major published visual culture 'readers' (eg. Mirzoeff 1998/2002 and Evans and Hall 1999) includes excerpts from Derrida, although Althusser, Barthes, Lacan, Foucault and Baudrillard are well represented.

The transformative effect of the linguistic turn can hardly be overstated and the linguistic model still has many powerful adherents. However, the recognition of an emergent paradigm of visual culture can, in retrospect, be seen as coincident with the atrophy of the linguistic model's allure. As the sovereignty of language diminished, a complex irreducibility of the visual and material came to the forefront of critical consciousness. The 'pictorial turn' – as one of its more sceptical champions, W.J.T. Mitchell, termed it – marked the emergence of the image as 'a central topic of discussion in the human sciences in the way that language [once] did' (1994: 13). This new turn will be considered in more detail in the fourth section.

THE VISUAL AS EXTRA-MUNDANE

Susan Buck-Morss, in a characteristic provocation, has declared that 'the production of a discourse of visual culture entails the liquidation of art as we have known it' (1996: 29). As a consequence of this liquidation 'museums would then need to become double encasings, preserving art objects, and preserving the art-idea.

Art history departments would be moved in with archaeology' (1996: 29).

If art history is content with 'art' and its transcendent aspirations, visual culture can only accommodate the 'art-idea', that is, a sense of art as social fact. The 'art-idea' is visual culture's anthropological description of those cultural practices of art that have endowed it with the possibility of transcendence, what Paul De Man called the 'temptation to permanence'. Visual culture encompasses a scepticism towards the transcendent claims of the art-idea, 'anthropologizing' the mythography of art and the heroic artist. Nathalie Heinich's (1996) demythologization of Van Gogh, for example, explores in detail the religious dimension of the public hagiography of the artist and provides a detailed affirmation of Alfred Gell's claim that for a secular West the art gallery had become the new temple.

In Europe this has a long history. We need only recall Coleridge (for whom art represented the translucence of the eternal in the temporal), and Nietzsche (tragedy comes *before* history) to understand the particular modality of art's appeal to the extra-mundane – to a world before and beyond history and time. Paul De Man – a Derridean literary scholar – exhibits a generously 'anthropological' recognition of art's 'error'-generating capabilities. Whereas certain conceptions are 'mistakes' – just plain wrong – De Man suggests that the 'temptation to permanence' (that art's putative transcendence embodies) should be understood as a kind of cultural necessity (see Norris 1988: 12–13, 164–5).

That this discussion of visual culture as extra-mundane should be so abbreviated is explained by the dominance of the linguistic and contextual model outlined in the previous section. For the vast majority of commentators such a link between the visual and the transcendent can be only a delusion: as 'myth', the seduction of 'presence', or a theological mistake that can have no place in any sensible discussion of this as a *social* phenomenon. Any desire to find an 'outside' is critiqued. Thus Hal Foster in his observations on the artist as ethnographer cautions against the tendency of artists to invoke an ethnic or community 'elsewhere' in the absence of a tabooed 'permanence' (1995: 302). 'Values like authenticity, originality, and singularity, banished under critical taboo from postmodernist art, return as properties of the site, neighbourhood, or community engaged by the artist' (1995: 306).

However, to permit the visual to be situated solely within the mundane and the social, as a kind of language, discursively constituted, is to disallow any confrontation with the figural and resistant properties of certain visual forms. It may be that the question of which paradigm, or theoretical orientation is most appropriate for the analysis of images is misguided, since it assumes a stable category of the visual for which one simply has to find the best theory. Perhaps the visual should be conceived of as a continuum ranging across different qualities for which different paradigms are called. James Elkins describes what he terms 'beautiful moments' in the work of Louis Marin in which he is forced to abandon his desire to reduce images simply to language 'when some passage in the painting prevents a reading from actually taking place' (1999: 55). Likewise, in an inverted manner, some of the later work of Roland Barthes 'replay[s] Odysseus's encounter with the sirens: Barthes listens to the call of the purely visual object, he approaches and then he veers back into the safer waters of coded images' (1999: 55).

Such revealing moments of unease may indicate that the visual is neither one thing nor the other, but encompasses instead a diverse set of forms, differently constituted. Jean-François Lyotard's opposition of 'discourse' and 'figure' may allow us to investigate this. He contrasted an energetic domain of 'figure' with a closed and knowable realm of 'discourse'. This is a binary that transcends any simplistic distinction between image and text, since as he shows, certain forms of poetry may be highly figural and a visual diagram might be discursive. Rather than essentializing different expressive modalities these terms express latent potentialities in all cultural production.

Discourse, for Lyotard, is 'old, used-up, determined by a long historical-philosophical tradition and limited to what can be *read*, identified, and given meaning within a closed linguistic system' (Carroll 1987: 30). One can imagine numerous visual forms that would fit this description: the kinds of political cartoons that appear in daily newspapers, and traditions of formal painted portraiture, for instance. These all accede to an enormous burden of expectation and there are never any surprises, or affronts, of form. Figure, on the other hand, is free of that linguistic weight: it is 'disruptive of discursive systems and destructive of signification in general'. It manifests 'what discourse is unable to *say*' (Carroll 1987: 30). Figure, which exists as a node of alterity within discourse itself, is where intensities are felt, rather than communicated. Alongside this, Lyotard mounts a radical critique of Marxist and subsequent assumptions

that the aesthetic is simply the superstructural and epiphenomenal reflection of a more important infrastructure, an argument that resonates with claims made by analysts of the former Soviet bloc such as Boris Groys (1988) and Alla Efimova (1997).

Lyotard fragments the single domain of the visual into something far more complex and suggests that while some discursive forms may warrant the kind of linguistic analysis explored in the first section above, figural forms are characterized by a libidinous quality that will always escape any attempts to impose 'meaning'. From the perspective of analysts, for whom the visual should always be enframed by the social and linguistic, Lyotard's work, with its claim that art is 'ontologically outside the socio-political universe' (Carroll 1987: 27), rather like Adorno's, seems to reinvent an aesthetic purism from which they see themselves as trying to escape. Yet Lyotard raises key questions which visual culture, if it is to be anything other than a branch of a language-based semantics, must place at the centre of its concerns.

THE VISUAL AND POWER

In a chilling account published in 1937 the anthropologist Julius Lips described how he was forced to flee from Nazi Germany. Lips had been researching material for the book subsequently published as *The Savage Strikes Back*. Documenting African and Oceanic responses to European colonization, Lips sought to restore to much of the world's population its own visual history. One version of the history of the modern world system was well preserved in shrine-like art galleries and museums in Europe, America and the Antipodes. This history, materially preserved in oil paintings and sculpture, as well as other quieter media, celebrated the achievements of figures such as Columbus and Cook and documented indigenous peoples, new landscapes and alien fauna and flora. Lips was concerned to create a parallel archive, one which was infinitely more difficult to create but which was as important, if not more, than the familiar Western mode of picturing the world. It is easy to comprehend why the Gestapo should have responded with threats to such a project, but more difficult to understand why Lips's work has fallen into neglect and its challenge refused.

The idea that visibility and its relation to knowledge were essentially political questions demanding cultural and historical investigation (a commonplace of Foucauldian and Saidean theory) were implicit in other early works such as Bernard Smith's important body of writing (1960), Bernadette Bucher's flawed yet valuable structuralist study of de Bry's *Great Voyage* (1981), Partha Mitter's (1977) rigorous history of European reactions to Indian art between the Middle Ages and the early twentieth century and Schivelbusch's (1977/1986) study of the 'industrialization of time and space'. This pioneering work would be cannibalized to varying degrees by later work, which, armed with Foucault, Said and Fabian, saw clearly the mechanisms through which visibility, and being made visible, were connected with carceral, disciplinary and colonial projects.

Bucher's study of early European visual representations of the Americas (specifically through de Bry's remarkable copperplate engravings for the *Great Voyages*, published between 1590 and 1634) was a response to a suggestion by Lévi-Strauss that they might bear investigation for the '*pensée sauvage*' among those who subjugated the American Indians' (1981: xi). The end result is a dogmatic structuralist account that treats the images solely as documents of European preoccupations and has been subjected to devastating criticism by Tom Cummins (1994). However, Bucher raises intriguing questions about the specificity of visual representation, suggesting that, in the visual, 'negation as a means of expression is lost' (1981: 35). She contrasts the role of negation in speech and the manner in which Native Americans became what Europeans were not, a practice satirized in Montaigne's phrase 'Eh, quoi, ils ne portent pas de hauts de chausse!' ('What! They're not wearing breeches!'). In the figurative arts, Bucher argues, negation is impossible: 'it is impossible to portray a thing by what it is not: it is present or absent, and if it appears, it is always positively, in a certain shape' (1981: 35). Hence early visualizers of the people of the Americas (such as Theodor de Bry) were forced to inhabit an intrinsic positivity. An immediate riposte to this might point to Eisensteinian practices of montage which produce language-like effects that Umberto Eco once memorably described as 'syntagmatic concatenations imbued with argumentative capacity' (1982: 38), but Bucher's response would presumably be that this depends on a multiplicity of images constructed in such a way as to mimic language.

Bucher's approach is unusual in that it attempts to formally consider the intrinsic constraints and possibilities of certain precise visual practices. Most writing on the politics of picturing follows Heidegger and Foucault and invokes generic 'scopic regimes' as correlates or mechanisms of work views. A work such as Timothy Mitchell's *Colonizing Egypt* (1988) draws on Foucault and Heidegger (especially the latter's 'world as picture' essay) to explicate the centrality of visuality for the political history of Egypt in the late nineteenth century. Colonizing becomes a question, both literally and metaphorically, of 'seeing' in a world-conquering manner. Mitchell's concerns resonate with those raised in a broader frame by De Certeau (1986) and Carter's exploration of 'spatial history' in an Australian context (1987).

Foucault's *Discipline and Punish* with its panoptic model of disciplinary power inspired a significant body of writing on photography. A group of theorists associated with the then Polytechnic of Central London (especially Victor Burgin and John Tagg), the journal *Ten-8* and the impact of Stuart Hall's concerns with the politics of visual representation acted as catalysts for a flowering of work on colonial and anthropological photography by anthropologists (see Edwards 1992, 2001). Other works such as Stagl's (1995) and Rubies' (1996) powerful studies of the role of observation in methodologies of Western travel have explored histories so complex that they are difficult to assimilate to the narratives expounded by Foucault and Said.

The manner in which visual practices are viewed simply as vehicles for all-encompassing politico-economic forces is especially clear in the highly Foucauldian work of John Tagg, where the photograph is declared to have 'no identity'. It has no intrinsic formal, technological or semiotic qualities, he argues, these simply being the effects of the 'currency' they acquire under different regimes: 'Its nature as a practice depends on the institutions and agents which define it and set it to work ... It is a flickering across a field of institutional spaces. It is this field we must study, not photography as such' (1988: 63).

Edward Said's *Orientalism*, published in 1978, has had as significant an impact on visual studies as in the humanities and social sciences more generally (see Van Dommelen Chapter 7 this volume). Said's central argument, that Euro-american inquiry had created two phantasmatic territories, the Orient and Occident, which became sites for contrasting histories, philosophies and other ways of marking difference has been explored with reference to visual imagery in a number of studies, including Cohn (1998), Mignolo (1995) and McClintock

(1995). The starkness of Said's vision was usefully complicated by Homi K. Bhabha's (1994) suggestion that 'Orientalism' was never as straightforwardly successful as Said imagined it to be, for it was itself internally flawed – 'forked' or 'split' – by the entanglement of horror and desire that constituted it. Bhabha's re-elaboration of the complex urges driving colonialism also illuminated the ways in which those who had been 'orientalized' might work within the contradictions of 'orientalism' as a practice to partially overthrow it. Bhabha's most useful argument was that colonial power was never simply acted out upon the site of its intended operation but was always subject to infinite translation. Colonial discourses were necessarily hybridized at the point of their articulation. Whereas Said's model is suggestive of a mimesis in which colonialism is granted the power of the master copy, Bhabha's is more suggestive of Pandora's Box – the act of colonial enunciation immediately sets free a surplus of possible enactments ensuring unpredictable outcomes.

Homi Bhabha's critique of the assumption in Saidean analyses that colonial power was possessed entirely by the colonizer has inspired several studies such as Carolyn Dean's (1996) work on hybrid Peruvian painting, Stephen Eisenman's (1997) exploration of the interstitial position occupied by the 'third sex' Gauguin in Tahiti, and Pinney's account of chromolithography and politics in colonial India (2004). Other accounts which do not make explicit theoretical use of Bhabha's important work but which are certainly consonant with its main trajectory include Serge Gruzinski's remarkable work on the subtle political strategies that lay behind Mexican post-conquest codices, and Roger Benjamin's (1997) and Beaulieu and Roberts's (2002) explorations – with respect to 'Orientalist painting' – of the complex 'transculturations' or 'interlocutions' that often characterized relationships between artists, those they represented, and diverse consumers of these images.

THE VISUAL AS PRESENCE

One of the issues raised in the *October* Visual Culture Questionnaire, which I discussed at the opening of this chapter, was a concern with visual culture's predisposition to dematerialize the image. They solicited opinions as to whether 'the precondition for visual studies as an interdisciplinary rubric is a newly wrought conception of the visual as disembodied *image*, re-created in the virtual spaces of sign-exchange and phantasmatic projection' (1996: 25).

In response, the art historian Carol Armstrong agreed, lamenting the manner in which the 'distrust of the material dimension of cultural objects' (1996: 26) by an interdisciplinary visual culture reflected a fear of the 'fetishism of the old art history'. For some exponents of the new visual culture its allure lay in the prospect of converting *things* into circulating signs. Baudrillard was the chief spectre of this disembodiment, but only nine years after its publication *October*'s anxiety seems curiously misplaced, for many of the most significant contributions to visual culture published within the last few years have reasserted the sensuous particularity of objects and images.

Indeed, in the same year as the *October* questionnaire, Barbara Maria Stafford published a bravura critique of what she described as 'the totemization of language as a godlike agency in western culture' (1996: 5). Stafford identified the manner in which 'Saussure's schema emptied the mind of its body, obliterating the interdependence of physiological functions and thinking' (1996: 5) In a similar way, within anthropology, the rise of Geerztian 'thick description' may be seen as what Barbara Maria Stafford calls 'cultural textology', reducing communication to inscription and '[reconceiving] the material subjects of ... inquiry as decorporealized signs and encrypted messages requiring decipherment' (1996: 6). Within the linguistic paradigm reigning throughout the humanities, iconicity came to be treated 'as an inferior part of a more general semantics' (1996: 5).

In a parallel manner, W.J.T. Mitchell identified an emergent 'pictorial turn' as a reaction against the 'linguistic turn', suggesting that it is about time we stopped asking what images can do for us, and time that we started asking 'What do pictures really want?' (1996). By treating images (subjunctively) as 'subalterns' we might, Mitchell implied, escape from the seeming inevitability of writing their histories with evidence derived (as Carlo Ginzburg would say) 'by other means' (Ginzburg 1989: 35).

The relationship of the human sensorium to different political orders and regimes of taste has been most fully developed in Susan Buck-Morss's (1992) working through of Walter Benjamin's 1930s insights into the question of embodiment. Buck-Morss has laid an analytical pathway towards the recuperation of the corporeality of aesthetics. Arguing for the necessity of a recognition of aesthetics' earlier sense as *aisthitikos* (denoting 'perceptive by feeling'), Buck-Morss mounts a sustained critique of the Kantian abolition of the phenomenal through its privileging of 'distinterest'. This position, which resonates with Bourdieu's argument in *Distinction*, is elaborated in a more ethnographic context by David Morgan (1998), who, in a study of US Christians, reveals how devotees invoke a non-Kantian phenomenology to ease their suffering. His study, replete as it is with accounts of how certain images of Christ are chosen because (say) they are profiles, which allow the devotee to whisper into his ear, or (say) feature a direct visual projection which will exude a protective veil when hung over a child's bed, adumbrates a complex popular embodied 'kitsch' in which what matters in the adjudication of an image's worth is not a disinterested aesthetic but practical efficacy. Similar views have been described in the context of popular Hindu practices in India, where *darshan* denotes a process of seeing and being seen in which vision acquires a tactility that draws devotee and deity together in an intimate reciprocity (see Pinney 2001, 2002, 2004).

Other key figures who are pioneering a new embodied analysis of visual culture include the ethnographic film maker David MacDougall, whose exploration of the filmic implications of Merleau-Ponty's (1962) insights have profound relevance for all anthropologists. Phenomenology also informs the work of the art historians Joseph Leo Koerner and Alexander Nemerov. Koerner, in his superlative book on Caspar David Friedrich, asks always what the embodied relationship of the beholder is to the painting in the language of a deliberately naive empiricism. 'You are placed before a thicket in winter,' the opening sentence of the book, describes the mechanics of beholding Friedrich's 1828 'Trees and bushes in the snow'. 'It testifies that the network was and is this way, and no other way, and that you, therefore, are placed here, rather than elsewhere ... Somehow the painting places *you*' (Koerner 1995: 5).

Alexander Nemerov's wonderful interpretation of the visceral identifications in the work of the nineteenth-century American still life painter Raphaelle Peale rejects the 'move outward, into "context"' that characterizes most writing about images, focusing instead on 'art's particularities – the touch of a raisin upon an apple, for example, or the hovering of a berry just above a surface' (2001: 5). Nemerov traces what he terms the 'fantasy of embodiment' in Peale's uncanny still lives. This is not simply, Nemerov argues, 'the early nineteenth century's not-yet-severed relation of sight to body' (2001: 29, here referring to Crary's 1990 historicization) but a more fundamental – indeed, ontological – projection of materiality between humans and non-humans – what Nemerov terms 'sensuous identification' (2001: 89). Though Latour is never mentioned in Nemerov's analysis one can see in Peale's work a refusal to 'become modern' and an insistence on the sensuous particularity of the animate object.

The pictorial turn's engagement with embodiment also raises the issue of how corporeal images can be displayed to audiences burdened by this putative autonomization of sight. This was the problem confronted in an illuminating manner by Jacques Mercier in considering different ways of presenting Ethiopian healing scrolls to a Parisian public in an exhibition at the Musée National des Arts d'Afrique et d'Océanie. Mercier finally opted for an 'analogic installation' designed to 're-create the scroll's emotional quality, to put the visitor in the emotional position of the user' (1997: 111). Mercier's design brief noted that the healing scrolls which he sought to have displayed were 'made from the skin of an animal sacrificed in the patient's name. This animal is a substitute for the patient ... The animal skin doubles for the man's skin. Furthermore, the scroll is cut to the length of the patient's body, because he must be protected from head to toe ...' (1997: 111). Given the peculiarly powerful 'double business' (Girard 1988) which binds object and patient (spectator), Mercier was especially keen to avoid the annulment of these scrolls' sensuous particularity in the disembodied visual regime of the European gallery. Working with the theatre designer Charles Marty (significantly 'a man used to creating imaginary spaces' 1997: 112) Mercier developed an ingenious solution to the problem of how to convey the Ethiopian patient's experience of sacrifice to the European museum-goer. A two-way mirror allowed the visitor to recognize himself, before illumination behind the mirror revealed an Ethiopian scroll with its characteristic large eyes displacing the viewer's double. 'The disappearance of the mirror image was intended to suggest the visitor's death, the appearance of the double to evoke his relationship to the sacrifice, to the parchment of the scrolls, and to the sprit inhabiting the patient's body' (1997: 112).

Mercier's solution is an example of what Liza Bakewell has termed an 'image act'. Expanding J.L. Austin's notion of speech acts, i.e. those linguistic events which are actions, rather than simply descriptions, Bakewell argues that 'a theory of images ought to form part of a theory of action' (1998: 22). Such ideas resonate profoundly with Gell's argument in *Art and Agency* (1998; discussed elsewhere in this volume) and with Diane Losche's writing on Abelam (Papua New Guinea) concepts and practices of visuality (1995). Losche builds upon Anthony Forge's pioneering work which explored the ways in which Abelam visual culture came to act directly upon those who had been inculcated in it. No exegesis could be provided because it could not be 'translated' across the boundaries of initiates and non-initiates. Echoing Buck-Morss, Losche argues that 'aesthetics' are of little use: instead we should focus on the 'generativity' that the visual produces and, rather than looking for meaning as reference, we should explore the manner in which 'a structure of sentiment and desire is modelled through object associations'. A product of stressful initiation rites, Abelam visual culture has strong terroristic and erotic dimensions. To ask about its 'meaning' is to *misunderstand* its modality: it would be akin to asking a Euro-american 'What does your refrigerator mean?' (1995: 59).

This radical delinking of iconicity from semantics is taken even further in Marilyn Strathern's consideration of how another Papuan community (specifically Mount Hageners, but implicitly all Melanesians) construct self-knowledge through the idiom of images that have the quality of compressed performances which 'contain their own prior context' (1990: 33). She builds upon Roy Wagner's observation that for the Barok of New Ireland 'an image must be witnessed or experienced, rather than merely described or summed up verbally' (Wagner 1986: xiv, cited by Strathern 1990: 36). Language corrupts the effects of images rather than defining and constraining them, and the Barok are suspicious of talk about images. For Mount Hageners 'the very act of presentation constituted the only act that was relevant' (1990: 33).

Strathern contrasts these Melanesian engagements with the image with that of Euroamericans, for whom images can be only 'illustrations' of a knowledge produced as Carlo Ginzburg would argue 'by other [linguistic] means' (1989: 35). Strathern brings us full circle from the language-based approaches with which this account opened: Mount Hageners exemplify in a pure form an anti-semiotics, a resistance to any export of meaning outside the image and its event. Yet Strathern is not simply describing a topography of cultural difference. Rather she engages with Mount Hagener visual ontology as a possibility that may be

open to all of us. She suggests that anthropology used to be, in some sense, closer to Mount Hagen practice before it reduced the visual and material to an illustration of what had already been described in more privileged registers. In the anthropological case this might be religion or kinship, but in the broader field of visual culture with which we have been concerned here it would be language, history and culture – all those forces which are used to enframe the image and which, through movement away from the centre, attempt to neutralize the anxiety that images generate.

I've suggested above that 'visual culture' may be considered 'anthropological' in an ecumenical sense: it marks out a transdisciplinary space of concern with the social processes of visuality. But we should also explore the claim that it has been insufficiently anthropological in the sense that as an intellectual strategy it has ethnocentrically reinscribed dominant Euroamerican practices and theories.

This is the reproachful and revealing claim made by James Elkins. Visual culture, he argues, is 'too easy' (2003: 63). One of the various ways in which it must be made 'more difficult' is by making it 'multicultural'. Elkins narrates a thwarted attempt to run a panel at the 1998 College Art Association conference examining art history outside the West. His call for papers provoked three papers, only one of which addressed non-Euro-american practice. He cancelled the panel and was left to reflect on how 'in the flood of papers on multiculturalism and postcolonial theory, which accounted for perhaps fifty papers ... it appeared that very few people ... had been reading non-Western books on art history' (2003: 110).

Elkins notes that matters are, in some respects, slowly improving: visual studies are increasingly concerning themselves with matters that were 'once entirely neglected or known only to anthropologists' (2003: 110). Yet, just as Dipesh Chakrabarty (2000) has noted the subtle and tenacious ways in which historians still assume a non-Euro-american 'belatedness', so Elkins notes that visual studies applies 'Western methodology to non-Western material' in an intellectual imperium that in the name of decolonization simultaneously inscribes Euro-american academic norms. Elkins concurs with Chakrabarty in acknowledging the near impossibility of escaping these profoundly embedded expectations and notes that any account which repudiated the Euroamerican academy would 'risk not being taken *as* history at all' (2003: 111; emphasis in original).

Elkins provides a telling analysis of the tenacity of master narratives in the case of Gayatri Spivak's *Critique of Postcolonial Reason*, which concludes by suggesting that 'postcolonial and western discourses might approach one another as asymptotes do, never touching but running in parallel' (2003: 116). On her final page, in a footnote, Spivak attributes this to Derrida, and in particular *Glas*, which presents parallel texts, neither of which is privileged. Elkins describes his amazement 'to discover that an optimal model of cultural affinity is wholly Western' and to find it presented in a way 'as if it will not be possible to be sure until Derrida decides' (2003: 116).

Instead of compulsory references to Freud, Benjamin, Foucault and Said, Elkins suggests, we should decolonize our methodologies through a foregrounding of non-Euro-american interpretive paradigms. He briefly discusses two examples: Ken-ichi Sasaki's account of Japanese notions of extramissive vision that 'fuses the subject with a distant object' (Sasaki 1996: 170, cited by Elkins 2003: 119) and Diane Losche's work on the Abelam, discussed above.

Elkins appears to desire the impossible utopia of an escape from Euro-american epistemology into pure alterity: a consciousness of the visual that might be grasped, and written, from the 'native's point of view'. However, his recognition of the impossibility of this manoeuvre compels him to acknowledge a quasi-Derridean 'erasure' as the only possibility. Such an erasure can only provisionally 'cross out' what can never be fully deleted.

Elkins might also have adduced the testimony of the Cambodian art historian Boreth Ly, who in a powerful account of what he terms the 'Khmer Rouge scopic regime' characterized it as being concerned with the 'devastation' of vision. He described two metaphors of surveillance through which Khmer Rouge terror was disseminated: 'One common metaphor was 'Angka [i.e. Pol Pot and his regime] has the eyes of a pineapple.' That is, just as a pineapple has eyes that face in all directions, Angka has panoptic vision. The second metaphor was embedded in an often repeated phrase, 'If you want to live, grow a *koh* tree in front of your house.' The threat is implied by a play on words: *kobak*, the name of a tree (*Ceiba pentrandra*), is also a pun on the Khmer word *koh*, which means 'mute'. Angka's advice in both cases was to watch your words, stay mute and be blind' (Elkins 2003: 72).

Ly provides us with an 'ethno sociological' account of what it is to live under such a terroristic regime. As a tragic participant, Ly takes us closer to those monstrous events: we are told about the specifics of forced evacuations, executions and the linguistic idioms of oppression and survival. So we learn about pineapples rather than Foucault's interpretation of Benthamite panopticans. Elkins would be right to point out that we would be missing the point if we read Ly's account as a simple example of Foucault gone native. Elkins rightly seeks to persuade us that the decolonization of visual culture would entail the development of theory on the basis of particular, *singular*, accounts such as Ly's, and what this particular account suggests is *not* discipline as a modern substitute for *punir* but the collapsing of the two under Pol Pot.

But what is so striking about Ly's account is that, while its compulsion stems from (to mix sensory metaphors) having its ear to the ground, and its presentation of an account riven with a sensory particularity, rather than the exnominated placelessness of the kind of approach which Elkins rightly bemoans, it does not expound a 'genuinely different' interpretive practice' (Elkins 2003: 118). Ly describes neither an alterity, nor a cultural idiosyncrasy, but a peculiarly ruinous form of the terroristic state which brings forth idioms of surveillance, blindness and invisibility that have resonance with practices in numerous other political tyrannies.

Elkins's call for challenges to the hegemony of Euro-american disciplinary language is admirable but this very utopia of divergent world views attached to cultures might itself be seen as the product of a certain European epistemology. An alternative strategy might address Bruno Latour's question as to whether anthropology will be forever condemned to study 'territories' rather than 'networks' (1993). Culture then becomes an *ex post facto* essentialization of difference rather than an originary ground. A fine example of this is provided by Finbarr Barry Flood in a discussion of the Taliban regime's destruction of the Bamiyan Buddhas in Afghanistan in February 2001. Flood documents how for many commentators this act of destruction came to exemplify the congruence between Islam and iconoclasm: 'common to almost all accounts of the Buddhas' demolition was the assumption that their destruction can be situated within a long, culturally determined, and unchanging tradition of violent iconoclastic acts' (2002: 641). Against this, Flood places the Taliban's actions within what Latour would term a 'network' that links Mullah Omar with the Euro-American museum and sees Taliban hostility to the Bamiyan statues as an anomaly in demand of a historicized explanation. 'Network' here denotes a path of exchanges characterized by contingency rather than opposed territories from which cultures misrecognize each other.

Flood notes that Mullah Omar had earlier bolstered his power by the 'rediscovery' of the *burda* (cloak) of the Prophet in a museum in Kandahar. This facilitated his alignment with 'a chain of caliphs who had earlier laid claim to his cloak of legitimacy' (2002: 652) and the cloak was regularly publicly displayed by Mullah Omar. The destruction of the Bamiyan statues occurred at the end of a complex conversation between Mullah Omar and various real and imagined European and American interlocutors, and Flood argues that the fact that Western journalists were taken by the regime to witness the destruction 'suggests that the intended audience for this communiqué was neither divine nor local but global: for all its recidivist rhetoric, this was a performance designed for the age of the Internet' (2002: 651).

There is a central paradox: there were no practising Buddhists left in Afghanistan and the Taliban had announced that their presence would have guaranteed the images' perpetuity. This leads Flood to suggest that what was at stake for the Taliban in the Bamiyan images was not their 'idolatrous' nature but 'their veneration as cultural icons'. Phillipe de Montebello of the Metropolitan Museum of Art in New York suggested that the statues be removed to a museum where they might safely be neutralized as 'works of art and not cult images' (Montebello, cited in Flood 2002: 651). Mullah Omar's response, broadcast widely by radio to the broader international Muslim audience, 'Do you prefer to be a breaker of idols or a seller of idols?' was a knowing allusion to Mahmud of Ghazni's response to the Brahmans of the Somnath temple (in Gujarat, India) in 1025. Mahmud had looted the temple, stealing its revered *linga* (the phallic icon of Shiva), and responded to priestly offers to ransom the icon with the cry that he would rather be known as the 'breaker' than as the 'broker' of idols (2002: 650) before smashing the *linga* and incorporating it into the foundations of the entrance to the mosque in Ghazni.

Mullah Omar appropriated a millennium-old idiom, and directed it against the museo-logical purveyors of a culturally idolatrous present' (2002: 652). Flood draws on Freedberg (1989) and Gell (1998) to suggest that the difference between the temple and the museum (which Montebello imagined to be profound) is in practice far from clear-cut and suggests that Taliban iconoclasm was centrally a rejection of a pseudo-universalism of 'heritage' which disguised the hegemony of Euro-America. The statues' destruction was designed to consolidate a broader Islamic identity which disdained the Western museum's obsession with non-human artefacts: it was an event designed to dramatize the contempt for Enlightenment values and the Taliban's sense of the hypocrisy of Euro-american institutions (2002: 653). Flood sees an affinity between the declarations of the Taliban envoy to the United Nations, Sayed Rahmatullah Hashimi, and suffragette Mary Richardson, who famously slashed Velázquez's 'Rokeby Venus' in London's National Gallery in 1914. Richardson attempted to destroy 'the most beautiful [painted] woman' because the government was destroying the 'the most beautiful character in modern history', Emmeline Pankhurst. Hashimi declared that 'When your children are dying in front of you, then you don't care about a piece of art' (2002: 653). Both motivations were those of the classic iconoclast, enraged by false valuations rooted in a faulty ethics. Consequently, Flood concludes, the Taliban's actions should be understood not as 'cultural pathology' or the working out of a peculiarly archaic cultural/religious hostility to images but as 'a peculiarly modern phenomenon, an act that, "under the cover of archaic justifications, functioned according to a very contemporary logic"' (2002: 651, citing Jean-Michel Frodon). In the light of this we might wish to modify Elkins's suggestion that visual culture should inject more 'culture' into its vision of itself. Deborah Poole, for instance, in a study of photography in Peru, has advocated the use of the term 'visual economy' instead. The problem with 'culture,' she suggests, is that it invokes an inappropriate sense of 'shared meanings and symbolic codes that can create communities of people' (1997: 8). The contrasting sense of the visual as an 'economy' structured by inequality and conflict is much more appropriate to the reality of the Andean experience, she claims.

We might also note that the modality of vision which in its Indian incarnation has been described above as *darshan* can be found globally outside of cultural instantiation in South Asia. It might be said that it is a practice which is *less than universal but more than global*, for a similar desire for embodied reciprocity through vision can be found among US Christians (Morgan), among those adolescents the world over who desire portraits of sport and music celebrities characterized by a high degree of frontality, and many intellectuals (for instance, Merleau-Ponty and Nemerov) whose work has been discussed above. This modality of vision can hence be seen at work in a globalized network rather than within the historically and territorially constrained boundaries of specific cultures. This visual idiom exists as an untheorized practice in various non-elite groups (characterized by marginalities of age, class and academic capital), as what Bourdieu termed an 'anti-Kantianism', as a matter of theological elaboration within certain religious communities, and as theoretical speculation within sections of the academy.

This reveals the way in which the various 'types' of visual culture adumbrated in this discussion operate not as discrete approaches or genres, but as complexly intersecting practices, best described as networks, rather than territories.

REFERENCES

Alpers, Svetalana (1983) *The Art of Describing: Dutch Art in the Seventeenth Century*. Chicago: University of Chicago.

Appadurai, Arjun, ed. (1986) *The Social Life of Things*. Cambridge: Cambridge University Press.

Armstrong, Carol (1996) Response to Visual Culture Questionnaire, *October*, 77, pp. 27–8.

Bakewell, Liza (1998) 'Image Acts', *American Anthropologist*, 100 (1): 22–32.

Barthes, Roland (1957) *Mythologies*. Paris: Seuil.

Barthes, Roland (1967) *Elements of Semiology*. London: Cape.

Barthes, Roland (1982) *Camera Lucida*, trans. Richard Howard. London: Cape.

Baxandall, Michael (1972) *Painting and Experience in Fifteenth Century Italy: Primer on the Social History of Pictorial Style*. Oxford: Clarendon Press.

Baxandall, Michael (1980) *The Limewood Sculptors of Renaissance Germany*. New Haven, CT: Yale University Press.

Beaulieu, Jill and Roberts, Mary, eds (2002) *Orientalism's Interlocutors: Painting, Architecture, Photography*. Durham, NC: Duke University Press.

Benjamin, Roger (1997) *Orientalism: from Delacroix to Klee*. Sydney: Art Gallery of New South Wales.

Benjamin, Walter (1992) 'The work of art in the Age of Mechanical Reproduction', in *Illuminations*. London: Fontana, pp. 211–35.

Bhabha, Homi K. (1994) *The Location of Culture*. London: Routledge.

Brunette, Peter and Wills, David (1994) *Deconstruction and the Visual Arts: Art, Media, Architecture*. Cambridge: Cambridge University Press.

Bryson, Norman (1991) 'Semiology and visual interpretation', in Norman Bryson, Michael Ann Holly and Keith Moxey (eds), *Visual Theory: Painting and Interpretation*. Cambridge: Polity Press, pp. 61–73.

Bucher, Bernadette (1981) *Icon and Conquest: a Structural Analysis of the Illustrations of de Bry's Great Voyages*. Chicago: University of Chicago Press.

Buck-Morss, Susan (1992) 'Aesthetics and anaesthetics: Walter Benjamin's artwork essay reconsidered', *October*, 62: 3–41.

Buck-Morss, Susan (1996) Response to Visual Culture Questionnaire, *October*, 77, pp. 29–31.

Burgin, Victor (1982) 'Photographic practice and art theory', in Victor Burgin (ed.), *Thinking Photography*, Basingstoke: Macmillan, pp. 39–83.

Carroll, David (1987) *Paraesthetics: Foucault, Lyotard, Derrida*. London: Methuen.

Carter, Paul (1987) *The Road to Botany Bay*. London: Faber.

Chakrabarty, Dipesh (2000) *Provincialising Europe: Postcolonial Thought and Historical Difference*. Chicago: University of Chicago Press.

Cohn, Bernard S. (1998) 'The past in the present: India as a museum of mankind', *History, and Anthropology*, 11 (1): 1–38.

Crary, Jonathan (1990) *Techniques of the Observer: on Vision and Modernity in the Nineteenth Century*. Cambridge, MA: MIT Press.

Cummins, Tom (1994) 'De Bry and Herrera: "Aguas Negras" or the Hundred Years War over an image of America', in Gustavo Curiel et al. (eds), *Arte, Historia e identidad en America: visiones comparativas*. Mexico City: UNA de Mexico.

Dean, Carolyn (1996) 'The renewal of Old World images and the creation of Peruvian visual culture', in Diana Fane (ed.), *Converging Cultures: Art and Identity in Spanish America*. New York: Brooklyn Museum/Abrams, pp. 171–82.

De Certeau, Michel (1986) *The Practices of Everyday Life*. Berkeley, CA: University of California Press.

Derrida, Jacques (1976) *Of Grammatology*. Baltimore, MD: Johns Hopkins University Press.

Eco, Umberto (1982) 'Critique of the image', in Victor Burgin (ed.), *Thinking Photography*. Basingstoke: Macmillan, pp. 32–38.

Edwards, Elizabeth, ed. (1992) *Anthropology and Photography, 1860–1920*. New Haven, CT: Yale University Press.

Edwards, Elizabeth (2001) *Raw Histories: Photographs, Anthropology and Museums*, Oxford: Berg.

Efimova, Alla (1997) 'To touch on the raw', *Art Journal*, spring, pp. 72–80.

Elkins, James (1999) *The Domain of Images*. Ithaca, NY: Cornell University Press.

Elkins, James (2003) *Visual Studies: a Skeptical Introduction*. New York: Routledge.

Eisenman, Stephen (1997) *Gauguin's Skirt*. London: Thames & Hudson.

Evans, Jessica and Hall, Stuart, eds (1999) *Visual Culture: the Reader*. London: Sage.

Flood, Finbarr Barry (2002) 'Between cult and culture: Bamiyan, Islamic iconoclasm, and the museum', *Art Bulletin*, 84 (4): 641–59.

Foster, Hal (1995) 'The artist as ethnographer', in George Marcus and Fred Myers (eds) *The Traffic in Culture*. Berkeley, CA: University of California Press.

Freedberg, David (1989) *The Power of Images: Studies in the History and Theory of Response*. Chicago: University of Chicago Press.

Gell, Alfred (1998) *Art and Agency: an Anthropological Theory*. Oxford: Clarendon Press.

Ginzburg, Carlo (1989) 'From Aby Warburg to E.H. Gombrich: a problem of method', in *Clues, Myths and the Historical Method*. Baltimore, MD: Johns Hopkins University Press.

Girard, René (1988) *To Double Business Bound: Essays on Literature, Mimesis and Anthropology*. London: Athlone Press.

Gombrich, E.H. (1986) *Aby Warburg: an Intellectual Biography*, 2nd edn. Oxford: Phaidon Press.

Gombrich, E.H. and Eribon, Didier (1993) *Looking for Answers: Conversations on Art and Science*. New York: Abrams.

Groys, Boris (1988) *The Total Art of Stalinism: Avant-garde, Aesthetic, Dictatorship, and Beyond*. Princeton, NJ: Princeton University Press.

Gruzinski, Serge (1992) *Painting the Conquest: Mexican Indians and the European Renaissance*. Paris: Unesco/Flammarion.

Heinich, Nathalie (1996) *The Glory of Van Gogh: an Anthropology of Admiration*, trans. Paul Leduc Browne. Princeton, NJ: Princeton University Press.

Howells, Richard (2003) *Visual Culture*. Cambridge: Polity Press.

Jay, Martin Jay (1988) 'Scopic regimes of modernity', in Hal Foster (ed.), *Vision and Visuality*. Seattle: Bay Press, pp. 3–27.

Kaufmann, Thomas Dacosta (1996) Response to Visual Culture Questionnaire, *October*, 77, pp. 45–8.

Keane, Webb (1997) *Signs of Recognition: Powers and Hazards of Representation in an Indonesian Society*. Berkeley, CA: University of California Press.

Khare, R.S. (1993) 'The seen and the unseen: Hindu distinctions, experiences and cultural reasoning', *Contributions to Indian Sociology* (n.s.), 27 (2): 191–212.

Koerner, Joseph Leo (1995) *Caspar David Friedrich and the Subject of Landscape*. London: Reaktion Books.

Krauss, Rosalind (1986) 'Photography in the service of surrealism', in Rosalind Krauss and Jane Livingston (eds), *L'Amour fou: Photography and Surrealism*. London: Arts Council, pp. 15–54.

Latour, Bruno (1993) *We have Never been Modern*, trans. Catherine Porter. London: Prentice Hall.

Latour, Bruno and Peter Weibel, eds (2002) *Iconoclash: Beyond the Image Wars in Science, Religion, and Art*. Cambridge, MA: MIT Press.

Lips, Julius E. (1937) *The Savage Hits Back*. Cambridge, MA: Harvard University Press.

Losche, Diane (1995) 'The Sepik gaze: iconographic interpretation of Abelam form', *Social Analysis*, 38: 47–60.

Ly, Borteh (2003) 'Devastated vision(s): the Khmer Rouge scopic regime in Cambodia', *Art Journal*, spring, pp. 67–81.

MacDougal, David (1998) *Transcultural Cinema*. Princeton, NJ: Princeton University Press.

McClintock, Annie (1995) *Imperial Leather: Race, Gender and Sexuality in the Colonial Contest*. New York: Routledge.

Mercier, Jacques (1997) *Art that Heals: the Image as Medicine in Eithiopia*. Munich: Prestel/New York Musuem for African Art.

Merleau-Ponty, Maurice (1962) *Phenomenology of Perception*, trans. Colin Smith. London: Routledge.

Mignolo, Walter (1995) *The Darker Side of the Renaisannce: Literacy, Territoriality and Colonization*. Ann Arbor, MI: University of Michigan Press.

Mirzoeff, Nicholas, ed. (2002) *The Visual Culture Reader*, 2nd edn. London: Routledge.

Mitchell, Timothy (1988) *Colonizing Egypt*. Cambridge: Cambridge University Press.

Mitchell, W.J.T. (1986) *Iconology: Image, Text and Ideology*. Chicago: University of Chicago Press.

Mitchell, W.J.T. (1994) 'The pictorial turn' in his *Picture Theory: Essays on Verbal and Visual Representation*. Chicago: University of Chicago Press, pp. 9–34.

Mitchell, W.J.T. (1996) 'What do pictures *really* want?' *October*, 77: 71–82.

Mitchell, W.J.T. (2002) 'Showing seeing: a critique of visual culture', in Nicholas Mirzoeff (ed.), *The Visual Culture Reader*, 2nd edn. London: Routledge.

Mitter, Partha (1977) *Much Maligned Monsters: History of European Reactions to Indian Art*. Oxford: Clarendon Press.

Morgan, David (1998) *Visual Peity: a History and Theory of Popular Religious Images*. Berkeley, CA: University of California Press.

Nemerov, Alexander (2001) *The Body of Raphaelle Peale: Still Life and Selfhood, 1812–1824*. Berkeley, CA: University of California Press.

Norris, Christopher (1988) *Paul De Man: Deconstruction and the Critique of Aesthetic Ideology*. London: Routledge.

Peirce, Charles S. (1966) *Selected Writings*. New York: Dover.

Pinney, Christopher (2001) 'Piercing the skin of the idol', in Christopher Pinney and Nicholas Thomas (eds), *Beyond Aesthetics: Art and the Technologies of Enchantment*. Oxford: Berg, pp. 157–80.

Pinney, Christopher (2002) 'The Indian work of art in the Age of Mechanical Reproduction: or, What happens when peasants "get hold" of Images', in Faye D. Ginsburg, Lila Abu-Lughod and Brian Larkin (eds), *Media Worlds: Anthropology on New Terrain*, Berkeley, CA: University of California Press pp. 355–69.

Pinney, Christopher (2004) *'Photos of the Gods': the Printed Image and Political Struggle in India*. London: Reaktion.

Poole, Deborah (1997) *Vision, Race and Modernity: a Visual Economy of the Andean Image World*. Princeton, NJ: Princeton University Press.

Rorty, Richard (1979) *Philosophy and the Mirror of Nature*. Oxford: Blackwell.

Rubies, Joan-Pau (1996) 'Instructions for travellers: teaching the eye to see', *History and Anthropology*, 9 (2–3): 139–90.

Said, Edward (1978) *Orientalism*. London: Routledge.

Sasaki, Ken-ichi (1996) 'The sexiness of visuality: a semantic analysis of the Japanese word: eye and seeing', *Filozofski-Vestnik*, 17 (2): 159–70.

Schivelbusch, Wolfgang (1986) *The Railway Journey: the Industrialization of Time and Space in the Nineteenth Century*. Berkeley, CA: University of California Press.

Smith, Bernard (1960) *European Vision and the South Pacific*. Oxford: Oxford University Press. Second edition New Haven, CT: Yale University Press, 1985.

Spivak, Gayatri Chakravarty (1999) *Critique of Postcolonial Reason*. Cambridge, MA: Harvard University Press.

Stafford, Barbara Maria (1996) *Good Looking: Essays on the Virtues of Images*. Cambridge, MA: MIT Press.

Stagl, Justin (1995) *A History of Curiosity: the Theory of Travel, 1550–1800*. London: Harwood Academic.

Strathern, Marilyn (1990) 'Artefacts of history: events and the interpretation of images', in Jukka Siikala (ed.), *Culture and History in the Pacific*. Finnish Anthropological Society Transactions 27. Helsinki: Finnish Anthropological Society.

Tagg, John C. (1988) *The Burden of Representation: Essays on Photographics and Histories*. Basingstoke: Macmillan.

Thomas, Nicholas (1991) *Entangled Objects: Exchange, Material Culture and Colonialism in the Pacific*. Cambridge, MA: Harvard University Press.

Wagner, Roy (1986) *Asiwinarong: Ethos, Image, and Social Power among the Usen Barok of New Ireland*. Princeton, NJ: Princeton University Press.

Weiner, James (1997) 'Televisualist anthropology', *Current Anthropology*, 38 (2): 197–236.

9

FOOD, EATING, AND THE GOOD LIFE

Judith Farquhar

Consider the cookbook.[1] Meant for use, its modern form of writing combines the list and the procedure. Ingredients and instructions, things and actions for the cook, cooperate in the making of food. Once made, food eaten and food given to others to eat are essential to the construction of human collective life. Cookbooks may seem to be an archive of shared knowledge, but the usefulness of cookbooks in guiding the (re)production of life actually depends on a body of tacit knowledge held by only some readers: the difference between creaming and mixing, the point at which milk is scalded (but not boiled), the yellow color of sautéed onions – these kinds of knowledge are more assumed than articulated. And only those who have been personally involved in the labor of cooking, at least as an apprentice, know how to properly read a cookbook. Experience is crucial in the proper deployment of these objects and instructions.

I think of a recipe sent to me years ago by a Minnesota friend, from the *Redwood Gazette*, quoted here in full:

Sandwich Filling

1 can Spam
1 can tuna
1 can mushroom soup

Mix together. No seasoning. This keeps and will make about 3 doz. sandwiches.

The clipping was long enshrined on my refrigerator door, and visitors who read it found it hilarious. These sandwiches seem to be filled with unselfconscious social class. Our laughter was directed at the small town housewife who still buys Spam – that wartime food banished by most Americans to a more impoverished past – and who finds canned mushroom soup to be a sauce that needs no seasoning. We think immediately of soft white bread and church-lady coffees, small town women sharing kitchen short cuts and keeping pantries full of cans. Readers who cook also marvel at the brilliant terseness of the recipe. Should the Spam and tuna be ground? Chopped? Mashed? Should the mushroom soup be thinned? Should the crusts be removed from the slices of white bread? Some reactions are even more direct. Cosmopolitan tastebuds revolt at the thought of all that processed food, not even heated up to purify this sandwich filling of its low-down tastes.

Yet the very humility of this recipe has a certain dignity. This is the food of people who feed each other – why else would you need three dozen sandwiches, even if they do keep? It is the lunchtime fare of people who make do with the available and the affordable in a food system that privileges foods that keep. Over the years I have lost my readiness to laugh at the Minnesota cooks who contribute to the food pages of the *Redwood Gazette*. At times I aspire to a life like theirs.

In this chapter, after surveying some ways of studying food and eating in the human sciences, I will narrow the scope of my anthropological interest in eating, seeking answers to several questions: What roles are played by food in the production and reproduction of social life? What difference does it make that food knowledge, practices, and preferences differ by time and place? How do eating practices relate to historical experience? All of these questions relate to a simpler but larger issue: what sort of agency can be ascribed to food? Two anecdotes from my collaborative fieldwork on life cultivation practice (*yangsheng*) in Beijing will be explored to open up this question of agency. Ultimately I suggest that agency in everyday life is a form of craftwork involving intimate collaborations among embodied humans and material objects like food. Like recipes and the cooking skills on which they rely, like tasting food and savoring the company of others, the crafting of a good life is an improvisational project in which a great deal goes without saying. Ethnography draws attention to some of this embodied and built common sense.

READING ABOUT FOOD

Food and the technologies of producing and consuming it convey many messages and speak to us of many lifeways. Objects like the ingredients of food and actions like the practices of cooking have long coexisted on the human sciences menu.[2] The topic of food and eating has invited encyclopedic collation both within gastronomic traditions and as multicultural compilations of foodways.[3] The human diet, past and present, local and global, is extremely diverse, and the social practices associated with eating are as various as the world's communities. Moreover, variation in diet and particularity in eating habits practically define social diversity while giving concrete form to culture. Indeed, the mantra 'You are what you eat' continues to be invoked in studies ranging across the human sciences to remind us that food makes human form – it directly produces bodies and lives, kin groups and communities, economic systems and ideologies, while being produced in its turn by these formations.

Responding to the empirical diversity and formative power of food practice, the literatures of the human sciences offer numerous approaches to food, each claiming a certain comprehensiveness. For anthropology from its inception, food has been good to think with. Twentieth-century anthropology hardly improved upon one of its earliest classic texts in this regard, *The Religion of the Semites*, by W. Robertson Smith (1887). In his chapter on sacrificial meals, Robertson Smith contributed to anthropology the notion of commensality. This term has kept the question of who eats together, what they eat, and with what effects, very much on the anthropological menu. Robertson Smith framed the sociological problem of eating in a way that was already dynamic and relativistic: he analyzed the commensal practices reflected in his sources on

Middle Eastern tribal cultures as making and remaking social groups at many levels of complexity. Moreover, he noted that groups who ate together – commensals – included not just men but gods.[4] Interestingly, Robertson Smith's argument also denies the historical or theoretical primacy of the nuclear family as a commensal group, criticizing arguments that would presume the naturalness of the domestic circle as a commensal group and derive the structure of larger groups such as the Semitic tribes from it.[5] Rather he suggests that food taboos deriving from the relationship of individuals and groups to the sacred always already divide small coresident groups such as families, making it relatively unusual for all nuclear family members to eat together. In his account, crosscutting affiliations – expressed and constituted by eating practices – construct kinship beyond coresidence, blood, and even humanity. It follows that there are no 'natural' commensal units except for those that are made as people (and gods and ancestors) eat together.

Food became more central to the anthropological tradition with the first full-blown development of field-based ethnography. One could argue, for example, that Malinowski's classic treatments of the *kula* system of exchange in the Trobriand Islands extended the notion of commensality to address questions of who 'feeds' what to whom, with what particular timing, using what technologies of transport, and by what means of ritual and symbolic legitimation.[6] Though Malinowski was more interested in highly valued inedible exchange objects such as *kula* shells than in the yams and pigs that also circulate, Annette Weiner and Nancy Munn followed up this classic research with innovative studies that did turn attention to food, feeding, and eating.[7] An ethnography in this tradition, Brad Weiss's *Sacred Trees, Bitter Harvests*, organizes much of its wide-ranging argument around the consumable of coffee. Returning constantly to coffee itself (as crop, as exchange item, as global commodity, as target of colonial and national policies), Weiss explores practical and evaluative links from coffee to other objects and processes, including 'sacred' trees; bananas as crop and food; cowry, rupee, and iron hoe currencies; clothes; caravan trade and agricultural cooperatives; and forms of counting everything. This way of tracing networks of objects, meanings, and practices gradually builds a whole social world around 'globalizing coffee', and suggests that any form of food could similarly be perceived as the center of a lived world. It would, of course, be only one of many possible centers; but thorough ethnography of this kind suggests that the links connecting food to everything else are irreducible, and should not be analytically dissolved.

Many recent studies of food and eating have centered on the psychological and sociological question of identity, but this too is an old theme in classic anthropology. Missionary ethnologists Spencer and Gillen, in their study of Australian social and religious practices (1899) emphasized the identification of human actors with food sources through social systems enforced in part by food taboos. Their descriptions – and those of other early ethnologists such as Fison and Howitt – were taken up and extended by Durkheim and his students as they crafted a powerful sociology that sutured individuals into *sui generis* social groups in part through edible, but proscribed, totem animals and plants. If anything, these early considerations of the issues we now class under the heading of identity were less reductionist than some more recent efforts, in that they tended to insist on the simultaneous construction of nature and culture through knowledge and practice. Durkheim and Mauss's *Primitive Classification* (1903/1963), for example, explores the logic of a cosmo-social framework in which food taboos and thus eating practices figure as technologies of human production and reproduction.[8] As subsequent ethnography has shown, such frameworks are inherent to everyday life and the eating it entails, not just analytic abstractions from lived worlds.[9]

One could argue that the anthropology of the second half of the twentieth century was practically founded on food studies, with Lévi-Strauss's *The Raw and the Cooked* (1969/1983) and *The Origin of Table Manners* (1978/1990) occupying pride of place. It is also impossible to ignore Mary Douglas's early and still increasing interest in food and culinary forms. Structuralist anthropology in its several forms reaffirmed the centrality of eating to human social existence, yet, following in the Durkheimian tradition most clearly seen in *Primitive Classification* (Durkheim and Mauss 1903/1963), its topic was always more mind than body. Despite their differences, the analyses advanced by Lévi-Strauss and Douglas shared an interest in the significant structures that gave form to – in the final analysis – the life of the mind. Thus, though there are fascinating engagements with food in the work of both writers, the tastes of food, experiences of eating, and the particular sociality surrounding commensal life were seldom a central issue for them.[10]

Ethnographic studies of food since the 1980s have returned some phenomenological importance to eating and taste, locating them as processes taking place in a social environment and carrying rich psychological significance. David E. Sutton, as part of his ethnography of alimentary culture and its forms of social memory on the Greek island of Kalymnos, has provided a masterly review of the recent literature.[11] In his discussion he considers the various ways in which experience – of taste, sociality, time, and space – has recaptured the ethnographic center stage. His bibliographic and analytic efforts focusing on memory have been paralleled by Carole Counihan's extensive and sensitive explorations of identity construction through 'the cultural uses of food' both in Italy and the United States.[12] Studies of this kind are ambitious in their refusal to confine eating to the restricted domains of political economy, nutrition, social structure, or individual experience. They may not be strictly 'post-structuralist' but they are certainly post-functionalist in their efforts to explain the cultural forms of food use without reductionist reference to stabilizing mechanisms arising solely from some form of need. Desire, pleasure, and pain play through the pages of the new studies of food practice. I include my own study of post-Maoist Chinese eating cultures in this group.[13] In the food-related parts of this work, I sought to denaturalize both hunger and taste, taking up both famines of the past and the consumption boom of the present, in an effort to show how appetites vary historically and change their character rather rapidly in shifting sociopolitical conditions. All these anthropological approaches have advanced some argument about the forms and processes of social life far beyond, but in close relationship to, human alimentation. Indeed, it could be argued that anthropologists have had a hard time maintaining a focus on food itself. Attention always returns to the social forms, ranging from states to kin groups to identities to histories, that are expressed and constructed in food practice.

Historians have their own route through the archives of food to grasp the details of social practice and propose broader narratives of social form. *Longue durée* historians work from humble sources like early cookbooks to infer aspects of daily life that have not otherwise entered the historical record.[14] Following their lead, cultural and social historians have used recipes and cooking techniques to fill in material gaps in the written archive, linking economic history to the history of gender, for example, while enriching our understanding of the slow evolution of the practices and spaces of everyday life.[15] In parts of the world where there is a literate *haute cuisine*, there are more elaborate discourses that can be historically cataloged. Abstract principles may be articulated in writing about cooking and food in these traditions alongside lists of ingredients, techniques, and folklore. In Chinese or French gastronomic literature, for example, cookbook writing may be supplemented by reflections on the aesthetics of flavor, texture, shape, and color; and food practice may be explicitly crafted to forge connections with broader domains of taste, connoisseurship, and social class.[16] One kind of cookbook in China, for example, compiles foods and menus of the pre-twentieth century imperial court; people I know who own such books often own no other cookbook, and the charm of these recipes may have little to do with actual eating or food preparation. The food is not incidental, and people may derive ideas for use in their own kitchens from such books. But they know they cannot reproduce the life of which these recipes and stories are one part. As they read, then, it is more likely that the imperial cookbook provides something like a whole vision of the practice of lordship and the material social order of a remote but glamorous national past. An aestheticized historical sense that also stimulates the taste buds.

Still, the famous literatures of cuisine tend to hide or understate their most theoretical dimensions, presuming rather than explicating commonsense relations between sociality and materiality as they explore local gastronomic and aesthetic aspects of human social life. Since few food discourses articulate the practical logics that are built into the gastronomic systems they discuss, history tends to be rendered as nature.[17] That which normally goes unstated is taken to be both natural and universal. As a result, most writings on cuisine remain resolutely local, however well their techniques may travel. Ginseng tea can be brewed properly and deliver a nice buzz in Nanjing or Nashville. There are compendia of health advice published in China that list the efficacies and properties of ginseng tea, and even some Americans have found them useful. But these are poor sources to consult if the aim is to learn how – on what sort of bodies and in what sort of social worlds – ginseng makes its contribution to the crafting of a good life. What is for one eater or drinker an 'alternative medicine' or a New Age herbal stimulant is for another drinker one of the pleasures of old age or an opportunity to consume the good wishes of family and friends. The practical lives in which food takes on its powers differ in ways that the literature does not usually articulate.

The natural sciences literature on nutrition is theoretically more ambitious than cookbooks and compendia. Nutritionists operate a powerful analytic system that can locate and quantify properties of food such as vitamins, fats, calories, and carbohydrates. Based on the body known to anatomy and physiology, nutritional science advances knowledge about the articulation of the outside world – in the form of nutritional factors borne by food itself – with the internal processes of bodily life – a bewildering variety of activities that only begin with the physiology of digestion. Historically, knowledge of this kind has tended to be normative: the question 'How does food affect us?' has been informed from start to finish by the practical and ethical question 'What *should* people eat?' A flood of popular books about Paleolithic diet, for example, has drawn on archaeological research to bring evolutionary time depth to the question 'What is it most natural for *homo sapiens* to eat?'[18] To what foods is human physiology most fundamentally adapted? In addition, debates about the proper structure of the 'food pyramid' engage educators, parents, publishers, and government agencies in efforts to simplify and systematize expert advice on diet while, incidentally, seeking to have an important influence through primary school education and lunchroom management. In the process of such debates, received wisdom about the nature of human physiological needs is constantly being challenged, constantly under revision.[19] At the same time, while food remains a problem at the level of concrete phenomena, it is nevertheless analyzed into factors that remove its powers from the level of the experiential. Taste and the social relations of eating are no longer the point. In a move parallel to the displacements of the classic cultural anthropology of food, attention drifts away from food as object, eating as practice.

At the other end of the human sciences spectrum from nutrition studies are the fictional and *belles lettres* literatures that have also found food good to think with. In the United States M.F.K. Fisher is considered the foremost example of a genre of twentieth-century writing on food that expands the topic far beyond the physiology of digestion, the recipe, and even the gastronomic construction of identity.[20] Not confined by the disciplinary commitments of biological or sociological traditions, writers like Fisher range across a number of material and experiential terrains to re-enchant the symbolic, erotic, and convivial worlds that are sustained by eating. Works like hers precisely make the point that, rather than dividing and reducing human life, as would be the case for a biology or sociology, studies of food and eating unify and expand human life. The gourmet essayist can be holistic about the social, which is to say, the commensal. Still, every essayist is constrained by her/his social position. All eating is done in place and incorporates a point of view. In previous writing on late twentieth-century China, for example, I have shown how a fictional work, 'The gourmet,' by Lu Wenfu, weaves together and clarifies some irresolvable political and moral contradictions of the eating life: we cannot eat without exploiting the labor of others, we cannot eat morally and still 'eat well'. In this charming and maddening novella, however, the direct sensuous appeal of food at once supports and undermines the complex arguments developed by the narrative. Readers who have eaten in Suzhou, where the story takes place, perhaps can taste the 'over the bridge' noodles and the shrimp-stuffed tomatoes that drive the narrative.[21] Similar effects are discernible in food writing ranging from the essays of Calvin Trillin to Proust's *Remembrance of Times Past*, from the speculations in Brillat-Savarin (*The Physiological of Taste*, 1826) to the quirky commonplaces of the *Alice B. Toklas Cookbook*.[22] In writing where food is taken seriously as an irreducible component of human life, one reads not only with the eyes and the brain but also with the palate and eventually the whole body.

But what is this body? Anthropology may be the only discipline that has begun to ask the question in fully comparative and relativistic terms, turning to literatures beyond ethnography for inspiration. Studies of gastronomy, nutrition, and commensality are rich and tempting resources not only for an anthropology of eating but also, by extension, of the body. Scholarship on everyday life and materiality becomes especially helpful in this relativization of 'the body' when the contingency of bodies as lived formations of time and space is theoretically acknowledged. The rather Eurocentric literature on gastronomy and 'food culture' is paralleled around the world by equally complex but often less fully acknowledged alimentary cultures. It would seem that every people, even if they lack a traditional literature, has a more or less articulate body of lore about food, a history of eating and a way of remembering it, a geography that distinguishes neighbors and strangers by what they eat, an embodied understanding of food efficacies. Some traditions also offer a systematic dietetics, an ethics of eating, a nutritional therapeutics, even an indigenous

political economy concerned with hunger and waste.[23] All of these rich human archives display a process of slippage: one may start with food, but soon the topic has shifted to physiological agents, social form, cosmic forces, moral precepts, bodily health, or historical memory. It is precisely because the discrete anatomical functional body, the body with nutritional needs, the body that embodies an individual biography, is not a given piece of nature that this slippage takes place. We begin with a simple bodily process and we end up everywhere. Or at least, everywhere that is material.

In the face of this huge and slippery archive, how should an anthropology of food and eating proceed? How can it challenge mainstream common sense about bodies, causes, and human nature? Can contemporary ethnography deepen our understanding of human foodways in a world being transformed by commercialized consumption, transnational corporate agriculture, food biotechnology, ever more rarified gourmet habits, eating disorders that can be fatal, and a widening gap between the world's rich and poor with the accompanying scandals of waste and starvation? Can anthropology expand on the pleasures of eating while acknowledging its relationship to privation, inequality, and exploitation? What now demands to be better understood, and how can the relatively limited methods of field-and-archive anthropology contribute new, and specifically anthropological, knowledge?

As much of the discussion above has shown, one classic strength of anthropology stems from its holistic, relativist, and field-based past: ethnography clarifies the historical and geographic specificity of lived worlds, and it does so through an investigation of practice. The consequence of this empirical contribution, one hopes, is an expansion of the human imagination. When food and embodiment are at issue, cultural imagining might even be quite visceral and involve some interesting surprises. Thus, however similar a McDonald's may appear in Beijing or Seoul, the uses to which fast food and small tables are put in various places render these cheeseburgers and fries a culturally-specific social technology even as they alter the palates and physical dimensions of populations that have in the past little enjoyed animal fat and dairy products.[24] However alien, and thus amusing, a sandwich filling made of Spam may be to my cosmopolitan friends, an ethnography of its small-town origins would reveal much about a disappearing American way of life and the meaning of 'comfort' in food. These cultural worlds are part of the anthropological heritage that has long informed us of human capacities, if not 'human nature'. But cultures are not adequately illuminated by lists of edible objects and descriptive accounts of the behaviors that make up their 'social context'. Simply knowing what, where, and when Tibetans or Brazilians eat tells us relatively little about their lives.[25] To adequately, if not completely, understand fully commensal lives would require the attentiveness and the participatory enthusiasm of an M.F.K. Fisher or a Lu Wenfu paired with an analytic that seeks to escape their local and class character. Perhaps ethnography can attempt a return to the kind of holism that, like the best food writing, abolishes the division between foods and ideas, mouths and brains while linking these materialities to more global processes. The path to this goal is an anthropology of everyday practice, which can also be conceived as an anthropology of embodiment.

In the rest of this chapter, keeping the large questions posed by the food and eating archive in mind, and seeking to offer only those riches that can be gathered through ethnography, I will draw primarily from my own research in China to develop some insights into food and life.

CLASS, HISTORY, AND 'TRADITIONAL BEIJING' FOOD

In the fall of 2003 I was part of a team of investigators who interviewed residents of Beijing interested in 'the cultivation of life' (yangsheng).[26] The popular practices of yangsheng include exercise, nutritional regimes, and hobbies, and they are encouraged and supported by a large and historically deep literature on health, personal efficacy, and happiness. Among the longer interviews we undertook with middle-aged residents of a downtown district was a long talk with Mrs Hu, a retired buyer for a factory.[27] She now devotes her time to keeping house for her husband and nineteen-year-old daughter, and she volunteers in the office of the neighborhood committee. In reply to one of our routine questions about food habits, Mrs Hu said that in her household her husband cooks his own food while she does the cooking for her daughter and herself. This being a rather unusual arrangement for a Beijing family, we asked why.

She replied that she considers herself a traditional Beijing cook, with a preference for meat dishes. 'I cook for taste, not for nutritional value, and I love fried foods.' She feels that her diet is very good – 'I pay close attention to diet' – even though she volunteers the idea that the fatty foods she prefers increase her already high cholesterol level and make it harder for her to lose weight. Her daily cooking regime includes two eggs, noodles, and leftovers for breakfast, and several dishes with meat – pork or chicken – with a starchy staple food like rice or bread for both midday and evening meals. She also hastens to add that her family observes the 'traditional' holiday food customs of north China. On birthdays, for example, they always eat 'long-life noodles' as well as the more modern birthday cake. Mrs Hu's husband, on the other hand, prefers 'clear and plain' (qingdan) foods, which is why he cooks his own vegetables and light meat dishes while avoiding deep-frying, sweets, and strong flavors.

My colleagues and I wondered about this separate cooking arrangement, bearing in mind that the most telling traditional marker of a divided family was 'separate stoves'. Family division can be rancorous enough when grown children split off from their parents' stove. But separate stoves for a husband and wife? Of course, in the city there are all manner of practical domestic arrangements, and they need not generate anxiety just because they are unconventional. Several other features of Mrs Hu's daily life and history helped to make sense of these separate stoves, however. She had married her husband near the end of the Maoist period (the late 1970s), and, counter to the preferred practice, he had moved into her own family's household. The couple had continued to live with her parents, who came to require very intensive nursing care as the years advanced. Perhaps their presence also demanded that the proprieties of having an undivided family be met, and in these years Mrs Hu cooked for everyone.

Marriages made at this time were often socially asymmetrical, with those from intellectual and former business families seeking out working-class spouses in the hope that their own problematic background would not be held against them in the rectifying class logic of Maoist social administration. Mrs Hu's husband's rather austere food habits suggest that their marriage was just such an asymmetrical arrangement. He not only displays the preferences of the intelligentsia in seeking out lighter food, his preferences are more consistent with the scientific nutritional advice available from so many media sources in the city.

Mrs Hu and her husband had cooked apart only since her parents died in 1999. Up until then, she emphasized, their life had been quite hard, with too little income for the five of them and a heavy burden falling on her to provide nursing care for her parents while maintaining her factory job (which also involved occasional – unwelcome – out-of-town travel). Recalling these hard years, and the lack of control she had over her own time during that period, Mrs Hu equated *yangsheng*, the cultivation of life, with the achievement of a quiet and peaceful life, lived 'according to regularities of my own'. Presumably this control over her own time included not having to deal with her husband's demands about diet. But it also allowed indulgence in the (more expensive) comfort foods that she considered to be part of her Beijing tradition, without worrying too much about the health consequences. She was giving herself a break from self-sacrifice, one that had already lasted more than four years since the death of her parents.

She had not, however, ceased to look after her daughter. It was clear in the interview that this young woman, who had just tested into college at the time of the interview, was the center of Mrs Hu's life. We heard about the three full meals a day she cooked for the two of them, as well as the quiet evening regime of reading and clipping the newspaper she had devised so as not to disturb her daughter's studies. One wonders what the daughter's relationship with her father was like. Perhaps the whole family still shared one goal, to increase the educational level of the next generation. The father's contribution may have been somewhat more remote and abstract than the mother's, but Mrs Hu seems to have seen her job as making sure that the material conditions were in place to get her daughter's body (at least) into and through college. Was she also continuing to recruit the filial loyalty of this precious daughter, even against the father, with the delicious if fattening foods she offered up? I would be more sure of this gendered resistance if I had eaten at Mrs Hu's, but it did seem plausible to our group of researchers that there was an oppositional quality to these cooking and eating arrangements. Like some other households where I have eaten in China, when the stir-fried dishes are cold or skimpy, when the rice is undercooked, when the meal itself is much delayed, the principal cook is usually taking a stand in the context of family politics.

This interpretation of Mrs Hu's interview has been partly speculative, since she did not invite us to keep in touch and become acquainted with her family. But the guesses made here are quite consistent with the uses of food in Chinese families of the latter part of the twentieth century. Tastes for food and linkages to values like comfort, health, and virtue cannot be separated from social class, personal history, and ongoing projects of life construction. One could summarize all the multi-layered activity manifested in Mrs Hu's food practices as contributing to identity construction: retired, 'traditional', working-class, a Beijinger, quiet and respectable, and (like so many others we interviewed) bearing the marks of past struggle. But this would suggest that the natural goal for a person of Mrs Hu's sort is social and psychological identity, which I think rather understates the complexity of her purposes and the forms of agency that converge in her. In particular, to see identity construction as the goal locates her satisfactions in the wrong place. She is not taking pleasure in the mere fact of being a traditional working-class Beijinger; her goal in life is not the achievement of some kind of psychological or cultural center point for herself. Rather, her everyday life activity, in which she 'pays close attention to diet', both expresses and constructs a material form of life that is quite visible and effective for both her family and her community. The working-class comfort foods she enjoys cooking and sharing with her daughter (and, I suspect, her coworkers in the neighborhood committee office) compensate her for years of poverty and sacrifice, (re)materialize a social rift between herself and her husband, and contribute to her personal, cultural, and moral well-being.

Mrs Hu, even while she expresses a very proper concern about 'high cholesterol', assesses her regime as one that is centrally concerned with health, and she uses the topic of the cultivation of life (*yangsheng*) to justify her enjoyment of fatty foods and regular habits: 'Yangsheng,' she says, 'is a big help with the health of the body and the happiness of the spirit. If the spirit is happy then the body is healthier. If the body is good, then the spirit will be happier.' Noting that cancer arises from 'blocked-up Qi', she places happiness at the center of a feedback loop linking 'body' and 'spirit' in a healthful cycle. And what conduces to happiness more than good food?

Mrs Hu's comments demonstrate the efficacy of food in reproducing class, working on family form, altering a personal history, and generally serving the strategies and tactics of everyday life. It is not difficult for a middle-class American of about the same age to relate to her notion of comfort foods. These fatty, starchy, oily, and sweet staples compensate us for the complicated demands of work and family, they transport us back to a time when the macaroni and cheese or cocoa with marshmallows was prepared by our mother and given us to eat. As a child, Mrs Hu probably seldom ate the dishes she now prepares every day, but her nostalgic embrace of 'traditional' cooking doesn't really need to be supported by actual childhood experience. Like all nostalgia, her comfortable eating is a cultural imaginary that satisfies certain desires. But that's not all it is. It also makes a neo-working-class life in which her daughter can be upwardly mobile, both husband and wife can cling to their class differences, personal time can be controlled, and Mrs Hu can be compensated for a past she has experienced as difficult. As she makes the food, the food makes her newly enjoyable life.

THE FLAVORS OF FRIENDSHIP

The interviews our group conducted in 2003 sometimes led to sustained engagement with residents of the downtown district where we worked. One especially enjoyable interview was with a sixty-year-old widow, Zhang Li, and her best friend, Zhou Xiaomei.[28] These two lived across the street from each other. Both being 'retired housewives',[29] they had time to engage in a number of *yangsheng* activities together. In their interview there was much talk of food, and both of them urged any of us to come visit so they could cook for us; my mouth was watering as they talked of vegetable pancakes, spicy congee (rice gruel with flavorings), and wild mountain greens. Lili and I began to visit and we also arranged to join them for one of their frequent early-morning trips to the Western Hills for mountain-climbing.

The situations of these two women were complex, and I find it difficult to separate the wonderful eating we did together from the many contingencies of their lives. The fact that Sister Zhang, the widow, was the poorest person we interviewed, surviving on about $50 a month supplied by her two children, and that Sister Zhou was living in extremely cramped space – a room of $7\,m^2$ for her family of four – is inseparable in my experience from their boundless generosity and (almost) unfailing good cheer.

Take our mountain-climbing trip, for example: Lili and I had provided ourselves with the kind of food the ladies had told us they always carried: a little fruit, bottled water, and some sesame seed cakes (*shaobing*). Sister Zhang and Sister Zhou didn't appear to be carrying any more than we were when we met them at the bus stop, but the delicacies began to appear even on the bus trip out to the Fragrant Hills Park. Special hard candy unlike any I had seen in my neighborhood stores was pressed on us along with comments about its unusual flavor. Did we eat breakfast? Wouldn't we like a piece of fruit?

Disembarked from the bus and walking to the park entrance, we learned it was part of the ritual to stop at a sidewalk vendor's stand to eat flatcakes stuffed with greens and scallions, hot off the griddle. I was allowed to pay for these only after a considerable struggle. Sustained with this second breakfast, we headed up to the peak. Halfway up the mountain we encountered a park maintenance crew watering newly planted trees. Climbers had stopped to drink from the hose; Sister Zhang explained that the workers tapped mountain spring water for this task, and an opportunity to drink such pure water straight from the source should not be passed up. The flavor is so much better than that of boiled or distilled water. But there were a lot of people waiting to taste the water and I wanted to climb on; Sister Zhang was mystified by my nonchalance: how could I think of passing up this chance to taste really fine water?

By lunchtime we had learned that Sister Zhou's heart condition was acting up that day and we also heard quietly from Sister Zhang about the reasons for her ill health. She and her family occupied a small room in a house that had once belonged to her whole family. Her unemployed brother, whose family had several rooms, had become an adversary; he was building an additional room in the tiny remaining common area. Sister Zhou felt his hostility very deeply and her worries aggravated her symptoms.

But her friend would not let these concerns spoil her day, or her lunch. Once down from the mountaintop, we found a bench at Half Mountain Plaza and opened our food bags. Lili and I were not allowed to eat the *shaobing* or fruit we had brought, on the grounds that they were of inferior quality. Sisters Zhang and Zhou had coordinated their buying: one had gone to the best street baker in the district and bought plenty of truly superior *shaobing* – crispy on the outside and tender inside, with a rich wheat flavor – and the other had found fine Fuji apples. One had brought sliced spicy sausage, vacuum-packed, and the other had bags of sticky dried fruit. Both had been lugging much more bottled water than we needed. And of course there was the very special candy. We feasted, and Sister Zhou cheered up quite a bit. She explained her brother's bad behavior as a product of his envy of her: 'He can't stand it that my family is so happy, my son is such a good boy, and we will soon be able to move into our own apartment.' Clearly, she did not think of herself as poor and oppressed; rather she saw herself as more fortunate than most, and she often said as much.

In fact both of them had a rather superior attitude. Sister Zhang liked to comment on the 'low social quality' (*suzhi*) of certain neighbors. She had very decided opinions on the characteristics of the good life, which she seemed to believe she had achieved even on her unusually low income. Not all of her views involved consumption or commodities, though she certainly shared the obsession of middle-aged Beijing women with getting the best-quality goods for the lowest prices. Like the pure spring water she urged us to drink on the mountain, the west-facing windows of her single room in the interior of an old courtyard house provided precious afternoon light and warmth, unusual for Beijing's old one-story buildings. Even better, her tiny kitchen was hers alone. And now that her long-disabled husband was dead, her time was also her own. 'No wonder we're so happy,' she said of herself and Sister Zhou. 'We have all day to cultivate our own lives.'

The food talk was part of the view shared by these two friends that they knew better than most how to cultivate life. And, I hasten to add, they did. My last visit with them in 2003 was shortly before my return to the United States as winter was settling in over Beijing. The two women had spent the early afternoon making dumplings (*jiaozi*), but not just any dumplings. These were stuffed with pork and pumpkin, a combination I had never encountered in my assiduous personal research on Beijing's many varieties of dumplings. When the day's menu was announced, I even wondered if they could have any flavor at all. As the plates of steaming *jiaozi* began to issue forth from Sister Zhang's little kitchen, though, I was converted. The dumplings were divine. I praised them with genuine pleasure, a bit surprised that the humble pumpkin could turn out to be such a fine filling for the thin flour-and-water skins the two ladies had spent the afternoon rolling out and stuffing. Sister Zhang brought out the half pumpkin that remained from this project – not the large orange item we know in North America, but an equally bland and tough sort of squash – to show me how to grate it finely

enough to mix with minced pork for the filling. I said, 'The best thing about this filling is that it is exactly salty enough.' Sister Zhou beamed, turning to Sister Zhang to say, 'I did that part; you see I was right about the salt.'[30] This conversation and the dumplings themselves made it clear, if it had not been before: these two are epicures. They think of themselves as achieving degrees of pleasure in everyday life that even much richer and better-housed people cannot appreciate, and they take pride in doing it with the simplest of means.

This is a subtle and thoroughly embodied apprehension of class through distinction. These ladies do not pretend to be secret aristocrats. Their tastes run to the simple and the cheap: Zhang Li is mostly vegetarian and Zhou Xiaomei is an advocate of 'home cooking' (*jiachang cai*). No bird's nest soup or shrimp-stuffed tomatoes for these two. And like many other aging low-income city dwellers in China, they are well aware that, lacking health insurance, the good life they have built could be shattered with the first serious illness to attack them. But this vulnerability is precisely why they devote their time to life cultivation at the level of the body and material everyday life. They are good at maintaining a healthy lifestyle and they believe that their wholesome eating habits, exercise (not just mountain climbing but badminton, dancing, and long walks), and above all happy attitudes might just stave off the physical disaster of serious illness indefinitely. Like Mrs Hu, they know by the pleasure they derive from physical activity and simple delicious food that they are doing something right. Their enjoyments distinguish them socially, historically, and physically in positive material form.

The pumpkin dumplings and fresh shaobing that are actually eaten play a role in this ongoing life-cultivation project; but *talk* of food and pastimes is perhaps just as important. I never did get the vegetable pancakes with which Sister Zhang and Sister Zhou roped me into their lives, but we all enjoyed talking about them and the many other home-cooked delicacies of Beijing cuisine. One particularly interesting form of talk threaded through the food chat of many Beijingers involved memories of widespread famine and systematic food shortages between the late 1950s and the late 1970s. Some, like Mrs Hu, had adopted a compensatory approach to food, nowadays eating well (or even too much) to feed a past hunger that still gnawed. Others seemed to structure their concern with food around a positively valued asceticism that could be explicitly linked to the Maoist values of hungrier times. In addition, conversations with Sister Zhang and Sister Zhou betrayed their relish at recalling in detail exactly how many ration tickets were needed to get exactly how much oil, or rice, or gristly pork. They spoke as proud housewives who knew how to manage on very little and who competed successfully with too many mouths – the Chinese population is counted not as 'heads' but as 'mouths' – for too few edibles. Listening to them, I suspected that oil, rice, pork, and other rationed foods would never again be just the ingredients of meals. These commodities carried a thoroughly textured form of value, speaking not only of secure eating but also of personal efficacy, not only of present comforts but also of past worries.

AGENCY

It is common for anthropologists of food to remind us that we are what we eat; less common for them to explore just how practices of eating do the work of constructing a broader material (and, of course, lived) reality. The first theme does not seem to lead naturally to the second. The forms of agency that construct social position or subjective identity are not often theorized beyond some attention to quasi-consumerist questions of choice, even where the role of consumption in the pursuit of social distinction is taken into account. In other words, though the verbal form 'identification' (as opposed to an all too nominal 'identity') helps us discern processes of situating and constituting actors, we too seldom move beyond questions of expression of 'selves' and their recognition by 'others' to consider whole fields of activity, the powers that pervade them, and the solidarities and exclusions that arise in them. Where agency itself is under consideration, on the other hand, as it has been in science studies and actor-network theory, the particular powers of human beings – in a diverse field of human and non-human agents – become a problem rather than a given.[31]

'Agency' came to be a theme in recent anthropology in reaction against functionalism and structuralism, both approaches to explaining human action that seemed at times to assume excessive limits on human freedom. Anthropologists and sociologists since the deterministic social theories of the mid-twentieth century have tended to advance agency not as an analytical term, in need of rigorous definition, but as a value to be defended: the human individual became unimaginable to the liberal position if s/he was not accorded the power to act more or less autonomously, at least at times, at least in theory. Agency has thus taken on most of its meaning in anthropology as a relational term: structure and agency are opposed, and dynamic concepts like Giddens's structuration have been required to resolve the opposition and restore a commonsense middle ground to our sociological accounts (without, incidentally, abandoning the use of rather classic opposed terms).[32] Thus 'agency' derives much of its obviousness from the relative fixity and seldom challenged actuality of structures (governments, institutions, society),[33] which have also seemed to have a self-evident exterior reality. Often in anthropological treatments, agency is shorthand for whatever forces resist domination by social structures, any human powers that revise received social forms. Since it is usually individuals whose agency is being defended, the very capacities of humans for freedom, choice, and creativity seem to be at stake. High stakes indeed.

But when the topic is food, can we really expect so much freedom? Our Minnesota housewives learned to love canned foods because they were cheap, in the stores, and convenient to store and prepare. To some extent their daughters have adopted similar approaches to home cooking, finding as much comfort in continuities of taste (and smells, colors, textures) as in the convenience of canned mushroom soup. What is the exact nature of their choice, freedom, or creativity? Should they be seen as domestic drones, mere victims of a system that 'processes' food and offers little variety in America's small towns; or perhaps they are creative reinventors of a local 'identity' in which all terms – the Spam, the local newspaper publicity, the ladies' luncheons – take on new meaning? The closer we get to these processes that so resemble our own everyday lives the less useful a dualistic formation of victimhood and domination, repetition and creativity, becomes. The kind of agency that builds the good life in Minnesota or Beijing cannot be attributed solely to those who (if only at times) escape domination or find original ways to bring significance to life. The conservative reproduction of culture is also a form of action.

The field of science studies has advanced quite a different approach to the 'problem' of agency by demonstrating both theoretically and empirically that non-human agency is not so different from that of humans. In some recent ethnographic and historical studies, recognition of the dispersed agency of objects, texts, spaces – non-humans in general – has tended to once again reduce the scope of human agency while finding underdetermined activity everywhere (even, of course, among humans).[34] Agents, or 'quasi-objects' and 'quasi-subjects', deploy diverse kinds of effectiveness through networks that are always under construction and swarming with minor powers.[35] When agency is seen as dispersed, necessary, and underdetermined it can be explored as an empirical problem rather than an assumed property of human beings alone. And 'identity' becomes only one of the many social forms – or positions – that can result from a play of powers in complex and shifting networks. It follows that these social forms extend far beyond human society. Yes, we are what we eat; but maybe eating is not all about us.

In this reconsideration of the place of food and eating in the human sciences, I have sought to move beyond experience-centered identity studies and introduce insights from the actor-network analysis of some science studies. The material presented here does not lend itself, however, to adopting the bird's-eye view that any study of extended networks must adopt. Rather I have introduced anecdotes about commensality in contemporary Beijing (and, more speculatively, Minnesota) to draw attention to the forms of agency with which 'the good life' is built anywhere. Rather than asking 'Where is agency here?' (which presumes there are activities in which no agency can be found), this treatment has collapsed the poles of structure and agency, freedom and domination, to appreciate the gratifications, anxieties, purposiveness, and productivity of a mundane effectiveness which is not merely human.

In this I am inspired by Walter Benjamin's sustained effort, via the notion of craftwork, to overcome a polarized discourse on freedom in mid-twentieth-century Marxism and Continental philosophy. His essay on the storyteller is one place where these concerns are made explicit. 'Traces of the storyteller cling to the story the way the handprints of the potter cling to the clay vessel,' he says.[36] With late twentieth-century debates on agency behind us, this remark could be reversed to assert that the material character of the clay (or the tradition drawn upon in a story, or the pumpkin grated for dumplings) acts on both the pot and the potter, the story and the storyteller, the meal and the cooks. The agency of things-as-materials in the context of daily life projects is always collaborative, of course. But so are the powers of storytellers, potters, and cooks, who know all too well the extent to which they bend their desires and aims to the demands of their tools

and ingredients. Further, the craftsmanship involved in everyday life can be seen as action guided in part by an aesthetic even under conditions where real lives may fall far short of what might be desired.[37] The same could be said of the politics and ethics governing the giving and keeping, serving and eating of food. And finally, a certain agency can be accorded to the embodiments of memory and desire, sedimented in habitus, that make our notions of comfort so variable and yet so conservative.

Perhaps future research on food in the human sciences can inquire into what food does and what people do with food without either narrowing the question – to notions of identity, for example – or polarizing it – as in models of structure and agency. We have no evidence that human eating is anywhere undertaken for purely nutritional purposes or that its form and meaning are anywhere fully under the control of autonomous human agents. Rather, there is much evidence that even under conditions of extreme hardship human populations still maintain – collaboratively with material conditions – particular forms of culinary life, at least in the shape of 'feasts for the mind'.[38] As the scholars of a consumption-obsessed First World continue to explore the place of eating in human life, we should endeavor not to reduce the natural complexity of the events of getting, desiring, eating, giving, enjoying, narrating, remembering, and cooking food. In this work it should be possible to clarify the forms of agency in food practices that extend well beyond human society, while proposing an aesthetic, ethical, and political urgency for our understanding.

CONCLUSION

It is fitting for a reflection on the anthropology of the vast subject of food and eating that more questions have been asked here than can possibly be answered. The descriptions I have provided of daily life issues for Mrs Hu and the two friends Sisters Zhang and Zhou can be read to extend to, but only partially address, most of the questions I have raised. Thus we can see the place of histories of privation in the activities of these women as they buy, cook, share, and talk about food. The class positioning in which all three engage is also evident, even though it does not fit very well with any stratified system of strictly economic classes. The relationship of eating to health concerns is visible in the rhetoric they use as well as in their tactical nutritional choices. And it is very clear that food has power to express positions in a complex field of social differences, enhance local and global ties, compensate for old and new difficulties, and generally give form to life. Above all, the enjoyment provided even by the simplest food is palpable, for these women as well as for a great many of those interviewed in Beijing. It seems significant to me that the ladies Hu, Zhang, and Zhou are organizing the current form of their daily lives especially around the pleasure they derive from daily regimes that include both eating as they please and cooking to please others.

Reflecting on this question of pleasure, I have come to believe that the pumpkin dumplings I ate with Sisters Zhang and Zhou were not the same ones they ate. They may not have been the same ones Lili ate, given our different histories and orientations in the world. My sense of eating 'Chinese' food, my limited experimentation with dumpling fillings, my feeling of being not only free but obliged to eat more than I thought was really good for me, and my anxiety to find the right way to show my hostesses my appreciation as I was leaving the city – these elements would not have been present for Sister Zhou as she evaluated the proper saltiness and more than adequate number of the dumplings she had made with her friend. She had other things on her mind, some of which I have discussed here. Even if the dumplings were all quite similar – the ladies had made only one filling for them, after all – and even if we accord them the status of 'non-human agents', their roles in the network-lives each of us was living were all different. Appearing in a compendium of Beijing's traditional foods, pumpkin dumplings would appear to be one thing. But anthropologically decomposed into the shreds and threads of buying, cooking, eating, remembering, interpreting, and giving, they become multiple indeed.

NOTES

1   This phrasing harks not only to the famous essay by M.F.K. Fisher, 'Consider the oyster' (1990b) but also (as she must have intended) to the lilies of the field, which are worthy of consideration because they 'toil not, neither do they spin'. Here I wish to thank Sara Ackerman, Jessica Cattelino, Jennifer Cole, Kesha Fikes, James Hevia, Lili Lai, Danilyn Rutherford, Margaret Scarry, Barry Saunders, Mark Sorenson, Patricia Spyer, Wang Ling, Wu Xiulan, and Zhang Qicheng for helpful comments on aspects of this argument.

2   The getting of food through practices like hunting, gathering, and agriculture is as central to the cultural subject of food as are the techniques of cooking and experiences of eating that occupy me here. Indeed, a fully ethnographic approach quickly discovers the inseparability of food production from the experiences and efficacies of food consumption. In this chapter, however, I neglect farming, marketing, and other aspects of food systems that are somewhat less proximate to the experience of eating in order to focus on a certain range of literature concerned with eating as a practice.

3   See, for example, Counihan and Esterik (1997), Chang (1977), and Scapp and Seltz (1998).

4   Robertson Smith, *The Religion of the Semites* (1887/1972), p. 287 *et passim*. In *The Religion of the Semites* these arguments were meant to explicate materials relating to the history of 'the Semites', defined by Robertson Smith as 'the group of kindred nations, including the Arabs, the Hebrews, and the Phoenicians, the Aramaeans, the Babylonians and Assyrians, which in ancient times occupied the great Arabian Peninsula, with the more fertile lands of Syria Mesopotamia and Irac, from the Mediterranean coast to the base of the mountains of Iran and Armenia' (p. 1). At times Robertson Smith extended his arguments to all human societies at a parallel level of development within an evolutionary scheme. It is one of the achievements of this work that sociological principles of considerable comparative power were advanced to explain the fragmentary and largely scriptural historical sources available at the time.

5   Robertson Smith (1887/1972: 278–80). Patricia Spyer in comments on this chapter noted the 'furtive eating' that she was required to do as an ethnographer in a setting where commensality was structured quite differently than has been assumed by Euro-American traditions.

6   Malinowski (1922). Anthropology that extended the functionalist orientation founded by Malinowski has also made important contributions to scholarship on food. See, for example, Harris (1974, 1985). Also see Rappaport (1967). For a recent study of globalizing and world-making food exchange, see Bestor (2004).

7   Weiner (1976). Munn's penetrating study of the cultural logics and broad material

consequences of practices of growing, cooking, eating, giving, and receiving food in Gawa is paralleled in its depth and ambition by Jacques Derrida's reflections on the ethics and language of consumption and exchange. See Munn (1986); Derrida (1991, 2002). The second Derrida paper has been lucidly explored in relation to eating practices by Ackerman (2004).

8 Spencer and Gillen (1899); Fison and Howitt (1880/1991); Durkheim and Mauss (1903/1963). This latter work is hardly a study of practice, of course. The ethnological work of Franz Boas which began in the late nineteenth century comes closer to being a study of practice, with its elaborate detail about American north-west coast consumption practices, especially with regard to institutions of potlatch. See, for example, Boas (1966).

9 See, for example, Pierre Bourdieu's spare essay 'The Kabyle house, or, The world reversed' (1970/1990b).

10 Lévi-Strauss (1969/1983, 1978/1990); Douglas (1966, 1999).

11 Sutton (2001).

12 Counihan (1999a, b); Counihan and Kaplan (1998).

13 Farquhar (2002).

14 Flandrin and Montanart (1999); Forster and Ranum (1979).

15 Theophano (2002); Davidson (1982); Bennett (1996).

16 The classic work of this kind is Brillat-Savarin (1826/1949). Also see Dumas (1873/1958), Toklas (1984), and Joyant and Toulouse-Lautrec (1930/1995). Encyclopedic compilations in Chinese often focus on the efficacies of food; see, for example, Dou Guoxiang (1999).

17 Bourdieu (1977, 1990).

18 See Ungar and Teaford (2002). More popular works include Audette et al. (1999), Cordain (2001) and Shepard and Shepard (1998).

19 My thanks to anthropologists C. Margaret Scarry and Mark Sorensen for briefing me on this subject.

20 M.F.K. Fischer's most comprehensive compilation is The Art of Eating (1990a).

21 See Farquhar (2002); Gang Yue (1999). There are other important works of Chinese fiction that concern themselves centrally with food, not all of which are considered at length in Yue's important study. Fascinating examples include Mo Yan (2000) and Su Tong (1995). A new series of 'occasional writings' on food by well known Chinese intellectuals began to appear in 2001 from San Lian Press in Beijing; these are philosophical reflections and memories on eating in its social and cultural settings. See, for example, Che Fu (2004) and Zhao Heng (2001).

22 Brillat-Savarin (1826/1949), Toklas (1984). Calvin Trillin's books on eating include American Fried (1974), Third Helpings (1983), and Feeding a Yen (2003).

23 One could cite whole genres of books published in China that do these things. In addition to discussions of medicinal meals and Chinese medical technologies of flavor I have already provided in Appetites (2002), there are books like the compendium edited by Dou Guoxiang (1999) on food therapeutics; hybrid cooking and self-health books about medicinal meals; public health writing about nutrition and good housekeeping practices; and advice literatures on the food-related duties of citizens.

24 Watson (1997); see also Chase (1994).

25 This insufficiency reminds one of the problems inherent in an anthropology of everyday life. This is in a way another word for Bourdieu's word 'field' of practice. Why is everyday life 'elusive'? It is elusive to any apparatus of knowledge because to know one must ask a researchable, answerable question. This asking, this focusing of the gaze, from a point of view, selects a few strains of practice, thereby losing the sense of the totality of the field. In a sense, this choice of focus is always already (partly) made. We researchers (knowers) are enculturated beings, we can't perceive totalities, we can only posit them in theory. There is no 'antepredicative' experience of the field which is everyday life, either for livers or knowers. So it escapes, always. On the elusiveness of everyday life, see Lefebvre (1947/1991), Certeau (1984), and Highmore (2002).

26 This research was funded by an international collaborative research grant from the Wenner Gren Foundation. My co-principal investigator on this project is Professor Qicheng Zhang of the Beijing University of Chinese Medicine. We are both especially grateful to Shen Yi, Lili Lai, and Qiu Hao for their very substantive contributions during the 2003 field research for this project.

27 Long interview, subject No. 100. Personal names used in this chapter are pseudonyms.

28 Long interview, subject No. 29.
29 The woman I am calling Zhou Xiaomei had actually been a worker in a different province for a large part of her life, but having returned to Beijing in retirement she now considered herself to be a housewife. Zhang Li had devoted most of her life to caring for children and nursing her husband after a head injury.
30 Jiaozi filling, when it includes pork, cannot be seasoned 'to taste'. Careful cooks hesitate to eat raw pork.
31 A useful clarification of the 'problem' of agency in social theory is Smith (1988); theories of agency in actor-network theory have been developed by Bruno Latour (see especially 1988, 1999) and Michel Callon (1986).
32 Giddens (1979).
33 See Laclau (1990). Samuel Weber's study of processes of instituting in discourse is also an interesting anti-foundational reflection on the reality of the institutions we tend to perceive as stable, given, and external to individual humans. See *Institution and Interpretation* (1987).
34 For an excellent collection of innovative research in science studies, see Biagioli (1999).
35 Latour (1993).
36 Benjamin (1969: 92). In this reading of Benjamin I am indebted to Barry Ferguson Saunders's Ph.D. thesis 'CT Suite' (2000).
37 Clearly a gourmet aesthetic is local and limited, but cultural notions of the good life are very widespread. I once spent several days in a remote village in Melanesia with a team of medical investigators. It didn't take long to realize that local householders knew much better than we did how to keep themselves and their food clean in small palm-leaf houses with packed dirt floors. Under these conditions it was the foreign scientists who appeared to have no notion of how to achieve a good life.
38 This phrase comes from Gu Hua's novel *Hibiscus Town* (1981), which I have discussed at length in Farquhar (2002: 89–105). Part I of the latter presents a series of Chinese reflections on the disastrous famine of 1958–1961; in these writings authors demonstrate that, even while starving, people exercised considerable agency in preserving aesthetic, ethical, and political forms of life. See also Gang Yue (1999).

REFERENCES

Ackerman, Sara (2004) 'Reading Narratives of Veganism and the Play of Derrida's *Animots*'. Unpublished MS, 3 May.

Audette, Ray V., Gilchrist, Troy and Eades, Michael (1999) *Neanderthin: Eat like a Caveman and achieve a Lean, Strong, Healthy Body*. New York: St Martin's Press.

Benjamin, Walter (1969) 'The story-teller', in Hannah Arendt (ed.), *Illuminations*. New York: Schocken Books.

Bennett, Judith (1996) *Ale, Beer, and Brewsters: Women's Work in a Changing World, 1300–1600*. New York: Oxford University Press.

Bestor, Theodore (2004) *Tsukiji: the Fish Market at the Center of the World*. Berkeley, CA: University of California Press.

Biagioli, Mario, ed. (1999) *The Science Studies Reader*. New York: Routledge.

Boas, Franz (1966) *Kwakiutl Ethnography*, ed. Helen Codere. Chicago: University of Chicago Press.

Bourdieu, Pierre (1977) *Outline of a Theory of Practice*. Cambridge: Cambridge University Press.

Bourdieu, Pierre (1970/1990a) *The Logic of Practice*. Stanford, CA: Stanford University Press.

Bourdieu, Pierre (1970/1990b) 'The Kabyle House, or, The world reversed', in *The Logic of Practice*. Stanford, CA: Stanford University Press, pp. 271–83.

Brillat-Savarin, Jean-Anthelme (1826/1949) *The Physiology of Taste: Meditations on Transcendental Gastronomy*. New York: Counterpoint.

Callon, Michel (1986) 'Some elements of a sociology of translation: domestication of the scallops and the fishermen of Saint-Brieux bay', in John Law (ed.), *Power, Action, and Belief: a new Sociology of Knowledge?* London: Routledge, pp. 196–229.

Certeau, Michel de (1984) *The Practice of Everyday Life*. Berkeley, CA: University of California Press.

Chang, K.C., ed. (1977) *Food in Chinese Culture: Anthropological and Historical Perspectives*. New Haven, CT and London: Yale University Press.

Chase, Holly (1994) 'The *meyhane* or McDonald's? Changes in eating habits and the evolution of fast food in Istanbul', in Sami Zubaida and Richard Tapper (eds), *Culinary Cultures of the Middle East*. London and New York: Tauris.

Che Fu (2004) *Chuancai Za Tan* (Essays on Sichuan Food). Beijing: San Lian Press.

Cordain, Loren (2001) *The Paleo Diet: Lose Weight and Get Healthy by Eating the Food You were Designed to Eat*. New York: Wiley.

Counihan, Carole M. (1999a) *The Anthropology of Food and Body: Gender, Meaning, and Power*. New York and London: Routledge.

Counihan, Carole (1999b) 'The social and cultural uses of food', in Kenneth F. Kiple and Conee Kriemhild Ornelas-Kiple (eds), *Cambridge World History of Food and Nutrition*. New York and Cambridge: Cambridge University Press, pp. 1513–23.

Counihan, Carole and van Esterik, Penny, eds (1997) *Food and Culture: a Reader*. New York and London: Routledge.

Counihan, Carole M. and Kaplan, Steven, eds (1998) *Food and Gender: Identity and Power*. Newark, NJ: Gordon & Breach.

Davidson, Caroline (1982) *A Woman's Work is never Done*. London: Chatto & Windus.

Derrida, Jacques (1991) 'Eating well,' or, The calculation of the subject: an interview with Jacques Derrida', in Eduardo Cadava et al. (eds), *Who Comes after the Subject?* New York: Routledge, pp. 96–119.

Derrida, Jacques (2002) 'The animal that therefore I am (more to follow)', *Critical Inquiry*, 28 (4): 369–418.

Dou Guoxiang, ed. (1999) *Zhonghua Shiwu Liaofa Daguan* (A Complete Book of Chinese Food Therapeutics). Nanjing: Jiangsu Science and Technology Press.

Douglas, Mary (1966) *Purity and Danger: an Analysis of Concepts of Pollution and Taboo*. London: Routledge.

Douglas, Mary (1999) *Leviticus as Literature*. Oxford and New York: Oxford University Press.

Dumas, Alexandre (1873/1958) *Dictionary of Cuisine*. New York: Simon & Schuster.

Durkheim, Emile and Mauss, Marcel (1903/1963) *Primitive Classification*, trans. Rodney Needham. Chicago: University of Chicago Press.

Farquhar, Judith (2002) *Appetites: Food and Sex in Post-socialist China*. Durham, NC: Duke University Press.

Fischer, M.F.K. (1990a) *The Art of Eating*. New York: Wiley.

Fisher, M.F.K. (1990b) 'Consider the oyster', in *The Art of Eating*. New York: Wiley, pp. 125–84.

Fison, Lorimer and Howitt, A.W. (1880/1991), *Kamilaroi and Kurnai: Group-marriage and Relationship, and Marriage by Elopement, drawn chiefly from the Usage of the Australian Aborigines; also, the Kurnai Tribe, their Customs in Peace and War*. Canberra: Aboriginal Studies Press.

Flandrin, Jean Louis and Montanart, Massimo (1999) *On Food: a Culinary History from Antiquity to the Present*. New York: Columbia University Press.

Forster, Robert and Ranum, Orest, eds (1979) *Food and Drink in History: Selections from the Annales. Economies, Sociétés, Civilisations*. Baltimore, MD: Johns Hopkins University Press.

Giddens, Anthony (1979) *Central Problems in Social Theory*. Berkeley, CA: University of California Press.

Gu Hua (1981) *Hibiscus Town (Furong Zhen), Dangdai* 1: 157–231.

Harris, Marvin (1974) *Cows, Pigs, Wars and Witches: the Riddles of Culture*. New York: Random House.

Harris, Marvin (1985) *Good to Eat: Riddles of Food and Culture*. New York: Simon & Schuster.

Highmore, Ben (2002) 'Introduction' to *The Everyday Life Reader*. New York and London: Routledge, pp. 1–34.

Joyant, Maurice and Toulouse-Lautrec, Henri de (1930/1995) *The Art of Cuisine*. New York: Holt.

Laclau, Ernesto (1990) 'The impossibility of society', in *New Reflections on the Revolution of our Time*. London and New York: Verso, pp. 89–92.

Latour, Bruno (1988) *The Pasteurization of France*. Cambridge, MA: Harvard University Press.

Latour, Bruno (1993) *We have Never been Modern*, trans. Catherine Porter. Cambridge, MA: Harvard University Press.

Latour, Bruno (1999) *Pandora's Hope: Essays on the Reality of Science Studies*. Cambridge, MA: Harvard University Press.

Lefebvre, Henri (1947/1991) *Critique of Everyday Life*. London: Verso.

Lévi-Strauss, Claude (1969/1983) *The Raw and the Cooked*, trans. John and Doreen Weightman. Chicago: University of Chicago Press.

Lévi-Strauss, Claude (1978/1990) *The Origin of Table Manners*, trans. John and Doreen Weightman. Chicago: University of Chicago Press.

Lu Wenfu (1982) 'Meishijia', (The Gourmet), in Lu Wenfu Ji, *Collected Works of Lu Wenfu*. Fuzhou, China: Straits Cultural Press, pp. 1–85.

Malinowski, Bronislaw (1922) *Argonauts of the Western Pacific*. London: Routledge.

Mo Yan (2000) *Republic of Wine*, trans. Howard Goldblatt. New York: Arcade.

Munn, Nancy (1986) *The Fame of Gawa: a Symbolic Study of Value Transformation in a Massim (Papua New Guinea) Society*. Cambridge: Cambridge University Press.

Rappaport, Roy (1967) *Pigs for the Ancestors: Ritual in the Ecology of a New Guinea People*. New Haven, CT: Yale University Press.

Robertson W. Smith (1887/1972) *The Religion of the Semites: the Fundamental Institutions*. New York: Schocken Books.

Saunders, Barry Ferguson (2000) 'CT Suite: the Work of Diagnosis in the Age of Virtual Cutting'. Ph.D. dissertation, Department of Religious Studies, University of North Carolina.

Scapp, Ron and Seltz, Brian, eds (1998) *Eating Culture*. Albany, NY: State University of New York Press.

Shepard, Paul and Shepard, Florence R. (1998) *Coming Home to the Pleistocene*. Collingwood, Vic.: Shearwater Books.

Smith, Paul (1988) *Discerning the Subject*. Minneapolis, MN: University of Minnesota Press.

Spencer, Baldwin and Gillen, Francis James (1899) *Native Tribes of Central Australia*. London: Macmillan.

Su Tong (1995) *Rice*, trans. Howard Goldblatt. New York: Penguin Books.

Sutton, David E. (2001) *Remembrance of Repasts: an Anthropology of Food and Memory*. Oxford and New York: Berg.

Theophano, Janet (2002) *Eat my Words: Reading Women's Lives through the Cookbooks they Wrote*. New York: Palgrave Macmillan.

Toklas, Alice B. (1984) *The Alice B. Toklas Cookbook*. New York: Harper & Row.

Trillin, Calvin (1974) *American Fried*. Garden City, NY: Doubleday.

Trillin, Calvin (1983) *Third Helpings*. New Haven, CT: Ticknor & Fields.

Trillin, Calvin (2003) *Feeding a Yen: Savoring Local Specialties from Kansas City to Cuzco*. New York: Random House.

Ungar, Peter S. and Teaford, Mark F., eds (2002) *Human Diet, its Origin and Evolution*. Westport CT: Bergin & Garvey.

Watson, James L., ed. (1997) *Golden Arches East: McDonald's in East Asia*. Stanford, CA: Stanford University Press.

Weber, Samuel (1987) *Institution and Interpretation*. Minneapolis, MN: University of Minnesota Press.

Weiner, Annette (1976) *Women of Value, Men of Renown*. Austin, TX: University of Texas Press.

Weiss, Brad (2003) *Sacred Trees, Bitter Harvests: Globalizing Coffee in Northwest Tanzania*. Portsmouth, NH: Heinemann Publishers.

Yue Gang (1999) *The Mouth that Begs: Hunger, Cannibalism, and the Politics of Eating in Modern China*. Durham, NC: Duke University Press.

Zhao Heng (2001) *Lao Tao Manbi* (Literary Notes of an old Gourmand). Beijing: San Lian Press.

10

SCENT, SOUND AND SYNAESTHESIA

Intersensoriality and Material Culture Theory

David Howes

The importance of attending to the multiple sensory dimensions of objects, architectures and landscapes is quickly becoming a central tenet of material culture theory. This sensual turn – or better, 'revolution' (Howes 2004) – is evident in the various references to the sensuous made by the contributors to *The Material Culture Reader* (Buchli 2002). In 'Contested landscapes', Barbara Bender writes: 'landscapes are not just "views" but intimate encounters. They are not just about seeing, but about experiencing with all the senses' (2002: 136). In his chapter on 'Trench art', Nicholas Saunders discusses the heightened sensory experience of warfare,[1] and the ability of material objects (e.g. recycled munition shells) to 'act as a bridge between mental and physical worlds' (2002: 181). In 'Visual culture', Chris Pinney argues that the field of visual culture (as currently understood) 'needs to be superseded by an engagement with embodied culture ... that recognizes the unified nature of the human sensorium' (2002: 84–5).

Christopher Tilley devotes a chapter to an analysis of the sensory and social symbolism of Wala canoes. The Wala, a people of Vanuatu, traditionally attributed various sensory powers to their canoes and embodied this understanding by carving ears, mouths and 'moustaches' as well as male and female sexual organs on the prow and stern. According to Tilley: 'The power of [this] imagery resides in its condensation of reference linked with the sensual and tactile qualities of its material form and reference to the human body' (2002: 25).

The implication to be drawn from these highly stimulating references to the sensuous is that material culture, in addition to materializing social relations and symbolizing the cosmos, gives expression to a particular set of *sensual relations*. Thus, Wala canoes may be said to condense the sensory – as well as social and symbolic – orders of Wala culture. They are attributed sentience in the same way that they render sensible the cardinal ideas of Wala society. Otherwise put, Wala canoes, and their uses, embody Wala 'ways of sensing' (Howes 2003).

My aim in this chapter is to discuss the significance of scent, sound and synaesthesia for material culture studies. My account opens with a consideration of the model of 'synaesthesia' (literally, 'joining of the senses') advanced by Lawrence Sullivan, a scholar of comparative religion, in a seminal article entitled 'Sound and senses' (1986). It goes on to provide a synopsis of the burgeoning literature in the history and anthropology of the senses, pioneered by Constance Classen (1993a, 1998) and Alain Corbin (1986, 1994), among others, which highlights the multisensoriality embedded in the materiality of human existence.

The increasingly sensual orientation of material culture studies and the emergent focus on objects and environments within 'sensual culture studies' (a shorthand for the history and anthropology of the senses) represent a happy confluence.[2] Both developments may be linked to the interdisciplinary counter-tradition that has crystallized in recent years partly in reaction to the excesses of 'textualism' and 'ocular-centrism' in conventional social scientific accounts of meaning. Sullivan's 'Sound and senses' was, in fact, published the same year as *Writing Culture* (Clifford and Marcus 1986) – that is to say, at the height of the textual revolution (also known as 'the literary turn') in anthropological understanding. The latter revolution began in the 1970s, when Clifford Geertz (1973) introduced the suggestion that cultures be treated 'as texts'. The idea of 'reading cultures' proved tremendously productive throughout the 1970s and early 1980s, but then the idea of 'textualization' (ethnography 'as writing') took command. This had the untoward consequence of deflecting attention on to styles of text construction, and away from the sensuous realities those texts sought to convey. Indeed, in his contribution to *Writing Culture*, Stephen Tyler (1986: 137) went so far as to proclaim that: 'perception has nothing to do with it' (the 'it' being ethnography).[3] While it may be etymologically correct to hold that ethno*graphy* is tied to writing, it is not epistemologically sound to reduce the anthropological endeavour to an exercise in 'text construction'.

Sullivan intended his model of 'sensing' – as opposed to 'reading' (or 'writing') – culture to serve as a multisensory alternative to 'the model of the text' (Ricoeur 1970, cited in Geertz 1973). That his article has languished in such obscurity is testimony to the extraordinary power of logo-centric models in the humanities and social sciences, whether inspired by the Saussurean dream of a 'science of signs' (modelled on linguistics) or Wittgensteinian 'language games' or Foucauldian 'discourse analysis'. But 'the model of the text' no longer enjoys the same grip over the anthropological (or historical) imagination it once did. For example, while it was fashionable for a spell to consider consumer culture as 'structured like a language' following Baudrillard's lead in *The Consumer Society: Myths and Structures* (1970/1998) and *The System of Objects* (1968/1996), many voices now caution against such a 'simplistic equation between language and materiality, mainly due to the unordered and seemingly unstructured nature of consumption' (Blum 2002: 234, citing Miller 1998).

It will no doubt come as a surprise to some that: 'The limits of my language are *not* the limits of my world' – or in other words, that the evidence of our senses is equally worthy of attention. However, this observation would appear to be a point of increasingly widespread consensus among scholars of material culture: 'a design is not a word and a house is not a text:

words and things, discourses and material practices are fundamentally different', writes Tilley (2002: 23–4; see further Pinney 2002: 82; Tacchi 1998; Stahl 2002). It is also fundamental to sensual culture studies, which has long warned against the visual and verbal biases intrinsic to the dominant social scientific accounts of 'meaning' (Classen 1990; Howes 1991: 3). Setting aside linguistic models and attending to the multiple respects in which culture mediates sensation and sensation mediates culture can be a source of many insights into the 'interconnectedness' of human communication (Finnegan 2002). 'Society', in so far as it is grounded in 'consensus' – meaning 'with the senses' – is a sensory fact, just as the sensorium is a social fact.

THE MODEL OF SYNAESTHESIA

In 'Sound and senses', Sullivan presents a review of recent developments in performance theory, hermeneutics and information theory. His account culminates in the suggestion that: 'The symbolic experience of the unity of the senses enables a culture to entertain itself with the idea of the unity of meaning' (1986: 6). He goes on to apply his model of 'the unity of the senses' – or 'synaesthesia' – to the interpretation of the myths and rituals of diverse South American Indian societies.

Medically speaking, synaesthesia is a very rare condition in which the stimulation of one sensory modality is accompanied by a perception in one or more other modalities. Thus, synaesthetes report hearing colours, seeing sounds, and feeling tastes (see Marks 1982).[4] Such inter-modal associations and transpositions are also commonly reported by persons under the influence of hallucinogens. Sullivan's account is, in fact, centred on a variety of South American Indian societies which make ritual use of the hallucinogenic *Banisteriopsis Caapi* plant. However, he also extends the term 'synaesthesia' to refer to the ritual process of bringing many or all of the senses into play simultaneously. This makes his theory of 'cultural synaesthesia', as it could be called, potentially applicable to the interpretation of ritual and cosmological systems the world over.

The strength of Sullivan's model lies in the way it recognizes 'the unified nature of the human sensorium', as Pinney (2002) would say; but, from the perspective of the anthropology of the senses this is also one of its weaknesses. The weakness stems from Sullivan's presupposition of 'the oneness of meaning'. The latter presumption derives from the information theory approach to the study of ritual communication, which holds that 'although the receiver of a ritual message is picking up information through a variety of different sensory channels simultaneously, all these different sensations add up to just one message' (Leach 1976: 41). Such an approach imposes a spurious unity on ritual communication because of the way it treats 'meaning' as primary and the senses as so many arbitrary and basically interchangeable channels for the delivery of some hypostasized 'message'. It would be more consonant with what we now know about the materiality of communication to regard sensing (seeing, hearing, touching, etc.) as primary and meaning as mediated. The information theory approach also tends to deflect attention from the subject of the socialization of the senses through ritual, whereas it is precisely this sensual socialization that ought to occupy the analyst. These points of critique may be illustrated by analysing Sullivan's interpretation of the Tukano-speaking Desana myth of the 'origin of communication' through the lens of Classen's (1990) independent account of the Desana sensory order.

As Sullivan relates:

> For Tukano speakers of the Northwest Amazon the crying sounds of a mythic baby called Cajpi are also the tastes and visual images of the hallucinogenic drink made from his body (the magical plant, *Banisteriopsis Caapi*) 'for as soon as the little child cried aloud, all the people ... became intoxicated and saw all kinds of colours.' The divinity named Yepa Huaké commanded that the child be dismembered. A piece of his body was given to each social group. This distribution established not only the ranked hierarchy of groups in society today but also the different qualities of vision and modulations of sound that constitute each group's cultural existence as art, musical performance, and speech.

> (1986: 26)

Sullivan goes on to bring the Desana 'interpretation' of ritual and mythic communication into alignment with information theory:

> The significance of the ritual beverage and the visions induced by ritual acts arises originally from the crying sounds of the sacred child. That sound in the environment of the unspoiled mythic world is an image similar to the perfect noise-free channel that Corcoran, the communication theorist, described as lying beyond this imperfect world of noise and redundancy. It is a unique

message, a unique signal, which bears meaning for all the senses ... [The] Tukano-speakers would agree that that kind of clarity and wholeness of meaning no longer exists. The dismembered state of meaning in this world requires and causes the redundant messages sent through different senses and media.

> (1986: 26–7)

What Sullivan accomplishes by means of the above passage, which stages a conversation between Corcoran and an imaginary Tukano-speaker, is a translation of one cosmology into the terms of another (scientific Western) one. But this conversation is forced, and overrides the question of whether the Desana shaman would be willing (or able) to state his 'message' without recourse to the medium that models it – that is, without insisting that Corcoran ingest *yagé* (the Tukano name for the magical *Banisteriopsis Caapi* plant) first. Let us turn the conversation around, following Classen's analysis of the Desana sensory order in 'Sweet colors, fragrant songs' (1990).

In the beginning there was sound (the baby's cry), not a 'word' or 'score' (another favourite metaphor of information theory). This sound embodied smells and temperatures, as well as colours and tastes. These sensations are meaningful to different senses now, but were indistinguishable from each other in the mythic world. Thus, the sound of the baby's cry is viewed as having contained the Tukano 'sense ratio' (to borrow McLuhan's 1962 terminology) in embryo.

The division and distribution of the parts of the child's body modulated the original sound, just as it modulated society, partitioning the latter into ranked groups, each with its own style of singing, speaking and use of colours as well as other sensory media (odours, tastes). The division of sound, the division of the senses and the division of society, therefore, all arose together. Thus, the Tukano social and moral universe is structured in accordance with a model derived from the interrelation of the senses under the influence of *yagé*.

Social norms are sensory norms. This fundamental tenet of the Tukano sensory-social order finds expression in the way the different flavours with which each of the social groups were imbued at the moment of partition are to this day used to regulate marriage: 'Compatible marriage partners are those with opposite flavours' (Classen 1991: 249). It is also embedded in the contemporary ritual use of *yagé*: 'Through the use of hallucinogens, and a controlled sensory environment, shamans attempt to "make one see, and act accordingly," "to make one hear, and act accordingly," "to make one smell, and act accordingly," and "to make one dream, and act accordingly"' (Classen 1990: 728). The need for the shaman to control the sensory environment follows from the fact that each social group embodies a different modulation of the senses. A shaman would not want his patients to see red where they ought to be seeing yellow, or smell a pungent odour when they ought to smell a sweet one, for it is believed that were the senses to be crossed in this way people would commit incest and other contraventions of the Tukano moral order.

Sullivan suggests that Tukano-speakers would agree with information theorists that the 'wholeness of meaning' is gone. He also claims that: 'Wholeness is seen in retrospect and in mourning' (Sullivan 1986: 27). This is far from clear. If there were only one sense and one meaning – that is, if the Desana sensory ratio had remained in the embryonic form it had in the mythic world, and never unfolded – then the sound of, say, a flute would convey a wealth of meaning, but not be able to evoke images in other modalities the way it does today. The Desana appear to delight in the cross-sensory associations which the unfolding of the sound of the baby's cry into the other senses has made possible. When a boy plays a flute, for example: 'The odor of the tune is said to be male, the color is red, and the temperature is hot; the tune evokes youthful happiness and the taste of a fleshy fruit of a certain tree. The vibrations carry an erotic message to a particular girl' (Reichel-Dolmatoff 1981: 91). The multiple associations adduced here serve to multiply the perceived meaning (or connotation) of the tune. Alas, the only thing the information theorist can see in this concatenation of sensations is redundancy; that is, all the *resonances* of the Desana way of sensing would be lost on one such as Corcoran.

Hence, while the theory of cultural synaesthesia has the potential to illuminate many aspects of cultural performance, space must be made within this theory to allow for a more relational, less unified conception of the human sensorium. Specifically, while the notion of 'the unity of the senses' is a helpful point of departure, and certainly more culturally sensitive than 'the model of the text' or 'score', more attention needs to be paid to such issues as: (1) the weight or value attached to each of the modalities, instead of assuming equality and interchangeability; (2) the sequencing of perceptions, instead of assuming simultaneity; and (3) the way the use of different senses

may give rise to different meanings, instead of assuming redundancy. Each of these assumptions (which Sullivan imports into his interpretation of the Desana myth owing to his uncritical reliance on information theory) limits what we sense, whereas the Tukano material challenges us to *expand* our senses, to recognize their interplay, and thus discover more meaning instead of less.

THE MODEL OF INTERSENSORIALITY

A consideration of Dorinne Kondo's sensuous symbolic analysis of the Japanese tea ceremony will help concretize what is meant by the model of intersensoriality (in place of synaesthesia) advanced here. Kondo notes the emphasis on non-verbal symbolism in Japanese culture. The tea ceremony itself entails a cleansing and heightening of perception conducive to a state of silent contemplation. In the ceremony meanings are conveyed through sensory shifts, from garden to tea room, from sound to silence, from the odour of incense to the taste of tea. Kondo describes the aesthetic order of the tea ceremony as an 'unfolding, a sequence of movement with tensions, climaxes and directionality' (1983/2004: 197).

As is well illustrated by the sensory sequencing of the tea ceremony, intersensoriality need not mean a synaesthetic mingling of sensation. The strands of perception may be connected in many different ways. Sometimes the senses may seem to all be working together in harmony. Other times, sensations will be conflicted or confused. Either state may be employed as a social or aesthetic ideology.

Just as the model of intersensoriality does not necessarily imply a state of harmony, nor does it imply a state of equality, whether sensory or social. Indeed, the senses are typically ordered in hierarchies. In one society or social context sight will head the list of the senses, in another it may be hearing or touch. Such sensory rankings are always allied with social rankings and employed to order society. The dominant group in society will be linked to esteemed senses and sensations while subordinate groups will be associated with less valued or denigrated senses. In the West the dominant group – whether it be conceptualized in terms of gender, class or race – has conventionally been associated with the supposedly 'higher' senses of sight and hearing, while subordinate groups (women, workers, non-Westerners) have been associated with the so-called 'lower' senses of smell, taste and touch (Classen 1998: 154–6).

Within each sensory field, as well, sensations deemed relatively unpleasant or dangerous will be linked to 'unpleasant', 'dangerous' social groups. Within the field of smell, for example, the upper classes were customarily considered to be fragrant or inodorate, while the lower classes were held to be malodorous. George Orwell described this olfactory division of society forcefully when he wrote that 'the real secret of class distinctions in the West' can be summed up in 'four frightful words ... *The lower classes smell'* (quoted in Classen et al. 1994: 166). This perception of malodour had less to do with practices of cleanliness than it had to do with social status: according to the sensory classification of society a low social status translated into a bad smell. Thus Orwell stated that a nasty smell seemed to emanate from 'even "lower class" people whom you knew to be quite clean – servants, for instance' (Classen et al. 1994: 167). Here we can see how sensations of disgust are a matter not just of personal distaste but of social ordering (Miller 1997). The transformation of class distinctions into physiological sensations is a powerful enforcer of social hierarchies (see Corbin 1986; Classen 2001).

An instructive comparative example is provided by Anthony Seeger's analysis of the sensory order of the Suyà Indians of the Mato Grosso region of Brazil in 'The meaning of body ornaments' (1975). Suyà men pride themselves on their ear discs and lip discs. These ornaments are understood to make one 'fully human' (*me*). The faculties of speech and hearing are, in fact, 'highly elaborated and positively valued in Suyà society' (Seeger 1975: 215). For example, the Suyà word for hearing, *ku-mba*, means not only 'to hear (a sound)' but also 'to know' and 'to understand'. Thus, when 'the Suyà have learned something – even something visual such as a weaving pattern – they say, "It is in my ear"' (1975: 214). The ear is the primary organ through which the world is cognized. It is also the organ through which the human subject is socialized: both boys and girls are fitted with ear discs at puberty. A person who is fully social – that is, one who conforms fully to the norms of the group – 'hears, understands and knows clearly' (1975: 214). Only senior men and chiefs are permitted to wear lip discs, and (by virtue of this oral modification) engage in 'plaza speech' or 'everybody listen talk' as well as perform the songs which are so central to the Suyà symbolic order and sense of cultural identity.

Significantly, 'the eyes are not ornamented, tattooed or specially painted', nor is the nose (1975: 216). This diminution of the eyes and nose (in contrast to the extension of the lips and ears) is linked to the fact that only certain highly dangerous and elusive game animals are credited with a keen sense of smell, as well as 'strong eyes'. Related to this is the fact that adult men are presumed to be 'bland smelling' while adult women, who are deemed to participate more in nature than society, are said to be 'strong smelling' (Seeger 1981: 111). Witches are also credited with 'strong eyes', and their transgressive position within the moral (which is to say, aural) bounds of society is further underscored by the fact that they are poor of hearing and engage in 'bad' or garbled speech.

It is of historical interest to note that Seeger's analysis in the 'Body ornaments' piece was inspired in part by McLuhan's notion of media as 'extensions of the senses'. Whereas McLuhan's point in *The Gutenberg Galaxy* (1962) was that our media become us, Seeger's point is that body decorations do much the same. The ear-minded sensory order of the Suyà is precisely what one would expect of an 'oral-aural' (as opposed to chirographic, typographic or electronic) society, in McLuhan's terms. However, Seeger also complicates McLuhan's typology by attending to the different meanings and values of the different faculties in the Suyà sensory order, and in those of other Gê-speaking peoples of the Mato Grosso. For example, the neighbouring Kayapo mark the attainment of puberty by fitting boys with penis sheaths, and do not wear ear discs (only strings of beads). Adult Kayapo men do wear lip discs, but they are not very ornate. This makes them less than human by Suyà standards, and this ranking is, of course, mutual. The Suyà economy of the senses thus differs from that of the Kayapo, as regards the salience and direct/indirect regulation of aurality and tactility (or sexuality) respectively. This suggests that, contrary to McLuhan's theory, not all 'oral societies' are of one mind with respect to the ranking and uses of hearing relative to the other senses – a point which has been confirmed by numerous subsequent studies (Classen 1993a, 1997; Geurts 2002; Howes 2003).

SENSORY WORLDS

The field of material culture studies stands to be significantly enriched through attending to the multiple sensory dimensions of 'material worlds' (Miller 1998). As Daniel Miller observes in 'Why some things matter': 'through dwelling on the more mundane sensual and material qualities of the object, we are able to unpick the more subtle connections with cultural lives and values that are objectified through these forms, in part because of the qualities they possess' (1998: 9). My focus in this section shall be on artefacts as extensions of the senses and the emergent notion of emplacement, or the sensuous reaction of people to place.

Artefacts

Every artefact embodies a particular sensory mix. It does so in terms of its production (i.e. the sensory skills and values that go into its making), in the sensory qualities it presents, and in its consumption (i.e. the meanings and uses people discover in or ascribe to it in accordance with the sensory order of their culture or subculture).

The shell valuables (armshells and necklaces) which circulate in countervailing directions around the vast inter-island system of ceremonial exchange known as the 'kula ring' in the Massim region of Papua New Guinea provide a good example of artefacts as extensions of the senses. The sonic, kinetic and visual as well as olfactory characteristics of these objects (together with their attachments) are keyed to the Massim hierarchy of sensing and scale of self-constitution. The shell valuables provide a standard in terms of which the social status and persuasive powers of their (always temporary) possessors can be judged and communicated. In the Massim world, every man of the kula wants to progress from being a face with no name (i.e. admired for his visual and olfactory appearance when he goes on a kula expedition to visit his partner on a neighbouring island) to being a name with no face (i.e. have his name circulate quite apart from his body in concert with the named shells of note that have passed through his possession).

According to Annette Weiner's revisionist analysis of kula exchange, the kula is not about 'the love of give-and-take for its own sake', as Malinowski suggested, 'but creating one's own individual fame through the circulation of objects that accumulate the histories of their travels and the names of those who have possessed them' (quoted in Howes 2003: 67). The cardinal value of Massim civilization is, in fact, butu, which means both 'noise' and 'fame'. This value is condensed in the sensual qualities of the attachments which serve as an index of a

kula valuable's status or rank. The attachments consist of trade beads, seeds, other types of shells, and bits of plastic or tin, which are tied either to the valuable itself or to a frame. Basically, the attachments serve to augment the space of the valuable by extending its boundaries, by suggesting motility and by making a chiming or tinkling noise. It is fitting that the attachments enlarge the body of the shell, extending it outward in space, given the connection between beautification and exteriorization that is so fundamental to Massim aesthetics (Munn 1986; Howes 2003: 72–3). It is also fitting that they impart motion (specifically, a trembling motion) to the shell, since the essence of a valuable lies in its mobility – its being for transmission. The main function of the attachments, however, is to signify success in kula exchange through sound, hence the significance of the chiming or tinkling sound they make. (In many parts, kula transactions are in fact concluded at night, so that it is the sound of a kula valuable being carried off to the beach that signals success on the exchange.) As Nancy Munn observes, 'the mobile decor makes a sound that ramifies the space [of the shell] – as if putting it into motion – so that what may be out of sight may nevertheless be heard' (quoted in Howes 2003: 82).

The sensory meaning of an object or artefact may change over time. Consider the case of the rose. The transformation of the rose from a premodern symbol of olfactory and gustatory perfection to a modern symbol of formal visual perfection indexes the shifting balance of the senses in Western history – specifically, the visual eclipse of smell. While in pre-modern times 'A rose by any other name would smell as sweet' and rose petals were frequently used in cooking, in modern times, many varieties of roses look quite splendid but have, in fact, lost their scent owing to selective breeding. This shift did not go uncontested. William Morris, for example, railed against 'the triumph of surface over essence, of quantity over quality', represented by the way in which showy gardens had come to replace scented gardens in Victorian England (Classen 1993a: 31).

The sensory meanings of objects also vary across cultures. Analysing commodities as bundles of sensual relations, susceptible to multiple appropriations (or appraisals), can help elucidate the sensory as well as social biographies of things in the course of their domestication (see Dant 1999: 110–29). It can also can help to explain the often innovative meanings and uses ascribed to foreign products in contexts of 'cross-cultural consumption' (Howes 1996).[5]

For example, the Algonquin Indians traded furs for glass beads of various hues with the French in seventeenth-century Québec, and there was also a significant traffic in prayer beads. But the Algonquians did not admire the beads simply for their 'brilliance', they also occasionally ground them up and smoked them because 'the respiratory route' was the standard sensory channel for the ingestion of power-laden substances (von Gernet 1996: 170–6). To take a contemporary example, Johnson & Johnson's baby powder is a popular trade item in Papua New Guinea. Rather than being applied to babies, however, it is used for purifying corpses and mourners, asperging the heads of ritual performers, and for body decor.[6] This decorative use of baby powder (as a substitute for crushed shell) has the effect of intensifying the visual and olfactory presence of the person in ways that accord with the emphasis on exteriorization in the Massim aesthetic order, as discussed elsewhere (see Howes 2003: 217–18).

It is not only in contexts of cross-cultural consumption that commodities acquire new uses and meanings on account of local appraisals of their sensual qualities. Take the case of Kool-Aid – that icon of American middle-class family life – which is used as a (cheap yet colourful) hair dye by numbers of rebellious North American 'tweens' (i.e. those aged 10 to 13). Here tween subculture is the determining factor in 'making sense' of what Kool-Aid is good for, converting a taste into a sight.

Emplacement

The sensuous reaction of people to place has received increased attention of late thanks to the pioneering work of Yi-Fu Tuan (1974, 1995) and Steve Feld (1996), among others. Their example has led geographers and anthropologists alike to foreground the notion of sense-scapes in place of the conventional notion of landscape, with its primarily visual connotations (see Porteous 1990), and to pay heightened attention to processes of 'emplacement' (Rodman 1992; Fletcher 2004) as distinct from (but inclusive of) processes of 'embodiment' (Csordas 1990).

In his contribution to *Senses of Place*, Feld probes the seemingly transparent meaning of the word 'sense' in the expression 'sense of place' by asking: 'How is place actually sensed?' He goes on to argue that 'as place is sensed, senses are placed; as places make sense, senses make place' (1996: 91). Feld's point is nicely exemplified by numerous subsequent studies

of the sonic dimensions of social life (or sonorization of the material world), such as those collected in *Music, Sensation, and Sensuality* (Austern 2002), *The Auditory Culture Reader* (Bull and Back 2003) and *Hearing Cultures* (Erlmann 2004).

The odorization of the material world, both historically and across cultures, has also come under increased investigation (Corbin 1986; Classen et al. 1994; Rasmussen 1999; Drobnick forthcoming). Vishvajit Pandya's ethnography of Ongee 'osmology' (or science of scent) presents a particularly illuminating case study of the socialization of olfaction. Among the Ongee, a hunting and gathering people of Little Andaman Island in the Bay of Bengal, smell is the primary sensory medium through which the categories of time, space and the person are conceptualized. Odour, according to the Ongee, is the vital force which animates all living, organic beings, and life, for the Ongee, is a constant game of olfactory hide-and-seek. They seek out animals in order to kill them by releasing their odours, and at the same time try to hide their own odours both from the animals they hunt and from the spirits who hunt them.

Space is conceived of by the Ongee not as a static area within which things happen but as a dynamic environmental flow. The olfactory space of an Ongee village fluctuates: it can be more expansive or less, depending on the presence of strong-smelling substances (e.g. pig meat), the strength of the wind, and other factors. The Ongee smellscape, then, is not a fixed structure but a fluid pattern that can shift according to differing atmospheric conditions. The Ongee convey the fluid nature of odour by employing the same word, *kwayaye*, for both the emission of odours and the ebb and flow of tides (Pandya 1993; Classen et al. 1994: 97–9).

When Pandya observed that his official map of the island did not correspond with his experience of it among the Ongee, an Ongee informant replied:

Why do you hope to see the same space while moving? One only hopes to reach the place in the end. All the places in space are constantly changing. The creek is never the same; it grows larger and smaller because the mangrove forest keeps growing and changing the creek. The rise and fall of the tidewater changes the coast and the creeks. ... You cannot remember a place by what it looks like. Your map tells lies. Places change. Does your map say that? Does your map say when the stream is dry and gone or when it comes and overflows? We remember how to come and go back, not the places which are on the way of going and coming.

(Pandya 1991: 792–3)

Among the Ongee, space is as fluid as the odours which animate the world. How would a Western cartographer begin to map the complexities of the Ongee's fundamentally non-visual sense of place?[6]

A culture's sensory order is also projected in its architecture. A good comparative example would be the nineteenth-century European fashion for balconies versus the windowless walled domestic compounds found in many parts of Africa. The architectural form of the balcony allowed the bourgeois subject to gaze but not be touched while the walled compound inhibits sight and fosters tactile engagement. The latter arrangement is important to a people such as the Wolof of Senegal, for whom touch is the social sense and vision the sense of aggression and transgression (Howes 1991: 182–5). Another interesting comparative example is the Inuit snowhouse or 'igloo' versus the modern bourgeois home. According to Edmund Carpenter, 'visually and acoustically the igloo is "open," a labyrinth alive with the movements of crowded people' (1973: 25). By contrast, the proliferation of rooms within the bourgeois dwelling has had the effect of privatizing what were once more social functions (the preparation and consumption of food, the elimination of bodily wastes, sleeping) by confining each to a separate compartment. The fragmented understanding of the sensorium with which most modern Western subjects operate is at least partly attributable to this great nineteenth-century repartition of space and bodily functions.

Most studies of emplacement have tended to focus on the ordering or integration of the senses. However, it is important to consider the underside of emplacement as well – namely, the sense of displacement typically experienced by marginal groups within society. For example, Chris Fletcher (2004) has coined the term 'dystoposthesia' to describe 'the incompatibility of bodies to the space they inhabit' experienced by those who suffer from 'environmental sensitivities' (ES). For sufferers of ES, the visual world is dangerously deceptive. Through the eye-catching facades of modern life – furniture, paint, rugs, cosmetics – seep invisible toxic fumes, turning the dream worlds of consumer capitalism into corporeal nightmares. ES sufferers have no evident reason for their deranged sensations, for the world they perceive as threatening is judged by others to be safe. Indeed, ES is medically unrecognized and often

dismissed as a 'garden variety mental disorder'. In order to retain a sense of sanity, ES sufferers must 'work out a bodily logic of what remains illogical' (Fletcher 2004: 384).

The term dystoposthesia might also be applied to the life world of the homeless persons in Boston studied by Robert Desjarlais in 'Movement, stillness' (2004). Whether on the street or in a shelter the homeless are incompatible with their sensory environment. Both sites offer a continual series of sensory assaults; brutal in the case of the street, distracting in the case of the shelter, with its constant hum of activity. Desjarlais describes how the homeless develop various sensory techniques to cope with their situation. When a 'quiet place' cannot be found, the body itself becomes 'silent', numb to the world outside and the feelings inside: the homeless 'play dead', even though this strategy exposes them to additional risks.

SENSORIAL INVESTIGATIONS

Victor Buchli has drawn attention to the curious neglect of materiality in material culture studies. He observes that 'material culture' transforms 'a mostly inarticulate realm of sensual experience into the two dimensions of a scholarly text or the "*nature-morte*" of the museum display' (2002: 13). He wonders whether there is any alternative to this seemingly inexorable 'decrease in physicality' (or movement towards 'the dimensionless and ephemeral') when objects are reduced to writing or subject to classification and exhibition in glass cases.

I am in sympathy with Buchli's critique of the neglect of materiality in material culture studies, though I would be more inclined to speak of the sensuality of material culture. I am also in agreement with his attack on the ideology of 'conservation'. (Conservation, according to Buchli, conserves nowhere near as much as it 'produces' a particular order of things.) However, I also believe that a number of questionable assumptions remain embedded in Buchli's state-of-the-art critique, and that these have the effect of limiting what he is able to conceive of by way of alternative modes of presentation. Why suppose that artefacts are not for handling? Why prioritize the visual appearance of an object?[7] This last question is prompted by Buchli's observation that:

Most of our publications deny us any visual representation of the very physical objects we explore. This was never the case in the beautifully illustrated discussions of material culture in the past and their exquisite display when the affects of these objects were at their most problematic ... [from a contemporary postcolonial perspective]. Their visuality and form was the primary vehicle of authority and information, the text was merely supplementary and discursive.

(2002: 14)

To truly access the materiality of an object, I maintain, it is precisely those qualities which cannot be reproduced in photographs – the feel, the weight, the smell, the sound – which are essential to consider. As the previous sections of this chapter have indicated, these non-visual qualities are also often of key importance within an artefact's culture of origin. Appreciating the visual design of a Tukano basket would tell one nothing of the range of sensory characteristics which are meaningful to the Tukano, right down to the odour of the vines from which a basket is made. To access such non-visual qualities, however, often involves breaking one of the most sacred museological taboos and actually *handling* a collectible. This fear of touch is not intrinsic to the museum. Early museums often gave visitors tactile access to their collections, of which visitors took full advantage. Thus seventeenth and eighteenth-century diarists record lifting, feeling and smelling artefacts in the collections they visited (Classen and Howes forthcoming). It is certainly the case that most early curators did not share the modern preoccupation with conservation. However, it is even more true that the sensory values of the time gave an importance to tactile knowledge which has since been discounted. Even though it might endanger the collection, visitors were still allowed to touch because of the belief that touch was essential for appreciation. The current sensory order of the museum resulted from the confluence of a widespread hypervaluation of vision in modernity and a new emphasis on the preservation of the material past (Classen 2005).[8]

Owing to its association with museum studies and to its development within a particular culture of vision, material culture studies has tended to overlook the multisensory properties of materiality. While this is now changing, as we have seen, old habits die hard. Examining the sensuous worlds of non-Western peoples such as the Tukano and the Ongee brings out the importance of exploring all the sensory dimensions of material life, even the olfactory – the most denigrated sensory domain of modernity. The model of intersensoriality, in turn, compels us to interrelate sensory media, to contextualize them within a total sensory and social environment. While all media may not be conveying the same message, or given the same attention, they are nonetheless all playing on each other. The study of material culture, from this perspective, becomes the exploration of sensory relationships and embodied experience within particular regimes or systems of cultural values. It is only through such multisensory investigations that material culture studies can become a full-bodied discipline. After all, a material culture that consisted solely of images would be immaterial.

NOTES

1 Saunders's point is that the Great War of 1914–18 was a crisis of synaesthetic proportions, and not simply a 'crisis of vision', as others maintain (e.g. Jay 1993: 211–15).

2 The sensual revolution in material culture studies is not confined to the work of the University College London Material Culture Group, as the examples cited thus far might suggest. For example, Nadia Seremetakis makes an eloquent case for treating 'perception as material culture in modernity' in *The Senses Still* (1994), and David Sutton (2001), building on the work of James Fernandez (1986), has highlighted the sensory dimensions of memory and food. There is a whole sub-field of archaeology now dedicated to the 'archaeology of perception' (Houston and Taube 2000; Ouzman 2001). Other leading proponents of the sensory analysis of artefacts include Richard Carp (1997) and Jules Prown (1996).

3 In drawing out this logical implication of the 'writing culture' position, Tyler is, of course, exposing the limits of representation, unlike the other contributors to the Clifford and Marcus volume (1986), who would appear to condone and even celebrate them (see Howes 2003: 22–3).

4 There is a quality to synaesthetic expressions, such as 'crumbly yellow voice', which some perceive to be akin to metaphor. Similarly, one finds the term 'synaesthesia' being used interchangeably with 'metaphor' in the works of anthropologists such as Isbell (1985). This is untoward, for synaesthesia is a sensory process, not a linguistic one like metaphor, and its value as a theoretical concept may consist precisely in the way it enables us to analyse rituals from a perspective that is beyond metaphor – that

is, from a perspective which treats rituals as 'ways of sensing' the world (Howes 2003). Such an approach builds on the manifold senses of the word 'sense' – 'sense' as 'sensation' and 'signification', to which one might add 'direction' (as given in the French word *sens*).

5   Also of note in this connection are those studies which highlight the struggle for dominance of conflicting constructions of the sensorium in situations of culture contact (see Classen 1993b; Hoffer 2003).

6   Ongee osmology, in addition to defying cartography, poses a significant challenge to phenomenological approaches to the study of human-environment relations. To take a paradigm case, in *The Perception of the Environment* (2000) Tim Ingold dwells extensively on sight and sound and 'motion' (or action) but his text is virtually devoid of references to smell or taste or touch. The Ongee would thus find little or nothing to perceive in Ingold's phenomenologically reduced 'surroundings' – but then, this should not be so surprising, given that phenomenology comes from the Greek *phainein*, which means 'to appear'. Ingold's work, in addition to being open to critique for (uncritically) reflecting certain conventional Western perceptual biases in its account of 'the environment', must be challenged for the Eurocentrism with which it champions the theories of perception advanced by philosopher Maurice Merleau-Ponty and psychologist J.J. Gibson as if the universal validity of those theories were a given, instead of remaining to be seen (see Ingold 2000: Chapter 14; Howes 2003: 239–40 n. 8).

7   To these questions one might add: why assume that writing must be a two-dimensional medium? There exist counter-examples, such as the Inca *quipu*, which consists of a series of knotted strings, and is best characterized as a multidimensional and multisensorial form of writing (Classen and Howes forthcoming; see further Küchler 2002 and Connor 2003: 40–1 on the multisensory symbolic significance of knots and knotting). Given the unlikelihood of Inca writing ever being revived, much less becoming the lingua franca of the academy, it might be objected that our writing about material culture means continuing to frame it within a two-dimensional medium. To this objection I would respond that it is nevertheless possible to hone our powers of (verbal) description to the point that our words mingle

with their referents, thereby sensualizing language instead of merely verbalizing things. This path is suggested by the work of historian Alain Corbin who, by recuperating past phrases, such as *aura seminalis*, miasma, etc., has succeeded at rendering history sensible (see Corbin 2000: 62). It is also exemplified by certain contemporary writers, such as Seamus Heaney (1991) and Susan Stewart (2002), who exploit the materiality (or better sensuality) of language in untold ways. So too can what Buchli (2002) calls the dimensionless '"*nature morte*" of museum displays' be complicated sensorially by curating exhibitions for all the senses, as exemplified by the work of Displaycult (Drobnick and Fisher 2002).

8   For an account of the florescence of the 'exhibitionary complex', or visual eclipse of touch, in the mid-nineteenth century see *The Birth of the Museum* (Bennett 1995), and for an analysis of the prehistory and fallout of this transformation in perception see Classen (2005) and Candlin (2004).

REFERENCES

Austern, Linda P. (ed.) (2002) *Music, Sensation and Sensuality*. New York: Routledge.

Baudrillard, Jean (1968/1996) *The System of Objects*, trans. J. Benedict. London: Verso.

Baudrillard, Jean (1970/1998) *The Consumer Society: Myths and Structures*. London: Sage.

Bender, Barbara (2002) 'Contested landscapes', in V. Buchli (ed.), *The Material Culture Reader*. Oxford: Berg, pp. 141–74.

Bennett, Tony (1995) *The Birth of the Museum: History, Theory, Politics*. London: Routledge.

Blum, M. (2002) 'Remaking the East German past: *Ostalgie*, identity, and material culture', *Journal of Popular Culture*, 34 (3): 229–53.

Buchli, Victor, ed. (2002) *The Material Culture Reader*. Oxford: Berg.

Bull, Michael and Black, Les (eds) (2003) *The Auditory Culture Reader*. Oxford: Berg.

Candlin, Fiona (2004) 'Don't touch! Hands off! Art, blindness and the conservation of expertise', *Body and Society*, 10 (1): 71–90.

Carp, Richard (1997) 'Perception and material culture: historical and cross-cultural perspectives', *Historical Reflections/Reflexions historiques*, 23 (3): 269–300.

Carpenter, Edmund (1973) *Eskimo Realities*. New York: Holt, Rinehart and Winston.

Classen, Constance (1990) 'Sweet colors, fragrant songs: sensory models of the Andes and the Amazon', *American Ethnologist*, 17 (4): 722–35.

Classen, Constance (1991) 'Creation by sound/creation by light: a sensory analysis of two South American cosmologies', in D. Howes (ed.), *The Varieties of Sensory Experience*. Toronto: University of Toronto Press, pp. 239–55.

Classen, Constance (1993a) *Worlds of Sense: Exploring the Senses in History and Across Cultures*. London and New York: Routledge.

Classen, Constance (1993b) *Inca Cosmology and the Human Body*. Salt Lake City, UT: University of Utah Press.

Classen, Constance (1997) 'Foundations for an anthropology of the senses', *International Social Science Journal*, 153: 401–12.

Classen, Constance (1998) *The Color of Angels: Cosmology, Gender and the Aesthetic Imagination*. London and New York: Routledge.

Classen, Constance (2001) 'The senses', in Peter Stearns (ed.), *Encyclopedia of European Social History from 1350 to 2000* IV. New York: Scribner.

Classen, Constance (2005) 'Touch in the museum', in C. Classen (ed.), *The Book of Touch*. Oxford: Berg.

Classen, Constance and Howes, David (2005) 'The museum as sensescape: Western sensibilities and indigenous artifacts', in E. Edwards, C. Gosden and R. Phillips (eds), *Sensible Objects*. Oxford: Berg.

Classen, Constance, Howes, David and Synnott, Anthony (1994) *Aroma: the Cultural History of Smell*. London and New York: Routledge.

Clifford, James and Marcus, George, eds (1986) *Writing Culture: the Poetics and Politics of Ethnography*. Berkeley, CA: University of California Press.

Connor, Steven (2003) *The Book of Skin*. Ithaca, NY: Cornell University Press.

Corbin, Alain (1986) *The Foul and the Fragrant: Odor and the French Social Imagination*, trans. Miriam Kochan, Roy Porter and Christopher Prendergast. Cambridge, MA: Harvard University Press.

Corbin, Alain (1994) *Village Bells: Sound and Meaning in the Nineteenth-Century French Countryside*, trans. Martin Thom. New York: Columbia University Press.

Corbin, Alain (2000) *Historien du sensible : entretiens avec Gilles Heuré*. Paris: la Découverte.

Csordas, Thomas (1990) 'Embodiment as a paradigm for anthropology', *Ethos*, 18: 5–47.

Dant, Tim (1999) *Material Culture and the Social World*. Buckingham: Open University Press.

Desjarlais, Robert (2004) 'Movement, stillness', in D. Howes (ed.), *Empire of the Senses*. Oxford: Berg, pp. 369–79.

Drobnick, Jim, ed. (forthcoming) *The Smell Culture Reader*. Oxford: Berg.

Drobnick, Jim and Fisher, Jennifer (2002) *Museopathy*. Kingston, ON: Agnes Etherington Art Centre, Queen's University.

Erlmann, Veit (ed.) (2004) *Hearing Cultures: Essays on Sound, Listening and Modernity*. Oxford: Berg.

Feld, Stephen (1996) 'Waterfalls of song', in S. Feld and K. Basso (eds), *Senses of Place*. Santa Fe, NM: SAR Press, pp. 91–135.

Fernandez, James (1986) *Persuasions and Performances: The Play of Tropes in Culture*. Princeton, NJ: Princeton University Press.

Finnegan, Ruth (2002) *Communicating: the Multiple Modes of Human Interconnection*. London: Routledge.

Fletcher, Christopher (2004) 'Dystoposthesia', in D. Howes (ed.), *Empire of the Senses*. Oxford: Berg, pp. 380–98.

Geertz, Clifford (1973) *The Interpretation of Cultures*. New York: Basic Books.

Geurts, Kathryn Linn (2002) *Culture and the Senses: Bodily Ways of Knowing in an African Community*. Berkeley, CA: University of California Press.

Heaney, Seamus (1991) *Seeing Things*. London: Faber.

Hoffer, Peter Charles (2003) *Sensory Worlds in Early America*. Baltimore, MD: Johns Hopkins University Press.

Houston, Stephen and Taube, Karl (2000) 'An archaelogy of the senses: perception and cultural expression in ancient Mesoamerica', *Cambridge Archaelogical Journal*, 10 (2): 261–94.

Howes, David, ed. (1991) *The Varieties of Sensory Experience: a Sourcebook in the Anthropology of the Senses*. Toronto: University of Toronto Press.

Howes, David (ed.) (1996) *Cross-cultural Consumption: Global Markets, Local Realities*. London and New York: Routledge.

Howes, David (2003) *Sensual Relations: Engaging the Senses in Culture and Social Theory*. Ann Arbor, MI: University of Michigan Press.

Howes, David, ed. (2004) *Empire of the Senses: the Sensual Culture Reader*. Oxford: Berg.

Howes, David, and Classen, Constance (1991) 'Conclusion: sounding sensory profiles', in D. Howes (ed.), *The Varieties of Sensory Experience*. Toronto: University of Toronto Press, pp. 257–88.

Ingold, Tim (2000) *The Perception of the Environment*. London: Routledge.

Isbell, Billie Jean (1985) 'The metaphoric process', in G. Urton (ed.), *Animal Myths and Metaphors in South America*. Salt Lake City, UT: University of Utah Press, pp. 218–313.

Jay, Martin (1993) *Downcast Eyes: The Denigration of Vision in Twentieth-Century French Thought*. Berkeley, CA: University of California Press.

Kondo, Dorinne (1983/2004) 'The tea ceremony', in D. Howes (ed.), *Empire of the Senses*. Oxford: Berg, pp. 192–211.

Küchler, Susanne (2002) 'The anthropology of art', in V. Buchli (ed.), *The Material Culture Reader*. Oxford: Berg, pp. 57–80.

Leach, Edmund (1976) *Culture and Communication*. Cambridge: Cambridge University Press.

Marks, Lawrence (1982) *The Unity of the Senses*. New York: Academic Press.

McLuhan, Marshall (1962) *The Gutenberg Galaxy*. Toronto: University of Toronto Press.

Miller, Daniel (1998) 'Why some things matter', in D. Miller (ed.), *Material Cultures*. Chicago: University of Chicago Press, pp. 3–21.

Miller, William Ian (1997) *The Anatomy of Disgust*. Cambridge, MA: Harvard University Press.

Munn, Nancy (1986) *The Fame of Gawa*. New York: Cambridge University Press.

Ouzman, Sven (2001) 'Seeing is deceiving: rock art and the non-visual', *World Archaeology*, 33 (2): 237–56.

Pandya, Vishvajit (1991) 'Movement and space: Andamanese cartography', *American Ethnologist*, 17: 775–97.

Pandya, Vishvajit (1993) *Above the Forest: a Study of Andamanese Ethnoamnenology, Cosmology and the Power of Ritual*. Bombay: Oxford University Press.

Pinney, Christopher (2002) 'Visual culture', in V. Buchli (ed.), *The Material Culture Reader*. Oxford: Berg, pp. 81–104.

Porteus, J. Douglas (1990) *Landscapes of the Mind: Worlds of Sense and Metaphor*. Toronto: University of Toronto Press.

Prown, Jules (1996) 'Material/culture', in W.D. Kingery (ed.), *Learning from Things*. Washington, DC: Smithsonian Institution Press, pp. 19–27.

Rasmussen, Susan (1999) 'Making better "scents" in anthropology: aroma in Tuareg sociocultural systems and the shaping of ethnography', *Anthropological Quarterly*, 72 (2): 55–73.

Reichel-Dolmatoff, Gerardo (1981) 'Brain and mind in Desana shamanism', *Journal of Latin American Lore*, 7 (1): 73–98.

Rodman, Margaret (1992) 'Empowering place: multi-locality and multivocality', *American Anthropologist*, 94 (1): 640–55.

Saunders, Nicholas (2002) 'Memory and conflict', in V. Buchli (ed.), *The Material Culture Reader*. Oxford: Berg, pp. 175–206.

Seeger, Anthony (1975) 'The meaning of body ornaments', *Ethnology*, 14 (3): 211–24.

Seeger, Anthony (1981) *Nature and Society in Central Brazil: the Suya Indians of Mato Grosso*. Cambridge, MA: Harvard University Press.

Seremetakis, C. Nadia, ed. (1994) *The Senses Still: Memory and Perception as Material Culture in Modernity*. Boulder, CO: Westview Press.

Stahl, Ann B. (2002) 'Colonial entanglements and the practices of taste: an alternative to logocentric approaches', *American Anthropologist*, 104 (3): 827–45.

Stewart, Susan (2002) *Poetry and the Fate of the Senses*. Chicago: University of Chicago Press.

Sullivan, Lawrence E. (1986) 'Sound and senses: toward a hermeneutics of performance', *History of Religions*, 26 (1): 1–33.

Sutton, David (2001) *Remembrance of Repasts: An Anthropology of Food and Memory*. Oxford: Berg.

Tacchi, Jo (1998) 'Radio texture', in D. Miller (ed.), *Material Cultures*. Chicago: University of Chicago Press, 25–45.

Tilley, Christopher (2002) 'Metaphor, materiality and interpretation', in V. Buchli (ed.), *The Material Culture Reader*. Oxford: Berg, pp. 23–56.

Tuan, Yi-Fu (1974) *Topophilia*. Englewood Cliffs, NJ: Prentice Hall.

Tuan, Yi-Fu (1995) *Passing Strange and Wonderful: Aesthetics, Nature and Culture*. Tokyo and New York: Kodansha.

Tyler, Stephen (1986) 'Postmodern ethnography', in J. Clifford and G. Marcus (eds), *Writing Culture*. Berkeley, CA: University of California Press, pp. 122–40.

Von Gernet, Alexander (1996) 'Reactions to the familiar and the novel in seventeenth-century French-Amerindian contact', in L. Turgeon et al. (eds), *Cultural Transfer: America and Europe*. Québec: Presses de l'Université Laval, pp. 169–88.

ACKNOWLEDGEMENTS

I wish to acknowledge the support of the Social Sciences and Humanities Research Council of Canada and the Quebec Fonds pour la Formation de Chercheurs et l'Aide à la Recherche, as well as all the stimulation I have received from my conversations with Jean-Sébastien Marcoux and other members of the Concordia Sensoria Research Team (http://alcor.concordia.ca/~senses).

11

THE COLOURS OF THINGS

Diana Young

This chapter addresses the materiality of colours. In using the term *materiality* to designate colour I refer to the material stuff of colour, coloured cloth, coloured paper, coloured paints, coloured food etc. I will argue that colour is a crucial but little analysed part of understanding how material things can constitute social relations. Here, in emphasising their materiality I will consider what it is that colours can do, something which has been neglected even in material culture theory, as it has been in every other branch of anthropology. It is as much for what they do, as well as for what they can mean, that colours are so useful and worth attending to both in images and in things. Colours may be harnessed to accomplish work that no other quality of things can, especially in the hands of knowledgable practitioners. Colours may be combined to interact with one another producing an effect of vivacity and movement. Colours animate things in a variety of ways, evoking space, emitting brilliance, endowing things with an aura of energy or light. Conversely colours are also able to camouflage things amidst their context. Colours constitute badges of identity and connect otherwise disparate categories of things – red buses, red birds, red fruit, say – in expanding analogical networks. Colours can transform things and sequences of colour transformations employed to represent temporality. Colours are also linked with emotional expression. Lastly, in the phenomenon known as synaesthesia coloured mental imagery is linked with other senses, not just the visual – commonly sound, odour and tactility.

Colour figures across a vast array of contested theories in philosophy, psychology, art and brain science. (e.g. Davidoff 1992; Gage 1993; Goethe 1987; Hardin and Maffi 1997; Lamb and Bourriau 1995; Wittgenstein 1977). In all of these, bar Western art history, colour has been consistently dematerialized; it has been argued that the very entity 'colour' is itself a product of science.[1] In post-Enlightenment philosophy and science, colour has been considered as *qualia*, a qualitative, not quantitative, aspect of things that resists mathematical measurements, making it problematic as a subject of scientific investigation (Hardin 1988). But since colours are also self-evidently *there*, philosophers have seen them, from Locke onwards, as paradigmatic of empirical knowledge (Hardin 1988; Saunders 2002). Colour has thus earned the status of a 'given', an innate concept common to all human beings, but it is also considered as merely a 'sensation' (Rye, quoted in Saunders 2002). These sensations are held to require processing by some higher area of the brain. The search for *where* in the brain such processing might take place and what kind of links there may be between 'higher' and 'lower' processes have occupied psychologists and neurologists. As I will explore below, most often the higher processing has been assumed as linked with language. A further consequence of this idea of sensation has been that colours are considered as spontaneous and a 'froth' of consciousness. The difficulty arises as to how it is possible to represent such sensations as measured (cf. Saunders 2002). This has resulted in a wavelength of light becoming the standard measure of colours in colour science. All this may seem tangential to discussions of colour as materiality. Yet the way colour is discussed across all disciplines is heavily influenced by colour science and it is a necessity to be critical of this, not least because most of the things circulating in the world today are coloured using formulas produced by colour science (Saunders 1998).

There is then a tension in this construct called colour. Colour is quantified and calibrated in some arenas, and extravagantly expressive and intuitive elsewhere. Colour is on the one hand considered merely 'decorative', trivial, feminine, and on the other taken as the foundation of epistemology since Descartes. Anthropology has, for the most part, taken colour as a serious subject in two ways: as a matter of classification linked with language and as symbolism.

For studies in material culture colour presents a thicket of difficulties. First there is a long history of the dematerialization of colours in Western science. Anthropology has followed the dematerializing approach with its interest in colour as symbolic, and standing only for a meaning that lies elsewhere, beyond the colours of things. Then there is the 'problem', dependant on the idea that colour is a given, that colour perception is somehow related to language and the understanding of colour as pure 'sensation' which only needs processing by higher mental levels to become relevant and meaningful. The disembodiment of the experience of colour occures when colour is understood as only connected with processes that take place in the head as mediated through the eyes and brain/mind.

The reductionism of colours in science eschews the emotion and desire, the sensuality and danger and hence the expressive potential that colours possess. These last may lack evidence in scientific terms but are extensively harnessed by makers and artists across cultures in their work. Colours seem to be too many things at once. Perhaps that is why universal or at least generalizing frameworks are constantly created for colour. It has been suggested that there are different grammars of colour: Euclidian, pixellated and vernacular.[2]

If all human beings have the capacity to discriminate colours then the universality of the human cognitive apparatus is often cited as a reason to believe that perception is similarly universal or that colours are cognitively salient (Dedrick 2002; Sperber 1975). I follow here the argument that cognition is always mediated by other people and altered by social experience (Toren 1993). 'We are not *constrained* by the nature of our perceptual experience but ... [are] *users*' (Dedrick 2002: 63).

Here I want to move away from linguistic models of colour. I argue that the colours of things are both able to structure knowledge as well as affect ways of being. The idea that the experience of colours is an aspect of being in

the world has meant that phenomenology is often invoked to illuminate social colour practice, since it considers colour as embodied, eschewing the mind/body split of colour science (e.g. Jones and MacGregor 2001). Merleau-Ponty wrote:

> We must stop ... wondering how and why red signifies effort or violence, green, restfulness and peace; we must rediscover how to live these colours as our body does, that is, as peace or violence in its concrete form ... a sensation of redness and its motor reactions [are not two distinct facts] ... we must be understood as meaning that red, by its texture as followed and adhered to by our gaze, is already the amplification of our being.
>
> (Merleau Ponty 1962: 211)

Red as the amplification of being is a beguiling concept. At the same time, the emphasis on the individual's sensations offers little to an understanding of colours as social practice and relegates colours yet again to qualia that cannot structure things, that cannot be knowingly and strategically employed. On the other hand *being* colour, literally, wearing colour or consuming it, may be an immediate and emotional response to a particular social situation, something I will explore further below.

The experience that is called colour is a highly encultured construct. The 'period eye' and the 'cultural eye' are always at play in judgements of colour and colour combinations (Gombrich 1960; Coote 1992). Questions about aesthetics as a cross-cultural category are often raised with respect to colour: is a colour or combination of colours sought after because it is 'aesthetically pleasing', or grounded in a biographical and socially relational milieu from which it derives significance (Gell 1998; Ingold 1996)? A conventional Western sense of colour is highly biased and based on ideas of aesthetics. As Malraux observes, 'Athens was never white but her statues, bereft of colour, have conditioned the artistic sensibilities of Europe ... the whole past has reached us colourless' (Malraux 1956: 47–9).

Time-worn patina is what is generally valued in European art, an aesthetic exported into ethnographic collections. Authenticity resides in the faded surface and rarely, for example, in a coating of fluorescent acrylic paints. This presents a dilemma for conservationists. Should an object that was once highly coloured be restored to that state, producing the effect it was originally intended to have by those who made it, or should it be left 'as found' for museum or gallery display?

In Western art history, colours have often been a mere superficial adjunct to the more substantial *form* or, in drawing and painting, *line*, or *designo et colore* (cf. Gage 1993). Line is more telling, more sophisticated and *more like writing* and reinforces the logocentrism of anthropological enquiries. This opposition between line and colour has heavily influenced analyses of non-Western art (e.g. Munn 1973; Dussart 1999). A linearity of thought pervades many important studies of art in anthropology, where colours are often rendered as redundant, cluttering the elicitation of meaning through graphics or form. A privileging of colour, rather than a reference in passing, needs to be continually justified. Commentators are allowed some latitude in judgements about the colour use of the 'Other', seen conventionally as tending to combine colours 'garishly' or to limiting themselves wisely to what are held to be 'traditional' earth colours, thereby ensuring the desirability of their work for the colonizer's art markets (e.g. Michaels 1994).

I propose an anthropocentric view of colour that can engage not only the question 'Why does the object have the colours it does?' but also, importantly, 'What do those colours do for the object?' or, in other words, 'What kind of effect do they have?' I turn first to a consideration of some of the existing frameworks that have been constructed to 'contain' and dematerialize colour, before suggesting how material culture theory may offer fresh insights.

COLOUR AS A SCIENCE

Colour science has constructed particular versions of what colour is. Colour, it seems, is a highly problematic concept, one that philosopher J.J. Gibson refers to as '*one of the worst muddles in the history of science, the meaning of the term "colour"* (Gibson, in Malcolm 1999: 723). The received view is that colours are not a fundamental property of things at all (Thompson 1995). Following this orthodoxy, colour can only be a secondary quality of objects in contrast to form. Thus, modern popular accounts of colour and its pragmatic applications, in landscape and building, for example, seem to need to begin with an account of the perceptual apparatus that are deemed to conjure it, the eye and the brain, something which is not apparently necessary for an account of form.

This enduring orthodoxy, the understanding of colour as a secondary quality, dates from Newton and Locke (Thompson 1995). Newton's experiments refracted sunlight through two prisms, producing the spectrum which he

famously named as 'seven hues', a propitious number derived from Descartes's musical scales and a number that Newton took some years to decide upon (Gage 1993: 232–3). These colours are, Newton theorized, produced by the wavelength of light refracted. In this way, colour became a mathematically precise principle that took precedence over the painter's and dyer's knowledge of colour, practised during the preceding centuries; 'the seventeenth century was, for the student of optics, the century when colour had finally been relegated to a derivative, subordinate position ...' (Gage 1993: 191, 155). Colour had been dematerialized into light. In the Newtonian paradigm a surface appears red because it reflects more red light than any other: 'every body reflects the Rays of its own Colour more copiously than the rest, and from their excess and predominance in the reflected Light has its Color' (Newton 1730, in Hardin 1988: 187). Modern colour science, with its Newtonian legacy, dematerializes colour into wavelengths of light, which is both geometrically precise and empirically quantifiable.

Colours have been measured by a system, metaphorically called the colour 'space' because it has been given three dimensions. The most common of these systems is known as the Munsell. The three dimensions of the colour space are hue, or the identification of *what* colour; tone, or the measurement of how much grey the colour contains, and saturation, or how pure a hue is or, in other words, how intense it is.[3] Van Brakel (2002) provides a good overview of the gradual accretion over time of this model to its status as an objective fact. It is such systematized colour that moves from laboratory testing out into the fields of anthropology and anthropological linguistics as chips or swatches, thereby inhibiting the study of the colours of things themselves within their different social contexts. Van Brakel challenges the 'methodological fetishism' of linguistic anthropology regarding, which 'it is often suggested that only data collected with elaborately standardised methodology can be taken seriously' (2002: 148). This is a pertinent point, as anthropological studies that do not employ Munsell chips or something similar are, of course, of no interest whatever to colour scientists.

Both modern and ancient philosophical debates about colour have debated colour's relative subjectivity and objectivity. Is colour out there in the world, as it were, or merely produced in our brains as sensations, such that things only *appear* to have colours? The most radical position in the latter conceptualization theorizes colour as an exclusively brain-based experience (e.g. Hardin 1988). Dispensing with this subjectivist approach, that colour is merely a quality extruded by the brain, or the objectivist approach that finds colour as a physical quality of objects, the new orthodoxy in colour science, following Thompson's influential work, considers colours as mutually constituted by things and persons, following (selectively) the ecological psychology of Gibson (Thompson 1995). Thompson's work intends to dissolve the mind/body split (Saunders 1998). This is a more helpful construct for material culture studies. If things themselves may embody social processes, so too may colours. The mutual construction of colour and person resonates with recent critiques of the assumed divide between persons and things as a myth of modernity, from the assumption that certain things possess person-like qualities (Latour 1993; Gell 1998). The 'stickiness' of highly saturated colours, as Gell describes the adherence of things to persons through the quality of pattern, can also render things and persons interchangable. Pattern, after all, can exist only through colour, since without contrast there is no pattern. Paul Cezanne put it more precisely: 'colour is the place where our brains and the universe meet' (Merleau-Ponty 1964/2004: 180).

Although neurology is not interested in embodied and socially situated experience, because it considers colour as a given, it is worth noting some recent influential neurological findings that claim to have identified a colour centre in the brain in the area called the 'visual cortex'. This is in contrast to the refusal to countenance the presence of such an area in the preceding century (Zeki 1993). According to Zeki, the brain experiences the world in a state of constant flux. The brain must assemble or collate information from large parts of the visual field, compare different features and extract constants rather than break information down into its components.[4] It is an active process rather than the old idea of an image impressed on the passive brain (1993). Colour is seen before form, which is seen before motion (Zeki 1998: 75). How the brain decides *what* colour it is seeing must always be, Zeki argues, as a result of comparison with surrounding colour. On some occasions the brain decides that a colour is a constant despite the comparative information. This is known as 'colour constancy'.

The neglected problem of colour constancy has recently become the central problem within the study of colour vision (de Weert 2002; Zeki 1993). How is it that a leaf looks green to us whatever the weather conditions

may be? That is, contrary to Newtonian theory, it is thought now that no precise relation exists between the wavelength of the light reaching the eye from every point on a surface and the colour we see at that point. Colour constancy is invoked as crucial because without it there would be no biological signalling mechanism, that is, there would be supposedly no method for an ape or a human to distinguish a ripe fruit from a leaf (Mollon 1999).

COLOUR AND COGNITION; LANGUAGE AND PERCEPTION

What is the relationship between colour perception and language? Is colour cognition independent of language? Is there a direct link at all between what we know and what we can articulate about colour? (Hardin and Maffi 1997: 355). To write about 'colour' at all may seem presumptuous, given that there is no universal linguistic term for what we understand by colour. That position depends on assuming that the discrimination of hues is somehow linked with the existence of colour terms. These are questions that have dominated colour debates and influenced anthropology during the last half-century. There is an enduring assumption that to communicate with colours is to talk about them – in short, that language is culture (e.g. Kuschel and Monberg 1974). Such research also hinges on the received view that 'colour' is a given cognitive category, that is, somehow innately present in the brain. The problem is to find out how colour is divided up. Are there universal categories or are such divisions culturally relative or, according to the language as culture paradigm, relative to linguistic differences (Saunders 2002)?

Gladstone wrote a famous paper on the apparent lack of interest in colour shown by the ancient Greeks, citing the paucity of colour words in Homer (Gladstone 1858). In the 1880s Magnus noted that many primitive peoples have a well developed colour perception, and a comparatively limited colour vocabulary (cited in Gardner 1985). Van Wijk hypothesized that societies near the equator focus more on brightness in their lexicon, whereas those from higher latitudes he claimed, are more interested in hue (Van Wijk 1959, cited in Gardner 1985). The Sapir-Whorf hypothesis, 'a radical doctrine of linguistic relativity', assumed that colour perception is created by language (Kay and Willett 1984; Whorf 1956). Thus if a language contains no term for 'blue', say, then allegedly its speakers do not discriminate blue as a category. Berlin and Kay claimed to overturn this hypothesis in their much criticized but highly influential theory of Basic Colour Terms (BCTs). They claimed that their research with people from ninety-eight language groups, all living in the Los Angeles area, showed that all languages follow a universal evolutionary pattern of colour naming. There could be no culture that would only have a single colour term. If a language has only two colour terms, these are always black and white, and this was dubbed Stage 1. In Stage 2, where there are three terms, the third is always red. The fourth and fifth terms are always either yellow or green and comprise Stage 3, and the sixth and seventh terms are either blue or brown, which is Stage 4. Purple, pink, orange and lastly grey amounted to a total of eleven terms, a sophistication achieved only by Indo-European cultures (Berlin and Kay 1969). A basic colour term is one that does not refer to something but rather is an abstraction.

There have been numerous criticisms of Berlin and Kay, including, for example, that all their informants lived in the Los Angeles area; that they took their eleven colour terms derived from the American English lexicon as a universal evolutionary standard to which everyone, given time, would evolve; that they made words conform to English colour words – light and dark, for example, were translated as white and black. Moreover, what the precise meaning of a BCT might be has never been adequately explained (Saunders and van Brakel 1997: 168).

Nonetheless, Berlin and Kay are ubiquitously quoted across many disciplines as fact, by, for example, neurologists, psychologists and art historians, and their work has spawned a host of ethnographic comparative studies. The early part of the developmental sequence proposed by Berlin and Kay, the so-called Stage 2, caused excitement in anthropology because it concurs with much evidence from ethnographic research, where there is a well documented common ritual triad of the colours black, white and red, to which I return below (e.g. Turner 1967; Tambiah 1968).

Berlin and Kay's basic colour terms were, they claimed, invariably clustered around 'focal' colours, that is, colours chosen as the brightest and best example of a hue, and a further dimension of their original project involved other participants representing twenty more genetically diverse languages. These participants apparently selected the same group of hues as brightest, whatever their lexicon. That is, according to Berlin and Kay, these bright colours are universally recognized or salient, regardless of a person's language. Berlin and Kay regarded their work as counter-evidence to Whorf's theory, which was that language determines perception.

Berlin and Kay's findings seemed to be endorsed by the research of Rosch Heider. Rosch Heider's research started from the premise that focal colours were 'natural prototypes', perceptually more attention-grabbing and therefore more easily remembered. Her work with the Dani of the Indonesian part of New Guinea showed, she claimed, that people's recognition of focal colours was unmediated by language (Rosch Heider 1972, Rosch 1978). She concluded from her work with the Dani that the ease with which colours were remembered correlated with the BCT series of Berlin and Kay. Her methods and results have also been challenged (e.g. see Saunders and van Brackel 1997).[5] Lucy, an enduring critic of the universal colour theory, and Shweder claimed that their experiments reinstated the Whorfian basis of earlier studies (Lucy and Shweder 1979). There has recently been an attempt to replicate Rosch Heider's research with a neighbouring group, Berinmo-speakers, and this proposes the opposite of Rosch Heider's findings (Roberson et al. 2002).

According to this study, the Berinmo have a term, *nol*, which encompasses green, blue and blue-purple on the Munsell chart; a term, *wap*, that refers to almost all light colours; *kel*, which applies to most dark colours; and so on for five categories. These categories are not centred on focal colours as Rosch Heider had proposed as universal and the new researchers claim 'an extensive influence of language on colour categorisation' among the Berinmo (Roberson et al. 2002: 35).[6]

Others have suggested broadening the category of colour, proposing that a fixation with brightness, rather than hue, precedes Berlin and Kay's Stage 1, while a linguist claims that there is a universal term 'to see' rather than a universal of colour (MacLaury 1992; Wierzbicka 1999). Fundamental criticisms of Berlin and Kay, in particular, and colour science, more generally, have been made by Saunders and van Brakel. These authors argue that the whole theoretical structure of Berlin and Kay in particular, and colour science in general, is tautological in its assumption of colour categories as given *a priori* rather than acquired socially in practice (Saunders 2000; Saunders and van Brakel 1997). Why, they ask, should colour form a closed and static system and why should it be a universal (Saunders and van Brakel 1999)? This is the assumption of such tests, which are doomed to find only the parameters that they construct. Berlin and Kay's argument that proposed a universal linguistic evolution to the standard of complexity represented by the Indo-European eleven hues is without foundation. 'Colour' is produced by the experimental framework of the contextless 'colour space' and the dematerialized patches of light that are presented as 'stimuli' both in and out of laboratory settings (Saunders 1998). In short, 'Colour science explores the (changing) definition of colour science itself' (Saunders 1998: 702).

Nonetheless, the work of Berlin and Kay and Rosch spawned many engaging cross cultural studies in anthropology and archaeology, locating colour terms and aiming to compare them with the evolutionary colour stages. These comparative studies reveal no universal pattern, only an increasing tendency for all languages to align themselves with American English as the current global standard (van Brakel 2002: 150).[7] Still, it is repeatedly assumed in much of the colour literature, or the premise is re-examined again and again, that colour language constitutes colour knowledge and, by extension, the failure to categorize or name a hue constitutes, at one and the same time, also a failure to discriminate *between* hues (e.g. Gellatly 2002). Elsewhere the divergence between what people say and what they know has been presented as a central flaw in research that uses verbal reports (Lakoff and Johnston 1981: 125). The complaint is also heard that all non-Western languages are now in a transitive state and will soon all use English colour terms – leaving no intact 'other' for colour science to research (Levinson 2000). Adopting Anglo-American colour terms, however, does not necessarily mean adopting Anglo-American colour *practices.*

While colour is popularly linked with emotional expression, there is also laboratory testing of the link between colour and emotion. As should be clear by now, such testing is conceived along the same lines as colour science, employing decontextualized chips in these studies while colour is similarly regarded as necessarily mediated by language. For example, D'Angrade and Egan used Munsell cards and words referring to emotions in laboratory research with Tzetzal and English-speakers. Both groups produced similar results for the following associations: 'happiness' elicited the most saturated colours, 'sadness' the most unsaturated, 'strong' the most saturated, 'weak' the most unsaturated and 'anger' and 'fear' produced the widest spread between the two groups (D'Angrade and Egan 1975).

The problem of language is, then, one that scholars of material colour must constantly confront. The study of material colours may yield further insights into the relationship between words and things (Keane 1997). But colours themselves are an expressive communication as potent as music, and this expressive potential lies in colour being other than verbal expression, in its being an-other medium. Colours can be agentive and thus capable of effecting events and transformations. It is surely these qualities that make colours so amenable to symbolism. It is to the prevalent notion in anthropology of colour as symbolic meaning that I now turn.

COLOURS AS MEANINGS

In symbolic anthropology the existence of 'colour' was not a philosophical problem. But here, too, the impetus has been to find some universal rules as meanings for individual hues, notably for the triad of red, white and black familiar from ritual settings (Barth 1975; Sahlins 1977; Turner 1967; Tambiah 1968).

In symbolic theory colours are transcendent, they stand for something else beyond and in this sense are representational. Symbolism in anthropological analysis works iconographically, that is, by similitude: 'if we want to know what black means we need to know what black is the colour of' (Bousfield 1979: 213). In the struggle to systematize unruly colour there are echoes of colour science. Colour cannot have influence in itself but must always be subordinated to form and substance, and meaning is learnt through this route.

Victor Turner's essay on red, white and black as 'epitomising universal human organic experience' has been highly influential (Turner 1967). Extrapolating from his work on the Ndembu, Turner proposed that semen and milk are symbolized by white, blood is symbolized by red, faeces and dirt are symbolized by black. All these are invoked as not merely perceptual differences but 'condensations of whole realms of psycho-biological experience, involving reason, all the senses and concerned with primary group relationships' (1967: 91).

Turner has been criticized in many quarters for being totalizing in his approach to symbolism in general (e.g. Sperber 1975) and colour symbolism in particular (Tambiah 1968) but his bodily fluids theory has been embedded within anthropological and archaeological discussions of colour. As with Berlin and Kay's work, the evidence from cross-cultural comparisons does not support Turner's universalist theory. As Urry remarked of Turner – but the criticism applies equally to Berlin and Kay – such models have severely limited the attention given to colour in anthropology and archaeology, where it remains sufficient to compare one's data with these parameters, thus covering the topic of colour, and consider it closed (Urry 1971).

Barth's analysis of ritual and knowledge among the Baktamen of New Guinea is a good example of a Turneresque symbolic approach, or at least a reply to it (Barth 1975). Barth's ethnography follows the example of Turner in that the dominant ritual colours of red, white and black are treated singly and are ascribed basic referents from which meaning is derived. The particular referents, though, differ from Turner's universals, except for the correlation between the colour red and blood (1975: 177). Barth writes that he cannot show that meanings derive from the inherent properties of the colours. In later work comparing the different cosmologies of Mountain Ok societies, Barth notes the use of a recipe containing red ochre, red pandanas fruit, red bark juice and pig fat as an 'emphatically male' substance among the Baktamen, who consider menstrual blood as black. The neighbouring Teleformin, however, consider red ochre as menstrual blood. Barth concludes that there is an opposition in the Teleformin ancestor cult between 'tarokind' in that gardening and pigs are codified by white and 'arrowkind', where war and hunting are codified by red. Barth concludes that 'powerful transformative processes are represented in myth and in ritual as transformations between red and white' (1987: 51). For Barth the coloured symbols achieve meaning through 'the design and activities of persons rather than by virtue of their natural qualities' (1975: 173). He sees colours as one aspect of a closed system of representation that is understandable only to those encultured in its codified meanings (cf. Forge 1970). As well as the power of colour to express a social dynamic in the red-to-white transformation of ritual, Barth's analysis also shows the linkage between everyday and ritual that colours make possible, habitually and instantaneously.

The association of red with blood has been much discussed in the literature of symbolic anthropology. There are different kinds of blood; menstrual blood, for example, is frequently symbolized, as in the example above, by black (Urry 1971). Red ochres sprinkled around Neanderthal graves and with more frequency in later burial sites of *homo sapiens*

have been used to argue that red ochre was associated with life/blood (Wreshner 1980). This approach to colours has been criticized as too particular, one that would invalidate its polysemic symbolism (Jacobsen-Widdings 1980). Rather red might be associated with ambiguity, as it is in Central Africa, where it is neither one thing nor the other and thus stands for things that defy classification. Red is therefore endowed with dynamic properties and with magical powers (*ibid.*).

I suggest that while colours do have meanings which may *represent* knowledge (Munn 1973) or *communicate* it (Morphy 1991), these are not the only things that colours do. These approaches may also lead to foregrounding only certain arenas of analysis where conscious and highly constructed appearances such as ritual or art prevail, thereby neglecting the flux of colour in the more mundane areas of the everyday – cloth, cars and food, for example – and the ebb and flow of colours that compose daily existence. Having explored the two most influential approaches to colour in the social sciences, colour language and symbolic colour, I now turn to the colours of things. In doing so I wish to place less emphasis on the singularity of hues that is central to colour science and also marks out the linguistic and symbolic approaches to colour in anthropology. Rather, colours in a coloured context, that is, in the habitus of everyday life, might be considered as relational effects. The effect of colours taken together may be manipulated to produce a specific impact; for instance, in the use of four earth pigments to produce 'brilliance' by Yolgnu people in Arnhem Land, North Australia (Morphy 1989). Material colours may tell us about the relationship between things and people, whether certain objects are, for example, regarded as possessing an animation or agency, and what kind of spatial effect they are intended to produce, while other things are construed as passive. By using such an object-centred approach to colours, and by carrying out ethnography on the colours of things, we could learn about all sorts of levels of which meaning is only one dimension.

MATERIAL COLOUR

So far I have discussed the various dematerializations of colour, namely the reduction of colour to a measurable 'stimulus' in colour science and the dematerialization of colour as language and colour as symbolic meaning in anthropology. I have discussed how the very notion of 'colour' has been considered problematic, since the apparatus of colour science that is used to conjure it already presupposes its existence. Yet the world is now full of circulating coloured things produced industrially such as cars, cloth and clothing, cosmetics and paints. All such industrial goods are coloured, usually purposely coloured with particular markets in mind, by employing pigment formulas with international standard numbers, pigments that are manufactured by a few multinational companies. Even the landscape is subject to colour interventions with, for example, the introduction of oil seed rape in the United Kingdom whose brilliant yellow flowers have transformed the washed-out hues that were once emblematic of the landscape.

I have suggested that material colour in the social world might be better considered as a relational quality, and below I will consider in more detail just what those relations might consist of. Rather than asking what people *perceive* in response to a given stimulus, such as an asocial, decontextualized piece of coloured card (a Munsell chip, say), or privileging what people say, we might consider what they *do* with coloured material things within the dynamics of social practice. By focusing on changes in colour practices during periods of social upheaval, for example, the articulation of the role of things might be revealed.[8] Such situations might include the impact of colonization or post-socialism in the former Soviet bloc, for example, the question 'In what ways are colour relationships used to animate things?' could then be tested by examining the qualities of colour mixtures chosen before and after social upheaval.

For, alongside the intuitive idea of colour in phenomenology, I suggest that colours can be a compelling, exact and calculated medium for producing and reproducing power and for transmitting knowledge and an essential facet of knowledge systems. Further, colours have agency and can communicate and also effect complicated ideas and relationships instantaneously, following Wagner's writing on the power of images (Wagner 1987). But colours are also able to convey and embody a sense of becoming, and of being. Within these two generalized senses of colour, as knowledge, and as being, are further particularities. I will suggest some aspects of colour that might constitute new parameters for investigation. They are by no means offered as universals, rather they require careful comparative ethnographic fieldwork to show how colours embody social transactions. By researching exactly how people communicate with coloured things and imagery, networks

of connections may be revealed. These types of colour practices are not mutually exclusive. Colours can be distinguishing and emotive, they can structure space and create topographies of things.

First, then, since it seems colour's most simple application, there is *distinguishing* colour or the difference in hue used to differentiate things from one another–ginger cats from tabby ones, red lorries from green, territories on a map (itself a famous mathematical problem: what is the fewest number of colours needed to colour a map?) In evolutionary biology the necessity of distinguishing fruit from leaves is said to account for the co-evolution of trees and colour vision among primates (Lumsden and Wilson 1981; Mollon 1999). Distinguishing colour is the singular hue of colour science in that colour is the property which is used to discriminate this from that and, as I discussed above, is now linked with new ideas about colour constancy. It is colour categorized, codified, functional and reductive, yet also potentially of great social import. Distinguishing colour, often as sets of colours, signals social identity such as football or basketball strips and national flags and as such can be the focus of intense emotional expression, socially directed (Lutz and White 1986).

An extension or the inverse of distinguishing colour is colour as *analogy* in which the colours of things connect whole panoplies of otherwise disparate cultural categories, thereby constituting a network of resemblances (cf. Stafford 1999). It is one way of creating categories of things that are otherwise dissimilar, for example things and persons or green birds and green clothing and green cars. There may flow from this an expectation that things that are similarly coloured will produce the same effect on the grounds that if things have similar attributes then they will have other similarities (van Brackel 2002).

The colours of things may change (something that is generally neglected in the constructs of colour discussed above, where singularity and stasis of colour are mostly assumed), rendering such networks both unstable and dynamic. Land is apt to pass through changes in colour with seasonal variation, as do some animals and birds, producing and concealing analogies as they transform (Boric 2002; Young n.d.). In representations, things and persons can be shown as dynamic by a succession of differently coloured outlines around the original figure.

A colour change might also be thought of as the transformation itself not just as symbolic.

For example, Bailey has written of colour in the Hindu tradition as not 'merely an accident of matter' but an independent manifestation of the spirit that is part of the make-up of red cloth. 'Thus the spirit of red cloth, or redness, can combine with the moral substance of a particular person and transform it'. A man dressed in red was something more than this, he was a red man, a sorcerer. 'His costume did not symbolise a status acquired by other means; it was an essential component of the very transformation itself' (Seal, in Bayly 1986: 287). In south Indian ritual, coloured food is used to control the state of heat or coolness in the body. White is auspicious for stability, whilst red supersedes the ordinary and is necessary for innovation. But the instability of redness makes a further change to white desirable for well-being. The person undergoing purification is thus fed balls of coloured rice: the first is white, the second red, a quality achieved by adding lime or tumeric, and the third white (Beck 1969).

Among Pitjantjatjara and Yankunytjatjara people living in the central desert of Australia, greenness is consumed in the form of green tobacco harvested from land following rain. The becoming green of the land is echoed by wearing bright green clothing, thus re-embodying the attachment of persons to their 'country' and the equation of these as interchangeable (Young n.d.). The becoming green of the body, both inside and out, is a concrete articulation of the ties of people to their land. In the Melanesian *kula*, the white shell valuables become red with age and human handling and it is this transformation that indicates their history and increases their prestige and value (Campbell 1983). The transformative work of colour thus effects and produces a spatial and temporal dimension. Colours are arguably, in these cases, construed as having agency, altering events and/or persons. Among the Abelam of Papua New Guinea, Forge wrote of the yam cult where all magical substances are classed as paint and paint is the ceremonial medium through which initiates are turned into men (Forge 1962). By anointing both yams and boys with colour both grow large and hot.

Colours acting together may be employed to produce captivating effects (e.g. Albers 1963; Cennini 1954; Chevreul 1858). In one of the few systematic attempts during the twentieth century to document the interaction of colours, the artist and teacher Josef Albers wrote, 'colours present themselves in continuous flux, constantly related to changing neighbours …' (1971: 5). These effects might be said to produce the quality of animation, a sense of movement through colour juxtapositions, that fetishizes things and brings them alive. The production of brilliance and of space are the two specific effects that I will discuss briefly here. While there is an inclination to oppose form to colour, both in art history and in neuroscience, as discussed above, form can be created through colour relationships. Paul Cézanne, for instance, used colours to create form in painting. 'The outline and the colours are no longer distinct from each other. To the extent that one paints, one outlines: the more the colours harmonise, the more the outline becomes precise'.[9] Albers's colour experiments also show the particular and strong spatial pull together exerted by the combination of red, white and black, the contractive nature of black, next to expansive white and reds that seem to come forward (Albers 1963). I suggest that the cross-cultural predilection for the ritual combination of these colours has to do with the spatial effect created by their relationship to one another, an effect that is certainly embodied, an 'amplification of being' in Merleau-Ponty's words. With such examples in mind, the replacement of one colour by another when people obtain access to new coloured materials can be seen differently. The use of blue paint instead of black, frequently noted in the anthropological literature, is discussed in relation to Abelam cult houses (Forge 1970). Seeing the use of colour as codified, Forge is puzzled by the lack of distinction made by painters between black and recently obtained blues. It may be that for the Abelam the blues and blacks were similar in their spatial effect, something also implied by the description of initiated men working only on dark backgrounds using white outlines. The space created by the figure/ground relationship of white lines on a black ground is considered by Abelam men as distinct from black lines on white. Abelam children, however, were happier to paint on white paper (1970: 284). A possibility offered by this information is that adult men have acquired a different notion of space from children (cf. Toren 1993).

The structuring possibilities of colour in pattern applied to things and bodies are arresting, altering symmetries and spatial structures. Altering the colours of repetitive patterns also transforms their spatial orientation and adds ambiguity to symmetries, as Boas recorded for Peruvian weavers and embroiderers (Gombrich 1979).

If some assemblages of colours create strong spatial relationships, then others create an impression of luminosity and dazzle. An analysis of Byzantine mosaics shows them to act as light materialized. It is through the colour combinations and lustre of the mosaic pieces that the huge church murals created and manifested form, with the whole building seeming to produce light as well as capturing daylight through its apertures. The Byzantines are held to have valued saturation rather than hue (James 1996). Among the Yolgnu of northern Australia, 'brilliance' is produced through the particular skilfull combinations of earth pigments and expresses the powerful and dangerous presence of ancestors. In his influential paper Morphy declares the transfromation from dull to brilliant as a concept underlying all ritual (Morphy 1989). My argument here is that objects can manifest different kinds of effects through the relationship of colours.

The idea of colour as involving only the visual is also a limited and culturally bound conception. In addition to the three 'dimensions' of colour encompassed by colour space models like the Munsell system, that of hue, tone and saturation, colours can also be implicated with senses that in the West are conventionally separated such as odour and tactility (see Howes, chapter 10 in this volume).

Conklin's paper on Hanunoo colour categories formed the basis of Berlin and Kay's research. His analysis of the four 'basic' categories of the Hanunoo correlates white to black as lightness and darkness, and wetness/succulence to desiccation shows a more expansive idea of colour (Conklin 1955: 343). This last pairing of wet to dry was grouped broadly around colours containing green and colours containing red, or rather things that were greenish and things that were reddish. This wider construct of what colour words might encompass resonates with other case studies on ancient Egypt and also contemporary central Australia, where greenness and wetness or fecundity are linked with rain in a way which might be termed cultural synaesthesia (Baines 1985; Young forthcoming).

In many cultures the senses are thought to alter the world in the process of perceiving it, rather than simply registering it (Howes 1992). In classical Mayan culture the eye was held to emit images (Houston and Taube 2000: 281). Recent rereadings of Aristotle, on whose work much subsequent Western philosophy of perception relies, have also argued for a return to the idea of colour as mutually 'out there' and in the mind, as having a powerful presence that changes objects and persons together (Johansen 2002).

CONCLUSION

Whilst anthropology might deplore the framework that has produced the phenomenon of colour, I have argued that as a discipline it cannot afford to ignore the industrial colours in the contemporary social world which are very often the result of that framework or are at least modified by it. Colours have escaped the laboratory where they had been de-materialized and become a part of material social practices.

I have attempted to argue that it is possible to step outside the guiding principles of colour science that have also influenced the social sciences by concentrating not on the discrimination of singular hues but on the effect of colours together. I have suggested that the qualities that Western science has called 'colour' animate things and are therefore crucial in determining the role of things and persons in a social context. It is through a detailed and thorough examination of colour practices, as well as what people say about these, that particular intended animative qualities can be revealed.

If colour continues to elude definition, the evidence of its pragmatic application is nonetheless present without anyone knowing why colour does what it actually does. A treatment for dyslexia has used coloured gel overlays on the standard black text on white page to enable dyslexics to decipher words (Wilkins 2003). It may be the spatial shift that the overlays bring about that introduces the necessary clarity.

Colour, then, is at once knowledge and being. Colours can dispense with the distinction between subject and object and define how things/persons move in the world through their animation and spatial distinctions. Indeed, the mutual constitution of persons and things will soon be literal in new 'smart' buildings where walls react to the occupants' clothing and change colour to match as a person moves across the space. While colour is still considered by anthropologists as a narrow specialist field, or as one which is too superficial, too difficult or as tautological, a whole dimension of the social world has escaped them.

NOTES

1   See Saunders (1998).
2   Saunders (2001) following Heelan's (1983) theory concerning grammars of perception,

constructs Euclidian colour as the geometric and standardized colour of colour science; vernacular colour as that of the 'life world', meaning colour as part of the lived world, including socially situated colours, and pixellated colours refers to the growing body of work concerning the role of colour in computer displays.

3 Some sources refer to these axes as hue, value and chroma.

4 Zeki, illustrating the incestuous circularity of colour science, quotes from the work of Rosch Heider, see below, to bolster his argument.

5 Saunders and van Brakel, among others, challenge Rosch Heider's notion of focal colours which she herself selected and seem to have some correlation with the most saturated colours.

6 See Henselmans (2002) for a critique of Roberson's Munsell-based methodology.

7 See van Brakel (2002) for an overview of comparative studies.

8 I am indebted to Nicholas Saunders for this insight.

9 Merleau Ponty in 'Cezanne's doubt' (1964), quoting conversations with Emile Bernard.

REFERENCES

Albers, Josef (1963) *The Interaction of Colour*. New Haven, CT: Yale University Press.

Baines, Jeremy R. (1985) 'Color terminology and color classification: ancient Egyptian color terminology and polychromy', *American Anthropology*, 87 (2): 282–97.

Barth, F. (1975) *Ritual and Knowledge among the Baktamen of Papua New Guinea*. New Haven: Yale University Press.

Barth, F. (1987) *Cosmologies in the Making: A Generative Approach to Cultural Variation in Inner New Guinea*. Cambridge: Cambridge University Press.

Bayly, C.A. (1986) 'The origins of swadeshi (home industry): cloth and Indian society 1700–1930', in A. Appadurai (ed.), *The Social Life of Things: Commodities in Cultural perspective*. Cambridge: Cambridge University Press, pp. 285–321.

Beck, B. (1969) 'Colour and heat in South Indian ritual', *Man* (4): 553–72.

Berlin, Brent and Kay, Paul (1969) *Basic Colour Terms: their Universality and Evolution*. Berkeley, CA: University of California Press.

Boric, Dusan (2002) 'Apotropaism and the temporality of colours', in A. Jones and G. MacGregor (eds), *Colouring the Past*. Oxford: Berg, pp. 23–43.

Bousfield, John (1979) 'World seen as a colour chart', in *Classifications in their Social Context*. New York: Academic Press, pp. 195–220.

Campbell, S. (1983) 'Attaining rank: a classification of shell valuables', in J. Leach and E. Leach (eds), *The Kula*. Cambridge: Cambridge University Press, pp. 229–249.

Cennini Cennino d'Andrea (1954) *The Craftsman's Handbook: the Italian 'Il libro dell'arte'*, trans. Daniel V. Thompson. New York: Dover.

Chevreul, M.E. (1858) *The Laws and Contrast of color*, trans. John Spanton. London: Routledge.

Conklin, Harold C. (1955) 'Hanunoo colour categories', *South Western Journal of Anthropology*, 11: 339–44.

Conklin, Harold C. (1973) 'Colour categorisation', *American Anthropologist*, 75: 931–42.

Coote, Jeremy (1992) '"Marvels of everyday vision": aesthetics and the cattle-keeping Nilotes', in Jeremy Cootes and Anthony Shelton (eds), *Anthropology, Art and Aesthetics*. Oxford: Clarendon Press.

D'Andrade, R. and Egan, M.J. (1975) 'The colour of emotion', *American Ethnologist*, 1, 49–63.

Davidoff, J. (1992) *Cognition through Colour*. Cambridge, MA: MIT Press.

Dedrick, D. (2002) 'The roots/routes of color term reference', in Barbara Saunders and Jaap van Brakel (eds), *Theories Technologies Instrumentalities of Color. Anthropological and Historiographic Perspectives*. Lanham, MD: University of America Press, pp. 53–68.

De Weert (2002) 'Color vision; psychophysics and physiology – a brief historical sketch', in Barbara Saunders and Jaap van Brakel (eds), *Theories Technologies Instrumentalities of Color. Anthropological and Historiographic Perspectives*. Lanham, MD: University of America Press, pp. 327–342.

Dussart, Françoise (1999) 'What an acrylic can mean: on the meta-ritualistic resonances of a Central Desert painting', in Howard Morphy and Margo Smith-Boles (eds), *Art from the Land: Dialogues with the Kluge-Ruhe Collection of Australian*. Charlottesville: University Press of Virginia, pp. 193–218.

Forge, A. (1962) 'Paint – a magical substance', *Palette* (Geneva), 9: 9–16.

Forge, A. (1970) 'Learning to see in New Guinea', in P. Mayer (ed.), *Socialisation: The Approach from Social Anthropology*. London: Tavistock Press, pp. 269–91.

Gage, John (1993) *Colour and Culture: Practice and Meaning from Antiquity to Abstraction*. London: Thames & Hudson.

Gardner, Howard (1985) *The Mind's New Science: a History of the Cognitive Revolution*. New York: Basic Books.

Gell, Alfred (1998) *Art and Agency*. Oxford: Oxford University Press.

Gellatly, Angus (2002) 'Colour perception: processing of wavelength information and conscious experience of colour', in Barbara Saunders and Jaap van Brakel (eds), *Theories Technologies instrumentalities of Color: Anthropological and Historiographic perspectives*. Lanham, MD: University Press of America, pp. 77–90.

Gladstone, W.E. (1858) *Homer and the Homeric Age*. Oxford: Oxford University Press.

Goethe, Johannes W. (1987) *Theory of Colour*. Cambridge, MA: MIT Press.

Gombrich, E.H. (1960) *Art and Illusion: a Study in the Psychology of Pictorial representation*. London: Phaidon Press.

Gombrich, E.H. (1979) *The Sense of Order: a Study in the Psychology of Decorative Art*. London: Phaidon Press.

Hardin, C.L. (1988) *Color for Philosophers: Unweaving the Rainbow*. Indianapolis, IN: Hackett.

Hardin, C.L. and Maffi, L. eds (1997) *Colour Categories in Thought and Language*. Cambridge: Cambridge University Press.

Heelan, P. (1983) *Space–perception and the Philosophy of Science*. Berkeley and Los Angeles: University of California Press.

Henselmans, Arnold (2002) 'The Munsell constraint', in Barbara Saunders and Jaap van Brakel (eds), *Theories Technologies instrumentalities of Color: Anthropological and Historiographic Perspectives*. Lanham, MD: University Press of America, pp. 37–52.

Houston, S. and Taube, K. (2000) 'An archaeology of the senses: perception and cultural expression in ancient Mesoamerica', *Cambridge Archaeological Journal* 10(2): 261–94.

Howes, David (1992) 'The Sounds of Sense: an Inquiry into the Sensory Orders of Western and Melanesian Thought'. Unpublished Ph.D. thesis, Université de Montreal.

Ingold, Tim, ed. (1993) 'Debate: Aesthetics is a Cross-cultural Category', *Key Debates in Anthropology*. London: Routledge.

Jacobsen-Widdings, Anita (1980) 'Reply to Ernst Wreshner', *Current Anthropology*, 5: 637.

James, Elizabeth Anne (1996) *Light and Colour in Byzantine Art*. Oxford: Clarendon Press.

Johansen, T. (2002) 'Imprinted on the mind: passive and active in Aristotle's theory of perception', in Barbara Saunders and Jaap van Brakel (eds), *Theories Technologies instrumentalities of Color. Anthropological and Historiographic perspectives*. Lanham, MD: University Press of America, pp. 000–00.

Jones, A. and MacGregor, G. eds (2002) *Colouring the Past: The Significance of Colour in Archaeological Research*. Oxford: Berg.

Kay, Paul and Willet, K. (1984) 'What is the Sapir-Whorf hypothesis?' *American Anthropology*, 86: 65–79.

Keane, W. (1997) *Signs of recognition: Powers and Hazards of Representation in an Indonesian Society*. Berkeley, CA: University of California Press.

Kuschel, Ralph and Monberg, Tito (1974) 'We don't talk much about colour here: a study of colour semantics on Bellona Island', *Man*, 9: 213–42.

Lakoff, George and Johnston, Mark (1981) *Metaphors we Live by*. Chicago: University of Chicago Press.

Lamb, Trevor and Bourriau, Janine eds (1995) *Colour: Art and Science*. Cambridge: Cambridge University Press.

LaTour, Bruno (1993) *We have Never been Modern*, trans. Catherine Porter. Cambridge, MA: Harvard University Press.

Levinson, Stephen. C. (2000) 'YeliDnye and the theory of basic colour terms', *Journal of Linguistic Anthropology*, 10: 3–55.

Lucy, J.A. and Shweder, R. A. (1979) 'Whorf and his critics: linguistic and non-linguistic influences on color memory', *American Anthropologist*, 81: 581–605.

Lumsden, C. and Wilson, E. (1981) *Genes, Mind and Culture: the Co-evolutionary Process*. Cambridge, MA: Harvard University Press.

Lutz, Catherine and White, Geoffrey (1986) 'The anthropology of the emotions', *Annual Review of Anthropology*, 15: 405–36.

MacLaury, Robert E. (1992) 'From brightness to hue: an explanatory model of color category evolution', *Current Anthropology*, 33: 137–86.

Malcolm, Neil L. (1999) 'Continuing commentary', *Behavioural and Brain Science*, 22: 723–733.

Malraux, André (1956) *The Voices of Silence: Man and his Art*, trans. Stuart Gilbert. New York: Doubleday.

Merleau-Ponty, Maurice (1962) *The Phenomenology of Perception*, trans. Colin Smith. London and New York: Routledge.

Merleau-Ponty, Maurice (1964/2004) 'Cezanne's doubt' and 'Eye and mind', in Maurice Merleau-Ponty, *Basic Writings*, ed. Thomas Baldwin. London and New York: Routledge.

Michaels, Eric (1994) *Bad Aboriginal Art: Tradition, Media and Technological Horizons*. Minneapolis, MN: University of Minnesota Press.

Mollon, John D. (1999) '"Cherries among the leaves": the evolutionary origins of colour vision', in B. Funt (ed.), *Colour Perception: Philosophical, Psychological, Artistic, and Computational Perspectives*. Oxford: Oxford University Press.

Morphy, Howard (1989) 'From dull to brilliant: the aesthetics of spiritual power among the Yolgnu', *Man*, 24 (1): 21–39.

Morphy, Howard (1991) *Ancestral Connections: Art and an Aboriginal System of Knowledge*. Chicago: University of Chicago Press.

Munn, Nancy (1973) *The Walbiri Iconography*. Chicago: University of Chicago Press.

Roberson, D., Davidoff, J. and Davies, I. (2002) 'Colour categories are not universal: replications and new evidence', in Barbara Saunders and Jaap van Brakel (eds), *Theories Technologies instrumentalities of Color. Anthropological and Historiographic Perspectives.* Lanham, MD: University Press of America, pp. 25–36.

Rosch, Eleanor (1978) 'Color categorisation', in E. Rosch and B. Lloyd (eds), *Cognition and Categorisation.* Hillsdale, NJ: Erlbaum, pp. 29–49.

Rosch Heider, Eleanor (1972) 'Probabilities, sampling and ethnographic method: the case of Dani colour names', *Man,* 7 (3): 448–66.

Sahlins, Marshall David (1977) *Colours and Cultures in Symbolic Anthropology.* New York: Columbia University Press, pp. 165–80.

Saunders, B.A.C. (1998) 'What *is* colour?' *British Journal of Psychology,* 89: 697–704.

Saunders, Barbara (2000) 'Revisiting basic colour terms', *Journal of the Royal Anthropological Institute,* 6: 81–98.

Saunders, Barbara (2001) 'Grammar(s) of perception', in B. Babich (ed.), *Hermeneutic Philosophy of Science. From Van Gogh's Eyes and God.* Boston Studies in the Philosophy of Science. Dordrecht: Kluwer.

Saunders, Barbara (2002) 'Getting in touch with the world', in Barbara Saunders and Jaap van Brakel (eds), *Theories Technologies Instrumentalities of Color: Anthropological and Historiographic perspectives.* Lanham, MD: University Press of America, pp. 91–104.

Saunders, Barbara and van Brakel, Jaap (1997) 'Are there non-trivial constraints on colour categorisation?' *Behavioral and Brain Science,* 20: 167–228.

Saunders, B. and van Brakel, J. (1999) 'Color world trouble', *Behavioural and Brain Science,* 22: 725–729.

Sperber, D. (1975) *Rethinking Symbolism.* Cambridge: Cambridge University Press.

Stafford, Barbara M. (1999) *Visual Analogy: Consciousness as the Art of Connecting.* Cambridge, MA and London: MIT Press.

Tambiah, Stanley. J. (1968) 'The magical power of words', *Man,* 2: 172–208.

Thompson, Evan (1995) *Colour Vison: a Study in Cognitive Science and the Philosophy of Perception.* London and New York: Routledge.

Toren, C. (1993) 'Making history: the significance of childhood cognition for a comparative anthropology of mind', *Man* (n.s.) 28: 461–78.

Turner, Victor (1967) *The Forest of Symbols: Aspects of Ndembu Ritual.* London: Cornell University Press.

Urry, J. (1971) 'Symbolic colour: Victor Turner reassessed', *Journal of the Anthropological Society of Oxford,* 2: 9–17.

Van Brakel, Jaap (2002) 'Chromatic language games and their congeners', in Barbara Saunders and Jaap van Brakel (eds), *Theories Technologies Instrumentalities of Color: Anthropological and Historiographic perspectives.* Lanham, MD: University Press of America, pp. 145–68.

Wagner, Roy (1987) 'Figure-ground reversal among the Barok', in Louise Lincoln (ed.), *Assemblage of Spirits: Idea and Image in New Ireland.* New York: George Braziller and Minneapolis Instit. of Arts.

Whorf , B.L. (1956) 'The relation of habitual thought and behaviour to language', in *Language Thought and Reality.* Edited and with an introduction by John B. Carroll. Cambridge, MA: MIT Press, pp. 134–59.

Wiersbicka, Anna (1999) 'Universals of color from a linguistic point of view', *Behavioral and Brain Sciences,* 22: 724–5.

Wilkins, A.J. (2003) *Reading through Colour.* Chichester: Wiley.

Wittgenstein, Ludwig (1977) *Remarks on Colour.* Oxford: Blackwell.

Wreshner, E.E. (1980) 'Red ochre and human evolution: a case for discussion', *Current Anthropology,* 21 (5): 631–44.

Young, D.J.B. (n.d.) 'The Colours of Things: Memory Materiality and an Anthropology of the Senses in northwest South Australia'. Unpublished Ph.D. thesis, University College London, 2001.

Young, D.J.B. (forthcoming) 'The smell of green-ness: cultural synaesthesia in the Western Desert', *Ethnofoor.*

Zeki, Semir (1993) *A Vision of the Brain.* Oxford and Boston, MA: Blackwell.

Zeki, Semir (1998) 'Art and the brain', *Daedalus,* 127 (2): 71–103.

ACKNOWLEDGEMENTS

Research for this chapter was enabled by ESRC postdoctoral award No. T026271266 and ESRC-funded doctoral research from 1995 to 1999.

12

INSIDE AND OUTSIDE

Surfaces and Containers

Jean-Pierre Warnier

The archaeological and ethnographic record concerning surfaces, containers, ceramics, textiles, the human skin, its openings, movements from inside to outside and vice versa is considerable. Too vast to reduce to a short article on the topic which would amount to a laundry list unless one has some kind of key that will unlock various doors opening onto a common corridor.

My key will be the human body, for two reasons. First, it is itself a container, with its skin as a surface, with its openings conjoining an inside and an outside. Second, by acting in a material world, the human body supplements itself with innumerable surfaces and containers by means of which it extends beyond its own physical limits.

However, we encounter here a first difficulty. It has proved difficult to turn 'the body' into an anthropological object. The reasons for this were explored by Berthelot (1995). Basically, the social and cultural facts are not the body in itself, but the techniques of the body (see Mauss 1936), its uses, its social representations, and all the practices (sports, health care, dress, cosmetics, control, apprenticeship, etc.) attached to it. This difficulty has led most attempts towards an anthropology of 'the body' to an epistemological dead end. As a result, from an anthropological point of view, it is more efficient to focus on bodily conducts than on the body as such. Consequently, my argument will unfold as follows.

Bodily conducts are gestures accomplished by a given subject in which his/her subjectivity is involved. They can be limited in scope, to the point of being static, like holding one's breath and staying put while playing hide-and-seek, or quite mobile, as in riding a bicycle. Second, there is no motricity without the involvement of the seven senses, that is, the conventionally distinguished five senses, to which must be added proprioception and the vestibular sense of gravitation and spatial orientation.[1] The seven senses are interconnected in such a way that, according to the neuroscientist Berthoz (1997), they are all part and parcel of a single sense: the sense of movement. There is no perception without motricity, and no motricity without the involvement of the senses. So far, my key has been transformed from 'the body' to 'motor conducts', then to 'sensori-motricity'. The next step consists in introducing a third essential dimension. As Damasio (2000) rightly pointed out, any sensori-motor conduct involves both a drive and the emotions that correspond to it: pleasure, anger, satisfaction, curiosity, etc. – most of the time, a complex and volatile mix of affects accompanied and stimulated by the production of hormones (ocitocyn, dopamine, endomorphine) affecting the central nervous system. As a result, my key becomes the 'sensori-affectivo-motor' conducts of the subject.

Much like keys that are equipped with grooves, small balls and holes, this key has several components or dimensions to it. It has a psychic dimension, made of the cognitive (not necessarily 'conscious') and emotional aspects (including 'unconscious' as repressed in the Freudian sense) of all our actions. It has an anatomo-physiological component in so far as all our actions are mediated by bodily motions, as those who are disabled know only too well.

Last but not least, it has a material component, in so far as all our 'sensori-affectivo-motor' conducts are propped against, or articulated with, a human-made material culture that has been co-produced along with the relevant gestures. The keyboard with which I type the present chapter has been manufactured very precisely to fit a human hand and to adjust to its motions. Vice versa, through a protracted apprenticeship I have devised sensori-motor algorithms that allow me to incorporate the keyboard and write as if it were a component of my bodily schema.

So now my key becomes 'sensori-affectivo-motor conducts geared to material culture'. It may sound a bit complicated, but human motricity in a human-made material world is easier to contemplate than to analyse, and for analytical reasons we need the full constellation of concepts. From an analytical point of view, the components of the key can be considered apart from one another. In agency, however, they are essentially welded and mobilized together. An acting subject is always a 'subject-acting-with-its-incorporated-objects'.

One more comment of a historical nature. At the beginning of the twentieth century, Head and Holmes (1911) and others accumulated numerous observations that were synthetized by Schilder (1923, 1935) under the expression of *Körperschema*, 'bodily schema' or 'image of the body', as a kind of bodily synthesis acquired through a long apprenticeship. Schilder (1935) insisted that the bodily schema does not end with the human skin as a limiting boundary. It extends far beyond it and, from the point of view of motricity, perception and emotions, includes all the objects we use, and to which we are geared. It even includes all the material culture that lies beyond our immediate grasp. The walking stick of a blind person, following Schilder, is incorporated into the bodily schema, as is clear from the way that the perception of the environment is felt by the blind person to reside at the end of the walking stick rather than at the interface between the stick and his or her hand. Similarly, our bodily schema incorporates the domestic space, its furniture and all the appliances we can reach on a routine basis, to such an extent that, if we change the location of a given cabinet in our flat, we will have to retrain our motor algorithms to look for the cabinet in its new location instead of the previous one. Our bodily schema also incorporates the static and dynamic properties of the car we usually drive, the bicycle we ride, our favourite armchair, etc. In short, Schilder's notion of a bodily schema,

enriched with all the knowledge accumulated since his time by the neuro- and cognitive sciences provides the grounds for a praxeological approach to material culture.

This approach considers material culture not only in terms of its sign value within a system of communication but in terms of its practical value in a system of agency. It departs significantly from semiological or structuralist approaches but it does not contradict them. To be sure, material culture is good to think and to signify with, but it is also jolly good to act with, as part and parcel of any sensori-affectivo-motor conduct of the subject. This approach also departs significantly from most phenomenological approaches to 'the body' (e.g. Featherstone et al. 1991; Csordas 1994) in so far as these do not consider material culture as an essential component of 'the body' (read 'sensori-motricity') and tend to deal with 'meaning' and representations of the body rather than with the ethnography of bodily conducts. The latter would compel them to take material culture into consideration, whereas it does not have any place in their agenda. This short summary will suffice here, since I have developed the argument more fully elsewhere (Warnier 1999, 2001; Julien and Warnier 1999; Bayart and Warnier 2004).

The approach summarized here provides a key to opening doors on to various domains of material culture in which containers, inside, outside, openings and surfaces are all relevant. In all cases, they will be understood as essential correlates of bodily conducts and as part of the bodily schema.

THE PRAXEOLOGY OF CONTAINERS, OPENINGS AND SURFACES

The arch-container is the human skin. The classic work here is the synthesis provided by the psychoanalyst Anzieu (1985) in his book *Le Moi-peau*, or 'The Skin-self'. A wealth of data, provided by human and animal ethology, projective tests (like the Rorschach) and dermatological observations, converge in underscoring the basic role of the skin in the ontogenesis of the human subject. The psyche is constructed as an envelope by 'anaclisis' on the anatomophysiological functions of the skin. Anaclisis refers to the process by which many psychic experiences build upon or are propped against bodily motions and emotions. The skin provides many such basic experiences; it covers the body, its protects it, it sustains the muscles, it registers information, it is an organ of sensori-motor and of libidinal stimulation. The psychic self models itself on the experiences provided by the skin. It fulfils similar functions as regards psychic content; is constructed as a container which provides the basic tenets of the processes of introjection and projection studied by Ferenczi. Additionally, the skin is provided with openings through which the inside and the outside communicate and through which things, substances, informations, and emotions enter or leave the body and the psyche.

The sensori-motor conducts dealing with the skin, its openings and the traffic of substances are the most archaic and deeply grounded in the experience of the subject. They begin to operate before birth. Feeding, breathing, defecating, perceiving, being handled and held, washed, clothed, etc., are all activities that develop at one and the same time both the sensori-motor and the psychic components of containment and its correlates. Any subject–adult or child–will draw on such a basic repertoire in dealing with material containers that have been incorporated in bodily conducts. The main categories of material culture involved here are clothing as a second skin, all domestic containers, buildings and architecture, ships and means of transportation, or all constructions that are aimed at channelling substances: dams, canals, pumps, pipes, roads, traffic lights, and all the technology of human containment such as prisons, cells, airports, camps of various kinds.

The sensori-motor conducts associated with containment may be as diverse as opening, closing, pouring, filling, emptying, wrapping, regulating, maintaining the envelope or the limits, removing the blockages that prevent the transit of substances, mending leaks, forming a queue. Such conducts involve material, psychic and sensori-motor components in various proportions, depending on the circumstances, the social context, the material culture involved, etc. Besides, they are culturally shaped. In Maussian parlance, they are 'bio-psycho-social' phenomena.

All such conducts mediate between the material culture of containers, contents, openings and surfaces, on the one hand, and the acting subject, on the other. As a result, the concerns of the subject are displaced on to, or extended into, the embodied material culture of containment: health, morality, possession and property rights, safety and security, intrusion, group belonging, privacy.

CONTAINMENT AS A TECHNOLOGY OF POWER

Michel Foucault (1975, 2001) has aptly emphasized how power is directed at 'the body' (read: to sensori-motor conducts) precisely at the point where the subject governs him/herself. Let me also emphasize here that the subject Foucault speaks of is not the conscious subject characteristic of the Cartesian tradition through phenomenology. It is rather the divided subject of its desires. Basically, power rests on agency, by acting upon the subjects and directing or helping the subjects to act upon themselves, govern themselves and act upon other subjects. All those actions – billions of them – rest on the use of given technologies of power. Such technologies include material components and know-how like those of the hospital, the school, the army barracks, the means of transport, etc. In so far as they are historically and culturally specific, Foucault calls them 'governmentalities'.

In this respect, the technology of the skin, of containment, and the associated material culture provide techniques of the self that may act as the point of departure for the construction of fully-fledged technologies of power. I will illustrate this point with an ethnographic example.

The highlands of western Cameroon have been densely settled for the last millenium. In a territory about the size of Belgium are to be found some 150 kingdoms, the largest of which have been revitalized in the last two decades of the twentieth century as part of the spectacular 'return of the kings' at the forefront of contemporary African political life.

Such kingdoms are typical examples of African sacred kingship made famous by Frazer some 100 years ago.[2] The technology of power in such kingdoms involves the mobilization of sensori-affectivo-motor conducts applied to containers and their contents. The king's body is a container of ancestral substances such as breath, saliva and semen. These substances are complemented by palm oil, raphia wine and camwood powder, a crimson pigment rubbed on people and things.

Such substances are transformed into ancestral substances through the utterance of performative words by qualified persons in the proper context of ceremonial offerings to the dead kings, or a variety of speech of a kind that has been analysed by the philosopher Austin (1962) in his stimulating book *How to Do Things with Words*. As a result, the king, in his body as a material container, possesses all the physical substances necessary for the production and reproduction of his subjects. He disseminates the aforementioned substances by projecting his breath and speech upon his subjects, by spraying them with raphia wine from his drinking horn and his mouth, and by anointing the skin of his subjects and the surface of diverse objects with palm oil and camwood powder. Since he receives reproductive substances direct from the ancestors, he is held to be the most fertile male in the kingdom. Accordingly, at the beginning of the twentieth century, most kings had at least 150 wives, sometimes numbering several hundred. Nowadays the number has been reduced to a 'mere' ten to fifty wives.

The photograph of Abu'Mbi of the Bafut (Figure 12.1) illustrates this point well. It was taken by Diel – a German traveller – some time around 1910. It is a still photograph taken on a glass plate with the cumbersome apparatus in use at the time. No doubt the larger *mise-en-scène* had been arranged beforehand by agreement between the photographer and the king. Despite the fact that the photographer wanted to show off an African despot, a number of features of the photograph correspond very nicely with the ethnography of the kingdom. It also fits with Foucault's argument regarding governmentality and the way this, in turn, may apply to containers.

To wit: the king cultivates corpulence. His girth is emphasized by his demeanour and the ample gown which is a second skin expanding on the first one. To his right stand a dozen of his wives, pregnant (that is, full) and naked. To his left are the offspring that issued from the king as a mon(arch)-container and from his wives. He stands in front of the door (or 'mouth' in the local language) of his personal house, where he spends his nights and receives his wives on a couch lined with the pelts or skins of the leopards with which he identifies.

The people in the still photograph do not move. In that respect, the picture is inadequate to show the motions that are essential to the governmentality of containment and distribution. In what follows, I outline the dynamics of such governmentality that obtain in the neighbouring kingdom of Mankon where I did the bulk of my fieldwork (Warnier 1975, 1985).

The cycle of performances begins at the end of the agricultural cycle around November. People harvest the crops, put them in sacks and baskets and bring them to the house of each individual married woman. Subsequently, a number of actions are taken to rid the kingdom of its suspected sorcerers, who are believed to eat and consume the life and wealth of people. Those persons suspected of being sorcerers are subjected to an ordeal which consists of absorbing a poison taken from the bark of the tree *Erythrophlaeum guineense*. They drink the poison, validating this gesture with the following words: 'If the poison finds sorcery in my entrails, may it destroy it.' Then the convicts run out of the enclosure of the city, where they die and are abandoned in the wild, or vomit the beverage and are brought back into the city, having been declared not guilty. Let me explain: sorcery is a bad substance contained in the belly of the subject-container. It therefore has to be ejected from the city-container. This is effected by introducing a physical substance into the suspected sorcerer-container, and expelling both out of the city through its openings, to die in the wild or be recorporated within the limits of the city.

The city is one of the three bodies of the king, the others being the palace and the king's own 'skin', as the human body and the self are named in the local language. The sorcerers, expelled from the city, are treated like the excrements of the body politic, and therefore of the king, who incorporates in his person the corporate kingdom. This last point is very much in line with Kantorowicz's argument in *The King's Two Bodies* (1957).

Mid-way through the dry season, or around December, the king makes offerings on the dead kings' graves. He is believed to receive their life essence that, in turn, invests his own bodily substances and their extensions in the form of raphia wine, oil and camwood. Following these offerings, he gathers his people at the palace for a four-day festival during which he pours out the life substances from his own body-container in a variety of forms for the benefit of the people, and, quite literally, on to their skin, when he sprays raphia wine from his mouth on the dancers around him. As containers, the corporate king-palace-city are inalienable and therefore sacred, whereas their contents (bodily substances, goods, people) are alienable and therefore to some extent profane or mundane.

The material culture of the palace is very much focused on containers and on openings: kings' graves, dwelling and storage houses, huge pots in which the raphia wine from the different lineages of the kingdom is blended, bags, boxes and bowls for camwood or the

Figure 12.1   *The King of Bafut, Cameroon, c. 1910.* Photo *Diel,* courtesy *Photo-Archiv, Rautenstrauch-Joest-Museum, Cologne*

mixture of palm oil and camwood that is rubbed on people and things, bags of medicine, lodges and houses containing the paraphernalia of palace societies. The openings receive much attention: the necks of pots are shaped and decorated. The door frames of the lodges and of the councillors' hall are adorned with human and animal figures with their mouths gaping open in the act of projecting their breath and saliva on to the incomers. With respect to doors, these are noticeably small, with a high threshold and a low frame. Consequently, the act of entering a house and of extracting oneself from it amounts to an elaborate technique of the body. What is more, people bearing medicines, musical instruments or weapons must always enter the house through the narrow door walking backwards. Consequently, the material culture and the sensori-motor conducts that go along with it are shaped together in peculiar ways.

Accordingly, people, as subjects, are shaped and identified as containers. There is no word for body or self other than 'skin'. Immediately after birth the newborn is rubbed daily with baby lotion for about ten to fifteen minutes thoroughly all over the body, beginning with the shaven scalp, with particular attention paid

to the folds of the nostrils, ears, eyes, mouth, legs and arms. In the past, palm oil was used instead of industrial baby lotion, and every woman and child had his or her oil container (calabash or clay pot). Notables owned elaborate ones for ritual purposes. In daily life, men identified with their bag and women with their basket, very much along the lines described by MacKenzie (1991) for Papua New Guinea concerning the identification of both men and women with their gendered carrying bags or containers. Going about without a bag or a basket makes one uncomfortable, lacking in interiority and substance.

I am by no means suggesting that containers, openings and their associated sensori-motor conducts are part of a technology of power in all known societies. Quite the contrary. What I wish to suggest with the above example is threefold: first, that it offers an overview of the microphysics and overall paradigm of the historical governmentality specific to the sacred kingship of the highlands of western Cameroon. Second, in this particular instance, the material culture of containers should not be understood only in terms of its potential 'meaning' or for what it might 'signify' in a system of communication. Importantly, it should also be understood for what it enables in terms of perception, action, achievement, and performance on the part of the subject. The main question is to understand what this elaborate material culture of containers and containment does to the subject in terms of routinely incorporated motions, emotions and perceptions, that is, in terms of power. As a technology, it applies to the subject and shapes it. This action provides the subject with what Foucault (2001) calls 'technologies of the self' whereby one can fix one's identity and find ways of governing oneself. Besides, it submits the subject to a given 'governmentality'. A Cameroonian subject of the 'Pot-king' cannot easily operate in a contemporary Western democracy or in an acephalous society like those of the forest area of Cameroon.

However, the Mankon kingdom or the sacred kingship of Africa may not be the rare exception it seems to be at first. Hendry (1993) suggests that the Japanese have developed a 'wrapping culture' in which polite speech is a kind of wrapping of thoughts and intentions and may help in wrapping others and exercise control upon them. This dimension of social life has its material counterpart in gift-wrapping, in dressing in layers upon layers of garments, in constructions and gardens as wrapping of space, and in retinues of servants and officials as the wrapping of sorts for those wielding symbolic power. This layer of people shields them off from contact with the crowd. In fact, state formation is a process of social and spatial closure. The politics of wrapping bring us back to the material culture of containment.

TOWARDS A PRAXEOLOGY OF CONTAINERS

In my discussion I will proceed from the larger space of the frontier and the border to the smaller artefacts of pottery and household containers. In each case, sensori-motricity provides a key for the interpretation of the material.

The open space of the frontier and the closure of the border are our point of departure. Turner's analysis of the American frontier (1893/1961), picked up by Kopytoff (1987) and applied by him to Africa, emphasizes the essential role of movement. The frontier is a vast space within which one is not only free to move about but even invited to do so ('Go west, young man') in order to fill up the emptyness and colonize it. It operates very much as an inside without any relevant outside. In other words, the notion of a clearly drawn border with its

specific technologies of control is not essential to it.

In human history, the border assumes a specific dimension of control over people and things with the closure effected by the state. The state clearly imposes a limit between an inside and an outside that is provided with gates and openings through which people, animals and goods may pass in both directions. The Great Wall of China is one of the most ancient and spectacular of such material technologies; Hadrian's wall would be another example. The border is equipped with specific technologies of surveillance: patrols along its length and checkpoints at the gates where vehicles and people are searched, examined and taxed. Airport technology is the most sophisticated development of border control.[3]

Cities provide an example of a smaller kind of container or border. In human history, these seem to antedate the state and are usually understood as representing the earliest forms of political organization that are not based on kinship. Much like the state, the city is composite and consists of a congeries of people of different origins collected inside what is usually a bounded space.

As compared with the state, the city provides specific sensori-motor experiences. Hall (1966) has emphasized how the city constitutes a visual, acoustic, olfactory and thermic space of a particular kind, to the extent that a traveller moving in or out of a city through its gates crosses not only a social and political threshold, but a sensori-affectivo-motor one as well. The city, indeed, can claim to possess a specific inside.

The French acoustician Louis Dandrel (personal communication) claims that each contemporary metropolis has its own acoustic signature, made up of a particular mix of sounds that depends on the type of architecture, the means of transport and the habits of the local inhabitants. There are, of course, differences among the various neighbourhoods, communities or zones of a single city, but, by and large, New York does not sound like Moscow, Shanghai or Lagos. Dandrel made recordings of the acoustic signature of various major cities. This remark could be extended to the olfactory, visual, kinesthesic and other components of urban life. Moving as part of a crowd in New York City, Rome or Shanghai does not constitute the same kind of experience, nor does moving alone.

What I wish to stress is not only that the city is characterized by its limits between an inside and an outside, which can be quite fuzzy, as, for instance, is the case with London, but also by the content of the inside, which differs from one city to the next. Moving across the limit and moving from one town to the other provide different kinds of experiences. Hall indicates some of the implications of such sensori-motor and emotional differences, especially with regard to group interactions and what Bourdieu, following Elias, would call 'different bodily and social habitus'.

The next step is to move down, as it were, the scale of containers to the house or building, with its own specific kinds of surfaces and openings. At a structural level, one of the most revealing analyses has been provided by Cuisenier in the case of French rural houses (1991: 289–344). In each case, Cuisenier gives the layout of the house drawn to scale, and there is nothing new or striking about this. Juxtaposed, however, he provides a dendritic or 'tree' diagram showing the possible trajectories that allow access to a particular inner space (a vestibule, staircase, corridor, room), and from there, again, to other spaces. The diagrams show clearly the presence and potential of different patterns of movements and, therein, also, the internal organization of the content of the house.

Using the diagrams developed by Cuisenier, let me contrast the peasant house of the lower Loire valley (around the town of Saumur) with the larger farmhouse of the Jura mountains. Around Saumur, calcareous building material is readily available. In the past, builders extracted this material on the spot and trimmed it as needed. They would build several houses around a common courtyard equipped with a well and an oven for baking bread. Typically, there was a dwelling house with a door and two rooms—the kitchen and the bedroom. Around the courtyard a building for one or two horses, another for the cows, one for the cider press and casks, a shed for tools, and a couple of barns were commonly found. In the lower courtyard, there were latrines, a pigsty and a smaller building for keeping rabbits and poultry. With the exception of the bedroom with access through the kitchen, one had to pass through the courtyard to move from one building to another. The climate is notoriously mild, so that using the courtyard as an entrance hall does not present much of a problem. In this case, the dendritic diagram assumes the shape of a common exterior trunk, with separate branches, each of which gives access to a single different specialized bounded space.

In the Jura mountains, the farmhouse is a single, large, self-contained building, with everything inside: the livestock in the basement during the winter and, above, the barn, the cheese manufacturing unit, the workshop and the dwelling quarters of the household. To this day, the Jura mountains are still a livestock-rearing area known for its milk and cheese production. During the winter, the livestock, kept in the basement, served as a kind of central heating system, adding warmth to the farmhouse and feeding on hay stored in the barn. The dendritic diagram of the building shows two or three entrances into it. From these the branches bifurcate several times to give access to different spaces in succession. However, in addition, there are transversal passageways to ensure that any space within the farmhouse can be reached from any other.

In the Loire valley, the horses, cows, poultry and people were kept separate, each with their specific smells, sounds, food, space, and so on. In the large Jura farmhouse, they were all collected together within the same envelope/container. As a result, in terms of content and surfaces, the Loire peasant house and the Jura farmhouse differ significantly. All the dimensions of space occupation and perception underlined by Hall, such as distance, smell, sight, and so on, were organized differently in the two cases. Nor were exterior surfaces treated the same way. In the Loire valley, depending on the wealth of the peasant family, the dwelling house was far more stylish than the utilitarian buildings. This is evident from the high-quality slates, cornice, door and window frames of the dwelling house as compared with the ordinary, makeshift, somewhat poorer finish of the more utilitarian buildings. In the Jura farmhouse, there is a single surface/envelope for the whole content, and it may be rather elaborate. This is even more the case with the alpine 'chalet' with its decorated wooden balconies and window ornaments.

Towns and houses are Neolithic innovations. This suggests that the passage from nomadic to sedentary life was accompanied by a drastic change in the closure of space articulated with equivalent changes in techniques of the body. The trend, from the political and architectural points of view, seems to have been towards more closure, departing from the openness of the nomadic camp with its marked flexibility in spatial organization and social affiliation, as suggested in Lee and DeVore's classic *Man the Hunter* (1968). It is also worth emphasizing that the advent of food production was accompanied by a major change in the domestic technology of containment, namely pottery.

Pottery provides the archetype for the actions of containing, storing, pouring, mixing, cooking, melting, heating, and so on. Its articulation with sensori-affectivo-motor conducts must also be highlighted because of pottery's close association with all daily household activities. Pottery may be provided with handles for easy grasping and a lid for better closure and treatment of the content. It is the necessary extension of the body in eating, drinking, washing and (in many societies) urinating or defecating. Surface decorations usually emphasize the opening or neck of the pot and the surface of its walls. From the vast literature devoted to pottery, let me paraphrase simply Arnold (1985) and the book by Cumberpatch and Blinkhorn (1997) and suggest that such containers may be not 'so much a pot, more a way of life'.

The close relationship between pottery and basketry has often been emphasized. In turn, the latter is closely related to the techniques of weaving, carpet making and, more generally, the manufacture and use of textiles. In clothing, the textiles are in close contact with the body, and provide it with a second skin. Schneider's review of the literature (1987; chapter 13 in this volume) on the anthropology of cloth illustrates the emotional and aesthetic dimensions of surfaces that achieve their highest realization with cloth. Cloth and textiles are gendered, and, when set in motion, they alter the proprioception and the sensori-affectivo-motor conducts in unexpected ways: either to stiffen or contain the body, or to enlarge and efface its contours or, again, by providing bounded surfaces for rest, social encounter (the 'divan'), prayer, meals or work. For example, Alec Balasescu (personal communication) noticed that, in the Middle East, the large gowns worn by some women all day long, even at home, inhibit the perception of the outlines of the female body. Nowadays, the value put on slimness conflicts with the premium formerly put on female corpulence. In such a conflicting context, the large gown makes it difficult for some women to monitor the limits of their body, even when they want to do so, and Balasescu tends to attribute this difficulty to the envelope made by the gown. Conversely, the women who remove their gown at home and dress in clothes that fit the body more closely maintain better perception and control of their body weight.

SYMBOLIZING PASSAGES AND TRANSFORMATIONS

This necessarily succinct overview still requires a few concluding remarks. First, from a praxeological and psychic point of view, the sensori-affectivo-motor conducts shored up by the human skin and containers achieve what the psychoanalytical tradition, summarized by Tisseron (1999), calls 'symbolization' – following the term's etymological meaning: in ancient Greek, *sun – bôlon*, meaning to 'put together'. Making use of containers amounts to working with and on containment, that is, putting together the things, substances and people that are introduced into a common container. It also amounts to separating things that belong together from those that do not, whatever they may be – livestock, human beings, memories, materials, liquids, and so on. The examples of the Loire peasant house and the Jura farmhouse are cases in point: through movement, living in those houses amounts to symbolizing in different ways the relationships among human beings, domestic animals, foodstuffs, etc.

Consequently, the material culture of containment helps every subject to symbolize all the relevant actions of daily life. Yet such a repertoire of actions can characterize a given society only in so far as it amounts to a technology of power, that is, to a governmentality in the Foucaldian sense of the term. Thus, the kingdoms of western Cameroon, and Japan according to Hendry (1993), provide cases where the technology of power rests on the material forms of containing or wrapping.

But then, containment, as a means of symbolizing power, the subject and daily life, is based on two processes brought out by Tisseron (1999, 2000), and, following Anzieu (1985), namely passing through and transformation. Containment in itself is of little value unless things, substances or people can be put together inside the container by passing through the opening cut into the surface of the container. This is why the openings of the body, of pots, houses and cities are so important and receive so much attention. This is also why the surface of the containers is usually treated with much care. The surface is the essential correlate of the opening. It must be as solid and tight as the opening is broad enough to allow the passage, and narrow enough to keep the content inside. The surface is smoothed and decorated. It may be coated or receive a gloss or some other treatment to protect it or adorn it as well as to enhance the emotional dimension of its sensori-motor manipulation. It has to have style, both to facilitate its identification and for aesthetic satisfaction.

However, the process of passing through also entails the transformation of what passes through the opening; things will be mixed, cooked, digested, assimilated, and so on, or they will be expelled, transformed into rubbish, or combined with other materials in other containers. Thus, the process of symbolization is essentially geared to passing through and being transformed.

I have neglected many other domains that would deserve equal attention in their relationship to the sensori-affectivo-motor conducts as applied to containers. The most important one is the body itself as a container. I alluded to it only when discussing the 'skin-self' analysed by Anzieu. But this is not intended as an ethnographic survey of practices involving the skin and its openings. I have also ignored the domain of masks and masquerades, of musical instruments and the acoustic envelope provided by sounds and music, of health practices aimed at introducing substances within the body or extracting them from it, or differently, effecting a cure by treating the skin as an envelope. The same praxeological aproach could also be applied to animals in so far as they are domesticated and share with humans in the household, or in so far as they provide hides, pelts and fur as surfaces suited to all kinds of purposes. I have also neglected many kinds of containers like pieces of furniture, cabinets, suitcases, boxes, etc. Nevertheless, I expect the key constituted by the sensori-affectivo-motor conducts applied here to containers can be used to open those doors that have remained closed, allowing access to their contents. Thus, investigating surfaces, containers, openings, inside and outside as essential material correlates of sensori-affectivo-motor conducts may indicate promising future directions for research. These directions take us away from the semiotics and the 'meaning' of containers; away from the study of their utility as material contraptions; and more towards the study of different kinds of technologies of the self, different kinds of subjectivities, and different kinds of power, both at individual and at social levels. It also takes anthropology and ethnography closer to the cognitive and the neuro-sciences.

However, such a perspective does not take us away from style, aesthetics and sensory qualities of material culture. Quite the contrary. The technologies of the self and the technologies of power have style, materiality and aesthetics, especially when they concern the human body as a container in motion, emotion and the exercise of power.

NOTES

1 Proprioception refers to the perception we have of our own body by means of the billions of captors disseminated throughout all the bodily tissues. The vestibular sense, located in the inner ear, is the sense by which we perceive the position of our body in space and its equilibrium while on the move. Both senses are crucial in relating to the material world.

2 See Feeley-Harnick (1985) for a review of the literature.

3 The interpretation of the process of closure has given rise to much debate. Lightfoot and Martinez (1995) discuss various models drawn from the archaeological record. The most basic debate revolves around the question as to whether increased mobility of persons and things gave rise to the institutions that we today associate with the state, or else, does state formation rest on other processes and, once accomplished, will it induce inter-state exchanges? A tradition that runs from Marx to Bayart (2004) through Horton (1971), Friedman and Rowlands (1977) and Appadurai (1997) argues convincingly that, as genealogically unrelated groups exchange, move about and congregate, they need to devise new political means to regulate their interactions. Closure provides a technology for creating locality, an inside, an outside, a space, and a way of mooring people and things to the body politic. In the twenty-first century the globalization of trade and financial fluxes goes together with a reinforcement of state control on migration and borders, and an increasingly sophisticated technology of closure directed at the sensorimotricity – and the emotion – of the migrant.

REFERENCES

Alvarez, R.R. (1995) 'The Mexican–US border: the making of an anthropology of borderland', *Annual Review of Anthropology*, 24: 447–70.

Anzieu, D. (1985) *Le Moi-peau*. Paris: Dunod.

Appadurai, A. (1997) *Modernity at Large: Cultural Dimensions of Globalization*. Minneapolis, MN: University of Minnesota Press.

Arnold, D.E. (1985) *Ceramic Theory and Cultural Process*. Cambridge: Cambridge University Press.

Austin, J.L. (1962) *How to Do Things with Words*. Oxford: Oxford University Press.

Bayart, J.-F. (2004) *Le Gouvernement du monde : une critique politique de la globalisation*. Paris: Fayard.

Bayart, J.-F. and Warnier, J-P., eds (2004), *Matière à politique : le pouvoir, les corps et les choses*. Paris: CERI/Karthala.

Berthelot, J.-M. (1995) 'The body as a discursive operator, or, The Aporias of a sociology of the body', *Body and Society*, 1 (1): 13–23.

Berthoz, A. (1997) *Le Sens du mouvement*. Paris: Odile Jacob.

Csordas, T., ed. (1994) *Embodiment and Experience: the Existential Ground of Culture and Self*. Cambridge: Cambridge University Press.

Cuisenier, J. (1991) *La Maison rustique : logique sociale et composition architecturale*. Paris: Presses Universitaires de France.

Cumberpatch, C.C. and Blinkhorn, P.W., eds (1997) *Not so Much a Pot, More a Way of Life*. Oxford: Oxbow Books.

Damasio, A. (2000) *L'Erreur de Descartes*. Paris: Odile Jacob.

Featherstone, M., Hepworth, M. and Turner, B., eds (1991) *The Body: Social Process and Cultural Theory*. London: Sage.

Feeley-Harnick, G. (1985) 'Issues in divine kingship', *Annual Review of Anthropology*, 14: 273–313.

Foucault, M. (1975) *Surveiller et punir*. Paris: Gallimard.

Foucault, M. (2001) *L'Herméneutique du sujet : cours au Collège de France 1981–1982*. Paris: Gallimard.

Friedman, J. and Rowlands, M.J. (1977) 'Notes towards an epigenetic model of the evolution of civilisation', in J. Friedman and M.J. Rowlands (eds), *The Evolution of Social Systems*. London: Duckworth, pp. 201–78.

Hall, E.T. (1966) *The Hidden Dimension*. New York: Doubleday.

Head, H. and Holmes, G. (1911) 'Sensory disturbances from cerebral lesions', *Brain*, 1911–12, pp. 34–102.

Hendry, J. (1993) *Wrapping Culture: Politeness, Presentation, and Power in Japan and other Societies*. Oxford: Clarendon Press.

Horton, R. (1971) 'Stateless societies in the history of West Africa', in J.R. Ade Ajayi and M. Crowder (eds), *History of West Africa* I. New York: Columbia University Press, pp. 78–119.

Julien, M.-P. and Warnier, J-P., eds (1999) *Approches de la culture matérielle : corps à corps avec l'objet*. Paris: Harmattan.

Kantorowicz, E.H. (1957) *The King's Two Bodies: a Study in Medieval Political Theology*. Princeton, NJ: Princeton University Press.

Kopytoff, I. (1987) *The African Frontier: the Reproduction of Traditional African Societies*. Bloomington and Indianapolis, IN: Indiana University Press.

Lee, R.B. and DeVore, L., eds (1968) *Man the Hunter*. Chicago: Aldine.

Lightfoot, K.G. and Martinez, A. (1995) 'Frontiers and boundaries in archaeological perspective', *Annual Review of Anthropology*, 24: 471–92.

MacKenzie, M. (1991) *Androgynous Objects: String Bags and Gender in Central New Guinea*. Chur: Harwood Academic.

Mauss, M. (1936) 'Les techniques du corps', *Journal de Psychologie*, 32 (3–4); reproduced in *Sociologie et anthropologie*. Paris: Presses Universitaires de France, pp. 331–62.

Schilder, P. (1923) *Das Körperschema. Ein Beitrag zur Lehre vom Bewusstsein des eigenen Körpers*. Berlin: Springer.

Schilder, P. (1935) *The Image and Appearance of the Human Body: Studies in the Constructive Energy of the Psyche*. London: Kegan Paul.

Schneider, J. (1987) 'The anthropology of cloth', *Annual Review of Anthropology*, 16: 409–48.

Tisseron, S. (1999) *Comment l'esprit vient aux objets*. Paris: Aubier.

Tisseron, S. (2000) *Petites mythologies d'aujourd'hui*. Paris: Aubier.

Turner, F.J. (1893/1961) 'The significance of the frontier in American history', in R.A. Billington (ed.), *Frontier and Section: Selected Essays*. Englewood Cliffs, NJ: Prentice Hall, pp. 28–36.

Warnier, J.-P. (1975) 'Pre-colonial Mankon: the Development of a Cameroon Chiefdom in its Regional Setting'. Ph.D. dissertation, University of Pennsylvania; Ann Arbor, MI: University Microfilms, No. 76–3227.

Warnier, J.-P. (1985) *Echanges, développement et hiérarchies dans le Bamenda précolonial, Cameroun*. Stuttgart and Wiesbaden: Steiner.

Warnier, J.-P. (1999) *Construire la culture materielle : l'homme qui pensait avec ses doigts*. Paris: Presses Universitaires de France.

Warnier, J.-P. (2001) 'A praxeological approach to subjectivation in a material world', *Journal of Material Culture*, 6 (1): 5–24.

PART III

SUBJECTS AND OBJECTS

Within the social or human sciences, material objects have rarely been a focus of attention simply in and of themselves. Rather, they have been of special interest primarily for the insights they may provide into human social and cultural worlds. Emerging as these sciences did out of Western philosophical and religious traditions, they commonly formulated the relations of humans and material things with reference to the broader conceptual opposition between subject and object. To be sure, 'object' is a category which, in its fullest scope, is considerably more abstract and far-reaching than the word understood in its material sense. It can, for example, denote the patient of an action, the grammatical complement of a transitive verb, the cognized concept, or the phenomenological focus of attention. Approaches to material objects have, however, drawn heavily on these more abstract treatments of objects, and the correlative concepts of objectivity and objectification. The earlier approaches in social theory tended to presuppose some *a priori* opposition between subject and object, privileging the former as the locus of agency, meaning and ethical concerns. Later work has often sought to overcome the subject-object opposition, with varying degrees of success. Even analyses that refuse to treat subject and object as *opposed* are likely to find that some *distinction* between the terms stubbornly persists.

Four basic understandings of the relations between subject and object predominate in the classic traditions of social theory. These focus respectively on the (1) production, (2) representation, (3) development and (4) extension of subjects (in most cases identified with humans) through objects (primarily material things). The chapters in this part reflect these themes, indicate some of their limits and suggest new directions in which we might develop and go beyond them. This introduction begins with a brief critical review of the four classic approaches, showing some of the ways in which the chapters that follow it draw on and shed new insights into them. It then discusses the limits of meaning- and agency-centred approaches to objects. In conclusion, the introduction sketches out the case for a modified philosophical realism as a starting point for the social analysis of material things. I suggest that a fully social and historical understanding of objects demands a more robust appreciation of the relative autonomy of objects from human projects. Further, an understanding of this relative autonomy should point the way to a more vigorous, but dialectical and non-deterministic, approach to the place of causality in social phenomena.

The focus on *production* is exemplified by Karl Marx. According to Marx, subjects that had once, in pre-capitalist relations of production, realized themselves through the transformation of nature into artefacts now, under capitalism, confront objects as external to them. There are two aspects of this approach of particular relevance to thinking about material culture. First, *non*-artefactual objects are largely of analytical interest only as raw material for possible artefacts, as unmediated elements of nature such as water, wind, minerals, mountains, plants, undomesticated animals. Second, there is an implicit semiotic and, one might even suggest, a cognitive dimension to the subject's self-realization, since that self-realization depends on the subject's being able to read the traces of human labour in the material thing. Under capitalist relations of production, tools, for instance, may still serve as *practical* means to human ends, much as they had before, and products may still bear the marks of the *labour* that produced them, but producers no longer *recognize* themselves in either tool or product. The very concept of objectification, in dialectical analysis in the Hegelian-Marxian tradition, is one in which the outcomes of active processes congeal as so many static entities, appearing as mere givens within the experienced world. (To be sure, this is not purely a conceptual problem. Much depends, for instance, on new kinds of property relations, such that workers under capitalism are no longer full masters of the means of production, and the commodity form, such that products seem to be endowed with agency independent of producers. But recognition nonetheless plays a crucial role in accounting for the ultimate political consequences.)

This basic production-oriented narrative underwrites much subsequent analysis. In the chapters before us, for instance, Bender (Chapter 19) shows that the affective and cognitive power of landscapes derives, in part, from human activities that have shaped them. The traces of human activities are reflected back to their subjects as apparently natural environments. The modernist anxiety about homelessness described by Buchli (Chapter 16) seems to derive from notions of home that presuppose a prior, unalienated relation to the shaped environment. But, within this tradition in social theory, the purported relations of subject to object under unalienated conditions have tended more to be assumed as some prior condition, or aspired to as some utopian future, than themselves subject to close analysis.

The second classic approach focuses on the ways in which objects also serve as *representations* of and for subjects. Emile Durkheim and Marcel Mauss, for example, argued that so-called primitive classification is embodied in the physical layout of houses and settlements in ways that diagrammatically reproduce the cosmological and social order of a given society. As in the productivist tradition, the object is of interest mainly as an artefact of human labours, something that has implications for the acting and self-knowing subject. In a somewhat similar spirit, Max Weber explicitly defined the domain of interpretive sociology in such a way that it excluded those aspects of the objective world that did not enter directly into intentional actions, such as floods and demographic cycles. The underlying assumption is that there is a world of natural givens that remains distinct from that of humans, in so far as the latter are understood as acting and self-knowing subjects (and not, in this tradition, merely organic beings). Natural givens enter the picture only once they are transformed by intentional actions.

But in this approach, by contrast to those that focus on production, objects are of interest mainly in their capacity to express intentional projects, such that they then have cognitive effects on social subjects. The physical world, as a second nature for humans, a nature created by and for humans, is both an effect of human understandings of the social and, as an object of experience, reflects those understandings back to the human subject. Objects materialize and express otherwise immaterial or abstract entities, organizing subjects' perceptual experiences and clarifying their cognitions. The very materiality of objects, their availability to the senses, is of interest primarily as the condition for the knowability of otherwise abstract or otherwise invisible structures such as divinities, cosmological principles or relations among clans. (Underlying this approach tends to be a somewhat distinct assumption that the raw materials of experience do not themselves fully determine how they will be grasped even as mere elements of subjective experience. Rather, some further organizing force or principle aside from sensory percepts themselves is required for there even to be coherent objects of experience. The Durkheimians find that principle in a given society's collective representations. A somewhat similar view of the cultural contribution to what is otherwise underdetermined raw experience runs through much of the American cultural anthropology influenced by Franz Boas.)

An important twist on the Durkheimian view appears in Claude Lévi-Strauss's distinction between the *bricoleur* and the engineer in *The Savage Mind*. In his analysis, the material qualities of objects are indeed crucial mediators of human understanding: sweet, for instance, serves to form a distinct contrast to sour, smooth to rough. But whereas the engineer's tools in themselves express the intentional projects for which they were made, the bricoleur works with objects that have no such entailments. They are merely what happens to be at hand. One consequence, to whose significance I will turn shortly, is that the causal processes by which they come to be at hand have, for the analyst, no bearing on their ultimate disposition and thus, for those who follow this line of thinking, can be excluded from consideration.

The representational perspective underlies several of the chapters in this part. It is especially germane to the analysis of landscape and, as we can see in Blier's and Buchli's chapters, architecture. In addition, in so far as clothing and furnishings give material form to social categories and hierarchies, this analysis runs through the chapters by Schneider (Chapter 13) and St George (Chapter 14). The socialist modernism and other reformist movements discussed by Buchli seem to draw quite consciously on an inverted version of the representational perspective. If traditional settlements and dwellings expressed existing social structures, utopian architecture would bring into existence as yet unrealized social structures by making them available to the imagination, diagrammatically, it would seem. And of course representation is definitive of the category of Australian Aboriginal 'art' discussed by Myers. In contrast to objects defined in directly functional terms, those defined as 'art' have often been analysed in quite distinct ways. Their sheer materiality is often overlooked in favour of their representational character, including their capacity to index the social identity of the producer. This is one reason why it is a scandal when a non-Aborigine produces Aboriginal art; in material terms, such an object may be identical to one produced by an Aborigine, but its capacity to represent its maker has been transformed. Furthermore, once Aboriginal objects are reclassified as art, certain material qualities may emerge as the basis of future reclassifications. Paint may be viewed in formal terms, as abstract painting, rather than as by-products of certain no-longer-visible ritual activities. A similar reframing of materiality can occur in architecture. As Buchli observes, to treat architecture as a schema or diagram is to dematerialize it. The representational approach invites the analyst to see *through* the material of the object in the effort to grasp the more abstract structure it is supposed to express. The subject tends to be identified with the resulting abstractions, the object, as something material, remains apart.

A third tradition concerns the internal *development of subjectivities* in relation to objects. In various psychological and psychoanalytic traditions, subjects develop in part through encountering and appropriating objects within an environment of already existing artefacts. Things may serve as objects of fascination or of obsessive recuperations of loss, as in the classic model of the fetish. For example, Freud, like Marx, adapted the terminology 'fetishism' from early comparative religion to name a kind of misunderstanding. The agency of humans is imputed to things, and thereby things become objects of a self-displacing subject. A somewhat different psychoanalytic tradition focuses on the role objects play in the child's self-realization as an agent within a world of things that are separate from the self, can be manipulated, and which resist its actions. Both traditions are interested in objects in so far as they are encountered in experience as things to be felt, smelled, touched and worked upon. Material properties, such as weight, visibility, persistence and perishability, are crucial to the

formative character of these encounters. In many cases, the developmentalist approaches come closest to overcoming the *a priori* opposition of subject and object, postulating, for instance, a dialectic through which subjects and objects are mutually produced by acts of separation and reincorporation (see especially Daniel Miller's psychologically informed rereadings of Hegelian dialectic in *Material Culture and Mass Consumption* and *The Dialectics of Shopping*).

We could, perhaps, group with these approaches those that concern things (which, notice, are not necessarily confined to artefacts) as anchors for emotional attachment and memory. The role in the formation and transmission of memory of the very material qualities of things, such as temporal durability and both social and geographical portability, is hinted at in Connerton's discussion of memory. One especially lively field of research in which earlier psychological thought has taken new forms is the study of consumerism and commodities. Why are commodities objects of desire? In what ways are subjects realized through acts of possession and consumption, in what ways are they thwarted, their self-understanding displaced (as in the Marxist tradition)? St George's discussion of furnishings shows some of the ways in which the proliferation of kinds and qualities of goods fostered new forms of sociality and even of subjective interiority. Schneider's account of clothing points to the important role of physical qualities, such as softness, durability or sheen, in the desirability of things. Foster shows some of the global consequences of the circulating of commodities and the stimulation of new forms of desire. But commodities may be desirable for reasons beyond their qualities. Circulation of Aboriginal objects, for instance, expanded dramatically once they were recategorized and entered cosmopolitan art worlds. In part this is due to obvious market effects. But we might also surmise that the category of 'art' gave new relevance to certain of the existing material qualities of these objects, which thereby became newly available for perception and desirability.

In these three approaches, the two senses of 'object', as material thing and as that towards which an action or consciousness is directed, tend to converge. Often the latter sense of the word predominates at the expense of mere physical properties. A fourth approach gives special importance to the very materiality of objects. It concerns the ways in which material objects realize subjects by pragmatically *extending* them. In some sense, this aspect of subject–object relations runs through all the approaches just mentioned. But recent efforts to rethink or break down the distinction between subjects and objects place special emphasis on the object-like qualities of humans, and the ways in which objects seem to contain some of the attributes that define human agency. In *Art and Agency: an Anthropological Theory*, for instance, Alfred Gell proposed that the soldier's weapon is not merely an object that is appropriated by an acting subject. Rather, it is a necessary component of the soldier's agency; that is, the 'soldier' is a totality composed of the person plus the weapon. In a similar vein, Bruno Latour's *We have Never been Modern* argues that the very distinction between humans and things is the result of a historically specific effort at purification which denies 'hybrids'. The implication is that hybrids of humans and things (Latour's contemporary examples include psychotropic drugs, hybrid corn and frozen embryos) that mix nature and culture, things and humans are in some sense prior to the opposition of human subjects and thing-like objects. One virtue of such arguments is that they help shift the weight of analysis away from the role objects play in the self-knowledge of subject towards an examination of their practical role in mediating actions. Although the mediation of action had always been part of the other analyses, in this case the object is seen not just to facilitate the acts or point back to the actor, but to expand, or even bring into existence, the subject. By stressing new possibilities, Latour points out the ways in which subjects take on object-like qualities in the process of extending themselves into the world of other objects (an approach that, in some of its dimensions, was anticipated by earlier approaches, from Mauss to Bourdieu and Foucault, to the human body and its socially structured habits and disciplines). The subject is not simply constituted through its *opposition* to and encompassment of the object; rather, it is amplified by merging *with* the object.

The limits of meaning-centred approaches to objects are explored in several of the chapters that follow. Foster's discussion of globalization (Chapter 18) asks how space is mediated by the motion of things through it. This mediation involves production, representation, development and extension, but cannot be reduced to any of them. Globalization studies show how moving objects link local social and material effects to distant causes. Subjects are also set into motion. As Bender points out, studies that stress the meaning of familiar places tend to play down power relations. Victims of displacement, for instance, may struggle with spaces that remain recalcitrant to any meanings they

may attempt to construct. In space they may confront an object world opposed to subjects and their projects.

Studies of artefacts commonly treat them as objects that are encompassed by subjects, but globalization and landscape suggest forms of materiality that encompass their subjects. In a sense the house forms a transition between these and the small things over which humans seem to have greater mastery. In Blier's Chapter 15 we can see a struggle between these two aspects of subject–object relations, as houses seem at once to express relatively unconstrained human imaginings yet are determined as well by unyielding environmental requirements.

Even clothing and furnishings can be recalcitrant. The studies St George reviews (Chapter 14) begin by emphasizing how furnishings express human purposes, especially social differentiations and display. But a second theme emerges, how the phenomenal characteristics of furnishings, once they have become given components of peoples' objective contexts, shape persons, through comfort, demarcations of space, channelling movement and posture, and by making possible new forms of possession and interiority. Schneider shows how furnishing the body itself cannot escape the causal chains linking the politics of display and of production. For instance, the very meaning of certain kinds of goods may be inseparable from the prices they carry under certain labour regimes, or the difficulty of obtaining certain materials.

Objects may thus convey into the world of socially realized meanings the *indexical* traces of causal processes that remain otherwise unexpressed. (The semiotic concept of indexicality refers to actual links between signs and their contexts or causes, independent of any 'meanings' produced by such things as resemblance or social conventions.) Without in any way *determining* their cultural significance, objects may nonetheless be important vehicles of transformative pressure on, or provide openings to new possibilities for, systems of meaning and of pragmatic action. To see this requires attention to the sheer materiality of things in two respects. First, in what I call *bundling*, material things always combine an indefinite number of physical properties and qualities, whose particular juxtapositions may be mere happenstance. In any given practical or interpretative context, only some of these properties are relevant and come into play. But other properties persist, available for promotion as circumstances change. Consider, for instance, the highly venerated ancestor tablets that were once preserved in households across rural China. That they were often made of wood was not in itself significant until the Cultural Revolution fostered a contemptuous recategorization, and they were disposed of as cooking fuel. This story involves the second aspect of materiality, the inherent vulnerability of even the most meaningful things to brute causality. This tiny example illustrates a pervasive feature of things, artefactual or otherwise, that these two aspects of materiality play a crucial – but not deterministic – role in mediating human histories.

All four of the classic approaches discussed above take objects to be of interest in so far as they offer insight into (human) subjects. They therefore tend to give privileged attention to the artefacts of human production, among material things. Moreover, artefacts may be privileged for epistemological reasons as well. Following Giambattista Vico, it has been common to argue that knowledge in the human sciences derives from the maker's special insight into the thing made. Conversely, in so far as objects are uninterpretable or have not yet been rendered meaningful, they would seem to lie beyond our scope – irrelevant, perhaps even unknowable.

The opacity or ineffability of things prior to interpretation may lead, depending on one's ontological inclinations, to the sceptical assumption that objects cannot in any meaningful way be said to exist independent of experience and interpretation, or, at least, that this existence must be bracketed, in the sense proposed by some phenomenologists. Opposing this position are various forms of philosophical *realism*, the postulate that a world exists independent of – and perhaps beyond the ultimate reach of – any knowledge we may have of it. Both sceptic and realist may well agree that experience cannot, in principle, give humans direct, unmediated contact with the world of objects. But the realist may argue that we are nonetheless justified in positing the existence of objects, perhaps much as Kant required the noumenal in his analysis of phenomena. According to the creator of semiotics, Charles Sanders Peirce, for instance, we make suppositions about objects by means of abductions from experience. Abduction is the logical process of postulating that which must, or is most likely to be, the case such that what we actually *do* perceive has the character that it does. Abductions have neither the evidential security of induction, nor the logical necessity of deduction, but nonetheless form an important bridge between subjective experience and its objective sources.

The relevance of this foray into ontology for the social scientist is this: only by positing the existence of objects independent of human experiences, interpretations and actions can we allow, analytically, the possibility of unforeseen consequences. Otherwise, one risks reducing the world of things to their actually or previously existing meanings for humans, foreclosing as yet unrealized future possibilities or reducing those possibilities to human invention alone. Certainly I have no wish to deny the importance of the anti-positivist insights that led social thought to stress the processual and meaningful character of objects. But these insights have their limits too. To place too much weight on interpretation risks reducing our understanding to the retrospective glance. The idea of a realism grounded in abduction should help the analyst of material culture recognize that, by virtue of bundling, things always contain properties in excess of those which have been interpreted and made use of under any given circumstance. Material things thus retain an unpredictable range of latent possibilities. They do not *only* express past acts, intentions and interpretations. They also invite unexpected responses. Subjects do not just realize themselves through objects, as if the fully-fledged subject were already latent, a chrysalis simply awaiting the moment at which it will unfold. To the extent that objects *are* autonomous of human projects, they may allow subjects to make real discoveries about themselves. They form the grounds for subsequent modes of action whose limits, if any, are in principle unknowable. They also, of course, can resist human projects and interpretations, remaining opaque and even oppressive, a point made in the chapters by Bender, Buchli and Blier. The various ways in which material things can be oppressive, although perhaps somewhat underdeveloped in the classic social theories, are elaborated in a variety of contexts, such as the Frankfurt School critique of technological modernity, Jean Paul Sartre's earlier, more phenomenological, work, and, of course, the long tradition of religious reformers' attacks on materialism.

It is in this light that we can return to the question of subjects and objects. The classic social theories usefully draw our attention to the ways in which material things, as objects of human actions and experiences, mediate the realization of human subjects. Material things index the human productive activity that went into them, they materialize social and cosmological structures that would otherwise elude direct experience, they foster the development of the person's sense of separateness from a world that resists its desires and the self-motivated agency that acts on that resisting world, they serve as stable anchors and instigations for memory, feelings and concepts. In all these cases, the sheer materiality of objects, their formal properties and phenomenological qualities, tend to be of somewhat secondary importance, as media for significations, for instance, or as evidence of something recalcitrant outside the person. But if we stress as well the reality of the object and its contribution to as yet unrealized further possibilities, we can expand our analysis beyond human products. Moreover, our analysis becomes not only more historically attuned, *of necessity*, but also may lead us to be more attentive to the full range of qualities that are, as it were, *bundled* into a single thing. At this point, the concept of *causality* seems finally and, despite the philosophical conundrums it poses, unavoidably to return to the social analysis even of meanings.

Webb Keane

13

CLOTH AND CLOTHING

Jane Schneider

Cloth and clothing constitute the widest imaginable category of material culture, covering a spatial domain that extends from the miles of textiles annually produced by hand or factory to the most intimate apparel of the human body, and a temporal domain whose earliest moments, lost to archaeology because of poor preservation, pre-date the neolithic. Encompassed within the category are the familiar dualities of Western social thought: production versus consumption; utility versus beauty; the gift versus the commodity; symbolic communication versus the materiality of colors, designs, shapes, and textures. Many accounts of the historical processes leading up to, and following from, the capitalist industrialization and marketing of cloth and clothing center around the duality most integral to the triumphalist narrative of European civilization: the West versus 'the rest'. This chapter attempts to transcend these oppositions.

As a political-economic and cultural system, capitalism historically overlaid and displaced, but did not eliminate, arrangements that privileged elite consumption, in which the opportunities for self-enhancement were intensely hierarchically distributed. Rather than label these earlier arrangements 'pre-' or 'non-capitalist' – appellations that imply, in the first instance, their eventual disappearance and in the second, an absence or lack – we will (experimentally) refer to them as 'courtly', highlighting their elitism. Capitalist and courtly societies differ with regard to how cloth and clothing are produced and consumed, but the contrasts elude simple oppositions.

'Productivist' explanations for the emergence of capitalism center around technological innovation and the mobilization of wage labor in the

textile sector. Emphasis is also placed on the capture of raw materials through colonial and imperial projects. Yet these foundations for capitalist development are more compelling when juxtaposed to the special genius of capitalism, which is its ongoing democratization of the possibility for self-enhancement through consumption. Because this democratization presupposes low-cost goods, the two aspects – heavy-handed interventions in production and the cultivation of desire – are integrally related.

'Self-enhancement' loosely refers to energizing the self and close others, perhaps organized in small groups, through life-affirming practices and rituals. Examples involving cloth and clothes include transforming the body and its surroundings in ways considered aesthetically or sexually attractive; dressing well to accrue prestige, the respect of others, a sense of worthiness or empowerment; generously distributing textiles to consolidate friendships and followings; and signalling through clothes an identification with particular values or constituencies. Cloth and clothing consumption is always restless and multidimensional. The point is that, in modern capitalist society, its enhancing qualities are, or can be, within the purview of virtually everyone.

Whereas, in the consumption sphere, capitalism corrodes courtly hierarchies, in the sphere of production, an opposite kind of rupture has occurred. Different from the proletarianizing and colonizing strategies alluded to above, the courtly production of cloth and clothing hinges on the ability of elites to acquire precious raw materials and finished goods through deputized trade or tributary exactions, and to patronize or attach to their courts beehives of artisanal activity – skilled, knowledgeable, artistically inclined, selflessly dedicated as the case may be. Under such arrangements, manufacturers enjoy a meaningful sphere of autonomy; they control product design and decisions and, to a considerable degree, the organization and rhythm of work. As a result, courtly systems of production are less dehumanizing and exploitative than the system of capitalist manufacturing. These distinctions between courtly and capitalist dynamics help frame the following discussion.

THE SPIRITUALITY OF CLOTH AND CLOTHING

Two aspects of cloth and clothing – their spirituality and their aesthetic characteristics – are crucial to self-enhancement. That objects can have a spiritual dimension was long ago established by Marcel Mauss, who noted their capacity to stave off sentiments of envy or resentment otherwise leading to evil eye, and even to open warfare. Given as gifts, objects compel reciprocity because the spirit of the giver is embodied in them, adding moral weight (Mauss 1923–24/1954: 10). Objects often also encode the names, biographies, memories, and histories of past 'owners', deepening their significance. In the 1980s, Annette B. Weiner applied these ideas to cloth (Weiner 1985, 1989). One of her case studies was Western Samoa, where women soaked, dried, and plaited the narrow fibers of the pandanus to make fine mats. Accumulating significance through association with ancestors and mythical events over periods as long as 200 years, these linen-like constructions reinforced claims to the past and were desired, and kept, as treasure.

The spiritual properties of cloth and clothing, whether they derive from soaking up historical and mythical associations, or from artisans' incantations as described below, render these materials ideal media for connecting humans with the world of spirits and divinities, and with one another. In episodes of spirit possession, a returning or restless essence is frequently believed to seek not only a human body in which to dwell, but human apparel, and to reveal its identity through demands for specific items of cloth and clothing (e.g. Verger 1954; Feeley-Harnik 1989; Masquelier 1996). A transforming medium, cloth also delineates and adorns sacred spaces; bedecks ceremonial dancers; drapes temples, shrines, icons, chiefs, and priests; and enriches umbrellas and palanquins. Mayan brocaded blouses called *huipiles* clothe images of patron saints and the

Virgin Mary, while Andean herders propitiate mountain spirits with a special textile bundle (Morris 1986; Zorn 1985).

Cloth intensifies sociality in rituals of birth, initiation, and curing. As James J. Fox summarized for Indonesia's outer islands, it 'swaddles the newborn, wraps and heals the sick, embraces and unites the bride and groom, encloses the wedding bed, and in the end, enshrouds the dead' (1977: 97). In many societies, spouses provide each other's wedding attire and minimum future wardrobes, thereby figuratively tightening the knot (e.g. Kendall 1985). 'When a man receives raffia,' wrote Mary Douglas of the competitively polygynous Lele, 'he hopes to use it to acquire a wife, or to sweeten relations with his wife and her kin … raffia keeps its high value because it gives command over women' (1967: 120–1). Textiles that a bride prepares herself – spinning, weaving, embroidering, adding appliqué or lace – constitute her personal gift, her trousseau, to her new household and its eventual descendants.

The capacity of cloth to enhance who we are and deepen our social relationships is especially evident in ethnographies of mortuary rituals, in which the living wrap their dead for burial, reburial or cremation in textiles believed to ensure their continuance as social beings. More than any other 'grave good', the shroud perpetuates what Terrence Turner (1980/1993) so aptly labeled the 'social skin' – a covering that, by virtue of its physical proximity to the body, articulates self with other. So compelling is the idea of cloth constituting a continuing tie that often the dead are understood to demand it on pain of sorcery or possession (Darish 1989; Feeley-Harnik 1989).

Cloth is also central to investiture ceremonies conferring entitlements. According to Bernard S. Cohn (1989), the Mughal court of nineteenth-century India stored treasured piles of memory-saturated fabrics, considering them a medium for the transfer of essential substances and emblems of 'honor for posterity'. How appropriate, then, to place such fabrics on the shoulders of a successor. When a new emperor is installed in Japan, textiles crafted by the rustic method of laboriously soaking, rotting, boiling and beating coarse, uncultivated fibers convey a simultaneously material and spiritual blessing derived from the 'ancient core of Japanese culture' (Cort 1989).

In considering the spirituality of cloth and clothing, we have relied on ethnographers, historians, and archaeologists of societies we have defined as courtly, who not only conducted their research a few decades ago, but who also considered themselves at the time to be documenting 'traditional' practices. 'Pre-industrial' or 'non-commercial' clothes and fabrics have a dominant presence in their accounts, as does what most social theory would classify as a 'pre-modern' orientation toward religious phenomena, emphasizing their presence *in* the material world. We would argue, however, that the spiritual and the material are inseparable in the minds of humans everywhere, including those who inhabit industrial capitalist societies. Here too textiles received as gifts are kept and stored. Here too the clothes of deceased loved ones elicit intense affect, a feeling of connection, while ceremonial robes add substance to the wearer. Here, too, the idea lives on, despite two centuries of modern scientific discourse, that cloth and clothes shore up the person in magical ways, promoting his or her success as vital, loved, and admired.

According to Harvey Molotch (2003), objects gain sentiment from accumulated social and physical use, that is, from their worn surfaces, altered shapes, and odors. Because we always exist on the edge of existential chaos, they fix certain meanings for us, constituting a tangible sense of social reality. Mystery, religiosity, spiritual motivation, and sensuality are integral to 'things'; so too are expressivity, art, and fun. As we search for criteria by which to distinguish courtly from capitalist societies, we must join theorists like Molotch who explicitly reject the gift/commodity opposition, in which gifts are 'enchanted' but commodities are not (see also Carrier 1994; Roseberry 1997; Smart 1997; Thomas 1991; Weiner 1992; and Mauss, himself, 1923–24/1954). Other contrasts, discernible in the spheres of both production and consumption, are far more telling.

COURTLY SOCIETIES: ARTISAN PRODUCTION

The idea that cloth and clothing are spiritually imbued materials is reinforced by ethnographic descriptions of artisans performing rituals and observing particular taboos in the course of spinning, weaving, embroidering, brocading, dyeing and finishing their product. Pueblo men spun, wove and embroidered in their male ritual center, the *kiva*. Older Kodi women in Sumba, Indonesia, likely practitioners of midwifery and, more covertly, of witchcraft, specialized in the resist dyeing of warp yarns with earth tones and indigo. Supplying these yarns to younger women for the production of warp-faced ikats

on backstrap looms, they let it be known through song, lament, and ritual offerings that dyeing was analogous to childbirth. Pregnant women should refrain from looking into the dye pots, lest the sight of the dark, churning, foul-smelling liquid dissolve the contents of their wombs (Hoskins 1989).

Beyond contributing spirituality, artisans contribute beauty – another ingredient in the capacity of cloth and clothing to infuse persons with vitality and widen their social worlds. Nor are these aspects separable; design motifs such as 'god's eyes' and genealogical crests, and symbolically coded colors, are at once beautiful and the conduits of spiritual power. Essential elements in textile aesthetics are the interlacing of warp and weft; 'post-loom' decoration (e.g. embroidery, appliqué, reverse appliqué); and the feel and color harmonies of the finished piece. Clothing hinges as well on shape, whether the soft contours of wrapped and folded lengths of fabric or the sculptural architecture that is achieved by cutting, fitting, and sewing. Throughout the history of cloth and clothing, male and female artisans have elaborated on one or more of these variables, inspired by other arts, by the availability of raw materials, by rivalries with other producers, by the support of patrons, and through interaction with one another. No cloth or clothing tradition was ever static, although many traditions became known for their excellent or unusual qualities and are today collected by aficionados and museums – for example, Kuba raffia velvets, West African (men's) strip-woven *kente* cloth, the double ikats of Bali, the warp-faced ikats and batiks of broader Indonesia, Mayan brocades (found in *huipiles*), Oaxacan embroideries, Chilkat (Northwest Coast) dancing capes and leggings, San Blas Cuna appliqués, the ancient Paracas embroideries of the Peruvian coast, to name a few.

Artisans had to seize opportunities and overcome serious obstacles in order to produce such textiles. The difficulties of obtaining reliable and fast colors – yellows, blues, and above all reds – in the centuries before the invention of aniline dyes, compounded by the challenge that, although protein fibers (e.g. silk and wool) bond with dyestuffs easily, cellulose fibers (e.g. linen and cotton) repel them unless manipulated with other substances, guaranteed that historically dyers occupied a particularly auspicious position among cloth makers. The reputation of many renowned textiles, some of them objects of royal monopoly, depended on dyers' access to exotic substances, training, talent, and closely guarded secrets (Schneider 1978, 1987: 427–31).

Although we can only guess at the everyday quality of productive relations for courtly societies of the past, pockets of oppression surely existed. The most telling instances were based on gender. In the characteristic 'men's cloths' of West Africa, men brocaded imported (and colorful) silk or woolen yarn into a cotton ground whose fibers were cultivated, processed and spun by women. Especially in polygynous households, or where Muslim rules of female seclusion prevailed, the woman's role was subservient. In certain circumstances, however, women developed their own cloth styles such as the resist-dyeing of commercial cloth, and did not spin for men. Similarly, urban-centered Javanese batiking was a woman's craft. Nevertheless, in most historical societies, when men's and women's styles coexisted, women more often than men produced their cloth in rural households and villages, men in the towns and cities; and men more than women benefited from the opposite gender's dedication to tasks of minor aesthetic relevance, like processing fibers and spinning (Schneider 1987: 417–19).

Katherine Bowie describes two kinds of village weaving for northern Thai kingdoms of the nineteenth century: poorer women's onerous production of (home-grown) plain white cotton, and wealthier women's time-consuming introduction of colors and stripes. 'The more elaborate the design, the more likely the weaver was weaving for pleasure with a "cool heart"' (Bowie 1993: 148). In the courts of the aristocracy, war captives, slaves and the nobles' daughters wove cloth of (imported) silk, decorated with gold and silver thread. Three hundred slaves wove for the ruling lord of Chiang Mai in 1875. Besides glorifying the lord, pillows and robes made from the most exquisite textiles were exported for revenues or, in grand ceremonies, given away to merit-conferring monks.

Forms of enslavement appear in various accounts of artisanal cloth production. As shifting trade patterns enabled the Bushong Kuba to create their 'velvets' in what is now southern Zaire, royal men exercised their marital privileges to bring women to their court, tasking them with adding plush-pile designs to male-woven lengths of raffia. As with the Inka, the instruction of court-bound women in the textile arts – here the skill was embroidery (with the Inka it was tapestry weaving) – must have been controlling. And yet, even under these circumstances, because the artisans in question possessed admired skills and specialized knowledge, they can be presumed to have had the leverage to connect ideas about design, motif, and color with the movements of their own hands. Nor did most cloth artisans work under conditions of near enslavement. One should not, of course, romanticize their 'mode of production' – work could be extremely tedious, foul-smelling and even dangerous; apprentices were demeaned as much as they were encouraged; materials could fail, or fail to be available. The point is that, compared with factory laborers, artisans benefit in the production sphere from the treasured condition of autonomy – a 'gift' that industrial capitalism takes away.

COURTLY CONSUMPTION

In contrast, in courtly societies, the consumption sphere is all about hierarchy; the most beautiful cloth and clothing, and the most spiritually powerful, as well, circulate upward, toward the chiefs and royals and aristocrats at the top, from whence they may be redistributed as gifts. In a well known analysis of cloth and its functions in the Inka state, John Murra showed that surpluses of peasant cloth, woven with 'magical precautions' and mobilized through the tribute system, were piled so high in the royal warehouses as to stagger the Spanish conquerors (Murra 1962). The state further relied for cloth on weavers at court and in its administrative centers, all source points for fine, intricately patterned tapestries. Constructed of strong cotton warps acquired through exchanges with the coast, and softer, brightly dyed alpaca wefts obtained from the highlands, these textiles were in great demand for purposes of diplomacy and foreign exchange. Kings offered them as gifts to attract the fealty of lords in newly incorporated peripheries and forbade their wear or display in the absence of royal approval. Especially valued for this overtly political purpose were cloths from the royal wardrobe, steeped with associations of past rulers and deeds. An 'initial pump primer of dependence', suggests Murra, cloth of this sort was hoarded by the lords of the provinces for four or more generations, symbolizing at once their obligations to Cuzco and Cuzco's bestowal of citizenship in return.

In courtly societies, hierarchy rests heavily upon sumptuary paraphernalia to objectify and communicate rank, and to constitute material bonds between the past and the present, the rulers and the ruled. As noted above for the Mughals, inaugural regalia, passed on from generation to generation, is itself the substance of rule. Among the most famous instances of cloth distributions illustrating these principles was the Northwest Coast potlatch of the late nineteenth century, held to celebrate birth, adolescence, marriage, house construction, death, and accession to chiefly office. The most important chiefly prerogative at potlatch events was the right to distribute valuables. Because of the demographic collapse and economic disruptions set off by the fur trade, *nouveaux-riches* commoners of lower rank, viewed as 'scavengers' by the chiefs, claimed access to this right while the quantity of the circulating wealth – most commonly copper shields, canoes, boxes, dishes, food and slaves – multiplied exponentially (see Wolf 1982: 184–94).

One item, 'blankets', appears with special frequency in anthropological accounts of potlatching and is often also presented as a measure of value. The term conflates a commodity introduced by whites (Hudson Bay blankets) with precious capes, dance skirts, kilts and leggings that native women wove, integrating warps of strong cedar bark with wefts of soft goat hair. Dyed with yellow and a lovely blue obtained from Alaskan copper (later from boiling indigo-dyed commercial cloth), the weft yarns traced out the spiritually powerful zoomorphic figures that men carved and painted on totem poles and boxes, their symmetrically arranged oval-shaped eyes, multiple profiles, and distorted anatomical relationships filling every space. An over-the-top potlatching gesture for chiefs of any group was to tear capes and dance skirts into small pieces for distribution among lowly recipients, who might then reconstitute them as leggings and aprons (Drucker 1955, 1965). Georges Bataille, reflecting on the potlatch in the mid-1980s, added to Mauss's theory of the gift the almost metaphysical principle of 'expenditure' or squandering. Living in a world characterized by excess, chiefs were compelled to expend, 'willingly or not, gloriously or catastrophically' (Bataille 1988: 21, 67; see also Clarke 2003: 39 40).

We are reminded of the Sun King, Louis XIV, drawing the nobility to Versailles and compelling them to dissipate their revenues on, among other extravagances, garments sprouting layers upon layers of lace. Or of Grant McCracken's (1990) characterization of the sixteenth-century court of Elizabeth in England as an 'engine of sumptuosity'. This monarch, McCracken argues, communicated her aspirations for legitimacy, magistry, and godlike status by manipulating mythical, quasi-religious objects, and ensured the dependence of noble men and women by rewarding their self-indulgence at court. Such exploitation of the expressive power of things was entirely consonant with the potlatching chiefs of the Northwest Coast. As we will see below, so is today's consumerism, with the difference that today ordinary, everyday people also contribute to the exuberance and the waste.

ELITE EXUBERANCE AND THE DYNAMICS OF FASHION

The elitism of courtly societies generated the fundamental elements of fashion. American social philosopher and friend of Franz Boas, Thorstein Veblen considered this proposition in his 1899 book, *Theory of the Leisure Class*. Conspicuous display marked high position, although the content of the display might vary. The aggressive, trophy-hungry 'robber barons' of Veblen's day mimicked the pursuits of a leisured aristocracy, engaging in wastefully honorific expenditures such as hiring an excessive number of (well dressed) servants and ostentatiously abstaining from labor. Women, he proposed, consumed vicariously, beautifying their households and making themselves into ornaments for the sake of the household head. Uncomfortable, impractical, corseted garments advertised their idleness. By contrast, religious elites carried austerity to extremes, being cloaked in the ornate but severe garbs of exaggerated devotion.

Whatever the mode, Veblen argued, gratification depended at least in part on obtaining superior, beautifully crafted products, whose aesthetic qualities and obvious expense created a magnetic effect. Attraction is a critical element of fashion. So is being 'in vogue', a condition that required excluding status inferiors from the scheme (except as the indebted recipients of hand-me-downs and gifts). As the potlatching ethnography suggests, when envious commoners acquire the means to emulate, there unfolds a race to stay out in front, rendering fashion inherently unstable.

This approach to fashion, in which elites build themselves up through conspicuous pursuits and do not like to be copied, found resonance in Georg Simmel's 1904 definition of the phenomenon as evolving through a dialectic of conformity and differentiation, imitation and individuality, adapting to society and challenging its demands. But it also encountered criticism for being too reductive, narrowly defining goods as signifiers of status and assuming that innovations come only from the top (Slater 1997). In Bourdieu's more subtle 'practice theory', society's many groups are shown to articulate and deploy their own criteria for achieving distinction, their respective constituencies having grown up in a particular habitus, learned in an embodied way particular customs and dispositions, and acquired particular tastes. Arbiters of taste, armed with insiders' expertise, amplify the resulting differences, although not irrevocably. Under some conditions, the values accumulated in one hierarchy, say robber barons, can be converted into the values of another, say priests (Bourdieu 1979/1984).

In fairness to Veblen, he did recognize several kinds of hierarchy – economic, religious, military. Moreover, his insights about the drive for invidious glory – the dynamics of 'upward chase and flight' – are easily expanded to include other aspects of glory than merely communicating status. At the core of courtly sumptuosity is a complex of relations between persons and things in which persons make themselves, their surroundings and their close others, more vital through myriad ritual performances, through hospitality and generosity, through absorbing energy from the spiritual and aesthetic dimensions of objects, as well as through showing off. Overtly communicative displays are only one piece of the puzzle and perhaps not the most significant.

That courtly sumptuosity is a complex phenomenon of great historical significance is suggested by the widespread enactment of sumptuary laws following the late Middle Ages, when intensified commercial exchange between continents placed more wealth in circulation, in the service of developing polities. Minutely regulating items of dress in relation to social rank, the laws presumed to defend courtiers from the pretensions of newly rich merchant and trading groups. In Tokugawa Japan, sumptuary legislation went so far as to specify the number and material composition of the thongs that commoners could have on their sandals (Roach and Eicher 1979: 13). In Europe, Protestant reformers, scandalized by the explosion of consumption going on around them, supported sumptuary legislation out of a kind of anti-materialism.

How effective were the regulations is another question, even when violators were threatened with capital punishment. Renaissance Italy saw merchant elites brazenly overtake the courtiers in the latest styles. These included particolored doublets and hose of silk and wool in which the sleeves were of contrasting colors, the pants legs also, and the body of another color still. Slashed with hundreds of cuts to reveal a different color underneath, such garments invited individuals to design their own color schemes, causing (male) court fashion to change 'with a rapidity … unknown before' (Chamberlin 1967: 52–6).

A fascinating detail was the emergence, in this moment, of tailoring as an additional level of both cost and instability. In many of the early cloth traditions continuous weaving, sometimes yielding a tubular construction, was believed to harness a fabric's spiritual essence, or express the continuity of kinship and descent, so much so that cutting it was taboo. Fashioning lengths of cloth on the body was a matter of folding and draping. It was generally done, moreover, with all-purpose fabrics, suitable for covering a table or bed, swaddling an infant or shrouding a corpse, as well as adorning a living, adult body (Keane 2005). With tailoring, the line between cloth is clothing was fully crossed. Consisting of pre-cut pieces reassembled through sewing, tailored clothes opened up a whole new realm of crafting and variation, their architecture constituting an additional ingredient, over and above colors, motifs, and textures, for constructing an aesthetically attractive body, a vibrant and sexual person, a glorious elite. And shapes, too, could change with the fashion swirl, camouflaging or exaggerating the body's contours.

Europeans were not the first to tailor their garments. The narrow, brocaded men's cloths of West Africa were traditionally assembled with an eye for shape – an example of widespread Islamic (and Jewish) craftwork with needle and thread. Limb-encasing pants and jackets protected many peoples from the rigors of climate and warfare. Yet these examples stopped short of the perpetual mutation – the high-velocity turnover – that appears to have taken hold in the courts of the precociously mercantile cities of Renaissance Italy. Here, in the early sixteenth century, Baldassare Castiglione published what is considered the founding text of fashion history, *The Book of the Courtier* (1528/1953), which argued for treating the 'natural' body as a human creation, reflecting humans' ideas.

THE 'RISE' OF INDUSTRIAL CAPITALISM

Renaissance Italy's exquisitely dyed silk and woolen cloth, crafted by well regarded artisans, was a stimulus to manufacturers in England – cited by most social theory as the original capitalist land. An interesting textile-centric debate pits 'productionist' accounts of English capitalism against analyses that take consumption into account. In the former, the emphasis is on factory mobilization of alienated and unskilled labor; technological innovations in spinning and weaving; and harnessing colonial sources of raw materials – above all, cotton. For some, the prime mover was a burst of creative energy dating to the mid-eighteenth century and yielding the flying shuttle, spinning jenny, water frame, and spinning 'mule' (which combined the advances of the water frame and jenny). With the application of steam in 1790, spinners could accomplish in 300 hours what it had formerly taken 50,000 hours to produce (Wolf 1982: 273–4). Others highlight the putting-out system, through which merchants of the seventeenth and eighteenth centuries avoided the expensive labor of urban guild manufacturing, advancing raw materials, spinning wheels and looms to peasant households, organized for 'piecework'. More developed in Europe than in Asia (see Kriedte et al. 1981), in England, the putting-out system was an efficient source of household linens for colonial as well as home markets, and of the so-called 'new draperies' – light, woolen broadcloths, made from the long-staple fiber of sheep well fed on improved pastures, and inexpensive enough to permit the wastage of tailoring. The cotton entrepreneurs devised another organizational breakthrough, modeled on plantations in the Caribbean and Ireland, these in turn a source of strategic raw materials: a strictly disciplined labor force was concentrated in a factory setting, lowering production costs by a staggering amount.

The consumerist approach to the 'rise' of industrial capitalism is equally textile- and Anglocentric but directs attention to the 'sumptuosity engine' of the Elizabethan court, which stimulated desires throughout society but left them unrequited. With the abandonment of sumptuary legislation at the turn of the seventeenth century (see Freudenberger 1973), and the vast increase of wealth owed to colonial expansion, challenges to courtly elitism became both feminized and general. In the words of Chandra Mukerji, whose 1983 book *From Graven Images: Patterns of Modern Materialism* is an exemplary 'consumerist' text, fashion became, for the first time, an 'open cultural system'.

In tracing the origins of English capitalism to the mechanized spinning and weaving of colonial cotton, Mukerji argues, productionist theory neglects the contribution of painted floral chintzes and their less costly printed 'calico' equivalents that the British East India Company imported from India in the late seventeenth and eighteenth centuries. Light and soft when compared to the native woolen broadcloths (an asset in tailoring), and inexpensive when compared

to the figured silks and brocades of French and Italian provenance, these fabrics had 'a breadth of appeal and use that was unprecedented' (1983: 185–92). Indeed, feeling threatened, woolen textile artisans petitioned the government to block the entry of Indian imports and in 1719 took to the streets of London, 'tearing calicoes off the women's backs ...' (quoted in *ibid.*: 207).

Soon other textile artisans and entrepreneurs began to invest in the experimental dyeing of linens and cottons. A long-standing rivalry between England and Holland energized the experiments, these two powers having competed in the seventeenth century for Protestant dyers, exiled by regimes of the Counter-Reformation. By 1752, chemists allied with merchants in both countries had initiated copperplate printing on cloth; inspired by printing press technology, they were putting the plates on rollers by 1783. In other words, roller printers were no less central than steam-powered spinning and weaving to the industrialization of textile manufacture, a fact that points to consumer desire as an essential 'precondition'.

Certainly, the democratization of what was once courtly fashion continued apace, the more so as capitalist institutions and practices took hold in continental Europe. Images of Paris after 1789 suggest a spreading euphoria in which classes formerly in the shadows of courtly sumptuosity appeared on the streets in bright colors and captivating shapes. Under the Second Empire, bourgeois women acquired the new identity of 'shoppers', encouraged by an emergent institution: the department store. Offering luxurious-appearing goods at prices ordinary consumers could afford, this emporium also provided an exciting and beautiful space in which to look and dream (see Williams 1982).

Besides adding tailored shapes to the repertoire of distinction, modern capitalist society also differentiated clothes according to function. Machinery for cutting and sewing, together with Protestant and Victorian ideas regarding appropriate attire for work and leisure, day and night, worship and school, summer and winter, youth and adulthood, not to mention women and men, fired up an entire garment industry, churning out an ever broader range of function-sensitive styles. Sumptuosity was not only democratized by capitalism; its possibilities have endlessly proliferated, down to, for example, the differentiation of the (cut and sewn) sneaker according to sport. We might acknowledge, in passing, the corresponding mountains of left-over material piling up on the cutting floors.

CAPITALIST EXPANSION
AND ARTISAN PRODUCTION:
EUROPE AND BEYOND

The tension between productionist and consumptionist understandings of capitalism reappears in the vast literature on cloth and clothing as these manifestations of material culture have been affected by capitalism's spread (see Foster in Chapter 18). A rather pessimistic productionist bias is evident in characterizations of capitalism as a concatenation of forces that, rather like a juggernaut or steamroller, flattens everything in sight. Applied to cloth and clothing, this includes the idea that industrial manufactures are damaging to their hand-crafted equivalents and the artisans who make them.

Not that evidence for this hypothesis is lacking. Mission schools taught embroidery, sewing, and knitting to colonized women and children – textile arts that made extensive use of industrial materials while undermining the transmission of indigenous skills, above all patterned weaving (Schneider 1987: 434). Clever industrialists produced batiks expressly to compete with the Javanese craft, roller-printing copies so precise as to duplicate the hairline capillaries that occur in hand dyeing when the wax paste develops cracks (Matsuo 1970). They also made factory versions of *adinkra*, the terracotta mourning cloth of the Asante, simulating the *kente*-inspired embroidery that Asante artisans added for prestige (Polakoff 1982). Artisans who had been displaced from hand weaving and dyeing by the competition of machine-made goods often met an unhappy end, being forced into unemployment, migration, or the rather ironic situation of cultivating textile raw materials for manufactories in the metropole. Surely the most dramatic collapse of cloth traditions to occur in a context of fiber exports was that of plantation slaves in the Americas. Recruited in regions of Africa with important weaving and dyeing traditions, these laborers did not spin, weave or dye any of the cotton they grew, and were dressed in clothes made from factory yardgoods imported from Europe.

There are, however, a number of counter-indications to such a bleak picture. Far from always threatening a craft, industrially produced elements may stimulate it. Plain factory textiles contributed, like their commercial Indian forerunners, to the batik traditions of Java and Nigeria; their smooth surfaces meant that the wax or starch tracings of the designs could be applied with greater intricacy and precision, using finer instruments. Inexpensive

and smooth factory cottons were attractive to the saturation indigo dyers of Kano in Nigeria, while embroiderers on every continent welcomed synthetically colored, machine-manufactured thread. Consider, too, the crafts that depend entirely on commercial and factory textiles for their execution – the appliquéd mola blouses of the Panamanian Cuna Indians, the cut and drawn 'embroidery by subtraction' that Nigeria's Kalabari execute on commercial madras and gingham, and the quilted compositions of African-Americans in Surinam and the United States (Schneider 1987: 439–40).

Artisans' eagerness to acquire industrial yarn or cloth reflects not so much the steamroller effects of capitalism as the latent demands that are continually generated by the lively competitive processes of courtly sumptuosity, both within and across societies. As we have already emphasized, aesthetic competition placed a premium not only on skilled labor, constancy, and craft excellence, but also on access to raw and processed materials with good reputations. Because such characteristics as the range, saturation, and fastness of colors, the fineness and density of weaves, the tensile strength of warping threads, the intricacy of decoration, gave an edge in aesthetic rivalries, cloth and clothing makers characteristically pursued with interest newly available material possibilities, both before and during the expansion of European-generated capitalism. The response to newly available reds more than makes this case. Cloth artisans of colonial Africa and Native North America – areas on the margins of the Coccidae dyes – avidly unraveled cochineal and kermes-dyed commercial cloth so as to be able to add this color to their product (Schneider 1988).

Artisans in the path of capitalist expansion have also responded to emergent markets for hand-crafted cloth and clothing spawned by tourists, travelers, and others nostalgic for courtly styles, by concerned citizens attracted to 'ethnic arts' as a gesture of solidarity with oppressed or exiled minorities (see Myers in Chapter 17), and by the many movements of 'ethnogenesis' that have surfaced amidst independence struggles and in immigrant communities. But ethnographers' accounts of craft revitalizations are often ambivalent as antidotes to the bleak, productionist picture of juggernaut capitalism. On the one hand, they point to opportunities for indigenous textile artisans to regain income and dignity from meaningful employment, and for indigenous women and men to become entrepreneurs and leaders of ethnic claims. On the other hand, however, they dramatize a series of compromises.

For example, rural households, beholden to native entrepreneurs who 'put out' raw materials for piece-rated weaving, sewing, or embroidering during the slack season of the agricultural cycle may experience a degree of exploitation comparable to that of the European countryside on the eve of industrialization (Waterbury 1989). Often artisans lose artistic as well as economic control over the final product, modifying their wares in response to market pressures. Nor are consumers necessarily aware of this. Tourists purchasing 'Thamelcloth' hats and tunics in Nepal, or in shops in New York City, believe them to be the products of the 'righteous labor' of Tibetan refugees when in fact they are turned out in a Kathmandu factory (Hepburn 2000: 290–6).

In other examples, debasement and care coexist as producers apply high standards to the cloth they make for indigenous ritual and social purposes, for elite consumers of ethnic dress, and for discerning outsiders. Studying the 'craft commercialization' of Zapotec weaving in Oaxaca, Lynn Stephen (1993) learned that US intermediaries attempted to get local weavers to incorporate 'oriental' carpet motifs into their designs, just as they had given weavers in India Zapotec motifs to copy. The Oaxacan artisans resisted, worried that an 'inauthentic' product would lose market share. In the end, the viability of a textile craft often depends on the mediation of 'fair trade' and human rights organizations publicizing faithfulness to an 'authentic' ancestral tradition. Hendrickson's (1996) analysis of Pueblo to People catalogs promoting Mayan *traje* or dress is fascinating in this regard. Producers of *huipils* are represented as living in small, rain-forest villages lacking in modern technology. Personalized relationships with them are invoked, as if to convert alienated commodities into animated possessions. Seeing the people behind the goods suggests that their spirit resides in them and buyers are led to feel engaged in a social relationship across cultures.

Finally, social movements of 'sartorial' resistance have from time to time challenged juggernaut capitalism within the sphere of production. India, rich in its own cloth traditions, several of them quite commercialized, repulsed waves of Manchester cottons as part of its struggle for independence. Choosing a captivating symbol of both economic autonomy and spiritual worth – the spinning wheel – and defining women spinners as the core of the nation, Gandhi advocated the production and wearing of hand-spun and hand-woven white cotton *khadi* and the boycotting or burning of imported English textiles. Descriptions of his initiative (e.g. Bean 1989) point not only to the circumstances of cloth manufacturing but also to the consumption sphere, where, as we will see, the pessimistic outlook on Western capitalism has also been up-ended.

THE HEGEMONY OF 'WESTERN FASHION'

The processes through which industrial textiles and clothing challenged and displaced, yet also stimulated, artisanal cloth production are paralleled in the consumption sphere by the hegemony, the contradictory meanings, and the limits of 'Western fashion' – generally more tailored than other dress traditions, consisting of many more components and accessories, and strongly differentiated according to gender and function. Spanish and Portuguese colonists followed by northern Europeans set this process in motion, first and foremost by penetrating and disrupting existing courtly hierarchies, together with their ongoing practices regarding cloth and clothes.

Colonial histories draw attention to European colonizers' heavy-handed dumping of surplus merchandise, establishment of 'company stores', and habit of dazzling untutored audiences with machine-made wonders never seen before. Marketing research, credit advances, image promotion, and advertising also spread in the wake of colonization (see Burke 1996). In an apparent contradiction, missionaries and colonial officials criticized indigenous peoples for adopting Western finery, mocking as ridiculous their presumed desire to participate in the new order; yet these same missionaries and officials imposed Westernized standards of appearance and behavior as a criterion for religious conversion or 'civilizational' status (e.g. Thomas 2003). For this reason, too, elements of Western dress spread vigorously around the world.

And yet, there is no clear story regarding the gravity of the damage wrought by this stylistic invasion. To the Rhodes-Livingstone ethnographers of the 1940s, Africans' love of dressing up and going to dance clubs was an index of urbanization – of the steps being taken by migrants to Copperbelt cities to distance themselves from their rural past and engage with a wider, more cosmopolitan world, of which their white oppressors were the reference group (Wilson 1941). As a kind of life force, the new elegance promised to bestow power, or at least the respect of others, by symbolic means.

A less benign explanation was put forward by Bernard Magubane in 1971. For Magubane, as for Franz Fanon, adopting the oppressors' clothing styles showed the extent of Africans' suffering, and the depth of their pathological colonial psychology of self-hatred. The Société des Ambianceurs et des Personnes Élégantes (SAPE) – a tradition of Congolese urban youth competitively sporting Parisian finery – and *Oswenka* – a fashion competition for adult men working in South African mines and donning 'swank' suits, ties, shoes, socks, and shirts during their leisure hours – have provoked similar arguments over interpretation (see Ferguson 2002; Friedman 1994; Gondola 1999; Scheld 2003).

It is interesting and perhaps significant that Magubane wrote during the apogee of 'productionist' theory in anthropology when the Marxist concept of the fetishism of commodities – their magical capacity to mask the labor processes embedded in them – relegated the analysis of consumption to second place, a distraction from the project of workers' liberation. Add to this the contemporary influence of Frankfurt School scholars who considered the entertainment and consumer industries of capitalist societies to be the source of a deadening, unfulfilling conformity and escapism. That working people – and by extension colonial subjects – desired 'Western fashion' could only be because they were manipulated by images and promotions.

New and less pessimistic assessments of the diffusion of Western dress were unleashed by anthropology's turn toward cultural theory in the late 1970s. A preliminary move, accomplished by Mary Douglas and Baron Isherwood in *The World of Goods* (1979), was the legitimization of consumption as a respectable rather than trivial research topic. *The Social Life of Things*, edited by Arjun Appadurai in 1986, celebrated this shift, offering several case studies of 'consumer revolutions' shaped by cultural particulars (see also Miller 1995). There followed Marshall Sahlins's landmark essay 'Cosmologies of Capitalism' (1988/1994), which explicitly rejected the idea that the West's industrial, capitalist manufactures victimized non-Western peoples and adulterated their cultures.

To the contrary, local concepts of status, means of labor control, and aesthetic preferences dictated a range of outlooks on Western goods. Sahlins relished recounting that in 1793, in a letter to George III, the Chinese emperor famously expressed disdain for European fashions, deemed inferior to Chinese cloth and clothing. A different, but equally ironic, outcome emerged in the Sandwich Islands, where chiefs defined their European visitors as mythic figures descending from the sky to re-enact their ancestral Kahiki. Already obsessed with marking rank through spiritually animated adornments, they coveted the newly available English broadcloths, allowing Sahlins to quip that 'the capitalist mode of production is organized by *mana*'. Other instances of the courtly adoption of Western dress would seem to amplify his argument. The pre-1950s rulers of Nepal, a country that had not been colonized, classified Europeans, whom they knew from a distance, as 'barbarians'. Yet they avidly consumed European cloth and clothing, initially attracted to tailored garb for military purposes, and interdicted commoners' access to these exotic imports through sumptuary legislation (Hepburn 2000: 282).

Outside of anthropology, scholars attached to the Birmingham School of Cultural Studies interpreted the purchase and display of industrially produced goods by marginalized, working-class youth as acts of creativity and resistance. In 1979, Dick Hebdige, overturning Frankfurt school dismay over popular culture, declared that British Teddy Boys in their Edwardian jackets, mods in their Italian suits, and punks flaunting shirts held together with safety pins were engaged in a process of *bricolage*, expressing rebel identities through a re-articulation of what they bought. Hebdige did appreciate, however, the eagerness of capitalist fashion designers to reappropriate subcultural styles, newly configuring their edginess for wider markets. His work has been influential in recent analyses of Hip Hop culture showing clothing and music styles to intersect in an ongoing dialectic of rebellion and appropriation.

Rather than treat consumers as passive or manipulated subjects, and the non-Western consumers of Western clothing even more so, the developments in cultural theory of the last quarter of the twentieth century pointed in the opposite direction: consumers are active agents in the construction of their own histories, even when adopting the very fashions of those they seek to resist. Thus Jean and John Comaroff argue for the incubation of revolutionary potential in colonized Southern Africans' evolving Christian identity – an identity indexed by mission-prescribed Western clothes (Comaroff 1996; Comaroff and Comaroff 1997; see also Thomas 2003).

CONSUMERISM AND DESIRE

As the foregoing review implies, the arguments surrounding the hegemony of Western fashion generally have, as background, Western

European industrial capitalism and colonialism. More recently, the United States has fostered a *post*-colonial transformation of capitalism, variously labeled 'neo-liberal', 'global', or 'postmodern'. Core characteristics include the deregulation of financial markets and disinvestment in the original heartlands of industrialization. An interesting body of social theory discusses this shift in terms of the concept 'consumer society'. A forerunner lies in Jean Baudrillard's (1970/98, 1973/1975) idea that, whereas 'modern' capitalism disciplined the body of the worker, postmodern capitalism seduces its subjects, redefined as consumers, to cultivate and care for their bodies, and the images of their bodies, as if still driven by an ethic of work. Experiencing freedom, and possibly joy, they also exist in a realm of unfreedom, being influenced since childhood by a bombardment of commercial images and compelled to acquire money by whatever means. The consequence is a troubling juxtaposition of desire and fantasy with stress, anxiety, and violence. For Baudrillard, addiction, the compulsion to remake the self, and exclusionary commitments to narrow social groups, are hallmarks of consumer society. Most distressing is the impossibility of resistance, as voluntary simplicity movements and rebel boycotts of excessive fashion inevitably become the foundation for new 'niche markets'.

Of particular interest for this chapter, given its emphasis in earlier sections on artisanal cloth production, is Zygmunt Bauman's related argument (1983) that the initial impetus for seduction as a technique of societal control is traceable to the first negotiations, in Europe, between the captains of industry and restive 'labor aristocracies', attempting to preserve their craft specializations in the face of the consolidating factory system. In effect, many skilled workers traded their treasured autonomy for the (economic) power to purchase what the captains had to offer; their frustration in confronting the constraints of industrial production was 'diverted' into consumption. Because this compensatory mechanism could never fully satisfy, however, the quest for autonomy continued in surrogate form, sowing the seeds of insatiable demand. The consequence has been to drive the production process into an 'exacerbated' condition of interminable (and squandering) growth, reminiscent of potlatching.

Contemporary consumer culture reproduces courtly sumptuosity in other respects as well. Aggressively promoted logos and labels convey a kind of spiritual power not unlike the auspicious motifs woven into traditional textiles (which for their part now circulate as disembodied images advertising 'cultural' tourism). Apart from signaling the authenticity of the product, logos encourage imagined connections, as when wearers of sneakers with the Nike 'swoosh' fantasize partaking in Michael Jordan's athleticism. Between the microdynamics of fads (Molotch 2003) and the globalization of media that foster symbolic associations, such magical effects increasingly have a worldwide reach (see Klein 1999). If anything, the craze for the label – Lee, Wrangler, Tommy Hilfiger, Sebago, Timberland – exceeds demand for the product itself. In an ironic inversion of Manchester's imitations of Javanese batiks, consumers may be happy with knock-offs so long as the label is 'real' (see Scheld 2003).

It is possible that artisans, exchanging their skill-based autonomy for the capacity to purchase wondrous things, were motivated by a latent desire for sumptuosity, born of their long-standing tenure on the margins of punishing status hierarchies to whose sensual and aesthetic pleasures their respective crafts had contributed. With the dawn of consumer culture, the honorific logic of elite sumptuosity is, by contrast, a logic open to everyone (compare St George in Chapter 14). No 'consumer society' better illustrates this than the United States, where, already in the 1960s, the annual consumption of fibers was 47.9 lb *per capita* as compared with 11.5 lb *per capita* worldwide (AFF 1969: 49–50). In 1987, the number of US shopping malls overtook the number of high schools; during the three decades leading up to 2000, each American gained, on average, four times more retail space; by 2000, consumer spending had ballooned to account for an unprecedented two-thirds of US economic growth (Zukin 2004: 16).

Yet any comparison between this seeming excess and potlatching is limited by the elitism of the latter. Only chiefs had piles of 'blankets'; they alone commanded their distribution at feasts. Commoners went without, or received these items in humiliating shreds and patches. In the contemporary US system, giant mega-stores, most notably Wal-mart, pursue the merchandising strategy earlier pioneered by the Woolworth chain: offering minutely differentiated, fashion-conscious name-brand goods as well as generic items at bargain prices. Although US moneyed and power elites continue to engage in highly exclusive consuming practices, the rest of society seems not to care, having come to define shopping as 'a realm of freedom from work and politics, a form of democracy open to all' (Zukin: 2004: 34; see also Miller 1998).

Consumer culture is, further, the well-spring of freedom from gender systems that harness sexuality – above all, women's sexuality – to reproductive roles, and to the structuring influence of older generations: parents, in-laws, religious authorities, and the (generally male) leaders of national and ethnic groups. Certainly, the clothing icons of global consumerism – blue jeans, polo shirts, tank tops, mini-skirts, lingerie, and little dresses – have undergone an inexorable sexualization in recent years, exposing more of the midriff and breasts, clinging more tightly to the limbs, dissolving the boundary between under- and outer-wear – in general teasing 'respectable society' with more of Victoria's secrets. Youthful consumers throughout the world, many of them young women away from home and earning wages for the first time, experiment with purchases of this sort, or dream about making them, just as they confront the new circumstances of finding and keeping a partner in the brave new world of sexual liberation.

THE GLOBAL FACTORY

The democratization of shopping is integrally related to vast and growing inequalities in the sphere of production and in the 'life chances' of people around the globe. Associated with disinvestment in the first industrial societies, since the mid-1970s, the industrial production of cloth and clothing has spread to every continent, incorporating volumes of new workers, and sucking up Asian, African and Latin American as well as European capital. Increasingly, China is the 'workshop of the world'. Yet cloth and clothing manufacture have remained remarkably resistant to technological change. Synthetic fibers, made by forcing petroleum products through 'spinarettes' (resembling shower heads) render laborious spinning unnecessary, while their high tensile strength allows for accelerated weaving (Schneider 1994). Machine innovations have reduced wastage in cutting. Nevertheless, labor is, has always been, and probably always will be the largest cost factor in making cloth and clothing. Assembly and sewing in particular remain highly demanding of the human hand; most fabrics are simply too fluid to trust to machines alone. As of the late 1990s, 13 million people were formally employed in textile manufacture worldwide, 6 million in garment manufacture, and this is not counting the millions who work in the informal sector, at home or in clandestine workshops (Dicken 1998: 283–6).

Between 1970 and 1993, 420,000 jobs were lost in textiles in the United States, and 180,000 (mostly unionized) jobs in the garment sector, cutting and tailoring. In the same period, the 'revolutionary retailers' launched an assault on labor, paying substandard wages to clerks and stock persons in their own outlets, explicitly discouraged in the case of Wal-mart from unionizing; and contracting for product from export processing zones, *maquilladoras* and sweatshops around the world. In such locations, employees tend to be young and female, often pressed into spinning or sewing by rural families suffering from crises of agricultural dislocation. The fragmented nature of the contracting arrangements constitutes a formidable obstacle to regulating what are often appalling working conditions: seven-day weeks with twelve to fourteen hours a day at times of peak demand; poor ventilation; accidents related to speed-up; and vulnerability to disemployment as the contractors relocate to zones where wages are lower still.

According to geographer Peter Dicken (1998: 294–5), the concentrated purchasing power of the great chains gives them 'enormous leverage over textile and clothing manufacturers'. In effect, they have combined state-of-the-art communications technology, design capability, and far-flung 'parts producers' into a singular colossus – the extraordinarily unequal counterpart to the democratization of fashion. Ian Skoggard, an anthropologist who researched shoe production in Taiwan, notes that the images highlighted in Nike's New York shrine to athletes, with its Fifth Avenue address, Greek columns, and videos of sponsored players and teams, would be tarnished if a consumer campaign were to dwell on the working conditions of its Asian suppliers (Skoggard 1998). Yet, even when they are aware of the circumstances of production, most consumers feel gratitude for capitalism's incredible gift: the possibility for sartorial self-enhancement under the almost affordable combination of credit and bargain sales. What is more, the young women who work in the sweatshops desire, themselves, to partake of this gift.

THE PRESENT-DAY SARTORIAL ECUMENE

Given that, today, 'commercial' cloth and clothing are produced in the 'global factory', the old problematic of the hegemony of 'Western fashion' – its relation to unequal power and resistance – seems quite beside the point. Paris, Milan, New York and London continue to be the pre-eminent centers of high-end design, but Tokyo, Hong Kong, and Shanghai are credible competitors (see Kondo 1992; Li 1998; Skov 2003). Most important, the high end is generally less relevant to the overall picture. As Karen Tranberg Hansen puts it, an increasingly vast proliferation of styles has definitively squelched emulation as a significant ingredient in clothing decisions, encouraging an unfettered individualism as it ushers in processes of 'bricolage, hybridity, and creolization' (Hansen forthcoming: 4–5). And yet, the 'sartorial ecumene', to borrow Hansen's felicitous expression (*ibid.*: 10), is far from a level playing field, given the powerful engines of consumerism and the production relations that accompany it. Three broad developments suggesting, respectively, resistance, courtly revitalization, and full participation in consumer culture are sketched below.

Of immediate visual impact are the widening zones of morally 'conservative' dress, for example the sari in India. As Mukulika Banerjee and Daniel Miller (2003) document in their beautifully illustrated book on the subject, this garment is now made of industrially manufactured cloth, more often polyester than silk or cotton, and worn in conjunction with tailored blouses. As well, it has undergone a process of homogenization, promoted by entertainment celebrities as well as political leaders, in which divergent regional methods of folding and draping are subsumed under a common national style, 'the Nivi'. Emblematic of pride in the nation, the sari has convinced all classes of women, from village field workers to employees in offices, to wealthy women of leisure, that it augments their 'possibilities of aesthetic beauty, female mastery, sexuality and the cult of the maternal'. Putting it on, women try to live up to 'the kind and quality of person that the sari now requires and stands for' (2003: 235–6; see also Tarlo 1996).

Because the sari's potential to evoke sexuality has triggered the sort of anxiety that attaches to trendy, consumerist clothes, however, some Indian women prefer the Muslim-influenced *shalwar kamiz*, a garment of trousers and tunic that hides, rather than reveals, the body. (So do long skirts, the hallmark of female modesty in the Middle East, where, in contrast, the early twentieth-century introduction of trousers for women provoked censure and even riots. See Gillette 2000: 97.) Moral concerns are uppermost in veiling, a spreading practice in Muslim societies across the globe. Many of today's veiled Muslims are caught up in (male-led) political struggles addressing the Arab-Isreali conflict and US intervention in the Middle East. More broadly, veiling seems powerfully to symbolize women's subordination to men. At the same time, however, conservative Islamic dress is a reminder that, throughout history, unprecedented squandering associated with a suddenly yawning chasm between rich and poor has triggered moralistic responses focused on justice and fairness. Thus St Francis, the son of a prosperous leather merchant in a time of spreading opulence in Florence, held his rough, undyed robes together with a (pointedly not leather) rope belt. Several ethnographic studies point to the veil as similarly materializing a broad moral critique.

Following the 1970s emergence of an Islamic youth and student movement in Malaysia, for example, upwardly mobile, urban educated women adopted conservative dress, their apparent identification with 'revivalist ideals of motherhood [and] male authority' occurring despite the fact that neither veiling nor female seclusion had characterized their society in the past. According to Aihwa Ong (1990), the movement 'railed against the decadent lifestyles of *nouveaux riches* Malays, considered too secular and materialistic'. In adopting the *minitelekung*, a cloth that 'tightly frames the face and covers the head, hair and chest', and the long black robes or *hijab*, women both experienced and expressed a sense of moral righteousness in relation to the sensuality of consumer culture, and the polarization of wealth and extreme poverty that its capitalist foundations had spawned.

Java is another place where veiling spread among university students in the late 1970s, in the context of a pan-Islamist movement, the practice having had no roots in local clothing traditions. Because in Java, unlike in the Middle East, veiling is an obstacle to secular employment, is criticized by public opinion for communicating sanctimoniousness and fanaticism, was for a while prohibited by government decree, and is even disapproved of by parents, persisting in the practice is disruptive of significant social ties and is a matter of soul-searching and determination. In the narratives of women who wore *jilbab*, or Muslim dress, Suzanne Brenner (1996) discovered that a moral crisis had been set in motion by an unchecked and 'disgusting' consumerism on the part of moneyed elites, juxtaposed with the suffering of an increasingly destitute 'underclass'. For the morally anxious person, veiling bestows a sense of calm, self-mastery, and renewal (see also Abu-Lughod 1990; Gole 1996; Hoodfar 1991; Mernissi 1987).

Another set of images from today's sartorial ecumene presents 'ethnic dress' as a counterweight to consumer culture, but not in a very compelling way. For one thing, iconic elements of ethnicity are products of historical and continuing interactions with Western and commercial fashions. They are not themselves emblems of an authentic 'cultural heritage'. Second, adopting them in urban and modern contexts, although it elicits approval from some groups, invites stigma or opprobrium from others. Where governments of multi-ethnic states are seeking to create a national identity, overriding ethnic difference, government officials may propagate ethnically neutral models of dress or mandate uniforms for schools and other public arenas. Finally, to the extent that elements of an ethnic wardrobe are produced by artisanal labor, their cost may exceed by far the cost of commercial wear. This circumstance means that only ethnic leaders are able to acquire the full regalia demanded by life-cycle rituals and ceremonial events; others must borrow to enjoy the symbolically and materially transformative properties of 'traditional' dress. It should be noted that, through dense relations of borrowing and lending, ethnic communities manifest the principles of generosity and clientelism that underpin social solidarity in courtly social forms.

The 'sweeping and cumbrous' Herero dresses that Botswana's Tswana believe descended from German missionaries illustrate these aspects of ethnic attire. Better-off Herero women acquire them for weddings and funerals, and extol the quality of regal and stately movement, the sense of great weight and mass, that a long, billowing, and many-layered garment (ten yards of fabric plus petticoats) provides. Other women too poor to possess a Herero dress borrow one, or money to buy one, in order to attend important ceremonial occasions (Durham 1999). In Kaolack, a predominantly Wolof city in the Gambia, Senegal, *sanse* or dressing up involves urban women donning copious starched and folded garments adorned with matching headdresses and abundant gold jewelry. Ideally constructed of hand-woven, damasked strip cloth that has been elaborately embroidered, this grand *boubou* costs more than an average household's monthly income. Younger enthusiasts have tailors incorporate commercial elements – flounces, lace, and fitted bodices. Poor enthusiasts add their own embroidery, using ravelings from secondhand sweaters. And they seek the help of kin, friends, and patrons in meeting ceremonial expenses (Heath 1992).

The ambivalent status of ethnic dress is evident in Leslie Gill's (1993) analysis of women's clothing styles in La Paz, Bolivia, during the decades following the 1952 revolution. Some Aymara migrants to the city acquired refined *polleras* or skirts and bowler hats made by urban artisans – their ticket to prideful attendance at Aymara events and a way to set themselves off from their country cousins whose skirts and hats were more rustic. But possessing such items meant incurring debts and the condescension of many non-Aymara. Not surprisingly, other immigrants dispensed with ethnic dress, shopping for cheap commercial clothes in neighborhood popular markets. A woman's relationships with her employer, her family, the artisan-entrepreneurs of the Aymara community, and both older and more recent immigrants shaped the mix of styles to which she became committed.

In Maris Gillette's (2000) study, Hui (Muslim) brides in the predominantly Han city of Xi'an are increasingly attracted to the Western-style wedding gown with fitted bodice – a garment that is displacing the red silk *qipao* dress modeled on Confucian courtly styles and popular since the 1920s, when it overtook the much less fancy Hui trousers and tunic. The recent transition can be traced to the appearance, in the 1990s, of Western-style gowns in cosmopolitan magazines and on television, and by their availability for rent in local Han shops. It is propelled by the support that young women receive from their girlfriends and close female relatives as they pursue their desire to be 'trendy' and 'modern' and to associate with affluence. At the same time, locally situated religious and public authorities modulate the change-over, their disapproval evident in the selection of pink or coral rather than white as the favorite wedding-gown color.

Reviewing several decades of ethnographic research in Africa, James Ferguson (2002) proposes that non-Europeans' adoption of commercial dress codes has been an 'embarrassment' to anthropology, whose stock in trade is the viability of local cultures. Hence anthropologists' tendency to celebrate local reworkings of the codes, finding assertions of opposition or autonomy in them. Meanwhile, however, their anthropological subjects are increasingly caught up in the kinds of modernizing and urbanizing processes that so impressed the ethnographers of the Copperbelt in the 1940s. Why not conclude, Ferguson argues, that, in getting swept up in contemporary fads and fashions, people are expressing their desire, and their *right*, to participate in modernity? Wearing commercial clothes is a way to cultivate a modern consciousness appropriate to the modern condition. Hansen's remarkable study of used clothing in Zambia (2000) is a case in point. A global commodity chain originating in the charities of the first industrialized countries delivers a vast array of barely worn, up-to-date clothing to the rest of the world. (The squandering United States ships out no less than 50 million tons per year, much of it manufactured or partly manufactured 'off-shore'.) Zambians enthusiastically rummage through used clothing markets and frequent resident tailors who fashion the necessary and wished-for alterations. The thrust of Hansen's analysis is to save their love of doing so from the charge that it is externally driven. 'Cultural and subjective matters', rooted in a past of courtly arrangements in which elites' capacity for enhancement far exceeded that of commoners, is part of the motivation; the other part is the capacity of 'modern clothes' to empower their wearers, imbuing them with the confidence of accruing respect.

And yet, Hansen's study also communicates a deeper truth about the sartorial ecumene, one that brings us back to this chapter's insistence on integrating the spheres of production and consumption. If it weren't for the secondhand markets many Zambians would be in rags, because over the 1980s and 1990s, decent work almost disappeared. Rummaged fashion narrows the gap in appearance between rich and poor, rural and urban, North and South. Evoking hoped-for opportunities and chances – what Keane (2005) poignantly calls 'expectations of history' – it permits the well attired person to imagine a better future. Sadly, the author concludes, dreams of a better life can also be illusory – at best a transient and vicarious way to escape the economic powerlessness wrought by the downward spiral of current trends.

REFERENCES

Abu-Lughod, Lila (1990) 'The romance of resistance: tracing transformations of power through Bedouin women', *American Ethnologist*, 17: 41–56.

AFF (*American Fabrics and Fashions*), 1969.

Appadurai, Arjun (1986) 'Introduction: Commodities and the Politics of Value', in *The Social Life of Things*. Cambridge: Cambridge University Press, pp. 3–63.

Banerjee, Mukulika and Daniel Miller (2003) *The Sari*. Oxford: Berg.

Bataille, Georges (1988) *The Accursed Share: an Essay on General Economy* I, *Consumption*. New York: Zone Books.

Baudrillard, Jean (1970/1998) *The Consumer Society: Myths and Structures*. London: Sage Publications.

Baudrillard, Jean (1973/1975) *The Mirror of Production*. St Louis: Telos.

Bauman, Zygmunt (1983) 'Industrialism, consumerism, and power', *Theory, Culture and Society*, 1: 32–43.

Bean, Susan S. (1989) 'Gandhi and Khadi, the fabric of Indian independence', in Annette B. Weiner and Jane Schneider (eds), *Cloth and Human Experience*. Washington, DC: Smithsonian Press, pp. 356–83.

Bourdieu, Pierre (1979/1984) *Distinction: a Social Critique of the Judgement of Taste*. Cambridge, MA: Harvard University Press.

Bowie, Katherine A. (1993) 'Assessing the early observers: cloth and the fabric of society in nineteenth-century northern Thai kingdoms', *American Ethnologist*, 20: 138–58.

Brenner, Suzanne (1996) 'Reconstructing self and society: Javanese Muslim women and the veil', *American Ethnologist*, 23: 673–98.

Burke, Timothy (1996) *Lifebuoy Men, Lux Women: Commodification, Consumption, and Cleanliness in Modern Zimbabwe*. Durham, NC: Duke University Press.

Carrier, James G. (1994) *Gifts and Commodities: Exchange and Western Capitalism since 1700*. London: Routledge.

Castiglione, Baldassare (1528/1953) *The Courtier*, in Burton A. Milligan (ed.), *Three Renaissance Classics: The Prince, Utopia, The Courtier*, trans. Sir Thomas Hoby, 1851. New York: Scribner.

Chamberlin, E.R. (1967) *Everyday Life in Renaissance Times*. New York: Capricorn Books.

Clarke, David B. (2003) *The Consumer Society and the Postmodern City*. London and New York: Routledge.

Cohn, Bernard (1989) 'Cloth, clothes and colonialism: India in the nineteenth century', in Annette B. Weiner and Jane Schneider (eds), *Cloth and Human Experience*. Washington, DC and London: Smithsonian Institution Press, pp. 303–53.

Comaroff, Jean (1996) 'The empire's old clothes: fashioning the colonial subject', in D. Howes (ed.), *Cross-cultural Consumption: Global Markets, Local Realities*. London: Routledge, pp. 19–39.

Comaroff, John L. and Comaroff, Jean (1997) *Of Revelation and Revolution* II, *The Dialectics of Modernity on a South African Frontier*. Chicago: University of Chicago Press.

Cort, Louise (1989) 'The changing fortunes of three archaic Japanese textiles', in Annette B. Weiner and Jane Schneider (eds), *Cloth and Human Experience*. Washington, DC and London: Smithsonian Institution Press, pp. 380–415.

Darish, Patricia (1989) 'Dressing for the next life: raffia textile production and use among the Kuba of Zaire', in Annette B. Weiner and Jane Schneider (eds), *Cloth and Human Experience*. Washington, DC and London: Smithsonian Institution Press, pp. 118–42.

Dicken, Peter (1998) *Global Shift: Transforming the World Economy*, 3rd edn. New York and London: Guilford Press.

Douglas, Mary (1967) 'Raffia cloth distribution in the Lele economy', in G. Dalton (ed.), *Tribal and Peasant Economies: Readings in Economic Anthropology*. New York: American Museum of Natural History Press, pp. 103–23.

Douglas, Mary, and Isherwood, Baron (1979) *The World of Goods*. New York: Basic Books.

Drucker, Peter (1955) *Indians of the Northwest Coast*. New York: American Museum of Natural History.

Drucker, Peter (1965) *Cultures of the North Pacific Coast*. San Francisco: Chandler.

Durham, Deborah (1999) 'The predicament of dress: polyvalency and the ironies of cultural identity', *American Ethnologist*, 26: 389–412.

Feeley-Harnik, Gillian (1989) 'Cloth and the creation of ancestors in Madagascar', in Annette B. Weiner and Jane Schneider (eds), *Cloth and Human Experience*. Washington, DC and London: Smithsonian Institution Press, pp. 75–118.

Ferguson, James (2002) 'Of mimicry and membership', Africans and the 'New World society', *Cultural Anthropology*, 17: 551–69.

Fox, James J. (1977) 'Roti, Ndao and Savu', in Mary Hunt Kahlenberg (ed.), *Textile Traditions of Indonesia*. Los Angeles: County Museum, pp. 97–104.

Freudenberger, Herman (1973) 'Fashion, sumptuary laws and business', in Gordon Wills and David Midgley (eds), *Fashion Marketing: an Anthropology of Viewpoints and Perspectives*. London: Allen & Unwin, pp. 137–47.

Friedman, Jonathan (1994) 'The political economy of elegance: an African cult of beauty', in Jonathan Friedman (ed.), *Consumption and Identity*. Chur: Harwood Academic, pp. 167–89.

Gill, Leslie (1993) '"Proper women" and city pleasures: gender, class, and contested meanings in La Paz', *American Ethnologist*, 20: 72–89.

Gillette, Maris (2000) 'What's in a dress? Brides in the Hui quarter of Xi'an', in Deborah S. Davis (ed.), *The Consumer Revolution in Urban China*. Berkeley, CA: University of California Press, pp. 80–107.

Gole, Nilufer (1996) *The Forbidden Modern: Civilization and Veiling: Critical Perspectives on Women and Gender*. Ann Arbor, MI: University of Michigan Press.

Gondola, Didier (1999) 'Dream and drama: the search for elegance among Congolese youth', *African Studies Review*, 42: 23–48.

Hansen, Karen Tranberg (2000) *Salaula: the World of Secondhand Clothing and Zambia*. Chicago: University of Chicago Press.

Hansen, Karen Tranberg, (forthcoming) 'The world in dress: anthropological perspectives on clothing, fashion, and culture', *Annual Review of Anthropology*, 33: 369–92.

Heath, Deborah (1992) 'Fashion, anti-fashion, and heteroglossia in urban Senegal', *American Ethnologist*, 19: 19–33.

Hebdige, Dick (1979) *Subcultures and the Meaning of Style*. London: Methuen.

Hendrickson, Carol (1996) 'Selling Guatemala: Maya export products in US mail order catalogs', in D. Howes (ed.), *Cross-cultural Consumption: Global Markets, Local Realities*. London: Routledge, pp. 106–25.

Hepburn, Sharon (2000) 'The cloth of barbaric pagans: tourism, identity, and modernity in Nepal', *Fashion Theory: the Journal of Dress, Body, and Culture*, 4: 275–301.

Hoodfar, Homa (1991) 'Return to the veil: personal strategy and public participation in Egypt', in Nanneke Edclift and M. Thea Sinclair (eds), *Working Women: International Perspectives on Labor and Gender Ideology*. New York: Routledge, pp. 104–24.

Hoskins, Janet (1989) 'Why do ladies sing the blues? Indigo dyeing, cloth production, and gender symbolism in Kodi', in Annette B. Weiner and Jane Schneider (eds), *Cloth and Human Experience*. Washington, DC and London: Smithsonian Institution Press, pp. 142–79.

Keane, Webb (2005) 'The hazards of new clothes: what signs make possible', in Susanne Küchler and Graeme Were (eds), *The Art of Clothing: a Pacific Experience*. London: UCL Press, pp. 1–16.

Kendall, Laurel (1985) 'Ritual silks and kowtow money: the bride as daughter-in-law in Korean wedding rituals', *Ethnology*, 24: 253–69.

Klein, Naomi (1999) *No Logo: Taking Aim at the Brand Bullies*. New York: Picador Press.

Kondo, Doreen (1992) 'The aesthetics and politics of Japanese identity in the fashion industry', in J. Tobin (ed.), *Re-made in Japan: Everyday Life and Consumer Taste in a Changing Society*. New Haven, CT: Yale University Press, pp. 176–203.

Kriedte, Peter, Medick, Hans and Schlumbohm, Jurgen eds (1981) *Industrialization before Industrialization*. Cambridge: Cambridge University Press.

Li, Xiaoping (1998) 'Fashioning the body in post-Mao China', in Anne Brydon and Sandra Niessen (eds), *Consuming Fashion: Adorning the Transnational Body*. Oxford: Berg, pp. 71–89.

Magubane, Bernard (1971) 'A critical look at indices used in the study of social change in colonial Africa', *Current Anthropology*, 12: 419–45.

Masquelier, A. (1996) 'Mediating threads: clothing and the texture of spirit/medium relations in *Bori* (southern Niger)', in H. Hendrickson (ed.), *Clothing and Difference: Embodied Identities in Colonial and Postcolonial Africa*. Durham, NC: Duke University Press, pp. 66–94.

Matsuo, H. (1970) *The Development of the Javanese Cotton Industry.* Occasional Paper 7. Tokyo: Institute of Development Economics.

Mauss, Marcel (1923–24/1954) *The Gift: Forms and Functions of Exchange in Archaic Societies,* trans. Ian Cunnison. Glencoe, IL: Free Press.

McCracken, Grant (1990) *Culture and Consumption: New Approaches to the Symbolic Character of Consumer Goods and Activities.* Bloomington, IN: Indiana University Press.

Mernissi, Fatima (1987) *Beyond the Veil: Male-Female Dynamics in a Modern Muslim Society.* Bloomington, IN: Indiana University Press.

Miller, Daniel (1995) *Acknowledging Consumption: a Review of New Studies.* London: Routledge.

Miller, Daniel (1998) *A Theory of Shopping.* Ithaca, NY: Cornell University Press.

Molotch, Harvey (2003) *Where Stuff comes from: How Toasters, Toilets, Cars, Computers and many other Things come to be as They are.* London: Routledge.

Morris, W.F. (1986) 'Maya time warps', *Archaeology,* 39: 52–9.

Mukerji, Chandra (1983) *From Graven Images: Patterns of Modern Materialism.* New York: Columbia University Press.

Murra, John (1962) 'Cloth and its functions in the Inka state', *American Anthropologist,* 64: 710–28.

Ong, Aihwa (1990) 'State versus Islam: Malay families, women's bodies, and the body politic in Malaysia', *American Ethnologist,* 17: 258–77.

Polakoff, C. (1982) *African Textiles and Dyeing Techniques.* London: Routledge.

Roach, M.E. and J.B. Eicher (1979) 'The language of personal adornment', in J.M. Cordwell and R.A. Schwartz (eds), *From The Fabrics of Culture: the Anthropology of Clothing and Adornment.* The Hague: Mouton, pp. 7–23.

Roseberry, William (1997) 'Afterword', in James G. Carrier (ed.), *Meanings of the Market: the Free Market in Western Culture.* Oxford: Berg, pp. 251–61.

Sahlins, Marshall (1988/1994) 'Cosmologies of capitalism: the trans-Pacific sector of the "world system"', in Nicholas B. Dirks *et al* (eds), *Culture, Power, History.* Princeton, NJ: Princeton University Press, pp. 412–57.

Scheld, Suzanne (2003) 'Clothes Talk: Youth Modernities and Clothing Consumption in Dakar, Senegal'. Ph.D. dissertation in anthropology, Graduate Center, City University of New York.

Schneider, Jane (1978) 'Peacocks and penguins: the political economy of European cloth and colors', *American Ethnologist,* 5: 413–47.

Schneider, Jane (1987) 'The anthropology of cloth', *Annual Review of Anthropology,* 16: 409–48.

Schneider, Jane (1988) 'European expansion and hand-crafted cloth: a critique of oppositional use-value versus exchange-value models', *Journal of Historical Sociology,* 1: 431–8.

Schneider, Jane (1994) 'In and out of polyester: desire, disdain and the global fiber wars', *Anthropology Today,* 10: 2–10.

Simmel, Georg (1904/1971) 'Fashion', in D. Levine (ed.), *On Individuality and Social Form.* Chicago: University of Chicago Press, pp. 294–323.

Skoggard, Ian (1998) 'Transnational commodity flows and the global phenomenon of the brand', in Anne Brydon and Sandra Niessen (eds), *Consuming Fashion: Adorning the Transnational Body.* Oxford: Berg, pp. 57–71.

Skov, L. (2003) 'Fashion-nation: a Japanese globalization experience and a Hong Kong dilemma', in A. Brydon and S. Niessen (eds), *Consuming Fashion: Adorning the Transnational Body.* Oxford: Berg, pp. 215–42.

Slater, Don (1997) *Consumer Culture and Modernity.* New York: Polity Press.

Smart, Allen (1997) 'Oriental despotism and sugar-coated bullets: representations of the market in China', in James G. Carrier (ed.), *Meanings of the Market: the Free Market in Western Culture.* Oxford: Berg, pp. 159–95.

Stephen, Lynn (1993) 'Weaving in the fast lane: class, ethnicity, and gender in Zapotec craft commercialization', in June Nash (ed.), *Crafts in the World Market: the Impact of Global Exchange on Middle American Artisans.* Albany, NY: State University of New York Press, pp. 25–59.

Tarlo, E. (1996) *Clothing Matters: Dress and Identity in India.* Chicago: University of Chicago Press.

Thomas, Nicholas (1991) *Entangled Objects: Exchange, Material Culture, and Colonialism in the Pacific.* Cambridge, MA: Harvard University Press.

Thomas, Nicholas (2003) 'The case of the misplaced ponchos: speculations concerning the history of cloth in Polynesia', in C. Colchester (ed.), *Clothing the Pacific.* Oxford: Berg, pp. 79–96.

Turner, Terrence (1980/1993) 'The social skin', in C.B. Burroughs and J. Ehrenreich (eds), *Reading the Social Body.* Iowa City: University of Iowa Press, pp. 15–39.

Veblen, Thorsten (1899/1958) *The Theory of the Leisure Class: an Economic Study of Institutions,* in Max Lerner (ed.), *The Portable Veblen.* New York: Viking Press, pp. 53–215.

Verger, P. (1954) *Dieux d'Afrique : culte des Orishas et Vodouns à l'ancienne côte des esclaves en Afrique à Bahia, la baie de tous les saints au Brésil.* Paris: Hartman.

Waterbury, Ronald (1989) 'Embroidery for tourists: a contemporary putting-out system in Oaxaca, Mexico', in Annette B. Weiner and Jane Schneider (eds), *Cloth and Human Experience.* Washington, DC and London: Smithsonian Institution Press, pp. 243–71.

Weiner, Annette B. (1985) 'Inalienable wealth', *American Ethnologist,* 12: 210–27.

Weiner, Annette B. (1989) 'Why cloth? Wealth, gender and power in Oceania', in Annette B. Weiner and Jane Schneider (eds), *Cloth and Human Experience*. Washington, DC and London: Smithsonian Institution Press, pp. 37–75.

Weiner, Annette B. (1992) *Inalienable Possessions: the Paradox of Keeping while Giving*. Berkeley, CA: University of California Press.

Williams, Rosalind (1982) *Dreamworlds: Mass Consumption in Late Nineteenth Century France*. Berkeley, CA: University of California Press.

Wilson, Godfrey (1941) *An Essay on the Economics of Detribalization in Northern Rhodesia*, Part 2. Rhodes-Livingstone Papers 6. Manchester: Manchester University Press.

Wolf, Eric R. (1982) *Europe and the People without History*. Berkeley, CA and Los Angeles: University of California Press.

Zorn, Elaine (1985) 'Textiles in Herders' Ritual Bundles of Macusani, Peru'. Paper presented at American Anthropological Association, eighty-fourth annual meeting, Washington, DC.

Zukin, Sharon (2004) *Point of Purchase: How Shopping changed American Culture*. New York and London: Routledge.

14

HOME FURNISHING AND DOMESTIC INTERIORS

Robert St. George

To survey furnishings and interiors requires the neat modifiers of *home* and *domestic* as a means of limiting discussion. Whether one investigates these materials circulating in either historical or ethnographic time and space – or both – they share a common principle: namely, both furnishings and the ways in which particular artifacts – beds, chairs, tables, carpets, lighting devices, television sets, among others – are used to define interior spaces depend on domesticating objects made by others to one's own social position and expressive style. In order to situate their study, this chapter will first ground them in the historical process of enclosure, as we have come to understand its grip on the material life of England in the seventeenth century; with privacy and historically situated assertions of empire at stake, the decisions people make about furnishings and interiors are never simple. How, then, are we to know these material objects? Home furnishings warrant attention first, as historians and ethnographers have made distinct kinds of contributions to their study. But furnishings, as constructed objects, attributed things, emblems of an adherent realm of myth and cosmos, fit together to shape the interior spaces of domestic dwellings. Interiors are what the walls of dwelling houses define. But, unlike the totally empty floor plans published in many studies of vernacular architecture, domestic interiors are social spaces that shape human interaction according to the furnishings a given room contains. This chapter will then connect domestic interiors with the rise and fluorescence of consumer culture in England and America, and the new sense of interiority it sustained.

THE ENCLOSURE OF DOMESTIC FURNISHINGS

From the late sixteenth century through the mid-twentieth, the protracted process of enclosure has conditioned our understanding of both land management and social schism. In south-eastern England between 1580 and 1640 new landlords set up new fences that turned small, rented farms over to grazing and market capitalist agriculture. The class antagonisms felt by their ejected renters brought on riots. The enclosure movement represented for the bourgeois yeomanry a general world-view that linked upward social mobility and the attainment of a kind of spatial privacy previously cherished only by the gentry; to be sure, the profits garnered by this new class of landowners from enclosure allowed them to invest in improved standards of material life and line their interiors with a new panoply of goods. What historian W.G. Hoskins in 1953 called a 'revolution in housing' (Hoskins 1953/1963) was also a great refurnishing as well. As William Harrison described in 1577, those luxury furnishings (arras tapestries, silver vessels, elaborate cupboards) that had long been restricted to the households of nobility and gentry, were becoming more common across the English countryside:

> now it is descended [Harrison observed] yet lower, even unto the inferior artificers and many farmers, who, by virtue of their old and not their new leases, have for the most part learned also to garnish their cupboards with plate, their joint beds with tapestry and silk hangings, and their tables with carpets and fine napery, whereby the wealth of our country

(God be praised therefore and give us grace to employ it well) doth infinitely appear.

(Harrison 1968: 200)

Subsequent to Hoskins's initial treatment of the process, architectural and social historians have been able to prove that the business of rebuilding in some places continued into the early nineteenth century (Machin 1977; Hutton 1977). As rebuildings and refurnishings gained force, however, their net result was an increasing subdivision of interior functions and an underlying bourgeois concern for privacy. So just as houses were subdivided to afford new sleeping chambers, objects as mundane as storage chests were similarly enclosed into ever more specific forms that enabled the enclosure and more classification of individual possessions; first chests with added interior tills, then chests with one or two drawers underneath, and then, in the eighteenth century, full chests of drawers. The 'great refurnishing' is doubly important because its initial timing corresponded to the 'great migration' of English planters to Ireland, first, and then to Virginia, Maryland, and New England. From the perspective of these new planters, the logical end of the enclosure movement was the enclosure of those native peoples they encountered in the search for property, propriety, and a fenced-in sense of identity. The institution of a new and legalized concept of alien property defined the 'settlement' process itself: 'paling' in new territory meant claiming sovereignty, through objects, over newly possessed acreage and objectified peoples.

FURNISHING HOUSES

Historians and specialists in the decorative arts have looked at several kinds of furnishings in detail, and fortunately an impressive bibliography exists that provides overviews to major types – furniture, ceramic and glass, textiles, silver and other metals, among others (Ames and Ward 1989). For present purposes, furniture may serve as a focus for discussion. General social histories of domestic furniture typically argue that furniture forms have increased in number from medieval times to the present, and that as the numbers of chests, chairs, or benches proliferated, their ritual and display functions have decreased in emphasis (Mercer 1969). This argument raises two points of debate. The first presupposes that changes in domestic furniture represented a tension between aristocratic and vernacular traditions. (Consider

Harrison's claim of aristocratic privilege and then wide social diffusion.) In France, Germany, Holland, England, and the United States, furniture study since the mid-nineteenth century has stressed upper-class objects, a social bias in the collection, conservation, and publication of aristocratic artifacts that results in part from museum-sponsored research. From this perspective, curator-scholars (there are exceptions, to be sure) have contributed energetically to the worship of specific objects – their precious materials, innovative technologies of production, and patterns of exquisite workmanship (Symonds 1929; Kreisel 1968–73). Yet since the early 1970s a counter-movement in both England and the United States has shifted attention toward vernacular furniture. In the United Kingdom the effort was spearheaded by Christopher Gilbert (1974), Anthony Wells-Cole (1973), and Bill Cotton (1986), while the North American effort was led by such scholars as Benno M. Forman (1988), Robert F. Trent (1977), Jean Palardy (for French Canada), and Marian Nelson (for Norwegian traditions in Minnesota). After new groups of locally made furniture were documented, questions quickly turned to their use, and such social functions as family genealogy, bridewealth, and dowry. From the sixteenth through the early nineteenth centuries, both chests and cupboards (often with drawers) were made to mark a wedding; they bore the initials of the new couple and the date of their union. Moreover, carrying the symbolic gifts of bed linens, ancestral baptismal gowns, and finely worked underclothing, these movables could be transported from the house of the bride to her new, marital residence (Ulrich 1997).

The second point of debate raises the materiality of the furniture itself. In Anglo-American culture until ca. 1680–1700, almost all furniture was made of oak, with the framing members attached to one another using mortise-and-tenon joints. As a result, a chest made in this way was termed a 'joined chest'. But as anyone who has ever used a cross-cut saw on dried oak knows, there is no way a 'joiner' could have used dried stock and still come out with a tightly constructed final product. Instead, he made the chest using green oak or 'live' wood, which cuts more like butter than iron. For the final chest to dry without warping, the different pieces of a chest had differential moisture contents: a framing member in which a mortise was cut typically was more 'wet' when worked than the piece fashioned into a corresponding tenon. So when the tenon was driven home, it gradually gained moisture from the surrounding mortise and thus 'swelled' to make the joint tight. Dower chests made with this 'live' wood construction method also framed nature in a distinctive manner. A typical joined chest might have three carved panels surrounded by the framed rails and muntins across its front. Whether of flowers, vines, or birds, each carving is bilaterally symmetrical and is thus 'improved' from its natural condition. Such improved flowers, carved into dower chests, also made immediate reference to the cultivation of improved children by a young bride. Early furniture, then, is made of 'live' material and uses artifice to frame an improved Nature with polyvalent meaning.

At the end of the seventeenth century, in England and its colonies, furniture making changed. The mortise-and-tenon joint – the hallmark technology of the trained joiner – was eclipsed by the dovetail joint. Dovetail joints must be worked into wood that is already uniformly dried, and hence the woods commonly used changed from oak to maple, tulip polar, or pine. Dovetails were fashioned by a new specialist artisan, the cabinetmaker. From their advent ca. 1680 until the present, dovetails, once cut, do not shift. They must be totally dry or 'dead' from the outset, especially when surface veneers – expensive in the early eighteenth century, but the superficial stock in trade of Ikea and Ethan Allen alike – needed a steady substrate for the necessary adhesive to bond. Along with the dovetail – used both for case furniture made of dried boards as well as for drawer construction – the description of Nature changed as well. Whereas artifice framed an improved Nature in the earlier joined tradition, it now shifted to decorative detailing – delicate floral vines, painted tendrils, even the interconnected S-scrolls borrowed from gravestone iconography – that marked the edges of artifice executed from dead material.

If we return to question our beginning argument – that as chests, chairs, and benches increased in quantity between 1500 and 1800, their ritual functions decreased in emphasis – we can now sketch some alternative explanations. Perhaps as woodworkers shifted from 'live' (green) to 'dead' (dried) material in the fabrication of furniture, its ritual significance decreased as its semiotic openness to personification, moving from life to death, gradually closed down; after about 1700, the use of carved and dated dower chests, for example, almost disappeared. In a similar fashion, once the artificial framing of an improved, even perfected, Nature shifted to a more trivial, decorative border on dovetailed case furniture, perhaps the ritual incorporation of Nature lessened as well. The shift may be restated: from Art as a means

of improving Nature, to Nature – now glowing with a Romantic agency of its own – as a means of improving artifice. Since the middle of the eighteenth century, materials and designs may have changed and changed again, but the production of 'dead' artifacts in which Nature has a fetishized force of its own over Art continues, barely interrupted.

FIELDWORK ON FURNISHINGS

Alongside changes in the historical study of European traditions, fieldwork in furniture design and production has emphasized materials, construction, and technology in order to better comprehend creativity and community aesthetics; we have studies as diverse as Estonian furniture crafts, the production of Turkish framed *sandiklar* or chests by Mustafa Sargin, and the constant rearrangement of dressers in Northern Ireland (Viriis 1969; Glassie 1982: 362–70, 1993: 165–78). In addition, curators of ethnology and natural history museums own examples of North American Indian furniture forms. Many of these, including the wide range of quillwork boxes made by the Micmac in Nova Scotia, conform to indigenous storage forms – round baskets, oval and rectangular boxes with both flat and gently rounded lids – commonly placed on raised interior platforms. In other instances, native forms such as cradles and settees suggest the incorporation of European forms into local design vocabularies. For example, a nineteenth-century New England kitchen chair reaching the Kwakiutl was disassembled, its seat shaped into a beaver's back and splat carved as its tail, and then reassembled. Or a factory-produced side chair (ca. 1870–80) made in Halifax has a slip seat made from Micmac quillwork, effectively turning the object into a kind of trophy at the dining-room table of its owner (Whitehead 1982: 148). On occasion, specific furniture forms are even claimed to have mythological significance. Certain storage boxes made by the Haida and Tlingit peoples are decorated, according to one scholar, with 'a mythical sea spirit, Kow-e-Ko-Tate', the implication being that home furnishings played a role in diffusing mythology into daily life (Inverarity 1950: cat. No. 22 [unpag.]). Another scholar has suggested that the carvings are appropriate because the box is 'used to store items imbued with supernatural power' (Walens 1981: fig. 2 caption, fac. p. 82). The same thing could be said of seventeenth-century historical furnishings from

Anglo-America. Puritan poet Edward Taylor versified his beliefs;

O! Box of Truth! tenent my Credence in
    The mortase of thy Truth: and Thou in Mee.

These Mortases, and Tenents make so trim,
    That They and Thou, and I ne'er severd bee.
    Embox my Faith, Lord, in thy Truth a part
    And I'st by Faith embox thee in my heart.

(Taylor, 1977: 172)

Ordinary domestic furnishings perform the work of metaphor that ties the sensate present to a contingent realm of myth and cosmos. Interior spaces of domestic dwellings overlap with the interior spaces of belief and lived religion. On one hand, historical studies must rely on visual documentation of interiors in prints and paintings, and at times suffer from the same elitist social bias that conditions the images themselves (Thornton 1984; Saumarez Smith 1993). Some probate inventories did proceed room by room, and thus leave a rudimentary listing of room names as well as contents. But where a given chest was actually placed in a bedchamber, or where in a kitchen a television might be located, suggests that only ethnographic studies are able to document precisely what things – and in what positions – a room contained at a given point in time. Occasionally, work appears that so integrates close study of extant buildings, interior fittings, geographical transmission, and probate records that it nearly imagines the interiors back into existence. One such study examines the density of surviving materials in early Quebec houses (Leahy 1994); another, which focuses on migrant artisans from Anabaptist-Mennonite villages in Russia and Poland-Prussia to Nebraska, Iowa, and Kansas during the period 1870–1920, is able to connect houses, case furniture, and the routines of farm work. For these migrants, the interior was less a cosmic container than a space for family labor and enforced gender domains. In part, the Anabaptist-Mennonite society carried to the Great Plains the rigid division between men at large in society and women doing unpaid labor at home that they had safeguarded as part of Prussian peasant culture. At the same time, once in the United States they found this customary world supported by the conservative message of such parlor-and-kitchen theorists as Katherine Ward Beecher, who reinforced their understanding of maternal domestic nurture sanctioning the public, reputation-sparring prowess of male heads of households.

At nearly the same time that Mennonite families were settling the plains, the earliest anthropological studies sensitive to the description of domestic interiors began to appear. They explored the material culture of American Indians. In 1891 Victor Mindeleff published *A Study of Pueblo Architecture in Tusayan and Cibola*. While most of the text (and site plans) concentrates on the planning of large and densely settled Indian villages, specific sections of the book address 'interior arrangement' and 'stools and chairs' (Mindeleff 1989: 108–11, 213–14). Robert H. Lowie first described the interior of Crow tipis in 1922, with prompt amplification in his 1935 study *The Crow Indians* (Lowie 1922, 1935). Historic photographs gathered in anthologies on American Indian architecture make one point clear: indigenous peoples frequently adapted European and American furnishings to their own strategies for interior space and, in so doing, redefined the object being appropriated. Thus a late nineteenth-century photograph of the interior of Haida Chief Weah's 'Monster House' shows mass-produced kitchen chairs and tables stacked on the giant platforms arranged around the structure's central hearth (Nabakov and Easton 1989: 267). The same integration of consumer goods happened much earlier. In 1761 Rev. Ezra Stiles of Newport, RI, visited a series of Niantic wigwams along the Connecticut shore. He made a series of detailed drawings showing the plan of the house and its interior sleeping platforms. On the platforms were trade goods – a small table with turned legs, a chest of drawers, a frame box and, suspended over the hearth, a blacksmith-made pot hanging from a trade trammel (Sturtevant 1975). After studying the organization of Indian dwellings for a century, scholars now argue that interior layouts are often keys to both kinship and cosmic connection (Nabokov and Easton 1989: 32, 38–9). In other words, indigenous households pursued interior strategies under the pressures of split cultures. Instead of imagining any single means of cultural reproduction guaranteeing interior spaces as merely 'customary', American Indians had to appropriate new technologies and imported goods in such as way as to assemble a strategy for survival amid the mixed materialities of cultural colonization.

In the post-World War II years, the same concern for interior organization diffused from American anthropology into ethnological and folkloristic research. In 1951, Northern Irish geographer E. Estyn Evans included a brief discussion of house plans and the location of some basic household furnishings in *Mourne Country*, his portrait of south County Down. Six years later, his *Irish Folk Ways* illustrated variants of Irish two- and three-room plan houses with drawings of the precise placement of bed, dresser, table, bench, and churn (Evans 1951: 196, 1957: 42, 63, 66). Shortly after Evans's work appeared, it had an immediate impact on I.F. Grant, who included a chapter on 'Furnishings and plenishings' in *Highland Folk Ways*. While Grant did illustrate Scots chairs, dressers, and cradles, he made no effort to show their position in the rooms of a standard highland two-room cottage (Grant 1961: 167–97).

In south and central Europe during the same decades, work of a different sort was under way. In 1959 French sociologist Paul Chombart de Lauwe published his innovative *Sciences humaines et conceptions de l'habitation*. In many ways the book served up a critique of what modernist architects (including Le Corbusier) were promising in the 1920s and 1930s. The designers maintained that their visionary housing complexes could ameliorate the poor housing conditions of France's industrial working classes. Based on actual engaged work with families living in *habitations degradées*, Chombart concluded his argument with these words: 'No regeneration of architecture will be possible if it is not a direct response to the needs of families, and in the first place to the needs of those families which, while having modest financial means, nonetheless express their desire for a habitation that conforms to new necessities' (Chombart 1959: 97). Only when the actual needs of working families are known through ethnographic interviewing can adequate new architecture conform to their basic needs. Subsequent to Chombart's work, Christian Bromberger's nuanced treatment of 'Les manières d'habiter' of working people in rural Provence suggests a set of interior demands similar to those of Paris's laboring classes, including: maintaining the kitchen as *un espace polyvalent*, with a full complement of table, hearth, bedding; conceiving of the interior as an area of labor and petty production; and conceiving of the interior as a consecrated space where rituals attendant on birth, marriage, and death are celebrated and where images of revered saints may preside over certain rooms (Bromberger 1980: 98–9, 105–7, 110–11). In 1969, Hungarian ethnologists Édit Fél and Tamás Hofer illustrated two house plans and their rudimentary fixtures – stove, kitchen sink, bench – in a rural laborer's house built in 1876 (Fel and Hofer 1969: 80–1).

While research in Europe progressed during the 1960s, sociologist Pierre Bourdieu was working on the domestic layouts of Kabyle dwellings in North Africa. In a pair of drawings he prepared of a small dwelling that combined one room for people with a small stable under the same roof, Bourdieu detailed the location of furniture, food mill, and water jars on one side of the structure, and water and fodder troughs for animals on the other. He argued that human movement in the house was constant and mediated a fundamental pair of oppositions – one between internal and external space, the other between areas of gendered labor. Each of these divisions mediated additional oppositions: 'Thus, the house is organized according to a set of homologous oppositions: fire : water; cooked : raw; high : low; light : shadow; day : night; male : female; *nif* : *homa*; fertilizing : able to be fertilized; culture : nature. But in fact,' he concluded, 'the same oppositions exist between the house as a whole and the rest of the universe' (Bourdieu 1973: 102, 107–8).

Evans's and Bourdieu's studies, and their drawings – Evans's anecdotally rich, Bourdieu's descriptive of schematic process – have had a lasting effect, in part because they were direct influences on folklorist Henry Glassie as he began ethnographic work on a small district in County Fermanagh in the early 1970s. Glassie's *Passing the Time in Ballymenone* (1982) ranges across many expressive genres, but includes scale drawings of: 'Mrs Cutler's kitchen' and its artfully arranged dresser; a house in Derrygonnelly showing the placement of furniture and functional groupings for 'cooking', 'talking', 'eating'; and 'Change in the kitchen', with eight floor plans that show how furniture groupings change when a front hall is inserted in a house to buffer the kitchen from the public way (Glassie 1982: 355, 357, 396–7, 411–13). Through his emphasis on interiors, Glassie inserted gender in the center of his work. As he phrased it, this was a switch in his own *modus operandi*: 'In this chapter I improve upon my earlier studies of housing,' Glassie admitted, 'by moving from the outside to the inside, from form to use, from house to home. That shift entails a change of emphasis from male house builders to female home makers' (Glassie 1982: 760 n. 1). In other words, the shift was from people who make objects *qua* objects to those who create subjectivities from the object world. With his drawings Glassie set a standard for ethnographic studies of domestic interiors, as Gerald L. Pocius's study of 'everyday space' in Calvert, Newfoundland, made clear. Pocius's *A Place to Belong* (1991) augmented scale drawings with an actual listing of the furnishings used in the village ('Table 7: Major furniture items in three Calvert houses'); it is as if he were making a probate inventory of a house that was still in active use. His scale drawings of interiors include details previously overlooked. 'Tom and Ida Sullivan's kitchen', for example, shows such possessions in location as a television, garbage can, water heater, 'boots on rubber mat', daybed, and rocker, among other items. When Pocius turned his eye on the contents of the Sullivan's 'front room', he included chairs and couches as well as the 'clear plastic strips' that protect the floor, a stereo, and a 'portable TV' (Pocius 1991: 229, 231, 240).

Ranging from William Harrison's description of ordinary farmers owning tables, carpets, and bedsteads with silk hangings in the 1570s to the uses of dressers and stools in the Irish kitchens studied by Evans and Glassie to the oppositional logic that Bourdieu discovered in Kabyle dwellings, home furnishings describe many points in the protracted, historical process of symbolic enclosure. But what about the plastic strips and portable televisions found in the households that Pocius studied in Calvert? And what of the selective appropriation of ready-made furnishings and trade goods in American Indian dwellings from the 1760s through to the present? These latter questions suggest a second historical trajectory that defines domestic interiors: the beginnings and irregular expansions and contractions of consumer culture.

CONSUMING INTERIORS

Consumption provides our third approach to the study of interior furnishings and domestic space. Recall this key component of the enclosure movement: As market agriculture generated profits for new freeholders in the seventeenth century some yeomen farmers had sufficient capital to purchase new kinds of things in greater quantities. Historian Joan Thirsk argued in *Economic Policy and Projects* (1978) that the new zeal among country farmers as well as among London merchants for small purchases of ready-made goods moved England to a consumer economy by the 1640s. Inventories of estate provide clues to the rapidity of the new commercial market for furnishings. In mid-Essex between 1635 and 1690, for instance, the total number of chairs owned in the community by yeomen at their death rose from thirty five to 439 – even as the population decreased slightly – with a similar rise in the numbers of ordinary stools, from sixty six to 301. By the 1620s most yeoman farmers had invested between one-quarter and one-third of their wealth in household movables, including furniture, textiles, and plate. Seventy years later the percentage had risen in some rural parishes to almost one-half (Forman 1988: 85; St. George 1982: 229).

From its origins in early modern England, consumer culture has been steadily elaborated and consolidated through such techniques as mechanized production, advertising, and the rise of centralized commercial sales sites (department stores beginning in the mid-nineteenth century, shopping centers in the 1920s, and shopping malls in the 1950s). Thus studies of consumerism now range chronologically from the 1630s to the 1730s to the nineteenth century – with an emphasis on the articulation of *fin-de-siècle* opulence) – to the modern mall of the mid-twentieth century and its martial displays of anti-modernist nostalgia (Brewer and Porter 1993; Bermingham and Brewer 1995; Mukerji 1983; Lears 1981; Fox and Lears 1983; Shi 1985). Consumer culture thus spans the expanding geographies of the rise of mass marketing for clothes, shoes, and shovels, advertisements for soap and sex, and malls that promise a standardized contemporary faith in – as well as the predictable fault lines of – what one author has terms the 'consumer republic' of twentieth-century America (Lears 1994; Cohen 2003).

One effect of consumer culture on interior spaces has been to drive an awareness and desire for things ever inward; the path moves from such concerns as brand-name loyalism and direct-sales evangelicalism to the repeated wearing of 'lucky' shoes and pants, to an almost complete identification of one's inner desires and fantasies with advertisement imagery and (via radio, television, and the Internet) its seductive, endlessly rehearsed and jingled soundtrack, to the complete sublimation of self to external strategies of manufactured desire. Thus one path of new work has led to a new sense of how such disparate objects as paintings of interiors, advertisements for household appliances, visits to museums or retail stores with room settings, may each shape the interiority of individuals in accordance with a commodity aesthetic (Agnew 1989). It follows that a key element of such interiority depends on the articulation of a desire for things as an elemental part of a sense of self. Precisely where to locate the driving force behind interiorization has no easy answer. Stewart Ewen and Elizabeth Ewen argue that our consciousness has been the target of consumption media – advertisements, radio, television, to which we might now plausibly add the pop-up adds that often accompany e-mail and Web hosting clients. For the Ewens, the problem is so pervasive because consumerism has become 'a way of life' (Ewen and Ewen 1982/92: 23–52) though which we assimilate, fragment by fragment, the in-dwelling cohesion of commercial capitalism.

For other scholars of consumer culture, it has been the singular force of department stores and the seductive relationship between painting, display window decoration, and fantasy escapes into perfect 'dream worlds' of entertainment and consumption where material stability is shared but no rivalry exists. As William Leach has observed, it was no accident that L. Frank Baum, author of the *Oz* stories (think of the illusionary blue beauty of Munchkinland, or the outright hucksterism of those green glasses in Oz), began his working life as an actor in 1880, and then moved on to a dreamier kind of theater; he became was a window decorator and, in 1897, founded the successful trade journal *The Show Window*. The following year he launched the National Association of Window-Trimmers, a trade association hailed by such leading department store merchants as Marshall Field as 'indispensable' to the process of building year-round desire for consumer goods (Leach 1993: 59–60). As Field's comment suggests – and as Leach develops – responsibility for the interiority of commodity desire was (in part) orchestrated by merchants keen to shape popular consciousness in such a way as to keep people buying while remaining blissfully unaware of how their taste was already manipulated.

Perhaps, however, the relentless striving for self-fulfillment that interiority may privatize for evaluation is driven by demand, not coercive supply (Carson 1994). In a competitive post-*Wealth of Nations* neoclassical economy, individuals may search for objects to domesticate to their own self-interest. From this perspective, people *de jure* have whole concepts of the self; they interiorize a commodity aesthetic assembled from the flotsam and jetsam of circulating goods – like that beaver-seated kitchen chair, or the dining chair with a quill-work cushion. Chairs with beaver seats and quillwork cushions warrant attention in this regard precisely because they so effectively show the strength with which creativity in colonized cultures rises up against the forms of inevitable political subordination that condition their daily work and family life. Chairs of this hybrid sort are master works of aesthetic *bricolage*. Interiorized signs also offer the possibility that desire might shape a communicative logic from the buyer's perspective, thereby reinforcing Mary Douglas's insistence that the semiotic promise of commodities as communicative ciphers of moral significance, might trump their coercive or manipulative qualities (Douglas and Isherwood 1979: 59–62).

Finally, the architecture of private interior souls vindicates Richard Sennett's dark argument in *The Fall of Public Man* that public life in modern Western society changed dramatically between the eighteenth and the twentieth centuries (Sennett 1977). What began as a culture of market squares and of enlightened souls meeting in taverns and coffee houses to hammer out contemporary controversies in politics, the economy, and aesthetics gradually began to turn inward. A new sense of personal privacy – defined in part through evangelical religion and reform ideologies that focused on the individual *qua* individual – undercut the established sense of a public group consciousness. Indeed, as private souls searched for political safety, publicity evaporated into a series of more fully psychologized individual subjects who subtracted their visible status for a protected and therapeutically defined social being. It is no accident that the white noise humming beneath this new subtractive person was the teeming life of interior furnishings – beds, rugs, chests, lamps, televisions, laptops, cell phones, and Game-boys – and all those things that have gradually enclosed and consumed our lives.

REFERENCES

Agnew, Jean-Christophe (1989) 'A house of fiction: domestic interiors and the commodity aesthetic', in Simon J. Bronner (ed.), *Consuming Visions: Accumulation and Display of Goods in America, 1880–1920*. New York: Norton, pp. 133–55.

Ames, Kenneth L. and Ward, Gerald W.R. eds (1989) *Decorative Arts and Household Furnishings in America, 1650–1920: an Annotated Bibliography*. Charlottesville: University Press of Virginia for Winterthur Museum.

Bermingham, Ann and Brewer, John, eds (1995) *The Consumption of Culture, 1600–1800: Image, Object, Text*. New York: Routledge.

Bourdieu, Pierre (1973) 'The Berber house, or, The world reversed', in Mary Douglas (ed.), *Rules and Meanings: the Anthropology of Everyday Knowledge*. New York: Penguin Books, pp. 98–110.

Brewer, John and Porter, Roy, ed. (1993) *Consumption and the World of Goods*. New York: Routledge.

Bromberger, Christian (1980) 'Les manières d'habiter', in Christian Bromberger, Jaques Lacroix and Henri Raulin *L'architecture rurale Française, corpus des genres, des types et des variantes: Provence*. Paris: Musée Nationale des Arts et Traditions Populaires.

Carson, Cary (1994) 'The consumer revolution in colonial British America: why demand?', in Cary Carson, Ronald Hoffman and Peter Albert (eds), *Of Consuming Interests: the Style of life in the Eighteenth Century*. Charlottesville: University

Press of Virginia for the Unites States Capital Historical Society, pp. 483–697.

Chombart de Lauwe, Paul (1959) *Sciences humaine et conceptions de l'habitation*. Paris: Centre National de la Recherche Scientifique.

Cohen, Lizabeth (2003) *A Consumer's Republic: the Politics of Mass Consumption in Postwar America*. New York: Knopf.

Cotton, Bill (1986) *The Chair in the North West: Regional Studies in the Eighteenth and Nineteenth Centuries*. Burnley: Burnley Borough Council.

Douglas, Mary, with Isherwood, Baron (1979) *The World of Goods: Towards an Anthropology of Consumption*. New York: Norton.

Evans, E. Estyn (1951) *Mourne Country*. Dundalk: Dundalgan Press.

Evans, E. Estyn (1957) *Irish Folk Ways*. London: Routledge.

Ewen, Stuart and Ewen, Elizabeth (1982/92) *Channels of Desire: Mass Images in the Shaping of American Consciousness*. Minnesota: University of Minnesota Press.

Fél, Edit and Hofer, Tamás (1969) *Proper Peasants: Traditional Life in a Hungarian Village*. Chicago: Aldine.

Forman, Benno M. (1988) *American Seating Furniture, 1630–1730*. New York: Norton.

Fox, Richard Wightman and Jackson Lears, T.J., eds (1983) *The Culture of Consumption: Critical Essays in American History, 1880–1980*. New York: Pantheon.

Gilbert, Christopher (1974) 'Regional traditions in English vernacular furniture', in Ian M.G. Quimby (ed.), *Arts of the Anglo-American Community in the Seventeenth Century*. Charlottesville: University Press of Virginia, pp. 43–78.

Glassie, Henry (1982) *Passing the Time in Ballymenone: Culture and History of an Ulster Community*. Philadelphia: University of Pennsylvania Press.

Glassie, Henry (1993) *Turkish Traditional Art Today*. Bloomington: Indiana University Press.

Grant, I.F. (1961) *Highland Folk Ways*. London: Routledge.

Harrison, William (1577/1968) *The Description of England*, ed. Georges Edelen. Ithaca: Cornell University Press.

Hoskins, W.G. (1953/1963) 'Rebuilding of rural England', in *Hoskins' Provincial England: Essays in Social and Economic History*. London: Macmillan, pp. 131–8.

Hutton, Barbara (1977) 'Rebuilding in Yorkshire: the evidence of inscribed dates', *Vernacular Architecture*, 8: 819–24.

Inverarity, Robert Bruce (1950) *Art of the Northwest Coast Indians*. Berkeley: University of California Press.

Janzen, Reinhild Kauenhoven and Janzen, John M. (1991) *Mennonite Furniture: a Migrant Tradition, 1766–1910*. Intercourse, PA: Good Books.

Kreisel, Heinrich (1968–73) *Die Kunst des deutschen Möbels. Möbel und Vertäfelungen des deutschen Sprachraums von den Anfängen bis zum Jugendstil*, 3 vols. Munich: Beck.

Leach, William (1993) *Land of Desire: Merchants, Power, and the Rise of a New American Culture*. New York: Vintage.

Leahy, George W. (1994) *L'Ornamentation dans la maison québécoise aux XVIIe et XVIIIe siecles*. Quebec: Septentrion.

Lears, Jackson (1981) *No Place of Grace: Antimodernism and the Transformation of American Culture, 1880–1920*. New York: Pantheon.

Lears, Jackson (1994) *Fables of Abundance: a Cultural History of Advertising in America*. New York: Basic Books.

Lowie, Robert H. (1922) *The Material Culture of the Crow Indians*. Anthropological Papers of the American Museum of Natural History 21 (3). New York: Trustees of the American Museum of Natural History.

Lowie, Robert H. (1935) *The Crow Indians*. New York: Holt Rinehart.

Machin, Robert (1977) 'The great rebuilding: a reassessment', *Past and Present* 77 (November): 32–56.

Mercer, Eric (1969) *Furniture, 700–1700*. New York: Meredith Press.

Mindeleff, Victor (1891/1989) *A Study of Pueblo Architecture in Tusayan and Cibola*. Washington, DC: Smithsonian Institute Press.

Mukerji, Chandra (1983) *From Graven Images: Patterns of Modern Materialism*. New York: Columbia University Press.

Nabokov, Peter and Easton, Robert (1989) *Native American Architecture*. New York: Oxford University Press.

Pocius, Gerald L. (1991) *A Place to Belong: Community Order and Everyday Space in Calvert, Newfoundland*. Athens, GA: University of Georgia Press.

Saumarez Smith, Charles (1993) *Eighteenth-Century Decoration: Design and the Domestic Interior in England*. New York: Abrams.

Sennett, Richard (1977) *The Fall of Public Man: On the Social Psychology of Capitalism*. New York: Knopf.

Shi, David (1985) *The Simple Life: Plain Living and High Thinking in American Culture*. New York: Oxford University Press.

St. George, Robert Blair (1982) 'A Retreat from the Wilderness: Pattern in the Domestic Environments of Southeastern New England, 1630–1730'. PhD dissertation, University of Pennsylvania.

Sturtevant, William (1975) 'Two 1761 Wigwams at Niantic, Connecticut', *American Antiquity*, 40 (4): 437–44.

Symonds, R.W. (1929) *English Furniture from Charles II to George II: a full Account of the Design, Material and Quality of Workmanship of Walnut and Mahogany Furniture of this Period, and of how Spurious*

Specimens are made. New York: International Studio.

Taylor, Edward (1977) *The Poems of Edward Taylor*, ed. Donald E. Stanford. New Haven: Yale University Press.

Thirsk, Joan (1978) *Economic Policy and Projects: the Development of a Consumer Society in Early Modern England.* Oxford: Clarendon Press.

Thornton, Peter (1984) *Authentic Decor: the Domestic Interior, 1620–1920.* New York: Viking.

Trent, Robert F. (1977) *Hearts and Crowns: Folk Chairs of the Connecticut Coast, 1720–1840.* New Haven: New Haven Colony Historical Society.

Ulrich, Laurel Thatcher (1997) 'Hannah Barnard's cupboard: female property and identity in eighteenth-century New England', in Ron Hoffman, Mechal

Sobel, and Fredrika J. Teute (eds), *Through a Glass Darkly: Reflections on Personal Identity in Early America.* Chapel Hill: University of North Carolina Press, pp. 238–73.

Viriis, Anton (1969) *Woodworking in Estonia*, trans. J. Levitan. Jerusalem: Israel Program for Scientific Translation.

Walens, Stanley (1981) *Feasting with Cannibals: an Essay on Kwakiutl Cosmology.* Princeton: Princeton University Press.

Wells-Cole, Anthony (1973) *Oak Furniture from Gloucestershire.* Leeds: Temple Newsam House.

Whitehead, Ruth Holmes (1982) *Micmac Quillwork: Micmac Indian Techniques of Porcupine Quill Decoration, 1600–1950.* Halifax, NS: Nova Scotia Museum.

15

VERNACULAR ARCHITECTURE

Suzanne Preston Blier

DEFINING THE VERNACULAR

The term 'vernacular architecture' over the last half-century has come to represent a farrago of building traditions that lie outside canonical largely Western building exemplars created generally by formally trained architects. From the Latin *vernaculus*, meaning native, indigenous, domestic, or subaltern (*verna* referencing local slaves), vernacular connotes popular as opposed to elite idioms. In contexts of language, vernacular evokes not only spoken language and dialect in contradistinction to literary form, but also everyday language instead of scientific nomenclature. In architecture specifically, the term 'vernacular' embraces an array of traditions around the world – everyday domiciles, work structures, non-elite places of worship, and cultural sites (battlegrounds and tourist centers, for example) as well as both colonial/settler and settlements. The term also embraces a range of other architectural forms outside the West (elite and otherwise) that long have been overlooked in Western scholarly study. Thus in addition to comprising a large number of structures which generally have been excluded from the study of canonical Western architectural forms, the term 'vernacular architecture' also has provided a salient alternative for the larger grouping of buildings once called 'primitive' – a both pejorative and notably arbitrary classification which set apart the larger grouping of non-Western architecture from Western and Asian exemplars (see also Myers in Chapter 17). Forms of vernacular architecture in this way comprise a vast majority of the world's architecture, works remarkable at once for their geographical breadth, historical depth, and socio-cultural diversity. Vernacular forms include small-scale structures of hunter-gatherers as well as global exemplars of empire (see Buchli in Chapter 16), structures which have endured through millennia and those whose ephemeral features last for only a few weeks or months.

The study of vernacular architecture historically has been of broad cross-disciplinary interest. Related scholars and practitioners comprise not only anthropologists, archaeologists, architectural historians, and architects, but also historians with a range of interests, folklorists, geographers, engineers, museum curators, and community activists – some focusing on issues of materials and construction methods, others on socio-cultural concerns, still others on the history of form and the needs and practicalities of preservation. Vernacular architecture scholars have addressed questions of spatial use and planning, regional variations in form, race and/or ethnic variables in building typology, landscaping and land use (see Bender in Chapter 19), agricultural idioms, suburb enclaves, squatters' communities, and global urban settings. Increasingly energy sustainability and issues of climate also have become a significant feature of vernacular architecture discussion. Related analyses also have broached standard architectural questions with respect to structure, sources, symbolism, patronage, and the unique input of the designer, as well as larger issues of building use. (See also Myers in Chapter 17.)

Despite the importance of vernacular architecture within the larger discussion of built environment, the use of the term vernacular architecture has strong detractors, with

Norberg-Schulz (1971) and Bonta (1977) among others arguing that singling out 'vernacular' structures from other architectural exemplars represents a form of fallacious thinking. As Güvenç points out (1990: 285) 'By dictionary definition and popular use, "vernacular" and "architectural" suggest a semantic differential that may imply some kind of logical contradiction'. Architecture is architecture, they maintain, regardless of when, where, by whom, or for whom it is created. Güvenç adds (1990: 286):

> Before the so-called modernization of the architectural profession, a good portion of the built environment in the world was what today we would call 'vernacular.' It is fundamentally a human activity (although there are interesting comparable forms in nature), and as such addresses vital considerations at both the individual level and society as both narrowly and broadly concerned.

The complaints are valid. Indeed, vernacular, like other building taxonomies, reveals as much about modern (largely Western) classification values as about the salient issues addressed by the structures themselves. Among other things, the prominence of binary oppositions posited *vis-à-vis* 'vernacular' versus 'polite' architecture (Brunskill 1970), or what was once called 'primitive' (pre-literate, pre-industrial) buildings versus industrial, urban, and elite forms (Fitch 1990: 266) reveals the enduring nature of Western dualistic thinking. Similarly, tripartite classification schemes such as those which distinguish vernacular, folk, and modern traditions (Edwards 1979), and quadripartite taxonomies which differentiate so-called primitive (pre-literate), vernacular (pre-industrial and other), popular, and high style buildings (Rapoport 1969) all reflect prominent Western typological and classificatory considerations between self and 'other' framed to a large degree on social evolutionary grounds. Studies such as these have tended to see the largely non-Western, rural or ancient architectural expressions as framed by considerations of physical need (security, shelter) and environment (materials, climate), rather than technological know-how, innovation, and concerns with social and creative expression. If there is one thing that the case studies of global architecture have made clear, it is that buildings, even those of a seemingly rudimentary nature, are shaped fundamentally by decisions of individuals as well as communities and convey notable differences between them.

Vitruvius' *De Architectura* (*The Ten Books of Architecture*), written in the first century BCE – the earliest surviving text on the subject – sets out a trilogy of core architectural values, these comprising *utilitas* (suitability), *firmitas* (structure), and *venustas* (aesthetic consideration). Similar factors of function, technology, and visual primacy can be said to be at play in architectural traditions around the world – both vernacular and elite. Moreover, the imperative of building forms with respect to these elements features prominently in related scholarship. As Vitruvius noted: 'Architecture is a science, arising out of many sciences and adorned with much and varied learning ...' Extending in part from the above, Vitruvius maintains that the creators of these works should be acquainted with diverse fields of knowledge, among them astronomy, philosophy, and music. Those who study these architectural exemplars, it follows, similarly must seek to understand an array of factors – local theories concerning the natural world, taxonomies of thought, ancillary arts and ritual – among other factors.

EARLY AND INFLUENTIAL SCHOLARSHIP

From the earliest days of anthropology, forms that today have come under the broader rubric of vernacular architecture have figured prominently. Among the notable early anthropological texts which signaled this interest were studies of Native American architecture, most notably those of L.H. Morgan (1881), V. Mindeleff (1886–87), and Franz Boas (1888). In scholarly writings in other fields, too, the importance of building forms were being addressed, as for example E.S. Morse's (1886) exploration of Japanese homes and their surroundings. Through the eyes of these writers, architecture and other elements of the built environment were central to understanding society more generally.

Interest in vernacular form continued through the twentieth century, culminating in the establishment of the Vernacular Architecture Group in 1952 to promote the study of traditional buildings in varied world contexts. The Vernacular Architecture Forum was founded in 1980 (accessible now through the Web) pressing for documentation and preservation of local and regional building traditions. An extensive global and cross-disciplinary bibliography on related scholarship (*The Vernacular Architecture Newsletter Bibliography*) accessible also on the Web builds on the scholarly database first compiled by folklore scholar and vernacular proponent Dell Upton in 1979. Many vernacular architecture advocacy groups at both the local and regional level similarly have been established throughout the world and are also accessible through Web sites and publications. The study of vernacular architecture also now has its own journal, *Perspectives in Vernacular Architecture*, these volumes to date focusing largely on American vernacular traditions.

Peter Nabokov (1990) provides an overview of the diverse building traditions. Carol Herselle Krinsky's 1997 study of contemporary Native American architectural traditions looks at questions of cultural regeneration and creativity. Her volume looks at a broad sweep of building types, houses, religious and community structures, clinics, schools, office buildings, museums, and casinos. Among other issues she raises are the various strategies involved in defining an array of contemporary and historical cultural values. Other sources include Jett and Spencer's (1981) study of Navajo architecture with respect to form, history, and distribution as well as Patricia L. Crown's (1985) overview of morphology and function in Hohokam structures. (See also Lekson (1986) and Morgan (1994)). Pre-Columbian vernacular architecture has also seen both broad overview studies and local monographs. Among the former is Heyden (1975b) and Kowalski (1999). With regard specifically to Peruvian forms, see Gasparini and Margolies (1980) and Moore (1996) among others. Scholars interested in addressing related considerations in archaeological settings include Chang (1968), Hodder (1982), Hodder and Orton (1976) and Kroll and Price (1991).

There also have been two excellent review essays which address broad vernacular architecture interests, one by Lawrence and Low (1990) which appeared in the *Annual Review of Anthropology*, a second by Parker-Pearson and Richards (1994). An anthology concerned with the anthropology of space and place by Low and Lawrence-Zuniga (1988) also brings together a range of important articles on this subject with contributions by Miles Richards, Nancy Munn, Pierre Bourdieu, Deborah Pellow, James Fernandez, Margaret Rodman, John Gray, Hilda Kuper, Theodore Bestor, Akhil Gupta, Arjun Appadurai, Gary McDonough, Paul Rabinow, and Michael Herzfeld among others. Mari-Jose Amerlinck's 2001 anthology, *Architectural Anthropology*, also makes clear the global primacy of the built environment to the very fabric of society.

The publication of Paul Oliver's three-volume *Encyclopedia of Vernacular Architecture of the World* in 1997, which includes entries by some 750 authors from more than eighty countries, makes clear that vernacular architecture has come into its own as a field of study. The first volume of this comprehensive work focuses largely on theoretical issues and related principles – addressing a broad range of approaches to global building form. Included in this volume as well are explorations into variant thematic concerns, among these the impact of environment (climate and topography), the nature of building (craftsmanship and production), and critical concerns with architectural typologies (structural factors and technique). Among the other issues raised here is the role of color (the primacy of blood color in Swedish barns, for example) and the use of color triads in architectural decoration in many parts of the world. The second and third volumes of this encyclopedia are organized by larger geographic considerations, with associated essays providing a sense of the variety of architectural form, along with socio-political, environmental, historic and other considerations.

Studies of vernacular architecture have followed somewhat different paths across the disciplines. One of the most important anthropological volumes which also impacted the field more generally is Daryll Forde's groundbreaking *Habitat, Economy, and Society* (1934), which offers not only vital data from a range of cultures around the world, but also an interpretative model for the study of building traditions outside the West, addressing among other things the relationship between housing concerns, economic factors, environment, and social organization. Key examples taken up by Forde offer convincing evidence of both the complexity and diversity of building traditions of populations across the globe. The primacy of the socio-political in shaping the built environment is a particularly noteworthy part of Forde's exegesis, a work which countered long-standing views that climatic considerations and issues of shelter were the most salient determinants of building form in these cultures.

Three publications concerned with vernacular architecture were especially important in the fields of design and architectural history. The first is Sibylle Moholy-Nagy's *Native Genius in Anonymous Architecture* (1957), a book widely read by design students of the era which foregrounded the importance of vernacular architecture. A second is Alexander's *Notes on the Synthesis of Form* (1964) which sought to counter the long-standing myth that vernacular architecture constituted essentially unspecialized work and was created without conscious intervention. Vernacular works, Alexander suggests, even if one does not know the name of their designers, evoke genius and a deep understanding of the power and potential of form. In many respects, the most influential of the mid-century authors is Bernard Rudofsky, whose *Architecture without Architects* of 1964 accompanied a ground-breaking exhibition by the same name at the Museum of Modern Art in New York. This volume with its rich pictorial format promoted the aesthetic power of vernacular structures across the globe. In his discussion, Rudofsky further brought into the realm of elite architectural scrutiny buildings designed and built by ordinary people which had hitherto been ignored or dismissed in academic architectural circles. The title of his work, like that of Moholy-Nagy's above cited book, goes to the heart of the difficulties posed by prior Western classificatory schemas, and the general insistence that to be considered as 'architecture' buildings had to be designed by academically trained architects. By labeling these works as 'native' or 'anonymous', Rudofsky and Moholy-Nagy broadened the canon of what was considered as architecture. Moreover, as Rudofsky would insist in his 1977 study, 'non-pedigreed' building exemplars evidence a 'way of life' which has special aesthetic and moral value because they reflect greater popular input and appeal. Roger Scruton in his 1994 *The Classical Vernacular: Architectural Principles in an Age of Nihilism* goes on to suggest that vernacular exemplars not only are visually among the most powerful but also evince a moral integrity which should serve as a model for elite modern building forms.

Oliver has criticized (1990: 23) one aspect of this vernacular focus, namely its general insistence on anonymous design, suggesting that in global vernacular architecture, as in elite architecture in the West, trained individuals with technical know-how and design skills also are important, these figures serving roles in many ways analogous to architects even if they do not have academic degrees. Among others Oliver cites as providing functions analogous to Western-trained designers are Chinese diviners, Maori building *tujunga*, and Navajo singers involved in the Blessingway. Oliver adds with pointed reference to Rudofsky (1964):

> even in traditional societies 'architecture without architects' appears to be the exception rather than the rule: most durable cultures have developed, in one guise or another, the specialized interpretation of cultural values and norms through built form. The people who exercise this function, and who rarely bear the title *architect*, are often both 'designers' and 'contractors': They are custodians of the rules of both design and construction.

Central to this issue (and to the broader question of what constitutes 'architecture' is the role of a given 'architecture'. The phoneme *archi* refers to chief, deriving from the Greek *archos*, meaning ruler, suggesting perhaps less the underlying hierarchy of forms than the ways in which local individuals recognized for their experience in building (and design) activities play a prominent role in related traditions.

Technical knowledge is important too. Mitcham has noted in this regard (1979: 172) that the term 'architecture' historically has placed a primacy on core aspects of technique (*techne* in Greek). Thus the Greek word *techne* means craft or skill, deriving from the Indo-European *tekhn* (probably related to the Greek word *tekton*, which references woodwork and carpentry. The term also shares compliments with the Sanskrit *taksan* (carpenter, builder), the Hittite *takkss* (to build or join), and the Latin *texere* – to weave, as for example to construct a roof. Drawing on the importance of technique, Heidegger (1977) explores two complementary features of *techne*, in the first case the knowledge and practices of the principal actor (the craftsman or builder), and in the second, the primacy of the creative (the mind) and the aesthetic. Architecture, like other forms of expression in this sense, comprises at once process (acts) and results (products).

HISTORICAL FACTORS OF CHANGE, THE PRIMACY OF TRADITION, AND PRESERVATION

One of the larger issues that has shaped discussions of vernacular architecture over the last half-century is that of change. Related questions are important both to broader historical considerations of society and culture, and to the ways in which visual forms such as buildings evidence factors of both stasis and change which actively impact the societies that create and use them. Some authors have maintained that vernacular building and settlement forms are largely static idioms that cannot be studied historically. Other scholars see built form and settlements as evidencing epiphenomenal evolutionary changes as defined through adaptations to salient factors experienced by the society more generally. A third perspective views vernacular architecture as a dynamic mode of human expression, with related changes largely being 'purposeful'.

The perspective that vernacular architecture is a fundamentally static form shaped much of the scholarship on vernacular architecture through the 1960s and 1970s. In addition to Rapoport (1969), see also Rudofsky (1964) and Guidoni (1975). Characteristic of the second adaptive perspective of change are Hardie's 1985 analysis of Tswana house forms and settlements in southern Africa as well as Coiffier's 1990 overview of change in Sepik River architectural models. Other studies of this genre, among these Glassie's 1975 examination of Virginia house form over time, point to broader rules that may be reflected in these changes. Lawrence maintains (1990) in turn that vital differences exist between types of societies and how they respond to environment and other factors of change. Lekson (1990) uses a biological evolutionary model to suggest that change largely results from environmental disturbance, and that structures are at once adaptive constant and conservative (see also Lawrence 1990; Smith 1975).

Countering the stasis and adaptation models are a range of largely field-based analyses which suggest that major building changes are purposeful. Broad cross-regional studies of specific types of building forms make clear the complexity of related issues. (See also Roxana Waterson's 1989 analysis of migration and its impact on Indonesian vernacular architecture and Frishman and Khan's (1994) examination of the mosque in its historical and cross-cultural settings.) In Africa, studies of major architectural change, among these differences resulting from the expansion of the Manding (Dyula) across the Western savanna (see among others Prussin 1970 and Lane 1994) evidence how building typologies have altered over time. In some cultures (the Fon of Benin and the Dogon and Bamana of Mali), earlier housing forms sometimes were preserved as temples.

Many of these issues also impact the growing architectural and cultural preservation movement. As noted above, architectural preservation projects have been a particularly lively focus of local vernacular support groups and related journals, among these *Historic Preservation*. There also have been a range of related studies addressing this issue from a global perspective. Charles Anyinam notes (1999) how sacred space, practices of indigenous medicine, and concerns with ecosystem preservation intersect in East Africa. In Thailand, to the contrary, where historical preservation has not had broad acceptance, according to Alexander (1986), this is due largely to Buddhist views of the world, in which buildings, like people, are not meant to survive for ever. Hobsbawm and Ranger's ground-breaking

1983 anthology *The Invention of Tradition* explores the ways in which idioms of 'tradition' are created or given new shape in contexts of historic change. The issues raised in this volume also are important from an architectural preservation perspective. (See also Highlands (1990: 56) on the question of indigenousness.)

THEORECTICAL UNDERPINNINGS OF VERNACULAR ARCHITECTURE STUDY

That different methodologies shape our understanding of vernacular architecture is a given. With respect specifically to the Dogon of Mali, several studies suggest how scholarly perspectives impact related findings in fundamental ways. French anthropologist Marcel Griaule and his colleague Germaine Dieterlen brought Dogon architecture to the attention of the West through their elaboration of its rich cosmological symbolism (1954, 1965). Dutch anthropologist Walter Van Beek suggests (1991, 2001) that earlier ethnography concerning this and other factors of Dogon life is flawed. Unable to replicate Griaule's findings, Van Beek argued that, rather than addressing larger cosmological concerns, Dogon social expression (including architecture) was in key respects framed by questions of need. Adding to the fray have been two ethnoarchaeological analyses of the Dogon, one by Paul Lane (1994) the other by Jean-Christophe Huet (1994). Both studies, which address the temporal dimensions of Dogon architecture and settlements, maintain that the Dogon, rather than being an isolated population living at the very edge of Western Sudanese civilization, instead evidence notable cultural influences and architectural changes over the course of their history, the response in part to religious, political, and commercial shifts affecting this region of Islamic influence and empire expansion more generally. Indeed, rather than constituting an intact ancient civilization removed from the region's ebb and flow as promoted by Griaule and to some degree Van Beek, the Bandiagara escarpment inhabited by the Dogon seems to have been a sociocultural hodgepodge reflecting traditions of variant disenfranchised populations who over the centuries have sought the protective refuge of these mountains.

As Huet explains (1994: 48), the Dogon homeland in the Bandiagara represents not so much a site of 'origin' (as Griaule argues in largely cosmogonic and mythic terms) but rather a place of emergence and renewal. In short, these ethno-archaeological studies have allowed a more complex reading of this setting, suggesting that mythic idioms of 'origin' elaborated by Griaule with respect to Dogon architecture may have been promoted in part to cover a larger 'lack' within the social fabric. The long history of regional slavery in this area also seems to have impacted Dogon architecture and local perceptions of it, with many Dogon having been enslaved by nearby Islamic states, and these populations, once freed, returning to the Bandiagara cliffs in the late nineteenth and early twentieth centuries, seeking to promote in their built environment – even in their mosque architecture – a sense of homeland and shared ancestry (Blier 2004). Like the nature of society more generally, these studies suggest that vernacular architecture has been shaped by an array of concerns, including the variant perspectives of scholars who study them.

Functionalist approaches to building form, following on the work of British anthropologist E.E. Evans-Pritchard (1940) among others, has tended to highlight a broad range of practical considerations – environment, materials, sociopolitical factors, economy, and security – as determinants of form, siting, and signification. Among the numerous related studies which have addressed architecture are those of Prussin (1969), Rapaport (1969) and Van Beek (1991). While functionalist perspectives have tended to privilege the relationship between buildings and socio-economic practice, one of the problems with this approach is that many building forms are created which in whole or part lie outside broader functional considerations with respect to, among other factors, belief and aesthetics.

Beginning in the 1940s and continuing into the 1960s, French anthropologists drawing on the earlier writings of Émile Durkheim and Marcel Mauss (1967) with respect to the linkage between systems of thought and social practice focused on the symbolic aspects of traditional building form, saw these works as reflecting insights into *mentalités*, as evidenced in part through cosmological beliefs and idioms of the human body (see, among others, Lebeuf 1961 and the above cited works of Griaule). Such studies, however, in their overarching symbolic focus have often left an impression that everyday thought and actions are predominantly symbol-driven and ritualistic.

In the early 1960s, anthropologist Claude Lévi-Strauss began to reconfigure the above largely localized French academic studies of systems of thought into a broad cross-cultural theory of internal dualisms. Lévi-Strauss's influential *Structural Anthropology* (1963) and *Tristes Tropiques* (1974) showed the striking manner in which village plans, axiality, and notions of the body reveal comparables across a range of cultures and contexts. Irish anthropologist Mary Douglas left the largely secular functionalist orientations of her British colleagues, to promote the primacy of rituals of pollution in architectural and other dimensions of human experience central to Catholicism and many other religions in her seminal *Purity and Danger* (1966). Douglas addresses the related symbolic dimensions of domestic space (1972), and her works have provided important structuralist insights into how vernacular (and other architectural models) are shaped in their form, action, and belief through dualistic idioms. Pierre Bourdieu's study of the Berber house (1973), Hugh-Jones's elaboration of village planning and house forms in the Amazon river region (1979), Feely-Harnik's overview of Saklava domestic architecture in Madagascar (1980), and Cunningham's examination of Atoni houses in Indonesian Timor (1973), all are paradigmatic structuralist engagements with vernacular architectural form and signification. The applicability of structuralist theory to Western vernacular forms also has been addressed, as for example in Lawrence's (1987) investigation of the English house in both its secular and its sacred features.

One of the more innovative of these structuralist architectural studies is Fernandez's analysis of Fang architecture and village planning in Gabon (1977), which points to important complementarities between dualistic village planning considerations and the game of *mankala* within this largely acephalous political setting. The game itself, which is widely played both in Africa and the adjacent Islamic world, features a board or ground defined by a series of pockets along each side of a long rectangle, as well as two pockets at each end. In many respects, the Fang community with its two rows of buildings facing each other across a neutral space shows visual parallels with this game board (including the presence of structures at each end), complements which, as Fernandez points out, also find expression in how the village functions as a whole. Fernandez's game board/village parallel is a provocative one, if also calling up an array of questions, among these how the *mankala* game board, an import form in this region, came to assume architectural primacy for the Fang. Beginning in the early 1980s, structural analyses came under scrutiny with respect to their often overly deterministic dualistic and ahistorical tendencies, as well as their emphasis on structure at the expense of process and anomaly.

The languages of architecture also have been an important focus of scholarship with respect to vernacular and other forms of architecture. Some studies such as that of Basso (1996) examine the ways in which specific language use informs notions of place in specific cultural areas. Building terms, as well as the very structure of language (noun classes, for example) also offer insight into architectural meaning (Blier 1987: 226 ff.). Other scholarship informed by questions of language has sought to theorize architectural form in a more global way, particularly with respect to semiotic considerations first espoused by Saussure (1916), Peirce (1931–58) and later Eco (1976, 1980). Scholars addressing larger semiotic concerns have taken up, among other things, the ways primary architectural elements such as center points, symmetry, and means of access, carry, by their very nature, important elements of cross-cultural signification in the same way that certain grammatical considerations have broadly universal validity. Donald Preziosi's 1983 study of early Minoan building forms draws on grammatical elements of the semiotic to explore considerations of design, structure, and meaning. Criticism of semiotic models has been published by Leach (1978) and others. In addition to concerns with respect to the primacy of structure and stasis within many semiotic studies, other issues have been raised about how cogently a universal theory of signification can address complex variables at the local and individual level. In short, if center points, axial symmetry, and access points are universal, what do they really tell us about building and social variation?

The study of vernacular architecture also has been shaped in important ways by concerns with psychology, behavior, and issues of healing. Larger considerations of behavioral psychology and architecture have been published by Broadbent (1973), Heimsath (1977), and Hall (1990) amongst others. Research by these scholars has emphasized both the psycho-sensory characteristics of architectural form and the socio-psychological factors impacting architectural experience. Cooper (1974) takes up specifically Jungian architectural models in examining the house as archetype. The importance of vernacular architecture in contexts of healing is documented by Day (1990) in the examination of the ways in which the very form of architecture and related aspects of environment nourish the soul. See also Tuan et al. (1991) and Tuan and Hoelscher (1997/2001) on the emotional dimensions of space, and the core spiritual needs addressed by architecture. On memory and architecture see Yates's ground-breaking (1966) work on mnemonic factors with examples such as the Globe Theatre. Vital links between architecture and behavior also are explored in a broad-reaching anthology on space and human behavior edited by Grøn et al. (1991). Psychological disorders that find expression in spatial idioms also have been taken up. See among others Simmel's study of urbanism and mental life (1948/1971) and Bartlett's 1994 exploration into how spatial forms figure in psychiatric abnormalcies particularly vis-à-vis purification rituals and idioms of order. As a caution, it should be emphasized that while buildings can create conditions in which particular forms of behavior or response find expression (or may be fostered), it is individuals who are the ultimate determinants of how actions and ideas are addressed within any built environment.

The phenomenology of the built environment, or how experiences are shaped by the buildings in which we live, work, and worship also has been the subject of study, with variant authors arguing that the meaning of architecture is rooted fundamentally in our experiences of these structures (Rasmussen 1959). Because vernacular building forms often have been seen to be in some ways more 'honest' in expressing the needs and aspirations of their residents and builders, questions of ontology as evinced through the phenomenology of architecture have been accorded special value with respect to vernacular exemplars. Related scholarship draws in important ways on the writings of Heidegger (1977, 1978), Bachelard (1969), and Norberg-Schulz (1971/1980, 1985) among others, particularly with respect to links between the symbolic and the real. Anthologies rich in vernacular exemplars which have addressed the phenomenological dimensions of the built environment in everyday lived experience include Buttimer and Seamon (1980) and Seamon and Mugerauer (1985). At the same time it is worth noting that questions of architectural phenomenology have meant quite different things to scholars in diverse disciplines. In architectural history a greater emphasis on ontology and the lived experience of architecture broaden the dominant historical model of a field which has long privileged architects and design history over the users (residents) of these forms (Blier 1987). In other disciplines, such as anthropology, phenomenology has brought into play a greater consideration of the multidimentionality of these works and the changing nature of built form in new sociocultural arenas. See for example Bender's (1998) study of the ways in which Stonehenge has been reinvested with meanings by modern visitors.

Henry Glassie's contributions to vernacular and particularly domestic architecture (1975, 1995, 2000), are reflective of this larger phenomenological interest, as contextualized through the varied details of everyday lived experience. His 1995 study of culture and history in the Ulster community of Ballymenone is a striking exegesis, rich in ethnographic detail and critical insight. His descriptions of life in the Irish kitchen as seen in ceremonies of tea and the positioning of kitchen furniture offer vital insights into the relationship between place, practice, and both individual and social identity (see St. George in Chapter 14). From religion to Gaelic poetry, songs to work, the volume offers an insightful view into how homes define a people. To Glassie, a folklore scholar, vernacular architecture involves an ongoing social engagement with materials, technologies, and cultural knowledge. As he explains, vernacular architecture evidences not only the complexity of cultures but also their changing circumstances. In Glassie's words (1990: 280) 'Vernacular architecture records subtly but insistently the history of a people'. Glassie sees vernacular architecture in this way as providing vital evidence of a range of social and cultural values. He stresses the importance of seeing architecture as an accumulation of 'experiences through participation', with personal investment shaped by cultural need, these structures helping to construct unique visions of the worlds in which people live.

Post-structuralism, and the broad array of theoretical perspectives drawn largely from Frankfurt School critical theory, as framed around issues of resistance, the subaltern, colonial/postcolonial impact, and globalization have helped to define the study of vernacular architecture in important ways. The cojoining of psychology and political dominance as addressed by theorists such as Theodor Adorno has brought to the foreground vital connections between the aesthetic and political realms in architectural perspective; see among other sources *Aesthetics and Politics* and Fredric Jameson's forward to this work (1980) as well as Soja (1989). Neil Leach provides (1997) extracts from theorists who have focused on the built environment from this vantage, including not only Adorno, but also Gaston Bachelard, Georges Bataille, Jean Baudrillard, Jean François Lyotard, and Gilles Deleuze. Michel

Foucault (1973: 207) also has examined the oppressiveness of architectures of dominance, calling our attention to how building forms identified with brutal political systems (e.g. prisons, slave markets, and apartheid government complexes) impact the societies in which they were built. Borden (2002) has studied the way in which contested spaces and related social concerns have shaped the urban landscape. Davis (1992) elaborates vital dimensions of urban space conceptualization – the junkyard and fortress idioms – in Los Angeles.

Mark Wigley's *The Architecture of Deconstruction: Derrida's Haunt* 1993 looks at the unique problems posed by buildings within the broader sociopolitical arena. In addition to addressing core architectural dimensions of Derrida's discourse (idioms of place, space, and domestication, among others), he also points out the underlying dialectic between belonging to a home and desiring to break out of this enclosure. Humans do not build homes, he maintains, but act out in their architectonic exemplars deep concerns with invasion and destruction. Homelessness, nomadism, and destruction are among the considerations of desconstructionist scholars addressing vernacular and other architectures. There also have been an array of architectural studies which have focused on questions of poverty. See, among others, Hassam Fathy's 1973 overview of housing endeavors to address contexts of poverty in rural Egypt. See also James Scott (1998) on how certain state schemes to ameliorate the human condition often have failed.

Among the criticisms of post-structuralist and deconstructionist approaches to architecture is the concern that while purporting to privilege the native (local, subaltern) vantage in their focus on the global, these studies often promote the view that little other than resistance (response) is available to such populations at the macro level. Such studies also frequently overlook the ways in which local exigencies serve to fundamentally shape and give meaning to buildings in contemporary global contexts. These works at the same time have tended to emphasize the uniqueness of the postmodern situation, with little consideration of the long-standing importance of core global or resistance considerations in historic situations around the world. For example, Henry David Thoreau (1966) spoke eloquently of the importance of architectures (and lifestyles) of resistance in nineteenth-century America. Other related concerns are addressed below.

PHYSICAL ENVIRONMENT AND THE SHAPING OF ARCHITECTURE

Physical considerations of environment as defined by available materials, technologies, sites, and climatic considerations have been an important focus of scholarly considerations of vernacular architecture from a broad range of theoretical vantages. As noted above, Forde's *Habitat, Economy, and Society* (1934) presented a thoroughgoing challenge to core assumptions of the era that environment (climate) was the principal determinant of vernacular building form. Forde was able to show not only the striking differences between structures created in similar ecological conditions around the globe, the tropics for example, but also how buildings created from similar materials and techniques reference notably variant symbolic and sociocultural forms. Ecological perspectives nonetheless have continued to shape scholarly discussions such as those of Fitch and Branch (1960) and Rapoport (1969).

Typical of many environmental studies is Lee's 1969 geographical overview of house types in the Sudan, suggesting that architectural differences here reflect climatic variations, with round houses being built in the south because of heavy rainfall, and earthen rectilinear structures predominating in the north as a reflection of more arid conditions. As Aloba points out, however (1998: 127), not only are there important areas of overlap in Lee's examples, with circular and rectilinear house types being found together in certain areas, but also other factors are mentioned by Lee as impacting architectonic form, among these prestige, culture, and war history. Aloba's own (1998) study of borderland communities in the Yoruba area of southwestern Nigeria emphasizes the primacy of the age and history of the settlement as well as the owners' occupation, ethnic identity, and status. Archaeological and other evidence in areas of the western Sudan suggest a shift over the course of the last millennium from circular structures to rectilinear forms, suggesting that climate here too is not the most important determinant. Holahan (1978) presses for a more dynamic perspective of environment, behavior, and structure, suggesting that the impact of environment on built form is neither passive, direct, nor broadly predictable.

While it seems to be untenable to seek a purely environmental source for core vernacular architectural decisions and differences, there is little doubt that environment and geographical factors impact architectural form and community planning. Minge's 1991 study of how Acoma buildings relate to the land is an important contribution to this subject. Other scholarship on this issue includes Michael Coe's 1961 analysis of differences at Tikal (Mexico) and Angkor Wat (Cambodia), a comparative analysis which looks at variables in typology in these two tropical forest civilizations.

Questions of water also have received notable scholarly consideration. Wells, canals, drains, irrigation, water management, and the sociocultural significance of boats which serve as houses are among the many subjects raised. Water concerns go back to early settlement history, as explored in, among other works, M. Jansen's 1993 study of wells and drainage systems five millennia ago in Mohenjo Daro. The challenges posed by water also have been a factor of Mexican early settlement scholarship, as discussed by Coe (1964) on the transformation of wetlands in Mexico into gardens and settlements. In other regions, the challenge posed by exceedingly arid climates also has been taken up. In late Andean contexts, local irrigation forms have been addressed in Netherly's (1984) study of land use and settlement. J. Nicolais's (1971) investigation of water as an element in urban Nepal looks at these issues in contemporary design. On the use of canals see Adams (1982) for the Maya and Ortloff (1988) on pre-Inka Peru. Civil engineering and nautics in China are elaborated in J.A. Needham's multivolume introduction *Science and Civilisation in China* 1971. In these various works, the issue of technological skill in addressing variant environmental conditions is emphasized.

There also has been ongoing interest across a range of fields into broader ecological and architectural concerns with respect to larger energy considerations. Vernacular architecture often has been seen to offer an important model for addressing ongoing problems of scarce resources. Solar factors in architecture are taken up in Knowles's study of the Acoma (1974, 1981). Concerns such as passive cooling systems in hot and arid climates are addressed in Bahadori (1978), Shearer and Sultan (1986), and Prakash et al. (1991). The latter study of earthen construction in the north-west Himalayan area is published as part of the Sustainable Development series, an important forum (and consideration) in a number of similar publications. Issues of poverty and the larger problem of housing the world's poor through building models which are at once ecologically viable and cost-efficient have been a focus of a wide array of studies, among these Fathy's overview of housing in Egypt (1973, 1986). These authors often address not only design considerations but also questions of cost and return. What is important to emphasize with respect to these works is that the authors see environment not as a determinant of architectural form but rather as a given that builders creatively address through their selection of materials and effective design choices, related works sometimes serving as models for contemporary building practice in a range of comparable settings elsewhere.

Tim Ingold's (2000) study of architecture and environment argues that, instead of focusing our attention on the cultural variation of form, we should be looking at variation in skill in addressing the environment as framed by considerations of both biology and culture. Some of the most interesting work being done in this area is that being produced in the field of humanist geography (see among others, Adams et al. 2001). In this volume, the last few decades of geographical study are addressed, specifically with respect to how humans transform the world. Much of this work also reveals the longstanding impact of Yi-fu Tuan (1974, 1977, 1991), and his emphasis on human choice, with a range of insights – materialist, normative, and aesthetic – coming into play.

In the same way that environment can be seen to pose important challenges and potentialities with respect to vernacular architecture, so too nature more generally also has been addressed with respect to models in human building practice. A classic text in the exploration of these issues is C. Alexander's *A Pattern Language* (1977). Bees, hornets, termites, birds, and in some cases lower primates are among the many species who build structures remarkable for their technical expertise and aesthetic interest. Like the use and making of tools, one of the central concerns in these discussions is how to viably differentiate animal and human building imperatives, and the factors dividing the two. Following Marx, Yi-Fu Tuan (1977: 102) singles out awareness (consciousness and intent) as the most salient means of distinguishing human and natural construction. The question of choice (selection) here too is important. As Norberg-Schulz has noted 'what we select from nature to serve our purposes, we also call architecture. ... Our ability to dwell is distinguished from that of a bird living in a nest by our inherent awareness that we are not mere things'. (1971: 37) That said, it is also important to note that forms from nature – spheres, shells, termite mounds, nests, caves – have long provided vital visual and technical models for human building efforts. From this vantage one can also point to the primary

place that core mathematical constructs also may play in the conceptualization of form. See, for example, E. Baldwin-Smith's 1978 study of geometric modeling in domes.

HOUSE, HOME, DOMESTICITY, AND MOBILITY

By far the largest corpus of structures examined within the context of vernacular architecture comprises domestic or residential forms. The sociocultural dimensions of design are addressed by Rapoport (1969), Prussin (1969), Bourdier and Minh-ha (1997), Raulin and Ravis-Giordani (1977), and Benjamin and Shea (1995), among others. The inherent connection between social organization and domestic spaces also has been taken up by Ian Hodder in his 1978 anthology (see also his 1990 study of domestic structures and domestication in Europe), and the work of Birdwell-Pheasant and Lawrence-Zuniga (1999). Richards's contribution to Hodder's 1978 work provides a thoughtful overview of related issues, foregrounding the diverse ways that the social world imprints the built environment and the visual clues that connect the two. See also Myers (1986), Wilson (1988), and Duncan's cross-cultural anthology (1981) on housing and identity. Two other notable books on the spatial and socio-iconic primacy of domestic structures include Samson's (1990) volume on the social dimensions of housing in archaeological contexts and Kent's (1990) anthology on domestic architecture cross-culturally. Kent's own contribution to this latter study looks at the relationship between sociopolitical complexity and the built environment; see also her broad reaching 1991/1995a essay on the ethno-archaeology of the home. Larger issues of identity as expressed through housing are explored by C.C. Marcus (1993) with respect to the deeper meaning of dwellings. On identity factors in domestic architecture see also Sircar (1987), Arhem (1998), and Csikszentmihalyi and Rochberg-Halton (1981), the latter focusing on domestic symbols of self in different social settings. Gregory and Urry (1985) look at housing forms as sites where social relations are both produced and reproduced. Another work which looks at architecture, social structure, and considerations of space over time is Mark Horton's (1994) discussion of the Swahili built environment. On the global impact and issues of village modernity in Togo see Piot (1999). Wright's socially redolent analyses of housing in the United States (1981, 1985) examines how idioms of moralism shape American housing form. Issues of self-reference are taken up in the (1985) volume edited by I. Altman and C.M. Werner on home environments framed around concerns with not only housing, but also homelessness; E. Relph (1976) studies complementary issues of place and placelessness. For other factors of space, place, and politics see Doreen Massey (1993).

A broad array of scholars has addressed questions of gender and sexuality with respect to housing and spatial organization, among these Shirley Ardener (1981), Daphne Spain (1992), Beatriz Colomina (1992), and Diana Agrest et al. (1996). Sanders's anthology *Stud: Architectures of Masculinity* (1996) also looks at core spatial considerations of gender. Ethnographic studies of space provide vital and diverse details of gender in building form, use, and symbolism. Huntington (1988) examines these concerns in Madagascar and Houseman (1988) looks at Beti housing contexts. Townsend (1990) documents the ways in which settlement forms reflect gender and other concerns in the Sepik river of Papua New Guinea. Issues raised by Nast (1993) with respect to Hausa spatial conceptualization in Kano also look at gender, in this case shaped by both Islamic and local considerations. Celik Zeynep (1996) examines gender issues in colonial Algiers. The importance of gender in the construction of space in ancient contexts has been explored by Rendell et al. (1999) and Gero and Conkey (1991), among others. Lisa Nevett (1994) queries separation versus seclusion idioms in ancient Greek household contexts. With specific reference to contemporary forms of housing and implications for gender in the United States see Hayden (1982/2002) and Friedman (1998) on the roles of women in the making of design decisions. In Native America, the special roles of women as builders have been addressed by Wolf (1972) and Brasseur (1976) with respect to tipis.

Considerations of spatial mobility also have come to the foreground in a range of studies. Okley (1983) addresses nomadic considerations in life and settlement configuration within gypsy communities. Stone Age archaeological contexts of mobility in terms of strategies of space and site use are taken up by Susan Kent (1991). Margaret C. Rodman's (1985) essay on residential mobility in Longana, Vanuatu, is a provocative discussion of Polynesian patterns of spatial movement. The primacy of migration in Indonesia as well as its impact on local architectural and cultural forms is explored in Waterson (1989). Still another noteworthy

contribution is Humphrey's (1974) study of the Mongolian *yurt*, which examines the striking ways that Buddhist cosmological beliefs shape these native forms, with core elements suggesting at once local and broader Asian religious values.

Tent forms which predominate in the circum-Sahara region of south-west Morocco are examined by Andrews (1971). Labelle Prussin's 1995 overview of African nomadic traditions also makes particular reference to the prominent roles of women as builders and home owners. She also looks at the symbolic dimensions and adaptability of these forms. In southern Africa, Biermann's 1977 study of Zulu domed dwellings points to the primacy of symbolic considerations; Kuper (1993) looks at the ways in which Zulu nomadic forms also convey important political concerns. A sizable grouping of scholars also have addressed nomadic architecture among the Mbiti (Turnbull 1961) and the !Kung and other Kalahari residents, among the latter publications are works by Lee (1972), Silberbauer (1981), and Kent (1995b). In these case studies, we see the central socio-symbolic load that nomadic housing forms carry in communities in which material goods are often minimal.

Related theoretical issues also have been addressed in post-structuralist contexts. See especially Gilles Deleuze (with Felix Guattari 1987), a complex, theoretically provocative volume called *A Thousand Plateaus: Capitalism and Schizophrenia*. This work looks at how, in new global economies, transnational mobility has in some cases led to a sense of schizophrenic unease, in which housing insecurity is given heightened primacy. Lynette Jackson also has pressed this discussion into the foray of the new global economy in her provocative 1999 essay on 'stray women', mobility, and issues of disease in colonial and postcolonial Zimbabwe. Allan Wallis's (1989) study of house trailers and how they constitute exemplars of both innovation and accommodation is also of broad interest. Mobility now, as in the past, is shaping the lives of individuals and communities in ways that impact vernacular architecture and the perception of it.

The dominant emphasis on social factors and others has come under some criticism for privileging housing–social interconnections above other considerations. Shea (1990), for example, points out that sociological development cannot effectively be indexed by technological development, urban propensities, or population density, indicating that there are far too many exceptions to make for any viable rule. So too, as Shea explains (1990: 30), 'economic factors and, in particular, modes of production, are part of – not independent of – culture, and contribute importantly to vernacular settlement'. Studies also have made clear that buildings are part of larger regional and global interactions and that these factors also are important.

ANTHROPOMORPHISM, WORLD VIEW, COSMOLOGY, ASTRONOMY, AXIALITY

Not surprisingly in light of the primacy of the human as models of sociocultural construction, anthropomorphic idioms figure prominently in building symbolism. Anthropomorphism is one of architecture's universals, and in many cultures specific body-linked terminologies and actions are identified with core building parts. Bloomer and Moore's *Body, Memory, and Architecture* (1977) addresses the centrality of anthropomorphism in Western architectural contexts. House facades constitute the 'face' of the dwelling, garbage containers – like the end point of digestion – are placed often at the domicile rear, and the fireplace mantle – like the heart or soul – is a repository for family mementoes, a function also taken up in the kitchen (in particular the refrigerator) with its array of family snapshots and reminders. Among the broad range of ethnographic studies emphasizing anthropomorphism are Lebeuf (1961), Griaule (1965), and Malaquais (2002). Another important and influential text is Y-F. Tuan's eloquent *Topophilia* (1974) with its exploration of the intersection of the human body and a range of spatial considerations. Tuan, a geographer by training, offers a broadly philosophical analysis of the aesthetics of environment and the affinities which have long existed between humans and landscape.

The fashioning of world view finds widespread expression in building form as well. Interest in this question has been long-standing, as seen in, among other sources, William Lethaby's 1891 *Architecture, Mysticism and Myth* with its examination of the iconic elements of housing. Mircea Eliade's widely influential writings (see especially 1959) also have shaped related discussions in important ways with their highlighting of the connections between dwelling forms and features of sacred space. Paul Oliver (1975) brings together a range of scholarly contributions which address this from both theoretical and regional perspectives.

The importance of the house as an *imago mundi* is widespread too. In many contexts, a rich array of metaphoric elements come into play. See among others Littlejohn's (1967) examination of the Temne house, Bourdieu's 1973 elaboration of the interface between the Berber built environment and world view, Kuper's (1980) discussion of the symbolic dimensions of Bantu homesteads, and Tilley's (1999) provocative volume on metaphor and material culture, which includes important references to architecture. Dolores Hayden's (1976) thought-provoking work on seven American utopian communities and related architectural forms points to among other exemplars how Shakers convey vital attributes of their sect through design and related ritual practice. As Hayden notes, core features of simplicity and honesty as expressed in Shaker furniture reveal core religious tenets of material and spiritual 'truth'. Cities, in particular newly planned capitals, also express core utopian values. Such centers – among these Brasilia – also have been seen to have core problems (Holston 1989). Related concerns are also seen in architectural manifestoes (Conrads 1971), with texts by among others Adolf Loos (1982) on ornament and crime, Frank Lloyd Wright (1963) on the importance of organic architecture, and Buckminster Fuller (1973) on the architect as world planner.

With reference specifically to building traditions and world view in China, see Chang (1956) and Krupp (1989). Hindu traditions expressing factors of body, cosmology, and space are often cojoined in temple architecture (Beck 1976; Snodgrass 1985; Slusser 1982). Cosmological considerations in the Native American southwest also have been frequent subjects of scholarly interest, going back to, among other texts, White's (1962) discussion of cosmology in Pueblo life, Ortiz's (1969) examination of Tewa space, and Witherspoon's (1977) overview of Navajo *hogan* structures. Religious and other symbolism specifically linked to caves has been taken up as well, among these Vedic and Saiva contexts (Bäumer 1991). Heyden (1975a) shows the sacred importance of the cave in the central Mexican highlands site of Teotihuacan.

Axial positioning and ritual movement figure importantly as well. Lethaby's above cited 1891 volume makes particular note of the primacy of the rising sun in an array of communities and historical contexts around the world. Also see Irwin (1980) on axial symbolism in early Indian *stupas* and Meister (1991) on similar concerns in various Indian temple sites. Krupp's 1989 examination of axial positioning in early Beijing and Deal's 1987 analysis of Mayan ritual space and architecture also offer important insights. On the relationship between building traditions and astronomic perceptions see Aveni's publications on archaeo-astronomy in pre-Columbian America (1977) and architectectural dimensions of non-Western time keeping (1989).

Rykwert's *On Adam's House in Paradise* (1981) reveals how models of primeval house forms figure in later architectural exemplars in a range of contexts. Lord Raglan's *The Temple and the House* (1964) draws on a range of traditions to argue for the primacy of the house as temple (rather than shelter *per se*), drawing on idioms such as foundation rituals, hearth-fire symbolism, material use, and primary shapes (house form) to support this view. See also his 1965 discussion of the origin of vernacular architecture with respect to religious concerns in domestic architecture more generally, as well as Deffontaines's (1972) discussion of the links between vernacular built form and both belief structures and ritual practices. In addition to the role that domestic structures play in conveying religious concerns, specialized ritual structures are also important, among these Shinto shrines (Watanabe 1974), Meso-American ball courts (Scarborough and Wilcox 1991), Igbo structures erected in honor of local deities (Cole 1982), and Polynesian Marae and Heiau temple complexes (Emory 1969; Kolb 1992). In various areas of Melanesia, larger community-built structures also assumed vital religious significance. See Hauser-Schäublin (1989) on the rich symbolism of men's houses in the Sepik river area of Papua New Guinea and Waterson's 1990 examination of religious and other forms in Indonesia.

BUILDERS, TECHNOLOGIES, AESTHETICS, AND DECORATION

Some of the most enduring issues of vernacular architecture have been those of building technology and construction. The range of issues involved in the construction of a Malay house are addressed in Gibbs et al. (1987). Needham's 1971 exploration of engineering factors in Chinese architecture is important as well. See also Arnold's examination of building practices in Egypt (1991) and Stanier (1953) on cost considerations in building the Parthenon in early Athens. On Mayan building technologies see Pendergast (1988) and Abrams (1994). Protzen's 1993 volume on Inka architecture and construction techniques also addresses a range of related concerns. Paul Oliver (1990) takes up the critical

question of vernacular know-how in broader comparative terms, pointing to the ways in which construction knowledge necessarily embraces broader features of material experimentation and adaptation.

In addition to exploring the input of individual and community traditions of construction, a number of studies also have looked at the role guilds have assumed in building processes in certain areas. In the western Sudan, guilds established during periods of empire (Mali, Songhai, and Hausa, among others), which were comprised initially of persons forced into the service of the state, played an important role. Some guild members eventually rose to positions of power, status, and wealth (see Moughtin 1985). In the Djenne area of Mali, many of these guild-linked masons were members of the indigenous population who, because of their ritual primacy in the area, were seen to have unique abilities to address spirits of the land. The impact of African slavery populations on architectures of state not only in this Western Sudan area, but also in North Africa, and Spain also has been addressed (Blier 2003).

Another important factor of vernacular architecture is that of aesthetics. Whereas Rapoport's 1969 volume privileged social and environmental factors over aesthetic considerations, Rudofsky's 1964 text has been criticized for its overly aestheticized approach to vernacular building form to the exclusion of concerns such as building use and meaning. Most studies of vernacular architecture, however, have pointed to the interpenetration of aesthetic and sociocultural factors in architectural expression. Aldo van Eyck's (1968) discussion of Dogon architecture points out, for example, that the supplemental spanning elements of local Toguna structures are far greater than the related needs of load support, suggesting that these structural elements convey larger social and religious ideas – a notable feature also of the surfeit of load-bearing features in some vernacular Indonesian and South Asia building forms. Architectural style, aesthetics, and ethnicity are taken up by Herzfeld in Greece (1991). Decorative programs frequently convey important symbolic concerns. In Chios specifically, Politis (1975) has focused on how certain forms reflect religious values. Braithwaite (1982) on the other hand notes that decorative elements in Azande building contexts suggest social ambiguities, the hidden meanings of these motifs promoting political interests, and serving to denote exchange processes across the spheres of men and women. Donley (1982) has observed in turn how Swahili Coast trading houses on the east coast of Africa emphasize decorative motifs which reference protection and cleansing, attributes also addressed in West African Islamic facade decorations (Prussin 1986). Van Wyk (1993) has noted how decorative building motifs serve as forms of resistance for the Sotho-Tswana women painters who create them.

SETTLEMENT PLANS AND URBAN PLANNING

Approaches to rural and city planning also are of fundamental importance to vernacular building study. Numerous scholars have sought to chart social identity, ritual practice, patterns of connectedness and difference in an array of spatial contexts; among these works are Hodder's 1978 volume on typologies of spatial relations. On the wider implications for vernacular architecture, see also Ligget and Perry (1995). Littlejohn's 1963 and 1967 studies of Temne spatial concerns in Sierra Leone look at the ordering of space, numerical strategies in village organization, and larger questions of Temne versus European values of place. Perin's analysis of American suburbs (1977: 210, 216) elaborates the centrality of physical proximity, social and income homogeneity, and symbolic elements of house style, as well as larger values of cosmic order and salvation. Vital attributes of transitional factors of space are addressed by Nancy Munn (1983). She sees paths (of objects and individuals) as impacting centrally on social construction and change. Other studies which explore these issues include J. Hyslop's 1984 examination of the Inka road system, and Zeynep et al. (1994) on the nature of streets and public spaces more broadly. Transcending long-standing concerns with urban centers and formal planning features also have been several studies which take up post-structural questions framed around so-called 'non-places', i.e., transitional areas such as airports, highways, shopping malls which are important precisely because they are both everywhere and nowhere, popular and elite (Augé and Howe 1995).

Several volumes have set the stage for a broader consideration of settlement questions in village settings, among these Douglas Fraser's 1968 structural-functional overview of village planning forms in varied world contexts. Ucko et al.'s 1972 volume, *Man, Settlement and Urbanization*, is also an important contribution, the authors of this anthology exploring multiple factors of environment, planning, and settlement structure. Both cross-culturally and

transhistorically, settlement patterns show not only unique similarities and differences but also core concerns with materials, social relations, economies of scale, periodicity, and regional value. Among the important foundational studies of urban planning is Kevin Lynch's (1960) exploration into the image of the city, Jane Jacobs's 1969 study on the ecology of the city, and Joseph Rykwert's (1976) provocative cross-cultural examination of how towns historically have taken shape. See also Eisner et al. (1992) on issues of the urban fabric. Fustel de Coulanges explores (1896/1980) important ritual and other factors that have long shaped the city of Rome, suggesting the important ways that past and present intersect. Another notable study which addresses the urban experience from a cross-disciplinary vantage is Borden et al.'s (2002) anthology on architectural contestation and its social dimensions.

Broader historical considerations specifically in Meso-America are the focus of Hardoy (1973) and Vogt and Leventhal (1983). See also Ashmore's (1992) analysis of Mayan settlement organization, Danien and Sharer (1992) on Maya planning more generally, and Rust's (1992) overview of geography and social setting at the earlier Olmec site of La Venta. Urban considerations in the central highlands site of Teotihuacan are addressed in Bray (1972, 1983) and Berlo (1992), among others. For Peruvian urban settlement concerns see Garcilasco (1961), Zuidema (1964), and Kolata (1983).

Within the Islamic world, Hourani and Stern (1970) look at various dimensions of city planning, and Montêquin (1979) discusses how factors of morphology shape the Islamic urban fabric. In Asia, the conceptualization, shape, and architecture of the city also have been extensively explored. Wheatley (1971) provides insight into the roots and cosmological significance of the early Chinese city. Bacon (1974) focuses on the city of Beijing and its architectural forms; Steinhardt (1990) examines the Chinese imperial city and larger political issues at play with respect to planning. The nature of spatial organization in Nepal has been explored by Gutschow and Kölver (1975). A quite different, but also insightful, work is Blair's 1983 study of four Nepalese villages and the ways in which social values find expression. Theodore Bestor (1989) addresses neighborhood primacy in modern Tokyo.

In Africa, both pre-colonial city planning and modern metropolitan centers have been subjects of scholarly attention. While Hull (1976) focused attention on 'traditional' urban settings, Coquery-Vidrovich (2005) looks at the city more broadly defined in contemporary and historical contexts. Abdoul's *Under Siege* (2003) examines four contemporary African urban centers – Freetown, Johannesburg, Kinshasa, and Lagos – from the standpoint of infrastructure, transportation, informal architecture, open areas, issues of poverty, and new urban paradigms. The authors of this provocative volume include historians (Achille Mbembe), urbanists (AbdouMaliq Simone), architects (Rem Koolhaas), and others.

ARCHITECTURES AND THE SUBALTERN: EMPIRE, SLAVERY, COLONIALISM, AND GLOBALIZATION

It is well acknowledged that empires across history have employed architecture to convey values of power and perpetuity. Architectures of state which denote, by their very scale, permanence of materials, control of landscape vistas, and larger-than-life-size sculptural programs promote ideas of dominance in particularly notable ways. Lefebvre (1991) looks at the role that monumentality often assumes in promoting idioms of fear and dominance. He also looks at political economies, dominated versus appropriated space, abstract versus absolute space, housing versus residence, homogeneity versus fragmentation, and contradictory dimensions of space and power. Examples as varied as the Great Wall of China (Luo 1981; Waldron 1990) and Fascist period forms in Italy and Germany suggest how these architectures promote particular political concerns. The force of empire in the construction of building programs also has been provocatively explored by Butzer (1982) in the context of Ethiopia and both Grabar (1978) and Meeker (2002) with respect to Islamic states. (See also Geertz (1981).) In South East Asia, the complex nature of palace buildings is examined by Dumerfaya (1991). The role modern domestic and other building models play in both addressing and promoting fear is explored by Ellin (1997). Setha Low's (2003) overview of gated communities in the United States also investigates this, and how issues of security and fortress mentality shape suburban American life. Another notable investigation into these issues is Steven Robins's (2002) examination of planning and idioms of suburban bliss in Cape Town.

Attention also has turned to the architectures of slaves and other subaltern populations with respect to complementary concerns with dominance, resistance, mediation, and retension. The Americas have been a particularly

important focus of such research. Among the notable related studies are John Vlach's 1980 analysis of the US shotgun house form as a West African legacy. See Samford's (1999) overview of West African ancestor shrines and sub-floor pits in African-American quarters in the US. George McDaniel (1981) and Leland Ferguson (1992) also study vital issues of African American slave architecture. Focused primarily on early plantation life in South Carolina and tidewater Virginia, Ferguson demonstrates, through building and other evidence, the work and ritual spheres of slaves. Schuyler (1980) explores the archaeology of ethnicity with respect to both African American and Asian diaspora contexts in the United States. Sidney Mintz and Richard Price (1980) discuss Afro-American life in the Caribbean. Barton (2001) elaborates the role of race and ethnicity in constructing sites of memory. Bahloul (1996) and Slymovics (1998) address the importance of memory in Jewish and Muslim contexts in Algeria, on the one hand, and Palestinian communities on the other. These various studies are important in bringing to light the architectural contributions of historically disempowered and academically marginalized populations in various world contexts.

In many parts of the world, colonialism has left a fundamental imprint on the local built environment. Okoye (2002) offers an assessment of the colonial impact on southeastern Nigerian architecture. Ranger (1999) looks at the ways that colonialism and landscape have shaped each other in Zimbabwe. On colonialism and Egypt see Mitchell (1991). Neich (2003) examines colonial responses to Maori building forms, and Maori counter-responses. See also Purser's (2003) study of Fiji settler identities in the later colonial era and Yeoh's (2000) overview of contexts of colonial neglect in post-independence Singapore housing (2000). Issues of creolization as expressed through colonial building form also have been taken up by Edwards (2001), who encourages us to think broadly about sources and the ways in which cultures creatively draw on an array of forms which cross-pollinate each other.

Several important studies also have looked at how violence to architecture reflects broader political concerns (Bourgeois and Pelos 1989; Malaquais 1999, 2002; Roberts 2003). In key respects related forms of architectural violence share features in common with art iconoclasm, although, as Glassie has noted broader issues are at play as well: 'The decision to create a building is the decision to destroy some part of the material universe' (1990: 280). Related issues of violence and destruction also find expression in questions of urban planning (Blier in press). In the Dahomey kingdom in West Africa, city planners in the seventeenth century seem to have anticipated later-era destruction and renovation, creating a spatial plan which allowed and indeed encouraged each new monarch to raze buildings in a designated area of the city, with the king then establishing important family members, ministers, and attendants in the newly cleared areas. Such planned destruction conveys a unique sense of political imperative and temporality. The marked destructive impact of segregation – and its extreme extension, apartheid – also has been taken up by scholars. Among the many contributions to this subject are Lemon's multi-authored 1991 volume on South African segregated cities and Rakodi's 1995 analysis of Harare, Zimbabwe's capital, as a settler colonial city. Janet Abu-Lughod (1980) addresses issues of urban apartheid in Morocco. See also Delaney (1998) on issues of race, law, and segregation in the United States with specific attention to the geographies of slavery and the geopolitics of Jim Crow.

In many parts of the world, sprawling shanty towns fueled by massive population movements have reflected deeply entrenched poverty and disempowerment, while also conveying the unique ingenuity and creativity of related inhabitants. (See among others Berman (1988) and Hardoy and Satterthwaite's *Squatter Citizen* (1989).) Watson and Gibson (1995) examine adaptive space in postmodern cities and Harvey (1993) discusses an array of modernity factors. Development considerations are a significant focus as well, as elaborated by Potter and Salau (1990) with respect particularly to the Third World. Marshell Berman's *All that is Solid melts into Air: The Experience of Modernity* 1988 is a provocative text in theoretical and other terms, and addresses the tragedy of development and underdevelopment with specific reference to social theorists (Marx), philosophers (Baudelaire on modernism in the streets), literary sources (Goethe's *Faust*), and core cities (Petersburg). See also Venturi et al. (1972) on learning from Las Vegas.

CONCLUSION

In addition to the larger theoretical issues which shape scholarly perspectives on vernacular architecture in significant ways, building forms and meanings also are defined fundamentally by an array of local, regional, and global factors. Questions of domesticity and mobility, as well as symbolic dimensions such as world view, cosmology, axiality, and anthropomorphism are central to our understanding of the built environment. Core considerations are how the buildings are experienced by and further shape the lives of their varied occupants – urban, rural, suburban as well as nomadic and the homeless. These are increasingly important subjects of consideration as well, defined from the vantage of psychological, phenomenological and other viewpoints.

Power relations as embodied in architecture – class, ethnicity, political institutions, gender – figure prominently in building forms of various types. Contemporary social theory has paid particularly close attention to the ways in which political-economic factors and institutions – slavery, imperialism, colonialism, apartheid, nation-state considerations, and globalization impact lives through habitus.

Key divisions between 'elite' and 'vernacular' forms (and scholarship) are likely to dissipate in the years ahead as scholars across the disciplines continue to move to counter narrow West versus non-West considerations. The complex push-pull between society and individual, pattern and anomaly, is playing out in interesting ways as well. Increasingly scholars also are reaching beyond issues of resistance and response, as popular forms or works at the 'periphery' are seen to shape and reshape the center. Studies also are reframing narrow concerns with 'tradition' and 'change' (as well as 'historic form' and 'modernity') to a consideration of cross-cultural and quantitative factors. One of the tools which is seeing increasing use is global mapping software such as GIS/GPS, which allows broad consideration of settlement planning, environment, and other architectonic considerations regionally and historically. In practical terms, the needs of sustainable global development are also continuing to be explored.

REFERENCES

Abdoul, Mohamadou ed. (2003) *Under Siege: Four African Cities: Freetown, Johannesburg, Kinshasa, Lagos.* Documents 11, Platform 4. Cantz Pub.

Abrams, E. (1994) *How the Maya built their World: Energetics and Ancient Architecture.* Austin, TX: University of Texas Press.

Abu-Lughod, J. (1980) *Rabat: Urban Apartheid in Morocco.* Princeton, NJ: Princeton University Press.

Adams, P.C., Hoelscher, S. and Till, K.E., eds (2001) *Textures of Place: Exploring Humanist Geographies.* Minneapolis, MN: University of Minnesota Press.

Adams, R.E.W. (1982) 'Ancient Maya canals: grids and lattices in the Maya jungle', *Archaeology*, November–December, pp. 28–35.

Adorno, T., Benjamin, W., Bloch, E. and Lukacs, G. (1980) *Aesthetics and Politics*, trans. ed. R. Taylor. London: Verso.

Agrest, D., Conway, P. and Weisman, L.K., eds (1996) *The Sex of Architecture*. New York: Abrams.

Alexander, C. (1964) *Notes on the Synthesis of Form*. Cambridge, MA: Harvard University Press.

Alexander, C. (1977) *A Pattern Language*. New York: Oxford University Press.

Alexander, C. (1986) 'Dr Sumet Jumsai, Thailand's 'ancient town planner', looks to the future', *Sawasdee*, 15: 28–32.

Aloba, O. (1998) 'Evolution and factors influencing house-types in borderlands of southwestern Nigeria: the example of Ife–Ijesa frontier zone', in B. Amole (ed.), *Habitat Studies in Nigeria: Some Qualitative Dimensions*. Ibadan: Shaneso, pp. 121–41.

Altman, I. and Werner, C.M., eds (1985) *Home Environments*. Human Behavior and Environment: Advances and Research VIII. New York: Plenum.

Amerlinck, M.-J., ed. (2001) *Architectural Anthropology*. Westport, CT: Bergin & Garvey.

Andrews, P.A. (1971) 'Tents of the Tekna, southwest Morocco', in P. Oliver (ed.), *Shelter in Africa*. London: Barrie & Jenkins, pp. 124–42.

Anyinam, C. (1999) 'Ethnomedicine, sacred spaces, and ecosystem preservation and conservation in Africa', in *Sacred Spaces and Public Quarrels: African Cultural and Economic Landscapes*. Trenton, NJ: Africa World Press, pp. 127–46.

Ardener, S., ed. (1981) *Woman and Space: Ground Rules and Social Maps*. New York: St Martin's Press.

Arhem, K. (1998) 'Powers of place: landscape, territory, and local belonging in northwest Amazonia', in Nadia Lovell (ed.), *Locality and Belonging*. London: Routledge, pp. 78–102.

Arnold, D. (1991) *Building in Egypt: Pharonic Stone Masonry*. New York: Oxford University Press.

Ashmore, W. (1992) 'Deciphering Maya architectural plans', in E.C. Danien and R.J. Sharer (eds), *New Theories on the Ancient Maya*. Philadelphia: University Museum, University of Pennsylvania.

Augé, M. and Howe, J. (1995) *Non-places: Introduction to an Anthropology of Supermodernity*. London: Verso.

Aveni, A.F. (1989) *Empires of Time: Calendars, Clocks, and Cultures*. New York: Basic Books.

Aveni, A.F., ed. (1977) *Archaeoastronomy in pre-Columbian America*. Austin, TX: University of Texas Press.

Bachelard, G. (1969) *The Poetics of Space*. Boston, MA: Beacon Press.

Bacon, E.N. (1974) *Design of Cities*. Harmondsworth: Penguin Books.

Bahadori, M.N. (1978) 'Passive cooling systems in Iranian architecture', *Scientific American* 238 (February): 144–54.

Bahloul, J. (1996) *The Architecture of Memory: a Jewish–Muslim Household in Colonial Algeria, 1937–1962*. Cambridge: Cambridge University Press.

Baldwin-Smith, E. (1978) *The Dome: A Study in the History of Ideas*. Princeton, NJ: Princeton University Press.

Bartlett, A. (1994) 'Spatial order and psychiatric disorder', in M. Parker Pearson and C. Richards (eds), *Architecture and Order*. London: Routledge, pp. 178–95.

Barton, C., ed. (2001) *Sites of Memory: Perspectives on Architecture and Race*. New York: Princeton Architectural Press.

Basso, K. (1996) *Wisdom sits in Places: Landscape and Language among the Western Apache*. Albuquerque, NM: University of New Mexico Press.

Bäumer, B. (1991) 'From Guha to Asoka: the mystical cave in the Vedic and Saiva traditions', in K. Vatsyayan (ed.), *Concepts of Space Ancient and Modern*. New Delhi: Abhinav, pp. 105–7.

Beck, B.E.F. (1976) 'The symbolic merge of body, space, and cosmos in Hindu Tamil Nadu', *Indian Sociology*, n.s., 10: 213–43.

Beek, Walter E.A. Van (1991) 'Dogon restudied: a field evaluation of the work of Marcel Griaule', *Current Anthropology*, 32: 139–67.

Beek, Walter E.A. Van (2001) *Dogon: Africa's People of the Cliffs*. New York: Abrams.

Bender, B. (1998) *Stonehenge: Making Space*. Materializing Culture. Oxford: Berg.

Benjamin, D.J. and Shea, D. (1995) *The Home: Words, Interpretations, Meanings and Environments*. Aldershot: Avebury.

Berlo, J., ed. (1992) *Art, Ideology and the City of Teotihuacan: a Symposium at Dumbarton Oaks*. Washington, DC: Dumbarton Oaks.

Berman, M. (1988) *All that is Solid melts into Air: the Experience of Modernity*. Harmondsworth: Penguin Books.

Bestor, T. (1989) *Neighborhood Tokyo*. Stanford, CA: Stanford University Press.

Biermann, B. (1977) 'Indlu: the domed dwelling of the Zulu', in P. Oliver (ed.), *Shelter in Africa*. London: Barrie & Jenkins, pp. 96–105.

Birdwell-Pheasant, D. and Lawrence-Zuniga, D. (1999) *House Life: Place, Space, and Family in Europe*. New York: Berg.

Blair, K.D. (1983) *Four Villages: Architecture in Nepal*. Los Angeles: Craft and Folk Art Museum.

Blier, S.P. (1987) *The Anatomy of Architecture: Ontology and Metaphor in Batammaliba Architectural Expression*. New York: Cambridge University Press.

Blier, S.P. (2003) *Butabu: Adobe Architecture in West Africa*, with James Morris, photographer. New York: Princeton Architectural Press.

Blier, S.P. (2004) 'Trading and transcending places: a hybrid, multiplex approach to visual culture', in Mariet Westerman (ed.), *Anthropologies of Art*. New Haven, CT: Yale University Press.

Blier, S.P. (2005) 'Razing the roof: the imperative of building destruction in Danhomè (Dahomey)', in Tony Atkin and Joseph Rykwert (eds), *Structure and Meaning in Human Settlements*. Pennsylvania: University of Pennsylvania Press.

Bloomer, K.C. and Moore, C.W. (1977) *Body, Memory and Architecture*. New Haven: Yale University Press.

Boas, F. (1888) *The Central Eskimo: Sixth Annual Report*. Washington, DC: Bureau of American Ethnology.

Borden, I. et al. (2002) *The Unknown City: Contesting Architecture and Social Space*. Cambridge, MA: MIT Press.

Bourdier, J.-P. and Minh-ha, T.T. (1997) *Drawn from African Dwellings*. Bloomington, IN: Indiana University Press.

Bourdieu, P. (1973) 'The Berber house', in M. Douglas (ed.), *Rules and Meaning*. New York: Penguin Books, pp. 98–110.

Bourgeois, J.-L. and Pelos, C. (1989) *Spectacular Vernacular: the Adobe Tradition*. New York: Aperture.

Braithwaite, M. (1982) 'Decoration as ritual symbol: a theoretical proposal and an ethnographic study in southern Sudan', in I. Hodder (ed.), *Symbolic and Structural Archaeology*. Cambridge: Cambridge University Press.

Brasseur, T.J. (1976) 'Home, house, and temple among the Plains Indians', *Canadian Collector*, 11 (1): 31–4.

Bray, W. (1972) 'Land-use, settlement patterns, and politics in prehispanic Middle America: a review', in P. Ucko et al. (eds), *Man, Settlement, and Urbanization*. Cambridge, MA: Shenkman, pp. 909–26.

Bray, W. (1983) 'Landscape with figures: settlement patterns, locational models, and politics in Mesoamerica', in E.Z. Vogt and R.M. Leventhal (eds), *Prehistoric Settlement Patterns: Essays in Honor of G.R. Willey*. Albuquerque: University of New Mexico Press, pp. 167–93.

Broadbent, G. (1973) *Design in Architecture: Architecture in Human Sciences*. London: Wiley.

Buckminster Fuller, R. (1973) *Earth, Inc.* Garden City, NY: Doubleday.

Buttimer, A. and Seamon, D., eds (1980) *The Human Experience of Space and Place*. London: Croom Helm.

Butzer, K.W. (1982) 'Empires, capitals and landscapes of ancient Ethiopia', *Archaeology*, September–October, pp. 30–7.

Chang, A.I.T. (1956) *The Tao of Architecture*. Princeton, NJ: Princeton Architectural Press.

Chang, K., ed. (1968) *Settlement Archaeology*. Palo Alto, CA: National Press Books.

Coe, M.D. (1961) 'Social typology and the tropical forest civilizations', *Comparative Studies in Society and History*, 4 (November): 65–85.

Coe, M.D. (1964) 'The Chinampas of Mexico', *Scientific American*, 211 (July): 90–8.

Cohen, L.A. (1986) 'Embellishing a life of labor: an interpretation of the material culture of American working-class homes, 1885–1915', in D. Upton and J.M. Vlach (eds), *Common Places: Readings in American Vernacular Architecture*. Athens, GA: University of Georgia Press, pp. 261–78.

Coiffier, C. (1990) 'Sepik River architecture: changes in cultural traditions', in N. Lutkehaus et al. (eds), *Sepik Heritage: Tradition and Change in Papua, New Guinea*. Durham, NC: Carolina Academic Press and Wenner-Gren Foundation, pp. 491–7.

Cole, D. (1973) *From Tipi to Skyscraper*. Boston, MA: I Press.

Cole, H.M. (1982) *Mbari: Art and Life among the Owerri Igbo*. Bloomington, IN: Indiana University Press.

Colomina, B. (1992) *Sexuality and Space*. New York: Princeton Architectural Press.

Conrads, Ulrich, ed. (1971) *Programs and Manifestoes on Twentieth Century Architecture*, trans. M. Bullock. Cambridge, MA: MIT Press.

Cooper, C. (1974) 'The house as symbol of the self', in J. Lang, W. Moleski and C. Vachon (eds), *Designing for Human Behavior*. Stroudsberg: Dowden Hutchinson & Ross.

Coquery-Vidrovitch, C. (2005) *History of African Cities South of the Sahara*. Princeton, NJ: Weiner.

Crown, P.L. (1985) 'Morphology and function of Hohokam small structures', *Kiva*, 50 (2–3): 75–94.

Csikszentmihalyi, M. and Rochberg-Halton, E. (1981) *The Meaning of Things: Domestic Symbols and the Self*. Cambridge: Cambridge University Press.

Cunningham, C.E. (1973) 'Order in the Atoni house', in R. Needham (ed.), *Right and Left: Essays on Dual Symbolic Classification*. Chicago: University of Chicago Press, pp. 204–38.

Danien, E.C. and Sharer, R.J., eds (1992) *New Theories on the Ancient Maya*. Philadelphia: University Museum, University of Pennsylvania.

Davis, Mike (1992) *City of Quartz: Excavating the Future in Los Angeles*. New York: Vintage.

Day, C. (1990) *Places of the Soul: Architecture and Environmental Design as a Healing Art*. Wellingborough: Aquarian Press.

Deal, M. (1987) 'Ritual space and architecture in the Highland Maya household', in D.W. Ingersoll and G. Bronitsky (eds), *Mirror and Metaphor: Material and Social Constructions of Reality*. Lanham, MD: University Press of America.

Delaney, D. (1998) *Race, Place and the Law, 1836–1948*. Austin, TX: University of Texas Press.

Deleuze, G. with Guattari, F. (1987) *A Thousand Plateaus: Capitalism and Schizophrenia*, trans. Brian Massumi. Minneapolis, MN: University of Minnesota Press.

Donley, L.W. (1982) 'House power: Swahili space and symbolic markers', in I. Hodder (ed.), *Symbolic and Structural Archaeology*. Cambridge: Cambridge University Press.

Douglas, M. (1966) *Purity and Danger: an Analysis of the Concepts of Pollution and Taboo*. London: Routledge.

Douglas, M. (1972) 'Symbolic orders in the use of domestic space', in P.J. Ucko et al., *Man, Settlement and Urbanization*. Cambridge, MA: Shenkman, pp. 513–21.

Dumerfaya, J. (1991) *The Palaces of South East Asia: Architecture and Customs*, ed. M. Smithies. New York: Oxford University Press.

Duncan, J.S. (1981) 'Home ownership and social theory', in J.S. Duncan (ed.), *Housing and Identity: Cross-cultural Perspectives*. London: Croom Helm.

Durkheim, E. and Mauss, M. (1967) *Primitive Classification*, ed. R. Needham. Chicago: University of Chicago Press.

Eco, U. (1976) *A Theory of Semiotics*. Bloomington, IN: Indiana University Press.

Eco, U. (1980) 'Function and sign: the semiotics of architecture', in G. Broadbent, R. Bunt and C. Jencks (eds), *Signs, Symbols and Architecture*. Chichester: Wiley.

Edwards, J.D. (2001) 'Architectural creolization: the importance of colonial architecture', in M-J. Amerlinck (ed.), *Architectural Anthropology*. Westport CT: Bergin & Garvey, pp. 83–120.

Eisner, S. et al. (1992) *Urban Pattern*. New York: Van Nostrand Reinhold.

Eliade, M. (1959) *The Sacred and the Profane: the Nature of Religion*. New York: Harcourt Brace.

Ellin, M., ed. (1997) *Architecture of Fear*. New York: Princeton Architectural Press.

Emory, K.P. (1969) 'A re-examination of east Polynesian Mare: many Mare later', in R.C. Green and M. Kelly (eds), *Studies in Oceanic Culture History* I. Pacific Anthropological Records 11. Honolulu, HI: Bishop Museum, pp. 73–92.

Evans-Pritchard, E.E. (1940) *The Nuer: a Description of the Modes of Livelihood and Political Institutions of a Nilotic People*. London: Oxford University Press.

Eyck, Aldo van (1968) 'Kaleidoscope of the mind' (pp. 90–5); 'Houses and villages of the Dogon of Africa' (pp. 96–125); 'Images of ourselves' (pp. 125–9), *Via*, Volume 1.

Fathy, Hassam (1973) *Architecture for the Poor: an Experiment in Rural Egypt*. Chicago: University of Chicago Press.

Feeley-Harnik, G. (1980) 'The Sakalava house (Madagascar)', *Anthropos*, 75: 559–85.

Ferguson, L. (1992) *Uncommon Ground: Archaeology and early African America, 1650–1800*. Washington, DC: Smithsonian Institution Press.

Fernandez, J. (1977) *Fang Architectonics*. Working Papers in the Traditional Arts 1. Philadelphia: Institute for the Study of Human Issues.

Fitch, J.M. (1990) 'Vernacular paradigms for post-industrial architecture', in Mete Turan (ed.), *Vernacular Architecture: Paradigms of Environmental Response*. Aldershot: Avebury, pp. 261–70.

Fitch, J.M. and Branch, D.P. (1960) 'Primitive architecture and climate', *Scientific American*, 203 (6): 134–44.

Forde, C.D. (1934/1963) *Habitat, Economy and Society*. New York: Dutton.

Foucault, M. (1973) *Discipline and Punish: the Birth of the Prison*, trans. A. Sheridan. London: Tavistock Publications.

Fraser, D. (1968) *Village Planning in the Primitive World*. New York: Braziller.

Friedman, A. (1998) *Women and the Making of the Modern House*. New York: Abrams.

Frishman, M. and Khan, H.-U. (eds) (1994) *The Mosque*. London: Thames and Hudson.

Fustel de Coulanges, N.D. (1896/1980) *The Ancient City*. Baltimore, MD: Johns Hopkins University Press.

Gasparini, G. and Margolies, L. (1980) *Inca Architecture*. Bloomington, IN: Indiana University Press.

Geertz, C. (1981) *Negara: the Theatre in the Nineteenth Century*. Princeton, NJ: Princeton University Press.

Gero, J. and Conkey, M., ed. (1991) *Engendering Archaeology: Women and Prehistory*. Oxford: Blackwell.

Gibbs, P. et al. (1987) *Building a Malay House*. Singapore: Oxford University Press.

Glassie, H.H. (1975) *Folk Housing in Middle Virginia*. Knoxville, TN: University of Tennessee Press.

Glassie, H.H. (1990) 'Vernacular architecture and society', in M. Turan (ed.), *Vernacular Architecture: Paradigms of Environmental Response*. Aldershot: Avebury, pp. 271–84.

Glassie, H.H. (1995) *Passing the Time in Ballymenone: Culture and History of an Ulster Community*. Bloomington, IN: Indiana University Press.

Glassie, H.H. (2000) *Vernacular Architecture: Material of Culture*. Bloomington, IN: Indiana University Press.

Goody, Jack, ed. (1969) *Comparative Studies in Kinship*. London: Routledge.

Grabar, O. (1978) 'The architecture of power: palaces, citadels, fortifications', in G. Mitchell (ed.), *Architecture of the Islamic World: its History and Social Meaning*. London: Thames and Hudson, pp. 48–79.

Grabar, O. and Hill, D. (1964) *Islamic Architecture and its Decorations*. Chicago: University of Chicago Press.

Gregory, D. and Urry, J. (1985) Introduction to D. Gregory and J. Urry (eds), *Social Relations and Spatial Structures*. Basingstoke: Macmillan.

Griaule, M. (1965) *Conversations with Ogotemmili*. London: Oxford University Press.

Griaule, M. and Dieterlen, G. (1954) 'The Dogon of the French Sudan', in D. Forde (ed.), *African Worlds*. London: Oxford University Press, pp. 83–110.

Griaule, M. and Dieterlen, G. (1965) 'Le renard pâle', Tome I, Fascucule 1, Institut d'Ethnologie, Paris.

Grøn, O., Engelstad, E. and Lindblom, I., eds (1991) *Social Space: Human Spatial Behaviour in Dwellings and Settlements*. Odense: Odense University Press.

Guidoni, E. (1975) *Primitive Architecture*. New York: Abrams.

Gutschow, N. and Kölver, B. (1975) *Ordered Space Concepts and Functions in a Town of Nepal*. Nepal

Research Centre Publications. Leiden: Rijksmuseum vor Volkenkunde.

Güvenç, B. (1990) 'Vernacular architecture as a paradigm-case argument', in M. Turan (ed.), *Vernacular Architecture: Paradigms of Environmental Response*. Aldershot: Avebury.

Hall, E.T. (1990) *The Hidden Dimension*. New York: Anchor Books.

Hardie, G.J. (1985) 'Continuity and change in the Tswana's house and settlement form', in I. Altman and C.M. Werner (eds), *Home Environments: Human Behavior and Environment. Advances in Theory and Research VIII*. New York: Plenum.

Hardoy, J. (1973) *Pre-Columbian Cities*. New York: Walker.

Hardoy, J. and Satterthwaite, D. (1989) *Squatter Citizen*. London: Earthscan.

Harvey, D. (1993) 'From space to place and back again: reflections on the condition of modernity', in J. Bird, B. Curtis, T. Putman et al. (eds), *Mapping the Futures: Local Cultures, Global Change*. London: Routledge.

Hauser-Schäublin, B. (1989) *Kultheuser in Nord-neuguinea*. Berlin: Akademie-Verlag.

Hayden, D. (1976) *Seven American Utopias: the Architecture of Communitarian Socialism, 1790–1975*. Cambridge, MA: MIT Press.

Hayden, D. (1982) *The Grand Domestic Revolution: a History of Feminist Designs for American Homes, Neighborhoods, and Cities*. Cambridge, MA: MIT Press.

Hayden, D. (2002) 'Claiming women's history in the urban landscape: projects from Los Angeles', in I. Borden et al. (eds), *The Unknown City: Contesting Architecture and Social Space*. Cambridge, MA: MIT Press, pp. 56–369.

Heidegger, M. (1977) *The Question concerning Technology and other Essays*. New York: Harper & Row.

Heidegger, M. (1978) 'Building, dwelling, and thinking', in *Basic Writings: from 'Being and Time' (1927) to 'The Task of Thinking' (1964)*, trans. and ed. D.F. Krell. London: Routledge.

Heimsath, C. (1977) *Behavioral Architecture: Toward an Accountable Design Process*. New York: McGraw-Hill.

Herzfeld, M. (1991) *A Place in History: Social and Monumental Time in a Cretan Town*. Princeton, NJ: Princeton University Press.

Heyden, D. (1975a) 'An interpretation of the cave underneath the Pyramid of the Sun in Teotihuacan, Mexico', *American Antiquity*, 40: 131–47.

Heyden, D. (1975b) *Pre-Columbian Architecture of Mesoamerica*. New York: Abrams.

Highlands, D. (1990) 'What's indigenous? An essay on building', in M. Duran (ed.), *Vernacular Architecture: Paradigms of Environmental Response*, pp. 31–65.

Hobsbawm, E.J. and Ranger, T.O., eds (1983) *The Invention of Tradition*. Cambridge: Cambridge University Press.

Hodder, I. ed. (1982) *Symbolic and Structural Archaeology*. Cambridge: Cambridge University Press.

Hodder, I. (1990) *The Domestication of Europe*. Oxford: Blackwell.

Hodder, J. (1978) *The Spatial Organization of Culture*. London: Duckworth.

Hodder, J. and Orton, C. (1976) *Spatial Analysis in Archaeology*. Cambridge: Cambridge University Press.

Holahan, C.J. (1978) *Environment and Behavior: a Dynamic Perspective*. New York: Plenum.

Holston, J. (1989) *The Modernist City: an Anthropological Critique of Brasilia*. Chicago: University of Chicago Press.

Horton, M. (1994) 'Swahili architecture, space and social structure', in M. Parker Pearson and C. Richards (ed), *Architecture and Order: Approaches to Social Space*. New York: Routledge, pp. 147–69.

Hourani, A.H. and Stern, S.M., eds (1970) *The Islamic City: a Colloquium*. New York: Oxford University Press.

Houseman, M. (1988) 'Social structure is where the hearth is: a woman's place in Beti society', *Africa*, 58 (1): 51–69.

Huet, J.-C. (1994) *Villages perchés des Dogon du Mali: habit, espace et société*. Paris: Harmattan.

Hugh-Jones, C. (1979) *From the Milk River: Spatial and Temporal Processes in North-west Amazonia*. Cambridge: Cambridge University Press.

Hull, R.W. (1976) *African Cities and Towns before the European Conquest*. New York: Norton.

Humphrey, C. (1974) 'Inside a Mongolian tent', *New Society*, 630: 273–5.

Huntington, R. (1988) *Gender and Social Structure in Madagascar*. Bloomington, IN: Indiana University Press.

Hyslop, J. (1984) *The Inca Road System*. Orlando, FL: Academic Press.

Ingold, T. (2000) *Perception of the Environment: Essays in Livelihood, Dwelling and Skill*. London: Routledge.

Irwin, J. (1980) 'The axial symbolism of the early *stupa*: an exegesis', in A.L. Dallapiccola and S.Z-A. Lallemant (eds), *The Stupa: its Religious, Historical and Architectural Significance*. Wiesbaden: Steiner, pp. 12–38.

Jackson, L. (1999) '"Stray women" and "girls on the move": gender, space, and disease in colonial and postcolonial Zimbabwe', in P. Tiyambe Zeleza and E. Kalipeni (eds), *Sacred Spaces and Public Quarrels*. Trenton, NJ: Africa World Press, pp. 147–67.

Jacobs, J. (1969) *The Ecology of Cities*. New York: Random House.

Jansen, M. (1993) *Mohenjo Daro, City of Wells and Drains: Water Splendor 4,500 Years ago*. Bonn: Frontinus Society.

Jett, S.C. and Spencer, V.E. (1981) *Navaho Architecture: Forms, History, Distribution*. Tucson, AZ: University of Arizona Press.

Kent, Susan (1991) 'The relationship between mobility strategies and site structure', in E. Kroll and T.D. Price (eds), *The Interpretation of Spatial Patterning within Stone Age Archaeology*. New York: Plenum, pp. 33–60.

Kent, Susan (1995a) 'Ethnoarchaeology and the concept of home: a cross-cultural analysis', in D.J. Benjamin and D. Shea (eds), *The Home: Words, Interpretations, Meanings, and Environments*. Aldershot: Avebury.

Kent, Susan (1995b) 'Unstable households in a stable Kalahari community in Botswana', *American Anthropologist*, 97 (2): 287–312.

Kent, Susan, ed. (1990) *Domestic Architecture and the Use of Space: an Interdisciplinary Cross-cultural Study*. Cambridge: Cambridge University Press.

Knowles, R.L. (1974) *Energy and Form*. Cambridge, MA: MIT Press.

Knowles, R.L. (1981) *Sun Rhythm Form*. Cambridge, MA: MIT Press.

Kolata, A.L. (1983) 'Chan Chan and Cuzco: on the nature of the ancient Andean city' in R.M. Leventhal and A.L. Kolata (eds), *Civilization in the Ancient Americas*. Albuquerque, NM: University of New Mexico Press, pp. 345–71.

Kolb, M.J. (1992) 'Diachronic design changes in Heiau temple architecture on the island of Maui, Hawaii', *Asian Perspectives*, 31 (1): 9–38.

Kowalski, J.K. (1999) *Mesoamerican Architecture as Cultural Symbol*. New York: Oxford University Press.

Kroll, E. and Price, T.D., eds (1991) *The Interpretation of Spatial Patterning within Stone Age Archaeology*. New York: Plenum.

Krupp, E.C. (1989) 'The cosmic temples of old Beijing', in A.F. Aveni (ed.), *World Archaeoastronomy*. Cambridge: Cambridge University Press, pp. 65–75.

Kuper, A. (1980) 'Symbolic dimensions of the southern Bantu homestead', *Africa*, 50 (1): 8–23.

Kuper, A. (1993) 'The "house" and Zulu political structure in the nineteenth century', *Journal of African History*, 34: 469–87.

Lane, P.J. (1994) 'The temporal structuring of settlement space among the Dogon of Mali: an ethnoarchaeological study', in M. Parker Pearson and C. Richards (eds), *Architecture and Order: Approaches to Social Space*. London: Routledge, pp. 196–216.

Lawrence, D.L. and Low, S.M. (1990) 'The built environment and spatial form', *Annual Review of Anthropology*, 19: 453–505.

Lawrence, R.J. (1987) *Housing, Dwellings and Homes: Design Theory, Research and Practice*. Chichester: Wiley.

Lawrence, R.J. (1990) 'Learning from colonial houses and lifestyles' in M. Turan (ed.), *Vernacular Architecture: Paradigms of Environmental Response*. Aldershot: Avebury, pp. 219–59.

Leach, E. (1978) 'Does space syntax really "constitute the social"?' in D. Green, C. Haselgrove and M. Spriggs (eds), *Social Organization and Settlement: Contributions from Anthropology, Archaeology and Geography*. Oxford: BAR I International Series (supplement), 47.

Leach, Neil, ed. (1997) *Rethinking Architecture: a Reader in Cultural Theory*. New York: Routledge.

Lebeuf, J-P. (1961) *L'Habitation des Fali*. Paris: Hachette.

Lee, D.R. (1969) 'Factors influencing choice of house-type: a geographic analysis from the Sudan', *Professional Geographer*, 21 (6): 393–7.

Lee, L.B. (1972) '!Kung spatial organization: an ecological and historical perspective', *Human Ecology*, 1 (2): 125–47.

Lefebvre, H. (1991) *The Production of Space*. Oxford: Blackwell.

Lehner, E. (1996) *Sudsee-Architektur. Traditionelle Bautypen auf Hawaii, Tonga, Samoa, Neuseeland und den Fidschi-inseln*. Vienna: Phoibos.

Lekson, S.H. (1990) 'Cross-cultural perspectives on the community', in *Vernacular Architecture: Paradigms of Environmental Response*. Aldershot: Avebury, pp. 122–45.

Lemon, A., ed. (1991) *Homes Apart: South Africa's Segregated Cities*. Bloomington, IN: Indiana University Press.

Lethaby, W. (1891/1974) *Architecture, Mysticism and Myth*. London: Architectural Press.

Lévi-Strauss, C. (1963) *Structural Anthropology*, trans. C. Jacobson and B.G. Schoepf. New York: Basic Books.

Lévi-Strauss, C. (1974) *Tristes tropiques*. New York: Atheneum.

Ligget, H. and Perry, D.C. (1995) *Spatial Practices*. London: Sage.

Littlejohn, J. (1963) 'Temne space', in *Anthropological Quarterly*, 36 (1): 1–17.

Littlejohn, J. (1967) 'The Temne house', in J. Middleton (ed.), *Myth and Cosmos: Readings in Mythology and Symbolism*. New York: Natural History Press, pp. 331–47.

Lloyd Wright, F. (1963) *The Natural House*. New York: Mentor.

Loos, A. (1982) *Spoken into the Void: Collected Essays, 1897–1900*. Cambridge, MA: MIT Press.

Low, S. (2003) *Behind the Gates: Life, Security and the Pursuit of Happiness in Fortress America*. London: Routledge.

Luo, Z. (1981) 'How the wall was built', in *The Great Wall*. New York: McGraw-Hill, pp. 128–39.

Lynch, Kevin (1960) *The Image of the City*. Cambridge, MA: MIT Press.

Malaquais, D. (1999) 'Building in the name of God: architecture, resistance, and the Christian faith in the Bamileke highlands of western Cameroon', *African Studies Review*, 42 (1): 49–78.

Malaquais, D. (2002) *Architecture, pouvoir et dissidence au Cameroun*. Paris: Karthala.

Marcus, C.C. (1993) *House as a Mirror of Self: Exploring the Deeper Meaning of Home*. Berkeley, CA: Conari Press.

Massey, D. (1993) 'Politics and space/time', in M. Keith and S. Pile (eds), *Place and the Politics of Identity*. London and New York: Routledge.

McDaniel, G. (1981) *Hearth and Home: Preserving a People's Culture*. Philadelphia, PA: Temple University Press.

Meeker, M. (2002) *A Nation of Empire: the Ottoman Legacy of Turkish Modernity*. Berkeley, CA: University of California Press.

Meister, M.W. (1991) 'The Hindu temple: axis of access', in K. Vatsyayan (ed.), *Concepts of Space Ancient and Modern*. New Delhi: Abhinav, pp. 269–80.

Mindeleff, V. (1886–87) *A Study of Pueblo Architecture: Eighth Annual Report*. Washington, DC: Bureau of Ethnology.

Minge, W.A. (1991) *Acoma: Pueblo in the Sky*. Acoma, NM: Pueblo o Acoma.

Mintz, S.W. and Price, R. (1980) *An Anthropological Approach to the Afro-American Past: a Caribbean Perspective*. Philadelphia, PA: ISHI.

Mitcham, C. (1979) 'Philosophy and the history of technology', in G. Bugliarello and D.B. Doner (ed.), *The History and Philosophy of Technology*. Urbana, IL: University of Illinois Press, pp. 163–201.

Mitchell, T. (1991) *Colonizing Egypt*. Berkeley, CA: University of California Press.

Moholy-Nagy, S. (1957) *Native Genius in Anonymous Architecture*. New York: Horizon Press.

Montêquin, F.N.A. de (1979) 'The personality and morphology of the Islamic city', *Action*, 21: 6 ff.

Moore, J.D. (1996) *Architecture and Power in the Ancient Andes: the Archaeology of Public Buildings*. New York: Cambridge University Press.

Morgan L.H. (1881) *House and House Life of the American Aborigines*. Chicago: University of Chicago Press.

Morgan, W.N. (1994) *Ancient Architecture of the Southwest*. Austin, TX: University of Texas Press.

Morse, E.S. (1886/1961) *Japanese Homes and their Surroundings*. New York: Dover.

Moughtin, J.C. (1985) *Hausa Architecture*. London: Ethnographic.

Munn, N. (1983) 'Gawan *kula*: spatiotemporal control and the symbolism of influence', in J. Leach and E. Leach (eds), *The Kula*. Cambridge: Cambridge University Press, pp. 277–308.

Myers, F.R. (1986) *Pintupi Country, Pintupi Self: Sentiment, Place, and Politics among Western Desert Aborigines*. Washington, DC: Smithsonian Institution Press.

Nast, H. (1993) 'Engendering space: state formation and the restructuring of the Kano palace following the Islamic holy war in northern Nigeria, 1807–1903', *Historical Geography*, 2 (1–2): 62–75.

Needham, J.A. (1971) *Science and Civilisation in China* IV (3), *Civil Engineering and Nautics*. Cambridge: Cambridge University Press, pp. 125 ff.

Neich, R. (2003) 'The Maori house down in the garden: a benign colonialist response to Maori art and the Maori counter-response', *Journal of the Polynesian Society*, 112 (4): 331–68.

Netherly, P.J. (1984) 'The management of late Andean irrigation systems on the north coast of Peru', *American Antiquity*, 49 (2): 227–54.

Nevett, L. (1994) 'Separation or seclusion? Towards an archaeological approach to investigating women in the Greek household in the fifth to third centuries BC', in M.P. Pearson and C. Richards (eds), *Architecture and Order: Approaches to Social Space*. London: Routledge, pp. 98–112.

Nicolais, J. (1971) 'Nepal: water as element in urban architecture', *Architecture and Urbanism*, 1 (7): n.p.

Norberg-Schulz, C. (1980) *Genius Loci: Towards a Phenomenology of Architecture*. London: Academy Editions.

Okley, J. (1983) *The Traveller Gypsies*. Cambridge: Cambridge University Press.

Okoye, I. (2002) 'Against history? A Nimo-born architecture of Umu Nri (Enugu Ukwu)', *Ijele: Art Journal of the African World*, 2 (1): n.p.

Oliver, P., ed. (1969) *Shelter and Society*. New York: Praeger.

Oliver, P., ed. (1971) *Shelter in Africa*. London: Barrie & Jenkins.

Oliver, P. (1975) *African Shelter*. London: Arts Council of Great Britain.

Oliver, P. (1990) 'Vernacular know-how', in M. Turan (ed.), *Vernacular Architecture: Paradigms of Environmental Response*. Aldershot: Avebury, pp. 146–64.

Oliver, P. (ed.) (1997) *Encyclopedia of the Vernacular Architecture of the World*, vols 1–3. Cambridge: Cambridge University Press.

Ortiz, A. (1969) *The Tewa World: Space, Being, and Becoming in a Pueblo Society*. Chicago: University of Chicago Press.

Ortloff, C.R. (1988) Canal builders of pre-Inca Peru', *Scientific American*, December, pp. 100–7.

Parker-Pearson, M. and Richards, C., eds (1994) *Architecture and Order*. London: Routledge.

Perin, C. (1977) *Everything in its Place: Social Order and Land Use in America*. Princeton, NJ: Princeton University Press.

Piot, C. (1999) *Remotely Global: Village Modernity in West Africa*. Chicago: University of Chicago Press.

Politis, E. (1975) 'Decorated houses of Pyrghi, Chios', in P. Oliver (ed.), *Shelter, Sign and Symbol*. London: Barrie & Jenkins.

Potter, R.B. and Salau, A.T., eds (1990) *Cities and Development in the Third World*. London: Mansell.

Prakash, S. et al. (1991) *Solar Architecture and Earth Construction in the Northwest Himalaya*. New Delhi: Har-Anand (in conjunction with Viking).

Preziosi, D. (1983) *Minoan Architectural Design: Formation and Signification*. Berlin: Mouton.

Protzen, J. (1993) *Inca Architecture and Construction at Ollantaytambo*. New York: Oxford University Press.

Prussin, L. (1969) *Architecture in Northern Ghana*. Berkeley, CA: University of California Press.

Prussin, L. (1970) 'Sudanese architecture and the Manding', *African Arts*, summer, pp. 13–19, 64–67.

Prussin, L. (1986) *Hatumere: Islamic Design in West Africa*. Berkeley, CA: University of California Press.

Prussin, L. (1995) *African Nomadic Architecture: Space, Place, and Gender*. Washington DC: Smithsonian Institution Press.

Purser, M. (2003) The view from the Verandah: Levuka bungalows and the transformation of settler identities in later colonialism', *International Journal of Historical Archaeology*, 7 (4), special issue *Historical Archaeology and Vernacular Architecture of Levuka, Fiji*, pp. 293–314.

Raglan, Lord (1964) *The Temple and the House*. New York: Norton.

Raglan, Lord (1965) 'The origin of vernacular architecture', in I. Foster and L. Alcock (eds), *Culture and Environment: Essays in Honour of Sir Cyril Fox*, London: Routledge.

Rakodi, C. (1995) *Harare: Inheriting a Settler-Colonial City: Change or Continuity?* Chichester: Wiley.

Ranger, T.O. (1999) *Voices from the Rocks: Nature, Culture and History in the Matopos Hills of Zimbabwe*. Bloomington, IN: Indiana University Press.

Rapoport, A. (1969) *House Form and Culture*. Englewood Cliffs, NJ: Prentice Hall.

Rasmussen, S.E. (1959) *Experiencing Architecture*. Cambridge, MA: MIT Press.

Raulin, H. and Ravis-Giordani, G. (1977) *L'Architecture rurale française: corpus des genres, des types et variantes*. Paris: Berger-Levrault.

Relph, E. (1976) *Place and Placelessness*. London: Pion.

Rendell, J. et al., eds (1999) *Gender, Space, Architecture: an Interdisciplinary Introduction*. London: Routledge.

Richards, P. (1978) 'The spatial organization of culture', in J. Hodder (ed.), *The Spatial Organization of Culture*. London: Duckworth.

Roberts, A.F. (2003) 'An architecture of the word', in A.F. Roberts et al., *A Saint in the City: Sufi Arts of Urban Senegal*. Los Angeles: University of California Press, pp. 213–30.

Robins, S. (2002) 'Planning "suburban bliss" in Joe Slovo Park, Cape Town', *Africa*, 72 (4): 511–48.

Rodman, M.C. (1985) 'Moving houses: residential mobility and the mobility of residences in Longana, Vanuatu', *American Anthropologist*, 87 (1): 56–72.

Rudofsky, B. (1964) *Architecture Without Architects*. Albuquerque: University of New Mexico Press.

Rudofsky, B. (1977) *The Prodigious Builders*. London: Secker and Warburg.

Rust, W.F., III (1992) 'New ceremonial and settlement evidence at la Venta and its relation to preclassic Maya cultures', in E.C. Danien and R.J. Sharer (eds), *New Theories on the Ancient Maya*. Philadelphia, PA: University Museum, University of Pennsylvania, pp. 123–39.

Rykwert, J.H. (1976) *The Idea of a Town*. Cambridge, MA: MIT Press.

Rykwert, J.H. (1981) *On Adam's House in Paradise*. Cambridge, MA: MIT Press.

Samford, P. (1999) 'Strong is the bond of kinship': West African ancestor shrines and subfloor pits on African-American quarters', in M. Franklin and G. Fesler (eds), *Historical Archaeology, Identity Formation and Interpretation of Ethnicity*. Williamsburg, VA: Colonial Williamsburg Research Publications, pp. 71–91.

Samson, R., ed. (1990) *The Social Archaeology of Houses*. Edinburgh: Edinburgh University Press.

Sanders, J., ed. (1996) *Stud: Architectures of Masculinity*. New York: Princeton Architectural Press.

Saussure, F. de (1916) *Cours de linguistique générale*. Paris: Payot.

Scarborough, V.L. and Wilcox, D., eds (1991) *The Mesoamerican Ballgame*. Tucson, AZ: University of Arizona Press.

Schuyler, R.L. (1980) *Archaeological Perspectives on Ethnicity in America: Afro-American and Asian-American Cultural History*. Baywood Monographs in Archaeology 1. Farmingdale, NY: Baywood.

Scott, J.C. (1998) *Seeing like a State: How Certain Schemes to improve the Human Condition have Failed*. New Haven, CT: Yale University Press.

Scruton, R. (1994) *The Classical Vernacular: Architectural Principles in an Age of Nihilism*. Manchester: Carcanet Press.

Seamon, D. (1980) 'Body-subject, time–space routines, and place-ballets', in A. Buttimer and D. Seamon (eds), *The Human Experience of Space and Place*. London: Croom Helm.

Seamon, D. and Mugerauer, R., eds (1985) *Dwelling, Place and Environment: Towards a Phenomenology of Person and World*. New York: Columbia University Press.

Shearer, W. and Sultan, A., eds (1986) *Vernacular Architecture: Principles and Examples with Reference to Hot Arid Climates*. Chicago: University of Chicago Press.

Silberbauer, G. (1981) *Hunters and Habitat in the Central Kalahari Desert*. Cambridge: Cambridge University Press.

Simmel, G. (1948/1971) 'The metropolis and mental life', trans. Edward Shils, in *Social Sciences* III (2), *Selections and Selected Readings*, 14th edn. Chicago: University of Chicago Press, repr. *On Individuality and Social Forms*, ed. Donald Levine. Chicago: University of Chicago Press, pp. 324–39.

Sircar, K. (1987) 'The house as a symbol of identity', in D.W. Ingersoll and G. Bronitsky (eds), *Mirror and Metaphor: Material and Social Constructions of Reality*. Lanham, MD: University Press of America.

Slusser, M.S. (1982) *Nepal Mandala: a Cultural Study of the Katmandu Valley*. Princeton, NJ: Princeton Architectural Press.

Slymovics, S. (1998) *The Object of Memory: Arab and Jew narrate the Palestinian Village*. Philadelphia, PA: University of Pennsylvania Press.

Smith, P. (1975) *Houses of the Welsh Countryside: a Study in Historical Geography*. London: HMSO.

Snodgrass, A. (1985) *The Symbolism of the Stupa*. Ithaca, NY: Institute of Southeast Asian Studies, Cornell University.

Snyder, P.F. (1976) 'Socio-cultural modifications and user needs in Navajo Housing', *Journal of Architectural Research*, 5 (3): 4–9.

Soja, E.W. (1989) *Postmodern Geographies: the Reassertion of Space in Critical Social Theory*. London: Verso.

Spain, D. (1992) *Gendered Spaces*. Durham, NC: University of North Carolina Press.

Stanier, R.S. (1953) 'The cost of the Parthenon', *Journal of Hellenic Studies*, 73: 68–76.

Stea, D. (1990) 'The ten smudge pots of vernacular building: notes on explorations into architectural mythology', in *Vernacular Architecture: Paradigms of Environmental Response*. Aldershot: Avebury, pp. 20–30.

Steinhardt, N.S. (1990) *The Chinese Imperial City*. Honolulu, HI: University of Hawaii Press.

Thoreau, H.D. (1966) *Walden and Civil Disobedience*. New York: Norton.

Tilley, C. (1999) *Metaphor and Material Culture*. Oxford: Blackwell.

Townsend, P.K. (1990) 'Our women are okay: Aspects of Hiyeure women's status', in N. Lutbehaus et al. (eds) *Sepik Heritage: Tradition and Change in Papua New Guinea*. Durham, NC: Carolina Academic Press, pp. 374–79.

Tuan, Y.-F. (1974) *Topophilia*. Englewood Cliffs, NJ: Prentice Hall.

Tuan, Y.-F. and Hoelscher, S. (1977/2001) *Space and Place: the Perspective of Experience*. London: Edward Arnold.

Tuan, Y.-F. et al. (1991) *Place, Art, and Self*. Oxford: Blackwell.

Turan, M., ed. (1990) *Vernacular Architecture: Paradigms of Environmental Response*. Ethnoscapes 4. Brookfield, VT: Gower.

Turnbull, C.M. (1961) *The Forest People*. London: Chatto & Windus.

Ucko, P.J., Tringham, R. and Dimbleby, G.W., eds (1972) *Man, Settlement, and Urbanization: Proceedings of the Research Seminar in Archaeology and Related Subjects*. Cambridge, MA: Schenkman.

Venturi, R. et al. (1972) *Learning from Las Vegas*. Cambridge, MA: MIT Press.

Vlach, J. (1980) 'The shotgun house: an African architectural legacy', in D. Upton and J.M. Vlach (eds) *Common Places: Readings in American Vernacular Architecture*. Athens, GA: University of Georgia Press (1986), pp. 261–78.

Vogt, E.Z. and Leventhal, R.M., eds (1983) *Prehistoric Settlement Patterns: Essays in Honor of G.R. Willey*. Albuquerque, NM: University of New Mexico Press.

Waldron, A. (1990) *The Great Wall of China: from History to Myth*. New York: Cambridge University Press.

Wallis, A.D. (1989) 'House trailers: innovation and accommodation in vernacular housing', in

T. Carter and B.L. Herman (eds), *Perspectives in Vernacular Architecture* III. Columbia: University of Missouri Press, pp. 28–43.

Watanabe, Y. (1974) *Shinto Art: Ise and Izumo Shrines*. New York: Westerhill.

Waterson, R. (1989) 'Migration, tradition and change in some vernacular architectures of Indonesia', in J.-P. Bourdier and N. Al-Sayyad (eds), *Dwellings, Settlements, and Tradition: Cross-cultural Perspectives*. Lanham, MD: University Press of America, pp. 477–501.

Waterson, R. (1990) *The Living House: an Anthropology of Architecture in Southeast Asia*. Singapore: Oxford University Press.

Watson, S. and Gibson, K., eds (1995) *Postmodern Cities and Spaces*. Oxford: Blackwell.

Wheatley, P. (1971) *The Pivot of the Four Quarters: a Preliminary Enquiry into the Origins and Character of the Ancient Chinese City*. Edinburgh: Edinburgh University Press.

White, L.A. (1962) 'Cosmology and Pueblo life', in *The Pueblo of Sia, New Mexico*. American Ethnology Bulletin 184. Washington, DC: US Government Printing Office, pp. 110–22.

Wigley, M. (1993) *The Architecture of Deconstruction: Derrida's Haunt*. Cambridge, MA: MIT Press.

Wilson, P.J. (1988) *The Domestication of the Human Species*. New Haven, CT: Yale University Press.

Witherspoon, G. (1977) *Language and Art in the Navajo Universe*. Ann Arbor, MI: University of Michigan.

Wolf, Hungry (1972) *Tipi Life*. Fort MacCloud, Alberta: Good Medicine Press.

Wright G. (1981) *Building the Dream: a Social History of Housing in America*. Cambridge, MA: MIT Press.

Wright G. (1985) *Moralism and the Model House*. Chicago: University of Chicago Press.

Wyk, G. Van (1993) 'Secret resistance in the murals of Sotho-Tswana women', in M.H. Nooter (ed.), *Secrecy: African Art that Conceals and Reveals*. New York: Museum of African Art, pp. 93–7.

Yates, F.A. (1966/1999) *The Art of Memory*. London: Routledge.

Yeoh, B.S.A. (2000) 'From colonial neglect to post-independence heritage: the housing landscape in the central area of Singapore', *City and Society: Journal of the Society for Urban Anthropology*, 12 (1): 103–24.

Zeynep, C. (1996) 'Gendered spaces in colonial Algiers' in Diana Agrest et al. (eds), *The Sex of Architecture*. New York: Abrams, pp. 127–40.

Zeynep, C., Favro, D. and Ingersoll R., eds (1994) *Streets: Critical Perspectives on Public Space*. Berkeley, CA: University of California Press.

16

ARCHITECTURE AND MODERNISM

Victor Buchli

Of all the areas encompassed by Material Culture Studies, the area of architectural Modernism is peculiarly underdeveloped. That this should be so is remarkable considering the importance of anthropological and archaeological studies for the development of Modernism in general. From the very beginnings of these disciplines Ethnography and Archaeology's pre-occupation with built forms went hand in hand with the development of modern architectural principles and the eventual development of Modernism in the twentieth century. If we think of the origins of modernity within architecture as the historical move away from vernacular traditions and the emergence of architecture as seen in the Renaissance then it becomes evident how both the ethnographic 'other' and the archaeological 'past' served as a means of renewal, critique and development of modern non-traditional forms. The Renaissance development of classical studies with its concern for the architectural forms of classical antiquity used early archaeological works as a means for creating and grasping eternal architectural principles. As late as the eighteenth century archaeologists and architects were almost indistinguishable from one another because of their preoccupation with the discovery of classical forms to inspire modern architectural work. Archaeologists were yet to be properly distinguished from architects in terms of their classical studies as they were in the nineteenth century. Archaeology basically served as the means to understand architecture and develop it as part of the modernizing enterprises of Enlightenment era thought, the spectacular example of Pompeii on the development of both architecture and neo-classicism is an excellent instance as to how the two fields – later distinguished from one another – worked in tandem – flip sides of the same endeavour, the modernization of architectural forms through the study of classical antiquity.

Ethnography as well served the eighteenth-century imagination also as a source of inspiration and reform for the creation of new architectural forms with which to realize the social goals of European Enlightenment era thought. The works of Abbé Laugier, and his investigations of the primitive hut, saw in the archaeological 'past' of classical antiquity, as well as in the ethnographic 'other', the origins of pure elemental universal forms with which to invigorate the development of Enlightenment era architecture. The sources of modernity were seen in the distant archaeological 'past' and the ethnographic 'other'. The hut of the 'noble savage' was instructive for these Enlightenment era endeavours, as was the burgeoning body of remains with the development of classical antiquity. These investigations had a social reformist impulse as a means with which to question the present by positing alternative 'pasts' whereby one could then imagine alternative 'futures'.

The first proper systematic study of architectural forms from within an anthropological context was arguably Morgan's magisterial *Ancient Society* (1877). However, a happenstance of publication prevented Morgan's *Ancient Society* to be published with its architectural study, thereby prefiguring the separation of studies of architecture from other human activities in the study of human societies that was the focus of *Ancient Society*. The unilineal evolutionary framework of the work evinced the nineteenth-century preoccupation with the 'philosophy of progress' fuelled by a historically determined impetus for inexorable progress. As Morgan stated: 'Every institution of mankind which attained permanence will be found linked with a perpetual want' (quoted in Paul Bohannan 1965: xvi). This preoccupation with social change or rather social evolution in nine-teenth-century terms highlighted the emerging Modernist impulse that had preoccupied archaeological and anthropological studies of architecture. The enterprise was truly at its root a Modernist one, and as such it is all the more peculiar that the study of Modernism and archi-tectural form has barely held the interest of anthropologists.

The negation of this connection is even more evident in the tradition of architectural Modernism itself and the modern movement in the architecture of the twentieth century. This movement had an even more emphatic if not suppressed preoccupation with prehistory and ethnography as a means of further mod-ernizing classical forms as represented by the Vitruvian orders. Vogt's work on the pre-eminent Modernist architect of the twentieth century, Le Corbusier, demonstrates this link between prehistory and Modernism with his analysis of the discovery of the early Lake Dwelling cultures found in the late nineteenth century on the shores of Lake Zurich in Switzerland (Vogt 1998) and its influence on Le Corbusier's Modernism. Prehistory, while simultaneously fuelling the nationalist imagi-nary with a history and material culture of autochthonous forms, similarly offered an opportunity for the discovery of 'pure' and universal forms in the tradition of the Abbé Laugier. As the archaeological discoveries of the Lake Dwellers emerged and were incorpo-rated into the Swiss national curriculum to forge a common sense of Swiss origins for an otherwise ethnically and linguistically divided democracy, it also served as inspiration for the consideration of alternative architectural forms and later as alternative social forms that would 'correct' the classical inheritance. The case in point is Le Corbusier's own innovation of the *pilotis*, which, while harkening back to the classical Vitruvian orders, surpassed them, going further back into prehistory with their association with the pile dwellings found on the periphery of Lake Zurich. Le Corbusier's exercise of the archaeological imagination, though restricted to the development of typologies, was not restricted to such formal

exercises by others. Architects of the Soviet avant-garde – the acknowledged architects of the first utterly Modern and progressive, utopian and socialist state – pursued these explorations of the archaeological past and ethnographic 'other' but in particular those soci-eties believed to be characterized by a lack of class exploitation and possessing egalitarian social principles (Figures 16.1–3). The standard work on Soviet town planning from as late as the 1960s shows how the architectural foot-prints of egalitarian societies (Figure 16.4) relate to the Modernist reinterpretation of these egalitarian principles in the new indus-trialized Modernist forms being built by the post-war post-Stalinist state (Gradov 1968). These ethnographic and archaeological models served, as Rykwert has noted, as 'a guarantee of renewal: not only as a token from the past but as a guide to the future' (1989: 191). Here we see how the tradition of Morgan and the Modernist planning tradition of the Soviet Union were imaginatively linked in the Soviet Marxist Modernist imagination.

Within anthropology between Morgan and then the birth of the New Archaeology, and the rise of structuralism in anthropology, little had happened in general in terms of the develop-ment of anthropological thought on architec-ture, not to mention Modernism. One is tempted to speculate the happenstance of pub-lication that divorced architecture from the study of human evolution and hence 'moder-nity' and the decline of material culture in the face of British social anthropology conspired to minimize the significance of this area of work. Morgan's work on architecture fell out of the developing canon of anthropological thought in the late nineteenth century. However, the implications for built forms were not lost on nineteenth-century social reformers such as Marx and Engels,who were keen readers of his work. Engel's seminal work on the family (*Origin of the Family, Private Property and the State*, 1972) was to remain the classic work in communist traditions on prehistory. This was essentially an application of Morgan's princi-ples on the bourgeois family and the devel-opment of a unilineal framework of social evolution for the understanding of future social formations that were central to the development of leftist thought in the late nine-teenth and early twentieth centuries. However, in the wake of such figures as Henry Maine (Carsten and Hugh-Jones 1995) and the rise of British social anthropology in the first half of the twentieth century, the anthropological

Figure 16.1   *An African dwelling, Zhilishche*
Source: Ginzburg (1934)

Figure 16.2   *Green city*
Source: Ladovski (1929)

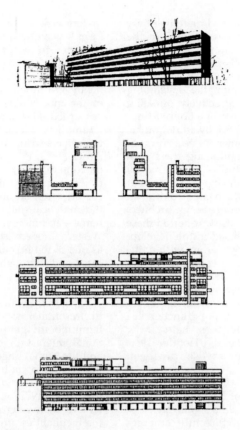

Figure 16.3   *The Narkomfin communal house*
Source: Soveremennaia Arkhitektura, 5 (1929): 158–61

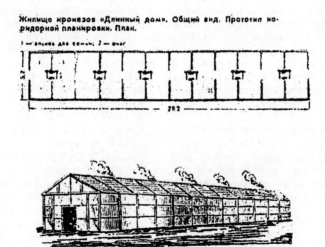

Figure 16.4   *An Iroquois dwelling, redrawn from Morgan (1881)*
Source: Gradov (1968: 30)

study of architecture remained marginal, only to re-emerge in the post-war period in the works of Edward Hall on proxemics (Hall 1959) and the structuralism of Lévi-Strauss (1973, 1983). However, in the intervening time architectural theorists within the developing canon of Modernism were actively pursuing their own empirical research into house forms, studying classical and especially ethnographic examples for the development of new forms of 'dwelling' as well as conducting their own sociologically inspired studies of use mostly deriving from the emerging management sciences of Taylorism which studied human behaviour in order to better design architectural forms. Later in the post-war period these concerns would be paralleled in the development of ethno-archaeology from within the New Archaeology, by studying the systematics of human movement and behaviour, particularly in relation to architecture and spatial use, to create analogues of material culture use in the present and past. Both functionalist and structuralist approaches held sway for their inherent systemness (Hodder 1986: 134–5) despite their otherwise divergent epistemologies.

Within this structuralist tradition, however, deriving from the work of Lévi-Strauss, architecture modestly reassumed a significance lost since Morgan's day. Architecture emerges as the social 'blueprint' according to which societies organize themselves and resolve their tensions and contradictions. It becomes a means of thinking through social life and as such becomes an important metaphor with which to conceive of oneself in the world and through which to behave, embodying 'deep structures' organizing human societies (Lévi-Strauss 1983). However, the materiality of built forms, unlike later studies (Humphrey 1974, 1988; Blier 1987; Bloch 1995), did not figure as prominently. What was significant was how these 'plans' structured how people thought and behaved.

Later figures, such as the American folklorist Henry Glassie, in the wake of Hall's proxemics and Lévi-Strauss's structuralism, further developed these ideas in relation to recent linguistic theories (especially those of Noam Chomsky 1968) to understand architecture as language-like, following similar forms of grammatical development and reflecting deeper cognitive processes that structure both language and material culture, especially architectural forms. What was to emerge within this understanding was an 'architectural competence' akin to linguistic competence. The materiality of form was reduced to its schematic outline as it pertained to the understanding of an abstract generative scheme (see Glassie 1975). In Britain, the impact of structuralism figured prominently in Caroline Humphrey's seminal work on the anthropological study of architecture in her structuralist account of the Mongolian *yurt* (Humphrey 1988). But it is probably Pierre Bourdieu's work on the Kabyle house of North Africa (1973, 1977) and his later work on taste in contemporary French society, *Distinction* (1979) that served more than anything to refocus attention on architecture – particularly at the analytical unit of the domestic sphere: the home – and more explicitly on the condition of Western 'modern' societies themselves, serving as one of the first and probably most sophisticated and thorough mediations on the experience of modernity, with an overt emphasis on material culture.

Later, in the wake of the feminist movement, the traditional association of the home with the feminine invigorated anthropology's traditional interest in dwelling, family structure and the home. Engels was reclaimed as a key intellectual forefather for thinking about social form, gender and by extension the home (see Engels 1972: preface). Thus domestic architecture increasingly became the site where the inequalities of gender could be addressed and studied. If subaltern groups and sexualities could not be studied directly, they could be approached in the almost forensic fashion of archaeology, ethno-archaeology and the re-emerging tradition of material culture studies (see Moore 1986 and outside of anthropology Duncan 1996; Sanders 1996).

The post-war response to Cold War antagonisms and radical social movements within Western democracies spurned a renewed Marxian-inspired critique of consumerism and its practices (de Certeau 1998; Barthes 1973; Baudrillard 1996). With the Western modern home as the key if not most important site of consumerist practices the dwelling in which these practices take place increases in significance (see Gullestad 1984; Csikszentmihalyi and Rochberg-Halton 1981; Miller 1987, 1988). Indeed, it is with Miller that the problem of modernity and consumption, particularly within the home, emerges as a central problem within anthropological thought and the re-emerging interest in material culture studies and the central role of consumption in the reproduction of social relations (see Miller 1987).

Alongside this trajectory of interest in consumption, the home and the perennial Modernist dilemma over 'dwelling', a broader focus on institutional and bureaucratic structures and cities emerges, owing a great debt to the philosopher and critical historian of intellectual thought Michel Foucault (1973). Within anthropology Paul Rabinow, Foucault's major anglophone translator and editor, worked on North African cities, particularly the impact of Modernist architects such as Le Corbusier and his role in town planning and bureaucratic colonial administration (Rabinow 1995). While in the wake of post-war critical interest in consumerism in the home, especially the suburban home, figures such as Setha Low refocused on the contradictions of modern urban life in the analysis of suburban communities (1999; see also Silverstone 1997).

The underlying modern preoccupation with architecture and the home has been of course its inherent 'unhomeliness'. This is the *unheimlich* derived from Freud and developed by the architectural theoretician Anthony Vidler – this is the flip side of the preoccupation with 'dwelling' by Modernist theoreticians and critics. The postmodern turn can be said to reflect this disillusionment and melancholy inherent within Modernist thought and its preoccupation with the terms of alienation within dwelling and the home. Marc Augé (1995) has refocused attention on new modern architectural forms within which this unhomeliness and alienation occur, focusing on those places such as airports, rest stops and spaces of transit that increasingly impinge on our troubled understanding of dwelling. Similarly, anthropological work has focused on the terms by which households are dissolved or divested (Miller 2001; Marcoux 2001). The implication of these works is that the almost melancholic obsession with the built forms of the home has suggested that the problem of 'dwelling' must be understood elsewhere and in different terms: in the ways we inhabit fragmented geographies and spaces, and the means by which new technologies such as the Internet, mobile phone use and SMS messaging create new dimensions of time and space which we inhabit.

Without doubt it was Modernism's myth of progress that required the suppression of this primitivist imaginary created within anthropological work (see Vogt 1998). Divergent methodologies and their attendant scales of analysis have been largely responsible for the relative dearth of ethnographic inquiries into architecture and Modernism. Anthropological inquiries regarding architecture have mainly focused on the dwelling, the architectural form most intimately associated with kin groups and households. This scale of inquiry has generally narrowed anthropological inquiry (ethnological, ethnographic and archaeological) to these architectural forms and scales. This is the scale anthropologists and archaeologists tend to work at by virtue of methodological constraints and their disciplinary focus and training. More complex structures and larger-scaled architectural assemblages tend to fall within the purview of archaeologists, with scales of analysis beyond the village level or face-to-face communities rarely taken up by ethnographers. At these greater scales, anthropologists have tended to give way to geographers, and students of urbanism.

This tendency to focus on dwellings, as opposed to other architectural forms, is also reinforced in the study of Modernism and its own preoccupation with dwelling. As Heynen notes, for Modernist theorists, philosophers, architectural theorists (and of course anthropologists) the home is the central problem of the experience of modernity (Heynen 2001). The two are inextricable when we think of Modernism and architecture. The Modernist break from tradition is a rupture with rootedness. At stake of course is the nature of dwelling and the home and modern anxieties over the inevitability of 'homelessness' (Heynen 2001). This is the problem that Heidegger identifies: 'The proper dwelling plight lies in this, that mortals ever search anew for the essence of dwelling, that they must ever learn to dwell' (1993: 363). This problem is what Morgan refers to in his preface to *House and House-life of American Aboriginals* (1881): 'Every institution of mankind which attained permanence will be found linked with a perpetual want' (quoted in Bohannan 1965: xvi). This restlessness is what characterizes the Modernist preoccupation with the architecture of dwelling. Transfixed as we are by this problem, as Heynen observes, we have tended to focus on the melancholic object of our restlessness and loss: dwelling – despairing to fix and grasp it (as with Heidegger) or more nihilistically despairing at our own despair (see Heynen on Adorno, Eisenman and Cacciari). It is worthwhile to reconsider Heidegger's suggestion that '[mortals] must ever learn to dwell'. How people cope with this problem is probably what students of material culture can address best and better enable but to do this also suggests a shift in the scale of analysis, a move away from the elusive artefact, the dwelling *per se*, to the process of dwelling itself: the physical house, dwelling and architecture of whatever form is a mere effect.

In light of these circumstances and their attendant splits in terms of method and disciplinary purview it is worthwhile considering how these historical breaks in analysis and method might be reconsidered. One problem that stands out is the question of materiality. The social terms and effects whereby the materiality of built architectural forms exist and are experienced in time and space are often overlooked – a consequence, I would argue, of this historical methodological and disciplinary division of labour and the driving myths of Modernism that this split has historically maintained. Materiality and its development over time are a crucial dimension towards resolving some of these issues that have been overlooked. These are the issues of housekeeping, within the critical feminist tradition, building maintenance, its organization and its social effects in terms of how such activities organize people's relationships to one another via the materiality of built forms. If buildings are about the construction of social forms, much of what has been written is about the exterior form, skeleton, or shell but not about how these relations are maintained. This is intended to mean everything from the maintenance of surfaces through the quotidian chores of housework to building maintenance overtime, to the issues of authenticity of form and surface relevant to cultural heritage. Social structure and architectural structure are presented as one-off givens. Such a static view of social structure is an effect of the anthropological preoccupation with the ethnographic moment: snapshots are by nature static, while similarly the architectural structure is subject to a similar stasis resulting from a preoccupation with form and the static nature of representation. Time depth and process are under-examined and architectural form and social life, though analysed in tandem, are rarely understood together in modern contexts. The two are presented as analytically separate and the embodied dimension of their interdependence (as can be seen in phenomenologically inspired studies of traditional forms) between the materiality of built forms, lived experience and maintenance and duration over time are overlooked. (See, however, Melhuish 2005.) Yet it is

precisely here where the politics and conflicts of preservation and cultural heritage management take place.

The materiality of built forms is often assumed, like the 'velvet folds' of Benjamin's description, unproblematically passively containing, circumscribing, enfolding and unambiguously signifying the social relations within. Similarly the act of building up these forms rarely moves beyond the one-off moment of construction when the analysis often stays focused on the means by which buildings create social relations among builders. Not often is the continuously lived interaction with built forms and their changing materiality engaged. (See the works of Bloch and Blier for especially good discussions of this ongoing process in non-Euro-American and non-Modernist contexts.) This interface is rarely engaged, while more consumption-based studies tend to ignore it altogether. Architectural form contains, maybe moulds, but it is presented as static by the constraints of the ethnographic moment. Work in the sociology of technology (Law 2002; Latour 1999; Yaneva 2003) suggests an enmeshed and deeply involved relationship between built forms in their changing dimensions and the various actors, both human, and non-human, that shape this continuous dynamic (see Yaneva 2003; Jenkins 2002). The physical qualities of buildings and their surfaces and materials and the social relations that the maintenance and presentation of these forms require and forge are often not glimpsed until critical moments, such as those that arise with conflicts over Heritage management (Rowlands 2002) and the negotiation of built forms. Otherwise this ongoing process between human agents both individual and institutional and material go unnoticed along with the critical dynamics of power forged within these processes and the social relationships thereby enabled.

For the most part this issue of materiality has been predominantly understood within domination and resistance models where home dwellers would 'appropriate' (the methodological domain of the ethnographer, see for instance Boudon 1979; Buchli 1999; Miller 1988) the dominant architectural forms created by architects and institutions (the methodological domain of the architectural historian and theorist). Materiality is seen as either/or: the product of two opposing social forces, methodologically segregated by the respective realms of surface and form and rarely seen as part of an integrative process that involves a constellation of actors, human and non-human, agents and time frames. There have been a few suggestions as to where such an approach might lead us and the nuances it might uncover (see Yaneva 2003 and Jenkins 2002). The significance of these approaches is evident in the way in which they are able to document the subtle play of micro-powers that forge the materiality of built forms we encounter and the social nature of their effects, which are generally lost or emerge as the intractable conflicts highlighted within preservation and cultural heritage disputes (Rowlands 2002).

Within material culture studies, visuality had been historically sidelined but more recently reincorporated (Thomas 1997, Pinney 2002), however textuality, since earlier understanding of material culture as text, has been similarly forgotten (see Tilley 1999; Buchli 1995) and not reconsidered. Recent work in literary studies has focused on the narrative tropes that shape perceptions of built forms and spaces. This narrative dimension has been generally overlooked in material culture studies. However, recent work has suggested how such narratives forms have very specific social effects. Ironic or satirical prose produces a sensibility towards materiality that can provoke a certain sensibility in the reader through the articulation of certain material qualities. Neutral empirical descriptions suggest a universality and interchangeablity (Guillory 2004) with their own effects and relationships, while satire produces others. These various dimensions along which materiality is produced have been demonstrated by Richardson in how satirical language used to describe the domestic spaces of Elizabethan drama serves to mediate a specific public and critical response to the significance of the home that only the satirical narrative style with its embellished materiality could render (Richardson 2004). This, like colour (Young 2004; Wigley 2001; also Dyer 1997) in more ephemeral but in very real ways produces certain materialities and sensibilities with direct significance for the ways in which people inhabit the built environment, create meaning and effect social relationships. This is not simply in terms of the sociological dimension of signification implied within narratives. Along this line of dimension, as within others, a material effect is produced that facilitates particular social relations: such as the work of satire through its highly particular and vivid prose which articulates a materiality that invites a certain relationship in a reading or listening audience, creating varying degrees of social engagement, in the way in which text and narrative style produce a particular way of dwelling and interaction within the narrative.

These different articulations of dimension are particularly significant in light of the fact that dwelling is understood increasingly in 'virtual' terms because of the impact of new technologies such as the Internet which spatially and temporally fragment the experience of contemporary dwelling (diasporic 'homes' maintained over diverse physical sites and times, Internet-based work/home relations mediated by time rather than space, remote dwelling via webcam video monitoring via computer or mobile video-phone, etc.). It is the case that dwelling is experienced 'virtually', that is, along different dimensions of materiality (such as visually mediated in two dimensions by digital technologies) such as the different dimensions in which materiality is experienced as in the engraving/print (Thomas 1997) dispersed over a wide essentially limitless area geographically in two dimensions as opposed to the three dimensions of the model, actual site or reconstruction experienced within in a very limited geographical area and by a limited audience. Similarly the social effect of architectural spaces and dwellings rendered linguistically within different rhetorical tropes (empirical descriptive, lyrically satirical) all function to render a certain materiality with specific social effects.

Within this set of issues arises the question of the ethnographic site. The legacy of the fossil has persisted with the site, be it the home or the building; the obviousness of the site is not questioned. The 'fact' of the 'interior' as an ahistorical and universal category still predominates. At a conference the suggestion by one speaker that the 'interior' as a self-evident analytical category was only a nineteenth-century invention was met with guffaws. The multifariousness of dwelling – the diasporic home, the space of the Internet, the simultaneity of different spatialities in architectural space and elsewhere – is under-analysed. There is a needed emphasis on material effects and the production of sites and multiple, fragmented sites. The prevailing fossil metaphor is no longer useful – a lingering effect of the work done to produce the myths of Modernism. Traditional ethnographic approaches have much to offer in terms of understanding how the multiplicity of dwelling occurs. If architecture is about dwelling as traditionally described then the multi-sitedness and increasing immaterial and virtual means of dwelling in the world require a reconsideration of this Heideggerian understanding. Buck-Morss (2002) observed how the progressive socialist Soviet state shifted the terms of Modernism from the conquering of space as part of the nation-building enterprise to the domination of time as part of the conquest of history and progress. This resulted in a very different materiality in terms of duration and presence that privileged the anticipation and control of socially progressive time over the domination of space, what Ssorin-Chaikov (2003) refers to as the 'poetics of unfinished construction' or alternatively (see Buchli forthcoming) as the indexes of continuity of varying materiality and dimensionality, depending on whether these index futurity or continuity with the past: two different means of reckoning continuity requiring different materialities and dimensions.

Similarly the Benjamin model of the *étui* containing the self within its 'velvet folds' presupposes the classical Cartesian individuated skin-enclosed self. But as such notions of individuation have been challenged not only in non-Western (Strathern 1998; Broch-Due et al. 1993) contexts as well as Euro-American, this distinction and division which have characterized much Modernist thought have little purchase. The relationship between architectural form, its materiality and the fragmented 'dividual' of late capitalism is obscured within this methodological division of labour and site. Within these late Modern settings the question of where the body and the building begin is fragmented and contested. How then is the materiality of built forms implicated in forging emerging notions of self and individuation? We have lost sight of the terms of dwelling identified by Heidegger, seeing them within the velvet folds of the discrete *étui*-like spaces that have held our attention. This boundedness is assumed (as those conference guffaws affirmed), but that is not merely an affirmation but a melancholic attachment that has fuelled the Modernist enterprise and its struggle with the unhomely terms of modern existence. As Internet studies (Miller and Slater 2001) and studies of diasporic communities suggest, all moderns are diasporic in relative terms of scale.

Within the question of the site is also the issue of homelessness, which has received little attention in relation to the study of Modernism and architecture within material culture studies. This is due in part I would suggest to an outmoded preoccupation with the 'fossil' and its ossified built forms partly deriving from anxiety over the fact that Modernism is by definition a condition of homelessness. We have abandoned the universality of the Western indigenous and Modernist Cartesian skin-enclosed unified self, but we have not adequately reconsidered the 'velvet-lined cases' in which it has been enfolded (Benjamin 1999): the dwelling; this has remained with us, much like the fossilized mould of long-dead life forms. As noted by Csikszentmilhalyi and Rochbert-Halton: 'Like some strange race of cultural gastropods, people build homes out of their own essence, shells to shelter their personality. But, then, these symbolic projections react on their creators, in turn shaping the selves they are. The envelope thus created is not just a metaphor' (1981: 138). In this sense the study of Modernism and architecture is a mournful preoccupation, the *étui* is really a death mask (as in *Rachel Whiteread's House*, Lingwood 1995) while at the same time it is an effort to, pace (but against) Heidegger, to learn how to dwell and thereby discern new forms of social life and individuation that are emerging.

The built and lived forms of Modernism are rarely studied together as part of an ongoing process. As dwellers are rarely ever builders this interrelatedness which characterizes ethnographic work on the dwelling of non-Modernist societies rarely looks at the imbrication of individuals, communities and institutions and their material practices which converge at the site of the 'home'. These spheres are segregated by the traditional methodological boundaries of disciplines and an imputed division of labour. The architectural 'shell', the building or dwelling, oftentimes is the subject of the architectural historian, theoretician or vernacular specialist. Little interest is expressed in activities inside, behind closed doors, and the lived forms that emerge. At best there is a strict division from the moment of construction to its appropriation – following rather rigidly a domination/resistance model. A dominant original form, the product of institutional works, is then appropriated (a good example is the work of Boudon (1979) in his ethnographic study of the inhabitants of Pressac designed by Le Corbusier). This is the traditional domain of the anthropologist and sociologist, who are often uninterested in the moment of construction when the structure emerges (see however Marchand 2001) and then exists indefinitely and unproblematically as an ideal type or background in which the ethnographic drama unfolds. In many respects Lévi-Straus's old observation that the house is the site where social tensions are negotiated, obscured and obviated needs further radical commitment.

There are two split moments, the dwelling/building at the moment of construction and the indwelt experience captured by the ethnographic moment. In between there is a whole process of change, modification and development, that is, a shifting nexus of interests that significantly shapes the materiality and social effects of built forms. The material and social effects of this shifting nexus are for the most part under-determined and fall out of analyses which privilege either built form or dwelt form and the snapshots that arise from the methodological restrictions of these forms of analysis and their disciplinary restrictions. Methodologically the two spheres have not been successfully approached as they have been in other non-Western and non-modern contexts (see Carsten and Hugh-Jones 1995; Bloch 1995; Riviere 1995; Blier 1987).

The Utopian ideal of dwelling which Modernism has longed for in its incessant and obsessive melancholic strivings should be set aside, to see what in fact homes 'do' as Lévi-Strauss long ago intimated. In my own work on Soviet Modernism I have attempted to try and discover how the materiality of built forms can be creatively and radically manipulated in order to overcome conflicting social tensions (Buchli 1999). Work by Young on housing and the London property market (2003) has gone a long way towards redressing this issue by focusing on the materiality of built forms in this case, namely colour, and the social effects it produces. In Young's work we see how the ideologies of transparency and neutrality that characterize the modern movement and its attempts to overcome the effects of industrialized capitalism in fact work in the opposite fashion by realizing the perfect, interchangeable universal commodity: one's real estate investment and home that enables the production of 'fluid' subjects (Bauman 2000) to exist within a highly fluid property market and thereby ensure the terms of constantly shifting subjectivity required by late capitalist modernity (Bauman 2000). Similarly Froud (2004) examines the materiality of neo-traditional built forms in English suburban communities and their simulacra of textures and architectural references. This work looks at the complex interaction of surfaces, environments and individuals and sees how the work of 'home', its agent-like qualities that generate homeyness and space, are the function not of any *a priori* understanding of material authenticity but of the complex interaction of these elements in the negotiation of social contradictions to create a contingent 'authentic' moment where it is possible to dwell in the Heideggerian sense. The preservation of the Modernist heritage of the recent past becomes equally problematic. Entirely new kinds of relationships are created between inhabitants, communities and local and national authorities through the creation and enactment of preservation guidelines. At times the preservationist impulse, focused on particular notions of material authenticity, flies in the face of the very well known architectural concepts supporting the structure – a building designed to be continuously added on to and expanded is suddenly threatened from being so by preservation guidelines which enforce an entirely new and different materiality and programme that were never intended by the original builders – two competing modern imperatives come into conflict with one another. These instances demonstrate the importance of both sides of the surface (inside and outside) as problematic and part of a complex nexus of shifting interests, institutions, agents and resistances that our melancholic Modernist preoccupation with home and dwelling has left us unable to describe adequately.

Similarly UNESCO's concern with the authenticity of built forms in its preservation guidelines creates a materiality that privileges a certain nexus of interests (globalized tourism, nation-building enterprises and various local elite interests) at the expense of other nexuses of interest groups, individuals and institutions that facilitate the contingent terms of dwelling by recourse to other materialities and orders of authenticity (see Rowlands 2002). As Rowlands notes, this is a means of asserting an objectified and mutually recognized form of authenticity with which to counter the various alienating historical processes of industrialization, de-industrialization, colonialism and post-socialist transition. The relationship between these nexuses and their competing constellations of social interests is only now beginning to be addressed. How this is achieved might be better addressed in terms of the nuances of power distribution and their material effects. The evident need of a twentieth-century Heritage (see Bradley et al. 2004) and its preservation presents many complex problems. The need to obsessively document and fix within the archive the disappearing worlds encountered in the nineteenth century with the birth of anthropology and archaeology was daunting but self-evidently urgent. If the pace of time and change dictated necessity in these nineteenth-century endeavours, then the experience of modernity in the twentieth century which is underfoot and amidst us dictates different terms of necessity. The role Modernism plays in the lived lives of communities needs to be more directly engaged and understood in terms of the material effects of Modernism and the social consequences of its preservation – not everything can or should be preserved. However, if the materialities of 'house' serve to negotiate social tensions, as Lévi-Strauss once observed, then it might be more profitable to identify those tensions, those areas of social conflict that require material intervention within the material legacy of Modernism to help negotiate these contingent issues. This requires a focused and nuanced approach that identifies micro-powers and their imbrication with macro-powers to help aid the new materialities constituted by our research into the experience of Modernism to do the relevant cultural work required of local interests as those needs arise (Bradley et al. 2004). A renewed attention to materiality and the imbrication of scales (micro-ethnographic, macro-architectural historical) might help to break this segregation which privileges one set of interests over another and thereby facilitates materialities that allow for a more inclusive and just intervention within these conditions.

REFERENCES

Augé, M. (1995) *Non-Places: an Introduction to an Anthropology of Supermodernity*. London: Verso.

Bachelard, G. (1994) *The Poetics of Space*. Boston, MA: Beacon Press.

Barthes, R. (1973) *Mythologies*. St Albans: Paladin.

Baudrillard, J. (1996) *The System of Objects*. London: Verso.

Bauman, Z. (2000) *Liquid Modernity*. Cambridge: Polity Press.

Benjamin, W. (1999) *The Arcades Project*. Cambridge, MA: Harvard University Press.

Blier, S.P. (1987) *The Anatomy of Architecture: Ontology and Metaphor in Batammaliba Architectural Expression*. Chicago: University of Chicago Press.

Bloch, M. (1995) 'The resurrection of the Zafimaniry of Madagascar', in J. Carsten and S. Hugh-Jones (eds), *About the House*. Cambridge: Cambridge University Press.

Bohannan, P. (1965) Introduction, in Lewis Henry Morgan, *House and House-life of the American Aboriginals*. Chicago: University of Chicago Press.

Boudon, P. (1979) *Lived-in Architecture: Le Corbusier's Pessac Revisited*. Cambridge, MA: MIT Press.

Bourdieu, P. (1973) 'The Berber house', in M. Douglas (ed.), *Rule and Meanings*. Harmondsworth: Penguin.

Bourdieu, P. (1977) *Outline of a Theory of Practice*. Cambridge: Cambridge University Press.

Bourdieu, P. (1984) *Distinction*. Cambridge: Cambridge University Press.

Bradley, A., Buchli, V., Fairclough, G., Hicks, D., Miller, J. and Schofield, J. (2004) *Change and Creation: Historic Landscape Character, 1950–2000*. London: English Heritage.

Broch-Due, V., Rudie, I. and Bleie, T. eds (1993) *Carved Flesh, Cast Selves: Gendered Symbols and Social Practices*. Oxford: Berg.

Buchli, V. (1995) 'Interpreting material culture: the trouble with text', in I. Hodder et al. (eds), *Interpreting Archaeology*. London: Routledge.

Buchli, V. (1999) *An Archaeology of Socialism*. Oxford: Berg.

Buchli, V. (forthcoming) 'Material interfaces', in C. Alexander, V. Buchli and C. Humphrey (eds), *Reconstructions of Urban Life in Post-Soviet Central Asia*. London: UCL Press.

Buck-Morss, S. (2002) *Dream World and Catastrophe*. Cambridge, MA: MIT Press.

Carsten, J. and Hugh-Jones, S., eds (1995) *About the House: Lévi-Strauss and Beyond*. Cambridge: Cambridge University Press.

Chapman, T. and Hockey, J. (1999) *Ideal Homes? Social Change and Domestic Life*. London: Routledge.

Chomsky, N. (1968) *Language and Mind*. New York: Harcourt Brace.

Chevalier, S. (1997) 'From woollen carpet to grass carpet: bridging house and garden in an English suburb', in D. Miller (ed.), *Material Cultures: Why some Things Matter*. London: UCL Press.

Csikszentmihalyi, M. and Rochberg-Halton, E. (1981) *The Meaning of Things: Domestic Symbols and the Self*. Cambridge: Cambridge University Press.

De Certeau, M. (1998) *The Practise of Everyday Life*. Minneapolis, MN: University of Minnesota Press.

Duncan, N., ed. (1996) *BodySpace: Destabilizing Geographies of Gender and Sexuality*. London: Routledge.

Dyer, R. (1997) *White*. London: Routledge.

Engels, F. (1972), *The Origin of the Family, Private Property and the State*. New York: Pathfinder Press.

Foucault, M. (1973) *Discipline and Punish: the Birth of the Prison*. London: Tavistock Press.

Froud, D. (2004) 'Thinking beyond the homely: countryside properties and the shape of time', *Home Cultures*, 1 (3): 211–34.

Ginzburg, M. (1934), *Zhilishche*. Moscow: Gosstroiizelat USSR.

Glassie, H. (1975) *Folk Housing in Middle Virginia*. Knoxville, TN: University of Tennessee Press.

Gradov, G.A. (1968) *Gorod i Byt*. Moscow: Literatury po Stroitel'stvu.

Guillory, J. (2004) 'The memo and modernity', *Critical Inquiry*, 31: 108–32.

Gullestad, M. (1984) *Kitchen Table Society: a Case Study of the Family Life and Friendships of Young Working-class Mothers in Urban Norway*. Oslo: Universitätsforlaget.

Hall, E.T. (1959) *The Silent Language*. Greenwich, CT: Fawcett.

Heidegger, M. (1993) 'Building, dwelling, thinking', in M. Heidegger, *Basic Writings: from 'Being and Time' (1927) to 'The Task of Thinking' (1964)*, trans. D.F. Krell. London: Routledge.

Heynen, H. (2001) *Architecture and Modernity: a Critique*. Cambridge, MA: MIT Press.

Hillier, B. and Hanson, J. (1984) *The Social Logic of Space*. Cambridge: Cambridge University Press.

Hodder (1986) *Reading the Past*. Cambridge: Cambridge University Press.

Humphrey, C. (1974) 'Inside a Mongolian yurt', *New Society*, 31: 45–8.

Humphrey, C. (1988) 'No place like home in anthropology', *Anthropology Today*, 4 (1): 16–18.

Jenkins, L. (2002) 'Geography and architecture: 11 rue de Conservatoire and the permeability of buildings', *Space and Culture*, 5 (3): 222–36.

Kent, S. (1990) *Domestic Architecture and the Use of Space: an Interdisciplinary Cross-cultural Study*. Cambridge: Cambridge University Press.

Latour, B. (1999) *Pandora's Hope: Essays on the Reality of Science Studies*. Cambridge, MA: Harvard University Press.

Law, J. (2002) *Aircraft Stories*. Durham, NC: Duke University Press.

Lévi-Strauss, C. (1983) *The Way of the Masks*. London: Cape.

Lévi-Strauss, C. (1995/1973) *Tristes tropiques*. Paris: Plon; trans. J. and D. Weightman (London: Cape).

Lingwood, J., ed. (1995) *Rachel Whiteread's House*. London: Phaidon Press.

Low, S., ed. (1999) *Theorizing the City*. New Brunswick, NJ: Rutgers University Press.

Marchand, T. (2001) *Minaret Building and Apprenticeship in Yemen*. Richmond, Surrey: Curzon Press.

Marcoux, J.-S. (2001) 'The *casser maison* ritual: constructing the self by emptying the home', *Journal of Material Culture*, 6 (2): 213–35.

Melhuish, C. (2005) 'Towards a phenomenology of the concrete megastructure', *Journal of Material Structure*, 10 (1): 5–29.

Merleau-Ponty, M. (1962) *The Phenomenology of Perception*. London: Routledge.

Miller, D. (1987) *Material Culture and Mass Consumption*. Oxford: Blackwell.

Miller, D. (1988) 'Appropriating the state on the council estate', *Man*, 23: 353–72.

Miller, D. ed. (2001) *Home Possession: Material Culture behind Closed Doors*. Oxford: Berg.

Miller, D. and Slater, D. (2001) *The Internet: an Ethnographic Approach*. Oxford: Berg.

Moore, H. (1986) *Space, Text and Gender: an Anthropological Study of the Marakwet of Kenya*. Cambridge: Cambridge University Press.

Morgan, L.H. (1877/1978) *Ancient Society*. Palo Alto, CA: New York Labor News.

Morgan, L.H. (1881) *House and House Life of the American Aborigines*. Contributions to North American Ethnology 4, Washington, DC: Government Printing Office.

Pinney, C. (2002) 'Visual culture: introduction', in V. Buchli (ed.), *The Material Culture Reader*. Oxford: Berg.

Rabinow, P. (1995) *French Modern: Norms and Forms of the Social Environment*. Chicago: University of Chicago Press.

Rappaport, A. (1982) *House Form and Culture*. Englewood Cliffs, NJ: Prentice Hall.

Richardson, C. (2004) 'Early Modern Plays and Domestic Spaces'. Unpublished conference paper. Literature and the Domestic Interior, Victoria and Albert Museum, London, 23 October.

Riviere, P. (1995) 'Houses, places and people: community and continuity in Guiana', in J. Carsten and S. Hugh-Jones (eds), *About the House: Lévi-Strauss and Beyond*. Cambridge: Cambridge University Press.

Rowlands, M. (2002) 'Heritage and cultural property', in V. Buchli (ed.), *The Material Culture Reader*. Oxford: Berg.

Rykwert, J. (1989) *On Adam's House in Paradise: the Idea of the Primitive Hut in Architectural History*. Cambridge, MA: MIT Press.

Sanders, J., ed. (1996) *Stud*. New York: Princeton Architectural Press.

Silverstone, R., ed. (1997) *Visions of Suburbia*. London: Routledge.

Spain, D. (1992) *Gendered Spaces*. Chapel Hill, NC: University of North Carolina Press.

Ssorin-Chaikov (2003) *The Social Life of the State in Subarctic Siberia*. Palo Alto, CA: Stanford University Press.

Strathern, M. (1998) *The Gender of the Gift*. Berkeley, CA: University of California Press.

Thomas, N. (1997) *In Oceania: Visions, Artifacts, Histories*. Durham, NC: Duke University Press.

Tilley, C. (1999) *Metaphor and Material Culture*. Oxford: Blackwell.

Vidler, A. (1992) *The Architectural Uncanny*. Cambridge, MA: MIT Press.

Vogt, A.M. (1998) *Le Corbusier, the Noble Savage: Toward an Archaeology of Modernism*. Cambridge, MA: MIT Press.

Wigley, M. (2001) *White Walls, Designer Dresses: the Fashioning of Modern Architecture*. Cambridge, MA: MIT Press.

Yaneva, A. (2003) 'Chalk steps on the museum floor: the "pulses" of objects in an art installation', *Journal of Material Culture*, 8 (2): 169–88.

Young, D. (2004) 'The material value of colour: the estate agent's tale', *Home Cultures*, 1 (1): 5–22.

17

'PRIMITIVISM', ANTHROPOLOGY, AND THE CATEGORY OF 'PRIMITIVE ART'

Fred Myers

In Sydney, Australia, in 1992, in a district near the old Rocks area now incorporated into a tourist district, the sign on the gallery door reads 'Aboriginal and Tribal Art Museum and Shop'. Inside, the objects range from New Guinea baskets and wood sculptures and Aboriginal boomerangs to bark and acrylic paintings. In 1994, Sotheby's catalog for their auction of 'Tribal Art' in New York changed the name it was using for its title, after protest from Indigenous Australians, from 'Churinga' (a word referring to sacred objects of Aboriginal people in Central Australia and specifically to one of the most important items in this sale) to the more general 'Tribal Art.'

Objects do not exist as 'primitive art'. This is a category created for their circulation, exhibition and consumption outside their original habitats. To be framed as 'primitive art' is to resignify – as both 'primitive' and as 'art' – acts that require considerable social and cultural work, and critical analysis of these processes has fundamentally transformed the study of art. In this chapter, I trace how the analysis of this process has taken place in terms of discourse, semiotics, and especially social life. Consideration of the circulation, exhibition, and consumption of objects – particularly of what Webb Keane (2005) has called 'the practical and contingent character of things' – shows how their materiality matters: the objects in question under the sign of 'primitive art' are more than mere vehicles for ideas. They are, as Keane notes in following Peirce's understanding of signs in contrast to the usual

Saussurean one, vulnerable to causation and contingency, as well as open to further causal consequences.

Critics have been drawn to the constructions of primitive art; they recognize that the display and circulation of objects through this register has been a significant form of social action, distributing value to cultural products. In turn, the material form of these objects shapes their semiotic constructions; for example, certain objects – especially the portable objects of 'primitive art', such as small carvings – can be more readily circulated, recontextualized, and reappropriated than others – such as cave paintings.

By the 1970s, as scholars recognized that the category 'primitive art' was problematic as an analytic frame, substitutes for the category have been sought – 'nonwestern art', 'tribal art', 'the art of small-scale societies', and so forth (see Anderson 1989; Rubin 1984; Vogel 1989). Nonetheless, the category persists within a significant market for objects, even as debates about the category continue to inform theories of material culture. The interest in 'primitive art' has shifted to the problem of 'primitivism' itself – emphasizing the categories of the West and the meanings they attribute to objects from elsewhere and also (but less obviously) to the ways that particular material objects instigate ideological effects (see Baudrillard 1968). In this chapter, I first argue that the existence of the category 'primitive art' as a framework for the curation of material culture is part of a taxonomic structure (Baudrillard 1968; Clifford 1988) shaped by an ideological formation. Along with this first argument, however, I wish to develop a second point through the notion of 'objectification', attending to the ways in which material qualities of objects suppressed within this categorical formation may persist and have potential for new readings and alternate histories.

PRIMITIVISM

The construction known as 'primitivism' has been considered by a wide range of scholars, in the past and in the present, and its origins have been found by some in the classical period (Lovejoy and Boas 1935; Gombrich 2002)[1] and by others more meaningfully in the concern of the Enlightenment to reconstruct the origins of culture shaped by a reaction against classicism (Connelly 1995). However they differ among themselves, the argument of these works is that particular attributes of objects are valorized as an alternative to that which is more refined, more 'developed', more 'learned' or 'skilled'. Thus, the 'primitive' is a dialogical category, often explicitly a function of the 'modern' (see also Diamond 1969); the current consideration of the category is inextricably linked to controversies about cultural and ideological appropriation launched from postmodern and postcolonial critiques. These critiques seek to identify the function of the category as part of Western culture.

As Clifford (1988), Errington (1998), and Price (1989) have shown, there have been significant consequences of this formation.[2] For much of the twentieth century, 'primitive art' defined a category of art that was, more or less, the special domain of anthropology – a domain differentiated from the general activity of 'art history' by virtue of being outside the ordinary, linear narratives of (Western) artistic 'progress' in naturalistic representation. Primarily, therefore, non-Western and prehistoric art, 'primitive art' (later to become 'tribal art', the 'art of small-scale societies', and even 'ethnographic art') was most obviously within the purview of anthropological study and was exhibited in ethnographic or natural history rather than 'fine art' museums. One consequence of this placement, noted by many, has been the popular identification of Native American cultures (for example) not with other human creations, but with the natural plant and animal species of a continent – suggesting that products are parts of nature, as if they had no history. Nonetheless, many particular analyses of non-Western art systems, the many detailed studies of local aesthetic organization and function, have value.

Because such studies were undertaken within a division of labor between art history and anthropology does not inherently make them part of the 'primitivist' ideological formation itself; essays in the well known collections edited by Jopling (1971), Otten (1971) and D'Azevedo (1973) can hardly be accused of imagining a unified 'primitivity'. Even so, the indirect influence of primitivism has remained all too often in other attempts to find local, ethnoaesthetic systems as if they were 'uncontaminated', or 'pure' of Western influence as well as 'allochronic' (Fabian 1983) and part of another era (see Clifford 1988; Thomas 1991).[3]

In a comprehensive survey, the art historian Colin Rhodes (1995) points out that the category 'primitive' is a relational operator:

> The word 'primitive' generally refers to someone or something less complex, or less advanced, than the person or thing to which it is being compared. It is conventionally defined in negative terms, as lacking in elements such as organization, refinement and technological accomplishment. In cultural terms this means a deficiency in those qualities that have been used historically in the West as indications of civilization. The fact that the primitive state of being is comparative is enormously important in gaining an understanding of the concept, but equally so is the recognition that it is no mere fact of nature. It is a *theory* that enables differences to be described in qualitative terms. Whereas the conventional Western viewpoint at the turn of the century imposed itself as superior to the primitive, the Primitivist questioned the validity of that assumption, and used those same ideas as a means of challenging or subverting his or her own culture, or aspects of it.

(Rhodes 1995: 13)

This relationality may help us to understand an extraordinary diversity of forms within the primitive, what Connelly has called 'the difficulty in discerning a rationale underlying the chaotic mix of styles identified as "primitive"' (1995: 3). Some critics have pointed out that the formulation of the primitive – as timeless, unchanging, traditional, collective, irrational, ritualized, 'pure' – has been configured against the notions of the individually heroic modern person as 'rational', 'individual', and so on. Others have emphasized the construction of 'primitive' expressiveness and directness as superior to classical and learned convention. A consideration of relationality further suggests that the operation of this category must be understood within a particular structure and in relation to the properties of the objects themselves. A perceived (or attributed) lack of refinement in the manufacture of objects might be conducive to the common view that 'primitive' art is more spiritual than Western art. Conversely, others regard such objects as providing a mere display of virtuousity and hence 'craft' (more material) compared to the philosophically loaded stuff of 'real art' (more ideational). My aim, then, is to illuminate the linkages between the ideological structure of an aesthetic doctrine of Modernism and notions of the 'primitive', and the materiality of the objects of 'primitive art'.

MOMA EXHIBITION: THE 'PRIMITIVISM' DEBATE

Much of the linkage between Modernism and the category of 'primitive art' was illuminated in the body of critical response to the New York Museum of Modern Art's 1984 exhibition '"Primitivism" in Twentieth Century Art: the Affinity of the Tribal and the Modern'.[4] The terms of the 'primitivism' debate as it developed in the art world should be understood initially as manifesting criticism of the famous Museum of Modern Art (MOMA) and its ideological construction of Modernism. In marking off 'capital M' Modernism, following Blake and Frascina (1993), I mean a *particular* aesthetic doctrine rather than the whole of what I should call modern art. (This is frequently identified with the doctrine of 'Modernism' that, in Clement Greenberg's famous (1965) formulation, strips away everything 'nonessential' to an artistic medium.)[5]

I have found it useful to distinguish two significant strands in the 'primitivism' critiques. By and large, critics of the varieties of what they see as a 'primitivist fantasies' paradigm have drawn on the Foucauldian association of power/knowledge to give theoretical shape to their efforts to discern the imposition of meaning and values on Native peoples. Those following this strand of analysis, best known through Said's *Orientalism* (1978), have emphasized how being represented as 'primitive' traps or subjectifies Others and has defining power (as dominant knowledge) over their identities. The exemplary case for such formulations has been the display of cultures in the museum or exhibition, a situation where local ('primitive', 'Native', 'indigenous') voices – if not entirely absent – were more muted. Indeed, a good deal of the recognition and criticism of these constructions follows from the emerging indigenous political project that involves critiques of the binding doctrines of 'authenticity' and cultural purity (see, e.g., Ziff and Rao 1997; Karp and Lavine 1991).

The second strand has drawn inspiration from the postmodern attack on the doctrine and practice of Modernism itself (its structures and codes) as a formation of hierarchy and exclusion that subordinates or manages cultural 'difference' that might be threatening to the values it instantiates (see Clifford 1988; Foster 1985; for a more general consideration of postmodernism, see Connor 1989). Not only does this variant of criticism manifest the struggle within art theory itself, about what 'art' or good art is, about what is 'art' and 'non-art' (Danto 1986). The significant insight of postmodern criticism has also been that art theory is not neutral and external, that formalist definitions of material culture as 'art' are themselves *part of culture*. They are projected and circulated as part of cultural struggle, as *defensive* responses to a surrounding context – to the threat to 'art', for example, of theatricality, entertainment, kitsch, and mass culture – threats specifically addressed in such well known formulations as those of Clement Greenberg (1961), Michael Fried (1967), and Theodor Adorno (1983).

It might well be argued that such formalism placed materiality itself (the quality of the 'thing', its very 'thingness') – its irreducibility to simple ideas – in the foreground, thereby contrasting with older views of art as the expression of ultimately immaterial intentions, meanings, and values. The rise of Formalism owed a great deal, historically, to the perceived need to sustain a place for 'art' after the rise of photography as the medium of naturalistic representation. In this regard, Roger Fry's (1920) theorization of 'significant form' rather than content as the basis of true art provides an important precursor of the theory and rescue work of later Modernist criticism, such as Greenberg's.[6]

In the criticized definitions of 'art' – definitions which are regarded by critics as sharing the Kantian ideal of aesthetics as somehow distinct from practical reason and morality – art is *qualitatively superior* (if not transcendent) to other cultural forms. Critically oriented postmodern theorists, such as Rosalind Krauss, Hal Foster, and Craig Owens, as well as more straightforward sociological critics such as Pierre Bourdieu (1984), asserted that art's defensive strategy of self-definition (art's autonomy from other spheres of culture) was not simply a neutral fact, but was a form of cultural production itself – an exclusionary, boundary-maintaining activity, a hegemonic exercise of power through knowledge.

From this point of view, the deployment of 'primitivism' was criticized – or deconstructed – precisely as a relational operator of Modernism itself. The art historian and critic Hal Foster (1985) argued that 'primitivism' (the framework through which certain cultural projects were experienced and understood) was an instrumentality of Modernist cultural formation, in the service of sustaining and producing a Western identity as superior. The sense of cultural hierarchy and exclusion as *defensive* strategies underlies much of the critical work of the 1980s and 1990s, and gives weight to Foster's characterization of it as 'fetishism' – that is, something made by people that appears to be independent of them and to have power over them, hiding its own source in the subject of whom it is really a part.

MOMA EXHIBITION: THE UNANTICIPATED CRISIS OF PRIMITIVE ART

Even in the more controlled domains, however, since those material qualities that are suppressed do persist, objects bring the potential for new realizations into new historical contexts (see, e.g., Thomas 1991).

(Keane 2005)

The contest of positions and ideas, however, was not a disembodied one, abstracted in space and time. It had everything to do with the cultural power of a particular institution – New York's Museum of Modern Art – to define artistic merit and value, and the struggle of those outside it – women, minorities – to establish a framework of recognition of their work and that of others who believed themselves to be excluded by MOMA's doctrines.

It should be clear that the dominant notion of 'art' that came under criticism was the notion of an aesthetic experience constituted through the *disinterested* contemplation of objects as *art* objects removed from instrumental associations (see Bourdieu 1984). This notion of the aesthetic was entirely compatible with the formalist emphasis of prevailing art discourses at the time, although the implicit hierarchies of value were at this time becoming the subject of challenge. Critics approached the MOMA show on grounds of the inapplicability of the Modernist, formal concept of 'art' itself as appropriate for universal application as a framework for interpreting or evaluating the value of material culture. They portrayed the exhibition not so much as a simply mistaken ethnocentric misrepresentation; rather, it was seen as actively constituting in its poetics a hegemonic ideological structure. The inspiration for such an analysis of the exhibition should ultimately be traced to Claude Lévi-Strauss's (1966) influential but now somewhat eclipsed discussion of the *bricoleur* and 'the science of the concrete'. The curator/*bricoleur* takes his or her elements from the world's material culture and recontextualizes their sensible or material properties by placing them within an exhibition or installation as a larger whole, itself standing indexically and iconically for the world outside it. From this recontextualization emerges a particular formation of 'primitive art' reflecting, instantiating, and 'naturalizing' the codes of modernism. That 'challenge' is possible, critical and/or political, suggests the instability of any such structure, its inability to hold the objects' material qualities to its singular ordering. Indeed, while the emphasis of Formalism might be seen as giving greater value to material form than to intentions, meanings, narratives, or other less material dimensions of the art work, since only the materiality *within* the art work was admitted to consideration, other qualities of the object could be made to challenge the structure.

The critiques of the MOMA show had precedents. Work that indicated this relationship between aesthetic theory and politics – e.g., Guilbaut's *How New York stole the Idea of Abstract Art* (1983) or Barthes's (1957) essay on the MOMA's early 'Family of Man' exhibition – informed their discussion of an ideology in which art practices and objects were made to represent a generic but problematic 'humanity'. The 'primitivism' debates pursued a series of questions about the complicity of Modernism – a supposedly progressive, emancipatory aesthetic doctrine – with projects of colonialist and imperialist hegemony. They implicated Modernism as an ideological structure in which value is constructed or denied through representation. That this ideological structure was embodied in the institution of MOMA – an institution with massive cultural authority and connection to collectors and dealers – was central to its effectiveness, far beyond anything that might have been produced, for example, through the discourse of anthropologists. Enacted within a controlled domain, this exhibition was a high stakes cultural performance of the relationship between the West and the Rest.

William Rubin, the curator of the exhibition, had gained his reputation as a Picasso expert. Not surprisingly, Rubin organized the exhibit around his understanding of Picasso, owing much to Picasso's own mythology – in which the artist's own internal history arrived at a situation (the critique of older models and conventions of art) that found African art/sculpture to exemplify formal properties important at that time in the West. Neither Rubin nor Picasso – nor Robert Goldwater, from whose earlier volume, *Primitivism in Modern Art* (1938), the idea came – saw the primitive as influencing the modern artist.[7] The evolution of modern art, according to the MOMA narrative, was supposed to be an *internal* dialectic of liberation from narrative content towards an emphasis on material form. The 'Primitivism' exhibition's fascination – and the first section of the installation – was with the objects that Picasso and his contemporaries had in their studios, what they could possibly and actually did see – a brilliant, historical exploration of the specific traffic in culture at the time – with an explicit consideration of how the particular objects entered into art (Rubin 1984). A salient example was the Picasso painting that portrayed a guitar resonating with the form of a Grebo mask – matching the specific mask then in his studio and its appearance in his painting.

The second part of the exhibition moved to 'Affinities', as they were called, or general resemblances – pairing a prominent Western art work (and artist) with a non-Western (or tribal) piece that presented the *same formal properties* (according to the curator's grouping). Clifford and others pointed out how this installation functioned ideologically. Following the famous Barthes (1957) essay on the ideology of 'The Family of Man' – an exhibition of photographs, curated by Edward Weston and circulated by MOMA in the 1950s, which saw human beings everywhere as subject to the same concerns and theme — Clifford argued that a 'Family of Art' was allegorized in the MOMA's 'Primitivism' exhibition. Especially in the pairing of unattributed non-Western works with the masterpieces of named Western Modernist artists, the exhibition emphasized creativity and formal innovation *as the gist of 'art' everywhere*.

Ideological critiques have long been suspicious of 'naturalizing' and regard such acts of representation not as innocent errors but as attempts to provide legitimacy for current formations of power. Thus, to represent so-called 'primitive' artists as having the same formal motivations and interests as those said to be central to the modern avant-garde was to assert that the particular art practices celebrated in twentieth-century doctrines (that seem conveniently resonant with bourgeois experiences and celebratory of individual and especially male heroic creativity) were a human universal and to support the Modernist narrative of contemporary Western art practice as representing the finest expression of human art. Those so-called 'primitive' artists whose work did not resemble the valued modern were not selected for display.

Postmodern critics have argued for a less linear, more decentered approach to 'art' – seeing 'art' as having less unity and having multiple histories, emphasizing a range of differences as equally 'art'. By seeming to discern 'affinities' that the exhibition itself constructed, the exhibition naturalized the MOMA doctrine of aesthetics while at the same time it abstracted non-Western objects from whatever context and function they might originally have had. By finding similarities where there should be differences, through this recontextualization MOMA's 'primitivism' operated, it was argued, to universalize the aesthetic doctrine of Western Modernism – emphasizing the formal, material dimensions of art objects as their central quality and indirectly supporting a separable or autonomous dimension of human life that was 'art'.

Anthropologists have been familiar with the potential that cultural comparison has for ideological deployment. Lacking historical connection and context for 'tribal' objects, the means of constructing typological similarities in the 'Affinities' section were very much like those involved in what was called 'the comparative method.' In the nineteenth century, in books and exhibitions, this method of cultural comparison undergirded the ethnocentric, universalist histories of unilineal evolution from 'primitive' (and simple) to 'civilized' (and complex).[8] However, at MOMA's exhibition, 'primitive art' had a different – but still ethnocentric – function, departing from the nineteenth-century construction of cultural hierarchy. The view of art implemented by the comparison at MOMA and more widely circulating, as Sally Price argued, was characterized further by what she called 'the universality principle' – a principle articulated in 'the proposition that art is a "universal language" expressing the common joys and concerns of all humanity' (1989: 32). Not only does such a principle of universality legitimate the view of aesthetics as universal, innate, and transcending culture and politics – the innate taste of the connoisseur who knows art (anywhere) when he or she sees it. But this proposition of universality is, in turn, based on another Western conceit – the notion that 'artistic creativity originates deep within the psyche of the artist. Response to works of art then becomes a matter of viewers tapping into the psychological realities that they, as fellow human beings, share with the artist' (Price 1989: 32).

While she was principally objecting to the ethnocentrism of viewers' presuming to know directly what is at stake in the objects, unmediated by knowledge of their context and function in the horizon of expected viewers, Price was drawing attention to another variety of 'primitivist' representation.[9] In this variant, the 'primitive' is more direct in expression, unmediated by tradition or reason – the polar opposite of the refined and inexpressive classical (see also Connelly 1995; Gombrich 2002).[10] There is no doubt that Western artists like Picasso had their own Romantic forms of 'primitivism', seeing so-called 'tribal' artists to be, as the art historian Paul Wingert (1974) said, 'more closely allied to the fundamental, basic, and essential drives of life' which Civilized or Western folks share but 'bury under a multitude of parasitical, nonessential desires'.

Along this fracture line, Thomas McEvilley criticized the exhibition for its effort to demonstrate the universality of aesthetic values. The implicit claim of universality, he observed, operated in the service of placing Formalist Modernism *as the highest criterion of evaluation*. To make his point, McEvilley invoked in positive terms another trope of 'primitivism' (endorsing the opposite side of the ideological dyad) – the Romantic and dark Otherness of non-Western art. McEvilley claimed the exhibition accomplished its construction of aesthetic universality through censorship of the meaning, context, and intention – the excessive materiality – of the exotic objects:

> In their native contexts these objects were invested with feelings of awe and dread, not of esthetic ennoblement. They were seen usually in motion, at night, in closed dark spaces, by flickering torchlight ... their viewers were under the influence of ritual, communal identification feelings, and often alcohol or drugs; above all, they were activated by the presence within or among the objects themselves of the shaman, acting out the usually terrifying power represented by the mask or icon. What was at stake for the viewer was not esthetic appreciation but loss of self in identification with and support of the shamanic performance.
>
> (McEvilley 1984: 59)

By repressing the aspect of content, the Other is tamed into mere pretty stuff to dress us up ... In depressing starkness, 'Primitivism' lays bare the way our cultural institutions relate to foreign cultures, revealing it as an ethnocentric subjectivity inflated to coopt such cultures and their objects into itself.

(McEvilley 1984: 60).

A number of historians have recognized the linkages in which, for example, 'the burden of sophistication' weighing on modern artists 'had necessitated their enthusiasm 'for every primitive period of art in which they could regain a sense of seeing with the uneducated gaze of the savage and the childlike eye' (Leo Stein, quoted in Price 1989: 33). This view of primitive art 'as a kind of creative expression that flows unchecked from the artist's unconscious' (Price 1989: 32) has potentially difficult ideological implications. While the implications for those valorizing 'directness' of expression or refusing the conventions of the past may point in one direction, the comparison of primitive art and children's drawings that valorizes this formation has also been recognized to underwrite some doctrines of racial inferiority.

TIME AND THE OTHER

Another significant criticism of the way the category 'primitive art' operates addresses the neutralization of Time, following Johannes Fabian's important (1983) discussion of allochronic and coeval perspectives. In the former, a temporal distancing technique exemplified by some kinds of traditional ethnographic writing, non-Western people are represented as existing in some other time than the writer, not as part of the same history. A coeval perspective, in contrast, emphasizes their copresence. Some connoisseurs have assumed that there were – at some time – isolated cultures projecting their own 'spirit' or cultural essence into their objects. In the MOMA show, and other exhibitions, Clifford (1988) pointed out, the objects of 'primitive art' were typically identified by 'tribal group', implying a stylistic consensus, without individual authorship (implying a collectivity), and without much temporal location. When operating in the project of defining – by contrast or similarity – 'us', the 'primitive' and his or her objects tend not to be seen within their own histories and contexts. The effect is to suggest that nothing happens over time in these homogeneous and apparently unchanging primitive, traditional societies. Such societies appear to exemplify Eliade's (1959) archetype of repetition in societies dominated by ritual rather than history.

The 'primitivism' debates revealed how the opposed categories of 'primitive' and 'modern', as 'tradition' and 'innovation' respectively, might regulate the fabricated boundaries between the modern West and a supposedly premodern Other. In drawing attention to the neutralization of Time, and borrowing from Fabian (1983), Clifford's criticism notes how this Other is distanced from *us* by being excluded from contemporaneous or coeval presence with 'us'. The skewing of temporality involves a chronotope that preserves the spatialized and temporal boundaries between sociocultural worlds and people who are in fact interconnected. Indeed, it requires denying or repressing the actual history of power, relationships, and commerce that resulted in collecting the objects in the first place. Are not such connections necessary for Westerners to have gotten the objects? And is their suppression necessary to the functioning of the category 'primitive art'?

For the purpose of the 'primitivist' alterity to modernity, such representations were valued for their contrast with the modern self-conscious, dynamism and challenge of conventions typical of Western society and Western art history. But for collectors of 'primitive art', this purity, association with ritual, and distance from Western influence are precisely the sources of value. Thus, the valorized 'primitive' usable in critique is nonetheless presumed to be ahistorical, timeless, unchanging, authorless. These qualities seem necessary to preserve the capacity of this formation to provide an alterity from the West. On the one hand, 'primitive art' is authentic, expressive of the truly different Other, only when it originates outside of Western contact, in a precolonial past. On the other hand, such modes of exhibition efface the specific histories and power relations through which non-Western objects became part of Western collections, available to display. Indeed, they typically exclude the contemporary representatives of these cultural traditions as 'inauthentic'.

Yet, as the critique of deconstruction provides in one way, these very meanings are also available in the presence of the objects and their exhibition – and they provide evidence of the cultural work (through recontextualization itself) in which objects have often been deployed – of remembering, forgetting, dismembering, obviating, and displacing histories and relationships. This is what Keane (2005) means in calling for attention to causality, attention to 'what things make possible' and not just what they 'mean'. At the same time, this quality has led to exhibitions – such as the one on Stewart Culin, an important collector of Native American art for the Brooklyn Museum – that place the objects of 'primitive art' precisely within the interconnections of their collection and display (Fane 1991) and also for analysis to relate the construction of exhibitions to

contradictions that, while general, are more specific and distinctive in the historical and geographical relationships mediated (Coombes 2001).

The debates themselves had a startling effect on anthropologists. For decades, after all, anthropologists and others had labored for official acceptance of non-Western visual arts and aesthetics as serious and deserving objects of consideration in the modernist canon of visual culture. Then, just when it appeared that so-called 'tribal art' was being recognized as having affinity with the work of the recognized geniuses of modern art, art critics pulled the rug from under the enterprise. Even more embarrassingly, perhaps, they did so on grounds that anthropologists ought to have anticipated: namely the inapplicability of the Modernist, formal concept of 'art' itself as a universal, interpretive, and evaluative category.

In this way, there has been a deconstruction both of the category 'art' and of 'primitive art' that is perfectly summarized in Clifford's influential review in the following comments:

> the MOMA exhibition documents a *taxonomic* moment: the status of non-Western objects and 'high' art are importantly redefined, but there is nothing permanent or transcendent about the categories at stake. The appreciation and interpretation of tribal objects takes place within a modern 'system of objects' which confers value on certain things and withholds it from others (Baudrillard 1968). Modernist primitivism, with its claims to deeper humanist sympathies and a wider aesthetic sense, goes hand-in-hand with a developed market in tribal art and with definitions of artistic and cultural authenticity that are now widely contested.
>
> (Clifford 1988: 198)

For many, this debate about 'the primitive' was principally a debate about Modernism and modernity, against Modernism's claim to universality and the insistent identification of art with formal, artistic invention. The debates have demonstrated the extent to which non-Western practices – or more often the extractable products of those practices – have become of theoretical significance for the massive and critical debates within the art world itself concerning aesthetics and cultural politics (Foster 1983; Lippard 1991; and see Michaels 1987). But this is not the only significance of the debates, because – fittingly enough in a world of globalization and boundary breakdown – the exhibition and debates provided an occasion for those cast into the 'primitive' category to protest and resist the ideological and practical effects of this representations.

UNIVERSAL ART PROCESSES?

These critical concerns about modernity and difference, constitutive in one sense of the meanings given to 'primitive art', have fitted very uncomfortably with the concomitant debates about the question of a cross-cultural and universal aesthetics as constituted in the disciplinary concerns of Anthropology. The ambivalence about comparison is of long standing in anthropology, but as suggested above, despite their *relativistic* suspicion of Western art theory's universality, anthropologists gave little *explicit* attention to the power of cultural hierarchy as an important component in the functioning of difference. [11]

While known for his 'historical particularism' and insistence on relativism, the 'father of American anthropology' and author of the seminal volume *Primitive Art* (1927), Franz Boas himself wrote that there is a common set of processes in art:

> The treatment given to the subject [primitive art] is based on two principles that I believe should guide all investigations into the manifestations of life among primitive people: the one the fundamental sameness of mental processes in all races and in all cultural forms of the present day; the other, the consideration of every cultural phenomenon as the result of historical happenings.
>
> ... So far as my personal experience goes and so far as I feel competent to judge ethnographical data on the basis of this experience, the mental processes of man are the same everywhere, regardless of race and culture, and regardless of the apparent absurdity of beliefs and customs.
>
> (Boas 1927: 1)

Brilliantly in this volume, Boas attempted to demonstrate technical virtuosity – emphasizing, thus, the materiality both of the worker's body and of the object on which it works – as the vital core of 'primitive art' and art more generally. By 1938, however, Joseph Campbell notes, similar passages were removed from Boas's updated *The Mind of Primitive Man* (1938): 'a tendency to emphasize the differentiating traits of primitive societies had meanwhile developed to such a degree that any mention by an author of common traits simply meant that he had not kept up with the fashion' (1969: 20).

It is not surprising that another component of the 'primitivism' critiques,[12] the discussions of aesthetic universality connected to the doctrine of Formalist Modernism, has cut across the older tradition of 'tribal art' studies that insisted at times simultaneously on (1) the existence of 'art' in all cultures and (2) their differences. This has been an area of ambivalence in the anthropology of art, sustained by an inadequate reflexive consideration of Western concepts of art (see Myers and Marcus 1995) and by the segregation of the market for non-Western objects from the larger debates. I don't mean to say that collectors of 'primitive art' were unaware of stylistic traditions and variations. (Indeed, some of them think they are collecting 'masterpieces'.) However, the participation of collectors in the discourse of 'authenticity' and 'purity' relates to the ideological functioning of the category 'primitive art' at another level – one in which the underlying forms of expression, psyche, and motivation are essentially one.

There are intrinsic contradictions here, and the emerging line of cleavage only reinforces the sense of the category's instability and involvement in ideological regulation. By 'instability' I seek to draw attention to conflation. The anthropological sense of difference is incorporated in concerns about cultural relativism; while concerned to grant some kind of equality or equivalence among cultural formulations, it does not address the difference among cultures in the same way as the postmodern suspicion of purported formal relationships between so-called 'primitive' and 'modern' artists. The postmodern concern is to draw attention to the existence of dominant Western cultural forms as *cultural*, rather than just natural and universal. They deride the effacement of what must be incommensurable differences in attempts at 'humanizing' or 'familiarizing' the foreign in terms of the dominant norm. They are further concerned with the way in which art theory has tended to deny the value of popular art practice and popular culture, in so far as they might differ from what Modernism presented as central and most valued. Skeptical of the strategy of 'humanism', Clifford (1988) – and in different ways Marianna Torgovnick (1990) – drew attention to these very tendencies in projects of comparison in distinguishing a humanistic ethnography of 'familiarization' (that finds similarities between them and us, but in our terms) from a surrealistic one that 'subverts' or 'disrupts' the all-too-familiar categories.[13] He called, famously, for attention to objects that are 'indigestible' by our own categories, especially 'hybrid objects', challenging to the frameworks of Western culture in ways resonant with the historical avant-garde.

The primitivism debates allow us to recognize that the doctrines that view art as autonomous from other domains of social life are not 'theories' external to their object (see Myers and

Marcus 1995; Myers 2002). As 'ethnotheories' these doctrines would be cultural products and linked organically to the same processes of modernization they seem to oppose. Just as 'antimodernism' has been identified by Jackson Lears (1983) as protesting 'modernity' and therefore part of it, so 'primitivism' is intrinsically connected to 'modernity' and 'Modernism'.

'MODERN ART'

The foregoing implies that the relationality of the category 'primitive art' finds its location within the changing meanings and valence of the category 'art' itself in the Western tradition. For many people engaged with the arts, 'art' remains a commonsense category of just this sort; and there is held to be something essential about these practices in terms of their value, their relation to the human psyche or creativity or spirituality. This has not, however, been merely a fact of art's universality, and social historians of art have pursued this strangeness, the particularity of Western art's own self-construction, from *within* the tradition. The research of Kristeller, Williams, and others (Baxandall 1972; Eagleton 1990) has pointed to the distinctiveness of this 'modern' notion of art, one in which quite distinct kinds of activity have come to be constructed (or recognized) as *separated from other cultural activity* and having something in common as 'art'. They have attempted to understand the transformations of European social life that led to the condition for our (Western) particular experience of an 'aesthetic dimension'.

The work of historians, no less than that of anthropologists and critics, has offered a challenge to the universality of the concepts of art and aesthetics familiar to Modernism. Raymond Williams (1977) famously outlined the changing meaning of the concept 'art', and its place in the history of industrialization (see also Baxandall 1972). From the Middle Ages to the nineteenth century, Williams pointed out, the concept changed from a reference to 'general skill' to one of a distinct sphere of cultural, aesthetic activity (a sphere distinguished by its combination of arts into art and by its transcendence of the instrumental, the merely material and mere bodily pleasure). Indeed, the Renaissance historian Kristeller somewhat earlier noted that there was no concept of 'art' that embraced the quite distinct forms of painting, music, sculpture, theater, and dance:

We have to admit the conclusion, distasteful to many historians of aesthetics but grudgingly admitted by most of them, that ancient writers and thinkers, though confronted with excellent works of art and quite susceptible to their charm, were neither able nor eager to detach the aesthetic quality of these works of art from their intellectual, moral, religious, and practical function or content, or to use an aesthetic quality as a standard for grouping the fine arts together or for making them the subject of a comprehensive philosophical interpretation.

(Kristeller 1951/1965: 174)

In considering what is called 'modernity', historians have explored what is involved in the binary constructions of 'primitive art'. The consideration of 'modernity' stresses the general context of institutional separation of distinct and abstract areas of interest – of kinship, politics, religion, economics, and art – taking place in the rise of capitalism's development, a line pioneered by Max Weber, or in the rise of the nation state (Eagleton 1990). There may not be much agreement about the timing of these developments as well as the definitive characterization of the separation, but most theorists agree that there is an important difference between art and these other domains, in that – as Daniel Miller sums it up, 'art appears to have been given, as its brief, the challenge of confronting the nature of *modernity* itself, and providing both moral commentary and alternative perspectives on that problem' (Miller 1991: 52, my emphasis). In contrast, surely, the anthropological emphasis on the *social* embeddedness of art practices in so-called 'traditional societies' is not a matter of simple difference but ends up constituting by contrast the distinctiveness of 'modern art' – in which the separation of an aesthetic sphere was constitutive of art and aesthetics as a particular mode of evaluating, or interrogating, cultural activity and its value.

The questions of mass culture and mass consumption, as well as that of cultural heterogeneity (high and low culture, fine art and popular or folk) are central questions addressed by modern ideologies of art. A hierarchy of discriminating value is organized through what is claimed to be a universalizing, interest-free judgment. What might be called 'modernisms', therefore, can be seen to develop in relation to the rise of industrial capitalism in Europe and the revolution in France in 1848 – a condition in which art comprises an arena in which discourses about cultural value are produced. Thus, modernization is the basis of 'modernism' – an ideology that engages with the conditions of the former. It is this dimension of 'modern art' – its complex and critical relationship to the concomitant 'modern' and emerging dominance of rational utility and money as the basis of all value – that has often shared with 'primitive art' an oppositional stance to the rational side of modernity. It is in this way that 'primitive art' has been able to operate as a basis for 'modern art'.[14]

Recruited in this way to the ideological project of 'modern art', a project built around the autonomy of art as a sphere of distinct experience, the resulting constructions of 'primitivism' were inevitably oriented to the concerns of those who used them. The relatively common view, therefore, that high art takes transcendence of the fragmented, dislocated nature of contemporary life in the industrial era as a central concern (see Miller 1991: 52) defines a 'primitive art' that functions as evidence of the existence of forms of humanity which are integral, cohesive, working as a totality. Such meanings do not simply provide the critical opposite to such an experienced world; rather 'primitive art' and its represented reality also permit the very characterization of the 'modern' *as* fragmented and a sense of contemporary mass culture as 'spurious' and somehow 'inauthentic'.

It should be clear that the signifying locations of 'primitive art' have varied with the particular narrative of 'loss' presumed to have occurred with modern life. But these signifying practices seem always to involve repressing or suppressing part of the phenomenon. If, in a certain sense, 'primitive art' supposes traditionalism – which violates avant-garde requirements for originality and self-creation – this opposition has had to be repressed to capture the organic opposite for modern fragmentation.

Thus, figures such as the 'primitive', the 'exotic', or the 'tribal' have offered a basis for challenging Western categories by defining 'difference', but they have done so principally, it would appear, *within* the ideological function of Western cultural systems. And it was this function – the continued support of the dominant Western cultural system that in fact might limit and misrepresent the works and meanings of non-Western practitioners – which postmodern theorists recognized and sought to disrupt.

The tropes of 'primitive art' continued to exercise considerable rhetorical power towards the end of the twentieth century, as demonstrated by the much publicized Parisian exhibition 'Les Magiciens de la terre' (see Buchloh 1989), by the continuing boom in the sale of 'genuine' African art that has not been in touch with the contaminating hand of the West or the market (Steiner 1994), and by the critical

responses to Aboriginal acrylic painting (Myers 1991, 2002).

PRIMITIVISM STILL

To conclude this chapter, I will remark on the opportunities I have had to see this myself, in writing about the representation of Aboriginal culture in the critical responses to an exhibition of Aboriginal acrylic paintings at the Asia Society in 1988, and to trace briefly some of the trajectories set in motion by the critiques.

In the responses to the exhibition of Aboriginal art at the Asia Society, I found (Myers 1991) that several evaluations suggested that the acrylics offer a glimpse of the spiritual wholeness lost, variously, to 'Western art', to 'Western man', or to 'modernity'. The well known Australian art critic Robert Hughes indulged precisely in the form of nostalgic primitivism, praising the exhibition lavishly in *Time* magazine and drawing precisely on this opposition:

> Tribal art is never free and does not want to be. The ancestors do not give one drop of goanna spit for 'creativity'. It is not a world, to put it mildly, that has much in common with a contemporary American's – or even a white Australian's. But it raises painful questions about the irreversible drainage from our own culture of spirituality, awe, and connection to nature.
>
> (Hughes 1988: 80)

In Hughes's estimation, their 'otherness' occupies a world without much in common with ours; the artistic values of individual creativity and freedom are not relevant. But this otherness, he maintained, was itself meaningful for us. Another line of evaluation asked if they could be viewed as a conceptual return to our lost ('primitive') selves, as suggested in the subtitle of another review: 'Aboriginal art as a kind of cosmic road map to the primeval' (Wallach 1989).

The conventions of their differences were also seen as morally instructive about some of our own associations, especially of our materialism. In his travels to Australia during the planning of the exhibition, Andrew Pekarik (then Director of the Asia Society Gallery) was reported as saying 'that these people with practically zero material culture have one of the most complex social and intellectual cultures of any society' (in Cazdow 1987: 9). In this Romantic – and Durkheimian – construction, a critique of Modernity, the paintings may represent the worthiness of Aboriginal survival and, consequently, the dilemma and indictment of modern Australia's history and treatment of their forebears as less than human.

POSITIONS FOR SIGNIFYING THE PRIMITIVE

The construction of 'primitivism' has a particular salience for the production and circulation of political and cultural identities. At the same time, recent work argues that 'primitivism' must be studied in its particular contexts, and it is increasingly realized that there is not a generic 'primitivism'. Nicholas Thomas (1999), for example, has written about the distinctive qualities of 'settler primitivism', which should be distinguished from other operations of the trope. One might note, for example, the importance of World War I – in the United States, Canada, and Australia – in leading these settler nations to pursue more actively an identity distinct from that of Europe, the role this played in the development of interest in 'primitive art', and the appropriation of each country's indigenous arts as part of the national cultural patrimony (see especially Mullin 1995).[15] Often, the effort to escape the anxiety of European influence and to express a unique experience has resulted in an appropriation of the 'native', the 'indigene', as a component of an authentic national culture, exhibited, sold, and collected in museums and markets of 'primitive art'. Objects marked as 'art' are not the only material for such cultural production, but their portability and circulability may allow such objects to bear special weight in these desires. The workings here seem to differ from the ideological function of 'primitivism' in the MOMA exhibition of 1984, which was concerned with making the Other legitimate the cosmopolitan Western (not national) construction of 'art' in its most essential form, as formal and creative, as a basic human impulse. In processes of nation building, a central activity of modernization, distinctive values may be imputed to the 'native'. Appropriation by nationalist culture represents different temporal and spatial juxtapositions. This occurs both by regional transposition and also by class and gendered positioning – but it is within this range of the ideological organization of 'difference' that 'primitivism' and modern art coincide.

Thus, suspicion about the uses of 'primitivism' has not been aimed only at the supposedly transcendent, autonomous aesthetic domain postulated by High Modernism. It has equally significant implications, however, for the way in which local identities might lose their integrity or have their distinctiveness subsumed within a grand narrative that does not engage *their* own histories. This may well be a problem of art at the periphery of the world system. Thus, the exhibitions of what were called 'Primitive Art,' while they emphasize form – in being displayed on the usual white walls without much information other than general date and probable 'tribal identity' – denied to these works the history and authorship which would be part of the Western context (see Price 1989).

For Aboriginal Australian and First Nation people in North America, 'primitivism' has a particular salience for the production and circulation of political and cultural identities (see Ziff and Rao 1997). Ames (1992), Clifford (1988, 1991) and some of the essayists in Karp and Lavine (1991) have eloquently made this point about museums particularly. But they do so in recognition of the active political projects of indigenous people and their representatives – in the practices of artists and curators such as Jimmy Durham, Jolene Rickard, Gerald McMaster, Fiona Foley, Brenda Croft, Tracey Moffatt, Paul Chaat Smith, and others – who reject the binding restrictions of 'authenticity' and cultural purity with their own insistence that 'We are not dead, nor less ['Indian', 'Aboriginal', etc.].' The fundamental rejection of the category 'primitive art' surely takes place in the creation of their own museums by indigenous communities in North America, Australia, and elsewhere – in museums such as the newly opened, indigenously curated and managed National Museum of the American Indian, twenty years old as an indigenous institution. Indigenous people are also, increasingly, reclaiming the objects made by their ancestors, through legislation relating to cultural property concerns such as the US Native American Graves Protection and Repatriation Act (passed in 1990) or the Aboriginal and Torres Strait Islander Heritage Protection Act of 1984. In reclaiming objects, indigenous people resituate the objects in *their* own histories, constructing a narrative of their presence and continued existence as part of a world that may include other cultures but also constituting themselves as a people through their claim. Indeed, the materiality of these objects enables their repatriation and history to be part of their continued presence. In July 2004, for example, under Aboriginal heritage protection laws, an Indigenous Australian group, the Dja Dja Wurrung, created a huge controversy in seizing some 150 year old artifacts that had been on loan from the British Museum to an exhibition in Melbourne at Museum Victoria. The contestation over this case exemplifies the collision of two different regimes of value, in which the values created by different forms of exchange – one in the market dominated by the West and the other in cosmological regimes of indigenous claims – are engaged in a 'tournament of values' (Appadurai 1986) fundamentally set in motion by an insistence on coeval presence.

THE INTERCULTURAL FIELD

Where are the 'natives', one must ask, in the primitivism debates, and why do they seem to be erased by the language of 'appropriation'? To be sure, the recognition that non-Western peoples 'had art' did result – and not inconsequentially – in their inclusion in the authorized 'Family of Man'. They were 'creative', 'humane', 'spiritual'. But the exhibitions promoting this inclusion – and the success of the intensified circulation of the products and images of non-Western Others – comprise a complex for recontextualizing objects that offers opportunities for varying engagement. In this sense, they are sites of ongoing cultural production (Bourdieu 1993), and it is important to understand them in this way.

I wish to draw on the analytic framework of 'recontextualization' first offered by Nicholas Thomas (1991; see also Myers 2001). It offers an opportunity for some suggestions beyond those imagined in the first round of Primitivism debates, suggestions more in keeping with the renewed approach to considerations of materiality (see Gell 1998; Miller 2005). It suggests that a larger frame for grasping 'primitivism' lies in the notion of intercultural exchange and transaction. This is a frame that can include the sort of 'appropriations' that have concerned critics, but the weight is placed not on the boundaries but on the charged social field that encompasses the actors. An emphasis on 'appropriation' and the primitivizing 'gaze' is not sufficient to understand what happens materially when such objects circulate into an international art world. Scholars such as Howard Morphy (1992), Ruth Phillips (1998), Richard and Sally Price (1999), Chris Steiner (1994), Nelson Graburn (2004), Charlene Townsend-Gault (2004) and I (among others) have asked what actually *does* happen in circulation, at the sites of exhibition – to ask how objects, identities, and discourses are produced, inflected, and invoked in *actual institutional settings*. These 'fields of cultural production' (Bourdieu

1993) have distinctive histories, purposes, and structures of their own.[16]

Further, this approach redresses one of the principal assumptions of 'primitivism', namely the temporal boundary that considered these cultures to be over, lacking a future, an assumption underlying the typical lack of concern to include the voices or actual subjectivities of those from these traditions.[17] In the Sotheby's auction, with which I began this chapter, the indigenous 'traditional owners' of the *churinga* attempted to bring it back – with the additional agency of the Central Land Council and the Federal Minister for Aboriginal Affairs – through purchase, and thereby to remove it from the realm of art commodity and replace it within their own tradition. Although they failed in the attempt, because the price exceeded the resources provided by the Australian government, the activation of their agency did succeed in redefining the social field and challenging the once easy placement of such objects within the domain of 'primitive art'. Even at the MOMA exhibition the indexical relationships of beautiful objects to their makers and heirs became a basis for the extension of 'native' agency: the so-called Zuni war god figures were withdrawn from the show when MOMA 'was informed by knowledgeable authorities that Zuni people consider any public exhibition of their war gods to be sacrilegious' (quoted in Clifford 1988: 209). As Clifford notes, this event shows that 'living traditions have claims on them' (*ibid.*), and a range of recent repatriation claims have made this process increasingly visible.

It is just such an 'Outward Clash' – as Peirce calls it (Keane 2005) – that forces us to attend to the broader materiality involved in such objects. In museums around the world, what was 'primitive art' is being resignified, reclaimed, re-exhibited as the patrimony of particular communities or peoples – bearing the trace, as well, of its history of 'collection' or 'alienation' (see Ames 1992; Clifford 1991; Cranmer Webster 1992; Saunders 1997; Kramer 2004). Research and writing on the nation and the native offer considerable insight into the problem.

In pursuit of this sort of specificity, it is clearly necessary to break down the very general notion of the 'primitive' that has tended to be deployed in analyses. In part, this involves recognizing that the processes of modernization are mediated through a range of distinctive institutions. Thus, scholars must continue to track the figure of the 'Indigenous Other' through the distinctive circuits of artistic, regional, and national institutions and identity, showing different mediations through time and place (Bakewell 1995; Cohodas 1999; Mullin 1995; Myers 2002; Phillips 1998; Thomas 1999).

There has been a *general* context for revaluing indigenous people and their products in the English-speaking settler states. It has often been noted that the recuperation of the indigenous culture in such appropriations may, however, value them only in ways defined by the dominant culture – that is, in terms of a hegemony that does not really accept 'difference' or that organizes difference in the service of another set of values. This is the effect of the effort at appropriation of the indigenous – the Indio – by Mexican fine arts in the service of the revolution's ideology of hybridization (Bakewell 1995); for such work to be 'fine art', however, it could not be made by those regarded as artisans – and certainly not by Indios themselves. Similarly, the resignifications of the Australian Aboriginal relationship to land embodied in their paintings may be resisted within the immediate region where they live (whose settlers compete for control of the land) or by immigrant minorities (who are threatened by a special Aboriginal status), but have a different meaning when they are 're-placed' in the context of emerging Australian nationalism, international tourism, and the new professional class that seeks to define itself.

However, while Aboriginal producers of the paintings – living in dilapidated and impoverished communities – may be stripped of their historical specificity and their images converted to signifiers in Australian national myth, their insistence on a return of value for their paintings also resists this incorporation. Objects lend themselves to recontextualization for an unlimited range of ideological purposes, an infinite number of desires, and so-called 'natives' appropriate, too – not just commodities and signifiers, but even the idea of art itself! The claim to be making 'art' – contemporary art – is a vital strand of the recent movement of acrylic painting and other forms of Indigenous expression in Australia, and significant parallels are clear in Canada – with Northwest Coast art (see Ames 1992) – and in the United States (Lippard 1991).

As a final comment, in recognition of the potentials of these interventions, I would like to reiterate what I have argued elsewhere (Myers 2001), therefore, that the language of 'objectification' – beyond the one-sided framework of 'appropriation' – may provide greater leverage in teasing out the complicated and subtle intersections of relative value and interests. If the appropriations of Aboriginal painting or decoration are objectifications of national identity, they are also objectifications of their Aboriginal makers, and we need to follow out the implications of their movement through a new system of value. In this movement, the media in which these objectifications occurred are a problem to be considered. Painting, sculpture, and dance may move very differently. But at the same time, we are forced to recognize that works of Aboriginal 'art' index their makers and their production history, even if the structure of an exhibition suppresses this by labels that present only tribe and century. Questions about the objects and how they got there are potentially present in any exhibition. Recent exhibitions – like 'Pomo Indian Basket Weavers: their Baskets and the Art Market' (organized by the University of Pennsylvania Museum of Archaeology and Anthropology and shown at venues like the NMAI, Gustav Heye Center in Manhattan in 1999) and the earlier 'Objects of Myth and Memory: American Indian Art at the Brooklyn Museum' (1991) that focused on the curator Stewart Culin's collecting – have reclaimed these histories and personages, and the networks linking, for example, basket makers in California and collectors in the Northeast through the display of baskets.[18]

Moreover, the objectifications of national identity are both variable and contextually limited in their stability. Aboriginal art's status as a commodity of consumption involves forms of commercial value that are potentially at odds with its capacity to articulate – as something spiritual, authentic, and attached to the land – national identity. It was nothing short of a scandal, then, when an Aboriginal bark painting in the Prime Minister's collection was discovered to be a forgery, painted by a white person! Furthermore, these paintings – and art itself – are not the only media in which national identity may be objectified. War memorials, automobiles, heritage sites, archeological formations, heroes, battlefields, natural history museums, symphony orchestras, and so on may offer very different – even competing – representations of the national self, representations that may circulate within different contexts and social formations.

These constitute the very different implications of what Thomas (1999) calls 'settler primitivism' from a more general primitivism such as that represented in European modernist art. The whole significance of settler primitivism is that the 'native' and the 'settler' *are* coeval. In this sense, settler primitivism depends on another contingency of the materiality of things – their spatial contiguity. The instabilities and the tensions come from the fact that indigenous communities are not only contemporaneous but also to some extent recognizably in the same space with so-called modern ones. While it draws on many tropes that are familiar, settler primitivism has a distinctive problem of context: the indigenous people cannot be fully relegated to prehistory as the predecessors of the settlers. There is a basic situation of copresence, even competing claims in the land. The logic of the more general primitivism – through which African cultural products were conveyed – differs in this regard, and is mediated through the constructions of the nation and national cultures in postcolonial states.

These recontextualizations – in this case of a hybrid formation of settler primitivism – are not just surprising or ironic juxtapositions, but reorganizations of *value*. The gain in value for native cultural forms should be conceptualized in terms that are relevant for anthropological theory more generally, and indeed such recontextualizations are increasingly common in the world.

NOTES

1 Gombrich wrote of 'the preference for the primitive' as having as early an appearance as the quotation he takes from Cicero, and sees it as an occasional and temporary rejection or disgust for the refined and the trajectory of mimesis.

2 Two other important collections have followed on the initial burst of interest in the primitivism debates – Karp and Lavine (1991) and Phillips and Steiner (1999).

3 A great exception to this preference for the pure exotic, of course, is Julius Lips's *The Savage Hits Back* (1937), while a more recent foray into such matters was Enid Schildkrout's and Charles Keims's exhibition of Mangbetu art (see Schildkrout and Keim 1990).

4 A further development of these discussions emanated in the wake of 'Les Magiciens de la terre,' an exhibition in Paris that attempted to transcend some of the difficulties faced by MOMA.

5 The Museum of Modern Art's approach is set forth in Alfred Barr's work. MOMA had considerable influence on the recognition of 'primitive art' as *art* through a series of exhibitions organized especially by René d'Harnoncourt. In 1936 he was appointed an administrator in the Indian Arts and Crafts Board, part of the Department of the Interior. D'Harnoncourt mounted one of the first national exhibitions of Native American arts at the Golden Gate International Exposition in San Francisco in 1939. D'Harnoncourt was responsible for other exhibitions of African art and that of North American Indians. In addition to being curator and later Director of MOMA, d'Harnoncourt also served as art advisor to Nelson Rockefeller's art collection and was vice-president for Rockefeller's Museum of Primitive Art from its beginning in 1957. D'Harnoncourt was closely involved with one of the major academic scholars of primitive art, Paul Wingert. Some important discussion of d'Harnoncourt can be found in Rushing (1995).

6 As Torgovnick writes of the critic Roger Fry, there was a great concern to 'rescue art from the morass of photographic representation and narrative' (1990: 87). Fry was one of the early critical enthusiasts for what he called 'Negro Art' (Fry 1920). The rise of photography and its greater capacity for naturalistic representation is commonly perceived as creating a crisis for 'art' and a need to 'make it new' by theorizing a distinctive function for it. If one account of Modernism and 'Primitivism' can be traced through the collection and exhibition of African and Oceanic art, as Rubin (1984) does and which Torgovnick follows, another account is traced by W. Jackson Rushing's *Native American Art and the New York Avant-garde* (1995) and his depiction of the unique critical contexts established in the United States in relation to Native American cultural products. The edited collection, *Primitivism and Twentieth-Century Art: a Documentary History* (Flam and Deutch 2003), provides many of the central documents for a history of primitivism and its controversies as well as a comprehensive chronology of exhibitions, publications, and events.

7 In *Primitivism in Modern Art*, published in 1938, Goldwater pointed to the important precedent set for much modern European art by the forms of children's drawings and other kinds of so-called 'primitive' art, as well as by artists' ideas about the nature of the creative process which lay behind those forms.

8 Such typological resemblance was what Boasian anthropologists once described as 'convergence' or forms of independent invention, although they functioned in the

exhibition to indicate the universality of the interest in form. For discussions of the 'comparative method' and debates about it, see Harris (1968) and Lowie (1937).

9 In this regard, there is still some ambiguity in anthropological concerns about context, which – art-oriented scholars have maintained – tend to subsume the material object to cultural meanings, claiming to see something *beyond* the object in itself.

10 In this form, the identification of the primitive with directness and expression could be mobilized to an avant-garde position that Gombrich delineates in Zola's review of Manet's 'Olympia', in 'Mon salon', in which he says he asks an artist to do more than provide mere 'beauty': 'It is no longer a question here, therefore, of pleasing or of not pleasing, it is a question of being oneself, of baring one's breast ... The word "art" displeases me. It contains, I do not know what, in the way of ideas of necessary compromises, of absolute ideals ... that which I seek above all in a painting is a man, and not a picture ... You must abandon yourself bravely to your nature and not seek to deny it' (Gombrich 2002: 206).

11 Miller has insisted, for example, that the claim of art as a transcendent realm was not something really taken seriously by anthropologists (see Miller 1991 and below), whose studies have tended to emphasize the embedding of aesthetics *in* everyday life (e.g., Witherspoon 1977). 'The separation and definition of art and aesthetics as something different and particular,' as Miller calls it (1991: 51), is rare in the world's cultures. Much anthropological ink was spilled in demonstrating the functional involvement of supposedly artistic forms – masks, sculpture – in political and religious activities, against an expectation of art for art's sake. At the same time, there were surely few anthropologists who wanted to claim that the communities they studied 'lacked art', since something unselfconsciously called 'art' remained the *sine qua non* of human status. Consequently, an anthropologist encounters the category of 'art' with suspicion and a sense of its 'strangeness'. Indeed, for most anthropologists, the concept of 'art' would be, as it is for Miller (1991: 50), 'subject to the critique of relativism, in that it stems from an essentialist foundation – that is, no absolute quality of the world – but has become an established perspective through particular cultural and historical conditions'.

12 See Dutton's 1991 review of Price (1989) as well as the Manchester debates on aesthetics (Ingold 1997).

13 In an excellent essay, Eric Michaels (1987) – no doubt sick of the repeated treatment of Aboriginal painters as 'so many Picassos in the desert' – argued that the practices of Aboriginal acrylic painting had more to offer postmodern art theory than that of Modernism. I cannot resist pointing out how these tendencies themselves draw precisely on the tropes of the historical avant-garde to tear away the familiar and to reveal, thereby, the world. An elegant example of this is to be found in Tony Bennett's (1979) discussion of 'estrangement' and 'defamiliarization' in Russian Formalism.

14 One must acknowledge that historians disagree in how they understand the emergence of such a set of discursive practices – with art as healing and the artist as heroic individual.

15 While I want to stress the development of an interest in and market for 'primitive art' here, I do not mean to say that this was the first time in which the settler societies appropriated their country's indigenous arts for the production of national identity. In the United States, this clearly occurred in periods earlier than World War I, although something distinctive does happen then.

16 I am indebted to Webb Keane for the reminder here that part of the value of Nicholas Thomas's (1991) book, *Entangled Objects*, rests in his effort to look in both directions, at Pacific peoples' recontextualizations of Western cultural objects. Obviously, this is not a level political playing field. At the same time, however, it is not a peculiarity of the West to resignify things.

17 Douglas Cole (1985), for example, describes a period of rapid accumulation around the turn of the nineteenth and twentieth centuries, justified in so far as Native cultures were thought to be vanishing. Others have insisted on the importance of Western custodianship of objects neglected or no longer of value in their 'home' cultures. These frameworks underlie the neglect of the possible attachment of these objects to living people.

18 The marvelous writing of Marvin Cohodas (1997) and Sally McLendon (1993, 1998) are exemplary of the work on collecting that has transformed the thinking about 'primitive art'.

REFERENCES

Adorno, Teodor (1970/1983) *Aesthetic Theory*. London: Routledge.

Ames, Michael M. (1992) *Cannibal Tours and Glass Boxes: the Anthropology of Museums*. Vancouver: UBC Press.

Anderson, Richard (1989) *Art in Small-scale Societies*. Englewood Cliffs, NJ: Prentice-Hall.

Appadurai, Arjun (1986) 'Introduction: commodities and the politics of value', in Arjun Appadurai (ed.), *The Social Life of Things*. Cambridge: Cambridge University Press, pp. 3–63.

Bakewell, Liza (1995) '*Bellas artes* and *artes populares*: the implications of difference in the Mexico City art world', in B. Bright and L. Bakewell (eds), *Looking High and Low: Art and Cultural Identity*. Tucson, AZ: University of Arizona Press, pp. 19–54.

Barthes, Roland (1957) *Mythologies*. Paris: Seuil.

Baudrillard, Jean (1968) *Le Système des objets*. Paris: Gallimard.

Baxandall, Michael (1972) *Painting and Experience in Fifteenth Century Italy: a Primer in the Social History of a Pictorial Style*. Oxford: Clarendon Press.

Bennett, Tony (1979) *Formalism and Marxism*. London: Methuen.

Blake, Nigel and Frascina, Francis (1993) 'Modern practices of art and modernity', in F. Frascina, N. Blake, B. Fer, T. Garb and C. Harrison (eds), *Modernity and Modernism: French Painting in the Nineteenth Century*. New Haven, CT and London: Yale University Press in association with the Open University, pp. 50–140.

Boas, Franz (1927) *Primitive Art*. New York: Dover Publications.

Boas, Franz (1938) *The Mind of Primitive Man*, rev. edn. New York: Macmillan.

Bourdieu, Pierre (1984) *Distinction: a Social Critique of the Judgment of Taste*. Cambridge, MA: Harvard University Press.

Bourdieu, Pierre (1993) *The Field of Cultural Production*. New York: Columbia University Press.

Buchloh, Benjamin J. (1989) 'The Whole Earth Show: an interview with Jean-Hubert Martin', *Art in America*, 77 (May): 150–9, 211, 213.

Campbell, Joseph (1969) 'Primitive Man as Metaphysician', in Stanley Diamond (ed.), *Primitive Views of the World*. New York: Columbia University Press, pp. 20–32.

Cazdow, Jane (1987) 'The art of desert dreaming', *Australian Weekend Magazine*, 8–9 August, pp. 6–9.

Clifford, James (1988) *The Predicament of Culture: Ethnography, Literature, Art*. Cambridge, MA: Harvard University Press.

Clifford, James (1991) 'Four northwest coast museums: travel reflections', in I. Karp and S.D. Lavine (eds), *Exhibiting Cultures: the Poetics and Politics of Museum Display*. Washington, DC: Smithsonian Institution Press, pp. 212–54.

Cohodas, Marvin (1997) *Basket Weavers for the Curio Trade: Elizabeth and Louise Hickox*. Tucson, AZ and Los Angeles: University of Arizona Press/ Southwest Museum.

Cohodas, Marvin (1999) 'Elizabeth Hickox and Karuk Basketry: a case study of debates on innovation and paradigms of authenticy', in R. Phillips and C. Steiner (eds), *Unpacking Culture*. Berkeley, CA: University of California Press, pp. 143–61.

Cole, Douglas (1985) *Captured Heritage: the Scramble for Northwest Coast Artifacts*. Seattle, WA: University of Washington Press.

Connelly, Frances (1995) *The Sleep of Reason*. College Park, PA: Pennsylvania State University Press.

Connor, Steven (1989) *Postmodernist Culture: an Introduction to Theories of the Contemporary*. Oxford and Cambridge: Blackwell.

Coombes, Annie, E. (2001) 'The object of translation: notes on 'Art' and autonomy in a postcolonial context', in F. Myers (ed.), *The Empire of Things*. Santa Fe, NM: School of American Research Press, pp. 233–56.

Cranmer Webster, Gloria (1992) 'From colonization to repatriation', in Gerald McMaster and Lee-Ann Martin (eds), *Indigena: Contemporary Native Perspectives*. Vancouver: Douglas and McIntyre.

Danto, Arthur (1986) *The Philosophical Disenfranchisement of Art*. New York: Columbia University Press.

D'Azevedo, Warren L., ed. (1973) *The Traditional Artist in African Societies*. Bloomington, IN: Indiana University Press.

Diamond, Stanley (1969) 'Introduction: the Uses of the primitive', in Stanley Diamond (ed), *Primitive Views of the World*. New York: Columbia University Press, pp. v–xxix.

Dutton, Dennis (1991) 'Sally Price on primitive art', *Philosophy and Literature*, 15: 382–7.

Eagleton, Terry (1990) *The Ideology of the Aesthetic*. New York: Blackwell.

Eliade, Mircea (1959) *Cosmos and History: the Myth of the Eternal Return*. New York: Harper Torchbook.

Errington, Shelley (1998) *The Death of Authentic Primitive Art and other Tales of Progress*. Berkeley, CA: University of California Press.

Fabian, Johannes (1983) *Time and the Other*. New York: Columbia University Press.

Fane, Diana (1991) *Objects of Myth and Memory*. Seattle, WA: University of Washington Press.

Flam, Jack and Deutch, Miriam, eds (2003) *Primitivism and Twentieth-Century Art: a Documentary History*. Berkeley, CA: University of California Press.

Foster, Hal, ed. (1983) *The Anti-aesthetic: Essays on Postmodern Culture*. Port Townsend, WA: Bay Press.

Foster, Hal (1985) 'The "primitive" unconscious of modern art, or, White skin, black masks', in *Recodings: Art, Spectacle, Cultural Politics*. Seattle, WA: Bay Press.

Fried, Michael (1967) 'Art and objecthood', *Artforum* 5 (summer): 12–23.

Fry, Roger (1920) 'Negro sculpture at the Chelsea Book Club', *Athenaeum*, 94 (16 April): 516. Repr. in *Vision and Design*. New York: Brentano's.

Gell, Alfred (1998) *Art and Agency*. Oxford: Clarendon Press.

Goldwater, Robert (1938) *Primitivism in Modern Art*. New York: Random House.

Gombrich, Ernst (2002) *The Preference for the Primitive: Episodes in the History of Western Taste and Art*. New York: Phaidon Press.

Graburn, Nelson (2004) 'Authentic Inuit art: creation and inclusion in the Canadian north', *Journal of Material Culture* 9 (2): 141–59.

Greenberg, Clement (1961) 'Avant-garde and kitsch', in *Art and Culture: Critical Essays*. Boston, MA: Beacon Press, pp. 3–21.

Greenberg, Clement (1965) 'Modernist painting', *Art and Literature*, 4 (spring): 193–201.

Guilbaut, Serge (1983) *How New York stole the Idea of Abstract Art: Abstract Expressionism, Freedom and the Cold War*, trans. A. Goldhammer. Chicago: University of Chicago Press.

Harris, Marvin (1968) *The Rise of Anthropological Theory*. New York: Columbia University Press.

Hughes, Robert (1988) 'Evoking the spirit ancestors', *Time*, 31 October, pp. 79–80.

Ingold, Tim, ed. (1997) *Key Debates in Anthropology*. London: Routledge.

Jopling, Carole F., ed. (1971) *Art and Aesthetics in Primitive Societies: a Critical Anthology*. New York: Penguin Books.

Karp, Ivan and Lavine, Stephen D. (1991) *Exhibiting Cultures: the Poetics and Politics of Museum Display*. Washington, DC: Smithsonian Institution Press.

Keane, Webb (2005) 'Signs are not the garb of meaning: on the social analysis of material things', in D. Miller (ed.), *Materiality*. Durham, NC: Duke University Press.

Kramer, Jennifer (2004) 'Figurative repatriation', *Journal of Material Culture*, 9: 161–82.

Kristeller, Paul (1951/1965) 'The modern system of the arts', in *Renaissance Thought and the Arts*. Princeton, NJ: Princeton University Press.

Lears, T.J. Jackson (1983) *No Place of Grace: Antimodernism and the Transformation of American Culture, 1880–1920*. New York: Pantheon Books.

Lévi-Strauss, C. (1996) *The Savage Mind*. Oxford: Oxford University Press.

Lippard, Lucy (1991) *Mixed Blessings: New Art in a Multicultural America*. New York: Pantheon.

Lips, Julius (1937/1966) *The Savage Hits Back*, trans. Vincent Benson. New Hyde Park: University Books.

Lovejoy, Arthur and Boas, George (1935) *Primitivism and Related Ideas in Antiquity*. Baltimore, MD: Johns Hopkins University Press.

Lowie, Robert (1937) *The History of Ethnological Theory*. New York: Holt Rinehart.

McEvilley, Thomas (1984) 'Doctor, lawyer, Indian chief', *Artforum*, 23 (3): 54–60.

McLendon, Sally (1993) 'Collecting Pomoan baskets, 1889–1939', *Museum Anthropology*, 17 (2): 49–60.

McLendon, Sally (1998) 'Pomo basket weaves in the University of Pennsylvania Museum collections', *Expedition*, 40 (1): 34–47.

Michaels, Eric (1987) 'Western Desert sand painting and postmodernism', in *Yuendumu Doors. Warlukurlangu Artists* (eds). Canberra: Australian Institute of Aboriginal Studies, pp. 135–43.

Miller, Daniel (1991) 'The necessity of the primitive in modern art', in S. Hiller (ed.), *The Myth of Primitivism: Perspectives on Art*. New York: Routledge, pp. 50–71.

Miller, Daniel (2005) 'Materiality: an introduction', in D. Miller (ed.) *Materiality*. Durham, NC: Duke University Press.

Morphy, Howard (1992) *Ancestral Connections*. Chicago: University of Chicago Press.

Mullin, Molly (1995) 'The patronage of difference: making Indian art "art, not ethnology"', in G. Marcus and F. Myers (eds), *The Traffic in Culture: Refiguring Anthropology and Art*. Berkeley, CA: University of California Press, pp. 166–200.

Myers, Fred (1991) 'Representing culture: the production of discourse(s) for Aboriginal acrylic paintings', *Cultural Anthropology*, 6 (1): 26–62.

Myers, Fred (2001) 'Introduction: the empire of things', in F. Myers (ed.), *The Empire of Things*. Santa Fe, NM: School of American Research Press, pp. 3–64.

Myers, Fred (2002) *Painting Culture: the Making of an Aboriginal High Art*. Durham, NC: Duke University Press.

Myers, Fred and Marcus, George (1995) Introduction, in George Marcus and Fred Myers (eds), *The Traffic in Culture: Refiguring Art and Anthropology*. Berkeley, CA: University of California Press, pp. 1–53.

Otten, Charlotte M., ed. (1971) *Art and Aesthetics: Readings in Cross-cultural Aesthetics*. New York: Doubleday.

Phillips, Ruth (1998) *Trading Identities: the Souvenir in Native North American Art from the Northeast, 1700–1900*. Seattle, WA: University of Washington Press; Montreal: McGill-Queen's University Press.

Phillips, Ruth B. and Steiner, Christopher B. (1999) 'Art, authenticity, and the baggage of cultural encounter', in Ruth Phillips and Christopher Steiner (eds), *Unpacking Culture: Art and Commodity in Colonial and Postcolonial Worlds*. Berkeley, CA: University of California Press, pp. 3–19.

Price, Richard and Price, Sally (1999) *Maroon Arts: Cultural Vitality in the African Diaspora*. Boston, MA: Beacon Press.

Price, Sally (1989) *Primitive Art in Civilized Places*. Chicago: University of Chicago Press.

Rhodes, Colin (1995) *Primitivism and Modern Art*. New York: Thames & Hudson.

Rubin, William (1984) 'Modernist primitivism: an introduction', in W. Rubin (ed.),*'Primitivism' in Twentieth Century Art: Affinity of the Tribal and the Modern*. New York: Museum of Modern Art, pp. 1–84.

Rushing, W. Jackson (1995) *Native American Art and the New York Avant-garde: a History of Cultural Primitivism*. Austin, TX : University of Texas Press.

Said, Edward (1978) *Orientalism*. New York: Pantheon.

Saunders, Barbara (1997) 'Contested ethnic in two Kwakwaka'waku museums', in J. MacClancy (ed.), *Contesting Art*. Oxford: Berg, pp. 85–130.

Schildkrout, Enid and Keim, Charles (1990) *African Reflections: Art from Northeastern Zaire*. New York: American Museum of Natural History.

Steiner, Christopher (1994) *African Art in Transit*. Cambridge: Cambridge University Press.

Thomas, Nicholas (1991) *Entangled Objects: Exchange, Material Culture and Colonialism in the Pacific*. Cambridge, MA: Harvard University Press.

Thomas, Nicholas (1999) *Possessions: Indigenous Art/ Colonial Culture*. London: Thames & Hudson.

Torgovnick, Marianna (1990) *Gone Primitive: Savage Intellects, Modern Lives*. Chicago: University of Chicago Press.

Townsend-Gault, Charlotte (2004) 'Circulating Aboriginality', *Journal of Material Culture*, 9 (2): 183–202.

Vogel, Susan (1989) *Art/Artefact. African Art in Anthropological Collections*. New York: Prestel.

Wallach, Ami (1989) 'Beautiful Dreamings'. MS (March), pp. 60–4.

Williams, Raymond (1977) *Marxism and Literature*. London: Oxford University Press.

Wingert, Paul (1974) *Primitive Art: its Traditions and Styles*. New York: New American Library.

Witherspoon, Gary (1977) *Language and Art in the Navaho Universe*. Ann Arbor, MI: University of Michigan Press.

Ziff, Bruce and Rao, Pratima, eds (1997) *Borrowed Power: Essays on Cultural Appropriation*. New Brunswick, NJ: Rutgers University Press.

18

TRACKING GLOBALIZATION

Commodities and Value in Motion

Robert J. Foster

The rhetoric of economic globalization invokes the movement of goods, money, information – usually rapid, sometimes promiscuous, always expanding. Images of hyper-mobility abound, for example, across the 'landscapes of capital' depicted in corporate television advertising since the 1990s (Goldman et al. n.d.; see also Kaplan 1995). Likewise, academic literature on the cultural dimensions of globalization, typified by Appadurai's influential 1990 essay, deploys the liquid trope of 'flows' – non-isomorphic movements of images, people, and ideas that describe shifting configurations or 'scapes': mediascapes, ethnoscapes, ideoscapes, and so forth. While questions have rightly been raised about the intensity, extent, and velocity of these movements, what concerns me here is how the current fascination with border-crossing mobility has prompted investigations into the social and geographical lives of particular commodities (Jackson 1999). This detective work is not restricted to specialists. Consider, for example, the spate of popular books devoted to tracking through historical time and geographical space such commodities as cod and salt (Kurlansky 1997, 2002), potatoes and diamonds (Zuckerman 1998; Hart 2002), coal and tobacco (Freese 2003; Gately 2001). (For global flows in the art market see Myers in the previous chapter.) It is as if renewed interest in the sociospatial life of stuff – in following tangible, ordinary things such as glass, paper, and beans (Cohen 1997) – has emerged as a therapeutic defense against the alienating specters of globalization.

Inside the academy, it is undeniable that 'the commodity is back' (Bridge and Smith 2003: 257). Commodities from bluefin tuna (Bestor 2001) to maize husks (Long and Villareal 2000)

have provided material vehicles for narrating economic change, political power, and cultural identity. Improvising upon Kopytoff's (1986) rich idea of 'commodity biographies', researchers have traced the movement of everyday things through diverse contexts and phases of circulation. Many of these exercises begin with the aim of demonstrating how such movement links geographically separate locales and connects producers and consumers stratified by class, ethnicity, and gender; they end with an argument about how the meaning of things shifts as a function of use by human agents in different social situations. Researchers thus do not simply trace the movement of commodities in the mechanical manner of a radar or a bar code scanning device; more important, they trace the social relations and material linkages that this movement creates and within which the value of commodities emerges.

At the same time, researchers emphasize the ways in which the active materiality of non-human things – the heterozygosity of apples (Pollan 2001) or the erucic acidity of rapeseed (Busch and Juska 1997) – constitute these very social contexts of use. That is, researchers acknowledge how materiality is an irreducible condition of possibility for a commodity biography – a condition that sometimes challenges or exceeds the attribution of meaning to things by human agents (Keane 2005). The overall result is a paradoxical form of self-aware, critical fetishism – an attitude of inquiry well suited to making sense of economic circumstances in which accumulation of wealth and creation of value seem mysterious and occult (Comaroff and Comaroff 1999). This attitude responds, moreover, to a world in which people's perspectives on distant others are often filtered through commodity consumption and/or its denial. Hence, tracking commodities and value in motion becomes a means for apprehending the 'global consciousness' (Robertson 1992) and 'work of the imagination' (Appadurai 1990) often associated with globalization.

Critical fetishism – a heightened appreciation for the active materiality of things in motion – entails certain methodological questions and challenges, which recent writings in anthropology and geography address. For anthropologists, the exigencies of tracking commodities define a mode of fieldwork that Marcus has identified as doing ethnography 'in/of the world system' (1995). This sort of fieldwork requires ethnographers to work in and across multiple field sites, to follow people (e.g., scientists and traders), images (e.g., Rambo and Pokémon), and commodities of all kinds (e.g., coffee and flowers) as they move from place to place and/ or from node to node within a network of production and distribution. Marcus asserts that 'Multi-sited research is designed around chains, paths, threads, conjunctions, or juxtapositions of locations in which the ethnographer establishes some form of literal presence, with an explicit posited logic of association or connection among sites *that in fact defines the argument of the ethnography*' (1995: 105, my emphasis). Tracking strategies thus bring anthropology closer to geography at the same time as they introduce an element of radical contingency into the ethnographic project, especially in cases 'where relationships or connections between sites are indeed not clear, the discovery and discussion of which are precisely in fact the main problem, contribution and argument of ethnographic analysis' (Marcus 2000: 16).

Geographers – long used to following things and mapping distributions as culture areas – have debated what sort of understanding of far-flung commodity networks critical fetishism ought to accomplish. Harvey's (1990: 423) exhortation to 'deploy the Marxian concept of fetishism with its full force' has been met with sympathetic rebuttals that 'getting behind the veil' of the market implies both a privileged position for the unmystified analyst and an undue emphasis on the site of production as the ultimate source of a commodity's value (see, e.g., Castree 2001). Instead of tracing a line from acts of guilty consumption to the hidden truth of exploited producers, some geographers have taken up anthropological preoccupations with symbols and meanings in order to emphasize the strategic interests and partial knowledges with which particular actors encounter and construct a commodity at different moments

in its circulation (for a brief review, see Bridge and Smith 2003). Critical fetishism, in this approach, begins with 'acknowledging the fragmentary and contradictory nature of knowledges through which commodity systems are imagined' (Leslie and Reimer 1999: 406; see, e.g., Cook and Crang 1996a).

Critical fetishism, in short, challenges a geographical view of globalization as 'a spreading ink stain' and instead promotes a spatial recognition of globalization as 'partial, uneven and unstable; a socially contested rather than logical process in which many spaces of resistance, alterity and possibility become analytically discernible and politically meaningful' (Whatmore and Thorne 1997: 287, 289). This view is an effect of switching metaphors, of abandoning the opposition between 'local' and 'global' in favor of the idea of networks – longer or shorter networks, always in the making, composed of people, artifacts, codes, living and non-living things (Law and Hetherington 1999). In this regard, both anthropologists and geographers extend the work of Bruno Latour's (e.g., 1993) science studies, including his emphasis on the role of nonhuman 'actants' in lengthening networks and sustaining connectivity. Tracking commodities in motion perforce becomes part of a larger strategy designed to identify the collective agency, distributed within a network, that enables action at a distance – one of the hallmarks of globalization (or global modernity) according to theorists such as Giddens (1990; see also Waters 1995).

Network methods and concepts have emerged as flexible means for historians and sociologists as well as geographers to question both the concept of globalization as a single, uniform process and the assumptions underpinning talk of a 'global economy' (see, e.g., Cooper 2001; Long 1996; Dicken et al. 2001; see also the journal *Global Networks*). At the interface of anthropology and geography, network methods and concepts have been used to bring exchange value and use value, markets and meaning, within a single analytical framework (Bridge and Smith 2003). An expanded definition of value creation is instrumental in this regard (see Munn 1986). Value creation refers to the practical specification of significance, that is, to actions that define and make visible relations between persons and things.[1] Value creation, in this expanded sense, encompasses both the political economist's preoccupation with human labor as activity that produces measures of (quantitative) value and the cultural anthropologist's apprehension of (qualitative) value as the product of meaningful difference.

What is at stake, then, in the strategy of tracking specific commodities in motion is the promise of a revised approach to culture and capitalism. Cultural analysis becomes less a matter of formulating a distinctive logic or code shared by a group of people living in one location and more a matter of tracing a network in which the perspectives of differently situated individuals derive both from their different network experiences and from their perspectives on other people's perspectives – 'their approximate mappings of other people's meanings' (Hannerz 1992: 43). This sort of analysis enhances appreciation of how commodities in motion engage desires and stimulate the imagination in the construction of both personhood and place (see, e.g., Weiss 2002). Economic analysis, in turn, becomes less a matter of charting the operations of institutions – whether transnational corporations (TNCs) or nation states – and more a matter of tracing a network of dispersed and disparate value-creating activities and relationships. This sort of analysis enhances appreciation of the extent to which culture figures in the construction of commodities (through design, branding, and marketing; see Cook and Crang 1996a) and in the production of monopoly rents (Harvey 2001). Following commodities in motion thus also leads to a politics of consumption emerging around contests over control of the knowledge intrinsic to value creation (see Maurer, Chapter 1 of this volume).

COMMODITY NETWORKS

The metaphor of the commodity network aims, above all, to foreground the connections between commodity producers and consumers, especially unequal connections between Northern shoppers and Southern growers of, for example, flowers (Hughes 2000), coffee (Roseberry 1996; Smith 1996), bananas (Raynolds 2003a) and tomatoes (Barndt 2002) (see also Redclift 2002 on chewing gum). Yet the metaphor lends itself to multiple glosses.[2] I here discuss three overlapping interpretations: commodity chains or value chains; commodity circuits or commodityscapes; and hybrid actor networks. The second of these interpretations, which I discuss in greatest detail, marks a convergence between anthropology and geography grounded in ethnographic practice and close attention to the meanings that people attribute to things.

Commodity Chains/Value Chains

Commodity chain analysis remains strongly associated with the world-systems theory of historical sociologist Immanuel Wallerstein (1974).[3] Hopkins and Wallerstein (1986: 159, quoted in 1994a: 17) define a commodity chain as 'a network of labor and production processes whose end result is a finished commodity' (see also Hartwick 1998, 2001). For Gary Gereffi, a sociologist and prominent proponent of global commodity chain (GCC) approaches, 'A GCC consists of sets of interorganizational networks clustered around one commodity or product, linking households, enterprises and states to one another within the world economy' (Gereffi et al. 1994: 2). Global commodity chains possess three main dimensions: an input-output structure; a territoriality; and a governance structure (Gereffi et al. 1994: 7; see Dicken et al. 2001: 98–9 for a summary). Gereffi's work has concentrated on governance structures, introducing an important distinction between producer-driven and buyer-driven chains. Buyer-driven chains, which Gereffi suggests are becoming more common in more industries, are chains in which 'controlling firms do not, themselves, own production facilities; rather they coordinate dispersed networks of independent and quasi-independent manufacturers' (Dicken et al. 2001: 99). These chains characterize and effect the spatial and temporal reorganization of production and exchange networks often associated with contemporary capitalism – just-in-time manufacturing systems and, more generally, the transition from high-volume, vertically integrated corporations to distanciated, high-value enterprise webs (Harvey 1989; Reich 1991). It is the contract structure of these chains that interests Gereffi, for this structure invests the ability to govern the chain not with firms producing the commodities, but rather with large retailers, brand-name merchandisers, and trading companies. Accordingly, the lead firms in buyer-driven chains focus on product development and marketing while outsourcing production and production-related functions to subcontracted suppliers.

Gereffi has been criticized for underemphasizing the other dimensions of commodity chains. Dicken et al. (2001), for instance, argue that Gereffi envisions the input-output structure of commodity chains in a way that obscures the complex vertical, hierarchical, and dynamic organization through which flow materials, designs, products, and financial and marketing services. Similarly, Smith et al. (2002; see also

Friedland 2001) accuse Gereffi of ignoring the role of state regulation and organized labor in affecting the governance and location of commodity chains. These critiques form part of a larger effort to complicate the understanding of commodity networks by recognizing territorially embedded strategic actions '*internal* to the "nodes" or sites of production and retailing within any chain' (Smith et al. 2002: 47) and by underscoring the 'complexities and contingencies that exist within and between actors' (Pritchard 2000: 789). This effort has been especially a feature of research on the global restructuring of agrofood industries (see, e.g., Arce and Marsden 1993; Busch and Juska 1997). Long (1996) accordingly proposes a model of 'global actor networks' that form and reform in response to the interests, options, and knowledge of the actors who comprise the networks. These 'interface networks' in turn form part 'of complex food chains that link producers to traders, state agencies, transnationals, supermarket businesses, agricultural input suppliers, research enterprises and eventually the consumers of the products' (Long 1996: 52).

One of the great virtues of commodity chain analysis besides its emphasis on process is that it puts the question of value creation and appropriation front and center; indeed, the term 'value-chain analysis' has been proposed as more inclusive of the variety of scholarly work being done on inter- and transnational economic networks (Gereffi, Humphrey et al. 2001; see Porter 1990: 40–4), and the privileged geographic scale of Wallerstein-inspired commodity chain analysis (see Smith et al. 2002). Nevertheless, Gereffi does not give explicit attention to the conceptualization of value in the input-output structure, that is, the 'value-added chain of products, services, and resources linked together across a range of relevant industries' (Dicken et al. 2001: 98–9). Gereffi, like other proponents of GCC approaches, imagines the repeated movement from input to output as essentially linear, a sequential process of value addition – of adding more products and services.[4] In this sense, of course, Gereffi's view is consistent with that of Hopkins and Wallerstein's (1994b: 49) view that any commodity chain contains a total amount of appropriated surplus value – a total amount of wealth that is unevenly distributed along the length of the chain. This uneven distribution practically distinguishes the periphery of the world system from the core, where surplus value is by definition accumulated.

The conceptualization of value addition in GCC analysis derives from the same 'continuist narrative' of value found in many Marxist accounts, as Spivak (1985/1996) has noted (see Anagnost 2004). This narrative – a narrative of incremental growth – is meant to identify inequalities and, in its development policy versions, to recommend how firms and/or countries can 'upgrade', that is, gain access to higher-value activities in a global commodity chain. For this purpose, it is of clear importance to measure value (or value-added increments) precisely, for example in terms of profits or prices. In doing so, however, the narrative privileges exchange value over use value or, put differently, quantitative value (unequal shares of the total appropriated value in the chain) over qualitative value (the meaning of commodities to the user/consumer). The continuist narrative refuses the possibility of *bricolage*, of putting commodities to uses for which they were not designed (Spivak 1985/1996; 128). This refusal effectively strips the definition of value of its historical and affective charge (Spivak 1985/1996: 126). In addition, I suggest, the continuist narrative obscures important aspects of value creation in commodity chains, especially in the buyer-driven chains becoming more common in complex assembly industries such as electronics and automobiles as well as consumer goods industries that produce food, clothing, and toys. The circuits of culture or commodityscape approach to commodity networks address this shortcoming directly.

Circuits of Culture/Commodityscapes

Gereffi has identified a reorganization of the input-output structure of value chains resulting from 'an increase in the importance of activities that deal with intangibles such as fashion trends, brand identities, design and innovation over activities that deal with tangibles, the transformation, manipulation and movement of physical goods' (Gereffi, Humphrey et al. 2001: 6). Put differently, tracking commodities and value in motion now requires far greater attention to culture – the transformation, manipulation, and movement of meanings. This requirement is obvious in the case of mobile commodities such as 'world music' (White 2000) and 'aboriginal art' (Myers 2002) which entail validations of cultural authenticity. But it is equally compelling in the case of commodities that now circulate in increasingly differentiated consumer markets, such as coffee and fresh fruits. The symbolic construction of these commodities through intensive marketing activities, including market research into everyday consumption practices, directs attention to both 'outside' and 'inside' meanings. While 'outside' meanings refer to the setting of the terms within which a commodity is made available, 'inside' meaning refers to the various significances that various users attribute to a commodity (Mintz 1986: 167, 171). The exercise of power impinges upon the shaping of both kinds of meaning. Hence the call of Cook and Crang (1996a: 134) for a 'focus on the *cultural materialization of the economic*, such that the cultural is increasingly [recognized as] what is economically produced, circulated and consumed'.

Within geography and cultural studies, a 'circuits of culture' approach has emerged for studying how the movement of commodities often entails shifts in use value, that is, shifts in what commodities mean to users (including producers) situated at different nodes in a commodity network (see Hughes 2000; Leslie and Reimer 1999 for discussions). This approach diverges from GCC analysis in three related ways. First, it refuses to treat production as the privileged moment or phase in the story of a commodity and instead traces the articulation of several distinct processes. For example, in their study of the Sony Walkman, du Gay et al. (1997: 3) contend that 'to study the Walkman culturally one should at least explore how it is represented, what social identities are associated with it, how it is produced and consumed, and what mechanisms regulate its distribution and use'. A prime concern of this strategy, which derives from media studies (Johnson 1986; see Jackson and Thrift 1995), involves demonstrating that the uses and meanings intended or preferred by a commodity's producers and designers are not necessarily the same meanings received or endorsed by a commodity's consumers/users. Consumption, in other words, is neither a terminal nor a passive activity, but is itself a source and site of value creation. In this sense, the 'circuits of culture' approach adopts a view of consumer agency characteristic of polemics in material culture studies that put consumption in 'the vanguard of history' (Miller 1995a; Chapter 22 this volume).

Second, as the metaphor of a circuit implies, the movement of a commodity is treated as reversible and nonlinear, without beginning or end. The circuit, moreover, is not a simple loop, but rather a set of linkages between two or more processes that is not determined or fixed. For example, advertisers and manufacturers convene focus groups and employ ethnographic fieldworkers in order to anticipate and modify how consumers will respond to product representations and designs; unanticipated consumer responses ensure that the research never ends and instead applies ever new techniques

(Gladwell 1997; Cook, Crang and Thorne 2000b). Cook and Crang (1996a: 132, 141) have thus argued for new cultural material geographies by developing the idea of 'circuits of culinary culture'. They view foods 'not only as placed cultural artefacts, but also as dis-placed, inhabiting many times and spaces which, far from being neatly bounded, bleed into and indeed mutually constitute each other' (Cook and Crang 1996a: 132–3). The notion of displacement emphasizes movement and interconnection, questioning any essential link between cultures or peoples and bounded places (Crang et al. 2003). More specifically, the notion of displacement emphasizes how although consumption (of food, for example) takes place in localized contexts, the definition of these contexts emerges through connections to spatially expansive networks or commodity-specific 'systems of provision' (Fine and Leopold 1993; Fine 1995). Furthermore, the materials moving through these systems are themselves represented (by retailers, for example) geographically – as of particular 'origin' or 'provenance': Jamaican papayas or Sumatran coffee (Crang 1996; Cook, Crang and Thorne 2000a ; Smith 1996).

The trope of displacement also implies historical and spatial variations in knowledge among people linked within a circuit of culture (or commodity network). Some geographers, such as Harvey (1990), treat these variations as the result of ignorance or mystification whereby consumers become oblivious to the traces of labor exploitation occurring at distant sites that mark the items on display in supermarket 'fresh' produce sections or on clothing store racks. The segmentation of knowledges (Arce 1997) is, in this view, effectively a result of suppression – a lack or absence of knowledge about, say, where a product comes from and why it is such a bargain. By contrast, the circuits of culture approach views situated or segmented knowledges as the contingent outcome of a variety of practices, including the active desires of consumers, the symbolic work of marketers, and the imaginative agency of producers who hold ideas about the people for whom they grow carnations or the places where the garments they stitch end up. This approach enjoins researchers to identify the means by which the whole variety of actors in a commodity network create and contest what any one actor in any one location knows. As a result, these researchers explicitly eschew the role of 'legislator' – of revealing an unknown structure visible only to the eyes of a trained social scientist, of exposing as a veil of illusion what most people regard as truth (Latour 2000: 118–19).

Instead, these researchers assume responsibility for representing things – things-in-motion – in all their complexity and uncertainty. As Cook and Crang (1996a) argue, critical intervention (or critical fetishism) here takes the form of working with the fetish rather than attempting to get behind it.

Lastly, while the GCC approach is not entirely indifferent to the place of consumption ('consumer demand') in a commodity chain (see, e.g., Collins 2000; Goldfrank 1994; Korzeniewicz 1994), the circuits of culture approach shows decisively how consumption matters. Empirically, this emphasis on consumption, along with the recognition of segmented knowledges, translates into a focus on the definition of 'quality', or what might be called the construction of qualitative value – value produced within a system of differences (see Myers 2001; Foster 1990). Cook (1994), for example, documents how trading managers working in the headquarters of major food retailing companies such as Safeway mediate the introduction of new, exotic fruits to UK shoppers by producing instructional materials. Glossy brochures and manuals 're-enchant' food commodities, qualitatively distinguishing kiwi and mango from ordinary fruits while simultaneously educating consumers about the proper features and uses of these foods. Furthermore, the bare fact of availability of exotic foods distinguishes some retailing outlets from others, thus generating qualitative value along another dimension of comparison.

The processes of constructing qualitative value ramify in circuit-like fashion, connecting retailers not only with shoppers but also with agricultural producers. Arce (1997: 180–2) relates the story of a group of women flower growers from Tanzania who were brought to the Netherlands in order to see firsthand the operation of flower markets and thus to learn well the importance of 'quality', that is, to learn well the perspective of Dutch flower consumers, as mediated by flower retailers (see Hughes 2000). Tracing the commodity network through which their flowers move, the women were invited 'to internalize the value of flowers' (Arce 1997: 181) and perforce to recognize as irrelevant criteria of texture, size, and so forth which informed their own enjoyment of flowers. Arce's commodity story indicates how dominant definitions of 'quality' – routinely attributed to the tastes and preferences of sovereign consumers – percolate through the often fragile links in a distanciated commodity network (Raynolds 2003b). The control by retailers over the definition of quality displaces growers from any privileged position in such a network; the

local production of globally competitive and marketable carnations, grapes, *mange-tout*, etc. requires awareness and knowledge of other actors in other places, what Hannerz (1992) calls a 'network of perspectives'. If re-enchanted commodities incite consumer fantasies about faraway people and places, then the product specifications of trade managers likewise incite producers to imagine their location in a spatially extensive network of relations.

Definitions of quality entrain unequal social, political, and environmental consequences, especially for contract farmers. Images of healthy eating in the United States and Europe translate into the use of health-damaging pesticides by Caribbean peasants and Central American proletarians striving to produce unblemished yellow bananas (Andreatta 1997; Striffler and Moberg 2003). The quality standards applied to export grapes from Brazil intensify labor requirements, which employers meet by hiring temporary, nonunion female workers at low wages to do the culling, trimming, harvesting, and packing – tasks with 'the most significance for the product's final quality' (Collins 2000: 104). Nevertheless, as Long and Villareal (2000: 743) insist, we ought not to lose sight of how the movement of a commodity within a network of relations entails myriad 'negotiations over value and its definition'. Quality as defined by retailers and trade managers is one among many definitions; other use values struggle to be realized. By adopting an actor-oriented perspective on transnational commodity networks, then, we are able to recognize the 'moments of value contestation that take place at critical interfaces wherein normative discourses and social interests are defined and negotiated' (Long and Villareal 2000: 726; see also Arce 1997; Long 1996).[5] These contests might hinge on a collision between incommensurable knowledges – say, the knowledges of scientists, bureaucrats, and peasants linked in a commodity network (Long 1996). But, more generally, multiplicities and ambiguities of value inhere in the workings of all commodity networks. A maize husk might thus have value for US consumers as an artifact of 'traditional ethnic cuisine'; for Mexican peasants as a flexible currency for securing harvest labor; and for Mexican migrants in the United States as festive reminders of home (Long and Villareal 2000). Ethnography – multi-sited or not – of a sort unassociated with the GCC approach is thus necessary to apprehend how 'the use and meanings of specific products' – their qualitative value – 'are continuously reassembled and transformed' within 'situated social arenas' (Long and Villareal 2000: 747).

By highlighting the construction of qualitative value, the circuits of culture approach both unites economy and culture within a single analytical framework and defines a point of intersection between current work in cultural/ economic geography and rural sociology, on the one hand, and anthropology, on the other. Anthropological attempts to track commodities and follow objects in motion derive from a rebirth of material culture studies during the 1980s that gave new attention to contexts and practices of consumption (see Miller 1995b for a review). Similarly, Appadurai (1986) and Kopytoff's (1986) use of the notion of commodity biographies, with its emphasis on the circulation of commodities, recovered consumption as an important activity through which people negotiate and renegotiate the meaning – or qualitative value – of things. To a large extent, this emphasis on circulation recalled classic anthropological discussions of exchange epitomized in Malinowski's famous (1922) account of *kula*. Appadurai (1986) not surprisingly drew explicitly on more recent ethnography of *kula* exchange in formulating his ideas about the 'paths' along which things moved and the 'diversions' to which they were subject.

Appadurai's essay also aimed to undo the conceptual dichotomy between gifts and commodities that informed many analyses of exchange in and beyond Melanesia (see, e.g., Gregory 1982; Strathern 1988). Instead of asking what is a commodity, Appadurai (1986: 13) asked *when* is any 'thing' a commodity, that is, in what situation or context is a thing's exchangeability a socially relevant feature. A thing's 'commodity candidacy' thus varies as it moves from situation to situation, each situation regulated by a different 'regime of value' or set of conventions and criteria governing exchange (see Bohannan 1955; Steiner 1954). Accordingly, 'all efforts at defining commodities are doomed to sterility unless they illuminate commodities in motion' (Appadurai 1986: 16). Control over this motion – its trajectory, speed, transparency, and very possibility – marks the parameters of a politics of value (see also Wiener 1992).

The notion of 'regimes of value' allows for the possibility that exchange situations differ in the extent to which the actors share social conventions and cultural criteria for evaluating commodities. Thomas exploits this possibility in his study of how Europeans and Pacific Islanders appropriated each other's things to satisfy divergent agendas; he thereby renders an historical account of these 'entangled objects' – muskets and soap, barkcloth and shell money – as a particular example of the 'succession of uses and recontextualizations' (1991: 29) that characterizes the social life of most things. Thomas, moreover, underscores 'the mutability of things in recontextualization' (1991: 28); and this theme of mutability pervades the work of many anthropologists who have tracked globalization through the movement of commodities across cultural boundaries. A good deal of this work, including Thomas's book, concerns the recontextualization of colonized people's material culture in the museums or homes of metropolitan art collectors and tourists (see Myers 2002; Steiner 1994; Phillips and Steiner 1999). But other work deals with everyday consumer goods that take on new meanings as they travel from their original sites of production/consumption. Weiss, for example, juxtaposes the lived experience of coffee in Tanzania and Europe, and situates the consumption of African-American hip-hop styles in the lives of Tanzanian youth (1996, 2002). Mankekar (2002) illustrates how brand-name commodities such as Hamam soap and Brahmi Amla hair oil enable diasporic shoppers at Indian grocery stores in California to create variable notions of homeland and family. Even branded commodities that commonly portend an imperialistic cultural homogeneity, such as McDonald's fast food (Watson 1997), Coca-Cola soft drinks (Miller 1998), Disney theme parks (Brannen 1992), and Barbie dolls (MacDougall 2003) have all been shown to be pliable, subject to domestication by users from Taiwan to Trinidad. Indeed, a double goal of anthropologists studying cross-cultural consumption has been to recover the agency of people often represented as passive recipients of foreign imports and to demonstrate, if not cultural resilience, then the emergence of new forms of cultural heterogeneity (Howes 1996; Tobin 1992).

Appadurai's conceptual framework easily lends itself to following 'roving commodities' (Inda and Rosaldo 2002) across spatially distinct social realms, to delineating a 'commodity ecumene, that is, a transcultural network of relationships linking producers, distributors and consumers of a particular commodity or set of commodities' (Appadurai 1986: 27; see Eiss and Pederson 2002). This sort of exercise in composing a commodityscape results in the mapping of a network of perspectives (or circuit of culture) that offers insight into how people's livelihoods and imaginations are shaped – rarely reciprocally – by the livelihoods and imaginations of people elsewhere (see Collins 2003). Multi-sited ethnographies organized along these lines are still few and far between – Mintz's groundbreaking historical (1986) study of sugar remains a model for many anthropologists – but their contours are becoming clearer. Hansen (2000), for example, explores the world of secondhand clothing as a system of provision, that is, a 'comprehensive chain of activities between the two extremes of production and consumption, each link of which plays a potentially significant role in the social construction of the commodity both in its material and cultural aspects' (Fine and Leopold 1993: 33). Her research took her to Salvation Army thrift shops in Chicago, sorting plants in Utrecht, warehouses and wholesale stores in Lusaka, and retail outlets and markets throughout Zambia. Accordingly, Hansen well recognizes the constraints involved in choosing vantage points from which to consider and compose the commodityscape of secondhand clothing. Hansen's own theoretical interests in the recontextualization of cast-off clothing as desirable fashion and in the ways in which Zambians selectively use clothing to construct and contest social identities lead her to foreground the 'hard work of consumption' (2000: 183).[6]

Steiner resolves the problem of studying the spatially extensive circulation of African art objects by focusing ethnographically on the activities of African traders, 'middlemen who link either village-level object-owners, or contemporary artists and artisans, to Western collectors, dealers and tourists' (1994: 2).[7] This focus accommodates Steiner's interest in documenting a crucial phase in the commodity biography of African objects, namely the moment in which traders move objects from 'a "traditional" sphere of value as ritual or sacred icon' to a '"modernist" sphere of value as *objet d'art*' (Steiner 1994: 13). In so doing, Steiner effectively illustrates how the commercial pursuits of traders simultaneously bridge and divide the segmented knowledges of producers and consumers. In other words, Steiner locates himself as a field researcher in the market places of Abidjan and the supply entrepots of the rural Ivory Coast in order to trace the interface of two distinct value regimes. Similarly, Myers (2001, 2002) has documented the emergence of an 'Aboriginal fine art market' by tracking the circulation of acrylic-on-canvas paintings through a transnational network of persons (Aboriginal artists, government advisors, gallery owners) and institutions (state agencies, mass media, art museums) that uneasily articulates radically different understandings of ownership, creativity, and personhood.

Anthropologists are deliberately applying a 'follow the thing' method to an ever-widening range of commodities – from mineral specimens (Ferry 2005) to marriage beads (Straight 2002) and shea nuts (Chalfin 2004). Bestor's (2001) ambitious research program mimics the movements of its highly migratory object, the bluefin tuna, propelling the anthropologist from the docks of Maine fishing villages to commercial tuna farms off the coast of Cartagena to Tsukiji, Tokyo's massive wholesale seafood marketplace. Like Steiner, Bestor focuses on middlemen, the various traders (buyers, dealers, agents) whose activities connect producers to markets and, through markets, to distant consumers. In this sense, his ethnography makes visible the political economy and fragmentary social structure of the global tuna commodity network. Like Hansen, moreover, Bestor chooses certain sites from which to compose the commodityscape, privileging Tsukiji because of its dominant effects in governing both the economic and cultural terms (i.e., the dominant definition of 'quality' bluefin tuna) of the global tuna trade. The creation of value, qualitative and quantitative, revolves around the management of segmented knowledges, that is, around the strategic deployment by traders of an image of superior Japanese culinary tastes and essentially inscrutable expertise in all things sushi (cf. Walsh 2004). Bestor, then, is as interested in describing the work of the imagination as in demonstrating the work of consumption, that is, in describing 'the imagination of commodities in trade, as items of exchange and consumption, as well as the imagination of the trade partner and the social contexts through which relationships are created, modified, or abandoned' (2001: 78). Foster (2002) similarly describes the ways in which transnational advertisers, Australian corporate officials, and Papua New Guinean consumers all variously imagine themselves and each other as part of a global soft drink commodity ecumene. Ramamurthy (2003) juxtaposes the contradictory yearnings of rural Indian women for polyester saris with the simple view of the 'needs' of these female consumer-citizens held by the male managers of the TNC which produces the saris. The big promise of multi-sited ethnography thus lies in its capacity to combine a synoptic view of commodity networks (the system) with the situated views of people whom the networks connect (multiple life worlds) (Marcus 1995). The contingency and contradictions of the situated views qualify the stability and coherence of the synoptic view.

Composing commodityscapes and tracing circuits of culture present a paradox. These approaches distinguish themselves from the GCC approach by their thicker descriptions, often ethnographically based, of the ramifying social processes and relations that generate and transform the value of commodities in motion. But the conventional methods of thick description – what Geertz (1998) calls 'localized, long-term, close-in, vernacular field research' and Clifford (1997: 58) dubs a 'spatial practice of intensive dwelling' – are at odds with the demands of following mobile things across multiple sites occupied by very different sorts of people speaking very different sorts of vernaculars. The risk, as Bestor (2001: 78) puts it, is that multi-sited research eventuates in 'drive-by ethnography', thin and superficial description. As ethnographers – geographers (Cook et al. 2004) as well as anthropologists – take up the challenge of tracking globalization, they will more and more confront the question of revising their field methods (Gupta and Ferguson 1997). They may perhaps even conclude that the conceit of the solitary and heroic fieldworker no longer serves well (Foster 1999) and that following commodities in motion inevitably invites team-based fieldwork (see Banerjee and Miller 2003 for an instructive example).

Hybrid Actor Networks

Constructing hybrid actor networks requires the researcher to thicken description beyond even the density of circuits of culture or commodity-scape approaches. This requirement stems from the radically deconstructive and non-essentialist (semiotic) approach of actor network theory (ANT), which recognizes no discrete and independently existing entities but, rather, only relational effects or outcomes.[8] These effects of network relations might include such familiar units of social analysis as 'firms' or 'nation states' (or even 'persons') as well as familiar everyday objects such as 'telephones' and 'tea'. Networks are, in other words, materially heterogeneous or hybrid, built of both human and non-human elements, each of which exercises agency (as 'actants') in affecting the length and stability of the network. Constructing hybrid actor networks is thus a way of telling stories, of narrating how networks take and hold shape (or not), enrolling new people and things. It is the ongoing and uncertain performance of networking – the network as actor – rather than the fixed morphology of networks that occupies the attention of the storyteller.

As a framework for thinking about globalization, ANT first of all provides a way of accounting for how action at a distance happens. Instead of postulating global forces or institutions (such as TNCs) that affect local situations, ANT encourages researchers to investigate empirically how networks of relations hold and extend their shape through geographical space. (Put differently, ANT encourages researchers to show how networking produces or makes space as a material outcome (Law and Hetherington 1999).) It is the creation of more or less lengthy networks, enabled in part through new communications technologies, that effects and sustains global reach – the connection of 'separate worlds' into a 'single world'. For example, Law (1986) has described the fifteenth and sixteenth-century Portuguese expansion in terms of the capacity of documents (maps and tables), devices (astrolabes and quadrants), and drilled people (navigators and sailors) to hold each other together in a continuous network. Since networking always occurs specifically and materially, following it step by step never takes one from the 'micro level' to the 'macro level' or across 'the mysterious *limes* that divide the local from the global' (Latour 1993: 121). Actor network theory thus obviates familiar binary distinctions between the global and the local – or between core and periphery; questions of network connectivity eclipse questions of spatial scale (Whatmore and Thorne 1997: 289–90).

By no means all ANT-inspired research on globalization adopts a strategy of tracking commodities in motion or delineating commodity networks (see, e.g., Olds and Yeung 1999). But such work that focuses on agrofood networks begins by recognizing that 'breaking down the global-local binary … is intricately tied up with breaking down the nature-society binary' (Whatmore and Thorne 1997: 292; Whatmore 2002). For example, Busch and Juska (1997) narrate the emergence and decline of the network that grew around post-World War II efforts of the Canadian Defence Board to change industrial rapeseed into edible (canola) oil, thereby securing a self-sufficient national market. The material properties of rapeseed, however, object-ed to the enrollment of rape plants in this network. That is, the desirable quality of the rapeseed was 'bundled' (Keane 2005) together with an undesirable but copresent quality, erucic acidity. Hence, as an effect of the rapeseed's materiality, the enrollment in the network of agricultural researchers who developed techniques for breeding low erucic acid rape (LEAR).[9] In turn, the successful production of LEAR enabled the extension of the rapeseed network during the 1970s when, under pressure, Japan opened its domestic market to imported oilseeds. The story of the rapeseed network thus traces shifting combinations (or hybrid *collectif*; Callon and Law 1995) of differently constituted 'actants' with varied material properties; neither nature nor culture, but states-of-being that fall somewhere in between. The notion of hybrid actor network consequently expands upon Marx's vision of nature as a product and condition of the labor of human beings – a product and condition that 'strikes back' (Latour 2000).

In one significant sense, ANT confounds the strategy of tracking commodities, for *only* as an entity – a rapeseed – comes to be 'enrolled, combined and disciplined within networks' (Murdoch 1997: 330), does it gain shape and function; its shape and function – materially as well as semantically – are not fixed. For example, Whatmore and Thorne (2000) narrate stories of 'elephants on the move' that show how the bodies of nonhuman animals become enmeshed in extensive networks of wildlife conservation and science. At different moments or nodes in these networks, the bodies of African elephants materialize as digital records in a computer database, romantic images in travel brochures, and corporeal presences in zoos and game reserves. Nevertheless, ANT is potentially applicable to commodity networks of the sort studied by GCC and circuits of culture approaches. Whatmore and Thorne (1997) describe the Fair Trade coffee network which links UK consumers and organizations with Peruvian cooperatives and producers. Their concern, besides identifying the heterogeneous actants – both human (customs officials, banking clerks) and non-human (coffee beans, earthworms) – in the network, is to demonstrate how, despite their differences (see Raynolds 2002), alternative agrofood networks enroll many of the same actants as dominant commercial networks in attempting to extend their reach and to keep their components ordered and strongly related.

As the discussion of Fair Trade coffee indicates, the hybrid actor network approach is not indifferent to issues of power, largely understood as asymmetries within or between networks. Actors do not always enjoy equal options with regard to enrolling in a network, and some actors may function more as intermediaries (enrollees) than as agents (enrollers) within a network. Some networks reach farther and endure longer than others. Unlike the GCC or circuits of culture approaches, however, the vocabulary of hybrid actor network studies does not formulate questions of value creation or accumulation (but see Busch and Juska 1997). Instead of adumbrating a theory of value adequate to the patterned inequalities of

distanciated commodity networks, the political economy of hybrid actor networks risks becoming an account of the masculinist strategies of (mostly human) actants to position themselves as efficacious agents. As Busch and Juska (1997: 704–5) note, because the hybrid actor network approach is empirically driven, it is 'relatively "modest" in its scope (what is explained) as well as in its potential for generalization (what can be explained)'. The most significant critical import of the approach might well lie in its capacity as a sophisticated language for challenging the knowledge practices and ontological dualisms performed by powerful people – politicians, scientists, and bankers – and encoded by authoritative nonhuman entities – laws, machines, and the engineered bodies of plants and animals (Whatmore and Thorne 1997: 301).

CONCLUSION: POLITICS AND PROSPECTS

All three approaches to commodity networks imply a politics of knowledge. For example, all three approaches offer the strategy of tracing networks as a tool for undermining representations of globalization as an inexorable totalizing process, and of 'the global economy' as an integrated whole. By treating the activity of building commodity networks as contested and contingent, these approaches counter representations of capitalism as a juggernaut or leviathan that induces hopeless acquiescence and political passivity. They open up other ways of knowing and perforce identify possibilities for active resistance – for destabilizing dominant networks and building alternative ones. It is in this general sense that following commodities and value in motion accomplishes critical fetishism.

Similarly, all three approaches offer network solutions to the problem of connecting consumers with producers, of overcoming spatial distance and gaps in knowledge in order to produce an ethical, more equitable relationship. Yet each approach raises worries about the potential of the others to effect progressive change – either in the working and environmental conditions of producers or in the everyday consciousness of consumers. In particular, critics wonder whether the thickened descriptions required by both circuits of culture and hybrid actor network approaches blunt the critical edge of commodity chain analyses informed by labor theories of value and committed to explaining social inequality. Leslie and Reimer

(1999: 407) ask if circuits of culture accounts, by not foregrounding exploitation and its causes, lose sight of the political motivation for tracing commodity networks. Hartwick goes further, characterizing as uncritical fetishism ANT's preoccupation with nonhuman actants and hybrid networks: 'another device for hiding the real relationships between consumers and producers' (2000: 1182). What, then, are the political dimensions of each approach to commodity networks, especially the implications for a new politics of consumption? What sort of alternative commodity networks does each approach envision? How might researchers intervene practically in the commodity networks that they track?

The political rhetoric of commodity chain-inspired analysis is one of unmasking and exposure, of revealing a network of connections hidden by spatial distance or the magic system of advertising or even, as in the case of hybrid corn seed (Ziegenhorn 2000), by the state-sanctioned force of trade secrecy. This rhetoric points to how the 'tension between knowledge and ignorance' determines both the trajectory and the value of commodities in motion (Appadurai 1986: 41; see Hughes 2000). Hence researchers and activists alike attempt to repair the disjuncture in knowledge that renders consumers of expensive apparel or toys or fresh fruits ignorant of the abuses suffered by the poorly paid producers of these commodities. The awareness and concern of educated consumers in the North can thus be harnessed to empower exploited workers in the South through a range of efforts to improve labor conditions. These efforts include various promising 'fair trade' and 'organic' labeling schemes that guarantee minimum producer prices as well as corporate campaigns to pressure retailers into ensuring that brand-name commodities are made under non-exploitative conditions (Gereffi et al. 2001; Hartwick 2000). Such schemes inevitably involve political contests over the definition of fair labor and environmental standards and remain vulnerable to cooptation by corporate niche marketing (Murray and Raynolds 2000). They rely, moreover, on faith in public education – on the belief that educating consumers about their responsibilities and educating producers about their rights are necessary if not sufficient means for creating long-distance cooperation and achieving social justice. Connecting and educating consumers and producers in this way will therefore require new forms of pedagogy and curriculum (for example, see Miller 2003; McRobbie 1997), media activism (Klein 1999), and labor organizing among workers, unions, NGOs, religious groups, and student activists (see, e.g., the Web site of the National Labor Committee).

There is much work to be done in mapping commodity networks that function without publicity, including networks of non-agrofood commodities such as pharmaceuticals (van der Geest et al. 1996) and recycled goods such as used tires and scrap steel. The goal is not to compile an exhaustive inventory of commodities, but rather to devise ways of understanding the worldwide circulation and accumulation of value that do not presume and privilege either nation states or TNCs as central actors (Dicken et al. 2001). There is even more work to be done tracking flows of illicit commodities such as drugs, 'blood diamonds' and weapons (van Schendel and Abraham forthcoming). The anthropologist Nancy Scheper-Hughes (2000) has begun to expose the networks that link organ donors, doctors, and transplant recipients in a shadowy transnational trade of human livers, kidneys, and other body parts. Scheper-Hughes has also created Organs Watch, an international human rights and social justice organization dedicated to producing and disseminating 'an accurate and evolving map of the routes by which organs, surgeons, medical capital, and donors circulate' (Organs Watch, http://sunsite.berkeley.edu/biotech/organswatch/). Her efforts have brought the operation of organ trafficking worldwide to the attention of a wide public audience (Rohter 2004).

If commodity chain analyses encourage defetishization by exposing the network to consumers, then circuits of culture/commodityscape approaches suggest how consumers enchant the network by reembedding it in relations of trust. In this sense, Fair Trade initiatives enable consumers and producers to overcome the disembedding effects of the impersonal market and to relate to each other in terms that go beyond price, terms that reembed an 'abstract system' (Giddens 1990) in social relations predicated upon other values (see Foster 2002). (Likewise, organic or Green standards enable consumers to reembed commodity production and consumption in 'natural processes' (Raynolds 2000, 2002).) Fair Trade brings consumers and producers closer together – not in pursuit of a common understanding of quality, as in the case of the Tanzanian flower growers, but in pursuit of an equitable distribution of value.[10] Fair Trade thus engages the imagination, enabling consumers to situate themselves in a spatially extensive commodityscape. Cook et al. (2004) have argued that geographers require new techniques to provide consumers with resources to imagine their location in commodityscapes, especially given that retailers and marketers compete to provide resources of their own design. These techniques might entail unconventional forms of writing commodity networks (compare Clifford and Marcus 1986) – forms that, like Cook's multi-sited ethnographic description of a papaya commodity network, might mimic strategies of montage pioneered by film makers (Cook and Crang 1996b). Similarly, Cook, Evans et al. (2004) also advocate new forms of non-didactic public education (see Miller 2003); they are as skeptical of the persuasiveness of the demystifications advocated by Hartwick (2000) as Hartwick is dubious about the obfuscations of ANT. The challenge Cook, Evans et al. (2004) identify is one of enabling consumers themselves (Cook's geography students, specifically) to deal with their own 'perplexity' (Ramamurthy 2003) – an awareness that their subjectivity exceeds and confounds all appeals to shop ethically, patriotically, or hedonistically.

Every hybrid actor network approach emphasizes the porosity of boundaries between people and things, and thus provides a consistent analytical language for discussing many of the anxieties provoked by contemporary commodity networks, such as concerns about genetically modified food and Mad Cow Disease (Whatmore 2002). This language similarly provides a way of discussing the efforts of many Fair Trade and Green activists to create alternative commodity networks – assemblages of people and things that exclude certain actants: chemical pesticides, growth hormones, voracious middlemen, and so forth. These efforts often encounter limitations imposed by working within and against dominant market arrangements such as commercial practices of certification (Raynolds 2003b). The emergence of community-supported agriculture (CSA) – in which community members share the harvest and its risks with local organic farmers (Henderson 1999) – can thus be understood as an attempt to shorten the network, that is, to shorten the food supply chain through which households provision themselves. In other words, hybrid actor network approaches potentially re-present 'things' to the public in such a way as 'to modify the representation the public has of itself *fast enough* so that the greatest number of *objections* have been made to this representation' (Latour 2000: 120). It is thus potentially a political language, one that motivates action based on a relational ethics (Whatmore 2002).

The language of hybrid actor networks – like the encompassing metaphor of commodity networks – offers a way of thinking critically about the flows of objects (and people) so often associated with globalization. But dialects of this language are also spoken across the 'landscapes of capital' conjured out of less critical representations of globalization. Hence a promotional text for the NYK (Nippon Yusen Kaisha) Group about the challenges of global shipping: 'Today the logistics of moving goods around the world is coordinated on an increasingly complex and immense scale. To answer specific customer demands, the NYK Group has expanded its global network while evolving its services and means of transport.' The NYK Group claims to focus always on *gemba* – 'it's Japanese for "on site," where goods are actually put in motion'. Here, then, is the language of ANT – lengthening the network, which always remains local, in order to effect action at a distance – spoken in a *New Yorker* magazine advertisement. Can, indeed, the study of commodity networks move *fast enough* in modifying the representation the public has of itself when it is only one of many competing 'global connectivity discourses' (Ramamurthy 2003)?

As techniques for tracking globalization, mapping commodity networks and following things in motion are not ends in themselves. The initial methodological emphasis on discrete things must give way to an emphasis on relations. Theoretically, the method ought to explicate how value – quantitative as well as qualitative – is variably created and unequally distributed in and through contingent relations or assemblages of persons and things. Politically, the method ought to extend the insights of material culture studies about consumer agency, moving beyond a celebration of the capacity for creative self-fashioning through recontextualization of commodities and toward a vision of responsible consumer-citizenship. This vision entails articulating consumer agency – in the practical form of Fair Trade or CSA – with networks of people and things that perform social justice and environmental care. Making both these conceptual and ethical linkages will redeem the promise of commodity network analysis as critical fetishism and avoid a devolution into unreflexive cartography.

NOTES

1   Or, more precisely, the manifold relations between things and things, things and persons, and persons and things.

2   Leslie and Reimer (1999), Hughes (2000), Raynolds (2003), Bridge and Smith (2003), and Hughes and Reimer (2004) all provide useful reviews.

3   Commodity chain analysis bears affinities with both commodity systems analysis and the French *filière* tradition in the sociology of agriculture (Friedland 1984, 2001; Raikes et al. 2000).

4   Gereffi does not assume, however, that more value-added always accrues at nodes in the chain where manufacturing and distribution (as opposed to raw material extraction) occur. The GCC approach 'explains the distribution of wealth within a chain as an outcome of the relative intensity of competition within different nodes' (Gereffi et al. 1994: 4).

5   At these interfaces which occur within as well as between regional settings, discontinuities in social life (and thus potential shorts in the circuit of culture) become visible: 'such discontinuities imply discrepancies in values, interest, knowledge and power … [T]hey depict social contexts wherein social relations become orientated towards the problem of devising ways of "bridging", accommodating to or struggling against other people's social and cognitive worlds' (Long 1996: 55).

6   Hansen's interests in consumption make the 'systems of provision' approach to commodity networks particularly congenial, especially given its attempt to consider consumer behaviour not in terms of some all-encompassing motivation (emulation, rationality, etc.), but rather in terms of the historical and social conditions under which specific commodities are made materially available (Fine and Leopold 1993).

7   Ethnographies of transnational women traders – 'higglers' or 'suitcase traders' (Freeman 2001) and 'shuttle traders' (Yükseker 2004) – have effectively linked (and critiqued) globalization studies with gender and women's studies (see also Barndt 2002; Ramamurthy 2003).

8   ANT originally developed in the 1980s as part of sociological studies of science; it is associated with the work of Bruno Latour, John Law and Michel Callon (see Murdoch 1997). For a plea to keep ANT messy and vital in the face of its success as portable theory, see Law (1999).

9   Mintz (1986) similarly pointed out how the intrinsic properties of sugar cane, which must be cut when ripe and once cut rapidly crushed in order to extract the juices, conditioned the factory-like labor of cultivating and processing the crop.

10 Hence the report in the *New Internationalist*, a magazine devoted to issues of global social justice, of the UK visit of a Ghanaian cocoa farmer on tour sites along the cocoa trail, including the large chocolate processing plant, Cadbury World (August 1998, Issue 304).

REFERENCES

Anagnost, Ann (2004) 'The corporeal politics of quality (Suzhi)', *Public Culture*, 16 (2): 189–208.

Andreatta, Susan (1997) 'Bananas, are they the quintessential health food? A global/local perspective', *Human Organization*, 56 (4): 437–49.

Appadurai, Arjun (1986) 'Introduction: commodities and the politics of value', in A. Appadurai (ed.), *The Social Life of Things: Commodities in Cultural Perspective*. Cambridge: Cambridge University Press, pp. 3–63.

Appadurai, Arjun (1990) 'Disjuncture and difference in the global cultural economy', *Public Culture* 2 (2): 1–24.

Arce, Alberto (1997) 'Globalization and food objects', in H. de Haan and N. Long (eds), *Images and Realities of Rural Life*. Assen: Van Gorcum, pp. 178–201.

Arce, Alberto and Marsden, T.K. (1993) 'The social construction of international food: a new research agenda', *Economic Geography*, 69 (3): 293–311.

Banerjee, Mukulika and Miller, Daniel (2003) *The Sari*. New York: Berg.

Barndt, Deborah (2002) *Tangled Routes: Women, Work, and Globalization on the Tomato Trail*. New York: Rowman & Littlefield.

Bestor, Theodore C. (2001) 'Supply-side sushi: commodity, market and the global city', *American Anthropologist*, 103 (1): 76–95.

Bohannan, Paul (1955) 'Some principles of exchange and investment among the Tiv', *American Anthropologist*, 57: 60–70.

Brannen, Mary Yoko (1992) '"Bwana Mickey": constructing cultural consumption at Tokyo Disneyland', in J. Tobin (ed.), *Re-made in Japan*. New Haven, CT: Yale University Press, pp. 216–34.

Bridge, Gavin and Smith, Adrian (2003) 'Intimate encounters: culture – economy – commodity', *Environment and Planning D: Society and Space*, 21: 257–68.

Busch, Lawrence and Juska, Aunas (1997) 'Beyond political economy: actor networks and the globalization of agriculture', *Review of International Political Economy*, 4 (4): 688–708.

Callon, Michael and Law, John (1995) 'Agency and the hybrid *collectif*', *South Atlantic Quarterly*, 94 (2): 481–507.

Castree, Noel (2001) 'Commodity fetishism, geographical imaginations and imaginative geographies', *Environment and Planning A*, 33: 1519–25.

Chalfin, Brenda (2004) *Shea Butter Republic: State Power, Global Markets and the Making of an Indigenous Commodity*. New York: Routledge.

Clifford, James (1997) 'Spatial practices: fieldwork, travel and the disciplining of anthropology', in *Routes: Travel and Translation in the Late Twentieth Century*. Cambridge, MA: Harvard University Press, chapter 3.

Clifford, James and Marcus, George E. eds (1986) *Writing Culture: the Poetics and Politics of Ethnography*. Berkeley, CA: University of California Press.

Cohen, Leah Hager (1997) *Glass, Paper, Beans: Revelations on the Nature and Value of Ordinary Things*. New York: Doubleday.

Collins, Jane L. (2000) 'Tracing social relations in commodity chains: the case of grapes in Brazil', in A. Haugerud et al. (eds), *Commodities and Globalization: Anthropological Perspectives*. Lanham, MD: Rowman & Littlefield, pp. 97–109.

Collins, Jane L. (2003) *Threads: Gender, Labor, and Power in the Global Apparel Industry*. Chicago: University of Chicago Press.

Comaroff, J. and Comaroff, J.L. (1999) 'Occult economics and the violence of abstraction: notes from the south african postcolony', *American Ethnologist*, 26 (2): 279–303.

Cook, Ian (1994) 'New fruits and vanity: symbolic production in the global food economy', in A. Bonnano, L. Busch, W. Friedland, L. Gouveia and E. Mingione (eds), *From Columbus to ConAgra: the Globalization of Agriculture and Food*. Lawrence, KS: University Press of Kansas, pp. 232–48.

Cook, Ian et al. (2004) 'Follow the thing: Papaya', *Antipode*, 36 (4): 642–64.

Cook, Ian and Crang, Philip (1996a) 'The world on a plate: culinary culture, displacement and geographical knowledges', *Journal of Material Culture*, 1 (2): 131–53.

Cook, Ian and Crang, Philip (1996b) 'Commodity Systems, Documentary Filmaking and New geographies of Food: Amos Gitai's Ananas'. Paper presented at the annual conference of the Institute of British Geographers/Royal Geographical Society, Glasgow. Draft copy available at http://www.gees.bham.ac.uk/people/index.asp?ID=118.

Cook, Ian, Crang, Philip and Thorpe, Mark (2000a) 'Regions to be cheerful: culinary authenticity and its geographies', in I. Cook, D. Crouch, S. Naylor and J.R. Ryan (eds), *Cultural Turns/Geographical Turns: Perspectives on Cultural Geography*. New York: Prentice Hall, pp. 109–39.

Cook, Ian, Crang, Philip and Thorpe, Mark (2000b) 'Constructing the Consumer: Category Management and Circuits of Knowledge in the UK Food Business'.

Draft copy available at http://www.gees.bham.ac.uk/people/index.asp?ID=118.

Cook, Ian, Evans, James, Griffiths, Helen, Morris, Becky, Wrathmell, Sarah et al. (2004) 'It's more than just what it is': Defetishising Commodities, Changing Pedagogies, Situating Ethics'. Paper presented at the 'Spaces of Responsibility' session, annual conference of the Association of American Geographers, Philadelphia, March. Draft copy available at http://www.gees.bham.ac.uk/people/index.asp?ID=118.

Cooper, Frederick (2001) 'What is the concept of globalization good for? An African historian's perspective', *African Affairs*, 100: 189–213.

Crang, Philip (1996) 'Displacement, consumption and identity', *Environment and Planning A*, 28: 47–67.

Crang, Philip, Dwyer, Claire and Jackson, Peter (2003) 'Transnationalism and the spaces of commodity culture', *Progress in Human Geography*, 27 (4): 438–56.

Dicken, Peter, Kelly, Philip, Olds, Kris and Wai-Chung Yeung, Henry (2001) 'Chains and networks, territories and scales: towards a relational framework for analysing the global economy', *Global Networks*, 1 (2): 89–112.

du Gay, Paul, Hall, Stuart, Janes, Linda, Mackay, Hugh and Negus, Keith (1997) *Doing Cultural Studies: the story of the Sony Walkman*. Thousand Oaks, CA: Sage.

Eiss, Paul and Pedersen, David (2002) 'Introduction: values of value', *Cultural Anthropology*, special issue 'Value in Circulation', 17 (3): 283–290.

Ferry, Elizabeth Emma (2005) 'Geologies of power: value transformations of minerals from Guanajuato, Mexico', *American Ethnologist*, 32 (3): 420–36.

Fine, Ben (1995) 'From political economy to consumption', in D. Miller (ed.), *Acknowedging Consumption*. New York: Routledge, pp. 127–63.

Fine, Ben and Leopold, Ellen (1993) *The World of Consumption*. New York: Routledge.

Foster, Robert J. (1990) 'Value without equivalence: exchange and replacement in a Melanesian society', *Man*, 25: 54–69.

Foster, Robert J. (1999) 'Melanesianist anthropology in the era of globalization', *Contemporary Pacific*, 11 (1): 140–59.

Foster, Robert J. (2002) 'Globalization: a soft drink perpective', in *Materializing the Nation: Commodities, Consumption and Media in Papua New Guinea*. Bloomington, IN: Indiana University Press, chapter 7.

Freeman, Carla (2001) 'Is local: global as feminine: masculine? Rethinking the gender of globalization', *Signs: Journal of Women in Culture and Society*, 26 (4): 1007–37.

Freese, Barbara (2003) *Coal: a Human History*. Cambridge, MA: Perseus.

Friedland, William H. (1984) 'Commodity systems analysis: an approach to the sociology of agriculture', *Research in Rural Sociology and Development*, 1: 221–35.

Friedland, William H. (2001) 'Reprise on commodity systems methodology', *International Journal of Sociology of Agriculture and Food*, 9 (1): 82–103.

Gately, Ian (2001) *Tobacco: a Cultural History of how an Exotic Plant seduced Civilisation*. New York: Grove Press.

Geertz, Clifford (1998) 'Deep hanging out', *New York Review of Books*, 22 October.

Gereffi, Gary (1994) 'The organization of buyer-driven global commodity chains: how US retailers shape overseas production networks', in G. Gereffi and M. Korzeniewicz (eds), *Commodity Chains and Global Capitalism*. London: Praeger, pp. 95–122.

Gereffi, Gary (2001) 'Beyond the producer-driven/buyer-driven dichotomy: the evolution of global value chains in the Internet era', *Institute of Development Studies Bulletin*, special issue 'The Value of Value Chains: Spreading the Gains from Globalisation', (ed.) Gary Gereffi and Raphael Kaplinsky, 32 (3): 30–40.

Gereffi, Gary and Korzeniewicz, Miguel, eds. (1994) *Commodity Chains and Global Capitalism*. London: Praeger.

Gereffi, Gary, Garcia-Johnson, Ronie and Sasser, Erika (2001) 'The NGO-industrial complex', *Foreign Policy*, July–August, pp. 56–65.

Gereffi, Gary, Humphrey, John, Kaplinsky, Raphael and Sturgeon, Timothy (2001) 'Introduction: globalisation, value chains and development', *Institute of Development Studies Bulletin*, special issue 'The Value of Value Chains: Spreading the Gains from Globalisation', Gary Gereffi and Raphael Kaplinsky, (eds) 32 (3): 1–8.

Giddens, Anthony (1990) *The Consequences of Modernity*. Stanford, CA: Stanford University Press.

Gladwell, Malcolm (1997) 'The Coolhunt', *New Yorker*, 17 March, pp. 78–88.

Goldfrank, Walter L. (1994) 'Fresh demand: the consumption of Chilean produce in the United States', in G. Gereffi and M. Korzeniewicz (eds), *Commodity Chains and Global Capitalism*. London: Praeger, pp. 267–79.

Goldman, Robert, Papson, Stephen and Kersey, Noah (n.d.) 'Landscapes of capital', URL: http://it.stlawu.edu/~global/, accessed 18 June 2004.

Gregory, C.A. (1982) *Gifts and Commodities*. New York: Academic Press.

Gupta, Akhil and Ferguson, James, eds (1997) *Anthropological Locations: Boundaries and Grounds of a Field Science*. Berkeley, CA: University of California Press.

Hannerz, Ulf (1992) 'The global ecumene as a network of networks', Adam Kuper (ed.), in *Conceptualizing Society*, New York: Routledge, pp. 34–56.

Hansen, Karen Tranberg (2000) *Salaula: the World of Secondhand Clothing and Zambia*. Chicago: University of Chicago Press.

Hart, Matthew (2002) *Diamond: the History of a Cold-blooded Love Affair*. New York: Plume.

Hartwick, Elaine R. (1998) 'Geographies of consumption: a commodity-chain Approach', *Environment and Planning D: Society and Space*, 16: 423–37.

Hartwick, Elaine R. (2000) 'Towards a geographical politics of consumption', *Environment and Planning A*, 32: 1177–92.

Hartwick, Elaine R. (2001) 'Commodity chains', in *International Encyclopedia of the Social and Behavioral Sciences* IV. New York: Elsevier, pp. 2276–9.

Harvey, David (1989) *The Condition of Postmodernity*. Oxford: Blackwell.

Harvey, David (1990) 'Between space and time: reflections on the geographical imagination', *Annals of the Association of American Geographers*, 80 (3): 418–34.

Harvey, David (2001) 'The art of rent: globalization, monopoly and the commodification of culture', in Leo Panitch and Colin Leys (eds), *Socialist Register 2002: a World of Contradictions*. London: The Merlin Press, pp. 93–110.

Haugerud, Angelique, Stone, Priscilla M. and Little, Peter D. eds (2000) *Commodities and Globalization: Anthropological Perspectives*. New York: Rowman & Littlefield.

Henderson, Elizabeth (1999) *Sharing the Harvest: a Guide to Community Supported Agriculture*. White River Junction, VT: Chelsea Green.

Hopkins, Terence and Wallerstein, Immanuel (1986) 'Commodity chains in the world economy prior to 1800', *Review*, 10 (1): 157–70.

Hopkins, Terence and Wallerstein, Immanuel (1994a) 'Commodity chains: construct and research', in G. Gereffi and M. Korzeniewicz (eds), *Commodity Chains and Global Capitalism*. London: Praeger, pp. 17–20.

Hopkins, Terence and Wallerstein, Immanuel (1994b) 'Conclusions about commodity chains', in G. Gereffi and M. Korzeniewicz (eds), *Commodity Chains and Global Capitalism*. London: Praeger, 48–50.

Howes, David, ed. (1996) *Cross-cultural Consumption: Global Markets, Local Realities*. New York: Routledge.

Hughes, A. (2000) 'Retailers, knowledges and changing commodity networks: the case of the cut flower trade', *Geoforum*, 31: 175–90.

Hughes, A. and Reimer, S., eds (2004) *Geographies of Commodity Chains*. New York: Routledge.

Inda, Jonathan Xavier and Roslado, Renato, (eds.) (2002) *The Anthropology of Globalization: a Reader*. Malden, MA: Blackwell.

Jackson, Peter (1999) 'Commodity cultures: the traffic in things', *Transactions of the Institute of British Geographers*, 24 (1): 95–108.

Jackson, Peter and Thrift, Nigel (1995) 'Geographies of consumption', in D. Miller (ed.), *Acknowledging Consumption*. New York: Routledge, pp. 204–37.

Johnson, Richard (1986) 'The story so far: and further transformations?' in David Punter (ed.), *Introduction* to *Contemporary Cultural Studies*. New York: Longman, pp. 277–313.

Kaplan, Caren (1995) '"A world without boundaries": the Body Shop's trans/national geographies', *Social Text*, 43: 45–66.

Keane, Webb (2005) 'Signs are not the garb of meaning: on the social analysis of material things', in D. Miller (ed.), *Materiality*. Durham, NC: Duke University Press.

Klein, Naomi (1999) *No Logo: Taking Aim at the Brand Bullies*. New York: Picador.

Kopytoff, Igor (1986) 'The cultural biography of things: commoditization as process', in A. Appadurai (ed.), *The Social Life of Things: Commodities in Cultural Perspective*. Cambridge: Cambridge University Press, pp. 64–91.

Korzeniewicz, Miguel (1994) 'Commodity chains and marketing strategies: Nike and the global athletic footwear industry', in G. Gereffi and M. Korzeniewicz (eds), *Commodity Chains and Global Capitalism*. London: Praeger, pp. 247–65.

Kurlansky, Mark (1997) *Cod: a Biography of the Fish that changed the World*. New York: Walker.

Kurlansky, Mark (2002) *Salt: a World History*. New York: Walker.

Latour, Bruno (1993) *We have Never been Modern*, trans. Catherine Porter. Cambridge, MA: Harvard University Press.

Latour, Bruno (2000) 'When things strike back: a possible contribution of "Science Studies" to the social sciences', *British Journal of Sociology*, 51 (1): 107–23.

Law, John (1986) 'On the methods of long-distance control: vessels, navigation and the Portuguese route to India', in J. Law (ed.), *Power, Action and Belief: a New Sociology of Knowledge?* Boston, MA: Routledge, pp. 234–63.

Law, John (1999) 'After ANT: complexity, naming and topology', in J. Law and J. Hassard (eds), *Actor Network Theory and After*. Malden, MA: Blackwell, pp. 1–14.

Law, John and Hassard, John, eds (1999) *Actor Network Theory and After*. Oxford: Blackwell.

Law, John and Hetherington, Kevin (1999) 'Materialities, Spatialities, Globalities'. Lancaster: Department of Sociology, Lancaster University. URL: http://www.comp.lancs.ac.uk/sociology/soc029jl.html, accessed 23 February 2004.

Leslie, Deborah and Reimer, Suzanne (1999) 'Spatializing commodity chains', *Progress in Human Geography*, 23 (3): 401–20.

Long, Norman (1996) 'Globalization and localization: new challenges to rural research', in H. Moore (ed.), *The Future of Anthropological Knowledge*. New York: Routledge, pp. 37–59.

Long, Norman and Villareal, Magdalena (2000) 'Small product, big issues: value contestations and cultural identities in cross-border commodity networks', *Development and Change*, 29: 725–50.

MacDougall, J. Paige (2003) 'Transnational commodities as local cultural icons: Barbie Dolls in Mexico', *Journal of Popular Culture*, 37 (2): 257–75.

Malinowski, Bronislaw (1922) *Argonauts of the Western Pacific*. New York: Dutton.

Mankekar, Purnima (2002) '"India shopping": Indian grocery stores and transnational configurations of belonging', *Ethnos*, 67 (1): 75–98.

Marcus, George E. (1995) 'Ethnography in/of the world system: the emergence of multi-sited ethnography', *Annual Review of Anthropology*, 24: 95–117.

Marcus, George E. (2000) 'The twistings of geography and anthropology in winds of millenial transition', in I. Cook, D. Crouch, S. Naylor and J.R. Ryan (eds), *Cultural Turns/Geographical Turns: Perspectives on Cultural Geography*. New York: Prentice Hall, pp. 13–25.

McRobbie, Angela (1997) 'Bridging the gap: feminism, fashion and consumption', *Feminist Review*, 55: 73–89.

Miller, Daniel (1995a) 'Consumption as the vanguard of history: a polemic by way of introduction', in D. Miller (ed.), *Acknowledging Consumption*. New York: Routledge, pp. 1–57.

Miller, Daniel (1995b) 'Consumption studies in anthropology', in D. Miller (ed.), *Acknowledging Consumption*. New York: Routledge, pp. 264–95.

Miller, Daniel (1998) 'Coca-Cola: a black sweet drink from Trinidad', in D. Miller (ed.), *Material Cultures: Why some Things Matter*. Chicago: University of Chicago Press, pp. 169–87.

Miller, Daniel (2003) 'Could the Internet defetishize the commodity?' *Environment and Planning D: Society and Space*, 21: 359–72.

Mintz, Sidney (1986) *Sweetness and Power: the Place of Sugar in Modern History*. New York: Penguin Books.

Munn, Nancy D. (1986) *The Fame of Gawa: a Symbolic Study of Value Transformation in a Massim (Papua New Guinea) Society*. Cambridge: Cambridge University Press.

Murdoch, Jonathan (1997) 'Towards a geography of heterogeneous associations', *Progress in Human Geography*, 21 (3): 321–37.

Murray, Douglas L. and Raynolds, Laura T. (2000) 'Alternative trade in bananas: obstacles and opportunities for progressive social change in the global economy', *Agriculture and Human Values*, 17: 65–74.

Myers, Fred (2001) 'Introduction: the empire of things', in Fred R. Myers (ed.), *The Empire of Things: Regimes of Value and Material Culture*. Santa Fe, NM: School of American Research Press, pp. 3–61.

Myers, Fred (2002) *Painting Culture: the Making of an Aboriginal High Art*. Durham, NC: Duke University Press.

Olds, Kris and Yeung, Henry Wai-chung (1999) '(Re)shaping "Chinese" business networks in a globalising era', *Environment and Planning D: Society and Space*, 17: 535–55.

Phillips, Ruth B. and Steiner, Christopher B. eds (1999) *Unpacking Culture: Art and Commodity in Postcolonial Worlds*. Berkeley, CA: University of California Press.

Pollan, Michael (2001) *The Botany of Desire: A Plant's Eye View of the World*. New York: Random House.

Porter, Michael E. (1990) *The Competitive Advantage of Nations*. New York: Free Press.

Pritchard, Bill (2000) 'The Transnational corporate networks of breakfast cereals in Asia', *Environment and Planning A*, 32: 789–804.

Raikes, Philip, Jensen, Michael Friis and Ponte, Stefano (2000) 'Global commodity chain analysis and the French *filière* approach: comparison and critique', *Economy and Society*, 29 (3): 390–417.

Ramamurthy, Priti (2003) 'Material consumers, fabricating subjects: perplexity, global connectivity discourses, and transnational feminist research', *Cultural Anthropology*, 18 (4): 524–50.

Raynolds, Laura T. (2000) 'Re-embedding global agriculture: the international organic and fair trade movements', *Agriculture and Human Values*, 17: 297–309.

Raynolds, Laura T. (2002) 'Consumer/producer links in Fair Trade coffee networks', *Sociologia Ruralis*, 42 (4): 404–24.

Raynolds, Laura T. (2003a) 'The global banana trade', in Steven Striffler and Mark Moberg (eds), *Banana Wars: Power, Production and History in the Americas*. Durham, NC: Duke University Press, pp. 23–47.

Raynolds, Laura T. (2003b) 'The globalization of organic agro-food networks', *World Development*, 32 (5): 725–43.

Redclift, Michael (2002) 'Chewing gum in the United States and Mexico: the everyday and the iconic', *Sociologia Ruralis*, 42 (4): 391–403.

Reich, Robert (1991) *The Work of Nations: Preparing Ourselves for Twenty-first Century Capitalism*. New York: Knopf.

Robertson, Roland (1992) *Globalization: Social Theory and Global Culture*. London: Sage.

Rohter, Larry (2004) 'Tracking the sale of a kidney on a path of poverty and hope', *New York Times*, 23 May.

Roseberry, William (1996) 'The rise of yuppie coffees and the reimagination of class in the United States', *American Anthropologist*, 98 (4): 762–75.

Scheper-Hughes, Nancy (2000) 'The global traffic in human organs', *Current Anthropology*, 41 (2): 191–224.

Schlosser, Eric (2001) *Fast Food Nation: the Dark Side of the all-American Meal*. New York: Houghton Mifflin.

Smith, Adrian, and Rainnie, Al, Dunford, Mick, Hardy, Jane, Hudson, Ray and Sadler, David (2002) 'Networks of value, commodities and regions: reworking divisions of labour in macro-regional economies', *Progress in Human Geography*, 26 (1): 41–63.

Smith, Michael D. (1996) 'The empire filters back: consumption, production, and the politics of Starbucks coffee', *Urban Geography*, 17 (6): 502–24.

Spivak, Gayatri (1985/1996) 'Scattered speculations on the question of value', in D. Landry and G. MacLean (eds), *The Spivak Reader*. New York: Routledge, pp. 107–40.

Steiner, Christopher B. (1994) *African Art in Transit*. Cambridge: Cambridge University Press.

Steiner, Franz (1954) 'Notes on comparative economics', *British Journal of Sociology*, 5: 118–29.

Straight, Belinda (2002) 'From Samburu heirloom to New Age artifact: the cross-cultural consumption of Mporo marriage beads', *American Anthropologist*, 104 (1): 7–21.

Strathern, Marilyn (1988) *The Gender of the Gift: Problems with Women and Problems with Society in Melanesia*. Berkeley, CA: University of California Press.

Striffler, Steven and Moberg, Mark eds (2003) *Banana Wars: Power, Production and History in the Americas*. Durham, NC: Duke University Press.

Thomas, Nicholas (1991) *Entangled Objects: Exchange, Material Culture, and Colonialism in the Pacific*. Cambridge, MA: Harvard University Press.

Tobin, Joseph J., ed. (1992) *Re-made in Japan: Everyday Life and Consumer Taste in a Changing Society*. New Haven, CT: Yale University Press.

Van der Geest, Sjaak, Whyte, Susan Reynolds and Hardon, Anita (1996) 'The anthropology of pharmaceuticals: a biographical approach', *Annual Review of Anthropology*, 25: 153–78.

Van Schendel, Willem and Abraham, Itty eds (forthcoming) *Illicit Flows: States, Borders and the Criminal Life of Things*. Bloomington, IN: Indiana University Press.

Wallerstein, Immanuel (1974) *The Modern World System*. New York: Academic Press.

Walsh, Andrew (2004) 'In the wake of things: speculating in and about sapphires in northern Madagascar', *American Anthropologist*, 106: 225–37.

Waters, Malcolm (1995) *Globalization*. New York: Routledge.

Watson, James L., ed. (1997) *Golden Arches East: McDonald's in East Asia*. Stanford, CA: Stanford University Press.

Weiss, Brad (1996) 'Coffee breaks and coffee connections: the lived experience of a commodity in Tanzanian and European worlds', in D. Howes (ed.), *Cross-cultural Consumption*. New York: Routledge, pp. 93–105.

Weiss, Brad (2002) 'Thug realism: inhabiting fantasy in urban Tanzania', *Cultural Anthropology*, 17 (1): 93–124.

Whatmore, Sarah (2002) *Hybrid Geographies: Natures, Cultures, Spaces*. Thousand Oaks, CA: Sage.

Whatmore, Sarah and Thorne, Lorraine (1997) 'Nourishing networks: alternative geographies of food', in David Goodman and M. Watts (eds), *Globalising Food: Agrarian Questions and Global Restructuring*. New York: Routledge, pp. 287–304.

Whatmore, Sarah and Thorne, Lorraine (2000) 'Elephants on the move: spatial formations of wildlife exchange', *Environment and Planning D: Society and Space*, 18: 185–203.

White, Bob (2000) 'Soukouss or sell-out? Congolese popular dance music as cultural commodity', in A. Haugerud et al. (eds), *Commodities and Globalization: Anthropological Perspectives*. Lanham, MD: Rowman & Littlefield, pp. 33–57.

Wiener, Annette B. (1992) *Inalienable Possessions: the Paradox of Keeping-while-Giving*. Berkeley, CA: University of California Press.

Yükseker, Deniz (2004) 'Trust and gender in a transnational market: the public culture of Laleli, Istanbul', *Public Culture*, 16 (1): 47–65.

Ziegenhorn, Randy (2000) 'The commodification of hybrid corn', in A. Haugerud et al. (eds), *Commodities and Globalization: Anthropological Perspectives*. Lanham, MD: Rowman & Littlefield, pp. 135–50.

Zuckerman, Larry (1998) *The Potato: How the Humble Spud Rescued the Western World*. Boston, MA: Faber.

19

PLACE AND LANDSCAPE

Barbara Bender

At first glance the word 'landscape' might seem to denote something 'out there', objective, as in 'a desert landscape' or an 'urban landscape'. But it will quickly be apparent that in describing a bit of world as 'desert' or 'urban' a particular aspect is being focused on, and a particular unit is being circumscribed. 'Landscape' is, therefore, 'the world out there' as understood, experienced, and engaged with through human consciousness and active involvement. Thus it is a subjective notion, and being subjective and open to many understandings it is volatile. The same place at the same moment will be experienced differently by different people; the same place, at different moments, will be experienced differently by the same person; the same person may even, at a given moment, hold conflicting feelings about a place. When, in addition, one considers the variable effects of historical and cultural particularity, the permutations on how people interact with place and landscape are almost unending, and the possibilities for disagreement about, and contest over, landscape are equally so.

On the other hand, although our engagement with the land is subjective, the land itself, because of its materiality, 'talks back' – it sets up resistances and constraints. It makes it *not possible* to do or to think or to experience certain things.

To say that landscape and time are subjective does not require a descent into a miasma of cultural relativity. It simply means that the engagement with landscape and time is historically particular, imbricated in social relations and deeply political.

(Bender 2002)

If I wanted you, the reader, to begin to understand about landscape, I would not start with the work of anthropologists, or geographers, or academics of any sort. I would begin with novelists and poets, because, long before reflexivity, or multivocality, or any other aspects of postmodern conceptualization were invoked by academics, writers were subsuming them, incorporating them, taking them more or less for granted. If you want a gendered understanding of landscape, read V. Woolf's *A Room of One's Own* (1929), or George Eliot's *Middlemarch* (1871–2/1965); for a diasporic view of landscape try Jamaica Kincaid's *Lucy* (1989); a dyspeptic, tormented but also passionate view of deracinated and colonial landscapes, V.S. Naipaul's *The Enigma of Arrival* (1987; Bender 1993). For landscapes of movement, displacement and a historical time depth there's none better than Amitav Ghosh's *In an Antique Land* (1992). For landscapes of memory, volume I of Marcel Proust's *In Search of Lost Time* (1954/1981) would be a good place to start, or W.G. Sebald's *Austerlitz* (2001) or *The Rings of Saturn* (1998) (see also Connerton's Chapter 20 in this volume). For landscapes of war-torn identity and terror there's Seamus Heaney's *Station Island* (1984). Readers will have no difficulty in adding their own titles to this list.

As well as recognizing that one is surrounded by writers teasing apart the meaning of landscape, the reader might also note the way in which the phraseology that we employ in both everyday speech and more formal communications is replete with landscape metaphors. Take any page of writing and see how often such metaphors are employed – 'a difficult road', 'unknown territory', 'barriers to', 'barren', 'prospects', moral 'high ground', an intellectual 'desert', 'views', 'viewpoints', and so on and on. What is interesting is that these metaphors are part of an historically particular understanding of the world (Tilley 1999). Anne Salmond (1982) suggests that these 'Western' metaphors amount to an assumption of 'detached intelligence working to domesticate and master an objectified world'. She goes on to demonstrate how different, and how differently contextualized, are those deployed in Papua New Guinea.

Landscapes refuse to be disciplined. One of the reasons why landscape studies are so interesting, variable and often cutting-edge is that, invoking both time and place, past and present, being always in process and in tension, they make a mockery of the oppositions that we create between time (history) and space (geography), or between nature (science) and culture (anthropology). Thus the consideration of landscape spills over between the disciplines and, in theory at least, geographers (Cosgrove and Daniels 1988; Gupta and Ferguson 1997; Jackson 1985, 1994; Jacobs 1996; Lowenthal 1985, 1996; Massey 1994; Olwig 2002; Pred 1990; Rose 1993) talk to historians (Schama 1995; Samuels 1994; Thomas 1983), philosophers (Casey 1993; Deleuze and Guattari 1988), anthropologists (Basso 1996; Basso and Feld 1996; Bender 1993, 1998; Clifford 1997; Gosden 1994; Herzfeld 1991; Hirsch and O'Hanlon 1995; Ingold 2000; Orlove 2002; Strang 1997; Tilley 1994, 2004; Ucko and Layton 1999), sociologists (Bourdieu 1977, 1971/1990; de Certeau 1984; Lefebvre 1974; Merleau-Ponty 1962), prehistorians (Barrett 1994; Bradley 1993, 1998; David and Wilson 2002; Edmonds 1999; Thomas 1996) and cultural or literary studies people (Barrell 1972; Williams 1973). In practice there are often time lags in this cross-disciplinary communication.

In what follows I have drawn out different strands of landscape conceptualization. This drawing apart is somewhat artificial – by the end it will become clear that I am just shifting/juggling the facets of something that forms a connected whole. I begin by sketching in some changing theoretical perspectives. Then move to a discussion of 'the Western Gaze' and alternative, and conflicting, ways of 'being-in' the world. In the third section I discuss landscapes of movement, dis-location, and terror. And, finally, I suggest some ways in which the study of landscape might develop.

THEORIZING LANDSCAPE

Landscape as Palimpsest, 'Structures of Feeling' and the Production of Space

Whilst the theorization of time and history has a long genealogy, the serious discussion of place and landscape has been slower to get under way. We might take as a reasonable starting point the work of W.G. Hoskins in the mid-twentieth century (Hoskins 1955). For Hoskins the landscape was the material embodiment of people's activities. It was a *palimpsest*, the attentive reading of which allowed one to decipher the scribbled signatures of earlier activities. Hoskins – pipe in hand, map under arm – avers that one could write a book about every few square inches of the Ordinance Survey map, about the imprints left by changing land use and residential patterns, by changing social and cultural attitudes. He shows the way in which a landscape that might at first sight appear to be primarily spatial is always, and irrevocably, shot through with time.

Hoskins was a brilliant popularist and was quick to recognize that television provided an excellent medium for his particular and passionate espousal of landscape studies. But his work was, by and large, unreflexive, and his underlying threnody – his espousal of a rooted sense of place and his loathing of contemporary change – has made him vulnerable to hi-jacking by conservative Little Englanders (Bender 1988: 30).

On the other side of the Atlantic, at much the same time, the seemingly more robust, though even more weakly theorized, approach of J.B. Jackson (his picture has him dressed in leathers astride a motor bike), creates an on-the-road landscape of movement, of interstitial places on the margins of cities (Jackson 1994). Jackson attempts to draw a sharp distinction between the law-like grids laid out across the land by governmental agencies and the vernacular landscape of 'ordinary' people that compromise conformity. He fails to understand that impositions from above and vernacular untidiness from below work off each other, and whilst his seems a more radical understanding of place than Hoskins, in reality he is equally nostalgic, following in the wake of Kerouac's *On the Road* and espousing a somewhat romantic notion of the American 'way of life' and the 'open frontier' (Cresswell 1992).

Placing Hoskins and Jackson alongside each other makes it very clear that people's delineation and understanding of landscape owe a great deal to the particular historical, social and political contexts in which they themselves live and work. The Cultural Marxist Raymond Williams was among the first to recognize the need for a proper sense of self-reflexivity. His self-portrait is a split one: a man in a study surrounded by books/a man standing by a signal box which is his father's workplace and a place of memory (Williams 1973). Like many other Western landscape writers he offers, towards the end of his seminal *The Country and the City*, a 'view from his window', but his 'view' is very differently constructed from the one that W.G. Hoskins sees and despairs of (Williams 1973: 3; Hoskins 1955: 299–300; Daniels 1989). And although Williams's view encompasses both the deep past and contemporary landmarks, and the landscapes of both rich and poor, it also retains a (very British) nostalgia for more traditional labour processes.

Williams's writings permit a very nuanced understanding of how cultural perceptions cross-cut influence, and are influenced by, social and political relationships (see also Daniels 1993; Berger 1972; Barrell 1972, 2002). Through his discussion of 'structures of feeling' he allows one to understand how the phrase 'a fine prospect' is both a view across the land *and* the social possibility of attaining control of such a view, or how the expression 'farmhands' forms part of a commoditization of labour. His writing permits an understanding of how different people, differently placed, 'see' things quite differently – thus, for example, Jane Austen, William Cobbett and Gilbert White all lived quite close to Farnham in southern England in the early nineteenth century and yet had utterly different understandings of the world around them (Daniels and Cosgrove 1993). He is also able to show how seemingly disparate places or landscapes are in reality soldered together – town and country, great house, slave plantation and factory place, and so on (Said 1989).

Henri Lefebvre, the French Marxist sociologist, works along somewhat similar lines: he creates an interwoven dialogue between what he calls 'spatial practice', the way spaces are generated and used (usually by those with power); 'representations of space' – the rhetoric of spatial practice – and 'spaces of representation' – lived spaces as produced and modified by the inhabitants. Such spaces of representation are also, often, the spaces of resistance (Lefebvre 1974;

Soja 1991; Stewart 1995 for an interesting reworking in the context of slave plantations; see also Blier and Buchli in this volume, Chapters 15 and 16).

Williams and Lefebvre are strong on class relations, less good on gender. Nonetheless, whilst the inquiry into identity and a more embodied sense of place has moved on, there remains (I believe) a need to ground such work within the sharply delineated sociopolitical, economic and cultural contexts espoused by these earlier writers.

Phenomenological Landscapes and Landscapes of Social Practice

An extract from bell hooks's account of what it means to be a child, black and female in North America, and how this maps on to a walk on the wrong side, serves as an introduction to a more embodied or phenomenological approach to landscape, one in which all the senses are involved:

It was a movement away from the segregated blackness of our community into a white neighborhood. I remember the fear, being scared to walk to Baba's, our grandmother's house, because we would have to pass that terrifying whiteness – those white faces on the porches staring us down with hate. ...

Oh! That feeling of safety, of arrival, of homecoming, when we finally reached the edges of her yard, when we could see the soot black face of our grandfather, Daddy Gus, sitting in his chair on the porch, smell his cigar, and rest on his lap.

(hooks 1992)

In the last twenty years or so there has been a much stronger focus on such embodied landscapes, and also more work on the *physicality* of landscape, the ways in which the topography of place and landscape are creative of, as well as created by, human sociality, and how such places and landscapes empower people (Bender et al. 1997; Massey 1995; Thomas 1997; Bradley 1993, 1998; Jones 1998; Edmonds 1999, 2004).

Bourdieu's notion of *habitus* conjures up a world of routine and repetitive social practices through which, within which, people experience and understand their place, often in ways that are completely inarticulate (Bourdieu 1977). Habitus is knowledge learned through the encounter with the world – by copying ... watching ... listening ... by attentive involvement. Habitus is about:

the preoccupied active presence in the world, through which the world imposes its presence, with its urgencies, its things to be done and said, things made to be said, which directly govern words and deeds without ever unfolding as a spectacle.

(Bourdieu 1971/1990: 52)

Through time-space routines of movement a person knows where she or he is in relation to familiar places and objects and 'how to go on' in the world.

(Tilley 1994: 16)

Bourdieu's habitus explains wonderfully well both the historicity and the reproduction of social relations. It does, however, focus rather tightly on the way in which the socially structured environment affects our going on in the world. In contrast, Giddens's *Structuration Theory* (1981) engages more dynamically with people's *active* creation of social structures. With *structuration* we recognize that at the same time that we are caught up in a world not of our own making we are also, through our thoughts and actions, creating and changing the socio-political and economic structures. People are agents; their agency creates the structures; the structures constrain and enable agency. There is no one-way causal arrow; and life and landscape are always in the process of *becoming* (Soja 1989: Chapter 6; see also Munn 1992).

Giddens also charts in some detail how our movements through space always involve time, and how there are many sorts of time – personal time, clock time, gendered time, cyclical time, and so on. And he talks of locales, of front stage and backstage, of formal and informal spaces (Giddens 1985). However, as in so many accounts of landscape, he fails to remark on:

the role of gendered spaces in the ordering of social experience ... the power relations that physically separate male and female practical (time-) spaces, [and] the power relations that are reproduced by men and women practising in separate (time-)spaces.

(Pred 1990: 25–6)

Rose and other feminist writers have gone some way towards rectifying these oversights (Gero and Conkey 1991; Gilchrist 1994; Mouffe 1995; Rose 1993: Chapter 2; Tringham 1994).

In more recent years there has been a tighter focus on the *embodied* way in which people actively engage with the world (Basso 1996; Basso and Feld 1996; Casey 1993; Ingold 1993, 1997, 2000; Massey 2000; Merleau-Ponty 1962; Richards 1993; Thomas 1996; Tilley 1994). In many cases the emphasis is on small-scale

societies – prehistoric or contemporary – or on neighbourhoods, rural or urban, in which people feel 'at home'. The emphasis has been on how people create a sense of familiarity, how they move around places and spaces, naming them, investing them with memories. Naming involves the transformation of:

the sheerly physical and geographical into something that is historical and socially experienced. ... By the process of naming places and things become captured in social discourses.

(Tilley 1994: 18)

By moving along familiar paths, winding memories and stories around places, people create a sense of self and belonging. Sight, sound, smell and touch are all involved, mind and body inseparable (Casey 1993; Basso and Feld 1996). Often, in these studies, experience is conceived of as a sort of 'stocktaking' at points along the way, but it might be more accurate to think in terms of 'ambulatory encounters'. As people go about their business things unfold along the way, come in and out of focus, change shape and take on new meanings (Ingold 1997, 2000). Both Ingold and Edmonds have also emphasized the importance of 'practical activities', the hands-on familiarization that derives from 'taskscapes' (Ingold 1993; Edmonds 1999, 2004).

It is the phenomenologists that have most carefully theorised the distinctions between space and place, and between place and landscape, suggesting on the one hand that space cannot exist apart from the events and activities within which it is implicated – that it derives its meaning from particular places (Casey 1993), and on the other, that: *A landscape is a series of named locales, a set of relational places, linking by paths, movements and narratives.*

(Tilley 1994: 44, my emphasis)

These phenomenological approaches to landscape owe much to Heidegger's earlier conceptualizations – to his recognition of the importance of an embodied experience of the world, his challenge to the Cartesian split of mind and body, of nature and culture, his conceptualization of *being-in-the-world* and of *dwelling* (Heidegger 1962; Thomas 1996 Thomas, Chapter 3 of this volume). Nonetheless there is a danger in some of his writings, and in that of some of the practiners following in his wake, of creating a romantic, almost ahistorical sense of being–in–the–world, one that is rooted in seemingly 'timeless' activities and movements (Bourdieu 1991; Bender 1998: 37). There is a danger of focusing too sharply on social practices or practical activities and of failing to note their embeddedness in often deeply unequal and widely disseminated power relations. One needs to be continually reminded that:

> Representations of space and time arise out of the world of social practices but then become a form of regulation of those practices.

(Harvey 1996: 212; Harvey and Haraway 1995)

And that:

> Place is the reproduction of a particular set, a particular articulation of ... power-filled social relations ... There is always a history that is brought to each situation of political practice.

(Massey 1995)

We need also to continue to recognize that even the most familiar of landscapes is usually the precipitate of (unfamiliar) movements – of people, labour and capital between town and country, between country and country (Gupta and Ferguson 1997: 14). Even the most familiar places are webbed around with unfamiliar ones, and even within the familiar setting there lurks the possibility of Freud's 'uncanny' experience (Gelder and Jacobs 1995). With even more urgency we need to recognize that, both in the past, and on an ever increasing scale in the present, people are on the move, live in 'unfamiliar' places, are forced to juggle memories of old places with incomprehensible new ones (Ghosh 1992; Bender and Winer 2001). The study of these sorts of dislocated landscapes is discussed in the third section of this review.

SUBVERTING THE WESTERN GAZE

The Gaze

There was an early Anglo-Saxon word, corresponding to the German word *Landschaft*, that referred to a small patch of cultivated ground, a mere fragment of a feudal estate, an inset in a Breughel painting, something that approximated a peasant's view of the world (Jackson 1985). But this word went out of use, and when the word 'landskip' or 'scape' re-emerged in the Low Countries and Italy in the seventeenth and eighteenth centuries it was under conditions of emergent capital and carried very different baggage. Now it came to denote a very particular masculine and class-conscious way of 'seeing', and controlling, the world. One that created a divorce between 'nature' and 'culture', with culture understood to be active and nature passive, with culture gendered male and nature

female. (See Olwig 2002 for a very sustained discussion of the roots and derivative usage of nat-ure, nat-ion, nat-ive, etc.) This post-Enlightenment engagement with the world emphasized the visual, and 'the gaze' fanned out across the surface, creating a *self*-centred perspective. At first the word 'landscape' was used to denote a particular genre of perspectival paintings, then expanded to include 'correct' ways of viewing 'nature' – involving, on occasion, turning one's back on the desirable view and framing it in a Claude glass. Eventually it also encompassed the active creation of desired landscape effects (Daniels 1993).

The 'gaze', even in a Western context, even at the moment when patrician notions of landscapes held maximum sway, was never the only way of engaging the world. Barrell's study of the worker-poet Clare describes the tensions between an elitist aesthetic 'viewpoint' and an alternative, labourer's close-up landscape of open field and droveway, and a further tension between the proprietorial attitude to land in which there were 'sensible' economies to be made through enclosure and the anguished view of those whose land and livelihood were being curtailed or destroyed in the process (Barrell 1972, 2002).

Western Maps

The Western Gaze, whether it be at home, looking out over a 'fine prospect', or abroad, encroaching upon other people's places and understandings, is a colonizing gaze (Mitchell 1989; Pratt 1992; Blunt and Rose 1994). And the mapping of landscape was not just an adjunct to exploration and colonization, it helped create the conditions for such enterprises. Equally, Western cartography was not just an aid to the establishment and monitoring of different sorts of property and of national and regional boundaries, but a force in the creation of changing social configurations (Bender 1999; Harley 1992a; Ingold 2000).

Maps may attempt to assert control, but, just as with 'the gaze', they are always open to subversion (Crouch and Matless 1996; Harley 1992b). The meticulous detail of the Ordinance Survey map (a detail that nonetheless is never quite complete as the nuclear power station, the bunker disappear from view) makes it open to renegotiation. The field marshal's map may be annotated with forbidden places (sexual and political) (Benjamin 1985; Sontag 1983); the official government map may 'talk past' the unofficial peasants' 'sketch' (Orlove 1991, 2002); the boundary may become a symbol and thus a focus of resistance – whether in Berlin, Northern Ireland (Jarman 1993) or in Palestine (Selwyn 2001). It may become the locus of myth and storytelling (Jacobs 1993; Morphy 1993); or become a 'line' open to renegotiation in non-Western, Aboriginal terms (Byrne 2003).

> To find out where he stands the traveller has to keep listening – since there is no map which draws the line he knows he must have crossed
>
> (Heaney 1987: 10)

Landscapes of Contestation

Whether over the map, or on the ground, there are, in most parts of the world, and at most times, conflicts that arise because of people's different understandings, preoccupations, engagements with places and landscapes. There is a considerable literature about such conflicts in 'Western' contexts. To take a few examples, Edholm (1993) discusses the class and gendered cityscape, and the subversive interstices, of Haussmann's Paris (Edholm 1993); both Soja (1989, 1999) and Davis (1990) provide readings of Los Angeles which contextualize the development of gated communities, no-go parks, new ghettoes and new forms of surveillance and incarceration; Jarman (1993) charts a Northern Irish urban landscape of political antagonisms – the materiality of barbed wire and blocked view. He shows too, how murals (with changing political and gendered import) may be for internal consumption within a community or may mark the edge of territory, whilst the Orange marches involve a more direct physical appropriation of space.

In colonial settings, or postcolonial settings, the contestations may cover the brutal landscapes of plantation slavery (Stewart 1995; Upton 1985); or the contemporary landscape of terror around Freeport, Irian Jaya (Ballard 2002). They may involve, as under apartheid in District 6 in Cape Town, the tearing down of a whole neighbourhood, and then, much later, the emergence of new forms of identification with old places (Hall 2001). Or they may involve, as in Palestine, the creation of new settlements and arterial roads that slice through, dismember and dispossess the indigenous population (Selwyn 2001; Said 2003; Barghouti 2000).

Although landscapes of heritage and tourism are seemingly more benign, they too can arouse strong and sometimes violent confrontations. Aziz (2001) maps the radical and very gender-specific effects of tourism on the Bedouin landscape of the southern Sinai. Bender (1998),

Hetherington (2000) and Worthington (2004) discuss fierce stand-offs between Heritage purveyors and New Age Travellers in Britain. Johnson (1996), in the context of the highly contested histories surrounding the great houses in the republic of Eire, asks questions about whose story is being told? By whom? For whom? And discusses an alternative display strategy in which different, and conflicting, accounts lie side by side.

Small-scale Indigenous Societies

Some of the worst and most unequal confrontations have occurred between colonizing and small-scale indigenous societies. And here we may pause to recognize that the mutual incomprehension engendered by totally different social, political and economic practices extends to include the inability to recognize or at least to tolerate a completely different understanding of place and landscape.

Some of the earliest accounts of quite different ways of being-in-the-world were written in the first half of the twentieth century by anthropologists working in Australia. Whilst they had begun by focusing rather narrowly on kinship and social organization, the Aboriginal people soon made it clear that these things could not be understood without an understanding of the relationship between human beings and the land (Morphy 1993). The Aboriginal landscapes had been created in the Dreamtime by the ancestral beings, and human beings were dependent upon – were nurtured by – the work of the ancestors. But, equally, the ancestral beings were nurtured by humans. In stark contrast to the 'Western gaze', there could be no divide between nature and culture (Morphy 1995; Layton 1997).

The contrast between the gaze and a quite other way of being in place is reiterated in the difference between the Western map and Australian Aboriginal representations – the Yolngu bark paintings, the *daragu* boards, the Walbiri sand paintings. The Western map appears non-indexical:

> In the Western tradition the way to imbue a claim with authority is to attempt to eradicate all signs of its local, contingent, social and individual production.
>
> (Turnbull 1989: 42)

In reality, it is just as 'indexed' on a people's history as the Aboriginal maps (Gell 1985). The latter offer a more open and wonderfully polysemic understanding of people's relationship to the land. Thus, for example, the Yolngu paintings are, at one and the same time, topographic maps, mythological maps, maps of sacred knowledge, and maps of social relationships (Morphy 1989, 1999). As topographic maps they allow people to locate resources, camps, hunting grounds, to know where they are and where they might be travelling. As mythological maps they detail stories of ancestral activity and creativity – thus turning temporal accounts into spatial grids. These grids in turn locate the individual and the clan and allow them to renew their ancestral inheritance. At the same time, the paintings' symbolism and the associated rituals and ceremonies are forms of restricted knowledge that require initiation, and are therefore part of the way in which people create and sustain status and identity. Finally, both map and knowledge are always open to adjustment: 'The ancestral past is subject to the political map of the present' (Morphy 1989; Jacobs 1993).

It does not really matter where one looks at small-scale societies in the contemporary world, they are almost invariably going through a process of rapid change, and the anthropological accounts, be they the kinscapes of Amazonian Indians (Gow 1995), the mobile herding landscapes of chiefly or shamanistic Mongolian people (Humphries 1995), American Indian societies in the high Andes rewriting history upon the ground (Rappaport 1988) or the spirit landscapes of Papua New Guinea (Harrison 2001), cannot afford to airbrush out the effects of variable scenarios of oppression, subversion, contestation, and of uneasy coexistence and ways of getting by.

Küchler's account of the Malangan funerary carvings of New Ireland (off the north-east coast of Papua New Guinea) indicates not only how variable the forms of mapping can be, but how indigenous understandings are reworked in the face of colonial dislocation (Küchler 1993; see also Myers in Chapter 17). The people of New Ireland create elaborately carved funerary images which are abandoned shortly after they have been completed and exhibited. This art is a form of mapping that regulates, through what is incorporated and what is excluded, the transmission of land. Although it seems timeless, and, as such, was thought to be harmless by the German colonizers, it is, in fact, a relatively recent development resulting directly from the break-up of clan territory, a process which began in the eighteenth century and intensified under late nineteenth-century German colonial rule. The Germans, failing to understand the import of these objects, collected and exhibited

them as pieces of 'indigenous art' and thus, unwittingly, permitted – even encouraged – an indigenous form of resistance.

LANDSCAPES OF MOVEMENT, EXILE AND TERROR

Resistance and opposition have shifted from the settled, established and domesticated dynamics of culture to its unhoused, decentred and exilic energies, energies whose incarnation today is the migrant (Said 1993: 403):

> Routes and rootedness ... identifications not identities, acts of relationship rather than pre-given forms ... 'tradition' [as] a network of partially connected histories ... globalisation from below.
>
> (Clifford 1994)

Although there has been increased emphasis on embodied landscapes, and recognition that people's memories and sense of place are shaped in movement, there has been a tendency to focus on movement within familiar places and spaces. But, as noted earlier, human beings have always moved out beyond the familiar terrain, have had to engage with unfamiliar places and find ways to create links between places they have known and new places. In many cases, as with the tourist or explorer, such movement is voluntary and the 'unknown' sits (reasonably) happily alongside the 'left behind'. Sometimes, as with travelling people, the home (caravan or *yurt*) becomes the stable centre of a world which is, in part, made familiar through well worn routeways, but is always, in part, alien because of the reception of those whose land is passed through.

But, increasingly, there are more turbulent landscapes – the landscapes of the dispossessed, the migrant, the exile. Whilst there has been much work on the politics and economics of diasporic movement, there has been less attempt to 'place' these movements. The trope of nomadology (Deleuze and Guattari 1988), whilst it hammers the privileged Western emphasis on roots and belonging, also threatens to flatten the huge diversity of experiences (Aug 1994; Cresswell 1997). We have to recognize that though people may be *dis*-placed or *dis*-located they are never no-where. They are always – somehow, and however desperately – in place (Smith and Katz 1993; Bender and Winer 2001; Minh-ha 1994). Closer attentiveness to how people-on-the-move *re*-create their landscapes will permit a more grounded sense of what is involved in diasporic movement

(Clifford 1997; Harding 2000), and will also move beyond simple victimology – the silent and silenced people have their own biographies. As Massey (2000) suggests, there is as much variety, as much potential for good or evil, for suppression or omission, among the silenced as among the silencers.

Our accounts of how people relate to unfamiliar and often hostile worlds, how they carve out a place for themselves, create bridges between what is and what has gone before, wind memories around 'here' and 'there', and how they cope with the often desired but often traumatic journey 'home', need to be highly contextual (the particularities of time and place matter) and biographical (past, present and in process). We need to work with the particular, and, at the same time, the general. Despite being gender-blind, Berger puts it well:

> To see the experience of another, one must do more than dismantle and reassemble the world with him [sic] at the centre. One must interrogate his situation to learn about that part of his experience that derives from the historical moment. What is being done to him, even with his won complicity, under the cover of normalcy?
>
> (Berger and Mohr 1975: 104)

Berger's *The Seventh Man* (1975) offers an astonishingly empathetic account of the male world of Turkish gast-arbeiters in Germany or Switzerland, but their experiences need to be placed alongside those of Indian migrant workers in the Persian Gulf (Osella and Osella 2000), or of women migrant workers in Italy (Andrijasevic 2003). Accounts need to be carefully gendered and attentive to age, ethnicity and so on. Eva Hoffman's *Lost in Translation* offers a very personal account of a child's view of exile, the sense of being lost (literally and figuratively) in a new place, and the way in which, in adopting a new language, words without memory baggage lose their resonance (Hoffman 1997, 1998). Barghouti (2000) allows us an insight into the bewilderment of return to a place that, by definition, has moved on, and Basu (2001) indicates how, even after several generations, a yearning for roots leads people back to (selected) 'homelands'. Often the selected personal history is one of having been 'driven forth', and the return is a sort of redemption, an assuaging of generational wounds.

One of the things that emerges from such studies of movement and exile is that places of transit – airports, bus and train stations and so on – are often places of trauma, leave taking, news gathering. They are the very opposite of the 'non-place' used by Marc Augé to evoke a deracinated, restless world (Augé 1995).

Landscapes of movement and exile are often shadowed by landscapes of terror. There are occasions when we need to recognize that there are landscapes that are beyond words. We (academics) have a tendency to believe that one of our tasks is to explore the hidden depths of exploitation and contestation, and to create spaces for those that are silent/silenced. But there may be times or contexts when people's memories, wound around particular places, are too raw, too private for the outsider to intrude upon. It is perhaps salutary to recognize that in a world in touch with fear, torture and genocide, talking, remembering, memorializing may not only be dangerous activities but may involve emotions that cannot be expressed – or can be expressed only at certain times and places, or with certain people (Byrne 1999; Sebald 2003). Sometimes people will wish to stand witness (Levi 1958), sometimes, after a lapse of time, people may feel the need to recollect, to bring out memories or mementoes that make possible a present-past (Parkin 1999), but sometimes it may be important to simply acknowledge the silent places, the spaces of absence (Ballard 2002).

MOVING ON

Briefly: where should landscape studies be heading? I'm not a great believer in guidelines, and what follows are simply my personal inclinations. I do believe that our theoretical, as well as our practical, understanding of landscapes should espouse acceptance of disorder and untidiness. Our theories of landscape should embrace ambiguity and contradiction, eschew closure, recognize that people, things, places are always in process, and that the boundaries between them are permeable and imbricated.

We should be suspicious of the contemporary passion – institutional and personal – for theoretical innovation, for discarding and moving on. We might note how snugly this practice fits within a wider set of present-day political, economic and social relationships. It might be more useful to recognize and contextualize the swing of the theoretical pendulum, and to consider how, when it swings back, it incorporates, but also transforms, earlier conceptualizations. Thus, for example, one might want to consider how and why, in the earlier twentieth century, the prehistoric social landscape of Europe was premised on migration and movement; how and why, in the late 1960s and 1970s, the pendulum swung towards a much more parochial (regional) conceptualization of in-place development; and how and why the pendulum is now swinging back towards migration and movement. What links our contemporary understanding with the earlier one, but also how has it changed?

Theoretical composting might go hand in hand with more cross-fertilization between theories. We might create something more consistent with the untidy vagaries of human existence if, instead of insisting that things, in theory or practice, are *either* this *or* that, we understood them to be *both* this *and* that. Undoubtedly there are theoretical positionings that are deeply incompatible, but there are many that could be more closely aligned. They could be brought together within a capacious and encompassing narrative, or could lie alongside each other so that a given landscape might be regarded first through one prism, then another, and another. It would be good to see research projects that knit or facet the political and economic integrity of Williams's structures of feeling or Lefebvre's production of space, Giddens's knowledgeable agency and spatial temporalities, Bourdieu's habitus, more coherent gendered approaches, a properly embodied or phenomenal approach, and more besides.

In terms of subject matter, I would suggest that we need to shake up the notion of landscape and consider it as both in place and out of place. On the one hand, even landscapes that appear rooted and familiar operate, in fact, within larger fields of social and economic relationships that are less familiar. What are the variable contexts – social, geographical, biographical/temporal – that tension the known and the familiar?

On the other hand, and perhaps more urgently, we need a more vivid understanding of how people on the move locate themselves. How do people – wherever, whenever – come to terms with movement and exile, with dislocation and relocation, with loss or re-entry (which may also be loss)? How do the people left behind work a landscape of absence and change? We have to rework some of our notions of landscape within more volatile settings: how are memories recharged? How are old understandings reworked in new surroundings? What happens when the familiar becomes unfamiliar, or when being 'at home' connotes danger? How do people, however uncomfortable it may be, or minimal, or even unbearable, make some sense out of, and create some sense of, both place and landscape?

REFERENCES

Andrijasevic, R. (2003) 'The difference borders make: (ill)legality, migration and trafficking in Italy among Eastern European women in prostitution', in S. Ahmed, C. Castaneda, A.-M. Fortier and M. Sheller (eds), *Uprootings/Regroundings: Questions of Home and Migration*. Oxford: Berg.

Aug, I. (1994) 'On not speaking Chinese: postmodern ethnicity and the politics of diaspora', *New Formations*, 24: 4.

Augé, M. (1995) *Non-places: Introduction to an Anthropology of Supermodernity*. London: Verso.

Aziz, H. (2001) 'Cultural keepers, cultural brokers: the landscape of women and children – a case study of the town Dahab in south Sinai', in B. Bender and M. Winer (eds), *Contested Landscapes: Movement, Exile and Place*. Oxford: Berg, pp. 121–32.

Ballard, C. (2002) 'The signature of terror: violence, memory and landscape at Freeport', in B. David and M. Wilson (eds), *Inscribed Landscapes: Marking and Making Space*. Honolulu, HI: University of Hawai'i Press, pp. 3–26.

Barghouti, M. (2000) *I Saw Ramallah*. Cairo: American University in Cairo Press.

Barrell, J. (1972) *The Idea of Landscape and the Sense of Place, 1730–1840*. Cambridge: Cambridge University Press.

Barrell, J. (2002) 'Mr and Mrs Equivalent', *Times Literary Supplement*, 8 November, pp. 20–1.

Barrett, J. (1994) *Fragments from Antiquity*. Oxford: Blackwell.

Basso, K. (1996) *Wisdom sits in High Places*. Albuquerque, NM: University of New Mexico Press.

Basso, K. and Feld, S., eds (1996) *Senses of Place*. Albuquerque, NM: University of New Mexico Press.

Basu, P. (2001) 'Hunting down home: reflections on homeland and the search for identity in the Scottish diaspora', in B. Bender and M. Winer (eds), *Contested Landscapes: Movement, Exile and Place*. Oxford: Berg, pp. 333–48.

Bender, B., ed. (1993) *Landscape: Politics and Perspectives*. Oxford: Berg.

Bender, B. (1998) *Stonehenge: Making Space*. Oxford: Berg.

Bender, B. (1999) 'Subverting the Western gaze: mapping alternative worlds', in P. Ucko and R. Layton (eds), *The Archaeology and Anthropology of Landscape*. London: Routledge, pp. 31–45.

Bender, B. (2002) 'Time and landscape', *Current Anthropology*, 43 (supplement): pp. S103–S112.

Bender, B. and Winer, M. eds (2001) *Contested Landscapes: Movement, Exile and Place*. Oxford: Berg.

Bender, B. Hamilton, S. and Tilley, C. (1997) 'Leskernick: stone worlds, alternative narratives, nested landscapes', *Proceedings of the Prehistoric Society*, 63: 147–78.

Benjamin, W. (1985) *One Way Street and other Writings*. London: Verso.

Berger, J. (1972) *Ways of Seeing*. Harmondsworth: Penguin.

Berger, J. and Mohr, J. (1975) *The Seventh Man*. Harmondsworth: Penguin.

Blunt, A. and Rose, G., eds (1994) *Writing Women and Space: Colonial and Postcolonial Geographies*. London: Guilford Press.

Bourdieu, P. (1971/1990) 'The Berber house, or, The world reversed', in P. Bourdieu, *The Logic of Practice*. Oxford: Polity Press, pp. 271–83.

Bourdieu, P. (1977) *Outline of a Theory of Practice*. Cambridge: Cambridge University Press.

Bourdieu, P. (1991) *The Political Ontology of Martin Heidegger*. Cambridge: Polity Press.

Bradley, R. (1993) *Altering the Earth*. Monograph Series 8. Edinburgh: Society of Antiquaries of Scotland.

Bradley, R. (1998) *The Significance of Monuments*. London: Routledge.

Byrne, D. (1999) 'Traces of '65: sites and memories of the post-*coup* killings in Bali', *The Archaeology of Feeling*, 5 (1): 36–52.

Byrne, D. (2003) 'Nervous landscapes: race and space in Australia', *Journal of Social Archaeology*, 3 (2): 169–93.

Casey, E.S. (1993) *Getting Back into Place*. Bloomington, IN: Indiana University Press.

Clifford, J. (1994) 'Diasporas', *Cultural Anthropology*, 9: 302–38.

Clifford, J. (1997) *Routes: Travel and Translation in the late Twentieth Century*. Cambridge, MA: Harvard University Press.

Cosgrove, D. and Daniels, S., eds (1988) *The Iconography of Landscape*. Cambridge: Cambridge University Press.

Cresswell, T. (1992) 'Mobility as resistance: a geographical reading of Kerouac's *On the Road*', *Transactions of the Institute of British Geographers*, 18: 249–62.

Cresswell, T. (1997) 'Imagining the nomad: mobility and the postmodern primitive', in G. Benko and U. Strohmayer (eds), *Space and Social Theory*. Oxford: Blackwell pp. 360–79.

Crouch, D. and Matless, D. (1996) 'Refiguring geography: parish maps of common ground', *Transactions of the Institute of British Geographers*, 21: 236–55.

Daniels, S. (1989) 'Marxism and the duplicity of landscape', in R. Peet and N. Thrift (eds), *New Models in Geography* II. London: Unwin Hyman, pp. 000–00.

Daniels, S. (1993) *Fields of Vision*. Cambridge: Polity Press.

Daniels S. and Cosgrove, D. (1993) 'Spectacle and text', in J. Duncan and D. Ley (eds), *Place/Culture/ Representation*. London: Routledge, pp. 57–77.

David, B. and Wilson, M. (2002) *Inscribed Landscapes*. Honolulu, HI: University of Hawai'i Press.

Davis, M. (1990) *City of Quartz*. London: Verso.

de Certeau, M. (1984) *The Practice of Everyday Life*. Berkeley, CA: University of California Press.

Deleuze, G. and Guattari, F. (1988) *A Thousand Plateaus*. London: Athlone Press.

Edholm, F. (1993) 'The view from belong: Paris in the 1880s', in B. Bender (ed.), *Landscape: Politics and Perspectives*. Oxford: Berg, pp. 139–68.

Edmonds, M. (1999) *Ancestral Geographies of the Neolithic*. London: Routledge.

Edmonds, M. (2004) *The Langdales*. Stroud: Tempus.

Elliot, G. (1871–72/1965) *Middlemarch*. Harmondsworth: Penguin.

Feld, S. and Basso, K. (1996) *Senses of Place*. Santa Fe, NM: School of American Research Press.

Gelder, K. and Jacobs, J. (1995) 'Uncanny Australia', *Ecumene*, 2 (2): 171–83.

Gell, A. (1985) 'How to read a map: remarks on the practical logic of navigation', *Man*, 20 (2): 271–86.

Gero, J. and Conkey, M. (1991) *Engendering Archaeology*. Oxford: Blackwell.

Ghosh, A. (1992) *In an Antique Land*. London: Granta Books.

Giddens, A. (1981) *A Contemporary Critique of Historical Materialism* I, *Power, Property and the State*. London: University of California Press.

Giddens, A. (1985) 'Time, space and regionalisation', in D. Gregory and J. Urry (eds), *Social Relations and Spatial Structures*. Basingstoke: Macmillan, pp. 265–95.

Gilchrist, R. (1994) *Gender and Material Culture*. London: Routledge.

Gosden, C. (1994) *Social Being and Time*. Oxford: Blackwell.

Gow, P. (1995) 'Land, people and paper in western Amazon', in E. Hirsch and M. O'Hanlon (eds), *The Anthropology of Landscape*. Oxford: Clarendon Press, pp. 43–62.

Gupta, A. and Ferguson, J. (1997) *Anthropological Locations*. Berkeley, CA: University of California Press.

Hall, M. (2001) 'Cape Town's District Six and the archaeology of memory', in R. Layton, P. Stone and J. Thomas (eds), *Destruction and Conservation of Cultural Property*. London: Routledge, pp. 298–311.

Harding, J. (2000) 'The uninvited', *London Review of Books*, 3 February.

Harley, J. (1992a) 'Deconstructing the map', in T. Barnes and J. Duncan (eds), *Writing Worlds: Discourse, Text and Metaphor in the Representation of Landscape*. London: Routledge, pp. 231–47.

Harley, J. (1992b) 'Re-reading the maps of the Columbian encounters', *Annals of the Association of American Geographers*, 82/83: 522–42.

Harrison, S. (2001) 'Smoke rising from the villages of the dead: seasonal patterns of mood in a Papua New Guinea society', *Journal of the Royal Anthropological Institute*, 7: 257–74.

Harvey, D. (1996) *The Condition of Postmodernity*. Cambridge: Blackwell.

Harvey, D. and Haraway, D. (1995) 'Nature, politics and possibilities: a debate and discussion with David Harvey and Donna Haraway', *Environment and Planning D: Society and Space*, 13: 507–27.

Heaney, S. (1984) *Station Island*. London: Faber.

Heaney, S. (1987) *The Haw Lantern*. London: Faber.

Heidegger, M. (1962) *Being and Time*, trans. J. Macquarrie and E. Robinson. Oxford: Blackwell.

Herzfeld, M. (1991) *A Place in History: Social and Monumental Time in a Cretan Town*. Princeton, NJ: Princeton University Press.

Hetherington, K. (2000) *New Age Travellers*. London: Cassell.

Hirsch, E. and O'Hanlon, M., eds (1995) *The Anthropology of Landscape*. Oxford: Oxford University Press.

Hoffman, E. (1997) 'The new nomads', in A. Aciman (ed.), *Letters of Transit*. New York: New Press, pp. 35–63.

Hoffman, E. (1998) *Lost in Translation*. London: Vintage.

hooks, b. (1992) 'Representing whiteness in the black imagination', in L. Grossberg et al. (eds) *Cultural Studies*. London: Routledge, pp. 343–46.

Hoskins, W.G. (1955) *The Making of the English Landscape*. Harmondsworth: Penguin.

Humphrey, C. (1995) 'Chiefly and Shamanist landscapes in Mongolia', in E. Hirsch and M. O'Hanlon (eds), *The Anthropology of Landscape*. Oxford: Oxford University Press, pp. 135–62.

Ingold, T. (1993) 'The temporality of landscape', *World Archaeology*, 25: 152–74.

Ingold, T. (1997) 'The picture is not the terrain: maps, paintings, and the dwelt-in world', *Archaeological Dialogues*, 1: 29–31.

Ingold, T. (2000) *The Perception of Environment*. London: Routledge.

Jackson, J.B. (1985) *Discovering the Vernacular*. New Haven, CT: Yale University Press.

Jackson, J.B. (1994) *A Sense of Place, a Sense of Time*. New Haven, CT: Yale University Press.

Jacobs, J. (1993) '"Shake 'im this country": the mapping of the Aboriginal sacred in Australia: the case of Coronation Hill', in P. Jackson and J. Penrose (eds), *Constructions of Race, Place and Nation*, Minneapolis: University of Minnesota Press, pp. 100–18.

Jacobs, J. (1996) *Edge of Empire*. London: Routledge.

Jarman, N. (1993) 'Intersecting Belfast', in B. Bender (ed.), *Landscape: Politics and Perspectives*. Oxford: Berg, pp. 107–38.

Johnson, N. (1996) 'Where geography and history meet: heritage tourism and the Big House in Ireland', *Annals of the Association of American Geographers*, 86 (3): 551–66.

Jones, A. (1998) 'Where eagles dare: landscape, animals and the Neolithic of Orkney', *Journal of Material Culture*, 3 (3): 301–24.

Kincaid, J. (1989) *Lucy*. London: Picador.

Küchler, S. (1993) 'Landscape as memory: the mapping of process and its representation in a Melanesian society', in B. Bender (ed.), *Landscape: Politics and Perspectives*. Oxford: Berg, pp. 85–106.

Layton, R. (1997) 'Representing and translating people's place in the landscape of northern Australia', in A. James, J. Hockey and A. Dawson (eds), *After Writing Culture: Epistemology and Praxis in Contemporary Anthropology*. London: Routledge.

Lefebvre, H. (1974) *The Production of Space*. Oxford: Blackwell.

Levi, P. (1958) *If this is a Man*. Harmondsworth: Penguin.

Lowenthal, D. (1985) *The Past is a Foreign Country*. Cambridge: Cambridge University Press.

Lowenthal, D. (1996) *The Heritage Crusade and the Spoils of History*. London: Viking.

Massey, D. (1994) *Space, Place, and Gender*. Minneapolis, MN: University of Minnesota, Press.

Massey, D. (1995) 'Thinking radical democracy spatially', *Environment and Planning D: Society and Space*, 13: 283–8.

Massey, D. (2000) 'Living in Wythenshawe', in I. Borden, J. Kerr, A. Pivaro and J. Rendell (eds), *The Unknown City*. London: Wiley.

Merleau-Ponty, M. (1962) *The Phenomenology of Perception*. London: Routledge.

Minh-ha Trinh T. (1994) 'Other than myself/my other self', in G. Robertson, M. Mash, L. Tickner, J. Bird, B. Curtis and T. Putnam (eds), *Travellers' Tales*. London: Routledge, pp. 9–26.

Mitchell, T. (1989) 'The world as exhibition', *Comparative Studies in Sociology and History*, 31: 217–36.

Morphy, H. (1989) 'From dull to brilliant: the aesthetics of spiritual power among the Yolngu', *Man* 34 (1): 21–40.

Morphy, H. (1993) 'Colonialism, history and the construction of place: the politics of landscape in northern Australia', in B. Bender (ed.), *Landscape: Politics and Perspectives*. Oxford: Berg, pp. 205–43.

Morphy, H. (1995) 'Landscape and the reproduction of the ancestral past', in E. Hirsch and M. O'Hanlon (eds), *The Anthropology of Landscape*. Oxford: Oxford University Press, pp. 184–209.

Morphy, H. (1999) 'Manggalili art and the promised land', in L. Taylor (ed.), *Painting the Land Story*. Canberra: National Museum of Australia, pp. 53–74.

Mouffe, C. (1995) 'Post-Marxism: democracy and identity', *Environment and Planning D: Society and Space*, 13: 259–65.

Munn, N. (1992) 'The cultural anthropology of time: a critical essay', *Annual Review of Anthropology*, 21: 93–123.

Naipaul, V.S. (1987) *The Enigma of Arrival.* Harmondsworth: Penguin.

Olwig, K.R. (2002) *Landscape, Nature, and the Body Politic.* Madison, WI: University of Wisconsin Press.

Orlove, B. (1991) 'Mapping reeds and reading maps: the politics of representation in Lake Titikaka', *American Ethnologist,* 18: 3–38.

Orlove, B. (2002) *Lines in the Water.* Berkeley, CA: University of California Press.

Osella, P. and Osella, C. (2000) 'Migration, money and masculinity in Kerala', *Journal of the Royal Anthropological Institute,* 6: 117–33.

Parkin, D. (1999) 'Mementoes, reality and human displacement', *Journal of Material Culture,* 4 (3): 303–20.

Pratt, M.L. (1992) *Imperial Eyes.* London: Routledge.

Pred, A. (1990) *Lost Words and Lost Worlds: Modernity and the Language of Everyday Life in Late Nineteenth Century Stockholm.* Cambridge: Cambridge University Press.

Proust, M. (1981) *In Search of Lost Time I, Swann's Way.* London: Vintage.

Rappaport, J. (1988) 'History and everyday life in the Colombian Andes', *Man,* 23 (4): 718–39.

Richards, C. (1993) 'Monumental choreography: architecture and spatial representation in late Neolithic Orkney', in C. Tilley (ed.), *Interpretative Archaeology.* London: Berg, pp. 143–78.

Rose, G. (1993) *Feminism and Geography.* Cambridge: Polity Press.

Said, E. (1989) 'Jane Austen and empire', in T. Eagleton (ed.), *Raymond Williams: Critical Perspectives.* Oxford: Polity Press, pp. 150–64.

Said, E. (1993) *Culture and Imperialism.* London: Vintage.

Said, E. (2003) 'A road map to where?' *London Review of Books,* 19 June.

Salmond, A. (1982) 'Theoretical landscapes: on cross-cultural conceptions of knowledge', in D. Parkin (ed.), *Semantic Anthropology.* London: Academic Press, pp. 65–88.

Samuels, R. (1994) *Theatres of Memory.* London: Verso.

Schama, S. (1995) *Landscape and Memory.* London: Harper Collins.

Sebald, W.G. (1998) *The Rings of Saturn.* London: Harvill Press.

Sebald, W.G. (2001) *Austerlitz.* London: Hamish Hamilton.

Sebald, W.G. (2003) *On the Natural History of Destruction.* New York: Random House.

Selwyn, T. (2001) 'Landscapes of separation: reflections on the symbolism of by-pass roads in Palestine', in B. Bender and M. Winer (eds), *Contested Landscapes: Movement, Exile and Place.* Oxford: Berg, pp. 225–40.

Smith, N. and Katz, C. (1993) 'Grounding metaphor', in M. Keith and S. Pile (eds), *Place and the Politics of Identity.* London: Routledge.

Soja, E. (1989) *Postmodern Geographies.* London: Verso.

Soja, E. (1991) 'Henri Lefebvre, 1901–1991', *Environment and Planning D: Society and Space,* 9: 257–59.

Soja, E. (1999) 'Thirdspace: expanding the scope of the geographical imagination', in D. Massey, J. Allen and P. Sarre (eds), *Human Geography Today.* Cambridge: Polity Press, pp. 260 78.

Sontag, S. (1983) *A Susan Sontag Reader.* Harmondsworth: Penguin.

Stewart, L. (1995) 'Louisiana subjects: power, space and the slave body', *Ecumene,* 2 (3): 227–45.

Strang, V. (1997) *Uncommon Ground.* Oxford: Berg.

Thomas, J. (1996) *Time, Culture and Identity.* London: Routledge.

Thomas, J. (1997) 'An economy of substances in earlier Neolithic Britain', in J. Robb (ed.), *Material Symbols: Culture and Economy in Prehistory.* Carbondale, IL: Center for Archaeological Investigation.

Thomas, K. (1983) *Man and the Natural World.* Harmondsworth: Penguin.

Tilley, C. (1994) *A Phenomenology of Landscape.* Oxford: Berg.

Tilley, C. (1999) *Metaphor and Material Culture.* Oxford: Berg.

Tilley, C. (2004) *The Materiality of Stone.* Oxford: Berg.

Tringham, R. (1994) 'Engendered places in prehistory', *Gender, Place and Culture,* 1 (2): 169–203.

Turnbull, D. (1989) *Maps are Territories, Science is an Atlas: a Portfolio of Exhibits.* Geelong, Vic.: Deakin University Press.

Ucko, P. and Layton, R., eds (1999) *The Archaeology and Anthropology of Landscape.* London: Routledge.

Upton, D. (1985) 'White and black landscapes in eighteenth-century Virginia', *Places,* 2 (2): 59–73.

Williams, R. (1973) *The Country and the City.* London: Chatto & Windus.

Williamson, T. and Bellamy, L. (1987) *Property and Landscape.* London: Philip.

Woolf, V. (1929) *A Room of One's Own.* London: Penguin.

Worthington, A. (2004) *Stonehenge: Celebration and Subversion.* Loughborough: Alternative Albion.

20

CULTURAL MEMORY

Paul Connerton

A girl born in 1950, in time to have witnessed the events of May '68 in Paris, or the other student demonstrations of that year in the United States, the Federal Republic of Germany, Italy, and Britain, would have reached adulthood at a time when the word 'memory' lacked the cultural resonance it now enjoys. Neither the 1968 edition of the *International Encyclopedia of the Social Sciences*, nor Raymond Williams's *Keywords*, published in 1976, thought fit to include an entry on the subject. The intervening years have seen a sea-change. References to memory are now omnipresent in scholarly discourse and in wider public debate. 'Social memory', 'collective remembrance', 'national memory', 'public memory', 'counter-memory', 'popular history making' and 'lived history' jostle for attention. Heritage, museology, ethnohistory, industrial archaeology, retrofitting, retrochic, *lieux de mémoire* and counter-monument all allude to a common constellation of interests.

Memory's new position as a key word is signalled by a cluster of symptoms, some closely connected, others related together more tenuously. First of all, there is the vogue enjoyed by books devoted to producing an inventory of the contents of national memory.[1] This vogue is, admittedly, less original than is sometimes claimed. For one thing, some of its exemplars derive inspiration from a work written long ago, Maurice Halbwachs's *Les Cadres sociaux de la mémoire* (1925); this and other texts by Halbwachs first began to exert a serious impact long after their author had died in Auschwitz in 1944. For another thing, many contributions to what is now perceived to be a new field of inquiry elaborate research agendas previously pursued vigorously under

other names; specialists have long explored the history of mentalities, or myth, or oral history, or popular culture, or commemorative rituals, or autobiography, without seeking to link these strands together, as is now commonly done, by subsuming them under the general, overarching concept of memory. The elevation of this category, the crystallization of a conscious discourse about memory, is marked, above all, by collaborative scholarly enterprises: the publication of the first volume of *Lieux de Mémoire*, under the direction of Pierre Nora, in 1984;[2] the translation of Nora's essay, 'Between memory and history', in a special issue of *Representations* dedicated to memory in 1989;[3] and the founding of the journal *History and Memory* in the same year.

Closely related to this are a number of historical controversies concerning particularly tragic episodes in the past: regarding the Third Reich and its place in German history; the Vichy regime in France and its policy towards the Jews; fascism in Italy; Japanese war crimes in China and Korea; communist regimes in the former Soviet Union and in the countries previously annexed to the Soviet bloc. For many participants these disputes represented an opportunity to come to terms with a disputed past, and nowhere more stridently so than in Germany. If the *Historikerstreit* of 1986 opened for the first time a discussion of the relative status of Nazism in the context of other contemporary state crimes, particularly those in the Soviet Union, what gave that debate its peculiar intensity, its sting, was the fact that it offered the participants what they most probably felt to be a last chance to settle accounts. Most of those involved in the dispute belonged to the same age group, the 'Hitler Youth generation'. They were the last group active on the public scene whose members had a personal memory of the Nazi period, and, for this reason, there was in this group a powerful impulse to fix that experience in some kind of final form.[4] The German controversy about the national past not only fascinated a larger public than that of professional historians, it also took other forms than that of historical writing. This was the case not only in Germany. Thus although in France the work of historians on France's collaboration with the policy to exterminate the Jews surfaced into the public realm when a particularly flagrant case, that of Klaus Barbie or Paul Tournier for instance, caught the headlines, the one indisputably great French work on the massacre of the Jews was not a book but a film, Claude Lanzmann's *Shoah*. The fact is symptomatic. The 1970s and 1980s witnessed the return of the repressed not only as history but also, and often more impressively, as film: in Rainer Werner Fassbinder's *The Marriage of Maria Braun*; in Helma Sanders-Brahms's *Germany, Pale Mother*; in Edgar Reitz's *Heimat*; and, earlier than all of these, in Marcel Ophuls's *The Sorrow and the Pity*, which created a new type of historical film, setting up a confrontation between what people said in 1943 and what they said some thirty years later, before the camera.

Then again there is the contemporary culture of retributive justice and public apology. Since the Second World War, and ever more insistently towards the close of the twentieth century, scenes of legal judgement, repentance and pardon have multiplied on the geopolitical scene. Judgements at Nuremberg, Tokyo, Buenos Aires, Paris, Lyons, Bordeaux and The Hague have generated a special branch of criminal legislation in international law defining crimes against humanity, among them the crime of genocide. In the aftermath of administrative massacre, the movement for recovery of the facts of injustices perpetrated has almost invariably appeared – in Russia, the former Soviet Bloc societies, Argentina, Chile, El Salvador and Guatemala. The damage claims recently brought by comfort women, forced to serve as prostitutes for Japanese soldiers in the Second World War, have received considerable public support in Japan. In the United States and in France there has been a plethora of apologies for past actions by politicians and Church leaders. In South Africa the Truth and Reconciliation Commission was charged with the task of collecting evidence of crimes committed under apartheid, of providing a forum where the victims could ventilate their hatred face to face with the offenders and in the presence of

witnesses, and of granting amnesty to those who admitted that they had committed political crimes. In the wake of these events, there already flourishes an international debate regarding the relative merits of the various options – official truth commissions, criminal trials, parliamentary inquiries, sponsored scholarly inquiry into newly opened government archives – which might be adopted in response to the clamour for retributive justice. The cumulative effect of all these public proceedings is that the process of how people are made to vanish has become a distinctive feature of the contemporary conception of what constitutes cultural memory.

People are not the only things to vanish. The material culture of former lives does too. Indeed, it disappears more rapidly as the value attached to it diminishes. Between Elizabethan and Victorian times, for example, goods once valued for evidence of durability were replaced by goods valued for disposability. In counterpoint to this, the strategy of cultural salvage, no less than that of retributive justice, now belongs to the memory boom. Increasing importance is attached to what is thought of as cultural patrimony. The number of museums multiplies, especially museums of local identity, of everyday life and of working practices. What is sometimes referred to by the unlovely term 'museumification' is no longer bound to the institution of the museum but is extended to all areas of everyday life: to the restoration of old urban centres; the preservation of museum villages and landscapes; the flourishing of retro fashions. As the acceleration of technical and scientific innovation produces ever larger quantities of obsolescent objects, the monument as a category is unloosed from its reference to the privileged objects of the cathedral, the castle and the stately home, to embrace also the vestiges of the agriculture, industry and habitat of the nineteenth century and the first half of the twentieth. In England, the number of designated monuments, 268 in 1882, had risen to some 13,000 by the 1990s; English Heritage, charged with the task of preserving historical buildings, is now responsible for an entire town, Wirksworth, in the lead-mining district of Derbyshire; and at Wigan Pier Heritage Centre you can pay to crawl through a model coal mine and be invited in by actors dressed as 1900 proletarians. In France the Commission for the Ethnological Heritage promotes studies of life on the narrow boats on the canals of the Midi and the production of an inventory of the first cinemas in the Ile de France area; and the term *la patrimoine*, having been extended to refer to songs, dialects and good local wines, now includes the marble counter top from the Café du Croissant at which Jaurès drank his last cup of coffee.

If this is the evidence for the memory boom – academic studies of national memory, historical controversies concerning tragic episodes in the recent past, the culture of retributive justice and the public apology, the strategy of cultural salvage and invented tradition – what of its causes? Two in particular deserve to be singled out.

The first is the repercussions of twentieth-century totalitarianism. Totalitarian regimes revealed the existence of a danger hitherto unsuspected in history, that of the intentional systematic effacement of memory. There had, of course, been systematic destruction of the documents and monuments of opponents previously. The Spanish Conquistadores burnt and extinguished all the material traces which might have remained as evidence of the greatness of the peoples they vanquished. But they attacked only the official sources which transmitted the memory of conquered peoples, and allowed many other forms of the memory of vanquished peoples to survive, for example their oral narrations and poetry.

Both the Third Reich and the former Soviet Union, by contrast, waged an obsessive and total war on memory. Himmler said that the Final Solution was a glorious page in history which had never been written and never would be. The Nazi apparatus of genocide was to be responsible both for the murder and for the forgetting of the murder. Under the pressure of defeat, starting in 1943, the Nazis burnt the corpses and systematically destroyed the weapons of their crime; hasty efforts were made to get rid of potential witnesses through death marches. Victims who did in fact survive have told how they were terrified that the attempted cover-up might in the end succeed. Compared with twelve years in Nazi Germany, a time span of many decades shaped the attempt to asphyxiate the memory of victims in the former Soviet Union. Remembering had been dangerous since the 1920s, and only with the beginning of *Glasnost* in 1986 did it become politically possible to initiate openly the project of collecting oral histories. In the countries of East Central Europe annexed by the Soviet Union, too, memory was censored, whether because it had a religious character, or because it testified to the crimes of the Soviet Union, or because it related to political forces which were judged by the state apparatus to be anti-communist, or nationalist, or Jewish. In East Central Europe, as in the Soviet Union, the history of the revolution had been mythologized and official memory was in conflict with a memory which could be transmitted only orally, in families, and could attain a public hearing only through the secrecy of *samizdat* or through emigration.[5]

Hence the high prestige of memory among all enemies of totalitarianism. Every act of recollection, every attempt to disinter and reconstitute the past, was perceived as an act of principled opposition to state power. There was always a group of people who, throughout their imprisonment, nurtured the determination that what had happened to them and to those with them should be recounted. Many of them felt an imperative need to tell an account of wrongdoings precisely because they were convinced that the loss of the capacity to tell was one of the meanings of annihilation. They wanted to survive as moral witnesses, witnesses to the fact of evil and to the suffering it produces. Some poets and writers who have broken their silence may have paid with their life for that deed: Celan, Améry, Levi, Bettelheim. But from their pens there issued, as Elie Wiesel has said, a new literary genre, that of testimony. So Memorial, a large movement of moral witness in the former Soviet Union, has set out to document the victims of Stalinism, collecting written autobiographies, records and photographs, and recording and transcribing interviews. So the Fortunoff Video Archive for Holocaust Testimonies was established at Yale. And so too the overthrow of regimes in East Central Europe led to the collective rewriting of the past, from retrials to the rehabilitation of those imprisoned by previous regimes, from the replacement of statues and the names of streets to the rewriting of school history books.

There has been at least one other major cause of the memory boom. This is the fundamental transformation in the means by which cultural memory is transmitted and sustained. If an educated European or Chinese had been asked 200 years ago how the memory of their culture was passed on from generation to generation they would most probably have singled out, in the first instance, the crucial role played by the handing down of canonic texts. But the last 150 years have witnessed a revolution in communication as radical as that which resulted from the invention of printing, and, long before that, the invention and diffusion of writing. Photography, phonography, the cinema, radio, television, video and the Internet have together created a new collective memory. Superimposing a new stratum of memory on to that circulated by writing, these inventions have made ever greater quantities of memory potentially accessible.

They have also introduced a qualitative change into the way in which memory is experienced, because, in the objective form of images, films, discs, magnetic tape and cassettes, they seem to allow us to relive parts of the past, to see it again and to hear again its sounds, so long at least as these have been registered by a mechanical apparatus; by conferring on parts of the past a sensory presence previously absent, they generate the powerful illusion that it is actually possible to be in the presence of this past reality itself. As a consequence, it has become no longer possible to think of any historical trauma as a serious political issue outside and apart from the ways in which it is assimilated by the manner it is represented in photographs, films, docu-dramas and Internet sites; and these new forms of representation are so variegated and so ubiquitous that it has become difficult to think of anything as being in any sense not a representation.

This type of what might be called 'prosthetic memory', when it takes a mainly visual form, can sustain the existence of imagined communities as effectively as does, according to Benedict Anderson, the diffusion of printing. Film and video, by virtue of their narrative sequence, their temporal immersion, insinuate the suggestion of 'being there'. An archive of images yields objects around which collective remembrance may coalesce by contextual association. It was in this way that the instant captured in the Zapruder film of President Kennedy's assassination acquired mythic status as representing the moment when the United States underwent the transformation from being a nation of promise and optimism to becoming one of cynicism and violence. Similarly, the collective viewing of television images of the *Challenger* explosion and of the first Gulf War made the explosion and the war national experiences. For those Americans who lived through the years of the Vietnam War the most iconic documentation of the time were black-and-white photographs: the 1968 photograph by Eddie Adams of the chief of the South Vietnamese National Police shooting a Vietcong suspect in the head at point-blank range; and the 1972 photograph by Huynh Cong Ut of a young girl running naked down a road towards the camera and away from a napalm explosion. And for an American generation too young to have witnessed the Vietnam War at the time on television, the history of the war is represented by Hollywood narrative film produced for popular audiences.[6]

Many studies of cultural memory have clustered around three main areas.

Few aspects of memory have received more sustained attention than has the work of mourning. It is central in the studies by Paul Fussell and Jay Winter on the universality of grief in Europe in the wake of the First World War; it is the key theme in post-Holocaust literature, as in Saul Friedländer's *When Memory Comes*; it reappears in George Santner's and Anton Kaes's studies of belated mourning in German films of the 1970s and 1980s; it resurfaces in the dissection of the way the post-liberation French have dealt with the skeletons in the nation's closet, what Henri Rousso calls the 'Vichy syndrome', dating from the episode between the fall of France in June 1940 and the liberation in 1944; and it is announced once again in Yosef Yerushalmi's demonstration that the Jews have explored the meaning of their history more directly and more deeply in the prophets than in historical narratives, and that their collective memory of diaspora, pogroms and expulsions has been transmitted more actively through ritual than through chronicle. Studies of trauma, by Shoshana Felman, Dori Laub and Cathy Caruth, among others, belong in this context. In his major work, *Remembering*, Edward Casey has contrasted habitual bodily memory and traumatic bodily memory; whereas the former implies the continual resynthesis of the body, the latter implies the dissolution of the intact body. One particular case of traumatic bodily memory as a process of mourning has been investigated in detail by Arthur Kleinman: this is the experience of those who suffered social disorientation and a crisis of cultural legitimation during the Chinese Cultural Revolution of 1966 to 1976. The most striking physical symptom suffered by the victims was dizziness. For them to experience dizziness was to relive the memory of trauma; for them to tell about their dizziness was to give voice to an oblique criticism of the Cultural Revolution. Theirs was no arbitrary somatic symptom, as Kleinman shows. Given a medical tradition where balance was understood as constitutive of health, dizziness has particular salience as a physical work of mourning and memory, and the narrative of that illness becomes a sanctioned piece of utterable memory.[7]

Topography – the study of monuments, buildings, and entire landscapes as media of memory – has also been a key concern in recent debate.[8] Perhaps this is in part a response to the fact that the last half-century has experienced, as has no other, an end to the tyranny of distance; place, as evocative of shared memories, has become a surrogate for the territorial belongingness previously so central to the life of the nation-state. But in any event the classic works of Maurice Halbwachs and Frances Yates prefigure this contemporary preoccupation. No reader can fail to observe the dominance of spatial metaphors – 'framework', 'place', 'space', 'localizing', 'situating' – in Halbwachs's descriptions of social memory, or to appreciate the persuasiveness with which Yates excavated a long tradition of Western rhetoric with its stress upon the explicit spatialization of sequences of argument in imagined loci as the support to a trained memory. Their stimulus has been taken up most comprehensively, of course, in the vast collection of studies partly available in three volumes in English under the title *Realms of Memory* and completed under the direction of Pierre Nora. As a celebration of national identity in an era of national decline the design of Nora's enterprise is easily discernible, as a study in the mnemonics of place its lineaments are more difficult to decipher. Nora's enterprise is a confusing cornucopia. When he speaks of *lieux de mémoire* the word *lieu* fulfils two distinct types of function. Sometimes it is used literally to refer to features of topography: Lascaux, Versailles, the Eiffel Tower, street names. At other times it is employed figuratively to refer to tokens of cultural identity: the *Marseillaise*, Bastille Day, gastronomy, the memoirs of Chateaubriand, Stendhal and Poincaré. Nora's enterprise loses in logical coherence what it gains in comprehensiveness of treatment. No such incoherence mars other studies of place as a site of memory: Rudy Koshar's *From Monuments to Traces*, or Raphael Samuel's *Theatres of Memory*, or James Young's *The Texture of Memory*.[9]

A further theme of discussion has been the experience of memory in the era of modernity. Beginning from the general assumption that memory has a history, a number of scholars have argued that the history of memory in the nineteenth and twentieth centuries is unlike that of any other period. Focusing on the generation and a half between 1870 and 1914, Matt Matsuda has documented the ways in which it was obsessed by the meanings and uses of memory: how clinics, hospitals and laboratories were staffed by psychologists and neurologists who located memory in the tissues, organs, muscles and structures of the human body; how print memory proliferated in the new availability of mass-circulation newspapers; how the cinematic image was able not only to represent but also to preserve visual reality; how knowledge of the file, the accumulation of documents and images, was increasingly an instrument of state. Others have suggested that there is a paradoxical relationship between remembering and forgetting characteristic of modernity. Andreas Huyssen has pointed to a major and puzzling contradiction in our culture: the undisputed waning of historical consciousness, the lament about political, social and cultural amnesia, and the various discourses about *posthistoire*, have been accompanied in the past twenty years by a memory boom of unprecedented proportions. Jacques le Goff joins him in linking the valorization of memory to cultural forgetting when he argues that the public at large is obsessed by the fear of losing its memory in a kind of cultural amnesia, a fear that is awkwardly expressed in the taste for the fashions of earlier times and shamelessly exploited by nostalgia merchants. Richard Terdiman, too, focusing on French culture, argues that, beginning in the early nineteenth century, people worried both about forgetting and about difficulties which seemed to be associated with a persistence of recollection, so that we could say that, from the nineteenth century onwards, disquiet about memory crystallized around the perception of two principal disorders: too little memory and too much.[10]

If one were to assemble a list of all the books and articles worthy of consideration on the subject of cultural memory written between 1900 and the present day in English, French, German and Italian, fifty pages would hardly be adequate to contain the rich harvest. If one were to do the same for forgetting, a mere five pages would certainly suffice. Anthropologists and historians have paid a great deal of attention to the role of memory in transmitting knowledge and forming identity, but comparatively little attention has been devoted to what people forget, how they forget and why they forget.[11] It seems possible that this disparity will be rectified, to a degree, in the foreseeable future. It may be helpful, therefore, to conclude by proposing some preliminary discriminations between types of forgetting.

1. Forgetting as *structural amnesia* was identified by John Barnes in his study of genealogies.[12] By this he meant that a person tends to remember only those links in his or her pedigree which are socially important. Thus in the genealogies of the strongly patrilineal British peerage, as in those of the Nuer and Talensi, the ascending male lines are far more memorable than the associated female lines; the names of ancestors who do not give their names to units within the lineage structure tend to be forgotten. Among the Lamba, on the other hand, the matrilineal line of descent is more important than the

patrilineal; accordingly, the ascending female lines could be traced for three to five generations, whereas the ascending male lines could be traced back for only one or two generations. The same general principle of structural amnesia is exemplified by the history of cooking, in the sense that the availability of printing systematically affects what recipes are transmitted and what are forgotten. The number of recipes that can be held in written form is unlimited, whereas the number that can be held in the oral memory is limited. Both the standardization and the elaborateness of the modern cuisine depends, therefore, on the production of cookbooks and the literacy of cooks. The attraction of regional cooking, on the other hand, is tied to what Grandmother did, and the methods of country cuisine are acquired by observation rather than by reading. In these circumstances recipes are systematically forgotten.[13]

2. The concept of structural amnesia illustrates a more general point, namely our deeply held conviction that forgetting involves a loss. This conviction is found in our European and American background, even if it may not be held more widely. But could not forgetting be a gain, as well as, or perhaps more than, a loss? This appears to apply to a particular type of forgetting, the kind of forgetting that is *constitutive in the formation of a new identity*. The emphasis here is not so much on the loss entailed in being unable to retain certain things as rather on the gain which accrues to those who know how to discard. Forgetting then becomes part of the process by which newly shared memories are constructed because a new set of memories are frequently accompanied by a set of tacitly shared silences. Many small acts of forgetting which these silences enable over time are not random but patterned: there is for instance the forgetting of details of grandparents' lives which are not transmitted to grandchildren whose knowledge about grandparents might in no way conduce to, but rather detract from, the implementation of their present intentions; or the forgetting of details about previous marriages or sexual partnerships which, if attended to too closely, could even impair a present marriage or partnership; or details about a life formerly lived within a particular religious or political affiliation which has been superseded by consciously embracing an alternative affiliation. If the sections in Augustine's *Confessions* devoted to forgetting read less persuasively than those on memory, that may be due, aside from the greater intractability of the topic, to the fact that for him to have thought too hard or long about what he forgot, or half forgot, might have been

to disturb his projects in the present. Not to forget might in all these cases provoke too much cognitive dissonance: better to consign some things to a shadow world. So pieces of knowledge which are not passed on have a negative significance by allowing other images of identity to come to the fore. What is allowed to be forgotten provides living space for present projects.

The cognatic societies of South East Asia exemplify this.[14] Ethnographic studies of these societies, in Borneo, Bali, the Philippines, rural Java, frequently remark upon the absence of knowledge about ancestors. Knowledge about kinship stretches outwards into degrees of siblingship rather than backwards to predecessors; it is, so to speak, horizontal rather than vertical. It is not so much a retention of relatedness as rather a creation of relatedness between those who were previously unrelated. The crucial precipitant of this type of kinship, and the characteristic form of remembering and forgetting attendant upon it, is the high degree of mobility between islands in the South East Asian area. With great demographic mobility it is no longer vital to remember ancestors in the islands left behind, whose identity has become irrelevant in the new island setting, but it becomes crucial instead to create kinship through the formation of new ties. Newcomers to islands are transformed into kin through hospitality, through marriage and through having children. The details of their past diversity, in the islands they have now left, cease to be part of their mental furniture. Their forgetting may be only gradual and implicit, and above all no particular attention may be drawn to it, but it is necessary nonetheless. Forgetting is part of an active process of creating a new and shared identity in a new setting.

In the same sense, no narrative of modernity as a historical project can afford to ignore its subtext of forgetting. That narrative has two components, one economic, the other psychological. There is, first, the objective transformation of the social fabric unleashed by the advent of the capitalist world market which tears down feudal and ancestral limitations on a global scale. And there is, secondly, the subjective transformation of individual life chances, the emancipation of individuals increasingly released from fixed social status and role hierarchies. These are two gigantic processes of discarding. To the extent that these two interlinked processes are embraced, to that extent certain things must be forgotten because they must be discarded. This long-term forgetting as discarding in the interests of forming a new identity is signalled by two types of semantic evidence, one the emergence of a new type of vocabulary, the other the disappearance of a now obsolete vocabulary. On the one hand, certain substantives, which refer at once to historical movements in the present and to projects for the future, enter the currency: History, Revolution, Liberalism, Socialism, Modernity itself.[15] On the other hand, certain words previously employed by writers in English cease to be used and are no longer easily recognizable: memorous (memorable), memorious (having a good memory), memorist (one who prompts the return of memories), mnemonize (to memorize), mnemonicon (a device to aid the memory).[16] Could there be a more explicit indication than that signalled in these two semantic changes of what is thought desirable and what is thought dispensable?

3. Forgetting as *repressive erasure* appears in its most brutal forms, of course, in the history of totalitarian regimes, where, in Milan Kundera's often quoted words, 'the struggle of man against power is the struggle of memory against forgetting'.[17] But repressive erasure need not always take such transparently malign forms; it can be encrypted covertly and without apparent violence. Consider, for instance, the way in which the spatial disposition of the modern art gallery presents the visitor with nothing less than an iconographic programme and a master historical narrative; by walking through the museum the visitor will be prompted to internalize the values and beliefs written into the architectural script.[18] Entering the Great Hall of the Metropolitan in New York, for example, the visitor stands at the intersection of the museum's principal axes. To the left is the collection of Greek and Roman art; to the right is the Egyptian collection; directly ahead, at the summit of the grand staircase that continues the axis of the entranceway, is the collection of European paintings beginning with the High Renaissance. An entire iconographic programme establishes the overriding importance of the Western tradition and the implicit injunction to remember it. But the collection of Oriental and other types of non-Western art, as well as the medieval collection, are invisible from the Great Hall. They are included, yet they are also edited out. In exhibiting a master narrative, the museum's spatial script is overt in its acts of celebratory remembrance, covert in its acts of editing-out and erasure. Here too the struggle of man against power is the struggle of memory against forgetting.

4. *Politically expedient forgetting* is distinct from this. Like erasure, it is precipitated by an act of state, but it differs from erasure because it is believed to be in the interests of all parties to the dispute and because it can therefore be acknowledged publicly. Whether after international conflict or at the resolution of civil conflict, the formulation of peace terms has frequently contained an explicit expression of the wish that past action should be not just forgiven but also forgotten. The Treaty of Westphalia, which brought the Thirty Years' War to an end in 1648, contained the injunction that both sides should forgive and forget for ever all the violence, damage and injuries that each had inflicted upon the other. After the return of Charles II to the English throne in 1660, he declared 'An act of full and general pardon, indemnity and oblivion'. When Louis XVIII returned to occupy the French throne in 1814 he declared in his constitutional charter that he sought to extinguish from his memory all the evils under which France had suffered during his exile, that all research into utterances of opinion expressed before his restoration was to be forbidden, and that this rule of forgetting was enjoined upon both the law courts and the citizens of France. Sometimes at the point of transition from conflict to conflict resolution there may be no explicit requirement to forget, but the implicit desire to do so is nonetheless unmistakable. For example, societies where democracy is regained after a recent undemocratic past, or where democracy is newly born, must establish institutions and make decisions that foster forgetting as much as remembering. Not long after the defeat of Nazism, for instance, it became evident that West Germany could not be returned to self-government and civil administration if the purge of Nazis continued to be pursued in a sustained way. So the identification and punishment of active Nazis was a forgotten issue in Germany by the early 1950s, just as the number of convicted persons was kept to a minimum in Austria and France. For what was necessary after 1945, above all, was to restore a minimum level of cohesion to civil society and to re-establish the legitimacy of the state in societies where authority, and the very bases of civil behaviour, had been obliterated by totalitarian government; the overwhelming desire was to forget the recent past.[19] Again, the Spanish transition to democracy, after Franco's death in 1975, was eased by what Semprun called a collective and willed amnesia; and a similar desire to forget was put into practice when the personal files of the old Stasi, the former East German secret service, were shredded after 1989.

5. There is yet a further type of forgetting in which, though an element of political expediency may be involved, it is not the primary or

defining characteristic. This type of forgetting is certainly not solely, and may in large part be not at all, a matter of overt activity on the part of a state apparatus. It is manifest in a widespread pattern of behaviour in civil society, and it is covert, unmarked and unacknowledged. Its most salient feature is *a humiliated silence*. Perhaps it is paradoxical to speak of such a condition as evidence for a form of forgetting, because humiliation is so difficult to forget: it is often easier to forget physical pain than to forget humiliation. Yet few things are more eloquent than a massive silence. And in the collusive silence brought on by a particular kind of collective shame there is detectable both a desire to forget and sometimes the actual effect of forgetting.

Consider for instance the destruction of German cities by bombing in the Second World War.[20] This left some 130 cities and towns in ruins; about 600,000 civilians killed; 3.5 million homes destroyed; and 7.5 million people homeless at the end of the war. Members of the occupying powers report seeing millions of homeless and utterly lethargic people wandering about amidst the ruins. From the war years there survive a few accounts in which German citizens speak of their stunned bewilderment on seeing for the first time the appearance of their ravaged cities. Yet throughout the more than fifty years following the war the horrors of the air bombardment and its long-term repercussions have not been brought to public attention either in historical investigations or in literary accounts. German historians have not produced an exploratory, still less an exhaustive, study of the subject. With the sole exception of Nossack, and some passages on the aerial bombardment in the writings of Heinrich Böll, no German writer was prepared to write or capable of writing about the progress and repercussions of the gigantic campaign of destruction. A colossal collective experience was followed by half a century of silence. How is this to be explained? Sebald retells a story which hints at the nature of some of the emotions involved. A German teacher told him in the 1990s that as a boy in the immediate post-war years he often saw photographs of the corpses lying in the streets after the Hamburg firestorm brought out from under the counter of a second-hand bookshop, and that he observed them being examined, surreptitiously, in a way usually reserved for pornography. We are faced here with the silence of humiliation and shame. The conspicuous paucity of observation and comment on the subject of the bombing and its long-term effects amounts, in other words, to the tacit imposition of a taboo. Confronted with a taboo, people can fall silent out of terror or panic or lethargy or because they can find no words. We cannot, of course, infer the fact of forgetting from the fact of silence. Nevertheless, some acts of silence may be an attempt to bury things beyond expression and the reach of memory; yet such silencings, while they are a type of repression, can at the same time be a form of survival, and the desire to forget may be an essential ingredient in that process of survival.

Or consider the Great War and modern memory. The colossal loss of human life gave rise to an orgy of monumentalization; memorials went up to commemorate the fallen all over Europe. But were these sites of memory the places where mourning was taking place, as the title of Jay Winter's book on the subject implies? The International Labour Organization estimated in 1923 that about 10 million soldiers from the German, Austro-Hungarian, French and British armies walked the streets of their countries. These were some 10 million mutilated men: half or totally blinded, or with gross facial disfigurements, or with a hand or arm or leg missing, hobbling around the streets like ghosts. They were badly cared for. The war wounded went financially unrewarded for their pains, in millions of households who rarely received the material assistance they needed from the political states on whose behalf they had fought. The war dead were annually remembered at memorial sites, and, until 1939, in a ritually observed two minutes of silence, people stopped wherever they were in the street, stood still, and reflected on the loss. But 10 million mutilated survivors still haunted the streets of Europe. They were dismembered – not remembered – men; many were subject to chronic depression, frequently succumbed to alcoholism, begged in the street in order to be able to eat, and a considerable number of them ended their days in suicide. All sorts of institutional provisions were put in place to keep those mutilated soldiers out of public sight. Every year the war dead were ceremonially remembered and the words 'lest we forget' ritually intoned; but these words, uttered in a pitch of ecclesiastical solemnity, referred to those who were now safely dead. The words did not refer to the survivors. The sight of them was discomfiting, even shameful. The living did not want to remember them; they wanted to forget them.

There may be in some cases an overlap between these different types of forgetting, and the discriminations suggested here are intended only as preliminary; they are offered as a set of suggestions regarding directions which future thinking about remembering and forgetting might take.

NOTES

1 For an overview of recent studies on memory see Fentress and Wickham (1992), Ricoeur (2000), Megill (1998) and Klein (2000).
2 Nora (1996–98).
3 Nora (1989).
4 On the *Historikerstreit* see Maier (1988) and Evans (1989).
5 See Passerini (1992). See also her *Fascism in Popular Memory* (1986).
6 On the new visual media and memory see Sturken (1997).
7 Fussell (1975); Winter (1995); Friedländer (1979); Santner (1990); Kaes (1989); Rousso (1991); Yerushalmi (1982); Casey (1987); Kleinman (1986); Kleinman and Kleinman (1994). See also Friedländer (1992); Felman and Laub (1992); Lacapra (1994); Caruth (1995, 1996).
8 See Said (1999–2000).
9 Halbwachs (1925, 1941); Yates (1966); Nora (1996–98); Koshar (2000); Samuel (1994); Young (1993). See also Lowenthal (1985); McCracken (1988); Boyer (1996); Assmann (1999).
10 Matsuda (1996); Huyssen (1995); Le Goff (1992); Terdiman (1993).
11 But, for a distinguished study of forgetting which treats a wide range of literary texts, see Weinrich (1997). Klein (1997) examines the process of memory erasure in the context of city building. See also Yerushalmi et al. (1988), Augé (1998), Forty and Küchler (1999) and Ricoeur (2000).
12 Barnes (1947).
13 See Goody (1977), pp. 135 ff., 140–3.
14 See Carsten (1996).
15 See Koselleck (1985).
16 See Casey (1987: 5–6).
17 Kundera (1980: 3).
18 See Duncan and Wallach (1980).
19 See Judt (1992).
20 See Sebald (2003).

REFERENCES

Assmann, A. (1999) *Erinnerungsräume. Formen und Wandlungen des kulturellen Gedächtnisses*. Munich: C.H. Beck.

Augé, M. (1998) *Les Formes de l'oubli*. Paris: Payot et Rivages.

Barnes, J.A. (1947) 'The collection of genealogies', *Rhodes–Livingstone Journal*, 5: 48–55.

Boyer, M.C. (1996) *The City of Collective Memory*. Cambridge, MA: MIT Press.

Carsten, J. (1996) 'The politics of forgetting: migration, kinship and memory on the periphery of the Southeast Asian state', *Journal of the Royal Anthropological Institute*, (n.s.) 1: 317–35.

Caruth, C., ed. (1995) *Trauma: Explorations in Memory*. Baltimore, MD: Johns Hopkins University Press.

Caruth, C. (1996) *Unclaimed Experience: Trauma, Narrative and History*. Baltimore, MD: Johns Hopkins University Press.

Casey, E. (1987) *Remembering: a Phenomenological Study*. Bloomington, IN: Indiana University Press.

Duncan, C. and Wallach, A. (1980) 'The universal survey museum', *Art History*, 3: 442–69.

Evans, R.J. (1989) *In Hitler's Shadow: West German Historians and the Attempt to Escape from the Nazi Past*. New York: Pantheon.

Felman, S. and Laub, D., eds (1992) *Testimony: Crises of Witnessing in Literature, Psychoanalysis, and History*. London and New York: Routledge.

Fentress, J. and Wickham, C. (1992) *Social Memory*. Oxford: Blackwell.

Forty, A. and Küchler, S. (1999) *The Art of Forgetting*. Oxford and New York: Berg.

Friedländer, S. (1979) *When Memory Comes*. New York: Farrar, Strauss, Giroux.

Friedländer, S., ed. (1992) *Probing the Limits of Representation*. Cambridge, MA: Harvard University Press.

Fussell, P. (1975) *The Great War and Modern Memory*. Oxford: Oxford University Press.

Goody, J. (1977) *The Domestication of the Savage Mind*. Cambridge: Cambridge University Press.

Halbwachs, M. (1925) *Les Cadres sociaux de la mémoire*. Paris: F. Alcan.

Halbwachs, M. (1941) *La Topographie légendaire des Evangiles en Terre-Sainte*. Paris: Presses Universitaires de France.

Huyssen, A. (1995) *Twilight Memories: Marking Time in a Culture of Amnesia*. New York and London: Routledge.

Judt, T. (1992) 'The past is another country: myth and memory in postwar Europe', *Daedalus*, 121: 83–118.

Kaes, A. (1989) *From Hitler to Heimat: the Return of History as Film*. Cambridge, MA and London: Harvard University Press.

Klein, K.L. (1998) 'On the emergence of memory in historical discourse', *Representations*, 69: 127–50.

Klein, N.M. (1997) *The History of Forgetting: Los Angeles and the Erasure of Memory*. London: Verso.

Kleinman, A. (1986) *Social Origins of Distress and Disease: Depression, Neurasthenia and Pain in Modern China*. New Haven, CT and London: Yale University Press.

Kleinman, A. and Kleinman, J. (1994) 'How bodies remember: social memory and bodily experience of criticism, resistance, and delegitimation following China's Cultural Revolution', *New Literary History*, 25: 707–23.

Koselleck, R. (1985) *Futures Past: on the Semantics of Historical Time*. Cambridge, MA: MIT Press.

Koshar, R. (2000) *From Monuments to Traces: Artifacts of German Memory, 1870–1990*. Berkeley, CA, Los Angeles and London: University of California Press.

Kundera, M. (1980) *The Book of Laughter and Forgetting*. Harmondsworth: Penguin.

Lacapra, D. (1994) *Representing the Holocaust: History, Theory, Trauma*. Ithaca, NY: Cornell University Press.

Le Goff, J. (1992) *History and Memory*. New York: Columbia University Press.

Lowenthal, D. (1985) *The Past is a Foreign Country*. Cambridge: Cambridge University Press.

Maier, C. (1988) *The Unmasterable Past: History, Holocaust, and German National Identity*. Cambridge, MA: Harvard University Press.

Matsuda, M.K. (1996) *The Memory of the Modern*. New York and Oxford: Oxford University Press.

McCracken, G. (1988) *Culture and Consumption*. Bloomington, IN: Indiana University Press.

Megill, A. (1998) 'History, memory, identity', *History of the Human Sciences*, 11: 37–62.

Nora, P. (1989) 'Between memory and history: *les lieux de mémoire*', *Representations*, 26: 7–25.

Nora, P., ed. (1996–98) *Realms of Memory*, 3 vols. New York: Columbia University Press.

Passerini, L. (1986) *Fascism in Popular Memory: the Popular Experience of the Turin Working Class*. Cambridge: Cambridge University Press.

Passerini, L., ed. (1992) *Memory and Totalitarianism: International Yearbook of Oral History and Life Stories*. Oxford: Oxford University Press.

Ricoeur, P. (2000) *La Mémoire, l'histoire, l'oubli*. Paris: Editions du Seuil.

Rousso, H. (1991)*The Vichy Syndrome: History and Memory in France since 1944*. Cambridge, MA: Harvard University Press.

Said, E.W. (1999–2000) 'Geopoetics: space, place, and landscape: invention, memory, and place', *Critical Inquiry*, 26: 175–200.

Samuel, R. (1994) *Theatres of Memory*. London and New York: Verso.

Santner, E.L. (1990) *Stranded Objects: Mourning, Memory, and Film in Postwar Germany*. Ithaca, NY and London: Cornell University Press.

Sebald, W.G. (2003) *On the Natural History of Destruction*. Toronto: Alfred A. Knopf.

Sturken, M. (1997) *Tangled Memories: the Vietnam War, the Aids Epidemic, and the Politics of Remembering*. Berkeley CA, Los Angeles and London: University of California Press.

Terdiman, R. (1993) *Present Past: Modernity and the Memory Crisis*. Ithaca, NY and London: Cornell University Press.

Weinrich, H. (1997) *Lethe. Kunst und Kritik des Vergessens*. Munich: C.H. Beck.

Winter, J. (1995) *Sites of Memory, Sites of Mourning: the Great War in European Cultural History*. Cambridge: Cambridge University Press.

Yates, F.A. (1978) *The Art of Memory*. Harmondsworth: Penguin.

Yerushalmi, Y.H. (1982) *Zakhor: Jewish History and Jewish Memory*. Seattle, WA and London: University of Washington Press.

Yerushalmi, Y.H., Loraux, N., Mommsen, H., Milner, J-C. and Vattimo, G. (1988) *Usages de l'oubli*. Paris: Editions du Seuil.

Young, J.E. (1993) *The Texture of Memory: Holocaust Memorials and Meaning*. New Haven, CT and London: Yale University Press.

PART IV

PROCESS AND TRANSFORMATION

The chapters in Part IV bring together diverse perspectives on the processes and transformations that have continued to place objects at the heart of social inquiry. These perspectives are distinguished not on the grounds of disciplinary or analytical orientation alone, but also in the time frame they cast on the social life of objects. From a snapshot of objects in production and use to biographies which cast a light on objects across decades or even centuries, objects will be shown to reveal the dynamics of social change through the complex resemblances they strike with the processes and transformations that shape persons and societies alike.

Made, not born, and of a shape and form that may outlast the life of an object, objects are pivotal to transforming matter and energy in ways that leave the world we inhabit changed forever. Not just does this transformation impress upon us the need to consider the dynamics of the relation between how objects are made and society, it also forces us to pay attention to the form given to things, for matters of design bring issues of shape and function up against the material realities of production. Across all of the chapters in this part we find, moreover, a concern not with individual objects, but with the factors that allow us to group objects into 'communities' of things, either in terms of the way they are made, their form and function, or the manner in which they change as they age, as they are consumed, passed on as gifts or sold as commodities, only ultimately to be disposed of as remains. What appears to bind artefacts together into 'communities of objects' (see Gosden in Chapter 27) is not a pre-existing classificatory scheme that is external to objects, but is an effect of the processes and transformations, which extend the materiality of things to persons in a distinctly analogous manner. The idea that it is communities of objects that allow

us to trace biographies of things and persons alike will be shown to be crucial to extending our understanding of what objects do to the object-worlds of both past and future societies. For it is the explanatory force carried by communities of objects that alone will enable us to capture the dynamics of long-term change.

This part commences with a review of the study of technology and its unrivalled importance to material culture. Whether the technology comes in the form of a loom or in the form of cutting-edge nano-technology, why we make what we make in one way rather than another and the difference that making things creates in society have been the most persistently asked questions to date. Ron Eglash shows in Chapter 21 on 'Technology as Material Culture' how deeply entrenched an awareness of the relation between technology and society is in the history of modern Western thought; from the nineteenth century onwards, writers across the disciplines of anthropology, history and political science employed observations on technology as evidence to support their theory of society. The way matter and energy are transformed into artefacts has been subject to the most detailed comparative descriptions of classical studies whose theoretical frameworks (evolutionary, economic, diffusonist, etc.) are discredited today, while their shared assumption that technology does have an impact on society arguably still fuels theory even if it is designed to disprove the premise upon which this assumption rests.

This classical theory which is known as 'technological determinism' gave way in the 1980s to a large number of different theoretical frameworks that have in common to largely accept as a premise that there are social influences in technology, having replaced the earlier impact-driven theory with a notion of a 'seamless web' of social and technological dynamics. The new studies of technology are concerned with writing the histories of innovation and of technological forms, which now appear much more contingent on social factors than previously assumed. The notion of contingency allowed a theory of 'technological systems' to be developed whose models set out to reveal the social dynamics of innovation by tracing networks of relations between social groups and groups of artefacts. More recently the concern with technology *per se* has given way to a more general concern with the social construction of science, showing social forces at work in everything from particle physics to mathematics.

The most crucial question asked today of technology concerns the possible synthesis of distinct analytical paradigms, as this alone is seen to have the capacity to drive forward our understanding of the complex factors that come into play in the success or failure of technological innovations in given social contexts. Moving across Third and First World contexts of technology, both in analysis and in the application, studies are beginning to intervene on behalf of indigenous knowledge against development projects. A wider concern with the sometimes difficult to explain 'efficacy' attributed to the knowledge of materials and their transformation into objects has brought back into the foreground another early modernist preoccupation – this time with consumption.

As Miller outlines in Chapter 22 on 'Consumption', the study of consumption is paradoxically oriented around the dissipation of material culture in processes that use up things. Consumption, therefore, lays waste to attempts at producing society through innovation in the technical realm. He shows how the debates that dominate this using up what technology allowed producing are both older and deeper than the concern with the contemporary critique of materialism, emerging from within the modern framework of anti-materialism. The promotion of consumption as a good thing, or its denigration as an ailment that is characteristic of the instability and shallowness of material culture as an analytical tool, both have to be taken into consideration when approaching the question of the 'nature' of consumption beneath the taken-for-granted rationale of a set of structures and practices that are abstracted as economy.

People have always consumed, a fact that explains why it was archaeology which has been at the forefront of consumption studies in material culture. Objects found in the ground and studied by archaeologists tell us not just about how they were used, but also about what people desired to possess. The early influence of social psychology on these studies, tracing the behaviour of social groups by following patterns of consumption, has given way since the 1970s to a general influence of social science and historical research in studies of consumption that have at the same time consistently moved away from archaeological data to observations of what consumption patterns can tell us about the dynamic of social and historical processes. Studies of consumption, thereby, observe as much what material culture can tell us about a moment in time, such as the observation of a general shift in the consumption of groceries and consumer durables in the Anglo-American world, as they trace patterns of change in consumption over longer periods of time. More recently, consumption has also preoccupied the disciplines of Economics and Business Studies where the focus was for the most part on the impact of economic models on the developing world.

Considerations of consumption have taken on new dimensions when applied to modernity, supported by studies which point up a transformation in the relation between persons and things: mass-produced consumer goods, which once stood for persons and relationships, have now come to replace these relations, be they symbolic of class or gender.

The centrality of consumption in the study of material culture today has arguably grown out of a 'post-structural' preoccupation with the fluidity of process, practice and performance, which acknowledges the transformation of objects and persons. Objects are not just buffers for our imagination, nor are they merely there to produce society, but they can also be used up or transformed in ways which make relations manifest materially in the relations between things. As the form given to objects or the material used is a vital indication of consumption patterns, it is clear that the study of consumption is inextricably linked to the study of design.

The concern with form and materiality in design is the theme of Margaret Conkey's Chapter 23. Like the study of consumption, approaches to design in material culture link biographies of objects produced and used at a particular time with the study of how form and material used change over time. Just as the design of an object is comparable to a snapshot of society at a particular time and place, offering us a glimpse into the social dynamics of response that labels certain things to be desirable as it consigns others to the dustbin, so the fact that certain objects move between places and between people has been fuelling inquiry into the role of material culture for much of the twentieth century.

It is now widely accepted not only that people live in society, but that they also produce society in order to live. To produce society, people use objects in different ways and for different purposes; in every society at every time, there must be certain objects that are given, others that are sold or bartered, and still others that are kept for good. In our societies, buying and selling have become the main activities, while in others the giving of things or even intangible entities such as services, names or ideas predominates. Yet why are there some things one sells, others one gives, and yet others that can neither be sold nor given, but which must be kept and transmitted? Reasons may not reside in the things themselves – as the same object may successively be bought as a commodity, circulated in gift exchange, and ultimately be hoarded in a clan treasure and as such withheld for a time from circulation.

James Carrier, in Chapter 24 on Exchange, opens up for us a perspective on why things move, developed by social anthropology where the study of the exchange of objects has framed the theory of social relations from its inception as a discipline in the early twentieth century. The basic model for understanding why exchange may be crucial to building society is still today derived from the classical study *The Gift* by Marcel Mauss which also here in our chapter forms the starting point for assessing contemporary theoretical developments which place at the centre not so much society at large as the person. A fundamental break with approaches which centred on the separation of gifts, as things which are lent or exchanged, from commodities, which are readily sold or bartered, was made by the anthropologist Marilyn Strathern. Summarizing evidence gathered from detailed field studies in Melanesia, one of the classical areas of gift exchange, she presented a model of societies where neither persons nor objects are independent entities, but where objects serve to externalize and carry for a time personal substances in a process which crucially defines, maintains and builds social relations.

As objects move in exchange, their flow links givers and receivers into social networks; often it is the idea exchanged which outlasts its physical medium and is called upon to defend economic or social relations. While networks based on gift-exchange analyses tend to focus on individuals whose actions are crucial for the shape of the network, so-called 'commodity chains' link people and institutions in the life of an object, from its creation to its consumption.

It is the transformation of commodities into things which are received not freely, but with an obligation to both accept and reciprocate, which has been shown to redefine anonymous relations into relations of attachment in British and American societies. Such a transformation of the way an object is perceived can involve physical manipulation of the objects, such as its wrapping, or just a subtle change of attitude brought out in the personal way one talks about its acquisition as a form of self-sacrifice.

This concern with the material transformation of the body, of things and of space is at the centre of Jonathan Mitchell's Chapter 25 on Performance. He outlines for us how the most extensive studies of performance-based transformation have been concerned with the human body. The transformative capacity of performance, in which the body is less the object of ritual performance than the subject, was supported in particular by detailed, ethnographic studies of initiation. It is now widely accepted that as performing subjects of transformation, those who undergo a rite of passage are not merely acting out roles in a wider dramatisation of their transition into adulthood, but are themselves the performing subjects of their transformation. Recent theorists have extended the argument from the body refigured as performative subject to artefacts, which for long were seen as mere objects and analysed with a semiological approach, which uncovered the relationship between materiality and meaning. Now artefacts could be revisited as active subjects in a web of relationships between persons and things. Agency as the central underlying driving force of all things is a common feature of conceptions of the universe and explains the predominant use of masks in performances that are synonymous with life-cycle stages. If performance involves a transformation of the person and the object, the same is true for space, which is transformed through performance. Performance is thus one of the most privileged contexts in which the interaction between the material and the conceptual can be observed in the transformations that weld together persons and things.

The processes and transformations which give rise to and which ultimately obliterate artefacts, leaving ideas they may have carried behind, are of crucial interest to ethno-archaeologists, who use insights derived from the study of material culture within living societies to build analogies that can be extended to archaeological contexts. Most crucially, it is through such attempts at uncovering analogies between archaeological remains and contemporary practices involving objects as well as the use of space that assumptions about the time depth of 'traditional' practices have come to be questioned. By searching the present for resemblances to the past, we can begin to ask why and how the present differs from the past in ways which will ultimately pave the way for questions directed to the historical value ascribed by different societies to the physical world. This critical inquiry into the challenges presented to ethno-archaeology is developed by Paul Lane in his chapter on 'Present to Past'.

Although specific in its focus on material culture as a physical link between past and present, Paul Lane introduces a theme that was resonating throughout the chapters of this part: the long-term histories carried by things which stand in for persons and communities long after they have gone, enabling us to render the world, or as some may more modestly argue,

the dynamic of social change intelligible to the people of tomorrow. For artefacts often have longer lives as collectivities than people do, forming, as Chris Gosden tells us in Chapter 27, 'Material Culture and Long-term Change', 'communities of their own through similarities of form and decoration'. Understanding where the future will take us demands in large measure an understanding of the processes and transformations recorded in material culture from both a short-term and a long-term perspective. If there is a lesson to be learned from the chapters in this part, it is to remind us of the challenges that lie ahead in understanding better what it is about objects that enables us to draw out analogies and to 'see' the connections through which we form attachments in the world.

Susanne Küchler

21

TECHNOLOGY AS MATERIAL CULTURE

Ron Eglash

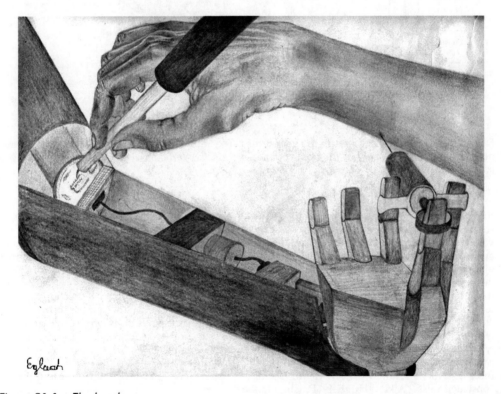

Figure 21.1 *The hands*

The term 'technology' can be defined in terms broad enough to encompass many of the chapters in this book – architecture, clothing, art, even the body in Foucault's sense of 'technologies of the self'. But even in its narrowest sense of machines, it remains a powerful cultural actor. From looms to linear accelerators, nanotech to the *Titanic*, the artifacts that transform matter and energy hold a special place as troubling objects of social inquiry. Part one of this chapter begins with a review of classics in social analysis of technology, including Ellul, Krober, Kubler, Marx, Mumford, Washburn, White, and others. While these theorists vary in

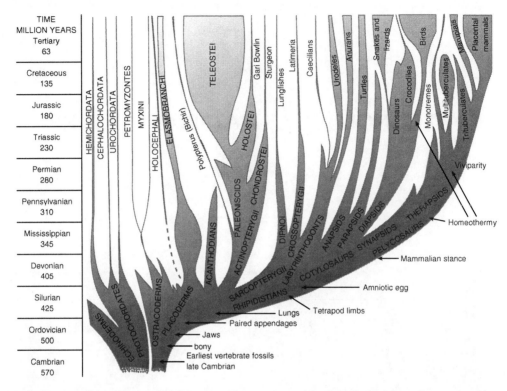

Figure 21.2 *Phylogenetic tree of the vertebrates. The width of the branches indicates the relative number of recognized genera for a given time level on the vertical axis. (Time in millions of years indicates the beginning of geological periods).*

disciplines (anthropology, history, political science, systems theory, etc.), encompass a wide variety of theoretical frameworks (evolutionary, economic, diffusionist, etc.), and lead to opposing conclusions (techo-optimist, techno-pessimist, instrumentalist, etc.) they are similar in their tendency to take an 'impact' view of technology: technological change brings social change, and social influence is primarily a 'bias' or 'contamination' of what would otherwise be governed by universal technical concerns. Part two of the chapter contrasts these traditional frameworks with the social constructionist (Bijker, Hughes, Pinch, etc.) and social power (Winner, Barnes, Mackenzie etc.) frameworks. Introduced in the 1980s, these frameworks highlight a 'seamless web' of social and technological dynamics; here there is no purely technical domain, even at the 'pure science' end of the techno-science spectrum. Rising at the same time, and in various relations to these new perspectives, are actor network theory (Latour, Wolgar), boundary object studies (Star, Henderson), evolutionary

economics (Arthur, Nelson), and a variety of technological analyses based on cultural politics (feminist, anti-racist, queer theory, etc.). The final section of the chapter examines the synthesis arising from new cross-cultural comparisons, appropriation studies, emerging technologies (information technology, biotechnology, nanotechnology, etc.) and other sources which highlight the ways in which technology destabilizes the very social categories we seek to apply to its analysis, and show the need for a new interdisciplinary hybridity in which technology and society will be engaged in mutual analysis.

MODERNITY AND SOCIAL ANALYSIS OF TECHNOLOGY

Many authors have noted that modernity itself seems deeply embedded in an awareness of the social significance of technology. Nineteenth-century writers on both sides of the political spectrum employed relations between technology and society as evidence to support their theories. One obvious outcome of such writing is the anthropological framework assigning cultures to various 'levels of advancement'. For example, Morgan's *Ancient Society*, published in 1877, posited that human society had passed through three major stages: savagery, barbarism, and civilization. Thus cultural differences from Europe were to be explained as societies which were still at a previous level along this unilineal chain. The role of technology in these portraits is vividly detailed in Adas (1989), who provides detailed descriptions of the writings of colonialists comparing indigenous and European material culture. But it is important to recognize that such comparisons also served the liberal and radical discourse of those eras, supplying Rousseau's noble savages and Marx and Engels's portrait of progressive social evolution.

There is an interesting parallel between biological and social frameworks in the late nineteenth century, as both posit a unilineal sequence. Lovejoy (1922) notes that the image of a 'great chain of being' from animals to people to God is quite ancient in European history, and was quickly (and mistakenly) applied by early biologists. Contemporary biologists view the philogenetic trajectories as a tree, not a ladder. The octopus, an invertebrate, has a highly developed nervous system, greater in some cognitive capacities than that of some vertebrate species. There are no 'primitive' species; all contemporary organisms are equally well adapted to their ecological niche. Similarly, contemporary anthropology no longer assumes a unilinear ladder of advancement for cultures. Even 'old-fashioned' anthropologists like Diamond (1996) will argue that the cognitive demands of hunter-gatherer economies are at least as complex, if not more so, than those of 'high-tech' societies.

In addition to the problematic aspects of this ethnocentric, unilineal model for cross-cultural comparison, Marx and Engels also used the social relations of technology to argue for the need for political centralization. Just as a ship cannot run without a captain, the ship of state needs a single hand on its rudder. This is merely one version of a wide variety of technological determinism themes seen throughout social studies of technology. Another, also starting in that modernist era, is the theme of technology as progress. Contemporary historian Leo Marx (1987) maps out the evolution of that theme. He begins with the Enlightenment era prescriptions for moral and social progress. By the eighteenth century writers such as Benjamin Franklin and Thomas Jefferson were using examples of technological progress as evidence

for such ethical changes: if stoves and printing presses could improve, so could societies. They also made connections between liberation from authority and the autonomy offered by certain technological innovations (but not others, most notably the factory). But, with industrialization in the nineteenth and twentieth centuries, the lines between social and technological progress became blurred in much of the political discourse. New inventions – the railroad, the telegraph, etc. – were hailed as 'social progress', regardless of their actual impact on people or the environment. Much social analysis of technology of the mid-century period was written in this celebratory view (e.g. Lillenthal 1944); at one point it even formed its own 'technocracy' social movement (Elsner 1966). More subtle versions of this thesis are often grouped by its contemporary critics under the category of 'technological determinism' – an account of technologies as having 'social impact' but little in the way of social origins, and with developmental trajectories that are either entirely obscured or seen as governed by a sort of natural law which makes their forms (and presence) seem inevitable.

The unilineal development model was challenged by twentieth-century writers. Biology's replacement of the unilineal development model with adaptative diversity inspired anthropologists such as Alfred Kroeber, who associated cultural differences with differing ecological conditions ('culture areas'). However, Kroeber (1917) also viewed culture as a 'superorganic' realm of autonomous change, and noted that variations in material style could occur independent of historical events. Leslie White also retained this dual view of both local adaptation (in Julian Steward's terminology a 'cultural ecology') and superorganic autonomous change, but placed a much stronger emphasis on technology as the source of change – essentially a technological determinist view. White attempted to quantify these relations by assessing *per capita* energy use (actually power, since he was measuring energy use per unit of time), and showing the variation of this measure with transitions across the spectrum from low-tech hunter-gatherer to high-tech industrialism.

HIGH MODERNITY AND TECHNOLOGICAL CRITIQUE

A revolt against such conflations between technological and social progress began earlier, most famously in the writings of Emerson and

Thoreau. Although there are many technology critics writing in relation to this romantic tradition (and some outside of it, e.g. Max Weber's 'iron cage of rationalization'), it was not until the high modern era, following World War II, that scholarly social analysis of technology uses 'technocracy' (Ellul 1954/1964) as an explicit framework for critique. Mumford (1964) made a distinction between 'authoritarian' technologies and 'democratic' technologies, but saw a strong historical progression towards the authoritarian, culminating in the replacement of people with automation and 'cybernetic direction'. Mumford, Ellul, and others such as Paul Goodman, Herbert Marcuse, and Theodore Roszak emphasized this negative view on the repressive, destructive, and authoritarian aspects of technological society. Embedded in much of this analysis was an implicit assumption that only a radical social break – a Marxist revolution, a romantic turn to nature, or a Luddite rejection of machines themselves could provide any solution.

The 1970s saw a new direction for technology critics in its understanding of possible technological alternatives. Emerging more from practice than from scholarly research, the 'appropriate technology' movement promoted solar energy, recycling, and 'soft energy paths'. Social analysts writing at this time primarily absorbed these changes within their current theoretical frameworks (Marxism, Keynesian economics, etc.). Information technology was undergoing a similar revolution at this time. Just as groups such as the New Alchemists in the United States and Intermediate Technology in the United Kingdom included grassroots innovation, hackers of hardware and software were also tinkering in garages and at the margins of universities or other institutions. It has taken scholarship some time to catch up with such challenges to the deeply embedded notion that democratizing or life-enhancing technological change can come only from Marxist or other social revolutions. Even some contemporary authors seem to be lagging behind: in his 1993 review of Feenberg (1991), Sclove (p. 399) notes that although Feenberg's construction of a critical theory of technology based on Heidegger, Habermas, Lukács and the like is conceptually powerful, 'one might want to descend from the lofty heights of continental discourse to consider carefully the ideas and actions of appropriate technologists, ecotechnologists (the New Alchemy Institute researchers), feminists, communitarians, physically disabled design critics ... [and others]'.

Despite this lag between practice and theory, several authors did deliver innovative social analyses of technology during this time. One body of work that stands out in the 1970s is the studies of women in development. In the 1960s 'green revolution' proponents assumed that specialized monocropping with chemical fertilizers would dramatically improve rural African lives. Instead, these schemes often led to soil depletion, over-dependence on insecticides, loss of genetic variation, and other social and ecological crises. The problems were exacerbated by ignoring the gendered division of labor in African societies. Starting with Boserup (1970), development organizations began to pay attention to the critical role of women in traditional societies, and to the social relations of technology at this intersection between gender, race and class.

Another body of work began with Langdon Winner's (1977) *Autonomous Technology*, culminating in his *The Whale and the Reactor* (1986). Writing in a 'technocritic' vein similar to Mumford and Ellul, Winner upended their assumptions on the primacy of politics, and instead claimed that there is a politics of technology itself. His classic example was the work of Robert Moses in bridge construction on Long Island, NY. Winner notes that there were low-pass bridges going to beaches and parks, and that this could be attributed to Moses's desire to eliminate the presence of poor people (with both racist and classist intent) in these public spaces. (The poor would travel by bus, which would be blocked by the low-pass bridges.) Strong empirical support for Winner's framework was provided by Noble (1979), in his classic study of numerical control (NC) machine tools. Noble showed that NC machine tools, and their computer predecessors (CNC), were introduced in an attempt to increase managerial control over the shop floor.

While Winner, Noble and like-minded colleagues forefronted technology in terms of the need for social change, a similar body of work with less political focus – although still appreciating the paradoxical concept that 'artifacts have politics' – began to appear under the rubric of social construction. The essential difference between social construction and previous work is the contention that 'it could have been otherwise' – that technological forms and histories of innovation are far more contingent on social factors than the technological determinist position indicates. The first major work of this constructivist genre was MacKenzie and Wajcman (1985), and it held many examples compatible with Winner and Noble's emphasis on political embedding (e.g. gendered labor in the printing industry). But the 1987 anthology edited by Bijker et al., *The Social Construction of Technological Systems*, became the definitive text, and it placed greater emphasis on a more abstract social dynamics of innovation: the topology of networks of relations between social groups and artifacts, the presence of 'reverse salients' in the developmental flow, etc. Abbreviated SCOT (Social Construction of Technology), it was strongly influenced by the British social construction of science (e.g. Bloor 1976).

The social construction of science is a much more radical proposition than the social construction of technology. Technological determinism was never a strong position in the first place. (Who could claim, for example, that the wide diversity of automobile designs was destined by some natural law?) But to say that F = MA is 'socially constructed' demands the possibility that 'it could have been otherwise' – how could that be possible for a universal law of physics? Surprisingly, the constructivists of science have been able to make a good case for exactly that proposition, showing social forces at work in everything from particle physics (Pickering 1984) to mathematics (Restivo et al. 1993). Thus SCOT was a much easier claim to make, and the framework of social construction had even greater clarity in its application to technology than its original domain of science. But SCOT's greater abstraction and lack of political grounding generated conflict with the earlier Winner-Noble framework. Winner responded with a 1993 essay titled 'Opening the black box and finding it empty', in which he questioned why it was necessary to import the powerful apparatus of social constructionist frameworks if one fails to reveal the relations of political power embedded in the artifacts under investigation. Woolgar and Cooper (1999) responded by suggesting that Winner's approach was asymmetric, demanding an unreflective realism on the social side while allowing constructivism on the technological side, and backed up their critique by providing a copy of the Jones Beach bus schedule.

ANTHROPOLOGICAL PARALLELS TO SCOT

While SCOT has been primarily the province of historians, political scientists, philosophers, and sociologists, anthropologists have been in conversation with the body of work associated with SCOT, and have provided some of the most richly detailed cases. Pierre Lemonnier's *Technological Choices* (2002) provides a classic anthology of this sort. For SCOT theorists the challenge is to explain how the form of new innovations could be driven by anything but technological considerations (at base the laws of physics). The thesis of constructivism is to reject determinism, and demonstrate that 'it could have been otherwise'. But anthropologists are often faced with a bewildering array of variation in low-tech indigenous settings.[1] The challenge for anthropologists is not to dislodge the singularity of one form, but rather to avoid the simple adaptation assumption for the multiplicity of forms. Just as historians have been tempted by a technological determinism that assures us that it could not have been otherwise, the temptation for anthropologists is to use a kind of reductive ecological determinism to explain this variation. Thus Lemonnier's title of technological *choices* signals an emphasis on non-deterministic views of this material variation. That is not to say ecological adaptation is irrelevant to their views, any more than the laws of physics are irrelevant to SCOT theorists; the question is how contingency and necessity co-evolve.

Cresswell's contribution to Lemonnier's anthology beautifully illustrates this co-evolution in his account of the cultural variation in mill waterwheel design. Western readers are used to seeing waterwheels of the *Mill on the Floss* variety, in which a stream falls over or under horizontal blades set into a wheel, but this is just one of a vast number of arrangements in which water is converted into mechanical rotation. From the twisted propellers of Nepal to the spoon-shaped blades of Corsica, waterwheel design is clearly driven by more than just the laws of physics. But Cresswell's careful study of the physics of waterwheel engineering – the balance, for example, between the need to maximize the force of the water on the blade and simultaneously limit the shearing stress on the blade's insertion into the axle – brings these considerations into play with other factors (such as the variety of grain being milled, domestic versus commercial production, the amount of moisture in the grain, etc.). His conclusion bears some striking similarities to Pickering's (1995) account of the social construction of science. In Pickering's view scientists encounter 'resistance' in their attempts to test the validity of their hypothesis – the resistance of nature, of technology, of other factors as well. They respond with an 'accommodation', by which he means not a correction from flawed model to perfected model, but rather inventing one of many possible creative solutions that reconfigures various elements of the model. Similarly, Cresswell describes how the interplay of physics in the water-wheel allows a kind of accommodation, but that these interrelated forces create 'resistance' to certain design trajectories. A social need to increase rotational speed, for example, might be met by adding more blades, lengthening the blades, changing their shape, changing the water flow, etc., but change in one parameter then creates greater limitation in the variation possible in other parameters – and thus less room for further accommodation.

Another theme encountered in Lemonnier's anthology is that of modernization – technological choices not highlighted by internal cultural difference, but rather external importations which are either imposed or marketed (or both). Akrich's account of a wood-powered electrical generator (gazogene) in Costa Rica gives a striking portrait of one such technological choice. She begins by noting that when studying technology transfer it is necessary to avoid the 'technologism' trap of viewing failure in adoption as merely due to cultural barriers, or success as their lack. Conversely, she also rejects the opposite 'sociologism' account in which technology must 'fit' a predetermined immutable social order. Akrich's thesis is that we artificially separate the technical and the social to begin with, and thus doom our analyses to that dichotomy. She begins by describing the partnership between the Organization of American States (OAS) and the Costa Rican Electricity Institute in Central America (CREI), and their analysis of conditions for bringing a gazogene pilot project to one village (nearby biomass, distance from central electrical grid, etc.). She notes that the original description mentioned only social barriers as problems (conflicts, economic disparity, etc.). But immediately after installation, it became apparent that the humidity in the wood was far too high to allow operation. A drying oven was built, but then additional problems appeared. Each fix – lighting system, airflow regulation, heatproof cement problems, filter maintenance – appeared to reveal other difficulties. Some symptoms (current instability) did not have clear causes, and some suspected causes (excessively dirty motor) did not have clear relations to symptoms. The villagers described it as lack of support from the CREI, the OAS described it as tacit knowledge that the French engineers were unable to transmit to the local technicians, and the CREI described it as a technology that was not yet mature enough to be transferred. As the need for accountability increased, a complex web of interpretations emerged (villagers accused of lacking motivation, CREI accused of bureaucratic elitism, the machine accused of technological flaws, etc.). Akrich makes a convincing case for how the imbrication of the social and the technical is the true *a priori*, and how portraits of isolated technical or social forces emerge as rhetorical tropes in this 'decoding competition'.

Other contributions to Lemonnier's anthology – in particular Pfaffenberger's analysis of factories in Sri Lanka, and Bedoucha's contrast of the wristwatch and the water clock in Tunisia – highlight the role of global political and economic change in local technological decisions. Pfaffenberger is an excellent example of a scholar who straddles the gap between anthropology and SCOT traditions. Outside of Lemmonnier's anthology, many other researchers have occupied both worlds. Hakken, for example, draws on materialist anthropological traditions in his studies of computing (cf. Hakken 1993, 1999). A relatively large number of researchers – Sarah Franklin, Linda Layne, Emily Martin, Rayna Rapp, Monica Casper, Valerie Hartouni, and Adele Clarke, to name but a few – have forged a strong synthesis through their research on reproductive technology (cf. Franklin and Ragone 1997 for a collection of case studies).

POSTMODERNIST ANALYSES

While social construction is widely regarded as a framework of the postmodern era, few of the authors mentioned in the previous 'high modern' section would regard themselves as postmodernists: their citations are to Weber and Durkheim, not Derrida and Foucault. For the purposes of this book postmodernism presents a unique challenge: generally postmodernism takes the 'semiotic turn' in analyzing material objects as sign systems. In that sense there is very little that is actually material to be found in the material culture analysis of postmodernism. Take, for example, Traweek's famous (1988) analysis of particle detector technology. She provides a detailed analysis of the symbolic meanings of such detectors in the lives of the physicists – as symbols of the relations between nature and culture, male and female, life cycles of both laboratories and scientists, etc. But there is very little mention of the actual physical substance of these machines. It is for that reason that Haraway (1996) takes pains to persistently point to technology as a 'material-semiotic hybrid'. Her point is not merely applying a fashionable label. Take, for example, the previously mentioned work by Boserup (1970) and others. Standard 'mismatch' of technologies' frameworks (cf. Khor 1999) would provide an analysis on purely material terms. Applying a more anthropological framework such as the 'technototems' of Hess (1995) would provide an analysis on purely semiotic terms. Haraway takes the well known example of high-yield variety (HYV) rice, which required rental of mechanical rice harvesters (due to the thickness of the stem) and artificial fertilizers – thus creating additional farmer debt – but focuses her analysis on the genetics within the rice seed: the 'congealed labor' of the laboratory embedding particular sets of practices within the informatics of a modified genetic code; a material-semiotic hybrid viewed through the analytic hybrid of both traditional Marxist analysis and postmodern semiotic apparatus.

There was also a blossoming of feminist and anti-racist analyses of technology during this time, but it would be inaccurate to say that they were consistently allied to postmodernist analysis. The feminist strand has several 1960s origins – Rachel Carson's environmentalism, women's health care collectives, and women in labor movements – and some of these have had an uneasy fit with the emphasis on semiotics and playful hybridity in postmodernist work. Indeed, what is often thought of as the foundational text for postmodern feminist technology analysis – Haraway's Cyborg Manifesto (1991) – ends in the phrase 'I would rather be a cyborg than a goddess,' a confrontational (or at least contrarian) reference to the organic romanticism of much feminist analysis from that era. Hacker (1989) for example provides a brilliant account of the intersections of race, gender, and technology in labor displacements, of sexism and technology in utopian workers' collectives, etc., but without any gestures towards the flexibility of postmodern interpretive frameworks. (Indeed, she holds a particularly modernist, conservative line when it comes to diversity in sexual practices, cf. p. 214.) Wajcman (1991) similarly provides a sharp modernist analysis of women and technology, but at a price (in her case the lack of race as a component of social construction).

Conversely, some of the explicitly postmodernist feminist works, such as Plant (1997) are celebrated for their 'high theory' abstraction and conceptual flexibility, but criticized for having neither history of organized resistance (the kind of labor connections that someone like Hacker excels at) nor any future direction (in contrast to the wonderful 'alternative outcomes' provided by Wajcman). Several anthologies have attempted to provide a broader survey in which both feminist and anti-racist critique, with both high theory and practical implications, can provide multiple perspectives for a social analysis of technology. Recent examples include Nelson et al.'s (2001) examination of race (primarily covering ethnic identity and technologies of everyday life), and Eglash et al.'s (2004) examination of the 'appropriation' of technology (reinterpretations, adaptations, and reinventions by users).

While many of the studies mentioned above can be viewed as arising out of analysis of identity (race, class, and gender), the actant network theory (ANT) approach of Latour and others (cf. Callon and Latour 1992) has offered a postmodernist challenge that is as often as criticized for its lack of political commitment as it is celebrated for going beyond constructivism. Latour and his colleagues see social construction as accepting the debate within the scientists' own framework. That is, science long ago constructed a nature/society divide (often characterized by the Hobbs/Boyle debate). Scientists will speak for the world of things – for Nature – and humanists will speak for humanity. But from the ANT approach, things are also actors (or at least actants) which must be recruited as allies, refuted as enemies, or otherwise dealt with in the web of relations that constitute scientific and technological development. For example, in his description of Aramis, a proposed semi-automated transportation system in France, Latour (1996) allows the technology itself to be one voice in the narrative. Thus the constructionist simply gives more causal emphasis to the social side, whereas a description in terms of ANT undermines the very division. '[W]e wish to attack scientists' hegemony on the definition of nature, we have never wished to accept the essential source of their power: that is the very distribution between what is natural and what is social and the fixed allocation of ontological power that goes with it' (Callon and Latour 1992: 348).

COMPLEXITY THEORY

Based on the previous sections, one might have the mistaken impression that although social

Figure 21.3   *Low-rider: An appropriation of standard automobile technology in the US Latino Community*

analysis of technology was originally dominated by mainstream technological determinists, once that determinism was defeated the entire field became entirely dominated by a small group of social visionaries. Of course that is not true. The mainstream of social analysis of technology did not sit idly by while sticking to its determinist roots, and nowhere is this more vividly portrayed than in the synthesis between complexity theory and technology analysis. If readers will pardon a brief digression, I will explain the mathematical basis for complexity theory before proceeding to its technosocial application.

In ordinary speech, 'complex' just means that there is a lot going on. But for mathematicians the term is precisely defined, and gives us a new way to approach the concept. Prior to complexity theory mathematicians had defined complexity in terms of randomness; primarily based on the work of Soviet mathematician A.N. Kolmogorov, and Gregory Chaitin and Ray Solomonoff in the United States. In this definition, the complexity of a signal (either analog or digital) is measured by the length of the shortest algorithm required to produce it. This means that periodic numbers (such as 0.2727272 ...) will have a low algorithmic complexity. Even if the number is infinitely long, the algorithm can simply say, 'Write a decimal point followed by endless repetitions

of "27",' or even shorter: '3/11.' Truly random numbers (e.g. a string of numbers produced by rolling dice) will have the highest algorithmic complexity possible, since their only algorithm is the number itself – for an infinite length, you get infinite complexity. In analog systems a periodic signal, like the vibration from a single guitar string or the repetitive swings of a pendulum, would have the lowest algorithmic complexity, and random noise, like static from a radio that has lost its station (what is often called 'white noise') would have the highest algorithmic complexity.

One problem with defining complexity in terms of randomness is that it does not match our intuition. While it's true that the periodic signal of a ticking metronome is so simple that it becomes hypnotically boring, the same could be said for white noise – in fact, I sometimes tune my radio between stations if I want to fall asleep. But if I want to stay awake I listen to music. Music somehow satisfies our intuitive concept of complexity: it is predictable enough to follow along, but surprising enough to keep us pleasantly attentive. Mathematicians eventually caught up with their intuition, and developed a new measure in which the most complex signals are neither completely ordered, nor completely disordered, but rather those which are half-way in between. These patterns (which

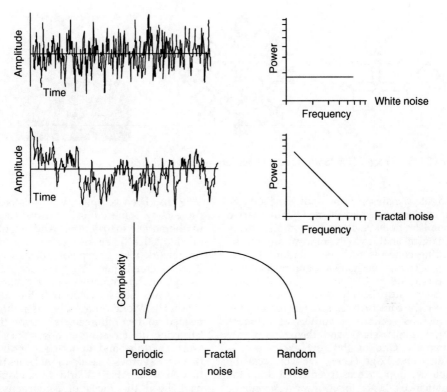

Figure 21.4 *Postmodern era (post-1970s) view: complexity as between random and ordered (Crutchfield–Smale measure)*

include almost every type of instrumental music) also happen to be fractals – in fact the new complexity measure exactly co-coincides with the measure of fractal dimension.

While such complexity measures were first applied to abstract systems such as cellular automata, it soon became apparent that there were a large variety of phenomena in biology, physics, and economics that matched this model. The economic models are where technosocial analysis has had its strongest connection. Economists themselves see the connection to mathematical complexity theory happening quite late in the game, and typically cite Schumpeter's evolutionary view as the essential concept, with Nelson and Winter (1982) as the first to forefront the evolutionary model in contemporary analysis. The concept of 'increasing returns', as promoted by Brian Arthur (first published as a working paper of the International Institute for Applied Systems Analysis in 1983, see Arthur 1994 for a collection of his work) at the Santa Fe Institute, provided the basis for forging a strong synthesis with computational frameworks (although this history is disputed

by Krugman 1998). The essential contrast is that while classical economics emphasized negative feedback – competition on an even playing field, where the best products and services win out – an evolutionary view could account for the positive feedback that takes place when more popular products and services generate sub-industries. The competition between Microsoft and Apple, for example, was not won because DOS was a superior operating system – its graphics looked positively primitive compared to the Apple – but rather because DOS allowed any vendor to create software for it – and with more vendors came greater usability, which attracted more vendors (hence the phenomenon of 'lock-in'). Rather than the white noise of the level playing field, economic portraits have now taken on the fractal contours of an evolutionary landscape.

Technological development has played a key role in these first portraits by Arthur and others; lock-in examples, for instance, included not only the Apple/Dos contrast, but also the QWERTY versus Dvorak keyboards, the rotational direction of clocks, Betamax versus VHS

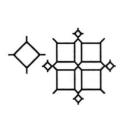  

Figure 21.5   *Fractal Simulation for an Ethiopian professional cross*

video, etc. Analyses from both the Santa Fe computational side and the neo-Schumpterian economist side have created a complete array of biological analogs to the innovation process, including concepts such as mutation of innovation, selection mechanisms, and measures of fitness (see Nelson 1995 for a review). But there has been surprisingly little conversation between the constructivist scholars highlighted in previous sections – politics of artifacts, SCOT, feminist, etc. – and these complexity economists. One of the few exceptions is Williams and Edge (1996), who criticize the complexity approach as 'predicated upon the maintenance of a stable set of social, economic and technical forces, which serve to generate the necessary uni-directionality of technological development'. A more optimistic outlook on the possible synthesis has come from Loet Leydesdorff and his colleagues at the University of Amsterdam (cf. Leydesdorff and Van den Besselaar 1994). But here the use of systems theory terminology has created little appeal for the constructivists.

SUGGESTIONS FOR FUTURE RESEARCH

Creating a synthesis between these powerful paradigms – the simulations and quantitative of complexity scholars and the progressive social vision of constructivism – is a dream we have yet to realize. But there are hopeful signs of convergence. Lansing's brilliant work on computational models of water temples in Bali has intervened on behalf of indigenous knowledge against development projects, similar to constructivist analysis of local knowledge and political critique, but using the tools and techniques of complexity theorists. My own work on fractals in African material culture (Eglash

1999) has been accepted, with relatively little protest, by some educational institutions for mathematics instruction. And Douthwaite et al. (2002) make use of an evolutionary framework for participatory design of Third World technologies. What is odd is that the convergence of constructivism and complexity approaches seems to happen, in the main, outside of First World contexts. Just as anthropology needed to revolutionize its perspectives for 'studying up' (creating ethnographies of First World middle- and upper-class individuals), this new synthesis needs to make its transformation to the First World technologies that have been the focus of constructivist and 'complexivist' analysis.

But complexity theory is just one of many bodies of research with which constructivism needs to forge a synthesis. Constructivist views alone have become, in the opinion of this author, rather sterile. At one time it was a tremendous challenge to express any view outside that of the technological determinist. But social influences in technology are now well accepted. To say that the purpose of one's research is to defeat the portrait of purely technical determination is to invoke a straw target. Winner's 1993 essay 'Opening the black box and finding it empty' is still relevant for those who wish to push constructivism towards more productive challenges. Yet the would-be successor to constructivism – ANT – is not generally viewed as having filled that box. And Winner's own framework is sometimes criticized as overly deterministic: while technologies do indeed have politics, they also embody political dynamics, and our analysis needs to be capable of keeping up with the shifts in such social relations.

Take, for example, the process of participatory design (PD). This is not an analytic framework, but rather a program for carrying out one analytic framework's implications. PD is a bold

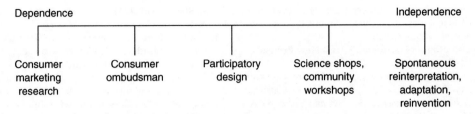

Figure 21.6 *Spectrum of lay user relations to expert production*

claim as to the politics of artifacts: it assumes that those technologies created more democratically, with the participation of the potential users, will have better impact on the lives of those using them. But it also assumes some rather static categories. Suppose, for example, that the utopian design is judged vastly superior by the users, but turns out to be unaffordable once manufactured. Or suppose that one group's ideal technology involves maintaining its race, class or gender privilege over others? What is at first a simple proposition becomes a complicated mess as our analytic categories start to unravel. When our 'Appropriated Technology' group (Eglash et al. 2004) began to examine PD, we came to the conclusion that it needed a more flexible framework for examining the relations between users and the social forces of interest (Figure 21.6).

When examined in such a space of social forces, we find PD is not a utopian extreme, but rather one point along a spectrum of practices in which users have various kinds of 'voice' in the design process. And rather than see the right end of the spectrum, user independence, as an ultimate goal (cf. Figure 21.3), we found that various user needs are best met by contextually determined positions in the spectrum, and that these positions shift through time. But this is only one of a potentially vast array of possible conceptual tools, of flexible technosocial spaces that could help us map out such dynamics.

The fact that computers could be an emblem of the military-industrial establishment in 1967 and an emblem of counter-culture zeal in 1997 says much about the need for understanding these kinds of flexible dynamics. Whether via constructivist synthesis with another discipline, Haraway's material-semiotic hybrids, ANT's celebration of the agency of things, or mapping dynamics in technosocial space, we need a materialist analysis that is decisive enough to enable action, and yet has

the flexibility for avoiding overdetermined conclusions.

NOTE

1 Unfortunately some anthropologists still use the term 'primitive' to make this distinction. Many biologists, having recognized that all contemporary organisms, regardless of their anatomical complexity, are the result of millions of years of evolution which left them well adapted to their contemporary ecological niche, no longer use the term. There is nothing anachronistic about the amoeba; indeed, it might be that humans are only a temporary 'blind alley' in the long run.

REFERENCES

Adas, Michael (1989) *Machines as the Measure of Men: Science, Technology, and Ideologies of Western Dominance*. Ithaca, NY: Cornell University Press.

Arthur, W. Brian (1994) *Increasing Returns and Path Dependence in the Economy*. Ann Arbor, MI: University of Michigan Press.

Bijker, W.E., Hughes, T.P. and Pinch, T.J. (1987) *The Social Construction of Technological Systems*. Cambridge, MA: MIT Press.

Bloor, David (1976) *Knowledge and Social Imagery*. London and Boston, MA: Routledge.

Boserup, Ester (1970) *Woman's Role in Economic Development*. London: Allen & Unwin.

Callon, Michel and Latour, Bruno (1992) 'Don't throw the baby out with the bath school!', in Andrew Pickering (ed.), *Science as Practice and Culture*. Chicago: University of Chicago Press, pp. 343–68.

Diamond, Jared (1996) *Guns, Germs, and Steel: the Fates of Human Societies*. New York: Norton.

Douthwaite, B., Keatinge, J.D.H. and Park, J.R. (2002) 'Learning selection: an evolutionary model for understanding, implementing and evaluating participatory technology development', *Agricultural Systems*, 72 (2): 109–31.

Eglash, Ron (1999) *African Fractals*. New Brunswick, NJ: Rutgers University Press.

Eglash, Ron, Croissant, Jennifer, Di Chiro, Giovanna and Fouché, Rayvon, eds (2004) *Appropriating Technology: Vernacular Science and Social Power*. Minneapolis, MN: University of Minnesota Press.

Ellul, J. (1964) *The Technological Society*. New York: Vintage Books. (French edition 1954).

Elsner, Henry, Jr (1966) *The Technocrats: Prophets of Automation*. Syracuse, NY: Syracuse University Press.

Feenberg, Andrew (1991) *Critical Theory of Technology*. New York: Oxford University Press.

Franklin, Sarah and Ragone, Helena, eds (1997) *Reproducing Reproduction: Kinship, Power, and Technological Innovation*. Philadelphia, PA: University of Pennsylvania Press.

Hacker, Sally (1989) *Pleasure, Power, and Technology: Some Tales of Gender, Engineering, and the Cooperative Workplace*. Boston, MA: Unwin Hyman.

Hakken, David (1993) *Computing Myths, Class Realities: an Ethnography of Technology and Working People in Sheffield, England*. Boulder, CO: Westview Press.

Hakken, David (1999) *Cyborgs@Cyberspace? An Ethnographer looks to the Future*. New York and London: Routledge.

Haraway, Donna (1991) 'A cyborg manifesto: science, technology, and socialist-feminism in the late twentieth century', in *Simians, Cyborgs and Women: the Reinvention of Nature*. New York: Routledge, pp. 149–81.

Haraway, Donna (1996) *Modest_Witness@Second_ Millenium. Femaleman©_Meets_OncoMouse™. Feminism and Technoscience*. New York: Routledge.

Hess, David (1995) *Science and Technology in a Multicultural World: the Cultural Politics of Facts and Artifacts*. New York: Columbia University Press.

Khor, Martin (1999) 'Global economy and the Third World', *International Journal of Rural Studies*, October.

Kroeber, Alfred (1917) 'The superorganic', *American Anthropologist*, 19: 163–213.

Krugman, Paul (1998) 'The legend of Arthur: a tale of gullibility at the *New Yorker*', Online at http://web. mit.edu/krugman/www/legend.html.

Lansing, J. Stephen (1991) *Priests and Programmers: Technology of Power in the Engineered Landscape of Bali*. Cambridge, MA: Princeton University Press.

Latour, Bruno (1996) *Aramis, or, The Love of Technology*. Cambridge, MA: Harvard University Press.

Lemonnier, Pierre (2002) *Technological Choices: Transformation in Material Cultures since the Neolithic*. London: Routledge.

Leydesdorff, Loet and Van den Besselaar, Peter, eds (1994) *Evolutionary Economics and Chaos Theory: New Directions in Technology Studies*. London: Pinter.

Lillenthal, David (1944) *TVA: Democracy on the March*. New York: Harpers.

Lovejoy, Arthur O. (1936/1971) *The Great Chain of Being*. Cambridge, MA: Harvard University Press.

MacKenzie, Donald and Wajcman, Judy, eds (1985) *The Social Shaping of Technology: How the Refrigerator Got its Hum*. Milton Keynes: Open University Press.

Marx, Leo (1987) 'Does improved technology mean progress?' *Technology Review*, January, pp. 33–41, 71.

Mumford, Lewis (1964) 'Authoritarian and democratic technics', *Technology and Culture*, 5: 1–8.

Nelson, Alondra, Tu, Thuy Linch N. with Hines, Alice Headlam (2001) *Technicolor: Race, Technology and Everyday Life*. New York: New York University Press.

Nelson, R. (1995) 'Recent evolutionary theorising about economic change', *Journal of Economic Literature*, 33: 48–90.

Nelson, R.R. and Winter, S.G. (1982) *An Evolutionary Theory of Economic Change*. Cambridge, MA and London: Belknap Press.

Noble, David (1979) 'Social choice in machine design: the case of automatically controlled machine tools', in A. Zimbalist (ed.), *Case Studies on the Labour Process*. New York: Monthly Review Press, pp. 18–50.

Pickering, Andrew (1984) *Constructing Quarks: A Sociological History of Particle Physics*. Edinburgh: Edinburgh University Press.

Pickering, Andrew (1995) *The Mangle of Practice: Time, Agency, and Science*. Chicago: University of Chicago Press.

Plant, Sadie (1997) *Zeros + Ones: Digital Women and the New Technoculture*. New York: Doubleday.

Restivo, Sal, Van Bendegem, J.P. and Fischer, Roland (1993) *Math Worlds: Philosophical and Social Studies of Mathematics and Mathematics Education*. Albany, NY: SUNY Press.

Traweek, Sharon (1988) *Beamtimes and Lifetimes: the World of High Energy Physicists*. Cambridge, MA: Harvard University Press.

Wajcman, Judy (1991) *Feminism Confronts Technology*. Cambridge: Polity.

Williams, Robin and Edge, David (1996) 'The social shaping of technology', *Research Policy*, 25: 856–99.

Winner, Langdon (1977) *Autonomous Technology: Technics-out-of-Control as a Theme in Political Thought*. Cambridge, MA: MIT Press.

Winner, Langdon (1986) *The Whale and the Reactor: A Search for Limits in an Age of High Technology*. Chicago: University of Chicago Press.

Winner, Langdon (1993) 'Social constructivism: opening the black box and finding it empty', *Science as Culture*, 3 (3) 16: 427–52.

Woolgar, Steve and Cooper, Geoff (1999) 'Do artifacts have ambivalence? Mose's bridges, Winners' bridges and other urban legends in S&TS', *Social Studies of Science*, 29 (3): 433–49.

22

CONSUMPTION

Daniel Miller

The aim of this chapter is not simply to review work on the topic of consumption, it is to investigate the specific consequences of thinking about consumption as an aspect of material culture. I will try and show how a material culture perspective is particularly relevant to the study of consumption, but this includes not only showing the positive implications of adopting this perspective, but also acknowledging the degree to which several other approaches to consumption are founded upon a peculiarly anti-material prejudice. This chapter begins with a discussion of those approaches which for various reasons stand in opposition to material culture. I will then briefly summarize a wide range of studies that reflect the diversity of disciplinary and regional approaches. The final section will be concerned with those studies that exemplify the contribution of material culture in particular and their potential future impact on the study of consumption.

THE OPPOSITION TO MATERIAL CULTURE

Apart from approaches that come from Material Culture Studies itself and some economists' perspectives, most academics who have written about consumption, and most especially those who have theorized about consumption seem to assume that consumption is synonymous with modern mass consumption. They note the vast scale and materialism associated with mass consumption and view this primarily as danger to both society and the environment. As such mass consumption has been regarded more as an evil than as the good. There has been very little

acknowledgment of the degree to which the rise of mass consumption could also be seen as synonymous with the abolition of poverty or of the desire for development. The reason why consumption studies have adopted this unusually moral or normative aspect compared to the study of most other phenomena is not, however, necessarily a result of any attribute of modern mass consumption itself.

The perception of consumption as an evil or antisocial activity is rather more profound and existed long before modern mass consumption. The very term 'consumption' suggests the problem is rather intrinsic to the activity itself. To consume something is to use it up, in effect to destroy material culture itself. As Porter (1993) noted the alternative meaning of the term 'consumption' as tuberculosis is no coincidence. Consumption tends to be viewed as a wasting disease that is opposed to production, which constructs the world. This is why in Munn's (1986) account of people on an island within New Guinea there is the exhortation never to consume what you yourself produce. Goods must first have been involved in exchange, which is productive of social relations. Merely to consume them is to destroy their potential for creating society, or what she conveys as the local desire for increasing the fame of Gawa – the island where she conducted fieldwork. I have argued that the same logic lies behind the centrality of sacrifice to most ancient religions (Miller 1998a). Sacrifice tends to come just prior to the consumption of what people have produced. First an idealized segment of that production must be given to the gods to forestall its destructive impact. Indeed, at least one approach, associated with Bataille (1988), celebrated this definition of consumption as inherently destructive. So the starting point for a consideration of consumption has tended to view this process largely as the ending point of material culture.

While production, in turn associated with creativity, as in the arts and crafts, is considered to be the manufacture of value, for example in the work of Marx, consumption involves the using up of resources and their elimination from the world. The moral debates that dominate this topic are then both older and deeper than the concern with contemporary materialism, but they have taken on new dimensions when applied to modernity. For example, with respect to the contemporary environmentalist critique, the same moral perspective has become ingrained at a semantic bias where consumption is again synonymous with destruction. For example, the environmentalist critique might have been largely directed at the destruction of the world's resources associated with the production such as the impact of heavy industry or agro-industry rather than consumption. But this is not what happens. Destruction is first identified with the stance to consumption itself, with the consumer viewed as using up scarce or irreplaceable resources, and production in this instance is seen as the secondary handmaiden to consumption.

This makes it quite unsurprising that the earliest discussions of consumption look remarkably similar to contemporary discussions (for which see typically the majority of contributions in Crocker and Linden 1998 or Goodwin et al. 1997). Both early and current commentary critiques attempt to define and condemn that portion of consumption which was held to go beyond what is deemed necessary according to some moral standard of need. Even within periods, such as medieval Christianity, which we certainly do not think of as profligate times, the consideration of consumption was directed largely to the issue of luxury. This is made clear in the contribution by Sekora (1977), who also introduces us to the notion of sumptuary laws. It should be noted that such laws, which existed in ancient China and India as much as in the West, were hardly ever based on an absolute standard (e.g. Clunas 1991: 147–55). Rather morality was relative to what was viewed as the natural hierarchy of society, such that what a commoner was allowed to wear was defined in opposition to a nobleman. Even today much of the disgust at consumption is directed specifically at products such as McDonald's and Barbie dolls deemed vulgar or in bad taste and associated with mass in contrast to elite consumption (see also Hebdige

1981). It is therefore hardly surprising that one of the first major anthropological studies of consumption by Bourdieu (1979) investigated the way in which class and consumption became naturalized as taste. It is only in recent times that need becomes more of an absolute than a relative quality.

Perhaps the strongest expression of this anti-materialism comes in the form of various South Asian religions such as Hinduism, Buddhism and Jainism which took a much more profound interest in the centrality of desire and materialism to the condition of humanity and its relationship to the world than did Judaism, Christianity or classical teaching. It was in these religions perhaps most clearly developed the idea that fulfilment of desires through consumption led to the wasting away of the essence of humanity in mere materialism. In India the avoidance of materialism which came to cover almost any involvement with the material world became essential to the quest for spiritual enlightenment. Any hope for spiritual rebirth or enlightenment depended upon the repudiation of the material world, which was seen as more or less synonymous with illusion. Once again this opposition to material culture was associated with a hierarchy, although this was theologically sustained in Hinduism (Dumont 1972), while it emerged more through practice in Buddhism.

So it is perhaps not surprising that the origins of the modern study of consumption lie within an essentially moral framework of anti-materialism. The evident founding ancestor is Veblen (1899/1979), though as Horowitz (1985: 1–8) makes clear a whole swathe of US commentators, reflecting perhaps the foundation of that state in Puritanism, tended to constantly subsume the topic of consumption within the issue of the morality of spending. Terms such as vicarious and conspicuous consumption that were coined by Veblen remain as critiques of the expression of wealth as material culture. There is remarkable continuity between the arguments of Veblen at the start of the twentieth century and critics of consumption such as Schor (1998) at the end. Slater (1997: 74–83) documents an alternative route to this critique in Europe, which emphasized not so much consumption *per se* but the effects of affluence in loosening social regulation and ties. For thinkers such as Durkheim and Rousseau the primary cause of anxiety came from their sense that humanity was thereby losing its integrity. Quite extreme versions of these ideas can be found in the writings of Lasch (1979) and Marcuse (1964; see also Preteceille and Terrail 1985) all influenced by what became a highly ascetic version of Western Marxism. A version of Marxism curiously out of synch with Eastern Marxism, where the Soviet Union proclaimed it would outdo capitalism in bringing wealth to the people. But the critical edge was also strong in other perspectives, such as those influenced by Weber, one of which by Campbell (1986) became an important contribution to more recent attempts to define modern consumerism, in this case as synonymous with hedonism.

Those writings within Western Marxism in turn developed a more general critique of consumption as simply the end point of capitalism. This is evident in the more recent writings of influential sociologists such as Baudrillard (1988), though others such as Bauman (1991) would also fit this characterization (see Warde 1994). According to this perspective the massive spread of consumer goods as acts of symbolizing has reached such a level that while goods once stood for persons and relationships, for example symbolic of class and gender, they now come to replace them (Baudrillard 1988). Such is the power of commerce to produce social maps based on the distinctions between goods that actual consumers are relegated to the passive role of merely fitting themselves into such maps by buying the appropriate signs of their 'lifestyle'. Humanity has become merely the mannequins that sport the categories created by capitalism.

The combination of these critiques has led in turn to a characterization of the modern world as an endless circuit of superfluous 'signs' leading to a superficial postmodern existence that has lost authenticity and roots. Both Baudrillard and Bauman have been powerful influences behind this stance. The tenor of such contributions is in some ways surprising. If this century has seen whole populations identifying themselves through consumption rather than production, this might have been viewed as progress. We might have welcomed a shift from identity being founded in something most people do for wages and under pressure (see Gortz 1982) to finding identity within a process over which they have far more control. We might have argued that capitalism has far more direct control over people's identities as workers than as consumers. The problems of people being defined by their labour also extended to women being relegated to domestic labour as their natural domain. But Marx and other writers that were foundational to critical studies actually welcomed such identification with labour as a more authentic form of humanity. One result of this critique of consumption

has been a tendency of contemporary academics to romanticize manual labour, something most academics show no inclination whatsoever to actually engage in, and denigrate precisely the consumer culture that they conspicuously do engage in.

The critique of materialism is extraordinarily basic.[1] There is an abiding sense in this literature that pure individuals or pure social relations are sullied by commodity culture. Indeed, the central plank of the colloquial term 'materialism' is that it represents an attachment or devotion to objects which is at the expense of an attachment and devotion to persons. This is of importance to the whole of material culture studies, since it exposed an underlying ideology in the stance taken, even to an academic interest that is potentially viewed as a mistaken emphasis on objects as opposed to persons. One of the problems with this as a moral stance that has underscored the academic representation of the topic is that it stands in direct opposition to a quite different morality, an ethics based on a passionate desire to eliminate poverty. There is no acknowledgment within this literature that we live in a time when most human suffering is still the direct result of the lack of goods. There are whole continents, such as Africa, where the vast majority of people desperately need more consumption, more pharmaceuticals, more housing, more transport, more books, more computers. So this critique of consumption tends both to be a form of self-denial, ignoring the degree to which these very same writers appear to favour in their private lives that which they refute in their writing, and a denial of the condition of poverty as a root cause of human suffering.

In practice the desire to give credit to the way consumers consume and the authenticity of some of their desire for goods need not detract from the academic critique of the way companies attempt to sell goods and services, or exploit workers in doing so. So it is quite possible to embrace acceptance of goods as potentially an integral aspect of modern humanity without actually contradicting the tenets of some of the most strident critics, such as Klein (2001). Overall I would suggest, however, that the appropriation of the study of consumption for the purpose of self-denigration of the modern or the West as superficial and deluded has amounted to what I have called 'the poverty of morality' on a par with Thompson's (1978) critique of Althusser in his *Poverty of Theory*, in that it essentially abstracts us from any actual study of consumption or consumers and replaces this with a theoretical projection of what might be called the 'virtual' (Miller 1998b) consumer. The problem is not the morality itself, which is no doubt often proclaimed with the most honourable of intentions, but that we learn almost nothing from any of this about the nature of consumption.

The critique of consumption as the using up of material culture is common to both modernity and other times and places. By contrast, what was perhaps unique to Western modernity, and which emerges clearly in Appleby (1993), is that during the eighteenth century there arose a powerful counter-discourse which asserted that consumption might also be beneficial to the commonwealth by stimulating what was then becoming abstracted as the economy. This strand leads to what has become almost the dominant ideology of the modern world, the flip side to the critique of materialism, where in our daily news broadcasts we hear economic reports telling us that our national economies are in need of a boost, which can be provided only by consumers spending more. As is often the case with ideologies, this promotion of consumption becomes effective largely because it become the taken-for-granted rationale behind a set of structures and practices. Just as the critique of consumption needs to be unpicked for its underlying moral stance, so does the advocacy of consumption. In this case, however, the problem has tended to be not so much the naturalization of consumption as an activity as the naturalization of one particular means for securing consumption, which is capitalism. The main form taken by this naturalization is the discipline of economics, which teaches as axiomatic a whole series of quite extraordinary claims about the relationship between consumers and capitalism. This naturalization of capitalism, though at least as pernicious, since vastly more powerful, than the critique of consumption, is, however, less germane to the question of consumption as material culture, since what is remarkable about it is its lack of concern with the specificity of goods or with the wider nature of materiality and its effects. Academic and philosophical writings therefore remain dominated by the older, more negative strand (though see Lebergott 1993 for the 'exception that proves the rule').

I have started with these underlying moralities involved in this topic, since it seems to me better to expose the ideological underpinnings of research in this area than to leave these unexplored, and they will have a considerable bearing upon the impact of material culture studies that will be discussed below.

Nevertheless it would also be unfortunate if consumption studies were simply reduced to this often rather empty debate over whether they are good or bad. So before looking at the very different perspective that has arisen from material culture studies, I want to briefly mention something of the vast literature that has arisen primarily from a disciplinary or regional perspective, and which is not necessarily positioned within this wider debate (see also Miller 1995).

DISCIPLINARY AND REGIONAL PERSPECTIVES

The history of a moral stance to consumption should not be confused with the history of consumption itself. People have always consumed goods created by themselves or others. Consumption is a topic that is emerging therefore in archaeological studies associated with the rise of concern with material culture more generally (e.g. Pyburn 1998, Meskell 2004). If we are to understand the diversity of consumption we need to remember the satirist Juvenal's attacks on consumption in ancient Rome, or the importance of luxury objects in the eleventh-century Japanese *Tale of the Genji* as cautions against assertions about the centrality of consumption in the rise of the modern world in general and, one might add, colonialism in particular.

One of the very best studies of consumption to have been carried out in recent years, *Fish Cakes and Courtesans* (Davidson 1999), is based largely on materials from fifth-century BC Athens. This remarkable study does many things that ought to be emulated. Materiality is to the fore from the beginning, since the opening chapters are particularly concerned with the consumption of fish. But consumption is an activity, so it is addressed to the question of locating the distinction between appropriate consumption of fish and gluttony. But equally the issue of materiality is raised with respect to the conceptualization of personhood. This is the critical issue identified in the other side of the book's title, the courtesan, and the way the Greeks of the time understood the distinction between a person's humanity and their commoditization. But the book does still more than this. It also shows how the issue of consumption when taken broadly becomes fundamental to all those other issues whose discussion is the legacy of fifth-century Athens to today. That is the meaning of democracy and the place of philosophy and other cultural arenas as an element of the emergent political process.

Not surprisingly, given the topic of consumption, a particular focus in historical research has been the early modern period. For example, Mukerji (1983) with respect to Europe, examines the move from elite to popular arts (for a parallel in Japan see Akai 1994), while Shammas (1993) examines the more general shifts in the consumption of groceries and consumer durables in the Anglo-American world. There is also growing historical work on non-European regions such as Clunas (1999) on China, for example, including an extended examination as to why mass consumption arose in Europe as opposed to China (Pomeranz 2000). This has been an important corrective to what otherwise has been a largely Euro-centred literature.

For these historical researches the key early publication was *The Birth of a Consumer Society* (McKendrick et al. 1983), which stimulated a large literature both as to whether there is a distinctive form to contemporary consumption and, if so, when it began. Crucial to this debate is the question as to whether modern consumption is actually a different kind of activity in intention and nature from merely the use of goods in prior times. The most powerful advocate of such a periodization is Campbell (1986), who defines modern consumption around the issue of unprecedented hedonism, although historians such as Schama (1987) (working under a parallel inspiration from Weber), suggest something closer to older forms of ambivalence.

The two disciplines that have retained more or less continuous interest in this topic have been Economics and Business Studies. Both represent the traditional view of consumption as essentially the study of people's relationships to the market place. In practice economics has concentrated upon theory and modelling, based largely upon aggregate data, and Business Studies has developed a more empirically focused set of studies often concerned with an isolated micro-environment of consumer choice. Lancaster (1966) may be seen as a classic example of more typical economic concerns, featuring highly abstracted and generalized models of consumer decision making which are starting to be attacked even within that discipline (e.g. Fine 1995). In effect these are the models of what consumption needs to be for other aspects of neoclassical economic theory to 'work'. There has grown up a kind of economistic imperialism which tries to project these approaches on to other disciplinary concerns with consumption, as for example in the work of Becker and some of his followers (Becker

1996; see Fine 1998). This may explain why the social sciences much more often make reference to nineteenth-century political economy and in many cases largely ignore the economics that has developed over the twentieth century. The concerns analysed by Perrotta (1997) seem to come closer to their interests in the development of consumption as a practice. On the other hand there are several branches of economic theory which, because they include an applied element, are currently more engaged. James (1993) exemplifies an approach that has shown consistent concern with the impact of economic models of consumption on the developing world and with the need to bring more general approaches to consumption within the framework of economic modelling.

Consumer studies based in business schools have produced perhaps the single largest body of material on this topic, and it is not particularly healthy that this has been largely ignored by more recent developments in consumer research within the social sciences. Much of the work done in business schools is premised on narrowly positivistic lines of hypothesis testing on issues such as which shelf in a supermarket is scanned by shoppers most often. As such there tends to be a split between on the one hand Economics, Business Studies and Psychology, which support the epistemological foundations of such research, and the other disciplines represented in this volume that eschew the underlying epistemology in preference for more open-ended contextualization of consumer behaviour. Of more interest to material culture studies is the rise of more qualitative and interpretive studies that are gaining authority within business schools. McCracken's (1988b) concept of the Diderot effect is a widely cited consideration of the implications of one particular consumer choice upon subsequent goods that need now to acknowledge the as it were incumbent object. Fournier's (1998) work on the relationship between consumers and their brands also became quickly influential as a new approach within the field. Finally Sherry and McGrath (1989) exemplify the rise of qualitative approaches which focus upon topics such as the nature of gifts or of cultural capital that tend to cut across disciplinary interests. Perhaps the most widely cited business studies researcher within the social sciences has been Belk (e.g. 1993, 1995), but there have been other engagements, e.g. Holt's (1998) commentary upon Bourdieu.

Both economics and business studies have been much influenced by psychology in their initial development, especially social psychology. Books such as Bowlby (1993) and articles such as Miller and Rose (1997) indicate just how powerful these influences were in the past. Psychological work still continues apace, as summarized by Lunt (1995), and certain work, such as that of Csikszentmihalyi (1993), continues to have considerable influence, but I think it is fair to say that the dominance held by psychology until around the 1960s has considerably declined. Instead what we find is the rapid rise in influence of social science and historical research on consumption that only really began in the 1970s.

Sociology has already been discussed in some detail as a major contributor to the wider ideological debates around consumption. Other influential work has included that of Ritzer (2004), whose ideas about McDonaldization have spawned many clones. Another theme developed by Cross (1993) and evident in Schor (1991) identifies consumption with the pressure that draws us back into longer hours as workers in order to pay for new consumption desire, again a particularly US theme. There has also been considerable work devoted to development and welfare perspectives, often in conjunction with others, such as the economist Sen (1998), or a political scientist such Etzioni (1998) writing about voluntary simplicity. At a more mundane level there is a considerable amount of detailed work around particular topics, for example Warde (1997) and many others on the consumption of food. Savage et al. (1992: 99–131) represent the kind of statistical analysis of taste that is a close cousin to the work of Bourdieu. There have also been theoretical contributions that don't entirely fit within the dominant ideology, as by Slater (1997). Ritzer and Slater combined to edit the *Journal of Consumer Culture*, the first on the topic that is not primarily oriented towards commercial imperatives.

ANTHROPOLOGY AND REGIONAL PERSPECTIVES

Influenced by the rise of structuralism (Lévi-Strauss 1972) and the application of semiotics to commodities (Barthes 1973), the study of consumption was revolutionized by two books published in 1979. Douglas (Douglas and Isherwood 1979) advocated an approach to goods as a system of communication on analogy with (but in critical respects also distinct from) language. Once consumer goods are thought of as a symbolic system then this opens up the possibility for in some ways 'reading' society itself through the pattern found among goods. This was the premise of the other book published that year, by Bourdieu (1979), who focused upon goods not just as reflections of class distinctions but as a primary means by which these were expressed, and thus reproduced, without it being apparent. The power of consumption as a means to reproduce social patterning was hidden by an ideology which viewed consumption as merely an expression of individual taste. This mapping of many social distinctions (especially that of gender) through the study of goods as a cultural system has become something of an industry in its own right (see also Sahlins 1976). It tends to dominate approaches in cultural studies, and semiotic analysis has been highly influential within commerce, for example as part of a constant search for a gap in such social maps that could be filled with some well targeted product.

This first tranch of more semiotically minded studies was consolidated into an established anthropological approach to consumption in the late 1980s with the publication of a further three books (Appadurai 1986; McCracken 1988a; Miller 1987). Of these three Appadurai represented a trajectory emerging from the study of gifts and commodities in social anthropology, McCracken was concerned with the contribution of anthropology to commercial studies such as marketing, while my own book attempted to ground such studies in the core concerns of material culture. Although all of these contributed to the wider theorizing of consumption, because they arose under the auspices of anthropology they have also spawned a larger literature on regional consumption and comparative consumption which examines the often quite different trajectories taken to becoming part of a consumer society. This has been an important antidote to the hegemony of particular regions such as the United States and United Kingdom in most other disciplines. It helps us avoid a stance that views, for example, one society using computers and wearing blue jeans as less authentic than another.

Many aspects of consumption emerge from this area of research. To take one region, that of South Asia, Gell (1986) presents a tribal population whose consumption is being affected not by foreign imports but by the neighbouring Hindu communities. As such these people need to find a way to 'tame' what are seen as the negative consequences of new wealth. As Cohn (1989) shows, the colonial consumption of the British in India had often to be very aware of their potential articulation with previously existing forms of consumption, which in some ways could 'outwit' the meanings which colonial authorities wished to impose upon the way people dressed and appeared in public. Finally through careful ethnography Osella and Osella (1999) demonstrate that such localization of consumption becomes if anything more important for people such as those they worked with in Kerala who, as in many regions peripheral to metropolitan capitalism, are greatly affected by remittances from those working abroad. They may use the money to develop their consumption practices along highly specific lines that can be understood only in terms of the particular structures and concerns of each of the many groups that make up a particular region.

The evidence from East Asia has been particularly important in challenging assumptions about globalization inevitably meaning homogenization. Even such icons of globalization as McDonald's are given a particularly Chinese inflection by Yan (1997) through his study of their consumption in Beijing (see also Miller 1997 on Coca-cola). For example, Davis (2000) indicates through her summary of a whole series of articles the many nuances and contradictions we would have to take into account in assessing the rise of affluence in a particular region, in this case the area around Shanghai, which has become the vanguard of mass consumption within contemporary China.

Sometimes this influence is highly nuanced. So, for example, a study by Burke (1996) based on historical materials from Zimbabwe shows that there certainly are cases where the rise of demand, in this case for soap, does seem to develop in accordance with the pressure of advertising and marketing, while other demands, as for margarine, come from cultural practices that remain outside capitalist authority. Other studies accord more easily with the emphasis in sociology upon capitalist hegemony. For example, also in Africa, Gunilla and Beckman (1985) document an indigenous and readily available staple food being replaced by the rise of an expensive imported staple (see also Weismantel 1988). These are of particular consequence in such areas, given the huge inequalities in income and power.

This concern with the impact of capitalism brings out the other side to the anthropological coin. As well as examining specific locations, the discipline has also contributed to the rise of new studies of globalization. Following from historical work such as Braudel (1981) and Wallerstein (2000), one of the clearest examinations of the way production in one region

became linked with consumption in another was Mintz's (1985) pathbreaking study of sugar, now echoed in many other products such as coffee (e.g. Pendergrast 1999; Weiss 1996a). Other studies have emphasized the complex interplay between growing heterogeneity and homogeneity in these encounters. Sometimes this interplay rests upon quite specific aspects of style (e.g. Wilk 1995), in other cases consumption becomes important in the forging of national identity, as in Foster's (1995) study of New Guinea. Equally, consumption may become a means, as Heinze (1990) shows with respect to immigrant Jews in the United States, by which groups come to identify with the larger national project of development. But this does not always occur outside of contrary forces and contradictions. The people living on the border between the United States and Mexico studied by McHeyman (1997) may have aspirations towards forms of consumption which only exacerbate their ambiguous geographical position. In other cases phenomena such as consumer co-operatives that were of huge importance historically in Europe, but now largely diminished, remain central to consumption in another area, in this case Japan (see Furlogh and Strikwerda 1999). A final example of the complexity of these processes comes with the consumption of new technologies that are assumed to be instruments of globalization that demolish local or national boundaries. In practice, Miller and Slater (2000) argued that in its consumption the Internet become one of the most important elements of localization.[2]

CONSUMPTION: THE APPROACH FROM MATERIAL CULTURE

It was suggested at the beginning of this chapter that most approaches to consumption took a decidedly anti-material culture stance, seeing materiality as itself a threat to society and in particular to spiritual or moral values. In this section I will show how a material culture approach does quite the opposite from that imputed to it. Material culture studies work through the specificity of material objects in order ultimately to create a more profound understanding of the specificity of a humanity inseparable from its materiality. In one of the most influential studies that initiated this approach to consumption Hebdige (1981/1988) examined the use of motor bikes and motor scooters by subculture groups such as mods and rockers. Hebdige argued that consumption was not just about buying goods but often involved a highly productive and creative appropriation of those goods which transformed them over time. But equally that it was through this practice devoted to material transformation that certain social groups were themselves created, for example the rocker in association with the motor bike and the mod with the motor scooter respectively.

My own early contribution (Miller 1987) was to theorize consumption, using examples such as this study by Hebdige. At that time consumption was generally regarded as simply the end point and thus expression of capitalism which produced these goods for sale. Instead, I argued, while this may sometimes be the case, there was also the possibility that consumption could be viewed as the negation of capitalist production. Since, following Simmel (1978), it was argued that consumption returned goods back to the creation of specificity and relationships after extracting them from the anonymous and alienated conditions of their production. This theorizing should be viewed against the backdrop of a time when anthropology was dominated by a particular version of Marxism that had led to a focus entirely upon production and goods as expressive of capitalism. Such a stance is no longer required today. I have written more recently on why I think commonly consumption does not achieve this potential, but itself can become a medium for further abstraction and alienation in the form of virtualism (Miller 1998b).

Nevertheless the emergence of a series of studies that looked at the productive potential of consumption through a focus on the transformation of commodities produced an extensive literature which turned away from consumption as a general sociological trope, and towards the specificity of particular forms of consumption and particular genres of commodity. The virtue of theorizing consumption at that time was that it released the topic from being merely the handmaiden to the characterization of capitalism, and allowed one to turn back to its specificity, which in many respects also meant a return to its materiality. Because, if the theory was to be of any substantive use, it implied that there were many disparate ways in which consumption could manifest itself as productive of social groups, and that these had to be examined each in its own right.

There are many ways in which this could be done, but, to highlight the contribution of material culture, I want to briefly mention several genres of object and look at ethnographic research which has been dedicated to showing how each has, in its own way, contributed to this larger theoretical point. After considering each genre in turn I will end by briefly mentioning new work which is at the vanguard of such material culture studies, partly because it rearticulates the link with production and exchange and partly because it leads through a rethinking of materiality back to a consideration of the nature of humanity within a consumer society.

One of the reasons that the material culture approach to the home and possessions has been so influential is that it demonstrated the extraordinary blindness to consumption in the two disciplines most responsible for the form of our contemporary material culture – that is, architecture and design. In effect this meant that people produced the built environment with very little sense of the consequences those objects would have for those who used them, or the processes by which consumers might try and appropriate and transform them. There were many anecdotes about building projects that won prizes, but no one actually enjoyed living within. Indeed, it is largely through the influence of material culture studies that those working in design and design history have started to turn their attention to these larger consequences of their discipline, e.g. Attfield (2000) and Clarke (1999).

Buchli (1999) provides an extended case study of an apartment block in Moscow with a sense of its successive transformation by users under the impact of various ideological regimes. The equivalent in terms of an ethnographic treatment of this subject was Gullestad's path-breaking ethnography (1985) of the use of the home by Norwegian working-class housewives. In Miller (2001a; see also Chevalier 1998) it is the home itself that becomes the focus of inquiry. Much of contemporary consumption is concerned with the home either as the object of consumption or as the setting for the arrangements and use of commodities, and the contributors to that book take a wide range of perspectives upon the relationship of homes and their possessions. These range from the topic of moving house (Marcoux 2001) and arranging the furniture (Garvey 2001) to questioning assumptions about the tidy house in Japan (Daniels 2001) and the home as an expression of the discrepancy between aspiration and practice (Clarke 2001). Other collections, including Birdwell-Pheasant and Lawrence-Zúñiga (1999) and Cieraad (1999) include work on consumption. Despite all this, the impact upon architecture is still limited and the need for architects to acknowledge the consequences of their work for consumers remains.

The same general point – that any genre of commodity needs to acknowledge its implications for the effects it has on consumers – stands for a wide range of other topics. For example, clothing studies have traditionally been just as obsessed with the study of designers, especially *haute couture* designers, to the almost complete neglect of the effects of clothing upon users. Although there is good historical work that shows the integrity of clothing and the sense of the self (e.g. Sennet 1977) and also anthropological work on non-industrial societies making a similar point (e.g. Küchler in press; Henare in press), only recently has this been applied to the study of the mass consumption of clothing. What was required was more ethnographic work that sought to consider clothing from the point of view of actually what it means to wear particular clothes (e.g. Banerjee and Miller 2003; Clarke and Miller 2002; Dalby 2001; Freeman 2000; Woodward 2005). There has also been some *rapprochement* with new writing in clothing history, ranging from Summers' (2001) valuable study of the Victorian corset through Breward's (1995) historical work on clothing more generally in Britain. Recent work on the relationship between style and being gay has also contributed to this new work (e.g. Mort 1996; Nixon 1996). A final way in which the materiality of clothing has also come to the fore is through new writing about second-hand clothes either sold as garments (e.g. Hansen 2000) or in particular the implications of its materiality when it is shredded and remanufactured for resale (e.g. Norris forthcoming).

Perhaps even more surprising than the neglect of housing as something lived in and clothing as something worn has been the same lacuna with respect to the consumption of media. Given that while the consumption of clothing has not been seen as worthy of journalistic attention in its own right, the effects and consequences of the media are front-stage in so many discussions of contemporary society. Yet this concern only really arose with the development of audience research represented by figures such as Morley (1992) and Ang (1985). Once again, students of material culture have sought to broaden these changes by paying greater attention to the role of materiality in specific forms of media and the subsequent impact upon the creation of sociality. An example of this is Tacchi's (1998) work on the consumption of radio in the home. This is a particularly private activity, especially as she concentrated on single mothers and the quite personal relationship they feel with the radio. What Tacchi thereby demonstrated is how much media research requires this kind of encounter if it is to be serious about understanding consumption of the media. Increasingly globalization of the media may be matched by increasingly private consumption of the type highlighted by ethnographic studies of the media as material culture. The contrast is with more conventional media studies, where the tendency had been to reduce the study of consumption to the study of audiences. There are also important contributions from media studies that have concentrated on the materiality of particular media such as Manuel (1993) on the cassette and McCarthy (2001) on ambient television.

Given the close relationship between new studies in material culture and the wider concerns of anthropology, one of the consequences of applying a material culture perspective to the study of consumption has been the simultaneous application of anthropological relativism. In effect a quest to understand the specific consumption of an object is often most effectively addressed by demonstrating the diversity of that consumption. For example, faced with a general sense that a car is always just a car, there was very little attempt in mainstream anthropology to subject the car to relatavisitic perspectives. It is mainly through the material culture of its consumption that we start to appreciate that the car is not the same to Australian aboriginals (Young 2001) as it is to West African taxi drivers (Verrips and Meyer 2001) and this is partly because of the extensive transformations that tend to take place to the car itself.

These four examples – housing, clothes, the media and the car – suggest that the development of a material culture approach is one that helps tease out the specificity of consumption, and show that the materiality of each genre matters in its own right. That is to say, we can eschew technological determinism but still manage to consider the specific potentials of, for example, new computer technologies in the workplace (e.g. Garsten and Wulff 2003; Lally 2002) as against the marketing of sex aids (e.g. Storr 2003) or the way visitors respond to a particular design of museum display (e.g. Macdonald 2002). In turn ethnographic approaches do not reduce down to give sociological parameters such as gender and class. Rather we have material categories such as office workers using computers but becoming 'geeks' or teenagers that adopt a particular style and lifestyle to become 'goths' that cut across more conventional social parameters.

It would, however, be a pity to reduce this contribution to conventional categories of objects even if avoiding conventional categories of subjects. Much of the most recent and important work on the material culture of consumption has been more concerned with a series of theoretical and analytical contributions and concerns that apply to almost any such genre of materialized subject or personalized object. One of the most important themes to have developed and one that is likely to expand still further in the future develops from two trends in the material culture approach to consumption. On the one hand there has been a realization that, having had two decades which under the influence of Marxism emphasized the study of production followed by two decades that concentrated upon consumption, what is most needed today are approaches that emphasize the relationship between these two. There are many divergent approaches to this question. For example, Fine and Leopold (1993) argued for what they called vertical chains of integration by which the particular system of consumption of, for example, clothing or food was in large measure an outcome of the particular mode of production that pertained to the clothing industry or the food industry. Miller (1997) argued, by contrast, using the example of the soft drink industry, that there could be a surprising degree of autonomy in these various area, and consumption could not often be understood as a determinant of production. Various researchers at University College London have conducted Ph.D. theses intended to look more closely at this issue. For example O'Connor (2003) has shown the degree to which producers may fail to understand the nature of markets, such that production cannot be assumed to follow consumption, while others such as Petridou (2001) have emphasized the importance of the links in areas such as marketing and retail that tend to be neglected if we just concentrate upon production and consumption.

This approach then dovetails with another, in which the material culture aspect is paramount, since it follows from a strategy in which the object itself is acknowledged as that which unites often far-flung populations. This is commodity chain analysis, which has been developed particularly in human geography (see for example Leslie and Reimer 1999; Hughes and Reimer 2004). For example, a study of foodstuffs in Jamaica (Cook and Harrison 2003) may involve not just concern for the relationship to labour in production but needs to appreciate also the impact of consumption in the United Kingdom, the political economy of retail, and the various middlemen involved in areas such as transport and the treatment of the foods in between. The overriding point here is that it is the commodity that in effect produces the relationship both between itself and the various people who work with it but also the relationship between those people along the chain.

Ultimately there is a failure in education if we continue to live in a world in which in continuation of Marx's critique of fetishism we cannot see the patterns of labour and social relationships that link by link follow the various events through which goods create this chain between production and consumption. The material culture of consumption seems to be the ideal point of reference for engaging with the continued fetishism of the commodity, not only at a theoretical level (e.g. Spyer 1997) but also at the practical level of trying to consider what transformations in knowledge and production are required to make consumers acknowledge the products they purchase as among other things the embodiment of human labour (Miller 2003).

This moral issue of how to bring back our consciousness of the human element of consumption and its consequences takes us full circle to the initial accusation with which this chapter begun. This implied that consumption is an aspect of materialism that reduces our humanity by its focus upon the object. What we have seen is that, by contrast, it is precisely a material culture approach with its focus upon the object that helps us gain a much richer sense of humanity, one that is no longer divorced from its intrinsic materiality. This is why one of the most common points of affinity between material culture and social anthropology is Mauss's work on the gift, where the role of the object in the formation of social relations is paramount.

In many of the studies discussed here the same argument is made with regard to consumption. Shopping, for example, is transformed into an approach that allows us access to the technology of love, the way care and concern are expressed within the household (Miller 1998a; also Chin 2001; Gregson and Crewe 2002). An appeal is made to a commodity chain analysis in which the aim is to defetishize the commodity and show the human links that are created through capitalism, not to valorize them, but to acknowledge them and understand the responsibilities that arise when we benefit as consumers through low prices at the expense of others. One of the most poignant examples of the logic behind this material culture approach to understand how we constitute ourselves as humanity may be found in a study which balances the acquisition of objects with our relinquishing of objects. Layne (2000, 2002) focused upon women who had suffered from late foetal loss or stillbirth. She found that the main concern of the parents who had suffered such loss was to demonstrate that for them what had been lost was not simply a thing but a real person, a relation, a child. The most effective way they could achieve this constitution of their loss as that of a person was through the relationship with the things they had purchased in expectation of the birth and were therefore the possessions of the deceased: though their gradual separation from these objects and their continued inclusion of the lost individual in gifting, such as purchases of objects for what would have been their birthday, or on behalf of the dead for their own birthdays. They were able to constitute and then separate from those they had lost. What this study demonstrates is how a genuine material culture approach to consumption is one that starts from and ends with the understanding of humanity as enhanced rather than reduced by also recognizing its intrinsic materiality (Miller in press).

NOTES

1   This and the next two paragraphs are part of an argument that may be explored in more detail in Miller (in press).
2   Much of the above section is based on the selection of readings found in Miller (2001b).

BIBLIOGRAPHY

Akai, Tatsuro (1994) 'The common people and painting', in C. Nakane and S. Oishi (eds), *Tokugawa Japan*. Tokyo: University of Tokyo Press.

Ang, I. (1985) *Watching Dallas*. London: Methuen.

Appadurai, Arjun, ed. (1986) *The Social Life of Things*. Cambridge: Cambridge University Press.

Appelby, Joyce (1993) 'Consumption in early modern social thought', in John Brewer and Roy Porter (eds), *Consumption and the World of Goods*. London: Routledge, pp. 162–173.

Attfield, Judy (2000) *Wild Things*. Oxford: Berg.

Banerjee, M. and Miller, D. (2003) *The Sari*. Oxford: Berg.

Barthes, R. (1973) *Mythologies*. London: Paladin.

Bataille, G. (1988) *The Accursed Share*. New York: Zone Books.

Baudrillard, J. (1988) *Jean Baudrillard: Selected Writings*. Stanford, CA: Stanford University Press.

Bauman, Z. (1991) *Modernity and Ambivalence*. Cambridge: Polity Press.

Becker, G. (1996) *Accounting for Tastes*. Cambridge, MA: Harvard University Press.

Belk, Russell (1988) 'Possessions and the extended self', *Journal of Consumer Research*, 15: 139–68.

Belk, Russell (1993) 'Materialism and the making of the modern American Christmas', in Daniel Miller (ed.), *Unwrapping Christmas*. Oxford: Oxford University Press, pp. 75–104.

Birdwell-Pheasant, D. and Lawrence-Zúñiga, D., eds (1999) *House Life*. Oxford: Berg.

Bourdieu, P. (1979) *Distinction: a Social Critique of the Judgement of Taste*. London: Routledge.

Bowlby, R. (1993) *Shopping with Freud*. London: Routledge.

Braudel, F. (1981) *The Structures of Everyday Life*. London: Collins.

Breward, C. (1995) *The Culture of Fashion*. Manchester: Manchester University Press.

Buchli, V. (1999) *An Archaeology of Socialism*. Oxford: Berg.

Burke, Timothy (1996) *Lifebuoy Men, Lux Women*. Durham, NC: Duke University Press.

Campbell, C. (1986) *The Romantic Ethic and the Spirit of Modern Consumerism*. Oxford: Blackwell.

Carrier, J. (1995) *Gifts and Commodities*. London: Routledge.

Chevalier, S. (1998) 'From woollen carpet to grass carpet', in D. Miller (ed.), *Material Cultures. Why some Things Matter*. London: UCL Press.

Chin, E. (2001) *Purchasing Power: Black Kids and American Consumer Culture*. Minneapolis, MN: University of Minnesota Press.

Cieraad, I., ed. (1999) *At Home: An Anthropology of Domestic Space*. Syracuse, NY: Syracuse University Press.

Clarke, Alison (1999) *Tupperware: the Promise of Plastic in 1950's America*. Washington, DC: Smithsonian Institution Press.

Clarke, A. (2001) 'The aesthetics of social aspiration', in D. Miller (ed.), *Home Possessions*. Oxford: Berg, pp. 23–45.

Clarke, A. and Miller, D. (2002) 'Fashion and anxiety', *Fashion Theory*, 6: 1–24.

Clunas, Craig (1991) *Superfluous Things: Material Culture and Social Status in Early Modern China*. Cambridge: Polity Press, pp. 166–73.

Clunas, C. (1999) 'Modernity global and local: consumption and the rise of the West', *American History Review*, 104: 1497–511.

Cohn, Bernard (1989) 'Cloth, clothes and colonialism: India in the nineteenth century', in A. Weiner and J. Schneider (eds), *Cloth and Human Experience.* Washington, DC: Smithsonian University Press, pp. 312–21, 331–53.

Cook, I. and Harrison, M. (2003) 'Crossover food: rematerialising postcolonial geographies', *Transactions of the Institute of British Geographers,* 28 (3): 296–317.

Crocker, D. and Linden, T., eds (1998) *Ethics of Consumption: the Good Life, Justice, and Global Stewardship.* Lanham, MD: Rowman & Littlefield.

Cross, Gary (1993) *Time and Money: the Making of Consumer Culture.* London: Routledge.

Czikszentmihalyi, Mihaly (1993) 'Why we need things', in S. Lubar and W. Kingery (eds), *History from Things.* Washington, DC: Smithsonian Institution Press, pp. 20–9.

Dalby, L. (2001) *Kimono: Fashioning Culture.* New York: Random House.

Daniels, I. (2001) 'The "untidy" house in Japan', in D. Miller (ed.), *Home Possessions.* Oxford: Berg, pp. 201–29.

Davidson, J. (1999) *Courtesans and Fish Cakes: the Consuming Passions of Classical Athens.* London: Perennial.

Davis, Deborah, ed. (2000) *The Consumer Revolution in Urban China.* Los Angeles: University of California Press, pp. 1–22.

Douglas Mary (1992) 'Why do people want goods?' in S. Hargeaves and A. Ross (eds), *Understanding the Enterprise Culture.* Edinburgh: Edinburgh University Press, pp. 19–31.

Douglas, M. and Isherwood, B. (1979) *The World of Goods.* London: Allen Lane.

Dumont, L. (1972) *Homo Hierarchichus.* London: Paladin.

Etzioni, Amitai (1998) 'Voluntary simplicity: characterization, select psychological implications, and societal consequences', *Journal of Economic Psychology,* 19: 619–43.

Fine, B. (1995) 'From political economy to consumption', in D. Miller (ed.), *Acknowledging Consumption.* London: Routledge, pp. 127–63.

Fine, B. (1998) 'The triumph of economics; or "rationality" can be dangerous to your reasoning', in J. Carrier and D. Miller (eds) *Virtualism: a New Political Economy.* Oxford: Berg, pp. 49–74.

Fine, B. and Leopold, E. (1993) *The World of Consumption.* London: Routledge.

Foster, Robert (1995) 'Print advertisement and nation making in metropolitan Papua New Guinea', in R. Foster (ed.), *Nation Making: Emergent Identities in Postcolonial Melanesia.* Ann Arbor, MI: University of Michigan Press, pp. 151–81.

Fournier, S. (1998) 'Consumers and their brands: developing relationship theory in consumer research', *Journal of Consumer Research,* 24: 343–73.

Freeman, C. (2000) *High Tech and High Heels in the Global Economy.* Durham, NC: Duke University Press.

Furlough, E. and Strikwerda, C. (eds) (1999) *Consumers Against Capitalism? Consumer Cooperation in Europe, North America and Japan 1840–1990.* Lanham, MD: Rowman and Littlefield.

Garsten, C. and Wulff, H., eds (2003) *New Technologies at Work.* Oxford: Berg.

Garvey, P. (2001) 'Organised disorder: moving furniture in Norwegian homes', in D. Miller (ed.), *Home Possessions.* Oxford: Berg, pp. 47–68.

Gell, Alfred (1986) 'Newcomers to the world of goods; consumption among the Muria Gonds', in Arjun Appadurai (ed.), *The Social Life of Things.* Cambridge: Cambridge University Press, pp. 110–38.

Goodwin, N., Ackerman, F. and Kiron, D., eds (1997) *The Consumer Society.* Washington, DC: Island Press.

Gortz, A. (1982) *Farewell to the Working Class.* London: Pluto Press.

Gregson, N. and Crewe, L. (2002) *Second Hand Worlds.* Oxford: Berg.

Gullestad, M. (1985) *Kitchen-Table Society.* Oslo: Universitetsforlaget.

Gunilla, Andrae and Beckman, Bjorn (1985) Introduction to *The Wheat Trap: Bread and Underdevelopment in Nigeria.* London: Zed Books, pp. 1–12.

Hansen, K.T. (2000) *Salaula: the World of Second Hand Clothing and Zambia.* Chicago: University of Chicago Press.

Hebdige, D. (1981) 'Towards a cartography of taste, 1935–1962', *Block,* 4: 39–56.

Hebdige, D. (1988) 'Object as image: the Italian scooter cycle', in *Hiding in the Light: On Images and Things.* London: Comedia, pp. 77–115.

Heinze, Andrew (1990) 'From scarcity to abundance: the immigrant as consumer', in *Adapting to Abundance.* New York: Columbia University Press, pp. 33–48.

Henare, A. (in press) 'Nga Aho Tipuna (ancestral threads): Maori cloaks from New Zealand', in S. Küchler and D. Miller (eds), *Clothing as Material Culture.* Oxford: Berg.

Holt, Douglas (1998) 'Does cultural capital structure American consumption?' *Journal of Consumer Research,* 25 (1): 1–25.

Horowitz Daniel (1985) *The Morality of Spending: Attitudes towards the Consumer Society in America, 1875–1940.* Baltimore, MD: Johns Hopkins University Press, pp. 1–8.

Hughes, and Reimer, L. (2004) *Geographies of Commodity Chains.* London: Routledge.

James, Jeffrey (1993) 'Positional goods, conspicuous consumption and the international demonstration effect reconsidered', in J. James, *Consumption and Development.* London: Macmillan, pp. 111–46.

Klein, N. (2001) *No Logo.* London: Flamingo.

Küchler, S. (in press) 'Why are there quilts in Polynesia?' in S. Küchler and D. Miller (eds), *Clothing as Material Culture.* Oxford: Berg.

Lally, E. (2002) *At Home with Computers*. Oxford: Berg.

Lancaster, K. (1966) 'A new approach to consumer theory', *Journal of Political Economy*, 74: 132–57.

Lasch, C. (1979) *The Culture of Narcissism*. New York: Norton.

Layne, L. (2000) 'He was a real baby with baby things', *Journal of Material Culture*, 5: 321–45.

Layne, L. (2002) *Motherhood Lost*. New York: Routledge.

Lebergott, S. (1993) *Pursuing Happiness: American Consumers in the Twentieth Century*. Princeton: Princeton University Press.

Leslie, D. and Reimer, S. (1999) 'Spatializing commodity chains', *Progress in Human Geography*, 23: 401–20.

Lévi-Strauss, C. (1972) *The Savage Mind*. London: Weidenfeld & Nicolson.

Lunt, P. (1995) 'Psychological approaches to consumption', in D. Miller (ed.), *Acknowledging Consumption*. London: Routledge, pp. 238–63.

Macdonald, S. (2002) *Behind the Scenes at the Science Museum*. Oxford: Berg.

Manuel, P. (1993) *Cassette Culture*. Chicago: University of Chicago Press.

Marcoux, J.-S. (2001) 'The refurbishment of memory', in D. Miller (ed.), *Home Possessions*. Oxford: Berg, pp. 69–86.

Marcuse, H. (1964) *One-dimensional Man: Studies in the Ideology of Advanced Industrial Society*. London: Routledge.

McCarthy, A. (2001) *Ambient Television*. Chapel Hill, NC: Duke University Press.

McCracken, G. (1988a) *Culture and Consumption*. Bloomington, IN: Indiana University Press.

McCracken, Grant (1988b) 'Diderot unities and the Diderot effects', in *Culture and Consumption*. Bloomington, IN: Indiana University Press, pp. 118–29.

McHeyman, Josiah (1997) 'Imports and standards of justice on the Mexico-United States border', in B. Orlove (ed.), *The Allure of the Foreign: Imported Goods in Postcolonial Latin America*. Ann Arbor, MI: University of Michigan Press, pp. 151–83.

McKendrick, N., Brewer, J. and Plumb, J. (1983) *The Birth of a Consumer Society*. London: Hutchinson.

Meskell, L. (2004) *Object Worlds in Ancient Egypt*. Oxford: Berg.

Miller, Daniel (1987) *Material Culture and Mass Consumption*. Oxford: Blackwell.

Miller, Daniel, ed. (1995) *Acknowledging Consumption: a Review of New Studies*. London: Routledge.

Miller, Daniel (1997) 'Coca-cola: a black sweet drink from Trinidad', in D. Miller (ed.), *Material Cultures*. London: UCL Press and Chicago: University of Chicago Press, pp. 169–187.

Miller, D. (1998a) *A Theory of Shopping*. Cambridge: Polity Press.

Miller, D. (1998b) 'A theory of virtualism', in James Carrier and Daniel Miller (eds), *Virtualism: a New Political Economy*. Oxford: Berg.

Miller, D., ed. (2001a) *Home Possessions*. Oxford: Berg.

Miller, D., ed. (2001b) *Consumption*, 4 vols. London: Routledge.

Miller, D. (2003) 'Could the Internet de-fetishise the commodity?' *Environment and Planning D: Society and Space*, 21 (3): 359–72.

Miller, D., ed. (in press) *Materiality*. Durham, NC: Duke University Press.

Miller, D. and Slater, D. (2000) *The Internet: an Ethnographic Approach*. Oxford: Berg.

Miller, P. and Rose, N. (1997) 'Mobilizing the consumer: assembling the subject of consumption', *Theory Culture and Society*, 14: 1–36.

Mintz, S. (1985) *Sweetness and Power*. New York: Viking.

Morley, David (1992) 'The gendered framework of family viewing', in *Television Audiences and Cultural Studies*. London: Routledge, pp. 138–58.

Mort, F. (1996) *Cultures of Consumption*. London: Routledge.

Mukerji, Chandra (1983) *From Graven Images: Patterns of Modern Materialism*. New York: Columbia University Press.

Munn, N. (1986) *The Fame of Gawa*. Cambridge: Cambridge University Press.

Nixon, S. (1996) *Hard Looks: Masculinities, Spectatorship and Contemporary Consumption*. London: UCL Press.

Norris, L. (forthcoming) *The Secret Afterlife of Clothing in India*.

O'Connor, K. (2003) 'Lycra, Babyboomers and the Immaterial Culture of the new Midlife'. Ph.D. thesis, University College, London.

Osella, Filippo and Osella, Caroline (1999) 'From transience to immanence: consumption, life-cycle and social mobility in Kerala, South India', *Modern Asian Studies*, 33, 989–1020.

Pendergrast, M. (1999) *Uncommon Grounds*. New York: Basic Books.

Perrotta, C. (1997) 'The preclassical theory of development: increased consumption raises productivity', *History of Political Economy*, 29 (2): 295–326.

Petridou, E. (2001) 'Milk Ties: a Commodity Chain Approach to Greek Culture'. Ph.D. thesis, University College, London.

Pomeranz, K. (2000) *The Great Divergence*. Princeton, NJ: Princeton University Press.

Porter, R. (1993) 'Consumption: disease of the consumer society', in J. Brewer and R. Porter (eds), *Consumption and the World of Goods*. London: Routledge, pp. 58–81.

Preteceille, E. and Terrail, J.-P. (1985) *Capitalism, Consumption and Needs*. Oxford: Blackwell.

Pyburn, A. (1998) 'Consuming the Maya' *Journal of Dialectical Anthropology*, 23: 111–29.

Ritzer, G. (2004) *The McDonaldization of Society*. London: Sage.

Sahlins, D.M. (1976) *Culture and Practical Reason*. Chicago: University of Chicago Press.

Savage, M., Barlow, J., Dickens, P. and Fielding, T. (1992) *Property, Bureaucracy and Culture*. London: Routledge.

Schama, S. (1987) *The Embarrassment of Riches*. London: Fontana.

Schor, J. (1991) *The Overworked American: the Unexpected Decline of Leisure*. New York: Basic Books.

Schor, J. (1998) *The Overspent American*. New York: HarperPerennial.

Sekora, John (1977) *Luxury: the Concept in Western Thought, Eden to Smollett*. Baltimore, MD: Johns Hopkins University Press, pp. 29–39.

Sen, Amartya (1998) 'The living standard', in David Crocker and Toby Linden (eds), *Ethics of Consumption: the Good Life, Justice, and Global Stewardship*. Lanham, MD: Rowman & Littlefield, pp. 287–311.

Sennett, R. (1977) *The Fall of Public Man*. New York: Knopf.

Shammas, Carole (1993) 'Changes in English and Anglo-American consumption from 1550–1800', in John Brewer and Roy Porter (eds), *Consumption and the World of Goods*. London: Routledge, pp. 177–205.

Sherry, J. and McGrath, M. (1989) 'Unpacking the holiday presence: a comparative ethnography of two Midwestern American gift stores', in E. Hirschman (ed.), *Interpretive Consumer Research*. Provo UE: Association for Consumer Research, pp. 148–167.

Simmel, Georg (1978) 'Culture and the quantitative increase in material culture', in *The Philosophy of Money*. London: Routledge, pp. 446–50.

Slater, Don (1997) *Consumer Culture and Modernity*. Cambridge: Polity Press.

Spyer, P., ed. (1997) *Border Fetishisms: Material Objects in Unstable Places*. London: Routledge.

Storr, M. (2003) *Latex and Lingerie*. Oxford: Berg.

Summers, L. (2001) *Bound to Please*. Oxford: Berg.

Tacchi, J. (1998) 'Radio texture: between self and others', in D. Miller (ed.), *Material Cultures*. Chicago: University of Chicago Press, pp. 25–45.

Thompson, E.P. (1978) *The Poverty of Theory and other Essays*. London: Merlin Press.

Veblen, T. (1899/1979) *The Theory of the Leisure Class*. Harmondsworth: Penguin Books, pp. 22–34.

Verrips, J. and Meyer, B. (2001) 'Kwaku's car: the struggles and stories of a Ghanaian long-distance taxi-driver', in D. Miller (ed.), *Car Cultures*. Oxford: Berg, pp. 153–84.

Wallerstein, I. (2000) *The Essential Wallerstein*. New York: New Press.

Warde, A. (1994) 'Consumption, identity-formation and uncertainty', *Sociology*, 28: 877–98.

Warde, A. (1997) *Consumption, Food and Taste*. London: Sage.

Weismantel, M. (1988) *Food, Gender and Poverty in the Ecuadorian Andes*. Philadelphia, PA: Pennsylvania University Press.

Weiss, B. (1996a) 'Coffee breaks and coffee connections: the lived experience of a commodity in Tanzanian and European worlds', in D. Howes (ed.), *Cross-cultural Consumption: Global Markets, Local Realities*. London: Routledge, pp. 93–105.

Weiss, B. (1996b) *The Making and Unmaking of the Haya Lived World*. Durham, NC: Duke University Press.

Wilk, R. (1995) 'Learning to be local in Belize: global systems of common difference', in D. Miller (ed.), *Worlds Apart: Modernity through the Prism of the Local*. London: Routledge.

Woodward, S. (2005) 'Looking good – feeling right: aesthetics of the self', in S. Küchler and D. Miller (eds), *Clothing as Material Culture*. Oxford: Berg, pp. 21–39.

Yan, Yunxiang (1997) 'McDonald's in Beijing: the localization of Americana', in James Watson (ed.), *Golden Arches East*. Stanford, CA: Stanford University Press, pp. 37–66.

Young, D. (2001) 'The life and death of cars: private vehicles on the Pitjanjatara lands, South Australia', in D. Miller (ed.), *Car Cultures*. Oxford: Berg, pp. 35–58.

23

STYLE, DESIGN, AND FUNCTION

Margaret W. Conkey

How can one address these three topics – style, design and function – in a single chapter? Of course they are interrelated; perhaps one cannot really discuss one without both of the others? How can there be style without a function? How can there be style without design and design conventions? These three entangled concepts have been core concepts, but with a variable history of use and centrality in our study of material culture. They have been addressed in a multiplicity of ways, and have been both responsive to and, less frequently, defining of many shifts in material culture theory and interpretation over the past century or more. The primary players in the study and uses of style and design have been art historians and, within anthropology, archaeologists. Social and cultural anthropology has been less concerned with such concepts, if only because their engagement with the material world of human life has been notably erratic, coming to some fruition and promise primarily in the past few decades.

The main objective of this chapter is to provide historical perspectives on how design and style have been used in the study of material culture, especially within an anthropological and cultural framework. I will suggest that this history has been directly influenced by shifting anthropological approaches to the study of both technology and 'art'. These trends have also directly impacted the place and understandings of the function(s) of material culture. I will conclude with just a few of the social and cultural insights that have been generated through the study of design and style, with particular reference to recent studies of cloth.

Although there has been an impressive 'turn' to the object world in the past two decades, the social scientists who study material culture have primarily been concerned with the *relationships* between people and things, more so than in the things themselves. Thus, it is not surprising to see fewer studies of design and style than might be expected with this new materiality. As the title of Sillitoe's (1988) article says so succinctly, our concerns have shifted 'from [the] head-dress to head-messages', and Ingold (2004) has expressed concern that we have often lost the material in our studies of materiality. Additionally, recent studies have also been more focused on how objects construct and express social identities without, however, simply referring to these as the functions of the objects. This is primarily because the studies have simultaneously been concerned with the social practices in which objects are embedded, and, in a quite new direction, with 'the dynamics of recontextualization, valuation and reinterpretation they (objects) undergo along their trajectories through different cultural and historical contexts' (Leite 2004). In a way, objects today are more 'on the move' and 'in circulation'; they are not standing still long enough, perhaps, for a more traditional (and often static?) stylistic analysis, functional interpretation and/or capturing of principles of design. As Wobst says so succinctly in his important reassessment of his own very influential work on style (Wobst 1977), style 'never quite gets there', it 'never stays'. It is 'always in contest, in motion, unresolved, discursive, in process' (Wobst 1999: 130).

While the *trajectories* of material culture and objects have been revealed and inferred with new theoretical perspectives (e.g., Appadurai 1986; Kopytoff 1986; Thomas 1991; Miller 1998; Spyer 1998; Phillips and Steiner 1999;

Myers 2001), there has also been a theoretical trajectory of material culture studies themselves within anthropology and related fields, including an important new kind of connection between sociocultural anthropology/ethnography and archaeology (Brumfiel 2003). These often mutual dialogues may perhaps best be seen in the approaches to the study of 'technology' (see Eglash in Chapter 21 or in Dobres and Hoffman 1999), and to the study of 'art' or image making. Intra- and interdisciplinary connections may also be heightened by the current widespread recognition, and perhaps growing importance in our globalized worlds, of the increased value and power of objects from the past or from 'the other' (e.g., Hobsbawm and Ranger 1983; Lowenthal 1985; Handler 1988; Price 1989), especially in the creation and support of national and other political identities and negotiations. Although this chapter will dwell more on the anthropological trends, concerns and accomplishments, it goes without saying that the re-engagement with the object world has been strikingly – but not surprisingly – interdisciplinary; just note the 'disciplines' represented by the authors of articles in the *Journal of Material Culture* (Leite 2004).

One reason to focus primarily on the anthropological approaches to material culture and the object world is because anthropology has had an erratic history, an on-again/off-again, often distancing relationship with 'things'. This makes for a interesting inquiry into why it was distanced and then re-engaged: what are the theoretical or disciplinary influences or promoters of such re-engagement that might yield insights into the field of material culture studies? There will also be a tendency toward the anthropological here because anthropological inquiry distinctively balances (or tries to) two dimensions: on the one hand, the local-level, small-scale studies using most often (in ethnography and ethnoarchaeology) the participant observation method. On the other hand, anthropology attempts a holism that prefers to not take separate slices of the cultural 'pie' but to understand the intersectionalities and situatedness of human life, behaviors and meanings in an as-complete-as-possible social and cultural context (after Pfaffenberger 1988: 245), That is, the very multi-scalar nature of the anthropological enterprise allows us to consider the material world and objects at multiple scales as well. And, as many recent studies have shown, this is precisely one fascination and excitement of material culture studies at the turn of the twenty first century.

SOMETHING OF A HISTORICAL OVERVIEW

Of course, Franz Boas (1927, see also Jonaitis 1995) is usually the anthropological baseline for the study of objects and 'primitive art', although contemporary material culture studies today would go back to major theorists of culture (e.g., Marx, Veblen, Simmel). Even though Boas's (1927) chapter 5 was on 'style', anthropologists usually trace their roots in the study of style to Kroeber (e.g., 1919, 1957) and the art historical roots to scholars such as Wölfflin (1932; see also Gombrich 1960; Saüerlander 1983). Lemonnier (1993b: 7) identified the 1930s as the period when there is a noticeable decline in an interest in material culture; it was only in France, he points out, that an institutionalized study of the anthropology of techniques took hold. Thus, the work of Mauss (e.g., 1935) on *techniques du corps* as well as his more well known study *The Gift* (1967/1925) may provide an important bridge between this time period and what would become, by the 1980s, an increasingly robust field of technology studies (e.g. Lemonnier 1986, 1993a; Pfaffenberger 1988, among many; see Eglash, Chapter 21 in this volume). Lemonnier notes (1986: 181 n. 3) that in one valiant attempt at recuperating the anthropological study of material culture, Reynolds (1983) astutely 'marvels justly at the immediate disinterest of ethnologists for the objects they confer on museums as soon as they are deposited'.

This is not to say, though, that within this so-called 'gap' there was little being done; it's just not of major focus in an anthropology of objects that is waiting backstage for certain trends to pass on and for the curtain to be opened on to a more robust engagement with the object world. First, archaeology does not really experience a gap, but this is not surprising, given its dependence on material culture. However, despite the momentum established with the rise of the so-called New (or processual) Archaeology with its emphasis on understanding the nature and significance of variability in the archaeological record (Binford 1962, 1965), and the studies that linked stylistic attributes to social phenomena (e.g., Hill 1970, Longacre 1970 and chapters in Binford and Binford 1968), the primary flurry of archaeological discussion and debate on style, for example, came in the two decades between 1970 and 1990. In fact, if we look for review or overview articles on the concepts, use, and study of 'style', for example, these are primarily (only?) in archaeology (e.g., Plog 1983; Hegmon 1992; Conkey 1990; Boast 1997;

Wobst 1999) and in art history (e.g. Schapiro 1953; Saüerlander 1983; Davis 1990).

However, with some notable exceptions, archaeological studies of style, design, function, material culture and technology can be said to share with other approaches the general characteristic that they have tended to look primarily (and sometimes only) at the *effects* of material culture systems (style, design, technology) *on* culture or society or, more often, to look primarily for what/how/why humans *communicate* with material culture and artifacts. That this has changed as a primary approach will be considered below, and a notable early exception, at least in regard to technologies, would be the pioneering work by Heather Lechtman (1977) that identifies and illustrates the concept of 'technological style' (see also Lechtman 1984; Dobres and Hoffman 1994; Stark 1999; Dobres 2000), that is, that the technologies, materials and making of objects themselves have 'style'.

In cultural anthropology, the development of structuralism (e.g., in Lévi-Strauss 1963) brought forth a spate of material culture studies (e.g., Fernandez 1966; Munn 1966; Faris 1972; Adams 1973), which linked objects and other dimensions of culture. Semiotic approaches, broadly speaking, were also being developed (e.g., Forge 1966; 1970; Munn 1973) stressing how fundamental concepts could be visibly encoded in artifacts, objects and art. In fact, there was a notably renewed interest in the 'anthropology of art' (e.g., edited volumes by Jopling 1971 and Otten 1971a). In each of these volumes, for example, the editor has brought together articles primarily dating to the 1950s and 1960s, suggesting that the so-called 'gap' is one of quantity and attention, not complete absence. Otten (1971b) suggests that the renewed engagement with art was stimulated by the then current interests in the nature and evolution of human communication and in the approach to culture as a human value system. A key paper in 1969 that signaled an emergent engagement with an anthropologically more productive approach to material culture would be that by Ucko on penis sheaths. His concern 'was to unite the social and technological approaches to the study of material culture such that a detailed examination of the material object would lead to information about the non-material aspects of the producing culture' (MacKenzie 1991: 23).

However, as will be discussed further below, the ways in which anthropologists now view 'art' and how to study it – as a (problematic) 'category' of the material world – have

shifted since this 1970s reappearance on the anthropological stage (e.g., Sparshott 1997; Gell 1998; Townsend-Gault 1998; Graburn 2001). By the 1990s anthropological studies of art (despite many differing definitions), nonetheless 'become more numerous and informed by theoretical concerns such as gender and colonialism (Morphy 1991; Thomas 1991)' (Cannizzo 1996: 54). Of course, this is not the first appearance of a theoretically informed approach, but the theoretical approaches now at hand are ones that do more than look only at the effects of the objects and forms (whether they are called 'art' or not) on culture or society. This itself derives from 'a revival of interest in material culture as exegesis and evidence' (Cannizzo 1996: 54). With the wider developments in the study of material culture, 'things' and/or representations have been shown to be *crucial* to the articulation of debates on gender, power relations, colonialism, exchange, possession, consumption, tourism, perceptual knowledge, and more (after Townsend-Gault 1998: 427).

Thus, while one would be hard-pressed to find, in the cultural anthropological literature, many (or any?) overviews that summarize the state of approaches to and understandings of the study of style and design, much less the relationships to function, there is a burgeoning literature both on the anthropology of 'art' and, even more so, on the anthropology of material culture, which, perhaps like technology, has fortunately become less likely to be taken as a given and lacking intrinsic value (as Pfaffenberger suggests in 1988 for the anthropology of technology).

ABOVE ALL, THERE IS STYLE

Even a brief survey of the literature will confirm that the subject of 'style' is the most prominent of our three concepts to be treated on its own, with individual articles (e.g., Plog 1983; Hegmon 1992), especially in archaeology and art history, or as an important subheading in a review article (e.g., in Silver 1979; Schneider 1987). Recall that Kroeber considered 'Style' to be important enough to warrant its own chapter in his *Anthropology Today* volume (Schapiro 1953), even though the author is an art historian, not an anthropologist. Although there are fine studies that focus on design (e.g., Schevill 1985; Washburn 1977), 'design' and 'function' are not likely to be individual headings or topics to be covered in encyclopedias of anthropology or the social sciences. For many, style itself is methodologically taken as a set of 'design conventions' or 'formal attributes'. There are no major volumes addressing the concept and theory of design or function, but such do exist for 'style' (e.g., Conkey and Hastorf 1990; Carr and Nietzel 1995). Yet, most discussions of style almost inevitably engage with design or aspects of it. So many studies of material culture are concerned with function(s), even if the authors prefer a more complex understanding of the use(s), context(s) and significance(s) of material objects or forms. Assessments of style are usually in agreement that style is a central concept in any analyses of the material world; 'style is involved in all archaeological analysis' (Conkey and Hastorf 1990: 1).

Yet to take this foundational concept apart is a major historical and epistemological endeavor. At one level, it is a 'self-evident' concept (after Gadamer 1965: 466, cited by Sauerländer 1983: 253), but few seem to be able to agree on what it 'means'. For many studies up to the 1960s, style was taken as some sort of a 'key' that made cultural materials accessible to us, and in some sort of cultural ways. This was especially the case in archaeological studies, as the understandings and delineations of style were usually the foundation on which typologies and classifications were constructed. And, until the 1960s, at least in Anglo-American archaeologies, classifications and typologies, as well as their use in defining 'culture areas', were absolutely originary in any understandings of culture and culture history. With interpretive goals more focused on establishing chronologies and on tracing interactions, influences and pathways of diffusion, style was a crucial component of any culture historian's repertoire.

This entire chapter could be taken up with the relatively recent history (post-1960s) of the concepts and uses of style, especially as they have been the subject of definitional debates and reworkings by archaeologists alone (e.g., Plog 1983; Hegmon 1992; Carr and Nietzel 1995; Boast 1997; Conkey 1990; Wobst 1999). Perhaps this is because of the archaeological dilemma – or challenge – in the study of the material world, given the absence of informants and often, the absence of texts or other documents. Perhaps it is because of greater dependence upon providing a plausible and compelling 'reading' of the material record. Or perhaps it is because archaeologists have long been concerned with both epistemological and ontological premises and practices. It was not until the 1960s that archaeologists really began to 'push' with style – into an arena whereby more social and cultural inferences were attempted and sought, using style and design. The inferences of interest were now at a more refined scale than the general ebb and flow of 'cultures'. One might say that this was the time when style was seen as a 'key' to the social, and it was the social that was of particular interest.

These 1960s were the heady days of suggesting such things as how we could reveal postmarital residence practices using distributional patterns of variation in ceramic designs both within and between sites, assuming that mothers taught the designs to their daughters. As is now well documented, many of these early 'ceramic sociology' projects (e.g., Deetz 1965; Hill 1970; Longacre 1970) had problematic assumptions (e.g., Stanislawski 1969, 1973; Friedrich 1970). And, as Graves (1998) details so well, there were numerous precursors in such design and stylistic analyses in the US Southwest. Nonetheless, they set into motion core debates about what style measures, what it reflects, or can be used for in archaeological interpretations, as well as what the relationship between style and function was all about (e.g., Sackett 1982; Dunnell 1978). Style, well into the 1980s, was often taken to be (in what we now see as rather depersonalized and objectifying jargon) one aspect of coded information about variability in the functioning of past cultural systems.

In his 1979 review of 'Ethnoart', Silver is one of the relatively rare cultural anthropologists to address the topic of 'Style' under its own heading (but see in Layton 1991: 150–92, an entire chapter on 'Style' in a text on the anthropology of art). Silver noted the two problems of style for the social scientist, with its definition being one. But, unlike for most archaeologists, the definition of style is not the problem he will address explicitly. Rather, he prefers to wrestle with the problem of the relationship between art styles and the civilizations that produce them (Silver 1979: 270). He recognizes style as being operative at different levels, and refers the reader to Bascom's (1969) systematic overview for types of style. Silver's own preference is to consider the general theoretical approaches that would link style to its 'civilization': diffusion and evolution (e.g., Munro 1963); style, psyche and civilization (e.g., Bunzel 1927; Kroeber 1957); and the cross-cultural approach (e.g., Fischer 1961; Barry 1957; Wolfe 1969). As is evidenced in other cultural anthropological approaches to style (e.g., Schneider 1987), Silver comfortably accepts and works with the 'intensive' treatment of the concept of style put forth by art historian

Schapiro (1953) in Kroeber's *Anthropology Today*. Layton's (1991: 150) introductory text also follows Schapiro. Other studies (e.g., Van Wyck 2003) never define 'style' or 'design' but assume it.

In concluding his section on style, Silver anticipates what we see today were perhaps the two major dimensions that characterize the concern with style in the 1970s and 1980s, no matter what the field or sub-field. First is the emergent recognition that, while a style may be conveying 'considerable information about its producers and their culture', there is not yet a firm differentiation between the audiences to whom this information is being conveyed: to the other members of the cultural group under consideration or to the anthropologists who are using the style to infer information (see also the Sackett-Wiessner debate in Sackett 1985)? This query, as phrased in the information theory jargon that Silver also anticipates, would be 'To whom is the style signaling, and what is it signaling?' (e.g., Sterner 1989). Thus, the second dimension to the study of style at this time was the convergence of thinking about style in anthropological contexts with the parallel developments in information theory and linguistic metaphors for the interpretation of culture. In the 1970s and 1980s, for example, it would have been hard to miss the idea that style in material culture was transmitting information (for the classic expression of this, see Wobst 1977), an approach that has not disappeared but only, perhaps, become more nuanced (e.g., Van Wyck 2003). Not surprisingly, more recent studies of material culture – its styles, designs and functions – have challenged (or eschewed) the primacy of the linguistic and language metaphors (e.g., artifact as text), and a somewhat bald communication approach (e.g., McCracken 1988; Dietler and Herbich 1989; Conkey 1990: 10–11; MacKenzie 1991: 24–5; Gell 1998; Stahl 2002).

THE STORY OF STYLE, BRINGING ALONG DESIGN AND FUNCTION

It seems that there have been two recent trends in the study of style that followed the foundational uses of style by culture historians. At first, there were those who considered style explicitly and definitionally and who therefore set out specific concerns: how to analyze style, where to locate style in specific objects or forms; what, in fact, is stylistic variation (e.g., Plog 1983)? Are there different classifications or types of style (e.g., Bascom 1969, Plog 1983)? Does style have any function or is style a primary way to 'do' certain cultural things, such as communicate, negotiate, or reinforce ethnicity or identities? Can we use style to classify different so-called 'cultures' and to chart them through space and time?

The second trend has been either to not worry about any definitions of or specific analytical methods for the study of style and just assume it, and go on to other anthropological questions, or to reconceptualize style completely. Two innovative and intriguing approaches here would be Wobst's (1999) notion of style as 'interventions', or Wilk's (1995, 2004) concept of 'common difference'. As well, some other theoretical trends, such as the uses of practice theory, have implications for concepts, such as that of 'traditions', which have long been rooted in concepts of style (e.g., Lightfoot 2001). Let us first turn to one summary historical account, starting with the foundational culture history approaches and then move to consider 'what's new?'

As noted above, style became rooted in anthropological analyses with the culture historical approaches of the 1930s to 1960s, approaches that have not really gone away. To culture historians (e.g., Kreiger 1944) style was in the service of chronology and the typologies that were developed to order the material world were explicitly time-sensitive. For both art history and anthropology, 'stilus' (style) and 'chronos' (time) would intersect (Sauerländer 1983). Style was a self-evident concept upon which historical understandings were based. Archaeologists, at least, still depend upon the products of the culture-history approach and its concept and uses of style: the past, and even 'other cultures' ethnographically, are often divided into spatial and temporal units with labels and these, in turn, have allowed the construction of unquestioned periodizations (e.g., the Mesolithic) that are based on and thus privilege certain tools, technologies, 'styles' of ceramics or of other materials.

The ethnographic study of 'things' was somehow delegated or fell to the museological world, which had similar concerns to diligently catalog material objects, with, perhaps, an overemphasis on the form of the objects, with function or context infrequently of consideration. With such approaches, there are elegant typologies and closely honed studies of the formal relationships among the material objects themselves, but, in general, 'the artefact becomes recontextualized as an object of scientific analysis within a Western discourse, and its meaning is divorced from its origin as an indigenous product' (MacKenzie 1991: 23). Style has continued to be a specific analytical tool but beyond just to locate social units and to chart them through time and space or in order to organize objects in museums. Style was used to infer, measure or inform on more specific social and cultural processes, such as social interaction (e.g., Friedrich 1970) and social exchange (see Plog 1978 for a review). In archaeology, at least, the debates were more about what the given 'formal variation' that is style referred to or derived from.

There seem not to be many debates these days about how to 'measure' style, where to 'locate' style, or the function(s) of style. On the one hand, some have suggested two dismissive directions: Boast (1997) is ready to get rid of style; it is 'not a meaningful analytical category in the hermeneutic account of social action' that he outlines (Boast 1997: 189). Or, according to many (but not all) contributors to one edited volume (Lorblanchet and Bahn 1993), we have moved into what they call the 'post-stylistic era', at least in the study of rock art. This is attributed not so much to any new theoretical frameworks, but to such things as more viable dating techniques, pigment studies, and questions that go beyond establishing artistic chronologies based on mere stylistic impressions (Lorblanchet 1990: 20). This is a reaction to the persistence of how 'stilus' and 'chronos' have intersected; how chronologies have been all too unquestionably based on assumed notions and identifications of style. Some studies explicitly refuse to produce a chronological scheme based on changes in style, which had led previous researchers away from careful study of the content of images or 'arts' (e.g., Garlake 1995).

On the other hand, perhaps ironically, there is something of a return to some of the more culture-historical understandings of style and variation in material culture, and a less programmatic approach to the uses and concepts of style. First, the very general idea of style as being 'a way of doing' has reappeared (e.g., Wiessner 1990, but contrast with Hodder 1990), if it ever really went away. This, however, is a notion that is much more complex than a passive normativism that perhaps prevailed in traditional culture-historical studies. Style is taken now as 'a way of doing' but also as something more than that; style is part of the means by which humans make sense of their world and with which cultural meanings are always in production.

To a certain extent, these approaches, concerns, new labels and even dismissals actually signal

a continued engagement with 'style' – how could we ever *not* work with aspects of variation in material culture that are produced in and constitutive of human cultural and social life? These trends are a quiet way of rethinking style, and of framing it within new theoretical approaches (e.g., practice theory, culture-as-production, technological and operational choices, communities of practice), new methodological possibilities (e.g., chronometric dating techniques), and richer and more nuanced understandings of material culture, of humans as being simultaneously symbolists and materialists, and of the 'social life of things' (e.g., Appadurai 1986). But, once again, there is no one comprehensive theory of style, nor a call for one; neither is there a specific analytic tool kit that one can just pick up and apply to a set of things.

This is not, however, to abandon discussion and suggestions for how to use some understandings about style in the study of material culture. Taking the extreme approach of Boast (1997), for example, one could argue that he is not really dismissing style completely, but, rather, critiquing that the past uses of the concept of style have perpetuated the Cartesian boundaries between humans and objects, 'between the active *us* from an inactive *its*' (1997: 190; see also, he suggests, Latour 1992 and Akrich 1992). He is not alone in arguing for a different and more 'active' or agential dimension to objects, images and things (e.g., Gell 1998). He is also suggesting that a concept of style is 'dependent upon a specific set of assumptions about how the social world works' with 'little conceptual use beyond a vernacular distinction between social forms distinguished within a consumerist society' (Boast 1997: 190, 191). Both concerns are worth discussion; some of us can readily accept the first but perhaps not the second. In any event, such ideas have found their way from Boast and from other authors into contemporary debates and studies (e.g., for discussions and critique of Gell's agency theory of art, see in Pinney and Thomas 2001 or Layton 2003).

So what's new? Here again, although the focus is on style, it is not really possible to avoid inquiries into function and studies of design. First, there are several intriguing new ways of conceptualizing 'style', and I mention only two here. In the long awaited update from Wobst (1999) concerning his contemporary thoughts about 'style' now that we are some twenty-five years from his paradigm-setting paper of 1977, he embraces style more ambitiously and enthusiastically: style is that aspect of our material world that talks and interferes in the social field (1999: 125); 'stylistic form on artifacts interferes materially *with humans*' (p. 120, emphasis his). Since his original view stressed the communicative functions of style, style as 'messaging' through especially visible features, Wobst reports now on his 'mellowed functionalism' (1999: 124). He takes up Giddens's notion of enstructuration, which 'allows for contemporaneous social actors to arrive at different optimal solutions (even in the same social context), something that is very difficult to accommodate in many of the overly functionalist paradigms' (Wobst 1999: 125). He elaborates as to how even the most obvious and apparent functional aspects of an object (such as the working edge of a tool) are inseparably interwoven with social dynamics; after all, these functional features themselves help 'constitute, constrain or alter the social field' (1999: 126). Lastly, his discussion on the deeply problematic implications of the effects of certain long-standing methodological approaches to style, especially in archaeology, is particularly provocative, although substantive consideration here is not possible. Wobst shows how the predominant uses of style have promoted a focus on 'sameness' ('structuring data into internally homogeneous types' and the 'suppression of variance'), and this has not just reduced social variance in the human past, but serves certain social and political agendas in the present (1999: 127–9). After all, don't administrators of all sorts strive for 'docile underlings' who manifest 'similarities in template, action and symbols'?

Another provocative approach is that by Rick Wilk (e.g., 1995, 2004) in which he seeks to understand the processes whereby what is often called 'style' comes into existence and is worked out and appears to 'spread' or, as we used to think, 'diffuse'. Rather than invoking 'style', Wilk coins the term of 'common difference', which is a code and a set of practices that narrow difference into an agreed-upon system, whereby some kinds of difference are cultivated and others are suppressed. An art style, especially a widespread one (his 2004 example is the famous Olmec style in early Meso-America) is really an arena within which differences can be expressed, yet many of these are delimited, and a system of common difference is produced. And the really interesting questions are the agential ones: who controls what the 'rules' will be, and how are these accepted and agreed to? His own ethnographic work (on beauty pageants in Belize) suggests that there may be what appears as a resulting

hegemony of form but not necessarily of significances. What might appear as some sort of 'tradition' or even a cultural adoption may well be much more dynamic, and such a concept – as elucidated in the specifics (e.g. Wilk 2004) – resonates with the rethinking of the very concept of tradition (e.g., Hobsbawm and Ranger 1983; Pauketat 2001). Traditions, styles and systems of common difference are being shown as diachronic phenomena, as loci for political innovation and even resistance, as cultural productions through daily practices (e.g., Brown 1998; Lightfoot 2001). As we recognize that globalization is just a current variant of the long-standing circulation of objects within and through social forms and social relations, we are increasingly drawn to more dynamic notions about the 'mutability of things in recontextualization' (Thomas 1989: 49).

Thus, things and styles are not the (essential) things they used to be. The pervasive understandings of objects as being referable to some (usually single) essential categories or phenomena has been quite successfully challenged, at least among many scholars. It is difficult to sustain, for example, that all the Neolithic figurines of females can be referred to some essentialized, transhistorical concept of 'fertility' (e.g., Conkey and Tringham 1995; Goodison and Morris 1998), that Paleolithic cave art is all referable to (hunting) 'magic', or that string bags (*bilum*) among the Telefol-speaking people of the Mountain Ok (New Guinea) are merely women's (and therefore unvalued) 'things' (MacKenzie 1991). The long-standing tendency to view objects, through their styles and forms, as absolutes of human experience has given way to the idea that objects, forms, styles and functions are evolving, more mutable, and multivalent, without essential properties. And while this has certainly made the interpretive task more complicated and challenging, it nonetheless has simultaneously opened the door to new and hopefully more enlightening perspectives. For example, rather than assuming that many objects and forms cannot be explained because we cannot readily substantiate empirically such things as symbol and meaning – especially in archaeological contexts – it is now possible to use empirical work – such as in technological processes (e.g., Lechtman 1984; Dietler and Herbich 1998; Stark 1999) or studies of pigments and colors (e.g., Boser-Sarivaxévanis 1969) – to reconceptualize objects, forms and images as material practices and performances with linkages to social facts and cultural logics (e.g., Ingold 1993, among many).

RECENT APPROACHES TO TECHNOLOGY AND 'ART' THAT HAVE INFLUENCED UNDERSTANDINGS AND USES OF STYLE, DESIGN AND FUNCTION

As already suggested, trends in the study of our three characters – style, design, and function – have been integrally enmeshed in, produced by and yet contributed to shifts and concerns in the broader anthropological and cultural interests in the study of technology, on the one hand (e.g., Lemonnier 1986, 1993a; Dobres and Hoffman 1999; see Eglash, Chapter 21 in this volume) and 'art', on the other (e.g., Morphy 1994). In some ways, the trends in the study of technology may have had more of an impact on our three characters; perhaps this is due to the growth of social studies of science and technology (e.g., Jasanoff et al. 1995). From Lechtman's (1977, 1984) important work that argued for the place and power of technological practice and therefore of veritable technological styles in the making and meanings of objects, to the engagement with technology (*sensu latu*) as cultural productions, material culture has not been thought of in quite the same way, and certainly no longer as just the 'forms' or end products of previously unspecified, often assumed or ignored practices and social relations of production. For a concept of 'style' in the manner of Schapiro (1953), with a focus on forms, on form relationships, there was no immediate attention to an understanding of the practices and social relations that brought such forms into existence. One illustrative case study that might attest how far we have come in the integration of technologies, productive practices and social contexts in the making of 'things' and in the definition of style would be the continuing work by Dietler and Herbich (e.g., 1989, 1998) on Luo pottery making. Here, they remind us of not just the distinction between *things* and *techniques* (cf. Mauss 1935), but of the two (often conflated) senses of style: *style of action* and *material style*. From several decades of new approaches to understanding technology (e.g., Lemonnier 1986, 1993a; Pfaffenberger 1988, 1992; Ingold 1993; Dobres and Hoffman 1994; Dobres 1995, 2000), and from Bourdieu's (1977) concept of habitus, Dietler and Herbich (1998) put together a compelling case study of a more dynamic and deeply social understanding of what had previously often been a focus on a static concept of style and a mechanistic set of assumptions

about the uses of style either to 'mark' social boundaries or, on the part of the analyst, to infer them (see also, e.g., Hegmon 1998, among others). In fact, to talk today about an understanding of 'style' cannot be separated from our understandings both of 'technology' and of the practices and production of social relations. And, as Dietler and Herbich discuss, these approaches extend to the design conventions and decorations that so often stand for 'style': 'An understanding of the social origins and significance of material culture will not come from 'reading' the decorations as text (see Lemonnier 1990). It requires a dynamic, diachronic perspective founded upon an appreciation of the contexts of both production and consumption (see Dietler and Herbich 1994) ...' (Dietler and Herbich 1998: 244). Because of the intertwined reconsiderations of style and of technology, neither will be understood in the same ways again.

Especially since the 1950s, anthropological approaches to art, especially in small-scale societies, have focused on 'the mechanisms and nature of the messages carried by art', drawing upon either psychological or linguistic (textual, semiotic, communication) models, and following in 'the functionalist and structuralist modes of anthropology' (Graburn 2001: 765). Many of these were, of course, more synchronic, ahistorical and normative, and the diachronic, temporal and historical potentials of material culture were yet to be recognized, much less realized. With psychological approaches, style might be conceptualized as 'aestheticized versions of social fantasies' (Graburn 2001: 765) that give security or pleasure, as in Fischer (1961), who proposed that different (evolutionary) types of societies (egalitarian or hierarchical) tended to produce designs that were material and visual correlates of their prevailing social structure. However, it has been the linguistic approaches in art, as well as to material culture more broadly, which have prevailed, including structuralist (inspired by Lévi-Strauss 1963: 245–76); semiotic (e.g., Riggins 1994); and art-as-communication (e.g. Forge 1970, Munn 1973 as early, if not somewhat precocious, examples). Morphy (1994) identifies two primary influences that fostered the re-entry of art into the anthropological mainstream. On the one hand, a more culturally oriented archaeology was spawned, especially at Cambridge in the 1980s; many of today's most active material culture researchers have had this kind of archaeological background. On the other hand, but not, in fact, distinct from the so-called 'post-processual' archaeologies, was the expansion of an anthropology of meaning and symbolism: 'content was joined with form' (Morphy 1994: 659).

Perhaps the most significant aspect of the 'turn' to art and material culture has been the conjuncture with what we might call colonial and postcolonial sensibilities, which have promoted, first, the 'ah ha' understandings that much of the material world observed by anthropologists could not be considered in ahistorical, static or normative terms (e.g., Graburn 1999); the 'arts' were already enmeshed in colonial projects and trajectories when they were first encountered. (See especially Thomas 1991, who notes that his own project on 'entangled objects' was necessarily about 'recasting [these] issues in historical terms and with respect to the cultural constitution of objects', 1991: xi.) Beginning perhaps with the pioneering work of Graburn (1976) on ethnic and tourist arts, one might say that the anthropology of material culture, and all that it entails, including style, design and understandings of function, itself experienced a 'colonial encounter': a more widespread recognition of the previously unconsidered contexts of colonial domination. Not only has there been more attention to the historical depth and sociocultural complexity of art production in colonial and postcolonial, often touristic, contexts (e.g., Marcus and Myers 1995; Phillips and Steiner 1999), but fundamental concepts such as the functions of objects, the maintenance of or changes in style, and the cultural generation and deployment of designs, have had to be rethought. Furthermore, any studies of style, function and design have benefited from these deeper understandings of historically situated cultural practices, including observations on the ways in which local styles, for example, are actively reworked for new markets, global desires, and ever shifting political and cultural audiences and goals. Thus, approaches such as Wobst's notions on style-as-interventions, or Wilk's interest in the constructions of common difference, resonate with these new directions.

Certainly, Stahl's elegant (2002) critique of the prevailing (logocentric) linguistic and meaning-based models for understanding material culture, and her emphases on the practices of taste (after Bourdieu 1984), especially in understanding colonial entanglements, attest that what initially may have stimulated renewed interest in the anthropology of art and the object world – namely, the engagement with meaning and symbolism – has now been challenged and soundly critiqued. From both archaeological directions (e.g., Dietler and Herbich 1998) and those of a more historical anthropology (e.g., Phillips and Steiner 1999; Stahl 2002) art, style, design and functions have been reframed away from such a focus on finding 'the' meaning(s). Even those still engaged with a semiotic preference have advocated not the Sassurian semiological approaches, but those of C.S. Peirce (e.g., Peirce 1955; Singer 1978; Parmentier 1997; Preucel and Bauer 2001; Layton 2000, 2001: 329). What is heralded about such an approach is the way in which it almost necessarily 'accounts for and directs inquiry into the multiple meanings of a single artefact or sign' (Preucel and Bauer 2001: 91). In an interpretive world where inferring or understanding the possible functions and meanings of things is now thoroughly more open-ended and multivalent, discussions are necessarily more directed to the 'limits of interpretation' (e.g., Eco 1990, 1992).

ON DESIGN

The debate and shifts in our understandings about style, the influences from technology studies and the new approaches to the anthropology of art have all made their mark on the study of design. The studies of designs and decorations on objects are obviously integral to most ways in which style has been approached. There is often an unconscious slippage from one to the other. Pye (1982) argues that anyone studying material culture must understand the fundamentals of design; without design – in some form or another – one cannot really make anything. This is to consider design at the highest level; that is, how an object is conceived of and put together. In a difficult and somewhat classic essay, Pye proposed six requirements for design. As stated in the helpful editorial notes by Schlereth that precede Pye's essay, what Pye wants to do is to 'distinguish design as philosophical concept from solely sociological considerations'. In particular, Pye challenges the presumedly uncomplicated and causal relationship between design and function; design is not conditioned only by its function. Furthermore, it's not clear there even is such a thing as the 'purely functional'. How a number of factors affect design are Pye's focus: use, ease, economy and appearance. An early archaeological study of this type of design (McGuire and Schiffer 1983) wanted to focus on design as a social process, while noting that the treatment of the design process is usually subsumed by discussions of either style or function (1983:

277–303). McGuire and Schiffer are intentionally, as is Pye, considering design at a higher level than those who study 'the designs' incorporated into baskets, pots, masks painted on to houses, and the like.

For these latter designs, there are classic studies of material objects of ethnography and archaeology, such as Barrett's 1908 Ph.D. dissertation 'Pomo Indian Basketry' (republished 1996). Today this kind of work is hailed, including by contemporary Pomo Indian basket makers, for its relative lack of theoretical overburden; it is thoroughly a descriptive exposition on the designs of a certain set of Pomo baskets (Smith-Ferri 1996: 20). To this day, there are comparably meticulous studies of design, with lists of motifs, technologies and materials used, but most of them have a much wider tale to tell, an account of how such designs and their making are embedded in and constitutive of social relations (e.g., DeBoer's, e.g. 1990, excellent ethno-archaeological work with Shipibo-Conibo designs; MacKenzie 1991 on string bags and gender dynamics in central New Guinea; and Chiu 2003 on Lapita pottery designs and 'house societies' in Polynesia).

Among the more persistent approaches to design over the past several decades has been the study of symmetry (Washburn 1977, 1983; Washburn and Crowe 1988, 2004), which owes its heritage to structuralist approaches to material culture. Washburn began trying to access underlying cultural concepts in archaeological contexts by developing an analytical system based on universal principles of plane pattern symmetry (1977; for another example, see Fritz 1978 or in Washburn 1983). This has continued in collaboration with a mathematician as to 'how to' undertake such analyses (Washburn and Crowe 1988), leading to an edited volume with a wide variety of case studies (Washburn and Crowe 2004). In his somewhat radical challenges to the anthropology of art, the late Alfred Gell (e.g., 1998) accepts the idea of a universal aesthetic based on patterned surfaces – such as the symmetry analyses – even if one of his primary challenges is to aesthetics as the basis for a theory of art (*contra* Morphy 1994, Coote 1992, 1996, Price 1989; see Layton 2003). In fact, Gell can accept this because he views 'relationships between the elements of decorative art … [as] analogous to social relationships constructed through exchange' (Layton 2003: 450).

Although Gell is perhaps even more radical in his rejection of the view of art as a visual code, as a matter of communication and meaning (after Thomas 1998: xi–xiii; see also Layton 2003: 449), he does accept some studies of decorative art

and design as being of anthropological interest (e.g., Kaeppler 1978; Price and Price 1980; Hanson 1983). Furthermore, decoration, to Gell, is often an essential aspect of what he terms the 'technology of enchantment'; it is the decorations on objects and their designs that can weave a spell (see also Gell 1992; Layton 2003: 450)!

As already noted, one can properly credit the emergence of structuralism with a powerful rejuvenating effect upon material culture studies, including such approaches to design as symmetry analysis. In fact, linguistic approaches to design have been paramount since the early 1960s, at least. Munn's classic (1973) work on the design elements of Walpiri art suggests in this case that the designs are, in fact, parasitic on the language for the 'telling' of the sand drawing stories. Other early approaches to design include Bloch's (1974) ideas that designs and their organizational principles (such as repetition, symmetries, fixed sequences, delimited elements) may be some of the formal mechanisms whereby cultural 'authorities' may be empowered and might be enabled to control ritual, rhetoric and the arts, and may enact power over those who are enculturated to the patterns (after Graburn 2001). Another early and important use of the linguistic models was the work of Friedrich (1970), who viewed design generation and design sharing as part of interaction communities and how design makers (in this case, ethnographically produced designs on ceramics) did or did not participate in learning communities that themselves were specified sets of social relations. This kind of work anticipates one of the current very useful approaches based on the concepts of 'communities of practice' (after Lave and Wenger 1991).

Yet such structuralist, linguistic, communication and correlative approaches have been set to one side with the lure of context, the destabilization of the so-called 'concept of culture' (e.g., Fabian 1998: xii), and an engagement with history in a world of transnationalisms and globalized commodities where material objects are not, and have not been, just caught up in an ever shifting world but are actually creating, constituting, materializing and mobilizing history, contacts and entanglements.

One of the more interesting approaches to design in these contemporary circumstances within which material culture studies are situated is that by Attfield (1999, 2000), who comes to a material culture approach (as she calls it) from the perspective of professional designer herself, an approach that for her avoids the duality between art and design and makes central such issues as materiality and experience (Attfield 2000: xii). Attfield is particularly interested in the issues of identity and even individuality within a cultural context, even if these are not the usual domains of concern for the study of design. With an approach that is specifically focused on 'understanding design as an aspect of the material world as a social place', where we have as much to learn from rubbish and discarded things as from things of value, Attfield's book is explicitly and celebratorily interdisciplinary, bridging the views from the history of design and material culture studies. Her introduction provides a most useful understanding of design history and, by the end of Chapter 3 design has come to life. By placing the understanding of design in the contexts of time, space and the body, Attfield opens up the study of design to dimensions not often considered over the years of anthropological and archaeological studies of design.

ON FUNCTION

Some of what there is to say about function is mentioned above, and yet this is a grand topic in any aspect of the social sciences and in the study of the material world. This is notably so due to the importance of functionalism as an approach for many decades (e.g., Eisenstadt 1990). If one goes looking for 'function' as a topic, there are instead plenty of references to 'functionalism'. On one hand, the study of 'art' and the material world was not very central to mainstream developments (such as structural functionalism) in anthropological theory until the 1990s, and, on the other hand, there's very little material culture in classic functionalist social anthropology (but see, e.g., Firth 1936). As well, most anthropological definitions of 'art' have to do with the aesthetic, rather than sacred or functional qualities (Graburn 2001). Yet much work was concerned with how art styles, designs and forms function, particularly how they function to maintain the social (e.g., Sieber 1962; Biebuyck 1973).

In the debate over the function(s) of style, style came to take on communication as one of its functions. And style became more substantive than 'just' a residual dimension of material culture that was left over once we had identified what was functional about an object or class of objects (e.g., Wobst 1977; Sackett 1982, *contra* Dunnell 1978). Although early attempts at using style in this way often produced quite functionalist interpretations where style was assumed to

be 'adaptive' or functioned to maintain cultural equilibrium, further analyses have suggested how, in some cases, a materialist view on style *in* societies – as a means for political manipulation, for example – can be put to work (e.g., Earle 1990). A great deal of ethnographic work with art took this turn (see in Anderson 1989: 29–52): art and objects as a means for social control, art and objects as homeostasis, objects and the social order, objects as forms of legitimation, objects as symbols of power.

Nonetheless, there persisted a view that the object/artifact is almost autonomous and that stylistic analysis was primarily about the analysis of patterns of material culture, patterns often floating free of anything other than a generalized notion of 'function'. It was a view like this that accentuated some of the gaps between archaeology (often with its head in the stylistic sand) and sociocultural anthropology and ethnography (often completely unaware of the material world).

MacKenzie, in her brilliant study of string bags and gender in New Guinea (1991), notes that when anthropologists approached the study of artifacts from the perspective of their social functions in exchange systems, they often focused not so much, if at all, on the things that are exchanged, but on the social context of the transactions. Their emphasis on function, context and relations was at the expense of any consideration of the objects themselves (see, e.g., in Sieber 1962).

In contrast, archaeologists were perhaps over-dependent upon the objects and their inferred functions in overly generalized cultural or 'processual' terms (exchange, interaction, political manipulation) at the expense of objects-in-social-action. Given a predilection for categories and types, archaeologists have generated 'types' of function. For example, Binford (1962) suggested ideotechnic or sociotechnic objects and their implied functions (in a systems view of culture). Schiffer (1992) is even more specific with his categories of technofunction, sociofunction and ideofunction. For the more philosophically inclined, Preston (2000) brings in the philosophical studies of function in relation to how materiality matters, with particular reference to archaeology. She weds two different philosophical conceptions of function: Millikan's (1993) theory of 'proper function' and Cummins's (1975) conception of 'system function' that are not rival conceptions but instead complementary ones; both are 'required for an understanding of function in material culture' (Preston 2000: 46). Proper function, she reports, is function as a normative phenomenon – as a matter of what artifacts are supposed to do. Whereas system function is function as a matter of what artifacts in fact do in the way of useful performance.

As recently as 1994, Morphy suggests that 'the most productive initial approach to the explanation of form is through function' (1994: 662), hoping to 'wed content with form' (p. 659). But two divergent approaches can perhaps best sum up attitudes today towards function. On the one hand, there is the pervasive critique by Gell (1998), who bases his attitudes towards function through the lens of his primary objection, that is, to aesthetics as a foundation for a theory of art. Thus, because art is not always about aesthetics, the function of art is not to express a culturally specific aesthetic system. The anthropology of art and of objects should be interested, then, in how aesthetic principles are mobilized in social action. In fact, Gell's theory, as one rooted in social relationships and on 'the social' (rather than on culture; Gell 1998: 7), provides an important (albeit often conceptually challenging) new approach to 'the social' that, as Layton writes (2003: 448), differs from structural functionalism in important ways (see also Thomas 1998).

On the other hand, the reframing of 'the social' is also heralded in the view articulated by MacKenzie (1991: 27): the value of an object and even its function(s) are not inherent in the object but are 'multivalent and variously realized'. It is objects themselves that give value to social relations, yet the social values of objects are culturally constructed. Function, then, like style and design, is integrally caught up in expanded views on the ways that objects are linked to concepts of the world through cultural praxis (Morphy 1994: 664), and not just through but *as* social action.

SOMETHING OF A SUMMARY: THE STUDY OF CLOTH

In this section, I want to point to two primary features of current studies of the style, design and function of material culture: the centrality now of attending to issues of 'choices', and the destabilization of the communication functions and language metaphors. Embedded in the recent trajectory of material culture studies have been new approaches to and debates about the anthropology of cloth, where both of these features can be seen clearly. In the key volume that took up the 'social life of things', edited by Appadurai (1986), three (of eight)

chapters on specific materials focus on cloth. The study, analysis and interpretation of cloth have been a bridge between anthropology, art history and semioticians (Schevill 1992: 38), and the literature on cloth is enormous and instructive (e.g., Cordwell and Schwarz 1979; Tedlock and Tedlock 1985; Schneider 1987; McCracken 1987, 1988: 62 f.f; Weiner and Schneider 1989; Hendrickson 1993; Renne 1995; Eicher 2001). Additionally, the metaphors of textiles, and especially of weaving, are common in the study of material culture (e.g., Jarman 1997; Ingold 2000).

This multitude of publications on cloth since the mid-1980s conveys the shifts in how dimensions like style and design, even function, are conceptualized, especially as more nuanced and complex phenomena. Style cannot be 'read' in some of the more essentialized ways. Rather than a focus on the identification or characterization of 'a style', it is the dynamics of style or the mutability of style as embedded in contexts of social life and social relations that has captured the attention of and been elaborated by most cloth researchers. In what can be characterized as a key article, Schneider and Weiner (1986) make the point that while cloth is an economic commodity, it is also – and often just as much – 'a critical object in social exchange, an objectification of ritual intent, and an instrument of political power' (1986: 178). It is simultaneously a medium for the study of style, technology, function and design! In a subsequent review article, Schneider (1987) explicitly takes on what she calls the 'dynamic of style', drawing for her baseline concept on that put forth by Schapiro (1953). Those concepts of style as a homogeneous and uncontested expression of a discrete culture's world view, or 'as propelled by its own logic', obscure the ways in which such materials as cloth are relevant to the enactment of power through time. Schneider is particularly concerned (1987: 420–4) with the aesthetic options in cloth production; options that are tied in, to be sure, with 'designs' and 'technological style' (loom types, fiber types, etc.). What are the aesthetic choices that shape historical cloth styles?

This issue of 'options' or 'choices' is perhaps the key aspect in the contemporary approaches to style, design, and function. Although long recognized as one way to think about style (e.g., Sackett's isochrestism 1977, 1982), it is now the particular *conjuncture* of, on the one hand, a concern with choices all along the trajectory of material culture – from materials, aesthetics, technologies, production and consumption – with, on the other hand, a concern for cultural praxis, habitus and the dynamics of taste that best characterizes current approaches to style, design and function. A 'starter' reading list here would include Schneider (1987), Lemonnier (1993b), Dietler and Herbich (1989, 1998) and Stahl (2002), and the references therein.

The second feature of present approaches to our three characters of style, design and function would be the critique and alternatives to the communication models and the linguistic metaphors. The issue of using clothing as a metaphor for language (or vice versa) has both its supporters and its critics, but all might agree by now that a communication system cannot work without 'contextual knowledge'. Schevill, for example (1987, 1992), is motivated to 'rehabilitate' the approach to cloth and clothing as a communication system as an expressive system (1992: 9). But material culture theorists, such as McCracken, would disagree (1987; see his chapter 'Clothing as language' in McCracken 1988), even if a 'rehabilitation' of this concept is one of his options. He argues that we need to jettison the metaphor (clothing as language, as communication), which has been so over-used (and putatively without any depth or critical assessment) that it is, to McCracken, a 'dead metaphor' and a 'fixity of conventional wisdom' (1988: 62).

In the study of cloth and clothing, we can see how an approach to one kind of material culture embodies many of the issues being discussed and debated in regard to other kinds of material culture. The point that McCracken insists on is one reaction to a somewhat simplistic view of 'X as communication', especially as understood through its style and design. The McCracken view holds that it is precisely because material culture, in its styles, designs and even functions, is more limited than language in its expressive possibilities that it instead holds power; it is 'inconspicuous', has the potential to convey in more subtle ways, and allows a certain ambiguity that can be mobilized situationally and even more efficiently than language.

The domain of style, design and function is today more mutable, and ripe with more choices for us to make in how we study and understand it. There is no single new 'paradigm' and, if anything, our understandings are necessarily more nuanced, complex and situational. History has made a strong appearance, and our key concepts have been complicated. Style can no longer be equated with decoration; choices in the technologies of production must be attended to. Material culture 'does' much more than communicate, and the agency of both people and the objects that are used to intervene into everyday practices, identities and social worlds is now in focus.

REFERENCES

Adams, M.-J. (1973) 'Structural aspects of a village Art', *American Anthropologist*, 75: 265–79.

Akrich, M. (1992) 'The description of technical objects', in W. Bijker and J. Law, eds, *Shaping Technology/Building Society: Studies in Sociotechnical Change*. Cambridge, MA: MIT Press, pp. 205–24.

Anderson, R. (1979) *Art in Primitive Societies*. Englewood Cliffs, NJ: Prentice-Hall.

Anderson, R. (1989) *Art in Small-scale Societies*. Englewood Cliffs, NJ: Prentice-Hall.

Appadurai, A., ed. (1986) *The Social Life of Things*. Cambridge: Cambridge University Press.

Attfield, J. (1999) 'Beyond the pale: reviewing the relationship between material culture and design history', *Journal of Design History*, 12 (4): 373–80.

Attfield, J. (2000) *Wild Things: the Material Culture of Everyday Life*. Oxford and New York: Berg.

Barrett, S.A. (1908/1996) *Pomo Indian Basketry*. Berkeley, CA: Hearst Museum of Anthropology.

Barry, H., III (1957) 'Relationships between child training and the pictorial arts', *Journal of Abnormal and Social Psychology*, 54: 80–3.

Bascom, W. (1969) 'Creativity and style in African art', in D. Beibuyk (ed.), *Tradition and Creativity in Tribal Art*. Los Angeles, CA: University of California Press, pp. 98–119.

Biebuyck, D. (1973) *The Lega: Art, Initiation and Moral Philosophy*. Berkeley, CA: University of California Press.

Binford, L. (1962) 'Archaeology as anthropology', *American Antiquity*, 28 (2): 217–25.

Binford, L. (1965) 'Archaeological systematics and the study of culture process', *American Antiquity*, 31: 203–10.

Binford, S. and Binford, L., eds (1968) *New Perspectives in Archaeology*. Chicago: Aldine.

Bloch, M. (1974) 'Symbols, song, dance, and features of articulation: is religion an extreme form of traditional authority?' *European Journal of Sociology*, 15: 55–98.

Boas, F. (1927) *Primitive Art*. New York: Dover.

Boast, R. (1997) 'A small company of actors: a critique of style', *Journal of Material Culture*, 2: 173–98.

Boser-Sarivaxévanis, R. (1969) *Aperçus sur la teintureà l'indigo en Afrique occidentale*. Basel: Naturforschenden Gesellschaft.

Bourdieu, P. (1977) *Outline of a Theory of Practice*. Cambridge: Cambridge University Press.

Bourdieu, P. (1984) *Distinction: a Social Critique of the Judgement of Taste*. Cambridge, MA: Harvard University Press.

Brown, S.C. (1998) *Native Visions: Evolution in Northwest Coast Art from the Eighteenth through to the Twentieth Century.* Seattle, WA: University of Washington Press.

Brumfiel, E. (2003) 'It's a material world: history, artifacts, and anthropology', *Annual Review of Anthropology*, 32: 205–23.

Bunzel, R. (1927) *The Pueblo Potter: a Study of Creative Imagination in Primitive Art.* New York: Columbia University Press.

Cannizzo, J. (1996) 'Art', in A. Barnard and J. Spencer (eds), *Encyclopedia of Social and Cultural Anthropology.* London and New York: Routledge, p. 54.

Carr, C. and Nietzel, J.E. eds (1995) *Style, Society, and Person.* New York and London: Plenum Press.

Chiu, S. (2003) 'The Socio-economic Functions of Lapita Ceramic Production and Exchange: a Case Study from Site WKO013A, Kone, New Caledonia'. Ph.D. dissertation, Department of Anthropology, Berkeley, CA: University of California.

Conkey, M.W. (1990) 'Experimenting with style in archaeology: some historical and theoretical issues', in M.W. Conkey and C.A. Hastorf (eds), *The Uses of Style in Archaeology.* Cambridge: Cambridge University Press, pp. 5–17.

Conkey, M.W. and Hastorf, C.A. eds (1990) *The Uses of Style in Archaeology.* Cambridge: Cambridge University Press.

Conkey, M.W. and Tringham, R.E. (1995) 'Archaeology and the goddess: exploring the contours of feminist archaeology', in D. Stanton and A. Stewart (eds), *Feminisms in the Academy.* Ann Arbor, MI: University of Michigan Press, pp. 199–247.

Coote, J. (1992) 'Marvels of everyday vision: the anthropology of aesthetics and the cattle-keeping Nilotes', in J. Coote and A. Shelton (eds), *Anthropology, Art, and Aesthetics.* Oxford: Clarendon Press, pp. 245–75.

Coote, J. (1996) 'Aesthetics is a cross-cultural category: for the motion', in T. Ingold (ed.), *Key Debates in Anthropology.* London and New York: Routledge, pp. 266–75.

Cordwell, J. and Schwarz, R.A., eds (1979) *The Fabrics of Culture: the Anthropology of Clothing and Adornment.* The Hague: Mouton.

Cummins, R. (1975) 'Functional explanation', *Journal of Philosophy*, 72: 741–64.

Davis, W. (1990) 'Style and history in Art History', in M.W. Conkey and C.A. Hastorf (eds), *The Uses of Style in Archaeology.* Cambridge: Cambridge University Press, pp. 18–31.

DeBoer, W. (1990) 'Interaction, imitation, and communication as expressed in style: the Ucayali experience', in M.W. Conkey and C.A. Hastorf (eds), *The Uses of Style in Archaeology.* Cambridge: Cambridge University Press, pp. 82–103.

Deetz, J. (1965) *The Dynamics of Stylistic Change in Arikara Ceramics.* Urbana, IL: University of Illinois Press.

Dietler, M. and Herbich, I. (1989) 'Tich Matek: the technology of Luo pottery production and the definition of ceramic style', *World Archaeology*, 21: 148–64.

Dietler, M. and Herbich, I. (1994) 'Ceramics and ethnic identity: ethnoarchaeological observations on the distribution of pottery styles and the relationship between the social contexts of production and consumption', in D. Binder and F. Audouze (eds), *Terre cuite en société : la céramique, document technique, economique, culturel. XIVe rencontre internationale d'archéologie et histoire d'Antibes.* Juan-les-Pins: APDCA, pp. 459–72.

Dietler, M. and Herbich, I. (1998). 'Habitus, techniques, style: an integrated approach to the social understanding of material culture and boundaries', in M. Stark (ed.), *The Archaeology of Social Boundaries.* Washington, DC: Smithsonian Institution Press, pp. 232–63.

Dobres, M.-A. (1995) 'Gender and prehistoric technology: on the social agency of technical strategies', *World Archaeology*, 27 (1): 25–49.

Dobres, M.-A. (2000) *Technology and Social Agency.* Oxford: Blackwell.

Dobres, M.-A. and Hoffman, C. (1994) 'Social agency and the dynamics of prehistoric technology', *Journal of Archaeological Method and Theory*, 1 (3): 211–58.

Dobres, M.-A. and Hoffman, C., eds (1999) *The Social Dynamics of Technology: Practice, Politics and World View.* Washington, DC: Smithsonian Institution Press.

Dunnell, R. (1978) 'Style and function: a fundamental dichotomy', *American Antiquity*, 43: 192–202.

Earle, T. (1990) 'Style and iconography as legitimation in complex chiefdoms', in M.W. Conkey and C.A. Hastorf (eds), *The Uses of Style in Archaeology.* Cambridge: Cambridge University Press, pp. 73–81.

Eco, U. (1990) *Limits of Interpretation.* Bloomington, IN: Indiana University Press.

Eco, U. (1992) *Interpretation and Overinterpretation.* Cambridge: Cambridge University Press.

Eicher, J. (2001) 'The cultural significance of dress and textiles', *Reviews in Anthropology*, 30 (4): 309–24.

Eisenstadt, S.N. (1990) 'Functional analaysis in anthropology and sociology: an interpretive essay', *Annual Review of Anthropology*, 19: 243–60.

Fabian, J. (1998) *Moments of Freedom: Anthropology and Popular Culture.* Charlottesville, VA: University of Virginia Press.

Faris, J.C. (1972) *Nuba Personal Art.* London: Duckworth.

Fernandez, J.W. (1966) 'Principles of opposition and vitality in Fang aesthetics', *Journal of Aesthetics and Art Criticism*, 25 (1): 53–64.

Firth, R. (1936) *We, the Tikopia: a Sociological Study of Kinship in Primitive Polynesia*. London: Allen & Unwin.

Fischer, J. (1961) 'Art styles as cultural cognitive maps', *American Anthropologist*, 63: 79–93.

Forge, A. (1966) 'Art and environment in the Sepik', *Proceedings of the Royal Anthropological Institute of Great Britain and Ireland for 1965*. London: RAI, pp. 23–31.

Forge, A. (1970) 'Learning to see in New Guinea', in P. Mayer (ed.), *Socialization: the Approach from Social Anthropology*. London: Tavistock, pp. 269–91.

Friedrich, M.H. (1970) 'Design structure and social interaction: archaeological implications of an ethnographic analysis', *American Antiquity*, 35: 332–43.

Fritz, J.M. (1978) 'Paleopsychology today: ideational systems and human adaptation', in C. Redman, M.J. Berman, E.V. Curtin, Jr. W.T. Langhorne, N.M. Versaggi and J.C. Wanser (eds), *Social Archaeology*. New York: Academic Press, pp. 37–60.

Gadamer, H.-G. (1965) *Warheit üind Methode*. 2nd edn. Tübingen: Mohr.

Garlake, P. (1995) *The Hunter's Vision: the Prehistoric Art of Zimbabwe*. Seattle, WA: University of Washington Press and London: British Museum.

Gell, A. (1992) 'The technology of enchantment and the enchantment of technology', in J. Coote and A. Shelton (eds), *Anthropology, Art, Aesthetics*. Oxford: Clarendon Press, pp. 40–67.

Gell, A. (1998) *Art and Agency: an Anthropological Theory*. Oxford: Clarendon Press.

George, K.M., ed. (1999) *Objects on the Loose: Ethnographic Encounters with Unruly Artefacts*, a special issue of *Ethnos*, 64 (2).

Gombrich, E. (1960) *Art and Illusion: a Study in the Psychology of Pictorial Representation*. New York: Pantheon Books.

Goodison, L. and Morris, C. eds (1998) *Ancient Goddesses: the Myths and the Evidence*. London: British Museum Press.

Graburn, N., ed. (1976) *Ethnic and Tourist Arts*. Berkeley, CA: University of California Press.

Graburn, N. (1999) 'Epilogue: ethnic and tourist arts revisited', in R.B. Phillips and C.B. Steiner (eds), *Unpacking Culture: Art and Commodity in Colonial and Post-colonial Worlds*. Berkeley, CA: University of California Press, pp. 335–53.

Graburn, N. (2001) 'Art: anthropological aspects', in N.J. Smelser and P.B. Baltes (eds), *International Encyclopedia of the Social and Behavioral Sciences* II. Oxford: Elsevier, pp. 764–68.

Graves, M. (1998) 'The history of method and theory in the study of prehistoric Puebloan pottery style in the American southwest', *Journal of Archaeological Method and Theory*, 5 (4): 309–43.

Handler, R. (1988) *Nationalism and the Politics of Culture in Quebec*. Madison, WI: University of Wisconsin Press.

Hanson, F.A. (1983) 'When the map is the territory: art in Maori culture', in D.K. Washburn (ed.), *Structure and Cognition in Art*. Cambridge: Cambridge University Press, pp. 74–89.

Hegmon, M. (1992) 'Archaeological research on style', *Annual Review of Anthropology*, 21: 517–36.

Hegmon, M. (1998) 'Technology, style and social practices: archaeological approaches', in M. Stark (ed.), *The Archaeology of Social Boundaries*. Washington, DC: Smithsonian Institution Press, pp. 264–79.

Hendrickson, C. (1993) *Weaving Identities: Construction of Dress and Self in a Highland Guatemala Town*. Austin, TX: University of Texas Press.

Hill, J. (1970) *Broken K Pueblo: Prehistoric Social Organization in the American Southwest*. Anthropological Papers 18. Tucson, AZ: University of Arizona Press.

Hobsbawm, E. and Ranger, T., eds (1983) *Inventing Tradition*. Cambridge: Cambridge University Press.

Hodder, I. (1990) 'Style as historical quality', in M.W. Conkey and C.A. Hastorf (eds), *The Uses of Style in Archaeology*. Cambridge: Cambridge University Press, pp. 44–51.

Ingold, T. (1993) 'The reindeerman's lasso', in P. Lemonnier (ed.), *Technological Choices: Transformations in Material Culture since the Neolithic*. London and New York: Routledge, pp. 108–25.

Ingold, T. (2000) 'Making culture and weaving the world', in P.M. Graves-Brown (ed.), *Matter, Materiality and Modern Culture*. London and New York: Routledge, pp. 5–71.

Ingold, T. (2004) 'Materials Against Materiality'. Paper presented at the Theoretical Archaeology Group annual meetings, Glasgow, December.

Jarman, N. (1997) 'Material of culture, fabric of identity', in D. Miller (ed.), *Material Cultures: Why Some Things Matter*. London: UCL Press, pp. 121–45.

Jasanoff, S., Markle, G.E., Petersen, J.C. and Pinch, T., eds (1995) *Handbook of Science and Technology Studies*. Thousand Oaks, CA: Sage.

Jonaitis, A. (1995) *A Wealth of Thought: Franz Boas on Native American Art*. Seattle, WA: University of Washington Press.

Jopling, C., ed. (1971) *Art and Aesthetics in Primitive Societies*. New York: Dutton.

Kaeppler, A.L. (1978) *Artificial Curiosities: Being an Exposition of Native Manufactures collected on the Three Pacific Journeys of Captain James Cook at the Bernice Puahi Bishop Museum*. Honolulu, HI: Bishop Museum Press.

Kopytoff, I. (1986) 'The cultural biography of things: commodization as a process', in A. Appadurai (ed.), *The Social Life of Things*. Cambridge: Cambridge University Press, pp. 64–91.

Kreiger, A. (1944) 'The typological concept', *American Antiquity*, 9: 271–88.

Kroeber, A. (1919) 'On the principle of order in civilization as exemplified by changes of fashion', *American Anthropologist*, 21 (3): 235–63.

Kroeber, A. (1957) *Styles and Civilizations*. Ithaca, NY: Cornell University Press.

Latour, B. (1992) 'Where are the missing masses? The sociology of a few mundane artifacts', in W.E. Bijker and J. Law (eds), *Shaping Technology/Building Society: Studies in Sociotechnical Change*. Cambridge, MA: MIT Press, pp. 225–58.

Lave, J. and Wenger, E. (1991) *Situated Learning: Limited Peripheral Participation*. Cambridge: Cambridge University Press.

Layton, R. (1991) *The Anthropology of Art*, 2nd edn. Cambridge: Cambridge University Press.

Layton, R. (2000) 'Intersubjectivity and understanding rock art', *Australian Archaeologist*, 51: 48–53.

Layton, R. (2001) '"Things that signify and things that work": recent studies in material culture', *Reviews in Anthropology*, 30 (4): 325–42.

Layton, R. (2003) 'Art and agency: a reassessment', *Journal of the Royal Anthropological Institute* (n.s.) 9: 447–64.

Lechtman, H. (1977) 'Style in technology: some early thoughts', in H. Lechtman and R. Merrill (eds), *Material Culture: Styles, Organization, and Dynamics of Technology*. St Paul, MN: American Ethnological Society, pp. 3–20.

Lechtman, H. (1984) 'Andean value systems and the development of prehistoric metallurgy', *Technology and Culture*, 25 (1): 1–36.

Lechtman, H. and Merrill, R., eds (1977) *Material Culture: Styles, Organization, and Dynamics of Technology*. St Paul, MN: American Ethnological Society.

Leite, N. (2004) 'Material Culture: Objects, Trajectories, Value: A Course Proposal'. Berkeley, CA: Department of Anthropology, University of California.

Lemonnier, P. (1986) 'The study of material culture today: towards an anthropology of technical systems', *Journal of Anthropological Archaeology*, 5: 147–86.

Lemonnier, P. (1990) 'Topsy-turvy techniques: remarks on the social representation of techniques', *Archaeological Review from Cambridge*, 9 (1): 27–37.

Lemonnier, P., ed. (1993a) *Technological Choices: Transformation in Material Cultures since the Neolithic*. London and New York: Routledge.

Lemonnier, P. (1993b) Introduction, in P. Lemonnier (ed.), *Technological Choices: Transformation in Material Cultures since the Neolithic*. London and New York: Routledge, pp. 1–35.

Lévi-Strauss, C. (1963) *Structural Anthropology*. New York: Basic Books.

Lightfoot, K. (2001) 'Traditions as cultural production: implications for contemporary archaeological research', in T. Pauketat (ed.), *The Archaeology of Traditions: Agency and History before and after Columbus*. Gainesville, FL: University Press of Florida, pp. 237–52.

Longacre, W. (1970) *Archaeology as Anthropology: a Case Study*. Tucson, AZ, Anthropological Papers 17. Tucson, AZ: University of Arizona Press.

Lorblanchet, M. (1990) 'The archaeological significance of palaeolithic pigments in the quercy, France', *Rock Art Research*, 7 (1): 19–20.

Lorblanchet, M. and Bahn, P., eds (1993) *Rock Art Studies: the Post-stylistic Era, or, Where do we go from Here?* Oxbow Monograph 35. Oxford: Oxbow Books.

Lowenthal, D. (1985) *The Past is a Foreign Country*. Cambridge and New York: Cambridge University Press.

MacKenzie, M. (1991) *Androgynous Objects: String Bags and Gender in Central New Guinea*. Chur: Harwood Academic.

Marcus, G. and Myers, F., eds (1995) *The Traffic in Culture: Refiguring Art and Anthropology*. Berkeley, CA and Los Angeles: University of California Press.

McCracken, G. (1987) 'Clothing as language: an object lesson in the study of the expressive properties of material culture', in B. Reynolds and M.A. Stott (eds), *Material Anthropology: Contemporary Approaches to Material Culture*. Lanham, MD, New York and London: University Press of America, pp. 103–28.

McCracken, G. (1988) *Culture and Consumption: New Approaches to the Symbolic Character of Consumer Goods and Activities*. Bloomington, IN: Indiana University Press.

McGuire, R. and Schiffer, M.B. (1983) 'Theory of architectural design', *Journal of Anthropological Archaeology*, 2: 277–303.

Mauss, M. (1935) 'Les techniques du corps', *Journal de Psychologie*, 32, 271–93.

Mauss, M. (1967/1925) *The Gift: The Form and Reason for Exchange in Archaic Societies*. trans. Ian Cunnison. New York: Norton Press.

Miller, D., ed. (1998) *Material Cultures: Why Some Things Matter*. Chicago: University of Chicago Press.

Millikan, R.G. (1993) *White Queen Psychology and other Essays for Alice*. Cambridge, MA: MIT Press.

Morphy, H. (1991) *Ancestral Connections: Art and an Aboriginal System of Knowledge*. Chicago: University of Chicago Press.

Morphy, H. (1994) 'The anthropology of art', in T. Ingold, (ed.), *Companion Encyclopedia of Anthropology*. London and New York: Routledge, pp. 648–85.

Munn, N. (1966) 'Visual categories: an approach to the study of representational systems', *American Anthropologist*, 68: 936–50.

Munn, N. (1973) *Walbiri Iconography*. Ithaca, NY: Cornell University Press.

Munro, T. (1963) *Evolution in the Arts*. Cleveland, OH: Cleveland Museum.

Myers, F. (2001) *The Empire of Things: Regimes of Value and Material Culture*. Santa Fe, NM: School of American Research.

Otten, C., ed. (1971a) *Anthropology and Art: Readings in Cross-cultural Aesthetics*. American Museum Sourcebooks in Anthropology Q13. Garden City, NY: Natural History Press.

Otten, C. (1971b) 'Introduction', in C. Otten (ed.), *Anthropology and Art: Readings in Cross-cultural Aesthetics*. Garden City, NY: Natural History Press, pp. xi–xix.

Parmentier, R.J. (1997) 'The pragmatic semiotics of culture', *Semiotica*, 116: 1–115.

Pauketat, T., ed. (2001) *The Archaeology of Traditions: Agency and History before and after Columbus*. Gainesville, FL: University Press of Florida.

Peirce, C.S. (1955) 'Logic as semiotic: the theory of signs', in J. Buchler (ed.), *The Philosophy of Peirce: Selected Writings*. London: Kegan Paul, pp. 89–119.

Pfaffenberger, B. (1988) 'Fetishized objects and humanized nature: towards an anthropology of technology', *Man* (n.s.), 23: 236–52.

Pfaffenberger, B. (1992) 'Social anthropology of technology', *Annual Review of Anthropology*, 21: 491–516.

Phillips, R.B. and Steiner, C.B., eds (1999) *Unpacking Culture: Art and Commodity in Colonial and Postcolonial Worlds*. Berkeley, CA: University of California Press.

Pinney, C. and Thomas, N. eds (2001) *Beyond Aesthetics: Art and the Technologies of Enchantment*. Oxford: Berg.

Plog, S. (1978) 'Social interaction and stylistic similarity: a reanalysis', in M.B. Schiffer, (ed.), *Advances in Archaeological Method and Theory* I. New York: Academic Press, pp. 143–82.

Plog, S. (1983) 'Analysis of style in artifacts', *Annual Review of Anthropology*, 12: 125–42.

Preston, B. (2000) 'The functions of things: a philosophical perspective on material culture', in P.M. Graves-Brown (ed.), *Matter, Materiality and Modern Culture*. London and New York: Routledge, pp. 22–49.

Preucel, R. and Bauer, A. (2001) 'Archaeological pragmatics', *Norwegian Archaeological Review*, 34 (2): 85–96.

Price, S. (1989) *Primitive Art in Civilized Places*. Chicago: University of Chicago Press.

Price, S. and Price, R. (1980) *Afro-American Arts of the Surinam Rain Forest*. Berkeley, CA: University of California Press.

Pye, D. (1982) 'Six requirements for design', in T. Schlereth, (ed.), *Material Culture Studies in America*. Nashville, TN: American Association for State and Local History, pp. 153–61.

Renne, E.P. (1995) *Cloth that Does Not Die: the Meaning of Cloth in Bunu Social Life*. Seattle, WA: University of Washington Press.

Reynolds, B. (1983) 'The relevance of material culture to anthropology', *Journal of the Anthropological Society of Oxford*, 14 (2): 209–17.

Riggins, S.H., ed. (1994) *The Socialness of Things: Essays in the Socio-semiotics of Objects*. Berlin: Mouton de Gruyter.

Sackett, J. (1977) 'The meaning of style in archaeology: a general model', *American Antiquity*, 42 (3): 369–80.

Sackett, J. (1982) 'Approaches to style in lithic archaeology', *Journal of Anthropological Archaeology*, 1: 59–112.

Sackett, J. (1985) 'Style and ethnicity in the Kahalari: a reply to Wiessner', *American Antiquity*, 50 (1): 154–9.

Sauerländer, W. (1983). 'From stilus to style: reflection on the fate of a notion', *Art History*, 6 (3): 253–70.

Schapiro, M. (1953) 'Style', in A. Kroeber (ed.), *Anthropology Today*. Chicago: University of Chicago Press, pp. 287–312.

Schevill, M.B. (1985) *Evolution in Textile Design from the Highlands of Guatamala*. Seattle, WA: University of Washington Press.

Schevill, M.B. (1987) *Costume as Communication*. Seattle, WA: University of Washington Press.

Schevill, M.B. (1992) *Maya Textiles of Guatamala*. Austin, TX: University of Texas Press.

Schiffer, M. (1992) *Technological Perspectives on Behavioral Change*. Tucson, AZ: University of Arizona Press.

Schneider, J. (1987) 'The anthropology of cloth', *Annual Review of Anthropology*, 16: 409–48.

Schneider, J. and Weiner, A. (1986) 'Cloth and human experience', *Current Anthropology*, April, pp. 178–84.

Sieber, R. (1962) 'The arts and their changing social function', *New York Academy of Sciences*, 96 (2): 653–8.

Sillitoe, P. (1988) 'From head-dress to head-messages', *Man* (n.s.), 23: 298–318.

Silver, H. (1979) 'Ethnoart', *Annual Review of Anthropology*, 8: 267–306.

Singer, M. (1978). 'For a semiotic anthropology', in T.A. Sebeok (ed.), *Sight, Sound, and Sense*. Bloomington, IN: Indiana University Press.

Smith-Ferri, S. (1996) 'Introduction: the human faces of Pomo Indian basketry', in S. Barrett (ed.), *Pomo Indian basketry*. Berkeley, CA: Hearst Museum of Anthropology, pp. 1–66.

Sparshott, F. (1997) 'Art and anthropology', *Journal of Aesthetics and Art Criticism*, 55 (3): 239–43.

Spyer, P., ed. (1998) *Border Fetishisms: Material Objects in Unstable Places*. New York: Routledge.

Stahl, A.B. (2002) 'Colonial entanglements and the practices of taste: an alternative to logocentric approaches', *American Anthropologist*, 104 (3): 827–45.

Stanislawski, M.B. (1969) 'The ethno-archaeology of Hopi pottery making', *Plateau*, 42: 27–33.

Stanislawski, M.B. (1973) Review of William A. Longacre, *Archaeology as Anthropology: A Case Study*, *American Antiquity*, 38: 117–21.

Stark, M. (1999) 'Social dimensions of technical choice in Kalinga ceramic tradition', in E. Chilton, (ed.), *Material Meanings: Critical Approaches to the Interpretation of Material Culture*. Salt Lake City, UT: University of Utah Press, pp. 24–43.

Sterner, J. (1989) 'Who is signalling whom? Ceramic style, ethnicity and taphonomy among the Sirak Bulahay', *Antiquity*, 63: 451–9.

Tedlock, B. and Tedlock, D. (1985) 'Text and textile: language and technology in the art of the Quiche Maya', *Journal of Anthropological Research*, 41: 121–47.

Thomas, N. (1989) *Out of Time: History and Evolution in Anthropological Discourse*. Cambridge: Cambridge University Press.

Thomas, N. (1991) *Entangled Objects: Exchange, Material Culture, and Colonialism in the Pacific*. Cambridge, MA: Harvard University Press.

Thomas, N. (1998) Foreword, in A. Gell *Art and Agency: An Anthropological Approach*. Oxford: Clarendon Press, pp. vii–xiii.

Townsend-Gault, C. (1998) 'At the margin or the centre? The anthropological study of art', *Reviews in Anthropology*, 27: 425–39.

Ucko, P. (1969) 'Penis sheaths: a comparative study', *Proceedings of the Royal Anthropological Institute for 1968*. London: RAI, pp. 27–67.

Van Wyk, G. (2003) 'Illuminated signs: style and meaning in the beadwork of Xhosa- and Zulu-speaking peoples', *african arts*, autumn, pp. 12–33, 93–4.

Washburn, D.K. (1977) *A Symmetry Analysis of Upper Gila Area Ceramic Design*. Cambridge, MA: Harvard University Press.

Washburn, D.K., ed. (1983) *Structure and Cognition in Art*. New Directions in Archaeology. Cambridge: Cambridge University Press.

Washburn, D.K. and Crowe, D.W. (1988) *Symmetries of Culture*. Seattle, WA: University of Washington Press.

Washburn, D.K. and Crowe, D.W. eds (2004) *Symmetry Comes of Age: the Role of Pattern in Culture*. Seattle, WA: University of Washington Press.

Weiner, A. and Schneider, J. eds (1989) *Cloth and Human Experience*. Washington, DC: Smithsonian Institution Press.

Wiessner, P. (1990) 'Is there Unity to Style?' in M.W. Conkey and C.A. Hastorf (eds), *The Uses of Style in Archaeology*. Cambridge: Cambridge University Press, pp. 105–12.

Wilk, R. (1995) 'Learning to be local in Belize: global systems of common difference', in D. Miller (ed.), *Worlds Apart: Modernity through the Prism of the Local*. London: Routledge, pp. 110–33.

Wilk, R. (2004) 'Miss Universe, the Olmec and the valley of Oaxaca', *Journal of Social Archaeology*, 4 (1): 81–98.

Wobst, M. (1977) 'Stylistic behavior and information exchange', in C.E. Cleland (ed.), *Papers for the Director: Research Essays in Honor of James B. Griffin*. Papers of the Museum of Anthropology 61. Ann Arbor, MI: University of Michigan, pp. 317–42.

Wobst, H.M. (1999) 'Style in archaeology or archaeologists in style', in E. Chilton (ed.), *Material Meanings: Critical Approaches to the Interpretation of Material Culture*. Salt Lake City, UT: University of Utah Press, pp. 118–32.

Wolfe, A. (1969) 'Social structural basis of art', *Current Anthropology*, 10: 3–44.

Wölfflin, H. (1932) *Principles of Art History*, 7th edn. London: Bell.

24

EXCHANGE

James G. Carrier

A crucial way that people deal with the objects in their lives is by exchanging them with others. We exchange money for things in shops, we give and receive gifts and favours with others throughout our lives, we transact with co-workers on the job, we pay taxes to states and receive government services in return. Because exchange pervades social life and takes so many forms, it could be approached in a range of different ways and used to address a range of different questions about people and the groups in which they live. Neoclassical economics, for instance, is the consideration of exchange from a certain perspective, in which people are seen as relatively autonomous individuals who transact with each other things of value that are identified as bearers of utility, effectively as offering more or less gratification to those individuals.

Social anthropologists generally have approached exchange differently. Conventionally, they have been concerned with how the transaction of things is related to the nature of the relationships between people and social groups. Compared with economists, they have been less concerned with the utility of objects and less interested in seeing exchange as the result of decisions by individuals to increase their utilities; indeed, they are less willing to see individuals as autonomous in the first place. As a part of this, they tend to reject the idea of utility, which speaks of person, object and gratification. They replace it with the idea of meaning, which speaks of more or less collective perceptions of the nature and significance of objects.

My purpose in this chapter is to consider exchange from an anthropological perspective, which is appropriate, given that this is the discipline that has devoted the most attention to it. This chapter does not, however, pretend to a comprehensive review of the relevant literature, which is too vast and diffuse to permit ready summary. Rather, it begins with a set of classic anthropological works and debates, and uses these to lay out a set of issues and perspectives that they define. It then uses the works, issues and perspectives to frame some of the more recent streams of work on exchange, some from within anthropology and some from elsewhere. Presenting work on exchange in this way serves two purposes. First, it allows us to see the ways that the classics are reflected in current work, and so reminds us that what is in those classics encompasses much of what has attracted scholarly interest in the more recent past; continuing awareness of this helps us avoid the task of reinventing the wheel. Second, it allows us to see an important trend in work on exchange that emerged over the past few decades and that seems likely to continue. That trend is to broaden the context in which exchange is considered. While the classic works sought to view exchange in a broad perspective, that vision was realized only gradually. The shapes of this realization are the main plot embedded in the tale this chapter tells.

Exchange necessarily involves the movement of things from one social actor to another, though those social actors are not necessarily individual people acting on their own behalf. Quite often they are groups of one sort or another; occasionally they can be immaterial entities like deities. Because exchange involves the movement of things, it is part of people's material culture. However, the things that are transacted are not always material objects, though most of them are. In accord with this, I use 'thing' and 'object' in an extended sense, to refer to physical objects, services and even intangible entities like ideas, knowledge, names and the like.[1]

THE GIFT

Exchange has been an important topic in social anthropology for about as long as the discipline has existed; after all, it was the focus of one of the founding works in the field in its modern form, Bronislaw Malinowski's *Argonauts of the Western Pacific* (1922). Inevitably, different anthropologists have drawn on different intellectual resources as they have considered exchange. However, the work that probably has the greatest influence is Marcel Mauss's *The Gift* (1925/1990), the starting point of this chapter.

Mauss's slim book is an effort to identify forms of the exchange of objects in different societies, ranging from Polynesia and Melanesia to modern France. His was a comprehensive vision, and he was interested in placing exchange in the context of social organization and belief more generally. The work uses a core model to explore a core question: how does exchange serve to help build social groups, both the groups that exist within society and society itself?

The core of *The Gift* is a discussion of societies in which the gift form of exchange predominates, societies of the gift. However, Mauss's overall approach is broadly developmental, in which it echoes much early social science. So Mauss was interested in the distinction between Western industrial societies and pre-industrial societies, which he (1925/1990: 47) saw as stages 'in social evolution' that mark a number of general changes. One is the decreasing significance of large-scale, organized giving. A second is an increasing cultural separation of objects from people and social relationships: 'We live in societies that draw a strict distinction ... between things and persons' (1925/1990: 47). A third is a change in the nature of and motivation for giving. For modern Western societies, gifts tend to be seen as an expression of individual sentiment. On the other hand, in gift societies, occasions of gift giving are '"total" social phenomena ... [in which] all kinds of institutions are given expression at one and the same time – religious, judicial, and moral ... likewise economic' (1925/1990: 3). Mauss's approach in *The Gift*,

then, locates exchange in a broad sociocultural context. However, until the last quarter of the twentieth century, much work on exchange took a narrower view, focusing on the gift transaction and the sociocultural factors that appeared to motivate transactors. This narrow focus reflects Mauss's assessment of the core of exchange.

For Mauss, that core is a trio of obligations that appears to exist in all societies: to give, to receive and to reciprocate in the appropriate ways on the appropriate occasions, where 'appropriate' is defined in large part by the social relationship between the parties involved. In other words, in all societies there is a link between social relationships and exchange, though the details will vary from place to place. I can illustrate this with a society in Papua New Guinea, Ponam Island, in Manus Province. When a Ponam couple marry, the occasion, its anticipation (in betrothal) and its aftermath (in the birth of children, the maturity of the marriage, its end in the death of each partner) are marked by the exchange of gifts. The name of the gift and its occasion, the items given and the details of the givers and recipients vary over the life of the marriage (see especially Carrier and Carrier 1991: Chapter 4). However, the failure of the appropriate party to give, like the failure of the appropriate counter-party to receive and to reciprocate in the appropriate way, would cause comment and dismay, as people would wonder what caused this breach in the relations linking giver and recipient.

For those who pursued this element in Mauss's book, the focus is narrower than the broad context he invoked in his consideration of exchange. The issue that they pursued was the way that the gift and the giving embody the parties involved and their relationship. An important cultural manifestation of this is what Mauss called the 'spirit' of the gift. He presents this in terms of the *hau*, a Maori term. Mauss says that, for the Maori, the giver has a claim on whatever accrues to the recipient through the use of the object. To illustrate this, Mauss reports the words of Tamate Ranaipiri. Ranaipiri said that if you give me a valuable item and I then give it to someone else, and if that someone else later reciprocates with a second item, I must return it to you, for it embodies the spirit of what you gave me in the first place. If I fail to do so, 'serious harm might come to me, even death' (Mauss 1925/1990: 11). Mauss's discussion of this has generated a substantial body of commentary and dispute (e.g. Parry 1986: 462–6; Sahlins 1974: Chapter 4). However, at its core is the point that the gift represents the relationship between giver and recipient. To fail to give, to receive or to reciprocate would be to deny, or at least redefine, that relationship.

In *The Gift*, Mauss took a critical view of modern France and, by extension, modern Western capitalist societies more generally, though his broadly developmental approach made this criticism difficult to sustain and obscured it somewhat. That critical view has two aspects. First, he suggests that the distinction been modern societies and societies of the gift is not as radical as some might think. While these societies may be dominated by the gift, modern societies also contain it. This assertion is, however, somewhat wistful, as Mauss describes an attenuated set of practices among the French peasantry or laws that are not enforced (1925/1990: 66–7, 154 n. 5), or refers to reforms that are 'laboriously in gestation' but have yet to bear fruit (for example 1925/1990: 67–8, 78). Second, he approaches pre-modern societies as forms to be understood on their own terms and, more important, he uses them to illustrate an aspect of transaction that tended to be ignored in the economistic ideology that pervades modern life (e.g. Dumont 1977). In effect, Mauss was objecting to Adam Smith's (1776/1976: 17) famous assertion of people's innate 'propensity to truck, barter, and exchange one thing for another'. For Mauss, there is nothing innate about the sort of exchange that Smith meant. It emerges from social circumstance, and if we forget this, we cannot understand people's lives and societies. In spite of these elements in his work, however, Mauss's approach stresses the differences between types of societies that are part of a developmental or evolutionary sequence: societies of the gift developing into modern societies 'of purely individual contract, of the market where money circulates, of sale proper, and above all of the notion of price reckoned in coinage' (1925/1990: 46).

Mauss's treatment of types of transactions and types of transactors in gift societies attracted criticism from one of the anthropologists whose work he drew on, Malinowski and his description of exchange on Kiriwina, in the Trobriand Islands of Melanesia, in *Argonauts*. This criticism is interesting, because it identifies a tension in the anthropological treatment of exchange that persisted throughout the twentieth century, a tension that, moreover, helped restrict the context in which researchers placed exchange.

In *Argonauts* (1922: 177), Malinowski included a list of the sorts of exchange transactions that he observed on Kiriwina, which to Mauss (1925/1990: 73) evidently run 'from pure gift to pure barter', from the social and normative, on the one hand, to the impersonal, egocentric and calculating on the other, and Mauss invoked the social and normative end in his treatment of societies of the gift. Malinowski bridled at this. Shortly after *The Gift* was published, he said that Mauss had got it wrong:

> The honourable citizen is bound to carry out his duties, though his submission is not due to any … mysterious 'group sentiment', but to the detailed and elaborate working of a system … [in which there] comes sooner or later an equivalent repayment or counter-service.
>
> (Malinowski 1926: 42)

In pointing to the equivalent returns, Malinowski was asserting that there was no truly social and normative, non-egocentric gift in Kiriwina. In saying this, he was portraying exchange 'as essentially *dyadic* transactions between *self-interested individuals*, and as premissed on some kind of *balance*' (Parry 1986: 454).

On its face, this may appear to be a dispute about the details of the ethnography of a handful of people in a minor part of the world. However, it is much more than that, for it is the manifestation of differences between fundamental approaches to and assumptions about social life. For Mauss, exchange, and by implication social life generally, is a manifestation of society as a whole, an entity that may or may not encourage individualism and egocentric calculation (Mauss 1938/1985). Thus, for Mauss, it 'is not individuals but groups or *moral persons* who carry on exchanges' (Parry 1986: 456). For Malinowski, on the other hand, society in some sense came second. People and their needs and desires came first, and these resulted in the social organization and practices that an observer sees. Because people come first, transactions need to be explained not in terms of social rules and understandings of the sort Mauss described, but in terms of that equivalent repayment that transactors expect to get in return, and do typically get in return, for what they give. For Malinowski, then, what Marx said of bourgeois society appears to apply as well to Melanesia, where there rules:

> Freedom, Equality, Property and Bentham. Freedom, because … [they] are constrained only by their free will … Equality, because … they exchange equivalent for equivalent. Property, because each disposes only of what is his own. And Bentham, because each looks only to himself.
>
> (From *Capital* I, Chapter 6, in Tucker 1978: 343)

This tension between a more person-centred and a more society-centred approach to transaction has not gone away, and it is unlikely that it will go away, though it takes different forms at different times. Its most self-evident expression in the twentieth century among anthropologists was the debate between formalists and substantivists, which was important especially in the United States in the 1950s and 1960s (see Dalton 1967; LeClair and Schneider 1968). While this debate was about many things, formalists generally manifest Malinowski's concern to start with individuals, their calculations and transactions, while substantivists tended to echo Mauss, looking more at the ways that systems of belief and social order shaped people's actions. More generally, the difference between these two orientations is reflected in the difference between economists, especially neoclassical economists, and anthropologists. The former start with individuals and their desires, and build system and regularity on that foundation. Anthropologists, by contrast, are prone to reverse the analytical process, and see in people's actions the consequences of system and regularity, whether these spring from the logic of the social order or of people's beliefs and values.

The Gift and the debate it generated are not simply of historical interest, for they help define a set of questions and disputes that have shaped subsequent investigation and discussion and that help tie together and make sense of much current work related to exchange. A number of features of the work are important here. First is Mauss's developmental sequence, and especially the broad distinction between those societies where gifts are important and modern societies, where they are not. Second is the point that transactions reflect and help define the relationship between transactors. Third is the spirit of the gift, which points to the importance of people's understandings of objects and their place in exchange and transaction.

GIFT SOCIETIES AND MODERN SOCIETIES

I said that the first point Mauss's work raises is the distinction between gift societies and modern societies, which are dominated by the transaction of commodities. This distinction is elaborated most cogently in the work of C.A. Gregory, who has presented a comprehensive description of gift and commodity exchange, cast in ideal-typical terms.[2] He says that gift

exchange occurs between transactors who are related to each other, it is obligatory and it involves inalienable objects, which carry the identities of giver, recipient and their relationship (see Gregory 1980: especially 640). Alternatively, commodity exchange occurs between transactors who are otherwise independent of each other, it is voluntary (at least formally) and it involves alienated objects.

In gift systems, then, the parties to a gift exchange are identified in terms of their durable relationship with each other. A clear form of this is relations based on kinship, but it is apparent as well in durable non-kin relations, such as those linking trade partners or people who see themselves as coming from the same place. On the other hand, in commodity systems the parties to a commodity exchange are identified as autonomous individuals linked to each other only through the transaction at hand. A clear form of this is the transient relation between customer and store clerk, one which dissolves once the purchase is completed.

In gift systems, as indicated already, social expectations spring from the nature of the relationship that makes giving obligatory in the appropriate circumstances. In commodity systems, on the other hand, the transaction is voluntary: people are not obliged to work for one employer rather than another, to shop at one supermarket rather than another or to take their purchases to one checkout clerk rather than another. Finally, in gift systems the object given uniquely carries the identity of the giver, the recipient and their relationship, which can be summarized as the spirit of the gift. On the other hand, the things transacted in commodity systems are indifferent objects: one package of cereal or bag of sugar is the same as all the others piled on the shelf.

Gregory's work has been influential for identifying and elaborating the distinction between gifts and commodities (for an extended discussion, see Carrier 1995: Chapter 1). For my purposes here, however, it is significant because it relates sorts of transactions clearly to sorts of societies and forms of social relation, and hence fills a gap in *The Gift*, which was concerned more with identifying gifts, describing and making sense of them.

Gregory holds that gift and commodity societies differ in the fundamental ways that people are organized, and the ways that people and objects are conceived. Gift societies are organized in terms of kinship, archetypally descent, organized as clan members; and descent is a qualitative social relationship between people. Further, such societies are oriented toward the social reproduction of people, not just as individual humans, but as members and embodiments of kin groups. On the other hand, commodity societies are oriented toward the social production of things, not just material objects but their identity and meaning as indifferent commodities. In these societies, people are organized in terms of that production, which means class relations and the division of labour, and hence in terms of quantitative social relationships (see generally Gregory 1982).

It is possible to criticize what Gregory has to say by pointing to the importance of personal transactions in commodity-based societies (e.g. Carrier 1992) and of impersonal transactions in gift-based systems (e.g. Gell 1992). However, it is important to see that he has made a sustained and persuasive effort to link social and cultural, and even economic, aspects of exchange to the broader social context in which they occur. With Gregory, then, we move beyond Mauss's descriptive assertion that, in societies of the gift, gifts express religious, judicial, moral and economic values and processes to a coherent statement of how and why both gifts and commodities do so in their respective sorts of societies. We also see a broadening of the context in which exchange is viewed, as Gregory points us to much more than the obligation to give, to receive and to reciprocate.

Gregory was not alone in seeing links between forms of exchange and forms of social life. Marilyn Strathern addressed such links as well, in *The Gender of the Gift* (1988), though her focus is narrower, being what she describes as Melanesian societies. These are classic societies of the gift, and Strathern elaborates on the ways that people in such societies see the transactors and the objects transacted in gift exchange as intensely unalienated. She says that in these societies neither people nor objects are independent entities. Rather, both are conceived in terms of the social relationships that brought them about, and in terms of the people, things and relationships that they help to create. The pig given in exchange, like the person who gives it, is an embodiment of the people involved in its past: the women who fed the pigs and reared the children, the men who cleared the gardens and built the houses, the men and women who carried out the exchanges that shaped the histories of all that is involved in the exchange that we see today.

While Gregory and Strathern link exchange to broader analytical issues, they still restrict their concern to the field of beliefs and processes within the society in which exchange occurs. Claude Meillassoux (1981) represents a contemporaneous broadening, but in a different direction, for he points to the ways that understanding exchange can lead us beyond that society. In his analysis of village societies in colonial Africa he argued that these societies exist in a symbiotic, if unequal, relationship with urban areas and the capitalist relations and processes that characterize them. Those villages rear children, who commonly migrate to wage work for part of their adult lives. These migrants are the embodiment of the processes of child rearing, including the exchanges and other transactions involved. In return for sending them off to urban areas, villages typically receive a portion of the wages that they earn, in the form of remittances, cash that allows villagers to purchase objects otherwise unavailable. From the perspective of the organizations that employ them, these migrants are cheap labour. They are paid less than they would be in metropolitan countries, where their direct and indirect wages would have to cover not just their subsistence while they worked, but also the costs of reproducing the labour force that are borne by villagers (see Meillassoux 1981: 99–103).

It is worth noting that Meillassoux's concern with relations between village, city and the larger political-economic order appear in other areas of anthropology. For instance, one important stream in the study of peasant societies investigates the survival strategy of households. Some work in this stream has argued that households produce things and sustain their members in ways that resemble what Meillassoux describes. Because of the costs borne by the households in which they are produced, these objects and members' labour can be sold on the market cheaper than would be possible if they were produced in a fully monetized system (e.g. Harris 2000; Harriss 1982; Wolf 1966; see more broadly Gudeman and Rivera 1991).

Meillassoux's work, like the peasant studies I have described, raises issues that lead to a further broadening of the context in which exchange exists. We are well beyond the place and time of the exchange, beyond the obligation to give, receive and reciprocate, even beyond the society in which the exchange occurs. The village migrant working in an African gold mine is involved in an exchange of labour for money that speaks not just of the labour and the pay. As well, it speaks of the worker's past and future in his home village, and the company's position in global markets and the ways that this is made more secure by the availability of cheap labour. Moreover, this exchange speaks of more than societies of the gift or of the commodity, for it is concerned with the relationship between them. That miner's labour (like the peasant's produce brought to market) embodies both its antecedents in the gift system of village life (and of peasant households) and its consequences in the commodity world of the gold market (and First World supermarket shelves).

The writings that I have described in this section illustrate, albeit in a way he would not have foreseen, Mauss's (1925/1990: 3) point, that in exchanges 'all kinds of institutions are given expression at one and the same time – religious, judicial, and moral ... likewise economic'. With Gregory, we are concerned with society's prevailing economic and social organization, common understandings of people and their relationships, and the ways that people understand the objects that surround them. With Strathern, we are concerned with the people, objects and relationships in the past that constitute the actors and objects in exchange. With Meillassoux we are concerned with actors and relationships that are distant in both time and space from the exchange that we see.[3]

Talk of exchange, then, ends up leading us away from the social practice that we observe. The sections that follow illustrate aspects of this. In doing so, they incorporate other and more recent work, and point to some of the important ways that the study of exchange is changing.

TRANSACTIONS AND TRANSACTORS

I said that the second point that Mauss's work raised is the relationship between the transaction and the transactors. This relationship can be approached in two different ways, one concerning the identity of the transactors, the other concerning the organization of the transactors.

The Identity of Transactors

Because I have presented aspects of this issue already, I will deal with it only briefly here. Recall that, in gift systems, parties to an exchange are related to each other in durable ways and are obliged to transact, while in commodity systems they are neither related nor obliged. One way to get at this difference, and to complicate the ideal-typical contrast between gift and commodity systems, is through Marshall Sahlins's writing on exchange, based on Melanesian materials (especially Sahlins 1974: Chapter 5).

Sahlins argues that villagers tend to manifest three different approaches to their exchanges. At one extreme is the open-handed and generous giving and sharing that, he says, characterize relations within the immediate kin group, typically the family. Next is honest and even-handed transaction with those within the society but not within the immediate kin group, the realm that includes most of the gift exchanges that Mauss, Strathern and Gregory describe. At the other extreme is exchange with outsiders. Here there is no openhandedness or evenhandedness, but tight fistedness, the desire to get at least as good as you give, which shades into sharp dealing and even theft. For Sahlins, then, the type of exchange marches with the type of transactors: there may be no single identity that is typical of transactors in societies of the gift, and by implication in societies of the commodity.

It appears, in fact, that the situation is more complex than Sahlins's model indicates. This is apparent if we consider societies of the commodity, Western capitalist societies. They are notorious for the value they place on their economy (Dumont 1977) and the free market (Carrier 1997). And in the free market, as Gregory indicates, transactors are seen to be autonomous individuals motivated by their private resources and internal desires. Even so, in such societies gift transactions are frequent: the mass celebration of Christmas giving is only the most obvious example (Miller 1993). However, the identities associated with such gift transactions are ambivalent. This giving is an obligatory expression of the relations in which people find themselves, and the object given must be appropriate to the giver, the recipient and their relationship. This much is apparent to all those who have neglected to give appropriately to someone with whom they are in a close relation, just as it is apparent to all those who have had a gift rejected or questioned by a close relative (e.g. Carrier 1995: 26–7). At the same time, what can be called the ideology of the gift appears to deny the obligation, just as it denies that the thing given is significant (after all, the thought is what counts). Under this ideology, the giving and the object given are spontaneous expressions of the giver's sentiments, which means that they spring from the same internal factors that motivate commodity transactions (e.g. Carrier 1995: Chapter 7). As Parry (1986: 466) puts it, 'free and unconstrained contracts in the market also make free and unconstrained gifts outside it'.

The Organization of Transactors

I said that the relationship between transactions and transactors could also be approached in terms of the organization of transactors. By this I mean the ways that the flow of things between the parties to an exchange can generate or recreate sets of people. To a degree, this is implicit in Sahlins's discussion of types of exchange in the previous section, for the different sorts of transaction map on to the different sorts of transactors that an individual confronts: family, neighbours, strangers. Of course, one person's close relative is another person's stranger, so that the sorts of people vary with the individual transactor whose perspective we are assuming. Other work on exchange indicates how transactions can reveal or even create sets of people relatively independently of the perspective of any given transactor.

Perhaps the classic case of this in anthropology is the *kula* exchange that Malinowski observed in the Trobriand Islands and described in *Argonauts*. A *kula* exchange takes place between a pair of individuals, and involves the exchange of ceremonial necklaces (*soulava*) and armshells (*mwali*). If we look at *kula* exchange from a different perspective, however, we see something more than individual pairs of transactors and transactions. That is because, in these transactions, armshells are always given in one direction and necklaces are always given in another. The consequence, given the geographical distribution of transactors, is that the *kula* defines a structure linking people and places who may be distant, and even unknown, to each other. In effect, it is a giant circle covering much of the Milne Bay area, with armshells moving one direction around the circle and necklaces moving in the other.

The *kula* system is the result of a mass of actions by a mass of individuals, and in this sense resembles the classic construction of commodity markets with their mass of individual buyers and sellers. However, there are also systems of exchange that are focused much more on key actors and that define and reflect groups in different ways than does the *kula* (cf. Polanyi 1957). An important instance of this is the big-man system, common in the societies of the New Guinea Highlands (see Sahlins 1963; Strathern 1971).

In these societies exchange is common, and it is also common for individuals to seek prestige through their exchange activities, and particularly through engaging in competitive exchange; which is to say, to seek to become big men. Competitive exchange can emerge out of almost any exchange. It occurs when the person who receives a gift makes a return gift that is noticeably larger than what is normally expected. This large return gift can be taken as a challenge, and at some future date the recipient of this return gift may make another gift that is larger still, setting off a cycle of ever larger giving and counter-giving that lasts until one of the parties is unable to amass a gift of the requisite size, and so becomes indebted, and hence subordinate, to the other party.[4] I have described this from the perspective of the aspiring big men involved. Things look different if we take a broader perspective.

The aspiring big man does not produce the items given in an exchange (classically pigs and shell valuables). Instead, he solicits them from others. In the early stages of the competitive cycle these are likely to be his close kin. However, as the cycle continues he will recruit others, typically by judiciously distributing the gift that he has received from his competitor. Some will go to those who contributed to the gift that was reciprocated, and some will go to other people whom he wishes to recruit. Commonly this is done by contributing to these other people's own exchange obligations, which induces them to contribute to his next exchange payment in due course. The timing and balance of the debts and obligations these activities involve are difficult, and aspiring big men need time and skill to carry things off. If they are successful, however, they become the focus of an expanding web of social relations and obligations, generated by the exchange cycle and the flow of contributions to the big man and distributed by him. In a region where social groups are small and unstable, this social web can be a source of significant relations and obligations that transcend the immediate locality and kin group.

I have described two ways in which the flow of objects in exchange links givers and recipients into social networks and units of different sorts. One is the big-man system of competitive exchange, where the networks and units are focused on an individual whose actions are crucial for the shape of the network. The other is the *kula*, where the networks have no focus but result from the actions of individual transactors and their exchange partners, who commonly act in ignorance of what many other transactors in the *kula* system are doing. The second sort of network characterizes the focus of study of another set of exchanges that unite dispersed people into an overall system, commodity chains (e.g. Fine 2002; Leslie and Reimer 1999; Lockie and Kitto 2000; from a somewhat different perspective, see Carrier and Miller 1999).

Commodity chains are defined by the links between people and institutions in the life of a marketed object, from its creation to its consumption. Farmers, food processors, shippers, distributors, retailers and shoppers are the links in a chain through which the beans are grown, harvested, processed, tinned, shipped, put on store shelves, purchased, brought home and eaten. These chains lie somewhere between the *kula* and big-man systems I have described, their actual position being a matter of empirical investigation. These chains can be long and complex, so that a significant portion of the people and institutions involved commonly act in ignorance of what many others are doing (rather like those in the *kula*). Equally, however, in some chains one or another institution will have a significant grasp of the chain as a whole. In some food chains, for instance, large retailers will seek to control or directly influence many links in the chain, and will seek knowledge about the others (rather like an aspiring big man). Likewise, the rise of 'ethical consumption', most visible in the Fair Trade line of products, marks an effort by some to increase consumers' knowledge of and influence over links in the chain (e.g. Raynolds 2002).

In this section I have described work, some drawn from fields wider than anthropology, that bears on two important points in Mauss's *The Gift*, the ways that exchange is related to the identity of transactors and to the organization of transactors. The more recent work that I have mentioned does not spring from a conventional anthropological approach to exchange, though clearly it resonates with its concerns. And, like some of the other work I have described in this chapter, this work illustrates an important current trend in approaching exchange, broadening our field of vision beyond the place and time of the transaction itself, to include its antecedents and consequences.

UNDERSTANDINGS OF TRANSACTED OBJECTS

I said that the third issue that Mauss's work raises is the ways that people understand the objects transacted. Of course, because these objects are part of the identities of and relationship between the transactors, their understanding of themselves and the object and their understanding of the relationship will affect each other.[5] I want to begin to consider this

issue by returning to the distinction between gifts and commodities.

This distinction is especially important around Christmas. People give gifts then, but almost universally the things that they give are commodities. Because of the way gifts are understood in British and American societies (the two that I know best), these purchased commodities are risky gifts: to give something that is too obviously a commodity is to redefine the relationship between giver and recipient as being something like a commodity relationship: relatively impersonal and indifferent.

So people redefine these commodities by their practices and their talk. In terms of their practices, they remove the price tag and wrap the object in festive paper, which together hide, if not transform, its status as a commodity (indeed, in some settings the wrapping may be more important than the object wrapped; see Hendry 1995). In terms of their talk, they tell each other how hard it is to shop for Christmas gifts: the stores are crowded, the staff are overworked and grumpy and often enough are hired temporarily for the season and so know little about their work or the store, the store displays are a mess, it takes hours to find anything worth getting. In portraying the shopping as arduous, people obscure the commodity identity of the object beneath an overlay of their personal effort, which invests it with the identity of the giver and the giver's relationship with the recipient (see Carrier 1995: Chapter 8).

In these societies, Christmas is the most intense collective time of shopping and converting commodities into a form suitable for use in gift relations. In this heightened form it is a ritual that affirms and celebrates people's ability to perform the task that they carry out in mundane ways throughout the year. Everyday shopping, after all, is not simply acquiring objects for use; it is acquiring objects for use in personal relationships, which means gift relationships: even those who live alone are prone, it seems, to imagine a relationship in which the objects will be used (Miller 1998; see also Carrier 1995: Chapter 5).

Christmas shopping is a striking instance of the way that objects in exchange carry the meaning of their past: the Christmas present that obviously carries its past meaning as a commodity is inappropriate as a gift in a close personal relationship. In different circumstances, of course, the significant meanings and their implications will be different. A further example from Ponam Island will illustrate some of the complexities of this.

In their ceremonial gift exchanges surrounding marriage, death and the like, Ponams regularly give large quantities of uncooked starch, most commonly bags of rice (an introduced and purchased foodstuff) and bundles of sago flour (a traditional foodstuff prepared by people in villages near by). Where the immediate family that leads the ceremonial giving includes an adult male who has migrated to work in one or another of the country's cities, that person will play a prominent part in accumulating the gift to be given, a part that will reflect the social relationships that the migrant has built in the city. The successful and conscientious migrant will have established a network of close relationships with other migrants from the province who are also working in the city, including those from the villages near Ponam where sago is produced. The less successful and conscientious migrant will not. When the ceremonial exchange takes place, watching Ponams do not simply assess the quantity of starch given, they also see in it the social relationships that surrounded its acquisition. A generous supply of traditional sago bundles from nearby villages reveals a migrant who has successfully engaged in the Western world of city work; a generous supply of bags of purchased rice reveals a migrant who has been less successful, and so can contribute nothing but money.

The heap of gifts at the door of a house on Ponam is not, of course, the only place where the objects exchanged carry a significant meaning that attaches to the person who acquired them. People often judge stores by the quality of the commodities on their shelves. Likewise, they often judge people by the quality of the things associated with them, whether these be things they possess, like the clothes they wear or the car they drive, or the things they give.[6] Consider, for instance, a couple with a small child who is in day care while the parents work. That care can come through purchase, through state provision, through a neighbourhood cooperative arrangement, through a grandparent or other relative. Each of these ways of acquiring child care speaks of the parents, in a variety of possible ways.

The parents who pay for private provision may thereby attest to their relative wealth, but equally they may attest to a social isolation that means that they are unable to arrange child care through neighbours or relatives. The couple who participate in a neighbourhood child-care pool may attest to their poverty, or perhaps to their integration into the social networks in their area (see Narotzky 2005). The point is not that one or another interpretation is necessary or necessarily correct. Rather, it is that when the hypothetical couple engage in the exchanges to secure child care, like other exchanges that are part of the provisioning of their household, whether those exchanges are commercial, social or otherwise, they are likely to be judged by others who are party to those exchanges.

CONCLUSION

I have used a set of issues arising from Mauss's *The Gift* to describe important features in the ways that anthropologists and others have approached exchange. In doing this, I have tried to indicate the ways that those issues and approaches can take us very far from the conventional image of people giving to and receiving from each other, whether in a marriage exchange in the plains of southern Africa or on Christmas morning in Birmingham. I want to use this concluding section to reflect on the places that these studies of exchange have taken us.

Conventional anthropological work on exchange has focused primarily on the people transacting and the situation in which they transact: who gives what to whom, why, and how they think about it. In addressing these issues, this work has necessarily extended the area of interest beyond the immediate time and place of the exchange, but relatively little, and generally these extensions are still linked closely to the transacting parties.

However, I have tried to show that the recent history of work on exchange has involved addressing these same questions – who, what, why and how they think about it – in terms that extend far beyond the conventional focus on the time and place of exchange. These extensions effectively trace the social and cultural causes and consequences of the exchange to ever broader times and places. While it is true that conventional anthropological work devoted relatively little time to these issues, it will not do to say that it was blind to them. For instance, I have shown how Malinowski looked to broader places when he related individual *kula* transactions in the Trobriands to a regional system, and how Sahlins looked to broader times when he related competitive exchange in the New Guinea Highlands to the rise and fall of sociopolitical groups.

When scholars have situated the people and places they study in larger fields, the net is cast even wider. I have shown, for instance, how Meillassoux related the forms of exchange in African village societies to the forms of exchange in urban capitalist societies. This point is echoed in work on peasant societies, which persist in part, perhaps, because of the way that they ease the operation of capitalist firms. This wider net is not restricted only to the social dimensions of exchange, but appears as well in work on the cultural dimension. When I described work on gift giving in Western societies, I showed how people's understandings of the objects that they give and receive reflect their understandings of those objects' past and future contexts. The same point emerges, of course, in work on commodity chains and on Fair Trade, ethical consumption and sustainable commodities.

Neither my summary here nor the issues I described in the body of this chapter can pretend to be exhaustive. My purpose has been more modest. It is to indicate both the classic foundation of anthropological consideration of exchange and an important trend in the modern work relating to exchange. The goal in this tale is to indicate the ways that considering people's give-and-take can help us to understand their lives and the social and cultural worlds in which they exist. It is also to suggest a growing concern to place these social and cultural worlds in broader contexts, contexts linked by the material that people transact with each other.

NOTES

1   As this might indicate, the physical attributes of objects in exchange are relatively unimportant in considerations of exchange. Every so often, anthropologists are told that they really should look at those attributes, rather than seeing objects simply in terms of their social and cultural corollaries. Just as often, the advice is ignored (but see Keane 2001). Attention, then, remains fixed on how people interpret the things exchanged, whether in terms of the relationship in which they are transacted or in terms of cultural ascriptions of scarcity, gender, history or the like.

2   Gregory has rejected the idea that he meant to use 'the distinction between gifts and commodities to classify societies', adding 'nor have I ever suggested that "we" are to commodities as "they" are to gifts. Such an approach is anathema to me' (Gregory

1997: 47). Even so, such a distinction seems to be justified by various passages in his writings.

3   Much of the work I have described in this section makes the sort of points often associated with Appadurai's influential (1986) collection, *The Social Life of Things*. That volume appears to have crystallized the trends in the study of exchange that are the concern of this chapter.

4   Here, each party competes to give an amount larger than the other can reciprocate. In some systems, however, each party competes to destroy more than the other can match, the most famous of these being the potlatch of the Pacific Northwest (e.g. Codere 1950; Drucker and Heizer 1967; see Mauss 1925/1990: 6–7).

5   In some cases, the relationship between object and person or group is so strong that efforts are made to keep the object out of exchange altogether (e.g. Weiner 1992; this issue is addressed in different ways in Bloch and Parry 1989; Gudeman 2001).

6   To point to the cultural meaning of objects given in exchange leads us into important work in the study of consumption. This is a vast topic, far beyond the scope of this chapter. Foundational works on the issue include Baudrillard (1981), Bourdieu (1984), Douglas and Isherwood (1978), Sahlins (1976) and of course Veblen (1927).

REFERENCES

Appadurai, A., ed. (1986) *The Social Life of Things*. New York: Cambridge University Press.

Baudrillard, J. (1981) *For a Critique of the Political Economy of the Sign*. St Louis: Telos Press.

Bloch, M. and Parry, J. (1989) 'Introduction: money and the morality of exchange', in J. Parry and M. Bloch (eds), *Money and the Morality of Exchange*. Cambridge: Cambridge University Press, pp. 1–32.

Bourdieu, P. (1984) *Distinction: a Social Critique of the Judgement of Taste*. London: Routledge.

Carrier, A.H. and Carrier, J.G. (1991) *Structure and Process in a Melanesian Society*. London: Harwood Academic.

Carrier, J.G. (1992) 'Occidentalism: the world turned upside-down', *American Ethnologist*, 19: 195–212.

Carrier, J.G. (1995) *Gifts and Commodities: Exchange and Western Capitalism since 1700*. London: Routledge.

Carrier, J.G., ed. (1997) *Meanings of the Market: the Free Market in Western Culture*. Oxford: Berg.

Carrier, J.G. and Miller, D. (1999) 'From public virtue to private vice: anthropology and economy', in

H. Moore (ed.), *Anthropological Theory Today*. Cambridge: Polity Press, pp. 24–47.

Codere, H. (1950) *Fighting with Property: a Study of Kwakiutl Potlatching and Warfare, 1792–1930*. Seattle, WA: University of Washington Press.

Dalton, G., ed. (1967) *Tribal and Peasant Economies: Readings in Economic Anthropology*. Garden City, NY: Natural History Press.

Douglas, M. and Isherwood, B. (1978) *The World of Goods*. Harmondsworth: Penguin Books.

Drucker, P. and Heizer, R.F. (1967) *To Make my Name Good: a Reexamination of the Southern Kwakiutl Potlatch*. Berkeley, CA: University of California Press.

Dumont, L. (1977) *From Mandeville to Marx: the Genesis and Triumph of Economic Ideology*. Chicago: University of Chicago Press.

Fine, B. (2002) *The World of Consumption: the Material and Cultural Revisited*. London: Routledge.

Gell, A. (1992) 'Inter-tribal commodity barter and reproductive gift-exchange in old Melanesia', in C. Humphrey and S. Hugh-Jones (eds), *Barter, Exchange and Value: an Anthropological Approach*. Cambridge: Cambridge University Press, pp. 142–68.

Gregory, C.A. (1980) 'Gifts to men and gifts to God: gift exchange and capital accumulation in contemporary Papua', *Man* (n.s.), 15: 626–52.

Gregory, C.A. (1982) *Gifts and Commodities*. New York: Academic Press.

Gregory, C.A. (1997) *Savage Money: the Anthropology and Politics of Commodity Exchange*. Amsterdam: Harwood Academic.

Gudeman, S. (2001) *The Anthropology of Economy*. Oxford: Blackwell.

Gudeman, S. and Rivera, A. (1991) *Conversations in Colombia: the Domestic Economy in Life and Text*. New York: Cambridge University Press.

Harris, M. (2000) *Life on the Amazon: the Anthropology of a Brazilian Peasant Village*. Oxford: Oxford University Press.

Harriss, J., ed. (1982) *Rural Development: Theories of Peasant Economy and Agrarian Change*. London: Hutchinson.

Hendry, J. (1995) *Wrapping Culture: Politeness, Presentation and Power in Japan and other Societies*. Oxford: Clarendon Press.

Keane, W. (2001) 'Money is no object: materiality, desire, and modernity in an Indonesian society', in F.R. Meyers (ed.), *The Empire of Things: Regimes of Value and Material Culture*. Santa Fe, CA: School of American Research Press, pp. 65–90.

LeClair, E.E., Jr and Schneider, H.K., eds (1968) *Economic Anthropology: Readings in Theory and Analysis*. New York: Holt Rinehart.

Leslie, D. and Reimer, S. (1999) 'Spatializing commodity chains', *Progress in Human Geography*, 23: 401–20.

Lockie, S. and Kitto, S. (2000) 'Beyond the farm gate: production-consumption networks and agri-food research', *Sociologia Ruralis*, 40: 3–19.

Malinowski, B. (1922) *Argonauts of the Western Pacific*. London: Routledge.

Malinowski, B. (1926) *Crime and Custom in Savage Society*. London: Routledge.

Mauss, M. (1925/1990) *The Gift: the Form and Reason for Exchange in Archaic Societies*. London: Routledge.

Mauss, M. (1938/1985) 'A category of the human mind: the notion of person; the notion of self', in M. Carrithers, S. Collins and S. Lukes (eds), *The Category of the Person*. Cambridge: Cambridge University Press, pp. 1–25.

Meillassoux, C. (1981) *Maidens, Meal and Money*. Cambridge: Cambridge University Press.

Miller, D., ed. (1993) *Unwrapping Christmas*. Oxford: Oxford University Press.

Miller, D. (1998) *A Theory of Shopping*. Cambridge: Polity Press.

Narotzky, S. (2005) 'Provisioning', in J.G. Carrier (ed.), *A Handbook of Economic Anthropology*. Cheltenham: Elgar, pp. 78–93.

Parry, J. (1986) '*The Gift*, the Indian gift and the "Indian gift"', *Man* (n.s.), 21: 453–73.

Polanyi, K. (1957) 'The economy as instituted process', in K. Polanyi, C.M. Arensberg and H.W. Pearson (eds), *Trade and Market in the Early Empires*. New York: Free Press, pp. 243–70.

Raynolds, L.T. (2002) 'Consumer/producer links in Fair Trade coffee networks', *Sociologia Ruralis*, 42: 404–24.

Sahlins, M. (1963) 'Poor man, rich man, big-man, chief: political types in Melanesia and Polynesia', *Comparative Studies in Society and History*, 5: 285–303.

Sahlins, M. (1974) *Stone Age Economics*. London: Tavistock.

Sahlins, M. (1976) *Culture and Practical Reason*. Chicago: University of Chicago Press.

Smith, A. (1776/1976) *An Inquiry into the Nature and Causes of the Wealth of Nations*. Chicago: University of Chicago Press.

Strathern, A. (1971) *The Rope of Moka*. Cambridge: Cambridge University Press.

Strathern, M. (1988) *The Gender of the Gift*. Berkeley, CA: University of California Press.

Tucker, R.C., ed. (1978) *The Marx-Engels Reader*, 2nd edn. New York: Norton.

Veblen, T. (1927) *The Theory of the Leisure Class*. New York: Vanguard Press.

Weiner, A.B. (1992) *Inalienable Possessions: the Paradox of Keeping-while-giving*. Los Angeles: University of California Press.

Wolf, E. (1966) *Peasants*. Englewood Cliffs, NJ: Prentice Hall.

25

PERFORMANCE

Jon P. Mitchell

Performance is ... concerned with something that anthropologists have always found hard to characterize theoretically: the creation of presence: Performances, whether ritual or dramatic, create and make present realities vivid enough to beguile, amuse or terrify. And through these presences, they alter moods, social relations, bodily dispositions and states of mind.

(Schieffelin 1998: 194)

INTRODUCTION: THE THREE Ps, ANTHROPOLOGY AND MATERIAL CULTURE

Theory in anthropology since the sixties, wrote Sherry Ortner in the early eighties, had begun to move away from static metaphors of structure and system towards a more historicizing concern with process and practice (Ortner 1984). Since then there has been added a third theoretical P to describe culture and society as an unfolding rather than fixed reality – performance.

Performance has entered the anthropological lexicon via two related routes. First, through an expansion of Goffman's (1959) work on self-presentation, to focus on social identity – and particularly gendered identity – as performative. Such work provides a powerful critique of essentialized gender classifications, as it locates the processes of gender identification in bodily performance (see Butler 1990; Connell 1995; Herzfeld 1985). In doing so it also proposes a recasting of the gendered body as performative subject rather than material object. The second avenue for anthropology's incorporation of performance comes from the interdisciplinary area of Performance Studies, and its focus not on everyday performance but on performative events. Here, the impetus has come from theatre practitioners who wish to explore the relationships between theatre and ritual, and from anthropologists who – in a reciprocal move – have emphasized the theatrical performativity of ritual (see Barba 1995; Schechner 1985, 1993; Barba et al. 1991).

This chapter suggests that neither of these two perspectives on performance is entirely satisfactory on its own. Whilst it is true that performativity is a property of – at least some aspects of – everyday life, there is nevertheless an important distinction to be made between everyday performance and the more extraordinary performance of theatrical or ritual events. In particular, ritual events have the ability to effect major transformations of character or status on persons, things and places. However, such events should not be seen as entirely separate from everyday life, bracketed off as discrete ethnographic objects (see Coleman and Collins 2000). Rather, attention should be paid to the interrelationship of everyday and extraordinary performances, and particularly the extent to which transformations in the latter effect transformations in the former. This is the first theme of this chapter.

The contemporary study of material culture[1] has developed alongside – and indeed has arguably been born out of – the 'post-structural' preoccupation with process, practice and performance. In emphasizing the 'social life of things' (Appadurai 1986), the creative and active practices of consumption (Miller 1995), and the 'agency' of material objects as they are embedded in systems of social relatedness that they are both constituted by and constitute

(Gell 1998), material culture studies have at their centre not the fixity of structure and system but the fluidity of process, practice, performance which in turn emphasize transformation – of objects and, reciprocally, persons (see especially Kuechler 2002). It is transformation, then, that provides the second theme of this chapter.

The chapter focuses on three types of material transformation: of the body; of things; and of space. In each case, it explores the ways in which the relatively extraordinary performances of ritual create transformations that are carried forward into everyday contexts. Ethnographically, it examines initiation – particularly in Papua New Guinea; masking and masquerade – in West Africa; and public procession/parading – in Northern Ireland and southern Europe. It explores the ways in which the bodily transformations of initiation transform everyday personhood such that, although initiation involves a period of withdrawal from everyday life, the experiential qualities of ritual performance endure in the longer term, affecting everyday performance. It examines the ways in which the transformation of wood into mask, and then mask into artefact of power, creates enduring political legitimacy for those entitled to make, own and perform the masks. Finally, it examines the ways in which parading transforms political and religious geography to establish and reinforce territorial claims which endure after performance is finished. The chapter therefore emphasizes the long-term effects of ritual performance on the everyday order of material things.

The third theme of the chapter is the extent to which, in and through performance, objects of material culture become subjects. The transformations dealt with here, then, are not merely the transformation of inert material from one category to another, but a more substantive transformation in which the material is endowed with the power to act – with agency. In the case of initiation, it is the agency of the experiencing body that is critical, which generates salient memories of terror that endure in the initiand after their initiation. In the case of masks, it is the agency of the mask itself that is significant, which is produced through careful craftsmanship, the correct combinations of 'medicine' and performance itself. In the case of space, it is the agency of spatial precedence created by previous performance. Where decisions are made and spatial precedents established by a parade, these will not only generate political geography in the everyday but also require the reperformance of 'correct spatiality' in subsequent parades (see Pina-Cabral 1984).

It is these three themes, then, that inform this chapter: the relationship between extraordinary performative contexts and everyday; the transformation of objects and persons through performance; and the agency of material objects conceived as subjects, rather than objects, of ritual performance.

THE MATERIAL BODY: OBJECT AND SUBJECT

At the centre of a material culture approach to performance must be the body. Minimally, performance requires a body to act – to perform. Yet the relationship between body and performer is not so straightforward as one might imagine. The problem – like many in the study of material culture – stems from an over-reliance on semiological-representational theories that see the body as representation of something other than itself. At the heart of this assumption is the Cartesian separation of mind and body that places the body at a conceptual remove from the conscious self, thereby objectifying it.

The performing body can be thought of as object in two distinct but related ways. First, the body as object of the will of its possessor – a position that suggests that the body enacts processes determined by the person, either consciously – as in the case of theatrical performance – or unconsciously – as in the case of 'body language'. Born of social psychology, this quasi-linguistic metaphor is widely invoked in popular discourse to describe and ascribe the meaningful actions of the body, which are said to utilise a subconscious – some would argue primordial – grammar of action (Beattie 2003). By this logic, the body *enacts* the person, either the self or – in the case of theatrical performance – another.

Second, in contrast to this focus on the body as object of the self is the more anthropological understanding of the body as object of sociocultural process. This sees the physical body as both metaphor for and expression of the body social (Lock 1993: 135). Mary Douglas (1970), for example, argues that the body is a microcosm of society, and serves as a source of symbols through which society is expressed. The relationship between body and society, though, is reciprocal, such that although the natural body provides a source of 'natural symbols', the nature of the body is nevertheless subordinated to – and becomes the object of – society. It is subordinated both in the sense that the metaphorical possibilities of the body – the choice about which metaphors are used, and how – are determined by society, and in the sense that particular bodies – the bodies of persons living in society – are subordinated to, and so become objects of the social. This position presents the body as *tabula rasa* upon which society signifies the social person – most obviously through scarification, circumcision and other forms of body modification.

Such forms of body modification are normally associated with initiation in 'non-Western' societies.[2] In such contexts, the transition of a person from one social category to another is marked by their participation in compulsory ritual activities. There is also, however, a wealth of recent research on body modification in 'Western' societies in which it is associated less with the formalities of ritualized initiation and more with the informal processes of 'youth culture' (Featherstone 2000; Pitts 2003), in which body modification is seen less as a mark of society's action on the body and more as a performance of self and subjectivity (Jones 1998). The two contexts can therefore be contrasted as on the one hand societies in which personhood is socially ascribed through the performance of ritual, and on the other hand those in which it is achieved by the self; on the one hand analysts who have seen the body as a social object and on the other hand those who have seen it as an object of the self.

Recent developments in the anthropology of ritual – and particularly rituals of initiation – have challenged this dichotomy of Western/non-Western society through regarding the body not as an *object* of either society or the self, but as *subject*. The approach takes its cue from a broader rethinking of the nature of body in society, brought about partly by the rehabilitation of Marcel Mauss's (1973) piece on 'Techniques of the body' and particularly the adoption and expansion of the notion of *habitus* by Pierre Bourdieu. For Mauss, habitus was fundamentally social, and transcends mere habit or custom (1973: 73) to describe 'the ways in which from society to society men know how to use their bodies' (1973: 70). In a famously opaque statement, Bourdieu redefined habitus as:

> systems of durable dispositions, structured structures predisposed to function as structuring structures, that is, the principle of generation and structuration of practices and representations which can be objectively 'regulated' and 'regular' without in any way being the product of obedience to rules, objectively adapted to their goal without presupposing the conscious orientation towards ends and

the expressive mastery of operations necessary to attain them and, being all that, collectively orchestrated without being the product of the organising action of a conductor.

(Bourdieu 1977: 73)

His aim was to construct a non-deterministic sociology that somehow accounts for a mediation of on the one hand social structure and on the other hand modes of individual agency or instrumental rationality. Habitus describes the central mechanism of this dialectical process and is – critically – located in the body. But this is not a straightforwardly imitative body; and neither is it a body whose primary characteristic is representational – it is not a body-object. Bourdieu's focus on *dispositions* rather than obedience to social rules or laws confirms the status of the body as subject, rather than object, of social determination. Moreover, his explicit rejection of the social psychological focus on 'body language' takes us beyond the simplistic Cartesian dichotomy of mind-subject/body-object to suggest an embodied social process that locates the body in a dialectic of incorporation:

> Social psychology is mistaken when it locates the dialectic of incorporation at the level of representation … [rather] … the process of acquisition – a practical mimesis (or mimeticism) which implies an overall relation of identification and has nothing in common with an imitation that would presuppose a conscious effort to reproduce a gesture, an utterance or an object explicitly constituted as a model – and the process of reproduction – a practical reactivation which is opposed to both memory and knowledge – tend to take place below the level of consciousness, expression and the reflexive distance which these presuppose. The body believes in what it plays at: it weeps if it mimes grief. It does not represent what it performs, it does not memorize the past, it enacts the past, bringing it back to life.

(Bourdieu 1990: 72–3)

Somewhat controversially, given Bourdieu's adamant disavowal of phenomenology (1977: 81–3), Thomas Csordas (1990) has combined his approach to the body and habitus with Merleau-Ponty's phenomenology to construct a paradigm of 'embodiment' for the analysis of bodily being in society. Like Bourdieu, he rejects the notion of the body as object, stressing instead the pre-objective state of 'being-in-the-world' that for Merleau-Ponty demonstrates the influence of the body *qua* body over human existence – the body's own 'subjectivity'. What Bourdieu adds to this phenomenology of being is his insistence that the constitution of habitus is a political process. Throughout his work he uses the metaphor of the game. Habitus constitutes a 'feel for the game' that enables people to participate in the various 'fields' – or areas of social life – that they occupy. Where this feel for the game becomes naturalized such that it is utilized in a spontaneous manner by all participants – where players becomes 'experts', one might say, and where the techniques are uncontested – *doxa* prevails. This is a condition in which the terms of social hierarchy – of social power – are uncontested, for example in the modern education system, which exists for Bourdieu not to expand or enlighten but to ensure the reproduction of doxa. Fields, then, create the mechanisms for the reproduction of habitus that in turn ensure faith in doxa. They also create mechanisms for monitoring and managing entry into the field:

> Practical faith is the condition of entry that every field tacitly imposes, not only by sanctioning and debarring those who would destroy the game, but by so shaping things, in practice, that the operations of selecting and shaping new entrants (rites of passage, examinations, etc.) are such as to obtain from them that indisputed, pre-reflexive, naïve, native compliance with the fundamental presuppositions of the field which is the very definition of *doxa*.
>
> (Bourdieu 1990: 68)

The significance of initiation, then, is less to do with the physical scars it places on the body as object of society, and more to do with the creation of particular types of subject who are capable of acting in the social world – endowed with habitus and commitment to doxa. Often without directly drawing on Bourdieu's work, recent anthropologists of initiation have also moved towards this position. Whilst the 'classic' work on initiation – drawing on Van Gennep's pioneering *The Rites of Passage* (1960) – had emphasized its sociological significance in moving persons from one social category to another – a process of transition through what was conceptualized as relatively static social space – more recent work has focused not on social transition but on the transformation of the person in and through initiation – on the acquisition of bodily capacities or habitus through initiation.

THE TRANSFORMATION OF BODY AND PERSON: INITIATION

For Van Gennep (1960), rites of passage are all about marking the transition of a person from one social category into another – for example, childhood to adulthood – as they move through life. Each transition is marked by a series of rituals that have a distinct, tripartite structure involving rites of separation, rites of transition and rites of incorporation. At separation, an initiand is removed from everyday material life and placed in a *liminal* state in which transition rites are carried out before (re)incorporation into the everyday.

Using a slightly different terminology, Turner (1967, 1969) developed this tripartite schema, focusing more explicitly on the symbolic content of ritual, but again on the function of ritual in achieving social transition, reproducing social categories and with them society itself. Turner gives us the example of the installation ritual of an Ndembu senior chief (1969). This involved building a small shelter a mile from the chief's capital village, where the chief was taken, following separation rituals that both symbolize and achieve his physical detachment from everyday life. While there he was systematically jostled or insulted by ritual functionaries. His status at this stage was made deliberately ambiguous, even negated. He was symbolically dead. This was a period of liminality: literal and symbolic marginalization which established him as *tabula rasa* on which his new identity could be inscribed on his jubilant return to the village. In characterizing the initiand as *tabula rasa* Turner reinforces the idea that the person – and the body – are objects of the social, rather than its subjects. The installation ritual, he argues, not only marked or celebrated the transition of the initiand into senior chief, but also allowed reflection on the *social* nature of the new role he was adopting in Ndembu society. In having his identity negated during the liminal phase, then reinscribed on reincorporation – or reaggregation, as Turner terms it – the initiand was subjected to the authority of the community, and of society as a whole.

Turner emphasizes the functional, integrative features of this ritual process, but also begins to set the agenda for an exploration of the experiential elements of initiation rituals, and therefore for a reorientation of body and self as subjects, rather than objects of the ritual process. In particular, he is concerned with exploring the depredations of the liminal phase, which produce what he terms *communitas* – a commonality of purpose, or communal spirit that is born both of the acknowledgement of ritual as a social activity, and of the experience initiands share: that is often painful, frightening and revelatory.

It is this experiential element of ritual that Bloch (1992) pursues in a general theory of ritual that places initiation at its centre and argues that rites of passage do not merely effect the *transition* of an initiand from one social category to another, but should be seen above all as rites of (experiential) *transformation*. Through initiation, a person is endowed not only with new status but also with the permanent – what Bloch calls transcendental – properties of their new, transformed selves, which may be material possessions – objects of ritual knowledge, for example – physical modifications – scarification, circumcision, etc. – and, critically, cognitive-bodily orientation to the world – what Bourdieu would call habitus. This latter feature ensures that it is not only a transformation of the self that is achieved through initiation, but also a transformation of society:

> the initia[nd] does not merely return to the world he left behind. He is a changed person, a permanently transcendental person who can therefore dominate the here and now of which he previously was a part. The return is therefore a conquest of the kind of thing which had been abandoned but, as if to mark the difference between the going and the coming back, the actual identity of the vital here and now is altered.
>
> (Bloch 1992: 5)

For Bloch, rites of passage are characterized by violence, which enacts and achieves the conquest of the vital here and now by the transcendental. There are two critical moments of violence: at the point of separation; and at the point of incorporation or reaggregation. On the one hand is the symbolic and experiential violence inherent in removing initiands from everyday life and expunging their vitality – through denying their personhood or marking them as dead, as in the case of the Ndembu chief. On the other hand the 'rebounding violence' inherent in initiands' return to the everyday, in which the old vitality is conquered by the newly transformed and transcendental initiand. He explains the process experientially in terms of an internal division within the ritual subject between the vital and the transcendental, which in the initial moment of violence – of separation – sees the vital eclipsed by the transcendental, but in the rebounding violence of reincorporation sees a return of vitality – albeit conquered vitality:

> The first part of the rituals involves an experiential dichotomisation of the subjects into an over-vital side and a transcendental side. Then … the transcendental drives out the vital so that the person

becomes, for a time, entirely transcendental. This victory of one side of the person over the other is what requires the first element of violence in the rituals. This violence is, however, only a preliminary to a subsequent violence which involves the triumphant experiential recovery of vitality into the person by the transcendental element. However … this recovery of vitality does not compromise the superiority of the transcendental identity, because the recovered vitality is mastered by the transcendental.

> (1992: 5)

This is more than simply marking a transition or reproducing the social. It constitutes an experiential embodiment of the transformation of self, through experiencing the conquest of the vital by the transcendental.

Bloch's leading example is drawn from Iteanu's work on the Orokaiva of Papua New Guinea (1983, 1990). Initiation involves children – both boys and girls – in a ritual the details of which are secret to the uninitiated (Iteanu 1990: 46) and which serves to construct Orokaiva personhood in terms of social relations – particularly exchange relations (1992: 36). In the initial stages of the ritual, the children are driven out of the everyday, mundane world of the village into the bush, which is considered the domain of spirits, by people who come from the bush dressed as spirits, in birds' feathers and pigs' tusks (Bloch 1992: 9). The 'spirits' act as if they are stalking wild pigs, shouting 'Bite, bite, bite.' The children are then rounded up on to a platform reminiscent of the ones on which dead bodies are placed, are blindfolded and taken into a hut in the bush where they stay for between three and seven years (Iteanu 1990: 46). In the hut, they are forbidden from eating normal food, to wash, speak out loud or to look outside (Bloch 1992: 9). In time, they are taught a variety of secrets, including how to play the sacred flutes and bullroarers that represent the voices of the spirits. They are also given the feathers of the spirit masks they will be permitted to wear after initiation. After their time in seclusion, the children return to the village, wearing feathers and themselves shouting 'Bite, bite, bite.' They climb on to a platform similar to the one they were on before their seclusion, and distribute pig meat.

The cycle of the initiation transforms the Orokaiva children from prey into hunter, turning them initially into pigs, representing an over-vitality that is subsequently killed as the children mimic their own death. This initial violence sees the children becoming entirely transcendental, negating their own vitality while they live in the initiation hut and are there given the permanent elements of the transcendental that they will take back with them into the vital, everyday world after initiation. After the period of seclusion, the children return, with the transcendental element dominant. They are now part spirits and can themselves conquer the vitality of the pigs which are killed in the ritual's phase of rebounding violence. The ritual, then, entails a movement from children being 'like pigs', because vital, to being 'like spirits' because transcendental, and in doing so acknowledges the presence in the Orokaiva person of pig-like vitality and spirit-like transcendence at one and the same time. It therefore mediates the relationship between the very mortal processes of growth, reproduction and decay on the one hand, and the transcendental institutions of human life on the other. It also substantively reconfigures the social world, not only through the transformations inherent in ritual experience, but also through reordering the world of social relations to accommodate the exchange relations entered into by the newly initiated at their final distribution of pig meat:

> When the ritual is over, the society, in both its material and relational aspects, has thus been completely renewed. The universe appears then as a dense network of freshly constituted relations.
>
> (Iteanu 1990: 48)

Bloch concludes his argument with a return to the social implications of the rites of passage, emphasizing their social integrative function in an ultimately Durkheimian fashion (Gellner 1999: 144). Other scholars of Papuan society have pursued in different ways the experiential element of initiation rituals, focusing more centrally on experience *qua* experience. For all his emphasis on experience, Bloch's analysis is ultimately a symbolic one, in which the experiential is a secondary phenomenon to the more significant play of symbolisms of vitality and transcendence. As Whitehouse points out:

> A problem with Bloch's interpretation ... is that it does not capture very much of the conscious experience of participants. According to Bloch ... violence is part of a bifurcation process, as cognitively simple as it is ideologically powerful. In the context of this irreducible core of religious thought, the terror of Orokaiva novices seems to be superfluous, a mere side-effect of the particular choreography which happens to be involved. One gains the impression that an equally satisfactory result could be achieved ... by symbolically killing the novices *without actually frightening them.*
>
> (Whitehouse 1996: 705, emphasis in original)

This position threatens to reinforce the Cartesian dichotomy of cognitive-symbolic and affective-experiential and thereby once more characterize ritual participants and their bodies as objects rather than subjects of the ritual process. With some support from other analysts of Orokaiva initiation (Chinnery and Beaver 1915; Schwimmer 1973), Whitehouse suggests that rather than being a secondary phenomenon, terror – as experiential rather than merely symbolic – is integral. The significance of the ritual outlined above, then, is not so much the enactment of conquest of the vital by the transcendental as the opportunity it delivers for the initiands to be scared. Indeed, terror appears to be at the centre of a whole regional complex of initiation involving a number of different Papuan societies and a baffling range of ritual practices that are nothing if not inventive in their brutality – burnings, piercings, beatings, forced ingestion of various substances, vomiting, etc. As Tuzin argues of Ilahita Arapesh initiation, for example, the whole ritual was 'carefully and successfully designed to inspire maximum horror in its victims' (1980: 74). Among Bimin-Kuskusmin, there is a similar emphasis on the experience of fear within initiation:

> revelation is a consequence not only of others' communications but also of one's participatory experience: experience that cannot entirely be communicated, it must be undergone.
>
> (Poole 1982: 110)

Undergoing such rituals invokes in participants salient memories – which Whitehouse refers to as 'flashbulb memories': 'vivid recollections of inspirational, calamitous, or otherwise emotionally arousing events' (Whitehouse 1996: 710). Significantly, flashbulb memories appear to strengthen with time, rather than fade, and are a particularly effective means of transmitting religious knowledge (Whitehouse 1995, 2000, 2004). Such memories are 'sedimented in the body' of the initiand, to use Connerton's (1989) suggestive terminology, and effect transformation through encoding 'a set of very particular events, experiences and responses' (Whitehouse 1996: 712) which serve as a means of ordering subsequent reflections upon that transformation.

In Baktaman initiation (Barth 1975, 1987) there is a similar preoccupation with pigs as among the Orokaiva, and a ritual process that sees initiands 'turned into' pigs – but importantly *wild* pigs rather than domesticated (Whitehouse 1996: 706). Thus it is less the domestic pig's vitality that is emphasized, and more its wild cousin's destructive, violent virility. Most of the time, wild pigs are seen as enemies because of their destructive tendencies, but during initiation they are shown in a more ambivalent light – as possessing properties necessary for success as a father or warrior, of bravery and fierceness. Central to the initiation cult is the mandible of a pig that has been killed while copulating and then carried into successful battle by a group of Baktaman warriors, which according to Whitehouse is a key to the message of initiation:

> A clue to the meaning of the mandible is likely to be picked up by the novice in contemplating the aggressiveness and virility of wild male pigs. In addition to mulling over the paradoxical character of this revelation, the novice is likely to associate the mandible with other items of temple sacra: the bones of the ancestors, and the blackened ceiling of the cult house which in turn connotes the blackened vine used to tie the novices together – an even more explicit image of male solidarity (Barth 1975: 67). Above all, the first encounter with the pig mandible will be associated with the tortures and privations of third degree initiation, which are among the most terrifying of all Baktaman rites.
>
> (Whitehouse 1996: 708)

The salient memories, then, are of initiands having come close to – even themselves *become* – a terrifying, potent and potentially dangerous power but having nevertheless survived the ordeal. It might be said, then, that the ritual dramatizes less the conquest of the transcendental over the vital within the person, and more the vital person's conquest or control over their emotions when confronting the transcendental – emotions which are not *caused by* the encounter with the transcendental, but rather are evidence of the transcendental itself *within* the person: they *are* the transcendental. In such a scheme, the person – and indeed the body – is less the object of ritual performance, and more its subject.

In Bimin-Kuskusmin initiation, emphasis lies squarely on the mastery of emotions – fear and anger – that are provoked by the initiation process and constitute an embodied engagement with a man's legacy of agnatic blood, semen and *finiik* spirit – the spiritual property of socially appropriate adult masculinity (Poole 1982: 137–8). Initiation involves boys being transformed from 'people of the women's houses' into those who are 'becoming new men', through the systematic ingestion of male substances and their analogues – agnatic blood in the form of (wild) boar's blood and red pigment; semen in the form of semen-infused taro and pus (1982: 113) – and the extrusion of female substances – through vomiting female foods

such as sweet potato and weakening of the body's female areas by their being smeared in a domestic sow's blood (1982: 124). The boys' arms are burned with hot pig fat to produce pus that they must eat, they are whipped with nettles and have a series of incisions made in their nostrils and on their heads. Yet the effects on the body go beyond the scars that symbolize their status as 'becoming new men', to create a heightened awareness of the body, and particularly the difference between men's and women's bodies that is at the centre of their transformation. The body is not merely an object upon which initiation is marked, but a subject within it.

This is perhaps demonstrated more clearly in the example of Gisu initiation (Heald 1999). This group lives in Uganda and male initiation centres around the *imbalu* circumcision ritual. Again, though, the emphasis is less on the physical scars inflicted on the body-as-object and more on the subjective transformation inherent in control of fear and of powerful masculine force. *Lirima* – glossed by Heald as a kind of violent emotion (1999: 13) that is also a powerful creative force (1999: 28) – is like the wild pigs of the Baktaman example generally thought of as a dangerous or harmful element, but nevertheless a necessary element of adult masculinity. *Lirima* enables initiands to overcome the fear of circumcision – both of the pain and of the encounter with the ancestral power *imbalu* – but also in the process they learn how to control their *lirima*. It is not present in boys prior to *imbalu* but is systematically 'fermented' within the initiands in the build-up to circumcision. Although on the face of it not so brutal as the Melanesian examples, *imbalu* is also a ritual involving pain and fear, and significantly the conquering or mastery of fear in encounter with both a transcendent power and power within. Throughout *imbalu*, initiands are implored to 'be firm for *imbalu*' (1999: 24), controlling and conquering their emotions. What is more, there is a profound emphasis on the voluntary nature of *imbalu*. Initiands must *want imbalu* to take place, a feature of the ritual which emphasizes their active performance of initiation – not merely in the sense of their acting out roles in a wider dramatization of their transition, but as performing subjects of their transformation.

THE MATERIAL SUBJECT: ART AND AGENCY

If the evidence from Gisu and diverse Melanesian initiation suggests we move from seeing the body in performance as material object to performative subject, then the same might be said of material artefacts in performance. As with the body, recent theorists have suggested that we move away from seeing artefacts as objects and rather see them as active subjects in a web of relationships between persons and things. Part of this movement, as with the rethinking of the body, involves a movement away from principally semiological understandings of the relationship between materiality and meaning – in which the former is seen to stand for or symbolize the latter – to understand material artefacts as things-in-themselves. As Pels et al. put it:

> it is not so much what materials ... symbolise within social action that matters but their constitutive agentic effects within the entangled networks of sociality/materiality ... materials are not given meaning by a volitional will but are taken as 'actants'; their agency is understood as constituted as a relational and non-volitional 'will-as-force'.

> (Pels et al. 2002: 2)

The argument is nowhere better developed than in Alfred Gell's posthumous *Art and Agency* (1998) in which he also rejects semiological and 'comparative aesthetics' approaches to art which seek to locate the meaning of art within given 'cultural' systems of meaning and value (1998: 5–6). In particular, he problematizes the semilogical importantion of linguistic models of meaning into the understanding of art (see Layton 2003). The power of artefacts, he argues – and here his argument goes beyond art *stricto facto* to encompass broader material culture – is not that they convey meaning but that they are social agents in and of themselves. Using the relatively trivial example of the anthropomorphizing of motor cars – what he wryly calls 'vehicular animism' – Gell demonstrates artefacts' possession of intentional capacity to initiate causal events (by breaking down, for example) (1998: 18); a capacity it is made possible to adduce because of a cognitive 'module' of 'theory of mind' which attributes to social persons psychological intentionality (1998: 125–9). Where an object or artefact is also a 'social person' this intentionality can be and is extended also to the artefact as part of the same cognitive process. The thrust of Gell's argument is that this is a perfectly normal and sensible thing for a person to do – it therefore does not demand the perplexed incredulity of the ultimately condemnatory theories of reification or fetishism to account for its existence (see Pels et al. 2002). Rather, it is a routine part of people's everyday encounters with the material world around them.

If the attribution of agency to artefacts is a routine part of life, this is particularly so – for Gell – with artefacts that resemble the body (1998: 132, see also Looper 2003). Such artefacts – or idols – achieve their effectiveness in invoking a projection of mind through an iconicity of internality/externality. The two prime modes of such iconicity are orifices and enclosures, both of which communicate a property internal to the artefact; the former through offering a 'window to the soul',[3] the latter through offering a homology: idol : container/temple :: mind : body (1998: 136). In each case psychological intentionality, or agency, is attributed through the invocation of an 'inside' beyond the surface of the artefact. Idols that have orifices – and particularly eyes – and those which are contained in boxes, caskets, temples Gell sees as particularly agentive.

These insights help us to understand the significance of a range of different artefacts, but here I focus on masks in West Africa, which not only have eyes, but are also often contained – in between masquerade performances – in shrines, and indeed are also themselves containers. Moreover, as with the initiands, they undergo transformation through and within performance, rendering them like the performing body agentive subjects rather than objects.

THE TRANSFORMATION OF OBJECTS: MASKS

As Layton (2003) suggests, the focus on agency necessarily draws us towards Giddens's theorization of agency, and particulary his linkage of agency with questions of power. In the context of West African masks, and particularly those of the Dogon in Mali, Hoffman asks very similar questions to those of Gell in attempting to account for the quality of art objects – though rather than focusing on agency she emphasizes power as a property of artefacts we consider noteworthy or 'masterpieces' (1995). Power understood as an underlying but central driving force of all things is a common feature of West African conceptions of the universe (Arens and Karp 1999, Horton 1997). This is often linked to ideas about sorcery and witchcraft as technologies of harnessing this power (Geschiere 1997), and to initiation cults, secret societies and masquerade associations as legitimate custodians of the means to invoke power. Such power is evident in masterpieces or, as the Dogon sculptors say, works that make everyone 'stop breathing' (Hoffman 1995: 56). These works are the product of a moment in which the sculptors experience an internal 'wholeness' (1995: 57), in which the creative mind is subordinated to the hands (1995: 56); or, put another way, the agency of the sculptor is subordinated to the process of production in such a way as to endow the sculpture itself with agency:

> a magical object is able to put the viewer in contact ... with something buried deeply in each of us which crosses the line between culture and nature, both in the maker and the viewer of the object ... such an art object's ability to make the viewer stop breathing is an example of its ability to act, perhaps independently of the intellectual agency of explication and text.
>
> (1995: 58)

In his classic account of *The Mande Blacksmiths* and their place in Mande society, western Sudan, McNaughton (1988) explores in greater detail the nature of power in the artefacts they produce. As well as being smelters and metalworkers, the blacksmiths are wood carvers, initiators, circumcizers; both producers and performers of the important *komo* masks that lie at the centre of male Mande initiation and contain power to destroy sorcerers and criminals (1988: 130–1) but also convey important messages about nature, the spirit world, sorcery and about society and humanity as a whole (1988: 19). The masks are revealed to young men of the *ntomo* initiation association during a liminal phase of the process that, if perhaps not so overtly physically brutal as the Melanesian examples, is nonetheless terrifying. It involves, like the Gisu initiation, a temporary engagement with dangerous levels of a powerful creative force, *nyama*, which McNaughton describes as a kind of natural energy that governs the universe (1988: 16).[4] *Nyama* is the active ingredient in powerful amulets made by priests and blacksmiths and at the centre of the powerful *komo* association, that is owned and led by blacksmiths (1988: 130–1). Indeed, blacksmiths are among the clans referred to as *nyamakala* – 'handles of power, points of access to the energy that animates the universe' (1998: 18–19).[5] Blacksmiths alone make the *komo* masks that harness the energy of *nyama* and control it. They are also almost invariably those who wear the masks in performance.

The source of the mask's power is its status as a container of medicine and *daliluw*, 'the thing that can make something work' (1998: 43). At the root of *daliluw* is the idea that information

and materials can be arranged in such a configuration as to make them effective; to allow people to accomplish things with them. *Komo* masks embody and contain such effectiveness:

> An individual *komo* mask is, in reality, a wooden scaffolding onto and into which are packed a potent array of highly effective *daliluw*. They are very complicated amulets that are, simultaneously, an organized body of highly suggestive symbols.
>
> (1998: 131)

These symbols invoke a general animal nature that is a property of the bush – it is potent, dangerous and evasive (1998: 138) but controllable through *daliluw* and a necessary feature of initiation. The *komo* masks are large horizontal objects with huge jaws and horns, often topped with feathers and bird quills and smeared with sacrificial materials that are themselves a kind of *daliluw*. *Daliluw* amounts to an indigenous Mande conception of the object's agency. *Komo* masks, as instantiations of *daliluw*, possess agency as objects – they are effective, and this is because they are made by smiths who have access to the knowledge, skills and lineal authority to do so. Individual smiths have their own repertoire of *daliluw* which in turn enable the development of particular agentive capacities in the mask. Masks 'should do all the things the owner wants' (1998: 133).

The masks are not only effective in and of themselves, though. Their potency is operationalized – and indeed enhanced – through performance. As both Picton (2002) and Tonkin (1979) observe, a distinction can and should be made between mask as object *qua* object and mask-in-performance. For Picton, this is supported by his informants' – Nigerian Ebira – distinction between object-masks, *opo*, and masks-in-performance, *ebu* (2002: 53–4). The latter accrues power *through* performance. For Tonkin, the distinction is a theoretical one, which she marks by the use of the lower-case 'mask' to designate the mask-as-object and the upper-case 'Mask' for the mask-in-performance (1979: 240). For the Mande too performance is essential. Although masks will begin life possessing and operating through the producer's *daliluw*, the subsequent smearing of additional *daliluw* which occurs in performance ensures that the power of the mask develops and strengthens: 'These coatings are a kind of visual record of power harnessed through knowledge. They become energy symbolised and energy actualised' (McNaughton 1988: 138).

When first made, a mask will be worn by the mask maker alone, because he alone knows the exact configurations of *daliluw* he has included. Any other smith would have difficulty controlling the mask and harnessing the particular flows of *nyama*. It is possible that such attempts might end in death for the wearer (1988: 133–4). Masks are therefore initially inseparable from their maker and their wearer – so much so that when a *komo* leader/mask wearer/masquerade performer dies, his mask is carefully hidden until a new leader is found who is strong enough and knowledgeable enough to wear the mask. There is a symbiotic relationship between masks and their performers. Through performance, masks acquire power as they take on the properties of their successful deployment, which increases their *nyama*, giving them increased capacity for action (1988: 135). Older masks are therefore more powerful. Similarly, older *komo* leaders – older performers – are more powerful, as knowledge and experience generate potency and the capacity for success. Thus, through performance, both mask and masker are transformed. The mask, already transformed from its raw materials – from an object into a subject with power – acquires greater power, greater agency, greater capacity to act. The masker is transformed, both permanently through the acquisition of power from, in and through the mask, and temporarily during the performance itself: 'Many makers and users of African masks ... seem to regard their creations not as a mere disguise, nor as the semiotic representation of some spiritual feeling, but as a real transformation of the mask carrier's personality' (Tonkin 1979: 240).

Such transformation links back to the transformations of Melanesian and Gisu initiation, for, as well as being intiators, masking associations such as the Mande *komo* association also have their own initiation processes. Such processes also entail a transformation that links persons to wider sources of power and authority, as embodied in the masking association or society. In Nunley's (1987) treatment of Sierra Leone Ode-lay societies – masquerade societies based on Yoruba ideas and practices – initiation involves the ingestion by initiands of secret-society medicine – *juju* or *ogun* – after which they become an organic part of the group. Like the Mande *daliluw*, *ogun* is a power or capacity to effect change in both natural and supernatural realms, and is characterized more by what it *does* than what it *is* (1987: 68). It is what makes the society, its members and its masks effective. *Ogun* is contained in both masquerader and mask, ensuring that they are 'far more than mere symbols of the group; they are

the metaphysical extension of each individual member and of the group as a whole' (1987: 61). In a successful masquerade, person, society and *ogun* become one as participants – masker and audience – enter what Nunley describes as an 'ecstatic' state (1987: 176, see Lewis 1971). In this process, the performing body becomes homologous with the body politic (Nunley 1987: 188).

The Ode-lay societies are youth organizations associated not only with the control of *ogun* but also with antisocial and illegal activities – excessive alcohol drinking, marijuana smoking, petty crime (McIntyre 2002). Their masquerades are high-spirited public performances that although deriving much of their aesthetics and form from Yoruba *Egungun* and Hunting societies, are hybrid manifestations developed in the new urban and multi-ethnic context of Freetown (Nunley 1987: 132). In particular, the Ode-lay societies have combined in their masks the aesthetics of 'fancy' costumes – a feature of both *Egungun* masquerade and colonial fancy-dress balls – with 'fierce'. The latter comes from the Hunting societies and is inspired by the warlike Yoruba god of iron, Ogun, but is also a necessary element of urban youth style (1987: 137).

Ode-lay societies are competitive in their masquerades, which are an important enactment and instantiation of the society's autonomy and control (1987: 226), and their power to affect the world. They involve 'pulling a devil' – dressing a masquerade performer in a large and ornate costume that is paraded through the streets to the accompaniment of loud jazz music and sometimes other, privately owned devils. The society devils begin in the society shrine, where, as with the Mande *komo* masks, animal sacrifices provide raw materials for the masks' embellishment (1987: 177). Masks and costumes develop reputations as devils endowed with agency. Nunley cites examples in which the police have confiscated devils and denied permits to perform in order to curtail the power that devil and masquerade confer on the Ode-lay society (1987: 88). Such power is dependent on the society's ability to 'take it to the streets' (1987: 186) – to perform the masquerade in public. For although the mask is powerful in and of itself, in order to fully realize and instantiate the society's power, it must be mobilized in space. Masquerades that are unable to 'take it to the streets' are regarded as a failure, as they are unable to establish autonomy from the state government and appropriate public space. As such they are unable to effect the successful transformation of space that is necessary for successful Ode-lay, and indeed is a prominent feature of performance in general.

THE TRANSFORMATION OF SPACE: ORANGE PARADES

If performance involves a transformation of the person and of objects, then the same is true of space. Through performance, space is transformed from the relatively neutral space of a lived environment to the symbolically and often politically charged space of performance. Building on Eliade's (1959) account of religious performance, and broadly within the framework of geographical approaches to religion, Holloway (2003) argues that performance effects a sacralization of otherwise profane space through what Eliade calls 'hierophany' (see also Kong 2001) – the manifestation of the sacred, or, in Schieffelin's terms, the 'creation of presence' (1998: 194). Holloway, however, like many before him, seeks to question the legitimacy of the sacred–profane binary, suggesting a more dialectical relationship in which sacred performances and spaces affect the profane and vice versa (see, for example, Coleman and Collins 2000). This is clear from the examples of initiation and masquerade. The former is not a sacred performative event bracketed off from the more profane everyday, but one which transforms both the initiand and the everyday world they occupy. Similarly, although a distinction is made between mask-in-performance and unperformed mask, the performance is not an event that leaves the mask unaffected; it accrues power that it maintains after the performance, in its non-performative life.

If this is true of the person in performance and of objects in performance, then the same is true of space. Space is transformed through performance, but the post-performance space retains the characteristics of the transformation. For example, in Ode-lay, and other West African masquerades, which in 'taking it to the streets' effectively also claim those streets as spaces over which social groups have legitimate hegemony, through their ability to channel ancestral force in performance. Pratten (forthcoming) links these spatial claims to the politics of people–state relations in rural southern Nigeria, where vigilantism has become one of a series of ways in which these relations are mediated by Annang youth, and where vigilante groups are also masquerade groups (see also Fermé 2001; McCall 1995). The (sacred) masquerade

performance effects a transformation in (profane) political space that endures beyond the performance event itself, creating a new politico-religious geography.

One of the clearest examples of this process in action comes from Northern Ireland, where Orange parades don't merely reflect but also create new geographies of sectarianism (Bryan 2000; Jarman 1998). Orange parades have their origins in late seventeenth-century commemorations of the Protestant King William's victory over the Catholic James II at the river Boyne in Leinster, eastern Ireland. This was regarded as the final act of the Glorious Revolution that saw William (Prince of Orange) replace the Stewart James on the English throne. By the late eighteenth century these commemorations were being organized throughout the north of Ireland by the newly established Orange Institution or Orange Order, and were until the late nineteenth century instrumental in establishing a conflictual Protestant–Catholic sectarianism, but after that more concerned with consolidating Protestant Unionist identity (Jarman 1998). Before the 1870s the parades had also been considered 'rough', unruly affairs (Bryan 2000: 13). After then, they gained a respectability that was partly derived from the Protestant middle classes' attempts to maintain power through manipulating them (*ibid.*). By the late twentieth century, Orange parades were a politically sensitive manifestations and consolidations of the Protestant community in Northern Ireland. Their effectiveness in this role, and their sensitivity, derives from their ability to claim space, demarcating the boundaries of claimed Protestant hegemony and envisioning that hegemony as absolute. As Jarman says of the important Twelfth (12 July) parade in Belfast:

> While this is a commemoration … [of the Boyne] … the Orangemen simultaneously mark out the extent of Protestant South Belfast as they walk to the boundaries that separate the adjacent loyalist communities from their nationalist neighbours … these divisions are symbolically reaffirmed by the act of processing. Marking the boundaries also serves to facilitate the symbolic unity of the four distinct geographical communities in the Sandy Row Orange district.
>
> (1998: 98)

Since their very beginnings, Orange parades have involved a triumphalist militarism that signalled commemoration and celebration of military victory. They retain the hierarchized structure of a military parade and many of its trappings – marching bands, militarist colours, etc. Such triumphalism has been controversial – and was arguably intended to be so – since the early days. There is contemporary controversy over parade routes, and this I would argue has its origins in earlier disputes about the material culture of the parades. In the early nineteenth century, the routes began to be embellished with archways erected over the roads for paraders to pass through (Jarman 1998: 48). These began as floral displays, incorporating orange lilies, laurels and evergreen, and topped with a painting of King William – King Billy – at the Boyne; they later developed into more elaborate iron structures with several arches topped with more explicit contemporary political references (1998: 49).

The arches were derived from the ancient Roman idea of the triumphal arch, which endowed those passing through it with the qualities and virtues of the decoration – in this case, Orangeism (1998: 48). They therefore marked a claim over space such that all those who passed through the arch were considered complicit in the celebration of the original victory. Inevitably, the Catholic populations objected to the Orange arches, erecting their own Green arches to mark off Catholic nationalist territory. As Jarman confirms: 'these developments mark the beginnings of the visible sectarianism of space' (1998: 49).

In time, these arches became unfashionable, but were replaced by more permanent manifestations of sectarian hegemony. In the early twentieth century the first murals appeared in the streets of Belfast, initially located in the same places as – and replacing – the triumphal arches (1998: 70). Similarly, the temporary bunting hung from lamp posts and houses along the parade routes was supplemented by the more permanent painting of kerbsides and lamp posts with the colours of political loyalty (1998: 209). As with the arches, the Catholic communities responded with their own colour-coded demarcations, which permanently inscribed sectarianism in space – red, white and blue for Protestant loyalist areas; green, white and orange for Catholic nationalist areas. This contributed to the ghettoization and mutual exclusivity of the two communities, establishing effective 'no go' areas for Catholics and Protestants respectively. Here, practices originating in the temporary spatiality of the Orange parades come to permanently transform the everyday space of Belfast and Northern Ireland.

Although the parades lead to the fixing of sectarian spatial zones, the Orange parades

also challenge them – or, more specifically, challenge the legitimacy of Catholic areas. The Orange Order see it as one of their fundamental human rights to be able to parade wherever they wish within Northern Ireland (1998: 121–2), and so effectively 'reclaim' as Protestant areas that are classified as Catholic. The justification for this is the spatial precedent of 'traditional'[6] marching routes, the appeal to which confirms the reciprocal dialectic of space and performance – if performance transforms space, as demonstrated above, so too does space transform performance, as it generates correct, traditional routes which must be adhered to, despite changing political geography: 'The fight to maintain traditional routes in areas with a large Catholic population is an attempt to deny or to ignore the demographic and political changes that have been taking place in Northern Ireland in the past few decades' (1998: 128).

A case in point is the parade at Portadown, which in 1996 sparked a conflict that was to be long-lasting and violent – known subsequently as Drumcree, after the church to and from which the parade went. The 'traditional' route of the parade back into town from the church was along Garvaghy Road, controversial since the building of housing estates there in the 1960s which had effectively become Catholic ghettoes (McKay 2000). In 1996, for the second year running, a ruling that the parade be rerouted to avoid sectarian confrontation led to a stand-off with police as the Orange marchers were blocked from exerting their 'rights'. When for the second year the authorities capitulated under threat of major Protestant violence, there was widespread violent unrest as Catholics protested and Protestants celebrated. Over a period of four days, a Catholic taxi driver was killed, there were over 100 incidents of intimidation, ninety civilian injuries, 758 attacks on the police, 156 arrests made and 662 plastic baton rounds fired by the police (http://cain.ulst.ac.uk/issues/parade/develop.htm#2).

That all this conflict could have been generated 'just to walk down one bit of road' (Bryan 2000: 6) reveals the significance of the spatial in performance. Writing against tendencies within the anthropology of ritual to overemphasize the verbal, Parkin redefines ritual performance thus, to focus on its spatiality: 'Ritual is formulaic spatiality carried out by groups of people who are conscious of its imperative or compulsory nature ...' (Parkin 1992: 18). Such spatiality is central not only to Protestant parades in Northern Ireland, but also to Catholic processions in southern Europe, and particularly those associated with the feast days of saints.

Writing of religious processions of the Alto Minho in northern Portugal, Pina-Cabral (1986) argues that they should be seen, above all, as rituals of correct motion; rituals which must abide by the 'correct' spatial formula or spatial structure – what Lewis (1980) refers to as a 'ruling' – in order to be successfully performed.

To regard such ruling as strictly compulsory, and ritual performance as slavish obedience to it, however, would be misleading. As with the Orange parades, the 'traditional' procession is as much an object of innovation as of conservatism. As Catherine Bell (1992) has argued, such performative innovation is always situational and strategic – situational because it emerges in given, specific contexts; strategic because it is aimed at and serves to either reinforce or reconfigure the order of power in the world (1992: 83–5). Such an approach assumes that conflict over ritual form is not only possible but in some senses endemic to ritual itself. Even in situations where the grand structural conflict over ritual form is absent – the disputes about the routeing of an Orange parade – the myriad petty conflicts over the details of ritualization persist: what costumes, banners, slogans, music to use on any particular occasion. Such conflicts themselves lead to transformation of the 'ruling', and are achieved only in and through performance.

TRANSFORMATIONS OF SPACE, OBJECTS AND PERSONS: MALTESE *FESTA*

The Maltese saint's feast – or *festa* – is a procession rooted in such conflict. There are sixty five parishes in the predominantly Catholic Maltese islands, each of which celebrates at least one *festa* each year. Many of these *festi* directly compete with one another to produce the best *festa*, with the most innovative forms of ritualization: procession, street decorations, brass band marches, fireworks, etc. *Festa partiti* – competing *festa* factions – are also political factions, such that contest between *festi* is political contest (Boissevain 1965, 1993). Moreover, *festa partiti* themselves are divided between the often antagonistic authorities of clergy and laity, which means that the *festa* is rooted in the struggle for both secular and spiritual power.

The example of *festa* – the final example of this chapter – brings together the three themes – transformation of space; transformation of objects; and transformation of persons – in the context of competition over power. This thematic unification is not unique to *festa*.

The other examples used here could also have provided such an analysis: initiation involves the transformation of objects and space, as well as persons; masquerade involves the transformation of persons and space, as well as objects; and Orange parades involve the transformation of persons and objects, as well as space. However, this unificatory approach to the three transformations is not one that immediately suggests itself when reading the material on initiation, masquerade and Orange parades – partly because of the theoretical angle taken by ethnographers of these performances, and partly – consequently – because of their concentration on certain types of ethnographic evidence over others.

This final section focuses on my own ethnographic research in Malta, on the *festa* of St Paul, held every year in February in Malta's capital city, Valletta (Mitchell 2002). The *festa* itself is opened some two weeks before *festa* day, 10 February, when the monumental statue of St Paul – some 10 ft tall and made of solid wood – is taken out of its normal home in a niche in the parish church and placed on a pedestal in the main body of the church. From that day onwards, the parish streets are elaborately decorated with flags, banners and bunting. The five days leading up to *festa* day see a combination of solemn liturgical functions inside the church and more playful, ludic celebrations outside – including processions, brass band marches, fireworks displays, discos. On *festa* day itself, the statue is taken into the streets in procession around the parish, accompanied by lively brass bands and a formal liturgical procession.

Conceptually, the *festa* is divided into 'inside' and 'outside' festivities, which are the respective responsibilities of the clergy and the lay organization in charge of *festa* – the Ghaqda tal-Pawlini (Association of Paulites). This division is mediated by the statue of St Paul, particularly during the final procession, which involves taking the statue – which belongs to the church and is normally inside – outside. Whilst outside it is the responsibility of the Ghaqda, which takes contractual responsibility for its safety during the procession. In taking the inside outside, the outside is transformed – from mundane, everyday space into transcendent, ritual space (see Mitchell 2004; Figure 25.1). In the process, the divisions which exist between the different 'ritual constituencies' (Baumann 1992) involved in *festa* – clergy and laity; younger and older *Ghaqda* members; higher and lower-status participants – are mitigated in a moment of Durkheimian effervescence that informants themselves describe as genuinely unifying (Mitchell 2002).

Figure 25.1   *The transformation of space: Valletta streets decorated for the festa*

This transformation of space is not limited to the duration of the procession. The procession ensures the enduring patronage of St Paul over the parish, and is like the Orange parades governed by a significant spatial 'ruling' that for example frames the way the statue should be carried – swaying from side to side as though the saint himself is walking the streets – and requires that where the procession passes streets down which it will not pass the statue is turned around so that the saint looks down the unwalked streets. Above all, though, the ruling dictates that the procession must, if possible, take place. The mitigating factor is the weather, and where this prevents the procession there is always conflict and controversy, followed by anxiety – even depression – among parishioners until the procession can be expedited at a later date.

The key to understanding the procession as not merely a symbolic act but a substantive transformation of parish space – and its spiritual rejuvenation – is to recognize that the statue itself is more than a symbol (Mitchell 2004; Figure 25.2). Like the West African masks, it is more than a representation of the saint, but is rather a substantive embodiment, with its own agency. During the period of the *festa*, when the statue is in the church, parishioners engage with it as with an actual person – they will talk

Figure 25.2   *The transformation of the object: St Paul during the procession*

to it directly, and apologize when turning their back to it. During the procession, the statue is animated by the 'walking' action of the statue carriers, and its spiritual agency is confirmed by its 'looking' down the streets it patronizes. The *festa* therefore involves not only a transformation of space, but also a transformation of the object – and, like the West African masks, this is a double transformation: from wood into statue, and from statue into saint.

The final transformation is that of the body. Bodily transformation during *festa* reconfirms the agency of the statue-saint, not merely as a spiritual agency that ensures patronage and the promise of intercession but as a felt agency that is inherent in the bodily experience of proximity to the saint himself. This agency is most felt by the statue carriers, or *reffiegha,* for whom the physical trauma of bearing the statue's incredible weight is seen as a kind of penance but also as a status-enhancing, status-changing experience that constructs a particular form of masculinity (Mitchell 1998; Figure 25.3). The trauma is marked on the body in the form of large callouses that develop on the shoulders of a *reffiegh* as bodily manifestations of their proximity to and experience of the saint's agency. This transformation of body and person is particular to those chosen as *reffiegha* – who must be not only physically able, but also morally appropriate.

The experience, however, is 'democratized' at the end of the procession when the *reffiegha* leave the statue and allow other men to experience proximity to the saint. Like the ideal Odelay, this enables a union of performer and audience; performing unity through the transformation of space, object, body and person.

CONCLUSION

This final example demonstrates the multiple transformations brought about by and through performance: of space, of objects, of persons. The analysis of performance might pick up on this approach, to establish an agenda for future research on similar multiple transformations – and perhaps others: of time, for example – and their interrelation.

What this chapter has focused on are examples that demonstrate the fluidity of performance – and its role in transformation. It has therefore focused less on performances *per se,* and more on the transformative potentialities of performance. Performance is consequently not bracketed off as a separate activity, nor yet is performance expanded out into a metaphor for action in everyday life. Rather, the intention has been to explore the ways in which performative

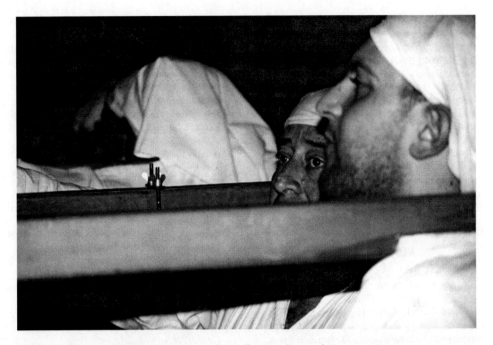

Figure 25.3   *The transformation of the body:* reffiegha *during the procession*

activities or events – initiation, masquerade, parade and *festa* – interact with everyday life to effect transformation.

Each transformation addressed here involves an intersection/interaction of the material and the conceptual; but the material things – bodies, things and space – are not treated here as *objects*. Rather, this chapter explores the extent to which they become *subjects* within the performative process – through their performative deployment. Thus, the person and body of the initiand are the subject of their own transformation; the medicine-rich mask (dually transformed, from wood into mask and from mask into powerful mask) is a powerful agent of the masquerade performance; and the transformed, politicized sectarian space of the Orange parades generates 'tradition' and an imperative to maintain a particular spatial, ritual form.

This focus on the interaction between the material and the conceptual, and the resultant transformation, is a position I see more in keeping with the lessons of material culture studies than either the bracketed 'performance studies' approach that looks at performance *qua* performance or the more generalizing Goffmanesque approach to 'everything-as-performance'. Material culture focuses not on entities, but on relationships between persons and things, where those things can equally be bodies or spaces as things *stricto facto*. Performance is a privileged context in which to observe these relationships as they are constructed through, and give rise to, transformation.

NOTES

1   As exemplified by the work of the Material Culture Group at University College London (see Buchli 2002).

2   Clearly, given the globalization of contemporary society, the distinction between 'non-Western' and 'Western' societies is problematic, particularly when associating them with societies that on the one hand are characterized by body modification in initiation and on the other hand are not. In Jewish contexts, for example, initiation and body modification are present within 'Western' society. Nevertheless, in as much as the two traditions of objectifying the body are linked respectively to a social anthropology of 'non-Western' society and a social psychology of 'Western' society, it is useful to maintain the distinction, at least heuristically.

3   Attributed to Karsh of Ottowa, http://www.quotationreference.com/quotefinder.php?strt=1&subj=+Karsh+of+Ottawa&byax=1&lr=.

4   *Nyama,* like many such West African concepts of power or energy, is notoriously difficult to define, and McNaughton, following Zahan (1960), cautions against too rigid a definition.

5   Blacksmiths – and indeed the other specialized professional clans – are regarded ambivalently, though, and *nyamakala* also means filth or manure (McNaughton 1988: 18).

6   'Tradition' is an important element in the politics of Orange parades, as it creates a justification for insisting on particular routes and asserting the right to parade (Jarman 1998: 25–8).

REFERENCES

Appadurai, A., ed. (1986) *The Social Life of Things.* Cambridge: Cambridge University Press.

Arens, W.W. and Karp, I. (1999) *Creativity of Power: Cosmology and Action in African Societies.* Washington, DC: Smithsonian Institution Press.

Barba, E. (1995) *The Paper Canoe: Guide to Theatre Anthropology.* London: Routledge.

Barba, E., Savarese, N. and Fowler, R. (1991) *A Dictionary of Theatre Anthropology: the Secret Art of the Performer.* London: Routledge.

Barth, F. (1975) *Ritual and Knowledge among the Baktaman of New Guinea.* (New Haven, CT: Yale University Press.

Barth, F. (1987) *Cosmologies in the Making: a Generative Approach to Cultural Variation in Inner New Guinea.* Cambridge: Cambridge University Press.

Baumann, G. (1992) 'Ritual implicates "Others": rereading Durkheim in a plural society', in D. de Coppet (ed.), *Understanding Rituals.* London: Routledge.

Beattie, G. (2003) *Visible Thought: the New Psychology of Body Language.* London: Routledge.

Bell, C. (1992) *Ritual Theory, Ritual Practice.* Oxford: Oxford University Press.

Bloch, M. (1992) *Prey into Hunter: the Politics of Religious Experience.* Cambridge: Cambridge University Press.

Brissevain, J. (1965) *Saints and Fireworks: Religion and Politics in Rural Malta.* London: Athlone Press.

Boissevain, J. (1993) *Saints and Fireworks: Religion and Politics in Rural Malta,* 2nd edn. Malta: Progress Press.

Bourdieu, P. (1977) *Outline of a Theory of Practice.* Cambridge: Cambridge University Press.

Bourdieu, P. (1990) *The Logic of Practice.* Cambridge: Cambridge University Press.

Bryan, D. (2000) *Orange Parades: the Politics of Ritual, Tradition and Control.* London: Pluto.

Buchli, V., ed. (2002) *The Material Culture Reader.* Oxford: Berg.

Butler, J. (1990) *Gender Trouble.* London: Routledge.

Chinnery, E.W.P. and Beaver, W.N. (1915) 'Notes on the initiation ceremonies of the Koko, Papua', *Journal of the Royal Anthropological Institute,* 45: 69–78.

Coleman, S. and Collins, P. (2000) 'The "plain" and the "positive": ritual, experience and aesthetics in Quakerism and charismatic Christianity', *Journal of Contemporary Religion,* 15 (3): 317–29.

Connell, R.W. (1995) *Masculinities.* Berkeley, CA: University of California Press.

Connerton, P. (1989) *How Societies Remember.* Cambridge: Cambridge University Press.

Csordas, T. (1990) 'Embodiment as a paradigm for anthropology', *Ethos,* 18: 5–47.

Douglas, M. (1970) *Natural Symbols: Explorations in Cosmology.* New York: Random House.

Eliade, M. (1959) *The Sacred and the Profane: the Nature of Religion.* New York: Hartcourt Brace.

Featherstone, M. (2000) *Body Modification.* London: Sage.

Fermé, M.C. (2001) *The Underneath of Things: Violence, History and the Everyday in Sierra Leone.* Berkeley, CA: University of California Press.

Gell, A. (1998) *Art and Agency: an Anthropological Theory.* Oxford: Oxford University Press.

Gellner, G. (1999) 'Religion, politics and ritual: remarks on Geertz and Bloch', *Social Anthropology,* 7 (2): 135–53.

Geschiere, P. (1997) *The Modernity of Witchcraft: Politics and the Occult in Postcolonial Africa.* Charlottesville 1997: University Press of Virginia.

Goffman, E. (1959) *The Presentation of Self in Everyday Life.* New York: Doubleday.

Heald, S. (1999) *Manhood and Morality: Sex, Violence and Ritual in Gisu Society.* London: Routledge.

Herzfeld, M. (1985) *The Poetics of Manhood: Contest and Identity in a Cretan Mountain Village.* Princeton, NJ: Princeton University Press.

Hoffman, R. (1995) 'Objects and acts', *African Arts,* summer: 56–9, 91.

Holloway, J. (2003) 'Make-believe: spiritual practice, embodiment, and sacred space', *Environment and Planning A,* 35 (11): 1961–74.

Horton, R. (1997) *Patterns of Thought in Africa and the West: Essays on Magic, Religion and Science.* Cambridge: Cambridge University Press.

Iteanu, A. (1983) *La Ronde des échanges: de la circulation aux valeurs chez les Orokaiva.* Cambridge: Cambridge University Press.

Iteanu, A. (1990) 'The concept of the person and the ritual system: an Orokaiva view', *Man* (n.s.), 25 (1): 35–53.

Jarman, N. (1998) *Material Conflicts: Parades and Visual Displays in Northern Ireland.* Oxford: Berg.

Jones, A. (1998) *Body Art: Performing the Subject.* Minneapolis, MN: University of Minnesota Press.

Kong, L. (2001) 'Religion and technology: refiguring place, space, identity and community', *Area*, 33 (4): 404–13.

Kuechler, S. (2002) *Malanggan: Art, Memory and Sacrifice*. Oxford: Berg.

Layton, R. (2003) 'Art and agency: a reassessment', *Journal of the Royal Anthropological Institute* (n.s.), 9 (3): 447–64.

Lewis, G. (1980) *Day of Shining Red*. Cambridge: Cambridge University Press.

Lewis, I.M. (1971) *Ecstatic Religion: a Study of Shamanism and Spirit possession*. London: Routledge.

Lock, M. (1993) 'Cultivating the body: anthropology and epistemologies of bodily practice and knowledge', *Annual Review of Anthropology*, 22: 133–55.

Looper, M.G. (2003) 'From inscribed bodies to distributed persons: contextualizing Tairona figural images in performance', *Cambridge Archaeological Journal*, 13: 25–40.

Mauss, M. (1973) 'Techniques of the body', *Economy and Society*, 2: 70–88.

McCall, J. (1995) 'Rethinking ancestors in Africa', *Africa*, 65 (2): 256–70.

McIntyre, A. (2002) 'Politics, war and youth culture in Sierra Leone', *African Security Review*, 11 (3): 7–15.

McKay, S. (2000) *Northern Protestants: an Unsettled People*. Belfast: Blackstaff Press.

McNaughton, P.R. (1988) *The Mande Blacksmiths: Knowledge, Power, and Art in West Africa*. Bloomington, IN: Indiana University Press.

Miller, D. (1995) *Acknowledging Consumption: a Review of New Studies*. London: Routledge.

Mitchell, J.P. (1998) 'Performances of masculinity in a Maltese *festa*', in F. Hughes-Freeland and M. Crain (eds), *Recasting Ritual: Performance, Media, Identity*. London: Routledge.

Mitchell, J.P. (2002) *Ambivalent Europeans: Ritual, Memory and the Public Sphere in Malta*. London: Routledge.

Mitchell, J.P. (2004) 'Ritual structure and ritual agency: "rebounding violence" and Maltese *festa*', *Social Anthropology*, 12 (1): 57–75.

Nunley, J. (1987) *Moving with the Face of the Devil: Art and Politics in Urban West Africa*. Urbana, IL: University of Illinois Press.

Ortner, S.B. (1984) 'Theory in anthropology since the sixties', *Comparative Studies in Society and History*, 126: 126–66.

Parkin, D. (1992) 'Ritual as spatial direction and bodily division', in D. de Coppet (ed.), *Understanding Rituals*. London: Routledge.

Pels, D., Hetherington, K. and Vandenberghe, F. (2002) 'The status of the object', *Theory Culture and Society*, 19 (5): 1–22.

Picton, J. (2002) 'What's in a mask?' in F. Harding (ed.), *The Performance Arts in Africa: a Reader*. London: Routledge.

Pina-Cabral, J. de (1986) *Sons of Adam, Daughters of Eve: the Peasant Worldview of the Alto Minho*. Oxford: Oxford University Press.

Pitts, V. (2003) *In the Flesh: the Cultural Politics of Body Modification*. London: Palgrave.

Poole, F.J.P. (1982) 'The ritual forging of identity: aspects of person and self in Bimin-Kuskusmin male initiation', in G.H. Herdt (ed.), *Rituals of Manhood: Male Initiation in Papua New Guinea*. Berkeley, CA: University of California Press.

Pratten, D. (forthcoming) 'The politics of vigilance in south-eastern Nigeria', *Development and Change*.

Schechner, R. (1985) *Between Theatre and Anthropology*. Pittsburg, PA: University of Pennsylvania Press.

Schechner, R. (1993) *The Future of Ritual*. London: Routledge.

Schieffelin, E.L. (1998) 'Problematizing performance', in F. Hughes-Freeland (ed.), *Ritual, Performance, Media*. London: Routledge.

Schwimmer, E. (1973) *Exchange in the Social Structure of the Orokaiva: Traditional and Emergent Ideologies in the Northern District of Papua*. London: Hurst.

Tonkin, E. (1979) 'Masks and power, *Man* (n.s.), 14 (2): 237–48.

Turner, V.W. (1967) *The Forest of Symbols: Aspects of Ndembu Ritual*. Ithaca: Cornell University Press.

Turner, V.W. (1969) *The Ritual Process: Structure and Anti-structure*. New York: Aldine.

Tuzin, D.F. (1980) *The Voice of the Tambaran: Truth and Illusion in Ilahita Arapesh Religion*. Berkeley, CA: University of California Press.

Van Gennep, A. (1960) *The Rites of Passage*. London: Routledge.

Whitehouse, H. (1995) *Inside the Cult: Religious Innovation and Transmission in Papua New Guinea*. Oxford: Oxford University Press.

Whitehouse, H. (1996) 'Rites of terror: emotion, metaphor and memory in Melanesian initiation cults', *Journal of the Royal Anthropological Institute* (n.s.), 2: 703–15.

Whitehouse, H. (2000) *Arguments and Icons: Divergent Modes of Religiosity*. Oxford: Oxford University Press.

Whitehouse, H. (2004) *Modes of Religiosity: a Cognitive Theory of Religious Transmission*. Walnut Creek, CA: AltaMira Press.

Zahan, D. (1960) *Sociétés d'initiation bambara: le Ndomo, le Koré*. Paris: Mouton.

26

PRESENT TO PAST

Ethnoarchaeology

Paul Lane

Ethnoarchaeology is a sub-field of archaeological research concerned primarily with investigation of the role of material culture and the built environment within living societies, and the processes which effect and affect their transformation to archaeological contexts. The ultimate objective of such research is to improve methods and procedures of archaeological inference, and particularly the use of analogical reasoning. A wide range of subject matters has been examined by ethnoarchaeologists, including different technologies of artefact manufacture; the nature, meaning and spatial consequences of artefact discard; the social and symbolic structuring of space; the locus and meaning of artefact style; and processes of site maintenance, abandonment and decay. This chapter examines the origins and development of ethnoarchaeology as a distinct sub-discipline; the range, strengths and weaknesses of different theoretical perspectives within ethnoarchaeology; its contributions to more general theories of material culture; and past, present and future research priorities. Drawing on a wide range of case studies from different parts of the world, the chapter also discusses the contributions of ethnoarchaeology to the discipline of archaeology and broader studies of material culture. The chapter concludes with a discussion of the main ethical issues raised by ethnoarchaeology as currently conceived, and in an effort to address these will offer an alternative definition and research agenda which gives more credence and weight to indigenous, non-Western epistemologies of the material world than has been the case in previous formulations of the sub-field.

Ethnoarchaeology emerged as a distinct sub-field of archaeology (and some would even say it qualifies as a sub-discipline) in the 1960s, as part of broader changes in archaeological method and theory that were associated with what came to be known as 'processual' or 'new' archaeology. Archaeologists, and their antiquarian predecessors, however, had always made use of ethnographic data to assist their interpretation of archaeological remains. What was distinctive about the development of ethnoarchaeology as a concept was that it sought to transform the way in which archaeologists utilized ethnographic data in two fundamental ways. First, rather than relying on the published accounts of ethnographers and anthropologists, as had been the norm among previous generations (with some notable exceptions – such as the British field archaeologist O.G.S. Crawford, e.g. 1953: 218–31), archaeologists themselves became actively involved in the collection of pertinent ethnographic information through participant observation among living communities. Second, the unstructured and random selection of ethnographic 'parallels' that had tended to characterize earlier uses of ethnographic data in archaeological interpretations were challenged, and in their place efforts were made to establish robust analogies that could stand up to critical testing and had some validity across both time and space. (For discussion of the history of using ethnographic parallels, see Charlton 1981; Daniel 1950; Orme 1973, 1981. For discussions on the use of ethnographic analogy in archaeology see Ascher 1961; Binford 1967; David and Kramer 2001: 33–62; Gould

1980: 29–47; Gould and Watson 1982; Hodder 1982a: 11–27; Lane 1994/95; Lyman and O'Brien 2001; Poor 1999; Stahl 1993; Stiles 1977; Wobst 1978; Wylie 1982, 1985.)

THE ORIGINS AND GROWTH OF ETHNOARCHAEOLOGY

The precise origins of 'ethnoarchaeology', as is often the case with intellectual advances in any discipline, are diffuse. The term 'ethno-archaeologist' is known to have been used as early as 1900, by Jesse Fewkes in connection with the use of local traditions and knowledge dealing with Native American migrations so as to interpret remains in the south-western United States (see Hodder 1982a: 28; David and Kramer 2001: 6) – a tradition that subsequently became popular among archaeologists and ethnographers based in the Bureau of Ethnology in the United States. However, as discussed above, similar approaches were being used by Fewkes's predecessors as early as 1845, whereas systematic ethnoarchaeological research *with clearly defined objectives and methodology* did not begin until much later. Kleindienst and Watson's study of what they termed the 'archaeological inventory of a living community' (1956), also conducted among a group of Pueblo Indians, is often cited as the crucial turning point, since this aimed to illustrate the extent to which an archaeologist might be able to infer the non-material elements of a particular society from its material traces. This was followed soon afterwards by a similar study by Ascher among Seri Indians in Mexico (1962). Both studies were designed explicitly to test the validity and reliability of the inferential procedures then used in archaeology, and to try to account for the resultant biases and misinterpretations of the material evidence. David and Kramer, on the other hand, while recognizing the important contribution made by these authors, have suggested that Donald Thompson's study of the influence of seasonality on the material culture and adaptations of the Wik Monkan tribe of Australian Aborigines (Thompson 1939) may represent the first truly 'modern' ethnoarchaeological study (2001: 6). However, Wauchope's study of Maya houses, conducted explicitly for 'collecting data to facilitate interpretation of ancient dwelling sites' (1938: 1), would seem to be an equally deserving candidate. Irrespective of which study qualifies as the 'first' piece of ethnoarchaeological research, there is no doubt that its origins as a distinct sub-discipline are directly associated

with the rise of *anthropological* approaches to archaeology in North America during the late 1950s and early 1960s (e.g. Binford 1962; Willey and Phillips 1958), and the simultaneous concern to introduce 'scientific' procedures of analytical reasoning and explanation (e.g. Binford 1964; Clarke 1968; Watson et al. 1971). Both aspects lay at the heart of what became known as the 'new archaeology', which placed greater emphasis on the reconstruction of cultural processes in the past (hence the term 'processual archaeology') as opposed to earlier concerns with the reconstruction of cultural histories. Since processes cannot be directly observed in the static arrangement of archaeological materials, and different processes might well generate the same spatial and physical patterning of material culture, it seemed highly appropriate to investigate the operation of different dynamic processes and their material traces in the present in the hope that it might reveal ways of distinguishing between them.

This being said, precisely what constituted ethnoarchaeology, as opposed to more general studies of material culture in contemporary contexts, was still very much a matter of opinion and inclination. In their major review of much of the relevant literature in English, French and German, David and Kramer provide a variety of published definitions, out of the myriad available (2001: 6–13), and their own particular view on the issue. The variability reflects, in part, the diversity of research strategies, research objectives and ultimate goals of different ethnoarchaeologists. Nevertheless, many have a number of elements in common, that are listed in Table 26.1.

Undoubtedly other archaeologists and ethnoarchaeologists might want to add extra clauses or subtract certain elements from this. The point, however, is not to offer a 'comprehensive' definition but rather to highlight the main components of ethnoarchaeological research on which there is at least some broad if not entirely unified consensus. Far more important is the need to recognize different trends and the philosophies of material culture and human 'behaviour' that underlie them.

For instance, after an initial period of fairly diverse research philosophies and the use of a wide range of terms, that included 'living archaeology', 'action archaeology', 'actualistic research', 'archaeoethnography', 'ethnographic archaeology' and 'modern material culture studies', to describe what would now be simply categorized as ethnoarchaeology, from the mid-1960s until at least the mid-1980s, a great many ethnoarchaeological studies were essentially

Table 26.1   *An outline of the core characteristics of ethnoarchaeology based on commonalities of the majority of published definitions given in David & Kramer 2001*

Core Defining Characteristics of Ethnoarchaeology

- A research strategy, not a theory.
- Conducted among living societies by archaeologically-trained individuals.
- Involves the combined use of anthropological methods of participant observation and common archaeological procedures for recording sites, structural features and artefacts.
- General purpose is to gather information directly relevant to assisting the interpretation of archaeological remains and for answering archaeological questions.
- Developed in particular to investigate and document:
  a) the processes whereby material culture and residues enter into and create archaeological records;
  b) the causes of variability in material culture and its spatio-temporal organisation;
  c) the relationships between such variability and human behaviour/action, systems of meaning, social organization, and/or patterns of belief.

concerned with establishing the various 'material correlates' of different categories of human behaviour (e.g. Gould 1980: 4; Kramer 1979a: 5; Rathje 1978: 49; Stanislawski 1978: 204). Ideally, such correlates need to be universal in nature, or at least common under certain cross-cultural conditions, if they are to have predictive value and to allow correct inference of meaning and significance from the static remains of the archaeological record (e.g. Binford 1980). Under these broad terms, the majority of ethnoarchaeologists subscribed to the belief that material culture and its patterning reflect behaviour, although they differed widely as to the specifics of this relationship. (See, for instance, the debate on whether the archaeological record represents a *distorted reflection* of past human activity, e.g. Schiffer 1985, or the *normal consequence* of the operation of behavioural systems, e.g. Binford 1981a.) Accordingly, during these two decades (*c.* 1965–85) considerable attention was given in particular to identifying and describing the various processes that contribute to the formation of archaeological records; the various mechanical and physical processes involved in the manufacture of different types of artefact, especially pottery and iron; and the nature, causes and social referents of stylistic variation in artefacts. Examples of some of the most significant of these studies and the debates they engendered are given below.

From the late 1970s and early 1980s, a contrary position began to be forwarded which posited that material culture stands in a recursive relationship to human agents. This stance is widely associated with, at least in the first instance, the work of Ian Hodder (1982b) and several of his students. Strongly influenced by the 'practice' or 'action' theories of Bourdieu (1977) and Giddens (1979, 1981), that emphasize

the contingent nature of social structures and norms, along with various anthropological analyses, and especially structuralist and semiotics-oriented analyses, of material objects and the organization of space (e.g. Barthes 1973; Douglas 1966; Glassie 1975; Hugh-Jones 1979; Leach 1976; Lévi-Strauss 1968, 1970; Tambiah 1969), these researchers tended to see the relationship between material culture and human action as being essentially 'recursive'. By which, it was generally meant that while the patterning of material culture indubitably results from human activities and intentions and thus might be said to 'reflect' these, material culture (including architecture and 'constructed space') through its very materiality can also constrain, condition, generate and facilitate certain kinds of meaningfully informed behaviour and beliefs. While many of the early studies of this 'post-processual' approach to ethnoarchaeology (e.g. Braithwaite 1982; Crawford 1987; Donley 1982; Lane 1987; Miller 1985; Moore 1982; Parker Pearson 1982; Welbourn 1984) sought to illustrate in more detail how material culture and its spatial organization worked in a recursive fashion in particular ethnographic contexts, far less attention was given to how such a concept might be used to interpret specific archaeological contexts and materials other than in an fairly abstract way. Because of this lack of attention to how this theoretical perspective on material culture might be applied archaeologically, criticisms were commonly couched along the lines of 'So what?' Alongside such general reactions, other common criticisms of 'post-processual' ethnoarchaeology were that it lacked 'methodological rigour', that rather than offering cross-culturally valid analogies it was overly 'particularistic', and 'anti-scientific' (e.g. Stark 1993; Watson and Fotiadis 1990).

Since the early 1990s, there has been a certain diminishing of ethnoarchaeological research, and most particularly work conducted from a 'post-processual', 'post-structuralist' perspective – although some of the current work on *chaînes opératoires* and 'technological style' represents an emerging trend that has some intellectual affiliation with such studies. One reason for this may be increasing concern within archaeology with disciplinary ethics. Fewster (2001), for instance, has argued that ethnoarchaeologists face two particular ethical concerns in addition to those common to archaeology in general and those shared with social and cultural anthropologists. (For a review of these shared ethical concerns as they pertain to ethnoarchaeology, see David and Kramer 2001: 63–90.) The first dilemma, according to Fewster, concerns the issue of 'representation' and more particularly the morality of studying '"other" societies with the sole intention of making analogies to those of the past' (2001: 65) (Plate 26.1). Fewster's second concern relates to the role and responsibilities of ethnoarchaeologists to the communities among whom they work 'with regard to active participation in programmes of economic

development' (*ibid.*). To resolve such dilemmas, Fewster argues, there is a need to develop a 'responsible epistemology' of the ethnoarchaeological subject centred on Giddens's (1979) notion of the role of agency in structural change in ways in which agency is 'neither relegated to the margins nor transliterated into symbolic material representations' (Fewster 2001: 67).

Another likely contributing factor has been the burgeoning of studies of material culture in contemporary contexts by scholars from other disciplines – including the revival of interest in, and concern with, material culture among anthropologists. Somewhat bucking this trend, to judge from David and Kramer's review, is the number of ethnoarchaeological studies being conducted by non-Western archaeologists, whose work may well open up new avenues of inquiry and different perspectives as to what constitutes material culture. Another feature of ethnoarchaeological research in recent years has been the increasing regionalization of approaches, whereby different themes and methodologies are increasingly being developed to address archaeological questions specific to a particular geographical area. (For reviews of

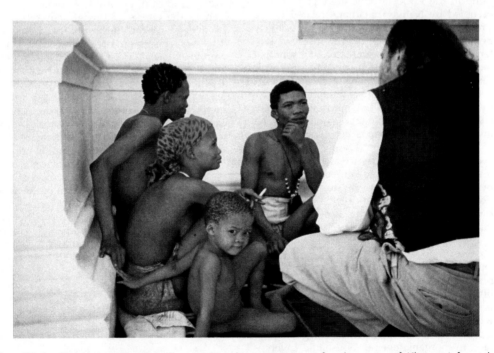

Plate 26.1   *Imagining the 'Other' – a journalist interviews a family group of Khomani from the Kagga Kamma Tourist Reserve, on the steps of the South African National Gallery, Cape Town at the opening of the Miscast: Negotiating Khoisan History and Material Culture exhibition, 1996 (see Buntman 1996; Lane 1996a); cf: Figure 26.3. Photo. P. Lane*

the history of ethnoarchaeological research on different continents see, for example, Atherton 1983, MacEachern 1996 and Schmidt 1983 on Africa, especially sub-Saharan Africa; Griffin and Solheim 1998/99 on Asia generally and Allchin 1985 and Sinopoli 1991 on South Asia; and Allen 1996 on Australia). This may well relate to the more general awareness of the need to establish the relevance of any particular ethnographic analogy on both the source (i.e. ethnographic) and subject (i.e. archaeological) sides of the equation. (For further discussion of the issue of relevance, see Wylie 1985.)

FORMATION OF ARCHAEOLOGICAL SITES AND ASSEMBLAGES

One of the most common concerns of ethnoarchaeologists during the heyday of processualist approaches was with the wide range of human activities and natural events and actions that can contribute to the formation of archaeological sites and deposits. Many of the earliest studies of this kind were simple 'cautionary tales', or 'spoilers' as Yellen termed them (1977a: 9–11). For instance, in his study of an abandoned camp in the Rocky Mountains that had been occupied by Native Canadians related to the Cree, Bonnischen found that his 'intuitively derived interpretations' of the observed patterning resulted in a combination of errors that included misidentification of items and their functions, false associations between objects and their users, and incorrect definition of activity areas and their relationship to one another (1973: 286). Comparable studies encompassed investigations of an abandoned Apache *wicikup* or living site in Arizona (Longacre and Ayers 1968), comparisons of the artefact assemblages found at occupied and abandoned camps used by Turkana pastoralists in northern Kenya (Robbins 1973), and study of the recycling of dwellings and other structures in a Fulani village in Cameroon (David 1971).

The object of such studies was essentially to observe the operation of particular processes and events in the present, so as to draw out broader implications of value to the interpretation of remains from the past. Aside from ethnocentric bias, other suggested reasons for why errors in interpretation might occur include the relative proportion of organic artefacts to inorganic ones in household inventories (the latter being more likely to survive and thus to be 'over-represented' in archaeological assemblages); the conditions under which a site was abandoned (for instance, a planned abandonment would be more likely to result in fewer artefacts being left behind than one which took place in response to some catastrophic event); the secondary use of buildings and other features, especially as locales for disposing of refuse; and the effects of various post-depositional process ranging from the activities of children to different natural weathering processes. (For a detailed summary of the literature, see Schiffer 1987.)

Another category of site-formation studies developed during the same period relied more on uniformitarian assumptions[1] pertaining to the natural world. A classic example of this kind is McIntosh's ethnographic study of house wall collapse and decay in Ghana near the archaeological site of Begho, and subsequent controlled excavation of a recently abandoned structure (1974, 1977). Additional examples of site-formation studies focusing on the operation and physical consequences of different processes governed by natural laws include Schmidt's investigation of iron-smelting furnaces in Buhaya, Tanzania (1980; Schmidt and Avery 1978; Schmidt and Childs 1996) and Friede and Steel's experimental burning of Nguni huts (1980; see also Plate 26.2). To some extent these cross-cut more strictly taphonomic[2] studies of natural formation processes such as the effects of fluvial activity on site assemblages, or the effects of dogs, hyenas and other scavengers on bone preservation. (For overviews, see Gifford 1981; Hudson 1993.) Some more recent approaches to the reconstruction of activities and activity areas (see below) have also begun to investigate various microscopic by-products of human activity, such as phytoliths, diatoms, spherulites, rock polish, soil micromorphology and micro-fauna, using a combination of ethnographic observation and various techniques of scientific analysis, with promising results (e.g. Boivin 2000; Brochier et al. 1992). The strength of the analogies developed in these cases also rests on the fact the various microscopic traces; although a consequence of human or humanly managed activities such as stock herding, are similarly governed by natural laws.

RECONSTRUCTING DISCARD, ACTIVITY PATTERNS, AND BUTCHERY PRACTICES

During the initial stages of the new archaeology, there was a widespread assumption that the spatial patterning of material on archaeological sites reflected the patterning of activities

a

b

c

(Continued)

Plate 26.2   *Stages in house collapse at Tswana farming (masimo) settlements – a) typical masimo compound and Tswana cone-on-cylinder rondavel, SE Botswana 1992; b) cone-on-cylinder rondavel in early stage of collapse, showing pattern of roof collapse, N Botswana 1994; c) Example of a Tswana rondavel after several years of abandonment, showing surviving residual wall stumps, SE Botswana 1992; d) House daub scatter marking remnants of a 17th century Tswana house, excavated near Ranaka, SE Botswana 1992. Photos: P. Lane*

and the use of space at the site during its period of occupation or use. By mapping the distribution of this material, it was believed, aspects of the organization of the society that produced these remains could be simply 'read off', thereby providing insights into such issues as room function (e.g. Longacre 1970), whether certain areas were associated with different social categories (e.g. Hill 1970; Clarke 1972), and even the prevailing rules of post-marital residence (e.g. Deetz 1968; Ember 1973). Largely as a consequence of ethnoarchaeological research in a variety of settings on discard behaviour, activity patterns and butchery practices, few archaeologists would now accept such one-to-one correspondences. Regarding discard practices, for example, at least three broad categories of 'refuse' need to be distinguished from one another – namely, 'primary refuse' discarded at its location of use or production, 'secondary refuse' discarded away from its use location, and *'de facto'* refuse that consists of material (often still usable) left behind when structures and sites are abandoned (see Schiffer 1976, 1987). A range of other processes may also account for the formation of particular deposits, including the caching, curation and recycling of materials and structures, accidental loss and deliberate deposition. Attempts have also been made, for example, to distinguish between 'nuclear' and 'communal' areas (e.g. Yellen 1977a; Bartram et al. 1991), and animal 'kill sites' and 'processing sites' at hunter-gatherer sites (e.g. Binford 1978b; 1991; see also Plate 26.3).

The ethnoarchaeological literature on these topics is vast. The following example, however, illustrates some of the principles involved. Specifically, at the late Upper Palaeolithic open site of Pincevent in northern France, occupied between some 12,300–10,700 years ago, scatters of flaked stone tools and waste material with reindeer bones and fragments were found in association with three hearths in an area designated Section 36 by the excavators (Leroi-Gourhan and Brézillon 1966). In their interpretation of the site, Leroi-Gourhan and Brézillon suggested that each of the hearths lay within a circular hut constructed from skin and poles that overlapped with one another to form a larger structure with a common gallery and several entrances, and that the site probably represented a base camp. Drawing on his observations at Nunamiut hunting stands and base camps, Binford argued that only one hearth (hearth 1) may possibly have been situated within a tent, while the other two (hearths 2 and 3) were outside hearths, and that the site was a 'logistic' camp rather than a residential one (1978b, 1983: 144–60). Binford's principal

Plate 26.3   *Elephant butchery and meat processing by a group of Bugakhwe (Northern Khoe Bushmen) in the Okavango Delta, Botswana 1996–a) Men butchering a juvenile elephant shot as part of a Government controlled culling programme; b) Bugakhwe woman hanging up strips of elephant meat on a wooden frame so as to make biltong (sun-dried meat): Photos. P. Lane*

reasons for suggesting this were as follows. First, the patterning of debris around hearths 2 and 3, in his view, resembled the structure and size composition of 'toss' and 'drop' zones created by Nunamiut while seated around open hearths. 'Drop zones' are generally composed of small waste items that accumulate when people are seated around a hearth, while 'toss zones' (which can be either in front or behind the seated persons) typically comprise larger debris deliberately thrown away from the seating area so as not to interfere with the activities being performed there. After even a short period of hearth use, two concentric semicircles of size-sorted debris are created. This patterning of discarded material does not occur around hearths inside huts or tents, principally because people are inclined not to throw away large bits of rubbish within their dwelling and sleeping space. Instead, they are more likely (as in the case of the Nunamiut) to put these objects beside the hearth for subsequent disposal as 'secondary refuse' outside the structure. Open hearths occur on both base camps and temporary work and logistic stations among the Nunamiut. However, Binford noted that Nunamiut home bases could be differentiated from hunting stands owing to the absence of activities directed towards the maintenance (i.e. tidying up) of living space at hunting stands, with the result that whereas patterned 'toss' and 'drop' zones tend to survive at sites used for only a short period of time before being abandoned, at base camps further sweeping up and redeposition of items occur that effectively restructure the patterns initially created around open hearths. The fact that a pattern resembling 'toss and drop zones' survived archaeologically at Pincevent, therefore, suggested to Binford that hearths 2 and 3 were not inside a tent and that the site was not a base camp, but instead some form of logistic station (for alternative assessments, see Carr 1991; Johnson 1984).

Many other comparable studies have been conducted among mobile hunter-gathers (e.g. Binford 1981b, 1982; Gould 1968; Yellen 1977b, 1993; O'Connell 1987; O'Connell et al. 1991), pastoralists (e.g. Cribb 1991; Hole 1978; Mbae 1990) and agro-pastoralists (e.g. Kent 1984; Graham 1994; Nandris 1985) as well as settled fishing communities (e.g. Pétrequin and Pétrequin 1984) and agriculturalists (e.g. Deal 1985; Hayden and Cannon 1983; Gorecki 1985), and on task- or gender-specific groups (e.g. Chang 1993; Gallay 1981; Gifford 1978; Gifford and Behrensmeyer 1977; Stewart and Gifford-Gonzalez 1994; Tobert 1985; Vidale et al. 1993). Inevitably, these studies have been motivated by a wide range of specific research questions. Many of the studies among hunter-gatherers, for instance, have been ultimately concerned with how mixed assemblages of 'bones and stones' found in Plio-Pleistocene depositional contexts on the African continent may or may not have been related to the behaviour of early hominids. (See Binford 1983, Gallay 1999 and Isaac 1984 for synopses of this debate.) Whereas, for instance, parallel studies among pastoralists have been concerned with identifying various material 'signatures' that might be used to detect evidence of pastoralism in the archaeological record and to distinguish between sites occupied during different seasons.

The most obvious conclusion to be drawn is that the patterning of remains uncovered on an archaeological site is rarely the material equivalent of a snapshot taken while the site was in use. Instead, on most sites and in most contexts, there is progressive 'smearing and blending' of different depositional events (Stevenson 1991: 294). More significantly, these studies challenge the view that all sites experience a progressive reduction in the quantity and quality of information over time, culminating in a state of entropy (e.g. Ascher 1968; Binford 1981a: 200). Instead, it is now recognized that degradation is caused by specific *processes* rather than simply the passage of *time*, and as critically, archaeological site formation processes may add information as well as removing it. Consequently even the most degraded deposits still retain information about how they were formed. The real interpretive challenge, therefore, lies in trying to establish whether different modes of discard, uses of space, butchery events and so on leave sufficiently diagnostic physical 'signatures' that would enable archaeologists to distinguish between them. The only way of establishing this is through detailed comparative study of the operation of such processes in the present, where causes and effects can both be observed.

SOCIAL AND SYMBOLIC USE OF SPACE

One criticism that can be levelled at many, but by no means all, ethnoarchaeological studies of discard practices and activity areas is the lack of attention given to cultural context. Thus, although Binford's observations regarding the different intensity of maintenance activities at base camps and hunting stands provides a useful interpretive model for understanding hunter-gatherer sites, to imply, as he does, that patterns generated by discard at hunting stands *in general* are not subjected to tidying up simply because they are non-residential introduces several ethnocentric assumptions about 'domestic space' and attitudes to discarded materials. It also fails to explain *why* this conceptual division is important to the Nunamiut. Moreover, even if it could be demonstrated that particular discard strategies are common to all modern mobile 'hunter-gatherer' groups, as has been suggested by some (e.g. Murray 1980), the possibility that hunter-gatherer groups in the past behaved differently must always be kept in mind (Wobst 1978).

Several of the early post-processual ethnoarchaeological studies were directed at addressing precisely these concerns over the lack of attention to cultural context. In her study of discard among the Marakwet in Kenya, for instance, Moore noted that they distinguished three types of 'refuse', namely ash from cooking fires, chaff produced during the winnowing of millet and sorghum, and dung from the goat pens found in most compounds (1982, 1986). As well as being conceptually and semantically distinguished, these categories of rubbish tended to be spatially segregated as well. Thus ash was normally thrown behind the woman's house, chaff and household sweepings dumped downslope from the compound, and goat dung also down-slope but behind the man's house. Care was taken to ensure that these different types, and especially ash and goat dung, did not become mixed deliberately. All three categories would constitute what processualist archaeologists might simply designate 'secondary refuse', and as Moore observed their spatial patterning did indeed 'reflect' the activities and uses of the various structures closest to them. However, although clearly influenced by functional requirements and the maintenance of living space, Moore found that these practices also related to a broader ordering of Marakwet society on age and gender lines, and that the different categories of refuse carried a number of symbolic associations that related in particular to the positive and negative values Marakwet placed on the roles of men and women within society. Following Bourdieu's analysis of the Kabyle Berber house (1977: 91, 1979), Moore argued that the symbolic loading of each category of refuse, the spaces where it accumulated and the gendered task with which it was associated acted as mnemonics for the wider cultural order. Thus, for instance, the practical separation of Marakwet women from tending goats has the effect of restricting access to, and control over, material wealth to men while simultaneously generating a particular symbolic capital

which men can deploy in various social and political strategies to their own advantage (Moore 1986: 91–120).

Similar arguments about the intersection of agency, relations of power and symbolic meanings in the material world featured prominently in other post-processual studies of discard practices (e.g. Hodder 1982b: 125–63, 1987) and the use and production of space (e.g. Crawford 1987; Donley 1982; Herbich and Dietler 1993; Kus 1982; Lane 1994; Smith and David 1995). More generally, post-processual approaches tend to emphasize the recursive nature of material culture and architectural forms in the constitution and reconstitution of meaning that is derived, in part, from their central role in the routinization of daily practice. Thus, for instance, in her study of Swahili town houses in Lamu, Kenya, Donley noted that newly born infants are taken on a tour of their parental home and 'told who is to use each item of furniture and on what occasions' (1982: 70), thereby establishing the 'ground rules' of a symbolic scheme that are re-enacted through the temporal and spatial ordering of daily activities during the course of their lives.

Envisaging how such meanings might change, however, requires recognition of the potential for different 'readings' of the material world and the symbolic schemes associated with it, by individuals who occupy different positions of power, status and authority. In this sense, it can be argued that the spatial and formal qualities of the material world exhibit certain text-like properties, and like conventional texts are 'open to a multiplicity of different interpretations' (Moore 1986: 86; see also Hodder 1986). This polysemic quality, by virtue of the power of meaning to guide, stimulate and condition everyday practice ensures that spatial arenas become a nexus of ideological discourse and concern, and as a cultural representation, any spatial order is 'completely bound up with the conduct of a continual process of argumentation' (*ibid.*). To offer one reading out of many, or to challenge a dominant reading, thus requires not simply a rhetorical, but also a *practical* autonomy over the formulation and articulation of the spatial order. In such formulations individuals are seen to be not merely passive observers of rules (as was the case in many processualist approaches) but active creators, through their agency, of a world imbued with meaning.

Alongside these symbolically oriented studies of the use of space, other ethnoarchaeologists have been more concerned with investigating the possibility of accurately inferring the

principles of social organization, population
size and/or variations in wealth and status from
such variables as settlement layout, room size,
architectural features and house floor artefact
inventories. By and large, despite an initial
optimism that robust material correlates might
be identified (often inspired by cross-cultural
studies based on the Human Resources Area
files), many of the correlates that have been
proposed (e.g. Jacobs 1979; Smith 1987; Sumner
1979; Watson 1979; Wilk 1983), have all been
found to be generally context- or culturally specific, and as open to symbolic manipulation as
any other element of the material world.

The complexity of the relationships between
compound or room area, wealth and household
size are drawn out, for example, by Kramer
(1979b, 1982) with reference to the architectural space of a Kurdish village. Accepting the
premise that 'residential space reflects variation
in both compound population and economic
status' (1979b: 158), Kramer, nevertheless, noted
that certain architectural features were of relevance to different socio-economic variables.
Specifically, the number of dwelling rooms provided a good indication of the number of co-
residing married couples, whereas estimates of
household size were more adequately derived
from the metric area of dwelling space, although
the number and/or volume of facilities such as
ovens and grain bins also provided a coarser
indication. Finally, compound size, rather than
the area of the dwelling space, correlated positively with the economic prosperity of the principal resident (1979b: 153–8, 1982: 104–36).
Watson, on the other hand, in a comparable
study of another village in the Iranian Zagros,
with a much lower total population, found that,
along with its size, the furnishings and condition
of the living room were also good indicators of
family size and relative wealth or poverty (1979).
In fact, Kramer also noted that across south-west
Asia the relationship between settlement size
and population density exhibits considerable
variation (1982: 160–8). Also of relevance are the
observations by Audoze and Jarrige (1980) that
in Baluchistan compound size was determined
by the types of domestic animals that were kept
rather than wealth, and by Horne (1994), who
found, also for an Iranian village, that such relationships were further complicated by the
system of inheritance, which allowed members
of the same kin group to occupy several spatially
dispersed compounds simultaneously, while
Friedl and Loeffler (1994) have drawn attention
to the need to also consider the life histories of
individual rooms and buildings. (See also Lane
1994 for an African illustration of this.)

ARTEFACT TECHNOLOGIES AND CRAFT ORGANIZATION

A third cluster of ethnoarchaeological studies
concern those that deal with issues relating to
the manufacture of objects, their formal properties, the meanings of their stylistic variation and
the social context of their production. As with
the other main themes of ethnoarchaeological
research, such issues have been addressed from
a combination of broadly processual and post-
processual perspectives, and are reviewed
below along these lines. That said, such categorization masks considerable variation in the
overall theoretical perspectives of the different
researchers involved.

By far the largest number of artefact-focused
ethnoarchaeological studies have been concerned with documenting the techniques and
processes of their manufacture, with the bulk of
these being concerned with potting (for a synopsis, see Kramer 1985) metalworking, especially iron (for summaries concerning Africa
see, e.g., Childs and Killick 1993; Schmidt 1996)
or stone working (e.g. Brandt 1996; Clark 1991;
Gould 1980; White 1967), with other crafts being
rarely investigated (Plate 26.4). The principal
value of these studies is the information they
provide on variations in techniques of artefact
manufacture, the processes involved, and the
range of physical, chemical and mineralogical
characteristics that can be used to distinguish
between the use of different techniques in a particular craft. However, given the pace of social
change and the growing impact of globalization
on non-Western cultures (a subject that has also
received some ethnoarchaeological investigation, e.g. Moore 1987; Rowlands 1996; Sargent
and Friedel 1986), such that even seemingly
robust craft traditions are now rapidly dying
out, these studies are also useful pieces of historical ethnography.

Only rarely have ethnoarchaeologists approached the investigation of a particular technology from a holistic perspective, incorporating
the insights gained from ethnographic observation with those obtained from the use of material science, historical inquiry, anthropological
analyses and archaeological excavation, best
illustrated in the work by Schmidt and Childs on
iron smelting, its symbolism and long-term
history in the Buhaya region of north-western
Tanzania (see Schmidt and Childs 1996; Schmidt
1997, and references therein). More specifically,
by deploying a range of disciplinary approaches
and by comparing their ethnographic data with
the historical and archaeological record of iron

Plate 26.4   *Different stages in the manufacture of a large, open bowl, using a combination of the coil-technique and a tournette (hand-operated potter's wheel), Dia, Mali 2001. a) placing of the first coil on a clay dish sitting on the tournette; b) the pot wall is then built up by the addition of further coils; c) once all the coils have been added, the vessel wall is drawn up with one hand while the tournette is operated with the other; d) the vessel walls are then drawn outwards during the final stages of the forming process. Photos: P. Lane*

production in the same area, they were able to demonstrate, for instance, that the Haya and their ancestors possessed a sophisticated 'folk' understanding of the chemical and physical processes involved in iron smelting, that encompassed a knowledge of which clay sources produced the most suitable refractory ceramics, which types of reed provided the best carbon flux, how to raise the internal temperature of furnaces by 'pre-heating' the air being pumped in by bellows, and a host of other technical details. This knowledge, which on archaeological grounds has been shown to have been locally discovered rather than introduced from elsewhere, meant that the inhabitants of this part of the Lake Victoria basin invented techniques for producing low-grade carbon steel hundreds of years before similar capabilities were developed in Europe. Parallel studies conducted by Schmidt and Childs also demonstrated that the craft of iron smelting here, as elsewhere across much of sub-Saharan Africa (see Herbert 1993), was enmeshed within a complex web of symbols that focused on concerns about sex and gender, production and reproduction, power and authority.

Other predominantly processual ethnoarchaeological studies of artefact production and craft specialisation have considered such issues as the spatial and social organization of workshops (e.g. Annis 1988; Nicholson and Patterson 1985), patterns of household production and learning networks (e.g. DeBoer 1990; Hayden and Cannon 1984; Herbich 1987; Stanislawski 1977), the distribution and exchange of finished products (e.g. Mohr Chávez 1991), the causes of stylistic and technological innovation and standardization (e.g. Arnold 1985; Dietler and Herbich 1989; Longacre et al. 1988), among others. More recently, there have been productive attempts to examine the interplay between technical processes and requirements, cultural practices, and social context and meanings in the production of technical 'style' (e.g. Childs 1991; Dietler and Herbich 1998; Gosselain 1998; Hegmon 1998; Lechtman 1977).

At the core of these developments is the basic observation that objects which serve similar functions can take a variety of different forms. This suggests that while artefact form is partly constrained by functional considerations, the range of suitable forms is quite open-ended, with the result that the ultimate selection of one form out of many possible ones is a product of cultural or individual choice. Sackett (1977) has termed this type of variation 'isochrestic variation', meaning 'equivalent in use'. Careful examination of the manufacturing process involved in producing an object has the potential to reveal the logic to the sequence of decisions taken at each stage. Such sequences of technological choices are increasingly referred to as *chaînes opératoires* (Lemmonier 1986), or operational sequences. It has been suggested that cross-cultural comparisons of the different logics and operational sequences employed in a particular technique, such as potting, has the potential to reveal longer-term cultural and historical linkages between even geographically distant populations (e.g. Gosselain 1998, 1999). Moreover, as Lechtman demonstrated in her paper on Andean metallurgy which first introduced the notion of technological style (1977), the same stylistic logics to artefact production may be exhibited within several different crafts within a particular social context. Thus, in the Andean case, Lechtman noted that just as the incorporation of designs in gold and silver into the structure of metal objects is a defining aspect of local metallurgical traditions, the same principle also applies to cloth manufacture and may well relate to a wider set of cultural ideals (1993; for somewhat similar possibilities, see Collett's 1993 discussion of correspondences between the decoration of iron-smelting furnaces, pots and women's clothing in southern Africa). There is also a close similarity between these ideas and Connerton's (1989) concept of 'incorporation' as one of the primary means of social memory (the other being 'inscription'), and Bourdieu's (1977) more general notion of habitus (see Dietler and Herbich 1998). This latter concept, best described as a system of durable dispositions derived from active participation within a cultural tradition that result in members of the same social group acting in a particular way, was also at the core of most post-processual ethnoarchaeology studies of the use of space, artefact categorization and the social uses of artefact style conducted during the 1980s.

ARTEFACT CATEGORIZATION AND STYLISTIC VARIATION

The definition of style, what it constitutes, how stylistic variation might differ from variation attributable to functional requirements (Plate 26.5), the implications this has for the classification of artefacts, and what style might signal have been extensively debated within archaeology (for overviews, see e.g. Boast 1997; Conkey and Hastorf 1990; Hegmon 1998; Shanks and Tilley 1987: 86–95). The results of various

Plate 26.5 *The problems of inferring function from form alone – examples of five out of a possible eight stone Dogon artefacts with similar forms but different functions a) Upper & lower grinding stones for producing millet flour; b) top – stone anvil and hammer-stone used during potting, bottom – tobacco grinding stone; c) worn and abandoned grinding-stone for making gunpowder; d) rain-making altar. Photos. P. Lane: Banani Kokoro and Sanga, Mali, 1980–83*

ethnoarchaeological studies have contributed significantly to these debates.

Regarding artefact typology and systems of categorization, most studies have been concerned with testing the degree of correspondence between indigenous folk taxonomies and the typologies produced by archaeologists. This kind of contrast forms part of a broader etic: emic debate – the former term referring to the external observer's view and ordering of the world, the latter to the insider's own culturally constructed categories. The basic questions in this context centre on determining the extent to which the analytic categories used by archaeologists, from which a wide range of functional and social inferences are often drawn, correspond with the lived 'reality' of the subjects of archaeological analysis, and whether it is necessary that the two should be closely similar (e.g. Arnold 1971; White et al. 1977). Miller's study of artefact categorization, specifically pot types, in a predominantly Hindu village community in Madhya Pradesh, India, also reviews the differences between his own predominantly symbolic framework for analysing the observed variation and that of the villagers among whom he worked (1985: 142–8). More significant, however, is his analysis of the role of emulation in the broader process of stylistic change. Specifically, Miller found that in this community of thirty Hindu castes plus some Muslim residents, with marked economic differences and occupational roles, the copying and appropriation of ceramic styles previously associated with higher-status groups was a particularly effective means for lower-status castes to effect upward movement within the caste hierarchy. Such copying, in turn, encouraged the elite to commission new styles for themselves from the village potters.

Similar concerns with the symbolic meanings of things and places, and how these contribute to the construction of age, gender, class and ethnic identities feature in numerous other ethnoarchaeological studies. Hodder's work on such issues among the Tugen, Pokot and Ilchamus (Njemps) around Lake Baringo, Kenya (1982b), was one of the first of this kind, and has been particularly influential. Two of his primary goals were to examine the degree of correspondence between the spatial distribution of specific ethnicities and material culture patterning, and to establish the conditions under which isomorphic correspondences occur. More specifically, whereas Wobst (1977) had argued that the greater the interaction between groups the greater the similarity in their material culture styles, Hodder found the converse to be the case in the Lake Baringo area. Thus, despite frequent interaction between the three groups, their material culture exhibited a number of distinct stylistic differences (1982b: 13–57). Rather than attributing such patterning simply to 'cultural' norms, Hodder argued that material culture styles were used strategically to maintain notions of difference between the three groups, and that in this sense material culture could be said to play an *active* role in the creation and recreation of identities. (For a contrasting example where a similarly long history of interaction between different ethnic and linguistic groups, in this case along the Sepik coast of northern New Guinea, *has* resulted in more generalized and less sharply bounded stylistic distributions, see Welsch and Terrell 1998.)

Wiessner's study of the formal variations of arrowheads between different San groups in Botswana (1983) also examined the assumption that formal variation in material culture conveys information about personal and social identity. Whereas Wiessner found that this was indeed the case, she noted that artefact style communicated information about both individual identity – which she characterized as 'assertive style', and group identity – or 'emblemic style'. Thus, for instance, she found that !Kung projectile points differed from those made by !Xo and G/wi, and that members of all three groups could differentiate their arrows from those of others, suggesting that these items of material culture were recognized as emblems of the different socio-linguistic groups. However, informants from all three groups were typically unable to identify which linguistic groups had made the arrows they recognized as 'different'. Moreover, 'no single attribute carried information about linguistic group affiliation' (1983: 270). Among the !Kung the critical variable was size, whereas for G/wi and !Xo tip and body shape were more significant.

Larrick's analyses of spear forms and their social correlates among the Lokop section of the Samburu of northern Kenya (1985, 1986) is another useful illustration of similar issues. The focus here was on variations between different age sets within Lokop society rather than between different ethnic or language groupings. Spears are the pre-eminent symbol of warrior status and each age set has a preferred spear style. Typically, each newly initiated warrior age set adopts its own style of spear, and fashions change frequently, partly in response to changing technical needs and partly in response to more expressive concerns. As with San projectile points, Lokop 'spear style' can be read at a variety of social levels ranging from that of the individual to the entire ethnic group. However, spears alone cannot be used to define Lokop identity, not least because there is frequent borrowing of traits from other neighbouring groups for 'assertive' stylistic reasons. Contrary to commonsense expectations, these include the Turkana, who were once perceived by the Lokop to be their fiercest enemies. All of these studies, and numerous others, indicate that different artefact attributes can convey different types of meanings within any group, and that the significance and meaning content of a particular attribute can vary between groups and individuals, and across different social, spatial and temporal contexts.

CONCLUSION: HISTORICIZING AND INDIGENIZING ETHNOARCHAEOLOGY

The use of ethnographic analogies is an inescapable element of archaeology, and the past half-century of systematic ethnoarchaeological research has done much to strengthen how such analogies are formulated and applied. Their use nevertheless introduces a fundamental paradox. Specifically, by drawing on ethnographic data to aid the interpretation of archaeological remains, archaeologists necessarily transform 'the past' into something 'other' than their own world, from which they are removed not just in a temporal sense, *but also spatially*. In this way, to invoke L.P. Hartley's famous phrase, the past becomes 'a foreign country [where] they do things differently' (1953). This notion that 'the past' is somewhere from which we have escaped is further reinforced by the widespread tendency to categorize the disparate remains of past societies into some form of evolutionary framework. It is precisely such concerns that lie at the heart of the ethical dilemmas voiced by Fewster (2001). However, while her recommendation that the notion of human agency should be at the core of any ethnoarchaeological enquiry is certainly an apposite one, there needs to be a far more fundamental reassessment of what the ultimate goals of ethnoarchaeology should be.

Several possibilities suggest themselves. First, instead of searching the present for resemblances to the past, ethnoarchaeology, combined with some form of historical archaeology, could be used to examine why and how the present differs even from the most recent past. As Stahl has observed, far too often ethnoarchaeologists have assumed that the material practices they study are of considerable antiquity (Stahl 1993). Indeed, it was precisely such a belief in the time depth of so-called 'traditional' practices that initiated the growth of ethnoarchaeological research in the first place. Only rarely, however, have ethnoarchaeologists attempted to verify such a fundamental assumption, and as Stahl's recent work in the Banda region of Ghana illustrates there are good reasons as to why they need to do so, not least because of the considerable transformations effected in many parts of the non-Western world as a result of the encounter with European colonialism (Stahl 2001). Second, and in line with broader trends within anthropology, ethnoarchaeologists might aim to act more as enablers for their ethnographic subjects, rather than as interpreters of them. The narrative about iron-smelting practices given to Terry Childs by her principal Toro informant, Adyeri (Childs 2000), may well be the only example of its kind – but is surely a good precedent to follow.

Finally, an alternative (and more etymologically correct) type of 'ethnoarchaeology' concerned with how different societies ascribe historical values and meanings to the physical world and employ these material traces in their construction and representation of individual and collective memory could be developed (Lane 1996b). From this, two separate, but potentially highly connected, benefits might be derived. First, as is widely recognized within archaeology, historic landmarks, archaeological sites, monuments and individual artefacts are often used by various sections of society in their efforts to legitimize their social position or to support a particular view of the past (e.g. Gathercole and Lowenthal 1988; Meskell 1998). Such historical valuations can as easily result in the destruction of sites and monuments as in their conservation. Consequently, improved understanding of how contemporary communities in different parts of the world ascribe historical value to the physical remains of the past they encounter is of critical importance to developing appropriate cultural resources management (CRM) strategies that give due regard to local sensitivities and understandings of the past. Without such efforts, CRM policies will continue to be perceived by a great many non-Western people as yet further examples of state intervention in their affairs and the imposition of alien value systems (Miller 1980).

The second reason, only now being recognized by archaeologists working in various regions (e.g. Bradley 2002; Van Dyke and Alcock 2003; Williams 1998), is that all societies both past and present can be shown to have ascribed historical value to objects from the past. Moreover, the manner in which this is or was done has a direct consequence not only on *what* enters the archaeological record, but also *when* it enters that record, since some objects are conserved well beyond their use life precisely because they have historical value to either individuals or social groups. An obvious example is that of family heirlooms, which are curated partly as a means of sustaining the memory of an individual and so enter the archaeological record, if at all, well after other objects produced coevally with them have been discarded (Lillios 1999). Burials, hoards and storage facilities can also be considered integral aspects of the process of creating social memory, as can body ornamentation and other methods of inscribing identity (Hendon 2000).

Two further observations follow from this. First, archaeologists must begin to give due consideration to the effects the *historical* value of objects and structures can have on the formation of the archaeological record of an area. This is because decisions such as those entailing repair, modification, replacement, curation, preservation or discard are not just driven by the kind of utilitarian concerns generally emphasized by ethnoarchaeologists, but also draw on cultural understanding of the historical value of the object or building in question (Lane 1996b, 2005; Rowlands 1993). Second, archaeological study of continuities and changes in these mundane practices over the long term may well have the potential to provide insights into the nature of historical practice in past societies, and hence, if one accepts an aspect of archaeology to be 'the creation and representation of the past through material remains', how societies *in the past* practised their own kind of 'archaeology'.

NOTES

1   The term 'uniformitarian assumption' refers here to the premise that because past processes and events are unobservable, to learn about them we must compare their effects with those processes observable in the present that operate in comparable ways – an approach sometimes termed 'methodological uniformitarianism' (S.J. Gould 1965). However, whereas we can be confident that processes governed by the natural laws of physics, chemistry and biology operating in the past had identical consequences in the past to those observable in the present, defining universal laws of 'human behaviour' that go beyond broad generalities is far more problematic, and many would argue completely unachievable.

2   Taphonomy involves the study of the processes that affect the transformation of organic remains (bones, plants, etc.) from the biosphere to the lithosphere, with particular focus being placed on those which leave traces analogous to ones observable in the fossil record.

REFERENCES

Allchin, B. (1985) 'Ethnoarchaeology in South Asia', in J. Schotsmans and M. Taddei (eds), *South Asian Archaeology 1983*. Naples: Instituto Universitario Orientale, pp. 21–33.

Allen, H. (1996) 'Ethnography and prehistoric archaeology in Australia', *Journal of Anthropological Archaeology*, 15: 137–59.

Annis, M.B. (1988) 'Modes of production and the use of space in potters' workshops: a changing picture', *Newsletter of the Department of Pottery Technology, Leiden*, 6: 47–78.

Arnold, D.E. (1971) 'Ethnomineralogy of Ticul, Yucutan potters: emics and etics', *American Antiquity*, 36: 20–40.

Arnold, D.E. (1985) *Ceramic Theory and Cultural Process*. Cambridge: Cambridge University Press.

Ascher, R. (1961) 'Analogy in archaeological interpretation', *Southwestern Journal of Anthropology*, 17: 317–25.

Ascher, R. (1962) 'Ethnography for archaeology: a case from the Seri Indians', *Ethnology*, 1: 360–9.

Ascher, R. (1968) 'Time's arrow and the archaeology of a contemporary community', in K.-C. Chang (ed.), *Settlement Archaeology*. Palo Alto, CA: National Press, pp. 43–52.

Atherton, J.H. (1983) 'Ethnoarchaeology in Africa', *African Archaeological Review*, 1: 75–104.

Audoze, F. and Jarrige, C. (1980) 'Perspectives et limites de l'interpretation anthropologique des habitats en archéologie, un example contemporain: les habitats de nomades et de sedentaires de la plaine de Kachi, Baluchistan', in M.T. Barrelet (ed.) *L'Archéologie de l'Iraq*. Paris: CNRS, pp. 361–81.

Barthes, R. (1973) *Mythologies*. London: Paladin.

Bartram, L.E., Kroll, E.M. and Bunn, H.T. (1991) 'Variability in camp structure and bone refuse patterning at Kua San hunter-gatherer camps', in E.M. Kroll and T.D. Price (eds), *The Interpretation of Archaeological Spatial Patterning*. New York: Plenum Press, pp. 77–148.

Binford, L.R. (1962) 'Archaeology as anthropology', *American Antiquity*, 28: 217–25.

Binford, L.R. (1964) 'A consideration of archaeological research design', *American Antiquity*, 29: 425–41.

Binford, L.R. (1967) 'Smudge pits and hide smoking: the use of analogy in archaeological reasoning', *American Antiquity*, 32: 1–12.

Binford, L.R. (1978a) *Nunamiut Ethnoarchaeology*. London: Academic Press.

Binford, L.R. (1978b) 'Dimensional analysis of behavior and site structure: learning from an Eskimo hunting stand', *American Antiquity*, 43: 330-61.

Binford, L.R. (1980) 'Willow smoke and dogs' tails: hunter-gatherer settlement systems and archaeological site formation processes', *American Antiquity*, 45: 4–20.

Binford, L.R. (1981a) 'Behavioral archaeology and the "Pompeii premise"', *Journal of Anthropological Research*, 37: 195–208.

Binford, L.R. (1981b) *Bones: Ancient Men and Modern Myths*. London: Academic Press.

Binford, L.R. (1982) 'The archaeology of place', *Journal of Anthropological Archaeology*, 1: 5–31.

Binford, L.R. (1983) *In Pursuit of the Past*. London: Thames & Hudson.

Binford, L.R. (1991) 'When the going gets tough, the tough get going: Nunamiut local groups, camping patterns and economic organization', in C.S. Gamble and W.A. Boismer (eds), *Ethnoarchaeological Approaches to Mobile Campsites*. Ann Arbor: International Monographs in Prehistory, Ethnoarchaeological Series 1, pp. 25–138.

Boast, R. (1997) 'A small company of actors: a critique of style', *Journal of Material Culture*, 2: 173–98.

Boivin, N. (2000) 'Life rhythms and floor sequences: excavating time in rural Rajasthan and Neolithic Çatalhöyük', *World Archaeology*, 31: 367–88.

Bonnischen, R. (1973) 'Millie's camp: an experiment in archaeology', *World Archaeology*, 4: 277–91.

Bourdieu, P. (1977) *Outline of a Theory of Practice*. Cambridge University Press, Cambridge.

Bourdieu, P. (1979) 'The Kabyle house, or, The world reversed', in P. Bourdieu, *Algeria 1960*. Cambridge: Cambridge University Press, pp. 133–53.

Bradley, R. (2002) *The Past in Prehistoric Societies*. London: Routledge.

Braithwaite, M. (1982) 'Decoration as ritual symbol: a theoretical proposal and an ethnographic study in southern Sudan', in I. Hodder (ed.), *Symbolic and Structural Archaeology*. Cambridge: Cambridge University Press, pp. 80–8.

Brandt, S.A. (1996) 'The ethnoarchaeology of flaked stone tool use in southern Ethiopia', in G. Pwiti and R. Soper (eds), *Aspects of African Archaeology*. Harare: University of Zimbabwe Publications, pp. 733–8.

Brochier, J.E., Villa, P. and Giacomarra, M. (1992) 'Shepherds and sediments: geo-ethnoarchaeology of pastoral sites' (with an appendix by A. Tagliacozzo), *Journal of Anthropological Archaeology*, 11: 47–102.

Bunn, H., Bartram, L. and Kroll, E. (1988) 'Variability in bone assemblage formation from Hadza hunting, scavenging, and carcass processing', *Journal of Anthropological Archaeology*, 7: 412–57.

Buntman, B. (1996) 'Bushman images in South African tourist advertising: the case of Kagga Kamma', in P. Skotnes (ed.) *Miscast. Negotiating the Presence of the Bushmen*. Cape Town: UCT Press, pp. 271–79.

Carr, C. (1991) 'Left in the dust: contextual information in model-focused archaeology', in E.M. Kroll and T.D. Price (eds), *The Interpretation of Archaeological Spatial Patterning*. New York: Plenum Press, pp. 221–56.

Chang, C. (1993) 'Ethnoarchaeological survey and pastoral transhumance sites in the Grevena region, Greece', *Journal of Field Archaeology*, 20: 249–64.

Charlton, T.H. (1981) 'Archaeology, ethnohistory, and ethnology: interpretive interfaces', *Advances in Archaeological Method and Theory*, 4: 227–43.

Childs, S.T. (1991) 'Style, technology and iron smelting furnaces in Bantu-speaking Africa', *Journal of Anthropological Archaeology*, 10: 332–59.

Childs, S.T. (2000) 'Traditional ironworking: a narrated ethnoarchaeological example', in J.O. Vogel (ed.), *Ancient African Metallurgy: The Socio-cultural Context*. Walnut Creek, CA: Altamira, pp. 199–253.

Childs, S.T. and Killick, D. (1993) 'Indigenous African metallurgy: nature and culture', *Annual Review of Anthropology*, 22: 317–37.

Clark, J.E. (1991) 'Flintknapping and debitage disposal among the Lacandon Maya of Chiapas, Mexico', in E. Staski and L.D. Sturo (eds), *The Ethnoarchaeology of Refuse Disposal*. Anthropological Research Papers 42. Tempe, AZ: Arizona State University, pp. 63–78.

Clarke, D.L. (1968) *Analytical Archaeology*. London: Methuen.

Clarke, D.L. (1972) 'A provisional model of an Iron Age society and its settlement system', in D.L. Clarke (ed.), *Models in Archaeology*. London: Methuen, pp. 801–69.

Collett, D.P. (1993) 'Metaphors and representations associated with pre-colonial iron-smelting in eastern and southern Africa', in T. Shaw, P. Sinclair, B.W. Andah and I.A. Okpoko (eds), *The Archaeology of Africa: Food, Metals and Towns*. London: Routledge, pp. 499–511.

Conkey, M.W. and Hastorf, C.A., eds (1990) *The Use of Style in Archaeology*. Cambridge: Cambridge University Press.

Connerton, P. (1989) *How Societies Remember*. Cambridge: Cambridge University Press.

Crawford, O.G.S. (1953) *Archaeology in the Field*. London: Phoenix House.

Crawford, S. (1987) 'Iconography, sacred and secular: visions of the family', in I. Hodder (ed.), *The Archaeology of Contextual Meanings*. Cambridge: Cambridge University Press, pp. 20–30.

Cribb, R. (1991) *Nomads in Archaeology*. Cambridge: Cambridge University Press.

Daniel, G.E. (1950) *A Hundred Years of Archaeology*. London: Duckworth.

David, N. (1971) 'The Fulani compound and the archaeologist', *World Archaeology*, 3: 111–31.

David, N. and Kramer, C. (2001) *Ethnoarchaeology in Action*. Cambridge: Cambridge University Press.

Deal, M. (1985) 'Household pottery disposal in the Maya highlands: an ethnoarchaeological interpretation', *Journal of Anthropological Archaeology*, 4: 243–91.

DeBoer, W.R. (1990) 'Interaction, imitation and communication expressed as style: the Ucayili experience', in M.W. Conkey and C.A. Hastorf (eds), *The Use of Style in Archaeology*. Cambridge: Cambridge University Press, pp. 82–104.

Deetz, J. (1968) 'The inference of residence and descent rules from archaeological data', in S.R. Binford and L.R. Binford (eds), *New Perspectives in Archaeology*. Chicago: Aldine, pp. 41–8.

Dietler, M. and Herbich, I. (1989) 'Tich Matek: the technology of Luo pottery production and the definition of ceramic style', *World Archaeology*, 21: 148–64.

Dietler, M. and Herbich, I. (1998) 'Habitus, techniques, style: an integrated approach to the social understanding of material culture and boundaries', in M.T. Stark (ed.), *The Archaeology of Social Boundaries*. Washington, DC: Smithsonian Institution Press, pp. 232–63.

Donley, L.W. (1982) 'House power: Swahili space and symbolic markers', in I. Hodder (ed.), *Symbolic and Structural Archaeology*. Cambridge: Cambridge University Press, pp. 63–73.

Douglas, M. (1966) *Purity and Danger*. London: Routledge.

Ember, M. (1973) 'An archaeological indicator of matrilocal versus patrilocal residence', *American Antiquity*, 38: 177–82.

Fewster, K. (2001) 'The responsibilities of ethnoarchaeologists', in M. Pluciennik (ed.), *The Responsibilities of Archaeologists: Archaeology and Ethics*. Oxford: BAR International Series 981, pp. 65–73.

Friede, H. and Steel, R. (1980) 'Experimental burning of traditional Nguni huts', *African Studies*, 39: 175–81.

Friedl, E. and Loeffler, A. (1994) 'The ups and downs of dwellings in a village in west Iran: the history of two compounds', *Archiv für Völkerkunde*, 48: 1–44.

Gallay, A. (1981) *Le Sarnyere Dogon: archéologie d'un isolat (Mali)*. Paris: Éditions Recherche sur les Civilisations, Mémoire 4.

Gallay, A. (1999) 'À la recherché du comportement des premiers hominides', in A. Gallay (ed.), *Comment l'homme? À la découverte des premiers hominides d'Afrique de l'Est*. Paris and Geneva: Errance/Géo-Découverte, pp. 9–94.

Gathercole, P. and Lowenthal, D., eds (1988) *The Politics of the Past*. London: Unwin Hyman.

Giddens, A. (1979) *Central Problems in Social Theory*. London: Macmillan.

Giddens, A. (1981) *A Contemporary Critique of Historical Materialism*. London: Macmillan.

Gifford, D.P. (1978) 'Ethnoarchaeological observations of natural processes affecting cultural materials', in R.A. Gould (ed.), *Explorations in Ethnoarchaeology*. Albuquerque, NM: University of New Mexico Press, pp. 77–101.

Gifford, D.P. (1981) 'Taphonomy and palaeoecology: a critical review of archaeology's sister disciplines', *Advances in Archaeological Method and Theory*, 4: 365–438.

Gifford, D.P. and Behrensmeyer, A.K. (1977) 'Observed depositional events at a modern human occupation site in Kenya', *Quaternary Research*, 8: 245–66.

Glassie, H. (1975) *Folk Housing in Middle Virginia*. Knoxville, TN: University of Tennessee Press.

Gorecki, P. (1985) 'Ethnoarchaeology: the need for a post-mortem enquiry', *World Archaeology*, 17: 175–91.

Gosselain, O. (1998) 'Social and technical identity in a clay crystal ball', in M.T. Stark (ed.), *The Archaeology of Social Boundaries*. Washington, DC: Smithsonian Institution Press, pp. 78–106.

Gosselain, O. (1999) 'In pots we trust: the processing of clay and symbols in sub-Saharan Africa', *Journal of Material Culture*, 4: 205–30.

Gould, R.A. (1968) 'Living archaeology: the Ngatatjara of Western Australia', *Southwestern Journal of Anthropology*, 24: 101–22.

Gould, R.A. (1980) *Living Archaeology*. Cambridge: Cambridge University Press.

Gould, R.A. and Watson, P.J. (1982) 'A dialogue on the meaning and use of analogy in ethnoarchaeological reasoning', *Journal of Anthropological Archaeology*, 1: 355–81.

Gould, S.J. (1965) 'Is uniformitarianism necessary?' *American Journal of Science*, 263: 223–8.

Graham, M. (1994) *Mobile Farmers: An Ethnoarchaeological Approach to Settlement Organization among the Rarámuri of Northwestern Mexico*. Ann Arbor, MI: International Monographs in Prehistory, Ethnoarchaeological Series 3.

Greene S.E. (2002) *Sacred Sites and the Colonial Encounter: A History of Meaning and Memory in Ghana*. Indiana, IN: Indiana University Press.

Griffin, P.B. and Solheim, W.G. (1988/9) 'Ethnoarchaeological research in Asia', *Asian Perspectives*, 28: 145–62.

Hartley, L.P. (1953) *The Go-between*. London: Hamiish Hamilton.

Hayden, B. and Cannon, A. (1983) 'Where the garbage goes: refuse disposal in the Maya highlands', *Journal of Anthropological Archaeology*, 2: 117–63.

Hayden, B. and Cannon, A. (1984) 'Interaction inferences in archaeology and learning frameworks of the Maya', *Journal of Anthropological Archaeology*, 3: 325–67.

Hegmon, M. (1998) 'Technology, style, and social practices: archaeological approaches', in M.T. Stark (ed.), *The Archaeology of Social Boundaries*. Washington, DC: Smithsonian Institution Press, pp. 264–79.

Hendon, J.A. (2000) 'Having and holding: storage, memory, knowledge and social relations', *American Anthropologist*, 102: 42–53.

Herbert, E. (1993) *Iron, Gender, and Power: Rituals of Transformation in African Societies*. Bloomington, IN: Indiana University Press.

Herbich, I. (1987) 'Learning patterns, potter interaction and ceramic style among the Luo of Kenya', *African Archaeological Review*, 5: 193–204.

Herbich, I. and Dietler, M. (1993) 'Space, time and symbolic structure in the Luo homestead: an ethnoarchaeological study of "settlement biography" in Africa', in J. Pavúk (ed.), *Actes du XIIe Congrès international des sciences préhistoriques et protohistoriques, Bratislava, Czechoslovakia, September 1–7*. Nitra: Archaeological Institute of the Slovak Academy of Sciences, pp. 26–32.

Hill, J. (1970) *Broken K Pueblo*. Anthropology Papers 18. Tucson, AZ: University of Arizona.

Hodder, I.R. (1979) 'Economic and social stress and material culture patterning', *American Antiquity*, 44: 446–54.

Hodder, I.R. (1982a) *The Present Past*. London: Batsford.

Hodder, I.R. (1982b) *Symbols in Action*. Cambridge: Cambridge University Press.

Hodder, I.R. (1986) *Reading the Past*. Cambridge: Cambridge University Press.

Hodder, I.R. (1987) 'The meaning of discard: ash and domestic space in Baringo, Kenya', in S. Kent (ed.), *Method and Theory for Activity Area Research: An Ethnoarchaeological Approach*, New York: Columbia University Press, pp. 424–8.

Hole, F. (1978) 'Pastoral nomadism in western Iran', in R.A. Gould (ed.), *Explorations in Ethnoarchaeology*, Albuquerque, NM: University of New Mexico Press, pp. 127–67.

Horne, L. (1994) *Village Spaces: Settlement and Society in Northern Iran*. Washington, DC: Smithsonian Institution Press.

Hudson, J., ed. (1993) *From Bones to Behavior: Ethnoarchaeological and Experimental Contributions to the Interpretation of Faunal Remains*. Carbondale: Southern Illinois University, Center for Archaeological Investigations, Occasional Paper 21.

Hugh-Jones, C. (1979) *From the Milk River*. Cambridge: Cambridge University Press.

Isaac, G. (1984) 'The archaeology of human origins: studies of the Lower Pleistocene in East Africa, 1971–1981', *Advances in Old World Archaeology*, 3: 1–87.

Jacobs, L. (1979) 'Tell I Nun: archaeological implications of a village in transition', in C. Kramer (ed.), *Ethnoarchaeology: Implications of Ethnography for Archaeology*. Columbia University Press, New York, pp. 175–91.

Johnson, I. (1984) 'Cell frequency recording and analysis of artifact distributions', in H. Hietala (ed.), *Intrasite Spatial Analysis in Archaeology*. Cambridge: Cambridge University Press, pp. 75–96.

Kent, S. (1984) *Analysing Activity Areas*. Albuquerque, NM: University of New Mexico Press.

Kleindienst, M.R., and Watson, P.J. (1956) '"Action archaeology": the archaeological inventory of a living community', *Anthropology Tomorrow*, 5: 75–8.

Kramer, C. (1979a) 'Introduction', in C. Kramer (ed.), *Ethnoarchaeology: Implications of Ethnography for Archaeology*. New York: Columbia University Press, pp. 1–20.

Kramer, C. (1979b) 'An archaeological view of a contemporary Kurdish village: domestic architecture, household size and wealth', in C. Kramer (ed.), *Ethnoarchaeology: Implications of Ethnography for Archaeology*. New York: Columbia University Press, pp. 139–63.

Kramer, C. (1982) *Village Ethnoarchaeology: Rural Iran in Archaeological Perspective*. London: Academic Press.

Kramer, C. (1985) 'Ceramic ethnoarchaeology', *Annual review of Anthropology*, 14: 77–102.

Kus, S. (1982) 'Matters material and ideal', in I. Hodder (ed.), *Symbolic and Structural Archaeology*. Cambridge: Cambridge University Press, pp. 47–62.

Lane, P.J. (1987) 'Reordering residues of the past', in I. Hodder (ed.), *Archaeology as Long-Term History*. Cambridge: Cambridge University Press, pp. 54–62.

Lane, P.J. (1994) 'The temporal structuring of settlement among the Dogon: an ethnoarchaeological study', in M. Parker Pearson and C. Richards (eds), *Architecture and Order: Approaches to Social Space*. London: Routledge, pp. 196–216.

Lane, P.J. (1994/5) 'The use and abuse of ethnography in the study of the southern African Iron Age', *Azania*, 29–30: 51–64.

Lane, P.J. (1996a) 'Breaking the mould? Exhibiting Khoisan in southern African museums', *Anthropology Today*, 12: 3–10.

Lane, P.J. (1996b) 'Rethinking ethnoarchaeology', in G. Pwiti and R. Soper (eds), *Aspects of African Archaeology*. Harare: University of Zimbabwe Publications, pp. 727–32.

Lane, P.J. (2005) 'The material culture of memory', in W. James and D. Mills (eds), *The Qualities of Time*. Oxford: Berg: pp. 19–34.

Larrick, R. (1985) 'Spears, style and time among Maa-speaking pastoralists', *Journal of Anthropological Archaeology*, 4: 206–20.

Larrick, R. (1986) 'Age grading and ethnicity in the style of Loikop (Samburu) spears', *World Archaeology*, 18: 268–83.

Leach, E. (1976) *Culture and Communication*. Cambridge: Cambridge University Press.

Lechtman, H. (1977) 'Style in technology: some early thoughts', in H. Lechtman and R.S. Merill (eds), *Material Culture: Style, Organization, and Dynamics of Technology*. New York and St Paul, MN: West Publishing, pp. 3–20.

Lechtman, H. (1993) 'Technologies of power: the Andean case', in J.S. Henderson and P.J. Netherley (eds), *Configurations of Power: Holistic Anthropology in Theory and Practice*. Ithaca, NY: Cornell University Press, pp. 244–80.

Lemmonier, P. (1986) 'The study of material culture today: towards an anthropology of technical systems', *Journal of Anthropological Archaeology*, 5: 147–86.

Leroi-Gourhan, A. and Brézillon, M. (1966) 'L'habitation magdalénienne No. 1 de Pincevent près Montereau (Seine-et-Marne)', *Gallia Préhistoire* 9: 263–385.

Lévi-Strauss, C. (1968) *Structural Anthropology*. London: Allen Lane.

Lévi-Strauss, C. (1970) *The Raw and the Cooked*. London: Cape.

Lillios, K.T. (1999) 'Objects of memory: the ethnography and archaeology of heirlooms', *Journal of Archaeological Method and Theory* 6: 235–62.

Longacre, W.A. (1970) *Archaeology as Anthropology.* Anthropology Papers 17. Tucson, AZ: University of Arizona.

Longacre, W.A. and Ayers, J.E. (1968) 'Archaeological lessons from an Apache wickiup', in S.R. Binford and L.R. Binford (eds), *New Perspectives in Archaeology.* Chicago: Aldine, pp. 151–9.

Longacre, W.A., Kvamme, K.L. and Kobayahsi, M. (1988) 'Southwestern pottery standardization: an ethnoarchaeological view from the Philippines', *The Kiva*, 53: 110-21.

Lyman, R.L. and O'Brien, M.J. (2001) 'The direct historical approach, analogical reasoning and theory in Americanist archaeology', *Journal of Archaeological Theory and Method*, 8: 303–42.

MacEachern, S. (1996) 'Foreign countries: the development of ethnoarchaeology in sub-Saharan Africa', *Journal of World Prehistory*, 10: 243–304.

Mbae, B. (1990) 'The ethnoarchaeology of Maasai settlements and refuse disposal patterns in the Lemek area', in P. Robertshaw (ed.), *Early Pastoralists of South-western Kenya.* Memoir 11. Nairobi: British Institute in Eastern Africa, pp. 279–92.

McIntosh, R.J. (1974) 'Archaeology and mud wall decay in a West African village', *World Archaeology*, 6: 154–71.

McIntosh, R.J. (1977) 'The excavation of mud structures: an experiment from West Africa', *World Archaeology*, 9: 185–99.

Meskell, L., ed. (1998) *Archaeology under Fire: Nationalism, Politics and Heritage in the Eastern Mediterranean and Middle East.* London: Routledge.

Miller, D. (1980) 'Archaeology and development', *Current Anthropology*, 21: 209–26.

Miller, D. (1985) *Artefacts as Categories.* Cambridge: Cambridge University Press.

Mohr Chávez, K.L. (1991) 'The organization of production and distribution of traditional pottery in south highland Peru', in G.J. Bey III and C.A. Pool (eds), *Ceramic Production and Distribution: An Integrated Approach.* Boulder, CO: Westview Press, pp. 49–92.

Moore, H.L. (1982) 'The interpretation of spatial patterning in settlement residues', in I. Hodder (ed.), *Symbolic and Structural Archaeology.* Cambridge: Cambridge University Press, pp. 74–9.

Moore, H.L. (1986) *Space, Text and Gender.* Cambridge: Cambridge University Press.

Moore, H.L. (1987) 'Problems in the analysis of social change: an example from the Marakwet', in I. Hodder (ed.), *Archaeology as Long-term History.* Cambridge: Cambridge University Press, pp. 85–104.

Murray, P. (1980) 'Discard location: the ethnographic data', *American Antiquity*, 45: 490-502.

Nandris, J.G. (1985) 'The Stina and the Katun: foundations of a research design in European highland zone ethnoarchaeology', *World Archaeology*, 17: 256–68.

Nicholson, P.T. and Patterson, H.L. (1985) 'Pottery making in Upper Egypt: an ethnoarchaeological study', *World Archaeology*, 17: 222–39.

O'Connell, J.F. (1987) 'Alywara site structure and its archaeological implications', *American Antiquity*, 52: 74–108.

O'Connell, J.F., Hawkes, K. and Blurton-Jones, N. (1991) 'Distribution of refuse-producing activities at Hadza base camps: implications for analyses of archaeological site structure', in E.M. Kroll and T.D. Price (eds), *The Interpretation of Archaeological Spatial Patterning.* New York: Plenum Press, pp. 61–76.

Orme, B. (1973) 'Archaeology and ethnography', in C. Renfrew (ed.), *The Explanation of Culture Change: Models in Prehistory.* London: Duckworth, pp. 481–92.

Orme, B. (1981) *Anthropology for Archaeologists.* London: Duckworth.

Parker Pearson, M. (1982) 'Mortuary practices, society and ideology: an ethnoarchaeological study', in I. Hodder (ed.), *Symbolic and Structural Archaeology.* Cambridge: Cambridge University Press, pp. 99–113.

Pétrequin, A.-M. and Pétrequin, P. (1984) *Habitat Lacustre du Bénin: Une approche ethnoarchéologique.* Paris: Editions Recherches sur les Civilisations, Mémoire 39.

Poor, M. (1999) 'Archaeology, analogy, material culture, society: an exploration', in L.R. Owen and M. Porr (eds), *Ethno-analogy and the Reconstruction of Prehistoric Artefact Use and Production.* Tübingen: Mo Vince, pp. 3–15.

Rathje, W.L. (1978) 'Archaeological ethnography ... because sometimes it is better to give than to receive', in R.A. Gould (ed.), *Explorations in Ethnoarchaeology.* Albuquerque, NM: University of New Mexico Press, pp. 49–75.

Robbins, L.H. (1973) 'Turkana material culture viewed from an archaeological perspective', *World Archaeology*, 5: 209–14.

Roberts, M.N. and Roberts, A.F., eds (1996) *Memory: Luba Art and the Making of History.* New York: Museum of Modern Art and Munich: Prestel.

Rowlands, M. (1993) 'The role of memory in the transmission of culture', *World Archaeology*, 25: 141–51.

Rowlands, M. (1996) 'The consumption of an African modernity', in M.J. Arnoldi, C.M. Geary and K.L. Hardin (eds), *African Material Culture.* Bloomington, IN: Indiana University Press, pp. 188–214.

Sackett, J.R. (1977) 'The meaning of style: a general model', *American Antiquity*, 43: 369–80.

Sargent, C.F. and Friedel, D.A. (1986) 'From clay to metal: culture change and container usage among the Bariba of northern Bénin, West Africa', *African Archaeological Review*, 4: 177–95.

Schiffer, M.B. (1976) *Behavioral Archaeology.* London: Academic Press.

Schiffer, M.B. (1978) 'Methodological issues in ethnoarchaeology', in R.A. Gould (ed.), *Explorations in Ethnoarchaeology*. Albuquerque, NM: University of New Mexico Press, pp. 229–47.

Schiffer, M.B. (1985) 'Is there a "Pompeii premise" in archaeology?' *Journal of Anthropological Research*, 41: 18–41.

Schiffer, M.B. (1987) *Formation Processes of the Archaeological Record*. Albuquerque, NM: University of New Mexico Press.

Schmidt, P.R. (1980) 'Steel production in prehistoric Africa: insights from ethnoarchaeology in West Lake, Tanzania', in R. Leakey and B.A. Ogot (eds), *Proceedings of the Eighth Pan-African Congress of Prehistory and Quaternary Studies*. Nairobi: International L.S.B. Leakey Memorial Institute, pp. 335–40.

Schmidt, P.R. (1983) 'An alternative to a strictly materialist perspective: a review of historical archaeology, ethnoarchaeology and symbolic approaches in African archaeology', *American Antiquity*, 48: 62–79.

Schmidt, P.R., ed. (1996) *The Culture and Technology of African Iron Production*. Gainesville, FL: University of Florida Press.

Schmidt, P.R. (1997) *Iron Technology in East Africa: Symbolism, Science and Archaeology*. Bloomington, IN: Indiana University Press.

Schmidt, P.R. and Avery, D.H. (1978) 'Complex iron smelting and prehistoric culture in Tanzania', *Science*, 201: 1085–9.

Schmidt, P.R. and Childs, T.S. (1996) 'Actualistic models for interpretation of two early Iron Age industrial sites in northwestern Tanzania', in P.R. Schmidt (ed.), *The Culture and Technology of African Iron Production*. Gainesville, FL: University of Florida Press, pp. 186–223.

Shanks, M. and Tilley, C. (1987) *Social Theory and Archaeology*. Cambridge: Polity Press.

Sinopoli, C.M. (1991) 'Seeking the past through the present: recent ethnoarchaeological research in South Asia', *Asian Perspectives*, 30: 177–92.

Smith, A. and David, N. (1995) 'The production of space and the Xidi Sukur', *Current Anthropology*, 36: 441–71.

Smith, M.E. (1987) 'Household possessions and wealth in agrarian states: implications for archaeology', *Journal of Anthropological Archaeology*, 6: 297–335.

Stahl, A.B. (1993) 'Concepts of time and approaches to analogical reasoning in historical perspective', *American Antiquity*, 58: 235–60.

Stahl, A.B. (2001) *Making History in Banda: Anthropological Visions of Africa's Past*, Cambridge: Cambridge University Press.

Stanislawski, M.B. (1977) 'Ethnoarchaeology of Hopi and Hopi-Tewa pottery making: styles of learning', in D.T. Ingersoll, J.E. Yellen and W. McDonald (eds), *Experimental Archaeology*. New York: Columbia University Press, pp. 378–408.

Stanislawski, M.B. (1978) 'If pots were mortal', in R.A. Gould (ed.), *Explorations in Ethnoarchaeology*. University of New Mexico Press, Albuquerque, pp. 201–27.

Stark, M. (1993) 'Re-fitting the "cracked and broken façade": the case for empiricism in post-processual ethnoarchaeology', in N. Yoffe and A. Sherratt (eds), *Archaeological Theory: Who sets the Agenda?* Cambridge: Cambridge University Press, pp. 93–104.

Stevenson, M.G. (1991) 'Beyond the formation of hearth-associated artefact assemblages', in E.M. Kroll and T.D. Price (eds), *The Interpretation of Archaeological Spatial Patterning*. New York: Plenum Press, pp. 269–99.

Stewart, K.M. and Gifford-Gonzalez, D.P. (1994) 'Ethnoarchaeological contribution to identifying hominid fish processing sites', *Journal of Archaeological Science*, 21: 237–48.

Stiles, D. (1977) 'Ethnoarchaeology: a discussion of methods and applications', *Man* (n.s.), 12: 87–103.

Sumner, W.M. (1979) 'Estimating population by analogy', in C. Kramer (ed.), *Ethnoarchaeology: Implications of Ethnography for Archaeology*. Columbia University Press, New York, pp. 164–74.

Tambiah, S.J. (1969) 'Animals are good to think and good to prohibit', *Ethnology*, 8: 423–59.

Thompson, D.F. (1939) 'The seasonal factor in human culture, illustrated from the life of a contemporary nomadic group', *Proceedings of the Prehistoric Society*, 5: 209–21.

Tobert, N. (1985) 'Craft specialisation: a seasonal camp in Kebkebiya', *World Archaeology*, 17: 278–88.

Tobert, N. (1988) *The Ethnoarchaeology of the Zaghawa of Darfur (Sudan): Settlement and Transcience*. Cambridge Monographs in African Archaeology 30. Oxford: BAR International Series 445.

Van Dyke, R.M. and Alcock, S.E., eds (2003) *Archaeologies of Memory*. Oxford: Blackwell.

Vidale, M., Kenoyer, J.M. and Bhan, K.K. (1993) 'Ethnoarchaeological excavations of the bead-making workshops of Khambat: a view from beneath the floors', *South Asian Archaeology 1999: Proceedings, International Conference of the Association of South Asian Archaeologists in Western Europe*, 9: 273–87.

Watson, P.J. (1979) *Archaeological Ethnography in Western Iran*. Tucson, AZ: University of Arizona Press.

Watson, P.J. and Fotiadis, M. (1990) 'The razor's edge: symbolic-structuralist archaeology and the expansion of archaeological inference', *American Anthropologist*, 92: 613–29.

Watson, P.J., LeBlanc, S.A. and Redman, C.L. (1971) *Explanation in Archaeology: An Explicitly Scientific Approach*. London: Columbia University Press.

Wauchope, R. (1938) *Modern Maya Houses*. Publication No. 502. Washington, DC: Carnegie Institution.

Weiss, B. (1997) 'Forgetting your dead: alienable and inalienable objects in Northwest Tanzania', *Anthropological Quarterly*, 70: 164–72.

Welbourn, A. (1984) 'Endo ceramics and power strategies', in D. Miller and C. Tilley (eds), *Ideology, Power and Prehistory*. Cambridge: Cambridge University Press, pp. 17–24.

Welsch, R.L. and Terrell, J.E. (1998) 'Material culture, social fields, and social boundaries on the Sepik coast of New Guinea', in M.T. Stark (ed.), *The Archaeology of Social Boundaries*. Washington, DC: Smithsonian Institution Press, pp. 50–77.

Werbner, R., ed. (1998) *Memory and the Postcolony: African Anthropology and the Critique of Power*. London: Zed Books.

White, J.P. (1967) 'Ethno-archaeology in New Guinea: two examples', *Mankind*, 6: 409–14.

White, J.P., Modjeska, N. and Hipuya, I. (1977) 'Group definitions and mental templates: an ethnographic experiment', in R.V.S. Wright (ed.), *Stone Tools as Cultural Markers*. Canberra: Australian Institute of Aboriginal Studies, pp. 380–90.

Wiessner, P. (1983) 'Style and social information in Kalahari San projectile points', *American Antiquity*, 48: 253–76.

Wiessner, P. (1984) 'Reconsidering the behavioural basis for style: a case study among the Kalahari San', *Journal of Anthropological Archaeology*, 3: 190–234.

Willey, G.R. and Phillips, P. (1958) *Method and Theory in American Archaeology*. Chicago: University of Chicago Press.

Williams, H. (1998) 'Monuments and the past in early Anglo-Saxon England', *World Archaeology*, 30: 90–108.

Wilk, R. (1983) 'Little house in the jungle: the causes of variation in house size among modern Kekchi Maya', *Journal of Anthropological Archaeology*, 2: 99–116.

Wobst, H.M. (1977) 'Stylistic behavior and information exchange', in C. Cleland (ed.), *Papers for the Director: Research Essays in Honor of James B. Griffin*, Michigan Anthropological Papers 61. Ann Arbor, MI: Museum of Anthropology, University of Michigan, pp. 317–42.

Wobst, H.M. (1978) 'The archaeo-ethnography of hunter-gatherers, or, The tyranny of the ethnographic record in archaeology', *American Antiquity*, 43: 303–9.

Wylie, A. (1982) 'An analogy by any other name is just as analogical: a commentary on the Gould-Watson dialogue', *Journal of Anthropological Archaeology*, 1: 382–401.

Wylie, A. (1985) 'The reaction against analogy', *Advances in Archaeological Method and Theory*, 8: 63–111.

Yellen, J.E. (1977a) *Archaeological Approaches to the Present: Models for Reconstructing the Past*. London: Academic Press.

Yellen, J.E. (1977b) 'Cultural patterning in faunal remains: evidence from the Kung Bushmen', in D.T. Ingersoll, J.E. Yellen and W. MacDonald (eds), *Experimental Archaeology*. New York: Columbia University Press, pp. 271–331.

Yellen, J.E. (1993) 'Small mammals: !Kung San utilization and the production of faunal assemblages', *Journal of Anthropological Archaeology*, 9: 1–26.

27

MATERIAL CULTURE AND LONG-TERM CHANGE

Chris Gosden

Long-term change, unfolding over decades, centuries or millennia, is hard to grasp or conceive of, existing as it does at a scale beyond that of the human life span. However, I shall argue here that cultural and material forms existing over long spans of time form a channelling for human being that helps orient and shape short-term processes and events. Looking at our lives at the biographical scale of the individual human life, we can see that each of us lives by sets of skills of making and discrimination which we learn in the course of our lives, with crucial learning taking place in childhood. How we make and use things in a manner which is appropriate both to the materials from which things are made and to their social purposes is fundamental to our lives as skilled social beings. How to walk, how to eat, what to give and when to receive are all things we need to know, such knowledge encompassing skills of making things, but also those of taste and discrimination which provide a sense both of the conventional and of impressive novelty. We are taught to make and use things by people through verbal instruction or emulation, but the crucial teachers are things in themselves. As a parent it is possible to prepare a child to ride a bicycle by talking about balance, speed and when to turn the handlebars. But the real teacher is the bike itself, which will tune muscles, set up the faculty of balance and provide the social expectations of what other bike riders will do. Textiles, hand axes and fish stews are other vital teachers in human history and it is only through action, or more particularly interaction, that we learn what will work and what will fail. Educative artefacts often have longer lives as collectivities than people do, forming communities of their own through similarities of form and decoration. In this chapter I want to explore the long-term histories of some of these communities of objects, how they behave and change, obeying logics of their own. The interaction between these long-term histories of things and the shorter-lived communities of people represents a vital and virtually undiscovered aspect of human history. When considering the prehistoric past, individual people drop away, so that things stand out, as do the means by which they render the world intelligible for people.

New work on the operations of the human body help render it a truly active element, unlike in many considerations of the body where it becomes a form of text or inscription. The intermingling of the body and of material things also becomes highlighted in a manner of relevance for all those interested in material culture. I shall start with a brief consideration of the nature of skills and intelligence, as developing in a number of areas, such as robotics and artificial life, which are coming to emphasize the distributed and extended nature of intelligent *action* (rather than the representational abilities of intelligent *thought*) before making the point that a concentration on material culture and its social lives, especially when considered over the long term, supplies a lack encountered in theories stressing the human body.

The approach I am favouring here is rather different from earlier analyses of long-term change within archaeology. Three main past approaches can be identified: social evolutionary approaches, structural-Marxist views and symbolic or post-structuralist archaeologies. In each case there is a crucial lack of a deep theory of material culture and its deep involvement with social forms. I shall look briefly at each in turn.

PAST ARCHAEOLOGICAL APPROACHES TO LONG-TERM CHANGE

All three of these approaches felt that they took material culture seriously, so that a definite argument needs to be made as to why such was not the case. Social evolutionary approaches derive ultimately from the nineteenth century, taking inspiration from Darwin. However, it is their twentieth-century incarnation I shall concentrate on mostly. Just as with other organisms when taken from a biological point of view, it was felt that the crucial element of human history was the ability to harness energy from the environment. Unlike most other organisms the human ability to produce tools and technology allowed a sophisticated capacity to gather and store raw materials and food which were then used to underwrite aspects of the social process. The complexity of social relations ultimately depended on a human ability to extract energy, so that the motor of human social and political history was technology. As technology advanced, so did social organization. The notion of advance was a key one for social evolutionists, who saw historical developments as taking the form of shifts from an early hunter-gatherer lifestyle in all parts of the world prior to 10,000 years ago to the development of farming in some areas, followed later by the move to cities and states which eventually saw the rise of industrialism in Europe in the eighteenth century. These changes in production and surplus were paralleled by social changes from hunter-gatherer bands to farming tribes or chiefdoms to urbanized states (Childe 1930; Sahlins and Service 1960; Service 1962, 1971; White 1959). Not dissimilar views of history were found in the nineteenth century (Tylor 1871). The main problems with such views were long ago identified and have been much discussed – a progressive view of history which works only for some parts of the world and a functionalist notion of technology, conceived of in terms of its physical impact and consequences. To a critical eye these suppositions about the manner in which human history works look like nineteenth and twentieth-century economic rationality and Western supremacy applied to human history as a whole. The emphases on functions and measurable outcomes leave a lot of human life out, assuming that structures of meaning, thought and feeling are epiphenomenal and weeded out by the long-term processes of human prehistory.

Also, taking inspiration from the nineteenth century, but with a much more compelling theoretical basis, is structural Marxism (Friedman and Rowlands 1978). Structural Marxism was an attempt to develop Marxist theory in a manner in tune with the record of a deep prehistory that had obviously been unavailable to Marx himself. As is well known, Marx took a historical view of human society, holding that no point in time could be understood without looking at the social forces which have led up to that point. He developed a general history of modes of production from primitive communism to present-day capitalism. Marx's view of a mode of production was that it was made up of the forces of production, which were the technological means by which society produced the goods it wanted, and the relations of production, which specified the relations between people pertaining to both the division of labour and the division of the items produced. With the exception of the influences from Morgan, Marx paid little attention to modes of production outside those known from the history of Europe. This has left Marxist anthropologists and archaeologists with a series of basic principles pertaining to the process of labour, and the social and ideological relations resulting from that process, but little in the way of specific models to apply to non-capitalist societies. Also over the century since Marx died there have been subtle currents within Marxist thought which have subjected principles drawn from Marx to constant criticism and revision.

Structural Marxism, as this trend is known, has been influential on the other main area of Marxist thought influencing archaeology. Recent Marxist writers have tackled a particular aspect of the base-superstructure problem: what sorts of relations of production are exercised in the absence of classes and how is the control over production translated into social power and standing? One answer given to this problem was that direct control was not exercised over production at all, but that power derived from the control of the flow of high-ranking items of exchange. These in turn were used to control the flow of people in marriage, which had important consequences for the demographic strength of a group. In societies dominated by kinship the conclusion consequently was that it was the relations of reproduction which were central to the social process rather than the relations of production. These ideas had a direct impact on archaeology and were worked into a general model by Friedman and Rowlands (1978). To accuse a Marxist approach of lacking a theory of material culture may seem ironic or misguided. However, I feel that the concentration on production inherent in many Marxist views stifled creative thought about more rounded relations between people and things, especially in the areas of exchange and consumption. As we shall see below, some of the most interesting aspects of contemporary thought concern the impact that things have on people through our sensory experience of them. Social relations shaped by the forms that objects take was immanent in Marxist thought, although the main emphasis was on the manner in which social relations shaped objects.

In books such as *The Domestication of Europe* (1990) Ian Hodder attempted a contrary view of long-term continuity and change focusing on structures of meaning and ritual (see also Hodder 1987). The coming of the Neolithic did not so much herald a change in subsistence from hunter-gathering to farming as it had for the social evolutionists or a shift in the relations of production as seen by structural Marxism, but rather a symbolic revolution. Sedentary life concentrated social tensions within the home and the village, so that relations between men and women, or worries about life and death, needed dealing with in new ways. Novelty was seen in ritual structures, such as greater care over burial or the symbolism inside the house playing with wild and domesticated forms. This revolution, although it had material expression through houses or pots, was ultimately a revolution of thought about the different categories of things that made up the world and the tensions between these. Material culture formed a series of texts to be read by the archaeologist and it was the ephemeral meanings that were interesting, open as they were to varying forms of interpretation by people in the past and in the present. This was an interpretive archaeology, whose solid material base gave rise to meanings and interpretations, and was thus ultimately fluid rather than solid. Fluidity of course was an emphasis of much post-structuralist thought. Much of this emphasis was liberating, opening up new possibilities of seeing the world. But it did ignore what Bourdieu called the non-discursive elements of human life, those habitual actions we are little conscious of and find difficult to talk about. Many of our non-discursive relations are with things and things have become ever more central to a range of disciplines over the last decade, as we shall see.

INTELLIGENCE: EMBODIED, DISTRIBUTED, EXTENDED AND MATERIAL

What is the quintessential marker of intelligence in a human being? An answer to this question until recently would probably have concentrated on abstract reasoning, the ability that humans have to represent the world through logical notation or geometrical forms. These days many might say that being able to pick up a plastic cup full of hot coffee on a moving train without injuring oneself involves a series of skills of a very complex, but uncelebrated, type. There has been a distinct shift over the last few years from the view that intelligence involves abstract reasoning that takes place in the mind to an approach which sees intelligence deriving from the actions of the human body and its interactions with the material world. Such ideas have important implications for the study of material culture, but these have not so far been spelt out in any detail. Ideas on embodied and distributed intelligence derive from a variety of literatures, ranging from neurosciences, which concentrate on the body, to robotics, which tries to simulate the actions of the body in relationship to external environments, to studies of artefacts, which tend to take the body and its skills as a vital background for production and consumption without focusing on the skills of the body as such. There is something of an inside-out structure to this spectrum of accounts starting with what happens inside the body and moving out into the world. Whilst ultimately wanting to break with this inside-out structure of thought, I shall use it initially to provide a direction for discussing current work and identifying the key weakness, which is a lack of real understanding of material culture.

Spinoza said that the mind is the idea of the body. This aphorism has been the basis of much recent work, which has provided empirical evidence for such a view. In Damasio's work, for instance, he makes a distinction between core consciousness and extended conscious, whilst saying that all kinds of consciousness arise from our awareness of our bodies. Core consciousness, which we share with many other animal species, derives from 'the creation of mapped accounts of ongoing relationships between organism and objects' (Damasio 2000: 197). Here mapping refers to the internal chemical and neurological systems of the body which provide a continuous set of charts of the states of the body and its external positioning and objects refer to elements of consciousness like memories. Such maps are updated enormously quickly, with impulses travelling through the body in a fraction of a second, so that many elements of core consciousness occur without us being aware of its unfolding. There is thus something of a paradox here – consciousness may well flux and unfold at speeds too fast for us to grasp or to put into words. We are always trying to catch up with ourselves. Extended consciousness gives rise to the biographical self in which memory is crucial in connecting up the here-and-now with past states of the body in its world, so that there is a complex tracking back and forth between immediate sense impressions and those recalled from other times, or anticipated in the future. Extended consciousness may not require language and might be something we share with other primates and other animal species. It is worth noting that Damasio uses the term 'extended' primarily to refer to time – past, present and future intermingle to create the true complexity of experience. However, his self is a somewhat isolated neurological being, undoubtedly in contact with the material world and with others, but lacking any real richness of social or material relations.

Damasio's notion of extended consciousness starts to move from the realm of neuroscience to philosophy, a move developed by Lakoff and Johnson in their attempt to create 'an empirically responsible philosophy' (1999: 3). In attacking the concept of an abstract, virtual, disembodied mind, they state three basic premises – the mind is inherently embodied, thought is mostly unconscious and abstract concepts are mostly metaphorical (Lakoff and Johnson 1999: 3). Thanks to the speed of bodily processes much of our awareness of the world and thought about the world are unconscious. What was taken, in the older paradigm of the mind, as the quintessence of human being, abstract thought, arises from the everyday operations of the body. Crucially, two elements of human being which used to be separate are now linked – perception and conception. Our concepts arise from our ongoing apprehension of the world, so that we need to know more about our visual systems, our motor systems and our neural binding to understand how we conceive of the world. An older definition of philosophy, as thinking about thinking, will no longer do, as acting and thinking are linked, so that metaphor has a consistent ontology rooted in the actions of the body. Metaphor is found when words are applied to things or events other than those which they normally designate. An idea may 'go over our heads' or a relationship may be 'at a crossroads' or we may fail to see 'the point of an argument', so that abstract circumstances or relationships are clothed in more concrete words. Rather than stressing a gulf between the mind and the body, Lakoff and Johnson are engaged in knitting together again physical existence and abstracted forms of consciousness, images and representations. As a slight aside, it was worth noting that there are issues

of timescales – many of the operations of the body occur so fast that they elude conscious awareness and indeed if we were aware of all we are doing all of the time, little space would be left for broader forms of awareness.

The embodied mind provides a concrete basis for abstraction and awareness. However, moving a little further out from the body are forms of thought that use terms like 'extended' and 'distributed' in a slightly different manner from their usage by Damasio. The most balanced of these accounts is that by Clark (1997), who develops the 'equal partnership hypothesis'. Work in robotics and artificial life, by Brooks (2003) and others, has shown that early attempts to create robots and animats with a large central processing unit (what would be known in a real creature as a brain) in which complex representations of the world can be assembled have generally failed to replicate intelligent behaviour. On the other hand, developing robots with a relatively simple set of sensors and motors can allow them to navigate around quite complex forms of terrain, performing tasks. Clark contrasts two sorts of projects. On the one hand is CYC (short for 'encyclopedia'), a project which started in 1984 with a budget of $50 million. The idea was to feed into a powerful computer a series of language-based rules, making explicit much of the tacit knowledge we have about the world ('most cars today have four tires. If you fall asleep while driving, your car will start to head out of your lane pretty soon' – Clark 1997: 3). It was thought that the big constraint on artificial intelligence was not inference, but knowledge, and once a sufficient knowledge base was assembled CYC would be able to read and assemble written texts and 'self-program' the rest of its knowledge base. Despite much money, a long period of time and the use of a powerful language for encoding logical relationships, self-programming and intelligent reasoning do not appear on the cards. The lack of success of these large, representational systems has been balanced by a more embodied approach, which creates creatures with little central processing power, but which are able to operate effectively (intelligently?) in the world. One such example is Brooks's robot, 'Herbert'.

Herbert was made up of a series of layers of behaviour which were influenced and directed by inputs from the environment in which they operated. Herbert's task was to collect drinks cans from a crowded and chaotic laboratory. A central processing approach to this problem would have been to create a rich map of the laboratory that Herbert could use to navigate and this would have had the disadvantage that the furniture, people and the cans kept changing configurations, so that the map would need constant updating. Herbert instead was made up of some simple navigating routines, using sensors to detect obstacles and motors to stop and reorient motion. Once a table-like outline was detected by the sensors, using a simple visual system, locomotion and obstacle avoidance routines were temporarily suspended and a laser beam and video-camera swept the table top. If a can outline was detected the robot moved so that the can was in the middle of its field of vision, extended an arm, which if a can outline was encountered activated a grasping routine and the can was removed. Herbert then moved on. Crucially, Herbert's relatively simple set of routines worked only through stimulus from the environment, so that in a sense Herbert's actions and intelligent behaviour derived partly from the mechanics of the robot and partly from the surrounding environment.

Such instances gave rise to Clark's notion of the equal partnership between organism and environment, where the boundaries of a creature or mechanical device are less important than its emplacement within a world and its ability to act with respect to specific elements of that world. Humans are rather more complex than Herbert, but some of the same ideas still apply. We are intelligent in interaction with the world around us and in this sense our intelligence may be said to be distributed or extended, as the material world provides a series of cues and prompts to action in special ways. Furthermore, many of our intelligent actions may not be directed by our central processing unit, that is, our brain, but may derive from a series of skills of the body working in partnership with the physical properties of the world around us. Human skills can be seen as a series of fragmentary abilities and skills, held together rather loosely by the patterns in the material world and our responses to them. Abstract representations do occasionally obtain and help us think about the world through words and images, Clark accepts, although truly abstract thought that is productive is very rare (Clark 1997: 174–5). I shall return to the issue of abstract representations below.

In the everyday encounter the flickering of attention between people and things constitutes both as elements of society and these complex interactions have been brought out well in what have been called 'joint attention studies' reported on by Tomasello (2000). Between nine and twelve months of age infants start to follow an adult's gaze, to engage in extended bouts of social interaction mediated by an object, to use adults as social reference points, modelling their reactions on those of others, and to act on objects in the way that adults are acting on them (Tomasello 2000: 62). The basic alchemy of human life is to transmute our relationships with material things into social relations, so that the values that attach to things help create the values that attach to people (and vice versa). Joint attention studies show how this may happen. We are starting to approximate in thought some of the true complexity of the human and material worlds. Joint attention studies show triadic relations between two (or more) human subjects and the objects they are using. Human and material relations unfold over time through a complex mutual referencing and sets of influence moving backwards and forwards in non-linear manners.

Recent views, whether from neuroscience or robotics, have started to provide empirical detail on physical interactions with the material world, either on the part of humans or other entities. Focus has shifted swiftly from the isolated human body and mind, separated from each other and at some distance from the world, to the embodied mind with the activities of the body rooted in the world. Conceptions and representations are actively created, not passively contemplated, with perception and conception being tightly linked. Action is the root of thought. Through views, such as Clark's equal partnership hypothesis, the link between humans and their world is highlighted. But here occurs a gap in people's current understanding, this gap being constituted by a lack of real grasp by many disciplines of the nature and social role of material culture. Many of these recent theories travel a path that leads to the material world and the intermingling of humans and other entities, but an absence occurs where there should be a rich material presence, that of material culture and the nature of the humanized landscape. If we follow Clark's desire to understand the equal partnership between people and the material world, we need to know what each partner brings to the relationship. Our newly enriched views of the human body throw into relief the thinness of many pictures of the world.

The obvious groups who can help make the equal partners truly equal, through a knowledge of material culture, are the archaeologists and anthropologists. But we are only just starting to engage in these larger conversations. Two thinkers are of considerable relevance here, but each has his own approach to the material nature of things. The first is Ingold, whose ecological approach has much in common with Clark; and the second is Gell's work, which has spawned much discussion of the agency of people and objects, but from which I want to take some thoughts about style as a starting point for later discussions. In *Art and Agency* Gell (1998) starts to consider the idea of effect, focusing on how objects effect and shape relationships between people. The forms things take and the impression they make on the senses are seen as integral to the manner in which people think and feel about the possessors of those things. A key example is Trobriand canoe prows, where the intricacy of the carving and brilliance of their painting have a stunning effect on potential exchange partners, making them much less able to resist the blandishments of the canoe's owners. Canoes are not just a passive but intricate backdrop to exchanges, but a vital element in those exchanges. Although canoe prows in this instance are especially compelling forms of art objects, many items falling within the category of 'art' will have effects on how people relate to each other, changing and channelling social relations. Gell's work causes us to think about singular objects: how people are halted and surprised by things, making them attend to the world with special care.

Ingold's ecological perspective enjoins holism and asks us not to look at the finished forms which things take, but rather at the rhythms that exist in different areas of life which help create and grow things within a series of echoing forms. Human energies, in Ingold's view, are part of a broader set of energy flows within the biosphere, parts of which are given shape and direction by the poetics of people's lives. Poetry and music are important elements in Ingold's thought, as well as walking, basket weaving or everyday speech. All are held together by a sense of rhythm, so that the rhythms of action become embodied in things: the structure of a basket can be seen as the outcome of the regular movement of hands directed in part by the pliability and resistance of the materials they are weaving. Ingold upbraids us for being more concerned with outcomes than with processes, seeing objects as solid presences of particular forms, instead of viewing each artefact as part of the overall flow of life, where flow and movement are ultimately more pervasive than the temporary forms that things take, which arrest our attention so much. There is much in common here with the views of both neuroscientists and philosophers, who are starting to emphasize the vital link between action and knowing: habitual acts and conscious knowledge of the world.

Gell and Ingold on superficial consideration seem to have opposite points of view, but they are in fact complementary. Ingold is trying to place the human subject within their overall flow of life and their total environment, one active element among many. He is thus suspicious of attempts to break up the flow or distance people from the world in which they dwell. Too much emphasis on the finished forms of things seems to provide too many breaks and barriers to the analytical attention, which becomes unappreciative of flows. Gell wants us to linger and attend to form, saying that the forms that artefacts take are vital to the manner in which they shape relations between people. Indeed, form is the means by which objects relate to each other, in the inter-artefactual domain, so that the forms things have taken constrain and direct the creation of new forms. Gell's key term 'stoppage' emphasizes the manner in which people and objects can pause in each other's company when especially important relations are being cemented, so that human attention is arrested by things which then redirect action. In this manner things can be agents too. By concentrating on the moments when people stop, overwhelmed by complexity of form, Gell does not allow himself to dwell on flows. Ingold stresses forgetfulness, the moments when people are so immersed in what they are doing, they become as one with the tools they are using and oblivious to anything but their own actions. Gell likes the power to shock – the moment when someone is taken aback by a thing, due to the virtuosity of its making or its originality against a general background of other things.

A currently pervasive form of thought emphasizes relations, saying that entities (both people and things) do not have essential properties of their own, but are given these properties through the relations into which they enter. We are also aware that entities help create and shape relations. A world of pure relations starts to look undifferentiated and shapeless. Taking a more dialectical view, we can see that the forms that things take help create relations between them and those relations affect the aspects of form that are taken as salient or influential at any one moment. A full view of the manner in which the world unfolds needs to take account of both flows and stoppages, a general pattern of action and individual things and people that occasionally stand out and redirect a flow of action. Owing to a quirk of how our understanding operates it is hard to appreciate both overall rhythms of life and more singular objects at once. It thus becomes an analytical question as to whether one temporarily emphasizes rhythms and flows (that is, relations) or stoppages (the forms that things take). Neither one allows a full sense of the temporality of human life: an understanding of the real sense of the shared attention between people and things. So far I have been discussing these issues in the same temporal register as Gell and Ingold, thinking about how life unfolds in the relatively short term of the here and now moment. Flows and stoppages of material culture also operate on time scales beyond that of the human life span. The longer-term unfolding of material forms is a vital, but largely unacknowledged, part of human life and it is to this I shall now turn.

FLOWS AND STOPPAGES OR ANALOGY AND TYPOLOGY

Archaeologists have thought about material culture in terms of both flows and stoppages, although they have rarely used these terms. Typological thought leads to a notion of stoppages, so that the series of types, it is assumed, are important markers of the history of a culture or social formation. Typology has been basic to archaeological approaches to material culture since the early nineteenth century, when it became the foundation for chronological understanding of Europe's prehistory in the shift from stone, to bronze to iron, providing the basis of the so-called 'Three Age system'. Typology and the Three Age system have both been roundly criticized for reifying basic types which then create an overly rigid distinction between one period and another when much continuity as well as change can be seen between the Neolithic and the Bronze Age or the Bronze and Iron Ages. The Three Age system undoubtedly produces a prehistory which is too compartmentalized, but this is not my concern here and I would rather celebrate the typological urge for a moment, owing to what it can tell us about things individually and as a mass.

To give some initial sense of how typology works let us take one of the most famous recent explorations of types and their changes: that of Deetz and Dethlefsen (1966, Deetz 1977) looking at gravestones on the eastern seaboard of the United States. They and others created a series of tombstone typologies for New England and the eastern seaboard more generally, which defined types of tombstones in terms of their decorations and epitaphs, together with their changes through time. The great advantage of tombstones for creating a time series is that they have on them the date of the person buried. Many can also be attributed to individual carvers, as some are signed and others provide indications of their activities through diaries, account books and other forms of archival record. Nor did tombstones move far from their point of manufacture, with a thirty-mile radius encompassing most movement of tombstones, which were usually made in a town and then exported out to the countryside. Between 1680, when the first stone tombstones were carved (before then memorials in wood were common) and 1820 three basic forms of design are found, each of which derives from a different form of religious sensibility. Tombstones help make links between people's feelings for the world and material forms. At the end of the generally austere seventeenth century winged death's heads predominated, reminding people of the fragility of life and the certainty of death. Early in the eighteenth century death's heads were replaced by winged cherubs as tombstones became more reflective of an ideology in which the personal qualities of an individual helped shape their life after death. Tombs shifted to becoming individual memorials, with epitaphs that reflected people's life and deeds. The decline of the death's head parallels the decline of Puritanism. At the end of the century the third style came in, which was a willow tree and an urn, a further softening of imagery and helped stress once again the possibility of salvation through good works on earth.

These overall trends can be described by so-called 'battleship curves' (see Figure 27.1) which chart the coming into being of a new style, its rise in popularity and its decline when succeeded by a further style. Such curves have been used to describe the history of styles in a whole range of artefacts, prehistoric as well as historical, seeming to capture general tendencies in the history of types. Styles often go through processes of initiation, florescence and decline, and analogies have been made with biological organisms. Deetz's work shows some complications to this pattern. Styles of tombstones were often introduced from England, arriving first in the major metropolitan centres such as Boston, MA, before spreading out to more rural areas. Taking the eastern seaboard as a whole at any one time, there would have been a mix of styles in operation, depending on proximity to urban influences spreading out from the towns like ripples across a pond. But not only was there conservativism in the countryside, there was also the more active creation of new local styles,

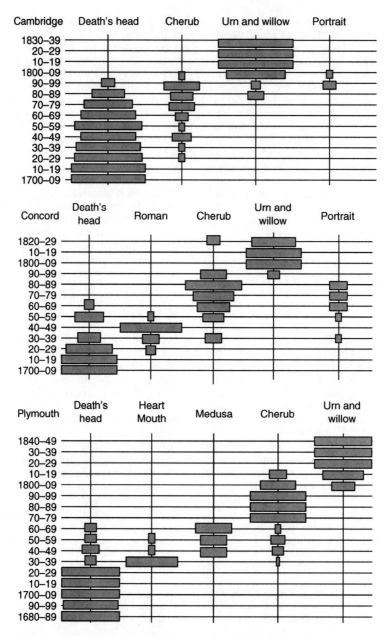

Figure 27.1   *Battleship curves describing the changing popularity of different grave-stone motifs at various places in New England, 1700–1830 (after Shennan 2002: Fig. 6)*

so that local influences and craft practices flowed into the overall mix of stylistic changes, with local diversity reaching a peak before 1760, when general forms of communication were most difficult. At a broad temporal and geographical scale, the shift between the three patterns happened sequentially; but looking at

the picture more finely there was a complex amalgam of material forms, depending on the biographies of craftspeople, the nature of religious belief within communities and the flow of ideas across the Atlantic and within the region generally. On this last point, Deetz's assumption, deriving from his structuralist orientation, is that material forms followed the structure of ideas abroad in society, so that the coming into being of the 'Georgian order' was part of Enlightenment thought expressed in rational principles of architecture and material forms. Greater reciprocal influence may well have been at work, so that the forms things took helped influence the manner in which people thought about the world, rather than just reflecting that thought, a point I shall return to below. We can see in general that people were born into worlds of material culture which lasted longer than it took to replace human generations. Each form lasted for at least forty years and often a lot longer, considerably more than the conventional time period given for a human generation of twenty-five years, although not quite as long as a human lifetime (although life expectancy may not have far exceeded it for some). We are able to see constant change, looking back in time, but for those contemporary with the things made and used things would have represented a series of stable or slowly changing entities through which to build social relations, or, as in this case, relationships with the divine. The nature of intelligent action was refracted and made effective through material forms of some stability and durability.

Types of things, such as tombstones, never existed in isolation, but were part of a complex cultural ecology of material forms. The tendency within archaeology to see material culture as a changing series of types has a long pedigree, but it is becoming counterbalanced by a search for linkages among forms of material which have otherwise been separated by our analytical categories. In an important study, Ortman (2000) has explored how meanings are generated, looking in particular at the links between pottery decoration and the structure of weaving and baskets. Ortman discusses Lévy-Bruhl and others who felt that 'primitive' thought was basically analogical, being especially fertile in making links between people, animals and things in a manner that would not occur to Westerners. Totemism, whereby an animal or bird is taken as the symbol of a clan and treated in a special manner as a result (it cannot be eaten, for instance), or animism, occurring when objects are seen to have capacities of movement, action and volition, both break down the divisions Westerners make between animate creatures possessed of some will and purpose and the inanimate and unwilled. It may well be that it is Western thought that is historically unusual, so that the distinction between inanimate objects and willed subjects is part of the process of objectification, itself a result of mass-production and

consumption found under capitalism. The more pervasive form of analogical thought manifests itself in the links between varying classes of objects and between people and things. Ortman is interested in metaphor as a means of mapping relationships (2000: 616), although these are ultimately relationships of meaning (see also Tilley's work on metaphor, 1999). Drawing on the work of Lakoff and Johnson (1980), he shows that metaphor moves from the concrete to the abstract, so that the words and images we use are often grounded in bodily experience. Taking the influence of his theoretical source material, Ortman's approach is dominated by linguistics and the manner in which meanings are shaped and conveyed through words. However, his analysis is impressively material.

Looking at the Great Pueblo period (AD 1060–1280) in the Mesa Verde area of the American south-west, Ortman concentrates on the links between textiles, which form the basis for much of the decoration on pottery. Textile forms include coiled basketry, plaited basketry, non-loom weaving and loom-woven cotton cloth. Each of these was made by a different technique. Coiled baskets were created by sewing successive circuits of an outward spiralling coil on to itself; plaited baskets were made from a plaited square mat of yucca leaves which was forced through a circular hoop and sewn up; non-loom weavings were created from a patchwork of warps and wefts often of very different materials (ranging from dog and human hair to cotton, yucca and other fibres); cotton cloth was woven on backstrap or upright looms to create warp-weft weaves purely of cotton (Ortman 2000: 621). The arid conditions of the American south-west have preserved a whole range of such materials, although obviously not the complete set of such materials from any place and time (Ortman 2000: table 2). Working from the analysis of pottery and published information, Ortman identified twenty-five analogous features of pottery decoration that originated in woven forms.

The decorative motifs found on sherds can definitely be seen to originate in textiles, as they mimic the techniques of construction of the textiles, which are thus integral to the textiles themselves. Some details of decoration were not intentionally woven into textiles, but derived from the weaving processes themselves (Figure 27.2). The motifs cannot have moved in the opposite direction. The processes of painting required the surface of the pot to be laid out and decoration applied in a consistent and structured manner, resulting in some systematic differences

Table 27.1   *Styles of pottery decoration in the Mesa Verde*

Source Industry	Rim	Decorative Zone Interior margin	Interior	Exterior
Coiled Basketry	1. Coloured rim coil 2. Rim stitching 3. Rim-stitch gaps 4. False-braided rim	5. Coil interstices 6. Alternating coloured and plain coils 7. Coloured coils and interstices 8. Stitch-marks	9. Coiled colour designs 10. Coiled texture designs 11. Coiled/non-loom triangle	13. Coiled surface texture
Plaited basketry			14. Simple plaited designs 15. Uncoloured twill-plaited designs 16. Coloured twill-plaited designs	17. Exterior selvage band designs
Non-loom warp-weft weaves			18. Pre-cotton non-loom band designs 19. Post-cotton non-loom band designs 20. Plain-tapestry terrace	
Loom-woven cotton Cloth			21. Twill-rib background 22. Twill-tapestry band designs 23. All-over twill-tapestry designs 24. Twill-tapestry terrace 25. Twill-tapestry triangle	

(after Ortman 2000: Table 3)

between the decorations on textiles and those on pots. Some combinations of motifs, never found together on a single textile, as they derive from different manufacturing processes, can be found combined on one pot.

The systematic sets of linkages between the two domains leads Ortman to conclude 'that POTTERY IS A TEXTILE describes an ancient mental phenomenon that really was shared among Mesa Verde potters and that is decipherable from archaeological remains alone' (2000: 637).

Such a conclusion raises the question of why pots and textiles should be linked in this way. Ortman feels that the broad category of container feeds through into other domains of *pueblo* life. A crucial aspect is the *kiva*, a circular subterranean structure, which had clay walls and a timber roof. 'This combination of a "coiled basket" roof with "pottery bowl" walls in the kiva suggests that textiles and pottery were linked in additional metaphorical concepts that defined the Mesa Verde Puebloan

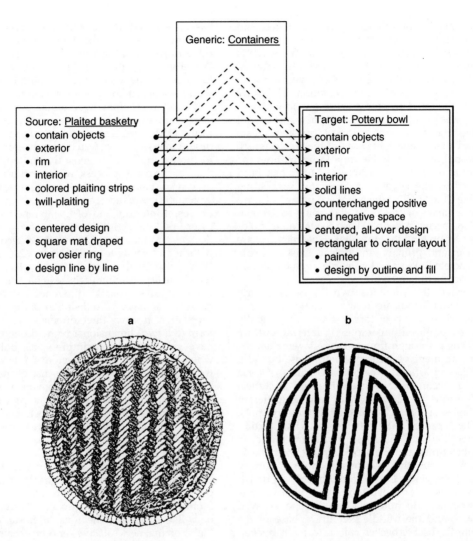

Figure 27.2   *The links between pottery and weaving styles in Mesa Verde (after Ortman 2000: table 3)*

world' (Ortman 2000: 638). Modern Puebloan views of the cosmos emphasize an earth-bowl below and sky-basket above, so that it might well be that pottery and textiles are combined in a broader conceptual system, as parts of a larger cosmological whole.

Ortman's analysis is compelling both in its detail and in its overall discussion of the importance of metaphor. Implicit in this discussion is the notion that concepts and sensibilities exist in a mental universe before they are applied to the material world, so that the links between pots and textiles were initially set up in abstract mental thought and through language (see the quotation in the previous

paragraph, that this was 'an ancient mental phenomenon') which was then applied to the material world. Following the general line of argument deriving from embodied cognition, we can see that the arrow of cause may be reversed – the creation of material forms and types of decoration could easily have given rise to mental representations. It is hard to see how a Puebloan cosmology of earth-bowl and sky-basket could have come about without the existence of pots (made from the earth) and baskets. We encounter a more subtle and complex causality here. Material forms give rise to abstract thought and representation; the ability to manipulate the world in an abstract manner through thought can help change and variegate the forms the world is made to take. Material forms don't just embody concepts they help create them, linking the habitual skills of the body in potting and weaving with domains of mental representation. The body and the mind become much more difficult categories to hold separate; material forms are not existing ideas made manifest, but help create and shape representations of the world which would not exist in the same forms without the prior existence of artefacts. Much has been made of the Vygotskian concept of scaffolding (see Clark 1997), which looks at material things as a means of creating and shaping social relations between people. Discussions of scaffolding again tend to imply that social relations are prior and primary, and objects exist to create concrete links between people, or to help more concrete human skills.

What the previous two elements of my discussion indicate is that people exist in a world made up of forms which are spatially and temporally complex. Material culture changes through time at rates slower than the replacement of human generations, but also exists in a field of complicated links of form and decoration, cross-cutting the analytical divisions we tend to make between different classes of materials, such as textiles and pots. The types of links between pots and textiles identified for the Mesa Verde are found in other times and places. Sherratt (1997: 366–7) points out that various Neolithic pottery assemblages in Europe are probably modelled on earlier forms of baskets and other organic containers. In north-western Europe grooved ware and the Middle Neolithic phase of the Nordic Trichterbecker culture contain bucket-like shapes with a decoration deriving from constructional techniques of stake-frame basketry. *Linearbandkeramik* pottery of central Europe may have been more influenced by coiled basketry traditions deriving from the Middle East. Later in the Neolithic and the Bronze the plasticity of clay is again put to use when pots echo metal vessels (Sherratt 1997: 381–2), this time maybe as an attempt at imitation by those unable to obtain high-value metal objects. Wengrow (2001) notes that between the early and late Neolithic in the Middle East there was a shift towards surface decoration on pottery and that much of this decoration derives from constructional forms of basketry. Baskets existed at least since early Neolithic times, using techniques of twining, coiling and plaiting. Indeed, basketry frames may have been used in the production of pottery. Making

baskets required control of rhythmical processes of weaving and provided knowledge of the three-dimensional geometry of shapes. As Wengrow says, 'the craft of hand-woven basketry would have equipped Neolithic potters with the applied knowledge of spatial relations and properties of number required to reproduce complex geometrical designs on ceramic forms' (2001: 179). It was not just the specifics of design that were transferred from one medium to another, but a more general set of appreciations of form and process, which included 'the division of patterns into uniform segments, the systematic use of radial and rotational symmetry on vessel interiors and of linear repetition on exteriors, the rigid geometry of figurative designs and the overall harmony of decorative pattern and vessel form' (Wengrow 2001: 179). Whilst visually the effects of pottery decoration may have been similar to those of baskets, there were important tactile differences. Pots and baskets may have looked similar (although the translation from a three-dimensional woven form to a two-dimensional painted one would have given a different impression), but they would have felt quite different in terms of weight, tactile qualities and a sense of fragility. The movement of decoration from one material to another took place through a process of decontextualization, whereby elements of design integral to basketry or weaving were reapplied using different materials and bodily movements in another medium.

Jones (2001: 342) uses the concept of citation to look at the metaphorical relationships between pottery, metal axes and the human body in early Bronze Age Britain. For Jones, objects can have body-like qualities. Chevrons in linear zones found on the 'neck' of a beaker echo ornamentation on a bronze necklet and also similar motifs on the central portion of a bronze axe. Ornaments are promiscuous, crossing categories of objects – pot, bronze necklet and bronze axe – but all have a possible central referent in the human body (Jones 2001: 342). We may see here a cosmology rooted in the human body, in contrast to the broader cosmology of Mesa Verde encompassing sky and earth. It may be that we have not learned to follow the trail of similarities of form, motif and materials which might link early Bronze Age bodies to broader sets of associations. Associations flow across material boundaries, linking pots, baskets and metal vessels.

A number of more general lessons can be adduced from these specific cases. First of all, metaphors deriving from and adhering to material forms may create a widespread set of connections which cross types of materials (and thus the boundaries between archaeological specialisms). Some connections might have a central cosmological focus, such as the human body, or a broader one linking heaven and earth. The forms that things take and the sets of links between them do not make manifest ideas with a prior existence, they may call these ideas into being. Such ideas may be very general ones, such as concepts of number, an appreciation of three-dimensional form or a sense of the correct sequence of actions. Alternatively, they can be quite specific, deriving from the actions needed to make baskets, pots or metal vessels and the forms these create. Crucially the links between objects can help understand the genesis of forms of abstract thought. The crucial element of a general form of representation (the idea of number or three-dimensional geometry) is that it can exist outside a specific context. Numbers work, if the rules of arithmetic are applied properly, irrespective of what they are applied to. The movement of one type of decoration or formal quality of an object out of its originating context (woven textiles, in the Mesa Verde case) to another (pottery decoration) involves a process of generalization and decontextualization, the very mark of abstract thought and representation. The arrow of cause is generally seen to run from a pre-existing realm of meaning in people's heads to types of decoration or forms of objects. On occasions where form and decoration escape a specific context they give rise to abstract forms that can then run wild across the material world, creating a much more recursive set of connections between action, material form and thought. It does mean that we have to attend much more closely to form and its ability to give rise to thought.

A tantalizing aspect of Gell's book *Art and Agency* is what he calls the 'inter-artefactual domain', an idea he mentions almost in passing and never gets a chance to fully develop. The inter-artefactual domain is a means of approaching the concept of style, as a set of relations between relations (Gell 1998: 215). Artefacts are decorated with motifs that are transformed one into another by regular and generally small modifications. Indeed, Gell feels that stylistic change occurs by the 'principle of least difference' – that is, differences occur between motifs through making the least modification that is possible in order to establish something as different. Such a field of tiny differences can be understood only once artefacts are looked at as a corpus from which it can be seen that the constraints governing production are the constraints governing the possibility of transforming a motif or form into

a related form. The Marquesan style of artefacts, for instance, is the 'sedimented product of tiny social initiatives taken by Marquesan artists over a long period of historical development' (Gell 1998: 219). Crucially Gell criticizes the view that culture as a whole dictates the practical or symbolic significance of artefacts, saying rather that the inter-artefactual domain is one in which artefacts obey rules set up by the style as a whole in some way removed from and different from the intentions of human makers and users. Although he doesn't explore the conceptual implications of this idea, Gell's view that artefacts form a world with its own logics somewhat independent of human intentions is vital in demonstrating that there may be many cases in which forms of abstract thought and mental representation take the shape suggested by objects, rather than objects simply manifesting pre-existing forms of thought. Decisions taken when making objects may occur without deliberate reflection on meaning, but never without some overall cognizance of the prevailing social context of material forms. One of the mysteries of things is that they take an infinity of forms, but often also have marked resemblances one with another, and the notion of style tries to probe the tension between similarity and difference which maintains and creates both.

Gell's ideas form part of an emerging attempt to take the material world seriously in terms of how it affects human relations. Such attempts are also found in disciplines such as art history where links between sociability and objects are eagerly sought, although the dangers of imputing sociability to objects are recognized. In his article 'What do pictures *really* want?' Mitchell (1996) feels that we should take the desires of objects seriously at an analytical level, as these are already taken seriously in everyday life. When pornography is seen not as a representation of violence against women, but as an act of violence; when style and substance become confused in a celebrity's presentation of self; when a painting is discussed in terms of what it does to the viewer, then we are imputing desires to things which we might otherwise see as inanimate. Objects with desires, rather than objects of desire, might seem to take us into the realm of fetishism, totemism, animism or idolatory, attitudes to the world acceptable in children or non-Westerners but dubious for sophisticated postmodernist actors to hold. But if these attitudes do exist – and Mitchell makes a convincing case for their presence in our lives – they demand some form of understanding. Ultimately his attempt to understand the desires of things is a little disappointing, but Mitchell does point out that objects are an important element in plays of recognition and knowing that pass between social actors all the time in daily life. What it means to know others depends on our ability to know others which are objects as well as others who are people. The conditions of knowing derive not just from mental schemes in people's heads, but from the forms taken by things, which require that we know them in particular ways. The independence of the style of objects from human cultural forms, discussed by Gell, allows us to talk about how things themselves create the grounds for our understanding of them. We know them in their ways, rather than purely on our own terms.

Setting objects free from immediate human influence and control has something of a heritage in archaeology. David Clarke (1978) felt that populations of artefacts had their own behavioural characteristics, which were more complex than simply combining characteristics of their components of style and form, but also more predictable than individual components looked at historically. Clarke was influenced by the battleship curves of Deetz and others within American archaeology and sought to explain why such regularities of change happened, pointing out that while some artefacts went through a sequence that could be glossed as birth, maturity and death, others changed more slowly into completely different types. Structure was found in types of artefacts partly because to create a type a repeated sequence of actions was needed, and these were in some sense implemented by the type. Some of the originality of Clarke's view was vitiated by his ultimate belief that artefacts arose as ideas in the makers' mind which then were substantiated in an object. Giving a degree of autonomy to things acting together in large numbers, which can change the pattern of people's thought as well as respond to the nature of those thoughts, would provide a much more rounded sense of our relationship with objects, especially as these unfold over the long term.

BECOMING ROMAN IN BRITAIN

One key way of understanding how objects influence human sense and sensibilities is to look at periods of dramatic change in both material and social forms. One such period occurred between 100 BC and AD 100 in Britain in the transition from the later Iron Age to the Romano-British period. A series of complex changes occurred in material forms during this period, which is more generally thought of in terms of the Roman invasion of Britain (AD 43) and the political and economic changes attendant upon that event. However, if we ignore the invasion, initially at least, and concentrate on the shifts in material forms, together with some continuities, a different picture emerges from the conventional one of barbarian Britain brought within the scope of the Roman empire by the might of the legions. Indeed, these two centuries stand out as one of the periods in Britain's (pre-) history which sees a most dramatic shift in the basic conditions of people's lives.

In 100 BC material forms in Britain were changing fast, against a background of some continuity. Continuity was provided by the basic circular form of houses and settlements, which had a long history back to the Neolithic (Bradley 1998). In most areas of southern Britain people were abandoning hill forts and moving into smaller enclosures in both upland and lowland areas, but keeping the circular nature of their houses. These, in turn, were the basis for a series of cosmological manipulations of the world, based on the orientation of the house (doorways often faced east or southeast towards the sunrise) with propitious and less propitious areas which must have arisen in part from the lived experience of dwelling in a circular house and not just from ideas arising in the abstract and then applied to the house. Continuity also existed in the digging of pits and ditches, and the very acts of digging such large features (many of the ditches were kilometres long) would have helped shape and cement social relations. Artefacts and the bones of people and animals were placed in subterranean features of all types, the forms of which again helped channel thoughts and links between people.

From the first century BC onwards things started to change, although there was a great deal of regional variability which can't be dealt with properly in a brief survey such as this. Rectangular buildings are first found in the mid-first century BC and the only previous noncircular structures had been temples and granaries, which might well have had sacred associations that came to infuse the new rectangular forms. Large, probably urban, settlements emerge as a novel feature in the immediately pre-Roman period. Silchester (which became the Roman *civitas* capital of Calleva Atrebatum) was founded between 20 and 21 BC prior to the Claudian invasion of AD 43 and had both rectangular buildings and an orthogonal ground plan from the start, features that were previously thought to have arrived only with the Roman invasion. The widespread nature of these novel forms of architecture is hinted at by similar plans at Heybridge and possibly also Abingdon. Claudian Silchester was laid out on an east-west axis, some 45° from the late Iron Age south-east-north-west axis, showing that the Iron Age innovations were not always seen as signs of beneficial progress by some Romans, who wanted to use town plans to reify their power and not to have the possibility undermined by innovating Iron Age dynasts. These new urban forms were central to emerging large-scale polities with a well defined elite and kings. The king's power was best exemplified and mobilized through objects like coins, which bore the king's name from the first century BC onwards, as well as various symbols derived from Rome or transformed from Roman originals. Early in the first century BC wheel-turned pots were made for the first time in Britain, bringing about a much greater range and standardization of forms, which in turn must have responded to new foodstuffs, sauces and wine stemming from Roman forms of dining and celebration. The new pots were often painted in designs quite unlike older Iron Age types, so that pottery and food together created a new set of sensibilities in people. Moving into the first century AD, Roman pottery types, such as Samian, quickly moved into households across Britain and these included houses still built on the older circular pattern as well as those in new rectangular forms. Not everyone wanted or could acquire such new forms, but even small rural sites in southern Britain yield up finds of Samian, indicating that the new types penetrated deeply (Millett 1990).

Richly decorated forms of metalwork show complex patterns of change. In the second and early first centuries BC much material labelled 'Celtic' art, that is, bronze, iron and gold work decorated with abstract and figurative motifs, concerned the human body, being made up of weapons and torcs (Hutcheson 2004; Jope 2000). Power seems to have resided in the body of the powerful person. This changed during the first century BC, when personal ornament became more mass-produced and less spectacular (torcs and weapons become less common and brooches are made in much larger numbers to standard designs). The emphasis of virtuoso craftspeople, in some areas of the country at least, is now on horse gear and chariot fittings, making power less personal and more generalized, a fact reinforced by the commonness of horses on coins. This emphasis on horses and chariots continues into

the Roman period, especially in areas like East Anglia, showing marked continuities before and after the Roman invasion. Also, in the first century AD, more complex forms of brooches make a comeback, often utilizing techniques developed initially in the Iron Age, such as enamelling as well as motifs derived from 'Celtic' art, like the triskele. For reasons that are poorly understood, people after the Roman invasion were drawing on forms and materials with a long history to them, grounding some of their claims to power and sociability in the past.

As should be obvious from this brief sketch there are complex histories here, involving both people and materials, as well as continuity and change. New forms imposed novel sets of sociability. The patterns of daily life in a rectangular stone-built structure were quite different from those in a round wattle-and-daub house, not to mention the smells, sights and sounds in the two cases. Wheel-turned pottery took production out of the hands of the majority, making it the preserve of a few specialists; the new food and drink contained within such pots presaged novel tastes, using the word in both its senses. For the elite and some of the less well connected there were subtle shifts in personal ornament and the panoply of power, with complex and contradictory changes across the two centuries. Clothing, furniture, roads and drains have not even been mentioned but burrowed deep into people's social beings. The introduction and deployment of so many different forms would have re-educated people in a fundamental manner, yielding up a new sensory and social universe in which the old and the new combined in exciting or disconcerting ways. Becoming Roman did mean thinking and feeling differently, but the introduction of novelty was not primarily through literature or rhetoric, but mainly through artefacts and a new stylistic universe. Roman forms were not imposed from the outside, but grew up in Britain as a combination of local types and materials with long histories with outside influences, from both Mediterranean culture and neighbouring Gaul (Gosden 2004).

To use an expression come down to us from the Roman period we can agree that *ars longa, vita brevis* (art is long but life is short), with material forms enduring in a way that people cannot. But occasionally human generations are played out in periods of rapid change, such as the one we feel ourselves to be living in at present, and during the course of a human lifetime people are called upon by objects to change their mode of being. Not everyone heeds such calls, with some sticking with the older ways, but even these would seem like deliberate conservativism, having quite a different impact from when they are a general norm.

CONCLUSION

The following points are key to the argument I have developed here. Artefacts can exist as a mass in which they follow stylistic and formal logics of their own. This is because individual makers operate within an overall tradition, working to originality within that tradition. The past forms that objects take help shape and channel the choices made in the present. Because objects exist to a degree independently of people they shake not just the actions of the makers, but also give rise to categories of thought and notions of sensibility. People as social beings can be shaped in how they think and how they feel by objects. Ideas and feelings do not exist in cultural forms in a manner prior to things, but are created partly by them. The process of moving forms or decorations from one medium to another, for instance from baskets to pots, decontextualizes them, making them suitable for abstract thought. Once elements of material culture exist in an abstracted form then they can be manipulated imaginatively, unconstrained by the nature of the materials from which they are made. Abstract representation and things exist in a complex dialectic, by which one can influence the movement between the concrete and the abstract. We can start to see the full complexity of this process. Material culture is vital to the notion of embodied or distributed intelligence. Ideas such as scaffolding are not sufficient in order to understand material things, with the equal partnership hypothesis making much better sense, as long as we have a real idea of what both people and things can contribute from their side of the partnership.

Looking at how artefacts act *en masse* and at a distance from people calls into question a whole range of entities that we take for granted, from individual people to larger abstractions such as culture. In almost all views of our social and cultural worlds, people and cultures in their various different ways have been seen as active elements and material things as passive. But if it can be shown that objects educate people's senses, and thus their basic appreciation of the world, they help shape and determine sequences of actions in making, using and exchanging things, and they also give rise to thought, then a very different notion of the relationship between people and things comes about, throwing into question many of our assumptions about the relations between people. What it means to be an intelligent human turns centrally on our ability to act as competent social beings. We need to be able to mobilize the material world in order to be an effective social actor and we do this not under conditions of our own choosing but partly through following sets of rules laid down by objects. Objects, in turn, have their own long-term histories beyond that of the individual life span, so that we are educated into a sense of what it means to be a social actor through our sensory and intellectual relations with things.

Artefacts create categories and forms of thought. Indeed, the general concept of a category may derive from containers, such as pots or baskets, with a category containing a series of individual instances joined by some form of resemblance. Similarly, an understanding of number, weight, geometry, sequence and duration arises from both making and using things, providing a broad material substrate for thought. Cosmologies, such as the earth-bowl and sky-basket found among Puebloan peoples, are more specific instances of thought shaped by materials. The power of artefacts to shape and direct our thought and speech should be no surprise when we think that many objects were made in contemporary forms before we were born and may continue in those forms after we die. Cars have changed in their details since the late nineteenth century but are still, in the twenty-first, recognizably descended from older forms. No one alive today pre-dates the car. How long such forms will last is unknown, but we can see that materially and socially effective forms may have considerable durability even in periods of rapid change.

Material culture, especially in its long-term manifestations, raises many challenges for how we conceive of ourselves as people, as participants in cultural forms and as historically grounded beings. We are just starting to assimilate the depth of our involvement with the material world and to glimpse its power to shape us. An openness to what objects require from us may be key to our intellectual and social lives in the present and future, as well as to a rounded understanding of the past. Much new work can and should be carried out following a new emphasis on material culture. Both the social evolutionary and structural-Marxist views discussed above had a definite view of politics and political relations (often judged through the degree of hierarchy between people). Politics has been lost from more recent approaches. If we take the view that politics concerns forms of association and also that associations always involve people and things, both elements of which have their requirements, then new views of politics are possible. The band, tribe, chiefdom and state model prevalent for so long in so many approaches to prehistory was something of a hybrid view in that material arrangements in subsistence and living space together with the use of surplus combined together with social relations. Relations between people were always primary and active, with the material role having a passive, supportive role at best. If we have to think what objects want and how these wants evolve over long periods of time then we are forced to consider new axes of association ranging from cultures of intimacy where relations between people and things are direct and unmediated to cultural forms in which interpretations of the object world are the province of the few, carried out on behalf of the many, who never have access to the full range of built or mobile forms of material culture. There is a shift in power structures of knowledge, from non-discursive forms of knowing and being deriving from direct sensory contact with the things to the interpretive structures possible and necessary once discursive knowledge and representation become key. The links between knowledge and power, so crucial since at least the work of Foucault, can be refined around varying forms of knowledge which implicate in turn different sets of relationships with the world. Politics and association could again become central issues in archaeology to the same degree, but in a different manner from how they figured for the social evolutionists.

The nature of and links between the senses, people's overall sensibilities and the emotions become key in a way that they have never been for archaeology (Edwards et al. in press; Gosden in press). It is less a question of what people felt (using that word in both its senses) about any particular object or event, but more an issue about the conditions of knowledge and their long-term generation and changes. Archaeology's great knowledge of material culture could be put to new uses if considered from the vantage point of the senses and the emotions, and the rather pernickety archaeological attention to material details (the squiggles on pots, the flanges on metal axes or stone tool knapping debris) could be put to theoretically informed use when thought of in terms of sense and sensibility.

It is hard to resist the impression that a new paradigm is emerging through a combination of neuroscience, robotics, artificial intelligence,

animal intelligence and an interest in material culture through archaeology and anthropology. These last two disciplines are ahead of some elements of the new game in that we have both theory and methods that can be applied to the material world and human involvements in it. The simultaneous creation of the social and the material is one of the miraculous aspects of human existence and is at last being given the attention it deserves.

REFERENCES

Bradley, R. (1998) *The Significance of Monuments: on the Shaping of Human Experience in Neolithic and Bronze Age Britain*. London: Routledge.

Brooks, R. (2003) *Flesh and Machines: How Robots will Change us*. New York: Vintage Books.

Childe, V.G. (1930) *The Bronze Age*. Cambridge: Cambridge University Press.

Clark, A. (1997) *Being there. Putting Brain, Body and World together Again*. Cambridge, MA: MIT Press.

Clarke, D. (1978) *Analytical Archaeology*. 2nd edn. London: Methuen.

Damasio, A. (2000) *The Feeling of What Happens: Body, Emotion and the making of consciousness*. London: Vintage.

Deetz, J. (1977) *In Small Things Forgotten: The Archaeology of Early American Life*. New York: Anchor Books.

Deetz, J. and Dethlefsen, E. (1966) 'Death's heads, cherubs, and willow trees: experimental archaeology in colonial cemeteries', *American Antiquity*, 31: 502–10.

Edwards, E., Gosden, C. and Phillips, R. (eds) (in press) *Sensible Objects: Colonialism, Museums and Material Culture*. Oxford: Berg.

Friedman, J. and Rowlands, M.J. (1978) 'Notes towards an epigenetic model of the evolution of "civilisation"', in J. Friedman and M.J. Rowlands (eds), *The Evolution of Social Systems*. London: Duckworth, pp. 201–76.

Gell, A. (1998) *Art and Agency: Towards a new Archaeological theory*. Oxford: Clarendon Press.

Gosden, C. (2004) *Archaeology and Colonialism: Cultural Contact from 5000 BC to the Present*. Cambridge: Cambridge University Press.

Gosden, C. (in press) 'Aesthetics, emotions and intelligence: implications for archaeology', in C. Renfrew, C. Gosden and E. DeMarrais (eds), *Rethinking Masteriality*. Cambridge: McDonald Institute.

Hodder, I. (ed.) (1987) *Archaeology as Long-term History*. Cambridge: Cambridge University Press.

Hodder, I. (1990) *The Domestication of Europe: Structure and Contingency in Neolithic Societies*. Oxford: Blackwell.

Hutcheson, N. (2004) *Later Iron Age Norfolk: landscape, metalwork and society*. British Archaeological Report 326.

Jones, A. (2001) 'Drawn from memory: the archaeology of aesthetics and the aesthetics of archaeology in earlier Bronze Age Britain and the present', *World Archaeology*, 33: 334–65.

Jope, M. (2000) *Early Celtic Art in the British Isles*. Oxford: Clarendon Press.

Lakoff, G. and Johnson, M. (1980) *Metaphors we Live by*. Chicago: University of Chicago Press.

Lakoff, G. and Johnson, M. (1999) *Philosophy in the Flesh: The Embodied Mind and its Challenge to Western Thought*. New York: Basic Books.

Lee, R.B. (1968a) 'What hunters do for a living, or, How to make out on scarce resources', in R.B. Lee and I. DeVore (eds), *Man the Hunter*. Chicago: Aldine, pp. 30–48.

Millett, M. (1990) *The Romanization of Britain*. Cambridge: Cambridge University Press.

Mitchell, W.J.T. (1996) 'What do pictures *really* want?' *October* 77: 71–82.

Ortman, S. (2000) 'Conceptual metaphor in the archaeological record: methods and an example from the American southwest', *American Antiquity*, 65: 613–45.

Sahlins, M.D. and Service, E.R. (eds) (1960) *Evolution and Culture*. Ann Arbor, MI: University of Michigan Press.

Service, E.R. (1962) *Primitive Social Organisation: an Evolutionary Perspective*. New York: Random House.

Service, E.R. (1971) *Cultural Evolutionism: Theory in Practice*. New York: Holt Rinehart.

Shennan, S. (2002) *Genes, Memes and Human History: Darwinian Archaeology and Cultural Evolution*. London: Thames & Hudson.

Sherratt, A. (1997) *Economy and Society in Prehistoric Europe: Changing Perspectives*. Princeton, NJ: Princeton University Press.

Tilley, C. (1999) *Metaphor and Material Culture*. Oxford: Blackwell.

Tomasello, M. (2000) *The Cultural Origins of Human Cognition*. Cambridge, MA: Harvard University Press.

Tylor, E.B. (1871) *Primitive Culture: Researches into the Development of Mythology, Philosophy, Religion, Language, Art and Custom*. London: Murray.

Wengrow, D. (2001) 'The evolution of simplicity: aesthetic labour and social change in the Neolithic Near East', *World Archaeology*, 33: 168–88.

White, L. (1959) *The Evolution of Culture*. New York: McGraw-Hill.

PART V

PRESENTATION AND POLITICS

In this part we survey how the collection and presentation of material culture play a role in the creation of personal and group identities. The right to have a cultural identity – or rather the problems encountered in not having one – is increasingly recognized in human rights cases, asylum law, in disputes over the repatriation of cultural property and the recognition of indigenous rights. It is becoming inconceivable for rights to resources and entitlements to be allocated outside a politics of recognition that asserts identity to be a prerequisite rather than the outcome of a claim to belong. This rise of a 'politics of belonging' privileges the possession of culture as a right that protects the interests of groups in both persons and things. In the last few decades we have seen a dramatic increase in claims over the possession of rights in cultural property, combined with a therapeutic sense that imbues such claims with an emancipatory aura. Such dual expectations, the jural and the therapeutic, can evoke a deeply ambivalent set of solutions to identity problems. Whilst material culture as property implies rights of ownership that close off access to it by strangers and others, it also has the allusion of things as inalienable and therefore to be acquired as an outcome of mobility and willingness to integrate. All of which has considerable implications for our future understanding of humanity, justice, citizenship and the avoidance and reconciliation of conflict.

An emphasis on material culture in these questions emerged in the 1970s and 1980s as rights to sacred sites; indigenous knowledge, land and the right of return of cultural property and human remains to 'peoples of origin' became a central argument in these disputes. Moreover, and somewhat ironically, recognizing how material culture was decontextualized, reified and authenticated, precisely those conditions that had led to its demise as a research and teaching practice at the beginning of the twentieth century, became part of its revival at the beginning of the twenty first. The chapters in Part V are all concerned with the implications of such claims to preserve, collect, own, exhibit and visit material culture and what these entail in pursuing issues of cultural property and cultural rights. In part, this also reflects those countless situations in which a difference in culture is used to explain conflicting values and practices and their misunderstanding. In other words we increasingly identify interests in culture as belonging to those groups or persons who recognize and mobilize themselves around the pursuit and defence of cultural property. Recognition of cultural difference relates these debates to the production of cultural property and its identification in terms not just of museums and heritage sites but also of anything that can be designated as 'cultural' in origin.

Material culture is treated here therefore as knowledge, either objectified or experienced, that can be defended and protected against abuse, exploitation and loss. As cultural property, we deal with collective knowledge or what might be termed 'habitus identities' (to follow Bourdieu's term) rather than the individual forms of creativity usually associated with intellectual property and indigenous technical knowledge rights. But as Strathern points out in her chapter, property implies the creation of value through ownership as if without Euro-American property forms and their global dissemination we face a future where a deliberate antipathy to property may be attractive but hard to contemplate. In our case, the notion of material culture as property through the possession or ownership of knowledge, objects, sacred sites, intangible heritage becomes deeply problematic as a means of ensuring the protection and conservation of creativity. There is a growing consensus that the jural domains of intellectual property, copyright and patents provide little security in practice when applied to cultural property. In the sense that these were all legal devices originally developed to encourage circulation and the spread of knowledge, it is not surprising to find that they would not be appropriate for those forms of cultural knowledge that are deemed secret and to be kept out of circulation. Strathern points to a creative ambiguity at the heart of Euro-American ideas of property that refer both to things and to social relations. Rights are held in things only to the extent to which others can be excluded from having possession of them. But most forms of material culture as heritage that Butler, for example, refers to would not respond well to the conditions of alienation implied in commodification, i.e. the submersion of ethical issues to ownership claims. The case of Yumbulul discussed by Strathern highlights the distinction between intellectual property rights as a legal instrument allowing economic exploitation through ownership of cultural knowledge and the inalienable character of cultural knowledge that, kept secret, cannot be mapped on to either public or private domains of knowledge. Yet what seems an obvious distinction in practice is rarely like this and whether we are talking about rights over things, over performances or intangible knowledge or the need to keep secret things separate from the wish to take advantage of their value through circulation, the issue remains a conflict over who gains access to them.

Nowhere is this issue of access more potently demonstrated than in the museum display, where, since the inception of the great public museums of the nineteenth century in Europe, it has been recognized that allowing people to 'see' cultural patrimony also defines how it will be ordered and secured in memory. This returns us to Butler's argument for a shift of heritage studies from a historical to a humanistic perspective that returns debate to moral-ethical issues of 'well-being'. Whilst we can see that this has been largely figured within a category of cultural loss and redemption, it is part of a growing recognition that contemporary acts of possession continue to be reserved for settings where knowledge can be judged as accessible and of benefit potentially to all. But this does represent a special area of material culture where the notion of patrimony implies origins that actively constitute both the present and the potential of having a future. That these did not necessarily follow the 'Western imaginary' of genealogical histories is described by Shelton in the case of Mexico as the 'affirmation of a radical non-Euro-American difference'. If we graft on to this Butler's argument about heritage constituting a sense of 'well-being' through the capacity to cure a sense of loss, we

have the resources to detect how alternative narratives and oppositions are used to create a parallel heritage of lasting difference. Museums like memorials have an alienating quality since they must refer both back to an origin, usually in some barbarous act, and to a space where the meaning we find in living together is reproduced. They have the transcendental quality of temples precisely because they ritualize patrimony into orders that demonstrate local conflicts and demonstrate that historical discontinuities are never arbitrary but follow some greater design. 'Every act of institution is a well founded delirium, said Durkheim, and an act of social magic,' concluded Bourdieu. The essence of cure, we are told, is effortlessly to enjoy museums and the social order and share them with everyone. Rather like having faith in the curative effects of a Truth and Reconciliation Commission, cultural heritage is a form of confession or witnessing in which acknowledgement and an apology may be possible. Whether the cultural goods so gathered together are available to all to achieve this is of course highly unlikely, shaped as it is by inequalities in the modes of transmission. Nevertheless the notion of material culture as patrimony lays less stress on ownership and possession and more on who can gain access to its legitimizing and curative principles.

But this only shows that material culture is always selectively and necessarily accompanied by amnesia. Whether memorializing takes place in the museum or in sites of commemoration, the selective forgetting of what is difficult or contradictory is well represented in the chapters on museums, conservation and monuments. The archaeology of monuments is particularly insightful in showing how returning to visit a monument or site is part of an ongoing process of instituting a lasting difference between those who are participants and those who remain outside. The blending of monuments into landscapes, the perception of qualitative differences in materials used in monument construction and how to respond affectively to their materiality are included within a *longue durée* of reflective reorganizing of a monument space. None of which is likely to be learned or open to a verbal exegesis, so how we empathize with such an environment as a matter of habitual action shapes the transformation of material culture into cultural heritage.

A politics which organizes how things should be seen suggests the existence of changing visual regimes that are more dispersed and less condensed than is usually conjured up by images of art or spectacle. It is the revitalization of the materiality of visual culture, which also implies radically different relationships between museums and their publics, objects and their communities of origin, that Shelton sees as constituting a radical redirection of the museum functions away from pure scholarship towards fostering social and political awareness. It might be thought that conservation is concerned principally with decisions that preserve and restore objects but this is to forget that the principal reason for doing so is to ensure that they may be seen. Ranging from how decisions are made to clean or not to clean to reconstructing the biography of an object, Eastop shows how conservation practice focuses on the essential nature of objects, their integrity and inherent truth and their social agency.

Another aim in this part is to explore how different practices of 'making' material culture relate to a politics of presence. Belk makes a rather Walter Benjamin-like point that collecting can be a magical act that singularizes and decommodifies a personal or social world. This re-enchantment of worlds through collecting has a modernist ring to it but can be seen as more pervasive by drawing our attention to any act of 'gathering' or bringing together persons and things. Descriptions of archaeological landscapes, notions of property, heritage crusades, conserving museum collections, the buying of 'instant collections' through e-Bay somehow gain a unity as various strategies in the making of presence. These may be mobile and nomadic or highly fixed and centralized but the implication that such acts of 'gathering' may be encouraged or hindered plays on the idea that belonging is not to do with claims and rights that remain separate from the more everyday sense of making and doing and, as such, 'being human'.

Mike Rowlands

28

INTELLECTUAL PROPERTY AND RIGHTS

An Anthropological Perspective

Marilyn Strathern

Under what circumstances might material culture become a focus of social activism, acquire political and economic salience? This chapter charts a trajectory of global interest: intellectual property rights (IPR).[1] The foundational notion is that certain immaterial or intangible aspects of material things can be the subject of rights and claims. The distinction (between the tangible and intangible) relates to property, and in the Euro-American tradition intellectual property law occupies a highly specialist niche. The distinction vanishes when one steps outside this tradition, at least for much of the developing world that is the field for this chapter. Here discussions about intellectual property feed different concerns. Rights initially developed to protect interests in innovation and originality promise to liberate defenders of cultural traditions. The 1980s and 1990s have seen the rise and fall of IPR as a potential set of international instruments by which expression could be given to 'indigenous' culture.

IPR has also been a source of ideas for scholars, stimulating fresh interpretations of artefacts and practices. For the observer or theorist of society, two areas have been of particular interest. This chapter might have pursued them through analogies with the two principal objects of IPR philosophy: the patent that recognizes the embodiment of knowledge and inventiveness in material things, and copyright that is concerned with the authorship of forms. The first area engages with the concept of traditional knowledge (TK) (Sillitoe 1998; Ellen and Harris 1997), and debates over (intangible) resource extraction, including advocacy of traditional

resource rights (TRR) (Posey 1996; Posey and Dutfield 1996), where the protection of 'indigenous' rights is often coupled with conservation and biodiversity issues (Swanson 1995; Blakeney 1999b; Moran et al. 2001), many first raised in Central and South America (Tobin 2000). The second area comprises ethnographic and theoretical interest in 'creativity' and claims to origination, in Melanesia and Australia among other places (Kingston 2003; Küchler 1997, 2002; Leach 2003a, b; Liep 2001; Harrison 1992; Morphy 1995; Myers 1991, 2004). Too important to be squeezed, these lines of inquiry are largely set aside.

Instead, the chapter focuses on circumstances under which material culture is treated as property. Property exists of course as a right. But precisely because it signals rights, people who might criticize Euro-American property forms – especially those who, in UN language, call themselves indigenous peoples – may be attracted to the notions of ownership and protection it also brings. One outcome has been the attempt to formulate instruments for protection in deliberate antithesis to property. Such weaving between stimulus (ideas that catch the imagination) and detachment (putting the ideas to purposes removed from their original locations) recurs over and over again.

HISTORICAL OVERVIEW

The recent history rehearsed here concerns the way IPR came into Social Anthropology in the 1980s and 1990s via indigenous rights movements. It was the time when this domain of the law found itself exposed to media attention and to popular and literary analysis (e.g. Woodmansee 1994; Rose 1993; McSherry 2001). New 'things' were creating new claims of intellectual input. One should not underestimate the explosion of biotechnology, whose objects included life forms. The domain of patenting was being stretched, first by the creation of informational or biogenetic entities which both did and did not conform to industrial artefacts (Pottage 1998), and second by clamours over the kind of rights themselves (e.g. Nuffield Council on Bioethics 2002; CIPR 2002). In copyright, technical developments in reproduction, especially in the communications and music industries, opened up questions about access and control (open source) (Okedji 2003), while cultural tourism swept up images of all kinds, both external and internal for their exotic origins (Kirtsoglou and Theodossopoulos 2004; Schröder 2003). Some prefatory comments on IPR itself are in order.

Modern IPR developed in eighteenth-century Europe and the United States as an adjunct of industry and commerce, though patents and copyright had no single rubric until later, and were then joined by trade marks, design rights, etc.[2] The aim was to invest intellectual creations with economic rights. The rationale of the patent is that short-term licences for the exclusive development of inventions will encourage inventors to spread knowledge rather than keeping it secret. More exactly, the licence is to give or withhold permission for exploitation, a negative right, for exploitation cannot proceed otherwise. The crucial (intangible) 'inventive step' must be demonstrably embedded in a (tangible) artefact capable of commercial application, and requires registration. Copyright requires no registration; it comes into being the moment expressions are fixed in tangible form (texts, photographs, recordings); invoked, it identifies the work/utterance with the originator of it. The form must thus be made present in the material world, it being rights to the (intangible) acts of its expression and reproduction that are owned. In both cases, economic rights are time-limited.

One should not underestimate, either, the extent to which IPR invites imaginative response. Competitive resource hunting uncovers new entities to which economic value can be attached, and patenting can be applied to things still in the making, to manufacturing processes as well as products. It invites 'prospecting' for future exploitable potential (Barry 2000, 2001; Hayden 2003).[3] At the same time, value put on knowledge as a creative resource leads to reflection on talent already made useful, and thus already embedded in artefacts (e.g. designs), persons (transferable skills), practices (medical remedies). Cultural devices such as ethnobotanical classifications may aid future discovery or point to past human creativity.

The assumption that economic growth is key to national survival underwrites agreements endorsing national sovereignities, and the relations state agencies have with aboriginal peoples ('first nations'). IPR flourishes in a social context energized by national aspirations to globalization and techno-commercial advance. Since the late 1980s/early 1990s, international policy instruments such as the Convention on Biological Diversity (CBD 1992) and TRIPS (1994, Trade Related Aspects of Intellectual Property Rights, emanating from the WTO) have invited the re-evaluation of the nature of resources of all kinds.[4] The World Intellectual Property Organization (WIPO) has helped draw up, for local national and regional adoption, model laws for implementing IPR legislation. Harmonizing provisions for patent law mean that all members of WTO, as signatories to TRIPS, will recognize one another's patenting procedures. World concern with the protection of intellectual rights also engenders organizations such as NGOs, and instruments beyond the state, including soft law[5] regulations. These encourage communication (learning what others are doing) and regulation (international agreements) beyond the state. Human rights arguments single out specific categories likely to be underprivileged and assist the formalization of interest groups.[6] This creates possibilities for enfranchising local interests through a global identity such as 'indigenous people'. It also challenges the expectation, as written into many international agreements, that national interests are people's interests.

So what is behind UNESCO's standard-setting convention in the area of 'intangible cultural heritage'?[7] 'Cultural property' has in effect moved from its location within the world of national monuments and heritage conservation to fuse with notions of 'cultural rights' (Cowan et al. 2001).[8] While there is 'nothing unusual about communities mobilizing what power they can command to protect a valued resource, [or] maintain a traditional practice ... What does appear to be new is asserting such claims on the basis of culture' (Winthrop 2002: 116). As we shall see, the fusion (of cultural property and cultural rights) simultaneously engages with the application of IPR to items of material culture *and* with many objections to so doing.

Questions of cultural appropriation belong to other fields as well, such as the politics of identity (e.g. Merry 2001; Eriksen 2001) and long-standing concerns in the politics of nationhood (e.g. Rowlands 2000; the cases in Cowan et al. 2001: Chapters 7–10). The link to intellectual property was initially made when UNESCO and WIPO joined forces in 1978/79 to agree an approach to the international protection of 'folklore' (Blake 2001). UNESCO was to concentrate on safeguarding intangible cultural heritage, WIPO to consider the application of IPR to expressions of culture. This resulted in a set of *Model Provisions for National Laws on the Protection of Expressions of Folklore against Illicit Exploitation and other Prejudicial Actions*, 1982; it has rarely been implemented. UNESCO's *Recommendation on the Safeguarding of Traditional Culture and Folklore* in 1989 also found it hard to gain momentum (Simon n.d.). Something of a turning point was Daes's 1993 *Study on the Protection of the Cultural and Intellectual Property of Indigenous Peoples* (Daes 1997), produced for the UN Working Group on Indigenous Populations.[9] It was not until 1998, however, that WIPO itself set up a Global Intellectual Property Issues Division in order to include 'indigenous peoples' within its purview (Roulet 1999: 129), and 'traditional knowledge' (TK) began to take over from earlier understandings of cultural and intellectual property as a matter of folklore. As Blakeney (1999a; 2000) remarks, this significantly changed the discourse. Folklore was typically discussed in terms of copyright – traditional knowledge points towards patent law and biodiversity rights.

Perceiving culture as encoding knowledge went hand in hand with recognizing biological, environmental and other knowledge-sensitive resources. Indeed, the question of *protection* as a matter of sustainability, alongside that of exploitation with just reward, arguably arose from the association of TK with protocols about natural resources that had figured in the CBD (e.g. Swanson 1995; Brush and Orlove 1996; Brush 1999). Indigeneity, originally tied to being of a place, now backed up people's claims as the original owners of resources – and therefore the appropriate guardians of them (Simpson 1997: 48; Muehlebach 2001). Despite the working definition of 'indigenous' used by UN agencies, which refers to non-dominant sectors of society; internal debate over the meaning of 'indigenous' ensued (Simpson 1997: 22–3).

Although left to one side here, biodiversity, especially via ethnobotany, was a significant point of entry for anthropology (e.g. Brush 1993, 1994; Posey 1996; Ellen and Harris 1997); it almost simultaneously widened into questions as to whether IPR could acknowledge practices and values that other legal instruments could not (Greaves 1994; Brush and Stabinsky 1996; Patel 1996; Taylor 2000). Greaves's study commissioned by the AAA (1994) was a pioneer here. Under the impetus of anthropological critique, among others,[10] a frequently cited position today is that 'tradition' refers less to the (tangible) products of cultural life than to (intangible) modes of transmission. Thus Dutfield goes back to a 1992 statement that the 'social process of learning and sharing knowledge unique to every culture is at the heart of its "traditionality."'[11] Kalinoe (1999: 35) writes of Papua New Guinea custom that it need not have existed from time immemorial, and is 'fluid, flexible and responsive to social change'. But there are larger questions too, such as those contained in the three terms forming the rubric to this chapter, where anthropologists can offer input.

Whether *property* was ever an appropriate mode for the negotiation of interests in resources was a question anthropologists raised from the outset in relation to developing countries or minority groups. What kinds of relations do property rights imply? Then there are questions about the appropriateness of conceiving of *intellectual* rights. Are the intangible resources gathered under the rubric of 'cultural property' most usefully described as intellectual (Gudeman 1996)? Daes's formula, 'intellectual *and* cultural property', was meant precisely to put the two terms in parallel. As to *rights*, the very terms in which rights are claimed already belong to the international community, as indigenous conceptualizations of 'law' or 'government' belonged to colonial regimes.[12] Interesting problematics: all three show how the Euro-American distinction between tangible and intangible renders material culture a catalyst for considering the immaterial forms it contains. From a large literature I take just one exemplar of each.

CONCEPTUAL AND THEORETICAL ISSUES

Property, Ambiguity and Auto-critique

Debates over IPR regimes frequently turn on the notion of 'property'. But while it is acknowledged that assumptions originating from Europe and North America inform many values that the international community takes for granted, less obvious is that from the same source comes fundamental opposition. Euro-American ambiguity towards property fuels both enthusiasm for and antagonism to IPR. Private property is a recurrent target of Euro-Americans' self-criticism: for 300 years they have railed against its individualistic connotations, their own ideas of its opposite generally pointing to communal forms of ownership. In the specific case of intellectual property, nineteenth-century protesters resisted the idea of treating knowledge as property, on both practical and moral grounds. You could not control the flow of ideas; equally important, 'ideas are in essence free goods and, therefore, common property' (Brush 1993: 655). Note the equation of common property not with collective identity but with unrestricted access.

Property has many connotations.[13] Macfarlane (1998) reminds us that Roman law identified ownership with the thing owned. Property (the thing) was capable of infinite division, as in continental peasant Europe, where things were divided between persons by being split into shares.[14] Title inhered in the thing owned (e.g. an estate), to which persons became attached, and only certain things were regarded as property (movable or immovable goods). English common law, by comparison, developed from the tenures of medieval feudalism, rendered the thing indivisible; what was divided was not the thing but rights between persons. Several persons might have ownership in different aspects of 'one' thing. People could thus buy and sell rights without altering the thing itself, a system that allowed intangible entities such as copyright and patents to be considered property. In turn, intangible components of material culture – design, expressions of lifestyle, information, ideas (e.g. Drahos 2000) – became potential candidates for property rights.

In the words of the CBD, intellectual property offered a route to recognizing holders of the 'knowledge, innovations and practices of indigenous and local communities embodying traditional lifestyles relevant for the conservation of and sustainable use of biological diversity' (CBD, article 8j). At the same time, the convention cautioned signatory nations over IPR agreements lest they run counter to rather than support its objectives (article 16.5). For what protects one person (claims to the usable products of their activities) may exploit others (disregard other kinds of claims). This contributes to the double-edged character of property as at once a highly moral and highly duplicitous construct. We find just such an equivocation in the soft law instruments noted in the previous section.

On the one hand rights are positively coupled with property. The 1994 UN Draft Declaration on the Rights of Indigenous Peoples saw it as a strength to talk of 'cultural, intellectual, religious and spiritual property' (Simpson 1997: 18; Roulet 1999). Blakeney (1999b) discusses the declaration from the viewpoint of the relevance of cultural traditions to indigenous people's property rights over plant genetic resources. Moreover, the 'right to own property is recognised in the Universal Declaration on Human Rights and the International Convention on the Elimination of All Forms of Racial Discrimination as a fundamental human right that extends to everyone' (Simpson 1997: 35). Adding that such international legal instruments 'do not draw on the principles of indigenous customary law', Simpson notes that they 'assume that the sovreignty of the National State and the concept of exclusive possession lie at the heart of property rights, thereby denying the existence of collective ownership and the non-transferability of ownership, which are central to indigenous property systems' (1997: 35).[15] On the other hand, rights are uncoupled from property. The UN Working Group on Indigenous Populations, participants at the WIPO Roundtables on Intellectual Property and Indigenous Peoples in the 1980s and 1990s, called for protection of the 'traditional knowledge' and 'cultural values' of indigenous peoples without presuming that the relationship was one of property ownership.

At the heart of Euro-American ideas lies a creative ambiguity: property refers both to things and to social relations (e.g. Hann 1998). It is equally the thing in which a person holds rights and those rights themselves. In the second sense, rights are held against other persons, and property points to the fact that claims are always made by persons in relation to others. Enthusiasm for and antagonism to IPR pick up both senses (and see Strathern et al. 1998).

Enthusiasm Things. IPR is seen as a legal instrument allowing indigenous communities to assert claims on the international stage in a manner hardly before possible.[16] What helps technology also helps indigenous activists.

Indigenous knowledge, historically scorned by the world of industrial societies, has now become intensely, commercially attractive. ... At bottom, intellectual property rights consist of efforts to assert access to, and control over, cultural knowledge and to things produced through its application. [And] ... the thought arises, why couldn't indigenous people *own* their cultural knowledge, and then, if they allow it to be used elsewhere, secure a just share of the money it generates.

(Greaves 1994: ix, 4; original italics)

Relations. IPR is premised on equity in the two-way flow of knowledge and recompense. It does not just create a legal arena to protect rights, it gives power to new social actors, those identified as inventor or author in whom economic rights are invested. Such persons are legal individuals, a concept that includes corporate bodies (government agencies, research institutes). Any social unit – individual, clan, village – could theoretically seek registration as a potential right holder.

Antagonism   Things. Not everything is appropriately turned into a thing to be owned, for in Euro-American thinking ownership implies the right of alienation (disposing of the thing to another, through sale, gift). The question of what can and cannot be alienated is often answered in terms of the kind of thing at issue. Thus many people regard 'nature' as a common resource that should not be allocated specific owners. But questions typically follow, here, for example, the question then becomes what nature is. The European Parliament directive on the legal protection of biotechnological inventions, giving companies the right to patent organisms created through microbiological processes, was referred to by one opponent as a charter to enslave nature.[17] In this thinking, organisms are not appropriately owned as property. This comes both from a Euro-American perception of things as objects of manipulation and from the idea of nature as a resource to be freely shared.[18]

Relations. The question of what can be alienated is answered in terms of people's relationships. Opponents of IPR may see it as asserting a form of private property that challenges the ethos of sharing they would attribute to collective ownership typical of indigenous communities where generations of people have built up cultural knowledge.

Contemporary intellectual property law is constructed around the notion of the author as an individual, solitary and original creator ... Those who do not fit this model – custodians of tribal culture and medical knowledge, collectives practising traditional artistic and musical forms, or peasant cultivators of valuable seed varieties – are

denied intellectual property protection. For members of indigenous peoples, knowledge and determination of the use of resources are collective and intergenerational.

(Bellagio and COICA statements, Posey 1996: 13)

But is the only counterpoint to private property the sharing of resources, and does the model of collective rights have to be that of communal ones? We will return to this. In the meanwhile, note that questions as to the organic or non-human character of 'nature' or of 'things' touch on some of the boundary conditions of material culture.

Intellectual Input, Broad and Narrow

How should we understand the intellectual content of material culture?[19] Broad and narrow claims to originality echo for copyright what has become a vigorous controversy over the breadth of patents.[20] In debate is the nature of the 'intellectual' contribution. New technologies have rendered obscure distinctions once at the basis of legal limits in patenting, primarily between invention and discovery.[21] Critics note that current legal artifices (arguments such as, when genes are isolated and purified, they can be regarded as no longer existing in nature and thus as patentable inventions) ignore the purpose of the original distinction, to promote the innovation of products, not of abstractions (Drahos 1999), or that doctrinal distinctions are used to disqualify political or ethical objections (Pottage 1998).[22] In relation to material culture, Brown (1998, 2003; and see Rowlands 2000) voices comparable criticism of 'the moral alchemy' by which broad questions about fair use and expression turn into narrow disputes over commodification; property discourse displaces debate about the morality of (say) subjecting people to unwarranted scrutiny or sequestering public-domain information, submerging complex ethical issues in favour of competing claims to ownership. Here I comment on the breadth of claims to originality or creativity, and take a well discussed example.

The case of Yumbulul versus the Reserve Bank of Australia has been seized on for the relationship it reveals between an individual artist and the source of his creativity (Barron 1998; Blakeney 1995, 2000; Kalinoe 2001, 2004). Terry Yumbulul granted an Australian collecting society administering reproduction rights in Aborginal art an exclusive licence with respect to the copyright he held in a decorated wooden pole. (The pole he had carved was on display in the Australian Museum.) The bank reproduced the design ('Morning Star') on its $10 note, under a sub-licence granted them by the collecting society. Yumbulul went to court to dispute the original licence, complaining that he did not really have copyright to dispose of, mainly because of pressure from his clan (Galpu from Yolngu), who claimed that the reproduction was a desecration. The Morning Star configuration on his pole was, in Kalinoe's words, 'clan heritage material'. Kalinoe focuses on the fact that the capacity to carve the pole did not indicate original creative work but had been bestowed through initiation rites. The carving only worked as a faithful reproduction of existing imagery. This is not simply a matter of 'traditional knowledge' owned by a 'group': through those rites Yumbulul had been placed into a specific position with respect to clan ancestors, co-members, related clans and other kin.[23] He had been through several ritual stages, including the critical one authorizing his production of the Morning Star design.

Writing from a Papua New Guinea perspective, Kalinoe dwells on the authorization individuals must seek from clan members, arguing that practical or mundane knowledge should be distinguished from secret or sacred knowledge. The economic exploitation of the former may be welcomed, but sacred assets demand protection from misuse. This leads him to propose that such cultural property should be treated for legal purposes simply as property, albeit of a special kind in being inalienably identified with its owners, but emphatically *not* as intellectual property. Regimes for the preservation of culture should be kept separate from the promotion of IPR. One reason is that IPR brings things into the public eye; the limited restriction guaranteed by IPR protection is nothing compared with exposure when the copyright (say) expires. The public domain aspect of IPR causes as many problems as its private property aspect (Brown 1998; Brush 1999).

The Australian Federal Court hearing the case in 1991 upheld (against Yumbulul's will) the appropriateness of copyright as a property relation between the Aboriginal artist and his carving of the sacred emblem (hence validating the subsequent licence). How had this legal recognition come about? Barron (1998) discusses broad issues in the air at the time that some thought relevant to the law even if not the basis of law. Aside from the newly discovered artistic value of Aboriginal 'art' were cultural assumptions about individual creativity and the genius of the Romantic individual. The law satisfied itself with a narrow view. Copyright was allocated to the artist as the originator of the work (he and no other carved it), without invoking any stronger sense of intellectual input.

Now what in the law was an easily settled question about 'breadth' of originality, on the Aboriginal side was an equally clear view on creativity. Creativity entails the capacity to (re)produce (life) forms. It engages issues of personhood, contingent for the law, central for Yumbulul's kin. Euro-Americans equate sources of potency with an origin in the person as a singular entity, the person in this respect being indivisible. Imagining how copyright ownership mapped on to Aboriginal concepts of clan ownership of images and designs, Barron (1998: 72) notes the distribution of relationships: 'Even if it could, the unification of copyright ownership in a single entity, albeit a collective one, would not mirror the distribution of rights among individual members of the clan' in their relations with members of other clans. Such rights are neither public nor private. Rather, they show how the design authorizes the carver by its identification with those persons variously embodied in it. A painting executed in reference to ancestral images contains its own conditions of reproduction: the design itself indexes who has the right to paint it. In this manner, artist belongs to painting rather than painting to artist.

To reproduce a design may involve sources of creativity apart from the owners. The procreative/exogamic model is evident: those who (help) bring forth need not be the owners.[24] The Director of the Papua New Guinea National Cultural Commission has concerns here (Simet 2000, 2001, n.d.).[25] Simet observes of the Tolai of New Britain (2000: 78):

> One idea, which might easily form part of the development of a mechanism for protection of indigenous knowledge, is the assumption that all traditional knowledge is communally owned. [In fact] ... people were very particular about acquisition, ownership, transfer, protection and use of knowledge. Only some kinds of knowledge belonged to the public domain, while the rest belonged to individuals and social groups.

Tolai individuals and groups are enmeshed in diverse relations with one another. Thus signs of a clan's identity are distributed between its masks (*tubuan*) and the magic (*palawat*) which makes the masks effective vehicles of power. A clan member who acts as manager for the clan holds the *tubuan*; a non-member, a custodian who deploys the magic on its behalf, holds the *palawat*. Clan members cannot use their own magic themselves.[26]

One might want to agree in a broad way with Posey and Dutfield (1996: 220): 'For indigenous peoples, life is a common property which cannot be owned, commercialised, and monopolised by individuals. Based on this worldview, indigenous peoples find it difficult to relate intellectual property rights issues to their daily lives.' But it becomes a narrow view when it overlooks how creativity channelled through artefacts is also channelled through specific persons, owed by others as it is owed to others. These others may be ancestors or bush spirits or members of other groups. And very often what is owed has to be paid for. Papua New Guinea shows many cases where payments are made against the flow of benefits. In this way intangible benefits (the power to reproduce forms) are rendered tangible (wealth given in return) (Strathern 2004). Thus the circulation of 'rights' over intangibles (knowledge, magic) is often bound up with 'rights' over performance (exchange, ritual). The accompanying transactions cut across the logic of both patenting (sustaining the flow of ideas) and copyright (copying unique artistic expressions) regimes.[27] 'Ownership' in these circumstances is not straightforward. People may wish to facilitate *both* the protection of items that belong to groups *and* the flow of exchanges guaranteeing that what is of value circulates and continues to receive the value that circulation (keeping up relationships) confers.

Holders of Rights: Communal or Multiple?

This section brings together Euro-American critiques of property and of private and public 'rights'. Its cue is the Model Law directive[25] that makes its case for setting up protection mechanisms outside intellectual property regimes by insisting on the claims of 'traditional owners', typically groups.[28] Collective ownership is thus addressed in the opposites familiar to Euro-American private-property thinking: 'community ownership', 'communal moral rights'. Based on explicit objections to Western forms, then, the Model Law sees the indigenous counterpart as 'communal': in its words, 'ownership and control over the reproduction of works are vested in the group, clan or community'. We have noted Simet's (2000) distinction between a 'community' as a kind of public domain in which certain types of knowledge

circulate on a non-exclusive basis and clans or groups that assert exclusive claims. Exclusive access does not mean that the clan has authority and control over all its property: aspects of *its* property may be under the control of *other* (non-member) custodians.

Let us look at the terms arising in Euro-American critique of rights regimes. The emphasis on originality and innovation in copyright and patent identifies individual persons as rights holders even where economic rights are held by publishers or employers who were not the creative source of the original work. This does not mean that no recognition is accorded the wider social context from which creations come, only that the context does not in itself create rights. It is a truism that inventions are either new ways of producing something old or old ways of producing something new, every invention a 'new combination of pre-existing knowledge' (Bainbridge 1999: 349).

Particularly in relation to scientific knowledge, a separate issue arises over the propriety of acquiring property rights in areas said to belong to people, 'the public', 'humankind', in general. It may be argued that because 'the building blocks of intangible work – knowledge – is a social product', no individual should have exclusive ownership of the shared knowledge of society (Moore 2000: 113). On this view, 'the commons' designate resources which should be kept freely available.[29] Unlike the commons, 'the public domain' is a residual category created by intellectual property regimes themselves (e.g. modern copyright created the public domain by limiting the period of copyright monopoly, beyond which the rights must lodge in a legal entity other than the copyright holder: Brush 1999: 541; McSherry 2001: 27), but in everyday usage the terms often converge. Thus it is argued that knowledge created from common resources should be put 'back' into the public domain. This is not knowledge from the past but new knowledge judged to be to the benefit of everyone; once public, it cannot be subject to proprietary claims.

Scientists have used the term 'gift exchange' for a prestige-reward system through which they both ensure the circulation of information and gain recognition (Biagioli 2000, quoting Hagström 1982). Sharing is critical. Unless scientific findings have circulated among co-researchers, they cannot be verified: truths about the world must become facts in a public domain. 'Scientists buttress their new claims by connecting them as much as possible to the body of previous scientific literature' (Biagioli 2000: 88, 2003); they form a community identified by common interests and responsibilities.[30] The logic of an intellectual property system is antithetical to this kind of accreditation: the contrast is both with patents, which are about utility, not about the factual status of knowledge, and with copyright, which is about original expression, not truth claims. The Royal Society's recommendation (2.8)[31] is that, 'rather than focusing on who owns the IPR', what needs encouraging is the appropriate environment for fair exploitation. In debates over IPR cross-licensing – negotiations between commercial interests – it is almost a mantra that the key is not ownership but access (Hill and Turpin 1995: 145).

Some of these ideas are echoed in descriptions of indigenous systems. When a people think of styles and practices that point to their identity, the collective character of these things may seem inseparable from (their possession of) themselves as 'a community' (Kalinoe 1999). Items handed on from previous generations impose an obligation on the holders to act as custodians:[32] on this view, 'heritage' held in trust couldn't be disposed of, nor collective interests ever extinguished. If people think of these encompassing sources of their identity as 'their property', then among themselves it becomes analogous to the common law idea of 'the commons'. This emphasizes the principle of inclusion by denying exclusion (no one can be excluded). Obviously, common identity may be asserted at several levels of inclusion, whether of all humanity, of the nation through national cultural property acts, or of a language group, or culture.

An exclusive emphasis is found in 'common property' that implies a specified owner, as when rights in common are shared among a body of co-owners forming a corporate entity. Clans and kin groups may be identified as corporations, members exercising rights to the exclusion of non-members. Common property rights imply co-equal ownership of the rights, not equal shares to resources. Often, where rights are vested in the corporate entity or group, the title holder, individual members hold rights of usufruct. Usufruct rights may be managed in diverse ways but the group's ownership cannot be extinguished by the actions of individuals; as in the Australian case, individual owners have no rights over disposal, because the right-holding 'individual' here is the corporation. Thus we may define corporate property *either* as a kind of collective property (ownership rights shared among the members) *or* as a kind of individual property (the corporate group acts an individual entity ['person'] in relation to others) (Foster 1995). Corporate

claims to group emblems or signs (dances, songs, carvings, myths) (Mosko 2002) are in practical terms 'inalienable'.

However, such rights may coexist alongside other regimes that define interests that are neither individual nor collective, but invested rather in sustaining relations.[33] Here people are acting neither as individuals, but as parties to an enduring relationship, nor with respect to a collectivity, but within the limits of obligation to specific others. Examples include alliances between intermarrying kin groups from which flow gifts between affines (artefacts as well as food or parcels of land); contracts between rulers and subjects (regalia, ceremony); obligations entailed in ritual duties (songs, magic) carried out on a reciprocating basis; exchanges or payments (ornaments, canoes, masks) valued for their own sake, where keeping up the exchange itself becomes paramount. Such relationships may be significant precisely because they cut across group alignments. Value lies in the fact that access to display or performance exists because of their origination in another person or social entity or domain of power. That is, the 'rights' are specifically to something *that has come from elsewhere*. Note the surprise with which it is reported that (for instance) shamanic knowledge can be bought, sold or stolen (Dutfield 1999).

Transactions thereby create a form of 'multiple ownership'.[34] In so far as they determine what is transactable they can also determine the parties to the transaction. Thus 'groups' may 'emerge' at the time of the interchange itself, identitified as parties to the transaction (e.g. Hirsch 2001, 2004). The gaining and disposal of things do not extinguish the parties' mutual interest in the things or in one another: in 'owning' the flow of items they 'own', as an intangible thing, the relationship between them. As a result, much indigenous knowledge is both embedded *and* transactable. There is no simple confrontation between communal versus individual rights: specific interests are embedded in relations between persons. That things reify relations is often misunderstood as mercenary. Yet transactions may sustain a flow of intangible benefits – 'life' or 'well-being' – of a spiritual as well as material nature. Persons identified as the source of such benefits may be said to 'create' rather than produce them (the benefits) so they are embodied in (the health and life chances of) persons who are thus 'created' by others. When benefits come from a particular social source (in other persons, other clans), that source is part of the benefit.[35] 'Payments' acknowledge the source, the form the 'payment' ranging from a purchase to recompense or compensation.[36]

TRENDS AND DIRECTIONS

Several pointers to further research are apparent in these examples. New technologies and new social expectations affecting IPR also affect how one might approach material culture itself. At the same time a lasting impact of indigenous rights activism is the politicization of research and its documentation apropos cultural performance and, indeed, knowledge. Here we give a very brief nod to the material culture created through the process of research itself. Fieldworkers and their notebooks compose a familiar conundrum; employees and their academic outputs are 'new' figures on the scene.

With the expansion of IPR activity of all kinds come increasing sensitivities over the basis of the claims on which individual property rights are made. In 1999, a Draft Declaration from the UK Association of Learned and Professional Society publishers opened: 'Academic authors communicate and share ideas, information, knowledge and results of study and research by all available means of expression and in all forms. They recognise that participants in the scholarly communication process include academic editors, publishers and presentation experts.'[37] One European impetus is a move to distinguish economic rights from moral rights – the ownership of rights in an intellectual resource, as a contractual and legal matter – and from the assertion of 'moral rights', the right to be named as author (recognition, accreditation and so forth). Economic rights can be bought and sold; moral rights are tied to the author as originator. The two sets of rights holders may coincide, but need not.

McSherry (2001) argues that the so-called 'knowledge economy' that has made universities aware of intellectual property challenges IPR and the academy at the same time. The two may even be dramatized as being in some kind of mutual crisis (Pottage 1998). *Battling for Control of Intellectual Property* is the subtitle of McSherry's book on academic output. (She opens with a case concerning the leaking of research results through a doctoral student who channelled information from the lab where she had studied to researchers in a pharmaceutical firm.)[38] If ethical objections to acquiring proprietory rights include the grounds that scientific knowledge is ultimately derived from 'common property', political and economic objections include the grounds that scientific knowledge is ultimately derived from public funding.[39] There are many contexts in which academics are urged to treat their output as something to be owned. Property rights over what they create should be made evident.

In the United Kingdom, urging comes from central government, and it is not only individual academics but their institutions that are exhorted to behave as owners. In the United States this was initiated by the University and Small Business Patent Procedures Act 1980, named Bayh-Dole after its protagonists. University bodies became empowered to hold patents arising from federally sponsored research. Universities would treat public funding as investment, return profits to the taxpayer and plough surpluses back into more research. Asserting property title in intellectual output is a way of ensuring this. Consequently, divisions between the market and the academy have become blurred by increasing pressure to bring intellectual protection into the scholarly reward system. In sum, the new stakeholder in knowledge production is a collective or corporate individual, not the community of scholars but the institution that employs them. Publicly funded bodies such as universities find that they have a positive duty to protect the investment made in them, thereby making sure benefits are to 'society'.[40]

In the United Kingdom, the Research Councils oblige universities to take on the ownership of intellectual property created in the course of research. Note the double public duty: to disseminate knowledge, as encouraged by IPR; to return public investment by allocating IPR to the university. At the same time, it has been accepted by the Court of Appeal that academic work is based on assumptions different from those imposed by other employer-employee agreements. Indeed, the special connection between academics and their work arguably requires protection from the institution. Here the institution is in its private guise, for it is feared that IPR would lead it to suppress what it did not favour. And here copyright steps in to protect the author. In most places, UK university staff own copyright in their publications, papers, lecture notes, one of the by-products being another way of encouraging the flow of ideas.[41] Traditionally academics may not have wished to create private property out of output, but they may have wished to exercise something akin to *personal* ownership. The academic anthropologist finds him or herself learning about material culture from unexpected sources.

NOTES

1 I use IPR as shorthand for an ideational domain that includes both the law and its philosophy.

2 In giving individual authors rights to the products of their exertions, IPR broke the monopolies of guilds.

3 Because of huge investments in biotechnological research, companies seek broad patents to cover future exploitation. Dating from the first filing of patents for gene sequences in 1991: 'Venter's applications were for DNA [gene] sequences *whose function was unknown*, a move that has led to a kind of 'gene prospecting' whereby companies apply for patents without really knowing what the scientific value of the DNA is' (Cunningham 1998: 229–30 n. 16, added emphasis).

4 For an early anthropological comment on TRIPS, see Coombe (1996: 245). Post-TRIPS, much has changed with the Doha Round agreement that placed development on the negotiating agenda, and the subsequent debacle at WTO's Cancun meeting in 2003 (www.ictsd.org).

5 'Soft law' refers to declarations of principles, codes of practice, recommendations, guidelines, standards, resolutions. Not legally binding, there is nonetheless an expectation that they will be respected by the international community. The evolution of 'customary international law' is accelerated by including customary principles in soft law agreements and non-governmental declarations; these become hardened through worldwide acceptance (Posey and Dutfield 1996: 120).

6 Posey and Dutfield include the following texts: Declaration of Principles of the World Council of Indigenous People; UN Draft Declaration on the Rights of Indigenous Peoples (1993); Kari-Oca Declaration and the Indigenous Peoples' Earth Charter (1992); Charter of the Indigenous–Tribal Peoples of the Tropical Forests (1992); Mataatua Declaration on Cultural and Intellectual Property Rights of Indigenous Peoples (1993); Recommendations from the Voices of Earth Congress (1993); UNDP Consultation on the Protection and Conservation of Indigenous Knowledge (1995); UNDP Consultation on Indigenous Peoples' Knowledge and Intellectual Property Rights (1995). On some of the diverse relationships between cultural rights and human rights, see the overview of works published since the 1990s in Winthrop (2002: 117–19); Cowan et al. 2001.

7 UNESCO, First Preliminary Draft of an International Convention for the Safeguarding of Intangible Cultural Heritage, 2002 (not adopted).

8 UNESCO's 1972 Convention concerning the Protection of the World Cultural and Natural Heritage demarcated specific sites of world cultural heritage, in the same way as cultural property laws are concerned with original artefacts or monuments, and thus with conservation and not with practices of reproduction (cf. Coombe 1993: 264).

9 Eriksen (2001) offers a sympathetic critique of UNESCO's efforts, and of the publication *Our Creative Diversity* (WCCD 1995; also see Arizpe 1996).

10 It was not lost on the anthropological community that property claimed in the name of IPR had the potential to impinge on those who make 'culture' their subject matter.

11 From a submission to the 1992 CBD by the Four Directions Council, an organization of Canadian indigenous peoples, 'what is "traditional" about traditional knowledge is not its antiquity but the way it is acquired and used' (cited by Dutfield 1999: 105, emphasis omitted).

12 For example, neo-Melanesian *kastom* ('custom') refers to practices flowing across the generations and is found in habits definitive of the present; in Bolton's (2003) words, *kastom* is not conserved but enacted, and may have a transactable value in relation to outsiders (Harrison 1999; Mosko 2002). Bolton argues for Vanuatu that it is 'the product of the *interaction* between expatriate ideas of culture and custom and ni-Vanuatu conceptualizations of their [own] knowledge and practice' (2003: 52, my emphasis). It does not, in this sense, refer to pre-colonial processes or representations.

13 Hann (1998); van Meijl and von Benda-Beckman (1999), as well as Carrier (1995); cf. Verdery and Humphrey (2004); Humphrey (2002); Rumsey and Weiner (2001); Filer (1997); outside anthropology, among others, Rose (1993); Radin (1996).

14 Macfarlane quotes the jurist Maine on the idea that no Roman lawyer could conceive of the feudal 'series of estates' – a number of owners entitled to enjoy the same piece of land, where a person's possession was protected by custom and no claim was absolute (1998: 113).

15 Exclusivity and transferability are taken, for example by Gray (1991), as conditions for propertization.

16 At the same time as introducing creativity as an explicit resource, IPR throws up a difference between *innovatory versus non-innovatory regimes* of production/reproduction. The international community may rehearse this as a contrast between invention and inventiveness, characteristics of technology-rich economies, and convention, which carries connotations of the static. Having to seek protection for the explicitly non-innovative means that the concepts 'tradition', 'custom' and 'heritage' must all be made to carry new freight.

17 Human genetics creates particular controversy over what can or cannot be patented. Article 5 of the 1998 Directive of the European Parliament and of the Council on the Legal Protection of Biotechnological Inventions specified that the human body cannot be a patentable invention, including gene sequences, but that 'an element isolated from the human body or otherwise produced by means of a technical process', including gene sequences, may be.

18 It is when it comes to buying and selling that some things are regarded as alienable and some as not. A person may have title but still be restricted as to how to dispose of property (e.g. in inheritance laws); the issue of monetary gain adds a further dimension to what are sometimes perceived as moral dilemmas.

19 An intellectual property rights system 'creates incentives for the accumulation of useful *knowledge*' or 'novel *information*' (Swanson 1995: 11, added emphasis). From a 1990s managers' guide (Irish 1991): IP is a general term for different types of *ideas* protected by legal rights, since the time spent on *originating new concepts* is an investment which needs protection. Or: 'Intellectual property is a generic term which refers to the rights attached to the products of *human creativity*, including scientific discoveries, industrial designs, literary and artistic works' (Tassy and Dambrine 1997: 193, added emphasis).

20 For example, the 'broad' and 'narrow' readings that the European Patent Office gives to aspects of the European Patent Convention (Drahos 1999). The US Patent Code defines standards for 'novelty' and 'non-obviousness' but the courts are said to apply these standards loosely (Barton 2000: 1933). The weakening of the principle that mental processes and abstract concepts are not patentable was evident in the 1998 US Court of Appeals ruling that determined that 'even abstract ideas constituting disembodied truth' could be patented provided they performed a useful function (Gleick 2000).

21 This distinction is one of the cornerstones on which the concept of patent rests, namely that it protects the human ingenuity that has gone into technical inventions and rules out the discovery or application of natural materials or processes. In the famous Moore *v.* Regents of University of California case (Rabinow 1996b), Moore failed to lay claim to the profits of a cell line developed from his spleen because 'the cell line was entirely attributed to the inventive art of the scientists who had identified and isolated his ... cells' (Pottage 1998: 750; cf. Moore 2000).

22 Example: 'A spokesman for the UK patent office says: "If you find something in nature, then finding some way to separate it and to make it into something useful can be an invention' (*The Guardian* [UK] 18 February 2000). This was apropos a Maryland firm securing rights over a gene that allows the AIDS virus to settle in the body: it can stake a claim to any AIDS medicine targeting the gene.

23 As Barron puts it, drawing on anthropologists Howard Morphy and Fred Myers, *knowing* (recognizing and caring for) the sacred evidence of ancestral Dreamtime carries obligations as well as rights. Yumbulul's entitlement was to paint and even sell the relevant designs – provided they were destined for an appropriate place such as a museum – but not to authorize their reproduction by others (Barron 1998: 48–51).

24 The animating spirit may come from outside, from another. Funerals, too, often divide people into 'mourners' (owners of the death) and 'helpers' (who enable them to mourn).

25 Primarily in relation to moves by UNESCO and WIPO on a Model law for the Protection of Traditional Knowledge and Expressions of Culture for the Pacific Region.

26 In this matrilineal system the relevant non-members are 'children' born to male members of a clan. Tolai land use repeats the division, between the 'owners' of land and the 'custodians' of its history, non-owner 'children' who keep it secure.

27   A view arrived at through a rather different route by Daes (e.g. 1997) and endorsed eloquently in the Maori case (Garrity 1999), and by the Deputy Director General of WIPO, Shozo Uemura, at the Geneva Roundtable on Intellectual Property and Traditional Knowledge in 1999.

28   Indigenous systems are purportedly characterized 'by trans-generational, non-materialistic, and non-exclusive or communal ownership of rights' (Puri 2001) that make IPR inappropriate. The Model Law confers a 'property right' on those who own traditional knowledge and expressions of culture and seeks to identify the 'true owners', including groups or communities.

29   Popular (Euro-American) usage equivocates as to whether this refers to property that belongs to everyone (a common resource in which there can be no private property) or the property of no one (resources open to conversion into private property) (cf. Dutfield 1999).

30   McSherry, dealing with science in the United States, argues that in so far as the twentieth-century research university developed as the primary producer of science, it was most useful to commerce and government in its apparent independence from them. Its role, to validate the autonomy of scientific facts, found a social form in an autonomous community of scholars – where it became 'inappropriate to identify one's creations as private property' (McSherry 2001: 74–5). Individual 'ownership' was antithetical to this ethos.

31   Royal Society, 2003.

32   'Caretaker' is the preferred term in Garrity's (1999) review of Maori concepts of intellectual property. ('Stewardship' or 'guardianship' assumes human beings have a right to control the environment in ways at odds with Maori understandings.)

33   Existing IPR categories point to multiple interests, but not necessarily in a relational mode. English copyright recognizes joint authors. They own the copyright severally, as 'tenants in common', holding independent rights that they may dispose of without reference to the other party. Each is a full owner in relation to the part of the work that was theirs or to the whole if it was produced jointly. While the several owners of the patent may also act as tenants in common, where an invention is the outcome of combined efforts, patent holders may be 'joint tenants'. Each is entitled to exploit the product individually but cannot dispose of the interest (rights) without permission from the others. A different potential for multiple ownership arises where the development of products depends on marshalling together elements that have been separately and individually patented by different companies (Heller and Eisenberg 1998).

34   The concept of multiple ownership emerged strongly from the Workshop on Intellectual and Cultural Property in the New Guinea Islands Region held in Rabaul (March 2000); see Sykes with Simet and Kamene (2001).

35   So persons and resources may be seen as the 'combined' outcome of multiple sources of substance or benefit (see Kalinoe and Leach 2001).

36   Opponents of IPR may claim that one cannot identify the individual author under indigenous regimes where innovations are cumulative, and then attack the whole idea of payment. But 'payment' in Papua New Guinea precisely means making intangibles tangible (material). Payment for intellectual property is criticized for imposing the Euro-American split of mind from body, as in the transformation of community economies to market ones. But where there is no division between persons and things the practice of eliciting specific knowledge or assets through the payment of things may be a *sui generis* mode of dealing with relations between persons. (Cf. Toft 1997.)

37   A well worked theorization of multiple authorship presents the postmodern text as a tissue of other texts, e.g. Coombe (1998: 284). One stimulus for Rose's (1993: viii) historical inquiry into the notion of the individual creator was his experience of the entertainment industry, where almost all work is both 'formulaic' and 'corporate', coming from well established routines. In patenting there always has been tension between all the work and networks of persons who were involved in developing a product and the final invention which brought a product to its conclusion. A notorious example is what eventually became the cancer drug Taxol (Goodman and Walsh 2001).

38   From the United States; her cases are largely informed by hierarchies in academia – juniors/seniors etc.

39   However, since 1980 the private appropriation (through patenting) of publicly funded research has been part of the US

government's agenda to revitalize American business (Eisenberg 1996). Note the timing of this move in the light of international politics: the prospect of military funding for technology research drying up with the end of the Cold War. (Thanks to Eric Hirsch, personal communication; see McSherry 2001: 152).)

40 But as the Royal Society paper asks (1.7), Which society? The United Kingdom, the European Union, the world ? And it raises the pertinent question of benefits actually accruing to some at the expense of others.

41 The right of university employees to assert ownership of copyright in a work 'written, composed or drafted' by them is interpreted by Cornish as a part of the employee's implicit contract with the university (Cornish report to Cambridge University on copyright, *Cambridge University Reporter*, 17 October 2001).

REFERENCES

ALPSP (1999) *Draft Declaration*. London: Association of Learned and Professional Society Publishers.

Arizpe, L., ed. (1996) *The Cultural Dimension of Global Change: an Anthropological Approach*. Culture and Development Series. Paris: UNESCO.

Bainbridge, D. (1999) *Intellectual Property*, 4th edn. London: Financial Times Management and Pitman.

Barron, Anne (1998) 'No other law? Authority, property and Aboriginal art', in L. Bently and S. Mariatis (eds), *Intellectual Property and Ethics* London: Sweet & Maxwell.

Barry, A. (2000) 'Invention and inertia', *Cambridge Anthropology*, 21: 62–70.

Barry, A. (2001) *Political Machines: Governing a Technological Society*. London, New York: Athlone Press.

Barton, John (2000) 'Reforming the patent system', *Science*, 287: 1933.

Biagioli, M. (1998) 'The instability of authorship: credit and responsibility in contemporay biomedicine', Life Sciences Forum, *The FASEB Journal*, 12: 3–16.

Biagioli, M. (2000) 'Rights or rewards? Changing contexts and definitions of scientific authorship', *Journal of College and University Law*, 2: 83–108.

Biagioli, M. (2003) 'Rights or rewards? Changing frameworks of scientific authorship',. in M. Biagiolo and P. Galison (eds), *Scientific Authorship: Credit and Intellectual Property in Science*. New York: Routledge.

Blake, Janet (2001) 'Developing a new standard-setting instrument for the safeguarding of intangible cultural heritage'. Paris: UNESCO (typescript: CLT-2001/WS/8).

Blakeney, M. (1995) 'Protecting expressions of Australian Aboriginal folklore under copyright law', *EIPR* 9: 442–5.

Blakeney, M. (1999a) 'The international framework of access to plant genetic resources', in M. Blakeney (ed.), *Intellectual Property Aspects of Ethnobiology*. London: Sweet & Maxwell.

Blakeney, M., ed. (1999b) *Intellectual Property Aspects of Ethnobiology*. London: Sweet & Maxwell and Queen Mary Intellectual Property Institute.

Blakeney, M. (2000) 'The protection of traditional knowledge under intellectual property law', *European Intellectual Property Review*, 6: 251–61.

Bolton, Lissant (2003) *Unfolding the Moon: Enacting Women's Kastom in Vanuatu*. Honolulu, HI: University of Hawaii Press.

Brown, M. (1998) 'Can culture be copyrighted?' *Current Anthropology*, 39 (2): 193–222.

Brown, M. (2003) *Who Owns Native Culture?* Cambridge: Cambridge University Press.

Brush, S.B. (1993) 'Indigenous knowledge of biological resources and intellectual property rights: the role of anthropology', *American Anthropologist*, 95 (3): 653–86.

Brush, S.B. (1994) 'A non-market approach to prospecting biological resources', in T. Greaves (ed.), *Intellectual Property Rights for Indigenous Peoples: a Sourcebook*. Oklahoma City: Society for Applied Anthropology.

Brush, S.B. (1999) 'Bioprospecting in the public domain', *Cultural Anthropology*, 14: 535–55.

Brush, S.B. and Orlove, B. (1996) 'Anthropology and the conservation of biodiversity', *Annual Review of Anthropology*, 25: 329–52.

Brush, S.B. and Stabinsky, D. (1996) *Valuing Local Knowledge: Indigenous Peoples and Intellectual Property Rights*. Washington, DC: Island Press.

Carrier, J.G. (1995) *Gifts and Commodities: Exchange and Western Capitalism since 1700*. London and New York: Routledge.

CIPR (2002) *Integrating Intellectual Property Rights and Development Policy*. London: Department for International Development, Commission on Intellectual Property Rights.

Coombe, R. (1993) 'The Properties of culture and the politics of possessing identity: native claims in the cultural appropriation Controversy', *Canadian Journal of Law and Jurisprudence*, 6 (2): 249–85.

Coombe, R. (1996) 'Left out on the information highway', *Oregon Law Review*, 75: 237–47.

Coombe, R. (1998) *The Cultural Life of Intellectual Properties: Authorship, Appropriation and the Law*, Durham, NC: Duke University Press.

Cowan, J., Diembour, M.-B. and Wilson, R., eds. (2001) *Culture and Rights: Anthropological Perspectives*. Cambridge: Cambridge University Press.

Cunningham, Hilary (1998) 'Colonial encounters in postcolonial contexts: patenting indigenous DNA and the Human Genome Diversity Project', *Critique of Anthropology,* 18: 205–33.

Daes, Erica-Irene (1997) *Protection of the Heritage of Indigenous People.* Human Rights Study Series. New York and Geneva: United Nations.

Drahos, Peter (1999) 'Biotechnology patents, market and morality', *European Intellectual Property Review,* 21: 441–9.

Drahos, Peter (2000) 'Indigenous knowledge, intellectual property and biopiracy: is a Global Collecting Society the answer?' *European Intellectual Property Review,* 22: 245–50.

Dutfield, Graham (1999) 'The public and private domains: intellectual property rights in traditional ecological knowledge', WP 03/99, *Oxford Electronic Journal of Intellectual Property Rights.*

Eisenberg, Rebecca (1996) 'Public research and private development: patents and technology transfer in government-sponsored research', *Virgina Law Review,* 82: 1663–727.

Ellen, R. and Harris, H. (1997) 'Concepts of Indigenous Environmental Knowledge in Scientific and Development Studies Literature: A Critical Assessment'. APFT Working Paper 2.

Eriksen, T.H. (2001) 'Between universalism and relativism: a critique of the UNESCO concept of culture', in J. Cowan, M.-B. Djembour and R. Wilson (eds), *Culture and Rights: Anthropological Perspectives.* Cambridge: Cambridge University Press.

Filer, Colin (1997) 'Compensation, rent and power in Papua New Guinea', in S. Toft (ed.), *Compensation and Resource Development in Papua New Guinea.* Canberra: Australian National University and Port Moresby: Law Reform Commision.

Foster, R. (1995) *Social Reproduction and History in Melanesia: Mortuary Ritual, Gift Exchange and Custom in the Tanga Islands.* Cambridge: Cambridge University Press.

Garrity, Brian (1999) 'Conflict between Maori and Western concepts of intellectual property', *Auckland University Law Review,* 8: 1193–210.

Gleick, James (2000) 'Patently absurd', *New York Times Magazine,* 12 March.

Goodman, Jordan and Walsh, Vivien (2001) *The Story of Taxol: Nature and Politics in the Pursuit of an Anti-Cancer Drug.* Cambridge: Cambridge University Press.

Gray, Kevin (1991) 'Property in thin air', *Cambridge Law Journal* 50: 252–307.

Greaves, T., ed. (1994) *Intellectual Property Rights for Indigenous Peoples: a Sourcebook.* Oklahoma City: Society for Applied Anthropology.

Gudeman, S. (1996) 'Sketches, qualms, and other thoughts on intellectual property rights', in S.B. Brush and D. Stabinsky (eds), *Valuing Local Knowledge: Indigenous People and Intellectual Property Rights.* Washington, DC: Island Press.

Hagström, Warren, O. (1982) 'Gift giving as an organising principle in science', in B. Barnes and D. Edge (eds), *Science in Context: Readings in the Sociology of Science.* Milton Keynes: Open University Press.

Hann, C.M. (1998) 'Introduction: the embeddedness of property', in C.M. Hann (ed.), *Property Relations: Renewing the Anthropological Tradition.* Cambridge: Cambridge University Press.

Harrison, Simon (1992) 'Ritual as intellectual property', *Man* (n.s.) 27: 225–44.

Harrison, Simon (1999) 'Identity as a scarce resource', *Social Anthropology,* 7: 239–51.

Harrison, Simon (2000) 'From prestige goods to legacies: property and the objectification of culture in Melanesia', *Comparative Studies in Society and History,* 44: 662–79.

Hayden, C. (2003) *When Nature Goes Public: The Making and Unmaking of Bioprospecting in Mexico.* Princeton, NJ: Princeton University Press.

Heller, Michael and Eisenberg, Rebecca (1998) 'Can patents deter innovation? The anticommons in biomedical research', *Science,* 280: 698–701.

Hill, Stephen and Turpin, Tim (1995) 'Cultures in collision: the emergence of new localism in academic research', in M. Strathern (ed.), *Shifting contexts: Transformations in anthropological knowledge.* London: Routledge.

Hirsch, Eric (2001) 'New boundaries of influence in Highland Papua: "culture", mining and ritual conversions', *Oceania,* 71: 298–312.

Hirsch, Eric (2004) 'Boundaries of creation: the work of credibility in science and ceremony', in E. Hirsch and M. Strathern (eds), *Transactions and Creations: Property Debates and the Stimulus of Melanesia.* Oxford: Berghahn.

Hirsch, Eric and Strathern, Marilyn (eds) (2004) *Transactions and Creations: Property Debates and The Stimulus of Melanesia.* Oxford: Berghahn.

Humphrey, Caroline (2002) 'Rituals of death as a context for understanding personal property in socialist Mongolia', *JRAI* (n.s.) 8: 65–87.

Irish, Vivien, ed. (1991) *Intellectual Property: a Manager's Guide.* London: McGraw-Hill.

Kalinoe, L. (1999) *Water Law and Customary Water Rights in Papua New Guinea,* New Delhi: UBS.

Kalinoe, L. (2001) 'Expressions of Culture: A Cultural Perspective from Papua New Guinea'. WIPO Subregional Workshop on Intellectual Property, Genetic Resources and Traditional Knowledge, Brisbane, Australia.

Kalinoe, L. (2004) 'Legal options for the regulation of intellectual and cultural property in Papua New Guinea', in E. Hirsch and M. Strathern (eds), *Transactions and Creations: Property Debates and the Stimulus of Melanesia,* Oxford: Berghahn.

Kalinoe, Lawrence and Leach, James, eds (2001) *Rationales of Ownership: Ethnographic Studies of Transactions and Claims to Ownership in Contemporary Papua New Guinea.* New Delhi: UBS.

Kingston, Sean (2003) 'Form, attention and a southern New Ireland life cycle', *JRAI* (n.s.) 9: 681–708.

Kirtsoglou, Elisabeth and Theodossopoulos, Dimitrios (2004) '"They are taking our culture away": tourism and culture commodification in the Garifuna community of Roatan Honduras', *Critique of Anthropology*, 24: 135–57.

Küchler, S. (1997) 'Sacrificial economy and its objects', *Journal of Material Culture*, 2: 39–60.

Küchler, S. (2002) *Malanggan: Art, Memory and Sacrifice*. Oxford: Berg.

Leach, James (2003a) *Creative Land: Place and Procreation on the Rai Coast of Papua New Guinea*. Oxford: Berghahn.

Leach, James (2003b) 'Owning creativity: cultural property and the efficacy of Kastom on the Rai coast of PNG', *Journal of Material Culture*, 8: 123–43.

Liep, J., ed. (2001) *Locating Cultural Creativity*. London: Pluto Press.

Macfarlane, Alan (1998) 'The mystery of property: inheritance and industrialization in England and Japan', in C.M. Hann (ed.), *Property Relations: Renewing the Anthropological Tradition*. Cambridge: Cambridge University Press.

McSherry, Corynne (2001) *Who Owns Academic Work? Battling for Control of Intellectual Property*. Cambridge, MA: Harvard University Press.

Merry, S.E. (2001) 'Changing rights, changing culture', in J. Cowan, M.-B. Dembour and R. Wilson (eds), *Culture and Rights: Anthropological Perspectives*. Cambridge: Cambridge University Press.

Moore, Adam (2000) 'Owning genetic information and gene enhancement techniques: why privacy and property rights may undermine social control of the human genome', *Bioethics*, 14: 97–119.

Moran, Katy, King, Steven and Carlson, Thomas (2001) 'Biodiversity prospecting: lessons and prospects', *Ann. Rev. Anthropology*, 30: 505–26.

Morphy, Howard (1995) 'Aboriginal art in a global context', in D. Miller (ed.), *Worlds Apart: Modernity Through the Prism of the Global*. London: Routledge.

Mosko, M. (2002) 'Totem and transaction: the objectification of "tradition" among North Mekeo', *Oceania*, 73 (2): 89–110.

Muehlebach, A. (2001) 'Making place at the United Nations: indigenous cultural politics at the UN Working Group on Indigenous Populations', *Cultural Anthropology*, 16 (3): 415–48.

Myers, F.R. (1991) 'Representing culture: The production of discourse(s) for Aboriginal acrylic paintings', *Cultural Anthropology*, 6: 26–62.

Myers, F.R. (2004) 'Ontologies of the image and economies of exchange', *American Ethnologist*, 31: 5–20.

Nuffield Council on Bioethics (1995) *Human Tissue: Ethical and Legal Issues*. London: Nuffield Council on Bioethics.

Nuffield Council on Bioethics (2002) *The Ethics of Patenting DNA: A Discussion Paper*. London: Nuffield Council on Bioethics.

Okedji, Ruth (2003) 'Development in the Information Age: the importance of copyright', *Bridges*, 18 (8): 15–17, www.ictsd.org.

Patel, S. (1996) 'Can the intellectual property rights system serve the interests of indigenous knowledge?' in S.B. Brush and D. Stabinsky (eds), *Valuing Local Knowledge: Indigenous Peoples and Intellectual Property Rights*. Washington, DC: Island Press.

Posey, D. (1996) *Traditional Resource Rights: International Instruments for Protection and Compensation for Indigenous Peoples and Local Communities*. Gland, Switzerland, and Cambridge: International Union for Conservation of Nature.

Posey, D. and G. Dutfield (1996) *Beyond Intellectual Property: Toward Traditional Resource Rights for Indigenous Peoples and Local Communities*. Ottawa: International Development Reseach Centre.

Pottage, A. (1998) 'The inscription of life in law: genes, parents, and bio-politics', *Modern Law Review*, 61: 740–65.

Puri, K. (2001) 'Draft Model Law for the Pacific' published as *Model Law for the Protection of Traditional Knowledge and Expressions of Culture*, in Working and Information Papers, Second Working Group of Legal Experts on the Protection of Traditional Knowledge and Expressions of Culture, Noumea, New Caledonia, 2003.

Rabinow, P. (1996a) *Making PCR: A Story of Biotechnology*. Chicago: University of Chicago Press.

Rabinow, P. (1996b) *Essays on the Anthropology of Reason*. Princeton, NJ: Princeton University Press.

Radin, M.J. (1996) *Contested Commodities: Trade in Sex, Children, Body Parts and other Things*. Cambridge, MA: Harvard University Press.

Rose, Mark (1993) *Authors and Owners: the Invention of Copyright*. Cambridge, MA: Harvard University Press.

Roulet, F. (1999) *Human Rights and Indigenous Peoples: A Handbook on the UN System*. Copenhagen: International Work Group for Indigenous Affairs.

Rowlands, M. (2000) 'The power of origins: questions of cultural rights', in V. Buchli (ed.), *The Material Culture Reader*. Oxford: Berg.

Royal Society (2003) *Keeping Science Open: The Effects of Intellectual Property Policy on the Conduct of Science*, policy document 02/037. London: Council of The Royal Society.

Rumsey, A. and Weiner, J. eds (2001) *Emplaced Myth: Space, Narrative, and Knowledge in Aboriginal Australia and Papua New Guinea*. Honolulu, HI: University of Hawaii Press.

Schröder, Ingo (2003) 'The political economy of tribalism in North America: neotribal capitalism?' *Anthropological Theory*, 3: 435–56.

Sillitoe, P. (1998) 'The development of indigenous knowledge', *Current Anthropology*, 39 (2): 223–52.

Simet, J. (2000) 'Copyrighting traditional Tolai knowledge?' in K. Whimp and M. Busse (eds), *Protection of Intellectual, Biological and Cultural Property in Papua New Guinea*. Canberra: Asia Pacific Press and Port Moresby: Conservation Melanesia.

Simet, J. (2001) 'Conclusions: reflections on cultural property research', in Karen Sykes (ed.) with J. Simet and S. Kamene, *Culture and Cultural Property in the New Guinea Islands Region: Seven Case Studies*. New Delhi: UBS.

Simet, J. (n.d.) 'Custodians by Obligation'. Paper given to pre-PTC Conference Workshop 'Becoming Heirs: Making Inheritance Self-evident', University of Manchester, 2001.

Simon, B. (n.d.) 'Global Steps to Local Empowerment in the Next Millennium: An Assessment of UNESCO's 1989, *Recommendation on the Safeguarding of Traditional Culture and Folklore*', www.folklife.si. edu/unesco/simon/htm.

Simpson, T. on behalf of the Forest Peoples Programme (1997) *Indigenous Heritage and Self-determination: The Cultural and Intellectual Property Rights of Indigenous Peoples*. Copenhagen: International Work Group for Indigenous Affairs.

Strathern, M. (1996) 'Cutting the network', *Journal of the Royal Anthropological Institute*, 2: 517–35.

Strathern, M. (2004) 'Transactions: an analytical foray', in E. Hirsch and M. Strathern (eds), *Transactions and Creations: Property Debate sand the Stimulus of Melanesia*. Oxford: Berghahn.

Strathern, Marilyn, Carneiro da Cuhna, Manuela, Descola, Philippe, Alberto Afonso, Carlos and Harvey, Penelope (1998) 'Exploitable knowledge belongs to the creators of it: a debate', *Social Anthropology*, 6: 109–26.

Swanson, Timothy, ed. (1995) *Intellectual Property Rights and Biodiversity Conservation: an Interdisciplinary Analysis of the Value of Medicinal Plants*. Cambridge: Cambridge University Press.

Sykes, Karen, ed., with J. Simet and S. Kamene (2001) *Culture and Cultural Property in the New Guinea Islands Region: Seven Case Studies*. New Delhi: UBS.

Tassy, J. and Dambrine, C. (1997) 'Intellectual property rights in support of scientific research', *European Review*, 5: 193–204.

Taylor, M. (2000) 'Foreword', in M. Busse and K. Whimp (eds), *Protection of Intellectual, Biological and Cultural Property in Papua New Guinea*. Canberra: Asia Pacific Press and Port Moresby: Conservation Melanesia.

Tobin, Brendan (2000) 'The search for an interim solution [Peru]', in K. Whimp and M. Busse (eds), *Protection of Intellectual, Biological and Cultural Property in Papua New Guinea*. Canberra: Asia Pacific Press and Port Moresby: Conservation Melanesia.

Toft, Susan, ed. (1997) *Compensation and Resource Development in Papua New Guinea*. Canberra: Australian National University and Port Moresby: Law Reform Commision.

Van Meijl, T. and von Benda-Beckmann, F.L. eds (1999) *Property Rights and Economic Development: Land and Natural Resources in Southeast Asia and Oceania*. London: Kegan Paul.

Verdery, Katherine and Humphrey, Caroline (eds) (2004) *Property in Question: Value Transformation in the Global Economy*. Oxford and New York: Berg.

WCCD (1995) *Our Creative Diversity: Report of the World Commission on Culture and Development*. (Javier Pérez de Cuéllar and others). Paris: UNESCO Publishing.

Whimp, Kathy and Busse, Mark eds (2000) *Protection of Intellectual, Biological and Cultural Property in Papua New Guinea*. Canberra: Asia Pacific Press and Port Moresby: Conservation Melanesia.

Winthrop, R. (2002) 'Exploring cultural: rights: an introduction', in *Cultural Rights and Indigenous Identity in the Americas*, special issue of *Cultural Dynamics*, 14: 115–20.

Woodmansee, Martha (1994) *The Author, Art and the Market: Re-reading the History of Aesthetics*. New York: Columbia University Press.

ACKNOWLEDGEMENTS

The work on which this is based was done largely in the course of the project 'Property, Transactions and Creations: New Economic Relations in the Pacific' (UK Economic and Social Research Council award R000237838, gratefully acknowledged). PTC publications on Melanesia include Kalinoe and Leach (2001); Sykes et al. (2001); Hirsch and Strathern (2004). Texts on which this is based include the introduction to Hirsch and Strathern above; Strathern's chapter in Whimp and Busse (2000); and the 2002 paper 'Divided origins and the arithmetic of ownership', presented to the University of California – Irvine Critical Theory Institute series, 'Futures of Property and Personhood'. Very special thanks for help to write the manuscript to Benedictá Rousseau.

29

HERITAGE AND THE PRESENT PAST

Beverley Butler

We are all too inclined as Lowenthal observes to populate the past with people like ourselves, pursuing the same aims and responding with similar feelings, albeit dressed up in different cultural costumes ... Whether the concern is with people of the past or of the present, otherness is here reduced to the cosmetic variety of consumer choice ...

(Ingold 1996: 204)

My chosen point of departure for this chapter is a debate which took place between the historian David Lowenthal and a group of anthropologists the proposition of which was: 'Is the past a foreign country?' This theme was prompted by a book written by Lowenthal, which is oft-cited as the foundational text of the heritage studies canon. Entitled *The Past is a Foreign Country* (1985), as Lowenthal explains, the volume takes as its guiding metaphor the opening lines of L.P. Hartley's novel *The Go-between*: 'The past is a foreign country. They do things differently there' (Lowenthal 1985: xvi). As such Lowenthal makes an intervention which privileges a model of the 'past' defined in 'difference' from the 'present' as the critical dynamic of his book (*ibid.*). The ensuing debate saw the above participants taking on a 'historical approach' and a 'memorial approach' to the 'past' respectively (Ingold 1996: 202). In so doing, as the chair of the debate Ingold highlights, 'fundamental issues', 'concerning the relationship between past and present, the construal of difference, the awareness of time' and the 'respective modes of history and memory as modes of

apprehending the past or of bringing it to bear in the present' emerge as core preoccupations (Ingold 1996: 201–2).

In what follows I take these key shifts accessed by the debate as the broad critical framework from which to review the main preoccupations of heritage studies (past, present, future) and to readdress the core question 'What constitutes heritage and heritage value?' My approach has been to critically rehearse the dominant explanatory models and metaphors put forward by various contributors, which, as my text illustrates, operate across theoretical and empirical understandings of heritage, across a number of different registers (for example, ideological, metaphysical) and across North-South paradigms and contexts. As such, the first part, critically rehearses the 'historical approach' to the 'past' in order to narrate the 'rise of heritage' within the 'Western imagination' and within the academy. The second, by way of contrast, uses the 'memorial approach' as a starting point to chart out 'alternative' or 'parallel' heritages. Writ large, this shift of focus takes me from a discussion of the 'past as a foreign country' to that of heritage as a powerful resource for 'creating a future' and to the recognition of how a fundamental reconceptualization of heritage is uniquely placed not only to address claims about identity, ancestry and cultural transmission but to engage with key moral-ethical issues to our times: notably, conceptualization of 'otherness' and the capacity for 'othering' and, as such, core qualities of 'what it is to be human'.

THE HISTORICAL APPROACH: HERITAGE IN THE 'WESTERN IMAGINATION'

Inside the Academy: Establishing the Canon

The standard means of reviewing the 'rise of heritage' is to begin by charting this 'rise' in terms of the emergence of 'heritage' as a 'new' discipline establishing itself within academia. This is achieved by tracing the aforementioned 'historical approach' in terms of formative intellectual links made by historians from the 1960s and 1970s onwards in their critical study of the 'past' and by mapping the increased interest in the related studies of 'tradition', 'landscape', 'identity' and 'nation' to the dynamics of 'nostalgia', 'authenticity' 'origins', 'time', 'place' (for example, Lynch 1972, Plumb 1973, Blythe 1969; see Merriman 1996 for a review). The initial focus of these authors' critical attention has typically been upon the Euro-North American academic context and upon an historical understanding of the 'construction' or 'invention' of heritage in the 'Western' imagination. Lowenthal's canonical text *The Past is a Foreign Country* (1985), as the author himself states, is influenced by these above scholarly shifts which also provided the chief motivation for his follow-up text *The Heritage Crusade – and the Spoils of History* (1996), which appeared over a decade later.

As previously stated, Lowenthal's specific mobilization of a model or metaphor of the 'past' defined in 'difference' from the 'present' is important. It allows him to take forward fellow historian Plumb's (1973) pronouncement on the 'death of the past' – a 'death' which is understood as synonymous with the shift from a pre-industrial to an ever increasingly industrialized, urbanized modernity – in order, more specifically, to address the subsequent resurrection and new commodifications of the 'past'. Lowenthal's critical focus thus engages with a certain paradox: 'to show how the past, once virtually indistinguishable from the present [i.e. pre-industrial revolution], has become an ever more foreign realm, yet one increasingly infused by the present' (Lowenthal 1985: xxv). His emphasis then is upon a certain popular 'turn to the past' increasingly expressed in the material objectification and 'preservation' of the 'vestiges of history' in the form of monuments, museums, sites which have come to characterize a dominant 'Eurocentric' definition of what constitutes 'the heritage' (*ibid.*).

Moreover, in order to interrogate this 'turn to the past' Lowenthal focuses upon key 'epochs' to emphasize how the 'Western' imagination has become bound up in the establishment of lines of cultural transmission and claims to ancestry across ancient and modern worlds. His focus thus highlights what are invested as nodal points of rupture and reinvention: the Renaissance, the Enlightenment; nineteenth-century 'Victorian' Britain and revolutionary and post-revolutionary America (Lowenthal 1985: xx–xxi). In critically rehearsing this trajectory I want to place alongside Lowenthal's text other 'heritage' texts similarly committed to developing these themes.

Heritage Revivalism and Redemption

Returning to the above-mentioned nodal points, the Renaissance is profiled by authors as an epoch synonymous with the often 'creative' reclamation of the 'archetypes of antiquity' which subsequently 'infused the whole of European culture' and in so doing secured the 'West' the acquisition of a 'past' notably in the form of a classical civilizational pedigree and ancestry (*ibid.*). A potent example here is that of the canonization of the ancient Alexandrina Mouseion/library as 'archetype' and 'ancient ancestor institution' (Butler 2001a, b, 2003: see also Findlen 2000). This act of reclamation in turn highlights core foundational features of traditional heritage discourse. A key dynamic here is that what has become known as the 'Alexandrina paradigm' is underpinned by a 'myth of return and redemption' (cf. Foucault 1964). As such, this canonization of Alexandria can be seen as a particularization of a more general sense in which the 'West' invests heritage discourse as a 'redemptive formula' and as a medium by which to mythologize, reclaim and repossess 'lost' pasts, imagined homelands, ancient Golden Ages and to re-engage with 'roots' and 'origins'.

This wider 'myth of return and redemption' also reveals a further core concern of heritage discourse: that which holds in tension an initial interest in a return to the 'past' as a resource for intellectual, literary, metaphorical and metaphysical projects of retrievalism and that which is concerned with heritage revivalism as synonymous with literal, material objectification of the past. The former position sees the 'past' invested as a resource for spiritual/metaphysical refuge and renewal, as a quarry for 'ideas' and 'ideals' and for the redemption of a 'lost' authenticity of self/self-group. It is then with the forward march of modernity that 'heritage' acquires its now dominant associations with more material substance and monumentality. As Lowenthal clarifies, in the pre-industrial revolution period the 'physical remains' of 'classical vestiges' suffered a certain neglect or even destruction when mined by the 'West' for its own 'works' rather than protected 'against pillage and loss' (Lowenthal 1985: xvi).

The specific and 'creative' reclamation of the 'Alexandria paradigm' has thus seen the ancient Alexandrina objectified as the point of origin and 'template' for archival and museum institutions from the Renaissance onwards (notably the British Museum and Louvre; see Lewis 1992: 10) and as the icon from which the traditional 'salvage' paradigm of heritage loss and preservation establishes its roots (Lowenthal 1985: 67). Crucially too, this act of canonization is motivated by what is characterized as the traumatic 'loss' of the ancestor institution, the result, it is argued, of an originary act of iconoclasm (ibid.). The event embeds the 'Alexandrina paradigm' in an entropic poetics of melancholy, nostalgia and loss which draws from Aristotelian and Platonic philosophical models and which is also the mechanism which gives birth to the repetitive desire to rebuild the institution 'on the ruins' (Butler 2003). In this wider process of what might be best termed as the 'Westernization' of the origins and roots of heritage discourse the broader foundational values of the classical world – as the 'birthplace', for example, of 'universalism', 'democracy', 'civilization' 'humanism' and 'cosmopolitanism' – are also essentialized as core heritage values (ibid.) and as key motivations underpinning modernity's ongoing 'heritage crusades' (Lowenthal 1996).

Heritage Enlightenment

It is with the coming of the Enlightenment that what is couched as the ongoing relationship or 'quarrel between Ancients and Moderns' is subsequently re-expressed as dialectic of 'reverence' and 'rejection' (Lowenthal 1996: xx–xxi). Lowenthal, for example, argues that the 'classical tradition' while remaining 'the font of veneration' is increasingly pitched in relationships with modernity's new loci of power and authority (ibid.). This sees authors characterize the 'rise of heritage' as inextricably bound up with the rise of science, the decline of religious authority and the establishment of the meta-narratives such as discourses of progress and rationality. Modernity and the 'West' as synonymous with

the forward march of history, of capital and of imperial ambition are highlighted as central to this context (see Walsh 1992). As such one can trace the complex interactions in the construction of heritage discourse across rational, romantic and colonial imaginations. Moreover, the crux of this interaction relates to experiences of rupture, displacement and the concomitant 'traumatization of temporality' synonymous with episodes of radical change (ibid.). The effects of revolution – both political and industrial – are, for example, credited with bringing crisis to notions of 'identity', 'place' and to notions of the 'past' (ibid.). Urban migration, the creation of new industrial landscape and ideals of nationhood and citizenship which notably the French revolution ushers in are understood as inextricably bound up in experiences of 'time-space compression' which exacerbate modernity's experiences of rootlessness, rupture, displacement and estrangement (ibid.; see also Lowenthal 1985).

Again these changes are seen to encompass both metaphysical and more literal experiences of 'loss' and 'dislocation' as both 'epistemological' certainties and 'traditional' modes of life are put into crisis in the face of the unprecented pace of change and trauma affecting both 'real' and 'ontological' worlds (Walsh 1992; Maleuvre 1999). This results in what is regarded as an overdetermined investment in the 'redemptive' aspect of heritage. This creates a certain paradoxical context which sees heritage bound up in both desires to 'revive' (or more clearly, as Hobsbawm et al. (1993) demonstrate, 'invent') 'tradition' and to 'nationalize' its monumental vestiges. The museum and the 'creation' of monumental heritage landscapes are credited as key 'emblems' of modernity and of the 'imagined community' of nationhood (Anderson 1991). Heritage as buoyed up on the ebullience and confidence synonymous with modernity's nation and empire building is, however, undercut by the recognition that the 'redemption' offered by a return to the 'past' is only ever partial (Maleuvre 1999: 1).

This, in turn, leads some authors to highlight the intellectual empathetic identification made by philosophers between the 'rise of heritage' and recognition of the impossibility of finding metaphysical comfort and cure capable of encompassing the metaphysical trauma synonymous with modernity's experience and intellectualization of the opening up of human and historical consciousness (ibid.). As such, heritage and archival spaces emerge as modernity's privileged medium for reflecting upon the human condition and for addressing the core question: 'What is it to be human?' (cf. Bazin 1967; Maleuvre 1999). For others it is poof that heritage is a 'transitory enchantment' amid a wider and more negative economy of 'Weberian disenchantment' (Walsh 1992: 58). It is here too that the death of the 'past' is bound up in anxieties regarding the death of the 'self' with the subsequent turn to heritage indicative of attempts to deny, displace – and possibly mediate and manipulate – the reality of mortality and/or to monumentalize 'oneself'/'self-group' as a strategy of securing a form of immortality (Huyssen 1995).

Nostalgia and Authenticity

It is from this complex context that authors highlight the deployment of certain motifs and metaphors which are regarded as central to the legitimation of 'Western' heritage concepts and to the subsequent development of heritage practice. Notions of 'nostalgia' and 'authenticity' – or more correctly a nostalgia for authenticity – are highlighted for particular attention as core heritage values and as key underpinning and motivating dynamics of modernity's escalating desire for roots and origins. The concept of nostalgia, for example, is analysed by authors etymologically – *nostos*, meaning 'return to the native land', and *algos*, meaning 'grief' – and placed in the context not only of relationships between modernity's sense of cultural nostalgia for its 'Greek' childhood but of different historical expressions (Lowenthal 1985: 10). Some authors, for example, have traced references to 'nostalgia' both within antiquity – for example, in the writings of Aristotle, more specifically Plato, and in the texts of Homer and Virgil in terms of their preoccupation with the 'heroic, pastoral past' (*ibid.*; see also Bazin 1967) – and the nostalgia for antiquity. In the latter category, authors include thinkers such as Petrarch, whose characterization of nostalgia reiterated the concept of the 'past as refuge' (Lowenthal 1985: 8).

Emphasis is also placed upon the seventeenth-century use of the term to describe a 'physical complaint' and an 'illness' diagnosed as 'common' in those who 'once away from their native land … languished, wasted away and even perished' (Lowenthal 1985: 10). A condition, authors argue, synonymous with displacement through war and economic rupture (Gregory 1998: 31). In this sense the disease can be seen as a symptomization of the 'physical and emotional violence that characterised the history of modernity' and the concomitant 'desire of homecoming' (*ibid.*). As critics show 'nostalgia' gained medical currency during the eighteenth and nineteenth centuries, where it was understood as part of a melancholic pathology and as such was used as a legitimate medical diagnosis until the Second World War (Lowenthal 1985: 11). What from Hegel through Darwin, Marx and Freud have been referred to as intellectual 'pogroms on nostalgia' have resulted in a 'negative', banalized version of nostalgia as a 'cultural pathology' related to a society's inability to cope with the present (Gregory 1998: 31). As Lowenthal has it: nostalgia is 'the universal catchword for looking back' (Lowenthal 1985: 4). Critical rearticulations of the term have, in turn, drawn out the oppressive colonizing aspects of this trope and are best expressed in Rosaldo's characterization of 'colonial nostalgia' (Rosaldo 1989). A specific and enduring connection, however, is made between the Romantic movement and nostalgia, which not only see this motif mobilized as a reaction and resistance to the rise of rational discourse but, as outlined below, is it bound up in the literalization of the search for authenticity (Lowenthal 1985: xvii).

The concept of 'authenticity' has similarly been analysed in terms of an initial affirmation of ancient 'Greek' culture as the space of origin, originality and thus authenticity (McBryde 1997). These dynamics are subsequently pitched in relationships to the Roman 'copy' and with notions of the 'imitation' and 'fake' (*ibid.*). The etymological term *authenticus* is also used to illustrate links between the notion of 'originality' and that of the 'author' and 'authority' (*ibid.*). Here the dynamic of the collective creative emulation of ancient archetypes synonymous with the Renaissance period becomes eclipsed by the construction of a science of preservation and conservation. Not only does 'authenticity' subsequently undergo rationalization to emerge as an 'objective' absolute category but custodial authority is given to a (first amateur and subsequently professionalized) 'expert' culture and to an emergent practice bound up in re-inscribing 'authenticity' within discourses of scientific proof and as legitimated in the material analysis, in particular, of artefacts and monuments (Lowenthal 1996: 385). Within this context emergent canons of taste and expertise are crucial too in legitimating the 'auratic' quality of the art work and the concept of the individual (male) genius as creator (cf. Benjamin 1968). It is here that a historical anti-heritage critique or intellectual museumophobia takes root and becomes preoccupied with the metaphysical implications of the obvious 'inauthenticity' as they see it of such domains (Maleuvre 1999; Huyssen 1995).

As previously stated, the search for authenticity does, however, become increasingly bound up in its 'territorialization' as heritage. The Romantic movement's own preoccupation with landscape, nature, the 'cult of the ruins', the 'relic' and the 'souvenir' are crucial here, as is the authentication of vernacular architecture and settings. Here, critics draw out the importance of the site established in 1873 by Artur Hazelius at Skansen (Lowenthal 1985: xvii). The objective of this 'proto-heritage' project was to salvage local buildings, artefacts and folklore traditions which were disappearing throughout Scandinavia owing to changes wrought by industrialization. Bolstering patriotism was a further aim of this and related projects which are seen as indicative of European and North American attempts to define nation heritage icons at both local (folk life) and (elite) state level (see Walsh 1992: 95–7). Selecting and authenticating national Golden Ages has seen, for example, the German Romantics privileging of the Middle Ages, for example, 'as a site of redeemed culture and future utopia' and as the 'bedrock of German nationalism' (Huyssen 1995: 19). It is with the shift into the twentieth century that the definitions of heritage which originated from legal concepts of 'inheritance' as personal wealth typically handed down through family units became aligned to a concept of public patrimony. As Lowenthal comments, not only did this lead to people 'conceiv[ing] of the past as a different realm' but this 'new role heightened concern to save relics and restore monuments as emblems of communal identity, continuity and aspiration' (Lowenthal 1985: xvi).

Heritage Crusades and Religious Metaphors

Lowenthal's text which follows fully centres upon 'heritage' in its late twentieth-century transformation from an 'elite preoccupation into a major crusade to save and celebrate all that we inherit from the past' '(Lowenthal 1996: 2). Mobilizing a powerful 'religious' metaphor, Lowenthal argues, 'heritage relies on revealed faith rather than rational proof (*ibid.*). Lowenthal's thesis echoes other theorists who have similarly positioned 'heritage' as a form of 'secular religion' (cf. Horne 1984; Duncan 1995). These texts have given further critical depth to the relationship of the 'rise of heritage' to modernity's experience of secularization, to the

reorganization of religious experience and to the redeployment of its 'civilizing rituals' and theological languages. As such critics draw out how this transfer of power and authority was made to serve the 'ideological needs of the emerging bourgeois' and to substantiate the nation state, civic democracies and reproduce 'good' citizens (Duncan 1995: 7–8).

In the contemporary context the museum as 'secular shrine' and 'sacrilized' heritage landscapes (cf. MacCannell 1978/1989)[1] are situated by such authors as 'stations' which map out a 'redemptive' course for the performance of modernity's heritage crusades. Horne's analysis of Europe as a 'great museum', for example, demonstrates how former European pilgrim routes are now populated by 'tourist pilgrims' armed with travel guides as 'devotional texts' (Horne 1984: 1). In his critical commentary on the then Cold War ideological polarizations of context he explores how communist and capitalist political cultures manipulate heritage in specific commodifications of power which see them inscribe their own 'ceremonial agenda' on the landscape and similarly on 'the people' (Horne 1984: 3). The patriarchal nature of heritage commodification is also highlighted, as Horne points out, in that apart from the 'Virgin Mary and Joan of Arc' there is an absence of female heritage figures (Horne 1984: 4). Moreover, unlike the stated aspiration of heritage as a vehicle of humanism, Horne concludes with the need to challenge the negative, alienating aspects of heritage tourism, which he characterizes as synonymous with human life 'drained of cultural meanings' (Horne 1984: 249).

Intellectual Ancestors and Heritage as Commodity

An exploration of the methodologies which underpin these texts and the emergent critical study of heritage shows that alongside historians preoccupied with historical conceptualizations of the 'past' are critics who engage with the broader intellectual shifts taking place within the social sciences and draw from, among others, Marxist, sociological, postmodern, post-structuralist and anthropological theories as alternative explanatory models. It is, however, the Marxist-influenced critiques (which Duncan 1995 and Horne 1984 share an intellectual engagement with) that are mobilized initially by authors to articulate more explicitly the political/ideological agendas which dominate the 'rise of heritage'. This genre of critique – led by what one critic refers to as the 'lure of polemics' – is regarded as 'as valid' for the analysis of heritage *vis-à-vis* 'the imperialist past' as it is 'in the Age of Corporate Sponsorship' (Huyssen 1995: 16). This early canon of 'ideological' critiques has, therefore, done much to challenge, problematize and politicize the assumed neutrality of culture and heritage and has been particularly effective in the analysis of the European and North American museum and heritage boom of the 1970s and 1980s. (See Huyssen 1995 and Merriman 1991 for a critical review.)

Ground-breaking papers in this canon include Marxist interpretations of heritage sites such as Colonial Williamsburg by Leone (1973) and Wallace (1981) (see Merriman 1991: 14–16). The application of Althusserian frameworks and the positioning of heritage and cultural institutions as 'part of "Repressive State Apparatus"' have likewise drawn out the use of heritage to legitimate 'top down' 'dominant ideology' (see Meltzer 1985 on the National Air and Space Museum, Washington; Merriman 1991: 16). From these critical positions the above authors show that heritage ideology is used variously to substantiate the 'American Dream' (*ibid.*). These critiques were also accompanied by a first wave of feminist critiques and texts which highlight the heritage culture's complicity in 'empire' and in oppressive characterizations of 'race' and cultural difference (see Simpson 1996 for a critical review). The rejectionism, pessimism and theoretical negativity of these critiques which see heritage as 'bad faith', 'false consciousness' and as 'social control' (see Merriman 1991: 16), as a 'patriarchal' construct (Porter 1996) and a 'racist' colonial enterprise thus have been noted (Coombes 1994).

Furthermore, while these studies were to be offset by others committed to highlighting the 'more positive and potentially liberating role' of heritage (Merriman 1991: 17) critics have claimed that the 'very bad press' given by intellectuals from both 'right and left, though especially perhaps the latter' to heritage is linked in turn to the aforementioned historical 'anti-heritage' discourse and intellectual 'museumophobia' (Huyssen 1995: 18–19). Not only are Nietzsche and Marx's characterizations of the 'past as burden and nightmare' regarded as major interventions within this critical genealogy but the Frankfurt school of critical theory has been identified as a highly symbolic 'intellectual' ancestor (*ibid.*). Critics draw out the importance of Adorno's characterization of the deathly 'museal' consciousness (Adorno 1981) and Benjamin's unveiling of the quasi-religious

rituals and 'auratic' qualities of the museum space to new intellectual explorations of 'authenticity' and 'ritual agenda' and in terms of critical concerns with both the negative and more 'liberating' aspects of technical/'mechanical reproduction' (Benjamin 1968).

Heritage critiques also need to be placed in the broader context of the Frankfurt school's radical critique of modernity. The famous characterization of the Enlightenment project as 'mass deception' and the complicity of its associated ideologies of 'progress', 'objectivity', 'modernization', 'universalism' in projects of totalitarianism have, as Huyssen states, revealed how heritage and museological commodification too are implicated in the 'complexities of fascism and Third International communism' (Huyssen 1995: 17). It is, however, the characterization and commodification of 'mass culture' as synonymous with a 'culture industry' and as ultimately bound up in the 'preservation of capitalism' that emerges as an ongoing critical theme (Walsh 1992: 64). For example, the strategic choice of a book title made by the journalist/academic Hewison allowed him to ground his specific rallying call to resist the massive commercialization and commodification of contemporary culture in the Frankfurt school critical genealogy. As such his *The Heritage Industry: Britain in a Climate of Decline* (1987) was a clear echo of Horkheimer and Adorno's *The Culture Industry* (1979) and is a text which has come to symbolize the most recent revival of the 'anti-heritage' thesis.

Hewison was one of a number of critics or 'heritage baiters' (cf. Samuel 1994: 259) (these included left-wing academics and media commentators) in the UK context, who together were responsible for the production of a series of polemics which drew out the complicities between the 'heritage boom' of the 1980s and new forms of political commodification inextricably linked to the rise of the New Right. Wright's *On Living in an old country* (1985), for example, characterizes Britain as 'a society which seemed to be making not just a virtue out of the past but a set of political principles' (Wright 1985: 1). The specific focus of what has become known as the 'heritage debate' was upon a context of rapid change in which the growth of profit-making heritage centres, open-air museums, heritage attractions at an unprecedented rate saw the vast 'heritagization' of both rural and newly redundant urban landscapes. Again in the UK context authors not only regarded this as symptomatic of a country in decline and of a society unable to face the future but identified specific falsifications of history motivated by new 'top-down' expressions of 'vulgar nationalism' and 'jingoism' in which the desire to manipulate a 'deep Englishness' gives substance not only to rampant Europhobia but also to a wider attack on multiculturalism and to the mobilization of an 'anti-foreign/anti-asylum' discourse which helped give political substance and a reality to 'Fortress Europe' (see Walsh 1992; Samuel 1994; Hall 2000). Concomitant analyses of European – notably German and French – and US contexts drew out the same major themes and collectively have critically defined the 'heritage debate' as a key contour of the Euro-North American 'culture wars' (see Sherman and Rogoff 1994; Lowenthal 1996; Huyssen 1995).

Postmodern Heritage

Related theorizations of the above dynamics have opened up further intellectual-political analyses by specifically positioning the 'heritage debate' and the 'policies of the new right' as symptomatic of the wider 'postmodern condition' (Walsh 1992: 61). As Huyssen states this stages the 'anti-heritage' debate as 'the latest instance of the *quarrel* [specifically recast as a] battle between moderns and postmoderns' (Huyssen 1995). Heritage commodification is subsequently pitched in relationships with what Walsh defines as 'the world of the "post"' – a 'world' simultaneously 'postmodern, post-ethical, post-moral' (Walsh 1992: 2) – and with what Huyssen further refers to as the 'end of everything discourse' (Huyssen 1995: 13). Here the broad characterization emerges of 'postmodernity' as synonymous with the New Right belief (cf. Fukyama 1992) that the 'capitalist West' has achieved a 'position of unparalleled supremacy in both space and time', thus signalling 'the end of history' and confidence in the assertion that the 'American Dream is now a reality' (Walsh 1992: 67). Authors have responded by mapping out the more nightmarish implications of a postmodern landscape in which the predominant motif/metaphor to emerge is that of the hyper-reality and simulated spectacles and of the 'theme park' (Walsh 1992: 113–15).

Baudrillard, dubbed the 'postmodern prophet of doom', and his genre of nihilistic hypercriticism are mobilized by authors alongside Eco's *Faith in Fakes: Travels in Hyperreality in the United States* (1986) in order to draw out how heritage emerges as empty-signifier exhibiting the crisis in which 'reality' has been lost to an 'inauthenticity' theorized as both a 'dehistoricization' and a simultaneous 'generation by models of a real without origin or reality' (Baudrillard, quoted in Walsh 1992: 58) and expressed as a 'collection of simulations and simulacra' synonymous with the simultaneous death of nostalgia and birth of 'hyper-nostalgia' (Walsh 1992: 58–9). Moreover, this postmodern 'themepark' is located within a genealogy which links Skansen as 'proto-heritage' and as the 'model' for Colonial Williamsburg and Greenfield Village (both of which are understood as, 'mythical place[s] built on the whims and dreams of the world's greatest capitalist', i.e. Rockefeller and Ford respectively): these latter sites, in turn, are seen as a 'prophecy of postmodern heritage' and as the 'prompt' for the development in 1955 of 'Walt Disney's theme park development' (Walsh 1992: 95–7).

The motif of 'Disneyfication' can also be linked to further theorizations of the 'museal sensibility'. The theorist Jeudy, for example, analyses a postmodern force of 'musealization' in terms of its commodification of 'whole industrial regions', 'inner cities' and in terms of the 'self-musealisation' synonymous with new technological consumptions of self bound up in new 'simulation apparatus' (Huyssen 1995: 30–1). For critics such as Walsh and Huyssen this critique is undertaken in order to draw out the neo-colonizing aspect 'time-space compression' at stake which, in turn, is used to legitimate the 'superiority of one culture [the West] over all others in space and time' (Walsh 1992: 67) simultaneously re-establishing them as 'cultural mediators' (Huyssen 1995: 35). It is here too that Walsh argues the need to return to the political 'real' in order to bring to bear the complicities of the heritage discourse in contemporary neo-colonial violence synonymous with 'society's unquestioning acceptance of the need to go to war' (Walsh 1992: 2).[2] Both authors ultimately seek to identify some critical role for heritage in the future. For Huyssen this is located in the 'opening spaces for reflection and counter-hegemonic memory' (Huyssen 1995: 15) and as a means to find an effective mode of cultural mediation 'in an environment in which demands for multiculturalism and the realities of migrations and demographic shifts clash increasingly with ethnic strife, culturalist racisms, and a general resurgence of nationalism and xenophobia' (Huyssen 1995: 35). While for Walsh (mobilizing Jameson's critical perspectives regarding the reclamation of the 'real' and of 'place') this is located in a certain strategic revivalism of heritage as a means to reinstate a 'temporal depth' and a sense of place (Walsh 1992: 150).

Sociological Critiques and Reinvestment

The above shifts also show a certain relationship with a broader critical shift from heritage rejectionism to reinvestment. Alongside the aforementioned 'ideological critiques' can be sociological critiques, for example, which position heritage and museum spaces as sites for the 'reorganisation of cultural capital' (Huyssen 1995: 17). These, in turn, have been responsible for a series of critiques which address 'reception theory' (influenced by the work of Bourdieu) in the form of visitor surveys – and increasingly non-visitor surveys – in order to reshape heritage to address objectives of access, empowerment and inclusion (see Merriman 1989; Hooper-Greenhill 2001).

An initial impetus for this transformation came from within the museum world and with calls for the definition of a 'new' museology (capable of spanning both theoretical (Vergo 1989) and practical worlds (Mayrand 1985)). This movement is synonymous too with the emergence of the 'eco-museum', a critical museological model conceived of as an 'anti-museum', which inverts the notion of the museum as classical temple and agent of decontextualization in favour of a reconceptualization of the museum within its 'authentic' contextualized landscape (see Walsh 1992: 161–4). Here then the concepts of the museum and site merge. In terms of intellectual shifts as Walsh expands further, 'The origin of the eco-museum and deconstruction are the same ...' Not only was this bound up in the 'desire to "deconstruct" the "totalization" of government' (and more specifically the French government) and as synonymous with the 'emergence of post-structuralism' but also, he argues, in the 'light of the failure of the radical politics of mid to late 1960s, the earlier war in Algiers, and the break-up of the Empire ...' (Walsh 1992: 162). While theorists support the 'democratization of access to the past' this eco-museum brings with it calls for the extension of such a vision to encompass heritage proper as a category reconceptualized beyond or away from its rejection as 'Disneyfied' ideology (Walsh 1992: 170).

The historian Samuel more recently reiterated this position by challenging the above rehearsed 'heritage baiters' polemical attacks on the 'heritage industry' by drawing out the emergence of alternative characterizations of heritage created 'by the "people"' and as such he argues these are a 'democratic force' which offers points of access to 'ordinary people' and constructs 'a wider form of belonging' and a strategy for constructing a 'pluralist society' (Samuel 1994: 259). His largely celebratory thesis can be placed, for example, alongside Hall's critical investigation of the issues at stake in the relationship between heritage, cultural diversity and inclusion (Hall 2000).

The formation of Heritage Studies within the academy has similarly had a troubled journey from rejectionism to reinvestment. As Huyssen argues, the museum 'changed from its role as whipping boy to favourite son in the family of cultural institutions' (Huyssen 1995: 14) and as such has undergone a radical transformation which has seen Museum Studies consolidate itself within the academy as a vocational, training course and increasingly as a subject for theorization across disciplinary divides. This process has in turn legitimated and been legitimated by the professionalization of the museum world. The museum culture in response initially defined itself in difference from heritage and as such the term held little credibility within the professional and academy worlds. (In the latter domain heritage was largely still regarded by many as a 'Disney' subject.) Newer shifts, however, have seen the growth of both postgraduate and undergraduate heritage courses which have signalled a new phase of engagement. Heritage has thus been recouped as an intellectualized dynamic within the academy while recognition has been given to heritage discourse as a crucial component of globalized futures not only in terms of job markets but as a medium, for example, of human and cultural rights.

As Lowenthal argues 'the search for heritage' dominates the contemporary global context. As such he argues that the once 'Western'/Eurocentric preoccupation with 'roots and origins' has now become an international phenomena as 'massive migration sharpens nostalgia' and the trauma of 'refugee exodus' has defined new 'heritage-hungry' constituencies (Lowenthal 1996: 9). Here, he argues, are not only African-Americans and Italian-Americans, for example, part of this context but 'Palestinians, Liberians, Rwandans and Bosnians' are also part of this contemporary heritage constituency (*ibid*.). One is, however, left with the struggle of opening up of the above largely 'Westernized' heritage discourse with its 'Eurocentric' base to a wider global context – it is this context I address in part two.

THE MEMORIAL APPROACH: 'ALTERNATIVE' AND 'PARALLEL' HERITAGES

To speak of the past as a foreign country is to make a metaphorical statement about difference. ... always caught between the twin poles of anodyne difference and absolute otherness. Remaining mindful of these poles we must steer a cause between them as best we can. To pretend that the differences highlighted by the metaphor are ephemeral is a delusion.

(Harvey, in Ingold 1996: 224).

Anthropologizing Heritage: 'Memorial' Approaches

As stated in my introduction, in this second part of the chapter I want to return to the debate staged between Lowenthal and anthropologists which critically addresses the question: 'is the past a foreign country?' in order to use this as a framework from which to draw out new and alternative concepts and models for the theorization of heritage discourse. At stake is a radical redefinition of 'what constitutes heritage' and 'heritage value' and a critical shift of focus away from Eurocentic models, frames and sources and from the 'Western' academy's intellectual preoccupations with internal identity crises – and pronouncements of its own 'death' and 'resurrection' (cf. Huyssen 1995: 33) and a movement towards understanding alternative models of cultural transmission, ancestry and memory work. Anthropological understandings of memory work, for example, crucially bring into view 'non-Western' contexts, concepts and practices and in so doing pose questions regarding relationships to the 'other' and the capacity for 'othering' which are central to this critical context. As such, the focus on the 'memorial approach' to the 'past' also provides a means to bring into focus what can be best be described as 'alternative' or 'parallel' heritages and alternative framings of 'difference'.

Feeley-Harnik, in defining the 'memorial approach', begins by making her own critical return to L.P. Hartley's novel in order to engage in a radical refocusing of issues. Here, she argues, 'the central theme of his [Hartley's] story is not the past as a foreign country, but how the past has come to seem that way, owing to energetic forgetting and desperate attempts to deaden feeling. And it is about the going-between from which new life

comes' (Feeley-Harnik, in Ingold 1996: 212). Highlighting relationships between the key dynamics of memory work, forgetting, embodiment and personhood, she continues, 'we have no knowledge of past *people* except through present people; we have no way of knowing others except through ourselves' (*ibid*.), with Ingold arguing further that the 'placement' of 'mind and body' in the 'world presupposes a history of past relationships. Enfolded in the consciousness of the self, as its memory, this past is active and present' (Ingold 1996: 204).

Calls for adoption of the 'memorial' approach also manifest as calls for 'a radical critique of the orthodox notion, in cognitive psychology, of memory as a *store*, a cabinet of images and recollections from which the mind can pull out whatever it needs for different purposes' and its underpinning Eurocentric schema (*ibid*.). The point is reiterated by Küchler when seconding the motion: 'we have also to do away with the idea contained in the notion that the past is "stored" in a distant, "foreign" place waiting to be opened up through selective recollection' (Küchler, in Ingold 1996: 226–7). She argues rather that 'The presenting of the past in memory is relevant in the sense that it is self-relational and thus involved in the fashioning of identity, but this in itself forms a predisposition for certain aspects of the past to be incorporated within personal or cultural history' (*ibid*.).

Moreover, the 'memorialist' anthropological concern with 'the presenting of the past in memory' is detailed further as a concern with various 'acts of recollection' and 'commemoration' – 'in which events which actually took place in the past are represented (literally made present again) whether in writing, oral narrative, monumental sculpture or dramatic performance' (Ingold 1996: 202). This approach highlights how so-called 'authentic reconstruction' synonymous with the dominant heritage forms outlined in section one 'far from bringing the past to bear in the present, tends to highlight the disjunction' (Ingold 1996: 203). It is here that Feeley-Harnik privileges alternative 'approaches to memory' (including 'ecological approaches') as a means to go beyond 'past'/'present' dichotomies ('old' universalisms and 'new' relativisms) to engage with 'non-Western' expressions of cultural transmission and memory work (Feeley-Harnik, in Ingold 1996: 213–4). Here, for example, she refers to the 'weeping "bird sound word" songs of Kaluli funerals and *gisalo* ceremonies' to illustrate alternative paradigms which, she states, 'evoke powerful images of landscapes, paths and places through which, as they "harden" in the course of the singing, living people reconnect with their ancestors in seen and unseen worlds' (*ibid.*). These practices can also be understood as alternative means of understanding a core heritage dynamic: that of reconnecting to ancestors. As such, this can be set alongside the aforementioned 'historical approach' and 'Western' meta-genealogies which in cultural-historiographic terms, for example, have seen the privileging of classical origins, 'Greek memory' and Aristotelian concepts of culture as a means to define and 'reconnect' to ancestry.[3]

The 'memorialist' approach is also crucial in problematizing further key concepts that underpin the 'historical approach'. Moreover, further core heritage motifs such as the directionality of 'time's arrows' and the 'redemptive formula' are highlighted for critical attention (Feeley-Harnik, in Ingold 1996: 217–18). While Feeley-Harnik rehearses how European 'past-to-present directional histories' are associated with bringing 'particular kinds of redemption in territorially defined states', she challenges this paradigm by arguing, 'I see no clear direction, no foreign country against which we might see or measure our redemptive nativity, as it were – our renewed becoming' (*ibid.*). Here the Holocaust is singled out for discussion as a powerful indicator of the 'controversy' concerning the 'ability to claim that the "past" exists at all' (*ibid.*). Questions of the relative merit of 'evidence' in terms of 'conventional historical data', 'archival documents' and the 'substantial convictions' of people 'whose memories are divisible from their flesh and blood' (*ibid.*) are critically discussed. She argues, 'For North Americans and Europeans, these are not remote questions: they are concretely embodied in people,' notably, survivors (*ibid.*). These discussions are placed within her wider call for an understanding of what she terms 'the placedness of time' (Feeley-Harnik, in Ingold 1996: 216). Here she states, 'The past is not a foreign or distant country; it is the very ground on which, in which, with which we stand, move and otherwise interact; out of which we continually regenerate ourselves in relations with others, partly through distanciation' (*ibid.*). Her illustrations focus upon other forms of traumatic pasts, for example Malagasy 'pasts' and experiences of slavery, and in so doing reject the dominant focus on 'space-time' relationships in favour of centring issues upon the 'appropriation of land' (*ibid.*).

A shared desire subsequently emerges in terms of how the political 'real' operates across these two 'historical' and 'memorialist' approaches. In critical support of Lowenthal's motion, Harvey intervenes to reiterate Eric Wolf's call for anthropologists 'to discover history' (Harvey, in Ingold 1996: 222). She thus attempts to offer an alternative understanding of the 'past' and of heritage to that operating at the level of international 'Expo' culture which she sees as promoting a 'tasteful, sanitised ubiquitous difference that we produce for ourselves, in the vicious circle of what has been called "postplural nostalgia" where the innovations and changes that produce variety have simultaneously destroyed tradition, convention and choice' (Harvey, in Ingold 1996: 220). She continues, '[Wolf] stressed, that he was not referring to "Western" history divided into separate nations ... but the contacts, connections, linkages and interrelationships' (Harvey, in Ingold 1996: 222–3). Harvey states her interest is rather in how 'memory operates to humanise' such interrelationships while also arguing the strategic benefits of retraining a model which addresses the 'nature of immensurability between the past and the present' as a means to more directly address attitudes to 'otherness' (Harvey, in Ingold 1996: 221–2). Here a study of the 'past' and of heritage is argued to be a means too of readdressing alternative and parallel understandings of 'first contact', the 'extremes of foreignness' and the 'image of absolute other' (*ibid.*). Issues which have re-emerged too in the wake of 11 September 2001 and the ensuing 'war against terror'.

Küchler, as Feeley-Harnik's seconder, consolidates these main critical trajectories by putting forward an 'alternative view which restores the past to its active engagement in the present, not as a fictional by-product of that present, but as a constituent of the real world' (Küchler, in Ingold 1996: 226–7). Here she reiterates her commitment to defining a 'model of cultural transmission' that can be mobilized in 'the shaping of the future' (*ibid.*). This model is subsequently placed alongside a complex therapeutics (rather than grand narrative redemption) of 'remembering' and 'forgetting' and questions concerning strategies for alternative reconceptualizations of 'past', 'present' and 'future' and of 'otherness' and 'othering' (Ingold 1996: 42–3). Beneath these core agendas emerges a sense in which any reconceptualization of the 'past' and of 'heritage' beyond Eurocentric paradigms is inextricably related to a certain 'humanization' of the discourse which is bound up in a contemporary politics of 'return', 'redistribution', 'respect' and 'recognition' and with a complex politics of memory work. In what follows I give detail to these dynamics.

Heritage as Memory

The above shifts of discourse give recognition to how dynamics both 'within' and significantly from 'outside' the academy have established lines of debate, action and have influenced, if not at times dictated, the radical re-vision of 'heritage value'. This alternative perspective, for example, highlights how the archival compulsion to 'return to origin' and to 'revive' 'tradition' is now not only seen as symptomatic of the profound sense of cultural loss and erosion in the 'Western' imaginary but is increasingly present in 'non-Western' contexts due to the feelings of cultural loss caused by contemporary experiences of globalization. The consequences of such experiences are capable of framing alongside the 'West's' 'invention of the past' and modernity's 'rise of heritage' and concomitant Eurocentric urges to 'build *lieux de mémoire* (places of memory) because there are no more *milieux de mémoire* (real environments of memory)' (Maleuvre 1999: 59) contemporary acts of repossession in which the dream to both define and repossess one's lost heritage endures, as does an increased faith in, and calls for, culture as cure (Butler 2003).[4]

In this sense new investments are being made in the archive as a place of return, diagnosis and cure and thus as a potent locus for the narrativization of traumatic loss. One can include here, for example, the South African Truth and Reconciliation Commission (see Derrida 2004). With a more critical edge the historical 'anti-archival' discourse has not only provided a mobilization of the more subversive models of memory (from, for example, Nietzsche, Benjamin and Adorno to Derrida) to destabilize modernity's dominant preoccupations with a 'stifling historicism' (see Maleuvre 1999) and its 'archival traumas' (Derrida 1996) as a searing internal critique of the 'Westernization' of heritage, but has seen critics raise questions about the 'haunting of the archive' by those constituencies exiled, marginalized and misrepresented within this sphere. Here, for example, case-study contextualizations take in 'non-Western' contexts such as China (Feuchtwang 2000a, b).

Similarly the memorialization of modernity's violent conflicts has not only witnessed the centring of Holocaust memory within heritage discourse (Young 1993) but has seen the definition of historical and contemporary sites of 'human suffering', genocide and terror across the globe (Duffy 2001). It is here too that heritage discourse is confronted with certain crises of the 'representation'. The notion of the 'crisis of representation', famously articulated by Adorno, Lyotard, Levinas and others following the Holocaust, has, for example, implicated the act of monumentalization as at risk of repeating the same totalizing logic that underpinned the rationalization of the Holocaust itself (see Adorno 1949/1973; Young 1993; Radstone 2000). These dynamics have, in turn, not only given rise to recent interventions synonymous with the 'counter-monument' (Young 1993) and discussions of 'post-memory' (Radstone 2000) but in other contexts of suffering, controversies have similarly raged over the appropriate strategies for the objectification of memory in architectural form and the moral-ethical framing of the ritual performance of memory work and mourning in contexts of murder (Duffy 2001). It is here too that psychoanalytic and other theories of memory and of trauma theory have generated a significant body of texts (Forty and Küchler 1999; Antze and Lambek 1998; Kwint 1999; Radstone 2000). These have offered an alternative means, for example, to investigate the impulse to commemorate as part of acts of sacrifice and healing (Rowlands 1999).

It is here, however, that the limits of memory discourse need to be brought into view. One can argue that memory and trauma, like heritage itself, can be seen as 'Western' concepts and emerging from a 'Eurocentric' base (see Yates 1978). As such, this raises questions concerning the need to apprehend specific cultural practices – in terms of both tangible and intangible rituals, performances and commemorative strategies – in 'non-Western' contexts of suffering. Das and Feuchtwang, for example, use the alternative conceptualization of 'critical events' and 'cataclysmic events' to explore local responses to experiences of violence in India's (Das 1995) and China's recent past respectively (Feuchtwang 2000a, b). The challenge of moving beyond what might be defined as a Holocaust paradigm of suffering and redemption and the problematization of terms, such as, 'trauma', 'loss', 'mourning' and acts of 'working through' and 'closure' cross-culturally is, however, still an outstanding agenda. With the memorialization of sites synonymous with transatlantic slavery, the Gulags, the Palestinian 'Nakba' (the 'catastrophe' of 1948) and of genocide, in among other contexts, Armenia, Croatia, Cambodia, Nigeria and Rwanda, these questions appear more urgent than ever (see Duffy 2001).

Heritage as Well-being

Alternative 'readings' of 'Eurocentric' sources have, however, successfully drawn out debates on 'otherness' and strategies of 'othering'. Freud's therapeutic schema and his preoccupation with notions of 'speaking cures' and, more particularly, his radical 'inversion' of dominant memory models in order to profile the dynamic of 'forgetting' have provided a basis for the radical rethinking of heritage across North-South. For postcolonial critics, for example, Freud's work not only offers significant insights into the relationship between heritage and the unconscious but as Said (2003), Spivak (1992, 1993) and Bhabha (1994) have demonstrated, into 'non-Western' identity work.[5] Moreover, Freud's theorizing of a 'disturbance of memory' (Freud 1936/1984: 443–56)[6] as an exploration of how the literalization of icons and images of the 'past in the present' has the potential to access submerged and repressed memories has been re-worked as a means to understanding the complex psychodynamics and interactions of, among other factors, materiality, memory and 'persons-object' relations, with the more revelatory dimensions of heritage rituals (see Rojek 1997).

Heritage as a site of 'contestation', conflict and in terms of competing interpretations of sites and monuments has also resulted in clashes in which the cultural heritage has become a scene of violence and even death (see Layton et al. 2001 on the destruction of the mosque at Ayodhya, India). Similarly dominant discourse on iconoclasm has not only met its radical 'other' in the Taliban's destruction of the Bamiyan Buddhas in Afghanistan (dubbed by UNESCO Director General Matsurra as a 'crime against culture') and in other 'cultural fundamentalisms' (Stolke 1995) synonymous with 'ethnic cleansing' but has been itself problematized by new characterizations of heritage as a 'renewable resource' (see Holtorf 2001). This shift is captured by calls to 'actively and responsibly' engage in 'renewing the past in our time' rather than simply preserve and conserve and thereby sustain the monumental vestiges 'left' by posterity (ibid.). The contemporary focus upon 'intangible heritage' similarly offers alternative conceptualizations of culture (see http://www.unesco.org).

What has not yet been fully centred within a critical heritage discourse is a broader cross-cultural exploration of concepts of well-being. Perhaps a concept such as 'heritage magic' could be called upon here in order to apprehend insights into diverse global contexts in which, for example, strategies for the prevention of 'shock' and 'fear' and everyday practices which seek to bring about cure, well-being and protection are an essentialized part of 'what it is to be human' (see Meneley 2004). This act of reconceptualization also holds the possibility of accessing further insight into contexts in which people (as 'tourists', 'restorers', 'refugees') attempt to create narrative to reveal and to potentially heal past suffering and engage objects and places in this process (Scarry 1998; Hoskins 1998; Parkin 1999).

UNESCO and new Global Constituencies

These above themes define the complex, hybridized nature of dominant and alternative heritage discourse in the contemporary global context. This is a context which has also been problematized by Derrida in his 'deconstructionist' 'reading' of the major global culture broker, UNESCO. Derrida argues the need for UNESCO to make a conceptual and moral-ethical break with its historical, cultural and metaphysical preoccupation with 'Greek memory' and 'Greek origins' (Derrida 2002b: 40)[7]. He further argues that UNESCO's origins are bound up in an Occidental ontological tradition whose violences have 'displaced', 'among others', 'Egyptian, Jewish, Arabic' memory' (ibid.). Derrida's point, however, is to make a claim that 'even at origin, in its Greek moment, there was already some hybridization, some grafts, at work, some differential element' within UNESCO's foundational philosophies (ibid.).

It is this hybridizing force which Derrida sees as UNESCO's subversive dynamic, as it reveals how the organization necessarily participates in an 'othering' of its foundational values. Derrida's final appeal is for the mobilization of a 'new ethics' capable of 're-envisioning' the institution as an essentialized part of a 'new internationalism' (no longer tied to exclusively Kantian universalizing values) which will 'open up UNESCO's logic and its existence' as a truly 'world institution' (Derrida 2002b: 74). He sums up this strategy in terms of a moral-ethical 'debt', 'duty', 'response' and 'responsibility' towards 'the archive of another' to 'difference' and to the simultaneous 'opening-up the self-validating aspect' of the institution to the 'voice of the other' (Derrida 2002b: 23) and to a remodelled future institutional cosmopolitics (Derrida 2002b: 40). Furthermore,

Derrida's broader discussions of cosmopolitanism and hospitality are rooted in both refugee and asylum rights and in critical reflections on amnesty, truth and reconciliation, which he regards as an integral part of his moral-ethical project of 'restoring … heritage to dignity' and creating a 'just' future (Derrida 2004: 5).

Indigenizing Heritage

This sense of heritage as a resource for defining a 'just' future is perhaps nowhere more pronounced and more contested than in the utilization and reworking of heritage by new constituencies – notably indigenous groups[8] – as a powerful metaphor by which to express historical – and ongoing – grievance and injustice and as bound up in accompanying demands not only for the restitution of cultural objects and human remains but of human dignity, justice and respect (Rowlands 2002). Contemporary debates on cultural rights and cultural property have moved hand in hand with subsequent attempts to 'indigenize' heritage, to reclaim land and to reinterpret sacred sites (see Niec 1998). This has often wielded a critical edge, confronting the heritage culture with its own complicity in the often violent appropriation of land, artefacts (including 'cultural treasures' and secret sacred material), human remains and in the scientific, cultural and intellectual colonization of other cultures (see Simpson 1996; Fforde 2004).

Here, for example, the development of 'culture' and 'ethnic'-specific cultural centres and indigenous meeting places has offered new engagements with alternative dynamics of cultural transmission (Simpson 1996). Not only have such institutions repossessed 'tradition' but have witnessed a hybridization of knowledge and cultural forms that has fundamentally problematized dominant motifs of spectatorship, authorship, control and exhibition (ibid.). Similarly, critical reconceptualizations of 'ethnographic representation' have drawn out alternative strategies of 'cultural reciprocity' in cultural spaces in, for example, in South East Asia and the Pacific (Stanley 1998). Heritage as 'living tradition' and as part of expressions of local control and empowerment has likewise defined the Vanuatu Cultural Centre (Geismar and Tilley 2003) and as a particular model of what a true 'post-museum' (cf. Hooper-Greenhill 2001) may represent. The strategy of 'anthropologizing the West' and the profiling of ethnographic methodologies have also resulted in research into 'Western' heritage contexts, such as Colonial Williamsburg (Handler and Gable 1997) and London's Science Museum (MacDonald 2001).

Provincializing Heritage

One is thus confronted with both the limits of traditional heritage discourse and its possible futures in terms of the ability to embrace the above and other parallel and alternative heritages. Here one can find a resonance with the postcolonial critic Chakrabarty's (2000) assertion that the key values, concepts and paradigms that emerged from European thought are 'inadequate' to understand non-European life worlds. Therefore, the future reconceptualization of a globally responsive and moral and ethically responsible heritage studies discourse depends on the ability to address Chakrabarty's broader project of 'provincializing Europe' and strategizing attempts to apprehend 'non-Western' histories, subaltern memories and other modernities (ibid.). This is accompanied by the need to look beyond the existing or 'established' canon of cultural heritage texts in order to refocus our attention upon a wider scholarship committed to further disrupting and displacing dominant heritage. The concept and reality, therefore, of a Chinese modernity or Arab identity and heritage as a product of these communities' own long-term history – not just of 'contact' – need to be considered alongside theorists' calls to 'provincialize' the place of Europe within our understanding of the dynamics of cultural power and influence and as a means to challenge the presumed universalism of human and cultural values (ibid.).

Postcolonial theory, although still a shamefully under-theorized area within mainstream heritage studies, offers a potent insight into key themes of identity, representation and the mediation of identity. To return to the work of Spivak (1988) and Bhabha (1994), the project apprehending the 'subaltern voice' and the critical reconceptualization of 'mimicry' have done much to challenge dominant Eurocentric notions of 'authenticity'. As such, these critics make it clear that the intellectual must resist 'nostalgic desires' to reconstruct the subaltern as a 'lost object' and to recover the 'pure form' and redeem the 'unified, true and unmediated voice' of the 'people' and instead argue the need for a more critical, subtle line in strategies of representation and in the mediation of identity (Spivak 1988). From this starting point both the tactical mobilization of forms of 'mimicry' and 'strategic essentialism' and more metaphysical preoccupations with 'Greek Jew' identities are addressed and problematized by these authors (Spivak 1992)[9].

Heritage as a 'New' Humanism

The broad shift of this chapter is a movement from the 'historical approach' to heritage and its focus on the 'past as a foreign country' to that of heritage as an essentialized resource for 'creating a future' in the contemporary global context. The need to define a set of new and alternative agendas, concepts, methodologies and research questions oriented towards engaging with this context, as the above also demonstrates, is a project still in its infancy. What is clear, however, is that this urgent need for a reconceptualization of heritage discourse at both intellectual and operational level is based upon alternative sets of values, critical approaches, theorizations and lived experiences which are located outside mainstream heritage studies and, as such, remain largely unrecognized. The question of 'what constitutes heritage?' therefore demands a shift towards a consideration of: what are current constituencies of heritage in the global context? How are these needs and futures to be communicated and represented in terms of heritage values? As such, these constituencies, which notably include displaced, diasporic, transnational, indigenous cultures and cultures in conflict, need to be fully centred as the basis for heritage studies' articulation of its own 'possible futures'.

As Chakrabarty argues, the failure to be responsive to lifeworlds 'not yet visible' within current framings would leave heritage studies in 'ignorance of the majority of humankind' and, as such, it would be a redundant force (Chakrabarty 2000: 29). With this in mind, heritage critics would do well to engage in wider calls from elsewhere in the academy for the definition of a 'new humanism' (cf. Said 2004), no longer tied to the oppressive filter of 'Western' liberalism, which is not only capable of critically apprehending alternative conceptualizations of 'otherness' and 'othering' but which is responsive to the 'besieged subject' (Said 2003). I would argue that a resonant starting point for 'remodelling' heritage discourse on these lines requires the enactment of a strategic return to the core preoccupation of heritage studies with the question of 'what it is to be human'. Thus alongside cultural and human rights discourse alternative experiences and

conceptualizations of 'personhood' need to be brought into view, as do the diverse modes of representation that 'being human' takes. Only once these had been fundamentally reconceptualized could one agree (cf. Ingold 1996) that heritage discourse is uniquely placed not only to address claims about identity, ancestry and cultural transmission but is equipped to take on the key moral-ethical issues of our times and to fully engage with, and assist with the definition of, emergent global heritage futures.

NOTES

1 MacCannell's text is a key part of the tourism theory canon, which also includes Smith (1989); Boniface and Fowler (1993); Cohen (1988); Urry (1990). See Selwyn (1996) for a review.

2 Walsh states how 'the heritage industry especially [has ...] to shoulder the shame for the movement towards [the 'first' Gulf] war' (Walsh 1992: 2).

3 This genealogy defines the still globally dominant 'salvage' or 'container' models of heritage. For Renaissance 'arts of memory' and the other 'nodal' points of this Eurocentric genealogy see Yates (1978); Samuel (1994); Forty and Küchler (1999).

4 See, for example, the contemporary revival of the ancient Alexandrina project initiated by the Egyptian government in co-operation with UNESCO (see Butler 2001a, b, 2003).

5 All three critics have used Freud to analyse the (colonial) fantasies of the 'Western psyche' and to outline potential postcolonial transformations of identity work.

6 Freud's first visit to Athens saw him experience a 'disturbance' when his literal confrontation with the Acropolis (repressed by Freud as an 'object of the imagination') brought about the possibility of accessing the unconscious' (Freud 1936/1984: 443–56).

7 Other UNESCO literature includes Lacoste (1994); Mayor (1995); O'Brien (1968); Hoggart (1978); Titchen (1996); Cleere (1995, 1996, 2000, 2001); Hylland-Eriksen (2001).

8 See Kuper (2003) and Kenrick and Lewis (2004) for critical debates on 'indigenous identity'.

9 Levinas in the pivotal post-war period issued a challenge to the dominant 'Greek' metaphysical position by arguing a place for the figure of the 'Jew' within the domain of philosophy/ethics (Levinas 1987). The possible stagings of a 'third position' to destabilize the 'Greek'–'Jew' binary have

engaged Spivak, Bhabha and also Derrida (see Bennington 1992).

REFERENCES

Adorno, T. (1949/1973) 'After Auschwitz', 'Meditations on metaphysics', in *Negative Dialectics*, trans. E.B. Ashton. New York: Continuum.

Adorno, T. (1981) *Prisms*, trans. S. and S. Weber. Cambridge, MA: MIT Press.

Anderson, B. (1991) *Imagined Communities*. Princeton, NJ: Princeton University Press.

Antze, P. and Lambek, M., eds (1998) *Tense Past: Cultural Essays in Trauma and Memory*. London and New York: Routledge.

Barthes, R. (1957/1992). *Mythologies*. St Albans: Paladin.

Baudrillard, J. (1988) 'Simulacra and simulations', in M. Poster (ed.), *Jean Baudrillard: Selected Writings*. Cambridge: Polity Press.

Bazin, G. (1967) *The Museum Age*, trans. J. Cahill. New York: Universe Books.

Benjamin, W. (1968) *Illuminations*, trans. H. Zohn. New York: Schocken Books.

Bennington, G. (1992) 'Mosaic fragment: if Derrida were an Egyptian ...', in D. Wood (ed.), *Derrida: A Critical Reader*. Oxford: Blackwell, pp. 97–119.

Bhabha, H. (1994) *The Location of Culture*. London and New York: Routledge.

Blythe, R. (1969) *Akenfield: Portrait of an English Village*. London: Allen Lane/the Penguin Press.

Boniface, P. and Fowler, P.J. (1993) *Heritage Tourism in the 'Global Village'*. London and New York: Routledge.

Butler, B. (2001a) 'Egypt: constructed exiles of the imagination', in B. Bender and M. Winer (eds), *Contested Landscapes: Movement, Exile and Place*. Oxford: Berg, pp. 303–18.

Butler, B. (2001b) 'Return to Alexandria: conflict and contradiction in discourses of origins and heritage revivalism in Alexandria, Egypt', in R. Layton and J. Thomas (eds), *The Destruction and Conservation of Cultural Property*. London and New York: Routledge, pp. 55–75.

Butler, B. (2003) '"Egyptianizing" the Alexandrina: the contemporary revival of the ancient Mouseion/ Library', in C. Price and J-M. Humbert (eds), *Imotep Today: Egyptianizing Architecture*. London: UCL Press.

Chakrabarty, D. (2000) *Provincializing Europe: Postcolonial Thought and Historical Difference*. Princeton, NJ: Princeton University Press.

Cleere, H. (1995) 'Cultural landscapes as world heritage', *Conservation and Management of Archaeological Sites*, 1 (1): 63–8.

Cleere, H. (1996) 'The concept of "outstanding universal value" in the world heritage convention', *Conservation and Management of Archaeological Sites*, 1 (4): 227–33.

Cleere, H. (2000) 'The World Heritage Convention in the Third World', *Cultural Resource Management in Contemporary Society*, 4 (3): 99–106.

Cleere, H. (2001) 'Uneasy bedfellows: universality and cultural heritage', in R. Layton P. Stone and J. Thomas (eds), *Destruction and Conservation of Cultural Property*. London and New York: Routledge, pp. 22–9.

Cohen, E. (1988) 'Authenticity and commodization in tourism', *Annals of Tourism Research*, 15 (3): 371–86.

Coombes, A. (1994) *Reinventing Africa: Temples of Empire: the Museum and its Publics*. New Haven, CT, and London: Yale University Press.

Das, V. (1995) *Critical Events*. Delhi: Oxford University Press.

Derrida, J. (1996) *Archive Fever: a Freudian Impression*, trans. E. Prenowitz. Chicago: University of Chicago Press.

Derrida, J. (2002a) *On Cosmopolitanism and Forgiveness*. London and New York: Routledge.

Derrida, J. (2002b). *Ethics, Institutions and the Right to Philosophy*, trans. P. Pericles Trifonas. New York: Rowman & Littlefield.

Duffy, T.M. (2001) 'Museums of "Human Suffering" and the struggle for human rights', *Museum International*, 53 (1): 10–16.

Duncan, C. (1995) *Civilising Rituals inside Public Art Museums*. London and New York: Routledge.

Eco, U. (1986) *Travels in Hyperreality*. London: Picador.

Feuchtwang, S. (2000a) 'Reinscriptions: commemorations, restoration and the interpersonal transmission of histories and memories under modern states in Asia and Europe', in S. Radstone (ed.), *Memory and Methodology*. Oxford: Berg, pp. 59–78.

Feuchtwang, S. (2000b) 'The avenging ghost: paradigm of a shameful past', in *Anthropology* II, *Beliefs and Everyday Life*. Third International Conference on Sinology. London: Academica Sinica, pp. 1–29.

Fforde, C. (2004) *Collecting the Dead: Archaeology and the Reburial Issue*. London: Duckworth.

Findlen, P. (2000) 'The modern muses: Renaissance collecting and the cult of remembrance', in S.A. Crane (ed.), *Museums and Memory*. Stanford CA: Stanford University Press, pp. 161–78.

Forty, A. and Küchler, S. (1999), *The Art of Forgetting*. Oxford: Berg.

Foucault, M. (1964) 'Le language et l'espace', *Critique*, 5 (7).

Freud, S. (1936/1984) 'A disturbance of memory on the Acropolis', in A. Richards (ed.), *On Metapsychology*. London: Penguin Books, pp. 443–56.

Fukuyama, F. (1992) *The End of History and the Last Man*. New York: Free Press.

Geismar, H. and Tilley, C. (2003) 'Negotiating materiality: international and local museum practices at the Vanuatu Cultural Centre and National Museum', *Oceania*, 73: 170–188.

Gregory, E. (1998) *H.D. and Hellenism*. Cambridge: Cambridge University Press.

Hall, S. (2000) 'Whose heritage? Unsettling "the heritage"', *Third Text*, 49: 1–12.

Hand, S. (1989) *Levinas Reader*. Oxford: Blackwell.

Handler, R. and Gable, E. (1997) *The New History in an Old Museum: Creating the Past at Colonial Williamsburg*. Durham, NC: Duke University Press.

Hewison, R. (1987) *The Heritage Industry*, London: Methuen.

Hobsbawm, E. et al., eds (1993) *The Invention of Tradition*. Cambridge: Cambridge University Press.

Hoggart, R. (1978) *An Idea and its Servants: UNESCO from Within*. London: Chatto & Windus.

Holtorf, C. (2001) 'Is the past a non-renewable resource?' in R. Layton, P. Stone and J. Thomas (eds), *Destruction and Conservation of Cultural Property*. One World Archaeology Series. London: Routledge.

Hooper-Greenhill, E. (2001) *Museums and the Interpretation of Visual Culture*. London and New York: Routledge.

Horkheimer, M. and Adorno, T. (1979) *Dialectic of Enlightenment*. London: Allen Lane.

Horne, D. (1984) *The Great Museum: the Re-presentation of History*. London: Pluto Press.

Hoskins, J. (1998) *Biographical Objects: How Objects tell the Stories of People's Lives*. London and New York: Routledge.

Huyssen, A. (1995) *Twilight Memories: Making Time in a Culture of Amnesia*. London and New York: Routledge.

Hylland-Eriksen, T. (2001) 'Between universalism and relativism: a critique of the UNESCO concept of culture', in J. Lowen, M.B. Dember and R. Wilson (eds), *Culture and Rights*. Cambridge: Cambridge University Press, pp. 127–48.

Ingold, T. (1996) *Key Debates in Anthropology*. New York and London: Routledge.

Kenrick, J. and Lewis, J. (2004) 'Indigenous peoples' rights and the politics of the term "indigenous"', *Anthropology Today*, 20 (2): 4–9.

Kuper, A. (2003) 'The return of the native', *Current Anthropology*, 44 (3): 389–402.

Kwint, M. (1999) *Material Memories: Design and Evocation*. Oxford: Berg.

Lacoste, M.C. (1994) *The Story of a Grand Design: UNESCO, 1946–1993*. Paris: UNESCO.

Layton, R. Stone, P. and Thomas, J. (2001) *Destruction and Conservation of Cultural Property*. World Archaeology Series. London: Routledge

Leone, M.P. (1973) 'Archaeology as the science of technology: Mormon town plans and fences', in C.L. Redman (ed.), *Research and Theory in Current Archaeology*, New York: Wiley, pp. 125–50.

Levinas, E. (1987) *Collected Philosophical Papers*, trans. A. Lingis. The Hague: Nijhoff.

Lewis, G. (1992) 'Museums and their precursors: a brief world survey', in J.M.A. Thompson (ed.), *The Manual of Curatorship: A Guide to Museum Practice*. Butterworth, pp. 5–20.

Lowenthal, D. (1985) *The Past is a Foreign Country*. Cambridge: Cambridge University Press.

Lowenthal, D. (1996) *The Heritage Crusade and the Spoils of History*. London: Viking.

Lynch, K. (1972) *What Time is this Place?* Cambridge, MA: MIT Press.

MacCannell, D. (1978/1989) *The Tourist: a New Theory of the Leisure Class*. London: Macmillan.

MacDonald, S. (2001) 'Behind the scenes at the Science Museum: knowing, making and using', in M. Bouquet (ed.), *Academic Anthropology and the Museum*. Oxford and New York: Berghahn.

Maleuvre, D. (1999) *Museum Memories: History, Technology, Art*. Stanford, CA: Stanford University Press.

Mayrand, P. (1985) 'The new museology proclaimed', *Museum*, 148: 2000.

Mayor, F. (1995) *The future of the past*. Paris: UNESCO.

McBryde, I. (1997) 'The ambiguities of authenticity: rock of faith or shifting sands? NARA conference on 'Authenticity in relation to the World Heritage Convention', in N. Stanley-Price (ed.), *Conservation and Management of Archaeological Sites*. London: Unwin, pp. 93–100.

Meltzer, D.J. (1985) Ideology and material culture', in R.J. Gould and M.B. Schiffer (eds), *Modern Material Culture: the Archaeology of Us*. New York: Academic Press, pp. 113–25.

Meneley, A. (2004) 'Scared, sick or silly?' in P. Antze and M. Lambek (eds), *Illness and Irony: on the Ambiguity of Suffering in Culture*. Oxford and New York: Berghahn, pp. 21–39.

Merriman, N. (1991) *Beyond the Glass Case: the Past, the Heritage and the Public*. London: UCL Press.

Merriman, N. (1996) 'Defining heritage', *Material Culture Journal*, 1 (3): 377–86.

Niec, H. ed. (1998) *Cultural Rights and Wrongs: A Collection of Essays in Commemoration of the Fiftieth Anniversary of the Universal Declaration of Human Rights*. Paris: UNESCO.

O'Brien, C.C. (1968) *The United Nations: Sacred Drama*. London: Hutchinson.

Parkin, D. (1999) 'Mementoes as transitional objects in human displacement', *Material Culture Journal*, 4 (3): 303–20.

Plumb, J.H. (1973) *The Death of the Past*. London: Penguin Books.

Porter, G. (1996) 'Seeing through solidarity: a feminist perspective on museums', in S. MacDonald and G. Fyfe (eds), *Theorizing Museums: Representing Identity and Diversity in a Changing World*. Oxford: Blackwell, pp. 105–26.

Radstone, S., ed. (2000) *Memory and Methodology*. Oxford: Berg.

Rojek, C. (1997) 'Indexing, dragging and the social construction of tourist sites', in C. Rojek and J. Urry (eds), *Touring Cultures: Transformations of Travel and Theory*. London and New York: Routledge, pp. 54–74.

Rojek, C. and Urry, J., eds. (1997) *Touring Cultures: Transformations of Travel and Theory*. London and New York: Routledge.

Rosaldo, R. (1989) *Culture and Truth: The Remaking of Social Analysis*. Boston, MA: Beacon Press.

Rowlands, M. (1999) 'Remembering to forget: sublimation in war memorials', in A. Forty and S. Küchler (eds), *The Art of Forgetting*. Oxford: Berg.

Rowlands, M. (2002) 'Heritage and cultural property', in V. Buchli (ed.), *The Material Culture Reader*. Oxford: Berg, pp. 105–10.

Said, E.W. (2003) *Freud and the Non-European*. Verso: London.

Said, E.W. (2004) *Humanism and Democratic Criticism*. New York: Macmillan

Samuel, R. (1994) *Theatres of Memory*. Oxford: Blackwell.

Scarry, E. (1998) *The Body in Pain*. New York: Oxford University Press.

Selwyn, T., ed. (1996) *The Tourist Image: Myths and Myth Making in Tourism*. Chichester: Wiley.

Sherman, D. and Rogoff, I., eds (1994) *Museum Culture: Histories, Discourses, Spectacles*. Minneapolis, MN: University of Minnesota Press.

Simpson, M. (1996) *Making Representations: Museums in the Post-colonial Era*. London and New York: Routledge.

Smith, V., ed. (1989) *Hosts and Guests*. Oxford: Blackwell.

Spivak, G.C. (1988) 'Can the subaltern speak?' in C. Nelson and L. Grossberg (eds), *Marxism and the Interpretation of Culture*. Urbana, IL: University of Illinois Press, pp. 296–97.

Spivak, G.C. (1992) 'Asked about myself', *Third Text*, 19 (4): 9–18.

Spivak G.C. (1993) 'Echo', *New Literary: A Journal of Theory and Interpretation*, 24: 17–43.

Stanley N. (1998) *Being Ourselves for You: the Global Display of Cultures*. London: Middlesex University Press.

Stolke, V. (1995) 'Talking culture: new boundaries, new rhetorics of exclusion in Europe', *Current Anthropology*, 36: 1–26.

Titchen, S. (1996) On the construction of "outstanding universal value": some comments on the implementation of the 1972 UNESCO World Heritage Convention', in *Conservation and Management of Archaeological Sites*, 1 (4): 235–42.

Urry, J. (1990) *The Tourist Gaze: Leisure and Travel in Contemporary Societies*. London: Sage.

Vergo, P., ed. (1989) *The New Museology*. London: Reaktion.

Wallace, M. (1981) 'Visiting the past: history museum in the United States', *Radical History Review*, 25 (3): 63–96.

Walsh, K. (1992) *The Representation of the Past: Museum and Heritage in the Postmodern World*. London and New York: Routledge.

Wright, P. (1985) *On Living in an Old Country*. London: Verso.

Yates, F. (1978) *The Art of Memory*. Harmondsworth: Penguin Books.

Young, J. (1993) *The Texture of Memory: Holocaust Memorials and Meaning*. New Haven, CT: Yale University Press.

WEB SITE

UNESCO: http://www.unesco.org.

30

MUSEUMS AND MUSEUM DISPLAYS

Anthony Alan Shelton

Museums and displays, together with the associated panoply of galleries, international exhibitions, theme parks, panoramas, arcades and department stores, have been closely connected since the nineteenth century by related and sometimes mutually reinforcing disciplinary power relations (Lumley 1988: 2; Hamon 1992: 73; Georgel 1994: 119; Bennett 1995: 59; Silverstone 1994: 161). Together, such institutions form what Bennett calls an exhibitionary complex, which, in its modernist manifestation, consist of:

> linked sites for the development and circulation of new disciplines (history, biology, art history, anthropology) and their discursive formations (the past, evolution, aesthetics, man) as well as for the development of new technologies of vision ... which might be productively analysed as particular articulations of power and knowledge ...
>
> (1995: 59)

Every exhibitionary complex involves ways of organizing and institutionalizing visual experience; specific conjunctions of technologies of representation, conventions and codes of understanding, associated ocular regimes, and their own particular exhibitionary narratives. Complexes are both dependent and supportive of markets, and through their unequal institutional engagements and relationships with audiences, classes, guilds or professions are complicit in the reproduction of social structures. Museums and their related institutions are not only technologies of representation but are proactive in the construction of social 'realities' (Kaplan 1994: 4; Macdonald 1996: 13; Porto 1999: 3–4). They are 'products and agents of social and political change' according to

Kaplan which a nation can use 'to represent and reconstitute itself anew in each generation' (1994: 4–5). Exhibitionary complexes are not coterminous with political ideologies, though that part of them sponsored by the state and considered part of a national or local patrimony may bear evidence of their imprint. In societies with high illiteracy rates, state-sponsored visual organizations of knowledge frequently reinforce the educational system by providing the scenography and motivation behind the mobilization of 'celebrations, festivals, expositions, and visits to mythic places'. What Garcia Canclini describes as 'an entire system of rituals in which the "naturalness" of the demarcation establishing the original and "legitimate" patrimony is periodically ordered, remembered and secured' (1995: 112). Even in literate cultures the role of museums and galleries in sponsoring exhibitions that reiterate the symbolic constituents underlying national hegemonic mythologies is crucial for their periodic renewal and reassertion (cf. Duncan 1991: 90; Luke 1992: 38). Museums disseminate public culture and through their architecture, decoration, arrangements, articulation with other institutions and sponsored rituals frequently disclose, as Duncan (1995: 8), Handler and Gable (1997: 221), Porto (1999: 133) and others have clearly demonstrated, as much about the societies of which they form part as the supposedly objectivist disciplines they institutionalize.

Although the meanings museums attribute their collections are historically specific, variations and differences are always found within any one period. Museums, according to Lumley (1988: 2) 'map out geographies of taste and values' to articulate, as Bourdieu (1993: 121) or Garcia Canclini (1995: 136) would have it, particular hierarchical organizations and valorizations of symbolic goods. In late modern period metropolises, to assist their ideological functions, museums are nearly always incorporated into wider institutional fields and relationships; in ceremonial processionways or malls connected with the display of governmental power, where they 'become necessary ornaments of the modern state' (McClellan 1996: 29), or what Paul Valéry called the 'geodesic signals of order' (in Hamon 1992: 43);[1] as systems of nodal institutions within an international deployment of similar organizations for the transference, reception and communication of global and local cultures;[2] or increasingly as co-ordinated, or jointly managed organizations with shared collecting, exhibition and public service provision.[3]

Acknowledging these mutual and changing disciplinary, organizational, functional and performative linkages historically, the role of former colonial museums has been linked with map making, census inventories and archives as technologies of classification and serialization, which were intended to visibly materialize the totality of a domain over which governmental power strove to assert mastery (Anderson 1991: 184–5; Richards 1993: 6). This fascination with totalization and transparency, the production of a seamless narrative of local, national or universal history, whether through the display of history and antiquities themselves, or ethnography, art or nature, continues to remain at the heart of most national and large regional museums. The diverse visual and political regimes of which museums form part require them not only to be studied as singular integral institutions, as has been the tendency in the past, but also as part of specific historically determined 'exhibitionary complexes'; what Garcia Canclini (1995: 137) calls 'patrimonies'or, more narrowly, what Bouquet (2001: 79) refers to as 'museumscapes'.

As a field, critical museology still remains an extraordinarily underdeveloped subject of study. Baring the pioneering work of Marcus (1990), Macdonald (1997, 2001), Macdonald and Silverstone (1992) and Handler and Gable (1997) it is deficient in both emic and etic ethnographic case studies. It requires enormous foci on such issues as the interrelation between 'front stage' and 'backstage' activities and modes of communication – descriptive and interpretative understanding of what happens inside museums; proper analysis of the different foundation narratives underlying the diversity of disciplinary and national institutions; greater focus on the politics and not only

the poetics of representations – the relations between business, politics and museum interpretation and the ensuing 'culture wars' being fought in institutions not only in the United States, but in Europe and elsewhere too; reassessment of the epistemological adequacy of semiotic interpretations of museum meanings; more attention to the role of memory, its integration with other structures of events, and the mechanisms responsible for its ideological inflections. Differences in the institutionalization of material culture from one country to another need to be acknowledged, described and interpreted, and systems of material classification, and changes in the wider contemporary and historical fields of which museums form part, need to be better appreciated. There is great urgency for a theory of genres, so museum exhibitions can be subject to better critical scrutiny. Closer study of the different administrative and organizational models of museums, the distribution of power and authority they imply and actualize, and their relationship to the control and deployment of knowledges, with few exceptions (Krug et al. 1999), also require close study. Critical museology remains an open discipline which, although in the process of defining its central problematics, has hardly began to theoreticize its object, and even less to begin to distinguish interconnected fields, or develop a comparative perspectives that this chapter would like to encourage.

GENEALOGIES AND FOUNDATION NARRATIVES

Collecting, together with the requisite conservation, classification, interpretation and display or storage of the assemblages it engenders, has until recently provided not only the foundation, but the universalist justification behind museums. 'While the museum,' according to Elsner 'is a kind of entombment, a display of once lived activity ... collecting is the process of the museum's creation, the living act that the museum embalms' (1994: 155). This common perspective relies on a genealogical view of history in which museums have been naturalized, through an essentializing legitimatory discourse based on a sometimes applauded or vilified common mental proclivity, traceable to our earliest human origins.

For Pierre Cabanne 'The origins of collecting are as remote and mysterious as those of art' and coincide with the recognition of beauty

(1963: vii), while Jospeh Alsop, basing his argument on cave deposits, traces this primordial drive to the Palaeolithic (1982: 71). The genealogical viewpoint has been incorporated into manuals and managerial and technical works published by museums and their related professional associations. In *The Manual of Curatorship* (1984), Lewis concurs that acquisitiveness and the desire to record and transmit knowledge are basic human proclivities traceable to the Palaeolithic. Museums, he speculates, are 'a reflection of an inherent human propensity towards inquisitiveness and acquisitiveness combined with a wish to communicate to others' (1984: 7). For Pearce:

> It is clear that institutionalised collecting in various modes ... is an activity with its communal and psychic roots deep in the prehistory of European society, and can be traced in detail through the centuries of later prehistory in the Iron and Bronze Ages back at least to the Neolithic communities of around 3000 BC ...
>
> (1992: 90–1)

This long established, and still current view of museums as the product of individual acquisitiveness (cf. Kaplan 1994: 2; Thomson 2002: 29) was celebrated and popularized in *The Museum Age* (1967: 12), in which Bazin traced the collecting impulse to the Hellenic world and the beginnings of the Chinese empire.

Although chronologies on the origins of collecting and its museum institutionalization differ and necessarily are never more than speculative, genealogical approaches to museum history were until recently widespread. The etymological association which relates the classic Greek *mouseion* to the activities and attributes of the nine muses, the daughters of Zeus, associated with the arts and sciences, is ubiquitous in most museum histories (Bazin 1967: 16; Mordaunt Crook 1972: 19; Boulton n.d.: 2; Alexander 1979: 6; Lewis 1984: 7). Mordaunt Crook succinctly exemplifies the genealogical view of museum development in the classical world: 'The Greek *mouseion* became first a shrine of the muses, then a repository for gifts, then a temple of the arts, and finally a collection of tangible memorials to mankind's creative genius' (1972: 19). Pearce completes this unilinear evolutionary view by noting the successive periods – archaic, early modern, classic modern and postmodern – coincided with specific institutionalizations of collections in medieval treasuries, cabinets of curiosities in eighteenth to mid-twentieth-century museums, and contemporary museums (1992: 90).

Concerned with the indiscriminate use to which the term 'museum' had long been applied, Alsop proposed a more restricted attribution to refer to 'a permanently established assemblage of works of art to which the public has a permanent right of entry'. This he exemplified by what he regarded as its first manifestation, the 1471 Museo Capitolino, founded to bring together the dispersed remnants of Rome's classical sculpture (1982: 163–4). This chronology is also supported by Pearce (1992: 1) and Cannon-Brookes, for whom, like Alsop, museum collections derived their uniqueness from the intellectual environment fostered by Renaissance humanism (1984: 115).

Genealogical history, therefore, legitimates museums by locating their origins within a cluster of activities and institutional exemplars, motivated by the presumed universal human disposition towards collecting, the enjoyment of beauty or rarity, and/or curiosity for knowledge. These are all criteria which have been used to define the uniqueness of humanity and distinguish it from the remainder of the animal kingdom and consequently the transcendental importance with which such proclivities are endowed, through their association with the Greek muses, attribute them divine origin and patronage. Whether collections are exhibited as aesthetic transcendental or as encyclopaedic models patterned on the greatness of nature, the value and worth ascribed their deployments are located in the trans-social domains to which they ultimately refer.

Accepting these presuppositions, broad agreement over the museum's most singular characteristics has been long established. George Brown Goode, in his *Principles of Museum Administration* (1895), advised:

> A museum is an institution for the preservation of those objects which best illustrate the phenomena of nature and the works of man and the utilisation of them for the increase of knowledge and for the culture and enlightenment of the people.
>
> (Cited in Mather et al. 1986: 305)

The essential basis of this definition has been reproduced until recent times. Pearce, for example, opines: 'Museums are by nature institutions which hold the material evidence, objects and specimens of the human and natural history of our planet' (1992: 1).[4] For Kaplan museums collect, conserve and display 'the "things" of culture, belonging to the material world ... and specimens or phenomena of the natural world' (1994: 1). David Wilson concurs with orthodox opinion in his unequivocal assertion that 'The primary duty of museums ... is not didactic' but related to the conservation, collection and display of material culture. Adding: 'A museum which does not collect is a dead museum' (1984: 57), a sentiment he shared with Goode, who, in a slightly different form, had insisted: 'A finished museum is a dead museum and a dead museum is a useless resource' (cited in Mather et al. 1986). The three primary functions reiterated by Wilson and Kaplan have been reproduced in almost every institutional definition of museums right up to the last decades of the twentieth century,[5] when they were supplemented, subordinated or replaced by some sort of public service provision. Though it may be argued that museums are essentially ideas rather than buildings and collections (White 1987: 12), and although some of their more assiduous critics might argue collections need to be subordinated to clearer mission statements and managerial resource bases, for the most part the value of their material assets as their most unequivocal distinguishing characteristic is seldom challenged (cf. Thomson 2002: 25).

Institutional recognition of a change in emphasis, from a scientific to a social role, in the way museums are defined was first raised in the 1974 ICOM declaration which saw them as a;

> non-profitmaking, permanent institution in the service of society and of its development, and open to the public, which acquires, conserves, researches, communicates, and exhibits, for purposes of study, education, and enjoyment, material evidence of man and his environment.
>
> (In Alexander 1983: 3)

This shift later influenced changes in definitions adopted by national professional associations. The Museums Association, for example, abandoned its earlier adage that 'A museum is an institution which collects, documents, preserves, exhibits, and interprets material evidence and associated information for the public benefit' (Museums Association 1991: 13) towards the end of the 1990s to replace its once considered 'disinterested' purpose with its explicit use value:

> Museums enable people to explore collections for inspiration, learning and enjoyment. They are institutions that collect, safeguard and make accessible artefacts and specimens, which they hold in trust for society.
>
> (UK Museums Association 1999)

This more pragmatic view has perhaps most eminently been argued by Keith Thomson, who emphasizes the importance of mutuality between museums and users over their function rather than their subordination to the utopian pretensions of their collections (2002: 106). Museums for Thomson 'act as brokers and suppliers in the world of information' (2002: 3). Their rationalization and narrative legitimation have therefore shifted, in Lyotard's terms, from a Humboldtian or philosophical (rationalist) narrative to a narrative of emancipation (1984: 31).

With diversification of the museum's purpose, the increasing difficulty of capturing, never mind rationalizing, its proliferating functions is saliently attested in the adoption of functional criteria in the literary structure of recent monographs describing them (cf. Alexander 1979; Weill 1983; MacDonald and Alsford 1989). Most works, however, while acknowledging contradictions endemic to museums' burgeoning agendas, seldom discuss their resolution.[6] Contradictions between contending museum functions are profligate; in their designation as repositories of heritage and their incorporation within modernising discourses (García Canclini 1995: 107); in their aspiration to be both educational and entertaining (MacDonald and Alsford 1989: 58); in their split identities as lofty temples for disinterested contemplation and their general educational provisions (Hooper-Greenhill 1989: 63, 1994: 133; Thomson 2002: 64); between their focus on a common public addressee, and their role in differentiating populations (Bourdieu and Darbel 1991: 107; Bennett 1995: 104); in the division between restrictive practices intended to conserve objects and the requirements of public display and use (Clavir 2002: 35); between their professed universality and the interdictions of local knowledge systems (Holm and Pokotylo 1997: 34; Ames 2003: 175; Clavir 2002: 139; Clifford 1997: 144–5), and the dependence of collecting on the free market, which it inevitably restricts and progressively exhausts (Thomson 2002: 41). Paradox, therefore, appears to be an essential characteristic of much contemporary museum organization and work.

Current doubts over the purposes and natures of museums are made more complicated still because of their sometime involution of form over content. In recent decades, with museums themselves re-entering the arena of prestigious architectural competitions, new buildings like Piano and Rogers's Centre Pompidou, Meier's High Museum, Geary's Gulbenkian or Eisenman's Wexner Centre have become avante-garde objects in themselves, showcases for the virtuosity of new design and materials, which invite artists to interact with them. Content easily becomes secondary to their foil, with architecture regarded as a 'catalyst' for the event-centred 'activities' that museums increasingly sponsor (Ritchie 1994: 12), or alternatively 'a membrane through which aesthetic and commercial values osmotically exchange' (Luke 1992: 230), a situation reminiscent of the buildings that housed nineteenth-century international exhibitions (Hamon 1992: 92). If the ambiguities existent within formal definitions, and changing simulacra, were not confusing enough, a comparison of the mission statements of say the British Museum with the more interventionist Museum of the American Indian, New York, or the Tyne and Wear Museums Service quickly dispels presumptions of similarity and reveals the poverty of generalist approaches which have long troubled museum studies. Museums, as Wilson (1984: 54) cautioned, with their diverse 'forms, functions, philosophy and policies', preclude useful comparison and consistently evade definition and classification.

MUSEUMS AS SITES OF MEMORY

Museums again call on classic mythology through the figure of Mnemosyne, the goddess of memory, the mother of the nine muses, the 'Remembrances'. Once genealogical narratives ignore specific chronological history and memory and collected objects are explained by attributing the activity of collecting to a common, archetypal, psychological complex, museums appear to de- and retemporalize objects and exhibitions in accordance with modern-period meta-narratives. Moreover, because material culture is usually embodied with meaning retrospectively, and reanimated through its role within particular exhibitions, displays are often infused with the 'air' of an 'other', expired, time. It is surprising how little attention has been focused on the way museums manage and construct different relations between history, or for that matter any rationalized disciplinary formation, personal memory, and different constitutive gradations between articulated and unconscious cognitive structures. Halbwachs (1980) noted long ago how in pre-modern societies, historical events are structured by familial and community memory, while Nora (1995: 635) has argued that it is only after the relation between personal memory and the past is broken, as in modern Western societies, that history emerges to fix the past in

a uniform manner to produce stereotypical fictions that it sometimes tries to conflate with remembrance.

Exhibitions, the clearest expression to the public of a museum's identity (Hughes 1997: 157), structure objects spatially to reactivate or create memory anew. Paraphrasing Stewart (1993) and Donato (1979), Silverstone is mindful that 'An object is nothing unless it is part of a collection. A collection is nothing unless it can successfully lay claim to a logic of classification which removes it from the arbitrary or the occasional' (1994: 165). Exhibitions, as temporary classifications, incorporate both spatial and temporal structures, which clearly disclose the museum's role in the construction and reconstruction of temporal orders (Durrans 1988: 145–6), or what Bakhtin calls 'chronotopes' (cf. Levell 2001a: 154). All exhibition involves the 'disorganisation of an order and the organisation of a disorder' (Borinsky 1977: 89). They 'pull together an unstable combination of fragmentary mythologies, polyvocal meanings, and diverse values' whose understanding is arbitrated by interaction between curators and diverse audiences (Luke 1992: 228–9). Once decontextualized and allowed to return to their ruinous state these fragmentary material ciphers of diverse histories and geographies readily induce melancholia (Boone 1991: 256; Shelton 2003: 187). Burgin describes art museums as 'machines for the suppression of history' (1986: 159); Adorno as 'family sepulchres of works of art' (1967: 175) and Kirshenblatt-Gimblett, more humorously, as 'tombs with a view' (1998: 57). Clifford notes museums save objects 'out of time' (1988: 231), while for Crane museums 'freeze time' to precipitate a state that lies beyond it (2000: 93). More melancholic still, Shelton has described them as 'vaults hewn of interstitial melancholia' (1995b: 13), while Harbison locates them between graveyards and department stores, concerned either with the entombment or the commodification of objects (1977).

Nor is this melancholic attitude confined to academics. Merriman's 1987 survey of visiting patterns found that the most common comparison of museums made by less frequent or non-visitor groups, were with monuments to the dead, although this changed among frequent and regular visitors, who more commonly made a connection with libraries. Surprisingly, only 8–14 per cent of his samples made a connection with the temple or church, and hardly any to department stores, despite the oft quoted similarities between them and their shared genealogical origins, evident in some museological literature (e.g. Harbison 1977; Harris 1990; Hamon 1992 (Merriman 1987: 156).[7] Deathly associations, far from literary or prejudiced, are frequently embodied in the design and decoration of older buildings (Harbison 1977: 144; Shelton 1995b: 13–14; Duncan 1995: 83).[8] In some cases, the museum and the tomb of its founder are combined, as at the Dulwich Picture Gallery; others, like Berlin's National Gallery, were built as personal monuments and became transformed into museums to commemorate their former patrons. Funereal associations sometimes accrue to privately sponsored galleries, museums or house museums after their benefactors have deceased; the Barnes Foundation, Merion; the Pitt Rivers Museum, Oxford; the Musée Fragonard d'Alfort and Musée Gustave Moreau in Paris, or the Kahlo House in Mexico. Here, by fusing historical narratives with personal recollections, representation and commemoration are combined, and sometimes catalysed by architecture, to establish potent emotional sites like the Hall of Testimony of the Museum of Tolerance in Los Angeles; or the Washington and Berlin Holocaust museums and the Terezín Museum in Prague. Neither should the spectral association of natural history, anatomical and medical museums be forgotten, most of which inculcate their objective lessons from piles of carefully classified, preserved and mounted dead animals, skeletons and human organs. Small wonder that Harbison opines that a museum's life is 'naturally ghost life, meant for those more comfortable with ghosts, frightened by waking life but not by the past' (1977: 140).

To refer to museums as detemporalizing, ahistorical or static organizations, while greatly oversimplifying their temporal dimensions, also points to their often forgotten temporal complexity. Lumley's (1988: 6) designation of museums as 'time machines' is both apt and precise, though Nora's focus on their double self-referentiality, in which simulation is achieved through them acting as a 'site of excess closed upon itself, concentrated in its own name, but also forever open to the full range of its possible significations' (Nora 1995: 641) opens richer and still hardly acknowledged research opportunities.

Museums stage temporalization of buildings and galleries through spatializing knowledge. Different architectural styles both functionally and symbolically frame and determine the dispensation of objects and collections. Spatial relations between galleries, corridors, floors and staircases structure the circulation and sequence of visits, provide breaks and continuities

between one area and another, and regulate fields of perception by establishing beginnings and closures of knowledge (cf. Harbison 1977: 142; Bal 1992: 561; Boyer 1994: 133; Bouquet 1996: 10–13). 'The museum converts rooms into paths, into spaces leading from and to somewhere' (Bennett 1995: 44); site museums assign different epistemic knowledges to different areas (Handler and Gable 1997: 15). If the Renaissance memory palace organized memory by creating mnemonic associations between classes of objects separated and associated with specific mental or real *topoi*, in the nineteenth century memory received material expression in modern museums (Dias 1994: 166; Boyer 1994: 133). Anderson already recognized the classificatory, totalizing grid which provided the warp and weft, constituted by the effect of serial replication in which the singular stood for the series in a surveyed 'landscape of perfect visibility', with limitless ability to absorb anything that enters the state's jurisdiction, and its pernicious determination of official, subaltern or even alternative identities (1991: 184–5; cf. Shelton 1994: 190). In a similar vein, Ernst acknowledges the changing functions of museums in arranging texts and objects to inscribe private or publicly valued memories seeing them, like Ernst, as '"occupying a position in the discursive field somewhere between bibliotheca, thesaurus, studio, galleria, and theatrum" possessed of their own museology, more concerned with "the disposition of things, the structural relationship that governs their placement, than to the positivity of collections as such"' (2000: 18).

Silverstone makes a distinction between the dominant temporal orientation a museum may avow and the way it consciously uses time through the exhibits and services it provides. Temporal orientation is a kind of museal patina formed over time that frames representations and organization of activities while what Silverstone refers to as 'clocking' concerns a shorter and more limited time perspective based on the visitor experience of sequence, frequency, duration and pace, that has been deliberately incorporated into an exhibition's staging (1994: 170). Thus different temporal order and apparent contradictions between the old and new can often be found uneasily or complementarily juxtaposed together, and may even provide criteria for a classification of museums. Museums like the Fragonard, Moreau, the national military museums in Lisbon and Brussels, the old evolutionary galleries of the Musée d'Histoire Naturelle in Paris, or its sister institution in Toulouse, are characterized by past temporal orientation and slow clocking and exert strong feelings of nostalgia for the past; museums, including the new gallery of the Musée d'Histoire Naturelle and the Musée d'Orsey, Paris, possess a past temporal orientations, but disclose inside an accelerated clocking which exerts a contemporary orientation. Other museums with present temporal orientation and accelerated clocking, like Le Veillet, the Centre Georges Pompidou or the thirteen museums opened in Frankfurt at the end of the twentieth century, appear to disclose a future temporal orientation. These latter sites, like the Tate Modern, achieve far higher visitor figures than sites belonging to other temporal categories.[9]

However, these are rather tidy, rationalized classificatory approaches to museums which hide their complex epistemologies, the different formations between narratives structured historically or by nationally consecrated memories, and the multiplicity of potential meanings they are capable of generating, discussed by authors like Handler and Gable in their study of Colonial Williamsburg (1997: 62); Kirshenblatt-Gimblett's (1998: 194–5) work on Plimoth Plantation, and Holo's description of the contemporary Spanish museumscape (2000: 15). Museums, like all sites of memory:

> are mixed, hybrid, mutant, bound intimately with life and death, with time and eternity; enveloped in a Möbius strip of the collective and the individual, the sacred and the profane, the immutable and the mobile whose purpose is to stop time, to block the work of forgetting, to establish a state of things, to immortalise death, to materialise the immaterial.
>
> (Nora 1995: 639)

Lowenthal (1996: 161) rightly insist commemoration is 'profoundly anti-historic', and along with Nora (1995: 635–6) and Handler and Gable (1997: 35), views museums, monuments, cemeteries, archives, libraries and dictionaries as *les lieux de mémoire*, dislocated fragmentary sites of memory, which history continues to rework and transform in its attempts to subject experience of the intimately lived past to contemporary rationalizing narratives harnessed to the interests of an emergent democratic, mass future. Societies that assured the transmission and preservation of collectively held values, that valued the preservation of specific objects that enshrined collective memory, and those ideologies that ensured a smooth transition from the past to the future, have all declined, necessitating '*lieux de mémoire*, sites of memory,

because there are no longer *milieux de mémoire*, real environments of memory' (Nora 1995: 632). Such sites not only unavoidably restructure memory into narrative configurations, but narratives themselves can be politically manipulated to re-imagine the nation. In her study of post-democratic Spanish museums Holo describes the political motives behind the construction of the Museo Nacional Centro de Arte Reina Sofia and the Museo Thyssen-Bornemisza in Madrid towards encouraging a more international public vision of art denied during the dictatorship to affirm the vitality of contemporary Spanish culture, and to demonstrate the viability and adoption to the corporate model of museum institutions. Older institutions, long identified with a fossilized and closed image repertoire of the nation, like the Prado, were long ignored, as older memorialized orders of values were constructed to encourage new, modern and democratic genealogies (2000: 197). At the same time, while Madrid's museums sought to re-establish the vitality and moral reformation of the nation state, new provincial museums, established by regional governments to rescue local histories on which their distinct identities have been rationalized for narrative expression, proliferated, creating a structure which acknowledged and sometimes attempted to incorporate national and local structures of memorialization (2000: 116–17).

Nora's view of memory and its intertwinement with historical narratives and less articulated and unconscious knowledge formations complicates, and even undermines, existent theories on the reception of curatorial interpretation in museums. While the relationship between museum narratives and ideology is a subject of frequent disquisition, little attention has been paid to how such narratives are structured to trigger memory, or how group memories mediate the process of interpretation, which has been frequently reduced to formal semiotic terms. The most coherent theoretical presentation of their view is given by Taborsky (1990) in her discussion of Peircean semiotics to the understanding of museums, though again while acknowledging the interplay of different denominations of signs in shaping perception, and the relativity of object meaning, depending on the community interpreting it, she nevertheless equates the interpretant with the community from which s/he is a member, and reduces memory, unconscious association, or 'anti-structure', to knowledge formations. For Taborsky 'the observer is always "grounded" in a specific society, which provides him with a conceptual base which he uses for developing meaning. There is no such thing as a free or cognitively unattached observer' (1990: 70). This position has been pervasive and is represented in the works of Pearce, Hooper-Greenhill and Jordanova among others. These authors not withstanding memory cannot simply be treated as homogeneous or reducible to articulate structures for incorporation into semiotic analysis (cf. Burgin 1986: 183; Zolberg 1996: 80).

Semiotic approaches also frequently ignore the political dimension of exhibitions, which as Macdonald (1997, 2001), Macdonald and Silverstone (1991) and Luke (1992) have convincingly shown, play a determinative role in structuring, organizing and the interpretation and timing of exhibitions. On the other hand, Stafford (1994: 263), Handler and Gable (1997: 7) and Shelton (2000: 162–3) have focused attention on the simultaneous coexistence of different interpretative projects within the same institution; curiosities and classified and standardized specimens in the mid-eighteenth-century royal Cabinet d'Histoire Naturelle in Paris, commercial and antiquarian interests in the nineteenth-century India Museum, London, or celebratory and New Social History displays in Colonial Williamsburg. The continual applicability of semiotic models needs to be comprehensively evaluated in relation to complications added to interpretive readings as a result of the factors discussed above.[10]

Semiotic reductionism holds further serious implications for better understanding some of the root causes of conflicts of interpretation within museum environments. It is the differences between group memories or a group's spatial-temporal articulations that combine memory with other forms of temporal ordering, and the narrative approaches of museums, that have provoked many of the more dramatic confrontations between them and their publics over interpretation (cf. Zolberg 1996: 70). Documented examples of such conflicts can readily be drawn from both the Canadian and US museological literature.

In the United States, the controversy surrounding the Smithsonian's proposed 1995 *Enola Gay* exhibition in which military and veteran lobbyists forced the focus away from the historical circumstances that resulted in the use of the atomic bomb and its effects on Hiroshima to a focus on the personal reminiscences of the plane's designers, makers, restorers and crew, although clearly part of a depoliticizing strategy, was also very personally motivated by the protagonists' own memories (Harwitt 1996: 427; Zolberg 1996: 70; Lubar 1997: 17). 'The West as America' (National Museum of American Art,

1991), an account of America's westward expansion, challenged a decade of dominant self-images underlying the nation's foundation narratives, origins, values and political destiny which had been repeatedly reiterated during the Reagan-Bush years in exhibitions like 'Frederic Remmington: the Masterworks' (St Louis Art Museum, 1988), 'George Caleb Bingham' (National Gallery of Art, Washington, DC, 1990), 'The West Explored: the Gerald Peters Collection of Western Art' (Roanoke Museum of Fine Art, 1990) and others, which ignited the so-called culture wars between conservative and critical supporters. The proposed *Enola Gay* exhibition, through its historicist interpretation, and 'The West as America', by acknowledging the relativist meaning of art works, both confronted and threatened the normative representation of the nation's imaginary narratives of continuity (Truettner 1997: 44). By threatening the neat border around a domain of accepted history, by disrupting established narratives, historiography ran contrary to nationally reproduced and accepted narratives (Nora 1995: 641; Handler and Gable 1997: 24). At another level, however, the controversy that both these exhibitions fell into, as well as some of the few other documented postmodernist shows in the late twentieth century, were also disputes between older institutionalized narratives concerning the foundation and nature of the nation, deconstructvist rereadings of such narratives, and the collision between this latter historiography with dominant or subaltern memories, which may have been influenced by the older historiography. These have been documented in Harwitt's (1996) and Zolberg's (1996: 79) reading of the *Enola Gay* affair, or, in the case of another much disputed exhibition, 'Out of Africa' (Royal Ontario Museum, 1989–90), Butler's (1999) equally revealing description and interpretation of the role played by Canada in British colonial history. It seems probable that to a large extent, the difficulties experienced by modern museum exhibitions primarily stem from the uneasy coexistence of original intention and its rearticulation and representation within memory; 'all *lieux de mémoire* are objects *mises en abîme*' (Nora 1995: 640).

Memorialization in museums is always selective and necessarily accompanied by amnesia. By ignoring colonial history Mexican museums not only focused more precisely on their pre-Hispanic past but were excused from explaining the relationship between it and the contemporary living Indian populations. After the Second World War, West German museums adopted aesthetic approaches to elude the militarism and totalitarianism, even though in the east, the ideological pretensions of such aestheticization were dismissed by the occupying regime in favour of confronting the lessons of historical materialism. Spanish museums, according to Holo (2000: 199–200), in the latter quarter of the twentieth century were successively employed to reformulate and represent an open, tolerant and modern nation state while ackowledging the plurality of previously repressed regional historical realities that constituted it. Bennett's study of Beamish open-air industrial museum finds all mention or effects of class, the trade union or co-operative movements, or women's suffrage or feminism, eluded in a narrative without ruptures and conflicts that favours continuity and the naturalization of people's relation to land and to each other (1988: 67–9). Even Colonial Williamsburg, which for thirty years has attempted to embrace constructivist history and give much greater visibility to the 'other half', still according to Handler and Gable falls back into objectivism and reaffirmation of America's national mythologies. Luke's discussion of exhibitions during the Reagan-Bush presidencies, treating the theme of America's conceptualization of its western expansion, draws attention to parallel imaginaries dominating political, military and business discourses. These reaffirm and renew themselves historically through rerunning exhibitions on iconic heroic views of the nation's history represented by Bingham and Remmington; alternatively they may be used to materially brand a region with lifestyle values independent of its real condition (the use of O'Keeffe); or substitute symbolic acknowledgement of minority cultures for programmes for the amelioration of their marginalized condition ('Hispanic Art in the United States: Thirty Contemporary Painters and Sculptors' (Museum of Fine Arts, Santa Fe, CA, 1988). Examination of other contested exhibitions (MacDonald 1997, 2001; MacDonald and Silverstone 1992; Bouquet 1997; Clifford 1997; Levell 2001a; Butler 1999; Riegel 1996; Zolberg 1996; Harwitt 1996; Luke 1992) illustrates the usual elusion of some part of history necessary to affirm the preferred institutional interpretation.

THE END OF GRAND FOUNDATION NARRATIVES

If the still largely unexamined literature discussed in the introduction to this chapter, along with its associated publications (histories, descriptions and inventories of museum collections, catalogues, exhibition reviews, marketing literature, professional guidelines, reports, etc.), once provided the successive bases for the practical organization and operation of museums, by the last quarter of the twentieth century it had began to lose much of its former legitimatory conviction. In 1970 the annual general meeting of the American Association of Museums was repeatedly disrupted by protesters demanding that museums should abandon their traditional prerogatives by breaking their ties with the 'establishment' and redirecting their resources to eliminate social injustice, war and repression. Although no coherent critique or reform programme in the early 1970s had been formulated, at least four diverse dissenting currents have since then radically changed assumptions regarding the purposes and functions of museums, the demarcation of their institutional boundaries, and the suitability of subjects that form the focus of exhibitionary presentation (cf. Macdonald 1996: 1). André Malraux, a precursor to the sustained criticism which was to follow, challenged the presuppositions underlying Bazin's *The Museum Age* (1967) by contrasting the freedom and inclusivity of the personal recollections of works we carry in our mind, his 'museums without walls', with the overdetermined, selective and partial works displayed in galleries (Malraux, 1976: 133). More important, when seen in relation to his earlier work, *The Voices of Silence* first published in 1953, there is a clear implication that the personal museum without walls could be materialized through print. The rise of 'print capitalism', which made possible the reproduction, serialization and dissemination of geographical domains, from the mid-nineteenth century changed the form and function of the museum's construction of the imaginary (Anderson 1991: 163–4), leading not only to its literary imitators (Georgel 1994: 114), but complementary technologies to perfect its hegemony (cf. Müller 2002). Malraux presented not a confirmation of the art museum's authority but a deeply subjective and individually more meaningful alternative whose implications museums continue to experience with the development and adoption of digital and other technologies (Levell and Shelton 1998; Müller 2002).

A more explicit front of criticism, crystallizing around Riviere in the 1980s, and clearly forming the first of the national critiques to be discussed here, became variously known as 'active museology', 'experimental museology', 'popular museology' and 'anthropological' or 'ethnographic museology'. The 'French new museology' called for the rethinking of the museum's social purpose and provided the impetus and justification for rural and urban eco-museums, community, special-interest, industrial and national park museums. It radically questioned the institutional boundaries between museum and non-museum spaces; the nature and relevance of the connection between museums and collections; and even the location of expertise (Mayrand 1985: 200; Poulot 1994: 67). Hoyau's observation in particular that 'once the notion of "heritage" has been cut free from its attachment to beauty, anything can be part of it ... so long as it is historical evidence' (1988: 29–30) anticipated the application of new cultural technologies to substantially extend the museum's competence to include landscapes and cityscapes, industrial and community complexes, archaeological sites and theme parks. Furthermore, the adoption of new technologies has radically changed the media, what Haraway (1984–85: 30) calls 'technologies of enforced meaning', by which collections are interpreted. No longer are collections only deployed to stage a metonymic representation of an aspect of the external world. Increasingly, they are undergoing a secondary capture and recontextualization through electronic media, which in science museums may supersede the physical integrity of objects (Silverstone 1994: 172). The adoption of new media is partly subsuming established oppositions between material culture and interpretation with virtual simulation, which while substituting the 'aura' of the authentic and unique work with extended levels of information opens a new epistemological field of representative practices (Boyer 1994: 66; Stafford 1997: 23; Müller 2002), hitherto ignored by most museologists. Simulations are increasingly exploited by museums – Bologna's Nuovo Museo Elettronico has no physical integrity but exists only as a simulated three-dimensional environment, which enables the city's history to become accessible, while the Dutch Identity Factory South-east (Identiteitsfabriek zuidoost), includes multiple narratives, collated from different cultural sites (museums, landscapes, monuments, etc.), to provide a heterodox inventory pertaining to Kempenland's cultural identity. Projects like these are not only establishing new ontological bases from which to understand reality, but are determining some of the most significant transformation of Western ocular regimes since the nineteenth century. According to one of the bleakest evaluations of such tendencies, 'We

live among the interminable reproduction of ideals, phantasies, images and dreams which are now behind us, yet which we must continue to reproduce in a sort of inescapable indifference' (Baudrillard 1993: 4).

In North America a second series of critiques developed among others by Weill (1983, 1990), Sturtevant (1969), MacDonald (1992), Ames (1992) and Haas (1996) challenged the museum's continual social and, in some cases, academic relevance, its functional crises, and called for new directions in museology. Vine Deloria Jr and Clavir noted the limited relevance Western museums have for First Nation peoples and the clashes over the interpretation, relevance and use to which such collections should be put. Studies highlighted how different ethnic groups memorialize events and the different significance and interpretations they bestow on objects: Abrams (1994), Saunders (1995), Merrill and Ahlborn (1997), Wilson (2000) and Clavir (2002), on First Nation Americans, and Hall (1995) and Coombes (1994) on Africa. Similar concerns, in countries like Nigeria, where colonial museums had not been rearticulated in the service of new nation states,[11] have preoccupied curators there (Eyo 1988; Nkanta and Arinze n.d.; Munjeri 1991), though Yaro Gella's new cultural policies in which culture became an integral part in the nation's political and economic development to 'give meaning and order to life' once promised notable changes in the continent's 'largest and most extensive museum system' (Kaplan 1994: 45). In South Africa, the voice of interpretation is being reclaimed by artists working with indigenous populations to replace older racist displays and dioramas by more open, interogative and critical exhibitions (Scotnes 2002). Similar changes are occurring elsewhere. In the Pacific (Anderson and Reeves 1994; Kaeppler 1994; Moser 1995; Clavir 2002) and Asia (Prösler 1996; Appadurai and Breckenridge 1992; Ghose 1992; Taylor 1995).

While Malraux focused on limitations museums placed on personal experience of works of art, Sturtevant, Ames, MacDonald and Haas concerned themselves with the technological, academic and institutional realignments which were beginning to erode their established justification and legitimacy, others have challenged whether the move from a rationalist to an emancipatory meta-narrative has been sufficient to preserve the intellectual basis underlying them. Sola (1992: 102) accused museums of adhering to nineteenth-century models and ignoring crises concerning their institutional identities and sense of purpose. A third series of critiques originated in Britain, where Vergo (1989) questioned the aims and effectivity of exhibitions, which soon widened to discussion of the history and limitations of an essentially methodological and practical non-reflexive museology and its insularity and lack of theoretical concern with museum's relationships to the wider society. At nearly the same time, Shelton published a series of articles (1990, 1992a, b, 1997, 2000, 2001c and d) intended to provide an extensive critique of operational museology, and advocated its replacement by what he termed 'critical museology'. British critical tendencies were accompanied also by a anti-intellectual movement, promoted by Hooper-Greenhill, that blamed the insularity of museums from their publics largely on historical curatorial attitudes and practices (cf. Hooper-Greenhill 1988). Despite Hooper-Greenhill and many of her students' support for a client-focused museology, the public reception of exhibitions is often more complex than most educationalists and lobbyists would admit. Kirshenblatt-Gimblett argues that the museum's scopic regime is used by visitors to also view urban landscapes, and forms a split representational category through which the self can reflexively re-examine itself (1998: 48). This museological conditioning has also been commented on by the artist Sonia Boyce after being confronted by a museum collection of ethnological objects from her native Guyana (1995: 4), and is also evidenced in the demand for *faux* colonial-style real estate development encouraged by the restoration of Colonial Williamsburg (Handler and Gable 1997: 42–3). Riegel suggests that, under certain circumstances the public can actually value their distance from exhibitions, and that while supporting educational programmes, they do not want displays so realistic that they revoke painful past memories (1996: 87). Scattered references like these suggest the complexity of the linkages between different level simulacra in the perception of an increasingly problematicized social 'reality' that require much more attention than has so far been given them.

A fourth, explicitly postcolonial critique emerged among artists and theoreticians like Rasheed Aarans, Sarat Maharaj, Paul Gilroy, Hommi Bhaba and others associated with the journal *Third Text*. These opposed the objectification, essentialization and marginalization of non-European cultural expressions and their exclusion from art history and the world's major museums and galleries (Deliss 1990: 5). The different critiques came together in settler nations where professional organizations and legal provision sought to promote new relationships between museums and originating communities from which their collections had been ceded. NAGPRA legislation in the United States, introduced in 1991, required most museums to make available comprehensive inventories of Native American holdings as a necessary prerequisite for future restitution claims; the Joint Task Force Report on Museums and First Peoples prepared by the Assembly of First Nations and the Canadian Museums Association in 1992 recommended the involvement of native peoples in curating and interpreting heritage, a position similarly adopted by the Australian Council of Museums Associations the following year.[12] With new ethical and juridical concerns affecting the opinions of the professional associations in these countries, different concerns and newly emerging work practices began to divide European museums from those elsewhere in the world.

Although, seven years after the publication of his initial critique, Vergo saw little change in the unreflexive way exhibitions continued to be curated (1994: 149), changes in mainstream professional attitudes became evident from at least 1989, when the Museums Association conference 'Museums 2000' departed from its normally staid insularity by acknowledging the pervasive crises in which museums were embroiled.[13] The crises, already articulated by younger curators, often ignored by the profession, became palpable in presentation after presentation which treated issues like political engagement (San Roman 1992: 26), the need for museums to be proactive in the generation of new cultures rather than passively representing the old (Ghose 1992: 88), demands for reinstitutionalization and new configurations of subject specialisms (Horn 1992: 66), the failure of traditional museology (Sola 1992: 101), crises in curatorship (Cossons 1992: 125; Sola 1992: 105), and problems of future funding (Moody 1992: 44; Perrot 1992: 154; Verbaas 1992: 170). Even the direction and definition of what museums were or were thought to be becoming was contested, with Sola for one proposing an almost unlimited expansion of the concept to include 'any creative effort of cybernetic action upon the basis of [the] complex experience of heritage' (1992: 108). Although then unorthodox, the proposition has nevertheless proved to be consistent with later Information Age perspectives, like those of Ernst (2000) and Müller (2002), as well as certain political initiatives such as the plans underlying France's Commission on the Ethnological Heritage, established in 1978 (Hoyau 1988: 28) and, more recently, the definition adopted by the 2001 European Meeting of Experts on cultural heritage in Antwerp (Capenberghs et al. 2003: 96).

Some of the issues raised by these different critical sources, from the 1970s, became institutionally articulated by the International Committee of Museums (ICOM). Vergo's and other critical works of the period coincided with ICOM's 1985 Declaration of Quebec affirming a new social mission for museums. This focused on community development, a commitment to embed museological actions in the wider cultural and physical environment, and an undertaking to promote a more interdisciplinary, active, communicative and managerially oriented museology in order to better engage visitors (Mayrand 1985: 201). Though it may not have directly influenced the intellectual critiques emerging in 1980s Britain, the declaration was heavily influenced by French critical tendencies, and became instrumental in providing a foundation for a postcolonial museology both among immigrant populations in Europe and among internally colonized peoples in Australia, New Zealand, Canada, Mexico and the United States.

Independently developed French, British North American and postcolonial critiques not only coincided and sometimes merged with the reforms being supported by ICOM, but converged intellectually with the overlapping analyses and arguments of Bourdieu (1993), Burgin (1986), Becker (1982), Carrier (1987) and, more recently, Marcus and Myers (1995), Luke (1992) and Corbey (2000) on the market, politics and class relationships endemic to museums.[14] Theirs, together with critical work over the more general crisis of representation elaborated over approximately the same period by Debord (1990, 1994), Baudrillard (1983, 1993) and Stafford (1994, 1996), bear deep-seated implications for museums, not least of which might suggest the incipient beginning of a new exhibitionary complex in which visual experience is becoming reorganized to reassume the primacy it once had over textual exegesis. For Debord this new complex is characterized by increasing autonomy and elaboration of form over content, while for Baudrillard it is the proliferation of signs and their autonomy over significations in what he calls a viral simulacra that is the cause for most alarm. For Stafford, on the contrary, such a revitalization of visual culture is welcome for its ability to encode information and experience more richly.

New discursive tendencies reinforce the widespread and fundamental reconfiguration of museal and non-museal spaces imputed and effected by the French new museology. Together they imply a consequent reorganization of visual regimes, intellectual paradigms and even perhaps the beginning of a new exhibitionary complex based on the reconstruction of history to create a live heritage, in which the past interfaces and shapes, while becoming itself shaped by, the present. Instead of the past being removed and isolated from the present in museums, new building, architectural and planning technologies are aimed at transposing it and knitting it back together with contemporaneous communities.[15] This has not everywhere received positive acclamation. As early as 1987 *New Society* included a special section on 'the museum mentality' which mildly bemoaned the abandonment and transformation of industry into touristic spectacle (White 1987: 10). Lumley notes the irony of Labour councils turning depleted industrial landscapes, like those of the lower Don valley, the Black Country or Tyne and Wear into nostalgic evocations of working-class pasts, while cities become the host to architecturally innovative, new media museums sponsored by successful entrepreneurs (1988: 17). Both processes are part of wider developments and need to be studied as aspects of a new museum simulacrum which is increasingly substituting the 'traditional' curator's play with metonymy and metaphor for the market manager's indulgences towards the staging of the hyperreal (Lumley 1988: 15, cf. Eco 1986: 1–58). Similar transformations have proliferated elsewhere; in the United States (Luke 1992: 57; Handler and Gable 1997; Kirshenblatt-Gimblett 1998: 131–200; Chappell 2002); throughout Asia (Hendry 2000; Errington 1998; Treib 2002; Stanley 2002), Australasia (Bennett 1995: 128–62) and Africa (Hall 1995). This new exhibitionary complex which includes theme parks, as well as designated buildings and whole cityscapes classified as world heritage sites, implies a radically different relationship between museums and their publics, as well as the publics from which objects have been collected and those where they are being exhibited. Together these new tendencies can be expected to redefine expert subject positions and the kind of knowledges from which exhibitions and spectacles, and multimedia events, will increasingly be based. This still emerging exhibitionary paradigm has been called 'the society of the spectacle' (Debord 1994), or the 'paradigmatic postmodern visual condition' (Stafford 1996) and complements what Phillips has called 'the second Museum Age' (Phillips 2005).

Such diverse critical tendencies are suggestive of a pervasive and global redirection of museum functions away from pure scholarship towards fostering social and political awareness (Mayrand 1985: 201), and correspondingly, it might be added, increased disingenuous symbolic engineering. More than the simple 'contact zones' proposed by Clifford (1997: 192), museums, have become essentially threshold institutions constructed between major intellectual, historical and social fault zones, at the intersections and between the interstices of conflicting, contradictory and paradoxical, pluricultural cross-currents in an increasingly globalized cultural and political economy, that still awaits serious theoreticization and concerted empirical study.

NOTES

1 The Mall, Washington, DC (Longstreth 1991); the National Gallery and National Portrait Gallery on the route between St Paul's Cathedral and Buckingham Palace, London; the museums on Unter den Linden, Berlin, or the national museums along Confederation Boulevard, Ontario/ Hull (MacDonald and Alsford 1989: 10).

2 In Spain and Portugal, for example, where visual culture appears to be undergoing reorganization, new contemporary art and photography museums have emerged which express global → regional integration, while history and folk life museums, rearticulated as ethnographic, community or ecomuseums, reflect the reverse, regional → global relationship.

3 The examples that come most to mind are the thirteen Swedish museums that joined together to research and document agriculture, fishing and forestry (Veillard 1985: 192), and more recently the four Stockholm and Göteborg museums of antiquities and ethnography that since 2000 make up the National Museum of World Cultures. In Spain most national museums are administered at ministerial level, resulting in a high degree of central control.

4 This is very similar to the French eighteenth-century idea of the museum discussed by Georgel (1994: 115–16).

5 Cf. Vergo (1987: 40), MacDonald and Alsford (1989: 34), Hooper Greenhill (1994: 135).

6 K. Thomson's *Treasures on Earth* (2002) and Stephen Weill's *Rethinking the Museum* (1990) are notable exceptions.

7 Bourdieu (1980) suggests that the freedom department stores give their customers to judge their merchandise makes them into 'the poor man's art gallery'. Morton (1988) notes that increased competition between museums and theme parks and malls leads to greater identification between them and the commoditization of visitor experience. The architects of Tate Modern planned the museum as a long street.

8 This arrested time orientation is captured in Richard Ross's *Museology* (1989), a collection of photographs of museum galleries and stores, and Pierre Berenger and Michel Butor's *Les Naufragés de l'Arche* (1994). It is also a reoccurring theme in Peter Greenaway's use of both filmic and museum medias.

9 In its first year Tate Modern exceeded all expectations by attracting 5 million (Thomson 2002: 9). The Centre Georges Pompidou predicted visitor figures in the early 1970s of between 2.5 million and 4.5 million per annum, while in the first year of opening it attracted 7.3 million (Heinich 1988: 201). The success of these museums when measured against a star American attraction like Colonial Williamsburg, which attracts approximately 1 million visitors per annum (Handler and Gable 1997: 19), is noteworthy.

10 Museum labels, which many institutions archive, constitutes a largely unexploited area for research and provides one arena in which past and coexistent interpretation of objects can be traced (Bouquet 1988; Lawrence 1990).

11 See for example the work of Taylor (1995) on Indonesian museums and Yoshida's (2001) description of Japanese museum movement. Also see Eyo (1988), Munjeri (1991), Hall (1995) and Scotnes (2002) for discussion of wider but related issues in the African context.

12 Articles by Peirson Jones, Tivy, Monroe, Bromilow and Terrell provide a good introduction to these issues (*Museums Journal*, March 1993, pp. 24–36). See also Abrams (1994) and Moser (1995).

13 Although museums continued to harbour very real resentment of theoretical critiques, Vergo's reaction may be exaggerated and from his article appears to be based on just one critical review, written for a narrowly defined, even peripheral craft magazine (1994: 159).

14 The steep rise in critical attention given to museums over the 1980s and 1990s, by curators, art practitioners, academics and disaffected minorities, is also clearly

reflected by the increased in conferences and related publications that have emerged in each of its sectors. In the case of ethnographic museums alone, in just eighteen years, major conferences and colloquiums have included: 'Making Exhibitions of Ourselves' (British Museum, 1986), 'Exhibiting Cultures' (Smithsonian Institution, 1988), 'Museums in Dialogue' (Museum für Volkerkunde, Berlin, 1993), 'Ways of Seeing, Ways of Framing, Ways of Displaying' (Museu Antropologico, Coimbra 1993), 'Du musée coloniale au musée des cultures du monde' (Centre Georges Pompidou 1998); 'The World Mirrored' (Nationalmuseet, Copenhagen, 2000), and 'Les arts premiers' (Centro Cultural Calouste Gulbenkian 2002). These conferences have stimulated an impressive literature, including edited collections (Karp and Lavine 1991; Karp et al. 1992) and special editions of journals (*Zeltschrift für Ethnologie*, 1976, and 118 (1), 1993; *Anales del Museo Nacional de Antropologia*, Madrid, 1994; *Cultural Dynamics*, 1995; *Antropologia Portuguesa*, 14, 1997; *Focaal*, 34, 1999; *Cahiers d'Etudes Africaines*, 155–6, 1999; *Ethnos*, 65 (2), 2000; *Folk*, 43, 2001; *Arquivos do Centro Cultural Calouste Gulbenkian*, 45, 2003).

15 Durrans called for the public to participate in curating their own exhibitions as early as 1988 (1988: 166). Hooper-Greenhill gives the examples of Glasgow's Open Museum, which encourages the use of the city's reserve collections by the public to curate their own exhibitions (1994: 134). In the decade since she wrote her article, community projects and renewed commitment to education can be seen throughout the sector in Britain, France and elsewhere. In Britain, Merseyside, Tyne and Wear, Croydon, Walsall and the Horniman Museum have all adopted innovative community and educational compromises.

REFERENCES

Abrams, G. (1994) 'The case for Wampum: repatriation from the Museum of the American Indian to the Six Nations Confederacy, Brentford, Ontario, Canada', in F. Kaplan (ed.), *Museums and the Making of 'Ourselves': the Role of Objects in National Identity*. London and New York: Leicester University Press, pp. 351–84.

Adorno, T. (1967) *Valéry Proust Museum: Prisms*. London: Spearman.

Alexander, E. (1979) *Museums in Motion: an Introduction to the History and Functions of Museums*. Nashville, TN: American Association for State and Local History.

Alexander, E. (1983) *Museum Masters: Their Museums and their Influences*. Nashville, TN: American Association for State and Local History.

Alsop, J. (1982) *The Rare Art Traditions: the History of Art Collecting and its linked Phenomena*. Princeton, NJ: Princeton University Press and New York: Harper & Row.

Ames, M. (1992) *Cannibal Tours and Glass Boxes: the Anthropology of Museums*. Vancouver: University of British Columbia Press.

Ames, M. (2003) 'How to decorate a house: the renegotiation of cultural representations at the University of British Columbia Museum of Anthropology', in L. Peers and A. Brown (eds), *Museums and Source Communities: a Routledge Reader*. London and New York: Routledge, pp. 171–80.

Anderson, B. (1991) *Imagined Communities: Reflections on the Origin and Spread of Nationalism*. London and New York: Verso.

Anderson, M. and Reeves, A. (1994) 'Contested Identities: Museums and the Nation in Australia', in F. Kaplan (ed.), *Museums and the Making of 'Ourselves': the Role of Objects in National Identity*. London and New York: Leicester University Press, pp. 79–124.

Appadurai, A. and Breckenridge, C. (1992) '"Museums are good to think": heritage on view in India', in I. Karp, C. Mullen Kreamer and S. Lavine (eds), *Museums and Communities: the Politics of Public Culture*. Washington, DC: Smithsonian Institution Press, pp. 34–54.

Bal, M. (1992) 'Telling, showing, showing off', *Critical Inquiry*, 18 (3): 556–94.

Baudrillard, J. (1983) *Simulations*. New York: Semiotext(e).

Baudrillard, J. (1993) *The Transparency of Evil: Essays on Extreme Phenomena*. London: Verso.

Bazin, G. (1967) *The Museum Age*. Brussels: Desoer.

Becker, H. (1982) *Art Worlds*. Berkeley, CA and London: University of California Press.

Bennett, T. (1988) 'Museums and "the People"', in R. Lumley (ed.), *The Museum Time Machine*. London and New York: Routledge, pp. 63–85.

Bennett, T. (1995) *The Birth of the Museum: History, Theory, Politics*. London and New York: Routledge.

Berenger, P. and Butor, M. (1994) *Les Naufrages de l'Arche*. Paris: Difference.

Boone, J. (1991) 'Why museums make me sad', in I. Karp and S. Lavine (eds), *Exhibiting Cultures: the Poetics and Politics of museum Display*. Washington, DC and London: Smithsonian Institution Press, pp. 255–77.

Borinsky, A. (1977) *Repetition, Museums, Libraries: Jorge Luis Borges*. Johns Hopkins Textual Studies 2. Baltimore, MD: Johns Hopkins University Press.

Boulton, W.H. (n.d.) *The Romance of the British Museum: the Story of its Origins, Growth and Purpose and Some of its Contents*. London: Sampson Low.

Bouquet, M. (1988) *Melanesian Artefacts: Postmodernist Reflections*. Lisbon: Museu de Etnologia.

Bouquet, M. (1996) *Bringing It All Back Home … to the Oslo University Ethnographic Museum*. Oslo: Universitetsforlaget.

Bouquet, M. (1997) 'On the Making of *Man Ape, Ape Man*: Pithecanthropus in het Pesthuis, Leiden', *Antropologia Portuguesa*, 14: 79–92.

Bouquet, M. (2001) 'Streetwise in Museumland. Folk', *Journal of the Danish Ethographic Society*, 43: 77–102.

Bourdieu, P. (1980) 'The aristocracy of culture', *Media, Culture and Society*, 2: 238.

Bourdieu, P. (1993) *The Field of Cultural Production*. Cambridge: Polity Press.

Bourdieu, P. and Darbel, A. (1991) *The Love of Art: European Art Museums and their Public*. Cambridge: Polity Press.

Boyce, S. (1995) *Peep*. London: Institute of International Visual Arts.

Boyer, M. (1994) *The City of Collective Memory: its Historical Images and Architectural Entertainments*. Cambridge, MA and London: MIT Press.

Burgin, V. (1986) *The End of Art Theory: Criticism and Postmodernity*. London: Macmillan.

Butler, S. (1999) *Contested Representations: Revisiting 'Into the Heart of Africa'*. Amsterdam: Gordon & Breach.

Cabanne, P. (1963) *The Great Collectors*. London: Cassell.

Canclini, N.G. (1995) *Hybrid Cultures: Strategies for Entering and Leaving Modernity*. Minneapolis, MN and London: University of Minnesota Press.

Cannon-Brookes, P. (1984) 'The nature of museum collections', in M. Thompson (ed.), *Manual of Curatorship: a Guide to Museum Practice*. London: Butterworth and the Museums Association, pp. 115–26.

Capenberghs, J., Cools, J. and de Rynck, P., eds (2003) *Visions of Heritage in Flanders and Europe*. Antwerp: Culturele Biografie Vlaanderen.

Carrier, D. (1987) *Artwriting*. Amherst, MA: University of Massachusetts Press.

Chappell, E. (2002) 'The museum and the joy ride: Williamsburg landscapes and the specter of theme parks', in T. Young and R. Riley (eds), *Theme Park Landscapes: Antecedents and Variations*. Washington, DC: Dumbarton Oaks Research Library and Collection, pp. 119–56.

Clavir, M. (2002) *Preserving What is Valued: Museums, Conservation and First Nations*. Vancouver: University of British Columbia Press.

Clifford, J. (1988) *The Predicament of Culture: Twentieth-Century Ethnography, Literature, and Art*. Cambridge, MA: Harvard University Press.

Clifford, J. (1997) *Routes: Travel and Translation in the Late Twentieth Century*. Cambridge, MA: Harvard University Press.

Coombes, A. (1994) *Reinventing Africa: Museums, Material Culture and Popular Imagination*. New Haven, CT: Yale University Press.

Corbey, R. (2000) *Tribal Art Traffic: a Chronicle of Taste, Trade and Desire in Colonial and Post-colonial Times*. Amsterdam: Royal Tropical Institute.

Cossons, N. (1992) 'Rambling reflections of a museum man', in P. Boylan (ed.), *Museums 2000: Politics, People, Professionals and Profit*. London and New York: Routledge and the Museums Association, pp. 123–33.

Debord, G. (1990) *Comments on 'The Society of the Spectacle'*. London, Verso.

Debord, G. (1994) *The Society of the Spectacle*. New York: Zone Books.

Deliss, C. (1990) 'Lotte, or, The transformation of the object', *Durch*, 8–9: 3–28.

Dias, N. (1994) 'Looking at objects: memory, knowledge in nineteenth-century ethnographic displays', in G. Robertson et al. (eds), *Travellers' Tales: Narratives of Home and Displacement*. London and New York: Routledge, pp. 164–6.

Donato, E. (1979) 'The museum's furnace: notes towards a contextual reading of Bouvard and Pécuchet', in J. Harari (ed.), *Textual Strategies: Perspectives in Post-structuralist Criticism*. Ithaca: Cornell University Press, pp. 213–238.

Duncan, C. (1991) 'Art museums and the ritual of citizenship', in I. Karp and S. Lavine (eds), *Exhibiting Cultures: the Poetics and Politics of Museum Display*. Washington, DC, and London: Smithsonian Institution, pp. 88–103.

Duncan, C. (1995) *Civilizing Rituals inside Public Art Museums*. London and New York: Routledge.

Duncan, C. (1996) 'Putting the "Nation" in London's National Gallery', in G. Wright (ed.), *The Formation of National Collections of Art and Archaeology*. Studies in the History of Art 47. Washington, DC: Center for Advanced Study in the Visual Arts, National Gallery of Art, Hanover and London: University Press of New England, pp. 100–11.

Durrans, B. (1988) 'The future of the other: changing cultures on display in ethnographic museums', in R. Lumley (ed.), *The Museum Time-Machine*. London and New York: Routledge, pp. 144–169.

Eco, U. (1986) *Faith in Fakes: Essays*. London: Secker & Warburg.

Elsner, J. (1994) 'A collector's model of desire: the House and Museum of Sir John Soane', in J. Elsner and R. Cardinal (eds), *The Cultures of Collecting*. London: Reaktion Books. pp. 156–76.

Ernst, W. (2000) 'Archi(ve)textures of museology', in S. Crane (ed.), *Museums and Memory*. Stanford, CA: Stanford University Press, pp. 17–34.

Errington, S. (1998) *The Death of Authentic Primitive Art and other Tales of Progress*. Berkeley, CA, and London: University of California Press.

Eyo, E. (1988) 'Conventional museums and the quest for relevance in Africa', in M.J. Arnoldi, C. Geary and K. Hardin (eds), *Proceedings of the May 1988 Conference and Workshop on African Material Culture*. Joint Committee on African Studies, American Council of Learned Societies and Social Science Research Council.

Fernández, L.A. (1993) *Museologia: introducción a la teoría e práctica del museo*. Madrid: Istmo.

Forster-Hahn, F. (1996) 'Shrine of art or signature of a new nation? The national gallery (ies) in Berlin, 1848–1968', in G. Wright (ed.), *The Formation of National Collections of Art and Archaeology*. Washington, DC: National Gallery of Art.

Gaehtgens, T. (1996) 'The museum island in Berlin', in G. Wright (ed.), *The Formation of National Collections of Art and Archaeology*. Washington, DC: National Gallery of Art.

García Canclini, N. (1995) *Hybrid Cultures: Strategies for Entering and Leaving Modernity*. Minneapolis, MN, and London: University of Minnesota Press.

Georgel, C. (1994) 'The museum as metaphor in nineteenth-century France', in D. Sherman and I. Rogoff (eds), *Museum Culture: Histories, Discourses, Spectacles*. London and New York: Routledge, pp. 113–22.

Ghose, S. (1992) 'People's participation in science museums', in P. Boylan (ed.), *Museums 2000: Politics, People, Professionals and Profit*. London and New York: Routledge and the Museums Association, pp. 84–8.

Goode, G. Brown (1895) *The Principles of Museum Administration*. York: Coultas & Volans.

Haas, J. (1996) 'Power, objects, and a voice for anthropology', *Current Anthropology*, supplement, 37: 1–22.

Habermas, J. (1983) 'Modernity: an incomplete project', in H. Foster (ed.), *The Anti-aesthetic: Essays on Postmodern Culture*. Washington, Bay Press, pp. 3–15.

Habermas, J. (1989) *The Structural Transformation of the Public Sphere: an Inquiry into a Category of Bourgeois Society*. Cambridge, MA: MIT Press.

Halbwachs, M. (1980) *The Collective Memory*. New York: Harper & Row.

Hall, M. (1995) 'Great Zimbabwe and the lost city: the cultural colonization of the South African past', in P. Ucko (ed.), *Theory in Archaeology: a World Perspective*. London and New York: Routledge, pp. 28–45.

Hamon, P. (1992) *Expositions: Literature and Architecture in Nineteenth-Century France*. Berkeley, CA, and London: University of California Press.

Handler, R. and Gable, E. (1997) *The New History in an Old Museum: Creating the Past at Colonial Williamsburg*. Durham, NC, and London: Duke University Press.

Haraway, D. (1984–5) 'Teddy bear patriarchy: taxidermy in the Garden of Eden 1908–1936', *Social Text*, 11: 19–64.

Harbison, R. (1977) *Eccentric Spaces*. London: Secker & Warburg.

Harris, N. (1990) *Cultural Excursions: Marketing Appetites and Cultural Tastes in Modern America*. Chicago, University of Chicago Press.

Harwitt, M. (1996) *An Exhibit Denied: Lobbying the History of Enola Gay*. New York: Copernicus Springer.

Hatton, R. and Walker, J. (2000) *Supercollector: A Critique of Charles Saatchi*. London: Ellipsis.

Hendry, J. (2000) *The Orient Strikes Back*. Oxford: Berg.

Hoffmann, D. (1994) 'The German Art Museum and the history of the nation', in D. Sherman and I. Rogoff (eds), *Museum Culture: Histories, Discourses, Spectacles*. London and New York: Routledge, pp. 3–21.

Holm, M. and Pokotylo, D. (1997) 'From policy to practice: a case study in collaborative exhibits with First Nations', *Journal Canadien d'Archéologie*, 21: 33–43.

Holo, S. (2000) *Beyond the Prado: Museums and Identity in Democratic Spain*. Liverpool: Liverpool University Press.

Hooper-Greenhill, E. (1988) 'Counting visitors or visitors who count?' in R. Lumley (ed.), *The Museum Time-Machine*. London and New York: Routledge, pp. 213–32.

Hooper-Greenhill, E. (1989) 'The museum in the disciplinary society', in S. Pearce (ed.), *Museum Studies in Material Culture*. Leicester: Leicester University Press, pp. 61–72.

Hooper-Greenhill, E. (1994) 'Museum education: past, present, future', in R. Miles and L. Zavala (eds), *Towards the Museum of the Future: New European Perspectives*. London and New York: Routledge.

Horn, D. (1992) '"Reading" Museums', in P. Boylan (ed.), *Museums 2000: Politics, People, Professionals and Profit*. London and New York: Routledge and the Museums Association, pp. 62–74.

Hoyau, P. (1988) 'Heritage and the "conserver society": the French case', in R. Lumley (ed.), *The Museum Time Machine*. London and New York: Routledge, pp. 25–35.

Hughes, E. (1997) 'The unstifled muse: the "All in the Family" exhibit and popular culture at the National Museum of American History', in A. Henderson and A. Kaeppler (eds), *Exhibiting Dilemmas: Issues of Representation at the Smithsonian*. Washington, DC, and London: Smithsonian Institution Press, pp. 156–75.

Joachimides, A. (2000) 'The museum's discourse on art: the formation of curatorial art history in turn-of-the-century Berlin', in S. Crane (ed.), *Museums and Memory*. Stanford, CA: Stanford University Press, pp. 200–20.

Kaeppler, A. (1994) 'Paradise regained: the role of Pacific museums in forging national identity', in F. Kaplan (ed.), *Museums and the Making of Ourselves*. Leicester: Leicester University Press, pp. 19–44.

Kaplan, F. (1994) 'Introduction', in F. Kaplan (ed.), *Museums and the Making of 'Ourselves': the Role of*

Objects in National Identity. London and New York: Leicester University Press, pp. 1–15.

Karp, I. and Lavine, S. (eds) (1991) *Exhibiting Cultures: The Poetics and Politics of Museum Display*. Washington, DC: Smithsonian Institution Press.

Karp, I., Mullen Kraemer, C. and Lavine, S. (eds) (1992) *Museums and Communities: The Politics of Public Culture*. Washington, DC: Smithsonian Institution Press.

Kirshenblatt-Gimblett, B. (1998) *Destination Culture: Tourism, Museums, and Heritage*. Berkeley, CA, and London: University of California Press.

Krug, K., Fenger, A.-M. and Ames, M. (1999) 'The face of MOA: a museum out of the ordinary', *Archiv für Völkerkunde*, 50: 249–63.

Lawrence, G. (1990) 'Object lessons in the museum medium', in S. Pearce (ed.), *Objects of Knowledge. New Research in Museum Studies: An International Series 1*. London: Athlone Press, pp. 103–24.

Levell, N. (2000) *Oriental Visions: Exhibition, Travel and Collecting in the Victorian Age*. London: Horniman Museum and Coimbra: Museu de Antropologia, Universidade de Coimbra.

Levell, N. (2001a) 'The poetics and prosaics of exhibition making: a personal reflection on the centennial gallery', *Antropologia Portuguesa*, 18: 151–94.

Levell, N. (2001b) 'Scholars and connoisseurs: knowledge and taste: the Seligman collection of Chinese art', in A. Shelton (ed.), *Collectors: Expressions of Self and Other*. London: Horniman Museum and Coimbra: Museu de Antropologia, Universidade de Coimbra, pp. 73–90.

Levell, N. and Shelton, A. (1998) 'Text, illustration and reverie: some thoughts on museums, education and new technologies', *Journal of Museum Ethnography*, 10: 15–34.

Lewis, G. (1984) 'Collections, collectors and museums: a brief world survey', in J. Thompson (ed.), *Manual of Curatorship: a Guide to Museum Practice*. London: Butterworth and the Museums Association, pp. 7–22.

Longstreth, R., ed. (1991) *The Mall in Washington, 1791–1991. Studies in the History of Art*. Washington, DC: Center for Advanced Study in the Visual Arts, National Gallery of Art.

Lowenthall, D. (1996) *The Heritage Crusade and the Spoils of History*. London and New York: Viking Press.

Lubar, S. (1997) 'Exhibiting memories', in A. Henderson and A. Kaeppler (eds), *Exhibiting Dilemmas: Issues of Representation at the Smithsonian*. Washington, DC, and London: Smithsonian Institution Press, pp. 15–27.

Luke, T. (1992) *Shows of Force: Power, Politics and Ideology in Art Exhibitions*. Durham, NC, and London: Duke University Press.

Lumley, R. (1988) 'Introduction', in R. Lumley (ed.), *The Museum Time-Machine*. London and New York: Routledge, pp. 1–23.

Lyotard, J.-F. (1984) *The Postmodern Condition: a Report on Knowledge*. Manchester: Manchester University Press.

MacDonald, G. (1992) 'Change and challenge: museums in the information society', in I. Karp, C. Mullen Kreamer and D. Lavine (eds), *Museums and Communities: the Politics of Public Culture*. Washington, DC: Smithsonian Institution Press, pp. 160–81.

MacDonald, G. and Alsford, S. (1989) *A Museum for the Global Village: the Canadian Museum of Civilization*. Hull, ON: Canadian Museum of Civilization.

Macdonald, S. (1996) 'Theorizing museums: an introduction', in S. Macdonald and G. Fyfe (eds), *Theorizing Museums: Representing Identity and Diversity in a Changing World*. Oxford: Blackwell and Malden: Sociological Review, pp. 1–18.

Macdonald, S. (1997) 'The museum as mirror: ethnographic reflections', in A. James, J. Hockey and A. Dawson (eds), *After Writing Culture: Epistemology and Praxis in Contemporary Anthropology*. ASA Monograph 34. London and New York: Routledge, pp. 161–76.

Macdonald, S. (2001) 'Behind the Scenes at the Science Museum, London Knowing, making and using', in M. Bouquet (ed.), *Academic Anthropology and the Museum. Back to the Future*. New York and Oxford: Berghahn Books, pp. 117–40.

Macdonald, S. and Silverstone, R. (1991) 'Rewriting the museums fictions: taxonomies, stories and readers', *Cultural Studies*, 4 (2): 176–91.

Macdonald, S. and Silverstone, R. (1992) 'Science on display: the representation of scientific controversy in museum exhibitions', *Public Understanding of Science*, 1: 69–87.

Malraux, A. (1974) *Picasso's Mask*. London: Macdonald & Jane's.

Malraux, A. (1978) *The Voices of Silence*. Princeton, NJ: Princeton University Press.

Marchand, S. (2000) 'The quarrel between the ancients and the moderns in the German museums', in S. Crane (ed.), *Museums and Memory*. Stanford, CA: Stanford University Press, pp. 179–99.

Marcus, G. (1990) 'The production of European high culture in Los Angeles: the J. Paul Getty Trust as artificial curiosity', *Cultural Anthropology*, 3: 314–30.

Marcus, G. (1995) 'The power of contemporary work in an American art tradition to illuminate its own power relations', in G. Marcus and F. Myers (eds), *The Traffic in Culture: Refiguring Art and Anthropology*. Berkeley, CA, and London: University of California Press, pp. 201–23.

Marcus, G. and Myers, F. (1995) 'The traffic in art and culture: an introduction', in G. Marcus and F. Myers (eds), *The Traffic in Culture: Refiguring Art and Anthropology*. Berkeley, CA, and London: University of California Press, pp. 1–51.

Mather, P. et al. (1986) *A Time for a Museum: the History of the Queensland Museum, 1862–1986.* Brisbane: Queensland Museum.

Mayrand, P. (1985) '*The New Museology Proclaimed*', *Museum* (UNESCO), 148: 200–1.

McClellan (1996) 'Nationalism and the origins of the museum in France', in G. Wright (ed.), *The Formation of National Collections of Art and Archaeology*. Studies in the History of Art 47. Washington, DC: Center for Advanced Study in the Visual Arts, National Gallery of Art; Hanover and London: University Press of New England, pp. 29–40.

Merrill, W. and Ahlborn, R. (1997) 'Zuni archangels and Ahayu:da: a sculptured chronicle of power and identity', in A. Henderson and A. Kaeppler (eds), *Exhibiting Dilemmas: Issues of Representation at the Smithsonian*. Washington, DC, and London: Smithsonian Institution Press, pp. 176–205.

Merriman, N. (1987) 'Museum visiting as a cultural phenomenon', in P. Vergo (ed.), *The New Museology*. London: Reaktion Books, pp. 149–71.

Moody, E. (1992) 'Art and politics', in P. Boylan (ed.), *Museums 2000: Politics, People, Professionals and Profit*. London and New York: Routledge and the Museums Association, pp. 42–6.

Morales-Moreno, L. (1994a) 'History and patriotism in the National Museum of Mexico', in F. Kaplan (ed.), *Museums and the Making of 'Ourselves': The Role of Objects in National Identity*. London and New York: Leicester University Press, pp. 171–91.

Morales-Moreno. L. (1994b) *Orígenes de la Museología Mexicana: fuentes para el estudio histórico del Museo Nacional, 1780–1940*. Mexico DF: Universidade Iberoamericano.

Mordaunt Crook, J. (1972) *The British Museum*. London: Allan Lane the Penguin Press.

Morton, A. (1988) 'Tomorrow's yesterdays: science museums and the future', in R. Lumley (ed.), *The Museum Time-Machine*. London and New York: Routledge, pp. 128–43.

Moser, S. (1995) 'The "Aboriginalization" of Australian archaeology: the contribution of the Australian Institute of Aboriginal Studies to the indigenous transformation of the discipline', in P. Ucko (ed.), *Theory in Archaeology: a World Perspective*. London and New York: Routledge, pp. 150–77.

Müller, K. (2002) 'Museums and virtuality', *Curator: The Museums Journal*, 45, 1.

Munjeri, D. (1991) 'Refocusing or reorientation? The exhibit or the populace: Zimbabwe on the threshold', in I. Karp and S. Lavine (eds), *Exhibiting Cultures: the Poetics and Politics of Museum Display*. Washington, DC: Smithsonian Institution Press, pp. 444–56.

Nkanta, M. and Arinze, E. (n.d.) *The Lost Treasures of Ancient Benin*. Benin City: National Museum.

Nora, P. (1995) 'Between memory and history: *les lieux de mémoire*', in Jacques Revel and L. Hunt (ed.), *Histories: French Constructions of the Past: Post-war French Thought I*. New York: New Press, pp. 631–43.

Pearce, S. (1992) *Museums, Objects and Collections: a Cultural Study*. Leicester: Leicester University Press.

Penny, H. (2002) *Objects of Culture: Ethnology and Ethnographic Museums in Imperial Germany*. Chapel Hill, NC, and London: University of North Carolina Press.

Perrot, P. (1992) 'Funding, sponsorship and corporate support', in P. Boylan (ed.), *Museums 2000: Politics, People, Professionals and Profit*. London and New York: Routledge and the Museums Association, pp. 148–54.

Phillips, R. (2005) 'Re-placing Objects in the Second Museum Age: Historical Practices of Retrieval and Performance', *Canadian Historical Review*, 86 (1).

Porto, N. (1999) *Angola a preto e branco: fotografia e ciência no museu do Dundo*. Coimbra: Museu Antropológico da Universidade de Coimbra.

Poulot, D. (1994) 'Identity as self-discovery: the eco-museum in france', in D. Sherman and I. Rogoff (eds), *Museum Culture: Histories, Discourses, Spectacles*. London and New York: Routledge, pp. 66–84.

Prösler, M. (1996) 'Museums and globalization', in S. Macdonald and G. Fyfe (eds), *Theorizing Museums: Representing Identity and Diversity in a Changing World*. Oxford and Malden: Blackwell and the *Sociological Review*, pp. 21–44.

Puloy, M. (1996) 'High art and National Socialism Part 1, The Linz Museum as ideological arena', *Journal of the History of Collections*, 8 (2): 201–16.

Richards, T. (1993) *The Imperial Archive: Knowledge and the Fantasy of Empire*. London and New York: Verso.

Riegel, H. (1996) 'Into the heart of irony: ethnographic exhibitions and the politics of difference', in S. MacDonald and G. Fyfe (eds), *Theorizing Museums: Representing Identity and Diversity in a Changing World*. Oxford: Blackwell/Sociological Review, pp. 83–104.

Ritchie, I. (1994) 'An architect's view of recent developments in European museums', in R. Miles and L. Zavala (eds), *Towards the Museum of the Future: New European Perspectives*. London and New York: Routledge, pp. 7–30.

Rodrigues, J. (2001) 'Un repositorio de la imagen de lo nacional', in *El Museo Nacional en el imaginario mexicano. Alquimia*, 4 (12): 4–5.

Ross, R. (1989) *Museology*. Santa Barbara, CA: University Art Museum and Aperture Foundation.

San Roman, L. (1992) 'Politics and the role of museums in the rescue of identity', in P. Boylan (ed.), *Museums 2000: Politics, People, Professionals and Profit*. London and New York: Routledge and the Museums Association, pp. 25–31.

Saunders, B. (1995) 'Kwakwaka'wakw museology', in A. Shelton (ed.), *Museums and Changing Perspectives on Culture: Cultural Dynamics*, 7 (1): 37–68.

Scotnes, P. (2002) 'The politics of Bushman repesentations', in P. Landau and D. Kaspin (eds), *Images and Empires: Visuality in Colonial and Postcolonial Africa*. Berkeley, CA, and London: University of California Press, pp. 253–74.

Shelton, A. (1990) 'In the lair of the monkey: notes towards a postmodernist museography', in S. Pearce (ed.), *Objects of Knowledge. New Research in Museum Studies* 1. London: Athlone Press, pp. 78–102.

Shelton, A. (1992a) 'The recontextualisation of culture in UK museums', *Anthropology Today*, 8 (5): 11–16.

Shelton, A. (1992b) 'Constructing the global village', *Museums Journal*, August, pp. 25–8.

Shelton, A. (1994) 'Cabinets of transgression: Renaissance collections and the incorporation of the New World', in J. Elsner and R. Cardinal (eds), *The Cultures of Collecting*. London: Reaktion Books, pp. 177–203.

Shelton, A. (1995a) 'Dispossessed histories: Mexican museums and the institutionalization of the past', in A. Shelton (ed.), *Museums and Changing Perspectives of Culture: Cultural Dynamics*, 7 (1): 69–100.

Shelton, A. (1995b) 'Museums: holds of meaning, cargoes of re-collections', in G. Hilty, D. Reason and A. Shelton, *Hold: Acquisition, Representation, Perception: Work by Shirley Chubb*. Brighton: Royal Pavilion Art Gallery and Museums, pp. 13–26.

Shelton, A. (1997) 'The Future of Museum Ethnography', *Journal of Museum Ethnography*, 9: 33–48.

Shelton, A. (2000) 'Museum ethnography: an imperial science', in E. Hallam and B. Street (eds), *Cultural Encounters: Representing 'Otherness'*. London and New York: Routledge, pp. 155–93.

Shelton, A., ed. (2001a) *Collectors: Self and Other*. London: Horniman Museum and Coimbra: Museu de Antropologia, Universidade de Coimbra.

Shelton, A., ed. (2001b) *Collectors: Individuals and Institutions*. London: Horniman Museum and Coimbra: Museu de Antropologia, Universidade de Coimbra.

Shelton, A. (2001c) 'Museums in an age of cultural hybridity', *Folk: Journal of the Danish Ethnographic Society*, 43: 221–50.

Shelton, A. (2001d) 'Unsettling the meaning: critical museology, art, and anthropological discourse', in M. Bouquet (ed.), *Academic Anthropology and the Museum: Back to the Future*. New York and Oxford: Berghahn Books, pp. 142–61.

Shelton, A. (2003) 'Curating African worlds', in L. Peers and A. Brown (eds), *Museums and Source Communities: a Routledge Reader*. London and New York: Routledge, pp. 181–93.

Sherman, D. (1994) 'Quatremére/Benjamin/Marx: art museums, aura, and commodity fetishism', in D. Sherman and I. Rogoff (eds), *Museum Culture: Histories Discourses Spectacles*. London: Routledge, pp. 123–43.

Silverstone, R. (1994) 'The medium is the museum: on objects and logics in times and spaces', in R. Miles and Lauro Zavala (eds), *Towards the Museum of the Future: New European Perspectives*. London and New York: Routledge, pp. 161–76.

Smith, W.H., ed. (1967) *Horace Walpole: Writer, Politician, and Connoisseur*. New Haven, CT, and London: Yale University Press.

Sola, T. (1992) 'Museum professionals: the endangered species', in P. Boylan (ed.), *Museums 2000: Politics, People, Professionals and Profit*. London and New York: Routledge and the Museums Association, pp. 101–13.

Stafford, B. (1994) *Artful Science: Enlightenment Entertainment and the Eclipse of Visual Education*. Cambridge, MA: MIT Press.

Stafford, B. (1996) *Good Looking: Essays on the Virtue of Images*. Cambridge, MA: MIT Press.

Stanley, N. (2002) 'Chinese theme parks and national identity', in T. Young and R. Riley (eds), *Theme Park Landscapes: Antecedents and Variations*. Washington, DC: Dumbarton Oaks Research Library and Collection, pp. 269–90.

Stewart, S. (1993) *On Longing: Narratives of the Miniature, the Gigantic, the Souvenir, the Collection*. Durham, NC, and London: Duke University Press.

Sturtevant, W. (1969) 'Does anthropology need museums?' *Proceedings of the Biological Society of Washington*, 82: 619–50.

Taborsky, E. (1990) 'The Discursive Object', in S. Pearce (ed.), *Objects of Knowledge. New Research in Museum Studies*, Volume 1. London: Athlone Press, pp. 50–77.

Taylor, P. (1995) 'Collecting icons of power and identity: transformation of Indonesian material culture in the museum context', in A. Shelton (ed.), *Museums and Changing Perspectives of Culture, Cultural Dynamics*, 7 (1): 101–24.

Tenenbaum, B. (1994) 'Streetwise history: the Paseo de la Reforma and the Porfirian State, 1876–1910', in W. Beezley, C. Martin and W. French (eds), *Rituals of Rule, Rituals of Resistance: Public Celebrations and Popular Culture in Mexico*. Wilmington, DE: Scholarly Resources Books, pp. 127–50.

Tenorio Trillo, M. (1996) *Mexico at the World Fairs: Crafting a Modern Nation*. Berkeley, CA, and London: University of California Press.

Thomson, K. (2002) *Treasures on Earth: Museums, Collections and Paradoxes*. London: Faber.

Treib, M. (2002) 'Theme park, themed living: the case of Huis Ten Bosch (Japan)', in T. Young and R. Riley (eds), *Theme Park Landscapes: Antecedents and Variations*. Washington, DC: Dumbarton Oaks Research Library and Collection, pp. 213–34.

Truettner, W. (1997) 'For Museum audiences: the morning of a new day?' in A. Henderson and A. Kaeppler (eds), *Exhibiting Dilemmas: Issues of Representation at the Smithsonian*. Washington,

DC, and London: Smithsonian University Press, pp. 28–46.

Veillard, J.-Y. (1985) 'The valueless object', *Museum* (UNESCO), 148: 191–93.

Verbaas, F. (1992) 'Options and unique commercial opportunities for museums now and in the future', in P. Boylan (ed.), *Museums 2000: Politics, People, Professionals and Profit*. London and New York: Routledge and the Museums Association, pp. 169–78.

Vergo, P., ed. (1989) *The New Museology*. London: Reaktion Books.

Vergo, P. (1994) 'The rhetoric of display', in R. Miles and L. Zavala (eds), *Towards the Museum of the Future: New European Perspectives*. London and New York: Routledge, pp. 149–59.

Weill, S. (1983) *Beauty and the Beasts: on Museums, Art, the Law, and the Market*. Washington, DC: Smithsonian Institution Press.

Weill, S. (1990) *Rethinking the Museum and other Meditations*. Washington, DC: Smithsonian Institution Press.

White, D. (1987) 'The born-again museum', *New Society*, 80 (1270): 10–14.

Wilson, D. (1984) 'National museums', in J. Thompson, D. Bassett, G. Davis et al. (eds), *Manual of Curatorship: a Guide to Museum Practice*. London: Butterworth, pp. 54–8.

Wilson, D. (2000) 'Realizing memory, transforming history: Euro/American/Indian', in S. Crane (ed.), *Museums and Memory*. Stanford, CA: Stanford University Press, pp. 115–36.

Yoshida, K. (2001) 'Tohaku and Minpaktu within the history of modern Japanese civilization: Museum collections in modern Japan', in T. Umesao, A. Lockyear and K. Yoshida (eds) *Japanese Civilization in the Modern World. Collection and Representation*. Osaka: National Museum of Ethnology.

Zolberg, V. (1996) 'Museums as contested sites of remembrance: the *Enola Gay* affair', in S. MacDonald and G. Fyfe (eds), *Theorizing Museums: Representing Identity and Diversity in a Changing World*. Oxford: Blackwell/*Sociological Review*, pp. 69–82.

31

MONUMENTS AND MEMORIALS

Michael Rowlands and Christopher Tilley

MONUMENTALIZING THE PAST

Monuments and memorials exist as a means of fixing history. They provide stability and a degree of permanence through the collective remembering of an event, person or sacrifice around which public rites can be organized. This is a fairly straightforward understanding of why tangible heritages of objects, archives, museums, monuments and memorials exist in order to make us believe in the permanence of identity. Moreover, following Nora's now classic work on *lieux de mémoires*, these sites of memory are consciously held ideas of the past, constructed usually in the midst of upheaval (Nora 1989). The rise of national memory emerged in Europe in the midst of a crisis of authority. The foundation of the Louvre museum in 1793 belongs to a revolutionary era in France, whose agents, in the midst of upheaval, needed to fashion a stable image of the past. As Lowenthal suggests, the projection of of an image of permanence on to a landscape serves to deny the realities of change (Lowenthal 1985). As history destroys the capacity for 'real memories', Nora argued that it constructs instead sites of memory as a social and encompassing symbiosis maintained through objects and performances (cf. Nora 1989; Connerton 1989). He draws attention to the alienated status of memory in modern times: an estrangement concretized in monuments, museums and sites of memory (Maleuvre 1999: 59).

The monumentalizing of time is therefore inseparable from changes in social memory. A monument is an object taken out of history, by history. Yet it stands for history in terms of what it has left behind, as a mnemonic trace that also separates it from the present. The nature of the monument lies in the distance it creates for the viewer from both past and present; it belongs neither to an original setting from which it has been abstracted or copied nor to the present, in which it resists assimilation (cf. Maleuvre 1999: 59). Monuments create uncanny spaces of public display and ritual that also function to perform what Boyer refers to as 'civic compositions that teach us about our national heritage and our public responsibilities and assume that the urban landscape is the emblematic embodiment of power and memory' (Boyer 1994: 321). Johnson also emphasizes the duplicitous character of monuments that are materially experienced memorially through the visual and other senses while simultaneously functioning as social symbols (Johnson 2004: 317). Monuments are powerful because they appear to be permanent markers of memory and history and because they do so both iconically and indexically, i.e. they can evoke feelings through their materiality and form as well as symbolize social narratives of events and sacrifices retold in public rituals.

Alois Riegl also argued that the appearance of the 'modern monument cult' depended on a combination of different value judgements; 'historical value' as time-specific and documentary and 'age value', which includes signs of temporal duration from patina and damage to incompleteness and everyday wear and tear. Both defer to time and yet lace it with anxiety over the consequences of change (Starn 2002: 51). Monumental time is constructed as an index of an unchanging value but does so only by losing touch with what is actually remembered. As such monuments and memorials resist memory as much as they celebrate it. On the one hand we have museums for everything from agricultural tools to space exploration as part of the fear that everything in our self-liquidating modernity is threatened with oblivion (cf. Berman 1982) and on the other, for anything to deserve to be preserved suggests that it has already been forgotten. The real becomes cultural heritage, because according to Nora, reality as unproblematic memory has already disappeared. As many have observed, the cult of modern monumental time is therefore imbued with nostalgia. 'Nostalgia is the repetition that mourns the inauthenticity of all repetition and denies the repetition's capacity to form identity' (Stewart 1984: 23). Instead the failures of the present must be apprehended through the acquisition of some redemptive history that promises eventual salvation. This combines with mourning for lost individual autonomy, loss of spontaneity and simplicity and the claim that monumental time is a form of historical consciousness that leads to alienation from our surroundings. Susan Stewart argues that nostalgia is a form of sadness without an object; that it always only exists as a narrative, which attaches itself to an impossibly pure belief in the experience of a utopian origin. As such 'This point of desire which the nostalgic seeks is in fact the absence that is the very generating mechanism of desire – nostalgia is the desire for desire' (Stewart 1984: 23).

A distinct fascination with things memorable is therefore a feature of modernity. 'Collective memory' emerged as an object of scholarly inquiry in the early twentieth century. In *The Social Frameworks of Memory* Maurice Halbwachs argued, against the neurobiologizing, individualizing or racial views of the time, that memory is a specifically social and collective phenomenon (cf. Connerton 1989). The boom in memory studies, as a feature of the 1980s, is witnessed by the appearance of influential works such as Pierre Nora's *Realms of Memory* volumes (1996) and David Lowenthal's *The Past is a Foreign Country* (1985). They share a dissatisfaction with historicist approaches which claim to provide objective, critical reconstructions of the past. In part the heritage debate relates to various anti-historicist trends in postmodernism, claiming that heritage is a late twentieth-century form of social memory which appeals to a sense of the popular and the sensory which had become lost to the objectivism of history. The most common strategy identified public memory with a collection of practices associated with material culture, most obviously in the form of public architecture, archives, museums and monuments, and with more everyday forms of material culture – domestic objects, photographs, mementoes and souvenirs, children's toys, etc. Memory

objectified in material culture becomes an active agent with therapeutic powers (cf. Hoskins 1998; Young 1993). Memory as re-enchantment merges with recent work on trauma theory to promise recovery from loss and denial (Feuchtwang 2003). Memory work is thought most likely to subvert the totalizing varieties of historicism because our epoch has been uniquely structured by trauma and its effects. Moreover Nora's belief that true memory has disappeared could be challenged by the growth of heritage studies showing that memory survived as an authentic mode of discourse in the use of material culture or as a counter-history that challenged the false generalizations of exclusionary history (Samuel 1994).

We have therefore several explanations for a new memorializing of the past. Klein (2000: 143) summarizes these rather well as, first, following Pierre Nora, that we are obsessed with memory because we have destroyed it with historical consciousness. Modern memory is a conscious construct projected on to a sense of place. A second holds that memory is a new experience that grew out of the modernist crisis of the self in the late nineteenth century and has evolved into current usage as part of a cure and a healing process. A third would identify memory as the pre-modern that, *contra* Nora, we still discover in the ethnographic periphery or as 'real-life' experience of the poor, of minorities and the oppressed. Fourth, and following on from the third, that memory is a mode of discourse natural to people without history and so its re-emergence is a salutary feature of decolonization. Finally that memory is now inseparable from identity politics as a post-1980s feature linked to postmodern crises in historical consciousness and the production of totalizing narratives.

MONUMENTS AND PUBLIC MEMORY

There is a large literature on how official urban landscapes of memory – e.g. museums, memorials and monuments – act as stages or backdrops in framing myths of national identity (cf. Johnson 2004; Till 1999: 254). It is practically impossible to conceive of any modern urban landscape which is not saturated with the materiality and style of public buildings and spaces, designed and built in a relevant phase of nation building (in Euro-America e.g. c. 1870–1914). Always they were intended to inculcate a sense of belonging, civic consciousness combined with the everyday familiarity of moving and working in an urban environment. The redesign of the Ringstrasse in Vienna (Schorske 1980) or Haussman's rebuilding of Paris (Edholm 1993) exemplify the monumentalizing of urban form in late nineteenth-cèntury Europe and North America as the expression of triumphant middle-class values. Mosse's study of the rise of German nationalism from the Napoleonic Wars to the rise of National Socialism shows how this 'new politics' drew people into a common sense of belonging through their participation in national rites and festivals (Johnson 1995; Mosse 1975). These spaces of public display and ritual are civic compositions that aim to teach us about national heritage and our public responsibilities and assume that the urban landscape is the emblematic embodiment of power and memory (Boyer 1994: 321). Cultural practices and rituals such as laying wreaths at national memorials or festive parades that take place along a prescribed route serve still to 'naturalize' a collective identity as citizens enact what is normal and appropriate for a group in a particular setting (cf. Till 1999: 254). More often still, the twentieth century became associated with totalitarianism and the transfixing of fantasies of total and enduring power in highly personalized monumental landscapes. Saddam Hussein's 'victory arch' in Baghdad, built to nearly twice the size of the Arc de Triomphe, was made from a cast of his forearms, showing every bump and follicle (Makiya 2004).

Dissident groups may not agree with these rhetorics and may fight to take them over or to create alternatives that are territorially and socially distinct. In the nineteenth century, there were many such disputes over the appropriate nature of monumental urban landscapes, (e.g. Johnson 1995). But disputes over who has the authority to create, define, interpret and represent collective pasts through the creation of place also serves to reinforce the principle that this is how identity should be framed (cf. Kaplan 1994; Mitchell 1988). The formation of nineteenth-century urban imperial landscapes was also inseparable from the building of colonial urban landscapes. The building of Delhi by Lutyens, for example, which grafted British imperial ambitions on to earlier Mughal architectural styles created built forms that were imported back into metropolitan colonial architecture in Britain and the construction of war memorials after the First World War.

Public memory can become even more 'entangled' with the very objects of its negotiation, including historical narratives, oral histories, street landscapes, films, photographs and other cultural productions of collective memory. By collective memory is meant the way in which groups map their myths about themselves and their worlds on to a specific time and place (Connerton 1989, and Chapter 20 in this volume). Collective memory is not an accumulation of individual memories but includes all the activities that go into making a version of the past resonate with group members. This borrows from Halbwachs (1950) the notion that personal recall is localized in specific social and spatial contexts and is reconstructed in the social environments of the present. Hence collective memories are always open to renegotiation and change. But as Till (1999), Sturken (1991) and others stress, 'the cultural arena rather than the academy is the domain of public memory' (Till 1999: 255). They contrast the production of public memory through the media, cultural landscapes, entertainment and public ceremonies and festivals with historical discourses relying on scholarly exegeses and formal university and other institutional networks. The struggle between social groups to gain cultural authority to selectively represent and narrate their pasts includes the production of these means and therefore the right to engage in a cultural politics and to participate in a democratizing process (cf. Hall 2000).

Since the 1980s this struggle has increasingly taken the form of 'heritage' to describe the expanding range of commemoration in our time (Bodnar 2000: 957). Lowenthal argues that heritage is at present much less about 'grand monuments, unique treasures and great heroes' and now 'touts the typical and the vernacular' (Lowenthal 1995). Samuel concludes that 'heritage' has become a nomadic concept that is attached to almost anything, including landscapes, houses, family albums, souvenirs, street signs and sport. The suspicion exists that an earlier nationalist link between public memory and official space is being drained of politics and inequality. A commodified 'heritage' may instead promote a pseudo-democracy where people are free to pursue a myriad of personalized pasts and leisure-time fantasies and thus be diverted from reality (Bodnar 2000: 957).

By contrast, Philippe Aries's description of the rise of commemorative monuments and practices in the nineteenth-century in Europe informs us that the passing of loved ones and their commemoration was related to a new personal awareness of the fact that lived experience of the past can never be directly recalled (Aries 1974; Hutton 1993: 2). 'Heritage' is part of collective memory and inseparable from the rise of a modernist identity politics. It is a modern and more conscious sense of past that promotes a politics of belonging by embedding it in personal narratives of loss, redemption and reconciliation. Aries argued that such a need for personal commemoration and longing for a past flowed over into various public acts of monumentalizing heroic figures and events in the nineteenth century as the personal was harnessed to galvanize the public realm (Aries 1974). Tensions and conflicts existed in harnessing the forces of tradition to promote a national culture but it became increasingly difficult for an alternative, more personal, desire for a future to exist without them. This relates to Nora's claim that the nineteenth century saw a transition from 'pre-modern environments of memory' where the personal was embedded in a living memory to 'sites of memory' as places designed to perpetuate a consciously held sense of the past (Nora 1989).

Bodnar argues that whilst the monumentalising of the public realm in the nineteenth century was consistent with the rise of civic consciousness and tensions over the relation of democracy and tradition in France and America, the twentieth century saw this uneasy relationship shattered by war. Violence and the demands of the state for personal sacrifice on a huge scale undermined a nineteenth-century 'naturalizing' of personal commemoration and the public sphere and replaced it with grief and a struggle to justify enormous loss through the iconography and presence of war memorials. (Bodnar 1992, 2000; Sturken 1991). The rise of 'heritage' as nomadic and detached from any particular sense of place or monument represents therefore a distinct change in the nature of public memory. A late twentieth-century turn towards the personalization of local groups and identities is inseparable from a growing recognition of cultural diversity, the objectification of cultural memory and increasingly a sense of crisis in claims to cultural authority (cf. Johnson 2004).

MOURNING AND WAR MEMORIALS

During the twentieth century, public memory became charged with the responsibility to recognise the suffering caused by warfare. Prior to this memorials and statues were built for war heroes or for military triumphs but the majority of those who died in war disappeared unrecognized into unmarked graves. Individual recognition of the dead from major conflicts begins with the American Civil War and the Boer War but was only fully recognized and demanded by the families of the dead as a consequence of First World War trauma (cf. Winter 1995). Aries recognized that commemorating the dead had become an increasing personal and family matter during the latter part of the nineteenth century and that this had enervated a sense of national belonging. (Aries 1974). It was also to become the basis for the refusal by the living survivors and families to accept lack of recognition of the sacrifice of loved ones. Recovery from death and trauma is invariably associated with the assertion of love and intimacy in the mourning process and twentieth-century mass death projected this on to a landscape of mourning and suffering.

In the aftermath of the First World War each combatant state attempted to inaugurate a landscape of national remembrance (Saunders 2004). In France, the state agreed, where possible, to pay for the return home of the bodies of the dead and frequently their individual names were inscribed on local memorials (Sherman 1994; Johnson 1995: 56). In Britain it was decided (controversially) to bury the bodies of the dead near the battlefields of the western front and resist any attempt to return them to their families. Instead enormous efforts were made to identify individuals, initially to be inscribed on monuments and subsequently on individual headstones in cemeteries of standard dimensions and materials regardless of status or rank. The recognition of individual dead continued after the Second World War where names were often added to First World War memorials. The Vietnam war memorial in Washington extends the principle of equality to the point of listing the dead chronologically by the day of the year of their death (Sturken 1991; Rowlands 1998).

First World War sites were grouped to form landscapes in which cemeteries, memorials, battlefield sites and museums are 'mapped' to facilitate the visitor's experience of an event that personally they can have little means of imagining at first hand. The principal site for war remembrance in the United Kingdom is the cenotaph, an empty memorial designed by Edwin Lutyens and placed in Whitehall. This was accompanied by the burial of the Unknown Soldier in Westminster Abbey and both are linked with rites conducted at the same time throughout the country at similar memorials in towns and cities (Lacqueur 1994; Johnson 2004). What was considered to be an appropriate monument to the dead was already hotly disputed immediately after the First World War (cf. Saunders 2004). The cenotaph was attacked as 'nothing more or less than a pagan memorial' (cited in Johnson 2004: 324) whilst a memorial to the Anzacs in Sydney was finally never accepted because of the public outcry over its lack of respect for the dead (Rowlands 1998). Controversy over the Vietnam war memorial also centred on what was considered to be (lack of) proper respect (Sturken 1991). Werbner describes the monument built outside Harare in honour of the dead who fought against white supremacy in Zimbabwe as a form of anti-memory, given its precise objective to 'forget' the mass slaughter of the Ndebele that also formed the basis of the creation of the state (Werbner 1998). The Peace Museum in Hiroshima is equally an attempt to break with a memorializing tradition that promotes acceptance of mass sacrifice and promotes instead a wish never to forget and recognition of the consequences of mass death. Disturbance and shock can be seen as the aims of the counter-monuments described by Young (1993) and more broadly those representations of mass trauma that lead inevitably for many to ask why so many had to suffer and die.

Of these, the Holocaust has undoubtedly been the focus both of an effective means to silence the past and to come to terms with it. The US Holocaust Memorial Museum, for example, has been criticized for the way in which the memories of survivors are appropriated for the display of an idealized and liberal American identity, for the way that Jews are exhibited only in death or as a people and culture that exist only as having a past (Crysler and Kusno 1997). Young also points out that, whilst America puts so much of its resources into a Jewish Holocaust Museum, it refuses a similar commitment to a museum of slavery or the genocide committed against Native Americans. Via the Holocaust America can remember its tolerance and liberalism and forget its own past (Young 1993). Post-Nine-eleven and the debate over the memorializing of the ground zero site has effectively transformed the issue of remembering into a more charged issue of what should never be forgotten regardless of any crimes or intolerances endured along the way. The state and its citizens are now united in the assertion of a single identity the future of which is seen to be in peril and in their intolerance of critique (cf. Kapferer 2002: 149).

DISGRACED MONUMENTS

Since the nineteenth century and earlier, monuments and statues have attracted controversy and hostility. If an imperial project could be pursued through developing an appropriate memory space where only the 'thinkable' would be allowed, equally the opposite can occur. In part this may be as much a question of neglect, since monuments, as supposedly permanent markers of memory and history, require both physical and symbolic maintenance. There is no reason to assume therefore that nineteenth-century national and imperial projects were always successful in achieving their purpose (Johnson 1995). In Dublin, for instance, statues celebrating overtly nationalist leaders like O'Connell and Parnell were erected side by side with existing statues to George II or Queen Victoria. As the latter were either destroyed or removed, Irish nationalism asserted itself through a lengthy process of transforming the urban memory space of Dublin (Johnson 1995).

Widespread destruction of a previously unwanted past is particularly a feature of post-socialist states in Eastern Europe and Russia. In Budapest the city council removed over twenty monuments erected in the previous communist era. Statues in Moscow, St Petersburg and elsewhere in Russia have been removed and taken to special parks or a heritage space where those who want to can come and see them. Forest and Johnson (2002) explore the formation of a post-Soviet national identity through a study of the political struggles over key Soviet era monuments and memorials in Moscow. They show how the new elites used the decision to preserve or remove these sites to define their own positions within the new political hierarchy and with the public in order to gain prestige, legitimacy and influence (Forest and Johnson 2002). By erecting memorials in a public space, attempts are made to define the historical figures and events that become the formative events of a national identity. Disgracing existing monuments is a process of redefining this agenda and replacing them with new narratives. For example, Till has described the conflicts between different groups that negotiated the redesign of the Neue Wache memorial in Berlin (Till 1999). The destruction of the Berlin Wall was a more overt expression of the public 'speaking back' to the state whilst the history of Tianeman Square and the events of 1989 show an alternative sequence when the state 'strikes back' (Wu Hung 1991). What they share is the power to transcend time, to bring historical events back into the present and make bodies, objects and monuments effective again in mobilizing social movements. Verderey, in the context of Romania, describes how the wielding of 'symbolic capital' by political elites is essential to political transformation. (Verderey 1999) and Coombes's discussion of the fate of the Vortrekker monument outside Johannesburg illustrates how even 'disgrace' may be an ambivalent notion when the monument is retained in a 'state of disgrace' to remind future generations (Coombes 2003). The aim is not to challenge the need for national identity nor the desire to create a sense of sacred identity through the manipulation of the past but to reassert that after a short period of struggle, identities crystallize again and become once more difficult to challenge.

Finally the destruction of monuments shades into descriptions of iconoclastic destruction of emotionally charged sites and objects. Barry Flood's description (Flood 2002) of the destruction of the Bamiyan Buddhas by the Taliban in Afghanistan specifically warns against some attributioin of atavistic fury to the destruction of images in Islam but rather their destruction as a consequence of a calculated act by Mullah Omar to make the point that the West was more concerned with the loss of a heritage site than the consequences of economic sanctions on the lives of Afghans. The destruction of the mosque at Ayodhya is an even more telling description of how the emotional attachment to objects and monuments can be manipulated for political nationalist purposes (cf. Layton et al. 2001).

COUNTER-MONUMENTS AND NON-MONUMENTS

The association of public memory with monuments and memorials is biased towards a particular historical experience. Although monuments are powerful because they appear to be permanent markers of history and memory, they can weigh heavily on the capacity to change and to allow alternative renditions of the past. We should not be surprised therefore to detect strong evidence that we are moving perhaps towards the end of monumentalizing the past. Young suggests that counter-monuments in Germany are more subversive than providing alternative modes of representing historical events and personalities. Counter-monuments serve more radically to destabilize the basic premise that the past is stable and enduring (Young 1993). Klein summarizes some of the evidence suggesting that we suffer from a 'surfeit of memory' and a politics of victimization at present. Memory and identity are typically yoked together in postmodernist discourse to replace history and to re-enchant our relation to the past and with the world (Klein 2000: 145).

Monuments and memorials, however, share some of the oppressive influence of historical discourse, shaping our sense of the past in definite and figurative ways. By contrast, much of the writing on memory evokes a tendency to employ it as a mode of discourse natural to people without history. The reification of subjectivity and the revival of a primordialism of origins is a view of authentic memory that resolves that it should no longer be consigned to a pre-modern world destroyed by history but recognized as still with us and capable of taking the place of the latter. The tension between history and memory is therefore being reborn as one between discourse and feeling, between secular critical practice and therapeutic practice (cf. Klein 2000). But it need not be so and we seem to be moving towards some kind of reconciliation. Memory has now subsumed what used to be called oral history or popular history into a single field, described as the leading term in the new cultural history (Megill 1998). It is not surprising that material culture has played a significant role in this reconciliation between history and memory. Objects provide more than a mnemonic device for memory to be attached but also the means to privatize and secularize memorial practice. The idea of building personal archives through photographs, mementoes and other mnemonic traces implies that this new 'historical consciousness' married history and memory in new personal and material terms. It links monuments, memorials and museums with a much more diverse range of non-monumental sites, including intangible forms of song, music, design, dance and cultural performance. The danger here perhaps is to reiterate an earlier dichotomy espoused by Nora, that memory in opposition to history and consciousness belongs specifically to the peoples of Africa, the Americas and the Pacific as pre-modern sensibility. But a more careful strategy can pursue the useful insights drawn on the relationship between memory and material culture to suggest that a continuity of forms exist, which subverts the dichotomies of both pre-modern/modern and memory/historical consciousness.

THE ARCHAEOLOGY OF MONUMENTS

Given the enormous number and variety of monuments worldwide any attempt to summarize the archaeological literature on monument building is impossible. Instead we review some innovative archaeological interpretative approaches to Neolithic and Bronze Age monuments in Britain and north-west Europe. Even just within this literature there is now an extraordinarily rich and varied discussion about different aspects of monument construction and use with regard to earlier Neolithic long mounds and megaliths, cursus monuments (long linear monuments defined by parallel banks and ditches), causewayed (circular interrupted ditched) enclosures, later Neolithic henge monuments (circular enclosures with an external bank and internal ditch broken by one or a number of entrances), Bronze Age stone circles, barrows and cairns. We consider five interlinked areas of inquiry: studies of monuments and landscapes, the architectural forms of monuments, monuments in relation to cosmologies, mortuary practices, time and memory.

MONUMENTS AND LANDSCAPES

There have been a number of recent archaeological studies which have suggested a mimetic relationship between monuments and landscapes, with the monument being a microcosm of the surrounding world. Tilley has argued that the megalithic tombs in Västergötland, central southern Sweden, reflect the landscape in which they are found in terms of the use of building materials and chamber and passage orientation. The megalithic tombs here rest on a flat plain composed of sedimentary rocks. Blocks of these materials were used for the orthostats of the tomb passages and chambers. The plain is broken up dramatically by steep-sided and flat-topped hills of igneous rocks. These were preferentially used for the roofing stones. Thus the choice of building materials duplicates the high/low contrast between the sedimentary rocks and the igneous hills towards which one faces entering the tomb. The tombs frequently occur in staggered north-south rows and their chambers are orientated north-south. This also duplicates a north-south axis of the landscape as defined by the orientation of the igneous hills and valley edges. The passages are low and orientated west-east, the chambers high. On entering the tombs a person metaphorically makes his or her way towards the mountain, crawling down the low passage but being able to stand up in the chamber (Tilley 1996a: 208ff).

Scarre has noted similarities in shape and profile between the mounds of some passage graves in Brittany and local land forms (Scarre 2000). He also notes the liminal sea edge locations of tombs and a preference for a marine backdrop in the lineal arrangements of cairns, and links this with the transformative power of the land/sea boundary (Scarre 2002a). Bradley (2000) and Tilley and Bennett (Tilley et al. 2000; Tilley and Bennett 2001) have discussed relationships between granite rock outcrops and chambered tombs in south-west England and whether the latter resembled the former or the former provided direct inspiration for the construction of the latter and the manner in which later prehistoric populations may not have found it easy to distinguish between natural features such as tors, or rock outcrops, and ruined monuments (see also Bender et al. 2005).

The orientations and locations of the mounds of Neolithic long barrows and long cairns and the passages and chambers of megaliths and Bronze Age cairns have been studied in relation to such topographic features as prominent hills, rock outcrops and ridges, hill spurs and valley systems (Tilley 1994, 1996b; Cummings 2002) and their relationship to topographic features of the coastline, waterfalls and river systems investigated (Bradley 1998; Fowler and Cummings 2003; Fraser 1998; Scarre 2002a; Tilley 1999; Tilley and Bennett 2001). The locations and significance of other types of Neolithic and Bronze Age monuments such as temples, henges and stone circles have also been studied in relation to their landscape settings (Bender et al. 2005; Berg 2002; Bradley 1998; 2002; Cooney 2000; Edmonds 1999; Edmonds and Seabourne 2002; Richards 1996; Tilley 1995, 2004a) and standing stones or menhirs (Calado 2002; Tilley 2004a). These studies have all suggested that in various ways the significance of the monuments and the activities that took place in and around them was dialectically related to their landscape settings: the land itself, its forms and features, gave power and significance to the monument and vice versa.

The materiality of the monuments themselves has been a significant point of departure for their study: the shapes, textures, colours, the hardness or softness and roughness or smoothness of the stones and other materials used to construct them (Jones and MacGregor 2002; Cummings 2002; Tilley 2004a). Cummings has shown how different parts of monuments were built of rough or smooth stones and argues that this relates metaphorically to the general role of such monuments in transforming human experience as one moves in and out of and around them. Tilley has contrasted the visual appearance and the feel of stone monuments as part of their phenomenological experience. For example, some Breton menhirs appear visually to be smooth yet feel incredibly rough and coarse. Others look rough, gnarled and cracked yet feel smooth and silky. He has related this to the changing forms of the stones, the manner in which they can look dramatically different when approached from different directions. White quartz, a substance that has very special properties (it glows when pieces are rubbed together, creates sparks, gives off an acrid smell, gleams and shines in the sun and artificial light) and is frequently found on mountain tops, was not only deposited in megalithic monuments but was frequently used to embellish their external appearance, the most famous example being Newgrange in Ireland (O'Kelly 1982; see discussion in Fowler and Cummings 2003).

Parker-Pearson and Ramilisonina (1998) have argued, on the basis of analogies with monument construction in Madagascar (see Bloch 1971; Feeley-Harnik 1991) that the hardness and durability of stone was symbolic of the fixed nature of ancestors and ancestral powers and in opposition to wood, associated with the living. They contrast the nearby henge monument of Durrington Walls with its internal wooden circles surrounded by earthen banks and ditches and the construction of the stone circle of Stonehenge, suggesting that the former was associated with feasting and the world of the living and the latter with the ancestral dead. They argue that a processional route led between the two, at first following the course of the river Avon, and then marked by the earthen banks and ditches of the monument known as the Avenue that runs from the river up to Stonehenge. The study of monuments in relation to paths of movement through the landscape has formed a major focus of research (see, e.g., Barclay and Harding 1999; Barrett 1994; Bradley 1998, 2000, 2002; Exon et al. 2000; Edmonds 1999; Tilley 1994, 1995, 1999).

For the construction of some monuments the materials came from some considerable distance away, the most famous example being the bluestones at Stonehenge, transported from the Prescelli mountains of south Wales (see discussions in Cunliffe and Renfrew 1997). Part of their significance was not only that they were of an exotic non-local material but also where they came from, their place of origin and its characteristics, their paths of movement, and the myths and stories associated with them. The sources for lithic materials used for constructing megalithic monuments in the Boyne valley, Ireland, were many and numerous, including quartz from the Wicklow mountains at least 40 km to the south and granite and siltstones from the Carlingford mountains about the same distance to the north, together with a variety of more local stones: greywacke, limestones and sandstones (Mitchell 1992; Cooney 2000: 136). Similarly numerous types of stones were used to construct Swedish passage graves (Tilley 1996a: 127). This bringing together of raw materials from different local and more distant sources suggests that these monuments had an integrative role, linking human experience of different local and distant landscapes in the form of the monument itself through the transported raw materials used to construct it.

MONUMENTAL ARCHITECTURE AND ITS EXPERIENCE

The recent use of a phenomenological perspective has stressed the sensuous dimensions of the human experience of monuments and its relationship to the manipulation of architectural space. Prior to this these monuments tended to be both archaeologically represented and interpreted *as* plans, providing an entirely abstract and somewhat surreal two-dimensional view of them in which the only questions that tended to be asked were of a typological or classificatory nature (Richards 1993: 147). The majority of passage tombs, such as Maes Howe on Orkney, have spacious chambers which contrast with low, narrow passages to move along which one must stoop, or crawl. This physically restricts movement into and out of the tomb and emphasizes the liminal character of the passage linking the outside world of the living with the world of the ancestral dead buiried in the chamber. Loud noise is dampened in the chamber but projected out down the passage to the outside like a megaphone. Such sound effects have been studied in detail (Watson and Keating 1999). Visibility and degrees of illumination by the sun at different times of the year have been shown to be crucial to the interpretation of the spaces (Bradley 1989b), as has passage orientation and mound orientation (see e.g. Burl 1987; Ruggles 1997) and the direction in which the passage entrance faces (Tilley 1994). The passage entrance to Maes Howe in Orkney faces north-east, allowing the rays of the setting sun to shine down it and into the chamber on the midwinter solstice. A special roof box constructed above the passage entrance at New Grange in Ireland allows the sun's rays to enter the chamber on the midwinter sunrise (O'Kelly 1982). Passages of other tombs are often aligned with relation to the equinoxes.

Such experiences of light and darkness, sound, and warmth and coldness, dampness and dryness, have been linked by some to trance experiences and altered states of consciousness, and the geometric art found in some tombs has been interpreted as entoptic images (Bradley 1989a; Dronfield 1995). The more general point is that the architecture of monuments acts on people. It structures where and how they can move, bodily posture, and so on, and thus may be a fundamental element structuring the interpretation and understanding of these places. This embodied perspective on monuments has been linked by a number of authors to the ideological legitimation of power, the masking of social inequalities and the reproduction of dominant discourses.

The idea that monumental architecture was often periodically remodelled in relation to the production of a new social order has been widely discussed (Barrett 1994: 24; Bradley 1998: Chapter 6; Thomas 1991: 43, 1996: 170 ff.). Tilley (1996a) has used an emulation model of social competition to explain the changes in architectural form of megalithic monuments from long dolmens to round dolmens to passage graves in southern Scandinavia in an attempt to account for (1) the close spatial groupings of these different tombs in some areas and (2) their great differences in size and morphology. He argues that initially different groups competed in terms of building longer and longer dolmen mounds with more and more chambers. This is subverted by one group building a new type of tomb, the round dolmen with a chamber in a round mound. A final phase in this model attempts to account for the fact that some large monuments have comparatively few artefacts deposited in and around them while much smaller ones may have many. He argues that social competition for prestige and power switches from monument building to ceremonies involving the deposition and ritual sacrifice of wealth in the form of artefacts.

In general the architecture of Neolithic funerary and ceremonial monuments divides up and creates segmented spaces with varying degrees of accessibility knowledge of which, deemed essential for the well-being of the social group, may have been socially restricted in relation to age and/or gender (e.g. Barrett 1994; Richards 1993; Shanks and Tilley 1982; Thomas 1991: 51, 1993; Tilley 1984). The basic argument is that human subjects were formed through their differential engagement with, and knowledge of, the material forms of these monuments, what the architecture *does*, rather than what it

might specifically mean. The power of certain individuals may have only been manifested in relation to particular types of monument in particular places (Thomas 1996). Many were the medium for different and competing discourses and interpretations (Bender 1998; Brück 2001; Edmonds 1999). Bender (1998) stresses the way in which Stonehenge has been during the past few hundred years a place radically open to different kinds of interpretation in relation to different interests of individuals and groups: 'a multitude of voices and landscapes through time, mobilising different histories, differentially empowered, fragmented, but explicable within the historical particularity of British social and economic relations' (1998: 131). In her account the 'contested' nature of the Stonehenge landscape is much more evident and nuanced in the present than in the past. Perhaps this is just simply a reflection of the far greater evidence available for interpretation today (we can see the people and hear the cacophony of contemporary discourses), or alternatively, it might suggest a fundamental difference between the ordering of social life and the relation of the individual to society in the past contrasting with the present.

Edmonds stresses the multiple possibilities for interpreting the evidence from monuments such as the Etton causewayed enclosure:

> There are bundles of cattle bone placed in ditches while still fresh. Some may have still held flesh when buried. Fragments of people were often treated in a similar manner, but there were also human bones that were overlooked. Scattered unnoticed from one part of the enclosure to another, these were weathered and gnawed at by dogs. It is difficult to make sense of the material. The residues of formal moments lie cheek by jowl with traces of domestic activity, an amalgam of ritual and routine. There is an entanglement of roles and values, as if different qualities of the monument were pulled in and out of focus over time.
>
> (Edmonds 1999: 111)

In relation to the Mount Pleasant henge monument Brück (2001) similarly argues that its meaning and social relevance would very much have depended on who visited and how and when, on their social role and status, and this might account for the 'messy' and often contradictory sets of artefacts and their associations: 'people would have experienced several parallel versions of social reality constructed through different kinds of knowledge and informed by different concerns and interests' (2001: 663). It seems quite clear that certain types of monument such as causewayed enclosures and henges had multiple meanings and identities, perhaps precisely because they had a wide variety of different uses criss-crossing any division between the 'domestic' and the 'ritual'. Other types of monuments such as long barrows or dolmens may have had a far more restricted range of meaning and greater formality and control in their use.

COSMOLOGIES

The cosmological significance of monuments has been widely discussed, their link with the seasons of the year, the passage of day and night, the rising and setting of the sun, and the movements of the moon, their relationship to land forms, etc., as mentioned above. Bradley has argued that the circular form of monuments in the British (Bradley 1998: Chapters 8–10) Neolithic and Bronze Age suggests that the circle was a basic template for understanding the world. The burial mounds and cairns are circular, surrounded by circular kerbs of stones or ditches, the ceremonial monuments: henges and stone circles are circular and may contain circular structures within their interiors, and so are domestic dwellings. The whole world was, in effect, circles within circles, and in some cases the internal organization of domestic houses and burials is very similar in terms of the locations of pits, entrances, burials, metal deposits, etc. The houses of the living and those of the dead appear to be a structural transformation of the other.

Bradley draws an interesting distinction between 'permeable' monuments such as stone circles where one can look out beyond and have a view of the world and the enclosed interior spaces of henges where the world is blocked out. Henges are generally located in lowland landscapes, stone circles in much more dramatic rocky and rugged highland landscapes. Stone circles, he argues, often acted as metaphors for the surrounding landscape (see also Richards 1996):

> the building of such permeable enclosures in such a varied topography made it possible for the features of these monuments to refer directly to the world around them. This is what seems to have happened through the astronomical alignments in the planning of some of these sites. They located the newly built monuments within a wider sacred geography.

> (Bradley 1998: 145)

Fieldwork on the Bronze Age of Bodmin Moor has again emphasized the importance of a circular template for making sense of the world. Ring cairns enclose not only burials but

rocky outcrops, or tors (Tilley 1995, 1996; Bender et al. 1997, 2005). The houses on settlement sites have entrances that are oriented so as to look out towards distant cairns and tors. Huge boulder spreads below the main rock outcrops, known locally as clitter, may have been deliberately manipulated so as to create different visual and experiential effects and 'monuments' that ambiguously transcend a nature/culture distinction (Tilley et al. 2000; Bender et al. 2005). Unaltered stones were just as significant and meaningful as culturally erected stones such as the stone circles and houses. The houses themselves incorporated large 'natural' stones, or grounders, in their perimeters at particular cardinal points or as back stones opposite the house entrances. Some abandoned houses were turned into cairns, or houses for the dead, and were modified by having their interiors and entrances altered or blocked (Bender et al. 2005).

The origins of European megalithic monuments and long mounds have created endless controversy and discussion. They have been variously argued to be objectifications of movements of people or religious ideas (e.g. Childe 1957), territorial markers erected along the Atlantic seaboard of Europe as a result of population pressure (Renfrew 1973a, 1976), or a new set of ideas involving house symbolism (Hodder 1984, 1990; Bradley 1998) and the manipulation of the body and the dead (Thomas 1991, 1999a; Tilley 1996a) in various ways. Despite huge variety in the forms of these monuments at a European or even at a local scale of analysis it is always assumed that something broader links them together (for a discourse analysis see Tilley 1999: Chapter 3). The most significant general points about these monuments are (1) their durability and the manner in which they mark the landscape and relate to it; (2) the variability in their architectural forms; (3) the burials and artefact deposits found in and around them. The first two points have been discussed above and we will now consider the third.

MONUMENTALITY AND DEATH

A close connection has been suggested between different ways of treating the dead and the architectural forms of Neolithic megalithic monuments. Often the dead were buried in sealed chambers in the earlier monuments. Many of these were single burials of intact bodies. Later monuments were constructed so as to permit access to the burial chamber via a shorter or longer passage. In these monuments collective burial was practised of unfleshed bones. This involved the selection, disarticulation, arrangement and rearrangement of bones in various ways (see e.g. Edmonds 1999; Jones 1998; Fowler 2001; Richards 1988; Shanks and Tilley 1982; Thomas 2000) Some of the 'absent' or 'missing' bones were taken out of these monuments to circulate as relics among the living or deposited in other monuments in a variety of ancestor rites (see e.g. Barrett 1988; Bradley 1998; Thomas 1991, 1999a; Tilley 1996a). The practice of collective burial has been variously interpreted – as a sign of an egalitarian society in which the individual on death becomes dissolved into the social body, as an ideological representation masking social inequalities in life (Shanks and Tilley 1982), or as citations of different types of personal relations in life, indicating agency as 'partible' or 'fractual' in which personal identity is in a continuous process of contextualization, as argued by Strathern (1988) in relation to Melanesia (Fowler 2001).

Homologies have been argued to exist between the treatment and circulation of human bones and the deposition of artefacts. Tilley notes that elaborately decorated pottery and stone axes were smashed up and sacrificed outside the entrances to Scandinavian passage graves, being disarticulated and rearranged in a comparable manner to the skeletal remains inside the tombs. These artefacts were 'persons' that were destroyed and turned into 'corpses' of their original forms (Tilley 1996a: 315 ff.). Edmonds has made similar arguments in relation to the deposition of artefacts in earlier British Neolithic monuments (Edmonds 1999: 124 ff.) while Thomas has argued that the circulation of people between places and monuments and the circulation of bones and artefacts were homologous in a variety of ways. For example, the 'quarrying and depositing of artefacts, extraction and backfilling of monumental building materials ... amounts to a set of relations of reciprocity with the earth itself in which extractive labour and acts of deposition brought meaning to place' (Thomas 1999b: 76). He contrasts the earlier Neolithic pattern with that in the later Neolithic, where contexts for social action multiplied and became mutually exclusive, objectified in a very different 'economy of substances and depositions' (Thomas 1996: Chapter 6).

A shift from Neolithic collective burials to individual burials under barrows and cairns in the early Bronze Age of Britain has been elegantly interpreted by Barrett as a movement from ancestor rituals to funerary rites (Barrett 1988, 1991, 1994). The two, he argues, are quite distinct in terms of their organization and purposes. The former bring the living into the presence of the ancestral dead located in special places – megalithic monuments. These rites need not necessarily involve fresh interments but presence ancestral remains in relation to the social strategies of the living. The architecture of these monuments including forecourts and accessible chambers containing ancestral bones, provided spaces for the congregation of the living and places for the deposition of offerings. It was during the Bronze Age that the landscape became filled up with thousands of round barrows and cairns many of which covered a single primary act of body interment. The funerary rituals associated with these places were explicitly concerned with the burial of the deceased and the realignment of social relations among the living. These graves represent the concluding moment in a complex series of funerary rituals and symbolically sever the ties between the living and the dead. Burial was thus a means of forgetting. Subsequently fresh burials, often cremations, might be inserted in the mound or cairn or others built in its vicinity leading to the development of a barrow cemetery. In each case these subsequent events related back to the first burial so that genealogical lines of descent could be traced in, for example, the spatial distribution of barrow lines or clusters. Barrett links these changes in burial practice to different ways of inhabiting the landscape, much more mobile and fleeting during the Neolithic, much more fixed and tenurial during the Bronze Age. In the Neolithic the ancestral dead were co-present with the living, during the Bronze Age they became part of the past, placing them in a genealogical relationship to the living. While this interpretation remains excellent as a general model it necessarily ignores and cannot cope with the enormous variability in the Neolithic and Bronze Age mortuary practices being discussed (Thomas 2000: 658 ff.) nor the distinctive regional relationships of the barrows and cairns to the landscape. (For recent work see Tilley 1996a, 1999: Chapter 6; Tilley 2004a,b; Woodward 2000; Exon et al. 2000.)

MONUMENTALITY, TIME AND MEMORY

Earlier 'processual' functionalist models of monument types attempted to slot and identify them in relation to an evolution of social types. So while long barrows and megalithic monuments and causewayed enclosures might represent small-scale segmentary 'lineage' type societies, henges were linked with the evolution of hierarchy and ranking in the form of chiefdoms (Renfrew 1973). For Barrett (1994) and others (e.g. Edmonds 1999; Thomas 1996) by contrast, monuments do not passively reflect changing social relations, they actively serve to produce those relations or bring them into being. Barrett succinctly puts it this way:

> architecture structures the possible dispositions employed between those who inhabit its spaces. It creates the physical conditions of a *locale* which are drawn upon by practices which, in turn, sustain their meanings by reference to the conditions which they occupy. Architecture is a material technology enabling the regionalization of a place to emerge through practice, creating different categories and moments of being.
>
> (Barrett 1994: 18)

Monument construction may have had intended consequences in terms of the effects it had on people. It also almost certainly had *unintended* effects on social practices. Interpretations of the structural sequences of monuments such as Stonehenge and Avebury (e.g. Cleal et al. 1995; Bender 1998; Bradley 1998; Pollard and Reynolds 2002; Whittle 1997) or Maltese temples (Tilley 2004a) have shown they were constantly being modified and altered and were often left unfinished. They were not realized and planned in the mind first and then constructed on the ground. Their architecture provided both 'affordances' and constraints which were modified through time in a continual dialectic between persons, practices and material structures.

Monuments are often fundamental to the persistence and direction of social memory, frames for the inscription and reproduction of social values. They can also be means of forgetting and reworking social relations. Edmonds puts it this way:

> recruited by the living, they can change in form and significance. They can bolster ideas or positions far removed from those which held sway at their first construction. They can even become a focus for competing visions of the order of things. At the same time, they retain a sense of the timeless and eternal. The assertion of new values often goes hand in hand with the evocation of continuity, of an unbroken line between present and past.
>
> (Edmonds 1999: 134)

His book is an outstanding exploration of these ideas in relation to the earlier British Neolithic monuments and causewayed enclosures in particular. Bradley (2002) has written an intriguing study of how past monuments might have been understood in the past. Ancient monuments would, of course, have been visible in the past, as they are today. How might people in the past have experienced and understood their past and how might they have used it as a resource to construct their future? They could be ignored, destroyed, reworked, renewed or reinterpreted in various ways, for example the ruins of earlier structures could be used in creating later ones or earlier structures incorporated in new monuments in new ways to create new structures of experience, as can be seen, for example in the relationship between Bronze Age stone rows and reaves (linear boundary systems), cairns and houses on Dartmoor (Bradley 2002: Chapter 3).

CONCLUSION

From the Neolithic onwards monuments and memorials have littered the landscapes of the past, and the present. Their material endurance is clearly fundamental to their power and significance. There are two major aspects to this: that which they signify, or can be interpreted to signify, and the effects their very material presence has in relation to persons, groups, nation states, etc. A key concept is memory, although mediated by current debates on its alienated associations with modernity. There are, of course, many cultures in the past and the present which have no need to publicly objectify their identities in this manner. These are exclusively cultures without history in the modernist sense and documented archaeologically and ethnographically. To characterize such cultures as somehow possessing authentic and non-alienated memory, and thus having no need for monuments, is clearly inadequate. To further complicate matters, cultures 'without history' also erect and use monuments. We still have a poor comparative understanding of why it becomes necessary to erect monuments in different social and historical circumstances. To simply link their construction to crises of legitimation, whatever form these might take, is an all too easy generalization. Perhaps part of the problem may arise from our own rather restricted cultural definition of what monuments are. Landscapes, or humanly unaltered features of those landscapes, such as significant hills, large trees, deep valleys, etc., might themselves be considered to be monuments: so why 'improve', alter or, quite literally, build on them?

A mimetic relationship between artefact and landscape may be part of the answer here in some circumstances: one draws attention to that which is already there and emphasizes it. Alternatively monuments may be significant by drawing attention towards themselves and away from the landscapes of which they are a part. They may thus gather together or differentiate place. They may also punctuate time by a stress on events, and the event of their own construction, or alternatively suggest the endless, the repetitive and the cyclical. The ways in which pyramids, classical temple architecture and other monumental forms continue to be reused as either replication or pastiche suggests a potency for decontextualized forms regardless of apparent meaning. Thinking about these relationships and how they relate to the individuality (or otherwise) of the material form of monuments and memorials ought to be a significant direction for research.

Another problem area, comparatively little considered, concerns the relationship between public and official discourses and the private and the personal. How do the former mediate the latter and vice versa? and how does the tangible heritage of monuments and memorials and performances using them intersect with the 'intangible' heritage of dance, and song, clothing, body decoration, etc.? For example, exactly what are the social, moral and political implications of UNESCO designating certain monuments and places as world heritage sites today and then discovering, in retrospect, that many nations or cultures apparently have none?

The entanglement of monuments and memorials with shifting social identities is no more obvious than in post-socialist societies and the postcolonial world with various attempts to incorporate, appropriate, destroy or simply abandon and neglect the monuments of the past. We need further comparative ethnographic study of what happens, and how, in these very different contexts. To what extent does these very different histories relate to similar or different relationships to different types of monuments from the past today: graveyards, buildings, public sculptures, parks and gardens?

REFERENCE

Aries, P. (1974) *Western Attitudes towards Death.* Baltimore, MD: Johns Hopkins University Press.

Barclay, A. and Harding, J., eds (1999) *Pathways and Ceremonies: the Cursus Monuments of Britain and Ireland.* Oxford: Oxbow Books.

Barrett, J. (1988) 'The living, the dead and the ancestors: Neolithic and early Bronze Age mortuary practices', in J. Barrett and I. Kinnes (eds), *The Archaeology of Context in the Neolithic and Bronze Age: Recent Trends.* Sheffield: Department of Archaeology and Prehistory, University of Sheffield.

Barrett, J. (1991) 'Toward an archaeology of ritual', in P. Garwood, D. Jennings, R. Skeates and J. Thoms (eds), *Sacred and Profane.* Oxford: Oxford Committee for Archaeology.

Barrett, J. (1994) *Fragments from Antiquity.* Oxford: Blackwell.

Bender, B. (1998) *Stonehenge: Making Space,* Oxford: Berg.

Bender, B., Hamilton, S. and Tilley, C. (1997) 'Leskernick: stone worlds; alternative narratives; nested landscapes', *Proceedings of the Prehistoric Society,* 63: 147–78.

Bender, B., Hamilton, S. and Tilley, C. (2005) *Stone Worlds: Narrative and Reflexive Approaches to Landscape Archaeology.* London: UCL Press.

Berg, S. (2002) 'Knocknarea, the ultimate monument: megaliths and mountains in Neolithic Cúil Irra, north-west Ireland', in C. Scarre (ed.), *Monuments and Landscape in Atlantic Europe.* London: Routledge.

Berman, M. (1982) *All that is Solid Melts into Air.* New York: Simon and Schuster.

Bloch, M. (1971) *Placing the Dead.* London: Seminar Press.

Bodnar, J. (1992) *Re-making America: Public Memory, Commemoration and Patriotism in 20th Century.* Princeton: Princeton University Press.

Bodnar, J. (2000) Pierre Nora national memory and democracy: a review', *Journal of American History,* December: 951–63.

Boyer, M.C. (1994) *The City of Collective Memory.* Cambridge, MA: MIT Press.

Boym, S. (2001) *The Future of Nostalgia.* New York: Basic Books.

Bradley, R. (1989a) 'Deaths and entrances: a conceptual analysis of megalithic art', *Current Anthropology,* 30: 68–75.

Bradley, R. (1989b) 'Darkness and light in the design of megalithic tombs', *Oxford Journal of Archaeology,* 8: 251–9.

Bradley, R. (1991) Bradley, R. (1998) *The Significance of Monuments.* London: Routledge.

Bradley, R. (2000) *An Archaeology of Natural Places.* London: Routledge.

Bradley, R. (2002) *The Past in Prehistoric Societies.* London: Routledge.

Brück, J. (2001) 'Monuments, power and personhood in the British Neolithic', *Journal of the Royal Anthropological Institute,* 7 (4): 649–68.

Burl, A. (1987) *The Stonehenge People.* London: Dent.

Calado, M. (2002) 'Standing stones and natural outcrops: the role of ritual monuments in the

Neolithic transition of the central Alentjo', in C. Scarre (ed.), *Monuments and Landscape in Atlantic Europe*. London: Routledge.

Childe, V. (1957) *The Dawn of European Civilization*, 6th edn. London: Routledge.

Cleal, R., Walker, K. and Montague, R. (1995) *Stonehenge in its Landscape*. London: English Heritage.

Connerton, P. (1989) *How Societies Remember*. Cambridge: Cambridge University Press.

Coombes, A. (2003) *History after Apartheid: Visual Culture and Public Memory in a Democratic South Africa*. Durham, NC: Duke University Press.

Cooney, G. (2000) *Landscapes of Neolithic Ireland*. London: Routledge.

Crysler, G. and Kusno, A. (1997) 'Angels in the Temple: the aesthetic construction of citizenship in the United States Holocaust Museum', *Art Journal*, 56 (1): 52–64.

Cummings, V. (2002) 'Experiencing texture and transformation in the British Neolithic', *Oxford Journal of Archaeology*, 21 (3): 249–61.

Cunliffe, B. and Renfrew, C. (eds) (1997) *Science and Stonehenge*. Oxford: British Academy.

Edholm, F. (1993) 'A View from below: Paris in the 1880s', in B. Bender (eds) *Landscape and Politics in Perspective*. Oxford: Berg.

Edmonds, M. (1999) *Ancestral Geographies of the Neolithic*. London: Routledge.

Edmonds, M. and Seabourne, T. (2002) *Prehistory in the Peak*. Stroud: Tempus.

Exon, S., Gaffney, V., Woodward, A. and Yorston, R. (2000) *Stonehenge Landscapes*. Oxford: Archaeopress.

Feeley-Harnik, G. (1991) *A Green Estate*. Washington, DC: Smithsonian Institution Press.

Feuchtwang, S. (2003) 'The transmission of loss and the demand for recognition', in S. Radstone and K. Hodgkin *Regimes of memory*. London: Routledge.

Flood, F.B. (2002) 'Between cult and culture: Bamiyan, Islamic iconoclasm and the museum', *Art Bulletin*, 84 (4): 641–59.

Forest, B. and Johnson, J. (2002) 'Unravelling the threads of history: Soviet era monuments and post-Soviet national identity', *Annals of the Association of American Geographers*, 92 (3): 524–47.

Foster, R. (1991) 'Making national cultures in the global ecumene', *Annual Review of Anthropology*, 20: 235–60.

Fowler, C. (2001) 'Personhood and social relations in the British Neolithic, with a study from the Isle of Man', *Journal of Material Culture*, 6 (2): 137–63.

Fowler, C. and Cummings, V. (2003) 'Places of trans-formation: building monuments from water and stone in the Neolithic of the Irish Sea', *Journal of the Royal Anthropological Institute*, 9 (1): 1–20.

Fraser, S. (1998) 'The public forum and the space between: the materiality of social strategy in the Irish Neolithic', *Proceedings of the Prehistoric Society*, 64: 203–24.

Halbwachs, M. (1950/1992) *On Collective Memory*, ed. L. Coser. Chicago: University of Chicago Press.

Hall, S. (2000) 'Whose heritage? Un-settling "The heritage"', *Third Text*, 49: 1–12.

Hodder, I. (1984) 'Burials, houses, women and men in the European Neolithic', in D. Miller and C. Tilley (eds), *Ideology, Power and Prehistory*. Cambridge: Cambridge University Press.

Hodder. I. (1990) *The Domestication of Europe*. Oxford: Blackwell.

Hoskins, J. (1998) *Biographical Objects*. London: Routledge.

Hutton, P.H. (1993) *History as an Art of Memory*. Middletown, CT: University Press of New England.

Johnson, N. (1995) 'Cast in stone: monuments, geography and nationalism', *Society and Space*, 13 (1): 51–65.

Johnson, N. (2004) 'Public memory', in J. Duncan, N. Johnson and R. Scheim, *A Companion to Cultural Geography*. Oxford: Blackwell.

Jones, A. (1998) 'Where eagles dare: landscape, animals and the Neolithic of Orkney', *Journal of Material Culture*, 3 (3): 301–24.

Jones, A. and MacGregor, G., eds (2002) *Colouring the Past: the Significance of Colour in Archaeological Research*. Oxford: Berg.

Kapferer, B. (2002) 'The new Leviathan and the crisis of criticism in the social sciences', *Social Analysis*, 46 (1): 148–52.

Kaplan, F. (1994) *Museums and the Making of Ourselves*. London: Leicester University Press.

Klein, K.L. (2000) 'On the emergence of memory in historical discourse', *Representations*, 69: 127–50.

Lacqueur, T.W. (1994) 'Memory and naming in the Great War', in J.R. Gillis (ed.) *Commemoration and the Politics of National Identity*. Princeton, NJ: Princeton University Press.

Layton, R., Stone, P. and Thomas, J. (2001) *Destruction and Conservation of Cultural Property*. London: Routledge.

Lowenthal, D. (1985) *The Past is a Foreign Country*. Cambridge: Cambridge University Press.

Lowenthal, D. (1998) *The Heritage Crusade and the Spoils of History*. Cambridge: Cambridge University Press.

Makiya, K. (2004) *The Monument: Art and Vulgarity in Saddam Hussein's Iraq*. London: Tauris.

Maleuvre, D. (1999) *Museum Memories*. Stanford, CA: Stanford University Press.

Megall, A. (1998) 'History, memory and identity', *History and the Human Sciences*, 11: 37–8.

Mitchell, G. (1992) 'Notes on some non-local cobbles at the entrances to the passage graves at Newgrange and Knowth, County Meath', *Journal of the Royal Society of Antiquaries of Ireland*, 122: 128–45.

Mitchell, T. (1988) *Colonising Egypt*. Cambridge: Cambridge University Press.

Mosse, G.L. (1975) *The Nationalization of the Masses*. New York: Fertig.

Mosse, G.L. (1990) *Fallen Soldiers: Reshaping the Memory of the World Wars.* Oxford: Oxford University Press.

Nora, Pierre (1989) 'Between memory and history: *les lieux de mémoires*', *Representations* 26 (spring): 1–10.

Nora, Pierre (1996) *Realms of Memory: the Construction of the French Past* I, *Conflicts and Division*, trans. Arthur Goldhammer. New York: Columbia University Press.

O'Kelly, M. (1982) *New Grange: Archaeology, Art and Legend*, London: Thames & Hudson.

Parker-Pearson, M. and Ramilisonina (1998) 'Stonehenge for the ancestors: the stones pass on the message', *Antiquity*, 72: 308–26.

Pollard, J. and Reynolds, A. (2002) *Avebury: the Biography of a Landscape.* Stroud: Tempus Renfrew, C. (1973a) *Before Civilization.* London: Cape.

Renfrew, C. (1973) 'Monuments, mobilization and social organization in Neolithic Wessex', in C. Renfrew (ed.), *The Explanation of Culture Change.* London: Duckworth.

Renfrew, C. (1976) 'Megaliths, territories and populations', in S. DeLaet (ed.), *Acculturation and Continuity in Atlantic Europe.* Bruges: De Tempel.

Richards, C. (1988) 'Altered images: a re-examination of Neolithic mortuary practices', in J. Barrett and I. Kinnes (eds), *The Archaeology of Context in the Neolithic and Bronze Ages: Recent Trends.* Sheffield: Department of Archaeology and Prehistory, University of Sheffield.

Richards, C. (1993) 'Monumental choreography: architecture and spatial representation in late Neolithic Orkney', in C. Tilley (ed.), *Interpretative Archaeology.* Oxford: Berg.

Richards, C. (1996) 'Henges and water: towards an elemental understanding of monuments and landscape in late Neolithic Britain', *Journal of Material Culture*, 1: 313–36.

Rowlands, M. (1998) 'Remembering to forget: sublimation as sacrifice in war memorials', in A. Forty and S. Kuechler (eds), *The Art of Forgetting.* Oxford: Berg.

Ruggles, C. (1997) 'Astronomy and Stonehenge', in B. Cunliffe and C. Renfrew (eds), *Science and Stonehenge.* Oxford: British Academy.

Samuel, R. (1994) *Theatres of Memory.* London: Verso.

Saunders, N. (2004) *Matters of Conflict: Material Culture, Memory and the First World War.* London: Routledge.

Scarre, C. (2002a) 'Coast and cosmos: the Neolithic monuments of northern Brittany', in C. Scarre (ed.), *Monuments and Landscape in Atlantic Europe.* London: Routledge.

Scarre, C., ed. (2002b) *Monuments and Landscape in Atlantic Europe.* London: Routledge.

Schorske, C.E. (1980) *Fin-de-siècle Vienna.* London: Weidenfeld & Nicolson.

Shanks. M. and Tilley, C. (1982) 'Ideology, symbolic power and ritual communication: a reinterpretation of Neolithic mortuary practices', in I. Hodder (ed.), *Symbolic and Structural Archaeology.* Cambridge: Cambridge University Press.

Sherman, D.J. (1994) 'Art, commerce and the production of memory in France after World War I', in J.R. Gillis (ed.), *Commemoration and the Politics of National Identity*, NJ: Princeton: Princeton University Press.

Starn, R. (2002) 'Authenticity and historic preservation: towards an authentic history', *History of Human Sciences*, 15 (1): 1–16.

Stewart, S. (1984) *On Longing: Narratives of the Miniature, the Gigantic, the Souvenir, the Collection.* Baltimore, MD: Johns Hopkins University Press.

Strathern, M. (1988) *The Gender of the Gift.* Berkeley, CA: University of California Press.

Sturken, M. (1991) 'The wall, the screen and the image: Vietnam veterans' memorial', *Representations*, 35: 118–42.

Thomas, J. (1991) *Rethinking the Neolithic.* Cambridge: Cambridge University Press.

Thomas, J. (1993) 'The hermeneutics of megalithic space', in C. Tilley (ed.), *Interpretative Archaeology.* Oxford: Berg.

Thomas, J. (1996) *Time, Culture and Identity: An Interpretive Archaeology.* London: Routledge.

Thomas, J. (1999a) *Understanding the Neolithic.* London: Routledge.

Thomas, J. (1999b) 'An economy of substances in earlier Neolithic Britain', in J. Robb (ed.), *Material Symbols: Culture and Economy in Prehistory.* Carbondale, IL: Southern Illinois University Press.

Thomas, J. (2000) 'Death, identity and the body in Neolithic Britain', *Journal of the Royal Anthropological Institute*, 6 (4): 653–68.

Thomas, J. and Tilley, C. (1993) 'The torso and the axe: symbolic structures in the Neolithic of Brittany', in C. Tilley (ed.), *Interpretative Archaeology.* Oxford: Berg.

Till, K. (1999) 'Staging the past: landscape designs, cultural identity and *Erinnerung* politics at Berlin's Neue Wache', *Ecumene*, 6 (3): 251–83.

Tilley, C. (1984) 'Ideology and the legitimation of power in the middle neolithic of southern Sweden', in D. Miller and C. Tilley (eds) *Ideology, Power and Prehistory.* Cambridge: Cambridge University Press.

Tilley, C. (1994) *A Phenomenology of Landscape.* Oxford: Berg.

Tilley, C. (1995) 'Rocks as resources: landscapes and power', *Cornish Archaeology*, 34: 5–57.

Tilley, C. (1996a) *An Ethnography of the Neolithic.* Cambridge: Cambridge University Press.

Tilley, C. (1996b) 'The power of rocks: topography and monument construction on Bodmin Moor', *World Archaeology*, 28 (2): 161–76.

Tilley, C. (1999) *Metaphor and Material Culture.* Oxford: Blackwell.

Tilley, C. (2004a) *The Materiality of Stone: Explorations in Landscape Phenomenology.*

Tilley, C. (2004b) 'Round barrows and dykes as landscape metaphors', *Cambridge Archaeological Journal*,

Tilley, C. and Bennett, W. (2001) 'An archaeology of supernatural places: the case of west Penwith', *Journal of the Royal Anthropological Institute*, 7 (2): 335–62.

Tilley, C., Hamilton, S., Harrison, S. and Andersen, E. (2000) 'Nature, culture, clutter: distinguishing between cultural and geomorphological landscapes: the case of hilltop tors in south-west England', *Journal of Material Culture*, 5 (2): 197–224.

Watson, A. and Keating, D. (1999) 'Architecture and sound: an acoustic analysis of megalithic monuments in prehistoric Britain', *Antiquity*, 73: 325–36.

Werbner, R. (1998) 'Smoke from the barrel of a gun', in R. Werbner (ed.), *Memory and the Postcolony*. London: Zed Books.

Whittle, A. (1997) 'Remembered and imagined belongings: Stonehenge in its traditions and structures of meaning', in B. Cunliffe and C. Renfrew (eds), *Science and Stonehenge*. Oxford: British Academy.

Winter, J. (1995) *Sites of Memory, Sites of Mourning: the Great War in European Cultural History*. Cambridge: Cambridge University Press.

Woodward, A. (2000) *British Barrows: a Matter of Life and Death*, Stroud: Tempus.

Wu Hung (1991) 'Tiananmen Square: a political history of monuments', *Representations*, 35: 84–115.

Young, J. (1993) *The Texture of memory: Holocaust Memorials and Meaning*. New Haven, CT: Yale University Press.

32

CONSERVATION AS MATERIAL CULTURE

Dinah Eastop

This chapter examines conservation as material culture. The conservation of objects, collections, monuments and sites is a practical and philosophical response to both material changes and the cultural dynamics related to these objects.[1] Conservation as a practice changes over time, constrained both by ideology and by the limits of technology. Thus, conservation provides an exemplary model of the material culture in action.

Objects change over time, in both their physical composition and their cultural salience. Conservation practices came into being in order to address problems associated with these changes. The recurrent problem of conservation is to decide on the 'best' method of intervention. This decision usually leads to questions about what aspects should be conserved and for whose benefit. Conservation interventions have changed over time; and interventions can change objects.

This chapter presents one conservation tradition, textile conservation, as material culture. Textile conservation is viewed as both part of material culture and as a commentary on it. For instance, the decision to conserve an object is an act within material culture; the decision about how to conserve is based on negotiating the complexities of an object's physical and social environment. This chapter argues that material culture is questioned, negotiated and reproduced when each object undergoes conservation.

Problems of definition arise immediately, as the terms 'conservation' and 'restoration' are problematic. The meaning of the terms 'curator', 'conservator' and 'restorer' differ significantly between franco- and anglophone regions. One resolution to this historical and linguistic dilemma is the adoption of the term Conservator-Restorer by the International Council of Museums. While this hybrid term may suggest that conservation and restoration are synonymous, conservation and restoration are often viewed as opposing ends of a spectrum. Conservation may be defined as measures intended to preserve original material (and later changes considered significant), while restoration involves returning an object to its presumed original appearance or function (Oddy 1994). In this chapter conservation is defined as a practice of preservation, investigation and presentation, which can involve elements of restoration.

Conservation is explored through consideration of textile conservation, the author's specialism.[2] Conservation and material culture have distinctive terminologies. An attempt will be made to relate the rhetoric of textile conservation with the discourse of material culture. An outline of the history and organization of conservation is given. This is followed by a discussion of core concepts which dominate the theory and practice of conservation. An integration of theory and practice is enacted when each object is conserved. This discussion is followed by two case studies, one real and one fictional: the conservation of an early seventeenth-century garment and the fictive treatment of a toy cowboy in the film *Toy Story 2*. These case studies have been selected for two main reasons. First, because they present a series of dilemmas which illustrate key aspects of conservation, which are explored from the perspective of material culture. Second, both are internationally accessible, the first via the World Wide Web and the second via film distribution networks. This allows you the reader to undertake your own material culture analysis of the material.

THE HISTORY OF CONSERVATION

The history of conservation is often traced to 1920s Europe, with influential publications appearing after the Second World War, e.g. Plenderleith's *The Conservation of Antiquities and Works of Art* in 1956. The historiography of conservation is small (e.g. Brooks 2000; Oddy and Smith 2002). Significant literature has been identified, reprinted and analysed in *Historical and Philosophical Issues in the Conservation of Cultural Heritage* (Stanley Price et al. 1996). Clavir provides a short and thought-provoking history of conservation to introduce her book on museums, conservation and First Nations (2002: 3–25). Various specialisms have evolved, often based on types of material (e.g. textile conservation and stone conservation) or object type or context (e.g. easel painting conservation and archaeological conservation). Each specialism has its own history of development and traditions. Easel painting conservation traces its origins to the art historical studies of nineteenth-century Europe. Archaeological conservation, which Caple (2000: 206) characterizes as revelation, investigation and preservation, has its roots in antiquarian studies related to issues of technology and authenticity (see also Berducou 1996; Cronyn 1990; Pye 2001). Textile conservation is often linked with long-standing traditions of housekeeping and the maintenance of ceremonial textiles, notably ecclesiastical vestments and flags (e.g. Trupin 2003).

The Development of Textile Conservation

The pioneering generation of European textile conservation emerged in the mid-twentieth century, and includes Karen Finch (see Finch and Putnam 1977), Mechtild Flury-Lemberg (1988) and Sheila Landi (1985). This generation established studios serving public and private museums, country house collections and the commercial art/antique trade. As conservators were trained by these founding women, a semi-profession emerged in the 1970s, part professional in relation to codes of practice and part craftswoman in relation to craft skills (von der Lippe 1985). Textile conservation moved rapidly from a needlework/gentlewoman/family business ethos to become institutionalized by incorporation within state museums and latterly the higher education sector, while still maintaining a range of independent studios. Textile conservation is integrated into national and international bodies, with a university-based career entry system and the journals and conference proceedings characteristic of a profession. Despite its incorporation into the mainstream conservation profession, textile conservation remains a largely female occupation.

Craft technology and housekeeping (e.g. Sandwith and Stainton 1984), and then materials science (Hofenk de Graaff 1968; Tímár-Balászy and Eastop 1998; Tímár-Balászy 2000) and recently material culture have successively acted as knowledge bases to address the rationale and practice of textile conservation. This is reflected in topics presented in publications and conferences, and in the language used (Drysdale 1999). Textile conservators attempt to answer the 'What and how to conserve?' question within a complex network of power relations centred on the object. The object has multiple provenance: the original maker, owner and user and their descendants; the museum or other custodial institution, headed by a curator and advised by other interested parties, and ultimately the government department or national or international funders. Together with this current power nexus there is the future nexus: future users (curators, scholars, museum visitors and other users). At times there is a power nexus of people claiming a relationship to the object in a distant or undocumented past. This nexus of power relations forms around the decision-making process about whether and how to intervene with objects. The dynamics of these power relations is played out between textile conservator and curator or benefactor (such as research council), usually referred to as the client. The negotiation is mediated through the exchange of money (either directly or through budget allocations) and via the exchange of information about the object. This information attempts to address these dilemmas through the analysis of materiality, such as micro-structure and chemistry, as well as putative history and current material culture.

The Institutions

Much conservation literature takes the form of specialist journals and conference publications issued by various national and international bodies, either state-funded institutes, e.g. the Canadian Conservation Institute (CCI) or the profession's membership organizations, e.g. the International Institute of Conservation of Historic and Artistic Works (IIC).[3] The international membership organization ICOM (the International Council of Museums) publishes the pre-prints of the triennial meetings of its international Conservation Committee.[4] The International Council on Monuments and Sites (ICOMOS) is an international non-governmental membership organization of professionals dedicated to the preservation of monuments and sites.[5]

There are many national membership organizations in the sector, e.g. the United Kingdom Institute for Conservation (UKIC), the American Institute for Conservation (AIC) and the Australian Institute for the Conservation of Cultural Material (AICCM). Some provide peer-reviewed journals for the publication of research and case studies, e.g. the *Journal of the American Institute for Conservation* (AIC) and *The Conservator* (UKIC).

There are several very influential international organizations in the heritage conservation sector, notably ICCROM and the Getty Conservation Institute. The International Centre for the Study of the Preservation and Restoration of Cultural Property, nearly always referred to by its old acronym ICCROM, was founded as an intergovernmental organization, based in Rome, in 1959 following the ninth UNESCO General Conference of 1956. It now has over 100 member states. ICCROM's worldwide mandate is to promote the conservation of all types of cultural heritage, both movable and immovable, by improving the quality of conservation practice and by raising awareness of the importance of preserving cultural heritage.[6] The Getty Conservation Institute (GCI), which is funded by the J. Paul Getty Trust, was created in 1982 to enhance the quality of conservation practice by promoting interdisciplinary co-operation between conservators, scientists and art historians. It provides a catalytic role through its own in-house activities and via partnerships with other institutions (Ward 1986).[7]

CONSERVATION CONCEPTS

The concepts *reversibility, minimum intervention* and *preservation of 'true nature'* act as governing principles in the ideology of conservation, while remaining open to wide interpretation and supporting a very broad spectrum of justified practice (Ward 1986: 13–24; Muñoz Viñas 2002, 2005). They act as legitimating terms within all conservation specialisms. The concepts are explained and elaborated below in

such a way that they are understandable within current material culture discourse.

The Integrity and 'True Nature' of the Object

Conservation has been described as 'the means by which the true nature of an object is preserved' (UKIC 1990: 8). 'True nature' includes 'evidence of its origins, its original construction, the materials of which it was composed, and information as to the technology used in its manufacture. Subsequent modifications may be of such a significant nature that they too, should be preserved' (*ibid.*). It is now widely recognized that 'true nature' is not a fixed state but varies with context, is socially determined and is subject to contestation. This means that different institutions and practitioners adopt different approaches to conservation, depending on the role determined for the object in question (Gill and Eastop 1997). This is most obvious when it comes to objects with moving parts, e.g. steam engines and clocks (or the renewal of a toy penguin's voice-box in *Toy Story 2* outlined below). For the long-term preservation of the components it may be best to stop the clock, but the ticking of the clock may be seen as 'true to its nature' in the setting in which it is displayed/used. If the decision is made to keep an engine in working order, it may be necessary to replace worn-out gaskets in order to preserve its 'true nature' as a functioning machine. Such replacements (restoration), if well documented and not intending to deceive, may be viewed as a way of reconciling the demands of both 'minimum intervention' and preserving 'true nature'. *Restoration: is it acceptable?* (Oddy 1994) provides a useful overview of such restoration practices. The conservation of IT software and hardware presents a modern example of the same problem (Keene 1998).

Reversibility

Objects are usually preserved on the premise that the objects constitute evidence. Therefore each object has actual or potential 'evidential value'. The primacy attributed to evidential value means that any interventions intended to preserve the object should not impair the evidence, and should be reversible, i.e. should be capable of being removed without damage to the object or without leaving residues. It is generally recognized within the conservation sector that, while reversibility is desirable, it is rarely possible. For example, cleaning cannot be reversed; slight molecular realignments result from water-based cleaning of textiles, and resoiling or recreasing are not considered reversals of cleaning treatments.

What constitutes evidence can be contested; it is subject to different points of view. Assessing the relative importance of different forms of evidence is a social act, which can have a great influence on the way objects are investigated, documented, preserved and presented. For example, it is only recently that the textile substrates of easel paintings have been documented, because it was assumed that only the painted surface and the under-drawing merited recording (Villers 2000).

Minimum Intervention

Reversibility is complemented, and in some instances replaced, by the concept of 'minimum intervention' (Corfield 1988), which has recently been questioned by Villers (2004). This means that the intervention is limited to the minimum consistent with effective conservation. In textile conservation this approach has led to fewer textiles being cleaned or bleached. It has also supported the expansion of preventive conservation, with fewer single items being treated in order to release resources for better storage and display conditions for larger numbers of objects. It has also led to greater interest in supporting objects by custom-made mounts and greater finesse in the design, materials and the construction of display forms (Lister 1997).

Documentation

Documentation has become a central part of conservation. It is no longer considered acceptable to undertake a conservation treatment without recording the object and the intervention. The preparation of a detailed object record is now the norm, where the materials, form and construction of the object are recorded in a systematic way, often in diagrams and photographs as well as text. For example, standard ways have been developed for documenting upholstery under-structures (Gill 2001). The object record will be complemented by a written assessment of the object's condition. Alterations, repairs and areas of loss are recorded, and their likely causes and effects noted. A written treatment proposal (often with an estimate of cost) will be prepared, as a basis for discussion between the conservator and the legal custodian of the object. The documentation can also be viewed as a 'surrogate object', and can therefore form part of preventive conservation strategies intended to enhance access to information while reducing the handling of objects. Digital technologies can extend access to this documentation and also to museum collections (e.g. Cameron 2003); they can also allow the creation of virtual collections of objects that can be united only on the Web (e.g. the virtual collection of garments deliberately concealed within buildings, introduced below).

Materials identification by careful observation and morphological examination under magnification, and by testing small samples with solvents and reagents, can enhance the 'evidential value' of objects. In some instances the preservation of the resulting information can appear more important than preserving the object itself (Brooks et al. 1996). Developments in instrumental analysis mean that the possibilities of materials identification have increased, and more conservators have access to such specialist services. The documentation and analysis of an eighteenth-century stomacher (a corset-like, stiffened garment worn by women) provides a good example of the results of such analysis (Figures 32.1–2). The internal structure and materials of the garment were documented by means of x-radiography, which revealed the 'whalebone' (baleen) strips which stiffen the stomacher. The distorted edges of the strips provided evidence of the way the garment was made, suggesting that the baleen strips were pushed into the pre-stitched channels of the stomacher. X-radiography also showed the extent of loss to the baleen, and that the baleen had been infested by invertebrate pests, which had been eating it. With the owner's consent, a sample of baleen was removed from the stomacher for DNA analysis. The extraction of DNA from the eighteenth-century baleen was successful, and the results showed that the baleen was from a North Atlantic right whale (*Eubalaena glacialis*), and from a previously unrecorded mitochondrial lineage of this species (Eastop and McEwing 2005).

Preventive Conservation

Preventive conservation describes both a philosophy and a range of monitoring and control measures, based on the belief that 'prevention is better than cure', i.e. preventing damage is better then trying to rectify it. The term is often used to distinguish these approaches from

Figure 32.1   *The Nether Wallop stomacher.* Courtesy *Textile Conservation Centre, Winchester*

Figure 32.2   *X-radiograph of the Nether Wallop stomacher.* Courtesy *Sonia O'Connor*

remedial interventions, e.g. dust reduction measures compared with cleaning interventions to remove dust. Current preventive conservation approaches have resulted from several trends. These include recognition of the drawbacks of some interventive approaches, which may include pesticide contamination of objects (e.g. Odegaard 2000; Sirois 2001); repeated treatments (e.g. Wadnum and Noble 1999); greater understanding of deterioration mechanisms; prioritizing the preservation needs of collections rather than individual objects; and, recognizing the effectiveness of long-standing housekeeping traditions, such as the use of window blinds to reduce light exposure. Preventive conservation measures include the monitoring and control of the environmental conditions of cases, rooms and buildings used to store and display objects (e.g. Roy and Smith 1994; Thompson 1978), as well as strategies developed to promote an integrated approach to collection management (e.g. Putt 1998; Waller 2002).

Interventive Conservation

Until the development of preventive conservation, most interventions known as conservation were of the remedial or interventive type, i.e. those acts of conservation which physically or chemically intervene with the object. The terms *interventive* or *remedial* conservation were developed to draw distinctions with preventive conservation. The range of remedial or interventive conservation treatments is large and varies with each conservation specialism, as shown by the following example drawn from upholstery conservation.

Two chairs were acquired to furnish a room in Chiswick House (the earliest Palladian style house built in England) as part of a programme to restore the house to its original appearance. Each chair has a gilded wood frame and arrived for treatment upholstered in a plain beige fabric (Figure 32.3). The chair frames are of a similar date to Chiswick House, while the beige top covers are a much later addition and were not considered significant in this context. The decision was therefore made to remove them and to display the chairs with 1730s-style covers. Examination of the chairs showed that none of the seat upholstery was original, and it was therefore documented and removed. The upholstery of one of the chair backs was original and it was retained *in situ*, secured by an overlay of a thin support material. The missing upholstery was recreated with layers of an inert polyester felt, which was used to create the seat and back profiles appropriate to a 1730s chair. The

Figure 32.3   *The Chiswick House chair before treatment. Courtesy Textile Conservation Centre, Winchester*

Figure 32.4   *The Chiswick House chair after treatment. Courtesy Textile Conservation Centre, Winchester*

modern top covers were replaced with replica covers made in a pattern-weave blue velvet, specially woven to replicate the wall coverings of the Blue Velvet Room at Chiswick House (Figure 32.4). The replica chair covers take the form of close-fitting, detachable covers, copied from early eighteenth-century covers preserved at Houghton Hall. The chairs are now displayed in the Blue Velvet Room at Chiswick House, where they help to restore the appearance of the room's original decorative scheme (Gill and Eastop 1997). The treatment of the Chiswick House chairs raised ethical and practical challenges addressed by a combination of treatments. These ranged from minimal intervention (to the surviving original upholstery on the chair back, treated *in situ* so as to retain evidence of its original materials and structure) to the removal of later additions (which, in the context of the Chiswick House restoration programme, were not considered part of the 'true nature' of the chairs), to restoring the chairs to their presumed original appearance via replica velvet covers.

The cleaning of historic textiles also illustrates significant ethical problems in interventive or remedial conservation. In textile conservation cleaning focuses on the removal of 'dirt'. The

decision to clean (i.e. remove or reduce soiling and creasing) may be made because it is considered harmful or unsightly; because the dirt presents a health risk to those who handle the textiles because they contain irritant mould spores, or the residues of fumigation treatments, e.g. arsenic and DDT. In some cases, they may be cleaned because their 'true nature' is linked with their clean appearance, e.g. table linen. The benefits of cleaning (the textiles' enhanced chances of preservation due to improvements in their chemical, physical and aesthetic state) are presumed to outweigh the technical risks (dye running, fibre loss, changes in dimensions and surface finish) and ethical constraints.

The decision 'to clean or not to clean' depends on the significance attributed to the soiling or creasing (Eastop and Brooks 1996). Soiling and creasing are retained when they are considered to be part of the 'true nature' of the artefact, e.g. the blood staining on the clothes of heroes or martyrs. Examples include garments worn by Admiral Nelson at his death and by a soldier returning from the muddy trenches of the Somme. Retaining evidence of use leads to retention of soiling and creasing, the blood on Nelson's uniform and the mud on the trench-war tunic. The decision whether or not to remove soiling depends on whether it is considered as dirt, i.e. 'matter out of place' (Douglas 1966/1995). In the case of the Somme uniform, the mud soiling was the very reason for its collection, because the mud demonstrated the misery of trench warfare. When the mud was found to be dusting away, it was carefully consolidated to reduce the risk of loss (Dodds 1988).

CASE STUDY 1 THE REIGATE DOUBLET, A LINEN GARMENT c. 1600

The treatment of this linen garment has been selected as a case study because it provides an excellent example of the effects of significance assessment on conservation.

Discovery, Documentation and Investigation

In the early 1990s building work was carried out inside a Tudor era timber-framed building in Reigate, Surrey. It involved the removal of plaster from the wall above a blocked-in fireplace. In the resulting mass of rubble and plaster, which had been swept to one side, someone noticed that the brown cloth found within the wall had buttons and buttonholes, and it was removed from the rubbish. It was later taken to a museum curator with specialist knowledge of the history of dress, who recognised it as the remains of an early seventeenth-century doublet, which would have been worn by a young man (see Figure 32.5).

Examples of working dress rarely survive, so this doublet provides important documentary evidence for the materials, construction and quality of everyday wear of c. 1600. The curator referred the doublet to the Textile Conservation Centre (UK), where it was investigated and prepared for display. A detailed object record was prepared, including precise details of its cut. The condition assessment confirmed that the doublet was heavily soiled and creased, and that the lower part of each sleeve was missing.

The significance of the doublet was assessed. Its rarity and importance as an item of dress were confirmed. It was also considered significant as an example of the widespread but seldom reported practice of deliberately concealing garments (and other objects, e.g. bottles, cats and bones) within buildings. The practice of deliberately concealing shoes is well documented (Swann 1969, 1996). Concealments are attributed a protective or auspicious function. So the garment was significant in two ways: as an item of dress and as an item of concealment. The owner's plans for the doublet were also significant. His long-term aim was to donate the doublet to a museum, but he had not decided which museum. In the short term he decided to lend the doublet to a local school museum.

As the institutional context was not fixed, it was impossible to establish whether the doublet should be conserved as an item of dress for display in a costume museum (in which case the removal of soiling and creasing arising from concealment might have been considered appropriate) or in a social history museum, where the evidence of concealment might be considered part of the doublet's 'true nature'. Following consultation with the owner, curators and archaeologists, the point of historical significance was selected as the time of the doublet's discovery in the building. The doublet was therefore retained in its soiled and creased state and placed in a shaped, custom-made mount (of the type noted below in *Toy Story* 2), which was fitted with a transparent, protective cover. (Figure 32.6) A replica of the doublet was made

Figure 32.5 *The Reigate doublet, c. 1600, shortly after its discovery. Courtesy Textile Conservation Centre, Winchester*

Figure 32.6 *The Reigate doublet in its display mount. Courtesy Textile Conservation Centre, Winchester*

Figure 32.7   Replica of the doublet. Courtesy Textile Conservation Centre, Winchester

to show its presumed original form, and is displayed alongside the doublet. The replica has proved very effective in generating public interest in the fragmentary original, and has been handled so much that by 2004 it required repair or renewal (Figure 32.7).

The Doublet in the Cycle of Production, Consumption, Exchange and Destruction

The doublet is made of woven linen, itself made from yarn made by spinning flax fibres. The flax must have been planted, harvested and prepared for fibre extraction, and then spinning and weaving. Once the cloth was produced, it may have been sold or exchanged before it was made into the doublet and worn. The doublet may have been exchanged during its life as everyday wear, before it was damaged and selected for concealment. After it was uncovered during building work, the doublet was swept up, and was lucky to escape disposal as rubbish. It has now entered a new realm of consumption as a museum exhibit and research tool.

The Doublet's Biography

The production and consumption of the doublet can be plotted as a 'biography', following the concept outlined by Kopytoff (1986). The doublet has creasing and soiling consistent with wear, so we can deduce that the doublet was

worn. It is not clear when or how the sleeve ends were removed; they may have become worn, or may have been torn off prior to concealment as some concealed items appear to have been deliberately damaged prior to concealment. At some point the garment was selected for concealment, presumably when the timber-framed building in Reigate was modernized by the addition of a chimney. Many caches are found at such locations. The doublet was then discovered, and passed into museum display via the finder, curator, conservator and school museum. The doublet has also achieved international circulation, e.g. via this chapter, other publications (e.g. Eastop 1998) and the Web site established to record concealment practices: www.concealedgarments.org.

The Doublet's Social Life

The brief account of the doublet's biography reveals the extent of the social network that has developed around the doublet. It has mediated relations between the owner and curators and conservators, between curator and conservators, and between conservators and custodians and the media. Within the school museum, the doublet performs an important didactic role for teachers, pupils and visitors. The replica, which is handled by schoolchildren, gives the doublet an active social life. The replica allows the presumed original form of the doublet to be presented, and the size and construction of the replica mean it can be worn by schoolchildren.

The Doublet's Agency

The doublet can be seen to be animated in the sense that it is attributed agency, in the way analysed by Gell (1998). Garments may have been chosen for the protective or auspicious practice of concealment because they bore the imprint of the wearer. It is believed that such garments, when placed near chimneys or other points of entry to buildings, would attract the attention of malevolent forces which might otherwise enter a house and harm the household. In this way the garments may be understood to have the agency of a lure. Some finders will insist that caches are replaced after discovery so that they may continue their protective role (Eastop and Dew 2003).

The Doublet as Time Piece

People negotiate time through objects, and the doublet is used at the school museum as a marker for the Tudor era for the UK national school curriculum. The doublet also marks a time when there was widespread belief in witchcraft, when protective practices were taken very seriously. For the Deliberately Concealed Garments Project it also represents a seminal moment in the development of the project, because the uncertainties about its institutional context led to debates about what constituted its 'true nature' (Eastop 1998).

CASE STUDY 2
TOY STORY 2

The film *Toy Story 2* (1999) has been selected as a case study because it provides a vivid illustration of key issues. Its distribution by Disney-Pixar's international network means that the film probably provides the most widely distributed representation of artefact conservation-restoration. This was recognized by Simon Cane, who selected the film as a referent for his analysis of public perceptions of conservation (Cane 2001). *Toy Story 2* enters material culture in a number of ways: the film and its subsequent VHS and DVD versions have been bought, sold and exchanged throughout the world. The toys represented in *Toy Story 2* have been mass-produced in a range of qualities and re-entered popular culture as toys and other commodities, such as books (e.g. Disney/Pixar 1999).

Toy Story 2 focuses on 'Woody', a toy cowboy fitted with a pull-string. He is the favourite toy of American schoolboy Andy. Andy normally takes Woody to cowboy camp, but when he rips Woody's right arm the toy is left behind on a dusty shelf. As his mother explains, 'Toys don't last for ever.' While Andy is away at camp, his mother arranges a yard sale, where a toy penguin called 'Wheezy', whose voicebox no longer works, is offered for sale. While attempting to rescue Wheezy from the sale, Woody the toy cowboy is spotted by Al, a dealer in collectible toys. As Woody is 'an old family toy', Andy's mother refuses to sell him to Al at any price.

The dealer kidnaps Woody and drives him back to his high-rise apartment. While considering how to escape, Woody meets other toys: Bullseye the horse and Jessie the cowgirl, and Stinky Pete, the prospector, still in his original box. They explain that they are all characters from a 1950s television puppet show, *Woody's Roundup*, sponsored by Cowboy Crunchies. Jessie tells Woody 'You're valuable property ... We are a complete set.' He learns that the toys

have been in storage for a long time and are being sold to a toy museum in Japan. Woody protests that he does not want to go to a museum, because he still has an owner, but Jessie protests that she is desperate not to be returned into storage.

Al returns, and accidentally catches a thread, which causes Woody's ripped arm to fall off. This is an emergency for Al, who is keen to finalize the sale of the toys. He phones an expert, the cleaner. He is an old man carrying a toolbox fitted with a small vice-cum-chair and a spray gun. Once he has treated Woody, Al is delighted, and so is Woody, who now looks 'as good as new'.

The *Roundup* gang persuade Woody to stay with them. Jessie tells the story of her rejection by her former owner, Emily, who was Jessie's whole world and who made her feel alive. Woody recognizes that Andy is growing up and that in time he will be rejected, and he decides to stay with the Roundup gang. As Al packs the collectible toys for the flight to Japan, Andy's other toys come to rescue Woody. 'Buzz Lightyear', a space ranger, explains, 'You're not a collector's item ... you're a child's toy.' Buzz asks Woody whether he wants to watch kids from behind glass and never be loved again. Woody decides to return with his friends when he rubs off the overpainting on his boot to reveal Andy's name on its sole. Woody, Jessie and Bullseye are finally rescued at the airport and return to Andy's bedroom. On Andy's return from camp he is delighted to find Woody, and also Jessie and Bullseye, and he labels them with his name. Andy also repairs Woody's arm, newly ripped by Stinky Pete. The story ends with Wheezy, with a replacement voicebox, singing 'You've got a friend in me'.

Toy Story 2 as a Commentary on Material Culture

The film animates toys and stimulates their commercial sale. There is layer upon layer of animation. The film makers animate the people and toys in the film. Andy attempts to animate the toys with fantasies of the Wild West and intergalactic travel. The toys appear to have lives of their own. They believe that the love of children gives them life. Woody has to choose between the adoration of many children (while safely immobilized in a museum case) and being damaged in play with Andy, while knowing that as Andy grows up he will become redundant and may find himself in landfill.

Objects in the Cycles of Production, Exchange, Consumption and Destruction

The toys can be seen within cycles of production, consumption, exchange and destruction. The results of mass production are evident in the rows of stacked toys in 'Al's Toy Barn', although the actual process of toy production is not witnessed, as is usual in post-industrial societies. However, origin myths are evident. Andy plays out the American cowboy myth, seen also in the 1950s television series. Buzz initially believes his origins lie in another planet but reads later that he was made in China (see *Toy Story*).

Toy Story 2 centres on the exchange of toys, either through gifts and possible inheritance: Buzz is a gift, while Woody is a family toy. When offered for sale to a museum, the toys re-enter commodity exchange, where they risk losing their individual toyish qualities to gain wider exchange value. The toys are consumed in the rough-and-tumble of their life with Andy and within their own society. Andy plays out a scene where Woody rescues Bo-peep. During this heroic act, Andy rips Woody's right arm. As a result, Andy chooses not to take Woody to cowboy camp, much to Woody's disappointment. As Andy's mother says, 'Toys don't last for ever.' Woody's arm gets ripped and Wheezy loses his voice. While repair is possible, so is total destruction. Objects can be recycled, as seen in Woody's dream of a hybrid toy made of recycled toy components, or end up in landfills.

Object Biographies

The central characters of Woody and Buzz Lightyear have multi-layered biographies. Buzz is from a distant planet, and is threatened by Zurg. Once treasured by Andy and befriended by Woody and his fellow toys, Buzz changes from a superhuman space ranger to the awareness that he is a toy. He acknowledges that his laser weapon is merely a light bulb. He recognizes his catch phrase, 'To infinity and beyond,' as ironic. He discovers that he is not unique on meeting a new Buzz Lightyear toy equipped with a better belt. This new Buzz Lightyear finally recognizes himself as a toy, and he plays catch with Zurg, his character's deadly enemy. These toys have complicated biographies because they are alive in the imagination of the older generation, as many were popular in the 1950s and 1960s.

Objects as Social Life

Just as objects can be seen to have biographies (Kopytoff 1986; Eastop 2003), they can be seen to be both the medium and the outcome of social relations. There is an active social life among Andy's toys; for instance, the rivalry of Buzz and Woody for the affection of Bo-peep. Toys also mediate the relations between people. Andy's family is portrayed as a standard North American family: his mother as home maker and his invisible father as the person who renews Wheezy's voicebox. In contrast the dealer is portrayed as a greedy, lazy, slovenly single man, living in a penthouse apartment, avaricious for the best deal. This contrasts the suburban gift economy of home with the capitalist economy of the city. In the end the toys choose the domestic of the all-American family home rather than the enterprise of the Japanese museum.

Objects and Agency

Toy Story 2 is a story of toys told by toys. From its perspective, each toy feels and acts as an individual. The toys are active characters, except in the sight of people, when they become passive recipients of outside forces. These material objects appear as film stars in stories of their own fate. Designed and produced by humans, they act independently of them, albeit dependent on their affection and care.

Buzz Lightyear is shocked by the hundreds of identical Buzz Lightyears on the shelves of 'Als's Toy Barn'. Each Buzz Lightyear, on release from its packaging, will feel itself to be *the* Buzz Lightyear. A section of the film debates who is the real Buzz Lightyear; the answer is the one with the 'Andy' written on his boot sole. Love, naming and branding give identities the real identity. Toys are given as presents; literally 'presentations'. When given as gifts each moves from being a mass-produced object to belonging to a child with the opportunity of being loved and cherished. Woody knows that he is a toy; he enjoys being Andy's favourite toy and leader of Andy's toys. When among the toys he enjoys playing the role of the cowboy and looks forward to perfecting this role with Andy when they are away at camp. Woody is in command of the play of representations until he discovers that he and a set of other toys were characters in a 1950s television series called *Woody's Roundup*, cancelled on the launch of the Soviet satellite Sputnik. He temporarily loses his agency in the play of representations.

Objects as Time Pieces

People negotiate time through objects. Woody is both a string puppet in a 1950s television series and a contemporary toy. Woody is a generational marker, as he is treasured as an old family toy; we may assume that he has been passed on to Andy's parental generation. Objects also act as markers of world events. *Woody's Roundup* was abruptly taken off when Sputnik, the Soviet space satellite, was launched. The success of Sputnik was seen as a threat to American technological supremacy. As Stinky Pete explains, space toys (such as Buzz) replaced cowboy characters. The toys suffer wear and tear, but do not age, although they recognize that their owners will grow up and they will be disposed of.

CONSERVATION-RESTORATION IN TOY STORY 2

The film *Toy Story 2* can be read as a document of conservation because it provides a dynamic representation of debates about an object's 'true nature' and the effect this has on how an object is conserved. Key issues are summarized in Figure 32.8. Although documentation is not referred to in *Toy Story 2*, Al the dealer demonstrates a keen awareness of the materials and technology of Woody's clothes, presumably as markers of the toy's authenticity and resulting commercial value, as well as of his own connoisseurship. Al is delighted by Woody's 'Original hand-painted face ... natural dyed blanket-stitched vest ... hand-stitched polyvinyl hat'.

Preventive conservation measures are clearly demonstrated in *Toy Story 2*. After treating Woody, the cleaner places the toy in a glass display cabinet, and the floppy toy is held securely by a shaped mount, where it will be protected from dirt and handling. As the cleaner closes the door on the display case, he announces, 'He's for display only ... You handle him too much, he ain't going to last.' Later in the story, Al prepares the Roundup gang for shipping to Japan by packing each toy separately into 'custom-fitted foam insulation'. The appearance of the foam is consistent with the closed-cell polythene type, approved for conservation use.

Repair features centrally in the film. Andy, having damaged Woody's right arm, leaves him at home while he goes to cowboy camp. On his return, Andy immediately repairs Woody's arm by sewing the ripped seam closed with thick, strong red thread. This leaves Woody with distinctive scar-like stitching, but does allow Woody to show off his biceps to Bo-peep. In contrast, the cleaner, an old man with glasses and specialist tools, had earlier made an invisible mend to Woody's arm, and rectified paint loss on Woody's cheeks and hair. Andy's repair can be seen as the user returning the toy to effective functioning (play) without concern for appearance. The cleaner performs his professional tasks with great care, often under magnification. He removes all sense of unique identity by overpainting the name Andy on Woody's boot and by masking the worn paint caused by everyday play. A contrast can be drawn between functional repair for a plaything and a service to remove all individual identity and return a toy to its 'as new' appearance. Each intervention is directed by what is seen as the role of the object.

The expert called in by Al is called 'the cleaner' and he sees his job as removing 'dirt'. He cleans Woody's eye and ear, and polishes his boots. Once Woody is safely installed in his display case, the delighted Al tells the cleaner, 'You're a genius ... he's just like new.' It is obvious from this exchange that, for both Al and the cleaner, the dirt on Woody is unwanted; its removal helps to return Woody to an 'as new' appearance. The lack of any documentation of Woody or the toy's treatment, rather than any aspect of its treatment *per se*, is what makes it clear that the specialist employed by Al would not be called a 'conservator'.

The kidnap/theft of Woody points to the international networks of illegal trade and fraud associated with collecting. Professional codes of conduct and recent publications prohibit conserving or giving expert advice on objects of unknown provenance (Brodie et al. 2000). Woody's theft also highlights the fact that some of the best conservation measures are those that protect against natural and man-made disasters (fire, flood, war, looting). Disaster preparedness plans are one outcome of effective collection management strategies.

Three overlapping networks of rhetoric emerge from this analysis. First, the discourse of Disney-Pixar of comfortable American nuclear families and the international commerce in toys, focused in cleanliness and dirtiness, new and old. Second, there is the rhetoric of conservation, with its focus on the essential nature of objects, their integrity and inherent truth, and the complexity of history and the need to leave evidence for future generations. Third, there is the newer discourse of 'material

WOODY'S ORIGINS
(Production)

Woody as a cowboy string puppet in a 1950s television film
Woody as cowboy doll for sale (television merchandise)
Woody as gift (passed from parents to their son Andy)

WOODY'S ROLES IN THE FILM
(Consumption)

Subject in his own right	*Object in relation to Andy*	*Object in relation to set of objects*
Woody as animated in the film is an independent character	Woody as a plaything is a cowboy doll fitted with a string-pull to activate its voice box	Woody as a collectable is stolen for sale to an overseas toy museum, where the doll completes a set
Woody acts as leader of Andy's toys when unobserved by human characters	Woody is Andy's favourite toy, animated by Andy during play	Woody is prepared for museum display in a glass case
Woody's broken arm is held in a sling	Andy repairs his doll's arm with big red stitches	Toy undergoes treatment by a specialist to make it 'as good as new'

Woody is rescued by the toys from Al's room
Woody resumes his role as Andy's favourite toy

WOODY'S FUTURE
Woody's future remains uncertain

Reproduction	*Disposal*	*Retention*
Woody will be reproduced at each showing of *Toy Story 2*	Andy will grow up and his cowboy doll may be passed to a younger sibling, suffer 'wear and tear', and may be put aside, sold or end up as landfill	The toy may be valued as an old family toy and retained, or valued as a collectible/museum exhibit
Film medium will age but Woody won't	The material of the doll will deteriorate	The rate of the toy's material deterioration may be reduced by preventive and remedial conservation

Figure 32.8 *Summary of Woody's life in Toy Story 2, presented to distinguish the phases of his life as a culturally salient cartoon character/toy/exhibit*

culture' focused on the dynamics of social life and the active mediating role of objects.

EMERGENT THEMES

As in other fields, technological changes structure much development. In conservation this is increasingly balanced by the influence of meaning-based social science, of which material culture is a part, and this chapter is evidence. The political economy of conservation appears more transparent, with social inclusion policies matched by increasing professional cohesion and control.

Dynamic Physical Environment

Developments in instrumental techniques mean that even the tiniest samples can now be analysed (e.g. Newman 1998; Wyeth and Janaway 2005). This means that the size of samples removed from objects undergoing investigation can be reduced to a minimum, and more information can be obtained from a single sample. Techniques which do not require sampling are also under development; deterioration mechanisms are better understood and pathways of deterioration can be monitored *in situ* (Garside and Wyeth 2003). Instruments are becoming smaller and cheaper, so more conservators and curators can benefit from materials analysis. Computer technology means that reference material and results are more widely accessible via the World Wide Web, and data can be processed to give more information. The technical capacity to identify materials raises ethical issues. For example, 'Wet with blood: the investigation of Mary Todd Lincoln's cloak' (Buenger 2000) describes a consultation process (including a conference underwritten by the Monsanto company) to consider whether or not to agree to a request for DNA analysis to authenticate a cloak allegedly worn by Mary Todd on the night her husband, President Lincoln, was assassinated.

Environmental conservation is having a significant effect on the rhetoric and practice of conservation. In particular, the idea of 'sustainable heritage' has gained ideological and practical importance (e.g. Krumbein et al. 1994). By coming under the 'sustainability' umbrella, conservation is becoming part of wider debates, e.g. about pollution monitoring and control, heritage site management and urban development, and public access to collections and sites, and is able to attract international funding. The reluctance to use environmentally damaging surfactants for conservation cleaning or toxic substances to inhibit wood decay demonstrates areas of common concern between environmental and heritage conservation.

Sensitivity to local environmental conditions is also growing. The rigid environmental parameters established as norms in Western Europe and North America are no longer viewed as universally applicable. For instance, local traditions of housekeeping are being analysed to develop control methods that are appropriate, say, to conditions of high humidity and can be implemented locally without huge investments in equipment or imported supplies (e.g. de Paulo 2003).

There is also overt recognition that even the best conservation interventions cannot protect everything from destruction or unwanted change. The concept of acceptable damage is being discussed, e.g. acknowledging that a certain level of colour change (dye fading) will result from the display of historic textiles. The sudden, rapid, irreversible deterioration of some early plastics is now widely recognized (Grattan 1993). Identification of unstable materials and monitoring for early signs of deterioration can help to ensure that vulnerable objects are identified and documented before they break up (e.g. Lovett and Eastop 2004), with documentation becoming a surrogate for the degraded object.

Dynamic Social Environment

Conservation is entering a phase where its policies and practices are being informed by greater understanding of its changing social context. The material-based perspective, founded on preserving the material 'integrity' of the object, is being questioned. The essentialist, Eurocentric view evident in the concept of 'true nature' is being questioned by asking, 'Are the qualities of object that conservation seek[s] to preserve and maintain intrinsic to that object or reflections on subjective cultural values?' (Clavir 1996: 102).

Odegaard has argued that one outcome of the United Nations' proclamation of the Decade of Indigenous People 1994–2004 was greater concern on the part of indigenous populations for their material culture (Odegaard 2000: 38). This has affected not only the 'front of house' activities of museums and galleries, such as exhibitions, but also behind-the-scenes activities such as conservation. Requests by First Nation groups for the return of museum-held material, e.g. for burial and for use, have led to questioning of the basic tenets of conservation. For example, the Native American Graves Protection and Repatriation Act 1990 (NAGPRA) in the United States requires recipients of repatriations to be informed if the objects have been treated with pesticides or other substances that represent a potential hazard to the objects or the persons handling them (Odegaard 2000: 39).

There is growing awareness that the non-tangible attributes of objects should be given as much consideration as their material properties. When artefacts are usually consumed or destroyed in normal use, preservation of an object's physical integrity may be contradictory to measures required to sustain the object's intangible attributes. For instance, collection management measures taken to provide a secure and environmentally stable storage environment may mean that artefacts are grouped according to their material type, rather than according to other categories. For example, following consultation with community groups, human remains and the funerary objects found with them may be housed together, irrespective of material types (Salazar et al. 2001: 30). Consultation mechanisms and guidelines are being developed (e.g. Salazar et al. 2001; Sullivan et al. 2003) and incorporated into conservation education. Odegaard (2000: 40) argues that 'greater awareness of the lifeways and value systems of indigenous groups whose work is being conserved has offered significant advantages to the conservation process'.

For instance, the perceived agency of objects (as discussed in relation to the Reigate doublet) is now more widely recognized. In the American First Nation context, some museums have changed their methods of object storage, so that objects which are attributed lifelike properties are no longer placed in airtight containers believed to suffocate them, and they are provided with food (Clavir 1994). The introduction of a food source into a museum store goes against established practices of preventive conservation based on the precept of conserving the physical integrity of objects, because such food may attract pests. Such 'feeding' is said to be consistent with the symbolic properties recognized and sustained by representatives of the communities whose ancestors made and used the objects. (Clavir 2002)

Different concepts of ownership are being more widely recognized, e.g. ownership meaning the right to use and/or reproduce an object (e.g. Stewart and Joseph 2000: 43) rather than the right to retain legal custody of it. One effect of this is that object conservation is now linked with the conservation of 'intangible heritage', e.g. dance traditions and craft skills. For instance, the risk of 'skills decay' is considered as important as wood decay for the conservation of historic timber structures (Larsen and Marstein 2000).

A related development is the importance attributed to 'artists' intent'. The conservation of art works by living artists is governed by laws which give the maker the right to make decisions about intervention (Garfinkle et al. 1997; Lennard 2005; Odegaard 1995; Roy and Smith 2004). For some artists, long-term preservation of their art work is unwelcome. For others, re-establishing the original appearance of their art works is prioritized over preservation of the artworks' original materials or construction, leading to the remaking and/or substitution of damaged parts. In such cases, preservation of physical integrity may come second to respecting the artist's intent.

'Taken for granted' conservation principles, often focused on preserving the physical properties of the object, are being questioned by consideration of the object's social salience. 'Significance assessment' is a formal mechanism which encourages documentation of the various meaningful associations attributed to the object (e.g. AMOL 2003). This has allowed the interests of different parties to inform and contribute to conservation decision making. As significance assessment becomes more overt and explicit there is also a trend, welcomed by this author, to document not only the object and the conservation intervention, but also the rationale for the intervention.

Conservation is becoming more responsive to context. The essentialist rhetoric is being opened up to debate, both within the profession and outside (e.g., Torre 2002). The borders of conservation are changing and becoming less distinct, and professional networks are being renegotiated. If the concept of 'risk assessment' is influenced and moderated by 'significance assessment', the practice of conservation will be informed by assessment of predicted changes to symbolic properties and social roles, as well as to material properties.

Bureaucratic Changes

As conservation has passed from a craft to a semi-profession to a profession, bureaucratic management has emerged. When selecting and implementing conservation strategies there is greater awareness of 'cost–benefit analysis', 'risk assessment' (Ashley-Smith 1999; Waller 2002) and 'community involvement', i.e. working with different 'user groups' (e.g. Eastop 2002; Putt 1998, 2001). For instance, archaeologists are now more likely to work with, rather than against, metal detectorists. These approaches have encouraged a wider discussion of what should be conserved and at what cost.

There is also greater co-operation between the various specialist national and international conservation bodies, supported in part by the rhetoric of sustainability. One outcome of such co-working in the United Kingdom has been the move towards institutional convergence, with several influential professional organizations agreeing to merge to form a new body, provisionally called the Institute of Conservation. The main motivation is 'strength in unity', so that the conservation sector becomes more effective in informing policies affecting conservation practices and funding, and is able to provide better services (e.g. monitoring and maintaining professional standards).

The incorporation of UK museums and galleries into the realm of libraries and archives to form the Museums, Libraries and Archives Council (referred to as MLA) in 2000 is a state-sponsored outcome of this mood. 'Museums, libraries and archives connect people to knowledge and information, creativity and inspiration. MLA is leading the drive to unlock this wealth, for everyone' (MLA 2004). It is clear that the concept of cultural capital is being adopted by government agencies in the United Kingdom.

CONCLUSION

This chapter has shown how conservation is a part of material culture as well as a being a commentary on it. What has emerged is how textile conservation is now responding to the wider cultural salience of objects, as well as to their physical integrity. It is now more widely recognized within all conservation specialisms that human social life gives meaning to the life of objects. The conservation of objects will remain contested as long as the objects of concern remain culturally salient. Culturally important objects are marked by the degree of contestation about their material and social significance. Sustaining mechanisms for debate within conservation is as important as are methods of investigation, preservation and presentation. Indeed, the debate about the social life of an object adds to the very cultural dynamic of which the object is a part.

NOTES

1 For the sake of brevity, the term 'object' is used throughout this chapter to refer to objects, collections, monuments and sites.
2 I am embedded within the culture of textile conservation: I am both a subject of textile conservation and a commentator on textile conservation as material culture. My entry into conservation-restoration was through an interest in history and a desire to work with my hands. As a conservator I began as a volunteer in a private textile conservation studio, combining an apprentice-style training with a conventional academic education. Over the last thirty years I have contributed to and witnessed the development of textile conservation as a profession. My interest in material culture was triggered

by the request to conserve textiles collected from the Iban in Borneo at the end of the nineteenth century and the attached labels of its collector, A.C. Haddon. The challenge was to preserve the Iban cloth as well as the collector's handwritten labels.
3 For example, IIC (established in 1950) publishes *Studies in Conservation, Reviews in Conservation* and biennial *Congress Preprints*, e.g. *Preventive Conservation* (Roy and Smith 1994), *Archaeological Conservation and its Consequences* (Roy and Smith 1996) and *Modern Art, New Museums* (Roy and Smith 2004). www.iiconservation.org.
4 Examples include the preprints of the meetings in Rio de Janeiro (2002), Lyons (1999) and Edinburgh (1996). www.icom. museum
5 ICOMOS was founded in 1965 in response to the adoption of the Charter for the Conservation and Restoration of Monuments and Sites (the so-called Venice Charter of 1964). www.icomos.org.
6 ICCROM's five main areas of activity are training, information provision (e.g. via its excellent library in Rome and its Web site iccrom@iccrom.org), research support, co-operation with other agencies, and advocacy.
7 The GCI supports the dissemination of research and experience in a number of ways, including the support of AATA Online, which provides abstracts of conservation literature (http://aata.getty.edu/ NPS/) and via the commissioning of publications. One notable initiative is the GCI's Readings in Conservation series, which brings together texts considered fundamental to an understanding of the history, philosophies and methodologies of conservation (Stanley Price et al. 1996; Bomford and Leonard 2005).

REFERENCES

AMOL, Australian Museums and Galleries Online (2003) Development of a Standard Methodology for Assessing the Significance of Cultural Heritage Objects and Collections. http://amol.org.au/craft/publications/hec/significance/sign_cultural_obj.asp (21 March).

Ashley-Smith, J. (1999) *Risk Assessment for Object Conservation*. Oxford: Butterworth Heinemann.

Berducou, M. (1996) 'Introduction to archaeological conservation', in N. Stanley Price, M. Kirby Talley, Jr, and A.M. Vacaro (eds), *Historical and Philosophical*

Issues in the Conservation of Cultural Heritage. Los Angeles, CA: Getty Conservation Institute.

Bomford, D. and Leonard, M., eds. (2005) *Issues in the Conservation of Easel Paintings*. Los Angeles, CA: Getty Conservation Institute.

Brodie, N., Doole, J. and Watson, P. (2000) *Stealing History: the Illicit Trade in Cultural Material*. Cambridge: McDonald Institute for Archaeological Research.

Brooks, H.B. (2000) *A Short History of IIC: Foundation and Development*. London: International Institute for Conservation of Historic and Artistic Works (IIC).

Brooks, M.M., Lister, A.M., Eastop, D. and Bennett, T. (1996) 'Artifact or information? Articulating the conflicts in preserving archaeological textiles', in A. Roy and P. Smith (eds), *Archaeological Conservation and its Consequences*. London: IIC, pp. 16–21.

Buenger, N. (2000) 'Wet with blood: the investigation of Mary Todd's Lincoln's cloak', in *Conservation Combinations*. Asheville, NC: NATCC, pp. 41–51.

Cameron, F. (2003) 'Digital futures I, Museum collections, digital technologies, and the cultural construction of knowledge', *Curator: the Museum Journal*, 46 (3): 325–40.

Caple, C. (2000) *Conservation Skills. Judgement, Method and Decision Making*. London and New York: Routledge.

Cane, S. (2001) 'Challenging the Discourse of Conservation: the Development, Function and Position of the Conservation Process in the Museum System'. Unpublished M.A. dissertation, University of Southampton.

Clavir, M. (1994) 'Preserving conceptual integrity: ethics and theory in preventive conservation', in A. Roy and P. Smith (eds), *Preventive Conservation Practice, Theory and Research*. London: IIC, pp. 53–7.

Clavir, M. (1996) 'Reflections on changes in museums and the conservation of collections from indigenous peoples', *Journal of the American Institute of Conservation (AIC)*, 35: 99–107.

Clavir, M. (2002) *Preserving what is Valued: Museums, Conservation and First Nations*. Vancouver: University of British Columbia Press.

Corfield, M. (1988) 'Towards a conservation profession', in V. Todd (ed.), *Conservation Today: Papers presented at the UKIC Thirtieth Anniversary Conference 1988*. London: UKIC, pp. 4–7.

Cronyn, J.M. (1990) *The Elements of Archaeological Conservation*. London and New York: Routledge.

de Paulo, T.C. Toledo (2003) 'Caring for collections in tropical environments: collecting and communicating data at Museu Paulista/USP, Brasil (1997–2000)', *Anais do Museum Paulista*, 8/9: pp. 193–278.

Disney Enterprises/Pixar Animation Studios (1999) *Toy Story: the Essential Guide*. London: Dorling Kindersley.

Dodds, W. (1988) 'Consolidation of mud on a World War I uniform', *Australian Institute for Conservation of Cultural Material (AICCM) Newsletter*, 25: 7.

Douglas, M. (1966/1995) *Purity and Danger*. London: Routledge.

Drysdale, L. (1999) 'The language of conservation: applying critical linguistic analysis to three conservation papers', in J. Bridgman (ed.), *Preprints of the Twelfth Triennial Meeting of ICOM's Conservation Committee, Lyon*. London: James & James, pp. 161–5.

Eastop, D. (1998) 'Decision-making in conservation: determining the role of artefacts', in Á. Tímár-Balászy and D. Eastop (eds), *International Perspectives: Textile Conservation, 1990–1996*. London: Archetype, pp. 43–6.

Eastop, D. (2000) 'Textiles as multiple and competing histories' in M.M. Brooks (ed.), *Textiles Revealed: Object Lessons in Historic Textiles and Costume Research*. London: Archetype, pp. 17–28.

Eastop, D. (2001) 'Garments deliberately concealed in buildings', in R.J. Wallis and K. Lymer (eds), *A Permeability of Boundaries? New Approaches to the Archaeology of Art, Religion and Folklore*. BAR (British Archaeological Reports) International Series 936. Oxford: Hedges, pp. 79–83.

Eastop, D. (2002) 'Conservation as a democratising practice: learning from Latin America', *ICOM UK News*, 63: 22–4.

Eastop, D. (2003) 'The biography of objects: a tool for analysing an object's significance', in *International Workshop on Flexible Materials in Asian Collections: Exchange of Approaches to Conservation, Presentation and Use*. Kuala Lumpur: Department of Museums and Antiquities Malaysia, pp. 100–13.

Eastop, D. and Brooks, M.M. (1996) 'To clean or not to clean: the value of soils and creases', in J. Bridgman (ed.), *Preprints of the Eleventh Triennial Meeting of the ICOM Conservation Committee, Edinburgh*. London: James and James , pp. 687–91.

Eastop, D. and Dew, C. (2003) 'Secret agents: deliberately concealed garments as symbolic textiles', in J. Vuori (ed.), *The Conservation of Flags and other Symbolic Textiles*. Albany, NY: NATCC, pp. 5–15.

Eastop, D. and McEwing, R. (2005) 'Informing textile and wildlife conservation: DNA analysis of baleen from an eighteenth-century garment found deliberately concealed in a building', in P. Wyeth and R. Janaway (eds), *Scientific Analysis of Ancient and Historic Textiles: Informing Preservation, Display and Interpretation*. London: Archetype.

Finch, K. and Putnam, G. (1977) *Caring for Textiles*. London: Barrie & Jenkins.

Flury-Lemberg, M. (1988) *Textile Conservation and Research*. Berne: Abegg-Stiftung.

Garfinkle, A.M., Fries, J., Lopez, D. and Possessky, L. (1997) 'Art conservation and the legal obligation to preserve artistic intent', *Journal of the American Institute of Conservation (AIC)*, 36: 165–79.

Garside, P. and Wyeth, P. (2003) 'Monitoring the deterioration of historic textiles: developing appropriate micro-technology', in J.H. Townsend, K. Eremin and A. Adriaens (eds), *Conservation Science 2003*. London: Archetype, pp. 171–6.

Gell, A. (1998) *Art and Agency: Towards a New Anthropological Theory*. Oxford: Clarendon Press.

Gill, K. (2001) 'Example of cross-section diagrams to document changes in upholstery layers before and after conservation treatment', in K. Gill and D. Eastop (eds), *Upholstery Conservation: Principles and Practice*. Oxford: Butterworth Heinemann, pp. 181–5.

Gill, K. and Eastop, D. (1997) 'Two contrasting minimally interventive upholstery treatments: different roles, different treatments', in K. Marko (ed.), *Textiles in Trust*. London: Archetype, in association with the National Trust, pp. 67–77.

Grattan, D.W., ed. (1993) *Saving the Twentieth Century: the Conservation of Modern Materials*. Ottawa: CCI.

Hofenk de Graaff, J. (1968) 'The constitution of detergents in connection with the cleaning of ancient textiles', *Studies in Conservation*, 13: 122–41.

Keene, S. (1998) *Digital Collections: Museums in the Information Age*. Oxford: Butterworth Heinemann.

Kopytoff, I. (1986) 'The cultural biography of things: commoditization as process', in A. Appadurai (ed.), *The Social Life of Things: Commodities in Cultural Perspective*. Cambridge: Cambridge University Press, pp. 64–91.

Krumbein, W.E., Brimblecombe, P., Cosgrove, D.E. and Staniforth, S., eds (1994) *Durability and Change: The Science, Responsibility, and Cost of Sustaining Cultural Heritage*. Chichester: Wiley.

Landi, S. (1985) *The Textile Conservator's Manual*. Oxford: Butterworth Heinemann.

Larsen, K.E. and Marstein, N. (2000) *Conservation of Historic Timber Structure: an Ecological Approach*. Oxford: Butterworth Heinemann.

Lennard, F. (2005) 'The impact of artists' moral rights legislation on conservation practice in the UK and beyond', *Preprints of the Fourteenth Triennial Meeting of the ICOM Conservation Committee, den Haag*. London: James and James.

Lister, A. (1997) 'Making the most of mounts: expanding the role of display mounts in the preservation and interpretation of historic textiles', *Preprints of Symposium '97: Fabric of an Exhibition: an Interdisciplinary Approach*. Ottawa: Canadian Conservation Institute, pp. 143–8.

Lovett, D. and Eastop, D. (2004) 'The degradation of polyester polyurethane: preliminary study of 1960s foam-laminated dresses', in A. Roy and P. Smith (eds), *Modern Art, New Museums*. London: IIC, pp. 100–4 and plates 42–5.

MLA (Museums, Libraries and Archives Council) (2004) *Renaissance News* (July) 3: 1–8.

Muñoz Viñas, S. (2002) 'Contemporary theory of conservation', *Reviews in Conservation* (IIC), 3: 25–34.

Muñoz Viñas, S. (2005) *Contemporary Theory of Conservation*. Oxford: Elsevier Butterworth Heinemann.

NAGPRA (The Native American Graves Protection and Repatriation Act) http://www.cr.nps.gov/nagpra/.

Newman, R. (1998) Review of W.C. McCrone, *Judgement Day for the Turin Shroud* (Chicago: Microscope Publications), *Journal of the American Institute of Conservation (AIC)*, 37: 228–30.

Oddy, A. (1994) *Restoration: is it acceptable?* BM Occasional Paper 99. London: British Museum.

Oddy, A. and Smith, S., eds (2002) *Past Practice – Future Prospects*. BM Occasional Paper 145. London: British Museum.

Odegaard, N. (1995) 'Artist's intent: material culture studies and conservation', *Journal of the American Institute of Conservation (AIC)*, 34: 187–93.

Odegaard, N. (2000) 'Collections conservation: some current issues and trends', *Cultural Resource Management* (published by the US National Park Service), 5: 38–41.

Plenderleith, H.J. (1956) *The Conservation of Antiquities and Works of Art*. London: Oxford University Press.

Putt, N. (1998) 'Preventive conservation through teamwork: different nations, different solutions', *Museum Practice*, 3 (1): 17–19.

Putt, N. (2001) 'Heritage conservation in the Pacific Islands', *Reviews in Conservation* (IIC), 2: 61–72.

Pye, E. (2001) *Caring for the Past: Issues in Conservation for Archaeology and Museums*. London: James & James.

Roy, A. and Smith, P. eds (1994) *Preventive Conservation Practice, Theory and Research*. London: IIC.

Roy, A. and Smith, P., eds (1996) *Archaeological Conservation and its Consequences*. London: IIC.

Roy, A. and Smith, P., eds (2004) *Modern Art, New Museums*. London: IIC.

Salazar, V., Roberts, A. and Bohnert, A. (2001) 'Cultural sensitivity and tribal authority in research projects and museum collection management', *Cultural Resource Management* (published by the US National Park Service), 7: 29–32.

Sandwith, H. and Stainton, S. (1984) *Manual of Housekeeping*. London: Allen Lane in association with the National Trust.

Sirois, J. (2001) 'Pesticide residues in museum collections', *CCI* [Canadian Conservation Institute] *Newsletter*, 28: 13.

Stanley Price, N., Kirby Talley, M. and Melucco Vaccaro, A., eds (1996) *Historical and Philosophical Issues in the Conservation of Cultural Heritage*. Los Angeles: Getty Conservation Institute.

Stewart, J. and Joseph, R. (2000) 'Validating the past in the present: First Nations' collaborations with museums', *Cultural Resource Management* (published by the US National Park Service), 5: 42–5.

Sullivan, T., Kelly, L. and Gordon, P. (2003) 'Museums and indigenous people in Australia: a review of *Previous Possessions, New Obligations:*

Policies for Museums in Australia and Aboriginal and Torres Strait Islander Peoples', *Curator,* 46 (2): 208–27.

Swann, J. (1969) 'Shoes concealed in buildings', *Northampton County Borough Museums and Art Gallery Journal,* 6: 8–21.

Swann, J. (1996) 'Shoes concealed in buildings', *Costume: the Journal of the* [UK] *Costume Society,* 3: 56–69.

Thompson, G. (1978) *The Museum Environment.* Oxford: Butterworth Heinemann.

Tímár-Balászy, Á. (2000) 'Wet cleaning of historical textiles: surfactants and other wash bath additives', *Reviews in Conservation* (IIC), 1: 46–64.

Tímár-Balászy, Á. and Eastop, D. (1998) *Chemical Principles of Textile Conservation.* Oxford: Butterworth Heinemann.

Torre, de la, M. (ed.) (2002) *Assessing the Values of Cultural Heritage.* Los Angeles, CA: Getty Conservation Institute.

Trupin, D.L. (2003) 'Flag conservation then and now', in J. Vuori (ed.), *The Conservation of Flags and other Symbolic Textiles.* Albany, NY: NATCC, pp. 55–62.

UKIC (United Kingdom Institute for Conservation) (1990) 'Guidance for practice', in *Members' Handbook.* London: UKIC.

Villers, C., ed. (2000) *The Fabric of Images: European Paintings on Textile Supports in the Fourteenth and Fifteenth Centuries.* London: Archetype.

Villers, C. (2004) 'Post Minimal Intervention', *The Conservator,* 28: 3–10.

Von der Lippe, Inger Marie (1985) *Profession or Occupational Culture? An Ethnological Study of the Textile Conservators' Working Conditions at the Museums.* Acta Univ. Upsala, Studia Ethnologica Upsaliensia 14. Uppsala: University of Uppsala.

Wadnum, J. and Noble, P. (1999) 'Is there an ethical problem after the twenty-third treatment of Rembrandt's "Anatomy Lesson of Dr Nicholaes Tulp"?' in J. Bridland (ed.), *Preprints of the Twelfth Triennial Meeting of ICOM-CC, Lyon,* I. Paris: ICOM, pp. 206–10.

Waller, R. (2002) 'A risk model of collection preservation', in R. Vontobel (ed.), *Preprints of the Thirteenth Triennial Meeting of ICOM Conservation Committee, Rio de Janeiro, 22–27 September 2002.* London: James & James, pp. 102–7.

Ward, P. (1986) *The Nature of Conservation: A Race against Time.* Marina del Rey, CA: Getty Conservation Institute.

Wyeth, P. and Janaway, R. (2005) *Scientific Analysis of Ancient and Historic Textiles: Informing Preservation, Display and Interpretation.* London: Archetype.

ACKNOWLEDGEMENTS

I am pleased to acknowledge the stimulating discussion with David Goldberg, Janet Farnsworth, Simon Cane and Mary Brooks which helped to develop the ideas expressed here. I thank the owners of the Reigate doublet and the Nether Wallop stomacher, and Nell Hoare, Director of the Textile Conservation Centre, for permission to publish. The photographs of the Chiswick House chairs are reproduced by courtesy of English Heritage. The x-radiograph is reproduced by courtesy of Sonia O'Connor, University of Bradford.

33

COLLECTORS AND COLLECTING

Russell Belk

Although museums and other institutions are certainly involved in collecting and raise a number of unique issues about the politics, ethics, and value of such activity, the focus of this chapter is on individual collecting activity. Perhaps it is fitting that this is the last chapter of the *Handbook of Material Culture*, because collecting may be seen to be both the epitome and the antithesis of vulgar materialism (Belk 1998). I once suggested that:

> Collecting is consumption writ large. It is a perpetual pursuit of inessential luxury goods. It is a continuing quest for self completion in the marketplace. And it is a sustained faith that happiness lies only an acquisition away.
>
> (Belk 1995b: 1; see also Bianchi 1997)

I still believe this to be true, but I have also come to believe that collecting may properly be seen as an essentially anti-materialistic activity. For the collector, acquiring an object for a collection is apt to be regarded as a singularizing and decommoditizing act (Abbas 1988; Appadurai 1986). When an object enters such a collection it ceases to be a fungible commodity and becomes a singular object that is no longer freely exchangeable for something of similar economic value. Its value instead lies in its contribution to the collection as a whole. The collection is the creation of the collector who has brought it into existence, often by either taking objects out of their former economic circulation or by rescuing them from unappreciative neglect and thereby sacralizing them as a part of the collection within which they become enshrined. This ritual act of reverence stands quite apart from the utilitarian view of material objects as mere commodities serving a fixed purpose. And it

suggests a view of the collector as a heroic and selfless savior of objects rather than as an acquisitive and selfish consumer.

This dialectical tension between collector as selfish consumer and collector as romantic hero is also evident in the research and literature on collecting, as will be seen. In the following review, I will begin by defining collecting and distinguishing it from several other activities with which it might be confused. I next attempt to situate collecting historically and culturally, focusing on its apparent origins and prevalence. The next section addresses more behavioral considerations of who collects, how collecting takes place, and on the individual and societal consequences of collecting. Research and theorizing about collecting are reviewed and differing approaches are distinguished. Finally, the areas that seem most in need of additional research are outlined.

COLLECTING DEFINED

If collecting is consuming, it is a special type of consuming. Consuming, in its most literal meaning, is using up, devouring, or burning. Collecting, on the other hand, is about keeping, preserving, and accumulating. Although it is possible to collect intangible experiences (e.g., a collection of countries visited, birds seen, or sexual partners experienced), even in these cases there must be the sense of an ensemble or coherent set of experiences that are preserved in memory as being interrelated. Still, this distinction may depend partly on the frame of mind of the person doing the collecting. To one person, meals may be all about devouring food and beverages, while to another person certain meals are about social and gustatory experiences to be savored and fixed in memory. For certain types of collections, like a wine collection, objects are both accumulated and consumed. For one such collector I have interviewed, each empty space where a wine bottle used to be in his collection is represented in memory in terms of the occasion, food, and companions with whom it was enjoyed. And for objects whose cost and size may preclude a large simultaneous collection (e.g., automobiles), the collection may instead be serial and composed not only of objects currently possessed, but of those previously possessed as well.

Even when there is an accumulation of consumer goods, we must distinguish collecting from several other types of accumulations and consumption activities. Consistent with others, including Alsop (1982), Aristides (1988), Belk et al. (1991), Durost (1932), Kron (1983), and Muensterberger (1994), I define collecting as:

> The process of actively, selectively, and passionately acquiring and possessing things removed from ordinary use and perceived as part of a set of non-identical objects or experiences.

> (Belk 1998: 67)

This definition separates collecting from more ordinary consumption, based on collectors removing objects from ordinary use and placing them within a defined set. While a collection may involve utilitarian objects like salt and pepper shakers, once they enter the collection they are no longer routinely used for dispensing spices. The definition also distinguishes collecting from mere accumulations or clutter in that the collection must be selective, normally based on the contribution of an object to the bounded set of objects that constitute the collection. And collecting also differs from hoarding, both based on the lack of ordinary use of the collected objects and based on the stipulation that the objects be non-identical. If someone is hoarding flour or toilet paper, the fact that each item is or is not identical matters little. But collectors normally employ a rule of 'no two alike' (Danet and Katriel 1989).

The definition of collecting given above also helps to determine whether common objects within a contemporary home such as musical recordings, books, and photographs are collections or not. If these items are freely listened to, read, or act as mementoes of family and experiences, these ordinary uses would disqualify them as part of a collection. If instead they are valued for their contribution to a set using either aesthetic or 'scientific' criteria, then they are indeed a collection. For instance, book collectors describe their reluctance to ever sully their treasured books by actively reading them (e.g., Brook 1980; Jackson 1989; Wright and Ray 1969). Ironically the bibliophile may justify their book collections on vaguely scientific grounds of archiving valuable specimens, even as they hermetically seal them within unread libraries.

One further contribution of the definition of collecting being used here is that it allows us to distinguish between the actively acquisitive collector and the more passive curator of a collection. The curator may have once been a collector engaged in the active acquisition of objects for a collection, but when such acquisition stops, collecting stops and only the curator's role remains. Likewise, someone who inherits or buys an intact collection without adding to it or replacing some items with others is a curator but not a collector. But the definition also suggests that a collection can continue to be a collection after the collector ceases to own it. As long as the objects were once selectively acquired in order to form part of a set of non-identical objects, the collection can outlive the collector. Indeed, this possibility of symbolic immortality through the continued existence of the collection is a goal of some collectors.

ORIGINS AND PREVALENCE OF COLLECTING

To the extent that collecting is a consumer activity, it might be expected that collecting tends to develop and flourish during places and times of flourishing consumerism. There is some evidence to support this expectation. While royal and temple collections or art, armament, and other treasures have existed for some time, I am speaking of more widespread individual collecting: collecting on a sufficient scale to support a commercial market in collectable goods without court or Church patronage. Extensive research by Rigby and Rigby (1944) suggests that such conditions prevailed after Greek unification by Alexander the Great in the fourth century BC. Collecting by Hellenistic Greeks was stimulated by an influx of luxuries from the East, especially Persia (Taylor 1948). Objects collected included secular paintings, sculptures, autographs, engraved gems, fine pottery, oriental carpets, wall hangings, and embroidered textiles. The city of Sicyon became a central location for the production and sale of art, aided by dealers who catered to newly wealthy traders. There was a rediscovery of early Greek statuary as the fields of collecting interest expanded.

In ancient Rome, it was the concession of art-rich Pergamum to Rome in 133 BC that stimulated popular interest in collecting (Rigby and Rigby 1944). While new interest in Greek art and Asian art began with the wealthiest Romans, by the start of the Roman empire in 27 BC, Rigby and Rigby (1944: 128) contend, 'everyone who could possibly manage to do so was collecting something'. This something included art, books, antiques, coins, sculptures, Corinthian bronzes, ceramics, tapestries, jewelry, gems, fine furniture, silverware, fossils, insects in amber, and more. Sicyon continued as a center for both legitimate and forged art. Roman tourists were apt to return home with supposed clothing of Odysseus and shields of Achilles (Rheims 1961; von Holst 1967).

During the Middle Ages in Europe, collecting was primarily an activity of the Church, royalty, and a wealthy few like Duke Jean de Berry and the Medici. However, the unearthing of ancient Rome between 1450 and 1550 did prompt collecting of medallions, sculptures, and other ancient artifacts (Hodgen 1964). But the real boom in mass collecting in Europe as well as China and Japan began in the sixteenth and seventeenth centuries. In each case, the growth of collecting coincided with rapid economic growth due either to internal or international trade. In Asia a somewhat different set of collectable objects emerged, including tea sets, lacquer furniture, calligraphy and ink stones, scroll paintings, landscape rocks, zithers, textiles, rare woods, incense burners, and ancestral bronzes. Other collectibles like gems, jewelry, weapons, and books were similar to those collected in Europe. For Japanese collectors in the Tokugawa Shogunate in the Edo period (1603–1868) Chinese and Korean objects (tea sets and ceremonies, music, calligraphy and poems) were also popular collectable objects (Guth 1989; Hayashiya and Trubner 1977). Prominent among Chinese collectors of the late Ming (1550–1650) were *nouveau riche* merchants who found it difficult to break through the artist-patron linkages found among the literati (Clunas 1991). In response to the shortage of genuine art works, the market responded with numerous forgeries. This was so common that only one in ten paintings was likely to be genuine (Clunas 1991).

An important impetus for collecting in Europe at about the same time was the introduction of treasures from the New World as well as from trade with Asia. During the sixteenth and seventeenth centuries, thousands of Europeans constructed *Wunderkammern* (wonder cabinets) filled with collectibles and curiosities from other lands (Mason 1994; Pomian 1990). Some of these treasures may not have been too dissimilar from the shields of Achilles and clothes of Odysseus brought back from Greece by credulous Roman collectors. The *Wunderkammern* of one Englishman reportedly included:

An African charm made of teeth, a felt cloak from Arabia, and shoes from many strange lands. ... A stringed instrument with but one string. The twisted horn of a bull seal. An embalmed child or *Mumia*. The bauble and bells of Henry VIII's fool. A unicorn's tail. Inscribed paper made of bark, and an artful Chinese box. A flying rhinoceros. ... a number of crowns made of claws, a Madonna made of Indian feathers, an Indian charm made of monkey teeth. A mirror, which 'both reflects and multiplies objects', a sea-halcyon's nest. A sea mouse (*mus marinus*), reed pipes like those played by Pan, a long narrow Indian canoe, with oars and siding planks, hanging from the ceiling.

(Mullaney 1983: 40)

Like the *Wunderkammern*, the public collections of newly established zoos and botanical gardens also show the fascination with the Other in contrast to the European self (Ellenberger 1974; George 1985; Hunt 1985; Tuan 1984).

While such *Wunderkammern* were extremely popular in the sixteenth and seventeenth centuries, such encyclopedic collecting was most common in Protestant Europe. In Catholic locales like Rome collections were more specialized, and eventually other collections came to follow this specialization, including the Cartesian divorce of science from art (Olmi 1985; Pomian 1990). While this split may reflect the tempering of passion that Max Weber called the 'disenchantment of the world' (Berman 1981), it has by no means eliminated delighted fascination with the fantastic in either collecting or consuming more generally (Stewart 1984).

Throughout Europe and the Americas, the growth of collecting has tended to follow the development of consumer culture (Belk 1995b; Stearns 2001). For instance, the widespread collecting of oil paintings, engravings, tulip bulbs, shells, coins, minerals, and other diverse objects in the Netherlands exploded during the seventeenth-century Dutch 'Golden Age' of abundance (Mackay 1932; Mukerji 1983; Schama 1987). A similar pattern of the popularization of collecting followed in other countries. Collecting became a popular activity for both children and adults, and as the practice grew, so did the informal rules defining a good collection. Like the labor force following capitalism and the industrial revolution, collecting became more specialized. Not only types of objects collected, but also historical periods, genders, genres, geographic locations, and other classifications were imposed. Even collections of dolls, comic books, beer cans, and match books developed nomenclatures and niches. In the process:

> An excessive, sometimes even rapacious need to *have* is transformed into rule-governed, meaningful desire. Thus the self that must possess but cannot have it all learns to select, order, classify in hierarchies – to make 'good' collections.

> (Clifford 1990: 143)

As we shall see, such distinctions help to justify the acquisitiveness and possessiveness that are conspicuously displayed in collecting.

But to suggest that collecting is merely a manifestation of consumer culture would be misleading. There are evidences of collecting in human prehistory during periods and places where daily survival must have been challenging. An apparent collection of interesting pebbles has been found in an 80,000 year old cave in France (Neal 1980). More extensive collections of fossils, quartz, iron pyrite, sea shells, and galena have been found in Cro-Magnon caves (Pomian 1990). And numerous collections of art and grave goods have been found in caves from about 30,000 BC (Halverson 1987; Pfeiffer 1982). To the extent that these sets of goods can be regarded as collections of individuals or groups (for we cannot know the intent with which these objects were brought together) the tendency to collect clearly pre-dates consumer culture. This is not to deny that there may well have been acquisitive and possessive feelings by early collectors. Indeed, the belief that someone should be buried with their possessions suggests that attachments to objects can continue *post mortem*. Even without entombment, certain collectible objects may gain provenance, in much the same way that Miller (2001) suggests that old homes may acquire ghosts.

The fact that collections often outlive their collectors also means that these sets of objects are increasingly prevalent in the world. While the parallel history of institutional collecting may spring from the same cultural, economic, and political forces that precipitate explosions of individual collecting, museum collections are also a repository for what society judges to be the best individual collections (Belk 1995b). Besides sanctioning such collecting, the museum provides a model of what a good collection is. These collections, once they are enshrined in the museum, also help define a sense of local, regional, or national identity (Delaney 1992). As individual collecting has grown, so have museums, sometimes exponentially (Vander Gucht 1991). The best estimates of the prevalence of collecting, as defined above, are that perhaps one of three people in affluent nations are active collectors and that many have more than one collection (O'Brien 1981; Schiffer et al. 1981). As collecting has grown, so have studies of collecting, but not at the same pace. Given its economic and behavioral significance, there is a surprisingly limited amount of research and theory directed at collecting.

PRIOR COLLECTING RESEARCH

Much of the early research into collecting was historical and focused on high-culture collecting activity, primarily art collecting. Rigby and Rigby (1944) provide a wide-sweeping historical review and also offer an account of collector motivations (e.g., competitiveness). Other useful historical studies of art collecting include Alsop (1982), Cabanne (1963), Haskell (1976), Hermann (1972), Impey and MacGregor (1985), Jackson (1989), Moulin (1987), Pomian (1990), Rheims (1961), Saarinen (1958), Taylor (1948), and von Holst (1967). There are also several interesting studies of prominent historical collectors (both biographical and autobiographical), including Walter Benjamin (e.g., Abbas 1988; Benjamin 1968b), Sigmund Freud (e.g., Barker 1996; Dudar 1990; Engelman 1976; Forrester 1994; Gamwell and Wells 1989), and Andy Warhol (e.g., Johnson 1988; Kaylan 1988; Pivar 1988).

There has also been a small amount of research examining collecting as an economic activity (Grampp 1989; Moulin 1987; Van Der Grijp 2002). While dealers and manufacturers of collectible objects may regard collecting in economic terms, most collectors do not. Collectors instead seem to derive other benefits from their collecting activity. Perhaps the greatest amount of collecting theory and research has been devoted to trying to understand what these other benefits are. The question of collector motivations is also addressed by a number of fictional treatments that generally portray the collector as strange, obsessive-compulsive, antisocial, or someone who prefers things to people (e.g., Balzac 1848/1968; Boyle 1994; Chatwin 1989; Connell 1974; Flaubert 1880/1954; Fowles 1963; Nicholson 1994; Pynchon 1966). Likewise, Jean Baudrillard (1994) characterizes collectors as infantile and deficient personalities and Muensterberger (1994: 9) suggests a parallel between collecting and 'fetishes of preliterate human kind'. There have been a few suggestions that collecting is a biological imperative from human evolutionary heritage (Burk 1900; Humphrey 1979; Rehmus 1988). These arguments most often rely on analogies to animal hoarding behavior, but also suggest that principles of discrimination derive from the necessity to distinguish prey from predator and edible from inedible. The definition of collecting given earlier distinguishes it from hoarding, making this connection unlikely. Furthermore, the sorts of distinctions collectors are prone to make and the sorts of ambitions they are likely to have distinguish collecting from animal behavior, as one writer to the *Times* of London put it in a 1910 letter to the editor:

> When a dog makes a store of old bones, old and entirely fleshless, he is like the Collector who keeps things because they are obsolete. A used postage stamp is to a man what a bone without flesh is to a dog: but the collector of postage stamps goes further than the dog, in that he prefers an old postage stamp to a new one, while no dog, however ardent a collector of bones without flesh, would not rather have a bone with flesh on it. There is more method in the human collector, however, since he always has before him the ideal of a complete collection, whereas no dog probably ever dreamed of acquiring specimens of all the different kinds of bones that there are in the world.
>
> (Quoted in Johnston 1986: 13, 15)

As this observation points out so graphically, collectors tend to develop preferences and judgments that lack any sort of evolutionary advantage. As Clifford (1985) observes, we teach children the rules of taste and nomenclature in guiding their collecting behavior, even as we encourage them in the acquisitive and possessive practices that collecting entails.

Another approach to collector motivations is more psychoanalytical. Interpretations here are a bit more diverse, if no less strained. Baekeland (1981) and Abraham (1927) suggest that collecting arises from sublimated sexual desire and that collectors' obsession with looking, acquiring, and fondling collected objects is a form of foreplay and coitus. Formanek (1991) also subscribes to libidinal theory to explain collecting, but also sees collecting as an aggressive

competitive activity similar to hunting or warfare. Jensen (1963) suggests that collecting is a mania or an obsession. Goldberg and Lewis (1978) and Muensterberger (1994) maintain that collectors are attempting to make up for the love they feel was missing in their infancy and childhood.

Educational psychology focused on children's collecting behavior during the first half of the twentieth century. A study in 1900 found that grade school children averaged between three and four collections each, with the incidence of collecting peaking between ages eight and eleven (Burk 1900). Collecting may have been a fad at this time, as in 1927 there was a lower frequency (Lehman and Witty 1927), although this could be a methodological artifact, as a 1929 study reported a greater incidence of collecting than the turn-of-the-century figures (Whitley 1929). During the Great Depression of the 1930s, Durost (1932) found that ten-year-old boys averaged 12.7 collections each. Gelber (1991, 1992, 1999) argues that during the Depression, collecting came to be seen as a substitute for lost jobs and lost hopes, and was regarded as an act of production rather than consumption. In Stebbins's (1979, 1982) vocabulary, such collecting is a form of 'serious leisure'.

We should not too strongly emphasize the productive character of collecting, however. In a consumer society, the consumption aspects of collecting are hard to deny. Cook (2000) treats children's often abundant collections of sports cards, Beanie Babies, and Pokémon trading cards during the 1990s as a lesson in acquisition for acquisition's sake. Butsch (1989) analyzes the commodification of leisure time with model airplanes in an earlier decade. And Danet and Katriel (1988) found that even religion has been commodified in the Rabbi trading cards collected by children in Israel. But collecting can become a consumption activity even without marketization. In the communist Soviet Union (Barker 1999; Grant 1995) as well as China (Dutton 1998; Liming 1993; Pan 1999) and Romania (Belk forthcoming), collecting of such items as stamps, Mao badges, and maps was common.

Campbell (1987) has suggested that the development of consumer culture was strongly tied to the Romantic movement. Some of the work on collecting has also found an element of romanticism among collectors, relating particularly to the passion they exhibit toward their collections (Belk 1995b; Danet and Katriel 1994; Rogan 1997; van der Grijp 2002). This passion is found both in yearning for adored objects to add to the collection and in feelings, alluded to above, that objects in the collection are priceless and participate in an economy of romance rather than an economy of commodities. They become singularized (Appadurai 1986). Collecting is a mythical realm involving sublime sets of objects, rituals, and sacredness (Belk et al. 1989). Within this mythology, the collector sometimes sees him or herself as a savior, risking much in order to rescue treasures that others fail to appreciate. The passionate collector escapes the critique that collecting is the epitome of materialism. It is the dealer in collectible objects who is seen as pursuing profit and gain, while the collector loves his or her treasures for which noble sacrifices have been made (Belk 1997). By romanticizing collecting activity and sacralizing collected objects the collector negates the charge of materialism.

After the peak of childhood collecting, collecting tends to decline as children enter puberty and turn their attention away from childhood collections. A study in Israel found that collecting for the first six grades in school 93 percent of children collected something, but that this figure dropped below 50 percent by the eighth grade (Danet and Katriel 1988). In the United States, collecting peaks about age nine or ten (McGreevy 1990). Although not all children give up their collections, the majority eventually do. Collecting activity resurfaces about middle age, especially among men (Ackerman 1990). This male bias in later age may be a reflection of greater male economic power, competitiveness, or mastery inclinations, even though collecting also invokes traits stereotypically thought to be feminine, including creation, preservation and nurturance (Belk and Wallendorf 1997). But gender differences in collecting may be diminishing. Forty-one percent of American coin collectors are women and they comprise nearly 50 percent of stamp collectors (Crispell 1988). Pearce (1995) finds that in the United Kingdom there are at least as many women as men collectors. And despite a historical tendency to disparage women's collections as being 'mere bibelots' (Saissalin 1984), there have been a number of famous women collectors in history as well as in contemporary times (Gere and Vaizey 1999). There nevertheless remain differences in the types of objects collected by men versus women (Belk 1995b; Belk and Wallendorf 1997; Belk et al. 1991; Pearce 1995), echoing stereotypical 'men's things' (e.g., mechanical objects, functional objects, weapons) and 'women's things' (e.g., decorative objects, household objects, sentimental objects).

CRITICISMS OF COLLECTING

Among the criticisms that have been directed at collecting, one is that collections are frivolous objects of consumption rather than creative objects of production. This is a criticism that has been particularly directed at women as collectors. Saisselin (1984) observes that in nineteenth-century France, men were taken to be serious collectors while women were disparaged as 'mere buyers of bibelots' (1984: 68). According with this stereotype, a husband-wife pair studied by Belk et al. (1991) were found to have collections that systematically differed such that the man's (firefighting equipment, African hunting trophies, fine art) collections could be seen as gigantic, strong, worldly, mechanical, extinguishing, scientific, serious, functional, conspicuous, and inanimate, while his wife's (mouse figure) collection could be seen as tiny, weak, homey, natural, nurturing, artistic, playful, decorative, inconspicuous, and animate. Pearce (1995) expands on this list, suggesting other gender biases in characterizations of men's and women's collections. Similar criticisms were directed at the Romantic movement that Campbell (1987) identifies as the impetus for consumer culture. Thus, we might characterize this criticism as charging an excess of romanticism among collectors.

A different sort of criticism that has been leveled at collecting is that it reveals the obsessive-compulsive personality of one who has lost control to an addiction to acquisition and possession (e.g., Danet and Katriel 1994; Freund 1993; Gelber 1999; Rogan 1997). Although a small number of collectors may be clinically obsessive-compulsive, clearly such is not the case for most collectors, who are well in control of their collecting activities (Belk 1995b; Pearce 1995). Here, too, we can see a link to romanticism, with the obsessed artist epitomizing the romantic ideal. Although it might be argued that the artist is engaged in more of a productive than consumptive activity, as noted earlier, it is indeed possible to see collectors as engaged in a creative productive activity as well.

Part of the difficulty with collecting criticisms such as these is that there appear to be diverse types of collectors and diverse reasons to collect. One distinction is made by Danet and Katriel (1989). They distinguish the Type A collector, who strives to complete a series comprising the collection (stamp collectors filling a pre-printed album are an example), and the Type B collector, who follows aesthetic impulses and has no fixed sense of a complete collection. Work by some analysts, like Baudrillard (1994) and Gelber (1999), focuses exclusively on the Type A collector, while work by other analysts, like Baekeland (1981) and Muensterberger (1994) focuses on the Type B collector. Criticisms of the Type A collector accordingly tend toward charges of obsessive-compulsiveness, while criticisms of Type B collectors tend toward charges of excessive romanticism.

REASONS, RATIONALIZATIONS, AND PLEASURES OF COLLECTING

The criticisms directed at collecting largely ignore the questions of why so many of us collect something and how we account for our collecting activity. The object collected is often not deliberately chosen, although some collectors have a personal tie-in to a nickname, national or ethnic heritage, occupation, or realm of experience. But sometimes a collection begins with a 'seed gift' from a friend or family member. More often, there is a realization that one has two or three of something and that it is the start of a collection. In my study of collectors (Belk 1995b), one common benefit cited from collecting was a feeling of mastery and competence. By collecting, the collector brings order to a controllable portion of the world. Collected objects form a small world where the collector rules. This is often enhanced by the miniature nature of many collectibles (Stewart 1984). Closely related were feelings of competitive success in a narrowly defined realm of rare objects. In pursuing additions to their collections there was both a reliance on skill, persistence, and connoisseurship, and an added thrill due to the element of luck in encountering a sought-after object by chance, ideally at a bargain price. Most collecting areas abound with treasure tales of fortuitous finds (e.g., Fine 1987). This adds to the excitement behind the 'thrill of the hunt' that many collectors describe (e.g., Benjamin 1968b; Rigby and Rigby 1944). Beyond the extended self derived from the collection (Belk 1995b; Dannefer 1980; Formanek 1991; Pearce 1998), the collector's knowledge and expertise are the source of status within circles of fellow collectors. For some, it is seen as making an important, if vaguely conceived, contribution to history, science, or art (even for collections of such humble objects as beer cans or elephant replicas: Belk 1995b). A prized provenance for pieces in the collection may also participate in the contagious magic that rubs off on the pieces from their previous owners. The

creative act of assembling and organizing a collection is pleasurable in itself, as well as a source of pride among other collectors with similar interests. Socialization with fellow collectors may also provide social pleasures as well as a sense of community (e.g., Christ 1965; Lehrer 1983).

For a number of collectors the items collected are toys, games, sports cards, dolls, or other objects from childhood. Here, in addition to the miniature size of these objects and their possible use as transitional objects (Gulerce 1991; Muensterberger 1994), the collection may reflect nostalgia for the remembered freedom and joys of childhood (Holbrook 1993; Stewart 1984). Some collectors try to recreate long-lost childhood collections. Because adult collectors are often those who have reached the 'empty nest' family life-cycle stage, they have both a void to fill that family previously occupied and extra disposable wealth to devote to the collection. But while sometimes family members share in the collecting activity or aid it ('co-dependants'), often family members begin to resent the time, love, effort, and money that the collector devotes to collecting and curating the collection rather than devoting the same attentions to them (Belk 1995a). When the collection becomes a rival or 'mistress' to which the collector seems devoted, these family members are unlikely to be willing to carry on the collection if the collector dies (thus quashing the hopes of immortality that some collectors seek through their collections). For this reason, some collectors attempt to cultivate heirs outside of the family for the collection.

Even though collectors may offer the rationalization that their collection is an economic investment, there are many better investment opportunities (Belk 1995b). Nevertheless, by claiming that their collections are their nest egg for retirement or a legacy for their children, collectors attempt to legitimize their collecting as a rational economic activity rather than something strange (Gelber 1992). The market for fine art, the existence of museum collections, and the media attention paid to famous collectors, all help to legitimize collecting as well.

The act of collecting something also sacralizes it and it should accordingly be 'priceless' for the collector, who is as unwilling to part with the object as they would be to part with a child. In fact, collected objects are often regarded as the collector's children. Freud uttered morning greetings to his collected antiquities, while Jung anthropomorphized the books in his collection (Belk 1995b). As suggested in discussing the romantic bases of collecting, and in comparing the materialistic and anti-materialistic aspects of collecting, it is possible to construe collecting as a decommoditizing activity that singularizes objects (Appadurai 1986). It does so by removing objects from market circulation and enshrining them within the collection. Collected objects are no longer fungible. When an object enters a collection it often becomes immune from monetary valuation, since the collector values it instead for its contribution to the collection. Since collected objects that once had a functional use are no longer used for that purpose, the use value of the objects is reconfigured and converted to more symbolic value. Collecting can even be seen as offering contact with the sacred (Belk et al. 1989). Like a gift from a loved one that has been ritually transformed from its marketplace origins to become a personal treasure, so objects within a collection are recontextualized and elevated to a place of reverence. To place marketplace objects in such a position is both to celebrate consumer culture and to deny it.

FUTURE RESEARCH DIRECTIONS

Collecting, whether by individuals or museums, is essentially a modernist project of assembling, organizing, and controlling a portion of the world. It is not simply hunting and gathering, as a novel by Nicholson (1994) suggests. Nor does it seem susceptible to postmodern fragmentation and loss of the narratives that sustain the collection. There have, from time to time, been *faux* collections meant to challenge and subvert the notions of a collection (Buchloh 1983; Crimp 1993; Grasskamp 1983; Pearce 1995; Weschler 1996). But the practice of collecting continues to thrive. One thing that has changed since the earliest collecting is the commodification of many collecting markets and the creation of 'instant collections' for sale in large limited editions to the public (Belk 1995b). Still, even in an era of instant food, instant Internet access, and increasingly instant gratification, the notion of an instant collection denies the pleasures of collecting, including the scouting and hunting for rare objects, the exercise of skill and luck in acquisition, and the creative pleasure of envisioning and achieving a collection. Instant collections by companies such as Franklin Mint, Danbury Mint, Lenox Collections, and Bradford Exchange may appeal to the would-be curator but unless serial acquisitions from such companies are sought, the purchaser is likely not a collector (Belk 1995b; Berman and Sullivan 1992; Pearce 1995; Roberts 1990; Slater 1997).

Nevertheless, the commodification, globalization, and commercialization of collecting deserve further attention, as do the effects of Internet auction companies like eBay (e.g., Pollock 2000). Likewise, the corporate facilitation of brand-related collecting is a recent phenomenon deserving attention (e.g., Kozinets 2001; Martin and Baker 1996; Slater 1997). The presence of intermediaries in collectibles markets goes back at least as far as ancient Greece and Rome, and prominent artists have long had patron-collectors. But the interpenetration of the market and contemporary collecting may mean that it is not only knowledge and capital that shape collecting, but also promotion and fads (witness Beanie Babies, McDonald's collectable toys, and Pokéman characters: Bosco 2001; Cook 2000; Danet and Katriel 1988).

More theoretically driven inquiries into collecting might further consider the boundaries between collecting and consuming and how they articulate with profane commoditization on one hand and sacred singularity on the other. It is perhaps ironic that Walter Benjamin (1968a) worried about the work of art in the age of mechanical reproduction while at the same time avidly pursuing a book collection and thereby enshrining mechanically reproduced consumer goods (Abbas 1988; Benjamin 1968b). Nevertheless, this apparent contradiction highlights the complexity of our relationship with material culture in a society of abundance. Shades of dedication and connoisseurship help legitimize collecting (Ger and Belk 1999) at the same time that they provide fodder for literary and popular portrayals of the collector as an asocial obsessed miser. Thus, if collecting is consumption writ large, then its dual nature as the epitome and antithesis of vulgar materialism suggests that material culture in a consumer society is also a complex field of representation, full of paradox and simultaneously comprising trivial obsession and transcendent profundity.

REFERENCES

Abbas, Ackbar (1988) 'Walter Benjamin's collector: the fate of modern experience', *New Literary History*, 20 (autumn): 217–38.

Abraham, Karl (1927) *Selected Papers: Traditions of Psychoanalysis*. London: Hogarth Press.

Ackerman, Paul, H. (1990) 'On collecting: a psychoanalytic view', *Maine Antique Digest*, May, pp. 22A–24A.

Alsop, Joseph (1982) *The Rare Art: the History of Art Collecting and its Linked Phenomena Wherever they have Appeared*. New York: Harper & Row.

Appadurai, Arjun (1986) 'Introduction: commodities and the politics of value', in Arjun Appadurai (ed.), *The Social Life of Things: Commodities in Cultural Perspective*. Cambridge: Cambridge University Press, pp. 3–63.

Aristides, Nicholai (1988) 'Calm and uncollected', *American Scholar*, 57 (3): 327–66.

Baekeland, Frederick (1981) 'Psychological aspects of art collecting', *Psychiatry*, 44 (February): 45–59.

Balzac, Honoré de (1848/1968) *Cousin Pons*, trans. Herbert J. Hunt. Harmondsworth: Penguin.

Barker, Adele Marie (1999) 'The culture factory: theorizing the popular in the old and new Russia', in Adele Marie Barker (ed.), *Consuming Russia: Popular Culture, Sex, and Society since Gorbachev*. Durham, NC: Duke University Press, pp. 12–45.

Barker, Stephen (1996) *Excavations and their Objects: Freud's Collection of Antiquity*. Albany, NY: State University of New York Press.

Baudrillard, Jean (1994) 'The system of collecting', in John Elsner and Roger Cardinal (eds), *The Cultures of Collecting*. Cambridge, MA: Harvard University Press, pp. 7–24.

Belk, Russell W. (1995a) 'Collecting as luxury consumption: effects on individuals and households', *Journal of Economic Psychology*, 16 (February): 477–90.

Belk, Russell W. (1995b) *Collecting in a Consumer Society*. London: Routledge.

Belk, Russell W. (1997) 'Collecting in fiction', *Brimfield Antique Guide*, fall, pp. 23+.

Belk, Russell W. (1998) 'The double nature of collecting: materialism and anti-materialism', *Etnofoor*, 11 (1): 7–20.

Belk, Russell W. (forthcoming) 'Collecting', in Gary Cross (ed.), *Encyclopedia of Recreation and Leisure in America*. New York: Scribner.

Belk, Russell W. and Wallendorf, Melanie (1997) 'Of mice and men: gender, identity, and collecting', in Kenneth Ames and Katherine Martinez (eds), *The Material Culture of Gender: the Gender of Material Culture*. Ann Arbor, MI: University of Michigan Press, pp. 7–27.

Belk, Russell W., Wallendorf, Melanie and Sherry, John F., Jr (1989) 'The sacred and the profane in consumer behavior: theodicy on the Odyssey', *Journal of Consumer Research*, 16 (June): 1–38.

Belk, Russell W., Wallendorf, Melanie, Sherry, John F., Jr, and Holbrook, Morris B. (1991) 'Collecting in a consumer culture', in *Highways and Buyways: Naturalistic Research from the Consumer Behavior Odyssey*. Provo, UT: Association for Consumer Research, pp. 178–215.

Benjamin, Walter (1936/1968a) 'The work of art in the Age of Mechanical Reproduction', in Hannah Arendt (ed.), trans. Harry Zohn, *Illuminations*. New York: Harcourt Brace, pp. 291–53.

Benjamin, Walter (1955/1968b) 'Unpacking my library: a talk about books', in Hannah Arendt (ed.), trans. Harry Zohn, *Illuminations*. New York: Harcourt Brace, pp. 59–67.

Berman, Morris (1981) *The Reenchantment of the World*. Ithaca, NY: Cornell University Press.

Berman, Phyllis and Sullivan, R. Lee (1992) 'Limousine liberal', *Forbes*, 150 (26 October): 168+.

Bianchi, Marina (1997) 'Collecting as a paradigm of consumption', *Journal of Cultural Economics*, 21: 275–89.

Bosco, Joseph (2001) 'The McDonald's Snoopy craze in Hong Kong', in Gordon Mathews and Tai-lok Lui (eds), *Consuming Hong Kong*. Hong Kong: Hong Kong University Press, pp. 263–85.

Boyle, T. Courghesan (1994) 'Filthy with things', in T.C. Boyles (ed.), *Without a Hero: Stories*. New York: Viking, pp. 41–63.

Brook, G.L. (1980) *Books and Book Collecting*. London: Deutsch.

Buchloh, H.D. (1983) 'The museum fictions of Marcel Broodthaers', in A.A. Bronson and Peggy Gale (eds), *Museums by Artists*. Toronto: Art Metropole, pp. 45–6.

Burk, Caroline F. (1900) 'The collecting instinct', *Pedagogical Seminary*, 7 (January): 179–207.

Butsch, Richard (1989) 'The commodification of leisure time: the case of the model airplane hobby and industry', *Qualitative Sociology*, 7 (fall): 217–35.

Cabanne, Pierre (1961/1963) *The Great Collectors*. London: Cassell (original, *Le Roman des grands collectionneurs*, Paris: Opera Mundi).

Campbell, Colin (1987) *The Romantic Ethic and the Spirit of Modern Consumerism*. Oxford: Blackwell.

Chatwin, Bruce (1989) *Utz*. New York: Viking.

Christ, Edwin A. (1965) 'The "retired" stamp collector: economic and other functions of a systematized leisure activity', in Arnold M. Rose and Warren A. Peterson (eds), *Older People and their Social World: the Subculture of Aging*. Philadelphia, PA: Davis, pp. 93–112.

Clifford, James (1985) 'Objects and selves: an afterword', in Goerge W. Stocking, Jr (ed.), *Objects and Others: Essays on Museums and Material Culture*. Madison, WI: University of Wisconsin Press, pp. 236–46.

Clifford, James (1990) 'On collecting art and culture', in Russell Ferguson, Marsha Gever, Trinh T. Minh-ha, and Cornel West (eds), *Out There: Marginalization and Contemporary Cultures*. Cambridge, MA: MIT Press, pp. 141–69.

Clunas, Craig (1991) *Superfluous Things: Material Culture and Social Status in Early Modern China*. Urbana, IL: University of Illinois Press.

Connell, Evan S., Jr (1974) *The Connoisseur*. New York: Knopf.

Cook, Daniel Thomas (2000) 'Exchange value as pedagogy in children's leisure: moral panics in children's culture at century's end', *Leisure Sciences*, 23: 81–98.

Crimp, Douglas (1993) *On the Museum's Ruins*. Cambridge, MA: MIT Press.

Crispell, Diane (1988) 'Collecting memories', *American Demographics*, 60 (November): 38–41.

Danet, Brenda and Katriel, Tamar (1988) 'Stamps, Erasers, Table Napkins, "Rebbe Cards": Childhood Collecting in Israel', paper presented at the eighteenth annual meeting of the Popular Culture Association, New Orleans, LA, March.

Danet, Brenda and Katriel, Tamar (1989) 'No two alike: the aesthetics of collecting', *Play and Culture*, 2 (3): 253–77.

Danet, Brenda and Katriel, Tamar (1994) 'Glorious obsessions, passionate lovers, and hidden treasures: collecting, metaphor, and the Romantic ethic', in Stephen H. Riggen (ed.), *The Socialness of Things*. New York: Mouton de Gruyter, pp. 23–61.

Dannefer, Dale (1980) 'Rationality and passion in private experience: modern consciousness and the social world of old-car collectors', *Social Problems*, 22 (April): 392–412.

Delaney, Jill (1992) 'Ritual space in the Canadian Museum of Civilization: consuming Canadian identity', in Rob Shields (ed.), *Lifestyle Shopping: The Subject of Consumption*. London: Routledge, pp. 136–48.

Dudar, Helen (1990) 'The unexpected private passion of Sigmund Freud', *Smithsonian*, 21 (5): 100–9.

Durost, Walter N. (1932) *Children's Collecting Activity related to Social Factors*. New York: Bureau of Publications, Teachers' College, Columbia University.

Dutton, Michael, ed. (1998) *Streetlife China*. Cambridge: Cambridge University Press.

Ellenberger, Henri F. (1965/1974) 'The mental hospital and the zoological garden,' in Joseph Klaits and Barrie Klaits (eds), *Animals and Man in Historical Perspective*. New York: Harper & Row (original 'Jardin zoologique et hôpital psychiatrique', in A. Brion and Henri Ey (eds), *Psychiatrie animale*. Paris: de Brouwer, pp. 559–78).

Engelman, Edmund, ed. (1976) *Bergasse 19: Sigmund Freud's Home and Offices, Vienna 1938: the Photographs of Edmund Engelman*. New York: Basic Books.

Fine, Gary Alan (1987) 'Community and boundary: personal experience stories of mushroom collectors', *Journal of Folklore Research*, 24 (September–December): 223–40.

Flaubert, Gustave (1880/1954) *Bouvard & Pécuchet*, trans. T.W. Earp and G.W. Stonier. New York: New Directions.

Formanek, Ruth (1991) 'Why they collect: collectors reveal their motivation', *Journal of Social Behavior and Personality*, 6 (June): 275–86.

Forrester, John (1994) '"Mille e tre": Freud and collecting', in John Elsner and Roger Cardinal (eds), *The Cultures of Collecting*. Cambridge, MA: Harvard University Press, pp. 224–51.

Fowles, John (1963) *The Collector*. Boston, MA: Little Brown.

Freund, Thatcher (1993) *Objects of Desire: the Lives of Antiques and those who Pursue Them*. New York: Penguin Books.

Gamwell, Lynn and Wells, Richard eds (1989) *Sigmund Freud and Art: his Personal Collection of Antiquities*. Binghamton, NY: State University of New York.

Gelber, Steven M. (1991) 'A job you can't lose: work and hobbies in the Great Depression', *Journal of Social History*, 24 (summer): 741–66.

Gelber, Steven M. (1992) 'Free market metaphor: the historical dynamics of stamp collecting', *Comparative Studies in Society and History*, 34 (October): 742–69.

Gelber, Steven M. (1999) *Hobbies: Leisure and the Culture of Work in America*. New York: Columbia University Press.

George, Wilma (1985) 'Alive or dead: zoological collections in the seventeenth century', in Oliver Impey and Arthur MacGregor (eds), *The Origins of Museums: the Cabinet of Curiosities in the Sixteenth Century*. Oxford: Clarendon Press, pp. 179–87.

Ger, Güliz and Belk, Russell (1999) 'Accounting for materialism in four cultures', *Journal of Material Culture*, 4 (July): 183–204.

Gere, Charlotte and Vaizey, Marina (1999) *Great Women Collectors*. London: Wilson.

Goldberg, Herb and Lewis, Robert T. (1978) *Money Madness: the Psychology of Saving, Spending, Loving, and Hating Money*. New York: Morrow.

Grampp, William D. (1989) *Pricing the Priceless: Art, Artists, and Economics*. New York: Basic Books.

Grasskamp, Walter (1983) 'Les artistes et les autres collectionneurs', in A.A. Bronson and Peggy Gale (eds), *Museums by Artists*. Toronto: Art Metropole, pp. 129–48.

Grant, Jonathan (1995) 'The socialist construction of philately in the early Soviet era', *Comparative Studies in Society and History*, 37: 476–93.

Gulerce, Aydan (1991) 'Transitional objects: a reconsider of the phenomena', in Floyd W. Rudmin (ed.), *To Have Possessions: A Handbook on Ownership and Property*, special issue of *Journal of Social Behavior and Personality*, 6 (6): 187–208.

Guth, Christine (1989) 'The Tokugawa as patrons and collectors of paintings', in Denise L. Bissonette (coordinator), *The Tokugawa Collection: the Japan of the Shoguns*. Montreal: Montreal Museum of Fine Arts, pp. 41–51.

Halverson, John (1987) 'Art for art's sake in the Paleolithic', *Current Anthropology*, 18 (February): 63–89.

Haskell, Francis (1976) *Rediscoveries in Art: Some Aspects of Taste, Fashion, and Collecting in England and France*. London: Phaidon Press.

Hayashiya, Seizo and Trubner, Henry (1977) *Chinese Ceramics from Japanese Collections*. New York: Asia House Gallery.

Hermann, Frank (1972) *The English as Collectors: a Documentary Chrestomathy*. London: Chatto & Windus.

Hodgen, Margaret T. (1964) *Early Anthropology in the Sixteenth and Seventeenth Centuries*. Philadelphia, PA: University of Pennsylvania Press.

Holbrook, Morris (1993) 'Nostalgia and consumption preferences: some emerging patterns of consumer tastes', *Journal of Consumer Research*, 20 (September): 245–56.

Humphrey, N.K. (1979) 'The biological basis of collecting', *Human Nature*, February, pp. 44–7.

Hunt, John Dixon (1985) ' "Curiosities to adorn cabinets and gardens" ', in Oliver Impey and Arthur MacGregor (eds), *The Origins of Museums: the Cabinet of Curiosities in the Sixteenth Century*. Oxford: Clarendon Press, pp. 293–02.

Impey, Oliver and MacGregor, Arthur, eds (1985) *The Origins of Museums: the Cabinet of Curiosities in the Sixteenth Century*. Oxford: Clarendon Press.

Jackson, Holbrook (1930/1989) *The Anatomy of Bibliomania*. Savannah, GA: Beil.

Jenson, Jens (1963) 'Collector's mania', *Acta Psychiatrica Scandinavia*, 39 (4): 606–18.

Johnson, Jed (1988) 'Inconspicuous consumption', in *The Andy Warhol Collection, Contemporary Art*, V. New York: Sotheby's.

Johnston, Susanna (1986) 'Introduction', in Susanna Johnston and Tim Beddow (eds), *Collecting: The Passionate Pastime*. New York: Harper & Row, pp. 13–15.

Kaylan, Melik (1988) 'The Warhol collection: why selling it is a shame', *Connoisseur*, 915 (April): 118–28.

Kozinets, Reobert V. (2001) 'Utopian enterprise: articulating the meanings of *Star Trek*'s culture of consumption', *Journal of Consumer Research*, 28 (June): 67–88.

Kron, Joan (1983) *Home-Psych: the Social Psychology of Home and Decoration*. New York: Potter.

Lehman, Harvey C. and Witty, Paul A. (1927) 'The present status of the tendency to collect and hoard', *Psychological Review*, 34: 48–56.

Lehrer, Jim (1983) 'And now a word of praise for the pack rats among us', *Smithsonian*, 20 (March): 58–67.

Liming, Wei (1993) 'Private collection highlights exhibition', *Beijing Review*, 36 (October): 4–10+.

Mackay, Charles (1841/1932) *Extraordinary Popular Delusions and the Madness of Crowds*. Boston, MA: Page (original *Memoirs of Extraordinary Popular Delusions*, London: Bentley).

Martin, Mary C. and Baker, Stacey Menzel (1996) 'An ethnography of Mick's sports card show: preliminary findings from the field', in Kim Corfman and John Lynch (eds), *Advances in Consumer Research*, XXIII, Provo, UT: Association for Consumer Research, pp. 329–36.

Mason, Peter (1994) 'From presentation to representation: Americana in Europe', *Journal of the History of Collections*, 6 (1): 1–20.

McGreevy, Ann (1990) 'Treasures of children: collections then and now, or, treasures of children revisited', *Early Childhood Development and Care*, 63: 33–6.

Miller, Daniel (2001) 'Possessions', in Daniel Miller (ed.), *Home Possessions*. Oxford: Berg, pp. 107–21.

Moulin, Raymonde (1967/1987) *The French Art Market: a Sociological View*, trans. Arthur Goldhammer. New Brunswick, NJ: Rutgers University Press (original *Le Marché de le peinture en France*, Paris: Minuit).

Muensterberger, Werner (1994) *Collecting: an Unruly Passion: Psychological Perspectives*. Princeton, NJ: Princeton University Press.

Mukerji, Chandra (1983) *From Graven Images: Patterns of Modern Materialism*. New York: Columbia University Press.

Mullaney, Steven (1983) 'Strange things, gross terms, curious customs: the rehearsal of cultures in the late Renaissance', *Representations*, 3 (summer): 40–67.

Neal, Arminta (1980) 'Collecting for history museums: reassembling our splintered existence', *Museum News*, 58 (May–June): 24–9.

Nicholson, Geoff (1994) *Hunters and Gatherers*. Woodstock, NY: Overlook Press.

O'Brien, George (1981) 'Living with collections', *New York Times Magazine*, 26 April, part 2, pp. 25–42.

Olmi, Guiseppe (1985) 'Science-honour-metaphor: Italian cabinets of the sixteenth and seventeenth centuries', in Oliver Impey and Arthur MacGregor (eds), *The Origins of Museums: the Cabinet of Curiosities in the Sixteenth Century*. Oxford: Clarendon Press, pp. 5–16.

Pan, Lynn (1999) *Mao Memorabilia: The Man and the Myth*. Hong Kong: Form Asia.

Pearce, Susan M. (1995) *On Collecting: An Investigation into Collecting in the European Tradition*. London: Routledge.

Pearce, Susan M. (1998) *Collecting in Contemporary Practice*. London: Sage.

Pfeiffer, John E. (1982) *The Creative Explosion: an Inquiry into the Origins of Art and Religion*. New York: Harper & Row.

Pivar, Stuart (1988) 'Shopping with Andy', in *The Andy Warhol Collection, Contemporary Art*, V. New York: Sotheby's.

Pollock, Barbara (2000) 'Net scrapes: buying art online is easy, fun – and wide open to potential fraud', *Forbes* 166 (25 December): 186.

Pomian, Krystof (1987/1990) *Collectors and Curiosities: Paris and Venice, 1500–1800*, trans. Elizabeth Wiles-Portier. Cambridge: Polity Press (original *Collection-neurs, amateurs et curieux*, Paris: Gallimard).

Pynchon, Thomas (1966) *The Crying of Lot 49*. London: Cape.

Rehmus, James M. (1988) 'The collector's mind', *Perspectives in Biology and Medicine*, 31 (winter): 261–4.

Rheims, Maurice (1959/1961) *The Strange Life of Objects: Thirty-five Centuries of Art Collecting and Collectors*, trans. David Pryce-Jones. New York: Atheneum (original *La Vie étrange des objets*, Paris: Plon, published in England as *Art on the Market: Thirty-five Centuries of Collecting and Collectors from Midas to Paul Getty*, 1961).

Rigby, Douglas and Rigby, Elizabeth (1944) *Lock, Stock and Barrel: the Story of Collecting*. Philadelphia, PA: Lippincott.

Roberts, Gwyneth (1990) '"A thing of beauty and a source of wonderment": ornaments for the home as cultural status markers', in Gary Day (ed.), *Readings in Popular Culture: Trivial Pursuits?* New York: St Martin's Press, pp. 39–47.

Rogan, Bjarne (1997) 'From passion to possessiveness: collectors and collecting in a symbolic perspective', *Ethnologica Europaea*, 26 (1): 65–79.

Saarinen, Aline B. (1958) *The Proud Possessors: the Lives, Times, and Tastes of some Adventurous American Art Collectors*. New York: Random House.

Saisselin, Rémy G. (1984) *Bricobracomania: The Bourgeois and the Bebelot*. New Brunswick, NJ: Rutgers University Press.

Schama, Simon (1987) *The Embarrassment of Riches: an Interpretation of Dutch Culture in the Golden Age*. New York: Knopf.

Schiffer, Michael, Downing, Theodore and McCarthy, Michael (1981) 'Waste not, want not: an ethnoarchaeological study of refuse in Tucson', in Michael Gould and Michael Schiffer (eds), *Modern Material Culture: the Archaeology of Us*. New York: Academic Press, pp. 67–86.

Slater, Janet S. (1997) 'Trash to Treasure: a Qualitative Study of the Relationship between Collectors and Collectible Brands', unpublished Ph.D. dissertation, Department of Mass Communications, Syracuse University.

Stearns, Peter (2001) *Consumerism in World History: the Global Transformation of Consumer Desire*. London: Routledge.

Stebbins, Robert A. (1979) *Amateurs: on the Margins between Work and Leisure*. Beverly Hills, CA: Sage.

Stebbins, Robert A. (1982) 'Serious leisure: a conceptual statement', *Pacific Sociological Review*, 25 (April): 251–72.

Stewart, Susan (1984) *On Longing: Narratives of the Miniature, the Gigantic, the Souvenir, and the Collection*. Baltimore, MD: Johns Hopkins University Press.

Taylor, Francis Henry (1948) *The Taste of angels: a History of Art Collecting from Ramses to Napoleon*. Boston, MA: Little Brown.

Tuan, Yi-Fu (1984) *Dominance and Affection: the Making of Pets*. New Haven, CT: Yale University Press.

Van Der Grijp, Paul (2002) 'Passion and profit: the world of amateur traders in philately', *Journal of Material Culture*, 7 (1): 23–47.

Vander Gucht, Daniel (1991) 'Art at risk in the hands of the museum: from the museum to the private collection', *International Sociology*, 6 (September): 361–72.

Von Holst, Niels (1967) *Creators, Collectors and Connoisseurs: the Anatomy of Artistic Taste from Antiquity to the Present Day*. New York: Putnam.

Weschler, Lawrence (1996) *Mr Wilson's Cabinet of Wonder*. New York: Vintage Books.

Whitley, M.T. (1927) 'Children's interest in collecting', *Journal of Educational Psychology*, 20: 249–61.

Wright, Louis B. and Gordon N. Ray (1969) *The Private Collector and the Support of Scholarship*, Los Angeles, CA: William Andrews Clark Memorial Library, University of California.

INDEX